The Corporate Reapers

The Book of Agribusiness

A.V. Krebs

Essential Books
P.O. Box 19405
Washington, D.C. 20036

Chapters Thirty-Three, Thirty-Four and Thirty-Five originally appeared in the booklet *Heading Toward the Last Roundup: The Big Three's Prime Cut*, published by Prairiefire Rural Action, 550 11th Street, Des Moines, Iowa 50309

Cover Photo by Bill Witt, © 1991
Designed by A.V. Krebs

Library of Congress Catalog Card Number 91-75817

ISBN #0-9621259-3-8

Dedicated
to the
stewards of the land:
those
men, women and children
who plant, nurture and harvest
nature's bounty of food.

Table of Contents

EPILOGUE: BRINGING THE CORPORATE STATE UNDER DEMOCRATIC CONTROL

APPENDIX

An Old Farmers' Tale?

"One day at our Catholic Worker farm, John Filliger, talking of drying up a cow a few months before she was about to calve, said, 'The only way to do it with a good cow like this is to milk her out on the ground. She gets so mad at the waste of her milk that she dries right up.' That may be an old wives' tale — or an old farmers' tale, in this case — but there is a lesson in it: if we waste what we have, the source of supply will dry up. Any long range view of the colossal waste of the resources of the earth and human life points to an exhaustion of our economy, not to speak of man himself."

- Dorothy Day,
"A Brief Flame," *The Catholic Worker*
November, 1965

Introduction:

America's Permanent Agricultural Crisis

"The point was food, quantities of food. It all looked so easy, that tractor driver in his air-conditioned cab, that wonderful machine crawling across the face of the same earth it would have taken my ancestors forty years to plow. What matter if a whole style of life was gone? What matter if the earth no longer served a single family, a small parcel of immortality for the common man? All that was lost to me, as lost as a cherry orchard in which people no longer knew the meaning of cherries, as lost as the unwritten language of a long-expired race of men.

"All that mattered was food, the wheat on the hill, the hay in the meadow, the mutton under my boot. Whatever method could raise them best and most efficiently would win the prizes of the earth."

"There was little beauty to it, in my mind. There was only sweat, and maybe a certain sense of unspeakable smallness in my soul in that of all the generations behind me, of all the lost tribes of my forefathers who had dug potatoes, milked cows, sown grain, picked fruit from primeval gardens, it had all come down to me in a knowledge I only wished to lose."

- **Douglas Unger, *Leaving the Land***
Harper & Row: New York, 1984

Introduction

America's Permanent Agricultural Crisis

Food, next to life itself, is our species' greatest common denominator. Its availability, quality, price, its reflection of the cultures it feeds and its moral and religious significance makes food quite literally history's "staff of life."

Regrettably, in the ongoing worldwide struggle to determine who will control food's production and delivery, it is no longer viewed primarily as a sustainer of life. Rather, food has become a major source of corporate cash flow and economic leverage, a form of currency, a tool of international politics, an instrument of power — a weapon!

By ignoring food's fundamental relationship to life itself, those "communities of economic interests" who now control its availability, quality and price have generated a plethora of heretofore unaddressed social, economic, political, environmental and moral questions. Sartaj Aziz, deputy director of the World Food Council, adroitly summarized such questions when he asked a 1976 Ames, Iowa international food conference: "Are we going to treat the world as a market, or as a community?"

While the argument of who will produce and distribute our food ensues, both developed and underdeveloped nations meanwhile work to achieve sustainable, self-sufficient, equitable agricultural programs. Along with this growing awareness, struggles over land and natural resource ownership continue to be waged. Yet, as the eminent Protestant theologian Dr. Walter Brueggemann notes, historically society's minds and hearts have been shaped by the city. Speaking to a National Council of Churches conference on the urban/rural land connection at New York's Riverside Church in November 1986, Dr. Brueggemann elaborated:

We begin our analysis by observing that all those who thought they owned the land, who said they owned the land, who chanted liturgies that assured them that they owned the land, they are all the people who lived in the city. The urban power elite imagined that they owned the land and on that presupposition they conducted their politics and their liturgy; and so I submit that this conference which confesses that the land is owned by Yahweh, is a doxology against urban pretensions. The fact of the city is at the center of the land crisis. It was so in ancient Israel and it is so in our farm

crisis because the city is not simply a place, the city is a way of thinking about social reality.

He continues,

...the city is a place of monopoly where everything important and valued is gathered and stored and administered and owned. The city exists by the concentration of what is valued in the hands of a few. Indeed, the city exists for the sake of concentration.

The concentration of wealth and value is the cause of the city and the city is the result of that concentration. When the city is healthy it exists in a respectful coming and going with the country. But when the city arrives at a pathological self-importance and an imagined self-sufficiency, it fails to respect the country. When there is no coming and going, no giving and taking, but only taking, there comes death.

Today, in the United States, ready access to food is taken for granted. *Starvation* is a problem endured by others in faraway villages, fly-flecked, sad-faced, gaunt images which appear with increasing regularity on our television screens.

Meanwhile, Americans remain well-fed, despite the fact that there is a growing recognition that in some of our own cities and neighborhoods, there exist major problems with *hunger* and the inequitable distribution and availability of a seeming cornucopia of food. Responding to this seeming paradox, we have seen many recent efforts to raise public consciousness concerning the prevalence of starvation and hunger in our world and in our own communities. Such efforts have ranged from hand-holding demonstrations by "new wave philanthropists,'" publicly underwritten by a self-serving "corporate populism," to numerous Live Aid music concerts.

Well-intentioned, but basically misdirected, such ephemeral remedial gestures have tended to obscure the fact that it is the very structure of our current food production and delivery system and the self-serving policies that it generates that cause starvation throughout the world and hunger in our own country, while at the same time methodically eroding many of our most cherished moral values and democratic ideals.

Susan George, author of *Feeding the Few*, puts it succinctly: "Transnational corporations are not there to feed people, they are not there to provide jobs, they are there to make a profit. Period! That's all! So one should not expect them to be feeding people who cannot pay."

Indeed, as we continue to harbor a number of damaging myths about world hunger (See Appendix A) we have come to witness the unfolding of a most curious paradox.

As developed nations relentlessly pursue state-of-the-art food production systems, which will enable them both to maintain a high standard of living at home and to enter the economic and politically lucrative world food market as exporters, less developed countries (LDC's) struggle vainly amidst domestic political, economic and social instability, to find expedient ways to feed their own growing numbers of malnourished, hungry and starving people. Not surprisingly, many of these same nations have turned to the United States, the richest, most productive agricultural nation on earth — "the world's bread basket" — convinced that it is the American agricultural system that will lead them to the promised land of food stability and abundance.

However, the best interests of the developed nations and the LDC's often operate in opposition to one another for paradoxically the more these nations seek to emulate the U.S. system of food production, the less sustainable and more economically and socially chaotic they become.

In an attempt to understand this apparent dilemma, *The Corporate Reapers: The Book of Agribusiness* seeks to examine the present condition of modern U.S. agriculture and our nation's food delivery system, considering both its goals and its current structure. Second, it will seek to trace our agricultural, historical, political and economic roots. Third, it will endeavor to identify just who and what have been the major forces in the development of our long-standing domestic and foreign farm and food policies.

A Deity Called "Agribusiness"

America's "family farm system" of agriculture today stands on the threshold of eradication. Throughout the 1980s, ever-mounting numbers of farm bankruptcies, foreclosures, and forced evictions reaped a grim harvest of suicides, alcoholism, divorce, family violence, personal stress, and loss of community. We have seen the very economic and social fabric of rural America being ripped asunder.

But this disaster extends far beyond the farm gate.

The latest chapter in what Northern Plains rancher/journalist Homer Ayres has so aptly called "America's permanent agricultural crisis," this continuing eradication of the nation's farm communities involves not only some two million farms and their families, but it is a disaster that could ultimately affect every person on the planet.

Today, as what we eat becomes more and more of a *manufactured* product to be processed, packaged, advertised, marketed, traded and used as another weapon in the high stakes game of geopolitical diplomacy, the centuries-old role of the farmer as the *prod-ucer* of our food is being consigned to the scrap heap of history.

It is the purpose of this book, therefore, to demonstrate that the major responsibility for this systematic eradication of our family farm system of agriculture belongs to a variety of self-serving "communities of economic interest" (See Appendix B) and their agricultural policy planners in academia and government who view food not as food but as the "bottom line" — a new way to increase cash flow, corporate profits, and gain tighter control over the direction of our nation and the world's economy.

One fact frequently held up for veneration by the champions of U.S. agriculture is that each American farmer today can feed 128 people (94.3 in the United States and 33.7 overseas). By contrast, in 1910 our farmers fed only 7.1 persons (6.1 in the United States and one abroad). That earlier agricultural system, however, was generally characterized by many individual efforts at husbanding the land, by personal responsibility for the decision making required for relatively efficient management, by labor-intensive, low capital-and-energy costs, and by a subsistence style of living.

Today, however, the American farmer (approximately 2.2 percent of our population) no longer stands alone. He/she has become but a single cog in a vast machine called agribusiness.

The term *agribusiness* means more than just owning and cultivating land to raise and produce crops and livestock (agricultural production). The term also refers to the financing of agriculture, and the manufacturing, transporting, wholesaling and distribution of farm machinery, fertilizers, chemical poisons, seed, feed and packaging materials (agricultural inputs). Agribusiness also manufactures, processes and markets food (agricultural outputs).

By 1990, agribusiness accounted for over 16 percent of the nation's gross national product (GNP) while farming, itself, accounted for slightly over one percent of the GNP.

Thus, as agribusiness continues to grow, becoming increasingly dominated by large corporations, often multinational in character, while solidifying its claim as the nation's number one industry, its apostles and political disciples never seem to tire of extolling its seemingly endless number of virtues: a model of agricultural "efficiency" — the very soul of the so-called "free market" system.

"Bigger Is Better"???

When corporate America discusses "efficiency" it is usually in terms of a ratio comparing outputs to inputs. Soil resource loss, environmental degradation, food security and sustainability and other such costs not specifically built into the market pricing system are generally ignored.

As University of Missouri Rural Sociology Professor William D. Heffernan points out,

Often in the process of quantifying input and output resources in monetary terms, a power relationship is hidden. Does the fact that operators of large farms buy fertilizer cheaper than operators of small farms indicate that from a societal perspective the large farms are more efficient in their use of society's resources? Or does it indicate that they have more economic power?

Heffernan goes on to suggest that in today's corporate agribusiness structure, "power is more important than efficiency for assuring organizational survival which becomes the major goal for organizations that have become institutionalized."

Others argue that because our current industrialized society is so materialistic it has come to measure success only in quantitative rather than qualitative terms. Thus, two of the family farming systems's most cherished characteristics — diversity and individuality — are actually seen by corporate agribusiness as enemies of the system.

Thus, since the end of World War II, it is the socalled "efficient farmer" which has been characterized as the "final solution" to America's permanent agricultural crisis. But "efficiency" cannot be measured in realistic terms merely by looking at a farm's financial ledgers. Real *efficiency* involves a much more overall, sophisticated analysis of a farm's impact upon the community in which it operates, the quality it brings to both rural and urban life, as well as the manner in which its owner/operator husbands its resources for the future.

Michael Perelman, a Chico State University economist, rightly points out that farming is not just technical or biological, but is part of a more general economic process in which human labor power is combined with land and other resources. Purely technical aspects of agriculture cannot be analyzed independently of the way these other key resources are treated.

American agribusiness, by gradually minimizing the use of labor and thus placing agriculture on a scientific and technological treadmill, relying on enormous fossil fuel subsidies and neglecting other valuable natural resources, has accelerated what it myopically calls "economic growth." But, as a 1967 Brookings Institution study correctly reports, "an economic system should be judged by how it affects the lives of its citizens, and not by how well it maximizes money profits or measured output."

The history of American agriculture as we shall soon see has been characterized by a continual restructuring of a rural society aimed not toward meeting its own worthwhile community needs, but rather at satisfying the needs of remote and self-serving "communities of economic interests." As, Perelman reflects, "We work, we consume, we live our lives so that business may prosper."

Free Enterprise! or Free Enterprise?

Invariably, lectures on the merits of "efficiency" include sermons on the virtues of the "free enterprise" system. Americans are told *ad nauseum* that it is only the "efficient farmer" who will survive the "rugged competition" of the today's "marketplace."

Yet, "free enterprise" in agriculture has always been predicated on the largely unproven idea that pursuing profits without government interference results in lower food costs to the consumer and high-quality products at fair prices for farmers.

Such free enterprise advocates as Ronald Reagan never tire of insisting that it is government "interference" that has caused most of our modern agrarian problems. To a degree they are absolutely correct, for the actual role of government in our current agricultural system has evolved to a large degree into being that of a handmaiden for corporate agribusiness.

In an August, 1986 Chicago press conference, for example, Reagan related to a national TV audience that he had always felt "that the nine most terrifying words in the English language" were "I'm from the government and I'm here to help." In that same press conference he also boasted that his administration had spent more taxpayer's money in one year on agriculture "than any previous administration spent during its entire tenure." He added:

We are trying to help in a situation that, I believe, was originally created by the federal government when the federal government back in the days of the Depression started *invading the farm community* with all its various programs. It has brought on most of the problems that bother farmers today. (emphasis added)

But, as University of Wisconsin-Eau Claire's Geography Professor Ingolf Voegler, has argued, "an alternative interpretation is that the state has intervened in an attempt to manage problems that have originated in the 'free-market economy' itself. In doing so, the state takes the blame off the private sector for its own mismanagement; instead of people rebelling against business, they rebel against government programs."

This book offers many such examples of how responsibility for America's permanent agricultural crisis has been frequently and adroitly shifted from its origins — corporate agribusiness — to the public sector.

As Voegler adds:

the general public must recognize that only after the *demystification* of U.S. agriculture will family farmers, labor, and consumers see beyond corporate agribusiness's manipulations to the point where they will recognize that both their mutual interests and the future of agriculture can be best decided through a system that not only practices political democracy, but economic democracy as well.

Yet, today, when agribusiness's corporate managers use such economic jingoism as "free enterprise," "efficiency," and "rugged competition" they are really telling farmers that the only way to maintain a sufficient farm income in today's industrial-agricultural system is to get big or get out!

Professor Milton Friedman of the University of Chicago has taken such an argument one step further, declaring that the only way corporations can meet their "social responsibility" in today's world is by *maximizing profits.* Corporate executives who adopt any other criterion, he maintains, are just kidding themselves and their shareholders, opening the door to political control and indirectly promoting "pure and unadulterated socialism."

Currently, many of our nation's farm programs contradict even corporate agribusiness's so-called "efficiency" principle. By granting various classes of farms generous taxpayer subsidies, for example, the government has traditionally based its largesse not on yields per worker or per acre, but rather on total farm production or on the amount of land owned. Such a system not only misconstrues true efficiency, but encourages needless farm expansion while increasing the profits of a dwindling number of absentee property owners under the guise of increasing productivity.

There is no better example of this type of thinking than in The Great Southeast Drought of 1986. As crop loss estimates began to exceed $2 billion the U.S. Department of Agriculture announced with great fanfare a $1 billion "drought relief package." However, what the Reagan administration chose not to tell the public was that of the $1 billion, only $32 million, or less than four percent of the money, was destined to go to farmers in the eight states that included counties designated as drought disaster areas.

The largest share, $143 million, was destined for farmers in Iowa, which had been receiving abundant rainfall and were about to harvest a bumper corn crop, while Illinois was scheduled to get $96 million. These amounts, of course, reflected the fact that frequently farm subsidies are based on volume of production. The Southeast, however, is a relatively small producer of major subsidized crops such as wheat, corn, and rice.

One might ideally expect that Federal law would ensure all farmers an equal opportunity to compete in the marketplace. Yet, the reality of past laws, as we shall be examining, show that a ready access to land, capital and technical know-how has been decidedly unequal among American farmers.

In studying corporate agribusiness' adoration of today's so-called "free enterprise" gospel, we shall likewise see that the nature and primary goal of the corporate interests that control agribusiness has little or nothing to do with freedom or individual initiative. Rather the main objective of corporate agribusiness is to maximize profits, minimize costs and conduct and maintain its business with as little public accountability as possible.

Often forgotten in such a process, however, is a fact which Rev. Maurice Dingman, one-time Catholic bishop of Des Moines, Iowa, calls to public attention:

There is a grave temptation in our system of capitalism that a corporation will use the land to its advantages to gain an undue profit. I'm not saying it's wrong to work for a profit, but I say it's terribly hard to control that profit motive. If they can make a dollar, they're usually going to make it. And if it destroys the land, it doesn't matter. But a farmer doesn't view land as a commodity. Farmers understand that land has a social signifi-

cance ... If corporations in Chicago own land in Iowa, do you think they care what happens to the land as long as they're making a profit and can tell their shareholders that they will get big dividends?

Through the large diversified and often absentee corporation, with relatively easy access to credit and tax advantages, and the ability to rapidly expand its production capabilities by diversifying and digging into the deep pockets of its non-agricultural subsidiaries, and a subservient federal farm policy, *corporate* agribusiness has now become the dominant force in the production and manufacturing of U.S. food and fiber.

Indeed, in its relentless effort to derive more profits from the food we eat while effectively destroying the U.S. family farm system of agriculture, corporate America not only continues to gain an ever-increasing control over the quantity and quality of our food, but also over the constantly changing and often arbitrary price we pay for it in our markets, restaurants *and* tax bills, *and* in our share of the public and private debt.

As this rush to economic concentration continues to accelerate unabated, some agricultural economists are beginning to recognize that our misnamed *cheap* food policy is coming to us today not so cheaply but with many additional hidden and exacting social, political and environmental costs. At the same time, our family farms are being relegated to nothing but cheap, raw material producers for a mammoth, cash-rich food manufacturing system. And, as that system — corporate agribusiness — grows ever larger it continues to seek new and more devious ways to slash production costs and increase its already enormous cash flow.

The Disposing of "Excess Human Resources"

For over a century corporate agribusiness and those "communities of economic interests" which tightly control its structure have gone about addressing American agriculture's never-ending (and often self-created) "surplus" production and\or "inefficiency" *problem* by relentlessly seeking to rid agriculture of its "excess human resources."

Stated more bluntly, there has been a deliberate effort to drive as many farm families off the land as possible, and that strategy has obviously worked. During the eight years of the Reagan administration alone, every eight minutes the nation lost another family farm, 180 times a day, 1,250 times a week, 65,000 a year.

Although their strategy has been infinitely more subtle than many of history's other forced migrations of people by totalitarian societies, corporate agribusiness shares a similar goal: clearing millions and millions of human beings off productive land and relocating them where they might better serve the interests of an economic and politically powerful elite.

In their process of eliminating such human resources from agriculture these "communities of economic interests" have been also ably assisted by various self-serving public and private policies and government tax-supported programs, all justified by contorted explanations of the current condition.

Consequently, farm debt in six short years grew from $166 billion in 1980 to $210.4 billion in 1986. Net farm income shrank from a deflated $34.9 billion in 1979 to $33.4 billion in 1986. Land values, between 1982 and 1987 decreased nationally by over 33 percent and over 50 percent in some Midwest states.

Faced with economic conditions, perhaps worse than the Great Depression, these same six years saw nearly 235,000 U.S. farms go out of business. In turn over 60,000 main street businesses including 2,000 farm implement dealers, and 403 primarily rural banks were closed, while the nation witnessed the loss of nearly 650,000 of its farm population. Some farm belt states lost nearly one percent of their farms *each month*, either to foreclosures, forced evictions or outside acquisitions.

Virtually unnoticed but equally alarming was the declining number of black-operated farms which shrank by 57 percent in just one decade, a rate of loss two and one-half times that of white operated farms, leaving black farmers today representing less than two percent of the nation's 2.2 million farmers.

Figures such as these occasioned a senior Farm Credit Association (FCA) official in 1984 to predict that by 1995 two of every three commercial farms (farms with sales in excess of $40,000 per year) then in existence would be absorbed by larger ones. Thus, before long 200,000 farms could well be producing 90 percent of our food and fiber, each farm having annual average sales of $695,000 and assets worth $3.8 million. As recently as 1987, less than 15 percent of the nation's then 2.27 million farms were producing over 75 percent of the gross farm income and realizing over 80 percent of the net farm income from the production of our food and fiber.

In early 1986 the Office of Technology Assessment (OTA) declared that if present trends continue the total number of farms will have declined from 2.2 million in 1982 to 1.2 million in 2000. "The number of small and part-time farms will continue to decline, but will still make up about 80 percent of total farms. The large and very large farms [$200,000 and above in annual sales] will increase substantially in number. *Approximately 50,000 of these largest farms will account for 75 percent of the agricultural production by year 2000.*" (emphasis added) A 1980 USDA study also concluded that by the year 2000 some 50,000 farms will account for over one-half of the nation's farmland.

As farm liquidations, bankruptcies and forced foreclosures bring our "family farm system" of agriculture closer and closer to extinction, the economic concentration of our entire farm and food economy by corporate America both in the United States and abroad continues to accelerate at a rapid pace.

Today, therefore, consumers as well as farmers are faced with a rapidly diminishing number of companies from which to sell or buy their food. Two companies — Cargill and Continental control 50 percent of the world's grain trade. Three corporate giants Iowa Beef Processors, Cargill and ConAgra — slaughter upwards of 80 percent of all our red meat; one company — Campbell's — controls nearly 70 percent of our soup market; four company's — Kellogg's, Philip Morris, General Mills and Quakers Oats — produce nearly 90 percent of all our cold cereal; and one private firm — Southland — controls nearly half of all our convenience food sales.

The dire situation facing thousands of our food producers and their workers who today toil in the fields and sheds of rural America did not, as some politicians and the media often suggest, occur overnight. Rather, America's permanent agricultural crisis stems from two basic long-standing facts:

1) the accelerated erosion and destruction of our nation's rural economy and its "family farm system" of agriculture is the result not of failed programs and policies, but precisely the opposite. It is the result of carefully developed and successfully implemented policies designed by corporate agribusiness to concentrate its own economic power and thereby eliminate from agriculture its abundant and productive human resources, and

2) U.S. farm policy has been based for over a century not on the reality of what was taking place in agriculture and within the national economy, but rather on self-serving, contorted explanations of that reality by various policy planners and implementors who represented an ever-narrowing body of "communities of economic interests."

Consequently, for many decades we have witnessed a wholesale exploitation of our agricultural system by corporate agribusiness and its "communities of economic interests" directed at driving farmers, workers and consumers apart and diverting the taxpayers' attention away from the root causes of the farm crisis.

It has done this by preaching about farming practices and "excessive" government regulations, by creating artificial divisions within the farm community, and by replacing a fair price in the marketplace with an ever-escalating unfair burden of debt.

At the same time, unfortunately, most farmers and consumers have failed to recognize or understand the ulterior motives of such corporate/government/land grant college planning in the past 100 years, and the success of these "communities of economic interests" in obtaining their primary goal — namely, *destroying farmers' economic and political power through forced liquidation caused by enforced low commodity prices.*

By denying farmers a fair price for their work, by robbing them of their equity in the land, by plunging them deeper into debt and by creating a tax system which prevents many individuals from entering farming, this nation's century-old agriculture problem, edges nearer and nearer to a "final solution" as its family farm system comes closer and closer to extinction.

Agribusiness Goes For the SOCOs

To ignore the pivotal role played by particular individuals who are in positions of power is to do violence to historical accuracy. A recognition that

the course of economic events can be influenced by individuals who have the imagination and the power to take advantage of prevailing conditions does not constitute acceptance of a "conspiracy" theory of history.
- John Blair, former Chief Economist, U.S. Senate Subcommittee on Anti-Trust and Monopoly

In any consideration of the plight of the American farmer we cannot merely examine the inefficiencies of concentrated economic power in agriculture. Rather, before we can fully comprehend this 20th century phenomenon called "corporate agribusiness," we must first clearly recognize its three "single overriding corporate objectives" (SOCOs):
1) substituting capital for efficiency and technology for labor,
2) the standardization of our food supply, and
3) the creation of manufactured, synthetic food.

In pursuing each of these objectives, corporate agribusiness has sought to diminish steadily the role of our family farmers in the production of our food, reducing them to a small group of economically and politically impotent raw material producers serving a nationwide food manufacturing system controlled from afar by a select number of giant corporations and economically powerful individuals.

So as agriculture has shifted more and more from a labor intensive to a capital intensive, highly technological system, agribusiness continues to incorporate itself more and more around concentrated economic power. At the same time, however, by promoting and accelerating such a shift, corporate managers have left to the government and the general public the task of paying the high social and environmental costs that have accompanied their efforts.

This book will identify these "communities of economic interests," take a closer look at their motives, analyze their contorted explanations of current conditions, and examine their carefully crafted and implemented policies conceived to concentrate their own economic power while eliminating as many human resources from agriculture as possible.

The Corporate Reapers: The Book of Agribusiness will also seek to expose the manner in which corporate agribusiness has diverted public attention from the real, continuing and fundamental issues of U.S. farm policy and show how so many of our nation's farmers and consumers have failed to recognize, understand and counteract such diversionary tactics.

Identifying and Understanding the Family Farm Myth

Farmers, consumers, labor and business have always had a very real interest in agriculture. For most consumers, however, that interest has seldom been expressed in concrete action, except when confronted with matters concerning health, cleanliness or excessive price increases.

Farmers and labor, however, in their never-ending struggle to organize and promote beneficial societal change, have exhibited varying degrees of mutual and

self-serving interests. The fact that farmers, consumers and labor have not consistently collaborated and acted in the pursuit of their common interests is one of U.S. agriculture's enduring tragedies and has unfortunately in recent history led to a patchwork and often conflicting series of public policy initiatives.

At the same time corporate America, has increasingly come to see agribusiness as one of its own most important vested interests and has fashioned its usual *status quo* policies accordingly.

As Professor Heffernan reminds us:

As the agribusiness organizations, including banks, with which commercial farmers interact to obtain supplies and markets for their products gain a disproportionate share of the power in the relationship, they do not necessarily use it to maximize profits. More often they use the power to enlarge their share of the market or gain more control of other parts of their economic, social and political environment to assure survival of the organization.

Meanwhile, the farmers' plight has been marked by the never-ending struggle to maintain a reasonable and fair degree of their economic and political power, a power which for decades they have seen being systematically stripped from them.

Historically, Americans have tended to mythologize and romanticize farming as a profession, while often denigrating the farmer as an individual. By attempting to capitalize on the "myth as power" concept, many farmers have at the same time unwittingly allowed themselves to become victims of the so-called "family farm" myth. In unmasking such a myth consider the thesis stated in Ingolf Voegler's excellent book, *The Myth of the Family Farm: Agribusiness Dominance of U.S. Agriculture*:

The conventional account of contemporary U.S. agriculture is widely accepted because it is based on the national ideal of the family farm derived from the Jeffersonian concept of agrarian democracy and from a small amount of truth. *When a myth is widely accepted, this small amount of truth is perceived as the whole truth!* (emphasis added)

Voegler further suggests that the "family farm" myth so persistently perpetuated by corporate agribusiness, is avidly supported by four other myths: the work ethic myth, the free enterprise myth, the efficiency myth and the equal opportunity myth.

Together these myths have come to form the basis of what many in agriculture call "conventional wisdom." Such so-called wisdom thus holds that family farmers operate in an economic system that is both moral and one that rewards individual initiative and effort.

At the same time, these identical myths also make family farmers susceptible to (and firm believers in) agricultural programs, services, technologies and research that promote "efficient," business-like farm

Chapter One

Where Have All the Farmers Gone

"I always preached to the kids that if you had a dream, you go for it and you don't let your dream die, but my dreams are dying."

Cathy Langer's tearful confession to a national TV audience in February 1986 was only one among many of those farm family voices that were heard throughout the 1980s.

The Eberle, Iowa farm wife, mother of three boys, was not alone in seeing her dreams die. If one listened closely to her lament one would have also heard the sounds of the widespread suffering that echoed throughout the decade from the plains, valleys and hills of rural America.

Characterized by a depressive price, and compounded by a near catastrophic weather drought, the 1980s saw the latest chapter in "America's permanent agricultural crisis" unprecedentedly splayed out before a sympathetic, but quiescent public. Meanwhile, the politicians and economists endlessly came and went, praising "free markets," "federalized farming," and "bigness."

Yet, as the disastrous decade drew to a close these same "communities of economic interests" were still seeking to prop up the nation's fragile farm economy by methods based on disproven theoretical economic and political flotsam.

"The recovery in agriculture is really non-existent," according to National Farmers Union (NFU) president Leland Swenson. Farmers "are unable to look at sound financing or a fair market price as a mechanism" to keep themselves afloat. "They are," he adds, "really forced to use every tool of the farm program, and to me that is not economic recovery."[1]

By repeatedly pointing to improvements in net farm income, corporate agribusiness apologists conveniently ignore the fact that such income was coming not from fair farm prices in the marketplace, but out of the taxpayer's pockets. In fact, a 1987 Council of Economic Advisers study pointed out that then current programs which cost consumers and taxpayers $25.2 billion actually yielded only $20 billion to producers.[2]

Further, in boasting about the increasing volume of agricultural exports, corporate agribusiness overlooks the fact that the dollar value of such exports has been decreasing. If, for example, one subtracts Export Enhancement Program (EEP) "subsidies," the decline in the export dollar value between 1985 and 1988 alone was 12 percent.[3] The EEP enables private exporters to sell grain abroad at prices lower than otherwise would be charged while collecting a "bonus" from the federal government to make up the difference in price.

Shoveling all of corporate agribusiness' furbelows aside, however, the 1980s was significant because the plight of rural America was laid bare; even more importantly, the decade was a testament to failed public policies that created what Prairiefire, the Des Moines, Iowa research and advocacy organization, termed "an entire class of 'new poor' — once modestly prosperous and exceptionally productive rural residents who now find themselves without food, without work, and without homes."

"Rural homelessness," according to Bill Faith, director of the Ohio Coalition for the Homeless, "is growing faster than we can keep track of it." Margaret Ann Sweet, a Charlotte, Michigan psychologist who counsels homeless people, adds, "They try to keep it secret as long as they can. Some are ashamed to tell their friends they've lost their farm. Owning land and working hard to keep it is central to self-esteem here."[4]

For those who managed to survive, 1986 figures alone show that in the previous ten years median family income had dropped ten percent in rural areas as compared to a one percent decline in urban areas.[5] In addition, it has been estimated that half of all farm households depend mainly on off-farm income for family living expenses, while two-fifths depend primarily on farm income.[6]

The federal government's "recovery" figures are deceptive. For example, it was reported that in Iowa in 1988 the state's per capita personal income was up 3.4 percent. However, the national growth rate was 6.2 percent. In addition, a more careful breakdown of those figures shows that the income of those Iowans not engaged in agriculture rose 6.6 percent while the per capita personal income of farmers fell 34 percent from the previous year.[7] In 1986 the USDA reported that one third of all farm households fell below the poverty level. In what *Newsweek* has called "America's Third World," median rural income is 73 percent of the median urban income. As nearly one fourth of all rural children now live in poverty the "legacy of poverty" is passed on to still one more generation.

Is it no wonder that Rural Voice, a non-profit group headed by Senator Patrick Leahy, D-Vt., found that three out of every five rural U.S. residents in 1988 feared that the lifestyle they loved and valued would soon disappear.[8]

Watching Lives Being Stripped Away

"The crops we grew last summer weren't enough to pay the loan
Couldn't buy the seed to plant this spring and the Farmers Bank foreclosed
Called my old friend Schepman up to auction off the land
He said John it's just my job and I hope you understand
Hey calling it your job of hoss sure don't make it right
But if you want me to I'll say a prayer for your soul tonight
And grandma's on the front porch swing with a Bible in her hand
Sometimes I hear her singing 'Take me to the Promised Land'
When you take away a man's dignity he can't work his fields and cows
There'll be blood on the scarecrow, blood on the plow
Blood on the scarecrow, blood on the plow"

-John Cougar Mellencamp/George M. Green,
Rain on the Scarecrow
© 1985 John Mellencamp

Near the northern Iowa farming community of Dunk-erton, only a few miles from the Minnesota border, a mailbox with the name "Gilbert Ivy" stands forlorn alongside a seldom-traveled gravel road which skirts a now dirty-white farm house, a weather-worn red barn, an old windmill and a huge cottonwood tree. For all too many of our nation's farmers that lone mailbox in the midst of America's heartland became in the decade of the eighties a prophetic landmark.

In reality "Gilbert and Jewel Ivy" were a young married couple on celluloid, sensitively portrayed by Sam Shepherd and Jessica Lange in the critically-acclaimed film "Country."

For many Americans, however, the Ivys' fictional plight mirrored the real suffering of the thousands of farm families seeking to cope daily with marital stress, suicide, child abuse and family drinking problems, while at the same time attempting to hold on to their two most precious assets — their human dignity and for many their generations-old, debt-plagued family farm.

Driving but a few miles from the "Gilbert Ivy" farm one could see the story of "Country" played out with frightening realism on an almost daily basis. Within five miles of the "Ivys," for example, three families were forced to leave their farms in the months immediately after the film's release, another nearby farmer was divorced and another, after failing to get refinancing help for his homestead, "went out and shot himself." Jerome Nie, who lived in nearby Jessup and served as one of the movie's consultants, was forced to sell his dairy operation. In an almost exact repeat of an episode from "Country," Nie and his wife, Toni, after returning home one cold Saturday (during the filming of the movie), found that 70 of their hogs had been trucked off, reclaimed by a Waterloo bank.

But stories such as these were the rule rather than the exception throughout rural America. As Lange, who was herself raised and still owns a farm in the area, told a 1985 Congressional committee hearing in emotional testimony, "I've spent countless hours talking with farmers about the effects of low crop prices and plummeting land values and they are being made to feel and made to believe they have failed; failed their families, their heritage, their country, and that they have failed their land. . . It is heartbreaking to witness their anguish as they watch their lives being stripped away."[9]

Describing America's permanent agricultural crisis as "a question of values," Lange questioned the Congressional panel: "Are we willing to allow the last remnants of our heritage to disappear or worse to see it systematically eradicated by an economic power structure that views small farming as obsolete?"

Another witness, actress Sissy Spacek, who starred in yet another farm movie, "The River," and with her husband owns a Charlottesville, Virginia farm, warned the panel: "If we think this catastrophe affects only the farmer, we are dangerously naive . . . the drugstore, the implement dealer, the grocery store and the bank in every agricultural community in this country is in trouble and that trouble arrives in the cities when homeless farmers with their wives and children come to town to look for a job."

And, she added, "we have a responsibility to ensure that our farmers make not only a fair living, but can afford to put back into the soil what they take out."[10] Throughout the nation during the 1980s agricultural extension offices reported increasing numbers of farm families seeking help in coping with the stress of keeping family, farm and hearth together. That struggle's effects on the younger generation was also crucial as described in *The Wall Street Journal*: "The tranquility of rural life is vanishing, and countless farm children now are growing up in the atmosphere of constant worry, hopelessness, alienation or outright fear."

"It's scary to see your folks scared," is the way Kristy Miller, an Ogden, Iowa 15-year old summed it up.[11]

Joan Blundall, a Northwest Iowa human development specialist, who has counseled hundreds of farm families in coping with the trauma of structured stress in recent years, tells of the fearful young children she has seen who refuse to board the school bus in the morning scared that one day they will get off that bus after school and find their parents have been herded away just the way their pet animals previously were.

As Prairiefire's David Ostendorf points out, "the fact is that people are not only losing their livelihoods, they're also losing generational ties to the past and generational possibilities for the future. It's always been a tradition that land and farming are passed on through the generations, and that kind of tradition is rapidly being broken as a result of this crisis."[12]

Blundall agrees, but quickly adds,

We've got to stop using the word crisis. It's cruel. Crisis by definition is short and intense, and you know as well as I do that there's nothing short-term about what we're facing. The families and the neighbors that we deal with have been in a condition of chronic stress and pain and grief for four or five years. So, I don't talk about the farm crisis. I talk about the rural condition and the problems it brings and the strategies that we've got to create in counseling farm families and the people so that they can start rebuilding.

Farm families, she continues, view their loss, or their anticipated loss, very personally.

They are breaking a generational trust, losing a valued possession which has been an integral part of the family. This sense of loss is complex for it is a loss of one's history, one's present, and one's future. During the grieving process, the meaning and value of life is called into question primarily because of the discrepancy between one's hopes/expectations and between the course of actual events.

There is a loss of confidence in the predictability and stability of the environment. The grief tends to be cyclical rather than linear, since before the grief process is completed, a new grief must be dealt with. Loss of machinery, land, operation, small business, church, school, neighbors are griefs that continue. For some families, there has been grieving for four or five years. In these instances of prolonged grief there is little energy to focus on recovery.[13]

Funded through church and rural advocacy groups and individual donations, some ten states established farm crisis hot lines which sought to help troubled farmers and their families with emotional, financial and legal problems as the economic squeeze on their farms became greater and greater. (In Oklahoma, for example, the state's Community Mental Health Centers report that admissions among farmers in recent years show a 79 percent increase with alcohol-related diagnoses up 143 percent, substance abuse-related diagnoses increasing by 200 percent.)[14]

"Rural people place great value on the idea of self-sufficiency, but now they operate in a framework that is anything but independent," Rural America's George Rucker has noted.[15] Until recently, the Washington, D.C. public interest researcher adds, federal regulation amounted to a low-priced subsidy of power, transportation, telephone and other services, acting often as a form of "social engineering." The Reagan era of deregulation however, began to change the character of that "subsidy" radically.

"The Ears Heard, But it Made No Difference"
In a week when the whole world is shocked and deeply dismayed at the senseless and tragic loss of life in an Oklahoma Post Office, four Oklahoma farmers committed suicide, one of whom killed his wife and two children, and set fire to the house before accomplishing his own death. . . A total of 32 farm-related suicides have occurred in Oklahoma since November, 1985. The stress increases.

- Dr. Max E. Glenn, Executive Director, Oklahoma Conference of Churches, September 2, 1986.

Most of our people go through the standard depression curve," is the way Rev. Tom Hotle, pastor of the Odebolt, Iowa Methodist Church, describes it:

The first step is that it can't happen to me because I've been told that if I work hard and am honest I'll make it. Then comes the thought that I haven't been working hard enough and so I try to work harder. Then comes anger. Then the loss of self-esteem, the feeling of no self-worth.

Our people feel threatened because their way of life is threatened and that's what they are trying to preserve. We tell them they're the same person, that they shouldn't tie their self-esteem to their economic circumstances.[16]

Washington Post reporter Paul Hendrickson vividly described how one community sought to cope with this threat to their self-esteem.

This past March [1985], in a place called Strawberry Point [Iowa] (population 1463), men with mud on their boots sat in St. Mary's Catholic Church and wrote names on small pieces of paper. Maybe it was the name of the person in the Federal Land Bank who killed their loan. Maybe it was the auctioneer who sold off the family possessions as if they were bingo cards. Maybe it was the smart-ass from John Deere who had said, sorry, this time he'd just have to have cash. How are you supposed to get your corn in when they won't give you credit?

One by one, these proud, humiliated men got up from their pews and walked to the altar and deposited their slips of paper into a coffee can wrapped in tinfoil. Then they sat it on fire. What they were trying to do was burn away their bitterness and anger before something worse happened. Yes, it was symbolism, but it was also an expression of community grief. The priest who ran it said it was an effort to find a spiritual dimension to so much suffering and loss.[17]

For some, like Dale Burr, the pressure became too much.

When Hills, Iowa banker John Hughes was being buried just before the Christmas holiday in 1985 after being shot by Burr, a debt-plagued local farmer who had also killed his wife, his neighbor and then himself, a local minister, Rev. Henry Greiner asked that "the cries of those who till the soil and feed the nation be heard. We ask that the sounds of these shots, so desperate and so insane, will rouse the conscience of this nation."[18]

Ms. Blundall tells of one farmer with a sick wife who called the Service's Ft. Dodge office. "Someone had suggested they get a divorce, then her medical bills would be taken care of and he wouldn't lose the farm. He said to me, 'Joan, there's another solution. I could blow my head off.'"[19]

One study in 1985 estimated that the current suicide rate was 30 to 40 percent higher among farmers than non-farmers. "When you get two or three suicides in one year in a small area, as far as I'm concerned, that's an epidemic," observed one mental health worker.[20]

A more recent five-state study by the Minnesota Center for Health Statistics updating suicide data for Minnesota, Montana, the Dakotas and Wisconsin, revealed according to the Center's director Paul Gunderson, "in each state, the suicide rates were more elevated than I would have expected them to be. We had not gathered suicide data since 1985 and were under the impression that conditions had improved."

Montana showed the highest suicide rate — 65 per 100,000 farmers — compared with the average of 10 to 11 per 100,000 for the general population in the five-state survey. Wisconsin had the second highest rate of 59 per 100,000. Of the 499 farm-related suicides during the 1986-1988 study period, 60 percent were farmers.

Blundall adds, "People feel they don't matter anymore. There is loose in the land a feeling of expendability. As one farmer told me, 'the earth is bleeding and I can't stop the hemorrhaging.' "It's as if we spoke and there were no ears to hear us. Or maybe worse: The ears heard, but it made no difference."

The Killing of Our Rural Communities

Not only have individual lives been stripped away, but entire rural communities are disappearing. The number of U.S. farms have declined from 6.8 million in 1935 to under 2.1 million in 1989. The years 1985-1986 alone saw the loss of over 112,000 farms.[21] A 1990 report by the USDA and the Department of Commerce reveals that the nation's farm population numbered 4.80 million, a 30 percent drop from 1980. Average population losses in the 1980s were about 2.5 percent annually. In 1987 alone 240,000 people left the land.[22] Census analysts have pointed out, however, that these dramatic declines in the nation's farm population resulted from "significant losses" of 16 percent each in farm populations of the South and West. Because the USDA has determined that in the 1980s 60 percent of the nation's financially troubled farms were in the Midwest, it has been predicted that there will be still further dramatic declines in the farm population in that region.[23]

In addition the Census Bureau notes that approximately three percent of the nation's farm residents were black, a drop of 94,000 alone between 1980 and 1984, with 99 percent of these people living in the South.[24] Three of five farm residents in the West were Hispanic.[25] According to the Department of Agriculture and the U.S. Civil Rights Commission a variety of historical and economic factors have significantly contributed to this mass exodus of black farmers from the South. They include:

• Black farmers in the South have traditionally been forced onto unproductive land because of discrimination, while white farmers have received the choice parcels.

• Black farmers often grow crops such as tobacco that are poor money producers.

• Black farmers generally have had only small plots of land, which limits the versatility they can bring to agriculture. An average black-operated farm has only about 100 acres compared with the national average of 400 acres.

• Black farmers are generally older and have little formal education. Many of the younger blacks in rural areas have been leaving their communities and seeking work in higher-paying urban jobs.[26]

Current USDA figures show that counties in the Midwest and Great Plains that are today most dependent on farming are also ones where farmland values declined during the eighties most sharply and prices for major agricultural commodities were the most depressed.[27] Such conditions assuredly meant more people leaving those counties in search of jobs elsewhere.

The Census Bureau, for example, has reported that in 1984 the South, traditionally the lowest-income section of the country, climbed past the Midwest in average after-tax household income. Contrasting 1987 median family income by regions shows not only regional differences but the economic gap between while and blacks in the United States.

Region	White Median Income	Black Median Income
Northeast	$35,262	$20,678
Midwest	$32,149	$16,755
South	$30,729	$17,302
West	$32,521	$20,627

Source: U.S. Census Bureau, Labor Dept.

In 1950 more than 2,000 counties had agriculture as their main source of income, but by the mid-1970s that number had dropped to 700 and today, according to figures developed by the Council of State Planning Agencies, only 19 counties nationwide have half or more of their residents working in agriculture.[28] USDA demographer Calvin L. Beale points out that since 1980 "solid blocks" of declining-population counties have shown up in central Iowa, northern Missouri, and across central Illinois into Indiana. Beale observes:

The more sparsely settled areas in the Plains states have held up best in the 1980-1983 period. But a lot depends on what an area had in the first place. If there is no hospital, no public support systems of that sort, people learn to go elsewhere for that kind of help. But when a county changes visibly, there is more of a sense of crisis and deprivation — more so than in a county that started with little.

He adds,

Once those leaving the land were tenant farmers, the smaller operators. Today, it's often the larger farmers, the main-line operators, well-educated pillars of the community, everyone's hard-working models. And the financial institutions are in trouble too this time, making the sense of crisis very real.[29]

One survey by *USA Today* showed that at least 15 Western and Midwestern states took in less money in 1985 than they expected and 17 states in fiscal year 1986 found it necessary to impose substantial spending cuts to avoid deficits.[30] One state, Oklahoma, found itself the victim of a "double whammy" as drastically reduced world oil prices and an already sagging farm economy contributed to what one state official called a "collective depression."[31]

As farmers go out of business so do local suppliers, implement dealers and town businesses (it has been estimated that for every six farmers that fail, one local business also disappears). Tax bases and public services vanish. Since 1981 nearly 2,000 farm implement dealerships have shut down throughout the United States and 56 percent of the unionized agricultural implement worker jobs have been eliminated.[32] "When you go into an area predominantly agricultural and a number of farms are failing so are the peripheral businesses," points out Don Buckner, head of Minnesota's $1.2 million retraining program. "So we are finding ourselves trying to find jobs for farmers where high unemployment already exists."[33] One 1984 Nebraska study estimated that farm towns with populations under 500 are now an endangered species.[34]

In 1986, a Senate Intergovernmental Relations subcommittee issued a report concluding that a permanent change in the quality of rural life in America had taken place. After studying the affects of the farm crisis on rural communities in six midwestern states plus Montana and Arkansas, it showed declining farm income and plummeting land values had put these areas in a worsening financial bind which the study concluded would inevitably lead to higher taxes and reduced services.

"Hard times are passed around in a rural community," is the way Washington, Iowa farmer Bruce Campbell describes it, "and it will affect the whole United States. They just don't know it yet."

The Senate subcommittee's study also pointed out that the $146 billion farm land-value fall between 1982 and 1985 was the equivalent to the total assets of 11 major U.S. corporations, including International Business Machines, General Electric, Kodak, and McDonald's. While federal aid to local governments rose slightly between 1982 and 1984, it declined 18 percent in agriculturally dependent areas.

Meanwhile, tax delinquencies multiplied sevenfold in Nebraska rural areas and more than doubled in the areas the study surveyed in Iowa, Kansas, Minnesota and Montana.

Prospects for a positive turnaround, the report added, were remote because of Reagan administration cutbacks in federal and state aid that traditionally had buttressed development and service programs in agricultural areas. If left unchecked America's permanent agricultural crisis "has the potential to seriously — and in some cases permanently — undermine the fiscal foundations of many rural communities."[35]

Prior to the passage of the 1985 Farm Bill a study conducted by the Food and Agricultural Policy Research Institute (FAPRI) at the University of Missouri and Iowa State University forecast that American farmers faced at least six more years of economic hardships if prevailing government policies were to continue, and that matters would become even worse if the changes in farm policy proposed at the time by the Reagan administration were adopted.[36]

Subsequent developments show that this grim account actually understated the situation. Faced with economic disaster many small farm towns have formed economic development commissions in an effort to recruit outside industry by boasting of low taxes, central location and a dedicated and ample supply of labor, many of them farmers who have lost their farms. Rural economists, however, note that there are simply not enough new businesses to go around.

The Midwestern states are not alone in their crisis. The Southern Growth Policies Board also reports that rural Southern towns are "finding that the farm crisis has reached beyond fields and barns to nearby hardware, clothing and implement stores. Banks are squeezed, schools are consolidating, and homes are up for sale as the rural economy suffers . . ."[37] Even more serious is a 1986 Ford Foundation-sponsored study commission report which describes the situation in the South as "ominous." It sees two souths — one of sparkling "urban showcases" like Atlanta, Georgia and Charlotte, North Carolina and the other south of dirt-poor towns and rural areas that have slid into Depression-like conditions. "For a majority of counties in the rural South — especially those far removed from a city and without access to an interstate highway — the economic forecast is dark and growing darker," the study concluded. "A rural version of our inner cities, bereft and abandoned," is the way George Autry, president of MDC Inc. of Chapel Hill, North Carolina, the non-profit research firm which conducted the study, describes these rural counties.

Haley Blanchard, a job training director for the South Georgia Planning and Development Commission, points out, that in Georgia, three-fourths of all new jobs created since 1981 have been in Atlanta. "If you take Atlanta out of Georgia, you have what amounts to a Third World country in some areas."[38]

What also saddens so many in rural America today is the future of their communities as represented by the disappearance of the young. Max Miller, a store owner in Canova, South Dakota, laments, "our church has no children anymore — none. When I was growing up, there were 100 kids at Sunday school." Today, the town's high school has just 28 students, seven below the minimum required for state funding. When the school's principal dared to raise the issue of closing the school, the school board suspended her.[39]

Medical and hospital care throughout rural America have also reached crisis proportions. Between 1980 and 1989 some 206 rural hospitals have been closed, 43 alone in 1988. It has been estimated that by the middle of the 1990s another 600 rural hospitals will have closed their doors.[40]

Watching States Die

By 1987 U.S. Senator from Iowa, Tom Harkin, saw his state "dying. We are literally dying. In the first six years of the Great Depression, Iowa lost 7.8 percent of its farmers. In 1985 we lost ten percent."[41] Between 1979 and 1987 the state's commerce declined nearly 20 percent, dragging down state tax revenues to the point that in 1985 Governor Terry Branstad ordered a 3.9 percent reduction in all state spending programs.[42]

Iowa state's demographer, James Taylor, reported that 120,000 more people left Iowa than entered it from 1980 through 1984, a decline of over four percent. In 1985 the rate increased with 34,000 more people leaving than settling in the state. In the 1980s in rural Iowa 35 percent of the gas stations and 20 percent of the grocery stores closed and since 1970 the state's rural school enrollment had dropped 49 percent.[43] Four out of five young people who graduated from Iowa's universities in 1986 indicated they were not considering the state for possible future job opportunities.[44]

Nebraska economists believe that some ten percent of that state's farmers will soon disappear. "It all ripples out through the rural community. It is a scenario for some major depopulation," declares agricultural economist Bruce Johnson. "Do we want that to happen? Is one farm operation per township what we really want? These questions simply aren't being asked. But it is much broader than the future of the family farm. The fact of rural America and the maintenance of a diverse setting is what we are talking about. We're now seeing a time of more structural change than anything in the last 50 years."[45]

Larry Swanson, former director of the Center for Great Plains Studies at the University of Nebraska in Lincoln, Paul Lasley, a rural sociologist at Iowa State University, Bishop Dingman and David Ostendorf, also remind us of some of the other dimensions to rural America's present depopulation crisis.

"If this continues," Swanson notes, "over the next ten years, we've effectively killed our rural communities. There's really no turning around. I don't know what we're gaining, but it isn't efficiency." And Lasley adds, "the other side of that is the resettlement issue — absorption of the displaced. Where do they go and what is society's capacity to absorb them? How do we deal with the psychological problems of rural people being uprooted."[46]

"Rural communities are important for the democratic future of our country," Bishop Dingman stresses, "rural interdependence gives us a rich plurality of social institutions, enhancing personal freedom and contributing to the vitality of rural communities."[47]

And Ostendorf concludes:

The issue we face in the heartland is essentially the "Central Americanization" of America. The same framework of land and resource control that was constructed in many Third World countries — high levels of concentration of control by corporate and financial interests — is being constructed here in the United States.

The farm crisis of the eighties is going to be the food crisis of the nineties. As that kind of concentration is manifested, a handful of corporate interests in this country will be able to overtake the food production and distribution system, which is already beginning. Major corporations are locking up control over key sectors of the food economy, and as that continues the possibility for those interests to get control of food from the ground to the grocery store is very strong. And the consumer and the poor are going to pay the price for it in the next 10 to 20 years. Some of our most productive agricultural counties in the country have poverty levels of 70 percent.[48]

It's a Homestead! It's a Ranch!! It's Super-Farm!!!

Tenneco Unit Sale To Castle & Cooke
Special to The New York Times

LOS ANGELES, Sept. 23 — In a move to broaden its line of foods and bolster its holdings in California real estate, Castle & Cooke Inc. said it would acquire substantially all of the operations of Tenneco West, Inc., a subsidiary of Tenneco, Inc. of Houston for $238 million in cash and debt. The sale includes 40,000 acres of farmland and home sites. The profitable unit generated $350 million in revenue last year. Tenneco would retain mineral rights on the land and would keep 270,000 acres of leased farmland in California and Arizona.

Indeed, as Ostendorf and others have been repeatedly warning us, the structure of American agriculture shows that fewer and fewer farms are dominating our rural economy (See Chart 1A).

The aforementioned 1986 OTA study projects that this changing structure of agriculture will result in approximately 1.2 million farms by the turn of the century with small and part time farms making up nearly 80 percent of the total while some 50,000 super-sized farms will account for 75 percent of all agricultural production by the year 2000.[49]

Such economic concentration, or what former Agriculture Secretary John Block euphemistically called "contraction," already sees today 1.5 percent of the nation's farms, according to the USDA, producing almost 38 of the total farm cash receipts. And over ten percent of those 346,000 farms are operated by hired managers. Nearly 14 percent of our super-farms are now being operated by hired managers.

An even more revealing study, this one in the May 1989 issue of *Successful Farming* shows that the 100 largest farms in America (based on gross sales) account for over 10 percent — $16.7 billion — of the country's gross farm sales. (See Appendix C)

It is no surprise to learn that between 1984 and 1987 farms under professional management rose from 72,000 to 108,000 and between 1969 and 1985 alone

Chart 1A: Structure of American Agriculture

Annual Sales	Number of Farms (thsnds.)	[% of All Farm	Average Levels for 1983-1987] % of Direct Govt. Pay- ments	% Gross U.S. Farm Sales	% of Net Cash Income Land	[1986] % of Acres	Average Size
Less than $40,000	1,635	72.0	15.0	10.1	1.0	30.1	258
$40,000-$99,999	321	14.1	23.9	14.9	13.3	20.4	702
$100,000-$249,999	218	9.6	32.9	24.1	25.6	25.8	1,238
$250,000-$499,999	72	3.2	18.0	18.1	32.8	23.7[a]	2,507[a]
$500,000 plus	27	1.2	10.1	32.8	38.5		
More than $100,000	317	14.0	61.0	75.0	85.7	49.5	1,873
All Farms	**2,272**	**100**	**100**	**100**	**100**	**100**	

a=Farms with Annual Sales of $250,000 plus

Source: Economic Research Service, USDA, *Economic Indicators of the Farm Sector, National Financial Summary,* 1987 and USDA Agricultural Statistics, 1986.

farms in the $500,000-plus sales class increased from approximately 4,000 to 32,000.[50]

By contrast, what has always been considered the cornerstone of our "family farm system," the $10,000 to $100,000 sales class, accounted for over 40 percent of our farms, but only 20 percent of the total farm sales; 85 percent of these farms were operated by farmers who reported farming as their chief occupation. As recently as 1974, this class comprised 41.3 percent of our commercial farms and had a corresponding 41.6 percent of the total sales.

Examining the "market share" of individual crop sales by the $500,000-plus "super-farms," their dominant role in our present-day farm economy becomes even more apparent. In 1984 these farms reported a 24 percent return on equity while their production expenses amounted to 69 percent of their gross farm income.[51]

Based on 1987 Census of Agriculture figures, the 32,000 U.S. farms with sales of $500,000 or more brought in 38 percent of all farm commodity sales. These same farms, who own about 13 percent of the land, accounted for:
• 70 percent of the vegetable, sweet corn and melon sales;
• 70 percent of nursery and greenhouse sales;
• 60 percent of poultry and poultry product sales;
• 55 percent of fruits, nuts and berries sales;
• 50 percent of cattle and calf sales;
• 38 percent of cotton and cottonseed sales;
• 24 percent of dairy product sales;
• 23 percent of hog and pig sales; and
• nearly 10 percent of all grain sales.

These same farms also accounted for 55 percent of all hired farm labor, 49 percent of the feed grains and 39 percent of all farm expenses. Nearly 17 percent of all these 32,000 farms were in California and reported 74 percent of the agricultural sales in that state.

As the aforementioned OTA study details, we are now seeing the adverse relationship between agricultural structure and the welfare of rural communities, particularly in areas like California, Arizona, Texas, and Florida (CATF) where so many super farms exist today.

Large-scale and very large-scale industrialized agriculture in these communities is strongly associated with high rates of poverty, substandard housing, and exploitative labor practices in the rural communities that provide hired labor for these farms. Very large-scale agriculture has been a strong source of employment in the CATF region for many years, although at very low wage rates. Emerging technologies may reduce the labor requirements throughout much of the CATF region by 2000. Increased unemployment will greatly increase the strain on these communities.[52]

In addition to turning out more than a quarter of the total value of U.S. farm production, this 2.09 percent of our farms now reaps an astounding three-fifths of the U.S. net farm income.[53] From $2.3 billion in 1969, which was 16 percent of the total U.S. net farm income that year, to $14.3 billion in 1982, these super-farms by their ability to amass more production units relative to their expenses continue to gain a more dominant position in U.S. agriculture.

USDA statistics further show that while gross sales of these farms increased from around 20 percent in the mid-1970s to 31 percent in 1985 their share of net farm income rose from about 25 percent to over 50 percent. But even these super-farms have an elite class, the one out of every 250 U.S. farms which are one-million dollar a year operations. In addition to taking in more than $1 of every $5 of farm receipts they control about 47 million acres of land and $52 billion worth of assets. Between

1978 and 1982, according to USDA economist Paul Velde of the Economic Research Service (ERS), their numbers increased nearly 50 percent from 6,290 to 9,190 farms. Half of this growth, he points out, came from inflation, but the remainder came from increased sales volume, new investment and expansion.

Not necessarily large in terms of acreage, one third of them have less than the U.S. average of 440 acres. Usually, these farms specialize in livestock, poultry, or egg production and other high value crops such as oranges, grapes, and commercial flowers. California's 2,398 such sized farms, one-fourth of the total number, led the nation with Florida (643) and Texas (618) in second and third position.[54]

Paying off the Welfare Queens

When pretending he believed in Reaganomics, ex-Office of Management and Budget (OMB) director David Stockman frequently railed about "over-investment" in agriculture while describing farmers "as the one group that has the least claim on the budget."

Luther Tweeten, Oklahoma State agricultural economist and a long-time staunch defender of the corporate reapers also frequently laments a "federal budget out of control."

What both men are attacking is one of the family farm system's last lifelines — federal subsidies.

Subsidies, usually in the form of deficiency payments, are frequently the center of controversy and the subject around which so much farm legislation revolves. When Reagan, Stockman, Tweeten, *et al.* denounce government's role in agriculture and extol their "market-oriented" agricultural policy, they are in effect calling for termination of the very Federal programs which were originally designed, but for over half of a century have struggled, often vainly, to maintain some form of an economic equilibrium in agriculture.

Deficiency payments, supposedly limited by Congress to $50,000 per farmer, go to wheat, feed grain, rice and cotton farmers who agree to take part in federal-control programs. After the USDA sets a target price for a certain crop a farmer is eligible for a federal loan on his crop. If market prices do not reach the loan price the farmer usually lets the government take the grain as payment for the loan. At the end of the year, the government will pay the farmer the difference between the target price and the loan price in the form of a "deficiency payment."

Farmers are eligible to take out loans on their crops, based on the rate set by Congress, and at the end of the year if the market price is above the loan rate, reclaim their collateral, repay the loan and interest and sell the crop on the open market. If the market price is below that of the loan price the farmer can simply forfeit the crop to the government. While most farmers would prefer earned income to a government subsidy, many agree with Senator John Melcher, D-Mont., when he reflects that "I have a problem with the whole scheme. Why do we have a program that pays farmers in lieu of getting a price from the marketplace? The only reason I vote for these things is to keep going until we come to

our senses in this country. Why don't we find other mechanisms?"[55]

During the debate on the 1985 farm bill, Senators David Pryor, D-Ark., and David Boren, D-Okla., illustrated just how inadequate the government's deficiency payment scheme has become:

> Deficiency payments make up some of the difference between the market price and the farmer's cost of production. *They don't give the farmer a profit or an income.*
>
> Using USDA figures and projecting the results under the bill now before the Senate, the average 600-acre family wheat farm would receive $27,800 in deficiency payments, but would average *only* $7,646 in *net income* for the family. This represents the total payment for the labor of the *entire* family for a year and *total* return on an investment of an average of $500,000. (emphasis added)[56]

By contrast, many large farms mine the Federal treasury for hundreds of thousands of dollars from such "income-support" payments. Provisions in the 1985 Farm Bill also made it easier for what Robert Thompson, former Assistant Secretary of Agriculture for Economics, described as "the welfare queens of 1987" to receive even more lucrative subsidies out of the U.S. treasury.[57]

In 1986 the GAO reported that the wealthiest four percent of U.S. farms — with sales over $250,000 — received more than a third of the government's largesse while the small farmer — with sales under $40,000 — saw only six percent of the loans.[58]

In 1987 the USDA reported that farms with sales of $500,000 plus and which had 15 percent of the total sales in the major commodities received ten percent of the government's record $16.7 billion in direct payments. Meanwhile, farms in the $10,000 to $39,999 sales category, who had seven percent of the total sales in major commodities, received 8.9 percent of the government's total payments.

Farms who were in USDA's "favorable financial position" received 62.6 percent of the government's total payments in 1987 while 10.3 percent of the "marginal income," 20.4 percent of the "marginal solvency," and 6.6 percent of the "vulnerable" farms received the remaining government payments.

USDA's Thompson has pointed out that the programs Congress fashioned in 1985 "opened more loopholes" in the $50,000 payment limitation and allowed many farmers to receive $1 million or more in direct subsidies. The same person can qualify for multiple benefits by entering more than one farming unit in the program.[59] By way of illustration two farmers could each qualify for a $50,000 subsidy on their farm, then form a corporation and participate in it as partners, each collecting $50,000.

"Million-dollar-plus cotton and rice payments will be significant," Thompson observed after passage of the bill. "There will be a small handful of wheat and feed-grain producers in the $1 million range, but payments of

$150,000 to $200,000 will not be uncommon in wheat and feed-grains. It will get obscene."[60]

Take for example, the Future Farmers of America (FFA) chapter at a rural high school in Princeton, California. In 1984 its members collected $7,087 in Federal subsidies. FFA was only one of 56 "tenants" of the Zumwalt Farms Inc. of Colusa, California. This 16,000 acre rice farm earned $3,540 from the Princeton High student's 60-acre enterprise, while collecting a total of nearly $750,000 from its other "tenants." Even though current law limits subsidy payments to $50,000 the USDA interprets the statute as limiting only the partnership from receiving more than $50,000, not each individual entity. In 1986 Zumwalt received $2.3 million in subsidies through the 68 individuals and small corporations that grow rice on its properties.[61]

In Arkansas a spot check by the GAO revealed that reorganizations of farms had increased by 50 percent in two rice-growing counties. In a Kansas wheat county some farms split into 15 or 20 units in an effort to gain additional payments and in California, a preliminary survey in 1986 showed that in six of the state's counties $1.3 million in subsidy payments were going to foreign owners.[62]

In 1986 alone 21,000 cotton farmers magically transformed themselves into 95,000 to 120,000 "persons" and collected over $1.5 billion in direct cotton "deficiency payments," not including another $930 million that could well have been lost by the CCC on cotton crop loans when farmers marketed their own cotton and redeemed crop loans at as much as 15 cents a pound below the loan rate. It is further estimated that the top 2,500 cotton farmers received $930 million in 1986 in deficiency payments alone, in addition to $530 million on crop loan redemptions.[63] J.G. Boswell, the nation's largest cotton grower and a perennial recipient of government largesse, may well have reaped in excess of $8.5 million in such cotton payments. ("It is ludicrous to believe that we will be sticking any Government money in our pockets," Boswell company spokesman Walter Brown told *Time Magazine.* "This is survival money.")[64]

Several major cotton merchants, warehouse operators, farmer cooperatives and textile mill operators also enjoyed this bonanza. Just four such entities received over 35 percent of the $728 million that went to these users of cotton in 1986. They included: Dunavant Enterprises of Memphis, Tenn. ($90.2 million); Allenberg Cotton Co. of Memphis, owned by Louis Dreyfus Inc. ($83.6 million); Calcot Ltd., a Bakersfield, California co-op ($54.5 million), and Hohenberg Bros. of Memphis, owned by Cargill Corp., ($28.7 million).[65]

In September 1986 Senator Harkin introduced an amendment in the Senate Appropriations Committee which would have clamped a $50,000 limit on federal subsidy payments to farmers. But Senator Thad Cochran, R-Miss., chairman of the subcommittee on agriculture and related agencies, cast his and seven proxy votes against it, and the measure was defeated by a narrow 12-11 vote.[66]

In the first six years of the Reagan administration, over $85 billion was spent on farm subsidies covering direct loan and payment programs, storage costs and the cost of purchasing dairy products. By 1985, the Federal government owned $6.9 billion worth of farm products, spending $394 million in fiscal 1985 alone to store these commodities.[67] It was estimated by the USDA that about one-fourth of U.S. farmers' net cash income came from government subsidy payments.[68] Seventeen cents of every subsidy dollar went to financially distressed farmers while 32 cents went to farms with sales exceeding $250,000.[69]

Interestingly, recent history reveals that government payments per farm in the Republican years, 1970-72, averaged $1,243, and in 1977-79, under the Democrats, only $850.[70] When the supposedly budget conscious Reagan's four-year farm bill passed in 1981 the projected cost was set at $11 billion. By 1986 that figure was near $63 billion for the prior four year period compared to the $57 billion for the previous 20 years.[71]

Lighting Up the Christmas Tree

Aside from the deficiency payment program, however, there are other subsidies ranging from the lucrative Agricultural Stabilization and Conservation Service (ASCS) land set-aside payments of the late 1960s and early 1970s to the enormously expensive Payment-in-Kind (PIK) programs of the early Reagan administration.

These subsidies in particular have become almost the life blood of the nation's super-farms. Despite the fact that they are repeatedly held up to public scrutiny and decried by politicians, they are allowed to continue dispensing ever more wealth to fewer and fewer farms.

Agricultural subsidies have thus come to play a large role in farm income figures. Based on a 1987 USDA survey of the 1.7 million farms which received $16.7 billion in direct government commodity program payments, figures show that farms with less that $100,000 in annual gross sales, got 32 percent of the Department's program payouts.

Farms in the $40,000 to $100,000 sales class received 21.6 percent of the payments, while farms in the $100,000-$249,999 bracket got 36.3 percent of the payments. Farms in the $250,000-$499,999 sales class got 21 percent, and farms with $500,000 plus got 10.2 percent of the total payments.

In 1982 a Senate Budget Committee study determined that a handful of the nation's largest farmers received disproportionate shares of the government's subsidies, and there were glaring disparities between different crops and regions of the country. Critics of such government largesse point out that because our current federal support program is keyed to production volume instead of the individual farmer's needs for income protection, those who produce the most tend to benefit the most. For example, the average participating corn farmer received $1,333 in federal subsidies while the average rice producer received $11,238 and the cotton farmer took home $7,767. In addition, the average payment to all farmers was $3,297, however, while Maine farmers received $228 on the average. Arizona's large growers received $27,040, nearly 100 times the size of the Maine farmer.

The Senate study also noted that 17 percent of farmers operating on 500 acres or more received 60 percent of these subsidies (Texas receiving slightly more than one-fourth of the total). This same 17 percent also accounted for 60 percent of the production figures included in the government programs. Average payments to farmers with less that 70 acres was $488 while farmers with 2,500 acres or more of cropland received an average of $27,204.[72]

While Federal law stipulates that deficiency payments, a direct subsidy calculated by the complex formula linking market prices with production costs, cannot exceed $50,000 per farmer, and disaster insurance payments, available in areas with no federal crop insurance, cannot be over $100,000, there are many ways for large farmers to circumvent these laws. A 1987 GAO Report reported to Congress that unless USDA closed some legal loopholes, more than $2 billion in unjustified federal subsidies could be dispensed by 1989.[73]

For example, in an effort to tighten the rules governing subsidies Congress has been urged in the past to revised the definition of "person," for while the current law limits direct payments to $50,000 per person, some "innovative individuals," the USDA reports, have found ways "to organize and reorganize in order to increase the number of 'persons'."

USDA payment rolls show that between 1984 and 1986 nearly 9,000 new "people" were "reorganized" and the number of persons receiving deficiency payments at or near the limit went from 4300 in 1983 to 29,000 in 1985.[74]

"Should the trend . . . continue, reorganizations since 1984 could be adding almost $900 million annually to program costs by 1989," according to Brian P. Crowley, a GAO senior associate director. By 1989 it was estimated by this government agency that 31,000 new farming entities alone had been established in a further effort to "farm" federal crop subsidies.[75]

One innovation in this area is the Mississippi Christmas tree, a lawyer's invention that has allowed land owners and farmers to subdivide and reorganize their farms into legal entities and qualify each entity for the maximum payment of $50,000.

Also exempt from the $50,000 limit are stateowned farm operations such as Montana's Department of State Lands (which has received a $912,000 payment), Washington State's Department of Natural Resources ($966,000), University of Arizona ($373,000), Reclamation District No. 108 of Grimes, California ($336,000), and the Texas Department of Corrections ($312,000).[76] Keenly aware that such loopholes in the federal subsidy program exist, a University of Iowa survey of that state's farmers discovered that 84 percent thought that the federal government should stop the abuse of the $50,000 cap by making sure no farms received more than Congress originally intended.[77]

Curiously many of the current critics of the subsidy program blame those very interests who are trying to save the U.S. family farm system of agriculture for the creation of these new "farms.

William Haw, president of the National Farms Inc., a giant hog and cattle producer headquartered in Kansas City, Missouri, is quick to point out that "This is the result of social legislation, not economic legislation and the motives behind it seem to have a welfare orientation rather than a goal of an efficient agricultural industry." And John Marten, a staff economist with *The Farm Journal*, a leading national agricultural publication, underscores Haw's point. "We are seeing shades of old-fashioned populist land reform in a modern setting. The politicians' willingness to spend money for farm programs seems to be centered on the small-farm family and the rural way of life. But the cold, hard facts are that economic reality has marched on beyond the old 160-acre farm."[78]

Some reformers have suggested that farm investors have increased involvement in farm operations so as to qualify for subsidy payments, thus putting more of an emphasis on an individual's financial interest in the farm.[79]

By contrast, the GAO reported that in 1985 foreign investors through ownership of U.S. farmland received more than $7.7 million in subsidies in 401 counties where the bulk of their land holdings are located. West German and Netherlands Antilles investors qualified for 50 percent of the subsidy payments while Swiss and Canadians each claimed almost ten percent while sharerenting their land to U.S. farmers, then dividing the government payments between themselves and their tenants.[80] One such recipient was the crown prince of Liechtenstein, a partner with International Paper Co. in Farms of Texas Co., 76,500 acres of Texas farms and more than 36,000 acres larger than his own country. In 1986, the prince received a $2.2 million subsidy, the largest in the state.[81]

Meanwhile, in a rather macabre twist, the USDA was preparing to confiscate crop subsidies due to nearly 7,000 U.S. farmers who had been judged "terminal credit risks" by the Farmers Home Administration.[82] In addition to foreign operations receiving U.S. agricultural crop subsidies, the GAO in a 1988 study determined that between 1983 and 1987 more than $14 billion in USDA agricultural payments had gone to non-farmers, including grain exporters and storage firms, food processors and railroad and barge lines. Such payments represented from 16 percent to 20 percent of total agricultural subsidy outlay by the federal government. In 1986 and 1987 respectively they totaled $3.9 billion and $3.8 billion.

These payments involved purchases by the government of surplus dairy and processed food products, mostly from commercial food processors, payments to transportation companies to move federally owned commodities, and storage and handling payments to grain elevators and warehouses.[83]

Nevertheless, when it comes to limitations on government farm subsidies USDA records substantiate that the time-honored axiom that where there's a will there's a way is alive and operative in the suites of corporate agribusiness.

As one Iowa farmer observes: "To put it bluntly, if you're not farming the government today, you're not doing a very good job."[84]

Chapter Two

Coporate America's Food Fight: Who Wins? Who Loses? Guess!

"We kill the cow and then wonder why we are not getting any milk even though we have the meat to eat for awhile.

- Robert Mercer
Chairman and Chief Executive Officer,
Goodyear Company.[1]

While thousands of family farmers were either going out of business or facing severe financial hardships in the 1980s, notable events took place in the United States's $240 billion food industry in the Indian summer of 1988, one more chapter in corporate agribusiness's ongoing megabuck food fight.

First, came the news of the unsuccessful $5.03 billion takeover bid of Kroger Co., the nation's second largest supermarket chain, by Kohlberg, Kravis Roberts & Co., the nation's largest leverage buyout firm.

Two years earlier, for $4.2 billion this same New York investment banking firm bought Safeway Stores, the nation's largest supermarket chain. Before that, in 1984, KKR had purchased Beatrice Foods Co., one of the United States's largest food manufacturers, for $6.4 billion and then promptly sold off many of its assets to help pay off its buyout debt and interest obligations. Despite their inability to take over Kroger, it was later learned that following their initial rebuff KKR had nevertheless accumulated a 9.9 percent stake in the Cincinnati-based firm "solely as an investment."[2] In May 1989, it would sell 7.8 million shares of its stock in Kroger's to an unidentified buyer.[3]

But, even while the Kroger-KKR sale was debated, Grand Metropolitan PLC, the world's largest liquor producer and Great Britain's fourth largest company, was bidding $5.23 billion for Pillsbury, the giant Minneapolis food producing company. Although it indicated at the outset that it sought a "friendly" takeover, Pillsbury immediately mounted a defensive recapitalization effort to maintain its independence and further hinted that it might even seek to become a private firm in a leveraged buyout control.[4]

Grand Met quickly retaliated by seeking to enlist the support of Pillsbury's financially troubled Burger King franchisees. By attempting to get them to support the British firm's bid and thereby send a message to Pillsbury shareholders that the company no longer had the support of the franchisees, Grand Met hoped that shareholders would come to see that it was in their best interest to tender their shares to Grand Met.[5]

Pillsbury countered with the threat of "spinning off" its Burger King subsidiary and thereby making it a considerably less attractive takeover target.

While the financial community watched in fascination as these two food giants battled it out, it was further rocked by the news that Philip Morris, with 1987 food, beverage and tobacco sales of $27.7 billion, was offering to buy out Kraft Co. for $11 billion, the second largest takeover attempt to date.

Kraft with 1987 sales in international foods, food service and ingredients, and consumer food products totaling $9.9 billion, initially opposed the Philip Morris offer, but after lengthy negotiations it finally accepted a $13.1 billion bid.* Thus, a company once known only for its tobacco products now became the world's number one consumer products firm, moving ahead of Europe's multinational giant, the Unilever Corp. "People may ultimately stop drinking or smoking, though I don't believe it," declared Hamish Maxwell, Philip Morris' deal-making chairman, "but you can bet your life they will keep on eating."[6]

The size of the Philip Morris acquisition, however, was nearly dwarfed only three days later. In a series of mind-boggling announcements, four members of the management team of RJR Nabisco announced that

---

* People familiar with the situation described both negotiators as "very relaxed," maintaining they "got along very well."

"Serious negotiations began around 10 P.M. Mr. [Hamish] Maxwell's [Philip Morris chairman of the board and CEO] first real offer, according to those at the scene, was $104; Mr. [John M.] Richman [Kraft Inc.'s chairman of the board and CEO] said he thought that $106 was 'more like it.' Mr. Maxwell said $104.50; Mr. Richman stuck to $106. Mr. Maxwell came up $1, to $105.50.

"On the basis of Kraft's 127.4 million shares on a fully diluted basis, even 50 cents would cost Philip Morris another $64 million.

"Mr. Richman held out for the other 50 cents and by 1 A.M. Mr. Maxwell, smiling broadly, stuck out his hand to shake on the deal and said $106... "

-"Kraft Being Sold To Philip Morris For $13.5 Billion," by Robert J. Cole, *The New York Times*, October 31, 1988.

they planned on taking the nation's 19th largest corporation private with a $16.9 billion leveraged buyout. Their offer was immediately topped by KKR with a $20.2 billion bid only to be countermatched by a $20.6 billion bid from a group that included not only RJR Nabisco management's "gang of four," but also a consortium of investment firms led by Shearson Lehman Hutton Inc., the American Express Co. subsidiary. KKR later again topped their bid with a $24.88 billion offer, which in fact was the final sale price.

Amidst all such wheeling and dealing, the public was left to wonder who actually profited and who in the end paid for all these acquisitions, mergers and leveraged buyouts and what effect such transactions would have on their finances, jobs and the food supply.

Making Money the Safeway

After Kohlberg, Kravis, Roberts & Co. managed a $4.1 billion leveraged buyout of Safeway Stores Inc. in 1985 *The Washington Post* graphically illustrated who were the big winners in this major financial transaction. What this chart does not show is that the Safeway buyout probably also cost the American taxpayer more than $100 million in 1987 and could eventually cost them more than $500 million. Former *Forbes* reporter Jonathan Greenberg explains,

In 1985, the last year Safeway was publicly traded, the company paid $28 million in federal taxes on net income of $231 million. In the first nine months of 1987 the new Safeway Stores, despite more than $300 million in operating profits, reported a loss of $103 million.

Under U.S. tax law, a company can deduct interest payments from profits before it pays taxes, and with $4.3 billion in additional debt, Safeway has plenty of interest to pay off. It will probably be ten years before Safeway pays taxes again...

Arguably, those who receive Safeway's interest payments who hold its debt — will eventually have to pay taxes on *their* income, but the typical creditor is generally a financial institution such as a bank or pension fund, which either pays no taxes or has its own tax loopholes... "[7]

Before the KKR-Safeway buyout the Haft family, in only one of their seven unsuccessful corporate takeover transactions, had bought up six percent of the Safeway's stock and then later sold it for $140 million. While many Wall Streeters and others were enriching themselves, Safeway was announcing that it probably would have to close or sell some of its key assets, including some of its most profitable stores, in an effort to raise enough money to use as collateral for the buyer's loan.

One store that was closed was in the Cleveland Park district of the nation's capital. One of its regular customers was political columnist Mary McGrory who pointed out after the closing that the Hafts had not only made off with $140 million, but also made off with her corner grocery store.

This, I am told, is greenmail. Greenmail, my eye. That's blackmail, and I hope that in 1988 we call it that. If the Safeway were a fruitstand and some hood came along and demanded protection money, we'd call the cops. On Wall Street, it's considered 'healthy capitalism.' I don't know if Haft *pere* and *fils* would have stocked Elberta peaches and raspberry vinegar, as I used to ask Wally to do, but I still don't think they should get $140 million for coveting their neighbor's goods and disrupting our lives."[8]

With the first news of the Safeway takeover the United Food and Commercial Workers International Union (UFCW) officials charged that the costly takeover "could likely cost Safeway workers their jobs and their standard of living" and they threatened a boycott and strike if the Company should start laying off employees and closing stores.[9] In fact, after Safeway was bought out it sold or closed more than 1,100 of the 2,400 stores it had previously owned, while laying off thousands of its workers, including the complete dismantling of its Dallas and Salt Lake City divisions.[10]

Parlaying Millions Into Billions

As we witness more and more corporate buyouts and mergers, we must keep in mind the scope of the amounts of money involved in these transactions. KKR's

A LOT OF LETTUCE IN THE SAFEWAY DEAL

Most Profitable U.S. Consumer Food Companies, 1988

Company	3rd Quarter Net Latest Fiscal Year (M)	Operating Pctg. 1987- 1988	Profit of Sales Margin
Kellogg	$3,793.0	21.2%	+22%
Ralston Purina	$5,868.0	16.3%	-12%
H.J. Heinz	$5,244.2	15.7%	+13%
Hershey Foods	$2,433.8	15.0%	+114%
RJR Nabisco	$9,420.0*	13.7%	+11%*
Campbell Soup	$4,868.9	12.7%	+3%
Quaker Oats	$5,329.8	12.0%	+18%
General Mills	$5,178.8	12.0%	+276%
Borden	$6,514.4	11.7%	+16%
Pillsbury	$6,190.6	11.1%	+26%
Kraft	$9,875.7	9.5%	+17%
General Foods (Philip Morris)	$9,946.0	8.1%	+27%*
Sara Lee	$10,423.8	7.7%	+22%
26 Food Firms			+39%
6 Beverage Firms			+16%
3 Tobacco Firms			+20%
490 U.S. Firms			+12%

* = Food Operations Only
+ = Total Company earnings

Source: *The Wall Street Journal*, November 7, 1988.

expectation that they can make them more valuable," according to John Lister, an industry consultant with the New York firm of Lister, Butler Inc.[62] Such product line diversification has its disadvantages. "It seriously discourages product innovation," claims Al Ries, "companies are convinced that the only way to go is to milk existing brand names instead of coming up with something new."[63]

One telling sign of this policy is the fact that in 1988 analysts at Bear, Stearns & Co., Merrill Lynch Capital Markets, Shearson Lehman Hutton Inc. and Dean Witter Reynolds began issuing regular reports providing their customers with the "breakup value" of companies in the food, energy and media industries.[64]

"If you can't eat it, drink it, smoke it or use it in the bathroom, you don't want to own it," explained Steven A. Kroll, president of S.L.H. Asset Management, the $30 billion investment management subsidiary of Shearson Lehman Hutton, Inc.[65]

One sector of the food industry that remains particularly vulnerable to acquisitions and buyouts, however, is the food retailing business. Indeed, industry analysts often refer to the entire food retailing industry as one giant LBO.

Publicly traded megachains with their lower profit margins, steady cash flows, valuable real estate and operations that can easily be split off and sold are ripe acquisition candidates. Corporate bidders today finding particularly alluring the fact that the parts have become worth more than the whole. Chainstore companies are uniquely vulnerable because their shares have been so widely held.

Buying Food From the Corporate Behemoth

Yet, even as this corporate concentration in the food industry continues seemingly unabated.

For consumers, these mergers and acquisitions will mean "an endless elaboration of the sizes and flavors," says Leo Shapiro, a Chicago-based food consultant. "Seeing the same brand over and over means you are shopping for differences that aren't meaningful in stores that are quite sterile."[66]

"When a company as large as Philip Morris buys a company as large as Kraft, it can concentrate on one product, like mayonnaise, and run all the other mayonnaise processors, large and small out of the market," said one Washington-area supermarket executive.[67] Such a development could eventually seriously affect pricing by restricting the availability of items at given outlets. The grocery executive adds, "there is no law that says that a Philip Morris has to sell to a given store."

Such a point was vividly illustrated by financial analyst Stephen Carnes of Piper Jaffray when, in speculating how the Philip Morris buyup of Kraft might effect our future eating habits, he observed that one "could well start with a Miller Lite beer, eat a whole meal, then light up a Marlboro after you get done" and never have to use a product outside the new behemoth."[68]

Or as Michael Pertschuk, former Federal Trade Commission chairman, speculates only half jokingly, the way tobacco companies are accumulating cash and diversifying, "by the year 2000, there will be two consumer goods companies in the United States: RJR Nabisco will be selling all the consumer goods west of the Mississippi, and Philip Morris will be selling all the consumer goods east of the Mississippi."[69]

In this era of multi-billion dollar corporate agribusiness acquisitions and buyouts Pertschuk's words are more than food for thought.

Section One:

Eliminating "Biologic Variables"

"When tractors are as big as barns — their machinery the size of groves. Then might shall have become right ... machines will have won. When there's one yard light in a Dakota night and one farmer waking in the morning sun. Then there by the grace of God went us and technology's logic is done."

- **"The Successful Farmer," Tim Ralston, Petersburg, North Dakota**

Iowa, for example, reported in March 1985 over $153 million in farm real estate assets, an increase of 33 percent from a year earlier.[29]

The Lender of Last Resort

No single agricultural lender has come under more fire for its practices and policies than the FmHA, ostensibly created to serve as farmers' "lender of last resort." Here farmers with "a reasonable prospect of success" were supposed to be able to get government loans anywhere from three to eight percent.

Events in recent years, however, tell a quite different story. In Mississippi, P.L. Blake owed the FmHA some $3.7 million in 1983 after enlarging a cotton planting operation with a net worth of $25,000 in 1978 to a corporate agribusiness empire of $1.7 million. Not only did his Dewitt Corp. own a 6,547-acre Delta plantation and a catfish processing plant, but it was also the nation's largest warehouser of surplus government-held corn utilizing several large Texas grain elevators, and earning Blake over $17 million in storage fees from 1980 to 1983. Yet, Blake claimed that he was still "trying to make ends meet" and depended on FmHA for that help.[30]

Numerous complaints have also been lodged against the FmHA for racial discrimination in lending practices, with one group of black southern rural activists charging that Agency practices were accelerating a trend that in 15 years could result in no blacks owning the land they farm. The 1982 U.S. Civil Rights Commission also recommended major policy changes within FmHA to help black farmers.[31]

In California, a USDA investigation found Donald T. Hallett, head of the state's FmHA and husband of a prominent Republican state assembly leader Carol Hallett, guilty of racial discrimination in processing housing-loan applicants.[32]

The Agency also has been repeatedly criticized for its inability to process loan applications in time to help farmers in financial need.

In September 1986 the FmHA further outraged many of its borrowers when in seeking to recover $630 million outstanding in loans hired Capital Credit Corporation, a New Jersey firm, to collect on its loans.[33] "I thought the FmHA had just about gone the limit in being hard-hearted. But this goes beyond anything I've seen," said Iowa's Tom Harkin. "It's the most idiotic case of bureaucracy running amok," added Senator Mark Andrews, R-ND, "Unseen bureaucrats, people who wouldn't know a steer from a heifer, using eastern big-city tactics."[34]

As the number of foreclosures and threatened foreclosures by FmHA began mounting in recent years many farmers banded together and even reinstituted the numerous "penny auction" sales of the 1930s. Here neighboring farmers rallied behind a fellow farmer faced with foreclosure and packed the auction — staring down any potential serious bidders — and buying the farmer's machinery and household goods for a few pennies and then returning the belongings to the threatened farmer at the conclusion of the auction.

Thus scenes such as that which greeted a farm auctioneer in Clear Lake, Wisconsin, in February 1986

occurred frequently throughout the nation's farming communities. Nearly 200 farmers and their supporters, chanting "no sale! no sale!" stood in below zero weather for 45 minutes amidst the clanging beat of kitchen pots and pans, forcing the auctioneer to declare that the sale of Mike and Lue Ann Croes' dairy farm would "not be held today."[35]

Amidst such increasing distress in 1983 a Federal judge in North Dakota imposed strict limits on any move by the FmHA to foreclose on delinquent borrowers or to force them out of farming. Farmers' attorney Sarah Vogel of Grand Forks, North Dakota, who pioneered the case through the Federal court and would later be elected the state's Commissioner of Agriculture, noted that

> the judge has not said there can be no foreclosures. He has said that legal principles of due process must be applied by the FmHA ... By making this a national class action, the judge has recognized that it was a futile task for farmers, one by one, to litigate against the power of the Federal government.[36]

In that suit Judge Bruce Van Sickle ruled that the FmHA was required to allow delinquent borrowers to defer making loan payments if they were financially strapped because of circumstances beyond their control. Despite the ruling, however, farmers continued to charge that the Agency's power to refuse to release money to farmers to cover living and operating expenses was used by FmHA to "starve out" delinquent borrowers.[37]

FmHA, arguing that it is an agency designed "to help people succeed in farming," denied that it was seeking to drive farmers out of business pointing out that it had foreclosed on very few of the nearly 300,000 farmers who owed it money. Its critics continue to argue that there are plenty of *de facto* foreclosures by the FmHA when the agency "accelerates" loans, telling farmers to repay all that's owed in 30 days or foreclosure will follow.

Shortly after Judge Van Sickle's two-year moratorium expired in late 1985, the FmHA renewed its effort to collect $5.8 billion in delinquent loans and began mailing out some 65,000 "notice of intent" letters to farmers more than three years behind in loan payments and those accused of defrauding the government.[38]

A previous study by the GAO, Congress's investigative arm, revealed that about half of the FmHA' $28 billion farm-loan portfolio was in jeopardy of default. A sampling of the Agency's records also found that about 20 percent of its borrowers were "technically insolvent," with more debts than assets and another 31 percent had debt-to-asset ratios between 70 percent to 99 percent. The GAO report went on to say that "the rather gloomy picture," resulting primarily from low prices received by farmers, would more than likely see nearly half of the aforementioned 65,000 farmers "have little chance of becoming current and most likely will fail."[39]

By June 1986 the FmHA was working with less money than it had in 1985. With $2.2 billion in direct loans and $1.7 billion in guaranteed loans, the government lending agency showed a decrease of $1.4 billion in direct loans and an increase of $600 million in guarantees.[40] By the beginning of 1989 the agency had written off $2 billion in bad debts in contrast to the $12.2 million it had written off ten years earlier.[41]

By 1986 the FmHA was also holding more than one million acres of repossessed land. In all it, along with life insurance companies and the Farm Credit System, held about six million acres of such land — a landmass the size of Vermont.[42] By early 1989 the FmHA alone held land (1.3 million acres) an area the size of the state of Delaware.[43]

Believing the agency's past performance so callous and hard-hearted that if he were the attorney general he would seek contempt-of-court citations against FmHA's officials, Harkin has observed: "In my ten years in Congress I have never seen anything so badly administered as the economic emergency loan programs. The court ordered them to implement the emergency program and they showed clear contempt of the court."[44]

Efforts by Congress to liberalize federal and private farm credit programs during the Reagan Administration were repeatedly blocked by the White House and FmHA chief Vance L. Clark, a former Bank of America executive. After the Senate subcommittee responded to the FmHA's hiring of a private collection agency by unanimously passing a Harkin-sponsored amendment barring it from using FY 1987 funds for hiring such agencies to dun farmers for overdue loans the Office of Management and Budget (OMB) informed the Senate that it opposed the amendment.[45]

In addition to sustained Congressional criticism, Missouri farmers furious with FmHA's callousness began a prolonged protest in March 1986 with a tractor barricade at the Agency's office in Chillicothe, Missouri demanding the removal of the local Livingston County Supervisor David Stallings, and attempting to draw the nation's attention to their plight. It became one of the longest sustained sit-ins in American history.

In Missouri at the time the FmHA had an inventory of 123,000 acres of repossessed farm land, more than any other state, and 80 percent of that land was kept off the market in an effort to forestall a further depression in land values. Also, over a fourth of the state's FmHA loans were delinquent at the end of 1985, with delinquency rates being double and triple that number in its northern counties.[46] Testifying before Senate Agriculture committee in March 1987 on the status of the FmHA's farm loan portfolio and loan-making criteria and policies, Brian P. Crowley, GAO's Senior Associate Director for Resources, Community and Economic Development Division gave the lawmakers the following facts:

• Half of FmHA's $28 billion farm loan portfolio remained delinquent as of June 30, 1986.
• Loan losses were continuing to escalate, as evidenced by a 275 percent increase between 1984 and 1986.
• Over the ten-year period from 1977 to 1986, FmHA's farm debt in its five major farm programs — farm ownership, operating, emergency disaster, economic emergency, and soil and water — increased about 370 percent, from $6 billion to $28 billion.

• From June 1985 to June 1986 the delinquent amount owed by borrowers over three years delinquent, increased from $4.8 billion to $5.4 billion, while their outstanding principal decreased from $7 billion to $6.9 billion.
• For the past ten fiscal years, annual FmHA direct farm loan losses (net of proceeds from sales of loan collateral) grew from $26 million to $490 million.[47] By June 30, 1986 of the $60 billion in debt acquired by the FmHA, over $26.6 billion was owed by farmers and the GAO reported that 36 percent of the Agency's 261,000 borrowers were delinquent on repayments of loans totaling $6.8 billion. Four of every five of these delinquent loans have been overdue for more than three years.[48]

From 1981 to 1983 alone the farm delinquency rate went from 13 percent to 21 percent while farm debt held by commercial banks was only 9.3 percent overdue during that same period of time. Of the remaining billions owed to FmHA, mainly in housing and rural development loans, only an estimated 6.9 percent was delinquent.[49] Because of that high delinquency rate and the deteriorating financial condition of many of its borrowers by the end of 1986 the FmHA was prepared to write off as uncollectible about $2 billion in loans to farmers. As Clark noted: "There are still some legal hoops to go through, but we ought to write off these loans. They are carried on the books as assets, but I am a realist — the majority is not collectible."

While announcing this write-off Clark further revealed that the Agency believed that land prices had bottomed out and that the moratorium on the sale of the majority of 1.4 million acres of FmHA-held land would be lifted in nine economically troubled agricultural states. Discussing the FmHA's loan situation with *The Washington Post*'s Ward Sinclair, Clark appeared to signal that the agency's long-stated role as lender of last resort was being reevaluated. "Even if you quadrupled [farm commodity] prices, many of these borrowers still could not recover. It should not come as a surprise. We're the lender of last resort to economically marginal farmers."

But, then the former bank executive added, "we no longer are going to be on a first-come, first-served basis, which is going to cause new problems. It means that those who have been turned down by other lenders and who now are coming to us will have to go to the end of the line."[50]

It appeared that Clark intended to remain true to his word for about the same time the GAO was releasing its latest delinquency findings in March 1987, the FmHA issued a 90,000 word, 100-page rule-change proposal intended to "streamline" the agency and improve its ability to make and service loans. Both federal and state legislators and officials immediately denounced the new regulations, charging that at least half of the current

275,000 borrowers would be barred from obtaining future loans.

Senate Agriculture Committee Chairman Patrick J. Leahy, D-Vt, led the charge: "The regulations are a dramatic shift away from the agency's mandate to provide supervised credit to farmers in trouble ... The FmHA is a bulwark in our defense against bankruptcy and foreclosure. I intend to make sure it stays that way."[51]

The FmHA announced that the new proposals would be "modified."[52] Meanwhile, on June 3, 1987 in another significant decision, Federal Judge Bruce M. Van Sickle ordered the FmHA immediately to halt foreclosure actions against some 13,000 financially troubled farmers and require renotification of an additional 65,000 delinquent farmers because the agency had failed to inform them of their legal rights.[53]

By early 1988 the FmHA was again revising its forecast and saying that it expected to write off $8.8 billion in delinquent loans over a two year period, an amount twice what had earlier been forecast. The combination of the deficit reduction plan and the lowering of farm income provisions contained in the 1990 Farm Bill suggest only an exacerbation of America's permanent agricultural crisis throughout the 1990s. (See Chart 3D)

Director Clark has also been warning Congress that the agency's new policy of "leniency" under the Agricultural Credit Act of 1987 would not save as many delinquent borrowers from foreclosure as had previously been hoped.

"It would be unrealistic to expect a wholesale rescue of our most troubled borrowers," Clark told a Senate agricultural subcommittee.[54] He pointed out that only 16,200 of FmHA's 118,000 delinquent borrowers "stand to benefit" from the 1987 law's write-down provisions as many farmers and ranchers "are in such bad shape that even writing down their debt won't save them." At the time, he added, of the agency's $9.6 billion in bad loans, $7.3 billion was more than four years overdue. "For all intents and purposes, that debt is uncollectible. Most of those borrowers are no longer even in farming," Clark concluded. In the ensuing months he expected, the FmHA would forgive about $2.1 billion owed by 16,200 borrowers who would qualify for write-downs. Meanwhile, over $6.7 billion would be written off because the agency did not expect 54,270 borrowers to have the cash flow to pay off their loans "even with the write down."[55]

In defending its actions in recent years the FmHA has claimed that it is only practicing "good loan management." However, journalists Stephen Kindel and Laura Saunders, writing in *Forbes Magazine* explain that beginning in August 1981 the FmHA began establishing "goals" of "reducing" farm indebtedness.

Obviously, farmers feel a certain amount of resentment toward the government. Oliver Hansen, president of the Liberty Trust and Savings Bank, a large Durant, Iowa-based agricultural lender, says 'I think that the government, the agricultural economists and such really led the farmer down the primrose path.'If he had been completely

candid Hansen might have added: '... and the banks.' When times were good, the banks were pushing loans at the farmers. But just at the right moment many of the banks shifted their weaker loans to the FmHA."[56]

Doing Business With "A Real Populist Villain"

To many farmers and people living in rural America the FmHA is not the only all-too-pervasive Federal institution that plays such an important role in their economic lives, nor the only one that they must humor, entreat, plead with, rage against, and often accept unilateral decisions from on an almost daily basis.

For over the years, as farmers have found themselves in a tighter and tighter cost-price squeeze, the Farm Credit System has become, in the words of investigative journalist/editor James Ridgeway, the "real populist villain."[57]

The FCS is an immense hidden banking operation (with roots in Wall Street) that reaches far beyond farmers to bondholders in commercial banks, insurance companies, pension funds and thousands of individuals, including many foreigners, the latter holding an estimated 18 percent of the system's securities as nest eggs.

The Farm Credit System consists of three independent banking networks which are regulated by the Farm Credit Agency, a federal agency. (See Chart 3E) These three networks are organized on a regional basis and owned by their farmer borrowers, providing three basic kinds of loans: long-term mortgages on farm land, offered by the Federal Land Banks; short-term funds to cover the costs of growing and harvesting crops, offered by the Production Credit Associations (PCAs); and loans for co-ops, made by the Bank for Cooperatives. This system, coordinated and audited by the FCA, which generally is supposed to regulate the farm banks in the same manner as the Controller of the Currency regulates commercial banks, played a major role in rescuing many farmers during the Great Depression.

Nebraska banker Vince Rossiter recalls,

the system was organized because the bankers back in the 1930s wouldn't loan enough money, so they organized their own financing system. We would have loaned the money. We had the money to loan. But there wasn't any security, there wasn't any profit, the loans couldn't be repaid. We couldn't loan, but they could.

Did they do it? No, they didn't do it. This New York Bank Consortium that you hear criticized arranged to have the Farm Credit System set up so that they could tap the market in the Midwest for farm loans, because legally they couldn't go across state lines and get this market any other way.[59]

Today the Farm Credit System ranks second only to the U.S. Treasury in the amount of money it borrows on Wall Street — nearly $100 billion a year. It also accounted for the single largest chunk — one third — of the nation's staggering $210 billion farm debt in 1986.

In 1985 the FCS lost $2.69 billion due to declining land values and low commodity prices.[60] Following this huge loss the GAO estimated in a September 1986 report that the FCS could post a loss of $2.9 billion in 1986 and that the system might well go broke by early 1987.[61]

In fact, the FCS lost $1.91 billion in 1986 for a total two year loss of $4.6 billion while its loan portfolio has been declining in recent years from $80 billion to $50.9 billion as of June 30, 1987. At the same time its overhead costs skyrocketed from $621 million in 1981 to $882 million in 1985.[62]

The record 1985 loss, the first since the FCS was established during the Great Depression, compared with a 1984 profit of $373 million. The value of its non-accruing loans also rose to $7.1 billion, compared to $1.84 billion in 1984, while the value of the property it took

Funding Corporation. He added that that figure could result in "significant" future losses to the banks.[66]

Noting that any government attempt to bail out the FCS would dwarf the 1984 $4.5 billion rescue of Continental Illinois which had only $40 billion in assets and a far more healthy and diversified loan portfolio than the FCS, John Urbanchuk, a Wharton Econometrics Forecasting Associates economist, warned: "In scope and in terms of implications for government policy, this is far and away the biggest financial blowup since the Depression." Some farm economists speculated that it would take in excess of $10 billion to revitalize the system.[67]

Donald Wilkinson, the governor of the FCA, has repeatedly told concerned Congressional leaders and Reagan administration officials that the System could not survive its "snowballing" credit problems without some direct federal support. "We've come to realize that

Chart 3D

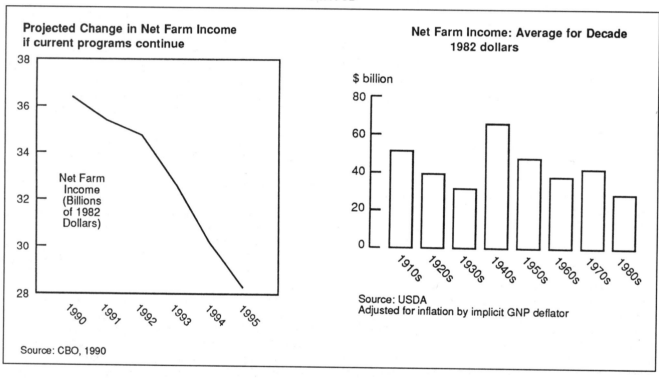

Projected Change in Net Farm Income if current programs continue

Net Farm Income (Billions of 1982 Dollars)

Source: CBO, 1990

Net Farm Income: Average for Decade 1982 dollars

$ billion

Source: USDA
Adjusted for inflation by implicit GNP deflator

over went from $505 million to $1.1 billion in two years.[63] In 1986 its actual net charge-offs for bad loans were $1.4 billion, up $300 million from 1985, while its portfolio continued to shrink, declining to $54.6 billion from the previous year's $66.6 billion. The FCS's $1.1 billion in property was obtained mostly through foreclosure proceedings.[64]

In 1985 nine of the System's 37 main banks had more problem loans than they had capital. A special credit review of the Federal farm banks also showed that about $6 billion of their $50 billion in loans were not properly secured by property and assets.[65] "The amount by which the undercollateralized loans exceed the collateral value was about $930 million," according to Peter Carney, who heads the Federal Farm Credit Bank

the deterioration in agriculture has grown beyond the ability of the [FCS] to handle it. We cannot absorb the losses we face."[68]

No Fair Prices! No Bailout!

In the closing days of its 1985 session, Congress did manage to pass legislation directing a reorganization of the FCS while holding out the possibility that some form of last-resort federal financial assistance could be forthcoming in case investor confidence was needed to restore faith in FSC bonds. But farmers like Nebraska cattle rancher Merle Hansen contended that any "bailout" of the FCA is futile "unless the root cause of the debt crisis — *government-enforced low farm prices* — is addressed now! No 'bailout' until fair prices are estab-

Chart 3E: Farm Credit System

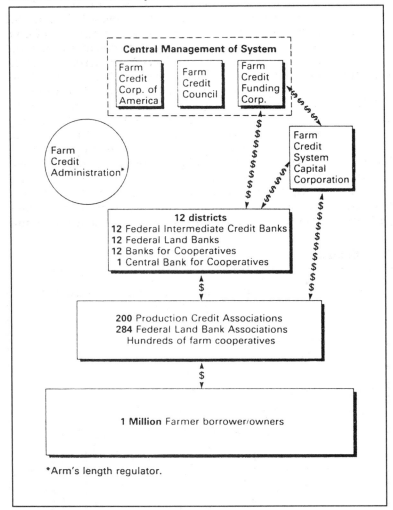

Central Management of System
- Farm Credit Corp. of America
- Farm Credit Council
- Farm Credit Funding Corp.

Farm Credit Administration*

Farm Credit System Capital Corporation

12 districts
12 Federal Intermediate Credit Banks
12 Federal Land Banks
12 Banks for Cooperatives
1 Central Bank for Cooperatives

200 Production Credit Associations
284 Federal Land Bank Associations
Hundreds of farm cooperatives

1 Million Farmer borrower/owners

*Arm's length regulator.

lished."[69]

And Jerry Hansen (no relation) of the Center for Rural Affairs in Walthill, Nebraska adds that these previously discussed "bailouts" by the Federal government "won't help farmers. It bails bondholders who supply the FCS with funds. Those bondholders are sophisticated Wall Street investors. They knew their investments were not guaranteed by the government."[70]

The FCS picture is further darkened by the fact that in recent years many of the banks in the System have seen their loan volume shrink as well as the number of borrowers, thereby necessitating an increase in interest rates. Yet, ironically, at the end of 1986 the FCS had $11.4 billion in cash and investment securities and a net worth of $5.6 billion.[71]

However, of that $5.6 billion, $1.5 billion was surplus and $4.1 billion was capital and "participation" certificates, or stock owned by FCS members which cannot be touched. The fact that the FCS estimated that its future losses would be near $400 million a quarter suggested that their $1.5 billion surplus was in real danger of rapidly drying up.

In the past FCS's bonds have been so highly regarded by the financial community that traditionally commercial banks, whose holdings of securities is strictly regulated,

have been permitted to hold unlimited quantities of the FCS bonds.

But, as Ridgeway explains,

when you look at its inner workings, the Farm Credit System is an oddity, and a dangerous one at that. It long ago paid back the government's depression era capital infusion, and is proud of its independence. But the system now operates in the market as if it were a branch of the Treasury. Because the farm banks are federally chartered, they have 'agency' status, trading as if they are backed by the U.S. government, offering exemptions from state and local taxes. In fact, the operations of the farm banks are not guaranteed by the federal government.[72]

By law if this system should ever fail, Congress could activate a bail-out. However, given the current political climate, in light of the staggering bailout of the Savings and Loan industry and the desire to reduce federal debt, it remains questionable whether such remedial action would be forthcoming without a prolonged political battle between the White House and the Congress.

In recent years, many farmers have also called into serious question the accountability of the FCS and its ambiguous ties to the Federal government. If a farmer whose land has been foreclosed upon should sue in a state court, the FCS insists that as an arm of the Federal government it cannot be sued. Yet, when farmers sue for forbearance on interest payments, arguing that the banks of the system are governed by Federal regulations, bank attorneys argue that they are private institutions.

Farmers who borrow from FCS banks are required to invest a portion of their loan proceeds into bank stock. Ostensibly, therefore, the entire System is owned and controlled by the farmer-borrowers. In practice, however, the stockholders seldom exercise their rights in a meaningful way. The FSC has no insurer like that of U.S. commercial banks, but rather is regulated by the Farm Credit Association, the FCA directors and its governor, who generally come from the nation's 12 Farm Credit districts. Thus the System is controlled by a self-perpetuating group of directors, most of whom are borrowers. The ultimate control of the System, however, lies with the agricultural committees of Congress, some members of which are actually borrowers. In short, there is no independent auditing of this huge multi-billion dollar financial system.

"The Fever Was On!"

As journalist Ridgeway recounts, it was during the 1970s, starting with the Nixon Administration, that the FCS banks began pumping money into the hands of farmers, rural businesses, and fishermen, wining and dining them and encouraging them to take out ever larger loans. In some cases, rules were bent to an incredible degree: one local bank in Kentucky actually financed the production of a Hollywood porno movie. As Ray Powell, a former Creston, Iowa loan officer, described it: "The fever was on."[73] Consequently, while farm debt in the United States grew from $103 billion in 1976 to $195 billion in 1981, outstanding FCS loans went from $20 billion in 1972 to $66.2 billion in 1980. As interest rates reached 16 or 18 percent farmers found themselves facing bankruptcy and foreclosure, as nervous FCS loan officers devalued land which only a few years previously their expansionist policies had helped to inflate.[74]

Largely because of actions like these, American agriculture now finds itself in economic and social chaos. Entire staffs and directors of FCS banks have been fired, PCA's are being combined, others closed and the System itself has been rocked by scandals.

One of the most serious of these cases involved an Omaha District bank which services 19,000 farmers and ranchers in the economically-depressed grain belts of Iowa and Nebraska, and in South Dakota and Wyoming. In 1985 the district lost more than $509 million with the Federal Land Bank operations losing $385 million, the Federal Intermediate Credit Bank of Omaha $23 million and the Omaha Bank for Cooperatives, $1.6 million.[75]

A Price Waterhouse report late in 1985 showed that in the first six months of the year the Omaha bank had $50 million in additional losses that the bank should have allowed for; including them would have converted the bank's reported $2.7 million first half profit into a $47.3 million loss.[76]

One result of this financial disaster was that the Omaha district loan interest rate went up to 16 percent in an effort to cover its losses. This in turn precipitated an exodus from the system by many of the more secure but frightened borrowers. This left the district with an even weaker portfolio, and forced it to seek bailout assistance from other banks within the System. As an increasing number of PCA member-farmers come face-to-face with foreclosure proceedings they discover that they have little or no voice in determining their fate or the course of their Production Credit Associations.

Many complaints about PCA procedures concern efforts by members to participate more fully in the Association's decision-making process. Requests for stockholder lists for the purpose of calling special elections, or efforts to discover the cause for abrupt cancellation of loans, are repeatedly rebuffed.[77]

After examining many cases throughout the Midwestern farm belt Ridgeway discovered that even when farmers threatened with foreclosure by a FCS bank managed to work out a deal for financial relief with another bank or the USDA, the FCS's practices "strongly suggested that there was a concerted policy to put farmers out of business."[78]

Prior to the 1986 GAO report, in July 1985 a panel of the FCS's top officials released a study which showed that it would collapse unless it undertook an immediate massive reorganization. It described numerous problems including illiquid assets, with $11.8 billion in capital assets of which only $6.8 billion was considered primary capital, and a deteriorating loan portfolio.[79]

The study recommended an ambitious overhaul by 1995, transforming the system into a centralized national bank holding company capable of catering to virtually all the credit needs of rural America, both on and off the farm.

But, as Charles F. McCoy points out in *The Wall Street Journal*, "many farmers and bankers oppose consolidation because they fear increased control in Washington will lead to tougher credit standards and other changes." Horace McQueen, president of the Federal Land Bank in Tyler, Texas is more outspoken on the matter: "This is just one more thing that they'll try to ram down our throats. We're not going to stand for it."[80]

Another Texas banker told McCoy that he had been asked to contribute about a quarter of his bank's $11 million in earned net worth, a major component of its primary capital. "That'll require me to raise my rates three-quarters of a [percentage point], and I'd lose a lot of my borrowers at those rates." In fact, it is estimated that the FCS has been losing about $1 billion worth of loans a month to its competitors because of these increased interest payments.[81]

Given such intense feelings it came as no surprise that, after the enactment of the 1985 law and the permitting of the strong parts of the system to aid the weaker ones, six banks sued the FCS claiming that they could lose all their assets under the new regulations which thus impaired their ability to provide customers with reasonable lending rates.[82]

In February 1987 a federal district court in Springfield, Massachusetts ruled that the system did not follow congressional guidelines in adopting its new regulations and could not transfer capital from its strong institutions to weak ones.[83]

Before a Senate Agriculture Committee hearing in September 1986, the FCS's head of banking operations, Brent Beesley, argued that "no financial institution can mount a recovery by charging noncompetitive rates ... [our] borrowers need rate relief." But, the FCA opposed proposed legislation to limit its power to cut interest rates, contending that the lowering of those rates would escalate the System's operating losses.[84]

Despite Congress giving the FCS the authority in 1985 to borrow money directly from the Treasury if needed, representatives of the FCS proposed some creative accounting changes to Congress in an effort to postpone its day of reckoning.

Ignoring some of the strict provisions of the 1985 legislation which included a requirement that it use generally accepted accounting practices, the FSC proposed that since the System estimated that it would lose an additional $1.8 billion over an 18-month period between June 1986 and December 1987, much of which would be due to provisions for loan losses, that it be allowed instead a 20-year write-off period.

As described by John M. Berry in *The Washington Post*, one major feature of such creative accounting was to allow the pretense that the FCS's $38 billion worth of high-yielding securities were paid off — by using new bonds. The System, therefore, would incur a one-time loss estimated by FCS officials at $2.8 billion by buying and retiring the higher yield bonds.[85]

Instead, by recording that loss all at once, Berry explained, the System would be allowed to write it off over a 20-year period at the rate of $140 million a year enabling it to reduce its cost of funds by enough to allow it to reduce the interest rates its borrowers are paying by between one and one-half and two percentage points.

Meanwhile, as the FCS sought ways to paper over its red ink, Congress and the Reagan Administration vowed to take rapid remedial action to save the system by injecting it with over $5-6 billion of aid, although some in Congress believe that up to $10 billion might eventually be needed.[86] In formally asking for a $6 billion bailout, the FSC noted that without such quick federal aid eight of the system's 12 district banks would be "nonviable" by the end of 1987 because of loans losses, failing land values, and low farm prices.[87] These same conditions suggested that the FCS was liable to incur a further $1.4 billion loss in 1987 and over $3.3 billion by 1989 after having already lost $4.8 billion since early 1985.[88]

Another Bailout, Another Billion

In April 1987, the GAO issued still another report on the subject, recommending that the federal government take control of the FCS. The cost of providing financial aid to the farm lending network might total "billions of dollars," but Charles Bowsher, comptroller general and head of the GAO, told a House Agricultural Committee, "we do not believe there is enough time to construct carefully thought out long-term solutions before the system's money crisis occurs."[89] He urged Congress to form a federal control board to oversee management of the system for at least 18 months.

By early 1989 the FCS showed signs that it might indeed survive. As its bad loans were foreclosed and its credit worthy borrowers paid off their loans the system's total loan volume went from $80 billion at the end of 1983 to $50.7 billion in early 1989.[90] Whether it will survive merely by shrinking in size, however, remains to be seen; forecasters have predicted that farm debt in 1989 probably increased 12 percent.[91]

Despite all these stop-gap proposals, however, the government is still faced with other financial lending crises. First, there is the call for taxpayer money to bail out hundreds of insolvent savings and loan associations, at an eventual estimated cost of at least a half trillion dollars.

Compounding the farm lending crisis, in December 1988 the GAO issued an updated audit on accumulated losses of $36 billion that it claimed the FmHA would be unable to recover. Farms loans it reported had grown from $60 billion in 1982 to almost $90 billion by 1987, with losses in 1987 alone increasing by $22 billion.[92]

"This crisis at Farmers Home is somewhere between Farm Credit and the thrift crisis," declared the GAO's Frederick D. Wolf. "People just don't realize how much money we are lending to farmers in this country. Congress is clearly going to have to deal with this problem."[93]

In the Reagan administration's desperate effort to save the FCS, however, perhaps no scheme was more revealing than its proposal to turn over a substantial portion of the FmHA's 1.5 million acres of land, acquired from farm foreclosures and forced liquidations, to the FCS to sell to the highest bidder to reduce its $6 billion deficit. In fact, in 1988 alone the Farm Credit Bank of Omaha sold over 898,500 acres of farmland in Nebraska, Iowa, South Dakota and Wyoming for over $229.2 million with another 101,500 acres for $25.9 million pending.[94]

Rather than use that land to help new and young farmers get started in American agriculture the Reagan plan would only have further consolidated land ownership in the United States As *The Post*'s Sinclair rightfully pointed out,

> It's a lousy idea, if only because the FCS already has roughly 2 million acres in its own land inventory and it has shown a notable inability to adequately manage its existing affairs. How the FCS would deal with additional property is certainly open to question.
>
> It's an even worse idea because, if recent FCS land-disposal patterns hold true, *it would put still more land in the hands of affluent farmers and outside investors, hastening the 20th-century movement toward larger farming units and adding to the growing class of farmers who in these troubled 1980s, have become tenants or employees.* (emphasis added)

Ironically, the resources of the FmHA, created as a last-resort lender to help low-income and minority farmers get into agriculture, would now be used to prop up the FCS, whose members historically have had little use for government-subsidized lending.

Sinclair adds,

> Worst of all, the plan would represent a missed opportunity to put land in the hands of people who have the ability and desire to farm, but do not have the capital or credit to do so. Despite the wrenching pain of foreclosure and low prices the farm sector has suffered since 1982, this is, in fact, an excellent time for entering farming, because land prices have stabilized and good used farm equipment is available.[93]

In an effort to prevent the FmHA and the FCS from carrying out this plan Senator Leahy and Representative Tim Johnson, D-SD, among others, proposed that the FmHA purchase the FCS's land with the money going directly to the FCS districts with the biggest inventories and thus the biggest cash-flow problems while the FmHA would make the land in its expanded inventory available to beginning farmers.[96]

The urgent questions concerning farm debt and who benefits and pays for that indebtedness are clearly related to who benefits and who suffers from an evolving technology-fueled structure of agribusiness that seeks to consolidate its sales and profits into a relatively few hands.

How these matters tie into an American agricultural system increasingly characterized by economic concentration and guided by a foresworn policy of ridding itself of "excess human resources," will be further seen as we examine the role of modern technology and the cost/price squeeze it has so effectively applied to millions of American farmers.

Chapter Four

Sweet Land of Opportunity

"The best fertilizer is the footsteps of the land-owner."

- Confucius

America has often been described as "the land of opportunity," yet today most of its citizens are becoming accustomed not to the footsteps of those who husband the land, but to the footprints of the slick soles of corporate America as it treads across our farmlands.

Land, of course, has always played a critical role throughout the nation's history not only in determining our agricultural priorities, but also in influencing the religious and philosophical framework of our communities. But as Peter Barnes reminds us in *The People's Land: A Reader on Land Reform in the United States*, it's more than the land itself that plays this role:

It is ownership — and the economics surrounding ownership — that determines whether land is farmed or paved, strip-mined or preserved, polluted or reclaimed. It is ownership that determines where people live and where they work. And, to a great degree, it is ownership that determines who is wealthy in America and who is poor, who exploits others and who gets exploited *by* others.

As noted in the Introduction, Protestant theologian Dr. Walter Brueggemann also had in mind the historical role of land ownership when he observed that while the majority of society's minds and hearts are shaped by the city, the city is remote from the land and therefore has largely misunderstood the land.

The city is a place of monopoly where everything important and valued is gathered and stored and administered and owned. The city exists by the concentration of what is valued in the hands of a few. Indeed, the city exists for the sake of concentration.

USDA statistics are often vague as to who actually owns or *controls* our farmland and about the true nature of the many super farms now involved in our agricultural production process. We do know, however, that such super farms exist and are not only increasing in number, but creating a growing number of economic, social and environmental problems.

1990 USDA figures show the size and sales of farms in the United States.[1] (See Chart 4A)

However, more detailed 1985 figures (Chart 4B) show that while only 2.09 percent of our farms operate nearly 13.5 percent of the land, nearly 60 percent of the nation's farms operate on less than 20 percent of our agricultural acreage. That same 2.09 percent utilizes nearly 85 percent of its land in growing crops while the 60 percent harvests 52.7 percent of its cropland. Non-family corporate ownership of farmland is statistically small (13 percent of the land and 3.7 percent of all owners) as 80 percent of the United States's farm cash receipts are earned on 53 percent of the operated acreage.

From 1974 to 1982 alone, according to USDA figures, there were dramatic increases in the land in farms (measured in current dollars) among the nation's large farms while the medium-size and small farm categories showed significant decreases.[2]

Yearly Sales	1974-1982
$500,000 or more	92.2%
$250,000 - $499,999	73.3%
$40,000 - $249,999	6.5%
$10,000 - $39,999	- 36.8%
Less than $10,000	- 31.1%

As Chart 4C shows the concentration of land ownership based on a 1988 ERS study is even more pronounced.

An exhaustive *Successful Farming* survey of the nation's 400 largest farms published in its January 1987 edition provides a rather recent useful insight into who some of the nation's largest farmland owners include. (See Chart 4D)

The Agribusiness Accountability Publication's *Directory of Major U.S. Corporations Involved in Agribusiness* (1976) also identified some of the top companies involved in agricultural production, such as Chevron (Standard Oil of California), Cargill, Tenneco, Beatrice Foods, General Foods, RJR Inc.. Burlington Northern, Ralston Purina, Southern Pacific, the Metropolitan Life and Prudential Insurance companies, and Coca Cola to name but a few.

Often these large corporations acquire agricultural or cattle grazing land for speculative purposes as the price of the land increases. Agriculture then becomes merely a subsidiary venture, as Tenneco Inc. characterized it when it bought the huge Kern County Land Company several years ago: "We consider land as an inventory, but we are still all for growing things on it while we wait for a price appreciation for development. Agriculture pays the taxes plus a little." [3]

Often when a corporation does sell its land for agricultural purposes it may then become a forward contractor, a vertically integrated operation where it does not necessarily own the land, but rather controls its use. Some companies, after such sales, even specify that the purchaser of the land must henceforth market crops through one of the company's own subsidiaries. As this trend continues we can expect to see more and farm tenancy.

Absentee Ownership

In recent years there has been increasing alarm about the foreign ownership of our agricultural land. Although, as one farmer notes, "you talk to folks in town and you hear all the stories about how the Arabs are buying up our land, when in fact it is mainly Canadians, Western Europeans and 'off-shore' tax syndicates."

Some of these "foreign" purchasers often do go to extraordinary lengths to conceal their identities. In one instance, a West German investor contacted a Canadian realty firm, which contacted a Wyoming broker, who contacted a Chicago bank, which hired a Kansas broker, who in turn found a local broker to handle the purchase of a 2,500-acre Kansas farm.

Although such sales as these are increasing, the overall figures are but a fraction of the total acreage of U.S. farmland. Foreigners own 12.9 million acres, slightly less than one percent of all U.S. agricultural acreage, with the Canadians (1.45 million acres) and West Germans (717,203 acres) the two largest owners. [4] In only five states — Maine (9.6 percent), Oregon (3.1 percent), Hawaii (2.7 percent) Louisiana (2.5 percent), and Arizona (2.5 percent) — is foreign ownership more than 2.5 percent of the total agricultural land.

Although in 1988 two Japanese firms — Sumitomo Corp. and a subsidiary of Toyota Motors — purchased hundreds of acres of Florida citrus groves, [5] that nation's total U.S. farmland investments amount to only 218,000 acres, a mere 2 percent of the foreign-held acreage. [6]

A more significant issue than foreign ownership, however, is *absentee ownership* — domestic *and* foreign. As Howard Hjort, former director of USDA's Office of Economics, Policy Analysis and Budget, told a House Agricultural subcommittee on the family farm, in June 1978. "Perhaps the single most important structural change which may be occurring in the agricultural sector today is the increasing frequency of the separation of ownership from operation, in some part encouraged by the attractiveness of farm land investment."

Hjort's concern needs no better illustration than the plight of the 10,000-acre Skyline Farms, ten miles northwest of Ontario, Oregon. Dug from sagebrush-covered desert, it was

originally started by H.J. Heinz's Ora-Ida Frozen Foods Division. In 1973, it was sold to J.R. Simplot Industries and continued to be used to raise potatoes. In May 1978, because the Oregon land had become "uneconomical for potato production," Simplot sold it for $5 million to the Prudential Insurance Co. [7]

Simplot Industries, which supplies the McDonald's Corporation with 80 percent of its french fries is one of the world's largest privately-held multinational corporations ($1.5 billion in sales in 1990). It is owned by J. R. Simplot whose net worth has been estimated at near $400 million. [8]

And then there is the little-known story of a particular 2,800-acre tract of land sitting in Sullivan County, Missouri which in 1978 changed hands three times within the space of three weeks.

Located in a fertile agricultural and cattle-producing area in north central Missouri, notorious for its tax-sheltered farming interests held by many out-of-staters and foreign investors, this particular 2,800 acres was from 1975 to 1978 jointly owned by R.P.F. Enterprises (with headquarters in Buenos Aires, Argentina) and My Dream, Inc., a Missouri corporation.

On August 2, 1978, the land was sold to Arlyn and F. Lucille Cady of Whiteside Co., Illinois. Less than a week later the same land was resold to a partnership of John W. Curry, George T. Clark and John R. Block, Ronald Reagan's first Secretary of Agriculture. Two weeks after this sale, on August 24, the same 2,800 acres of land was "traded" by the Curry-Clark-Block partnership to Richard R. and Betty M. Gerlach for 994 acres of corn in LeRoy, Minnesota.

Block, who later dissolved his partnership with Curry after he found himself with $4.4 million in assets and debts between $5.3 and $8.1 million, told a Senate confirmation committee in 1980 that he had sold the Minnesota property soon after moving to Washington, D.C. He noted that the Minnesota farm (approximately 300 miles from Block's Galesburg, Illinois "home" farm) was bought for his children, "but it's too far to drive to get there." Yet, the Sullivan County farm was only 200 miles from the Block farm. By trading the Missouri property for the Minnesota acreage, however, Block's partnership neatly avoided paying any capital gains tax on the transaction. [9]

But this is no isolated incident for much of our agricultural land is treated in a similarly reckless fashion, regarded more as a commodity to be financially mined than a natural resource to be husbanded. As Iowa's Bishop Maurice Dingman notes, there is increasing concern about the long-term effects of such practices.

Our values will ultimately determine how we respect and treat the land. If land is just a com-

Chart 4A: U.S. Farms Sales and Sizes

Gross Sales	Percentage of Farms	Percentage of Land
$1,000 - $9999	46.7	10.2
$10,000 - $39,999	23.2	17.1
$40,000 - $99,999	14.4	23.2
$100,000 - $249,999	10.0	26.0
$250,000 or more	4.8	23.5

modity, we will abuse it in our greed to make a profit. If land is just a means to make money, then we will lose sight of its ultimate purpose. But if land is a gift from God, then we will give that land the dignity and the sacredness that God has given it. Our economic system has little respect for land as a God-given resource. We seldom think that land must serve the needs of all God's people, not just a few.[10]

A 1980 farm-ownership report by the Senate Select Committee on Small Business predicted that if such abuse of our land continues "the land will be less carefully stewarded, farm-land will become the subject of price speculation and unwise farm development, and the family farm system as this country knows it will be undermined."[11]

The Senate committee's forecast is supported by the 1988 ERS figures that show an average of 45 percent of all U.S. farmland was leased from others (See Chart 4E).

The Senate committee's concern is further supported by the fact that from 1981 to mid-1986 the number of farms overseen by the nation's 1,000 farm management companies grew 40 percent from 78,000 to 110,000 with assets worth $12 billion including 59 million acres, an area nearly the size of the Colorado. It is also estimated that these farms have earned over $500 million for the farm management industry.[12]

Perhaps the largest of these farm management firms is the 69-year old Doane Agricultural Services. Once offering its services to 18 states, in the mid-eighties Doane's pared its operations to seven states. Currently, it manages 400,000 acres, with an increase of 100,000 acres between 1986 and 1987.

"We had to change," explains Joel McNeill, the company's president, because economic changes in farming necessitate the firm operate in geographic areas dominated by commercial rather than traditional farmer-operator farms. "Our primary business," he adds, "is supporting absentee owners and management of their properties. They basically are going to be owning the commercial-type farms."[13]

No longer family-controlled itself, Doane Farm Management is now owned by Arbor Acres of Glastenbury, Connecticut, a subsidiary of Booker PLC of London, England. Arbor Acres also owns Nicholas Turkeys, a major world-wide producer of broilers and turkeys.

As Prairiefire's Ostendorf points out:

The interest of farm managers is not necessarily to sell the land back to farmers, it's to sell the land to investors who will retain the companies to manage the farms. Our interest should be to keep farmers on the land, and land control is the fundamental issue in this struggle.[14]

In January 1986 the Prudential Insurance bought a 14-year old farm management subsidiary from Northern Bank & Trust of Chicago. Mutual of New York also purchased an investment company that owned Duff Farm Management Service, a 47-year old business that manages 200 farms. The biggest acquisition, however, was Metropolitan Life Insurance's purchase of Farmers National of Omaha, the nation's largest farm management firm, for $7 million. Farmers National at the time was managing 3,900 farms with over one million acres in nine states.[15]

A 1987 study by the Land Stewardship Project (LSP), a Stillwater, Minnesota public interest group shows the extent to which insurance companies benefit from farm foreclosures (Chart 4F). In addition, according to the American Council of Life Insurance's *Investment Bulletin*, between 1980 and June 1986 2,647 farm mortgages totaling $1.71 billion were foreclosed by life insurance companies.[16]

Chart 4B: U.S. Farm Characteristics by Sales, Operators and Land Ownership 1985 Percent of Total

Sales	% of Farms	% Cash Receipts	% Farming	Primary Occupation of Operators % Hired Manager	% of Acres Operated	% of Acres Harvstd
$500,000 and over	2.09	31.26	86.06	13.94	13.52	11.06
$100,000-$499,999	19.63	46.74	90.74	9.26	39.46	48.70
$40,000-$99,999	18.42	14.34	85.43	14.57	27.11	23.64
$20,000-$39,999	11.97	4.09	69.18	30.81	8.16	7.59
$19,999 and below	47.89	3.57	45.60	54.39	11.55	7.96

Source: "Financial Characteristics of U.S. Farms, January 1, 1986," USDA - ERS, Agricultural Information Bulletin #500.

Chart 4C: Percentage of U.S. Farm Land Owners, Acreage, and Value of Size by Holding, 1988.

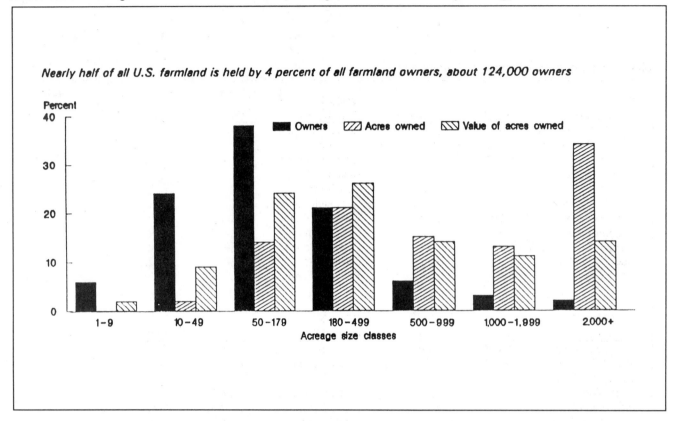

Nearly half of all U.S. farmland is held by 4 percent of all farmland owners, about 124,000 owners

In Iowa alone, the 12 largest insurance companies more than doubled their farmland inventory in value to $112 million on 130,000 acres by the end of 1986. These companies accumulated 294 parcels totaling 77,000 acres, the increase obtained exclusively through foreclosures and forced sales.[17]

Ostendorf observes:

These purchases show us just how profitable the farm management industry has become. Farm management firms often decide what seeds, what chemicals, what equipment a tenant farmer will use on the land. I say look a few years ahead.

Imagine what would happen if an oil company bought Hertz Farm Management [the nation's largest family-owned management company based in Nevada, Iowa]. Oil companies now own seed companies, and they have interests in equipment manufacturers and food processors and distributors. They could lock up agriculture from planting to the supermarket.[18]

Reflecting on the difference between owning one's land and renting or operating it for someone else, Kenneth Ver Steeg, a Rock Rapids, Iowa farmer notes:

I tried to do a good job when I was a renter, but it's different when you own it. I plan further into the future in terms of things like fertilizer and tillage; you give it the best care possible even if it costs extra now. But when you're renting, you just put in what you can get out this year.[19]

Cornelia Flora, a Kansas State University rural sociologist, has conducted studies which show that farm size has been increasing

the farm population did not decline. The number of hired persons increased. There were heightened class differences. We've had a tradition in this country that tenants and owners had more equal roles. Tenants have had the right to expect they will someday own land. That is now changing. Rural communities have also had a tradition of wonderful norms like underconsumption. In a highly stratified community you lose that. There is outstanding evidence that family farms are best for rural communities.[20]

In 1986 according to USDA figures, owner-operator farmers bought 58 percent of the land sold, down from the usual 80 percent-85 percent, while 32 percent to 38 percent of such sales were to outside investors, a figure that was up from the traditional 15 percent, according to a FCA spokesperson. These investors — doctors lawyers and other professionals — were attracted such purchases because bonds and CDs were earning only five to six percent whereas they saw a seven to ten percent annual cash return from renting their newly-bought land to tenants.[21]

The result of all this is that the United States is showing an even further degree of concentration in farm

Chart 4D: Largest U.S. Farms, by Commodity *

CORN			WHEAT		
Farm Name	Acres	State	Farm Name	Acres	State
First National Farms	21,635	Nebr.	Continental Corp.	40,455	Mont.
Virginia Beef Corp.	7,052	Va.	J.G. Boswell Co.	27,515	Calif.
Amana Farms Inc.	6,395	Iowa	Emmett Linnebur	22,358	Colo.
John Hancock			Diamond Ring		
Mutual	6,305	N.C.	Ranch Inc.	19,402	S.D.
K2H Farms, Inc	5,606	Wash.	Campbell Farming	15,272	Mont.
Carroll Olson	5,596	Nebr.	Westlake Farms	14,928	Calif.
Taggares Farms	5,550	Ore.	Lang Farms	13,425	Mont.
Gerald R. Kirwan, Jr.	5,451	Nebr.	Paloma Ranch	12,864	Ariz.
Rodney Horton	5,437	Mich.	David Ginz	12,210	N.D.
Dean Gigot	5,316	Kans.	Kalcevic Farms	11,247	Colo.

SOYBEANS			COTTON		
Farm Name	Acres	State	Farm Name	Acres	State
Morrison-Quick Grain	50,000	Nebr.	J.G. Boswell	80,914	Calif.
Mrs. J.W. Meyer	42,000	Ark.	Westlake Farms	22,914	Calif.
Louisiana Delta					
Plantation	37,500	La.	Paloma Ranch	21,961	Ariz.
E.B. Gee Co.	15,000	Mo.	Harris Farms Inc.	11,105	Calif.
Lloyd C. Wilken	15,000	Ill.	Jubil Farms	11,057	Calif.
Pacco, Inc.	14,000	Ark.	Airway Farms Inc.	10,922	Calif.
W.W. Moore	14,000	Miss.	Britz Inc.	8,386	Calif.
J.C. Chelette	12,000	La.	J.K. Griffith	7,893	Texas
N.H. Bruckerhoff	12,000	Mo.	O.O. Inc.	7,381	Texas
			Phoenix Agro		
J. Sam Brake Jr.	11,000	N.C.	Investment	7,108	Ariz.

* Lists do not include farm management companies

Source: *Successful Farming*, January, 1987.

Chart 4E: Percentage of Land Leased by Region, 1988.

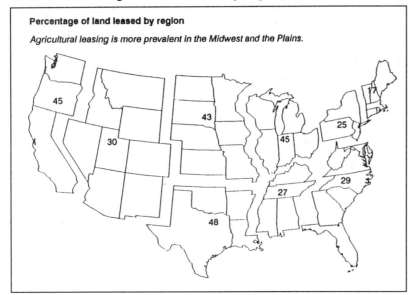

Percentage of land leased by region

Agricultural leasing is more prevalent in the Midwest and the Plains.

ownership. Ronald Knutsen, professor of agricultural economics at Texas A&M, believes this trend to be the "most uncertain and controversial issue in agriculture today — who is going to own the land?"[22]

There are those, however, who assert that tenancy is not necessarily detrimental. Economists like University of Minnesota's Michael Boehlje believe outside investor capital "may reduce the risk exposure and financial vulnerability of agriculture" and claims to see "no clearcut or distinct advantages for the owner-operator farm

structure."[23] Philip M. Raup, professor emeritus at the University of Minnesota, takes it a step further in explaining to *The Wall Street Journal*'s Marj Charlier that "the term 'family farm' was once interpreted to imply ownership of all the land farmed. *This is no longer a tenable definition.*" (emphasis added)[24]

Another long-time defender of corporate agribusiness, Donald Paarlberg, economics professor emeritus at Purdue University, echoes Raup's thinking. In decrying any farm legislation which would cut grain support payments by limiting production through supply management and tying such a program to production rights to the land, Paarlberg argues that such a plan resembles the "entailment of estates" — a system he maintains would foster a limited class of landowners.

He prefers rather the current direction U.S. agriculture is headed in: more land held by investors instead of single families. While he finds such a concept a little unsettling, he claims "it's inevitable."[25]

Others, like Neil Hamilton, director of the agricultural law center at Drake University in Des Moines, Iowa, sharply disagree with Paarlberg, Raup, Boehlje, *et al.*

I think we'd rather have land owned by the people who live nearby rather than feudal serfs on land owned by rich businessmen in New York City. You don't have to be a socialist or a crazy radical to say that. It's part of the American heritage and the agrarian ideals that Jefferson stood for.[26]

Or as one farmer described it to *The New York Times* Andrew H. Malcolm "generation after generation learned the lay of this land; which corners get too wet too often for early planting, how many years of hay make

Chart 4F: Major Insurance Company Farm Holdings

Company	Value of Assets (B)	Value of Acres of Farms (M)	Value of Mortgages Held (M)	Acres Holdings (T)
Travelers	$ 456.8	$ 1,974.8	$ 2,341.6	890,000
John Hancock	$ 419.5	$ 1,576.8	$ 1,996.3	590,000
Metropolitan Life	$ 82/$289.6	$ 1,604.8	$ 1,894.4	510,000
Prudential	$ 103/$570.0	$ 1,238.2	$ 1,808.2	920,000
Equitable (N.Y.)	$ 49/$91.2	$ 1,653.8	$ 1,745.0	175,000
CIGNA	$ 69.5	$ 725.7	$ 795.2	215,000
Aetna	$ 43/$168.7	$ 430.4	$ 599.1	415,000
Mutual Benefit	$ 50.1	$ 410.2	$ 460.3	47,000
Connecticut Mutual	$ 43.8	$ 364.7	$ 408.5	128,000
MONY	$ 53.9	$ 256.5	$ 310.4	87,000
Northwest Mutual	$ 8.9	$ 22.0	$ 294.4	50,000
Phoenix Mutual	$ 47.2	$ 87.4	$ 134.6	45,000
Kansas City Life	$ 2.5	$ 49.0	$ 51.5	n.a.
Northwest National	$ 8.9	$ 22.0	$ 30.9	n.a.
TOTAL	**$2,307.4**	**$10,608**	**$12,915.4**	**4,104,000**

Sources: 1986 Annual Insurance Reports *Fortune.*

that field grow more corn, which tractor sounds warn of impending failure."[27]

The love many farmers have for their land was tragically evident in Waynesboro, Georgia in February, 1986. L.D. Hill III, a 67-year old farmer and father of five, shot himself rather than see his 1,300 acres of farmland, which had been in his family for four generations, auctioned off to pay a debt of nearly $300,000. "He just couldn't stand to see his whole life go on the steps of the courthouse," daughter Deborah Jennings said later, "he was trying his best to pay his bills." He wanted to stop the sale of his land and he did.

"L.D. had a tremendous love for his land, and he wanted to save that land," recalls Bill Craven, the local county agricultural agent. "And he wanted to save it not for himself but for his heirs."

Noting that Burke County's farm debt in 1974 was $4.5 million and in 1986 was easily over $250 million with two or three farm auctions a month, Craven recalls that the scenes of those auctions were seared in L.D. Hill's memory. "I've been there with him. I know what it is. I've seen grown men cry. I've seen them sit on the rock wall around the courthouse and put their heads in their arms and weep."[28]

A Dying Minority

Nowhere is the decline in individual land ownership more starkly evident than in the plight of the black farmer in the south and southeast. Indeed, the recent anguish felt by so many of the nation's white farmers in the loss of their farmland has for most of the 20th century been the fate of the black farmer. Since 1920 almost 94 percent of the farms operated by blacks have been lost, compared with 56.4 percent of white operated farms. By 1978 the rate of land loss for blacks was two and one-half times the rate of loss for whites, with black farmers losing land at an astounding rate of nearly 1000 acres *a day*.[29]

In 1989, based on USDA and Census Bureau figures, 97.4 percent of farm residents were white and 1.8 percent were black, compared with 84 percent white and 12.5 percent black in the non-farm population. The Emergency Land Fund (ELF) reports that black landholdings declined from a peak of 15 million acres in 1910 to a 1974 level of 5.5 million acres, an annual average decline of 333,000 acres. Black landholdings are now at three-tenths of one percent of all privately held land despite the fact that Blacks constitute over 11 percent of the population.[30] Also accompanying this loss of land was an out-migration of over 4.5 million blacks from the rural South between 1940 and 1970, which occasioned former Secretary of Agriculture Orville Freeman once to observe:

Virtually every aspect of the urban crisis — poverty and welfare, employment, crime, housing and health — could be linked to a migration from rural America that resulted in too many people on too little space. ... There never has been any national recognition of what this pellmell change meant in terms of stresses on our communities, schools, governments, homes, churches, neigh-

borhoods, and on ourselves. ... The result has been a national crisis of environment — the relationship between the people and the land — and from this crisis others have erupted all around us.[31]

A 1982 U.S. Civil Rights Commission report, "The Decline of Black Farming in America," counted only 57,000 black commercial farms (sales above $2,500) who owned some 4.7 million acres. In addition, Black farmers were three times more likely to be poor than white farmers. The commission's study, with its shocking findings and urgent recommendations for constructive action, was all but ignored by Agriculture Secretary John Block.

Black-owned land traditionally has been the target of land speculators and developers. As the 1982 Civil Rights Commission report noted: "The frequent pattern is for land to remain in minority hands only so long as it is economically marginal, and then to be acquired by whites when its value begins to increase."

Ralph Paige, Executive Director of the Federation of Southern Cooperatives and Land Assistance Fund, elaborates:

Historically, landowners/farmers who are black have had to sell their land in the face of mounting financial and legal pressures. They have had to rid themselves of accumulated debt; been victimized by unscrupulous attorneys, realtors and speculators and have received separate and unequal treatment as a result of the South's land tax, partition sale and foreclosure system.

In addition, there is an underextension of program services and resources traditionally offered by the Federal government to black landowners. That is, as a farmer/landowner, the black landowner is at a distinct disadvantage when it comes to access to capital, markets and government-funded programs.[32]

Since the early 1970s, in an effort to materially assist black farmer/landowners, the privately funded Emergency Land Fund has organized affiliates in more than 100 counties in eight southern states, to lobby for less restrictive property laws, arrange for private funding to keep land in black hands and provide legal aid for black owners facing property loss. In 1985, financial problems forced the ELF to merge with the Federation of Southern Cooperatives.

As Earl Lewis, Sr., a black farmer from Earle, Arkansas told *The Washington Post's* Ward Sinclair: "It is important when you own something, you have a feeling of control. But the only way a black can buy land now, at least from white land owners, is to pay double the cost [because of discriminatory attitudes]. The black farmers is a dying breed."[33]

Following "Conventional Wisdom" Into Debt

As thousands of our food producers are unable to realize genuine income and must depend on borrowed capital merely to exist, their chief source of equity — the land — continues to ricochet in value. A May 1989 USDA report observed that "with real estate now accounting for about three-quarters of the farm sector's total assets, movements in land values dramatically affect net worth."

Meanwhile, a federal tax code that shelters high bracket individuals, mostly non-farmers, has conspired for some time to deny long-suffering farmers the relief they so desperately need during America's permanent agricultural crisis.

After the value of agricultural real estate skyrocketed from $216 billion to $756 billion in the 1970s,[34] while government officials like Agricultural Secretary Earl Butz urged farmers to plant "fence row to fence row," the 1980-1984 period saw a dramatic drop in prices.

Nationally, farm land values showed back-to-back annual declines of 12 percent in both 1984 and 1985. In 1986 in the eight state district of Iowa, Kansas, Missouri, Nebraska, Oklahoma, Colorado, New Mexico, Wyoming the decline was 14 percent, bringing the value 55 percent lower than the peak of 1981.[35] The 1985-86 figures were the largest two year drop since 1932/1933, when land prices dropped 17 percent and 19 percent respectively. (See Chart 4G)

The average value of farm land as of February 1, 1986 was $596 per acre, down from $679 in 1985 and a peak of $823 per acre in the early 1980s.[36]

By December 1, 1986, farmland values in Iowa had dropped by 17 percent, a record plunge of 63 percent from 1981.[37] 1986 USDA figures show that Nebraska, Illinois and South Dakota saw declines of over 25 percent, and the average farm estate decline for the year in 12 midwestern states was 23 percent. Even though farmland prices began to rise in 1988 with Iowa (20 percent), Illinois (10 percent), Missouri, Kansas and Nebraska (9 percent) leading the way average farmland values in 1989 remained 27 percent below the 1982 record.[38]

A 1985 Minnesota Department of Agriculture study further pointed out that since 1981 12 midwestern states had lost 73,500 farms, 316,000 farm family members, and 3.7 million acres of agricultural land. Nationally, the Department reports, farm assets, primarily land, fell $264 billion between 1980 and 1985, an average loss of $139,000 for every U.S. farmer.[40] In 1980 farm assets exceeded the $1 trillion national debt while in 1986 the United States's $2 trillion national debt grew to become two and one half times the value of farm assets.

A 1985 study by Iowa State University showed that midwest real estate brokers believed low commodity prices were the primary reason for reduced land values. Robert Jolly, a university economist, also points out that if declines in farm income are perceived as permanent, they will translate into lower land values, making the resolution of debt problems more difficult.[39]

Richard Krumme, editor of *Successful Farming*, comments:

> The way to get rich farming [in the 1970s] was to leverage, to borrow money and buy land *ad infinitum.* That was the strategy other farmers and

farm magazines and lenders and Extension service were telling farmers, so those who followed the accepted conventional wisdom at the time are those, ironically, the most hurt.[42]

Though many blamed the escalations in farm value in the 1970s on farmers' greed, banker Bud Newman believes that those farmers who found themselves in desperate shape because they borrowed to buy land were not necessarily to blame for their later plight. "I don't know who's to blame for that," the rural Nebraska banker reflects, "it wasn't a case of greed. It was a son buying a father's estate, or buying out his brothers and sisters, and a guy getting into farming when he shouldn't have. I don't know of anyone in this part of the farm belt who was 'trying to get rich'."[43]

In many states farmland fell to price levels at which the return on investment from renting the land was six to ten percent. Charles Schwab of Agrivest Inc., a firm specializing in farmland investments, notes that "contrarians are coming out of the woodwork, as in any security or investment that goes through a beating as agricultural land values have." Already with some $10 million in investments Schwab noted that people buying land not only could realize an immediate return of six to eight percent by renting their land to farmers, but would probably see it increase in value in a few short years.[44]

Many farmers rush to buy agricultural land cheaply because they fear that as a need for "outside" capital accelerates, major changes may take place in the 15 states that restrict corporate ownership and the 27 states that limit foreign ownership of farmland.[45]

What is considered a more immediate threat to the nation's farming communities, however, and one that highlights the gross inequities of the economic system in which today's agricultural producers must operate, is the continuing investment by limited partnerships in farmland for tax write-off purposes.

Nearly 70 percent of our farmland is owned by people over 50 years of age [46] and recent tax laws give such owners more incentives to keep their land in the family upon retirement, whether or not the heirs care to farm the land. The transfer of such land to a spouse tax-free and other recently enacted tax reductions have made such land especially attractive to investors, and thus increased tenancy.

"I think farmland will become a perfect shelter for people under the estate-tax changes," former Agriculture Secretary Bob Bergland told *The Wall Street Journal* in 1981. "We're going to see trust funds, pension funds and industrial buyers snap up farmland."[47]

"We'll see more absentee ownership," adds Dave Towns, farm management operations vice president for the world's largest agricultural lender, Bank of America, "because over the long haul, agriculture has been a good investment and has provided excellent tax advantages."[48] Professor Breimyer saw any declining value of farmland and the increase of heretofore outside tax-sheltered investment as making farming increasingly inaccessible to individual entrepreneurs.

Though preference for family farming is deep in American tradition, the fact is that most current landholdings by farmers was financed primarily by inflation — borrowing against the rising value of their land. It follows that deflation — or the drop in land value — forces farmers to sell their land. That land-price deflation now underway denies land-holding to newcomers and wrenches it from entrants of the last decade.

Now that inflation will not pay for a farmer's land, the alternate source of capital is tax-sheltered investment. Currently, income from farming denied the Internal Revenue Service (IRS) by tax shelters is almost twice the amount generated. If these conditions continue, most capital in agriculture will be of sheltered origin. And the economic consequence will be to speed the trend to deny ownership of farmland to those who will farm.[49]

Chart 4G: Decline in Land Values (1985-86)

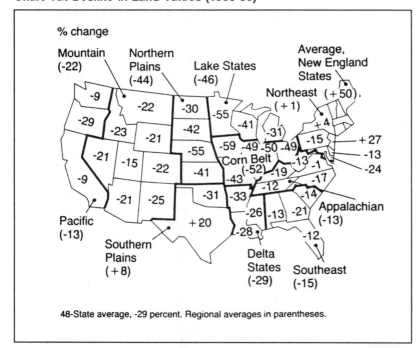

% change

Mountain (-22)

Northern Plains (-44)

Lake States (-46)

Average, New England States

Northeast (+50), (+1)

-9   -22   -30   -55

-29   -23   -21   -42   -41   -31   +4

-21   -15   -22   -55   -59 -49 -50 -49   -15   +27

Corn Belt (-52)   -13 -1   -13

-9   -41   -43 -12 -19   -17   -24

-21   -25   -31 -33   -14

Pacific (-13)   +20   -26 -13 -21   Appalachian (-13)

Southern Plains (+8)   -28   -12

Delta States (-29)   Southeast (-15)

48-State average, -29 percent. Regional averages in parentheses.

Our "Impermanence Syndrome"

The destruction of the environment, loss of topsoil and depletion of the water supply are among the worst consequences of increased tenancy and speculation in land and farming by outside investors even as our land and water become increasingly important in a world of finite food and energy supplies.

Misusing and abusing prime farmland on which all agriculture depends is like killing the goose of golden egg fame; once gone — down a river, into the air, under the asphalt or over the strip-mined hill — it is either gone forever or requires enormous time and money to reclaim. A Council on the Environment report issued in 1979 showed that an average of four square miles of our prime agricultural land *each day* was being taken out of

food production and assigned for residential, commercial or other development, mostly around the fringes of the nation's large urban areas. Of the 421 million U.S. acres of producing cropland, 250 million acres are considered prime (*i.e.*, of exceptionally high value in food production).[50]

New Jersey, for example, has been losing 20,000 to 30,000 acres of farmland each year.[51] Delaware, among the top eight states in the nation in percentage of land used for agriculture, lost nearly 50,000 acres of farmland between 1982 and 1987.[52] In that period New York lost ten percent of its farms and 800,000 acres while neighboring Connecticut lost 4.5 percent of its farms.[53] Meanwhile, in June 1988 the three most expensive states in terms of average value per acre of farmland were New Jersey ($5,321), Rhode Island ($4,217) and Connecticut ($4,056).[54]

American Farmland Trust (AFT) studies show that a majority of the highest market value farming counties in the United States are located within or adjacent to metropolitan statistical areas (MSA). MSAs are areas containing a city or urbanized area of at least 50,000 people with a total metropolitan population of at least 100,000 (75,000 in New England). The top fifth of counties in each state, ranked according to agricultural production values, are called High Market Value Farming Counties (HMVFC), They produce 48.7 percent of the nation's market value of agricultural products on 28.3 percent of U.S. farmland. A majority of HMVFC's are located on the urban fringe.[55]

"Every time you go through the checkout line at the supermarket on a weekly shopping trip, another 60,000 acres of American farmland has disappeared," is the way the Washington-based National Association of Counties research foundation has described this growing land use crisis.[56]

Another report, this one by the National Agricultural Lands Study (NALS), predicted that if our farmland continued to be lost to urban, industrial and transportation uses at the same rate as in the 1967-1977, period Florida, New Hampshire and Rhode Island would lose "nearly all" of their prime agricultural land. Other states are also expected to show dramatic decreases.

The United States has been converting agricultural land to nonagricultural uses at the rate of about three million acres per year — of which about one million acres is from the cropland base. This land has been paved over, built on, or permanently flooded, *i.e.*, converted to nonagricultural uses. For practical purposes, the loss of this resource to U.S. agriculture is irreversible.[57]

In Texas, for example, between 1977 and 1984 some 604,800 acres of prime productive farmland was lost to nonagricultural uses with perhaps three times that amount lost in total farmland.[58] Yet, despite such alarming statistics only 12 states (Connecticut, Maryland, Massachusetts, New Hampshire, New Jersey, New York [Suffolk County]), North Carolina, Pennsylvania, Rhode Island, Vermont, West Virginia and Washington (King County) buy land development rights from farmers to prevent development of farmland for other uses.[59] However, USDA researchers Ralph Heimlich and Douglas Brooks, noting that one-quarter of all U.S. farms in metropolitan areas account for 30 percent of farm sales, claim there has been "a recognition at the state and local level that the land preservation problem was important long before it became a national issue." Heimlich adds, "I think that in the future we will see even more activity to protect agricultural land."[60]

Nancy Bushwick, director of a farm and land preservation project for the National Association of State Departments of Agriculture believes that in the 1970s such preservation concern "was a movement, but if you look at the number of states that have passed laws, you see that it has become institutionalized."[61]

Due to what the NALS refers to as the "impermanence syndrome," this conversion of agricultural land to nonagricultural uses directly affects existing agricultural land. When the population

> on the fringe of urban areas increases, land values begin to rise as farms are broken into small parcels suitable for housing. As farmers look beyond their fences they understandably are tempted to sell their property at a large profit for nonagricultural uses especially when they see a bleak future for agriculture.[62]

As Don Ralston, co-director of the Center for Rural Affairs in Walthill, Nebraska reminds us,

> When a farm in a fringe urban area goes under, for whatever reason, that lost production is apt to be made up by a large investment type operation, where there are real opportunities for environmental abuse, both from large machinery and the farm's employees not having a real caring attitude about the land.[63]

The NALS report adds that conservation and building repairs are neglected, because continued investment would require long-term agricultural production planning. This "impermanence" begins to corrode the rural community and creates patterns of disinvestment such that other farm related businesses also begin to disappear.

> Tensions between farming and non-farming people often arise in rural areas with growing populations. The causes range from vandalism of crops and farm machinery to increased demands by new residents for public services, especially when the resulting tax increases to pay for these services fall heavily on the original residents.[64]

All this activity is creating what USDA researchers call a "new" and "diverse" look to rural landscapes.

Often in the process of this conversion of farmland into suburban development the long-term significance of such transmutation and the connection between local farms and food is lost on the public. Consider a letter-to-the-editor which appeared in the Connecticut weekly *Glastonbury Citizen* in December, 1987. The writer, self-described as "a poor, underpaid teacher," voiced objection to any zoning that would preserve

> unwanted and unnecessary farm operations in a growing and industrialized state ... The principle of perpetuating obsolete and undesirable operations in a clean, healthy environment is anathema to civil society ... No family wants a dusty, smelly farm in their neighborhood.[65]

Meanwhile, advertisements such as those appearing in southeastern newspapers with increasing regularity add to the disappearance of the nation's agricultural land.[66]

Commenting on such ads and after reading a *New York Times Magazine* article, "Magnificent Obsession," which told of the "growing number of middle and upper-middle class Americans whose pursuit of happiness has led them to the purchase of a weekend retreat" in the country, *The Washington Post*'s social critic Jonathan Yardley sagely noted in a column titled "Greed Acres: When the Rich Go Rural:

> **"The current land glut and how you can profit from 10 acre estates just 45 miles from 495"**
>
> "Despite the nation's glut of agricultural land, land within 50 miles of most major cities has generally risen in value due to housing pressures. The National Association of Home-builders reports that the cost of a developed lot now accounts for 25 percent of a new, detached home."
>
> **"Right now pockets of enormous value exist if you know where to look. This is because many investors and speculators are waiting for the new tax laws. Will tax shelters be removed on farmland and second homes? Such uncertainty has created a window of opportunity for you."**

If anything the words 'New York' and 'country' are mutually exclusive and oxymoronic. New Yorkers understand country approximately as well as country understands New York, which is to say not at all; the difference is that New York is convinced not merely that it understands country, but that it knows more about country than country itself will ever know.

Thus we have the ludicrous spectacle of motor-mouthed Manhattanites speeding to the sticks in their BMWs, decking themselves out in Laurenesque parodies of rustic garb and hunkerin' down to the pea patch. It's the ultimate Hick Chic fantasy, and fantasy is all it can ever be."[67]

As agricultural land continues to disappear we see what the NALS has referred to as "a matter of considerable uncertainty" growth in yield per acre. In the 1960s the U.S. crop yield per acre increased at an annual rate of 1.6 percent, sufficient to meet increases in demand. In the following decade the annual growth in yield per acre dropped to 0.76 percent. About three quarters of the nation's gain in total agricultural production, however, came from newly cultivated land; the rest from increased yield per acre.

Taking into account this data showing the conversion of cropland to other uses and the annual reduced yield per acre growth rates and looking ahead to the end of the century, NALS states:

To draw *into* agriculture sufficient resources to meet the projected level of demand in the year 2000, farmers and ranchers will require *incentives* in the form of *considerably higher* real profits from their commodities, either through *reduced* production costs or *increased* prices. Protecting productive cropland that otherwise would be converted to nonagricultural use will help mitigate upward pressure on production costs, and indirectly, consumer prices, as the demand for food and fiber mounts throughout the remainder of the century. (emphasis added)[68]

"Let's Stop Treating Our Soil Like Dirt"

According to former Secretary of Agriculture Bob Bergland, 15 million tons of topsoil or 93,750 acre-feet of land has been flowing out of the mouth of the Mississippi River *every minute* in recent years.[69]

Following the Dust Bowl days of the 1930s, much effort was made to institute good soil management on U.S. farms — contour plowing, cover crops, shelter belts of trees, rotation, strip cropping, etc. But, in recent years much of this soil care has been abandoned in favor of maximum production.

Environmentalists have frequently criticized farmers for abusing the land in this fashion. While it's true that modern farming practices take an exacting toll on the quality of farmland, the ultimate reason behind soil erosion is not wind or water, but economics. Driven to produce more to cover their mounting debts and expenses, farmers between 1979 and 1981 alone converted over 11 million acres to cropland. Some 2.3 million of those acres was land classified as highly erodible, over three quarters (1.9 million acres) planted to Federal farm programs.[70]

"There still is an ethic out here, and people will try to preserve their soil, but the economic pressures are so severe that many farmers must give conservation a lower priority," Bill Willis, an Atlantic, Iowa USDA Soil and Conservation Service (SCS) agent rightly points out.[71]

William K. Reilly, former president of The Conservation Foundation and head of the EPA in the George Bush administration, also reminds us, that

Soil conservationists often speak of the need for a land ethic. It is a noble, important ideal. But we indulge in selective moral assignment if we expect farmers to hold strictly to this ethic when their economic survival is at stake. We expect farmers to place social interest ahead of individual interest in a way that we expect from few other groups in society.[72]

In support of the argument that economics and the current cost/price squeeze compels many farmers to abandon a land ethic based on the preservation of the soil, some experts point out that erosion rates for cropland and permanent pasture land is 40 percent higher on rented than on owned land.[73]

An example came to light in January, 1985 in Millville, Minnesota when the John Hancock Insurance Co. took over a local 270-acre farm. Ed Hauck's dairy farm had long done a stellar job of soil conservation in the county with grassed waterways, hay strips, terraces to stop soil erosion, and planting in contours following the lay of the land.

Hancock, after hiring a farm manager, promptly utilized so-called "state of the art" heavy machinery, plowing over many of the strips, terraces and waterways that Hauck had installed. In a short period of time the insurance company turned one of the area's best conservation farms into one of the worst, prompting local citizens to form a Land Stewardship Project seeking to restore soil conservation practices on the farm.

Rallying behind the motto "Let's Stop Treating Our Soil Like Dirt" the Land Stewardship Project, through a series of community meetings and protests, mounted enough public pressure to get a reluctant John Hancock to restore soil conservation practices to the Hauck farm. Efforts to persuade Hancock to take the leadership in getting other farm management companies to practice good soil conservation measures, however, have not equaled the Project's success at Hauck's farm.[74]

It is necessary for people and landowners to understand that most of our nation's soil erosion problems, rooted in a complex web of economic and natural factors, are compounded by excessive plowing with heavy machinery, abusive irrigation practices and usage of chemical poisons and fertilizers, and the ever-increasing planting and harvesting of soil-depleting crops.

As American Farmland Trust's Robert Gray points out,

Few Americans realize that just slightly more than half of our current crop-land base of 421 million acres is prime agricultural land, which simply means that this land is the most productive and has the least sustainability. Because of its superior moisture-holding capacity, this land is less susceptible to drought.

Much of our remaining crop-land base has serious resource constraints, including high erosion levels, salinity problems, low fertility and lack of sufficient water for irrigation.[75]

The SCS has estimated that more than 3 billion tons of soil is washed and blown away annually from privately-owned crop land, in addition to another two billion tons from pastureland, rangeland and forests. It is also postulated that if the topsoil is one foot deep, there are approximately 160 tons per acre. Top-soil should erode no more than five tons per acre per year, according to soil scientists, if the long-term capability of the land to grow crops is to be maintained. A loss of eight tons a year means the complete eradication of that area's topsoil in 20 years.[76]

USDA figures in 1984 showed average annual sheet, rill, and wind erosion on U.S. cropland at an estimated 7.3 tons meaning that 44 percent of the cropland was eroding above rates needed to sustain high levels of production in the future. The conservationist's rule of thumb says that it takes 100 years to replace *one inch* of top soil by natural processes. After studying soil losses in the Corn Belt, one USDA researcher has estimated that each inch of topsoil loss also causes a six percent drop in yields.[77]

In some farm states in recent years the average erosion rate was as high as 14.1 tons per acre. In the Mid-Columbia wheat basin of southeast Washington State's Palouse hills, for example, the erosion rate has been 50 to 100 tons per acre.[78] On one day, October 7, 1985, Kansas farm lands lost 350,000 tons of topsoil during severe windstorms. A Federal conservation official estimated such a soil loss at between $5 and $6 million.[79]

In spring, 1988, after 11.9 million acres were damaged in 1987 due to wind erosion, the worst dust storms since 1955 and the second worst since the Dust Bowl of the 1930s struck the Great Plains. When they were over 14 million acres had been scoured with Kansas (5.1 million), North Dakota (2.3 million) and Texas (2 million) the hardest hit. In Kansas on March 14, winds clocked at 80 mph sheared off winter-wheat sprouts on 600,000 acres and swept topsoil off another 4.2 million acres.[80]

"Were losing fertility faster than Mother Nature can replace it," warned Charles Mumma, deputy director of conservation in North Dakota. "Landowners aren't only concerned about losing their crops this year; they're also concerned about losing their soil, because that's their livelihood."[81]

"When erosion occurs," adds Edward Skinner, a USDA soil scientist at Manhattan, Kansas, "we lose the most fertile part of the soil. The fines [nutrient-rich particles] are blown away and the sands are left behind. The topsoil gets thinner, and it doesn't hold water as well, either."[82]

And Away Goes Land Down the Drain

In the 1980s Iowa, the nation's leader in corn production, showed an erosion rate approximately ten tons per acre; its rich blanket of topsoil washed into the Mississippi-Missouri River system along with vast amounts of fertilizers, chemical poisons, animal wastes and other pollutants. Before it was tilled and planted

Iowa had an average topsoil layer of about 16 inches. Today, after only a 100 years of farming, that layer is half that thickness, leaving the Hawkeye state a scant eight inches of topsoil to maintain its place as one of the world's major food producers.[83]

According to a 1977 GAO report 84 percent of 283 farms the government visited at random at the time revealed a staggering fact: 84 percent of the farms were suffering soil losses that threatened crop productivity. It was thus calculated that one third of all the nation's farmland was suffering soil losses too great to be sustained without declining crop yields.[84]

James Risser, former Washington, D.C. bureau chief for the *Des Moines Register* and two-time Pulitzer Prize winner for his reporting on agricultural and environmental issues, fairly sums up this "other farm crisis:"

With the exception of the pesticide-regulation effort inspired by Rachel Carson, the environmental ills associated with modern big-time farming have been largely ignored. But the evidence has now become overwhelming that agriculture is the last of the largely uncontrolled big polluters.

Soil losses, caused by both water and wind, are greater now than in the Dust Bowl era despite the billions of private and government dollars spent on conservation. Silt, chemicals, and animal wastes wash into rivers and reservoirs, poisoning aquatic life and depriving the water of life-sustaining oxygen. Agricultural runoff is the nation's single greatest source of untreated water pollution. Eroded soil also settles in rivers, lakes and harbors, reducing navigability and making dredging necessary.[85]

Despite such dire forecasts, a 1986 study by 12 scientists published by the National Academy of Sciences (NAS) alleges that soil erosion is not likely to affect crop productivity in the twenty-first century, as soil erosion has been reduced in the 51 years since Congress established the nation's soil conservation program. (The study admitted, however, that environmental damage beyond the farm appears to be growing. More than 75 percent of the nation's 421 million acres of cropland, the study concludes, are eroding at rates low enough to sustain the production of crops indefinitely. The total erosion of cropland soil, the report declares, is approximately 2.7 billion tons as year.[86]

Robert Gray disagrees with the NAS conclusions. "I don't see how they could say this is an improved situation and that soil erosion rates are less than in 1935. There isn't any good scientific information from that period. A statement like that is based on pure speculation."[87]

Moreover the effects of soil erosion extend beyond the farm, according to Dr. Pierre R. Crosson, senior fellow with Resources for the Future, an environmental research group in Washington, D.C. He stresses that "studies have strongly indicated that considerably more important at this point than the damages to the productivity of the soil are damages to water."[88]

A May 1985 study by the Conservation Foundation estimates that soil sediment washed from farm fields causes from $3 billion to $13 billion in damage each year by clogging navigational channels, water conveyances and treatment facilities. The study concludes that if such soil losses continue, the nation's crop yields could be reduced by an average of ten percent over the next half century.[89]

Faced with the fact that over the past 15 years soil erosion had progressively worsened, in 1985 Congress approved five key conservation provisions as part the Conservation Title of the 1985 Farm Bill. Robert Gray believes the measures contained "the most significant shift in soil conservation policy since the inception of the Soil Conservation Service in the 1930s."[90]

The conservation provisions included sodbuster, swampbuster, conservation reserve, conservation compliance and conservation easement sections which provided incentives to remove highly erodible cropland from production and impose penalties to discourage additional fragile land from coming into production. It was estimated that the conservation reserve clause alone would remove up to 45 million acres of highly erodible cropland by 1990.

The ink on the legislation was hardly dry, however, before the bill was being attacked by Representative Jamie L. Whitten, D-Miss., chairman of the House Appropriations Committee. In seeking to lift several acreage restrictions and limits on reserve payments, he was accused by environmental groups of attempting to undermine the soil conservation reserve and penalize small family farmers while favoring bigger operators.

Whitten, the four-decade congressman who many consider the nation's "permanent Secretary of Agriculture," wanted to limit farmers enrolling in the program to no more than half of their cropland in the reserve, no matter how erodible the soil, and limit reserve payments to one-third the value of the previous year's crop. The latter provision, critics contended, would singularly penalize farmers who suffered from drought, flood or losses due to pests.[91]

It soon became clear the conservation plan was falling short of its goals, principally because another USDA program — the deficiency payment (crop subsidy) program — promised farmers more money if they cultivated erodible land. A combination of severe budget limitations and an inadequate promotional effort by the USDA to enroll farmers in the program resulted in only 75 percent of the five million acres of fragile land originally targeted in the first year of the program being brought in. By September 1987 the USDA was reporting that 22.9 million acres of highly erodible farmland had been placed in its conservation program.[92]

Had the USDA and the OMB raised the average initial bid acceptance levels only slightly from $44 to $50, Gray charged, enrollment by farmers in the conservation program would have been greater. "OMB is really cheap. For another dollar per acre they could have enrolled another one million acres. That is cheap. They just haven't analyzed what could be saved in spending on the other subsidy programs by raising bid acceptance levels."[93]

The Battle for Cool, Clear Water

Water — cool, clear water — plays an increasingly major role in today's agriculture. Without it very little in the way of crops, particularly fruits and vegetables, can be grown. To produce a pound of beef requires 5,214 gallons, while the grain in a loaf of bread takes 300.

American agriculture uses nearly 47 percent of our available water supply; 20 percent of the nation's over 51 million acres of irrigated farmland, receive water from Federal projects.[94] In 1982 the value of all agricultural products sold by irrigated farms exceeded $39.5 billion, although farms with less than 50 acres accounted for only about seven percent of those sales. (See Chart 4J)

Aside from the serious ecological consequences, two primary issues related to water as a resource for food production are: 1) the steady overdraft and depletion of ground water (that which lies beneath the surface and must be pumped out for irrigation) and 2) misappropriation of surface water at discounted rates from reservoirs constructed with public funds.

In each case millions of acres of farmland, much of it previously desert or low production cropland, are irrigated with these waters. Much of the increased food production from the Midwest and Western states since World War II is a direct result of this water, but as agricultural economist E. Phillip LeVeen cautions us, "the scientific literature on water supplies also confirms the dawning of a new era of 'scarcity,' especially in the arid regions of the West. Current water use exceeds average stream flows in most of the West's major watersheds, while groundwater is being depleted in many important basins."[95]

Two examples of the underground water crisis vividly illustrate the hidden inefficiencies of a modern corporate agribusiness structure aimed more at increased production than at care for the land and ecologically responsible water use.

The Ogallala Aquifer is an enormous underground water system underlying the western tier of the nation's midsection for a length of 800 miles, from South Dakota to northern Texas. This series of subterranean water pockets was formed millennia ago from rain water seeping through the earth and forming pools ranging in size from small ponds to vast lakes.

For the past 30 years, farms that once made up much of the old Dust Bowl region have tapped into this aquifer and used the water with such heedless abandon that the supply will soon either be exhausted or no longer economically feasible to pump to the surface from such a depth.

It is estimated that since 1950 over 65,000 irrigation wells have been drilled into this aquifer, primarily to accommodate the reckless expansion of giant computer-run center-pivot irrigation systems that distribute water over giant circles up to 160 acres in size.

"The Babe Ruth of Contradictions"

In the last 15 years, for example, such practices have taken place in what journalist Ward Sinclair has called "the Babe Ruth of contradictions" — the Sandhills region of central Nebraska.[96]

Chart 4J: Agricultural Products Sold by Irrigated Farms.

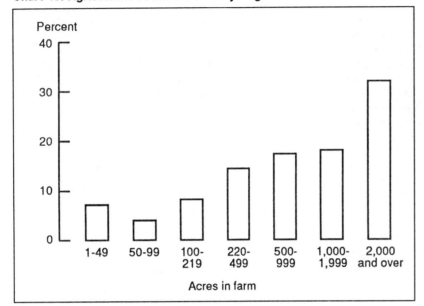

But today, we have hitched our star to exporting corn for the Japanese market. Now, we would much rather see Japanese automobiles sold in America [so the Japanese can afford to buy our corn] than worry about unemployed auto workers in Detroit. I think that is one of the things that's wrong about this industrial kind of agriculture that we're developing. Increasingly, there will be no loyalty to our own under it.[99]

To produce corn in this fashion requires heavy use of nitrogen fertilizer and chemical poisons which filter through the sandy soil, threatening both the aquifer's purity and the loss of the sand-holding grass, and adding immeasurably to wind erosion.

And Sinclair explains "a final twist to the contradictions" that allows an area such as the Sandhills to be changed from fragile prairie dunes to row crops.

The Sandhills region has become one of the state's most financially stressed farm areas. Farmer-run Production Credit Associations at O'Neill and Valentine went out of business in [1984], pulled into insolvency by their heavy commitment to expensive center-pivot irrigation development for growing corn.

Over the past four years, as corn prices stagnated and interest rates stayed high, land prices fell and the development thrill evaporated. The real estate promoters who transformed the Sandhills count on land turnover for their profits and tax benefits, and now, the land isn't moving.[100]

As if to punctuate the folly of such development in January 1986 in Omaha, Nebraska, a Larry Berryman announced that a "Sandhills Relief Fund" was being organized to collect money and food for distressed farmers still living in the Loup and Custer county areas of the Sandhills.[101]

Writing several years ago in *Environment*, Kevin Shea pointed out the wastefulness of agriculture's irrigation practices:

In spite of its long history, irrigation technology has remained fundamentally unchanged. In recent times, large inputs of energy and capital in the form of huge storage reservoirs, giant pumping stations, and concrete-lined canals have allowed irrigation systems to become more massive, but all systems, ancient or modern, still rely on gravity for distributing water. Unfortunately, the oldest and most widely used irrigation method, flood, or furrow, irrigation, is also the most wasteful and environmentally damaging. In flood irrigation, as much as 60 percent, and rarely less

For decades cattle ranchers grazed their cattle over these 19,000 square miles of grassland, the largest such expanse on the continent. Then in the 1970s, many outside real estate investors, including the Prudential Insurance Co., and the multimillionaire Bass Family from Texas — attracted by tax breaks on the land and equipment purchases, and on clearing costs and depletion allowances on water pumped from an estimated 10,000 wells drilled into the Ogallala Aquifer — turned the sand hills into acres and acres of corn. From some 2,500 center-pivot systems in the early 1970s Nebraska had over 24,000 in place a decade later.[97]

With such huge computer-operated center-pivot irrigation systems that sprayed water over hundreds of quarter-mile sections of land, a process some called "corporate hydroponics," corn production climbed from 95,000 acres to 500,000 acres. By 1975 over 35 percent of the center-pivot systems in Holt County alone were owned by outside investors with one firm — National Alfalfa Dehydrating & Milling Co. — owning and leasing some 23,000 acres.[98] This increased production soon led to a corn glut which helped depress corn prices, and increased the government's corn price support outlays. Whereas in the mid-1970s only about one percent of U.S. corn exports went to Japan, by 1981 over 13 percent of the nation's corn exports headed to Japan, with three quarters coming from Nebraska.

Marty Strange, co-director of the Center for Rural Affairs in Walthill, Nebraska which has documented this major shift in the state's exports, observes:

Unlike a few years ago, Nebraska's farm economy is not nearly so closely tied to the red-meat market. It used to be that we really cared about unemployment in Detroit because employed automobile workers tended to buy more red meat and that is where Nebraska got about three-quarters of its cash receipts from farming:

than 30 percent, of water delivered to a crop is not utilized.[102]

On 9.5 million acres — nearly one quarter of the irrigated farm land in the United States — crops are grown that nourish almost 40 percent of the nation's grain-fed livestock. As these wells dry up, momentous decisions about the future of American agriculture are under consideration: should we allow the region to revert to another Dust Bowl, or "seed" clouds to produce rain over the six-state area (with the sometimes disastrous flooding that follows), or divert some of the water from the Mississippi River to this region?[103]

Still another startling example of ground water being overdrafted by more than two million acre feet annually (an acre foot is enough water to cover one acre of land to a depth of one foot or 326,000 gallons per acre) is in California's Central Valley. Here, the water issue which has received the most attention from both farmers and the public in recent years is the long-standing controversy surrounding the enforcement of the Reclamation Law of 1902. Passed to break up the huge landholdings in the West and provide opportunities for families to settle on and till small parcels of land (160 acres), the law was never actually enforced in its 83-year history and by 1982 was radically changed in both letter and spirit.

Consequently, for years over 11 million acres of farm land in 17 western states have received irrigation water at a fraction of the actual cost of delivering it into the dams, canals and reservoirs built with public funds and administered by the Department of Interior's Bureau of Reclamation.

Much of this land has been and is now owned by nonresident "paper farmers," and cultivated in huge tracts of thousands of acres in direct contravention of the intent of the 1902 law's single-owner, 160-acre provisions. Banks, railroads, oil companies and other corporate landholders have been receiving this federal water for decades through various types of concealed ownership agreements and leaseback arrangements.

Today over 30 percent of our vegetables for fresh and processed markets is produced on this land, with major concentrations in California, Arizona and Washington. Also, approximately 18 percent of the nation's cotton, 14 percent of its barley, 12 percent of its rice and three percent of its wheat are grown on land now receiving federally subsidized water.[104]

Chapter Five

Trapped on the Technological Treadmill

Modern technology, widely acclaimed as the primary source of our nation's agricultural and industrial abundance, has in the 20th century now run the gamut: allowing us both the ability to realize mass production and/or mass destruction. In their relentless lust to manufacture two stalks of corn where one had grown before, in their quest to engineer bigger and more costly machines to plough up our fields and harvest our crops, and in their determination to eradicate pests and insects with ever-more-toxic chemicals, science and industry have also brought us to the ultimate technological denouement.

Buried in the earth of America's heartland, buried in that agriculturally rich and productive area that stretches from the Mississippi River to the Rocky Mountains and from North Dakota to Texas, are not only the seeds of a nation's cornucopia, but the instruments of its annihilation. Both are heralded as crowning achievements of modern technology, both ever ready to burst forth to fulfill their destiny.

Pondering such a grim paradox in her nationally-syndicated column, "The Silos That Don't Hold Wheat," Ellen Goodman reminds us that "in some ways North Dakota is like all of America. It's a land-based territory of plowshares and swords, giant combines and huge ICBMs, with resources to feed the world or destroy it. But it's more obvious here."[1] Here in North Dakota, for example, where over a reported 900 nuclear weapons were based on 300 Minuteman III missiles in addition to two squadrons of B-52 bombers,[2] is a state which also produces 12 percent of the nation's wheat and over $2.6 billion in total farm sales. It is also a state which some of its more zealous citizens tout as "North Dakota — World's Third Nuclear Power,"[3] where we have both at the same time enabled massive weapons of annihilation, in the words of the novelist E. L. Doctorow, "to partake of a life-giving symbol universally associated with regeneration," while allowing a faltering farm economy based on the sustaining of life to be preempted by a costly, wasteful and greedy industry built on death and destruction.[4]

As Doctorow explains,

Understand that when the farmers in North Dakota talk about being the world's third nuclear power, they are not talking as militarists, they are talking as a chamber of commerce... It's not that we love whatever it is that makes us special, it's that we have to take our identity where we can. The average human being's capacity for allegiance is indiscriminate, like pure sexual appetite, except that it increases with age... . Of course, among our most powerful allegiances are those relating to the sources of our income. The combined military and civilian [1978] payroll at Minot Air Force Base is more that $42,000,000 a year. For that kind of money, a community can work out any number of rationales for living in fields of missiles.[5]

Such an attitude, as Goodman has already pointed out, is a manifestation of the reliance all America has put on an unharnessed technology that could well destroy our planet.[6] It is not just the silos of nuclear destruction buried in the land that produces our food that now stand for us as macabre symbols of the dark side of modern technology: it is also the deadly waste from these silos' fissionable essence that modern technology suggests we use to process the food we eat.

As we shall later examine, there is today a growing movement within corporate agribusiness to utilize *irradiation* in the processing of our food. It is simply another way that modern technocrats seek further social justification for building more nuclear weapons while attempting to sell an uneducated public on a continued and expanded use of nuclear power.

In a 1970s essay "The Bomb Lives," Doctorow peered into a future built upon and dependent on such forms of nuclear energy and eloquently warned us of its possible promise.

We are extraordinarily sensitive now to the damage we do to the delicate web of life on earth simply by being ourselves. We used to fear the bomb, but now we fear everything. What can this be but the diffusion of our horror of this death-in-life weapon that we have given the world. For, of course, having buried our bombs, we are now seeing them stir and unwrap their mummy shrouds.

Conceivably, under the right circumstances, we may someday in our nuclear industry lose to the earth just the amount of radiant material necessary to effect a chain reaction. And then the failure of our vaunted adaptation will blaze upon us that what happened to the bomb was that it became the earth, and the earth became the bomb."[7]

But, whether we choose to praise, question or lament the precarious place in history to which modern technology has delivered us, we should not be lulled into believing that such a journey was one of "progress" or a mere evolutionary accident brought about by civilization's pursuit of the "better life."

As Oregon State sociologist Sally Hacker points out:

Technology — the way we organize energy and materials to get work done — can be and often is selectively developed to insure social hierarchy. Technology is not simply a collection of machines. It also includes social relations in the way that work is organized. Technology, then, is both social and technical. It doesn't simply emerge. It is not operating on its own internal principles. It is carefully selected and its development directed by those men who own and manage. And their choices are made in their own interests.

And, in discussing agriculture and agribusiness, she adds,

Hierarchy, with its related fear and uneasy relief, is a very effective source of control and characterizes most, but not all, forms of social organization. Agribusiness, compared with agriculture, exaggerates hierarchy in social relations... A rigid, divisive organizational structure — rural divided from urban, chicana/o from anglo, men from women, decision-making from labor — is brought to us by agribusiness and the companies it keeps.[8]

Who Gains? Who Loses?

Two decades ago Willard Cochrane, now retired agricultural economics professor from the University of Minnesota and former USDA director of economic research, described what he termed the "treadmill of agriculture," to explain the financial, structural and market effects brought about by technological changes in farming.[9] Any effort to understand America's permanent agricultural crisis should begin by examining Cochrane's analysis of the role of technology in agriculture and how that technology has played and is playing a decisive role in eradicating our nation's family farm system.

Cochrane's "treadmill" suggests that those who first adopt a new technology reap higher profits through lower costs per unit of output; that provides them with the motive and the opportunity to increase production, often by expanding the size of their operation.

The potential for higher profits attracts others to the technology. Soon, the spread of the technology affects overall supplies and prices, the value of land, and prices of production inputs. Eventually, Cochrane concluded, the "income gains to farmers are wiped out, and farmers are back where they started, in a no-profit position."[10]

Or as the Center for Rural Affairs's Marty Strange describes it,

The personality of our industrial system is materialistic. It is designed and expected to produce 'more.' The production process and the technology it employs conform to this expectation. Both diversity and individuality are its enemy.

The powerful, mysterious technology that fosters industrial agribusiness is directed at immediate materialistic objectives — more food and more profit with little concern for long-run sustainability.[11]

Dramatic proof of Cochrane's analysis has been reported by farm economist Lloyd Teigen of USDA's ERS after constructing an economic model to simulate the effects of technological change after a new technology is introduced and adopted.[12]

He launched his model with 100 farms, all utilizing a traditional technology, in an economic environment that he assumed would have the same competitive pressures and basic relationships among supply, demand and price as currently exists in U.S. agriculture today.

He then introduced a new technology, such as a new type of mechanical harvester. First, one farm adopts the new technology, increasing its output by using less labor and more land and chemical poisons, and realizing a much higher profit despite its higher production input costs. But sooner or later, Teigen explains, prices adjust for the adoption of the new technology by others which increases the supply of the product and reduces the market price.

Meanwhile, greater demand for land and chemicals raise farmland prices. These altered prices soon affect everyone in the system since those who haven't adopted the new technology have difficulty competing with the early innovators, who use their temporary advantage to bid for land and other resources from the more traditional farms.

As the new technology spreads, the profits of both the innovators and the traditional farms drop, as does the total net farm income. In Teigen's model, when 40 percent of the farms have adopted the new technology the average profit to each of the innovators is *less* than the profit made prior to the introduction of any change. By the time around half the farms in the industry have shifted from the traditional into the innovator category, profits fall below the level needed to keep farms in the industry.

When that happens, someone drops out, releasing resources to the others. The remaining farms expand, but they cannot completely make up for lost production from the exiting farms. The industry's overall output stops climbing and begins to decline. As a result, prices for its products stop dropping and begin to rise.

Although the innovators and traditional farms experience a brief increase in profits and the total net income grows for the first time since the process began, the upturn is brief, the pattern of declining profits and income quickly resume as more farms adopt the new technology.

When profits drop below the threshold again more farms drop out and the process repeats itself. Technological change expands industry output and reduces prices and profits, while structural change works in the opposite direction. It reduces the number of farms and the product supply, thus raising both industry income and profits. The combination leads to fewer and fewer farms whose profits converge to the threshold at which farms leave the industry.

As Teigen's model reaches a new equilibrium — a point at which no further change is taking place — only 88 of the original 100 farms remain. While all have adopted the new technology, the income of the industry is substantially lower than it was at the outset. However, this income is divided among fewer farms. Likewise, while output per farm is up sharply, output for the entire industry is only slightly higher than it was with the 100 farms in business. The price of the product is down while land and fertilizer prices are much higher than at the beginning.

While acknowledging that technological change is a continually evolving process that interacts with many other economic, political, social and institutional variables, Teigen claims that "in a competitive industry like agriculture, the gains from strategic information and innovation are never permanent.

"For that reason, technological change is like a narcotic. It creates a need for additional change because all subsequent people who adopt the new technology will be driving down your prices and your profits."

He also stresses that while it might be argued that technological change is necessary to maintain the "competitiveness" of the individual producer and U.S. agriculture as a whole, it does not necessarily improve the financial conditions of those who embrace it.

Strange also points out that farm technology in the United States has been fundamentally shaped by the perception that natural resources are plentiful and labor is dear. "But does that assessment remain accurate? he asks. "If it doesn't, then it is time for us to reconsider our technology base."

As we are about to see, those institutions within corporate agribusiness which own and control the major share of its natural and financial resources and which have the economic and political power to shape agriculture's research priorities are the ones which usually reap the largest rewards from such types of technological change.

"In the long term, the rewards will go to those farmers who ride the crest of each new technology, not those who adopt a technology and then hope to rest on their laurels," Teigen points out. Owners of land and other such assets benefit as the additional productivity of assets is capitalized into asset values, as happened during the 1970s.

Corporate agribusiness, meanwhile, never tires of proclaiming that consumers benefit most from this new technology. For example, a March 1985 report by the Office of Technology Assessment maintains that "the ultimate beneficiary is the consumer. Larger supplies, lower food prices, and better quality have almost invariably been the main results of agricultural research."[13] Teigen, however, cautions that such benefits do not necessarily accrue to consumers.

My model suggests that the structural effects induced by technological change might reduce the number of farms to the point where output of the remaining farms would not completely replace production from the original group. That could mean a smaller quantity of food on the market and eventually, a higher price to consumers. In other words, what technology gives, structural change may take away.

Strange wonders on a more fundamental level whether the social objective that our farm technology was supposedly designed to accomplish — to produce ever more food with fewer people — is still relevant.

The rationale for this objective is that if people can be freed from the burdens of working to produce their own food, they will be able to contribute to other economic development objectives.

In our society, only about 1 per cent of the population is directly involved in commercial food production and that 1 per cent supplies nearly all the food we eat, plus half again that much for export. A further reduction of the labor force in agriculture is not going to contribute much to increased economic development. Unemployment and poverty, not food shortages, are the social problems in America.

Balancing the Scales of Efficiency

The champions of modern technology frequently argue that farm "efficiency" and "economies of size" in agriculture are only enhanced by such progress and that while a few farmers might have to endure unfortunate side-effects, the overall economy and the society at large will benefit.

What modern technology in agriculture has brought about, however, is an increase in farm size, with ruinous side-effects: environmental disruption (from the increased use of large machines, more fertilizer, chemical poisons and herbicides); a mass migration of millions of small farmers and hired agricultural workers to cities ill-prepared to receive them; and the loss of the proven social, political and economic benefits of communities with a small farm base.

Meanwhile, state and Federal tax laws, regulations and controls favoring increasingly large farms have added to this disruption. As Michael Perelman and Kevin Shea observe:

Compounding the problem is the existence of two different concepts of efficiency in farming. One defines efficiency in terms of the accounting of dollar costs and profits; this is, an efficient farm makes money. The other defines efficiency in terms of effective use of human and natural resources; this is, the efficient farm realizes the greatest social and environmental good with the least expenditure of scarce resources.[14]

Debate about the attributes of modern technology often overlooks what California Resource Conservation Specialist Gil Friend calls "biological sustainability."

Speaking to a 1981 annual conference of the Agricultural Institute of Canada in St. Catherine's, Ontario, Friend explained:

> The question of sustainability is the question of whether, as we produce our food, we will leave our progeny gardens or deserts. And the challenge of a sustainable agriculture is to produce the food and fiber needed by people in a way that preserves — or improves fertile soils; that maintains — or expands — supplies of clean water; that protects — or regenerates — the biological diversity and health of the earth's ecosystems; that supports — or enriches vital, coherent human cultures; and that remembers the role of the farmer both as producer of food and fiber and as steward of natural resources.[15]

As Missouri's Professor Breimyer adds, we must recognize that "agriculture has an intergenerational dimension. It requires that a moral choice must be made between generations — ours, and those of the future."[16]

Efficiency in farming has traditionally been measured by comparing the number of hours worked with the amount of food produced. With the rapid development of ever-new technological inputs, we are now producing more food per hour than in 1940. However, when measuring the manner in which energy-based technology has replaced human labor with its high priced social, economic and environmental costs, serious doubts arise as to whether such productivity has genuinely been "cost-effective."

D. Gale Johnson, University of Chicago agricultural economist, in breaking down the USDA estimates of farm productivity, displays some revealing figures.

    1940-50 — 1.7 percent gain
    1950-60 — 2.4 percent gain
    1960-70 — 1.3 percent gain
    1970-80 — 2.1 percent gain[17]

The average rate of increase in productivity for the 1965-79 period was actually lower than the average for 1950-65. In figures submitted to Congress in the January 1987 *Economic Report of the President* farm productivity from 1981 to 1986 showed but a slight 1.3 percent increase.

We must ask at what cost is this corporate agribusiness concept of "efficiency?"

In the past we have been led to believe that "economies of scale" — that is, reducing unit costs by increasing the volume of production — will stretch indefinitely. But, in fact, beyond a certain point "bigger" is not more efficient — simply more powerful economically and able to control a larger market share.

Even corporate agribusiness giants like the oil, gas and land-company conglomerate Tenneco Inc. has recognized (at least on paper) that when it comes to long-term efficiency, which includes care of the land for several generations to ensure productivity, a family farm community is desirable. Tenneco has recognized that

economies of scale, which are so apparent in most lines of business, sometimes do not apply to agriculture.

> From the standpoint of efficiency, there is no effective substitute for the small to medium size, independent grower who lives on or near his farmlands, who is knowledgeable in the science of horticulture, who has a deep personal involvement in the outcome of his efforts.[18]

Numerous private and USDA studies have shown the family farm to be our most efficient agricultural production unit. Back in 1967 the USDA was claiming that the most efficient farms were "truly mechanized one-two man farms." Another USDA study indicated that even with current farming practices — heavy use of fertilizers, chemical poisons, mechanization, specialization, etc. — for most crops small acreages are the most efficient (20 acres for tobacco, 120 acres for peaches, 640 acres for mixed vegetables, and 1,000 to 2,000 acres for corn and wheat).[19] In July 1981 the USDA again concluded that "increasing farm size does not necessarily increase farm efficiency or productivity. In fact, small farms in many field crop [wheat, feed grains, and cotton] regions are nearly as technically efficient as large farms." And the report goes on to stress:

> Since medium-sized commercial farms with gross incomes from $41,000 to $76,000 achieve most technical cost efficiencies, society benefits *little* in terms of *lower real food costs* from further *increases* in farm size. Actually, many commercial farms now *exceed* the size necessary to achieve *all available cost efficiencies*. With current field crop production technology, *further growth in medium-size and larger farms will not likely improve overall food production efficiency.*" (emphasis added)[20]

The reality, however, is that super farms tend to dominate the marketplace, by producing a higher volume and thus reducing their unit costs vis-a-vis procurement costs. Meanwhile, small and medium size farms have been trapped in a vicious cost/price squeeze caused by a low net income coupled with even lower purchasing power.

A 1985 GAO report cautioned that the new technology and public policy threaten the survival of the moderate-size family farms which continue to be replaced by large farms that thrive on specialized equipment, computer management systems and genetic engineering as well as Federal tax laws and farm subsidy programs.[21]

These new technologies, the OTA's 1986 report stresses,

> are most likely to receive first adoption by farmers who are well financed and are capable of providing the sophisticated management required to make profitable use of the technologies. Most of these farmers will be associated with relatively large operations. Hence, the technologies will

tend to give additional economic advantages to large farm firms relative to moderate and smaller farms, accentuating the trend toward a dual farm structure in the United States.

In discussing the implications and policy options for agriculture resulting from these new technologies, the report adds that

> Without substantial changes in the nature and objectives of farm policy, the three classes of farms [large scale, moderate size, and small, predominantly part-time farms] will soon become two — the moderate size farms will largely be eliminated as a viable force in American agriculture. In addition, the problems of the small subsistence farms will continue to fester as an unaddressed social concern.[22]

Technology's "Logic"

In addition to the increasing concentration in agriculture itself, the market in the field of "new technologies" for the farmer today grows increasingly smaller, having become dominated by a few large major corporations. This is true with respect to borrowing of money from the bank, buying necessary seed and expensive agricultural chemicals or purchasing modern farm machinery.

Whereas the difference between consumer expenditures for domestic farm-originated food products and the value farmers received for the products was $111.4 billion in 1975 as compared with $261.2 billion in 1985 (an increase of 134 percent),[23] net farm income, expressed in real purchasing power was decreasing by 36.6 percent from 1975 to 1985.[24] As consumer food expenditures from 1975 to 1985 rose 107 percent, from $167 billion to $346.3 billion, the farmer's production expenses climbed even faster, doubling and tripling and in the case of interest expenses, multiplying fourfold. (See Chart 5A)

Just between 1980 and 1986 alone, the spread between the farmer's share of USDA's market basket of food and the retail cost of that basket rose 26.7 percent while the farmer's share dropped 19 percent.[25]

The high price of energy has certainly been a significant factor in triggering these increases, but, as we shall examine in the following chapter, the concentrated nature of the food and farm input industry, has played an even larger and virtually unnoticed role in increasing production costs and diminishing the real income of our farmers.

For example, the 23 corporations most deeply involved in agricultural inputs in 1986 came from the top 30 U.S. corporations in terms of assets. Indeed, of the $5.65 trillion held in corporate assets by the nation's top 500 businesses, 34 percent were in the hands of the largest 20 percent.[26]

First and foremost farmers need capital before one seed can go into the ground or a machine can move across an open field. In farm financing the top 100 banks in the United States issued $9.37 billion in agricultural loans (real estate and production) which were outstanding on March 31, 1986. Just ten of these banks, however, accounted for 45.6 percent of this total; the top three banks, all based in California, were responsible for 28.3 percent.[27]

And who are the customers of these major private farm lending institutions?

"There is no question that the big farmers command the largest proportionate share of all the credit outstanding to institutions," one FCA executive told *Business Week*. "We try to spread ourselves across the board, since we service all categories, but it is a fact that the bigger the farms become, the more credit they need. And they get it."[28]

As these larger and larger farms looking outside their own community for new capital to finance high tech agriculture local financial institutions find themselves unable to handle such sizeable loans. In recent years, therefore, many new large urban and foreign banks have begun to seek farm customers aggressively.

"Bankers from the heart of New York City are now looking at the heart of America" according to the FCA's Donald Wilkinson. "The day of the financial 'supermarket' may not be here just yet, but I don't think it's too far off. We are in a new era of banking and financing [for farmers]. And the question is whether or not we're ready and can handle a few 'mega-loans'."[29]

In the mid-1980s, for example, some small rural banks in 13 midwestern states were offered the services of a giant foreign financial institution, Rabobank of the Netherlands — a $40 billion Dutch cooperative bank. Through MABSCO Agricultural Services agricultural loans could be made available through a select number of local banks, which in turn sold up to 80 percent of those loans to Rabobank at a rate to be determined when the loan was made.[30]

For some farmers this interjection of foreign capital raises disturbing questions. As James Gutman, business news editor for the *Milwaukee Sentinel*, writes: "It all sounds good, but in the back of one's mind there is the specter already haunting many farm groups and agricultural policymakers — that even more of the nation's farmland could come under foreign *control or influence*." (emphasis added)[31]

The Seeds of Revolution

Farmers need not only "seed *money*" but seeds. In this important area we see still another example of the growing and alarming economic concentration in the farm input sector.

Today giant multinational corporations dominate the $13 billion seed trade, with nine out of ten of the world's major chemical poison manufacturers having become active in the seed industry.

Addressing this question, the Rural Advancement Foundation International's (RAFI) Cary Fowler and Pat Mooney, point out that,

> Through sheer size and economic power, the transnationals have come to dominate the commercial market for seeds. In industrialized countries this process has been facilitated by the passage of laws giving corporations patent-like

Chart 5A: Farm Expenses (in billions of dollars)

Year	Seed	Feed	Ferti-lizer	Chemical Poisons	Oil & Fuel	Elec-tricity	Machin-ery	Interest
1973	1.6	13.2	3.5	1.4	1.9	0.4	n.a.	4.7
1977	2.5	14.0	6.5	1.9	4.4	1.1	5.5	8.5
1981	3.9	18.8	10.1	3.6	8.9	2.0	10.2	19.9
1984	3.5	20.4	8.4	4.9	7.1	2.1	7.2	21.1
1985	3.4	18.0	8.9	2.4	6.5	2.0	5.8	20.4
1986	3.0	16.2	5.8	4.3	4.8	2.1	n.a.	16.9
1987	3.0	16.1	5.4	4.6	4.4	2.4	n.a.	15.5
1988*	3.0	21.0	6.0	5.0	5.0	3.0	n.a.	16.0

Source: "Farm Income Data: A Historical Perspective," Gary Lucier/Agnes Chesley/Mary Ahern, Economic Research Service, USDA, Statistical Bulletin No. 740. "1986 Agricultural Chartbook," USDA, Agricultural Handbook No. 663. "Agricultural Resources: Inputs (Situation and Outlook Report)," USDA-ERS, AR-5, January, 1987; "Economic Indicators of the Farm Sector: Farm Sector Review, 1986," ERS, USDA, ECIFS 6-3, January, 1988; "Agricultural Income and Finance: Situation and Outlook Report," USDA-ERS, AFO-33, May, 1989.

* USDA May, 1989 Forecast

control over new varieties they develop. Often called 'Plant Breeders Rights,'these laws allow corporations to own plant varieties and set the conditions of sale for those varieties.[32]

Fowler also expresses alarm over the fact that the multibillion seed industry has recently experienced a rash of mergers and corporate takeovers.

Many old family-owned seed companies have been bought out by large multinational corporations. The petrochemical and drug industries — major producers of pesticides and fertilizers — have been especially active. Their interest in the seed business raises three provocative questions.

First, will corporations who are big producers of pesticides and fertilizers encourage their new seed company subsidiaries to breed new plant varieties that require more or fewer pesticides and fertilizers?

Second, will the acquisition of small seed companies by corporations who are active around the world tend to create international seed companies that will be better able to spread their new varieties to regions where old varieties still predominate? Will they therefore speed up the process of driving these old varieties out of existence?

Finally, will the takeover of seed companies like Burpee by ITT bring slick, uninformative advertising to the seed business.[33]

Since 1970 some 500 seed houses around the world have been taken over by large transnational companies while another 300 appear contractually linked to the even larger firms. (Chart 5B)

World seed authority Pat Mooney, writing in the 1983 *Development Dialogue* on "The Law of the Seed: Another Development and Plant Genetic Resources," points out that, "three areas — seeds, pesticides and pharmaceuti-

cals — have a common ground in intensive research related to genetics and chemicals. With great new markets and patent security on the horizon, it was only natural for chemical concerns to become the world's new seedsmen."[34]

As more and more of these chemical and energy companies, grain traders and food firms become involved in seed sales and patents (between 1970 and 1980 some 28 such multinational corporations were awarded 51 percent of the total seed patents) we can expect increased concentration in this "new breed of farming."[35] Monsanto, for example, has announced plans to develop seeds which will "secrete a natural substance that kills soil-dwelling insects." "Farming," according to Howard Schneiderman, the company's vice president for research, "is becoming a higher and higher-tech business."[36]

One financial analyst predicts that by the year 2000 about two dozen multinationals will dominate the seed industry. "They are trying to solidify their links to the marketplace, and seed is the packet by which genetics research is delivered to the farmer," according to George Kidd.[37]

In expressing general alarm over the fate of our more traditional seed varieties, Fowler, who along with Canada's Mooney has co-authored *Shattering: Food, Politics and the Loss of Genetic Diversity,* stresses that the extinction of a seed variety does not come simply at the

Chart 5B: Top Ten Seed Houses (By Rank)

1. Pioneer
2. Sandoz
3. Upjohn
4. Limagrain
5. Cargill
6. Volvo
7. ICI
8. France Mais
9. Dekalb-Pfizer
10. Claus

time when there are no more seeds; rather extinction comes when their development process ceases to exist.

The authors of this, possibly the most significant book devoted to a specific environmental issue since Rachel Carson's *The Silent Spring*, point out that approximately 97 percent of the varieties given in a 1903 USDA vegetable list are now extinct.

Two years, for example, after the 1970 corn blight which destroyed over 15 percent of the U.S. crop, the U.S. National Academy of Sciences published a 307-page report titled *Genetic Vulnerability of Major Crops*. Fowler and Mooney emphasize that the study, in revealing that the U.S. was shockingly dependent on a handful of varieties of its major crops, concluded that U.S. agriculture was "*impressively uniform genetically and impressively vulnerable*."

Fowler and Mooney believe that five principles or "laws" of genetic conservation are necessary to preserve a healthy and diversified seed culture. These "laws" include:

Agricultural diversity can only be safeguarded through the use of diverse strategies. No one strategy can preserve and protect what it took so many human cultures, farming systems and environments so long to produce. Different conservation systems can complement each other and provide insurance against the inadequacies or shortcomings of any one method.

What agricultural diversity is saved depends on who is consulted. How much is saved depends on how many people are involved. Farmers, gardeners, fishing people, medicine makers, religious leaders, carpenters — all have different interests that foreign scientists could never appreciate fully. All segments of a community need to be involved to insure that the total needs of the community are met. The more involvement, the greater the potential to conserve.

Agricultural diversity will not be saved unless it is used. The value of diversity is in its use; only in use can diversity be appreciated enough to be saved. And only in use can it continue to evolve, thus retaining its value.

Agricultural diversity cannot be saved without saving the farm community. Conversely, the farm community cannot be saved without saving diversity. Diversity, like music or a dialect, is part of the community that produces it. It cannot exist for long without that community and the circumstances that gave rise to it. Saving farmers is a prerequisite of saving diversity. Conversely, communities must save their agricultural diversity in order to retain options for development and self-reliance. Someone else's seeds imply someone else's needs.

The need for diversity is never-ending. THEREFORE, OUR EFFORTS TO PRESERVE THIS DIVERSITY CAN NEVER CEASE. Because extinction is forever, conservation must be forever. No technology can relieve us of our responsibility to preserve agricultural diversity for ourselves and generations.

Thus, we must continue to utilize diverse conservation strategies, involve as many people in the process as possible, see that diversity is actively used and insure the survival of the farm community — for as long as we want agricultural diversity to exist.[38]

What is happening today in the seed industry throughout the world is but only one manifestation of a much more serious and encompassing revolution — the full-scale invasion of biotechnology into agriculture.

Striving to take the leadership in such a corporate dominated age of biotechnologically-engineered agriculture and food is the Monsanto Company, headquartered in St. Louis, Missouri. By setting out to change forever how food and fiber are produced, the near 90-year old chemical firm has asserted that as a corporation, "Monsanto is developing a way to use Mother Nature to modify organisms to serve us better."

"Research and development isn't part of the strategy. Research and development *is* the strategy," Richard J. Mahoney, the company's chairman and chief executive officer, emphasizes.

Congress's Office of Technology Assessment estimates that some 400 companies may now be spending over $2 billion a year on biotechnology research and development. Clearly, Monsanto is planning to be the leader in this growth industry.

"Two years from now, every crop in the world will be easily manipulated. Ten years from now, in some plant we'll know every gene, every protein, every function. The door is wide open. There are no longer any technical restraints," declares Robert T. Farley, who is in charge of the company's plant molecular biology group.

Monsanto's scientists are already predicting the first of its genetically engineered plants will be on the market by 1994 or 1995. At the same time, the company has reported that the "quality" of its products has been steadily improving and that productivity is 47 percent higher than it was four years ago. *Business Week*, however, observes that "in focussing on quality and productivity, [company] employees became less safety conscious, and injuries are more frequent."

Nevertheless, Mahoney's stated goal is to raise Monsanto's return on equity or investment from 15 percent to 20 percent by the mid-1990s.

Already the company has developed a variety of crops — tomatoes, potatoes, alfalfa, tobacco and cucumbers — that are resistant to viral infections. In addition, they have also altered cotton, tomatoes and potatoes with bacterial genes that produce proteins fatal to budworms, boil worms and other pests.

"The kind of biotechnology that Monsanto has embarked upon is silver-bullet technology that will prolong the system of agriculture we have now," warns Jack Doyle, author of the recently published *Altered Harvest* and director of the Friends of the Earth Agriculture and Technology Project.

"We have the potential to understand biological systems in agriculture as never before, such as understanding the entire cycle of how pests attack crops and how crops respond. But the way the very technology is being capitalized and developed, we're intervening for the convenience of a product."

"Monsanto sees all living creatures as resources to be subject to whatever manipulations are required for the market," adds the Foundation on Economic Trends' Jeremy Rifkin.

In *Altered Harvest*, a full and even-handed chronicle of the emerging agricultural genetics industry, Jack Doyle also tells us that:

> In this new era, food will be more finely shaped at its point of origin — at the level of the seed, the gene, and the molecule. Food will begin in the laboratory rather than the farmer's field. Crops will still grow in fields, but they will be given their biological marching orders by scientists who design them in the laboratory."[39]

Doyle also warns that with genetic engineering and biotechnology, this revolution is moving at astronomical speed, and it is shifting the practice and control of agriculture from farmers to scientists, and most importantly, *to those who own science.*

> If investment continues this way and if corporate entities begin producing foodstuffs that way, then natural resources are going to matter less. The real action is going to be the gathering of genes, not our concern about soil and the other basics of agriculture. And the farmer is in the middle, on his way to becoming a "tender" of genes owned by somebody else.

Doyle concludes,

> When you look at mergers and acquisitions of recent years, you see that the traditional lines of distinction between the seed companies, the drug and the energy and the chemical companies are made obsolete. At the base of all those industries is DNA [the genetic stuff of life]. It is a new power base for the superconglomerates.[40]

As noted nine out of ten of the nation's largest chemical firms are currently involved in genetic engineering and some experts predict that within the next 25 years biotechnology will become a $100 billion industry.[41]

Telling the Difference Between A Farmer and a Pigeon

After seeds go into the ground it is new and more powerful farm machinery, more toxic fertilizers and chemical poisons that modern farmers have been forced to rely upon to continue their crop's growth cycle.

Tractors, of course, have become essential to present-day farmers, but their choice of brands has been restricted, particularly in the past 15-20 years. As early as 1972 a Federal Trade Commission (FTC) study determined that such concentration accounted for farmers paying $251.1 million in monopoly overcharges.[42]

As rural life humorist Patricia Leimbach points out to delighted farm audiences: "the difference between a farmer and a pigeon today is that the pigeon can still make a small deposit on a tractor."[43]

By the early 1980s the market was dominated by Deere & Co. and International Harvester (now known as Navistar, Inc.), whose market share of the U.S. tractor market reached nearly 65 percent. They were followed by Massey Ferguson and Ford Motor, which together accounted for approximately another 26 percent of the market.[44] As the farm crisis began to worsen and farmers bought less heavy machinery, the industry became even further concentrated. In 1984 the giant multinational Tenneco, already in the market through its subsidiary J.I. Case, acquired most of the farm equipment business of International Harvester for $430 million of which only $260 million was in cash.[45]

In October 1985 Ford Motor Co. announced it was purchasing from Sperry Corporation for $330 million plus $110 million in liabilities its New Holland farm equipment business, further narrowing the number of U.S. tractor manufacturers.[46] Massey-Ferguson retrenched and restructured and another major firm, Allis-Chalmers, also disappeared from the tractor-manufacturing scene in 1985, having been acquired by a West German firm.[47] Later, in June 1987, the company filed for Chapter 11 bankruptcy protection.[48]

Boasting sales of more than 300,000 tractors, combines and other pieces of equipment in 1979 worth a total retail value of over $12 billion the industry saw its sales shrink to only $4.5 billion and 146,000 units sold by 1986.[49] In addition, unit sales of all major farm equipment items dropped 42 percent between 1979 and 1988.

The Allis-Chalmers acquisition by the German heavy industry firm of KlockneHumbodlt-Dentz AG also highlighted another dramatic shift in farm machinery manufacturing. In 1987 approximately 85 percent of the farm machinery sold in the United States was made in Japan and Europe, a startling 50 percent increase in just ten years.[50]

By the beginning of 1989 four firms — John Deere, (27 percent), Ford New Holland (19 percent), J.I. Case (17 percent), and Kubota (16.5 percent) controlled 79.5 percent of the North American market shares in farm machinery.[51]

Indeed, no one sector of the farm input industry has felt the impact of agricultural's current economic plight more than farm equipment firms. In the first five years of the 1980s its plants operated at less than 50 percent of capacity, the number of employees decreasing from 160,000 to 90,000. It has been estimated that the principal companies in the industry lost an aggregate of more than $2 billion.

Between 1979 and 1988 John Deere alone cut its worldwide employment 42 percent and now claims that it can make money even while its plants operate at only 35 percent of capacity, down from 65 percent to 70 percent earlier in the decade.[52]

The consequences of concentration in the oil and chemical industry, upon which so much of modern agriculture depends are, of course, well-known to both urban and rural Americans. Thus, in 1977 farmers were paying 57 cents per gallon for gasoline, 45 cents per gallon for diesel fuel and 39 cents for LP gas. By January, 1986 the respective costs were $1.14, $1.00 and 74 cents.[53]

At the same time fuel costs were skyrocketing, more and more energy was required to produce our food. For example, in 1950 it required slightly less than one-half barrels of oil (.44) to produce a ton of grain. By 1985 it took 1.14 barrels of oil to produce a like amount of grain.[54]

Better Living Through Chemistry?

The area where modern agribusiness technology claims to have made its biggest strides in recent years is in the production of fertilizers and agricultural chemicals. (See Chart 5C) By 1988 over 817 million pounds of herbicides, insecticides and fungicides had become available to American farmers.[55]

From 1950 to 1986 farmers increased their tonnage use of fertilizer by 141 percent, yet the cost of purchased fertilizers, as reported by the USDA, increased from $868 million to $6.5 billion.[56] In the 1983-84 period fertilizer consumption in the United States and Puerto Rico was up 20 percent from 1982-83,[57] however, 1985-86 brought a ten percent decline from the previous year's use.[58]

As in the other areas of the farm input industry, there is heavy corporate concentration in fertilizer manufacturing. Recent sales figures show that four firms produce 28.5 percent of ammonia nitrate fertilizer, 31 percent of all ammonia, 40 percent of the nitrogen solutions, 41 percent of urea, 45.7 percent of ammonium phosphate, 62 percent of phosphate rock, and 69 percent of the potash.[59]

At the conclusion of World War II the world's and United States's major chemical companies such as Dow, Shell and Du Pont found themselves with huge inventories of nitrogen used for making bombs during the war. Many of these chemicals and others produced for the war effort were soon packaged for agriculture for use both here at home and as one of the not coincidental cornerstones for the so-called "green revolution" abroad.

Fertilizer use throughout the world soared from 14 million tons in 1950 to 131 million tons in 1986. Even as cropland per person was declining by one-third, fertilizer use per person was going from 11 pounds per person in 1950 to 57 pounds in 1986.[60]

As world economic growth slowed in the 1980s and Third World debt grew with weakening agricultural prices and reduced fertilizer subsidies, the use of fertilizers dropped from six percent annual growth rate in the 1970s to less than three percent in the 1980s. At the same time between 1950 and 1980 the tons of grain produced per ton of fertilizer applied fell from 45 to 1 to 13 to 1 and remained at 13 to 1 throughout most of the 1980s.[61]

In the United States the use of herbicides grew over 175 percent from 1958 to the point that in 1981 farmers applied 625 million pounds to their land in an effort to destroy the hardy variety of weeds that often plague their fields. Herbicide sales now total over $2 billion in the United States and over $4.5 billion world-wide and account for over 60 percent of all chemical poison use in the United States[57]

The Chemical Poison Trade

Along with this dramatic increase in chemical fertilizers and herbicides in the post-war decades, there has also been an explosion in what the chemical industry euphemistically calls "pesticides" or "plant food," but which in fact are often highly toxic and deadly *chemical poisons.*

Today it is estimated that there are nearly 35,000 of these chemical poisons being manufactured from only some 600 different chemical components.[63] From 1950 to 1988 overall production of these poisons for agricultural use in the United States increased from 200,000 to 845 million pounds.[64]

The environmental and health consequences to farmers, farm workers and consumers from such massive use of these chemical poisons are bad enough; to make matters worse, despite an *11-fold* increase in the use of

Chart 5C: Agricultural Chemical Poison Use in the United States, 1985

Class of Chemical Poison	Expenditures in $ Millions	Amount Used in Pounds Millions
Herbicides	2,900	525
Insecticides	1,100	225
Fungicides	315	51
Other*	300	60
TOTAL	**4,615**	**861**

* Includes Rodenticides, fumigants, and molluscicides

SOURCE: Environmental Protection Agency, Economics Analysis Branch, Office of Pesticide Programs, Washington, D.C. 20460, September, 1986.

chemical poisons in the last 30 years, crop loss due to insecticide resistance has doubled.[65]

Researchers are beginning to report that these chemical poisons have only limited lifetimes of usefulness before nature adapts and makes them ineffective. More than 447 insects have become resistant to these poisons, along with seven animals, including rats. The United Nations further estimates the number of insect species resistant to chemical poisons has increased sixteen-fold between 1955 and 1980, meanwhile costing U.S. farmers $150 million a year in crop losses and increased chemical applications.[66]

"Shortsighted, irresponsible use of pesticides is producing strains of monster bugs. There are 30 that nothing can kill," notes Robert Metcalf, a University of Illinois entomology professor.[67]

In fact, a 1986 National Research Council report declared, "we see little justification in maintaining the polite fiction that pesticide resistance is solely a technical problem that can be readily overcome with the right new pesticide."[68] Long-time public interest and environmental critics of excessive use of chemical poisons are also raising the heretofore ignored question of their efficacy. Erik Jansson of the National Coalition Against the Misuse of Pesticides (NCAMP) points out:

> Because of past actions by the Congress, the pesticide user and the public have no real assurance that pesticides will perform as the manufacturer claims. With farmers operating on razor thin margins, inefficacious products threaten farmer's very existence. A 1979 report cites that most products tested for efficacy and passed by companies failed when tested by the EPA for registration purposes."[69]

Texas A&M researchers, for example, have discovered that the now-banned chemical poison Toxaphene was ineffective against cotton pests for which it had long been recommended by its manufacturer. Of 60 species of malaria-carrying mosquitoes, 51 have become resistant to the major poisons developed to control them.

The extremely toxic aldicarb has also been found increasingly ineffective in many areas of the country against a Colorado potato beetle.[70] Meanwhile its "mysterious" use on watermelons in 1985 in California caused the largest mass food poisoning in that state's history. Jansson concludes:

> Since efficacy testing is no longer an official program, researchers who discover that products no longer work or never worked, are generally harassed by government and manufacturing groups. The *farmer* is the real loser."[71]

Today, approximately 80 companies actually produce chemical poisons while another 5300 are formulators — companies involved in the combining and packaging of chemical poisons for specific uses.[72] Most of the top ten manufacturers (American Cyanamid, Dow Chemical, Du Pont, FMC Corp., Eli Lilly, Monsanto, Rohm & Haas, Stauffer Chemical, Union Carbide, and Uniroyal Inc.) that deal with chemical poisons are often very large and diversified firms with income from chemical poisons accounting for no more than 20 percent of company sales.

World Agrichemical Sales

Twenty corporations controlled 94 percent of the world agrichemical market in 1989, while the top ten companies commanded about 72 percent of total sales (see table below). Of the estimated U.S.$21,500 million of pesticides sold in 1989, over half were distributed in western Europe and the United States.

In April 1989, Dow and Eli Lilly, in an effort to gain an even larger share of the global market in chemical poisons, announced that they were joining forces to create Dow Elanco Inc., the sixth largest agricultural chemical company in the world with projected initial year sales of $1.5 billion.

On a world-wide basis the three West German chemical companies — BASF, Bayer and Hoechst,

Company	U.S.$ (million)
Ciba-Geigy	2,271
ICI	2,026
Bayer	1,862
Du Pont	1,684
Rhone-Pouknc	1,646
Monsanto	1,558
Dow Elanco	1,485
Hoechst	1,090
BASF	1,032
Shell	903
American Cyanamid	820
Schering	740
Sandoz	713
Kumiai	420
FMC	414
Rohm & Haas	367
Sankyo	344
Nihon Nohyaku	318
Takeda	268
Hokko	265

remnants of the once mighty post World War II German chemical monopoly I.G. Farben — today dominate the world market in chemicals. While the three now operate independently critics believe that they continue to behave like a cartel, each dominating specific areas and limiting head-to-head competition.

Foreign companies in 1988 also owned as much 30 percent of the United States's chemical assets, and industry analysts believe that West Germany's Big Three possess the economic muscle to acquire any U.S. chemical company, with the possible exception of Du Pont (who ranks fifth in world-wide sales) and Dow.[73] In 1982, for example, while pre-tax farm income was *dropping* 24 percent, the agricultural divisions of several major U.S. oil and chemical corporations showed sizeable pre-tax profit margins: Monsanto, 32 percent; Stauffer Chemical, 26 percent; Eli Lilly, 19 percent, and Rohm and Haas, 7 percent. Chevron (formerly Standard Oil of California) realized an over 200+ percent profit margin on its sales of the deadly Paraquat.[74]

A 1987 *Business Week* survey on the profits, research and development expenditures of a group of selected chemical firms showed that after-tax profits in 1986 exceeded research and development costs by 16 percent and that from 1982 to 1986 the industry increased its R&D expenses by only six percent, with Du Pont reporting only a one percent increase.[75]

The corporate value in the marketing of these chemical poisons was illustrated in 1984 when the Environmental Protection Agency (EPA) recommended the temporary lowering of the allowable dosage per acre of Lasso, a Monsanto produced weed killer for corn and soybean fields. The day prior to the government agency's decision Monsanto stock dropped 2 1/8 points on the New York Stock Exchange. Analysts pointed out that 20 percent of Monsanto's earnings came from Lasso.[76] Industry analysts have also noted that because chemicals like Lasso are intended for specific jobs, the "competition" between brands is "limited," *e.g.*, Monsanto's best selling herbicide "Roundup" had 1987 worldwide sales of $800 million and held about 10 percent of the $4 billion U.S. herbicide market.[77] Thus, producers are allowed to set prices well above their production costs.[78]

Poisons From Abroad

World chemical poison sales from the mid-1970s have nearly doubled to almost $18 billion a year with most of the growth coming in sales to Third World countries.[79]

In recent years as some chemical poisons have been restricted in their application or outright banned for domestic use in the United States their manufacturers have managed to find a lucrative market abroad. The GAO has reported that between 1977 and 1987 the international chemical poison market doubled in size to more than $17 billion. The United States, meanwhile, was annually exporting between 400 and 600 million pounds of domestically manufactured chemical poisons, accounting for nearly ten percent of that market. It is estimated that about a quarter of these products were not registered for use in the United States. Ironically, in the process the residues of these prohibitive poisons such as chlordane and heptachlor have been making their way back to the United States on the many cash crops this country imports from abroad. Some 4.8 million pounds of these two chemical poisons alone, manufactured by the Velsicol Chemical Corporation in Memphis, Tennessee, were shipped to at least 25 countries in 1988-1989.

In September 1986, the GAO reported to Congress that less than one percent of the $19.8 billion worth of fruits and vegetables imported annually into the United States are inspected for those chemical poisons that for safety and health reasons have been previously barred on domestic produce.[80] In defending itself, the Food and Drug Administration (FDA) said it did not believe that the amount of chemical poison residues on these imports were significant enough to pose any real danger to consumers.[81]

But, as an NCAMP staff scientist Diane Baxter was quick to add: "When the FDA inspects imported foods, they test for only about one-third (148 of 312) of known pesticides registered for use on food crops in the United States And there are unregistered chemicals, which can go undetected."[82] Representative Frank Horton, R-NY, who released the GAO report, claimed that "the rate of contamination found in imported foods is more than twice that found in domestic foods. Yet, enforcement actions involving contaminated imported foods are seriously deficient."[83]

An extensive study in 1981 also discovered that 70 percent of the chemical poisons used in the Third World are applied to export crops like coffee, tea, sugar, winter fruits and vegetables, or non-food crops like cotton and rubber. It is primarily large, multinational, corporate agribusiness firms (United Nations statistics show three percent of the landowners in 80 Third World countries control 80 percent of the land) who are growing such cash crops for shipment to the United States, Europe and Japan.[84]

Challenging the "Dirty Dozen"

No better example of how these chemical poisons are so widely used on crops sold in the United States can be found than in the Culiacan Valley in the Mexican state of Sinaloa. Here, on the valley's half-million acres of irrigated land are grown not only between one-third and one-half of all fresh tomatoes sold in the United States, as well as vast quantities of bell peppers, cucumbers, egg plants, zucchini, summer squashes, onions, garlic and chilies.[85]

When Angus Wright, professor of environmental studies at California State University in Sacramento visited that area he found the spraying rates of chemical poisons on the crops among the highest in the world. From January to May, fields are sprayed every three or four days, and some crops receive a dousing of these chemical poisons between 25 and 50 times during a growing season.

While many of the poisons used there are organophosphates, such as parathion, and less likely to persist at dangerous levels in the food chain over long periods of time, they are more toxic and readily absorbed through the skin by the workers who harvest the crops. Wright reports observing crop dusting planes flying directly over crews of workers, composed of 20 to 30 men, women and children. He recalled one conversation with an employee of the Culiacan Growers' Association who told him: "We try to tell them [workers] how to protect themselves, to wear the right clothes, to wash the tomatoes before they eat them, and *to exhale when the airplane passes over them while spraying.*"

As Wright later commented to Bryan Jay Bashin, executive director of the Center for Science Reporting, a science news service based in Sacramento, "When I walk into a supermarket and see the tomatoes that come from Culiacan, I get nauseous and angry, and I can't even look at them. It is so violent and brutal there, the most incredible kind of exploitation."[86]

The U.S. government estimates that fully 25 percent of all chemical poisons (500 million pounds) sold overseas by U.S. companies have either been banned, restricted or unregistered for domestic use.[87] EPA regulations require companies that manufacture these poisons not only to notify the agency concerning such shipments and their destination, but also to advise the receiving country of the U.S. ban. However, EPA has estimated that only 10 percent of such exports are in fact ever filed.[88]

Thus, since 1985, some 300 groups affiliated with the Pesticide Action Network (PAN) have embarked on an international campaign to call the world's attention to "the dirty dozen" of chemical poisons and enlist global efforts to eliminate their use from agriculture and provide for viable alternatives. Monica Moore, director of PAN's Pesticide Education and Action Project, explains the Network's purpose:

The "Dirty Dozen" Campaign is attempting to single out 12 extremely hazardous pesticides

[DDT, EDB, 2,4,5-T, DBCP, chlordane/hepta-chlor, toxaphene, paraquat, parathion, lindane, aldrin/dieldrin/endrin, pentachlorophenol, and chlordimeform] that should be banned, phased out, or carefully controlled everywhere in the world. Together, these 12 'worst case' pesticides are responsible for most of the pesticide deaths and much of the environmental damage that pesticides cause each year.

Accordingly, they have been banned or restricted in most industrialized countries as threats to the public health and the environment. Yet all 12 continue to be widely sold and heavily promoted in developing countries, where regulatory controls are fewer, and where the toll they take is proportionately high.[89]

Despite such efforts as PAN's "Dirty Dozen" Campaign, World Resources Inc. reports that generous foreign subsidies ranging from 19 percent to 89 percent of the retail price have "encouraged farmers to use more chemicals than they would if they had to pay the full costs. By the same token, subsidies discourage farmers from controlling pests by methods that rely less heavily on chemical applications."

Such subsidies are usually achieved through favorable exchange rates for importers, direct sales below cost to farmers by government agencies, favorable tax treatment and below-market interest rates on loans for purchases.[90] Robert Repetto, author of the study, also points out that none of the countries he surveyed — China, Columbia, Ecuador, Egypt, Ghana, Honduras, Indonesia, Pakistan and Senegal had collected data on chemical poison demand or the elasticity of their prices when demand changes that would have allowed analysis of the impacts of these subsidies on a domestic economy.

His data goes on to show that the per capita value of these subsidies was not trivial. Although the median expenditure was $1.70, Egypt's was $4.70. For perspective, the per capita Indonesian subsidy for chemical poisons, at about 80 cents, is half the government per capita expenditure on housing and water, and roughly a third of the government expenditure for health.

The consequences of such "salesmanship" by the three dozen U.S. and European chemical manufacturers which control 90 percent of the global chemical poison market has resulted, according to a British Oxfam study, in over 750,000 people per year world wide being poisoned to some degree, with a conservative estimate of 14,000 fatalities. Meanwhile, the equivalent of one pound of chemical poisons is produced each year for every man, woman and child on earth.[91]

It is no surprise, therefore, that blood samples of Guatemalans have registered 30 times more DDT than the average U.S. citizen's since the poison was banned in the United States in 1972.[92] And, in Nicaragua, until the Government of the National Reconstruction came to power, the cotton crop, which accounted for 40 percent of that nation's total exports in the 1970s, was so saturated with imported chemical poisons that it created alarming health and environmental problems through-out the countryside while adversely affecting food commodities, including substantial quantities of beef, which it was exporting to the United States.[93]

Challenging the "Corporate Lords"

In evaluating the use of the so-called modern technologies of agriculture, Wes Jackson, a 49-year old Salina, Kansas farmer, who heads the Land Institute, a privately financed research farm which advocates a growing movement called "alternative agriculture," believes high production, high tech, costly applications of fertilizers, herbicides and mechanization are all resulting in an "industrial agriculture."[94]

Jackson, who is fond of often comparing such farmers to medieval serfs, seeing how they are always wearing caps advertising their "corporate lords," argues that this so-called modern-day "industrial agriculture" erodes our soil and pollutes our groundwater while producing chemical runoffs and the bankrupting of farmers in the process.

Jackson and others clearly show that our "family farm system of agriculture" is pitted against a host of worldwide corporate giants in its struggle to produce crops efficiently while economically and environmentally attempting to survive.

Marian Lenzen, the wife of a Nebraska farmer, sees the nation's family farm system of agriculture as the last bastion against the total "corporatizing" of our society. "That's what 'agribusiness efficiency' does for farmers. It busts the small operators and forces them into the cities and it increasingly consolidates the production, processing and distribution of food in this country into the hands of a few big multinational corporations. Big business and big government now own or directly control all the resources and means of production in the world. The only holdout against complete corporate takeover today is the family farmer."[95]

Chapter Six

Killing the Environment

"There seem to be but three ways for a nation to acquire wealth: the first is by war, as the Romans did, in plundering their conquered neighbors — this is robbery; the second by commerce, which is generally cheating; the third by agriculture, the only honest way, wherein man received a real increase of the seed thrown into the ground, in a kind of continual miracle, wrought by the hand of God in his favor, as a reward for his innocent life and his virtuous industry. ".

-Benjamin Franklin[1]

In the over 200 years since Benjamin Franklin articulated the position agriculture deserved in calculating a nation's wealth it has come to play an unfortunate role in corporate agribusiness's efforts to control our farm and food economy.

Before we can fully understand corporate agribusiness, we must reassert once again its basic objectives. They are:
1) substituting capital for efficiency and technology for labor,
2) the standardization of our food supply, and
3) the creation of manufactured synthetic food.

Each of these goals has been carefully fashioned to not only diminish the role of farmers in producing our food, and, more importantly, to relegate the farmer to a small group of economically and politically impotent raw material producers within a food manufacturing system controlled from afar by a select number of corporations and individuals.(See Chart 6A)

Thus, as agriculture shifts from a labor intensive to a capital intensive, highly technological system, agribusiness continues to be characterized more and more by concentrated economic power. By promoting and accelerating such a shift this nation's corporate managers have left to the government and the general public the task of paying the high social and environmental costs that accompany their efforts.

Turning Family Farmers Into Technological Junkies

As already noted, more chemical poisons, fertilizers, bigger and more sophisticated machines, larger tracts of land, and plentiful capital to finance such purchases have become the rule rather than the exception. Meanwhile, as agriculture's yearly net income has gravitated between uncertainty and disaster, input costs have skyrocketed as corporate agribusiness continues to turn

family farmers into technological junkies. (See Chart 6B) In the first half of the 1980s alone prices received by farmers decreased 8.2 percent while prices paid by farmers increased 5.8 percent.[2]

There is no better example of how corporate agribusiness substitutes technology for labor in agriculture, despite the enormous and numerous environmental and health hazards engendered, than in its production, promotion and use of chemical poisons.

Not only do farmers put themselves at peril by repeated use of these poisons, but the lives and health of their family, their children's children, their workers and ultimately all consumers are threatened daily by the use of such dangerous chemicals. National Safety Council records since 1983 show that agriculture has accumulated the worst statistics in the United States for work-related deaths and injuries.

In 1987, the most recent year for which figures are available, U.S. farms experienced 49 work-related fatalities per 100,000 full-time workers, eight times the industry rate of six per 100,000, according to the National Safety Council. Such statistics did not include 300 children under the age of 16 who died in farm-related mishaps or the 23,000 injured on the farm.[3]

It is not uncommon to see such figures among children, when there is economic hardship among family farmers. First, farmers must rely increasingly on their children to help on the farm. Second, spouses must take jobs away from home; younger children are left on their own and thus more susceptible to injury.

Iowa farmers have shown a 32 percent greater risk than non-farmers of dying from cancer; the leukemia rate in Nebraska for farmers is 44 percent greater than non-farmers; cancer of the central nervous system for farmers is greater in Minnesota; a study of Kansas farmers has found a six-fold increase in certain kinds of cancers associated with prolonged contact with phenoxyacetic acids, a common ingredient in many herbicides used in wheat and corn fields, and cancer of the lymph system and multiple myeloma in Wisconsin is greater for farmers than non-farmers.

Research by the National Cancer Institute and several midwestern universities suggests that these rates are due to excessive use of chemical poisons and fertilizers in farming.[4]

For example, the previously mentioned Monsanto-produced weed-killer alachlor ("Lasso"), first marketed in 1969, of which more than 90 million pounds are used each year, has been shown to cause at least four types of tumors when fed to animals. The EPA has estimated that this number-one-ranked agricultural herbicide

Chart 6A: Food Sources

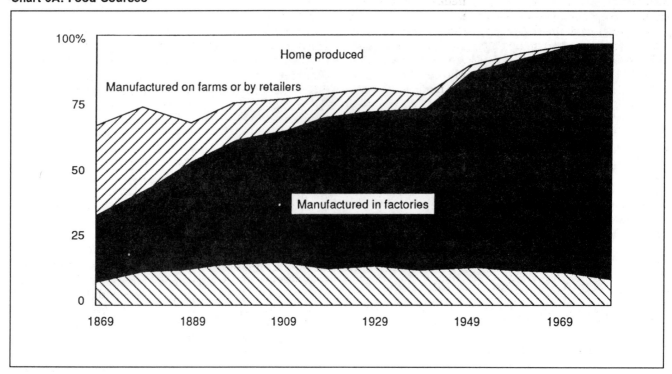

Chart 6A: Food Sources

could cause cancer risks to about 600,000 farmers and farm workers or as high as one in 10,000 from alachlor exposure. Reportedly EPA has no information on food residues.[5]

Meanwhile, it has been estimated that those large farms with annual sales of over $40,000 per year use chemical poisons on more than 30 percent of their acreage compared to a four percent use on smaller farms.[6] In addition the use of such chemicals by these large farms has profoundly influenced their smaller neighbors. As one Booneville, Iowa farm couple wrote to the *Des Moines Register*:

Chart 6B: Prices Paid and Received by Farmers

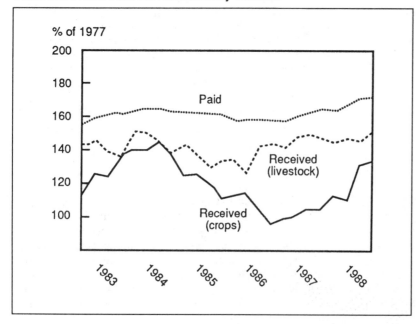

... we agree that it would be wonderful not to have to employ pesticides, chemical fertilizers and herbicides. Anyone who has seen and smelled these products (which are foul smelling and toxic to the skin) would undoubtedly [agree] that they can't help our bodies or the environment.

However, while raising our family and paying for a farm and equipment whose costs are exorbitant, our goal must be to make as much profit per acre as possible... Try telling your *banker* or *landlord* that you have not used any of these methods and that the yields will be cut appreciably because you want to save the environment. *Chances are you won't be farming next year.* (emphasis added)

Dramatic proof that the wide-spread use of chemical poisons by large farms affects small farms also came to light when the EPA issued a 1983 landmark environmental study of the Chesapeake Bay. It placed much of the blame for the bay's pollution on about 24,000 farmers from Maryland, Virginia and Pennsylvania whose chemical fertilizers, poisons and animal manure wash into the Chesapeake and its tributaries with the rain.[7]

The study also noted that many of these runoff problems stemmed in part from the agricultural traditions of Pennsylvania's many German and Dutch ancestry farmers. These farmers have traditionally divided their land among their children generation after generation. The result of this practice has been hundreds of increasingly smaller farms coming into existence.

Yet, each year these farms have to struggle harder and harder to earn an income by producing more crops and livestock, thus making themselves easy prey for the corporate agribusiness salespeople who constantly prey upon them to douse their land with more and more expensive chemical fertilizers and poisons in an often vain effort to increase their yields.

One has only to browse through the major farm publications to see how the chemical industry has propagandized farmers into believing that chemistry is a magic solution to their problems, and how the great majority of these publications have become mere shills for the chemical poison industry.

In 1986, for example, eight of the top ten farm publication advertisers were chemical companies, which spent nearly $40.3 million in peddling their wares to farmers.[8] Such advertising has reaped rich rewards for these companies as about 1.08 billion pounds of chemical poisons were used in the United States in 1984, nearly *double* the amount used in 1964, according to the EPA.[9]

"Healthy Hypochondriacs"???

Meanwhile, World Resources Institute, the policy research center concerned with environmental and resource issues, reported in its 1985 study that an estimated 300,000 American farm workers are affected annually by chlorinated hydrocarbons, like DDT, and organophosphates, like parathion; chemical poisons which display symptoms that include dizziness, nausea, contracted pupils and severe skin rashes. Delayed effects can also include sterility, cancer and birth defects. The Institute's report claimed that all of the four to five million field hands who come into contact with these poisons are "inadequately protected."[10]

In addition, the unwanted side-effects of these chemical poisons — human poisoning, livestock losses, pollution of the soil and water and air, and contamination of the food supply — according to one study, cost the United States an estimated $839 million in 1980 alone — an amount equal to about 20 percent of the annual sales of these poisons by U.S. chemical companies, a figure which "coincidentally" comes quite close to these same firms annual rate of profit in recent years.[11]

Meanwhile, the chemical industry and its apologists often seek to defend themselves by blaming a "sensational news media" for alarming farmers and consumers to the dangers of chemical poisons.

Lori Johnston, director of Pest Management for the California Department of Food and Agriculture, for example, told a meeting of the California Grape and Tree Fruit League in 1982 that "since the 60s debate over chemicals has become the order of the day. We have become a society consumed with fear despite the fact that we live longer. Today, we are a nation of healthy hypochondriacs."

She added that the media has "instilled fear" in the public by continually exaggerating the risks posed by "agrichemicals" and this fear is now a major obstacle to

rational and effective avenues of technology development and evaluation.[12]

Others would disagree with the California official. The GAO, for example, pointed out in April 1986 that the EPA was not using its full authority to protect the public from chemical hazards and was inadequately monitoring those new chemicals it had already approved.

To substantiate that charge, the GAO disclosed that 14 years after Congress had ordered the EPA to review the safety of hundreds of chemical poisons already on the market, the EPA, moving at what NCAMP's Director Jay Feldman has termed a "glacial pace," had not completed safety tests for long-term health effects on any of the 600 active ingredients used in 35,000 types of chemical poisons subject to the Federal Insecticide, Fungicide and Rodenticide Act (FIFRA).[13]

In May 1987 the National Academy of Sciences reported that in a study of 28 chemical poisons widely used on fruit and vegetables 23 were found potentially carcinogenic and exceeded the EPA's standard of acceptable risk — no more than one additional case of cancer for every one million people exposed.[14]

Jack Moore, EPA's assistant administrator for pesticides and toxic substances, admitted that these particular chemicals "need attention," but expressed the view that many of them would prove to be of "negligible risk" since the Council's projection "consistently overstates the degree of risk." "When we get the data, it'll show there's no risk," he added.

Environmentalists, however, estimate that based on the Council study, 1.45 million additional cancer cases could occur in the next 70 years, or about 20,000 per year.[15]

"The federal regulatory apparatus has been taken over by those it was designed to regulate," Russell W. Peterson, chairman of the President's Council on Environmental Quality (CEQ) from 1973 to 1976 has declared. "The national interest in a clean and healthy environment has been subordinated to the private profit-making interest of the favored few, often at the public's expense."[16]

In 1972 Congress passed the Federal Insecticide, Fungicide and Rodenticide Act in an effort to regulate the registration, production and use of chemical poisons in agriculture. Since that time most Americans have assumed that all chemical poisons are carefully examined by the EPA and have passed rigorous health and safety tests.

Such popular misconceptions aside, in the words of Nancy Drabble, director of Public Citizen's Congress Watch, FIFRA has become an "anachronistic statute" that is "riddled with loopholes and industry-oriented provisions."[17]

Persephone Rising From Hades

Recent attempts to improve FIFRA have been generally met with frustration, inaction and corporate delaying tactics. As former Chairman Representative George E. Brown, Jr., D-Calif., of the House Agriculture Subcommittee on Science and Technology said in 1985: "Just as Persephone rises from Hades to spring to the upper world, FIFRA rises from those same nether regions each year at this time to offset whatever joy I feel at spring's arrival." [18]

Even the EPA asked Congress in 1985 to make substantive changes in the law, despite the Reagan administration's recommendation for at least two more years of delay. "I think the current system needs change," Moore told a House subcommittee hearing in April 1985. "You can only go so far to make a silk purse out of a sow's ear."[19]

Five months later it was announced that a tentative agreement had been worked out between the chemical industry and a coalition of 41 environmental, labor and consumer groups. An attempt would be made to renew FIFRA while providing for an EPA review of all health and safety studies previously submitted by the industry — which industry would pay for in part — and new restrictions if necessary, including the regulation of those poison ingredients not now subject to review.[20]

Opposition to several of the coalition's proposals, however, was immediately voiced by the American Farm Bureau Federation, which expressed concern about provisions on ground water contamination and farmers' liability for chemical poison contamination.[21]

As a Reagan administration spokesperson told *The New York Times*, "it's going to be no cakewalk."[22]

Such a prediction would indeed soon come to pass when Senator Jesse Helms, R-NC, at the time chairman of the Senate Agricultural Committee, at the urging of the large food manufacturers sponsored an amendment to prevent states from adopting regulatory standards stricter than those of the federal government for monitoring the use of chemical poisons on food products.[23]

The amendment, which ultimately prevented the FIFRA reform package from passing out of a House-Senate conference committee at the end of the 1986 Congressional session, was supported by Jeffrey Nedelman, spokesman for the Grocery Manufacturers of America (GMA). Nedelman claimed that the GMA sought to ensure public confidence that food products have "a national stamp of approval" and that varying state standards would create "practical" problems because "we have a national food system in this country."

Al Meyerhoff, attorney for the National Resources Defense Council, disagreed.

Some of these big food outlets seem intent on preserving the right to contaminate the American food supply. Their only concern is profit, not human health. They're standing in the way of a major step forward for environmental protection.[24]

Maine's Governor Joseph Brennan in "unequivocally opposing" attempts to curb the state's authority on such matters declared:

The industry would have us believe that the food distribution system is so finely tuned that action by an aberrant state will crash it, emptying the nation's grocery store shelves. There is no readily apparent reason why the same skills that make and distribute foods to meet particular tastes cannot make and distribute foods to meet particular state standards.[25]

As if to underscore the critics' point concerning the EPA's failure to carefully examine the chemical poisons used today in agriculture, a Chicago, Illinois-based U.S. District Court jury in 1983 found the executives of what was once the most important chemical testing laboratory in the country, Industrial Bio-Test Laboratory (IBT), guilty of falsifying the results of many of the 22,000 safety tests that the firm performed for U.S. industry. According to government analysts, up to 80 percent of IBT's tests may have been phony.[26]

Despite the compromise of 1985, environmentalists and the chemical industry were still without any revisions to FIFRA and locked in heated controversy shortly after the opening of the 100th Congress in 1988. *The Washington Post*'s Michael Weisskopf reported that "whatever the rivals gave, they have taken away, and the partners once again are squabbling. Their differences underscore the divisions in Congress, dimming prospects for revision of a federal statue widely criticized as unwieldy and incomplete."[27]

Ultimately some changes were made in FIFRA in 1988. However, the Act's critics mockingly dubbed them "FIFRA Light" because the Act still failed to protect the public against dozens of pesticides that cause cancer and birth defects in laboratory animals.[28]

Changes in the Act included the calling for a review by EPA, not industry, of the 600 active ingredients used in the 35,000 types of chemical poisons licensed by the Agency, with industry paying one-half of the $42 million per year costs for the processing of the various data. It also partially repealed an existing requirement that EPA pay the manufacturer or users of chemical poisons for existing stocks banned by the Agency. In the future manufacturers would require specific Congressional approval on a case-by-case basis for any indemnification.[29]

Shortly after the House of Representatives approved these new FIFRA provisions the EPA announced a new policy to replace the "zero-risk" standard of the Delaney Clause. In the future all chemical poisons would be approved if they posed only a "negligible risk," increasing the odds of cancer by no more than one in one million.[30]

In processed food EPA is supposed to set chemical poison residue limits protective of health alone. In 1958, by passing the Delaney Clause, the Congress sought to tighten health standards by barring food additives that caused cancer in humans or animals.

As more and more of our food becomes processed, it has been unable to escape at least some of the carcinogenic chemical poisons used on the raw commodities. While Congress determined that the EPA need not set limits on residues in processed foods if the amount did not exceed levels allowed on the raw commodities, it did require the EPA to set limits on chemical poison residues that increased in concentration when cooked and rendered into finished manufactured products.

EPA argued that the new "negligible risk" policy was necessary if older, more carcinogenic chemical poisons were ever to be replaced. NRDC's Lawrie Mott, however, points out that the Agency's new policy "will put the public at greater risk" for as new carcinogenic chemical poisons, albeit chemicals of lower cancer risk, enter the scene, the EPA has announced no plans for removing the older, more dangerous ones. "I don't want to hear that they're going to add six without taking off six. You have to look at safety of the entire food supply."[31]

The Most Serious Hazard to Our Food
"Pesticides dwarf the other environmental risks the [EPA] deals with. The risks from pesticides are so much greater because of the exposures involved. Toxic waste dumps may affect a few thousand people who live around them. But virtually everyone is exposed to pesticides."[32]
-Steven Schatzow, Director
Pesticide Division, EPA

Aside from their efficacy, as discussed earlier, and their immediate threat to the health and safety of the thousands and thousands of farmers and farm workers who use them regularly, these chemical poisons also pose other dangers.

It is estimated that half of the American population gets its drinking water from underground sources. Nearly 20 percent of such systems have already been found contaminated to some degree by manufactured organic chemicals. Residues of 46 different chemical poisons commonly used in agriculture have been detected in the ground water in 26 states, according to the EPA.[33]

Likewise, two-thirds of the United States's 900 hazardous waste sites covered by the government's "Superfund" cleanup program have resulted in groundwater contamination as the organic-chemical industry, the nation's largest single source of hazardous wastes, now discharges 112 million pounds of such wastes a year.[34]

"As more and more states begin to test groundwater," points out NCAMP's Feldman, "pesticides not expected to show up in tests are being found in greater concentrations."[35]

In California, for example, the State Assembly Office of Research found 57 different chemical poisons in nearly 3000 wells in 25 counties.[36] In Iowa it is estimated that nearly half of the state's 800 municipal water systems have been tainted with such poisons.[37]

Perhaps no better description of the problem faced by agriculture and society in general today in dealing with the chemical poison industry has been offered than that which was offered nearly 15 years ago by the late, brilliant and outspoken University of California entomologist Dr. Robert van den Bosch.

Fundamentally, pest control as it is now practiced ... is essentially not an ecological matter. It is largely a matter of merchandising. In essence, we are using the wrong kinds of material in the wrong places at wrong times in excessive amounts and engendering problems which increase the use of these materials, adds to the pollution problem, adds to the cost of agricultural

pest control, and adds to what you might describe as the concern of the general public.[38]

The proof of such "concern of the general public" was clearly evidenced in a 1985 survey by the Food Marketing Institute (FMI) which found that 73 percent of 1,005 adult respondents saw chemical poisons as "the most serious hazard to our food."[39] Judging from recent findings there is good reason for the public to be so concerned. "The average consumer," the National Research Council reported in 1987, "is exposed to pesticide residues ... in nearly every food." The Council further notes that about 80 percent of the risk of cancer from such residues in food is estimated to come from only 15 foods (in order by level of risk): tomatoes, beef, potatoes, oranges, lettuce, apples, peaches, pork, wheat, soybeans, beans, carrots, chicken, corn and grapes.

When the National Bureau of Standards established a liver bank — a freezer where bureau scientists could keep specimens of human livers removed during autopsies for later study — it did not expect to learn that when livers were examined for evidence of agricultural chemical poisons they all contained measurable amounts of eight widely-used such chemicals, including DDT. As Stephen A. Wise, the bank's manager explains,

We initially thought we'd find high levels of pesticides for our study in an older farmer who might have been exposed to them over a number of years when his crops were sprayed. But we looked at a farmer's liver, and his levels weren't that high. So we suspect that the reason all the livers have some degree of exposure is that the pesticides were absorbed through the food chain.[40]

Although some of those chemical poisons found, according to Wise, were long ago prohibited for use in the United States, they probably showed up because of foods that were treated with the banned chemicals were still being imported into the United States.

In 1984 the NRDC commissioned a private laboratory to conduct a consumer survey to learn how much residue from chemical poisons used in agriculture was still on fruits and vegetables available to San Francisco, California food shoppers. Seventy-one samples of ten different products, ranging from strawberries to potatoes, were found to have residues of eight chemical poisons known or suspected of being carcinogens, five that are believed to induce birth defects and others that may be linked to reproductive problems.[41] While a majority of the foods tested had chemical poison levels below the EPA's set tolerance these residues, according to the NRDC, "may still endanger the public." Nearly half of the sampled produce bore traces of 19 chemical poisons, sometimes as many as four kinds on a single strawberry.

The national environmental group noted that a San Franciscan who ate broccoli, carrots, cucumbers, eggplant, lettuce, oranges, potatoes, spinach, strawberries and tomatoes over the two month period of time of its study might have unknowingly ingested a panoply of the chemical poisons found in the survey.

"This is significant because rarely, if ever, does the federal government consider synergism [a term referring to the multiple effect of two chemicals working together] when setting the maximum allowable residue limits, or pesticide tolerances," the report notes. In 1988 a study by the OTA, the bipartisan research arm of Congress, found that the methods the FDA was using to screen chemical poison residues in our food detected only 163 of the 316 chemical poisons registered with the EPA. In addition, USDA's Food Safety and Inspection Service which monitors meat and milk, the report added, was using tests that picked up only about 40 of the 227 chemical poisons listed for consideration.[42]

"In contrast to the general public's uneasiness over pesticide residues in food," the OTA notes, "the federal agencies responsible for regulating foods do not have the same level of concern for the situation as it exists."[43]

NCAMP's Feldman adds that "residue testing by private companies only gives the appearance of safety. The obvious problem is there aren't any national standards to measure the accuracy of the tests. And there is no public oversight to investigate the findings."[44]

Aloha!

The San Francisco study is not an isolated finding. On Oahu, Hawaii's most populous island, official state studies found that consumers had been drinking milk for an unknown length of time with levels of the chemical poison heptachlor nine to 15 times above the FDA ceiling. Heptachlor is manufactured by the Velsicol Corporation, a subsidiary of Northwest Industries, Inc., and can cause cancer at low levels in laboratory mice.[45]

How this chemical poison made its way into 73 percent of all of Hawaii's dairy products, 77 percent of its meat, fish and poultry supply, and most alarmingly into mother's breast milk, is instructive. After a state investigation and recall of the milk in March 1982 the source of the contamination was isolated to certain pineapple field plantations owned by Del Monte, once an RJR Nabisco Inc. subsidiary.

Del Monte sold its pineapple leaves sprayed with heptachlor to dairies for use as feed, commonly called "green chop." Dairy cattle that eat this "green chop," which was not supposed to be sold until one year had elapsed after the last spraying, passed the toxic substance along in the milk they produced. In turn, mothers who drank the heptachlor-contaminated milk fed contaminated breast milk to their babies.

Nearly five years later another heptachlor "incident" led to the contamination of over 100 dairy farms in Oklahoma, Missouri and Arkansas. An eight state region's milk supply became contaminated with as much as seven times the acceptable level of heptachlor, and traces of the deadly chemical poison were found in mother's milk and locally produced cattle. Apparently the heptachlor came from feed supplied to dairy farmers by Valley Feeds in Van Buren, Arkansas which was running a gasohol plant that turned grain into fuel alcohol and resold the "mash" from the distillation process as animal feed.[46] Heptachlor has been described by the EPA as both a "very persistent" and "very potent carcinogen" which "stays in the fatty tissues" of the human body. Yet, as Dr. Ian Nisbet, an Agency scientific analyst points out, heptachlor's effects on humans are unknown. Any data for people is "essentially nonexistent."[47]

Out of the Headlines and Into Our Food System

But heptachlor is not unique in this regard. As Feldman notes, "Beyond the extensive problem of products having been registered with faulty data generated by companies like IBT, data simply does not exist for most products' ability to cause cancer, genetic damage and birth defects."

Citing data drawn from EPA files by a 1983 House Agriculture Subcommittee staff report, Feldman shows that between 79 percent and 84 percent of the food products on the market today have not been adequately tested for their capacity to cause cancer; between 90 percent and 93 percent of the same products have also not been adequately tested for their ability to cause genetic damage; between 60 percent and 70 percent have not been fully tested for their ability to cause birth defects, and between 30 percent and 46 percent have not been fully tested for harmful reproductive effects.[48]

In addition, the National Research Council of the National Academy of Sciences released a 382-page report in 1984 entitled "Toxicity Testing: Strategies to Determine Needs and Priorities," which stated that complete health hazard assessments for chemical poisons and inert, or secret, ingredients of such formulations is possible for only 10 percent of the registered chemical poisons being used today.[49]

With respect to the Hawaii situation, as far back as 1974 the EPA was expressing concern about the effects of heptachlor and announced its intention to cancel the registration on the chemical poison. The Pineapple Growers of Hawaii — Del Monte, Castle & Cooke, and Maui Pineapple — along with Velsicol and other users challenged the government's ruling. In March 1978 all parties agreed to allow heptachlor to remain on the market for a maximum of *five years* and four months with each crop usage of the chemical given its own cancellation date. "The Pineapple Growers of Hawaii received one of the longest phase outs that anyone got," according to Jackie Cooper, an attorney for the Environmental Defense Fund (EDF). "It was less Velsicol than the Pineapple Growers Association that was instrumental in allowing extra time for its use in Hawaii."[50]

The action taken by the EPA in the heptachlor case, giving the company and users extended periods of time to withdraw such dangerous chemical poisons despite the danger to the health of the public, is not unusual and has been repeatedly and harshly denounced by environmental and public interest organizations.

Believed to pose "an unreasonable risk" of cancer to workers and to persons exposed to it, the chemical poison captan, *used since the 1950s* to prevent fungal diseases in fruit and vegetable crops, was banned from all food uses in 1985 after the EPA had reviewed its safety for five years.

The EPA, however, announced that the ban would not take effect for *at least two years*. Manufactured principally by Chevron Chemical and Stauffer Chemical, over ten million pounds of captan is used each year on dozens of U.S. fruits and vegetables.[51]

EPA's Moore has noted that while there are alternatives to captan, there is concern that the ban "may encourage users to switch to other fungicides that may be more toxic than captan," and Moore adds in classic Agency understatement, "our data seem to indicate that fungicides as a class present toxicological problems."

EDB [ethylene dibromide] is another prime example of a dangerous chemical poison allowed to stay on the market in the United States for nearly a decade, even after its cancer-causing properties had been confirmed. "Our sense is that the whole EDB debacle brought about no change," NRDC's Meyerhoff reflects. "EDB is going to be out of the news pretty soon, but it's not going to be out of the food chain."[52]

An Apple A Day Will ...

The EPA's action in seeking to ban daminozide, manufactured by the Uniroyal Corp. and sold under the trade name Alar, confirms the agency's maddeninglyslow review process, and again illustrates how well corporate agribusiness has used technology as a substitute for labor with little or no regard for long-term health consequences to consumers.

A plant growth regulator, daminozide has been on the market for nearly two decades. It has been used on nearly half of the nation's apples to delay ripening so that an orchard can be picked at one time in an attempt to cut labor costs. It is also used for cosmetic reasons (to make apples redder) and to increase apples' firmness and thus reduce shipping damage, which in turn gives them a longer shelf life. Alar has been used for similar purposes on peanuts, cherries, peaches, pears, plums, tomatoes, brussel sprouts and cantaloupes.

EPA's initial studies showed that it was a "potent" carcinogen that can cause kidney, lung and blood vessel tumors in laboratory animals; that the risk to adults is "high," increasing ten-fold for infants; that it cannot be removed by washing as it penetrates the fruit tissue, and that it has been found in apple juice and applesauce.

When daminozide-treated fruits are cooked the chemical degrades into UDMH, a more potent carcinogen that is chemically related to hydrazine rocket fuel.

"The primary group of concern is children," NRDC's Lawrie Mott stresses. "Besides, the benefits of this chemical are negligible. We're not talking about crop destruction or even reduced yields."[53]

Alar critics also pointed out that in late 1984, eight months before the EPA announced it was considering a ban on the chemical poison, the National Grape Cooperative, which was producing about half of the nation's Concord grapes and supplying the makers of Welch's grape juice and jellies, ordered its members to stop using Alar.[54]

Other major firms, including Safeway Stores Inc., soon followed the Co-op's lead. By 1987 apple growers had reduced their use of Alar to such a degree that apple processors and Uniroyal would claim that the chemical was used on only about ten percent of fresh apples and hardly at all on processed apples.[55]

Alar, however, was continuing to show up in the apple crop and nationwide publicity again spotlighted its use in the spring of 1989, principally through an Ed Bradley report on CBS-TV's *60 Minutes*, TV appearances by actress Meryl Streep representing Mothers and Others for Pesticide Limits, and a study by *Consumer Reports* showing that traces of the chemical were still being detected on apples in the nation's supermarkets.

(At the same time the U.S. Supreme Court was refusing to revive a suit by Ralph Nader and other environmentalists that a lower court had rejected on procedural grounds. The Nader suit came after EPA in January 1987 announced that it was lowering by one-third the allowable amounts of chemicals that could remain as residue on apples, while the Agency took more time to study Alar's effects. The Nader suit sought to force EPA to ban Alar.[56])

The attention generated by this spate of publicity soon produced noticeable results. Nationwide sales of apples dropped dramatically with estimated losses to the industry of $100 million or more.[57] Several school districts immediately stopped serving apples to their students.

Dennis Colleran, president and chief executive officer of Tree Top Inc., the nation's largest cooperative of apple growers headquartered in Selah, Washington, announced his resignation after angering his co-op growers by publicly stating that the co-op should not accept Alar-treated apples until tests showed them safe for human consumption.[58] Subsequently, four of the 13 members of the Washington State Apple Commission acknowledged that they had used Alar on their 1988 crop, despite the Commission's urging that its members not use the growth regulator.[59]

Meanwhile, Alar's manufacturer, Uniroyal, a subsidiary of Avery Inc., announced that it was "voluntarily" ending its U.S. sales of the chemical poison, the sales of which dropped by 75 percent since 1986. It would continue, however, to market the chemical, which accounted for less than one percent of its gross sales, in some 70 other countries throughout the world. In 1986, meanwhile, 50 percent of the apple juice concentrate used in the United States was imported.[60]

After the initial *60 Minutes* broadcast on the dangers of Alar and the EPA's reluctance to ban the chemical corporate agribusiness launched a widespread public attack both on the program and actress Streep. In a subsequent broadcast, reporter Bradley noted that a follow-up study by CBS found that in 200 random samples of apples found in supermarkets throughout the country 38 percent of red apples, 32 percent of all apples, and 30 percent of so-called Alar-free apples all showed traces of the growth enhancer.[61]

Despite all this publicity and even its own findings, the EPA has not completely suspended use of the chemical because it says the risks do not justify such action. Insisting that panic is unwarranted because risk figures assume a lifetime of exposure to the chemical, Paul R. Lapsley, an EPA review officer, has stated, "we don't believe the risks from this year's harvest presents

91

a significant risk, but we're interested in getting it off the market as quickly as we can."[62]

But alachlor, heptachlor, captan, and daminozide are only a few of many chemical poisons that comprise what former NCAMP Research Coordinator Sandra Marquardt has called a "chronology of catastrophe."[63] In a partial listing, since 1981, we have seen:

• Endrin contamination of game birds which had eaten contaminated wheat in Washington State in 1981.
• Paraquat used illegally on forest lands by the Drug Enforcement Administration in 1983.
• Dinoseb killed a Texas farmworker in 1983.
• EDB contaminated grain-based products and citrus found in 1983.
• Pentachlorophenol treatment of wood linked to illness and death in 1983.
• Methyl parathion spraying wiped out large colonies of bees in Illinois in 1983 and killed two children in Mississippi in 1984.
• Chlordane found to have contaminated 33 percent of 1,100 Long Island, New York homes tested in 1984.
• Aldicarb found in hundreds of wells in at least 15 states in 1984 and western states watermelons in 1985. (When asked to disclose the amounts distributed of this chemical poison in California after the watermelon scare a state official said such information was in the state's files but not available to the public because state law classified such information as a "trade secret.")
• Oftanol, Diazinon and Carbaryl sprayed for Japanese Beetle control sends California residents to hospital in 1983-1984.

Killing the Canaries

Despite such evidence of the dangers these chemical poisons pose, only major tragedies, such as the one in Bhopal, India, which killed over 2,500 people and injured thousands, and the near catastrophe in Institute, West Virginia in August 1985, (both plants operated by the Union Carbide Corp.) seem to create any sense of genuine public alarm.

Even aside from the dangers to farmers and consumers, one has to wonder about a chemical industry that has a 900 percent growth in production between 1947 and 1978, but, in the words of A. Karim Ahmed, NRDC's research director,

has essentially introduced an obsolete technology to the world. Most plants manufacture, store, process, and dispose of large volumes of highly hazardous substances while still employing 19th century concepts of industrial plumbing and plant design.

In addition, as the tragedies at Bhopal, India and Seveso, Italy, have shown, obsolete technology combined with poor maintenance, faulty equipment, lack of adequately skilled personnel, and the ever-present possibility of human error can be a deadly mixture.

And, Ahmed adds, "there is no comprehensive national regulation in plant safety, an area long neglected by both state and federal governments."[64] A preliminary EPA report in 1985 listed 135 deaths and 1500 injuries from 6928 toxic chemical accidents in the United States alone since 1980.[65]

Other studies have also cited the high cancer rates among people living near chemical plants. After the Bhopal, India tragedy a testy Union Carbide Board Chairman Warren Anderson offered a "novel" solution to such health risks, suggesting that "maybe the Third World ought to have rules and regulations so that people are not permitted to gather around your plant in clusters, because it's not a safe thing to do."[66]

EPA, while regulating only six toxic air pollutants, nevertheless lists 403 deadly chemicals. However, the agency leaves it to state and local officials to discover where they are produced and used. Consequently, public awareness of just what is produced in the nation's 5,000 chemical manufacturing plants remains minimal.

"Most Americans would be surprised to learn," Representative Henry Waxman, D-Calif., reminds us, "that the chemical industry is free to release into the air whatever quantities of whatever poisonous or cancer-causing chemicals it sees fit."[67] As these dangers become more evident various federal agencies are beginning to show concern. In June 1985 the EPA announced that it planned to seek nearly $7 million in fines against six major chemical companies that allegedly manufactured new chemicals without notifying the federal government.[68]

In April 1986 the Occupational Safety and Health Administration (OSHA) accused the Union Carbide Corporation of 221 violations of 55 Federal safety and health laws at its Institute, West Virginia plant and fined the company a record $1.4 million. In announcing the fines then-Labor Secretary William Brock indicated his department was prepared to "impose the full penalties of the law on those who blatantly or repeatedly violate safeguards necessary to protect American workers."

Brock said in the case of Union Carbide "we were surprised to find constant, willful, overt violations on such a widespread basis." By way of illustration, he noted that plant workers were "customarily" asked to detect the presence of the highly toxic phosgene gas — known as "mustard gas" in World War I and which can cause lungs to swell with often fatal results, but which now used as a dye and chemical poison — by sniffing the air after alarms had sounded indicating a leak.

"They used to use canaries for that," Brock angrily observed. Union Carbide indicated that it planned to appeal the fines.[69]

Such stories only underscore the need for public scrutiny of the chemical industry. Indeed, a 1987 survey by the Roper organization found that the three industries the public believes should be most subject to closer government regulation were chemical (44 percent), drug (43 percent), and food processing companies (37 percent).

As recently as 1984, the U.S. Supreme Court ruled in an 8-0 verdict that chemical companies cannot prevent the government from releasing health and safety data on their products. Monsanto had challenged the government's right to provide such information on grounds that such disclosures amounted to an unconstitutional seizure of private property. Justice Harry A. Blackmun, however, writing for the court, pointed out that Monsanto had essentially relinquished the exclusive rights to its scientific data when it sought the government's permission to market the poisons.

> As long as [Monsanto] is aware of the conditions under which the data are submitted, and the conditions are *rationally related to a legitimate government interest*, a voluntary submission of data in exchange for the *economic advantages* of a registration can hardly be called a taking. (emphasis added)[70]

Subsequent to this Court decision the EPA announced that it would henceforth require manufacturers of chemical poisons to submit more product information when seeking permission to sell their chemicals. In addition to requiring that all products, not just those used on food, be tested for possible genetic damage, EPA required manufacturers to submit data on the hazards of aerial drift by chemical poisons.[71]

Many farmers who have curtailed or refused to use chemical poisons in their fields and orchards have become increasingly vocal about the health problems they encounter from chemicals applied elsewhere that drift onto their property.

Poisons used on southern cotton have ended up in Chicago and in Great Lakes fish. In fact, a study by Michigan environmental biologist Wayland R. Swain found several different chemical poisons in the waters off Isle Royale, located in the pristine wilderness of Lake Superior in northeastern Minnesota. "It's such a remote island, so far removed from the industrial and cultural influence of man, that there's only one reasonable way the material could have gotten there. It had to have been the atmosphere."[72]

New deposits of DDT, presumably from Central America and Mexico, have been found contaminating the upper Great Lakes area even though this deadly chemical, the subject of Rachel Carson's classic *The Silent Spring*, was banned in the United States and Canada years ago.

The Arctic and Antarctic waters have also revealed traces of an insecticide used widely in Asia and southern Europe. "It isn't that difficult for the atmosphere to move chemicals thousands of miles," notes Steven Eisenreich, professor of environmental engineering at the University of Minnesota, ... nowhere are you immune from the effects of long-range transfer."[73]

Living and Working in the Cancer Clusters

As toxic as these chemical poisons can be to the applicators and the farmers that use them, they are even more threatening to the health and lives of millions of men, women and children who each day work among them and handle the crops on which they have been deposited. Citing the aforementioned World Resources Institute study stating that between four and five million farmworkers are exposed to these poisons while as many as 300,000 suffer from some kind of chemical poisoning, Cesar Chavez, head of the United Farm Workers (UFW), has made this issue central to the union's recent organizing efforts.

Although California has the toughest reporting standards in the United States most chemical poisonings in the state go unreported, making the actual extent of such abuse difficult to determine. Chavez cites evidence that in at least two California towns, Fowler and McFarland, cancer among children aged 3-12 years is 3,500 times higher in the area than the national average.[74]

Dr. Marion Moses, M.D., an assistant clinical professor at the University of California San Francisco School of Medicine and a long-time tireless worker as both a nurse and physician with farm labor organizations, stresses the field workers' right to information concerning the chemical poisons they are exposed to on a daily basis.

> Workers have a right to know what specific pesticides they are being exposed to, the potential health risks, both acute and chronic from their exposures, and the means to protect themselves and their families.
>
> Information that is specific and sufficiently comprehensive to be of practical use must be readily available and accessible to workers and their representatives. The agricultural and agrichemical industries have hidden behind the 'trade secret' argument long enough as a reason for denying access to information about specific pesticides and their use.
>
> ... If worker protection were as important as agribusiness and the agrichemical industry would like us to believe, many chemicals on the market today could not continue to be used.[75]

Energy Efficiency and Corporate Agribusiness

For over a century America's farms have gradually been shifting away from reliance on human labor and renewable energy to non-renewable petroleum fuels and energy-intensive petrochemical products such as fertilizer and chemical poisons. Thus, mechanical and chemical energy technologies are replacing human and animal energy resources resulting in serious harm to people and their natural environment, and threatens the very future of our natural resource supply.

The farm once was its own closed ecological cycle. Farmers used to feed their draft horses grain and grass from their fields. Later the waste was returned to the land as manure that would enrich the soil for the next crop.

Despite the many high-priced, petroleum-consuming machines on the market today there are still some farmers successfully using draft horses. One such farmer, in the Dry Creek Valley in Northern California's Sonoma County, Charles Richard, who grows the grapes and crafts the wine at Bellerose Vineyards in Healdsburg, notes that he and his wife Nancy were impressed by the spirit of the hard work of the people who had been here before us. I feel very strongly that we follow in the footsteps of these people. I see us as caretakers, not of a mere vineyard, not of a mere winery, but of land that someday will be farmed by someone else. We're interested in farming the land, in the *art* of farming.[76]

While it is estimated that there are some 20,000-40,000 non-chemical farmers who today produce but one percent of the nation's food,[77] most farmers continue to plow their land with high-powered tractors, spray their crops with chemical poisons, harvest their fields with more exotic gas-guzzling machinery, and haul their grain to a terminal elevator or local feedlot by gasoline or diesel-fueled trucks. By 1986 U.S. farmers were paying an annual projected bill of $18.4 billion for electricity/fuels/fertilizer/chemical poisons, up 32.6 percent from 1977, but down 22.9 percent from a record $23.9 billion in 1981.[78]

For example, in only one of the many paradoxes surrounding modern agribusiness, there frequently develops in large feedlots a volume of manure that can eventually lead to a huge disposal problem. Meanwhile, farmers are forced to use chemical fertilizers to replace missing organic manure, which in turn decomposes to inorganic nitrogen, causing a variety of continuing pollution problems in the local surface water supply.

In his book *The Poverty of Power: Energy and the Economic Crisis*, Barry Commoner elaborates on such absurdities:

> One can almost admire the enterprise and clever salesmanship of the petrochemical industry. Somehow it has managed to convince the farmer that he should give up the free solar energy that drives the natural cycles, and, instead buy the needed energy — in the form of fertilizer and fuel — from the petrochemical industry.
>
> Not content with that commercial coup, these industrial giants have completed their conquest of the farmer by going into competition with what the farm produces. They have introduced into the market a series of competing synthetics: synthetic fiber, which competes with cotton and wool; detergents, which compete with a soap made of natural oils and fat; plastics, which compete with wood; and pesticides that compete with birds and ladybugs, which used to be free.[79]

Beyond the farm, the packaging and transportation of farm products consume enormous amounts of fuel (See Chart 6C). In the shift from home-cooked to mass-prepared convenience foods, energy costs have skyrocketed. Sugar gets refined; grains are milled and baked; oil-bearing seeds are crushed and refined, and fruits and vegetables are canned, dried or frozen. Such changes require massive amounts of steel, glass, aluminum and plastic.

Today, over 93 percent of the energy that goes into American agricultural production comes from petroleum.

David Pimentel, Professor of Insect Ecology and Agricultural Sciences at Cornell University, has conducted studies which show that most grains in the United States yield two to three calories for

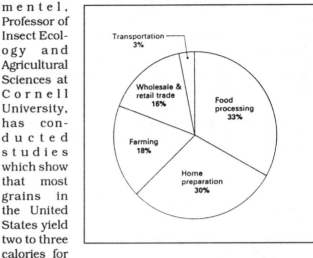

Chart 6C: Agribusiness Energy Use

- Transportation 3%
- Wholesale & retail trade 16%
- Food processing 33%
- Farming 18%
- Home preparation 30%

every calorie of fossil energy imputed. Ninety percent of that grain is used to feed livestock, the most energy consuming product of American agriculture.[80]

Over one third of the energy input into agriculture production is in the form of petrochemicals, chemical poisons and fertilizers. Nitrogen, phosphorous, and potassium are supplied by chemical fertilizers and the availability of these nutrients in the future is uncertain. Natural gas, used to produce nitrogen fertilizer, is becoming scarcer and more expensive; potassium supplies must be imported in large amounts and while we have large supplies of phosphate rock, it is a finite amount.

Only three percent of the total energy expended annually in the United States is devoted to agricultural production.[81] However, the food system as a whole consumes 16.5 percent, which results in the expenditure of 6.4 units of energy (most of it based on fossil fuels) for every unit of food that Americans consume.[82] (That is only an average; processed vegetables, for example, consume almost 16 units of energy for every food unit.[83])

It has been estimated that if the entire world were to adopt the present U.S. food manufacturing and delivery system it would require 60 percent of the total amount of energy that is commercially produced today worldwide; burning up all of the planet's known petroleum reserves within 13 years.[84] While food processors and packagers are using more energy than all the farms that produce our food, for every two dollars spent on energy to grow food, another dollar is spent on transporting it.[85]

A spokesman for the FMI told a Congressional Committee that during the 1979 fuel shortage, some food distributors "came within a day or two of not having enough fuel to deliver food. In other words, at any one time we are only days away from shortages on the shelves of grocery stores around the nation."[86] Moving food around not only costs money, but as we shall see, leaving that job to a relatively few corporations only intensifies the specter of possible food shortages.

Fuel and electricity costs in the food industry, according to the USDA's ERS, rose at more than 1.5 times the annual rate of other costs from the beginning of the sharp rise in energy prices in 1973 to 1981.[87] Increasing about 20 percent a year, these costs, which included only costs of electricity, natural gas, and other fuels used in food processing, wholesaling, and retailing, increased from two percent to four percent of retail food expenditures.[88]

Nearly 40 percent of these fuel costs were found in the food processing industry. Fuel and electricity costs went from $2.2 billion in 1970 to $13.3 billion in 1985, an increase of 504 percent.[89]

Consumers expenditures for the transporting by rail and truck of farm goods went up 213 percent from $5.2 billion to $16.3 billion.[90]

The Ozone and Toxic Fog

Ironically, the very pollutants from many of these same fuels are returning to haunt food producers. A 1988 EPA study showed that ozone pollution was reducing crop yields by $2.5 to $3 billion each year in the United States.[91]

"Farmers need to be aware that air pollution is out there and that it's become another cost of doing business, another piece out of their profits," warns John Laurence, the scientist who conducted the EPA study.[92]

A series of 1985/1986 University of California studies also showed that for both consumers and producers, the effects of ozone on agriculture are substantial.

When automobile exhaust and manufacturing plant emissions mix in the atmosphere they convert to smog or ozone through a photochemical process. In California, prevailing westerly winds carry this pollution into the state's agriculturally rich Central Valley. Increased industrialization has only exacerbated the region's air quality problems already burdened by air pollution resulting from agricultural burning.

One such study has shown that air pollution is a major stress causing yield losses in the state's crops, as many of California's fruits and vegetables are becoming more sensitive to ozone and are showing reduced yields and quality when exposed to these pollutants.[93] For example, 90 percent of the processing tomatoes grown in the United States are raised in the state's Central Valley. One area that grows a large portion of these tomatoes lies directly east, downwind from the San Francisco Bay Area, the nation's fourth most populous area where high humidity along with ozone has been shown to reduce the yields of the popular "Murrieta" tomato.[94]

Still another study indicates that for both consumers and producers, the effects of ozone on agriculture are "substantial" for at least 17 affected crops: alfalfa hay and seed, barley, dry beans, celery, corn, cotton, grain sorghum, lettuce, onions, potatoes, rice, fresh and processed tomatoes, and wheat.

While producers bear the brunt of the effects, consumers are also affected through changes in prices. Under significant air quality degradation (0.08 ppm) producers of crops known to be affected will have their returns to fixed costs reduced by almost 11 percent. Given the slim profit margins for many crops, ozone degradation will have much greater effects on farm profits."[95]

The ozone is not the only threat in the air. Research by Louis A. Liljedahl and Dwight E. Glotfelty of USDA's ARS division in Beltsville, Maryland, and James N. Seiber of UC-Davis indicates that there is also a very real danger to our environment from toxic fog.

The researchers, according to an article in the February 1987 issue of *Nature*, have found that fog samples taken near Beltsville and California's San Joaquin Valley bear concentrations of some toxic substances thousands of times higher than had been predicted by Henry's Law, a widely used law of chemistry. Among the 16 toxic compounds the researchers found were the chemical poisons diazinon, parathion and malathion and the herbicides simazine and alachlor.[96]

Subsequent research showed that the fog droplets can concentrate the vapors to far higher levels than exist in the air and that chemicals in the droplet or on its surface can make it easier for the droplet to take up other substances. "I think there is a very great potential for these water-borne organic compounds to damage crops and forests," observes Glotfelty. Liljedahl adds also that because many of the dissolved compounds are plant killers these new findings "give scientists a more solid basis for attributing low-level crop damage" to toxic fog.[97]

Farmer Block's "Dead End"

Meanwhile, as non-renewable fuels and energy-intensive agricultural chemicals become more expensive, many farmers are wisely beginning to question such new technologies and beginning to search elsewhere for alternative, low-cost technologies.

Some of the more popular methods adopted by these latter agricultural producers can be found in sustainable, low-input or organic farming.

But even as a growing number of the advocates of non-chemical agriculture seek to disengage themselves from the "pesticide treadmill," we see yet another prime example of how agribusiness can transform a seemingly serious threat to its corporate agenda into a grab for even more economic power in the marketplace.

In recent years the increasing public concern about the chemical dangers lurking in our food have triggered alarm bells throughout corporate agribusiness. Consequently, with one eye on their image and another on their sales figures we have seen significant sectors of corporate agribusiness attempting to co-opt the public perception of "organic" and/or "sustainable" agriculture, and to redefine it in self-serving terms.

In California, for example, Nunes Co., the Salinas Valley vegetable giant, Pandol Bros. Inc. and Marko Zaninovich Inc., two large San Joaquin Valley grape and produce growers, and Superior Farming Co., one of the world's largest grape and fruit growers, have all begun to experiment with so-called chemical-free methods in crop production on their thousands of acres of farmland.[98]

Meanwhile, the state's genuine 1,000 to 2,000 organic farmers, who till on the average between 60 and 70 acres of fruits and vegetables, voice legitimate and well-founded fears concerning the entrance of these corporate super-farms into organic agriculture.[99]

Such agribusiness behemoths are likely to skew much needed research in organic agriculture towards capital-intensive systems, and to legislate self-serving restrictive anti-competitive industry-wide standards. There is also the danger that they could, with their vast economic power, begin to flood existing markets with their produce, depress prices, and drive still more family farms out of business.

Farmers in Florida, which produces about half of the nation's fresh winter vegetables worth $1.3 billion, and other southern farmers who have come to rely on chemical poisons to fight the diseases and insects that thrive on high humidity and warm temperatures, now see the growth of chemical-free agriculture in the west and southwest as a serious economic threat to their survival.[100]

Contrary to what its critics charge, however, organic farming is not simply "farming without chemical fertilizers or poisons." Such advertisements as those that the Pennwalt Corporation, a major manufacturer of chemical poisons, have run in national magazines ("Natural farming is perfectly all right, as long as you believe in natural famine") have failed to discourage many farmers from experimenting with organic farming.

Most organic farmers would today subscribe to the definition offered by the *1980 USDA Report and Recommendations on Organic Agriculture*:

Organic farming systems aim at *working with* natural ecological systems rather than simply overriding these systems with outside 'inputs.' To the maximum extent possible, organic farming systems replace use of chemical pesticides and fertilizers with reliance on such methods as legume-based crop rotations, animal and green manures, mechanical cultivation and aspects of biological pest control to maintain soil productivity, to supply plant nutrients and to control pests.[101]

Many organic farmers have reported crop yields comparable to those obtained on nearby conventional farms, and despite studies using badly-dated 1944-46 USDA crop yield figures as a measuring device, organic farming could meet domestic food needs in small grains and soybeans while some exports could be continued and farm income would increase.[102]

More recent organic farm studies also show that in drought years, organic farms out-produced their conventional partners, while in favorable growing conditions they dropped only an average of 8.5 percent below their matched conventional fields. Net farm income on these organic farms also showed an increase due to lower "input" costs.[103]

In arguing for a "biologic sustainable" agriculture, organic farmers point out that if resource conservation and other ecological values are indeed important, they should be balanced against sheer production as a measure of the success of farm systems.

Neil Pashley, a Williamsfield, Ohio dairy farmer quit using chemicals in 1967 and, despite those who derided his organic farm efforts over the years, (including one County Extension agent who once called him a "medicine man") he has been quite successful. In 1983, for example, Pashley obtained 100 bushels of corn per acre compared to his home Ashtabula County average of 104. Ohio State University economists calculated that the typical corn farmer that year spent $99 an acre on chemical poisons and fertilizers. Pashley spent only $10 per acre, mostly on organic soil additives. Calculating four fewer bushels per acre he earned $12 less, but at the same time he spent $89 less per acre on input costs than his neighbors. Pashley reflects,

I say I've got $150 per acre in my pocket before I even plant. I'm putting money in the bank with my kind of farming. My rich soil is a good bank account. All these other guys think about is how much they can make off so many acres. To do what we are doing, you have to be strong and you can't let people talking about you hurt you. You dare to be different and sometimes it is painful. But eventually the so-called experts will have to admit they were wrong.[104]

Another farmer who has defied the "conventional" wisdom is Delmar Akerlund, who owns a 760-acre grain and cattle farm in Valley, Nebraska. For nearly 20 years he has been what is now called a "low-input" farmer, employing animal manure and crop rotation to suppress weeds and discourage harmful insects, boosting the fertility of his land by spraying mineral-rich sea kelp and fish emulsion on his crops. He recalls,

We had left all the decisions up to a chemical salesman. Our money went from one pocket to another. We just weren't farming anymore. The scariest thing was that the herbicides would not dissipate. Because of that we could not rotate crops in different fields and our disease problems increased. We were afraid of being locked into a monoculture.

Although going "cold turkey" at the beginning caused him to have decreased crop yields in the first three years, his costs also went down. Soon things began to change and in two decades Akerlund has seen his family farm not only produce ample harvests without the soil erosion that has periodically threatened his neighbor's fields, but because "our money comes in almost every day, like the filling station in town" Akerlund has not had to participate in government support programs to stay in farming.

As the *Post*'s Ward Sinclair has observed,

Then there is the matter of the earthworms, the songbirds and the wildlife. Long ago they had abandoned this farm, the environment was so forbidding, but now they are back in abundance. So populous are the worms, whose burrowings are vital to healthy soil, that during rain storms they will rise like a tide and cover the roads adjacent to Akerlund's fields.

Akerlund adds,

Many farmers know that something is wrong, that things are out of balance, because they are just not making it under conventional chemical farming systems. But it's almost a minute past midnight. We've almost run out of time for farmers to make the transition away from these powerful chemicals. The bankers now tell them they must farm with chemicals if they want their loans. They're between a rock and a hard place.[105]

Despite such optimistic projections and hopes the Reagan Administration, led by former Agriculture Secretary Block, who once termed organic farming "a dead end," consistently opposed government-sponsored research into such forms of alternative agriculture. First, by firing Garth Youngberg, who headed the Department's organic farming program and, in effect, gutting that program, and then by opposing the Agricultural Productivity Act, a bill that would have provided research and pilot programs in organic farming, Reagan & Co. sought to portray organic farmers as a fringe group, outside the agricultural mainstream.

Youngberg, now director of the Institute for Alternative Agriculture, a research group in Greenbelt, Maryland, disagrees with his former administration:

The fact that the Reagan administration ... opposed the Agricultural Production Act has created the impression that the agriculture establishment is not interested. That's, well, ... not an accurate portrayal of reality. We're trying very hard to build bridges to [Agricultural Extension Service] people. A lot of it is just lack of understanding. If they got out on these farms, they'd see something happening.[106]

Despite the Reagan administration's opposition, Senator Leahy, D-Vt., and then Representative James Weaver, D-Ore., were successful in getting language incorporated into the 1985 Farm Bill which directed the USDA to begin research that would demonstrate the conservation and production benefits of organic farming, although the term itself does not appear in the legislation.[107]

Subsequently, Department Deputy Secretary Peter C. Myers, Assistant Secretary Orville G. Bentley and others have shown signs of interests in such styles of farming. As Paul O'Connell, a USDA Cooperative State Research Service (CSRS) official who was named to coordinate such research, points out,

These low-input farmers have a hellva story to tell. And we need to show farmers that there are alternatives to their present situation and that this is one of them. I would promote this to the utmost, to lessen our surplus production, to cut farmers' costs, to save soil and the environment. It has all kinds of pluses.[108]

But, as Josh Andrew, a West Point, Indiana grain and livestock farmer, is quick to add,

... getting farmers to change is a slow process. Part of it is peer pressure; part of it is the ethic that says they have to have 'clean' weedless fields. You ask a chemical company what lower levels of herbicide use are acceptable and they can't tell you. The thing that really bothers me is the universities. I contacted Purdue a few years ago and they could give me no help at all about making the change. There was nothing there.[109]

In his "The Prospects of Small Scale Farming in an Industrial Society" agricultural economist Philip LeVeen concluded that when diminishing resources begin bringing highly mechanized agriculture to a grinding halt, small family farms will be the most "adaptable units" to scarcity.[110]

The question remains, however, whether there will be any such "adaptable" units left as corporate agribusiness continues to devise new and more subtle means towards achieving its vaunted goal of completely substituting technology for labor and capital for efficiency in the production of our food supply.

Section Two:

Controlling Our Food
From "Seedling to Supermarket"

"It's a food war out there and advertising is the weapon. TV is the bombers that have mass impact, and print media and couponing are the infantry for the hand-to-hand stuff. . . The reason the war analogy is so useful is that business itself is now in such a warlike mode. Business used to be, everybody made a lot of money and everybody was terrific and everybody was happy. Today, business has become pure competition, real war."

> - Jack Trout, president of the advertising
> firm Ries Capiello Colwell Inc.

Chapter Seven

Living with the "Vicissitudes of the Market"

Concentrated economic power and corporate mega-mergers have today become the chief characteristics of our current food delivery system.

Concentrated economic power in the hands of a dwindling number of giant, multinational corporations — and the economic, social, political and environmental costs that farmers, workers and consumers are forced to pay to sustain such power — should concern each and every person whose survival depends on food. To paraphrase a popular bumpersticker often seen on rural America's roads — "if you eat, you're involved in corporate agribusiness!"

No longer do producers, processors, manufacturers, wholesalers and retailers operate within a competitive "free market system" to bring food to our tables. Rather, our food delivery system is today dominated by highly capitalized, increasingly vertically integrated, industrialized and tightly concentrated corporations.

To the people who live in rural America the control of our food economy by large corporations has come to mean unavailable credit and oppressive market power by corporate interests, and unfair, uncontrolled and wildly fluctuating below cost-of-production prices for the products they must produce each year to survive.

Meanwhile, corporate agribusiness marches on, manufacturing less nutritious food in increasingly more artificial forms while consumers find themselves forced to pay an ever higher and more exacting quantitative and qualitative price for this rush to bigness.

Yet not a day goes by that we don't see in our newspapers or on the TV news still another abuse of corporate power. Nevertheless, we as a society stubbornly refuse to confront what authors Walter Adams and James W. Brock describe as "the unpleasant fact that concentrated power exists and that it has social consequences."

Writing in their book, *The Bigness Complex: Industry, Labor and Government in the American Economy*, Brock and Adams note that the United States is afflicted by a "structural malaise" which springs from the myth that "industrial giantism is the handmaiden of economic efficiency and consumer welfare."[1]

No one has offered a more insightful study of the characteristics and consequences of such economic concentration than the late John Blair, one-time chief economist of the Senate Anti-Trust and Monopoly Subcommittee, and author of the important book, *Economic Concentration: Structure, Behavior and Public Policy*.[2] Blair notes at the outset of his massive work that the primary reason behind the reluctance of business and government even to admit that such a phenomena

as economic concentration exists is the fact that few people have ever carefully studied its characteristics and consequences.

He adds, "a true understanding of concentration must embrace the structural and market-behavioral aspects of all four dimensions of concentration." Those four dimensions are: vertical, conglomerate, market and aggregate concentration.

Although Blair devotes comparatively little attention specifically to agriculture and to the food manufacturing industry, Purdue's John M. Connor and his fellow agricultural economists Richard T. Rogers, Bruce W. Marion and Willard F. Mueller later applied many of Blair's propositions to our modern-day food delivery system in their highly authoritative landmark work, *The Food Manufacturing Industries: Structure, Strategies, Performance, and Policies*.[3]

Food Needs From the "Womb to Tomb"

For many, the word "agribusiness" has replaced "farming" in the language of the marketplace. Vertical integration and/or "coordination," permits this structure called agribusiness to control food from "seedling to supermarket," as a Tenneco Corp. official once put it.

The term "vertical integration" generally applies to the holding of a share of an industry's output by companies also engaged in an earlier or later stage of production. In agriculture itself, vertical integration can take place at either end, *i.e.*, the input end, when a feed company produces hogs, or the consumption end, when a meat packing company produces its own hogs for slaughter.

Staking its claim to take care of people's food needs from the "womb to tomb," the Del Monte Corporation is a classic example of a vertically integrated multinational company. It is engaged in food and agricultural research, seed farms, agricultural production, inputs, processing, transportation, storage and distribution, marketing, advertising and food service.

Discussing the nature of vertical integration in their paper "Contract Production and Vertical Integration in Farming, 1960 and 1970," USDA researchers Ronald L. Mighell and William S. Hoofnagle first define vertical *coordination*:

It includes all the ways of harmonizing the successive vertical steps or stages of production and marketing. Vertical coordination may be accomplished through the market price system, vertical integration, contracting, cooperation, or any other means, separately or in combination. There is always some kind of vertical coordination if any production takes place.[4]

The authors then go on to define "vertical integration" as the coordination of many stages of production in one firm. Some of these stages may have previously been identified with separate firms that have merged into one.

Vertical coordination of farm production under agreements between farmers and the processors, dealers and others who sell to or buy from them, is known as "contract production." Frequently, such agreements are called "forward contracts" because they are made before a commodity is produced. Many farmers, before committing their resources to the production of a specific commodity, will reach an agreement with a contractor for the sale of their goods at a fixed, predetermined price. Such corporations, therefore, do not actually engage in farming, with all of its inherent risks, they simply "rent" a farm.

Economists like Eric Thor, former administrator of USDA's Farmer Cooperative Service, argue that farmers' interests are better served by their becoming part of the "coordinated production marketing system" rather than trying to break up large food firms. "In practice," he speculates, "breaking up large food companies would weaken the position of the American farmer."[5]

The thousands of U.S. farmers whose farms and businesses have come under the control of large food companies only to have those same markets either disappear or the company's production facilities move abroad, would undoubtedly take sharp issue with Thor. Those who watched Del Monte, for example, unceremoniously transfer the bulk of its peach production from Northern California to Italy and South Africa might question the beneficial effects of ever dealing with such large food processors in the first place.

USDA's ERS economist Kenneth R. Krause, citing in part researchers Mighell and Hoofnagleusing, claims that corporations "apparently" account for most of the vertical integration, which increased from 19 percent of farm output in 1960 to 22 percent in 1970 to about 30 percent in 1980.

"Contract production, however, was much more prevalent (22.9 percent of total farm output in 1980) than vertical integration (7.4 percent)."[6] Meanwhile, the American Agricultural Marketing Association was claiming in 1980 the figure was near 50 percent while projecting that by the end of the decade it would climb to almost 75 percent.[7] Even those estimates, however, may be deceivingly low because a close inspection of recent statistics reveals that production and marketing contracts already control:

- 98 percent of sugar beets
- 95 percent of fluid grade milk
- 89 percent of all broilers
- 85 percent of processed vegetables
- 65 percent of citrus fruit
- 80 percent of all seed crops
- 60 percent of potatoes
- 62 percent of all turkeys
- 52 percent of eggs

These above figures too must be viewed with some skepticism since they were compiled by the USDA's Economic Research Service commodity specialists in 1980. Noting how dated these figures may be, Krause, writing in December 1987, observes:

> While considerable work can be done to provide information on the importance of both family and wider shareholder ownership of corporations involved in farming, budget constraints will limit the work at least for the 1987 "Census of Agriculture" and perhaps longer.
>
> ... While special supplemental census studies have been done in the past, funding is unlikely to be available for special studies on corporate and vertically coordinated farming during the remainder of the 1980s.[8]

As Mighell and Hoofnagle have noted, vertical integration is most often used to define a situation in which several successive stages of production are coordinated within one firm:

> Nearly all firms have some inherent vertical integration. Hence, one could say that practically all production is vertically integrated to some extent. However, what we mean here by vertical integration is the situation in which two or more stages that were formerly handled by separate firms are merged into one firm. And we mean specifically, integration between farm and non-farm stages.[9]

A livestock feeder who buys or builds a packing plant to serve as an outlet for feed cattle, for instance, is vertically integrated. So, too, is a lettuce packer-shipper who also grows lettuce, as are broiler producers who build their own feed mills.

Blair rightly believed that vertical integration can affect competition adversely — a fact vividly illustrated by what happened to nearly all of the one-time small, independent chicken farmers in the south. In Mississippi, Georgia, Alabama and Arkansas in the 1960s, family farm poultry producers saw their industry go from 40 percent to 98 percent vertically integrated by the large feed companies.[10] When vertical integrators establish monopolistic control over scarce natural resources, non-integrated businesses eventually become cut off from materials or are forced to operate for far less profit.

Blair cites Carl Kaysen and Donald F. Turner's *Anti-Trust Policy — An Economic and Legal Analysis*:

> Finally, vertical integration offers opportunities for the use of market power not available to firms operating in a single-stage market. Both price and non-price discriminations are made possible by vertical integration, especially partial vertical integration in which a firm is both supplier and competitor of other firms. ... By narrowing the margin between the price at which it supplies its one-stage rivals and the price at which it sells the product with which their output competes, it can

limit their profits, their growth, and even drive them out of business ... By rationing the supplies of nonintegrated customers, or by simply refusing to deal with them, the same results can be brought about ...[11]

In addition to denying them supplies, the integrated producer can impose "price squeezes" on non-integrated rivals by narrowing the gap between the raw material and the finished product price.

Food processors and canners are among the major corporate integrators in agribusiness today, mainly through "contract production." However, because so many different companies are involved in processing and canning, it is not immediately apparent just how heavily concentrated that marketplace has become.

For example, there exists in the canning industry a high degree of specialization primarily because canners can such a variety of commodities. Yet, just as consumers are faced with two or three brands of any given item, farmers are often likewise faced with only two, three or possibly four markets for their product. Regionally, for most crops, four processors will handle 50 percent or more of the sales.

Before a spate of mergers in the late 1970s in which several canners were consumed by even larger corporations, the four leading fruit and vegetable canners — Del Monte, H.J. Heinz, Campbell and Libby, McNeil and Libby — sold more than 60 percent of the fruit cocktail, 57 percent of the applesauce, 82 percent of the canned figs, 52 percent of canned sweet corn, 58 percent of the vegetable juice, 53 percent of canned peas, and 72 percent of the tomato sauce. Campbell Soup Co., now alone, holds a 66.6 percent share of the nation's $2.3 billion soup market, including 82 percent of the condensed soup market, and can be found in 93 percent of American homes.[12]

On a national basis, these four processors had a "low-grade oligopoly," controlling approximately 40 percent of canned-goods sales nationally. According to a 1972 FTC study, to the consumer that control meant paying $143.6 million in monopoly overcharges for canned fruits and vegetables and $84.9 million in similar overcharges for frozen fruits and vegetables.[13]

Connor and Co. calculate that between 1972 and 1977 consumer overcharges due to the monopoly structure in canned fruits and vegetables was 3.5 percent to 6.9 percent of sales and 4 percent to 12.5 percent in frozen fruits and vegetables. Total consumer loss to monopoly in food manufacturing was projected to be $120 billion.[14] By 1981, the monopoly power of concentrated corporate power in food manufacturing alone was costing consumers an estimated $19-$22 billion a year in overcharges.[15] Meanwhile, between 1970 and 1977, profits for these four vertically integrated food processors skyrocketed: Campbell's went up 70 percent; Heinz' rose 156 percent; and Del Monte's leaped 254 percent.[16] Since Libby, McNeil and Libby was a subsidiary of Nestle Alimentana, a private Swiss multinational conglomerate, their profit and sales figures were not available for public inspection.

Conglomerate concentration has come to mean simply that a significant share of an industry's output is held by companies primarily engaged in an unrelated industry.

A chief characteristic of conglomerate concentration is cross-subsidization whereby profits earned in one industry subsidize sales in another at a loss or an abnormally low profit. Blair stresses that the single-line producer is frequently more efficient than the conglomerate operating in the same industry, but the single-line producer is reluctant to take any competitive action because the conglomerate can operate at a loss long enough to drive the single-line producer out of business.[17]

In discussing size and some of its drawbacks, Blair notes that large corporations' contribution to technical progress has often fallen short of what would have been expected in view of their resources. As an example, he points to the typically lengthy interval between the making of an invention and its introduction as an innovation.

Blair's position is borne out by a comment made by Archer-Daniels-Midland Corp. (ADM) CEO Dwayne O. Andreas in 1976 after ADM invested $80 million in the development and manufacturing of a new high-fructose corn syrup — a product destined to compete with then high-priced sugar.

As ADM increased its capacity ninefold to produce the new product the bottom fell out of the sugar market.[19] "We made a mistake with high-fructose," Andreas admitted. "We had the technology but delayed going into it because we thought the first people in should *develop* the market. We felt there was a timetable to market development." (emphasis added)

Despite the admitted delay and unlike the single-line producer, Andreas, as the head of a large, diversified corporation could afford the luxury of viewing his company's situation philosophically. He correctly believed that good profits would eventually be made in the high fructose business as the low price of sugar would almost certainly squeeze some sugar production from the market, producing a rise in prices. "Every year one of our businesses has some problems. For us, it's just *standard operating procedure* to live with *the vicissitudes of the market.*"[20] (emphasis added)

Indeed, as we shall see later, ADM has most certainly mastered the technique of living with such "vicissitudes."[21]

"Beatrice. You've Known Us All Along"

In his discussion of conglomerate concentration Blair explains that a conglomerate that competes vigorously in an industry affording an important source of profits to a rival conglomerate can expect retaliation.[22] Realizing this, the conglomerate usually won't make any competitive moves in the first industry. And the greater the number of industries in which given conglomerates confront each other, the stronger the rationale for mutual forbearance among each of them.

More than 3,300 food related companies between 1982 and 1988 alone have been merged or acquired by other corporations. As these larger companies buy smaller ones and become even bigger, they are less able and willing to do their own research and development, preferring to *purchase* new companies and new products. Frequently, these large companies will camouflage such takeovers with massive advertising campaigns. Corporate integrity is often the big loser.

Television viewers of the 1984 Olympics will remember seeing a variety of products, such as Culligan Soft Water repeatedly advertised, only to be reminded by a voice at the end of each commercial that it was "Beatrice. You've known us all along." No, in fact, most Americans didn't know it was Beatrice "all along," for in the previous decade the $13 billion firm has been buying one small, well-known, company after another (such as the family-owned Culligan firm).

In 1984, however, Beatrice had begun to sell off many of these newly-acquired subsidiaries in an effort to pay back the massive $2.8 billion it borrowed to buy Esmark, the giant meat packing and consumer products company.[23]

By 1985 Beatrice's directors approved a $6.4 billion takeover bid by the New York investment banking firm of Kohlberg Kravis Roberts & Co.. Beatrice's chairman Donald P. Kelly, also announced that in its first 18 months as a private corporation Beatrice planned on selling $1.45 billion more in assets in an effort to pay off the first two installments of its debt and interest obligations.[24]

At the same time it was revealed that Beatrice's former chairman and chief executive officer, William W. Granger Jr., and five other top company executives would receive "golden parachutes" in the form of hugh severance benefits totaling $23.5 million. A "golden parachute" is a provision in an executive's employment contract with the company guaranteeing substantial severance benefits if he should lose his job in a takeover.[25] Before Beatrice's takeover by KKR, however, a $23 million corporate-image advertising campaign touched off a heated debate between company officials and industry experts; the former arguing that the association with the company name would help Beatrice take regional brands national on the coattails of already popular products while the latter rightly believed such an advertising campaign to be a waste of money.

"Does it give them a better image within the consuming public for someone who buys Samsonite luggage to know that the same company also makes cat treats?" asks Smith, Barney financial analyst Ronald Morrow. "I don't think it is worth it."[26]

Less than two years after the KKR buyout of Beatrice it was announced that all of its non-food operations and even a few of its smaller food operations would be formed into a new company — E-II Holdings Inc. — which would sell shares on the open market. Beatrice, which had already sold eight of its divisions to other companies for $3.4 billion since going private in April 1986, became strictly a food company.[27] In mid-1990, Beatrice was subsequently purchased for $2.3 billion by the agribusiness giant ConAgra. "It's a good deal for ConAgra — they get size and presence in dry grocery in one fell swoop," observed Leonard Teitlebaum, industry

analyst with Merrill Lynch and Company on learning the news of the sale.

More than 50 percent of today's divestitures result from the merging of two companies in the first place, according to Willard Grimm, president of W.T. Grimm & Co., a firm which follows trends in mergers and acquisitions. "Usually these divestitures occur as a means of paying for the company just acquired" (as in the Beatrice purchase).[28]

Most of the companies now being divested, according to Arthur Burke, a Palm Beach, Florida mergers specialist, are

ugly ducklings but were star performers when they were purchased. But because the buyers *mismanaged them* — often because of their lack of sophistication — the new company failed to live up to its potential. And that *has cost society a high cost* — jobs, corporate profits and innovative products.[29] (emphasis added)

The Corporate Agribusiness Elite
(Top 12 U.S. Food and Food-Related Corporations, 1988)

Rank	Corporation	1988 Annual Sales (billions)
1	Cargill	$38.2
2	Kroger	$17.5
3	American Stores	$15.2
4	Continental Grain	$13.0
	Philip Morris	$13.0*
6	McDonald's	$11.3
7	Fleming Companies	$10.4
8	Safeway Stores	$10.2
	SuperValu	$10.2
10	RJR Nabisco	$ 9.2*
11	Winn Dixie	$ 9.1
12	Great Atlantic & Pacific	$ 8.2

* Food sales only

Source: *Food Marketing Review, 1989-90*, Commodity Economics Division, ERS, USDA, Agricultural Economic Report No. 639, November, 1990.

One food industry consultant, Richard Rakowski, estimates that big companies will not introduce a new product unless it will bring in $25 million in sales the first year.[30] Supporting this point, Willard Mueller, the University of Wisconsin economist, found that between 1971 and 1977 over 43 percent of the awards for process and product innovation went to companies with less than $10 million in sales.[31]

Professor Blair has also pointed out that if one selects an industry at random, there's better than a 40 percent chance that firms primarily engaged in some other category of enterprise will produce at least one-third of that industry's output and better than a one in six chance that they will produce two-thirds or more of its output.[32]

Market Concentration and "Freedom of Choice"

Market concentration is the control of an industry or market by a small number of producers exclusively or privately engaged in that industry. An industry is generally considered concentrated when the eight largest companies share more that 50 percent of the market.

However, in his studies, Blair uses the *four* largest companies because four is the smallest number for which Census concentration ratios are computed and, as he adds, "The four largest probably come closer than any other single figure to representing what economists usually have in mind when they think of oligopoly, [*i.e.*, many buyers confronted with few sellers.]"[33]

A 1966 Census of Manufacturing count, reveals that at that time the average four-firm control in the various industries that manufacture food and kindred products was 55 percent of the market, well into what economists call a "tight oligopoly" and subject to "non-competitive behavior practices."[34]

Twelve years later, the 1978 Corporate Data Exchange Agribusiness Ownership study showed many agribusiness categories well above 40 percent in four-firm control.[35]

The business pages of any daily newspaper confirm that this trend of corporate agribusiness toward concentration has not abated one iota in the past decade.

Another important indicator of the increasingly concentrated food industry is *Progressive Grocer*'s guide to the "175 Most-Used Super Market Grocery Products," which purports to be "an exclusive ranking of frequency of use and brand concentration and brand loyalty." Most revealing about the 1978 report was that within the 25 most-used items the share of users for the top *three* brands of food items was exceedingly high, *e.g.*, table salt, 92 percent; catsup, 86 percent; salad/cooking oil, 85 percent; canned soup, 84 percent; flour, 80 percent; peanut butter, 79 percent; mustard, 76 percent; mayo and mayo-type dressings, 69 percent; American cheese, 62 percent, and granulated sugar, 58 percent. Outside of the 25 most-used items, the share of users for the top *three* brands of many other food items was more than 80 percent.

The food industry calls such concentration "brand loyalty." The fact is that very often a consumer's "loyalty" is to just a few brands simply because they are the *only* ones available on the market shelves. Except when rare individuals speak out (like the New York money manager who publicly argued that Castle & Cooke Company should not sell its Dole banana subsidiary because Dole, R.J. Reynolds Industries and United Brands "are close to having a distribution monopoly in the United States[36]), the public is rarely reminded of such monopoly concentration.

Some food lines that were once only the business of anonymous neighborhood entrepreneurs have become almost completely taken over by large brand name corporations which now dominate the trade. Many local delicatessens, for example, where one can buy prepared salads and pasta are rapidly transforming themselves into showcases for such food giants as Sara Lee and Campbells.

It is estimated that 50 percent of the $500 million-a-year wholesale-prepared-salad business is controlled by about a dozen of the 70 companies in the industry.[37] And, as *The New York Times*' John Grossman learned, the top two — Brooklyn, New York's Blue Ridge Farms, with yearly sales of $100 million, and the Orval Kent Food Company in Wheeling, Illinois, with sales of $50 million — use brand identity as a weapon in their fight for market shares. Both try to convince supermarkets and delis that people want to buy salads by name.[38]

Likewise, when Americans go out for the $20 billion worth of pizza they collectively consumed in 1988 and wash it down with some of the 140.3 gallons of milk, soft drinks, juices and alcohol that each of them (on average) consumed in 1985,[39] they should harbor no illusions that they have a large measure of "freedom of choice" about the food they are purchasing.

At one time nothing was thought to be more "American" than steak 'n' brew. A wide variety of beers at the local tavern and red meat at the neighborhood butcher shop was an accepted part of many people's lives. (See Chart 7A)

Yet in just the past decade these two markets alone have experienced a profound structural "tastesgreatlessfillingflame-broiled" change.

The nation's brewing industry has been undergoing a major upheaval. "People buy brands now, not beer," is the way one old-time brewing industry executive describes the industry.[40] The original attraction of pure water and grain is gone. Today, companies want to be close to their major markets: California and the Sun Belt. "Transportation of the finished product, not the raw material is a primary criterion," remarks one industry analyst.[41]

What has happened in recent years in Wisconsin is now frequently held up as the model of what has taken place in the beer industry as a whole. Once there were 72 breweries in Wisconsin, today there are only seven.[42]

Milwaukee, where beers were brewed that made the city famous, today has but one brewery — Miller, now a subsidiary of Philip Morris, which brews beer "the American way."

The consequences of such an exodus are typical of what has taken place in communities throughout the nation as corporations merge and the food and beverage manufacturing business becomes more concentrated. When Schlitz Brewing Co. left Milwaukee the community not only lost 1,300 jobs, but lost corporate contributions to the area's hospitals, the zoo, the museums and the arts, the business each year of 100,000 tourists and what one city official termed "an intangible city spirit."[43]

"Milwaukee is just a larger version of what is happening to the beer industry as a whole," comments one industry analyst, citing both the declining sales nationwide and the fact that in recent years U.S. beer consumption has remained stagnant. "The name of the game now is market share, and the industry is in the final stage of contraction. In a few years we may end up

Chart 7A: Pizza and Beverage Corporate Market Shares (percentage)

Pizza Chains (1989)		Soft Drinks (1986)	
Pizza Hut	20.7	Coca-Cola	39.8
Domino's	17.0	Pepsi-Cola	30.7
Little Caesar's	16.7	Seven-Up	5.2
Pizza Inn/Pantera's	2.2	Dr. Pepper	4.8

Beer (1989)		Regular Coffee (1986)	
Anheuser-Busch	43.3	General Foods	42.6
Miller	22.4	Nestle	26.8
Stroh	11.3	Procter & Gamble	19.5
Coors	9.1	Borden	0.6

Chocolate Mix (1987)		Wine Coolers (1988)	
Nestle's	47	E.J. Gallo	31.9
Hershey's	17	Vintners Int.	7.0
Swiss	15	Canandaigua	5.2
Oveltine	4	Heublein	7.7

Orange Juice (1987)	Frozen	Ready-to-Serve
Tropicana (Seagram Co.)	22.0	27.3
Minute Maid (Coca-Cola)	20.5	17.7
Citrus Hill (P & G)	9.3	9.1

Source: (Pizza) Technomic Inc., *The Wall Street Journal*, April 21, 1989; (Soft Drinks) John C. Maxwell, Jr., *Advertising Age*, September 24, 1987; (Beer) *Modern Brewing Age, Chicago Tribune*, KRTN Graphics, *USA Today*, February 22, 1990; (Regular Coffee) *Advertising Age*; (Orange Juice) "An Orange Juice War Is Growing As Makers Vie for Fresh Markets," by Alix M. Freedman, *The Wall Street Journal*, April 27,. 1988 and "Seagram-Tropicana: Juicy deal," by Gary Strauss, *USA Today*, March 11, 1988; (Wine Coolers) *Advertising Age*, October 1, 1990; (Chocolate) Prudential-Bache Securities, *USA Today*, September 13, 1988.

with only two to four national breweries and a handful of good regional breweries."[45]

Likewise, we have seen a number of major moves in recent years by the leaders in the soft drink business — Coca Cola and Pepsi — to gain even larger shares of a market that provides each American with an annual average of 45.6 gallons of soft drinks.[46]

In June 1986 the FTC denied Coca-Cola the right to acquire Dr. Pepper and Pepsi to purchase Seven-Up. Had the mergers been allowed the two companies would have controlled 82 percent of the nation's soft drink market. "I'm pleased, of course, with the FTC decision," Representative Don Edward, D-Calif., ventured. "What worries me is that we had to face an extreme case, a merger that would have created a two-firm monopoly in a giant industry, before getting the FTC to enforce the antitrust law."[47]

After the Coca-Cola/Dr. Pepper and Pepsi/Seven-Up mergers were denied, the Dr. Pepper Holding Co. and the Seven-Up Holding Co. were purchased in 1986 by separate investment groups, both led by the Dallas investment firm of Hicks & Haas, and subsequently the management of the two companies was integrated in Dallas while their production facilities were centralized in St. Louis. In February, 1988 it was announced that the two holding company's would be merged, thereby creating the nation's third largest soft-drink maker. Because the two would now only control 13 percent-14 percent of the market, however, it was not expected that the FTC would oppose the merger.[48]

Immediately after Pepsi's unsuccessful bid to acquire Seven-Up the company sought to sooth its wounded pride by buying Kentucky Fried Chicken from RJR Nabisco for $850 million cash. While the purchase enabled Pepsi to run the world's largest restaurant group (it already owned Pizza Hut, Taco Bell, and La Petite Boulangerie) with 14,000 outlets, the group's $7 billion sales still left it behind McDonald's $20 billion. With the KFC acquisition Pepsi could lay claim to controlling three of the hottest fast-food markets — pizza, Mexican and chicken.[49]

With news of the Pepsi acquisition, however, Wendy's, the nation's third largest hamburger chain, annoyed about Pepsi's push into the restaurant business, announced that it would drop Pepsi-Cola from its menu at its company-owned outlets in favor of Coca-Cola. In corporate America you win some, you lose some![50]

Grocery Shopping: Is It a Safeway, Kroger, American, Lucky or 7-11?

After unsuccessfully trying to sell his idea for a "supermarket" to his superiors at the Kroger Grocery and Baking Co. in 1930, Michael Cullen, a branch manager, opened his own supermarket — "King Cullen" — in the New York City borough of Queens. Thirty-five years later 30,400 such U.S. supermarkets were selling $240.4 billion of food to the nation's consumers.[51] Yet, like so many of the firms that supply the supermarket industry, retail food marketing has also become increasingly concentrated.

Supermarket revenues in 1988 were $240 billion with $186.7 spent on food and $53.7 billion on non-food.[52] In 1988 the national market share for Safeway was 5.58 percent, for Kroger 7.96 percent, for American Stores 7.70 percent, and Winn-Dixie 3.75 percent, a misleading 29.2 percent total national market share.[53]

However, the latest available figures from Fairchild Publication's authoritative *Supermarket News* show alarming four-firm control in the major marketing areas in the United States where shoppers regularly buy their groceries. High on that list are cities such as Salt Lake City, Utah (100 percent); Des Moines, Iowa (95 percent); Denver, Colorado (94 percent); Phoenix, Arizona (88 percent); Miami, Florida (87 percent); Washington, DC

(86 percent); Pittsburgh, Pennsylvania (85.2 percent); Cincinnati, Ohio (83.2 percent); Milwaukee, Wisconsin (81 percent); Richmond, Virginia (80 percent); New Orleans, Louisiana (78 percent); Atlanta, Georgia (77.5 percent); Portland, Oregon (77 percent); Cleveland, Ohio (76.8 percent); Newark, New Jersey (76 percent); St. Louis, Missouri (76 percent); Dallas, Texas (75 percent); Philadelphia, Pennsylvania (72 percent); Nashville, Tennessee (72 percent); Houston, Texas (66 percent); Omaha, Nebraska (65.4 percent); Minneapolis, Minnesota (65 percent); Seattle, Washington (63.1 percent); Chicago, Illinois (64 percent); San Francisco, California (62.5 percent); Kansas City, Missouri/Kansas (59.7 percent); Nassau-Suffolk, New York (59.5 percent); and Los Angeles, California (59.4 percent).

A large metropolitan area like Boston, Massachusetts (47.9 percent), the nation's seventh largest marketing area, was also well above the oligopolistic four-firm, 40 percent market share standard. Even Detroit, fifth in the nation, where eight chains shared 45.3 percent of the sales, the top four hold 39.3 percent of the market.[54]

Testifying before a House Judiciary subcommittee in May 1988, University of Connecticut economist Ronald W. Cotterill warned that the nation's supermarket shoppers face "billions of dollars" of overcharges in the 1990s unless the federal government tightens its regulation of grocery chains. "Consumers," he stressed, "will face a wave of horizontal mergers ... with consequences that will be absolutely astounding."

"This is already happening," he added. He told committee chairman Peter W. Rodino Jr., D-NJ, that four mergers within the industry completed since 1986 and two proposed mergers promise to raise prices and force consumers in 16 metropolitan areas of New York and California alone "to pay one-half billion dollars more each year for food."[55]

Just a few short years ago American grocery shoppers were witnessing first hand the consequences of such tight market control, conveniently spurred on by spiraling inflation. Large chains had been able to build up huge inventories and as inflation went up stores raised the prices on goods that had been bought previously at much lower prices.

When inflation was up in the double-digit range, "prices were constantly marked up," Michael Drury, an economist with A. Gary Schilling & Co. in New York recalls. "Even companies that were not competitive could increase sales and profits," because they could pass their costs on to consumers.[56]

When inflation moderated and grocery shoppers became more cost-conscious supermarket chains feared that their high prices might drive shoppers to their competitors. They began to wage costly price wars with other chains and when that proved unsuccessful they began either closing their "non-profitable" stores or cutting operating costs — usually making labor the prime target for reductions.

In Detroit, for example, the Kroger Co., which ranked 23rd in the nation in total food retail sales in 1984, after waging an unsuccessful "price war" with its local competitors, asked its 4200 clerks and cashiers to give up $2.70 an hour in wages and benefits, which the company claimed would save it $65 million over several years. When the employees refused to go along with such demands Kroger closed the stores.[57]

Between 1985 and 1987, the supermarket industry earnings were but a penny or less on every dollar of sales (although unlike other businesses, supermarkets have a high yearly, if not monthly, turnover in sales). The chains claimed that to remain competitive they needed to expand; and a third of the nation's retail chains were either bought out by other firms or taken private. Explaining such high stakes activity, Pershing Bros. Jeff Siegel points out that one of the cheapest ways for large food chains to boost their sales is to push into or expand into another market by acquiring a well-established chain already in business.[58] (Grocers' stable cash flows — and extensive and often choice real estate holdings — make them natural targets for such buy-outs.[59])

In the Fight For Life, It's Shelf Space!

In addition, increased product proliferation among food manufacturers forces retailers to carry far more inventory than necessary and frequently to build ever larger facilities to accommodate the glut of products on the market. The retailer, in turn, passes such inventory and construction costs on to consumers who literally pay billions of dollars each year merely to warehouse and shelve this glaring superfluity of food.

The struggle most new products must now undergo to reach the shelves of our supermarkets is ferocious. The final arbiter of such choices is frequently the supermarket itself. "In the supermarket business, the fight for life is shelf space," states George Zimmerman, a food analyst for Gruntal & Co.[60]

To stock a new product on the supermarket shelf can cost a food company $2 million to $3 million, according to Keith Jones, a vice president of the Summa Group, a promotion consulting service owner by the A.C. Nielsen Co..[61]

These payments, called "slotting allowances," are charged by the supermarket to cover the costs of stocking a new product, and they do not exceed, according to the supermarkets, such expenditures. Such fees, however, may well lead to the "ruination of the grocery business," according to one salesman for a major food manufacturing system who talked to *The Washington Post*'s Caroline E. Mayer.

As manufacturers acquiesce to the slotting allowances, they are taking the eye off the consumer. They are giving too much money to the retail stores who in turn are putting it in their pocket. Meanwhile, the manufacturers are spending less money on advertising and couponing, which is necessary to get the customers into the store in the first place.[62]

It is estimated that it costs a chain of 40 stores about $1,500 to put a new item into its system, though the amounts demanded from the manufacturer are sometimes far more. Although "slotting allowance" figures are not made public, even by publicly-owned companies, some Northeastern city food manufacturers and brokers claim that it can cost as much as $20,000 to get a new product into a supermarket chain for a six-month period.[63]

In 1973 food manufacturers spent 75 percent of their advertising and promotion budget on consumers and 25 percent on supermarkets, according to Richard Furash, a partner in the Boston retail unit of Touche Ross & Co., an accounting firm. This figure contrasts with today's expenditures of 70 percent to supermarkets and 30 percent to consumers.[64]

In 1986 alone, manufacturers spent $15.3 billion on consumer promotions, excluding advertising, and $19.3 billion on promotions to supermarkets, such as new product allowances, discounts and funds for store advertising.[65]

The New York Times' Trish Hall notes that as a result of these practices "some supermarkets will in effect rent space to the highest bidder, resulting in higher prices and fewer choices. The system could make it difficult for innovative small companies to move their products to the market."[66] (Consumers concerned about freedom of choice should note that often when a new product is put on the supermarket shelf it usually *replaces* some other product.)

Guy Psychas, president of M&H Brokerage Inc. in White Plains, N.Y., for example, points out that it has become particularly difficult for small and medium-sized companies to get products into New York City. As for the food manufacturers who now complain bitterly about the "slotting allowances," it was they, in fact, who started offering the allowances a few years ago when competition among new products was intense. "They did it because of their anxiety to do business. All you need is a few to start the parade," Psychas adds.[67]

Throughout the nation the supermarket industry is undergoing profound changes introducing everything from fast foods to single's nights. "We're trying to overwhelm our customers with food products and food services," observes Seattle's Larry McKinley, owner of that city's Larry's Markets chain. "Any retailer today has to have a sense of theater to do what they do. To leave it out is a real mistake."[69]

Conscious that the amount of money consumers spend on food at home has dropped from 12.1 percent of disposable income in 1980 to 10.3 percent in 1986 (each percentage point amounting to tens of billions of dollars in lost business) supermarkets chains and convenience stores are rapidly becoming both food manufacturers and servers.[70] ConAgra Inc., formerly one of the nation's largest grain traders, has already established a new subsidiary to sell a complete line of traditional and prepared delicatessen products to these markets. According to ConAgra Deli Company president Jim Babka, "the deli business today is just a fraction of what it is going to be tomorrow."[71]

As a result of this development, fast food providers express concern for their future. "It is not a great threat now, but it is certainly something we are looking at," notes Joyce Myers, public and corporate relations manager of Burger King Corp. "It's an area that com-petes for the stomach, and that's where our business is."[72]

Computers and "Frequent Shopper" Cards

In the supermarket consumers will also soon be faced with a new concept — electronic marketing. Here computers will help consumers choose a wine, find the detergents through an electronic store directory, and pick out an appropriate menu for the evening meal. Some supermarkets are already using computers to "design" their display areas.

It is not outside the realm of possibility, therefore, that retailers will have still another means to promote impulse sales. They will push high-margin perishables, recommending them in specific recipes available to the shopper. The computer can also feature specific brand names in a recipe. The maker of one such computer system, Inter-Touch Cuisine Machine, notes that it has already been approached by some food manufacturers.[73]

In addition, computers are employed to provide detailed information on consumers buying habits and lifestyle. The introduction of "frequent shopper" cards is but one example of such new technology. The cards can be electronically scanned along with shoppers' purchases at the checkout counter, allowing the retailer to record what they buy, how much they buy, and how often they buy.[74]

This process can allow supermarkets to market directly to individual households, sending them coupons or other incentives to buy more of a certain kind of product — focusing their attention, for example, on products with higher profit margins.

"The supermarket industry is moving into an environment where they would like to be able to market more directly to customers," according to Bill Bishop, a retail industry consultant. Retailers recognize that "some customers are relatively more important than others and there are real advantages to knowing who your primary customers are and taking those actions that solidify your relationship with them."[75]

The collecting and utilizing of such information by supermarkets and food companies, however, raises important privacy questions among civil libertarians and consumer activists. As Janlori Goldman, a staff attorney on the American Civil Liberties Union's project on privacy and technology observes,

> I go to Giant Food to buy my food, not to provide marketing companies and retailers with information about what I buy and when. I think people have some expectations that the things that they buy, whether it's groceries or clothes or books or videos, should be kept confidential unless they choose to give out that information.[76]

Robert Ellis Smith, publisher of the *Privacy Journal*, a monthly newsletter that deals with computer-related privacy questions, also correctly points out that while businesses are using such technology to learn more about the consumer, "the consumer is not getting more information about the company."[77]

As each new product is introduced into markets it not only can bump off an existing product, but also affects the variety of foods available to shoppers in a different line. Frozen-food products replace dry foods and packaged food replaces canned foods, for example. This combination, along with a resurgence of fresh food products saw the American per capita consumption of canned food alone decline by almost half between 1980 and 1984, from 16.2 pounds to 8.9 pounds.[78] With some 20 percent of the total items a supermarket stocks each year being new ones, the introduction of optical scanners has enabled supermarkets to track sales of each product closely. As a former Campbell Soup Company executive explains it,

> As the information systems develop, the supermarkets will know the return on investment on each section in the store and which brand will give them the best margin and return. The people who are three and four and five in the marketplace will not be able to stay with it. The number one and two will stay in the stores.[79]

"The more new products that come out with [large amounts of] advertising," Abbott Wilson, a vice president of marketing for Larsen Co., a small food processor based in Green Bay, Wisconsin, adds, "the more difficult it becomes to get new products in. It also shortens the amount of time for new products to get acceptance." Space allocations have now become based solely on "shelf-movement."[80]

"Mom 'n Pops" Without Mom and Pop

Against this backdrop of growing concentration and ever-expanding technology in the retail food business, industry spokespersons see even more consolidation among supermarket chains with bigger stores ("hypermarkets") in the future.

Marvin Cetron, president of Forecasting International, told the 1989 National Grocers Association annual convention that

> we believe larger stores offering a wide variety of products and services — superstores, super warehouse stores, limited assortment stores, deep discount drug stores, combo stores, hypermarkets/hybrid discount stores and warehouse clubs — will be dominant in the future.[81]

Based on a survey his firm conducted for the NGA, Cetron expects that by 1995 there will be only about 200 wholesale companies left as the number of major food product distributors will be reduced by 20 percent.[82] "This does not mean that the number of wholesale facilities will decrease, simply that they will be owned by fewer companies."[83]

While one-outlet merchants still do 46 percent of the country's retail business, according to the Census Bureau, only 23 percent of our grocery sales originate from such merchants.[84] Such figures stem from the fact that supermarkets in the years following World War II rapidly forced thousands and thousands of smaller neighborhood stores out of business. In the last decade, however, we have seen the re-emergence of these neighborhood "mom n' pop" stores (but without mom n' pop) in the form of "convenience" stores.

The largest of these so-called convenience store chains is 7-Eleven ("7-Eleven — America's Convenience Retailer. Over half the U.S. population lives within two miles of a 7-Eleven ..."). A subsidiary of the Southland Corporation, the 6th largest food retailer in the United States,[85] 7-Eleven operates over 40 percent of all convenience stores in the United States and makes over half of all convenience store sales.[86]

However, many communities today, particularly in rural and sparsely populated suburban areas, find stores like 7-Eleven the only ones available for day-today shopping. Thus, high prices and a select number of products limit many such food shoppers in their purchases a fact not lost on the consuming public. After 7-Eleven announced that in deference to U.S. Attorney General Meese's anti-pornography crusade it would no longer sell *Playboy* and *Penthouse* magazines in its outlets, David Letterman astutely joked: "Well now, I guess, the only thing obscene left in those stores are the prices!"

In 1986 Southland had a marketing presence in 49 states and the District of Columbia, five provinces in Canada and ten foreign countries. This included 12,200 7-Eleven stores, each carrying 3,000 products, its food and beverage products accounting for over 52 percent of Southland's total $8.62 billion in sales and over 80 percent of its total operating profits.[87] Southland also owned 50 percent of the Citgo Petroleum Corp., the nation's largest independent refiner and marketer.[88]

The company was at one time also one of the nation's largest processors of dairy products and a leading manufacturer of "frozen novelties," operating under 11 well-known regional brand names which serviced customers in 46 states, the District of Columbia and Canada. Its purchase of the 350 outlets of the Maryland farmers' cooperative, High's Dairy, in November 1986 effectively eliminated its principal competitor in the mid-Atlantic area.[89]

But as we've seen so often in agribusiness in recent years, even a giant corporation like Southland can fall victim to takeover mania. In July 1987 in an effort to ward off potential "hostile" outside owners, the Thompson brothers, John P., Jere W. and Joe C. Jr., part of the family that already owned ten percent of the company, announced that they were planning a $5.1 billion leveraged buyout of the company stock.[90] And so Southland, like Beatrice and Safeway and other large food-related corporations, went private!

In addition to lining up $2.73 billion in bank financing from Citicorp, Bankers Trust Co., Manufacturers Hanover, Canadian Imperial Bank of Commerce, and Security Pacific National Bank and bridge financing from Goldman, Sachs & Co. and Salomon Bros, the Thompsons announced they were selling almost all the company assets, except 7-11 and Citgo, to help finance the buyout. Subsidiaries up for sale included Southland Dairies, one the nation's three largest, Chief Auto Parts and Reddy Ice, and its Snack Foods division.[91]

In March 1988 the Company announced that it was planning to sell 473 of its 7-11 stores for $147 million to its closest competitor, the Phoenix, Arizona-based Circle K Corp.. The sale helped reduce the number of 7-11 stores from 8296, before its acquisition by the Thompsons, to 7542 and boosted Circle K's total outlets to more than 4,000.[92]

Even as the number of convenience stores in the United States continues to increase (with 82,500 in operation in 1988 selling over $70 billion in merchandise),[93] the Southlands and Circle K's are confronted with a struggle for survival against an old and familiar corporate giant — the nation's oil companies.

Based on figures compiled by *Convenience Store News*, seven of the top 20 convenience store operators in the United States are oil companies with names like Arco, Exxon, Mobil and Shell. "The oil companies will control most of the industry within the next five years," predicts Monica Battagliola, the trade publication's editor.[94]

Industry analysts have pointed out that after years of "dabbling" in the convenience store business in an effort to attract gasoline customers, the major oil companies are now getting serious. As the *Dallas Morning News* Gary Jacobson's observes, "they have always understood how to sell gasoline and now they are learning how to sell milk, tobacco, soda, beer and other staples of the convenience business."[95]

Thus, market concentration, along with vertical coordination and conglomerate and aggregate concentration, continues to fire the imagination of corporate agribusiness, and ever widen the dimensions of its concentrated economic power.

Chapter Eight

What is This Thing Called Food?

A popular television "soap opera" in the 1970s chronicled the comical fortunes and misfortunes of a young married couple living in Fernwood, Ohio.

One evening as we joined Mary, her husband Tom and sister Kathy, Mary was preparing a pineapple pie for the family dinner. As she poured the somewhat grotesque-looking contents of a can of pineapple filling into a pie pan her sister Kathy, wondered aloud where the pineapple was?

Puzzled, they both proceeded to read the contents of the can as they appeared on the label. Amidst the various acids and flavorings and sugar no mention was made of pineapple, (except, of course, in the advertising portion of the label). Mary paused thoughtfully, and looking at her sister, remarked: "I don't see any pineapple listed here," to which Kathy replied, "they don't make food out of food anymore," provoking Mary to ponder, "what do they do with food, if they don't make food out of it?"

Mary Hartman, Mary Hartman, that's a good question, a good question!

Each day larger and more diversified corporations gain greater control of our food supply. Each day more and more of our traditional producers of food are forced off the land, replaced by the corporate geneticist, chemist, engineer, and manufacturer, who determine not only the quantity, quality, and cost, but even the very nature of our food supply.

Each day we see fewer and fewer and ever-larger agribusiness corporations seeking to cut costs and streamline production in their singular effort to gain a larger and larger share of the marketplace. And each day we see corporate agribusiness burrowing its way deeper and deeper into our stomachs and our pocketbooks. As *Fortune* magazine explains:

... food company managers look at the marketplace not as a whole, but by product category. A product category, in the consumer-goods sense defines a distinct, self-contained market, the battle ground upon which all the direct competitors of a product are to be found. What's important to the marketer is not what people are doing

with food, but what they're doing with frozen lima beans or single-layer cake mixes.[1]

While the struggle within the food industry for market shares continually escalates, we are also experiencing a certain national uniformity in our food. With increasing frequency we find ourselves asking the question, "what is this thing called food?" for whatever singular characteristics our food may now possess, they stem less from quality or taste than from the way our food is advertised and packaged. As the *Washington Post*'s William Rice has observed:

We don't taste, one is forced to conclude; or at best, we taste but don't bother to compare. Unless people care enough to think about the qualities of the food they chew, and unless they have a frame of reference (have tasted 'the real thing') how will they know — or care if they are being misled.

And Rice's colleague *Post* food columnist Phyllis C. Richman adds that

We are a curiosity. We eat all day long and talk about food at least that often, yet we are always on diets. We conduct wine tastings and ice cream tastings and chili contests. We are always comparing, judging, evaluating food. We memorize the best brands and travel great distances to buy a single product.

On vacation we will go clear across the city in rush hour because we heard the pasta is better than in the restaurant next to our hotel. Yet, we will buy — and eat — the most dreary and tasteless frozen pizza, polish every bite of food-shaped goo on an airplane, and support outlandishly expensive restaurants that look glamorous but serve rubberized, vinyl-flavored steak and lobsters. What does that say about us? ...[2]

Such questions have provoked Ward Sinclair, recalling the roots of that grand American institution — the county fair — to point out:

What we have now, as country fair season draws nigh and as rural America prepares to render its annual homage to the bounty of the land, is another phenomenon that Watson surely could not foresee. Much of the food and snacking fodder that fuels the fair-goer — the stuff of rich aroma and texture that excites the palate — is not food at all. Our annual celebrations of American agriculture have become monuments to concoctions of processor and chemist that have little, if anything, to do with the produce of the land.[3]

This lack of connection between what is produced on the land and what we eat gravely concerns not only many in agriculture, but also the general public in addition to many nutritionists and health professionals.

In their pursuit of larger and larger market shares the companies that manufacture and sell us food are endlessly attempting to develop new food gadgetry. They are also constantly meddling with our access to and supply of food as they advertise and package an ever-increasing number of "classy" and so-called "convenience" food products.

Indeed, in only one of the many ironies posed by corporate agribusiness's domination of our food system, we are today witnessing new food products advertised by companies as health antidotes — food as medicine — to combat the effects of the junk food those very same companies have been peddling to us for years.

We also see food manufacturers pitching their snack food wares to video stores with accompanying promotional brochures, radio ads, and a "That's Snackertainment" packet selling the store owners on the profitability behind selling snacks which tie in with movie themes: Psychedelic Dip for watching the films "Easy Rider," "Hair," and "Woodstock."[4]

As Michael McRae writes in *Harrowsmith*, "no task is more crucial than providing a family with its meals, but as a nation we have largely turned the chore over to the food processors, who are only too happy to conjure up recipes for us." In that process, these food manufacturers manage to "add value" to many of these products, *i.e.*, making the product supposedly easier to use by tailoring it to the needs of working people, smaller households or singles besides making it more attractive and profitable.

As one food analyst explains, by such food tailoring, "in the last ten years the [food] industry has shifted from commodities to value-added products, where margins are expanding at a nice clip."[5] Hedric E. "Pete" Rhodes, a Quaker Oats Co. executive vice president, sees the "add value" process as "trading consumers up. And it's why food companies are doing well right now."

Nancy Bauer, president of Bauer & Rosner, a marketing communications company, points out that "Twenty years ago stores and the names of the people behind the register stood for something. Now, after all the mergers and acquisitions, consumers need something to trust. The brand takes the place of the person."[7]

Bloom Company president Tony Wainright is quick to add,

when customers feel good about a brand, they'll buy line extensions. If people like JELL-O, they'll try JELL-O pudding. My mother would always tell me that the best soup was Campbell's. I remember asking why, and she said, 'They use home-

grown ingredients.' She played back the theme of their marketing campaign.[8]

A Philadelphia marketing consulting firm explains the process in terms of the belief that consumers are willing to pay a premium "for anything that will help them get control of their lives."[6]

But in reality, as we will shortly see, the way our food is manufactured, advertised, prepared and sold to us today gives us *less and less* control of our lives. As consumers we are gradually being deprived of not only our freedom of choice, but of our right to purchase economically-priced healthful and nutritious food.

"The Fragmentation of Eating"

Because low inflation throughout most of the 1980s blocked most food companies from raising prices, food retailers have become choosier, looking for products that will bring them a substantial profit in relation to their operating costs. It is also estimated that some of these new products, because they are considered unique, have a profit margin of 30 percent or more. It is estimated that big food companies today derive nearly half their yearly income from products less than three years old.[10]

Anthony J. Adams, director of marketing research for Campbell Soup Co. adds, "I think you'll probably see more of this kind of thing. Everybody is testing how high is high."[11]

Karen Bachmann, a Del Monte spokeswoman, is even more candid: "Pricing at retail year to year doesn't reflect supply and demand. You're going to have to charge the price the market can bear."[12]

Between 1980 and 1987 major U.S. food companies each introduced an average of 1.8 new food products *every day*, with Campbell Soup (688) and Philip Morris's General Foods (605) leading the way.[13] In 1988 alone, over 3440 new foods and beverages were introduced to the public.[14]

The *New York Times*' respected health and nutrition columnist Jane Brody disputes whether all this food gadgetry is necessary. "We don't need all those presweetened, heavily fortified cereals, fatty and salty processed meats, chips and dips, sugary soft drinks; and the endless stream of heat-and-serve, mix-and-match and eat-and-run products the American food industry foists on the public."[15]

Despite such warnings, what Linda Smithson, directory of Pillsbury's consumer center, calls "the fragmentation of eating" is rapidly becoming the norm rather than the exception. If current trends continue, according to her company's research, the traditional family meal may be all but dead by the next decade.

Her company's year-long study, which combined focus-group results with analysis of data on American eating behavior from 1971 to 1986, divided the public into five groups.[16]

Happy Cookers The fastest-shrinking and smallest group, which accounts for only 15 percent of the population and which has declined by 35 percent over the past 15 years, still cooks three meals day.

Down Home Stokers A significantly declining number of "modest" income and "modest" educated individuals who favor regional dishes in a traditional meal setting.

Functional Feeders Another traditional, but also rapidly declining number of blue collar people with above-average incomes who value convenience above all else.

Careful Cooks Well-educated, highly health-conscious, mostly retired people, who make up 20 percent of the population and whose numbers have increased in the 15-year period of the study by 122 percent.

Chase and Grabbits That segment, which comprises 26 percent of the population, which subsists on fast food, frozen dinners and carry-out pizza. To this group, which has grown by 136 percent in 15 years, the Pillsbury study notes, "even microwave popcorn can become a meal." It is with these people in mind that food manufacturers introduced some 7,866 new edibles, up from 4,540 in 1983, in 1987.[17]

"There's a general feeling these days that eating has to be combined with doing," observes Campbell Soup's Adams. People, he claims, feel guilty when they have to take time to prepare, enjoy and clean up after a meal. In fact, the aforementioned Pillsbury study found an unexpectedly large number of people within their focus groups who said they would rather just take a pill than eat a meal.

The *Wall Street Journal*'s Betsy Morris points out that conscious of such attitudes, Campbell's, instead of requiring that a new product go well with peas and potatoes, now requires that it be easy to eat one-handed while driving a car or operating a computer. Instead of fashioning food to a particular meal it fashions food to fit a mood.[18]

"Food is now trendy" says one New Jersey food marketer,[19] or as Elena Coccari, manager of consumer affairs for the Nestle-owned Stouffer Corp., puts it: "Sometimes consumers like food to look posh so they can one-up somebody else."[20]

Pillsbury, for example, markets 15 microwave pancakes for $1.59 so you can get "a real weekend breakfast ready in 90 seconds with no standing over the griddle."[21] Meanwhile, a two-pound box of Pillsbury's Hungry Jack pancake mix costs about $1.27; with a little egg, milk, some oil and a few minutes over the griddle you can turn out 80 pancakes.

Microwave cooking, in fact, has rapidly gained the attention of food manufacturers. More than 50 percent of the nation's households now have a microwave oven and industry experts predict that the figure could soon be as high as 90 percent. Between October 1986 and October 1987, according to SAMI/Burke Inc., a market research company, retail sales of microwave food reached $760 million.[22]

Having discovered the widespread use of microwaves, food companies like General Mills, Campbells, Pillsbury, General Foods, ConAgra, Kroger and others are rushing to get new products, such as hot fudge sundaes, on the market. "Food firms would cut their own mothers' throats to get their products out there. That's how fierce the competition is," according to Robert C. LaGasse, director of the International Microwave Power Institute.[23]

According to surveys by the Food Marketing Institute, consumers from almost every age and income bracket worry less about economizing on food than did their counterparts in previous years. The trade association notes that only four of ten shoppers routinely look for food specials advertised in newspapers, three in ten use discount coupons, and only 27 percent do price-comparison shopping.[24]

In light of such findings it is curious that corporate agribusiness continues to argue that any increase in price to farmers for raw materials would raise retail food prices to unacceptable levels. That claim still has political clout, however, despite studies showing that higher (and fairer) commodity prices for farmers would raise consumer food prices but a tiny fraction of the so-called "add value" price.

McFood

One principal byproduct of the "add value" syndrome has become the fast-food restaurant or food franchise business. It is estimated that in 1987 retail franchise outlets registered $591 billion in sales[25] with fast food restaurants having sales of $65 billion.[26]

While food spending in America since 1965 climbed by 46 percent to $476.6 billion in 1988, spending on food to be consumed at home grew only 20 percent to $264.1 billion. Meanwhile food eaten away at fastfood restaurants, delis and other such establishments went up 89 percent to $225 billion.[27]

Whether it's Breezewood, Pennsylvania; Everett, Washington, Odessa, Texas, or Anchorage, Alaska, under the golden arches we can now buy similar tasting hamburgers or cheeseburgers (in the time it will take you to say 499,999,999,999, 2,000 more of those same burgers will have been sold by the McDonald's Corporation),[28] the same textured french fried potatoes and the same flavored soft drink.

"Homogenized eating" is the way some people characterize today's fast food chain's fare. "I knew exactly what this cheeseburger would taste like before I even ate it," one marketing firm researcher told a *Wall Street Journal* reporter.[29] Nearly 17 million Americans eat at McDonald's 11,000 outlets *each day*; in a nine month period its sales could feed the equivalent of the world's population.[30] Since early 1985 it has opened a new branch every 15 hours in the United States.[31] It also operates and/or franchises 2,163 restaurants abroad.[32]

Today, one out of every ten Americans buys take-out food daily at one of the nation's 113,000 fast-food outlets,[33] with hamburgers, french fries and beverages accounting for 65 percent of such purchases.[34] Out of every dollar the American public spent on eating away from home in 1985, 44 cents was spent at fast food outlets.[35]

In 1988, McDonald's with $11.3 billion in sales was more than the combined sales of Burger King, Kentucky Fried Chicken and Pizza Hut.[36] In 1989, McDonald's spent $417.8 million in media advertising, more than the other three spent together for their media ads.[37] Since 1987 it has been the fifth largest TV advertiser in the nation.[38]

Whether it's on our highways and boulevards, in our inner cities, our shopping malls, department stores, casinos, corporate headquarters, or even in our hospitals, fast-food outlets appear everywhere. Whereas in the early 1970s the top 100 restaurant companies accounted for only 21 percent of the sales, in 1986 they had a 50 percent market share.[39]

The restaurant industry has not only welcomed such growth (which saw it gaining 41.1 cents out of every dollar spent on food in 1986, up from 25 cents in 1955,[40]), but other institutions have also recognized the potential gold under them there arches.

The credit card industry, for example, sees a bonanza market with the introduction of their cards and charge services at fast food outlets.

"For every point of market share we can swing our way," declares Daniel Brigham, a spokesman for Visa USA Inc., "we will move up to $1 billion through our system. Fast food and small payments are potentially a $100 billion market with fast food being around 55 percent of that."[41]

John F. Love, publisher of *Credit Card Management* magazine, explains the growing interest of credit card companies in the fast food industry.

"The traditional AmEx (American Express) card holder was an upscale male businessman and professional. AmEx wants to grow by expanding its card base. To do that, its got to increasingly appeal to the non-traditional AmEx card holder."[42]

In a test marketing sample conducted in the Phoenix, Arizona area, Arby's found that although the percentage of sales paid with credit cards leveled off at two to three percent, the average purchase was larger ($5.50) when a customer used a credit card than when paying cash ($3).[43]

A new age of credit cards and "power pizzas," however, has left some card holders perplexed.

"They've got us all convinced of the image of the debonair guy with the babe on his arm, getting into only the finest hotels and restaurants," Gerry Betterman, a bond salesman and AmEx member told *The Wall Street Journal* over lunch at a downtown Chicago Wendy's. "Now they want to get into McDonald's, Wendy's, and God forbid, White Castle? It doesn't compute."[44]

In 1988 four fast food companies held an 88.75 percent market share of the fast food restaurants:[45]

McDonald's	51.11%
Burger King	17.20%
Hardee's	10.71%
Wendy's	9.73%
Others	11.25%

All over America the scene at the intersection of Platt Avenue and Victory Boulevard in Southern California's San Fernando Valley is being replicated. As *USA Today's* Tom Green describes it, "such a visit would even be educational, inasmuch as these fast-food restaurants represent the nine basic food groups: McDonald's, Wendy's, Taco Bell, Kentucky Fried Chicken, Naugles, Sizzler, Pizza Hut, Carl's Jr., and Valley Dog."[46] Located either in the nearby shopping mall next door to where

millions buy their clothing and household goods, including the week's groceries, or on our community's highways and byways, or where we work, in a few short decades thousands of fast food establishments have become a permanent and widely accepted part of our modern day culture.

But again this convenience is not what it might seem. Jonathan Yardley, in *The Washington Post*, reminds us that,

in the malls and the franchise outlets alike, the operative word is control. The malls exercise a degree of control over the 'appearance, products and procedures of its business' that no downtown can match... The same is true of the franchises, where national headquarters exercise similarly dictatorial control, not merely over the design and operation of outlets, but also over the size and cut of french fries, the positioning of jeans racks, the crust of pizzas and the installation of mufflers.[47]

George Washington University Professor Amitai Etzioni points out yet another facet of the fast-food phenomena that plays an increasingly important and negative role in our modern culture:

As many as two-thirds of America's high school juniors and seniors now hold down part-time paying jobs, according to studies. Many of these are in fast-food chains, of which McDonald's is the pioneer, trend setter and symbol.

At first, such jobs may seem right out of the Founding Fathers' educational manual for how to bring up self-reliant, work-ethic-driven productive youngsters. But in fact, these jobs undermine school attendance and involvement, impart few skills that will be useful in later life, and simultaneously skew the values of teen-agers — especially their ideas about the worth of the dollar ... There is no room for initiative, creativity or even elementary rearrangements. These are breeding grounds for robots, working for yesterday's assembly lines, not tomorrow's high-tech posts.[48]

As if to prove Etzioni's point, the restaurant industry has announced that due to its estimates that the fast food industry remains 250,000 workers short of the six million needed to maintain its operations, it will in the years ahead look to use increasing numbers of robots and other "labor saving" devices.[49]

In his book *Roadside Empires: How the Chains Franchised America* (Viking Press), Stan Luxenberg writes about Burger King, one of the nation's major fast-food franchises:

Just as the movement of the workers is carefully regimented, the behavior of customers is engineered. Television ads prepare customers for new products, such as the pita salad, and show how they are eaten. In the store people line up, studying the brightly colored menu boards that highlight the limited choices.

Having been served, customers sit in seats that are deliberately hard. After eleven or twelve minutes their backsides begin to feel a little uncomfortable and patrons find themselves hurrying out. At various stations there are containers labeled THANK YOU. There are no signs instructing customers to dump their garbage, but most people do. The whole store is designed so that customers will quickly spend their money and leave.[50]

Luxenberg describes this process as "the goal of enforcing standards ... to achieve predictable mediocrity" and William Severini Kowinski, author of *The Malling of America: An Inside Look at the Great Consumer Paradise*, adds,

So now TV advertises 'your hometown Pizza Hut,' although about the only thing hometown about it is that there is probably one on the highway near where you live, pretty much like every other one in the country. Even the idea of a pizza 'hut' is neutralizing; not only is it devoid of ethnic content (unless you're thinking Polynesian), it doesn't even make sense.[51]

But, as Yardley concludes, making sense is beside the point when it comes to marketing modern day food products.

What we have here isn't sense but advertising, without the sublime and subliminal effect of which the malls and franchises are not, for the most part, selling products that we need; the function of advertising is first to make us want them generally — want fast-food hamburgers, that is, or blue jeans — and then make us want specific brands: Wendy's rather than McDonald's, Lees rather than Levis.[52]

Indeed, a 1985 consumer attitude poll by the Ogilvy & Mather advertising agency found that 84 percent of those questioned said ads "make people want things they don't really need," 72 percent believed "most advertising insults the intelligence of the average consumer," and 70 percent thought ads, in general, do not "present an honest picture of the product advertised."[53]

A subsequent national study in 1988 found that one-third of television audiences surveyed found ads misleading, insulting and boring, while only one-fifth found them informative.[54]

It's A Food War Out There!

Let them eat cake! The public be damned!

Competition among food manufacturers today has come to depend largely upon financial firepower to wage successful advertising campaigns; a food product now gets targeted by a Madison Avenue blitz until it somehow appears better than its competition.

Like a general describing a battle, Jack Trout, president of the advertising firm Ries Capiello Colwell Inc., explains: "It's a food war out there and advertising is the weapon. TV is the bombers that have mass impact, and print media and couponing are the infantry for the hand-to-hand stuff."[55]

As Trout and his partner view it, the aim of marketing is not to serve the customer, but to outwit, outflank, and outfight the competition, using strategies employed in the past by Alexander the Great to Napoleon to Dwight D. Eisenhower. "The reason the war analogy is so useful is that business itself is now in such a warlike mode," explains Trout. "Business used to be, everybody made a lot of money and everybody was terrific and everybody was happy. Today, business has become pure competition, real war."[56]

Testifying in 1973 before a House Subcommittee on Monopolies and Commercial Law, consumer advocates Ralph Nader and Beverly Moore best described the serious consequences of such food advertising:

Advertising powerfully influences consumers. First, to purchase different food items than those they would purchase if adequately informed of comparative price, product price and quality characteristics and, second, to spend more money on food than they would spend if the level of non-informative advertising messages were reduced ... to increase supply faster than demand will lower prices. But lower prices can also be achieved by decreasing demand while holding supply constant.

The effect of heavy advertising induces consumers to spend more of their dollars on food than they otherwise would is the same as an increase in demand, which creates a supply-demand gap that bids up prices. Thus, advertising inflates food prices by artificially increasing demand for limited food supplies as well as by inducing consumers to spend more for less value.

Using multi-billion dollar ad budgets as a weapon, large food firms drive smaller competitors out of the market and reduce the number of new firms entering the market. Traditional methods of competition, such as price and quality, are abandoned in favoring of creating "images."

Pepsi's signing of Michael Jackson to a three-year contract reportedly worth $15 million to act as its spokesman is one of the means image-conscious food corporations now use to sell their products. Jackson's image (Michael Raisin) has also been used in a 67-second movie theater ad by the California Raisin Advisory Board as part of its $6.8 million popular claymation ads.[57]

Prime time network advertising is not usually sold on a local or regional basis, so small firms (lacking the funds to advertize nationally) are denied exposure to this enormous audience. In addition, large volume advertisers usually enjoy substantial discounts from television networks. Obtaining the maximum discounts commonly requires annual expenditures of over $3 million on a single network.

In 1989, for example, among the United States's ten leading advertisers (network television advertising percentage of total media spending in parenthesis.): [1] Philip Morris, $443.4 million (21 percent); [2] Procter & Gamble spent $408.6 million (23 percent) on TV advertising (network, spot, and cable); [5] Grand Metropolitan $95.8 million (12 percent); [6] Pepsico Inc., $145 million (18 percent); [7] McDonald's Corp., $245.3 million (32 percent); and [9] RJR Nabisco, $230.7 million (33 percent).[58]

The average price of a 30-second commercial on prime time network TV in the first quarter of 1990 cost $122,000[59] while the highly rated Super Bowl XXV telecast charged $800,000 for a 30-second commercial.[60]

In 1975 these food advertisers were spending approximately $2.1 billion on TV commercials; 11 years later they were laying out $5.8 billion (34.5 percent) of their $16.9 billion advertising budgets[61] as the average 30-second spot for the three major networks earned $118,119 while NBC, the nation's top-rated network, gained an average of $134,092 for a 30-second spot.[62]

In a study on advertising's impact on the food manufacturing industry, the FTC has concluded that there is little or no cost justification for the volume discounts received by the largest food manufacturers.

Probably the most important anticompetitive effect of network television's discount policies for the economy as a whole, is the artificial stimulus to mergers which they provide. While real economies of integration may flow from some mergers, others may be prompted by simple strategic advantages of size, resulting in money savings to the firm which are not likely to be reflected in commensurate social benefits.[63]

Economists Leonard Kyle, W.B. Sunquist and Harold Guither quite candidly state the situation regarding modern food advertising:

The old simple concept of food as a staple, basic commodity and of a sovereign consumer with a clearly defined demand for food is being cast aside. Industry seeks to create consumer demand for differentiated products — and then to tailor the marketing and production processes accordingly. This is a process that has been used effectively in the production and marketing of automobiles, television sets, and numerous other consumer items.[64]

While some agricultural economists, like Cornell University's Olan D. Forker, have been predicting that "the agricultural industry of this country is about to take off on a big spending binge, spending huge sums of money on commodity promotion programs,"[65] others offer a more sobering picture. Janet Meyers in *Advertising Age* notes:

Eggs aren't cooking. Beef isn't big. Not enough people are bringing home the bacon. That's the bad news for some commodity groups watching consumption of their staples waning year after year despite sizeable ad budgets and skillfully carved campaigns. Yet major campaigns and even bigger budgets are on the drawing boards of other commodities' groups who think theirs will be the industry yanked back into boom times by Madison Avenue.[66]

The dairy industry is often held up as a case in point of the aforementioned "bad news." With a mandatory assessment program that funneled over $200 million into a promotional budget, the industry managed to boost sales. Beginning in 1983, sales of dairy products increased by ten percent — the largest three-year gain in the past 30 years — with cheese sales going up 20.8 percent, milk 10.3 percent, and frozen desserts 4.4 percent.[67] But, as Professor Forker's research shows, the law of diminishing returns sets in, and larger ad budgets become superfluous. In 1984, for example, dairy farmers realized a gain of only one dollar for every six spent on advertising and failed to see a hoped for reduction in price-depressing surplus products.[68] By 1989, per capita milk consumption was showing a 8.7 percent decrease from 1967.

Whereas generic advertising of commodities has been accepted in the past, some grower groups are now beginning to argue for a change in focus. For many years USDA marketing orders and generic food promotions have provided necessary protection to growers from potential anti-trust complaints. Now many of these same groups are arguing for mandatory assessment programs so that all producers who benefit from such an advertising program will also be participants in the program.

For many years Florida orange growers have engaged in generic advertising, however, the state now controls only about one-half of the U.S. orange-juice market. In recent years, due to four severe freezes since 1981 and an outbreak of a devastating bacterial disease known as citrus tanker, the state has lost over 200,000 acres of oranges which has noticeably crippled its $2.5 billion citrus industry.[69]

Capitalizing on these circumstances Brazil has dramatically increased its production of concentrated orange juice, and now imports enough juice concentrate to provide nearly 40 percent of all the concentrate used in the United States's frozen orange juice. Cargill Inc., the world's largest grain trader, which currently owns two processing plants in Brazil, supplies over 15 percent of this concentrate imported into the United States[70]

Because Brazil, Mexico and certain states (like California) have infringed on its sales, in recent years, Florida has embarked on an $11 million campaign to support branded orange juice rebate offers and other promotional programs in an effort to recapture lost sales.[71]

Meanwhile, food scientists have been seeking ways to produce laboratory juice. By removing juice cells from mature oranges and growing them in a test tube these scientists already have produced a juice chemical similar to that squeezed from tree-grown fruit.[72]

• Prior to the 1988 Alar scare, Washington State apple growers, who already control 46 percent of the nation's fresh apple market, spent $4 million on a magazine advertising campaign to explain apples' nutritional value, thus attempting to increase apple consumption from 18 pounds to 22 pounds per capita in a five year period.

"If it wasn't for the fact that we have this health and nutritional trend going with us, it would be impossible to achieve our goal," according to Tom Hale, the state's Apple Commission chairman. "We can hitchhike on that momentum."[73]

Advertising tactics such as these, which appear to make health claims, and ones like the Kellogg Co. launched in 1984 with its high-fiber "All-Bran" cereal, discussing on the package's back panel the role of a high-fiber diet in reducing the risk of cancer, are being sharply debated within the Federal government and the food industry. The permitting of such health-related messages, or "health claims," on food product packages could, without strict FDA guidelines, encourage an onslaught of misleading claims which exaggerate the benefits of various foods in preventing disease.

Currently, the FTC has no ban on health claims. The FDA says only that a food label cannot state that the product is *intended* for the cure, mitigation, treatment or prevention of disease unless the product has met the FDA's requirements for drug approval). However, this restriction doesn't prevent most health claims.

In January 1989, the FTC did manage to put the food manufacturing industry on notice concerning health labeling by charging Campbell Soup Co. with making deceptive claims in one of its advertisements.

The giant soup company, which dominates the nation's $2.3 billion soup market had advertised in magazines that its chicken noodle soup and "most of" its other soups were low in fat and cholesterol and thus helpful in fighting heart disease. The ad did not mention that "Campbell soups are high in sodium which may increase the risk of heart disease" the FTC said in its administrative complaint. According to the FTC, Campbell's failure to make available such information constituted a "deceptive" ad.[74]

Enhancing the Image

A 1972 FTC report on food manufacturing noted that "competition in this concentrated industry mainly occurs in terms of product variation, additional advertising and promotion."[75] In promoting their products food manufacturing companies have been spending enormous sums of money to protect and enhance their image. A few examples:

• Procter & Gamble, one of the nation's leading advertisers, announced in 1986 after months of considerable controversy, that it would take its famous man-in-the-moon trademark off its product packages because of recurring *false rumors* that P&G was somehow connected with Satanism.[76]

• Foodmaker Inc. announced in 1985 that it was changing the name of its 800 hamburger/fast food outlets from Jack In The Box to Monterey Jack's because in testing new names with consumers it found that young urban professionals ("yuppies") were attracted to a restaurant named for a cheese rather than a toy.[77]

• Quaker Oats in 1989 decided that the venerable Aunt Jemima, after nearly a century of portrayal as a large black woman with a bandanna wrapped around her head, will henceforth be shown "in a more contemporary light." Having already shed a few pounds she will now be outfitted in a red dress, pearl earrings and a "perky new perm."[78]

Perhaps no one figure in advertising, however, has come to represent a company more closely than the fictional Betty Crocker and General Mills. Born middle-aged in the 1920s and still unaged in her "seventh life" in the 1980s, she had become such a revered and trusted "person" by the late 1940s that popularity polls showed her to be the second-best-known woman in America, behind Eleanor Roosevelt.

In describing the newest version of the restyled First Lady of Food, the *Washington Post*'s Carole Sugarman has observed that "this woman doesn't look as if she bakes cakes; she buys them. Then again, she probably doesn't eat them. At least not after aerobics."[79]

Tony the Tiger, the Jolly Green Giant, Charlie the Tuna, Morris the Cat, Ronald McDonald and the Pillsbury Doughboy many of the most famous "personages" we see in ads today — have come to us from the food manufacturing business. These characters alone have been the creation of a single firm, Leo Burnett Co. Inc., the world's 14th largest ad agency in 1989.

Starting during the Depression with just one big account, by 1985 this agency claimed 27 clients, and they included many of the nation's major corporations. In 1984 alone, the Chicago-based company had $1.698 billion in worldwide bookings and $1.133 billion in the United States.[80]

The United States has roughly 14,200 firms that manufacture food. Through mergers and acquisitions the number of manufacturing firms has been cut by over 60 percent in just 40 years. More importantly, fifty of those same 14,200 firms (about-three-tenths of one percent of all firms manufacturing food) reportedly take home over 80 percent of the profits in the food industry.[81]

In 1989, 7 of the top 10 advertisers in the United States were food companies and they spent over $7.55 billion in advertising; 22.3 percent of the $33.9 billion spent by the nation's top 100 advertisers. Fifteen of the top 25 network TV advertisers were also food manufacturers.[82]

The Packaging and Merchandising of our Food

Successful advertising usually depends on "product differentiation," that is, the ability of the manufacturer to make its product *appear* different from competing lines through the use of a brand name, logo, or package shape familiar to shoppers.

In this process, the role of corporate agribusiness in reshaping the quantity and quality of our food supply becomes most apparent, as the food manufacturing industry wrests away control of the nation's food supply from farmers and food producers, relegating them to a handful of easily-manageable raw material producers economically subservient to a giant capital-intensive food manufacturing system.

Consequently, food and beverage packaging has become a $35 billion-a-year industry in this country, 66 percent of the value of all such packaging and container materials.[83] While between eight and 12 percent of the family food budget pays for packaging, it has been estimated that each person buys 660 pounds of packaging a year, 90 percent of which is discarded.[84] In 1985 alone, food packaging costs of $29 billion nearly equaled net farm income in the United States.[85]

Food packaging also accounts for 62 percent of all paper packaging, 71 percent of all metal cans, 96 percent of all glass containers, 80 percent of all textile bags, and 46 percent of all other materials. In ten food manufacturing industries, or one-fourth of all food and beverage products, the cost of packaging exceeds the cost of the food materials they contain (beer, soft drinks, breakfast cereals, frozen specialties, canned soups, baby foods and pet food to name a few).[86]

As food packaging continues to play an ever more important role in the way food is "presented" to the consumer, new and more complex products, such as new plastics, are being introduced.

For example, the fastest growing share of the U.S. "waste stream," are now plastics. They alone account for eight percent of U.S. household throwaways as each American uses almost 200 pounds annually, 60 pounds of that being in packaging. A Society of the Plastics Industry study has estimated that the use of plastics in food packaging will double between 1985 and 2000. Currently, the United States uses almost one million barrels of petroleum each year — enough to meet the nation's demand for imported oil for five months — just to manufacture its plastics.[87]

Cornell University's Joseph H. Hotchkiss has even suggested that before long it may be easier to find glass bottles and tin cans in museums than in supermarkets.[88]

In addition, other various packaging innovations include: boxes in which juices and fruit drinks can be sold; new uses for gas packaging — usually inert nitrogen flushed over dry food to increase shelf life, used for example, with potato chips; and more plastics and foil pouches. Hercules Inc. has announced its readiness to market a plastic container which contains a lung-like membrane that will regulate the inner atmosphere of a package and allow fruits and vegetables to remain fresh by lulling them into hibernation while they sit on supermarkets shelves.[89]

Today's packaging manufacturers argue that they are only responding to consumer desires for convenience items. Arguing that increased attention to packaging is well-founded, Elliott Young, who heads Perception Research Services, Inc. of Engelwood Heights, N.J., points out that when shoppers go to the store today they make out lists of products like "potato chips" and "butter," but when they're in the store they decide which brand to buy.[90]

"Packages must compete faster than a speeding cart," adds Frederick Mittleman, who heads the New York design firm that bears his name. Flavio Gomez of the consulting firm Sidjakov, Berman & Gomez underscores the point by noting that "there are so many new products that you have about five seconds to tell the consumer what your story is, you had better not give them a mixed message."[91]

Record numbers of new products now compete on supermarket shelves for space and electronic scanners are giving food retailers ever quicker readings on "what's hot and what's not." But, as Environmental Action Inc. has pointed out, "the consumers that the manufacturers are appeasing are not those who shop at the supermarkets, but rather the retailers themselves."

Writing in *Environmental Action*, Will Hitchcock and Rose Marie Audette raise some of the serious questions that bother environmental, health and consumer groups in respect to new types of packaging materials.

Many plastic products used with foods — such as meat and vegetable packages, bottles and bottle cap liners are made from polyvinyl chloride (PVC). Since by itself PVC is a hard, brittle resin, chemicals are added to make it flexible. The most common plastic additive is DEHP. Inexpensive and practical, DEHP is used in about 30 percent of all PVC products. About 400 million pounds of DEHP were used in 1981. The major producers in the $175-million-a-year industry are Tenneco, Exxon, Kodak, BASF and Pfizer.[92]

The authors go on to point out that DEHP can "migrate" from the plastic substance to the surrounding area and when disposed can also leach into the soil, air and water, creating a "considerable health risk to the general public." After a 1980 National Cancer Institute study found that mice and rats given DEHP-dosed food developed cancer, the EPA prepared a draft notice designating the chemical as a priority under section 4(f) of the Toxic Substances Control Act.

That section requires the EPA to "initiate appropriate action" within 180 days of receiving test data indicating "that there may be a reasonable basis to conclude" that a substance presents "a significant risk of serious or widespread harm to human beings from cancer, gene mutations, or birth defects." But, as Hitchcock and Audette report, "before final approval of this notice could start the clock on regulation of DEHP, Anne Gorsuch Burford assumed the helm of EPA, and she promptly bottled up the notice designating the chemical a priority."

Her action came after a letter from the president of the Chemical Manufacturers Association to the EPA denouncing the regulation and after a series of private meetings between EPA and industry officials — meetings that became publicly known only when a Congressional aide was mistakenly told of a session.[93]

The fears of environmentalists and others concerning the packaging of our food, however, has not gone unnoticed. Some major corporate agribusiness firms like Procter & Gamble, McDonald's, General Mills and Coca-

Cola have begun testing "environmentally friendly" products. It has been estimated that such products rose from 5,100 in 1985 to a projected 5,700 in 1989.

Harvard University's Ray A. Goldberg believes these "environmentally friendly" products are not just "a small market niche of people who believe in the 'greening of America'," but rather "a major segment of the consuming public." And, as befits the man who coined the word "agribusiness," Professor Goldberg notes that marketers also see such products as an additional means to help them differentiate their brands and receive premium prices.[94]

Consumers Play the Food Manufacturers "Shell Game"

One aspect of packaging that continues to surprise many consumers — and embarrass many advertisers — is the packaging of national brands, store brands and generics. As the *Post's* Sugarman reminds us,

> Product swapping, label switching and recipe imitating are common among manufacturers and packers. The result is a marketplace of products that may be more alike — or depending on your viewpoint, more different — than one might think. Sometimes you get what you pay for. Sometimes you don't.[95]

There are many examples of such a practice.
• Safeway's Town House brands of canned fruits are packaged by Del Monte; same product, according to Safeway, only the label and the price are different. Like many food processing companies, Del Monte usually provides the farmers who produce its brands with the seeds for the crop in addition to monitoring the growth of the commodity to determine if "it's Del Monte material." If it's not, Del Monte might well can it under two of its private label accounts — Grand Union or Kroger — and depending on the criteria set by these market chains, the canned product could well be the same in quality as Del Monte's own labeled brand.[96]
• Wine drinkers who drink wine from Modesto, California can almost be assured it is from the family-owned E.J. Gallo Co., no matter what the bottle's label reads. Over 27 percent of all wine sold in the United States in 1988 and over 40 percent of all wine produced in California today is by Gallo, including 45 percent of the nation's "jug" wine.

Gallo's E & J Brandy, Bartles & Jaymes wine cooler and Andre champagne all rank number one in sales throughout the United States, as seven of the nation's top 20 brands are produced by Gallo. The combined market shares of the next six national wine producers after Gallo fails to equal the Modesto firm's share. In 1985 *Fortune* magazine estimated that the winery earned $50 million from total sales of over $1 billion.[97]

A major reason for Gallo's dominance in the wine business is its size and vertical integration. While it grows only slightly above five percent of its grapes (it owns 20,000 to 25,000 acres in California's Merced County) it buys roughly 30 percent of California's annual wine-grape harvest from 1,500 of the state's growers. Its

storage capacity remains awesome as its four wineries have a capacity of over 330 million gallons.

But as *The Wine Spectator* has so aptly indicated,

> vertical integration gives Gallo its muscle. Gallo controls its entire destiny from vineyards to wineries to the glass plant and trucking lines, to sales, marketing, distribution and advertising. This alignment allows Gallo to control pricing because it can cut corners and save money in places its rivals can't. As Ernest said, "unlike our major competition, wine is our only business."[98]

Through such a process Gallo has cornered a major share of the $8.3 billion-a-year U.S. wine market. In 1986 it spent $72.3 million on advertising, 30.6 percent of the total money spent on U.S. wine advertising as compared with Joseph E. Seagram (12.8 percent) and Brown-Foreman Co. (10.2 percent) it two closest competitors.[99]

Forbes Magazine has further noted in a 1975 article:

> Above all, [Gallo's] products are absolutely consistent. [Ernest Gallo] sneers at Mother Nature and "vintage" years; his scientific approach makes one year's wine taste exactly like last year's. That's one reason he replaced the company's bacteria-breeding, wooden-aging vats with sterile stainless-steel containers that resemble one million gallon oil tanks. Whether his wine lacks 'character,' as critics say, or is the 'best,' as Ernest Gallo insists, the overriding point is that each year consumers vote yes with their tongues and swallow 100 million gallons of it.[100]

The Gallo brothers, Ernest and Julio, whose wealth is estimated by *Forbes* at $350 million apiece, are known throughout the wine industry for aggressively selling their products.[101] According to the FTC in 1976, the Gallos used their "dominant position, size and power to lessen, hinder or restrain competition in the sale and distribution of wines in the United States by engaging in various unfair acts, practices and methods of competition."[102]

"Ernest tries to persuade distributors to sell his wines exclusively," recalls a retired Gallo sales manager. "We never told distributors to throw out Gallo competitors, but we might have asked them how they planned to do justice if they carried two competing brands."[103]

Subsequently, Gallo was ordered to stop coercing 300 independent wholesalers into selling the more than 40 different brands of wine it produced.

Gallo was further required not to increase prices on its products once they were in transit or in wholesale warehouses and was restricted in the kind of financial information it could obtain from wholesalers. While Gallo signed a 1978 consent decree with the FTC, agreeing not to pressure its wholesalers, the order was rescinded in 1983.[104]
• Carnation, Pillsbury and Dean Foods are the only three manufacturers in the instant breakfast food business. If you buy an instant breakfast food product and it is not

from Pillsbury or Carnation it is, no matter what the name on the package might say, produced by Dean Foods, the only private-label packager of the product in the country.[105]

• Over 95 percent of the nation's grocery store-brand soup, including Safeway and Giant brands, is manufactured by the H.J. Heinz Co., which no longer sells the product under its own label.[106]

• Weaver Popcorn not only supplies approximately 40 percent of the nation's movie houses with concessionary popcorn, but also sells its product to General Mills, Planters and Pillsbury which market it under their own labels.[107]

• Friday Canning Co. in New Richmond, Wisconsin, cans vegetables for 500 private label firms throughout the United States. And Fritz Friday, the company's president, points out that sometimes when such major manufacturers as Green Giant or Libby experience shortages his company will also can for them.[108]

A measure of the success advertising achieves in attaching consumers to certain products is suggested by a Safeway spokesperson recounting what happened when the chain changed the name/label on a line of canned tomatoes from Garden Way to Scotch Buy. Despite the fact that they were packed by the same company and were identical, the supermarket received many complaints from people who preferred the taste of Garden Way.[109]

The popularity of private labels is suggested by the fate of "generic brand food." For a time in the late 1970s and early 1980s generics experienced a heyday when food prices were high. However, recent studies show that generics "are gradually phasing out," according to Sales Marketing Inc, a company that tracks buying trends. They account for only 2.2 percent of dollar sales of all food products in March 1985, down from a peak of 2.6 percent two years earlier.[110] Recognizing this trend many supermarket house brands, in an age of designer sneakers, bottled water and gourmet foods, have gone upscale with flashier labels, fancier packaging and exotic names. And while the stores may trumpet the brand's improved quality the key to these new house brands, as Booz-Allen Hamilton & Inc. vice president Barbara G. Cohen notes, is still packaging.[111]

"The retailer wants you to look at the label and believe that the bottle of olive oil is upscale. But consumer beware," she adds, because in some cases the quality may not be "all that much better. It may be just slight of hand."[112]

Michael Jacobson, director of the Center for Science in the Public Interest (CSPI), estimates that shoppers could save $7 a week on their groceries by buying generic brand food, a savings of $35 billion a year for American consumers.[113] He points out that because national brands are so heavily advertised consumers are apt to buy them for the wrong reasons, incorrectly thinking they're superior to store brands. The Consumer Federation of America's Stephen Brobeck adds that consumers may feel that it's socially unacceptable to buy a product that doesn't have national advertising recognition.[114]

It is not difficult to see why "product differentiation" through packaging is one major reason why food manufacturers reportedly use nearly 17 percent of the total U.S. energy output, up 65 percent from 1970. Food processing and the wholesaling and retailing of our food now accounts for almost one-half of the energy devoted to food in the United States.[115]

"Four Bowls !!! I'm Not That Hungry !!!"

When it comes to the question of "product differentiation" the major food industry model is the ready-to-eat cereal market. In that line, four corporations — Kellogg, General Mills, General Foods, Quaker Oats, and Ralston Purina — control over 84 percent of the market (See Chart 8A). In 1989, the hot cereal market was dominated by Quaker Oats (60 percent), Nabisco (13 percent) and General Mills (6 percent).

Basically, there is no competition on price or product quality nor on the efficiency of the manufacturers. The 2.37 billion pounds of cereal which the United States consumes annually is essentially the same,[116] with the only artificial differentiation usually being color, shape and degree of sugar content.

Yet, our major cereal manufacturers like to make the public believe that significant differences exist between various companies and brands.

A few years ago, after considerable controversy about the lack of nutritious cereals on the market (with some critics speculating that eating the box might have been more nutritious than eating what was inside) the Big Four quickly began marketing "fortified" cereals, introducing the new brands with 21-gun ad campaigns. Consumers were bilked by such campaigns. General Mills, for example, added less than two cents worth of vitamins to a 12-ounce box of "Wheaties" and marketed it as "Total." Yet, the shopper today pays almost 50 percent more for a box of "Total" than for a similar sized package of "Wheaties."

Using the methods — vitamin fortification and sweetening — that worked so well for selling cereal to children in the sixties and seventies, the cereal manufacturers today are emphasizing to adults, in a concerted effort to increase their market shares, the value of high-fiber content in their cereals.

Such emphasis came after the National Academy of Sciences report "Diet Nutrition and Cancer" suggested that dietary fiber might prevent certain forms of cancer. Ironically, until recently fiber was being processed out of many breakfast cereals: now it is back in and widely advertised. At the same time, in an attempt to differentiate their products the manufacturers are beginning to rely heavily on added dried fruit which may well be imitation.[118]

Cereal's leading marketers in 1989, for example, spooned out over $600 million dollars in advertising, with Kellogg ($373.3 million), General Mills ($68.1 million), Philip Morris Co. ($101.9 million) and Quaker Oats ($58.1 million) leading the way.[119]

The size and potential power of such advertising budgets became apparent in the late 1970s when the government investigated the possible break up of the "cereal trust" in what turned out to be a futile effort to bring more competition into the marketplace.

Cereal's Big Four, had little to fear over such an effort (later completely abandoned in the early years of the Reagan Administration's regime at the FTC), due in large measure to the fact that

Chart 8A: Ready-to-Eat Cereal Market Shares

Brand	1985 Pounds	1985 Sales %	1987 Pounds	1987 Sales %	1989 Pounds	1989 Sales %
Kellogg	42.4	41.6	42.5	42.0	39.0	39.6
General Mills	20.9	23.0	20.7	23.6	23.7	26.5
General Foods	13.3	12.4	12.8	12.1	10.6	10.0
Quaker Oats	7.3	7.7	7.8	7.9	8.1	7.8
Ralston Purina	5.8	6.2	5.5	6.1	6.1	6.6
All Others	10.3	10.7	8.3	12.5	9.5	

Source: *Advertising Age*, September 25, 1988; August 23, 1990.

their advertising budget alone at the time was *12.5 times* the size of the annual budget of the entire Anti-Trust Division of the U.S. Department of Justice and *nine times* that of the Federal Trade Commission.

Clearly, the power of advertising has led to greater concentration in the food industry by limiting a potential competitor's access to the consumer. No matter how tasty, how nutritious, or how efficiently produced an independent food product might be, it has to face competing with the multi-million dollar advertising and packaging budgets of the major food corporations.

How Cheap is Cheap?

It has been frequently noted by the devotees of corporate agribusiness that food expenditures consume approximately 11.6 percent of our income. What is

seldom mentioned by these same defenders of the faith, however, in boasting of such low food expenditures is how much of an income must be realized before such a 11.6 percent figure is applicable.

If a family of 3.2 persons earns between $40,000 and $50,000 a year, their household expenditures for food would be 11.6 percent of their income before taxes, while households with 3.2 persons earning over $50,000 a year would spend 8.7 percent of their income on food. However, households with 2.3 persons earning less than $15,000 would be required to use almost 20 percent of their income on food and households with 2.1 persons earning between $5,000 and $10,000 would find it necessary to spend almost 30 percent of their income on food.[120]

Chapter Nine

Every Trip to the Grocery Store — A Crap Shoot

The most effective way to cope with change is to help create it.

No other segment of our economy better illustrates this age-old marketing maxim than America's multi-billion dollar food manufacturing industry.

Whether it's the food we buy on the supermarket shelf or in the trendy new food "boutiques" which seem to spring up daily, the food manufacturing industry is targeting more and more specific markets in its effort to sell more and more "add-value" products.

Little attention is paid, however, to the fact that as so much of our "daily bread" is being reshaped, reformulated, reconstituted, fancy packaged and aggressively merchandised, our raw material producers have been relegated to but a minor role in this process. Not only are their numbers rapidly being decreased but those that are left are receiving less and less for their toil.

The chemical laboratory, the scientist's workshop, the corporate boardroom and the advertising agency's office are rapidly replacing our fields and orchards as the source of our food supply. Meanwhile, the corporate reapers pursue not only new ways to eradicate our family farm system, but also to change our food buying and eating habits dramatically and relentlessly.

It is imperative, therefore, that consumers understand what is happening to their food before it leaves the farm gate, that farmers understand what happens to their raw materials after they leave that same gate and that both consumers and farmers understand the whole process and how it affects each of their lives.

Much of our available food is the result not of nutritional, dietary or budgetary needs, but of careful research by corporate agribusiness into society's emerging lifestyles and tastes, lifestyles and habits which it would like us to believe it has no role in influencing through its own advertising and packaging.

Campbell Soup's research director Tony Adams calls this new trend a "general elevation of our tastebuds" as "adventuresome eating is becoming part of our lifestyle." He cites the public's "real preoccupation with the shapes, forms and textures of food" and notes that people are no longer satisfied with just being filled up, but now they want a "sensory 'hit', a reward."[1]

Indeed, as the aforementioned 1985 FMI study found, only 20 percent of its 1,005 respondents wanted less sugar, 19 percent less salt, 18 percent fewer chemical additives, 13 percent lower fat content, and 13 percent no preservatives. Meanwhile, only 14 percent wanted higher vitamin and mineral content and more nutritional value.

By 1987 only ten percent of consumers polled worry about chemicals or additives in their food while half of the surveyed shoppers were concerned about the nutritional content of what they were eating, down ten percent from 1986.[2] (Respondents to this food industry survey were free to choose more than just one of the above named categories.)

Likewise, in 1987 *The New York Times*, in one of the most comprehensive studies of eating patterns ever conducted, indicated that most Americans, regardless of age, have not responded in a "significant fashion to calls for decreasing fat in the diet, reducing sodium, taking in fewer calories or otherwise eating more healthfully."[3] This despite the fact that, as former Surgeon General C. Everett Koop reminds us, "there can no longer be any doubt about the link between diet and cancer."

Larry Schaeffer, editorial director of *Progressive Grocer*, a trade publication, points out that

> there's a real fixation on the part of consumers with foods in fashion so chains are using trendy foods as a lure for this market share. This means that more people will try a greater variety of new foods, and its from these that the next croissant will come.[4]

Based on USDA projections, for example, specialty food stores in 1986 captured approximately six percent of the $294 billion food store market revenues.[5]

While the move to "trendy food" excites many food manufacturers, others question whether, in their pursuit to gain newer and larger market shares of what promises to be a continuingly profitable area of business, these companies should allow such new products and new forms of retailing wholly to dictate and define the future of the entire food industry.

Katherine L. Clancy, an associate professor of Human Nutrition in the College of Development at Syracuse University who for five years reviewed food advertising for the FTC, calls attention to the effect food advertising and packaging has on the public, and illustrates how interconnected agriculture and ethics have become:

The morality of advertising foods both to children and to adults has been an issue for years. Advertisers so far have not been willing to share responsibility for the consumption (or overconsumption) of their products, preferring to place the burden solely on consumers.

Foods with high profit margins, *i.e.*, highly processed foods like soda, candy, snack foods, and convenience foods, continue to be the most highly advertised even though all recent dietary recommendations promulgated by the government and private organizations have stressed the need for all or part of the population to decrease the intake of foods high in refined substances like sugar, fat, sodium, etc.[6]

Underlying most food manufacturers' advertising campaigns is research that tracks and targets consumer tastes by utilizing demographic studies and a new and more sophisticated offshoot — psychographics. As USDA economist Larry Hamm explains, "while marketers can draw many important conclusions from demographic trends, the statistics alone do not explain why consumption patterns are changing." He elaborates:

People's decisions, including their purchase decisions, are conditioned by more than just economic variables. Sociological, political, theological, and economic factors all interact with personal histories and environments to form value-lifestyle preferences for most consumers. These lifestyle preferences affect all decisions.[7]

A rather subjective value and lifestyle classification system recently developed by Stanford Research Institute International (SRI), a California think-tank, helps us understand how corporate agribusiness has come to view consumers; its formulations and classifications also teach us about the long-range values and goals that our food manufacturing system currently finds desirable.

The SRI system defines nine categories which we can generalize into four groups.[8]
• *Belongers*: Roughly 35 percent of the population (according to 1980 Census figures) comprise this group of "stabilizers of social change ... characterized by people who are traditional, conservative, and conventional. Their central need is to fit in, not to stand out. They prefer brand names and they avoid experimenting with new foods and cooking methods."
• *Achievers*: This 33 percent of the population "are mostly middle-aged, white and working in successful managerial, professional, technical, or sales occupations. They are competitive, self-confident, and willing to try anything new, especially if it involves a technological breakthrough." They also prefer products and services that are top of the line and convenient. "They are the owners of microwave ovens, the ones who shop in the gourmet and specialty stores and spend a significant proportion of their food dollar on meals outside the home."
• *Inner-directed*: Roughly a quarter of the population, these people are mostly affluent and come from an "achiever" family background. They are highly educated and hold technical-professional jobs. Hamm adds, "These consumers are very socially concerned, and they are often active believers in holistic health and inner growth. Their food interest tend toward the exotic. Freshness, appearance, flavor, and health and nutrition are all important characteristic in the products they look for."
• *Need Driven*: Composed mostly of "money-restricted consumers" with few economic resources, this 11 percent of the U.S. population is "driven harder by need than by their preferences." Hamm believes this group is characterized by extremely low or poverty level incomes, greater numbers of minorities, high unemployment levels (especially among the young), and a high proportion of females.

The need-driven consumer segment is dominated by a sense of alienation, worry and mistrust of authority, but the older members of this group tend to be strongly traditional. Generally, price is the most important characteristic they look for in food items. They prefer private labels, shop for loss-leader items, use coupons, and often pay for food with food stamps, welfare, or Social Security checks.[9]

By neatly classifying consumers in these categories corporate agribusiness has made it easier to target and concentrate in certain markets, dominating them with appropriate advertising and packaging budgets. At the same time, by categorizing consumers as the "belongers," "achievers," and "inner directed" on one level and the "need driven" on another level, corporate agribusiness attempts to create a two-tier economic system reminiscent of the system it has traditionally sought and now seeks to perpetuate within our food production sector.

Creating Walking Chemical Laboratories
In its never-ending quest for maximum cash flow, large profit margins, "product differentiation," and a longer shelf life for its manufactured food, corporate agribusiness has successfully turned the consuming public into walking chemical laboratories. As McGill University's Dr. Ross Hume Hall cautions,

The general public may be only vaguely aware of what is happening, but the food engineers are even less aware of the effects of the changes they are helping to implement. Their insensitivity to these effects is typical of professionals immersed in their work: they are too close to it, too involved to understand or care about changes. Moreover, government agencies designed to guard the safety and wholesomeness of the nation's food, because they are equally involved in the industry, do not comprehend the effects of a transformed technology.[10]

For example, we ignore the fact that present-day humans, rely on just 22 crops for much of our food, although more than 20,000 edible plants exist worldwide.[13] Today we have over 5,500 chemicals in our food,[14] many of which we consume in the highly processed, fabricated, synthetic products that *Time* magazine food critic Mimi Sheraton has called "*trompe l'oeil* foods — foods that fool the eye and attempt to hoodwink the palate" — and which we now buy with regularity in our supermarkets and fast food outlets.[15]

Swanson markets "Take-out" frozen chicken which bought in the supermarket and fried at home, is designed to taste just like the chicken purchased from a take-out, fast-food chain (some of which advertise *their* chicken to be "as good as home fried")!

"White Chocolate with Almonds" soft drinks; "nacho cheese bagel dogs;" Coca-Cola's Minute Maid Orange Soda; "Love Buds" — edible long-stem roses; strawberry-flavored champagne mayonnaise; microwave cup cake mix which produces a final product that does not brown and has a moist top; "Faggots 'n Peas," (a product which occasioned television's David Letterman to wonder if its manufacturer Crosse & Blackwell "didn't look at the stuff and say to themselves 'God, it's so ugly we'll never sell it unless we come up with a really catchy name;'") Ocean Spray on a stick; Diet Squirt Plus, a soft drink spiced with vitamins; croissant pizza, and vanilla-flavored cigars; cinnamon-roasted peanuts that taste like Dentyne; tamari-flavored frozen yogurt; cheeseburger-flavored chips (to go with Borden's ketchup-flavored ones?); and bubble gum in Domino Pizza Pie packaging, are only a few of the "dazzling creations" which account for a ten to 12 percent increase in new food products offered to the public each year. According to *New Products News*, a trade publication in September 1985 alone 188 such new products were introduced by food manufacturers.[16]

It was our friendly "neighborhood baker," Continental Baking Co. (formerly a subsidiary of ITT and now a division of Ralston Purina), which first produced "Fresh Horizon" bread with 40 percent fewer calories than white bread and 400 percent more fiber than whole wheat. The fiber, which came from purified wood pulp, occasioned comedian Johnny Carson to speculate whether after eating 50 loafs of "Fresh Horizons" a person could expect protection by the Sierra Club. Despite an FTC warning in 1979 that requires bread manufacturers to list wood pulp by name as an ingredient, some firms are still using such terms such as "alpha cellulose" on their labels.

Standard Oil of Indiana (Amoco Farms) is manufacturing protein for commercial salad dressings from vats of petrochemicals. And McCormick & Co., the nation's largest seasoning company, has agreed to a $2.5 million joint venture with a Salt Lake City agricultural biotechnology firm to develop seasoning sources.[17]

General Mills, however, achieved a new level in product pizzazz in 1986 when it introduced its new "Rocky Road Cereal, the only cereal with the great tastes of Rocky Road! Special little marshmallows in a chocolaty, nutty coating, Plus crunchy chocolate and vanilla puffs, It's a delicious part of your children's nutritious breakfast."

The list goes on and on, new cereals, meat and dairy substitutes, etc. As Dr. Hall comments:

New food products rarely last more than two years, but each succeeding product represents a slight variation over the preceding one. The public is not aware of any major change in taste, texture, or appearance from one product to the next, but over successive product switches the change can become substantial.[18]

In 1940 there were 1000 food products on the market in North America, compared with 6,000 in 1965, and over 12,000 in 1975. In 1988, it's estimated that there were almost 50,000 processed food products sold in the nation's grocery stores.[19]

But the mere presence of so many "different" food products does not necessarily guarantee consumers real choice. As our fabricated and refined foods proliferate, the fundamental questions remain whether all these innovations are necessary, and who pays and who profits from such gadgetry?

Food Additives: Food or Drugs?

Using a list of nutritional categories provided by the Senate Select Committee on Nutrition and Human Needs, John Connor, former USDA economist and now a professor at Purdue University, has developed data showing that the greatest increases in concentration in food manufacturing over the past several decades occurred in those industries producing highly processed foods considered nutritionally suspect.[20]

"The strong association between poor nutritional quality with both high and increasing (corporate) concentration remains irrefutable," Connor declares.[21]

In his excellent book, *Guidelines for Food Purchasing in the United States*, Nick Mottern, former staff member of the Senate Select Committees, also points out that

The increase in concentration in highly processed foods, and their sales growth, is related to the growth strategy of major food corporations which, since the advent of television, have relied heavily on advertising for success ... This suggests that highly processed foods, which are also generally highly promoted, are essential to maintaining major food conglomerates at their current levels of profitability and scale.[22]

Clearly, food technology at the present time is primarily concerned with the preservation and manipulation of food. Such technology has developed faster as a science than the capacity of nutritionists to measure its impact on human nutrition. As Dr. Hall emphasizes:

Food engineers, who consider food in the same terms as a piece of steel, study the same properties in food products with the idea of reducing taste and texture to a set of mathematical formulas. If the science of physics can provide nuclear power and atomic blasts, surely it can provide the mathematical definition of eating a piece of bread.

Once they have acquired these formulas, technologists feel that they will be able to synthesize food products with predictable mouth feel and taste sensations.[23]

Writing in the *World Review of Nutrition and Dietetics* on "The Marriage of Food Technology and Nutrition," Drs. N.W. Tape and Zak Sabry comment:

The main objective of the food technologist is to improve food quality, to develop preservation methods and invent new foods and processes so that an expanding variety of products may be marketed in an ever-increasing geographic area at a reasonable price. To [them], food quality is primarily color, flavor, texture, appearance and stability.

Little attention is paid to the nutritive value of products — as affected by a new process, ingredient, additive, etc. The food industry appears to consider nutritionists *persona non grata* and seldom includes them in research and development teams, except perhaps in companies marketing pet food.[24]

Dr. Paul Spiers, a clinical neuropsychologist of the Behavioral Neurology Unit and the Harvard Medical School's Comprehensive Epilepsy Center at Beth Israel Hospital in Boston also adds this sobering reminder:

Now we have food additives that are more like drugs than foods, that are introduced into the dietary chain but have direct effects on the brain's neurotransmitter system. But the chemical industry is 20 years ahead of the regulators.[25]

It is estimated that in one day the average American eats one teaspoon of artificial colors, flavors and preservatives. That adds up to almost four pounds a year for every one person.[26]

Another important aspect of current food technology was the focus of attention of former Representative Benjamin Rosenthal, D-NY, and the CSPI's Michael Jacobson and Marcy Bohm in their 1976 study, "Feeding at the Company Trough."

Despite the compelling need for experts who can examine the food industry with a critical eye, the nutrition and food science communities have fallen under the $200-billion industry's influence. At our most prominent universities, eminent nutritionists have traded their independence for the food industry's favors. A recent survey of nutrition and food science departments ... [by the authors] has concluded that eminent nutritionists have prostituted their professional independence to curry the favor of the food magnates.[27]

The study cited Harvard University's Department of Nutrition, the University of Wisconsin's Food Research Institute, Oregon State University's Department of Food Science and Technology, and several other university departments and individuals as guilty of currying such favors.

As a consequence of all these actions, we are replacing more and more real foods with imitation and nutritionally suspect ones. We may soon, therefore, raise a generation which has never tasted a real tomato, a genuine cheese omelet, or freshly squeezed orange juice.

"Imitation foods do not necessarily have the nutrients of the mother food," Kathy King Helm, a registered Dallas, Texas dietician points out. "Many nutritionists, including me, encourage abstinence or moderation rather than fabricated foods."[28]

Let Them Eat Coke and Potato Chips!
I can't fool around in the market.
I have to read labels and think.
And look for the foods that are healthy.
The GOOD THINGS to eat and to drink. So -
You've gotta look hard for the good things
The oranges and the carrots and the whole wheat bread
Just walk on by all the sugary stuff
And find the GOOD THINGS instead.

GOOD THINGS
by Minnie O'Leary
© 1976

Identifying whether a food is "imitation" is a somewhat difficult chore for most consumers because the FDA currently does not require a food to be called "imitation" unless it is "nutritionally inferior" to the food it resembles. How the FDA determines "nutritional equivalence" has also been challenged by some nutritionists.

"Food labels (in their current form) are like dropping into a bridge game and not knowing what the bid means," according to Edward Dunkelburger, counsel for the National Food Processors Association (whose 600 member companies produce the nation's packaged food). "Reading them can only be helpful for our diets when we know the implications of the figures."[29]

Voicing even greater concern about modern food labeling is Marion Nestle, chairwoman, of the Department of Home Economics and Nutrition at New York University. "Right now, labels are worse than useless. They are dangerous."[30]

Nutritionally rich food is simply not a significant concern to corporate agribusiness. In the process of developing palatable products that sell well, with nutrition playing a relatively minor role, consumers have either been misled or left uneducated as to the ABC's of good nutrition.

A 1989 survey commissioned by Nutri/System Inc., for example, found that of 1,000 adults studied 41 percent incorrectly thought ketchup was a vegetable, 39 percent didn't know the marbling in raw meat is fat, 68 percent didn't know cholesterol is found only in products of animal origin, 61 percent mistakenly classified asparagus and broccoli as legumes, and 66 percent incorrectly identified honey, molasses and corn syrup (all sweeteners) as sources of carbohydrates and thus good foods.[31]

"Despite people's awareness of the risk of obesity and other nutritional diseases, they lack the knowledge to prevent and treat these diseases," comments Dr. Stuart Shapiro, Nutri/System's medical director. "They don't know the very basic facts about fats, carbohydrates and protein."[32]

General Mills' Arthur Odell once put it a little more bluntly: "You can't sell nutrition ... Hell, all people want is Coke and potato chips."[33]

Indeed, the USDA's basic philosophy in recent years is that it is useless to try to persuade people to eat nutritious foods; instead nutrition needs to be engineered into foods the public likes.

"What consumers really need," according to Public Voice for Food and Health Policy, a Washington, D.C. consumer group, "are mandatory nutritional labels on all food. The whole issue of labeling is one that the federal government is long overdue in making rational."[34]

Currently, 55 percent of the products regulated by the FDA carry nutritional labeling while 43 percent of processed meat and poultry products regulated by the USDA show such labeling.[35]

It has been noted by Public Voice that mandatory nutrition labeling was under consideration by the Carter administration, however, when Ronald Reagan became president "the impetus for regulation to do this was removed," according to Syracuse University nutritionist Kate Clancy.[36]

At a March 1989 conference in the nation's capital sponsored by Public Voice, FDA commissioner, Frank E. Young and many other speakers (including executives of food companies) all agreed that the time had come for mandatory nutritional labeling. However, there was relatively little agreement on just what information should be available on such labeling.

"Nutrition labeling is a good Republican program. People can make their own choices — their own informed choices," noted Carol Tucker Foreman, former Assistant Secretary of Agriculture for Food and Consumer Services in the Carter Administration.[37]

There exists some consensus that nutritional labeling should include levels of fat, saturated fat, cholesterol, sodium, calories, carbohydrates and fiber. Vitamin and mineral percentages are considered of relatively minor importance. Farm groups argue that the origin of the product's ingredients should appear also on the label.

One labeling process that has already received favorable reviews is that proposed by the Center for Science in the Public Interest. In an informal reader survey done by *The Washington Post* the CSPI sample label received 85 percent of the votes, while the American Heart Association model got 8 percent and the National Dairy Board's proposed label received no votes.[38]

CSPI has suggested that food labels, which about two-thirds of the American consumers reportedly read,[39] be presented in the following manner:
• A "stoplight system" on the front of the package of four individual colored squares showing the quantity of major nutrients (fiber, fat, sodium and calories) in colors of red (for high) and yellow (for moderate). If the product is low in a bad nutrient

or high in a good nutrient the blocks would appear in green.
• An ingredient's panel listing in descending order of prominence (as currently required), *but* including percentages of each ingredient as well (*e.g.*, sweeteners, which often appear in four different forms in a single product — sugar, corn syrup, molasses, and honey.)
• A pie-shaped chart, dividing the categories of each serving into wedges for the fat, sugars, protein and complex carbohydrates.
• Grams of cholesterol, sodium and fiber listed along with the percentages of U.S. Recommended Daily Allowances (U.S. RDA) of vitamins A and C, calcium and iron.

As Bruce Silverglade, the group's Director of Legal Affairs explains,

> people in this country mistakenly equate good nutrition with protein and vitamins. But protein and vitamin deficiencies are almost unknown in this country: they are Third World problems. What Americans should equate with good nutrition is a low fat, low salt, low sugar, high fiber diet.[40]

While the FDA has promised "sweeping" new proposals on food labeling, and Senator Howard Metzenbaum, D-Ohio, working with a coalition of health and consumer groups, likewise has promised new legislation on such labeling. After initially opposing any new label laws the food industry now claims it will back such legislation *if* states are prohibited from enacting their own food label laws.

Silverglade explains the industry's turnabout. "What the companies are worried about is tough state laws. They prefer a weak Federal law."[41]

Food industry officials, however, counter that without "national uniformity" confusion and uncertainty would be created in the minds of consumers, and interstate and international distribution of foods would be disrupted. "The consumer across the country needs to be fully informed across the board," claims John Cady, president of the National Food Processors Association. "We can't have 50 FDA's."[42] However, in the Campbell Soup "health claim label" case nine state attorney generals participated in the legal action prohibiting the company from making such claims.[43]

How Sweet It Is!

Sweeteners and sodium are two primary examples of consumers not always realizing exactly the amounts they are receiving in their food and drink.

In 1988 consumption of refined sugar in the United States was 62.6 pounds per capita, down over 30 percent from 1975. In this period, total consumption of sugar, corn syrup and other caloric sweeteners went from 132 pounds per capita to 152 pounds per capita as per capita consumption of soft drinks from 1975 to 1985 alone went from 31 to 45 gallons.[44] It is estimated that soft drinks and milk products provide over 30 percent of the sugar in our diets.

In the process of this surge, artificial sweeteners have become a $1 billion market, 60 percent of them being used in soft drinks, 15 percent in tabletop sweeteners, and 25 percent in other products such as powdered beverages, gelatins, etc.[45]

While consumers have to remain cautious about such new food sweeteners as aspartame, the beneficiaries are corporations like G.D. Searle & Co., purchased in 1985 for $2.7 billion by the Monsanto Corp. As one financial analyst pointed out, Searle's aspartame business will help Monsanto diversify from a two-product (Lasso and Roundup agricultural chemical poisons) into a three-product company, which is especially important because in 1986 the patent on Lasso expired.[46] By 1989 Monsanto was clearly the industry's leader in the production of artificial sweeteners with a 70 percent market share.[47]

In recent years four artificial sweeteners have appeared on the market — saccharin, which Congress, in overruling a proposed FDA ban in 1977, has kept on the market; cyclamate, which was banned in 1970 by the FDA and which has been further studied in recent years in an effort to reintroduce it into the artificial sweetener market; aspartame, which was approved for dry goods in 1981 and soft drinks in 1983; and Acesulfame, which has been approved for use in England, West Germany and Switzerland and is currently under study for use in the United States.[48]

Aspartame (now marketed as NutraSweet), 180 times as sweet as sugar, has created the most controversy among scientists and nutritionists. Currently consumed by over 100 million Americans each day in some 160 products,[49] it is charged that it might cause brain tumors, seizures, mood swings and headaches. Noting that the FDA had received 3,000 complaints from consumers since Aspartame appeared in 1981, Dr. Louis Elias, director of medical genetics at Emory University Medical school argues,

> They never asked the right questions about what it does to brain function in humans. They decided without data that you had to have enormous amounts of phenylalanine in your blood before it becomes a problem. We don't know that's the case.[50]

A 1987 GAO study remarked that although the FDA adhered to proper procedures by approving the sweetener, "we cannot comment on whether important issues surrounding aspartame's safety remain unresolved." The report noted that a survey it had conducted for Sen. Metzenbaum showed that over half of the 69 scientists it had polled voiced concerns about the sweetener's safety.[51]

Prior petition efforts by the Community Nutrition Institute's attorney James Turner to get the FDA to ban NutraSweet as an "imminent hazard to the public health" were rejected by the federal agency. Turner argued that medical records of a total of 140 NutraSweet users showed them to have suffered from epileptic seizures and eye damage after consuming products containing the artificial sweetener.[52]

Earlier, a 1987 study by a University of Illinois scientist indicated that using NutraSweet appeared to heighten chances of behavioral disturbances and birth defects. Dr. Reuben Matalon, a pediatrician and geneticist, argued that his test results suggested that large amounts of NutraSweet could affect small children and millions of people unaware of their body's inability to process phenylalanine fully. High concentrations of the chemical can cause reduced attention span and concentration and memory loss.[53]

In addition, some scientists claim that artificial sweeteners have the supposedly unintended consequence of increasing hunger. Studies on rats suggest that humans who use saccharin (for example) to lose weight may inadvertently increase their hunger, leading them to eat more.

As Alexandra Logue, a State University of New York at Stony Brook psychologist and author of *The Psychology of Eating and Drinking* points out, "the taste of any sweets, even artificial sweeteners, makes the body release insulin, which in turn leads more food to be stored, rather than be released as energy. That makes less energy available for immediate use, so the body craves more food to get the energy."[54]

"How many people even know that the FDA has attached a limit to aspartame consumption?" adds James Wagner, legislative aide to Sen. Metzenbaum. The FDA's limit of 50 grams per kilogram of body weight translates to about four liters of a diet drink for an adult, but only to about three cans for a 30 pound child.[55]

"Americans," he continues, "drink over 20 billion cans of diet soft drinks a year. And that doesn't count the gum, pudding, breakfast cereal, chewable vitamins, toothpaste juices, frozen pops — all sweetened with NutraSweet."[56]

CSPI's Jacobson sums it up: "Sugar leads to tooth decay and obesity. Saccharin has no calories but has been linked to cancer. Aspartame seems to be safer than saccharin but hasn't been tested well enough and some people have had bizarre reactions. The bottom line is to avoid them all as much as possible."[57]

Almost lost in the debate over the health risks involved in the consumption of aspartame are economic considerations: the wholesale price of aspartame in 1987 was about 35 cents a pound when adjusted to an equivalent amount of sweetening power as sugar. By comparison, the average price of all refined sugar offered for sale to manufacturers was near 26 cents and high fructose corn sweeteners, the most widely used kind of sweetener, were selling for between 14 to 18 cents a pound.[58]

Putting the controversy into proper perspective surrounding Nutrasweet and the other biotechnological food and agricultural products to be marketed by Monsanto, Margaret Mellon of the National Wildlife Federation points out, "the problem is that the private enterprise system which does so many things so well, has no incentive to come up with new *processes*; they have every incentive in the world to come up with new *products*."

The controversy surrounding aspartame thus highlights another important question: as many of the nation's food companies introduce a wide range of synthetic food additives, primarily sugar and fat substitutes, to the market, how will the Federal Government certify their safety?

Addressing this problem, Richard J. Wurtman, professor of neuroscience at the Massachusetts Institute of Technology, explains that to bring over-the-counter drugs to market, manufacturers must prove in exhaustive tests on animals and humans that the substances work as claimed and produce no harmful side effects.

By contrast, the 1958 laws that cover food additives fail to require *any* human testing. The law requires only tests with animals for toxicity and a few side effects, like the potential to cause cancer or genetic damage. Biochemical and behavioral effects are not considered, as they are for over-the counter drugs.[59]

"Common sense," Professor Wurtman believes, suggests that several changes in the approval system need to be made soon. They include: Congress should require the amount of synthetic additives in a product to be clearly stated on the label ("the FDA could order this immediately — joining virtually every country where aspartame is sold — but refuses"); Congress should require human tests and should establish an "early warning system" by requiring manufacturers to inform the FDA of reports suggesting that an additive is producing medical side effects; and Congress might "also consider transferring responsibility for synthetic food additives from the Bureau of Foods to the Bureau of Drugs and requiring that additives meet the same safety standards as over-the-counter drugs."[60]

Sodium, associated with high blood pressure, is also another food additive that increasingly concerns nutritionists and health experts. Yet, despite urgings from the FDA, the sodium content of most processed foods has not decreased significantly in the last several years. In fact, in a sodium count by CSPI of 165 lines of processed food, only 15 percent had shown a decrease, seven percent had increased and 75 percent had remained unchanged between 1985 and 1986.[61]

"Most of the sodium in the average American's diet comes from processed foods," CSPI's nutrition director Bonnie Liebman emphasizes, "and most corporate chefs show no signs of changing their cooking habits to protect the public's health."[62] By way of illustration, one bowl of Campbell's soup provides nearly all of an individual's recommended daily amount (RDA) of sodium.[63] Yet, Campbell's Jim Moran has explained that one of the reasons the salt is in there is that it is such a "low-cost flavor enhancer."[64]

While some manufacturers claim to be responding to the public's concern over a growing number of sweeteners, excessive amounts of fat or a high sodium content in their food, consumer surveys have shown that at the same time as these manufacturers reduce such suspect ingredients in some of their product lines, they are charging more for those same products.

One food company spokesman speculates that because some products have lower contents of fat, sweeteners and sodium, stores may alter the pricing structure because such products are "perceived as value-added products" and "people are willing to pay a higher price" for them.[65]

The effect of food additives on the health of Americans is revealed by the National Academy of Scientists' statistics: 36 percent of all cancers are diet-related;[66] obesity affects 20 percent to 30 percent of all Americans[67] while weight loss has become a $39 billion a year industry.[68]

Earl Mindell, author of *Earl Mindell's Vitamin Bible*, notes that "we are the most overfed, under-nourished country in the history of the world." He observes that the average person in the United States consumes 3,393 calories per day, highest in the world. We're also eating too much protein, consuming 106.3 grams each day.

I don't think the medical people know anything about nutrition. I don't think they really are into the concept of health at all. Our basic medical training is crisis medicine... It's about time we realize something the Chinese have known for 4,000 years: It's much cheaper to keep people well than wait until they get sick and pay for it.[69]

How Fresh Is Fresh?

In recent years, serious questions have also been raised about the quality and nutritional value of the types of food most commonly advertised, specifically on television. In 1975, the Northwestern Medical School surveyed Chicago television stations to see what types of food were most advertised.

The survey found that 40 percent of advertising air time was devoted to non-nutritive beverages; 11 percent to sweets, and 14 percent to oils, fats, margarines, baked goods, snacks and relishes. Overall, 70 percent of the time went to low-nutrient, high calorie foods. Fresh fruits, vegetables and juices received just seven-tenths of one percent of the Chicago TV ad time.[70]

One unusual byproduct of this advertising of non-nutritive food, is that while per capita consumption of fresh produce has risen by 12 percent, compared with 10 percent for frozen foods and a large drop in canned foods, many consumers lack knowledge about the selection and preparation of fresh produce.[71]

"They're like a species that's lost the use of its tail," observes Faith Popcorn, owner of BrainReserve, a New York marketing concern that specializes in the food industry. "They see the beautiful vegetables. They know they're supposed to do something with them, but what?"[72]

While most produce sections now stock about 250 items, compared to about 50 items ten years ago, many of these "fresh" items are still "in transit," undergoing their ripening process in specially designed rooms.[73] A U.S. Department of Defense report estimated that the average distance the nation's food travels before being eaten is 1,300 miles.[74]

In discussing what he terms "the freshness illusion," the Center for Science Reporting's Bryan Jay Bashin, writing in the January/February 1987 issue of *Harrowsmith* stresses:

This manna that is displayed daily on supermarket shelves has been bred for durability, picked green and waxed for show. It may be old enough to grow whiskers and have put on more miles than an average Airstream trailer in the summertime. It can be expensive, and by the time it arrives at the supermarket, its nutritional qualities are in decline.

And for those who reflect upon their actions, the implications of buying fresh can be troublesome indeed, as, increasingly, our winter produce comes from foreign lands, where farm workers labor under conditions so exploitative and inhumane that you probably do not want to know about them.

But nonetheless, those fruits and vegetables sitting on ice are always bought with the belief that they are somehow better for us than processed food and that they enhance our "lifestyle."[75]

He goes on to point out that while the average American eats 26 more pounds of fresh fruit and vegetables per year than he or she did ten years ago (annual sales of fresh produce have reached $35.9 billion), many people are missing an essential nutritional point: the American diet lacks not vitamins but minerals and fiber and "despite all the hoopla about fresh foods, there is no difference between fresh and frozen on that score." Much of the fresh produce we see in our supermarkets today has lost precious nutrients and flavor long after their frozen and canned counterparts have had those qualities sealed in at a processing plant.

Arguing for more regional-based agriculture Bashin notes that Philadelphia, which used to be surrounded by rich farmlands that supplied it with most of its food needs, today trucks in 70 percent of its food from out of state.[76]

A food delivery system which spends a dollar moving food for every $2 spent growing it can be quite expensive to consumers.[77]

In 1984, for example, New York area residents bought 24,000 tons of broccoli, most of it coming from California — 2,700 miles away at a transportation cost of $6 million. Hauling the refrigerated vegetable that distance also caused it to lose 19 percent of its vitamin C in 24 hours, 34 percent in two days. That same broccoli, which prefers cool growing weather, could have been produced in New York, not only saving Empire State consumers transportation costs, but also providing additional jobs and income for New York residents.[78]

Bashan also cites a 1986 report, "Status Summary on the Effects of Food Processing on Nutritive Values," issued by the 34,000-member Institute of Food Technologists concludes:

Foods which are processed with good manufacturing practices from high-quality, freshly harvested "garden-fresh" commodities will frequently have a higher nutrient content than freshly harvested "market-fresh" commodities which have been improperly handled during transportation and/or stored for a few days or more.[79]

In addition, mainly due to increasing volume and an inadequate number of Federal inspectors due to budgetary considerations, more than 50 percent of the food in supermarket produce sections gets from farm to store without government inspection. "What it comes down to," Mona Doyle, a Philadelphia-based marketing consultant notes, "is that consumers are the inspectors."[80]

As more fresh produce becomes available, supermarkets, which estimate that they throw away between 15 percent and 30 percent of their produce — over twice the amount of five years ago — are looking for ways to give such products longer shelf life. The major method employed to date has been "waxing." While this process is often used to prevent the shriveling of fruits and vegetables, it also adds to the cosmetic quality of the produce. Some health experts, however, worry about the repeated ingesting of this wax by the consumer.

"Waxing is just an embalming technique," Steve Pavich, a large California organic grower, told Bashan. "It allows the mediocre grower to do a mediocre job growing it and then pretty it up — and the consumer doesn't know the difference." The FDA has already approved a half-dozen waxes to be applied to some 18 varieties of fresh fruits and vegetables with some waxes containing the same ingredients as household floor and car waxes.[81]

Some shippers, Bashan adds, mix their wax coatings with sprouting inhibitors and fungicides such as orthophenylphenol, diphenyl and thiabendazole to slow decay. The latter chemical is also commonly used as a medicine for worming sheep.

"There isn't a banana or pineapple in any fruit bowl in this country that doesn't have thiabendazole in it," according to Mark Brian, a California consumer activist. "Nobody knows it exists, though, because the supermarkets destroy every trace of packaging that has information about it."[82]

FDA regulations specify that waxed produce must be labeled as such and that retailers must affix a card next to the price of the produce (when sold in bulk) which indicates the type and composition of the wax. The retailer may also simply display the original shipping carton alongside the produce. Fungicides and/or fumigants used on the produce must also appear on the box label.

But as Associate Professor Joe M. Regenstein of Cornell University's Food Science Department indicates, supermarkets routinely scoff at such regulations when they display their produce. "Nobody I know has ever seen an ingredient statement on fruits and vegetables."[83]

Further, a consumer survey reported in *The Wall Street Journal* found that 94 percent of respondents would be willing to switch supermarkets if they could find fresh food that wasn't "waxed." "Consumers want fresh products to actually be fresh, not just look fresh," Mona Doyle concludes.[84]

How Safe Is Safe?

Attempts by the Federal government to establish a national nutritional policy and alert consumers to the dangers of an improper diet have been repeatedly challenged by the food industry.

During the late 1970s the USDA, due mainly to the determined yet often-frustrated efforts of staff nutritionist Audrey Cross, published landmark guidelines calling for reduced consumption of foods rich in fats, cholesterol, sugar and salt; moderation in the drinking of alcoholic beverages; and emphasis on the importance of exercise in weight control.[85]

Although the Reagan administration later denounced guidelines establishing such a policy, a USDA committee headed by Bernard S. Schweigert, chairman of the Food Science and Technology department at the University of California, Davis, reaffirmed the earlier guidelines in a 1985 report.[86] In addition to the large amounts of fat, sugar, and salt that have been introduced into our food there are at least 2,700 different substances intentionally added to the U.S. food supply, according to FDA estimates. The greatest number of these additives are non-nutritive, used primarily to affect the appearance, texture and taste of our food.[87]

The ongoing controversy over Red Dye No. 3, now used in 2,000 different foods, and the latitude allowed by the Delaney Clause of the Food, Drug and Cosmetic Act, has focused considerable attention on the whole question of the 6.3 million pounds of artificial food dyes used in food products each year. The food industry claims that these color additives — called coal-tar dyes because they are derived from petroleum — present such a small risk to the public under current conditions of use that they can be considered "safe" according to the anti-cancer Delaney Clause.[88]

Few of these additives are used as preservatives. A GAO report, "Federal Human Nutrition Research — Need for a Coordinated Approach to Advance Our Knowledge," has stated: "A review of the 658 substances characterized in the current *Food Chemicals Code,* which sets standards of identity and purity for chemicals added directly or indirectly to foods, shows that the majority (79 percent) are used principally to color, flavor, cure, shape, texturize, or otherwise enhance the physical appearance or appeal of processed food items."[89]

Another report prepared in 1977 by the U.S. Department of Health and Human Services (then Health, Education and Welfare) notes that additive use in recent years has increased dramatically:

The enormous public demand for convenience tends to increase food additive use; so do substitute foods ... The Food and Drug Administration currently approves less than ten percent of all requests for new uses of food additives, yet the total use of additives has more than doubled in the last 15 years, significantly exceeding the rate of expansion of the food supply and the population.[90]

The FDA estimates that an additional 10,000 substances have been added "unintentionally" from such sources as packaging, chemical poisons and other environmental sources. As Nick Mottern points out, these additives need to be considered as a major concern to public health.

1) There is currently no accurate measure of the amounts of any single additive being introduced into the food supply.

2) All additives have not been tested for safety, and all testing has not been thorough or used up-to-date methods.

3) A major portion of the testing has been done by firms benefiting directly or indirectly from additive use, and the history of the industry testing is marred by cases of faulty test methods and suppression of adverse findings, and

4) There is extremely little knowledge of the impact of the interaction of additives and the effect of additives on the nervous system.[91]

More than just a few chemical additives are changing our food today. Indeed, throughout the country, government scientists, university researchers and food company engineers are virtually restructuring food.

"You're never going to convince people to only eat foods that are good for them. We have to make foods to fit people's taste preferences," is the way USDA chemist J. Michael Gould has characterized this food technology revolution.[92]

But the Environmental Policy Institute's Jack Doyle disputes that claim and expresses the concerns of many health professionals and nutritionists that these newly engineered foods do not bode well for consumers. Not only will they increase the mystification and the price of food, Doyle believes, but when food is developed in the confines of a fermentation tank or petri dish it weakens consumer input. "It leaves the high priest in the lab in control," rather than the marketplace, said Doyle who also voices suspicion about taking scientists' "word for it [safety]."[93]

Adding to this controversy is a 1989 study by the House Energy and Commerce Subcommittee on Oversight and Investigations finding much of the food imported into the United States unfit to eat by government standards.[95]

It is estimated that nine percent of the nation's food — produce and meat, canned and fresh — is imported and that the FDA tests only two percent of that food. Of that amount, according to Stephen Sims, one of the authors of the House report, 40 percent is rejected due to spoilage, faulty labels and the presence of salmonella, rodent feces and other contaminants. "That raises serious questions about the 98 percent they don't test," he adds. In addition, some importers re-import rejected food via a variety of ruses.[96]

Despite the increasingly dubious nature of our food, some government health officials still contend that U.S. food is the safest in the world, with the chances of a person getting sick from food about one in six each year.[97]

In an effort to reassure the public the Bush administration announced early on that it was inaugurating a review of American food-safety programs. Rather than drafting new regulations, however, the review promised to convince the public that the nation's food was safe to eat, according to Cooper Evans, special agricultural assistant to President Bush.

"We think the system now is very, very good," he emphasized. "The public needs to be reassured about that and given a better basis for making judgments."[98]

Others dispute such claims, noting for example, that the FDA has been stalling for some time on whether to ban ten color additives — six of which can cause cancer — used in food and cosmetics. Between 1981 and 1984 alone, 25 years after Congress told the agency to make such decisions, FDA law enforcement actions dropped by 49 percent.[99]

"Nutrition monitoring" by the USDA has also been called for in an attempt to discern new trends or changes in the American diet. One department official has claimed that "you need data every year to signal changes taking place."[100] Despite efforts by health and consumer groups, however, there has been little government initiative for establishing such a program.

As the *New York Times'* respected food critic Marian Burros notes:

In 1988 the safety and nutritional quality of the American diet took on the same urgency it had in the 70s. And now yesterday's Cassandras have become today's respected experts. The public is turning to public interest groups ... to expose the hazards in the food supply and tell them how to cope.

Many people don't believe that the Federal Government is doing its job, regulating the food supply to keep it safe; Government agencies acknowledge that they are understaffed, largely due to cutbacks during the last [Reagan] eight years.[101]

In 1984, for example, the Reagan administration's lobbying helped kill legislation authorizing a ten year program to gather continuous information on the dietary status of Americans. The measure fell 18 votes short of the two-thirds House majority needed for passage.[102]

The quality of nutrition information as its relates to many of the federal government's food assistance programs has also come under attack.

Joan Claybrook, president of the Washington, D.C.-based public interest group, Public Citizen, claims that former Agricultural Secretary Block "systematically sabotaged" the USDA's nutrition information programs.[103] Charging that "nutrition education programs already proven to be cost-effective were being threatened by arbitrary funding cutoffs, staff reductions and outright termination," Public Citizen noted that the availability of USDA nutrition publications for low-income consumers were "severely curtailed" by lack of publicity, budget cutbacks and the administration's policy of charging fees for materials previously distributed for free.[104]

Many critics of the Federal government's nutritional policies believe that the root of the problem is that the USDA constantly sends mixed messages concerning nutritional guidelines. Consider, for example, a 1989 interagency memo prepared by the USDA's dietary guidance working group which was charged with outlining principles that must be followed when dispensing dietary advice:

Guidance must not suggest that any food be eliminated from the diet or that some foods are "bad" and others are "good." Essentially any food can be combined with other foods in numerous ways in diets to conform to the Dietary Guideline principles of variety, moderation and balance.[105]

As food editor Burros notes, "These guidelines limit the department's ability to provide consistent advice and make judgments about which foods provide more nutritional value than others."[106]

Saturday Morning's Children

One glaring example of the problems with the USDA's "new" nutritional focus was a May 1985 rule formally allowing "junk foods" — sodas, candy and ice cream — to be sold in schools again. Despite objections from over 800 individuals and school officials during the "public comment" period, the USDA said it was issuing the new rule in compliance with an earlier Appeals court decision that over-turned the department's ban on the sale of junk foods in schools until after the final lunch period. The court, in a case brought by the industry-sponsored National Soft Drink Association, ruled that the USDA had exceeded its rule-making authority.[107]

No one segment of our society has been more cheated by the myriad conflicting policy decisions and mixed messages concerning food and nutrition emanating from the USDA than our nation's children.

Long victimized by junk and fast food manufacturers, by the 1980s an alarmingly large percentage of our children were exhibiting high cholesterol levels and weight problems. Yet, as Paula Zann reported on a 1988 ABC-TV special, "America's Kids: Diet of Danger," Saturday morning children's program sponsors, with their heavy diet of highly sugared cereals, soft drinks, gum, candy and fast food, continue to spend over $1 billion annually promoting their wares.[108]

(Capitalizing on the growing popularity of microwave ovens, "shelf-stable" foods — "My Own Meals," "Hormel's Kids Kitchen" and "Banquet's Kid Cuisine" — are being specifically designed for six to 14-year olds use. "They can do Nintendo better than most adults," Campbell's marketing research manager Bill Piszek notes, "the microwave is a lot easier."[109])

The New York Times insightful television critic John J. O'Connor also notes that the joys of junk and fast food may not be the only message conveyed to our children on Saturday mornings.

Certainly, the commercials specifically aimed at young audiences are, at the very least, suspect. They don't only sell products — sugar-saturated and grease-clogged junk food — that arrogantly ignore today's nutritional campaigns. They sell language ('Ain't life delicious,' says the candy spot). More to the point, they sell attitudes and values.

Equally as disturbing as the sexism on so many commercials is the racism, even if unintentional, although Madison Avenue puts so much research into its products that nothing is likely to be unintentional.[110]

Despite a growing concern among many parents and children's advocacy groups about the quality and quantity of advertising aimed at children, President Ronald Reagan in the closing days of his administration vetoed a bill that would have limited the number of television commercials aimed at children.

At the same time, that corporate agribusiness is targeting our nation's youth the USDA school lunch programs are forced to take from what Washington offers from its stock of surplus farm food purchases. As ABC reporter Bonnie Strauss sums up: "So the schools have become a dumping ground for high-fat whole milk, high-fat meats and high-fat cheese."[111]

The Reagan administration's attitude toward the question of nutrition was graphically illustrated in remarks by hog farmer John Block during his 1980 Agricultural Secretary confirmation hearings. He told a Senate Agriculture Committee hearing:

hogs are like people. You can provide protein and grain to a hog and he will balance his ration. People are surely as smart as hogs. I'm not so sure the government needs to get so deeply into telling people what they should or shouldn't eat.[112]

Block also attracted additional derision in 1983 when he and his family spent a week on a food-stamp budget of $58 after which he promptly pronounced that the family's diet was "quite adequate."[113]

Tainted Food

The FDA has also been repeatedly criticized for its slowness in seizing tainted food. A 1984 GAO study found that in 25 of 190 seizures reviewed by the agency's investigators, "all or a large portion of the food had been sold before it could be seized." Most of these cited cases involved food adulterated with "filth," meaning insect fragments and rodent or bird droppings.[114]

According to the GAO study, it takes the Federal government an average of 65 days to process a seizure order, including three reviews at the FDA district level, three more at the Agency's headquarters, and two at the Justice Department. In 76 of the seizures reported in its study, the GAO found that the food firms agreed to hold their product, but 19 reneged and "distributed or sold all or part of the food while awaiting FDA seizure action."[115]

Reviewing 82,000 samples tested by the FDA between 1983 and 1985 the GAO found that the inspection agency's 19 laboratories took an average of 28 calendar days to complete "product processing." These were not, however, ordinary tests, but rather urgent testing on product samples the FDA had good reason to believe had been tainted. The GAO concluded:

In a current review of pesticide residues in foods, we found that the FDA was not able to prevent any violative products from reaching the consumer because of untimely laboratory processing. By the time the FDA identified the products as violative, they were often no longer available because most agricultural products are perishable and therefore move rapidly from farms to consumers.[116]

Critics of the FDA approach note that the enormous size of food factories today, the length of the distribution chain, and the fact that fewer and fewer companies are acquiring larger and larger market shares by concentrating their manufacturing facilities means that food processed in one state is now sometimes eaten by persons on the other side of the continent. This leads to increased possibilities of mishandling along the way.

What Is That Glowing in the Kitchen?

In addition to these aforementioned problems modern technology now seeks to add yet another foreboding, new process in food manufacturing that raises a number of health questions medical experts have barely begun to understand.

Food irradiation, a process in which gamma rays, X-rays or electrons are passed through food or a food package to kill insects, molds or microorganisms that can lead to spoilage or disease, is rapidly gaining popularity among corporate agribusiness companies, which praise it for its safety and its extraordinary ability to extend the shelf life of foods.

Despite the fact that food irradiation has never been proven safe at even low doses, the FDA has approved its use on pork, wheat, flour, potatoes, fruits and vegetables, spices and vegetable seasonings — even though a Congressional amendment to the Food and Drug Act says that irradiation is to be treated as a food additive, subject to the same safety testing required of any new additives.

Meanwhile, a growing body of evidence suggests that irradiation on the food supply may have very serious health and environmental consequences, and severe economic effects as well. Critics contend that the issue of food irradiation turns on two major issues: safety and the consumer's right to know.

While claiming that food irradiation would end the need for chemical poisons in pest control, tests conducted on lab animals eating irradiated food have shown mixed results. According to an internal 1982 FDA review, 84 percent of 413 studies were inconclusive or inadequate while only one percent of the remaining 69 studies "appeared to support safety."[117] (Many of those tests, incidentally, were conducted by the aforementioned Industrial Biotest Laboratories, the company found guilty in 1983 of falsifying chemical poison tests for the EPA.)

It should also be pointed out that irradiation would not necessarily reduce the use of chemical poisons on food. The irradiation process would come after the harvest, so all the chemicals used in growing the food would continue to be used and no one really knows what would happen to those chemical residues after being irradiated.

Dr. John Gofman, professor emeritus of medical physics at the University of California in Berkeley and a world-renowned authority on low level radiation, further questions whether any genuine research on the matter of food irradiation has been carried out to date and even if such testing is possible.

> The kind of epidemiological study required to find out whether or not a diet of irradiated food will increase (or possibly decrease) the frequency of cancer or genetic injuries among humans simply has not been done. What is more, such a study is unlikely ever to be done, because it would require controlling the diets of at least 200,000 humans of various age-groups for at least 30 years, and following their health-histories for at least 50 years (preferably their full life spans).[118]

There are some fruits and vegetables, according to Sharon Bomer, chairperson of the Coalition for Food Irradiation and director of government relations for the United Fresh Fruit and Vegetable Association, that just do not irradiate well, or that actually become more sensitive to spoilage after being irradiated. She cites as examples sweet corn, green beans, cucumbers, grapes, lemons, limes, bell peppers and summer squash.[120]

"Radiation is a carcinogen, mutagen and teratogen," Dr. Geraldine Dettman, a safety officer at Brown University, points out. She notes that,

> at doses of 100,000 rads on fruits and vegetables, the cells of the fruits and vegetables will be killed, and most insect larvae will be destroyed, but fungi, bacteria and viruses growing on the fruit and vegetables will not be killed ... They will be mutated, possibly leading to more virulent contaminants.[121]

Whether consumers would even know that their food had been bombarded with gamma rays, X-rays, etc. is another crucial question. The FDA currently requires "any source of radiation" used in food processing or packaging to be labeled. However, the food industry is now seeking to change the definition of radiation from an "additive" to a "process," which is not required to be identified on food labels.

Proposals published in *The Federal Register* by the FDA would require that the words "treated with radiation" appear on all irradiated foods not sold in combination with other foods. Only "whole" irradiated foods such as fruits and vegetables are now required to be labelled, not the irradiated ingredients of processed products, such as certain fruits in cans of fruit salad.[122]

Massachusetts Institute of Technology's Department of Nutrition and Food Science professors Julius Coon and Edward Josephson argue that "labeling would tend to have an unfavorable psychological effect by implying that, in the view of health regulatory authorities, the safety of the labelled product is questionable, and the purchaser will be using it at his or her own risk."[123]

Sensitive to such pressure the FDA has announced that produce treated with low-level radiation were sold in supermarkets in the Pacific Northwest during the fall of 1986 in a limited-market test of consumer acceptance. However, it was noted that the sale locations were kept secret "because of fear of protesters."[124]

Grocery Communications, a food industry trade publication has further suggested that,

> one way of circumventing the labelling requirement, of course, would be to find a publicly acceptable euphemism for irradiation. "Picowave," "electron beam," and "ionizing energy" have all been suggested, though whether public fears would be pacified by a subterfuge is debatable.[125]

Or, as one labeling proponent noted "labeling would give irradiation the kiss of death."[126]

The health effect of food irradiation, however, is just one of the nightmarish consequences of utilizing such a process in the manufacturing of our food.

There are also environmental and safety issues relating to the dangers of trafficking nuclear materials through many of our communities. The Department of Energy (DOE), not surprisingly a supporter of food irradiation, has even advanced the idea of building *mobile* food irradiation units, which would move to different farm areas to irradiate crops immediately after harvesting. Not only would this lead to further centralization of agriculture as regional production would be required, but plant species would have to be further hybridized to facilitate radiation tolerance, thus increasing crop vulnerabilities.

Advocates of food irradiation have already begun to speak in terms of reducing the disposal costs of nuclear plant wastes whose byproducts could be utilized by 1,000 different food processing plants to be scattered throughout the nation. Currently, the Nuclear Regulatory Commission has licensed some 40 facilities to use nuclear materials in the manufacture or processing of commercial products, including food.

Robert Alvarez, past director of the Nuclear Weapons and Power Project at the Environmental Policy Institute, has pointed out that,

> much of the research on the safety of irradiated foods has been done by the U.S. Army.
>
> Thus, it comes as no surprise that the nuclear weapons FY1986 budget for the DOE contains the primary source of funds for research, development and commercialization of food irradiation. This is because the nuclear weapons program has generated enormous amounts of intensely radioactive waste byproducts from the production of nuclear explosive materials like plutonium. At DOE's Hanford, Washington facility, 80 to 90 million curies of radiocesium has been separated and has been encapsulated for commercial use.[127]

Testifying before a 1985 hearing of the Subcommittee on Department Operations, Research and Foreign Agriculture of the House Committee on Agriculture,

Alvarez voiced the EPI's opposition to H.R. 696. The bill, introduced by Representative Sidney Morrison, R-Wash., whose district includes the Hanford nuclear facility, forbad state and local governments from regulating food irradiation independently and forbad them to require consumer labeling or other consumer protection not required under federal law. Alvarez further noted:

> The irradiation of food involves an ultrahazardous technology which poses several types of risks to the public and workers ... one food irradiation facility will be generating as much as ten times more low-level radioactive wastes (in curie content) than all sources combined in the United States for the year 1981.[128]

Maine, New Jersey and New York have already adopted legislation restricting food irradiation and five other states are considering similar measures.[129] For example, the fear of exposure to such radiation provoked the citizens of Dublin, California to prevent the bid of a not-for-profit research group called National Food Processors (formerly the National Canners Association) from opening a pilot plant in their community, which they have proclaimed a "nuclear-free zone."[130]

Martin A. Welt, chairman and president of Radiation Technology Inc. and one of the nation's most outspoken advocates of food irradiation for the past 18 years, believes it is "*the* most important food-preservation technique for mankind" and that "no other method will do so much for public health." The public, however, does not agree with Welt. Survey after survey shows that a majority of people would not buy food that has been subjected to radiation.[131]

It is also worth noting that Welt's firm, which reported sales of $2.1 million in 1986, operating four irradiation plants in New Jersey, Arkansas and North Carolina, has been repeatedly cited by the Nuclear Regulatory Commission (NRC) for operating its Rockaway, New Jersey plant in a manner that could jeopardize the safety of its workers — and in one case resulted in a worker being severely exposed to radiation.

In March 1988 Radiation Technology pleaded guilty to charges that it submitted falsified documents to the NRC concerning safety procedures at its plant in Rockaway. It also admitted that its officials had lied to NRC investigators and radiation specialists about the length of time it operated without radiation safety monitoring equipment in place.[132]

Four months later Welt was found guilty by a federal jury of ordering his workers to bypass safety devices and lie about it to federal inspectors.[133]

Irradiating food would also further concentrate the food processing and manufacturing industry and rob many farmers of their traditional markets by making it infinitely easier for multinational corporate agribusiness firms to preserve a whole variety of *imported* previously perishable crops. This would allow food manufacturers to further exploit tenant farmers and peasant slave labor in other nations while accelerating their planned and continuing permanent displacement of U.S. farmers.

As we have seen, U.S. food producers already face competition from imports which are cheap because they are grown and harvested by workers paid the bare minimum wage. Irradiation of foreign produce would only add to this stream of imports while encouraging further exploitation of the poor in other lands. As Alvarez has pointed out:

> For several years, polls of the America public have consistently shown that shoppers are not interested in buying food if they know it has been irradiated... the Reagan administration is no doubt aware of this fact and is aggressively promoting food irradiation through its foreign aid programs, particularly the Agency for International Development (AID). Food irradiation facilities are being planned for several developing nations which lack even a minimal regulatory program for such an ultrahazardous industry.[134]

"The Solution Is To Stop!"

As corporate agribusiness continues to search for continued new ways to engineer food, extend shelf life, and enlarge market shares, Vicki Williams, King Features columnist, best summarizes growing public frustration over the claims and counterclaims regarding the integrity of those products it manufactures and that we eat:

> The only time I felt truly comfortable about the food I put on my table was when I lived on the farm and grew most of my own ... Now, I live in an apartment in the city, and am dependent on nameless, faceless strangers to grow, process and ship my food. It seems as if unethical and unsafe practices grow in direct proportion to how far we have lost the trail of accountability. So I don't always trust them to put my family's best interest over concern for their bottom line. I don't like feeling helpless, as if every trip to the grocery is a crap shoot. But I really don't know who to blame.[135]

What can be done about this alarming situation?

Several years ago Ross Hume Hall offered a rather unique but obvious suggestion to a national television audience on the NBC-TV produced-documentary "What Is This Thing Called Food": "You could put every scientist and biologist in the United States on this problem and there still would be no solution. *The solution is to stop!* To stop the technology. To hold it in abeyance until such time as we have an idea what is going on."

Section Three:

The Evolution of a Policy

A proud hog farmer had three sons, two of whom decided to attend the nearby state college while the third son remained on the homestead to help the family with the day-to-day chores. Like many of his neighbors the farmer was growing increasingly concerned as both his feed bills were skyrocketing while at the same time it seemed that an inordinate amount of the feed was getting wasted by the hogs at feeding time.

One Sunday afternoon when all the family was seated around the dinner table he expressed this growing concern to his three sons and his wife.

One son, who was studying to become an agricultural economist, suggested that his father redesign the feeding troughs so they were both narrow and deep. He further thought that when the family filled the troughs with feed they should only fill them half full so no feed would be spilled on the ground and get wasted.

The second son, who was studying to be a social scientist, promptly disagreed and suggested that a trough be built that was both wide and shallow and that the feed be filled right to the top so all the hogs could get plenty of feed and grow up to be big and fat.

The third son, who had been listening patiently and quietly to his two older brothers all this time slowly began shaking his head from side to side and turning to his father drawled, "Dad, the consumption and waste troubles we're having here on the farm are not going to be solved by the size of our feeding troughs or how much feed we put in those troughs, our main problem is the big hogs!"

Chapter Ten: Breaking the Plains

Chapter Eleven: A Populism Born and Bred in Agrarian Revolt

Chapter Twelve: Agriculture's "Golden Years"

Chapter Thirteen: An "Interplay of Economic Forces"

Chapter Fourteen: Fighting for "Equality for Agriculture"

Chapter Fifteen: "Oh Say to Him, Stuff and Nonsense"

Chapter Sixteen: A "New and Untrod Path"

Chapter Seventeen: Liberty Vs. Paternalism

Chapter Eighteen: War and Peace

Chapter Nineteen: Peace and War

Chapter Twenty: "Adapt or Die"

Chapter Twenty-One: "New Frontiers" and New Challenges

Chapter Twenty-Two: Ifs, Ands and Butz

Chapter Ten

Breaking the Plains

From the moment the first discoverer arrived in North America, the continent's bountiful agricultural system has involved a never-ending search by a few to mine its abundant natural resources, quantify them in monetary terms, and convert them into value-added, cash-rich manufactured commodities.

Throughout U.S. history we have seen government and business, with the latter's interests largely uppermost in mind, actively pursue policies and programs designed to exploit from "sea to shining sea" this nation's vast treasure-trove of natural and human resources.

But as Joseph Petulla stresses in *American Environmental History: The Exploitation and Conservation of Natural Resources*, the problem is multidimensional:

It is almost an understatement to assert that Americans have been all too willing to exploit natural resources to their limits for personal gain. But to decry America's materialism and greedy profit-seeking, its collective attitudes of waste, would be an oversimplified moralization. Attitudes — materialistic or otherwise — are born in history.

Economic, political and social institutions create a culture and a mentality which in turn live long after those institutions have given way to new structures. With them technologies are developed to meet new needs and engender habits, even new cultures of their own. Economies and politics, attitudes and beliefs, technologies and habits — these variables interact in a complex web of relationships in the creation of a culture.[1]

Breaking the Plains

In a very real sense, the history of American agriculture is less a series of revolutions than a continuing revolution based primarily on increasing productivity per dollar and per worker invested. For nearly 200 years the nation was wedded to a policy of land settlement based on an abundance of land and a scarcity of labor. Then from hand to animal power to tractor power to high technology this agrarian revolution became characterized by a dehumanization process which has worked in concert with the exploitation of natural resources exclusively for market profitability.

As Dr. Petulla points out, American exploitative attitudes:

were derived from the specific historical situations. Natural resources were available for the taking; social status came from rapid material advancement and affluence; economic opportunities encourage risk and the plunder of nature; national policy opened increasingly larger areas of land and subsequent markets; technologies to exploit and more resources followed the need; the 'good life' and economic security seemed to require an ever-increasing rate of resource exploitation.[2]

Land and Land Ownership

Land has always been agriculture's most valuable resource and this nation's cornerstone of individual wealth. How that land was to be used, who controlled its riches, and what the structure of American agriculture was to be were all issues that helped spark the American Revolution.

The prominent agricultural historian Wayne D. Rasmussen reminds us, that when we speak of such structures we are talking about the basic control and organization of societal resources. "Questions of farm structures have always related to the structure of the entire food and fiber system and, indeed to the total economic, social and political organization of the United States."[3]

When the early English colonists first settled in America, they faced the "quit-rent" system, a holdover from the centuries-old "land ownership" system in Europe. Under such a system tenants could only get title to land subject to a perpetual fee paid to an absentee landlord who usually resided in England.

In addition to this "quit-rent" system, the new farmers also came to resent the British government's efforts after 1763 to forbid the establishment of settlements west of the Alleghenies and its efforts to control the marketing of products from that area by imposing a series of unfair taxes. These three efforts by the British to regulate the structure of American agriculture became the basic causes for the American Revolution, a war that was led and fought mostly by planters and farmers.

Soon after independence was proclaimed and a federal constitution established, the fledgling government sought a land policy that would discourage sectionalism and provide an equal opportunity for citizens to become landowners. By developing a township and range land survey system the Federal government sought to divide blocks of property equally so as to provide equal access to the land. Feudal estates modeled after traditional Western European land holdings were already in existence, however, in the new land along with other various and sundry political and religiously organized villages, located principally in New England.

When the early settlers began to move inland at the end of the 18th century, small-scale farming began to dominate the agricultural scene. Such a trend alarmed industrialists, bankers and the large plantation owners because it signaled the effort by the new settlers to distribute the country's real wealth — its natural resources — into as many hands as possible.

The consequences of this conflict soon became apparent, for in this colonial period the dual U.S. agricultural economy that persists to this day first emerged. On the one hand there was the traditional subsistence form of agriculture while on the other hand was a system destined to become the forerunner of modern corporate agribusiness.

The Opening Struggles for an Egalitarian Land Base

Geographer Ingolf Voegler has pointed out that the land-settling efforts by early pioneers reflected a desire to achieve an egalitarian land base. He reminds us that it was that revolutionary concept through which economic democracy was meant to sustain political democracy. This same idea would come to inspire millions of people from abroad to settle in this new, rich nation and/or attempt to emulate its ideals elsewhere in the world.

For Jefferson and other eighteenth-century intellectuals, a nation of small farmers would provide political freedom, independence and self-reliance, and the ability to resist political oppression. In their minds, these goals were predicated on the right to own property, especially land. The right to land, the primary form of wealth in the eighteenth century, meant the right to a job and economic independence.[4]

Jefferson reasoned that in a democracy, access to the land must be provided by the national government.

Whenever there are in any country uncultivated lands and unemployed poor, it is clear that the laws of property have been so far extended as to violate a natural right. The earth is given as a common stock for man to labor and live on. If for the encouragement of industry, we allow it to be appropriated, we must take care that other employment be provided to those excluded from the appropriation. If we do not, the fundamental right to labor the earth returns to the unemployed.[5]

Unfortunately, the Ordinance of 1785 is an early illustration of America's enduring failure to ensure that land distribution shall be determined through a system that recognizes "equal justice under law." This ordinance, which authorized the survey of all U.S.-owned lands ahead of settlement into six-mile square townships and square-mile sections of 640 acres, was drafted by a committee chaired by Jefferson. Although the prevailing philosophy of agrarian democracy that motivated the

ordinance was a dominant influence for 75 years, in practice the ideal was poorly served.

From the start, for example, Alexander Hamilton envisioned speculators and land companies, not individuals, becoming the principal buyers of public land. In turn, such entities would then be free to sell off that land to actual settlers for a profit. In fact, this did happen and it was not until the Homestead Act of 1862 that this practice was changed.

The 1785 Ordinance also stipulated that one-half of the townships were to be sold as a whole and the other half in 640-acre sections. But, because such sales were by the auction system, it would become relatively easy for land companies and speculators to gain large tracts of land at cheap prices and then resell them at excessive profits to actual settlers. Over 220 million acres would eventually be bought and sold in this fashion.

Unfortunately Jefferson's belief that square grids were intrinsically democratic led him to overlook existing geographical differences, which from the start were a complicating factor — one that quickly led to the packaging of land parcels and the advent of a lucrative and flourishing real estate business in America.[6]

The government began selling land at prices considerably higher than its original purchase price, which discouraged actual settlers from purchasing it. The cost to the federal government, including interest, of the major and historic land purchases of the early 19th century was four and one-half cents per acre. Much of this same land, under the provisions of the 1785 ordinance, was in turn sold to settlers for over one dollar per acre. Revenue realized from these sales, of course, was a key means by which the Federal government, composed at the time of many large landowners, generated revenues.

A newly adopted Federal Constitution and an ever-expanding market for American goods prepared the groundwork for later technological innovations that would encourage new economic and social developments in agriculture. One has only to look at the composition of the delegates to the convention which drafted this Constitution to see that while future expansion of the national economy was important, protecting immediate selfish financial interests was vital to many of its drafters. Of the 55 delegates to the Constitutional Convention, 40 were holders of public securities, 14 were land speculators, 24 were moneylenders, 15 slave owners, and at least 11 were entrepreneurs. No one represented small farmers or artisans.[7]

The Advent of Commercial Agriculture

The Constitution's delegation of power to Congress to "pay the debts of the United States" provided the opportunity for Alexander Hamilton, the nation's first Secretary of the Treasury, to induce Congress to assume all of the Revolutionary War's debts.

By using tariffs and excise taxes on whiskey, Hamilton curried favor with Eastern merchants, manufacturers and other money lenders who profited from such federal largesse, but at the same time he angered and alienated small farmers, whose corn whiskey stills were being taxed, forcing them to pay higher prices for their imported goods. It was this action that fomented numerous small protests leading to uprisings such as the famous Whiskey Rebellion, which many regard as the first of this nation's farm protest movements.[8]

Further, in discharging the public debt through forced savings, Hamilton's policies put surplus capital in the hands of an aggressive entrepreneurial class seeking to reinvest in land speculation and manufacturing. Such actions so outraged Southern planters and yeoman farmers of the South and West that rather than allying themselves with the Federalist Party they became a restless faction of the Jeffersonian Republican Party, an alliance which endured for nearly half a century.

Throughout the early years of the republic farmers continued to strive for significant political victories, namely the effort to gain access to the ballot box (which they finally came to realize with the advent of Jacksonian democracy) in addition to searching for ways to transfer more of the public domain into many private hands and secure tariff laws that would protect and enhance their burgeoning economic system.

In the 1787 Constitutional Convention they managed to gain a general agreement on some duties on imported goods and the prohibition of tariffs on exports. At the same time, new roads, canals and railroads began opening up markets for agriculture and industry in the west. By 1820 about 80 percent of all food products grown on northern farms were consumed by rural populations.[9]

Until this time many farmers had mainly traded their surplus goods for cash in order to buy basic necessities for themselves and their families or to pay off loans on their equipment and land. In the early 1800s, however, they chose a more commercial type of agriculture, buying land and raising crops near urban areas, then near waterways where they could more easily transport their products to the east. By 1840 the era of regional specialization had set in.

In that process some farmers who found that they had already exhausted the soils in New England simply abandoned them and moved on to the more fertile, low-cost lands in the West. As one environmental historian remarked:

In the first two generations of the nineteenth century, almost everything happened to the land that could have happened to it. It was bought, sold, bloodied. Its soil was mined and abandoned, picked over, passed around and abused. It was also nurtured and cultivated, divided into lots great and small.[10]

Replacing Northeastern Indians with European settlers and the Indians' stable land-extensive system of rotating crops with a labor-and-land exhausting, highoff-the-food-chain system, farmers began to accelerate production rapidly, using horsepower, rather than oxen. By the outbreak of the Civil War, the percentage of farmers was already beginning to decrease as more money and more machines began producing a larger and larger share of the nation's food.

Precipitated Expansion and the "Squatters"

During this post-Revolutionary War period a pattern emerged which has persistently plagued American agriculture through the years. In each major war the nation has fought, increased demand on the farmer for food and fiber during the hostilities has led to inflated prices. This in turn has precipitated expansion based mainly on credit, which later takes its exacting toll as prices drop and money becomes scarce.

Here we see yet another of U.S. agriculture's recurring myths, *i.e.*, farmers should be able to eke out an existence for themselves on a day-to-day basis in not so prosperous periods on the profits they earn during periods when land values are high. Debunking such a myth, Fred A. Shannon points out in *American Farmers' Movements*:

In the first place, for nearly three centuries in America a good share of [the farmers] all were constantly on the move. Many were squatters on the public domain who ultimately had to buy their acres, surrender them to other purchasers, or, if lucky, receive pay for improvements. Land did, in the long run, increase in value, but along an irregular curve instead of an inclined plane.

The urge to expand operations in prosperous times resulted in contracts at high prices for land and equipment that could not be retained during the following depression. So the mortgage holders took the profits. When crops brought little, farmers had not the means to buy for speculative holding and therefore were not the ones who gained as times improved. More often, they lost their freeholds and became tenants.[11]

Although the land parcels available through the provisions of the Ordinance of 1785 were physically within the reach of most settlers, the price of that land frequently made it impossible for them to buy. Out of this dilemma a new class was born called "squatters."

Despite high prices for land, western migration was still an attractive alternative and many easterners and European immigrants began the search for property of their own on which to settle. Meanwhile, the presence of land jobbers was assuring the government of high prices for this new land, particularly for the cotton lands of the eastern Mississippi region. In Indiana and Illinois, however, where these jobbers were scarce, settlers were able to buy good farm land inexpensively.

As these new settlers moved west, classic battle lines were drawn among the business community, organized labor, rural people and farmers. It was farmers, however, who were often used as the unwilling, but principal and constantly manipulated economic variable in these struggles. The same battles continue to this day, although they have become far more subtle, sophisticated and complex skirmishes then those in the early 1800s.

It was after the 1818-19 inflation that the bottom fell out of the land buying business. Until that time speculative land buying was encouraged by several circumstances: high prices for goods, especially cotton, at home and abroad; ill-conceived efforts to establish state and private banks, which indiscriminately gave out credit, and the general westward movement after the War of 1812, which saw an unprecedented small labor surplus develop in the east.

Preparing the Ground for the Preemption Acts

When overproduction caused the price of cotton to fall to half its former price and the ensuing debt load became too great for many land buyers, banks failed and credit suddenly disappeared, along with paper money and specie. Land prices plummeted and crops began to rot in the fields. Relief was sought from Congress and by 1832 some 11 relief acts had been passed.[12]

As agrarian America began to discover its political muscle, Eastern manufacturers and their representatives in Congress became correspondingly alarmed. Their initial efforts to head off the formation of the new Democratic Party, which sought to bring together agrarian interests in the east and in the states south and west of the Appalachians along with a "shadow" labor movement, failed. Consequently, under the banner of the new party Andrew Jackson became president in 1832.

An early success of this new coalition was its role in the passage of the Preemption Act of 1830. This act made it possible for settlers to buy up to 160 acres of unsurveyed public land for $1.25 an acre after a 14-month residence on the land. Two years later 40 acre tracts became available under these same provisions.[13]

By encouraging these new settlers, northeastern labor organizations saw an opportunity to reduce the number of urban workers and thereby make it easier to demand higher wages for their members. Western politicians saw the new land owners and "squatters" as presenting an opportunity to add new wealth to the area and, with the influx of new people, to build farms, roads, schools and towns.

Northern industrialists and southern plantation owners, however, disliked the idea. A small urban work force would mean higher wages, better working conditions and less profits for the industrialist. Opportunities to start new farms would also provide a chance for blacks to escape the poverty of plantation slavery and the south.

Arguments against the Preemption Act of 1830 in Congress reflected these narrow concerns of established eastern wealth as opposed to the West's efforts to generate new capital. Preemption was resisted on the grounds that:

1) the government would lack the authority to enforce law and order;

2) the labor supply of the eastern states would diminish and thus wages would rise and profits fall for industrialists;

3) the principle of public lands as a source of revenue would be destroyed; and

4) preemption would provide a bounty to the new western states that was denied to the older, already settled eastern states.

Although the act was passed, squatters were actively discouraged from settling on new land; the federal government actually instructed the militia to evict them and burn their farms and cabins. The squatters, however, soon began to resist physically the Army's effort to deny them land and the other attempts to auction it away from them.

Despite the intent of the preemption acts fledgling farmers were progressively undermined and circumvented. For example, before the acts were repealed in 1891, in many states fraudulent entries ranged between 70 percent to 90 percent of all the land claims.[14]

Fostering Rural Poverty

Meanwhile, in an effort to avoid the force of the 1830s acts, over seven million acres of Indian lands, which were supposed to be held in trust by the federal government through executive treaties, were sold by the time of the Civil War. Still another scheme to circumvent the preemption act was the obtaining of land under Spanish and Mexican land grant claims.

Throughout what is now the Southwestern United States, Americans were in the process of claiming extensive Spanish and Mexican estates on territory bought, stolen and annexed by the United States. Protected by a Supreme Court ruling that stipulated "that the right of private property in land in the acquired territories should not be affected by the change in sovereignty regardless of treaty stipulation," over 34.6 million acres was kept out of the public domain.[15]

While a large measure of the claims on this land was later rejected due to fraud, or antedated and blatantly forged documents, or found contrary to Mexican law, many others were honored with last-minute land transfers clearly designed to avoid the preemption acts.

The south and southwest, notably California, Arizona and New Mexico, the site of vast land-based fortunes, areas historically dominated by the plantation system and the huge Spanish land grant estates, that have historically been the nation's two most persistent areas of rural poverty. It is principally in the northeast and midwest where, at least until recent years, a "family farm system" of agriculture, has prevailed.[16]

Fueling the War Between the States

These divisions in the structure of American agriculture were also major catalysts in provoking what historians still describe as this nation's most disastrous and traumatic war.

After the American Revolution a dying farm system in the south, badly hurt by the loss of its tobacco export markets, was struggling to recover. Eli Whitney revolutionized that effort with his invention of the cotton gin in 1793. Plantation agriculture began once again to dominate the economic, social and political structure of the entire region. The South's dependence on the export of "King Cotton," however, soon found the area economically exploited by northern industrialists, largely through the use of restrictive tariffs. The processing of southern farm commodities in the south, for example, was discouraged as high freight rate differentials were systematically biased against southern goods.

Using these heavy tariffs to control the flow of processed goods, the north rapidly subsidized its own industrial growth at the expense of the South's exports of cotton. Economist Michael Perelman notes that "by transferring the profits skimmed off the cotton and tobacco trade into manufacturing investments, the Northern bankers were able to transform the sweat of slaves into the vital fluids of industry."[17]

Northern family farms produced primarily for domestic consumption. Southern agriculture, centered around slave labor and its one cash crop — cotton — was sold solely for export, making the area almost wholly dependent on the north for its basic food stuffs. This clash of the two different agriculture structures and economic systems became a major factor in precipitating "the war between the states."

By the time the nation began spilling its own blood in the Civil War, regional specialization had also brought on a certain new affluence to a sizeable portion of the infant nation. The independent yeoman of earlier years in the west was no longer a pioneer. Money had to be borrowed from the bank, credit to buy machinery from farm equipment companies was necessary, commodities were sold to middlemen at unpredictable prices, livestock was taken by drovers to distant markets on commission, and crops were raised less for home use than to feed others.

U.S. food and fiber was now being sold in the world's markets, from the south's cotton to the wheat and livestock raised by a growing number of farmers west of the Appalachians. The mining and the processing of untapped natural resources also accelerated to such a degree that it would soon become a major U.S. industry.

As the war raged on, northwestern farming centers like Illinois, Iowa and Wisconsin faced severe depression resulting from several causes: there were huge agricultural surpluses since few if any foreign export markets were available; the nation's meager transportation facilities were almost being totally utilized as part of the war effort, and no crops, of course, were moving from the north into the Confederacy.[18]

The south, meanwhile, was suffering from critical food shortages. Believing that the price of cotton would remain high, southern planters had ignored repeated calls to grow subsistence crops. Famine soon threatened the entire Confederacy, civil chaos increased and eventually the scarcity of food became one of the major reasons for the South's defeat at the hands of the Union forces.

A War-Ravaged Nation Looks West

In near ruin and plagued by droughts in 1865 and 1867 family farmers were slow in restoring southern agriculture. To the dismay of many northerners, however, the region's plantations and large estates were not broken up, nor was the land distributed to the freed slaves and poor whites. Generally, the big landowners sold their other properties to pay off mortgages or taxes on the plantation, and thereby managed to keep most of their large estates intact.

Yet, the Civil War profoundly changed the character of farm politics, as it did politics in general. Southern farmers became Democrats, while in the North the Republican Party, until the 1896 election, became the party of hope, free land, anti-slavery and the U.S. "family farm system."

By the mid-1800s, Congress had begun passing laws to modify and in some cases even change the traditional structure of agriculture. The historic Homestead Act of 1862, an effort to reassert the Jeffersonian ideal and open the West for development, the establishment of the U.S. Department of Agriculture, the beginnings of the land grant college complex, and the subsidizing of the building of the transcontinental railroad all immediately and profoundly shaped the future course of American agriculture and the nation in general.

The latter project, which opened up the long-awaited direct route to the Orient for eastern industrial traders, also acted as an income "multiplier" for badly needed economic development for a war-weary nation.[19]

But, more importantly, this transcontinental railroad hastened regional specialization in agriculture by encouraging western settlement and assuring the industrial centers of the nation and a growing commodities market and food manufacturing industry a crucial degree of crop overproduction. Corporate planners began to see such a condition as vital to their long-term future success.

For if farming was destined to become a large corporate enterprise, creating crop "surpluses" while eradicating the independent producer of raw materials, it was also to be a key instrument in hastening that day when technology could be substituted for labor and capital for efficiency.

Chapter Eleven

A Populism Born and Bred in Agrarian Revolt

"We have come to claim our promise, O Oz."

"What promise?" asked Oz.

"You promised to send me back to Kansas when the Wicked Witch was destroyed," said the girl.

"And you promised to give me brains," said the Scarecrow.

"And you promised to give me a heart," said the Tin Woodsman.

"And you promised to give me courage," said the Cowardly Lion.

"Is the Wicked Witch really destroyed?" asked the voice, and Dorothy thought it trembled a little.

"Yes," she answered, "I melted her with a bucket of water."

"Dear me," said the Voice; "how sudden! Well, come to me tomorrow, for I must have time to think it over."

"You've had plenty of time already," said the Tin Woodsman, angrily.

"We shan't wait a day longer," said the Scarecrow.

"You must keep your promises to us!" exclaimed Dorothy."

- *The Wizard of Oz* by L. Frank Baum, from "The Critical Heritage Series with pictures by W.W. Denslow, Michael Patrick Hearn, Editor, Schocken Books, New York: 1983.

It was at this pivotal time in American history, with the U. S. western frontier rapidly expanding and a war-devastated South turning to "reconstruction," that the magnitude of the nation's deep-seated rural discontent manifested itself and evolved into a populist rebellion, born and bred in agrarian revolt.

University of Chicago historian Thomas C. Holt sees a distinct parallel between this chapter in the American saga and our lives in the 1980s. Writing in *The Washington Post's* "Book World" in May 1988 he observes:

The Reconstruction era, 1863 to 1877, bears an uncanny resemblance — in both trivial and profound aspects — to our own recent history. During each period, America, deeply scarred and uncertain, emerged from a divisive war. As the nation attempted to heal those scars, the pre-war generation's idealism turned rancid, moral fervor gave way to indifference, the reaction impulse was suffocated by an unembarrassed embrace of capitalist values and beatification of selfishness. And, most of all, in both periods the nation's commitment to achieve racial justice was left unfinished.

Certainly "in both trivial and profound aspects" the interests of today's corporate agribusiness stand in stark contrast to the concerns and values of family farmers, just as they did in the post-Civil War era.

As a burgeoning western agriculture increasingly found itself at the mercy of the Eastern railroads, grain elevator companies, money markets, industrial trusts, etc., so the South found itself almost totally dependent on the north for food staples and processing facilities. Laborless Southern planters and jobless blacks came together to form a system not too unlike the one they had been a part of before the conflict.

With "emancipation," sharecropping and the so-called "convict lease" system, the freedom of blacks consisted of little more than being able to move from place to place, but still very much *within* the plantation system. In some states, Black Codes even allowed marshalls to pick up and convict unemployed blacks and have them immediately sentenced to a year or more of work on roads or on a local plantation.

Sharecropping, on the other hand, was built on a "sharing system" where the farmer took the risk and the planter took the crop. This new arrangement provided other advantages for plantation owners. They were now assured of a supply of cheap, guaranteed labor, labor that would be available until "settlement time" which by its very nature reduced the threat of interplantation competition, particularly at harvest time.

"No Money Changed Hands"

Through this "crop lien system" planters were provided with ample opportunity to cheat their workers, if they so desired. This was often done by those operating plantation stores.

In *Democratic Promise: The Populist Moment in America*, Lawrence Goodwyn graphically portrays the scenes that occurred daily for decades in the South under the "crop lien system":

The farmer, his eyes downcast and his hat sometimes literally in his hand, approached the merchant with a list of his needs. The man behind the counter consulted a ledger, and after a mumbled exchange, moved to his shelves to select the goods that would satisfy at least a part of his customer's wants. Rarely did the farmer receive the range of items or even the quantity of one item that he had requested. No money changed hands; the merchant merely made brief notations in his ledger.

Two weeks or a month later, the farmer would return, the consultation with the ledger would recur, the mumbled exchange and the careful selection of goods would ensue, and new additions would be noted in the ledger.

From early spring to late fall, the little ritual would be enacted until, at 'settlin' up' time, the farmer and the merchants would meet at the local cotton gin, where the fruits of a year's toil would be ginned, bagged, tied and weighed, and sold. At that moment, the farmer would learn what his cotton had brought.

The merchant, who had possessed title to the crop even before the farmer had planted it, then consulted his ledger for a final time. The accumulated debt for the year, he informed the farmer, exceeded the income received from the cotton crop. The farmer had failed in his effort to 'pay out' — he still owed the merchant a remaining balance for the supplies 'furnished' on credit during the year.

The 'furnishing merchant' would then announce his intention to carry the farmer through the winter on a new account, the latter merely having to sign a note mortgaging to the merchant the next year's crop. The lien signed, the farmer, empty-handed, climbed in his wagon and drove home, carrying with him the knowledge that for the second or fifth, of fifteenth year in a row he had not paid out.[1]

These furnishing merchants, who often were paying 18 percent or more for credit extended by Northern banks, bought most of the needed supplies and equipment and then "furnished" them to penniless farmers, usually in excess of 100 percent annually, and often over 200 percent. They used a simple "two-price scale" — one price for cash customers and a higher price for credit customers. Farmers were often not aware of the disparity between the two prices since they were forced to do nearly all their business exclusively on credit.

For millions of Southerners this system was simply a modified form of slavery. "When one of these mortgages has been recorded against the Southern farmer," wrote one commentator,

he had usually passed into a state of helpless peonage ... with the surrender of this evidence of

indebtedness he has also surrendered his freedom of action and his industrial autonomy. From this time until he has paid the last dollar of his indebtedness, he is subject to the constant oversight and direction of the merchant.[2]

Both the furnishing merchants and the Southern planters were to a large measure dependent on northern capital. There is some evidence that several of the resurrected banks that began to do business at this time in the south were simply creatures of the furnishing merchants.

Not only had the end of the war invalidated all Confederate currency, but many Southern banks had failed. Massachusetts alone had nearly five times as much national bank circulation as the entire south. While the per capita figure in Rhode Island was $77.16, Arkansas had but 13 cents per capita.[3]

Farmers Fight a Contraction in the Money Supply

Of course, the North had fiscal problems of its own. The war had basically been financed by a combination of government loans and the issuance of paper currency (greenbacks). After hostilities ceased, the government sought to redeem these greenbacks with hard currency, thereby contracting the money supply.

Farmers immediately began a fight to prevent such contractions and their struggle would continue for nearly 30 years. They argued that such contractions not only increased the relative size of their debts incurred during the war, but did so at precisely the wrong time; during the harvest currency contractions depressed agricultural prices, which made it all the more difficult for farmers to earn enough income to reduce their previously acquired debt load.

During the Civil War a new national banking system was born, primarily designed to end the chaos of an earlier system dominated by state banks; to create a market for bonds to help finance the war; and to establish an institution of issue that would create a standardized national economy. Farmers were alarmed by this new system, seeing it as yet another effort to centralize the money supply. With local banks depositing reserves in larger banks, which in turn were depositing their reserves in huge Eastern banks, farmers argued that they would rapidly become entirely beholden to the industrial interests of the north and east.

Industry Flourishes, Agriculture Agitates

The Civil War, like the Revolutionary War before it, and World War I and II and the Vietnam War which followed, saw increased industrialization and dramatic changes in the utilization of the nation's natural resources.

The development of new manufacturing methods and the vertical and horizontal integration of the production, processing and marketing phase of many industries by such "captains of industry" as Rockefeller and Carnegie soon resulted in the concentration of the nation's wealth into fewer and fewer hands. The key to that process was the railroads. With the never-ending push west by the "iron horse," land became more valuable and a currency that would become more steadily and relentlessly pursued.

Individuals such as Gustavus F. Swift and James B. Duke were already establishing their own systems of national marketing and distribution for meat (Swift & Co.) and tobacco (American Tobacco Co.) even prior to their developing the production end of their respective businesses.[4]

As industry flourished, an over-productive agriculture, adapting innovations in farm technology, found itself laden with surpluses and in a constant search for new markets. Between 1866 and 1880 over 23 million additional acres were cultivated, increasing annual yields from 152 million to 499 million bushels of wheat alone. As early as 1870, the domestic agriculture market became glutted with corn and wheat, selling at 57 cents and $1.42 a bushel respectively in 1867 and dropping to 32 cents and 78 cents by 1868.[5]

By the early 1870s the nation was in the midst of the most severe depression in its history. A farm surplus, a drop in commodity prices and another sharp contraction in the money supply all were major contributors to this collapse.

On September 19, 1873 the mammoth Jay Cooke and Co. closed its doors due to overextension, trying to drive its Northern Pacific railroad deep into the Red River region of Minnesota and the Dakotas. The Panic of 1873 ensued: businesses failed, unemployment doubled and numerous strikes for higher pay and outbreaks of violence quickly followed.[6]

Agriculture began calling for a greater emphasis on expanding export markets by improving and regulating the nation's transportation system. The farmers' agitation with the railroads was reflected by Minnesota Governor Cushman Kellogg Davis's charge that the underlying troubles were caused by,

> capital — corporate and confederated — seeking its private interests through statutory means, and profaning every department of government in the effort... The expense of moving products has become the great expense of life and it is the only disbursement over which he who pays can exercise no control whatever ... the evil is a public one, affecting every citizen.[7]

In the South, cotton production started returning to its pre-war levels with the crop of 1876. A new slogan, "Bring the Cotton Mills to the Cotton Fields," was adopted as an effort was made to expand production and restore social and economic cohesion to the area.[8] By pushing for new overseas markets, cotton farmers and the area's city businessmen came together in an expansive mill building program. While the depression slowed the movement somewhat, southern exports dramatically increased in a five year period, jumping 300 percent between 1876 and 1881.

The rest of the country's farmers also began to see an increase in export trade. Commodity sales almost doubled from $271 million in 1877 to $520.4 million in 1880. The share of the gross national product supplied directly by agricultural exports averaged seven percent

for the same three years, and the farm share of all exports averaged over 82 percent.[9]

Europeans, particularly the British, became increasingly alarmed over the influx of American exports. Their strong negative reaction aroused Eastern financiers, industrialists and U.S. political leaders. Farmers had long contended that the financial leadership of the United States relied too heavily on its connections with British capital and that Wall Street was prone to follow the lead (and vetoes) of The City of London.

A New Order of Things?

Believing that agriculture was the sure road to domestic prosperity, farmers argued that it was time for the nation to assert its economic independence. The United States needed to seek world marketplace supremacy, but to do so it needed to wean itself from the gold standard and create its own monetary system, including the use of silver.

One editor declared that silver symbolized the "battle of the farmer versus the bondholder" and the "foreign influences" of the British and Western European metropolis. Remonetization would "go far toward restoring the debt-burdened West to something like equal footing with the East." He concluded that people had long enough "been hewers of wood and drawers of water to Eastern capitalists. ... The time has come for a new order of things."[10]

In general, however, the export bonanza of the late 1870s did not bring about "a new order of things," but rather, in the words of historian William Appleman Williams, turned an agricultural majority "and a metropolitan plurality toward a policy of active overseas economic expansion. The exports that prevented domestic upheaval became the exports that required an imperial foreign policy."[11]

By 1881 farm agitation for an expanding world market was in full voice. One Iowan declared that, "we are rapidly utilizing the whole of our continental territory. We must turn our eyes abroad, or they will soon look inward upon discontent."[12]

With new foreign markets discovered abroad and greatly expanded by the turn of the century, the nation now saw a need to safeguard these new sources of income. Thus, the United States began increasing its own military and diplomatic muscle in an effect to protect its worldwide ventures.

Meanwhile, the nation was undergoing a profound transformation, experiencing its own "industrial revolution." A Social Darwinism began to impose itself indelibly upon the American character, proclaiming that those who had "the vigor, capacity and talent for hard work, saving and shrewd investment are those who should and will prosper."[13]

This same "revolution" impressed on farmers the fact that while they had become increasingly dependent upon urban, industrial America, their living standards and income were often inferior to those in the city. The subsequent frustration and discontent that this attitude bred in rural areas quickly erupted into a movement unlike any seen in the United States since the founding of the Republic.

Homesteading

It was during this turbulent period that the Federal government no longer saw a need to depend on land as its principal source of revenue. In its zeal, however, to see settlers on free land it created a "homesteading" system that not only triggered decades of fraud and corruption, but laid the foundation for a narrow and self-serving philosophy regarding private property that exists in the United States to the present day.

With the Homestead Act of 1862 a citizen or a person intending to become a citizen could file a claim to parcels of unappropriated public land up to 160 acres. Upon paying a ten dollar fee and promising that the land would be settled on and cultivated, the person was granted permission to occupy the land. After a five-year period, dated from initial occupancy, the person would then receive title to that tract.[14]

An outspoken champion of homesteading, Galusha Grow, aptly described the basic issue in opening up land for settlement:

> the struggle between capital and labor is an unequal one at best. It is a struggle between the bones and sinews of men and dollars and cents; and in that struggle, it needs no prophet's ken to foretell the issue. And in that struggle is it for this government to stretch forth its arm to aid the strong against the weak?[15]

From the outset homesteading was opposed on several fronts. It would, President Buchanan proclaimed in his 1860 veto message, "introduce the dangerous doctrine of agrarianism and the pernicious social theories which have proved so disastrous (for the landed elite) in other countries (*e.g.*, France and Russia)."[16] Reaction in the Congress was both vocal and sharply divided along regional and class lines.

In 1862 the Homestead Act was finally passed, primarily because the southern plantation interests were no longer in Congress to block it and the northern capitalists had been satisfactorily assured by the General Land Office that the new land was no longer needed as a source of revenue for the Federal government.

The South had viewed the Homestead Act as creating a new yeoman class of farm families, working their own land. To the plantation owner such a creation meant an end to slavery and the south's traditional system of agriculture. Northern industrialists feared the act because income from the sale of such land had become a key federal revenue source, and its loss might well signal higher taxes.

By the time the Homestead Act was in place, however, no land was available in the public domain on the humid East Coast, and available land in the semi-arid Great Plains and arid west was not particularly suited to 160 acre tracts. Later, when many of these small farms defaulted, agriculture saw the birth of the bonanza wheat farms, particularly in the Northern Plains and in California.

By utilizing the new equipment that was rolling out of the eastern factories, these bonanza farms, with tenant managers and cheap labor, embarked on farming thousands of acres as single unit farms. The genesis of such units came from Illinois immediately after the war, but did not develop into a systematized operation until the late seventies when land started to be exchanged for worthless railroad securities in the Red River Valley.

The Northern Pacific Railroad would farm 100,000 acres while two Tidioute, Pennsylvania brothers put over 61,000 acres of land (that they had received from railroad securities) into wheat. Other such farms ranged from 17,000 to 40,000 acres and most were owned by Eastern business interests, since the capital investment was immense.[17] By 1885, when prices began to deteriorate again, the bonanza farms had an increasingly difficult time paying their taxes and were broken up and rented to tenant farmers. The environmental consequences of these mega-farms soon became apparent, as soil depletion began to affect many areas of the Great Plains.

"Over 21" and "14 x 16" Land Owners

Natural barriers, in conjunction with the Homestead Act's loopholes and corrupt administration made a mockery of the "equal justice under law" concept of land ownership.

One government commission estimated that nearly two fifths of these five-year homesteads were fraudulently obtained. Between 1881 and 1904, 22 million acres were assembled into large land holdings by using the Act's commutation clause, which allowed homesteaders in times of sickness, crop failure or the inability to make a living to postpone meeting the requirements of the Act. As so frequently happens to laws designed in the public interest, speculators used such clauses for personal gain.[18]

The Land Office reported:

> Actual inspection of hundreds of commuted homesteads shows that not one in a hundred is ever occupied as a home after commutation. They become part of some large timber holding or a parcel of a cattle or sheep ranch ... They are usually merchants, professional people, school teachers, clerks, journeymen working at trades, cow punchers, or sheep herders. Generally these lands are sold immediately after final proof.[19]

Two examples, offered by Ingolf Voegler, illustrate the lengths some speculators and companies went to in their effort to possess large parcels of the land.

Children would be picked up and placed over a chalk-drawn number 21 so that when the government agent asked if they were over 21 (a requirement of the Homestead Act) they could reply in the affirmative. Cardboard "houses" made from boxes, only 14 by 16 inches big, were placed on the land and "builders" would swear that a good board house "14 by 16" (the law assuming the dimensions to be in feet) had been built on the land as required by the Act. As Voegler points out, "in the end, the ineffectiveness of the Act was assured not so much by its own provisions or administration or even where it was applied, but rather by numerous simultaneous countervailing laws that were subsequently enacted."[20]

The renowned American historian and authority on land ownership in the Western United States, Paul Wallace Gates, summarizes the consequences of the laws's failings and the reaction to the Act's stated purpose:

> The retention of the Preemption Law and commutation clause of the Homestead Act made it possible for timber dealers, cattle grazers, mining interests, and speculators to continue to acquire lands through the use of dummy entrymen, false swearing, and, often, the connivance of local land officers. ... The Desert Land Act, the Timber Culture Act, and the Timber and Stone Act provided even greater opportunities for dummy entrymen to enter lands and assign them to hidden land engrossers. The palpable frauds committed and the large acres transferred under these acts and their interference with the homestead principle lead one to suspect that their enactment and retention were the results of political pressure by interested groups.[21]

As Professor Gates reminds us, it was not just the Homestead Act of 1862 which made this land bonanza available to the land speculators and corporations, but also many subsequent laws enacted by Congress. Since judges often interpreted these laws by whim, fancy or personal interest it was possible for a settler to take advantage of the Preemption, Homestead, and Timber Culture Acts and acquire 480 acres for about 50 cents an acre.

It has been estimated that about a tenth of all public domain land went to bona-fide homesteaders,[22] many of whom would later encounter financial difficulties. It was said that these farmers could succeed only if they immediately recognized their need for "a horse, a plow, a wife — and a mortgage," which occasioned Karl Marx to observe that the latter need would only assure that the homesteader's land would undoubtedly soon be back in the hands of the banks.[23]

Land granting laws passed after 1862 effected massive giveaways. The railroads gained over 128 million acres (an area equal to all the New England states, plus New York and Pennsylvania); wagon roads and canals got two million acres; states acquired 140 million acres (later sold to land companies, railroads and speculators), and unprotected Indian land, amounting to between 100 and 125 million acres, was sold with large tracts going to investors and the railroads. Only later were small tracts made available to settlers.[24]

Federal lands for cash sales saw 100 million acres disappear from the public domain, and the Agricultural College Act of 1862 saw eight million acres authorized for sale to pay for the construction of the land grant colleges.[25]

Once ownership of this land was concentrated by methods most historians agree to have been fraudulent, illegal, sanctioned by corrupt officials and frequently underwritten by laws specifically designed to benefit vested interests, the question became how best to make the land more profitable at the least social, economic, and political cost.

The Campaign to "Rationalize and Stabilize"

By the beginning of the 20th century the financial power of many corporations had come to rest in the money and banking centers of New York. As early as 1890 nearly three-fourths of the entire wealth of the nation was centered in urban areas and the gap between rural and urban, rich and poor was rapidly widening.[26]

In an effort to "rationalize and stabilize" the economic life of the country huge capital-rich corporations had formed holding companies designed to concentrate their wealth further. In combination with their markets, already coordinated by the wonders of the telephone, telegraph, transportation and other new technologies, monopolistic control of the industrial economy began to flourish.

In the depressions of the seventies and nineties these corporations had forced out weaker competitors by adopting cost-cutting technologies. By the turn of the century most key resource industries were controlled by one or two large corporations. Through price-fixing and increasing production these same corporations could avoid costly competition and focus on creating more demand for their goods while exploiting natural resources proportionately.

As these changes were taking place in urban areas, farmers struggled to refinance their operations to expand and to cover increasingly higher input costs. This struggle, which would come to plague rural America for an entire century, centered around the farmer's inequitable position within the economic system. Fred Shannon explains:

> The plain fact was that agriculture was hardly paying for the effort expended on it, and the gap between poverty and plenty seemed to be widening. Low prices for crops and livestock and the high cost of purchased necessities combined with scarce money, tight credit, towering interest rates, burdensome transportation charges, and the exactions of the middlemen — particularly the produce exchanges, grain elevator operators, and meat packers — to make agriculture a doubtful commercial venture and hardly even a way of life. ...
>
> The farmer's trouble was that in an erratically changing economy the supply of money lagged behind demand, his obligations deprived him of the supplementary medium of exchange that came to the aid of more favored businesses.[27]

Agriculture, unlike most other business ventures, was by its very nature ill-equipped to handle such rollercoaster rides between prosperity and depression. Farmers could not simply lay off labor (either themselves or their family) as factories do, nor could they make sudden decisions to reduce output when the market happened to collapse while crops were still in the ground or the livestock only half grown. Because farming depends on slow biological processes, it is much more difficult for farmers than businesses to synchronize their production schedules with abrupt swings in the economy.

Faced with low prices and high overhead, farmers have generally expanded their production, redoubled their efforts, and hoped and prayed that they would break even. In the late 1800s, however, while farm commodities were bringing in less money, prices for other goods, many of which were fixed by trusts and monopolies, were constantly on the rise.[28]

The Patrons of Husbandry Organize

In 1880, although agricultural and industrial income were both $5 billion, farm prices were being averaged with industrial prices to obtain a general curve. Prices of manufactured goods, however, were as far above the general curve as farm goods were below, nearly doubling the presumed distance of agricultural parity.[29]

Out of these conditions a variety of protest movements rapidly emerged, ranging from the National Grange in the 1870s to the Populists in the 1880s.

Originally organized as farm social clubs to sustain the certain richness in the texture of rural life, the Patrons of Husbandry, popularly known as the Grange, came into existence in 1867. Oliver Hudson Kelly, who conceived of the organization, once summed up its purpose:

Its grand object is not only general improvement in husbandry, but to increase the general happiness, wealth and prosperity of the country. It is founded upon the axioms that the products of the soil comprise the basis for all wealth; that individual happiness depends upon general prosperity, and the wealth of a country depends on the general intelligence and mental culture of the producing classes.[30]

Usually after their formal meetings they would adjourn, only to reconvene an "anti-monopoly" meeting which, although shunning partisan political activity, was largely devoted to discussing the railroads, the bankers' excessive interest charges and foreclosures, grain elevator operators, farm equipment companies and commodity middlemen. By 1875 some 21,697 Grange units in 33 states numbered an estimated 858,050 members and were directing most of their attention to the realization of cheap transportation and cheap money.[31]

Unless farmers had large amounts of capital and could afford to buy land near the railroads they found themselves at a distinct disadvantage when it came to shipping their crops. In addition, railroad companies often gave rebates to the large farms and large shippers to the East while charging inflated rates to farmers who shipped limited quantities of produce over short distances.

In an effort to overcome these economic hurdles the Grange began cooperative buying and selling while seeking legislation to control the abuses of the railroads. Unfortunately, its lack of business knowledge, capital

and cooperative experience led to an early demise for many of its cooperative ventures. It was successful, however, in securing many needed reforms in the railroad business, including reduced fare, freight and warehouse rates. From Grange's efforts also came the establishment of the Interstate Commerce Commission.

As the influence of the Grange diminished, the Greenback Party came to represent agrarian interests. Throughout the 1870s its candidates for local, state and federal office repeatedly declared that,

the right to make and issue money is a sovereign power, to be maintained by the people of the common benefit, not for the monopolies and international syndicates which force government policies of dear money, cheap labor, and weak people.[32]

Cheap Labor and High Tech

As a fundamental transformation in rural America was taking place in the late 1800s, largely fueled by overproduction in agriculture, an accelerated exploitation of natural resources and rapidly improving labor-saving technology, urban America was also changing. Cities were becoming crowded, poverty was increasing, huge factories seeking cheap labor were multiplying, and large corporations were replacing small businesses everywhere.

It is important to recognize the connections among these rapid transformations because what was happening in urban America — an ever-expanding cheap labor force in conjunction with high technology producing more consumer goods for concentrated capital — was soon to become the basic principle of U.S. farm policy. Perelman explains that process from the urban worker's perspective:

By increasing the area farmed by the average worker, labor-saving agriculture technology helped to absorb the reservoir of cheap, unused land. By increasing the amount of grain a single farmer could work, labor saving technology helped to glut the market with grain. As the price of grain fell, farmers' income suffered, making agriculture a less attractive venture. In short, labor-saving technology on the farm accomplished, to some extent, what employers had sought in vain to do by law and decree — namely, shut off the escape route from the factory.[33]

Even though some measure of recovery had occurred after the Panic of 1873 when thousands of farmers had run out of credit, there was a renewed effort by farmers in the eighties to open even larger markets abroad to prevent further declines in commodity prices. Two factors worried both farmers and many of the nation's businessmen:

1) the failure of the boom to improve the welfare of agriculture in general, still faced as it was with overproduction and weak prices, and

2) the renewed efforts by European interests to control, if not terminate, American efforts to promote exports.

Farmers were also angry that as "our exports increase, the cost of transportation augments in the same proportion, and the producer is left without profit."[34]

While American foods fs had played a significant role in relieving near famine abroad in the 1870s, many Europeans began to view the cure — in the form of price depressing commodities from the United States — as more damaging than the sickness, and anti-Americanism soon became pervasive. In attempting to combat this attitude in 1877 the United States embarked on a geopolitical course for the next two decades that transformed primary economic concerns with exports into "a demand for the kind of vigorous government action that produces imperial policy,"[35] — a "manifest destiny."

Toward the end of the 1880s the nation was faced with yet another depression almost as severe as the one in the 1870s. By 1893 a panic was on, followed by a depression that lasted into 1898. Unemployment quadrupled to over 18 percent and real earnings for the entire economy averaged 15 percent less for almost five years while gross farm income dropped by at least as much. Over 490 banks and some 15,000 businesses failed by the end of 1893.[36]

Market prices for corn went from 66 cents a bushel in 1866 to 28 cents at best and ten cents at worst in 1889, the price of wheat dropped from $2 a bushel at the end of the Civil War to 70 cents during this same period of time.[37] In some states prices were even worse. The desperate plight of many farmers at the time was captured in a story told by South Dakota State University historian, Dr. Robert Cherny[38].

A town in Kansas scheduled a community debate on the subject: Resolved that opportunities have never been better in Kansas. A lawyer from the town was invited to present the affirmative side of the question and he sought to do so in eloquent fashion. After he had completed his argument before a rapt audience a local farmer, a member of the Farm Alliance movement, was asked to present the opposing argument. Without a word he stood up, went over to the stove in the corner of the room, took a shovel and threw a load of corn on the fire, and then went back to his seat. "Everybody agreed," Dr. Cherny adds, "he had won the debate."

Coming at the end of a generation of instability and suffering, many believed the depression of the 1890s to be psychologically and politically more disruptive than its predecessors. The solution to this new disaster, government and business leaders contended, was to enlarge metropolitan or industrial exports, thereby creating more of a demand in the domestic market for the nation's abundant agricultural surpluses.

Most of the farm community, of course, viewed such thinking as another instance of eastern capitalist discrimination, and continued to argue for renewed efforts to expand overseas markets. They also believed that the key to "commercial independence from the East was to first become financially independent. That is ... dictate the financial policy of our government to [our] interests as the East has done." Silver, they believed,

was vital because it would "place the farmers of the South and Northwest upon equal footing in the market of the world."[39]

An Evolving Democratic Culture

As Southern farmers sought to escape the tyranny of sharecropping and the "furnishing merchant" system and western farmers fought the tyranny of burgeoning debt and mortgage foreclosures, both believed American agriculture was being driven into involuntary servitude. They also believed that the democratic promise was being destroyed and with it any possibility of individual respect and mass aspiration.

From a mass democratic movement, which had initially been generated by a cooperative crusade and which was to become the heart of the "agrarian revolt," to the formation of the National Farmers Alliance and Industrial Union, emerged a political movement that came to be called populism.

Populism, as historian Goodwyn reminds us, was characterized by an evolving democratic culture in which people could "see themselves" and therefore aspire to a society conducive to mass human dignity. In stark contrast to their efforts was the direction they saw being taken by the corporate state in the existing society.[40] One populist newspaper of the time described the issue in these blunt terms:

In the second fifty years of the republic a new power grew up, unobserved by most men. ... Seated in the east, it has dominated the west and south, has monopolized legislation, fortified itself in the citadel of national power and bids defiance of those who question its right.[41]

Populism clearly recognized this condition and thus believed that it was imperative to bring the corporate state under democratic control. "Agrarian reformers," Goodwyn points out,

attempted to overcome a concentrating system of finance capitalism that was rooted in Eastern commercial banks and which radiated outward through trunk-line railroad networks to link in a number of common purposes much of America's consolidating corporate community. Their aim was structural reform of the American economic system.[42]

The fact that populism achieved a high measure of political success for nearly a decade in the late 1800s explains why in the century since this "agrarian revolt," corporate America has reacted so strongly and swiftly to any renewed moves by the nation's farmers to assert that same degree of economic and political power they began to so forcefully apply in the late 1800s.

Built on the principle that "people need to see themselves experimenting in democratic forms," an "Alliance lecturing system" evolved. Farmers came together through hundreds of suballiances to learn not only the real causes of their economic plight, but also how they could gain strength through "cooperation and organization." Suballiances became classrooms with farmers addressing their condition and the task of explaining themselves and that condition to others.

The Alliance sought not only to reinforce members' commitment to their cause, but marched through towns and cities to exhibit their defiance of the local merchants whom they had come to view as an extension of the economic forces subjugating rural America.

Over 1,000 newspapers were published under the aegis of the National Reform Press Association. With news and opinions from the surrounding rural communities and with "ready print" inserts to bring news and commentary from their national office, these papers became the very center of populist revolt.

"In its underlying emotional impulses," Goodwyn tells us,

> populism was a revolt against the narrowing limits of political debate within capitalism as much as it was a protest against specific economic injustices. The abundant evidence that 'great aggregations of capital' could cloak self-interested policies in high moral purposes — and have such interpretations disseminated widely and persuasively through the nation's press — outraged and frightened the agrarian reformers, convincing them of the need for a new political party free of corporate control.[43]

Subsequently, where the suballiances were strong, where there was genuine "cooperation and organization" with a strong populist press reflecting these ideals, the movement sustained hardy roots which soon flowered into the People's Party.

At the heart of the Farm Alliance and populist platform for dealing with the enormous credit problem that plagued agriculture was their "sub-treasury plan." Although rejected at the time, it re-emerged some 40 years later as the genesis of Franklin Roosevelt's New Deal's agricultural program.

Under this plan, farmers could deposit their crops in government-financed storage facilities, receive a certificate of ownership and a loan in the amount of 80 percent of the crop's current market value plus a one percent interest rate. If the price of the crop rose, the farmer could sell the certificate of ownership and pay off the loan; if the price dropped the farmer simply retained the loan and the government eventually would sell the crop at auction. Although the plan had no provisions for support prices above current market prices or for holding surplus stocks, it would meet the producers' immediate need for cash while insuring that large harvest-time supplies of commodities would not depress the market.

Undertaking Basic Political Reform

Even though populism posed a number of specific economic solutions to the farm crisis, it is important to remember that the popular monetary issues of the day, *e.g.*, silver and/or gold were only ephemeral ones.

Reflecting on populism's analysis of the nation's emerging financial elite, Lawrence Goodwyn has pointed out that it is difficult to find a political doctrine narrower and more self-serving than the American banking hierarchy's fixation on "sound money."

> ... the artificially contracted currency of the gold standard had three undeniable and linked products: it curtailed the nation's economic growth; it helped measurably to concentrate the capital assets of the nation in the pockets of the nation's bankers; and it helped measurably to consign generation after generation of non-banking Americans to lives of hardship and dependence.
>
> Beyond this, the triumph of the political and cultural values embedded in the gold standard provided the economic foundation for the hierarchical corporate state of twentieth century America.[44]

The focus of Farm Alliance members, as declared in their Omaha Platform, was a rebellion against the American political party system. In order to restructure the nation's financial and economic system, the Alliance rejected both major parties, which they accused of being in "harmony with monopoly." (There were others at this time who also called themselves "populists" but were really a shadow movement; they sought to work within the Democratic and Republican parties and the existing economic system. The residue of their efforts would soon be absorbed by the Progressive movement.)[45]

Various noteworthy principles emerged out of the "agrarian revolt" of the 1880s. William Lamb, the leader of the Alliance radicals and perhaps populism's most articulate theoretician, spoke to one of those major principles in a historic 1886 open letter to the *Rural Citizen*.

Lamb believed society was dominated by manufacturers and their agents. The traditional image of the farmer as the "hardy yeoman" of the Jeffersonian era was quite out of place in the growing American corporate state at the turn of the century. He believed the farmer of the new industrial age was a "worker," the "labor question" was the central issue, and that the organized farmers of the Alliance should join with the organized workers of the Knights of Labor.

As business centralized, Lamb contended, farmers who continued to strive for friendship and parity with the commercial world simply failed to comprehend "what is going on against us." Members of the Alliance had to outgrow such naivete:

> We think all members should show the world which side they are on ... and we are looking forward for men that will advocate our interests, those who are working against us are no good for us ... we know of a certainty that manufacturers have organized against us, and that is to say if we don't do as they say, we can't get their goods ... Then for it to be said that we are unwise to let them alone, we can't hold our pens still until we have exposed the matter and let it be known what it is we are working for.[46]

Resisting Racism and Racist Propaganda

One other important characteristic of the early agrarian populist revolt was its resistance to racism and racist propaganda throughout the South. In a determined effort against incredible odds it sought to win political rights for blacks and defend those rights against white terrorism. Populists called for a spirit of tolerance so the races could work together to achieve some measure of economic and social justice. Historian C. Vann Woodward, portrays the results of that effort:

> The Populists failed, and some of them turned bitterly against the Negro as the cause of their failure. But in the efforts they made for racial justice and political rights they went further toward extending the Negro political fellowship, recognition and equality than any native white political movement has ever done before or since in the South.[47]

Because some elements within the farm communities generalized their attack upon the Eastern and English financiers and industrialists into an attack on Jews there is an assumption that the early agrarian populist movement was also anti-semitic in nature. Prominent American historian William Appleman Williams, however, disputes that assumption.

> Having read a vast number of Populist papers, letters and proceedings, it is my considered judgment that the incidence of anti-Semitism was very low. Those who maintain otherwise are unconvincing on two counts. First, they do not persuade one that they have done extensive research in the primary sources. Second, they do not conceptualize about the problem in a useful manner.

Williams continues,

> Jews did enjoy great power in European and American financial circles during this period. They further took great pride, as they had traditionally, in exercising that power. Hence to attack them for possessing and exercising that vast economic power is not *prima facie* evidence of anti-Semitism.
>
> To become such it would have to be supported by proof of an exclusive assault on Jewish financiers, and a general campaign against *all* Jews, whatever their wealth. The sources do not reveal such evidence. In a similar way, the rising opposition to immigration was due far less to any latent or overt racism than to the conclusions drawn from the analysis that established the end of the continental frontier.[48]

A Progressive Co-opt

Although many of the "populist" farm policy seeds would later flower in the form of constructive state and national farm and anticorporate legislation, the People's Party's demise as a political force came in the 1896 presidential election; the silverites captured control of the Party, amalgamated with the Democrats as William Jennings Bryan co-opted much of the "populist" rhetoric, and were beaten decisively by William McKinley and the Republicans.

During this era of populist revolt, however, the nation's farm community experienced profound change. From 1860 to 1900, while the average size of the American farm was declining from 199 acres to 147 acres, the proportion of farmers in the nation's labor force declined from 58 percent to 38 percent. Correspondingly, whereas farmers owned nearly 75 percent of the wealth of the nation in 1850, by 1890, they held barely a quarter of that wealth. In 1900 in the North Central group of states, the nation's richest agricultural region, 37.8 percent of all persons working on farms were wage laborers earning an average of $117 a year, while 19 percent were tenants, part-tenants and managers. Less than half (43.2 percent) owned or held an equity in their farms.[49]

In the south, in one favored section sampled by Fred Shannon, 276 out of 1,000 farmers earned over $500 a year and 84 received a "meagerly comfortable income" of $1,000 or more.

> One can imagine the raucous laughter of the 91.6 percent of all — those constantly aware of their precarious livelihood — if told that they really were prospering through the continuous rise in value of their land. They either did not own it at all, possessed so little that its gain in value was a mere bagatelle, or were living under the shadow of the mortgage so frequently commemorated in the stage plays of the era.[50]

Many men, women and children would leave their farms during this period to resettle in company mill towns or push further west in pursuit of the golden dream. Ironically, as each new invention (supposedly manufactured to ease and enrich rural life) reached farms from the nation's mighty industrial machine, farmers themselves were disappearing into the cities to provide a cheap labor pool for those same manufacturers.

Preaching the "Gospel of Success"

Clearly, the latter half of the 19th century was marked by considerable confusion and shifting values. The new materialistic "gospel of success" was replacing the ethics of the village, and powerful "captains of industry" like Andrew Carnegie, J.P. Morgan and John D. Rockefeller were the emulated heroes of the day. Responding to and representing this new breed of aggressive economic individualists, the so-called realists of the 1800s, was the Republican Party, which in 1896 had won a landmark political victory and control of the White House.

Meanwhile, with the increasing migration from country to city and the immigration from abroad, the demand for large amounts of storable and readily available food became an important part of the nation's burgeoning economy. This need gave birth to the giant food manufacturing, processing, transporting, wholesaling and marketing companies which in a few short decades would evolve into the nation's largest industry. As they grew farm technology also grew, but while productivity per person showed remarkable advances so also did farm debt.

As we examine the twentieth century transformation of agriculture into corporate agribusiness, we need to remember that this brief history was but the early stage of a specialized agricultural system designed to reward the few at the expense of the many.

In reviewing the major themes of his book on American environmental history Dr. Petulla, aptly sums up the early evolution of our farm economy:

> First, I suggest that the economic rationality of American democracy has tended to lead to economic concentration, a waste of natural resources; and environmental degradation (also an inequitable distribution of wealth ...).
>
> Second, business imperatives, rather than environmental or social concerns, and technological developments have increased the exploitation and processing of natural resources.
>
> Third, at the same time, the nation has become increasingly tied together through cheap transportation and regional specialization of resource extraction or processing.
>
> Fourth, American political policy and legal institutions have generally supported the logic of private enterprise development, promoting and defending individual private property rights over social and environmental concerns, eschewing control of private lands even for purposes of conservation; and also providing abundant government assistance for the profitable purposes of agriculture, lumber, oil and mining interests. The government has increasingly underwritten the needs of the larger companies representing the more "rationalized," efficient sectors of their respective industries.[51]

Chapter Twelve

Agriculture's "Golden Years"

"You could stick a banker, a grain trader and a railroad executive in a barrel and roll it down a hill and a son-of-a-bitch would be on top the whole time."

- A.C. Townley, Co-founder,
The Non-Partisan League

The decades from 1900-1920 have been called the "Golden Age of Agriculture." This period was, however, not without its problems; some of which would persist and fester.

The dawn of a new century brought relative prosperity and abundance to American agriculture after the recurring depressions of the late 19th century. By 1910 the purchasing power of farmers would at last equal that of urban, industrial workers, resulting in a four year period that would become in the decades following the basis for calculating "parity" prices for agriculture.

What happened in these first twenty years of the new century is crucial to America's permanent agricultural crisis. While these decades altered the character of American agriculture the social transformations that took place proved to be so rapid and profound for farmers and their communities they would never be able to adjust adequately.

Farm prices moved upward, in some cases more rapidly than the increase in the general price level. Steam power and broader-based education by the State Experiment Stations and USDA would also come to play important roles in increasing farm production.

Following the panic of 1893, a severe drought triggered a marked decline both in the number and quality of livestock and a dramatic increase in the price of two essential winter feed crops — corn and hay. These unfavorable weather conditions in turn accelerated the acreage devoted to grain production in 1895 and early 1896, leading to exceedingly low prices for both farm products. Prices remained low for the next year or so while the nation struggled with the currency question.

Several countries abroad, however, began to have short crops of grain and feed in 1896, so by the end of 1897 commodity prices began to rise. Soon thereafter the United States, still a debtor nation, resolved that the best method of meeting its foreign obligations was through exporting its agricultural products.

The influential Iowa farm editor, Henry C. Wallace, described this period, writing in 1900:

The farmer is the main element in national prosperity because there are so many of him. When the farmers prosper, have money to pay their debts, provide for their families, and make improvements, good times are clearly in sight, as they were in 1897. The farmer's money started the mills and factories all over the land. For two or three years they had been running on short time, the country was bare of manufactured products, the farmers had great need of them, and this farm prosperity started a wave of prosperity among all classes, which has continued to the present hour.[1]

What to do With Farm and Farmer Surpluses?

Some believed that a "surplus" of farmers created this new "wave of prosperity." "In very truth," one farmer had observed in 1845, "when enough [farmers] have been driven into manufacturing ... they would be numerous enough to manufacture two or three times as much as this country could consume and the surplus would have to find a foreign market."[2] Economists have even suggested that this surplus and its "wave of prosperity" contributed directly to World War I.

Once the farm surplus turned into a surplus of goods in general, the momentum generated in the drive for agricultural exports continued as a policy to expand manufacturing exports as well. The United States was eventually drawn into conflict with the other great industrial nations in a world struggle over markets which culminated in World War I.[3]

It was at this time farmers were also accelerating their struggle against the trusts and tariffs, believing that protectionism, which benefitted the trusts, raised farmers' costs and reduced their overseas markets.

A 1900 *Prairie Farmer* editorial declared:

Under the paternalism of a highly protective tariff that walls out foreign competition by putting an obstructive tax on trade, the trusts have become possible, the tariffs have become the citadel of their strength, and herein they have entrenched themselves. Some of our astute politicians aver that the trusts are not guilty of any moral obliquity, because they are amenable to any ethical rules or dogmas, nor do they come under the restraint of true civics, for it is claimed that they occupy a zone that is peculiarly their own, whose delimitation is that of business. Accepting this view of the case, then, why are not they conducted on business principles?

I apprehend that when this trust problem is divested of its surface covering, it will be found to be permeated with rottenness and fraud, a veritable robbers' roost, and the habitat of thieves. No legitimate business should ever be over capitalized. Any concern that issues industrial stocks that are half real and half water is a fraud, and in attempting to make dividends upon such capitalization, prices must be greatly inflated to the prejudice of the consumer.[4]

Proclaiming a "Manifest Destiny of Capitalism"

As suggested earlier, many of the inadequacies in the nation's political and economic structure at this time which the "shadow populists" had sought to remedy, were soon championed by the so-called Progressive movement. As Goodwyn points out:

The countervailing idea of the "progressive society" materialized slowly out of the symbolic values embedded in the gold standard. The "sanctity of contracts" and "the national honor," it soon became apparent were foremost among them. But, gradually, and with the vast distributional range afforded by the Republican campaign treasury, broader themes of "peace, progress, patriotism, and prosperity," came to characterize the [1896] campaign for William McKinley.

The "progressive society" advanced by Mark Hanna [McKinley's campaign manager] in the name of the corporate community was inherently a well-dressed, churchgoing society. The various slogans employed were not mere expressions of a cynical politics, but rather the authentic assertions of an emerging American world view.[5]

During the Progressive era, which reached full flower in the early 1900s in the first Theodore Roosevelt administration, it was widely acknowledged that the United States's "new wave of prosperity" was creating enormous social and economic problems; However, it was believed that that same system that created them could solve them. Consequently, progressives argued, if officeholders and businessmen were honest, upright, good and efficient, and applied the principles of science with the public good in mind, all the apparent evils of the time would disappear.

They also believed that scientific management and monopoly integration and power, if used wisely, could assuredly benefit all of society. To progressives, therefore, trusts were a fact of life; it was simply a matter of "good" and "bad" trusts.

The key to the monopoly question became one of motive rather than the existence of monopolies. When Edward Harriman and J.P. Morgan's fight for control of the Midwest railroads went to the Supreme Court and the Court ordered Morgan's Northern Securities Company dissolved because of its intent to restrain trade in interstate commerce, the "rule of reason" in anti-trust judicial opinion was introduced.

"Rule of reason" considered only motives, good or bad, behind monopoly, not the *de facto* economic effects of the monopoly. In dissenting from the court opinion, Justice Oliver Wendell Holmes wrote that common law precedents should be sought to distinguish between "reasonable" and "unreasonable" intent in restraint of trade. In writing for the majority, Justice John Marshall Harlan expressed the view that *every* monopoly restrains trade by its very nature and thus is to the public detriment.[6]

To the scientists, professional people, businessmen and politicians — the American elites — bigness and vertical integration was the assured means to a more efficient, stable and prosperous society. Further, they sincerely believed that vertical integration and/or monopoly was, in Professor Petulla's words, "the manifest destiny of capitalism."[7]

Ironically, however, while the Morgans and the Rockefellers preached this gospel from their Wall Street cathedrals many small businesses were rapidly growing and often proving themselves more efficient than the corporate giants. For that reason the elites soon began looking to the Federal government for relief and for the maintenance of their control in industry. As Petulla observes:

They became convinced that business and government could cooperate in 'rationalizing' the nation's economy for everyone's benefit. By the end of the first decade of the century, businessmen were actually initiating social reforms or at least suggesting national regulations when the demands of individual states and their laws regarding rates, competition or income taxes became oppressive.[8]

By way of example, as early as 1892, U.S. Attorney General Olney wrote to a close friend of a Burlington Northern rail lines executive that it would be wise for the railroads to use the Interstate Commerce Commission for their own purposes since:

the older the Commission gets to be, the more inclined it will be found to take the business and railroad view of things. It thus becomes a sort of barrier between the railroad corporations and the people and sort of protection against hasty and crude legislation hostile to railroad interests ... The part of wisdom is not to destroy the Commission, but to utilize it.[9]

A resolution of sorts to the trust and anti-trust arguments in the "Progressive Era" came in 1914 with the passage of the Clayton Act which sought to remove the ambiguities of the older Sherman Anti-Trust Act by more carefully defining what specific acts constituted an unfair competition. The Clayton Act also attempted to stress the value of competition even though it provided little ammunition against the huge monopoly conglomerates that by their very size kept competition out of the market. Curiously enough, labor and agricultural organizations were exempt from its provisions. To establish a means of enforcement of the Act the Federal Trade Commission was established within the year.

Answering the Siren Call

The dawn of the new century found prices for farm products increasingly attractive, although the agricultural community was still faced with its share of problems.

Tobacco and cotton prices were at a level that caused producers to engage in several, and on occasion violent, withholding operations. The Farmers Union and American Society of Equity were founded in 1902 in an attempt to improve and stabilize the economic position of farmers. The Equity society, a strictly business organization, emphasized buying rather than selling and soon drifted toward cooperative marketing activities. The Farmers Union began in Raines County, Texas as the Farmers Educational and Cooperative Union of America.[10]

Although it would later turn to the political process, the Farmers Union, known today as the National Farmers Union, originally stressed the importance of the "family farm system" to the social and economic health of the country. It also attacked farmers' price and market problems systematically.

In its first year, the NFU successfully negotiated cooperative contracts with cotton ginners to acquire a network of cotton warehouses. By 1904 it was withholding cotton from the market in an attempt to fix the price. Later it conducted a series of cotton acreage reduction campaigns. While it succeeded in building warehouses it failed to become a decisive force in the marketplace through control of crop production.[11]

Meanwhile, farm population continued to decline as the siren call of urban opportunity beckoned the young. In 1909 more than 10 million people were engaged in agriculture on six million farms which produced onefifth of the world's wheat crop, three-fifths of its cotton crop, and four-fifths of its corn crop. (All these commodities and the rest of the nation's agricultural harvest were being grown on less than one-half of the nation's farmland.)[12]

Reclaiming Arid Land in the West

Even though the land was bountiful and productive, the Progressives and Teddy Roosevelt saw a need to "reclaim" arid lands in the west through irrigation. Although midwestern and eastern farmers were alarmed by possible competition from new farmlands, eastern labor groups and many of the American elite and members of Congress from Western states applauded the idea.

Prior to Roosevelt's call for "reclamation," the Carey Act of 1894 had made a similar attempt to encourage irrigation, but no one devised a method to raise the capital needed to develop new irrigation systems.

When the Reclamation Act of 1902 was passed it contained important provisions designed by Roosevelt to stimulate the "family farm system" of agriculture. Landowners could apply for federally subsidized water on only 160 acres of their land and absentee landowners were not eligible for such water. While local water laws were to govern water distribution, the receipts from the

land sales covered by the Act were supposed to be applied to the construction of reservoirs and irrigation works.

In 1907 the new Reclamation Service was established as an independent Bureau under the Secretary of the Interior. It was soon apparent, however, that speculators, knowing the location of proposed irrigation sites, bought such land from their existing owners even before the Service had approved of the projects for the region. By the time they resold this land the price was so inflated that only highly capitalized farmers (and in many cases individuals who owned well beyond the allowed 160 acres) could afford to make the payments to the speculators or the Federal government.

When public officials objected to this trend, Reclamation Director Frederick H. Newell pointed out that the law intended only the reclamation of arid or semi-arid lands and made no distinction between private or public irrigable lands. By 1910 24 projects were under construction, but only a minute portion of the public was benefitting from the federal water.[13]

The Progressive Movement's attitude and handling of the "reclamation" water issue illustrates what Petulla describes as the "ambiguities" of the Progressive program itself.

> Although Progressives attacked monopolists as engrossers of the public domain, they allied themselves with monopolists who agreed on the necessity of a 'wise use' philosophy of scientific management and of economic growth and expansion. And although Progressives were committed to the fight for political and economic justice and to the idea of grassroots democracy, they did not hesitate to force the preservation of forest and mineral lands on smaller political units — the states and local governments — in the interests of a rational 'wise use' policy ('socialization of management') and in the name of all the people.
>
> In the final analysis they, rightly or wrongly, preferred their own ('scientific') counsel to that of the people, perhaps because they were convinced that powerful corporations would win out if these matters were put in the hands of the 'people'.[14]

The government's "scientific counsel" took the matter of federal water and reclamation out of "the hands of the people" and placed it part and parcel in the hands of the same "powerful corporations" which would soon come to dominate agribusiness. Probably no single federal law was so flagrantly abused and disregarded by both individuals and the Federal government as the Reclamation Act of 1902, until both its letter and spirit were drastically altered in 1982.

Examining the Country Life

Mindful of the many problems faced by American farmers and the vital role agriculture still played in the life of the nation, President Theodore Roosevelt appointed a Country Life Commission in 1908 to conduct a first-ever national effort to examine the structure of farming and farm life. In its 1909 report, the Commis-

The Corporate Reapers

sion praised agriculture for its productivity, its efforts toward self-improvement and its maintenance of the Jeffersonian ideal of "independent and strong citizenship." The report stated that "agricultural people constitute the very foundation of our efficiency." But, as agricultural historian Wayne Rasmussen notes:

> In spite of improvements that had been made, the Commission said that agriculture was not commercially as profitable as it was *entitled to be* for the labor and energy expended and risks assumed. Social conditions in the country fell far short of their possibilities. Rural people were not organized to work together to meet their needs.
>
> These problems existed because of a lack of knowledge of the exact agricultural conditions and possibilities of their regions, the lack of good education for country life in the schools, the *impossibility* of the individual farmer standing up against the *established* business systems and interests, the lack of good highway facilities, and continued depletion of the soils and other natural resources.(emphasis added)[15]

The Commission urged the Congress to: 1) Encourage a thorough survey of all agricultural regions as a basis on which to develop a scientific and economically sound country life; 2) Encourage a national system of Extension work through the land-grant colleges; 3) Undertake a thorough investigation of the middleman system of handling farm products; 4) Study the farmer's disadvantages in all parts of the general business system; 5) Inquire into the use of streams and other natural resources; 6) Develop effective and economically sound highway systems; 7) Establish a system of parcel post and postal savings banks; and 8) Encourage public opinion to favor a rural society resting directly on the land.[16] Each of these recommendations was aimed principally at the gradual rebuilding of a new agriculture and renewed rural life in America which would "develop and maintain on the nation's farms a civilization in full harmony with the best American ideals."

The Commission believed it essential that the entire nation be aroused to this need and attempt to make progressive efforts to realize such a goal.

But, because the Commission called for fundamental changes in the entire structure of American agriculture, many felt its recommendations were unrealistic. Certainly the national political struggles among the Democrats, Republicans and Progressives and between Congress and the White House during the ensuing three years did little to translate the Commission's work into legislation.

Promoting "Efficiency" in Rural America

A close look at the Country Life Commission's recommendations, however, shows the disruptive influence of the progressive era on American agriculture and clarifies some of the confusion among historians as to the nature of the Country Life movement itself.

The call for *efficiency* was a crucial element in the Country Life Movement's prescription for rural America, a fact carefully examined by David B. Danbom, an assistant professor of history at North Dakota State University, in a perceptive *Agricultural History* essay on "Rural Education Reform and the Country Life Movement, 1900-1920."

The Commission's preoccupation with efficiency stemmed from a decided urban bias. In comparing urban and rural systems the latter were found particularly inadequate and inappropriate for the modern age. The key to correcting that condition and creating an agricultural sector which could "efficiently" satisfy the needs of an industrial society and economy was massive rural education reform, the Commission declared.

Efficiency, it should be noted, had a variety of meanings in the Progressive era. It was used to connote "social harmony and the leadership of the 'competent.'" It was also used in "ominous terms like 'civic' and 'moral' efficiency." Rural reform educators, however, used the word mainly as an economic concept.[17]

Food prices were rising more rapidly than other consumer goods, which many feared posed a threat to the entire society's well being. Such price increases were largely attributed to what Progressives in the Country Life Movement defined as "agricultural inefficiency." In other words, without cheap food the competitive advantage of U.S. industry would evaporate, social and political unrest would ensue and the nation's favorable trade position would disappear.

The Country Life movement saw the school house, an important part of rural life, as a symbol of inefficient agriculture. They called for major reforms in the rural school system, including greater school consolidation and increased opportunities for a more rounded and "civilized" education. With a more varied curriculum the system could quell current discontent and the "efficient" farmer would not be tempted to abandon rural America. For them education spelled efficiency. Danbom elaborates:

> Rural education reformers, personifying the curious progressive conjunction between modern secular technocracy and traditional Protestant moralism, tended to tie the concepts of efficiency, social responsibility, morality and happiness together in a single package. For them, the socially responsible citizen was the moral citizen, and the moral citizen was a happy person.
>
> Hence, rural education reformers saw themselves as serving rural people by rendering them more socially responsible, more moral, and happier. And yet, the reformers invariably saw efficiency as the means to social responsibility, and the society to which one was responsible was always the larger, urban-industrial one. When they talked about the schools' new role of socializing rural people the education reformers usually meant creating efficient producers who could better supply the larger society with food.[18]

Cheap food!

Yet, the assumptions of the Country Life movement about rural America were not shared by the people who lived there. Farmers did not see inefficiency as the basic problem of agriculture, nor did they agree that in an urban-industrial society agriculture's role was to serve society efficiently from a subordinate position. Thus, they disagreed with the nation that the rural school's goal should be comprehensive socialization aimed at economic efficiency.

Basically rural people saw the Country Life movement as manipulative, condescending and misguided. One rural school board member said that its suggested recommendations for education reform seemed "to indicate that the country boy should be induced or compelled to do something toward lowering the cost of food."[19]

Faced with this rejection and their inability to implement their education reforms, many in the Country Life movement became frustrated with their powerlessness and assumed an elitist attitude, attacking rural people as ignorant or vicious. (It has been suggested that this same attitude has been assumed and perpetuated by a good many of our present agricultural economists.)

By 1920 interest in reforming rural schools had waned for various reasons. "But," Danbom notes,

it is my hypothesis that the most important cause for this declining interest is that rural inefficiency no longer seemed to be such a serious problem after 1920. High food prices had symbolized rural inefficiency to education reformers, and food prices fell after 1920.[20]

Speeding Up U.S. Agriculture

The beginning of World War I in 1914 and the United States's involvement in that war in 1917 not only profoundly changed the relationships among nation states and revealed their vulnerability to the ravages of modern warfare, but was also a crucial turning point for American agriculture. A.B. Genung, a one-time senior USDA economist, best summarized the war's effect on our food production system:

Instead of developing through long, quiet years of efficient farming, gauged to fit the needs of a rapidly growing nation and a prosperous world market, agriculture had to be adapted to the pressures and the disruptions of war. Developments that normally would have been spread over generations were packed into a half dozen years.

That was what the war did to our agriculture, as a first consequence it speeded it up, lifted it from its rational course of progress and forced it to an unnatural exertion in response to an abnormal demand. Under the stimulus of price and patriotism — finally of outright inflation — the farm business labored and expanded and provided the sinews. Then in the aftermath, it was left high and dry with its output up and prices down, its foreign market shrunken, its fixed charges a heavy burden.[21]

Stimulating the production of food became a major goal of the United States at the outbreak of the war. Correspondingly and quite rapidly, the nation witnessed a historic reversal of its position from a debtor to a creditor nation. In August 1914, for example, the balance of trade was running against the United States by over $19 million; September saw a dramatic turnaround as the trade balance showed $15 million in the nation's favor, and by the following December it was $132 million and still increasing.[22]

Wheat dramatically led the way in accelerating our agricultural trade abroad during the World War I period. While the United States had been an exporter of wheat ever since its founding, its acreage and yield having steadily increased from the Civil War to 1900, the pre-war decade had seen a slight decline in both acreage and wheat exports.[23]

At the war's outset Western Europe saw its biggest supplier of wheat, Russia, unable to export its crop due to the closing of the Dardenelles. Buyers turned to the United States The price paid to U.S. farmers for wheat began climbing. The market advanced by almost 80 cents a bushel from late 1914 to May 1915 as the nation exported nearly $55 million worth of wheat a month.[24]

Farmers responded to these changes by sowing five million more acres of wheat in the fall of 1914, and an additional two million in the spring of 1915. Some 60 million acres were harvested in 1915, and with per-acre yield setting new records, the United States had an unprecedented billion-bushel wheat crop.[25]

A black stem rust epidemic hit the wheat belt the following year and in conjunction with falling prices from the previous season quickly reduced the acreage harvested to 52 million and a yield of a 636 million bushels. Prices, however, advanced sharply, going from $1.50 to $2.40 by the spring of 1917 as wheat bins were vacuumed clean. With the value of wheat increasing, the public again became concerned about the effect of such prices on domestic bread stuffs and other foods.[26]

Lighting A Prairie Fire

Despite this apparent prosperity, some farmers were unhappy for many of the same reasons they had voiced in the 1890s. In North Dakota, like a summer prairie fire, the Non-Partisan League (NPL) came into existence.

Somewhat different in nature from other farm organizations, the League originated in the area in where it was to become most successful — the Northern Plains — and emphasized political rather than economic action. It was profoundly influenced by both socialism and organized labor.[27]

In North Dakota many farmers were particularly outraged because they felt they were being held hostage by the banks, the railroads, and grain companies — "the boys in St. Paul." They pointed out that wheat they were forced to sell at a cheap price to the local elevator because it was graded no higher than #2 and #3 was later sold in Minneapolis-St. Paul as the more expensive #1. They also charged that the real capital of the state was the St. Paul Merchant's Hotel suite of Alexander McKenzie, the Northern Plains representative of the Great Northern Railroad Co., and the leader of the so-called "McKenzie Machine."[28]

With the motto "We'll Stick, We'll Win," A.C. Townley, an ex-flax farmer who had gone broke, and his core of dedicated farm organizers, everywhere sought new members, many of them becoming known as "$16 suckers" — the amount of dues paid by each new member. When a farmer at a rally asked Townley what League members got for their $16 he replied, "you get the courage to stand up and ask that question."[29]

Townley also once reminded a farm audience:

I have been told all my life that you are independent American farmers. I know that you are independent farmers, because all those fellows that handle the wheat and potatoes say you are. They tell it from morning until night, that you are independent American farmers. You know that they never lie. I heard a farmer the other day say that his interpretation of an 'independent' American farmer was that he was 'in' about as far as he could get, and 'dependent' upon everything in sight.[30]

Advocating state-owned grain elevators and flour mills, the League succeeded in capturing most of the elective offices in North Dakota in 1916. It also succeeded in initiating many other state reforms including establishing the office of state inspector of grain, reassessing property taxes to favor farmers, and requiring railroads to give co-op elevators fair treatment.

In 1919, after capturing both houses of the state legislature, the NPL instituted the "New Day in North Dakota" which included the establishment of a State Industrial Commission, a state-owned bank, grain terminal and mill. The League also founded organizations in neighboring states and set up controversial industrial and banking programs.

During the war the NPL called for a fusion of agriculture and labor. It lobbied for price fixing and government operation of the food industry, both of which were called "Pro-German" by its enemies. Townley, in rebutting such charges spoke in words as applicable to Persian Gulf-conscious Americans in January 1991, as they were to the crowd in Jamestown, North Dakota on July 9, 1917.

It is absolute insanity for use to lead ourselves or anybody else to believe that this nation can succeed in war when hundreds of thousands of parasites, the gamblers in the necessities of life, use the war only for the purpose of exacting exorbitant profits. We are working, not to beat the enemy, but to make more multi-millionaires.

Nevertheless, members of the League were tarred and feathered and their homes painted yellow and red. Its leadership was branded as disloyal and soon became racked by internal dissension.

Although the League as a formal organization would die, its influence is still seen today throughout the Northern Plains as traditional roadblocks to farmer participation in the political and economic system continue to be challenged.

Agriculture Goes to War

Upon the U.S. entry into the war in the spring of 1917, the government took quick and unprecedented action to formulate a food policy that would carefully monitor both domestic supplies and exports. On August 19, 1917, one of the most drastic economic control measures in the nation's history, the Food and Fuel Control Act, was enacted into law.[31] The act gave the President power to control the entire food supply through provisions for licensing all handlers of food, fixing prices, punishing hoarding or limiting production, regulating trade practices, requisitioning supplies, operating manufacturing plants, railroads, etc., and the buying, selling and storage of certain specified foodstuffs.

At the outset, this act guaranteed a minimum price of $2 a bushel for the 1918 wheat crop, but President Woodrow Wilson fixed a minimum price of $2.20 for the 1917 crop of No. 1 Northern at Chicago, with differentials for other grades and markets. By adhering to such prices the United States Grain Corp., established a basic price for wheat for the duration of the war. Despite such price incentives and pleas of patriotism, 1917 was a poor growing season as only 45 million acres were harvested, with a yield increase of barely one million bushels from the previous year. The following 12 months were critical for Western world food production.[32]

A decade later, one commentator explained:

The most strenuous efforts had to be made during the winter and spring of 1917-1918 to keep Allied armies and civilians supplied with breadstuffs. No one will ever know the strain under which our own and Allied officials labored when, with practically a crop failure in this country, stocks of bread grains abroad fell below the danger point and the shortage and uncertainty of shipping rendered it doubtful if they could be replenished in time. February to April, 1918, marked the crisis in the bread supply of the Allied nations.

Conservation by the American people and close cooperation between officials made it possible to pass this turning point which, otherwise, might have changed the history of the war.[33]

In June 1918 the price of No. 1 Northern spring wheat was raised to $2.26 which was soon followed by a near record crop. Over 59 million acres were harvested, which produced some 921 million bushels, as growers ultimately realized a price slightly above $2 a bushel. 1919 saw several countries anxiously in need of more U.S. wheat. With a guaranteed price still in effect, the nation's farmers produced 952 million bushels, a crop that realized between $2 and $2.25 per bushel.[34]

Through five years of world war, U.S. wheat acreage increased from an average of 47 million acres from 1909-1913 to 74 million in 1919 and a crop of 690 million bushels to 952 million, a jump of more than half in acreage and 38 percent in production. By plowing up Western grasslands and converting from other small grains, flaxseed and corn, the nation's farmers had produced record amounts of wheat.[35]

Unlike wheat, other crops showed no great fluctuations during the war years. Corn advanced in price in 1916-1917, but since its price was not fixed by the government, acreage and output per capita remained stable. The only major effect of price changes in corn came in the hog industry, which was dependent on it for its feed grain.[36]

During the pre-war years approximately 12 percent of the United State's yearly production of pork and lard was shipped overseas. That figure rose to 24 percent during the war. After 1916, when hog prices began a marked increase, the Food Administration Board was unable to capitalize a stabilization effort, such as it was doing with the Grain Corporation. The board simply established a price yardstick and maintained it by using the weight of Allied, Belgian, Red Cross and Army purchases and by controlling the packers and exports. The stated objectives of the Food Administration in taking such action were:

1) to increase the number of hogs in the country;
2) to increase the export of pork products to the Allies;
3) to stabilize prices so that producers could be assured of a reasonable return for their efforts; and
4) to control the margin of profits to packers and distributors in order to protect consumers.

After the U.S. entry into the war, however, pork prices continued to climb dramatically from $15 per hundred weight in the fall of 1917 to over $19 in the summer of 1919. Beef cattle prices advanced by 53 percent from 1914 to 1919 while meat exports went from 150 million pounds to 954 million during this same period of time.[37]

The price of dairy products was about 70 percent above pre-war averages through 1917-1918. The war's stimulus on the dairy industry between 1914-1919 caused an increase in milk cows from 19.8 million to 21.5 million while total butter, cheese and concentrated milk production reached over 45 million pounds from a pre-war 42 billion.[38]

While cotton faced a series of economic hardships at the outset of this period, the overall effect of the war was to reduce world consumption of U.S. cotton from pre-war figures of approximately 12 percent, although domestic consumption showed a slight increase. At war's end, prices showed some stimulation, resulting more from domestic business activity, general inflation and moderately small crops, than from war demand.[39]

The conflict's major effect on the tobacco industry was increased production of smoking tobacco, specifically cigarettes. Although exports deteriorated during the better part of the war years, acreage and production gradually increased; acreage went from one and quarter million in 1914 to nearly two million in 1920. It was at the end of the war, however, that tobacco exports and production began to soar, with prices tripling from the ten cent pre-war average.[40]

Peace: Boom or Bust?

Because Europe was driven to abandon the gold standard during the war, it was now forced to finance its costly conflict by resorting to sharply inflated currency and credit structures which in turn forced a broad increase in all commodity prices. Between 1917 and 1920 the farm community immediately felt the severe post-war deflation that ensued throughout the world after the guns fell silent.

Farm prices lagged somewhat behind all commodity prices during the first two years of the war, but in the struggle's latter stages they jumped above general commodity prices and then joined the overall upward price curve at the end of 1919 until their peak in May 1920. It is generally believed that such commodity price increases are especially significant because when they exceeded the general price level they stimulated production.[41]

In the months following the May 1920 peak, as farm input costs remained high farm prices began to fall, falling faster than the price of other general commodities. Although in general, farm prices were higher at war's end than they were at the outset, production costs were also considerably higher. Neither farmers' prices nor profits during the war, however, matched those of industry.[42] As A.B. Genung reminds us:

The farmers of the world war period had about three really profitable years, 1917-1919. But neither their prices nor their profits were high as compared with those of the industrial community. They were sufficient to induce some expansion which threw out of gear no little of the favorable adjustment that had been achieved before the war. Moreover, any distortion of the settled pattern of production *is more difficult to deal with in agriculture than in urban industry, because agriculture is a biological industry with a slow turn-over. It takes at least a year and usually several years to make adjustments in cropping systems and in herds and flocks.* (emphasis added)[43]

By the early 1920s, the decline of agricultural prices had become more rapid and marked than with industrial goods and farmers were again faced with the all-too-familiar postwar cost-price squeeze.

When Johnny Comes Marching Home

A number of other social and economic problems compounded this difficult situation. In the early years of the war, as signs pointed to heightened American involvement, hundreds of thousands of farm families faced with high prices at home and better compensation in factories, deserted rural America for the cities. (Some were escaping poverty or racism, while others sought a bigger slice of the pie.) In 1917 this exodus was compounded by young men departing for the armed forces, leaving behind an unsettled and short-handed rural economy.

At the war's outset, the U.S. farm population numbered approximately 32.3 million and by 1916 reached a peak of 32.5 million. Net migration to the cities was about 400,000 a year. But, as noted above, economic conditions soon saw a dramatic change in numbers.[44]

Census studies indicate that between 1910 and 1920 over 300,000 black citizens alone migrated from the rural south to the major industrial cities of the north, swelling Detroit's black population, for example, by 611 percent.[45] The Bureau of Agricultural Economics (BAE) also estimated that over 1.1 million men left the nation's farms to join the military, one of every four U.S. servicemen in the war had a rural background.[46]

By 1919 the farm population had dwindled to 30.9 million as the rural to urban migration exceeded 1,350,000 a year, including the 500,000 who had left the farm to join the military. After the Armistice, the return of these hundreds of thousands of young men to their native soil to seek land and a career in farming only exacerbated a now rapidly growing economic crisis.[47]

While prices for farm land and farm equipment increased, commodity prices were beginning their deflationary dive, even as the farm tax bill soared from $222 million in 1914 to $510 in 1921 and continued to grow.[48] Consequently, thousands of new farms were bought and immediately plunged heavily into debt with ramifications that did not stop at the farm gate.

As the nation started its wild race through the roaring twenties, it also started to pay an escalating, but not immediately apparent economic, social and environmental cost for allowing its agricultural sector to carry the burden of what had become a failed, self-serving economic policy. The plight of the American farmer became the forerunner of a soon-to-be visited national depression.

Chapter Thirteen

An "Interplay of Economic Forces"

World War I, the "first world war," was unlike any other. Aside from its lasting psychological and emotional consequences, it left both victor and vanquished with serious and long-term economic, social and political problems which would soon lead to another even bloodier and more costly global conflict twenty years later. In retrospect, the war's carnage and the vicious recriminations that were to be visited upon the defeated in its aftermath severely damaged, if not all but destroyed, the West's long-held confidence in its own moral superiority.

Even in 1918 when victory was in sight, the post-war inflation period was already spurred by government policies encouraging reconstruction financing while attempting to meet the severe food shortages abroad. Both efforts were being built on a towering pyramid of credit.

Lost in the rush to satisfy Europe's demand for American goods and commodities was the fact that these markets ultimately depended not simply on a desire for such products, but rather on the ability of the buyer to pay for them with goods, services, gold or credit.

American farmers, confident they could meet the demands of a hungry world, were encouraged by the 1916 authorization of Federal Farm Loan banks, which had been an integral part of Woodrow Wilson's New Freedom agenda. They believed that loans from these banks would enable them to purchase tractors, improved farm implements and increased amounts of fertilizers; bolstered by guaranteed government support prices, they would be able to keep soaring production costs in balance with their revenues.

Angry Farmers

When farm commodity prices collapsed after May 31, 1920, as government supports came off and lower tariffs initiated in the Wilson era encouraged imports, it was a considerable shock to the agricultural community. Nonagricultural prices and wages remained high, so a noticeable disparity between farm income and input costs was immediately recreated.

Cropland values had soared between 1914 and 1918, spurred by inflated wartime prices creating a land boom in many farm areas, which in turn fueled an enormous expansion of credit at high wartime interest rates. The pressure during the war to expand production capabilities also accounted for the value of farm mortgages rose from $3.2 billion in 1910 to $10.2 billion in 1921.[1] By 1919 the average acreage value of the ten leading crops was $35.74; in 1921, it was $14.45, the ratio of prices received to prices paid falling from 109 to 75 (Base: 1910-1914 = 100).[2]

As farm prices fell on average to slightly more than half their wartime levels, nonfarm prices dropped only 25 percent before stabilizing. Five gallons of gas, for example, in 1919 cost the farmer a price equivalent to a bushel of corn; a year later the proceeds from that bushel could buy only one gallon of gas and by 1921 it would take two bushels of corn to buy that same one gallon of gasoline.[3]

Farm tenancy also showed a continuing steady increase from the late 1800s through the "golden years" to the point that in 1920, 38 percent of America's farmers did not own the land they farmed. Renters faced an uncertain future. "The trouble is," recalls one tenant farmer, "that just as sure as a tenant made a farm more productive, the owner boosted his rent."[4]

Farmers, encouraged to produce more during the war by the lure of high prices and calls for patriotism, naturally became angry. With markets overseas rapidly disappearing and domestic prices plummeting, they seemed set adrift by an indifferent, industrialized, urban-oriented nation complacently at peace.

Fred Shannon describes the times:

The loss of foreign markets as the world settled down to production instead of destruction, a decline in domestic consumption, and the fact that half of the people in the world could not buy what they needed to maintain a comfortable existence explained the presence of what was euphemistically called an "agricultural surplus."

But farmers could not solve the problem of world distribution. What they knew was that they had been encouraged to buy expensive machinery, and to till more acres more intensively, and now, like the snipe hunter of old, they were left holding the bag far out in the economic wilderness, while general business, envisioned as the pranksters who had instigated the hunt, were safe back at home basking in the firelight of prosperity.[5]

In 1921 Congress created a Joint Commission of Agricultural Inquiry to explore the roots of this farm crisis. The Commission was directed to "investigate and report" to the Congress upon the following subjects: 1) the causes of the present condition of agriculture; 2) the cause of the difference between the prices of agricultural products paid to the producer and the ultimate cost to the consumer; 3) the comparative condition of industries other than agriculture; 4) the relation of prices of commodities other than agriculture; 5) the banking and financial resources and credits of the country, especially as affecting agricultural credits; and 6) the marketing and transportation facilities of the country.[6]

The Commission also expected to make specific legislative recommendations, complete its work in the fall of 1921 and report to Congress in early December.

The report, later described both as "broad and important" but "limited and ineffectual" in its specific recommendations, was not favorably received by farmers.[7] It attempted to arrive at the causes of the current crisis by studying changes in the purchasing power of the farmer's dollar, the relation of prices of farm products to those of other commodities, and the physical output and the return to capital and labor in agriculture as compared with other industries, rather than addressing the overall price structure of farm commodities.

The inquiry noted that in May 1921 the purchasing power of the farmer's dollar was only 77 percent of its pre-war value. In addition, prices of farm products had declined more rapidly and to a lower level than prices of other commodities (although agriculture's physical output had not kept pace with other industries) and the return to farm capital and labor was still relatively low.

The report essentially blamed agriculture's plight on the general business depression, along with the decrease of U.S. exports and a strong protectionist trade program. Other contributing factors included the maintenance of unduly high freight rates, the lack of facilities for intermediate credit, and the need for an adequate and integrated warehouse system. The 1920 price decline, the Joint Commission declared, *was not due to overproduction or overmarketing of farm products.*

The Commission's recommendations to Congress included the granting of preferred legal status to cooperative marketing associations, a system of intermediate credits for agriculture, improved warehousing facilities and supervision, reduction in freight rates on farm products, extension of the statistical research and foreign-service functions of the USDA, better grades and standards for farm products, farm-to-market roads, and general rural life improvements.

The Commission concluded that a renewal of confidence and prosperity in the nation's agricultural sector depended on the readjustment of commodity prices, which "cannot be brought about by legislative formulas, but must be the result for the most part of the interplay of economic forces."

Repaying the War Debt

But it was this very "interplay of economic forces" that had played a major if uncritiqued role in causing the national farm depression, and was pointing to eventual domestic and world-wide financial chaos.

During the initial stages of the war many of the major financial institutions, both in the United States and abroad, were called upon by England, France, Holland, Italy and their allies to loan them huge sums of money to wage war against the Central Powers. Such international bankers as J.P. Morgan & Co., the Rothchilds of England, the Guggenheims of France and others responded to the Allies' appeal by making available an unheard of $15 billion in American money.[8]

When things did not go well for the Allies in the early years of the war, pressure on the United States to enter the conflict increased. When the United States finally joined the war, it not only sacrificed untold human life and material goods, but it was also asked to loan another $15 billion from its public treasury to prop up the faltering Allied effort. Now the Allies were indebted to the international bankers for $15 billion and to the U.S. government for another $15 billion, neither of which they could readily pay off after the Armistice in 1918.

It was clear at the time, particularly to international bankers, that given conditions in war-ravaged Europe, the debt would not soon be paid back. To collect on their loans the bankers needed to turn elsewhere. By carefully orchestrating an outcry from the American taxpayer ("Europe pay us what she owes us") the bankers successfully led people into believing that "us" was the taxpayer.

In fact, as the economic and political policies of the next decade proved, it was not the people of the United States who collected on the nation's war debt, but rather the Morgans, Rothchilds, *et al.*

By encouraging agricultural imports through lower tariff barriers while adopting strong protectionist measures against industrial goods and terminating credits to former European allies, these financiers began to collect on their loans. Meanwhile, American taxpayers were forced to dig deeper into their pockets to buy imported agricultural goods with money that went to the debtor nations and from there back into the pockets of the American bankers.

Importing Our Surpluses

From 1920 through 1930 the United States, according to government figures, imported goods worth $40.8 billion of which over 52 percent were agricultural.[9] This despite the fact that our factories were extremely capable of turning out all the manufactured goods people needed, our farmers were capable of producing all the food, fiber and feed that was necessary for the nation's well being, the labor supply was adequate and the country was beginning to enjoy an unprecedented prosperity as the economy adjusted to a high level of prices and volume.

With the aid of the compliant Coolidge and Harding administrations, however, a glut of surplus goods and commodities (the surplus coming primarily from foreign imports) soon flooded our markets. Twelve million Americans became unemployed and thousands of farmers were forced into bankruptcy as these agricultural imports began to take away a significant portion of the nation's domestic market from American farmers.

While agricultural products accounted for a yearly average of 52.8 percent of the value of total U.S. imports from 1920 to 1930, the average yearly value of our agricultural exports during this period was only 40.8 percent. In the six basic commodities wheat, corn, oats, barley, soybeans and cotton — which accounted for nearly 80 percent of the nation's total agricultural output, the United States imported the equivalent of 17.8 million acres worth of production during the 1920s — at the very time that surpluses were purported to be agriculture's number one problem.[10] (Other "cash crops," imported in the 1920s and on into the 1930s, not numbered among the aforementioned six, had also a direct effect on the planting and pricing of the many other domestic crops the United States was producing at the time.)

In effect, then, the United States actually imported its "surpluses" in agriculture. When cheap but substantial numbers of imports such as tomatoes, onions, buckwheat, dried peas and beans, lemons, dates, figs, almonds, mushrooms and the six basic crops mentioned above came into the United States during the 1920s they presented farmers with price-depressing "surpluses" not of their own making.

Corporate agribusiness, however, adroitly manipulated the "surplus" question, selling farmers on the idea that the world price, at which any surplus that existed after domestic consumption would be sold, should also dictate the domestic price, ignoring the fact that the so-called "surplus" constituted a relatively minor part of the total crop. One farm spokesman at the time aptly summarized this fallacious argument for a Congressional committee:

> In other words, the 3.8 percent of these grain crops which we sent abroad to meet the general trade price level of the world in competition with the products of the Hindus and peons and the peasants of Europe, and the cheaper labor and the cheaper lands of other countries, that little dinkey surplus automatically fixes approximately the price of the 96.2 percent of that crop which we consume at home, and regardless of the cost of production.[11]

Meanwhile, a select group of the world's bankers were reaping billions in "foreign debt" repayments.

When Herbert Hoover became president in 1929 he promptly issued an Executive Order declaring a moratorium on the collection of these war debts. In taking this long overdue action, however, Hoover conveniently overlooked the fact that England, France, Holland and Italy had credits worth over $3.5 billion in American banks. Rather than requiring these nations to convert this sum into U.S. Treasury notes as payment toward their war debt, Hoover allowed billions of dollars to remain subject to draft by these same countries. These countries, however, would exercise their right under international law to draw out their gold.[12]

Not surprisingly, however, this $3.5 billion in gold was more than the economy could spare and still maintain a legal gold reserve. It soon became necessary, therefore, for U.S. banks to reduce their deposits. This, in turn, forced the banks to make necessary collections from their customers to whom they had already loaned the depositor's money. Because these forced collections were often difficult to exact due to the heavy buying on margin taking place in a runaway stock market, many banks were forced to unload their own stocks and bonds, which had been held as security against such loans.

What followed was the great stock market crash of October 1929.

A Victory for the "Sound Money" Crusade

The nation's economic chaos was also attributable to the fact that in conjunction with the excessive surplus commodities imported during the 1920s and the ensuing depletion of the gold supply, the Federal Reserve Board in 1920 had deflated the currency and credits by an estimated $2 billion. The Fed's actions resulted in low prices which doubled the amount of goods it was necessary to import so other nations could "pay off" their war debts.

As late as 1913 the dollar had been worth as much as it had been in 1813 — $20 an ounce. Anyone from a farmer to a worker to a foreign government could present to the U. S. Treasury $20 and receive an ounce of gold. Thus for nearly a century people had some control over the value of their money. In 1913, however, that control was taken from them by the nation's banks with the passage of the Federal Reserve Act.[13]

Although the gold standard had been law since 1901, the financial panic of 1907 illustrated to the banking community the need for a flexible currency system. By pushing for and finally establishing the Federal Reserve, the banking community not only centralized and rationalized the nation's financial system, but insured that there would be no democratic influence over interest rates, such as had been suggested by the agrarian populists.

At the time these same "communities of economic interests" also sought to deflect public attention from their own manipulative actions by extending their "sound money" crusade of the previous decade.

The Panic of 1907 in part corroborated the earlier populist analysis that a contracted money supply could not provide adequate capital markets during a fall agricultural harvest. Calls on Eastern banks by Western banks at such times had traditionally created stringent shortages throughout the monetary system.[14]

Even though bankers capitalized on relatively high interest rates during these periods, the condition still depressed agricultural prices and eventually the whole banking system began to break down under this and other burdens.

Subsequent calls for reform were not primarily for agricultural's benefit, but rather were oriented toward the banking industry. As would happen so often in the ensuing years, the American public was not fully conscious that a real "crisis" existed in its farming sector until its banks begin to suffer economic hardships.

Even though the National Monetary Commission recommended legislation in 1912 to establish adequate credit for farmers the subsequent Federal Reserve Act failed to include them.

Gathering at the estate of J.P. Morgan at Jekyll Island, Georgia in 1910, the "Money Trust" conceived the plan for a Federal Reserve System. This group included Henry P. Davison, Senior Partner of J.P. Morgan & Co. and Morgan's personal emissary; Frank Vanderlip, President of the National City Bank of New York; Paul Warburg of Kuhn, Loeb & Co., Charles D. Norton,

President of the First National Bank of New York, along with Senator Nelson Aldrich, grandfather of David Rockefeller, Jacob Schiff of Kuhn, Loeb & Co.; A. Piatt Andrew, Assistant Secretary of the Treasury, and Benjamin Strong, also associated with Morgan.[15]

Fulfilling the Functions of a Central Bank

Although their plan was later presented to the Congress as the work of the National Monetary Commission, it was these bankers who actually conceived the Federal Reserve System. By naming it such they avoided the stigma of a "central bank" which long had been opposed by the American public dating back to the sharp debates on the plan between Jefferson and Hamilton.

The Federal Reserve System, nevertheless, was conceived to fulfill the functions of a central bank, namely, one owned by private individuals who could profit from ownership of shares, and as a bank of issue, control the nation's money and credit supply. The "Fed" was destined, in the words of one writer, to be "the guardian of credit and the currency."

The structure of the Fed would also insure that control remained in the hands of the Eastern banking establishment. The President would appoint the Board of Governors although the real work would be done by the Federal Reserve Council meeting with those governors. The Council would be selected by the directors of the 12 Federal Reserve Banks. In this manner the Eastern bankers, who were well aware of the popular resentment against them by farmers and small business people, would remain in the shadows.

Despite their efforts to avoid the public spotlight there was opposition to the "Aldrich Plan" in Congress. Senator Robert LaFollette, R-Wis., denounced the proposed system as a blatant effort by a money trust of 50 men to control the United States. Responding to these charges, George F. Baker, a partner of J.P. Morgan, told reporters that LaFollette was absolutely in error as he knew from personal knowledge that not more than *eight* men ran the country![16]

Aided by deception and propaganda, however, the Federal Reserve Act passed on December 12, 1913.

The System began as 12 regional banks. Each of these banks elected a member to the Federal Advisory Council, which would meet with the Federal Reserve Board of Governors four times a year in Washington, D.C. to "advise" the Board on future monetary policy. Very often, however, the small banks that made up the reserve district would simply be "correspondent" banks to their larger counterparts in New York and were often understandably reluctant to embark on policies of their own.

The fact that J.P. Morgan served as the chairman of the executive committee and high-powered financier Paul Warburg sat on the Advisory Committee during the Board's first four years, indicates the power that the New York banking establishment exercised in determining the nation's financial policies.

Clearly, the most powerful of the 12 Federal Reserve Banks was and to this day is the Federal Reserve Bank of New York. Despite the numerous claims of autonomy made both on its behalf and that of the Federal System, the New York bank is clearly the most powerful financial institution in America.

A look at the principal stockholders in that bank provides an excellent study in interlocking directors and multiple ownership. The majority stock (43 percent) of the Federal Reserve Bank of New York was purchased by five major New York banks: the First National Bank, National City Bank, National Bank of Commerce, Chase National, and Hanover National.[17] As of July 26, 1983 the top five surviving New York City banks had increased their ownership to 53 percent. In effect, therefore, America's monetary policy has been administered by a network of private banks which are regulated by institutions owned by these *same* commercial banks. (It has also been suggested that the principal stockholders in these banks, both in 1914 and today, bear a direct connection with banks abroad, specifically the House of Rothschild in England. Many of the United States's largest bank holding companies are multinational and they all maintain close relationships with foreign banks, including the House of Rothschild.)

It is most important in this regard to note here that from almost its inception, the Federal Reserve System, not to mention the entire U.S. banking system, has been the target of a variety of anti-Semitic charges that it is but a part of the alleged international Jewish banking conspiracy. There is no real evidence that that is the case.

In 1979, for example, only 15 of the 345 senior officers in the largest New York banks were Jewish, and only three of the top 86 were. Of the 22 officers of big New York banks who were members of their Board of Directors, none were Jewish. As of 1988, no one currently serving on the Federal Open Market Committee, which operates the Federal Reserve, is of Jewish descent.[18] So, despite what some may like the public and particularly farmers to believe, bankers make decisions based not on their religious beliefs but on what will earn them and their institutions the greatest profits.

In that regard, there is ample evidence that the Federal Reserve System has used its considerable financial power to influence U.S. economic policy profoundly throughout the years of its existence, while at the same time exerting a major influence in the decision-making process within the nation's "communities of economic interests," including corporate agribusiness, often to the detriment of the "family farm system" of agriculture.[19]

Using Debt to Inflate Real Money

In establishing the Federal Reserve System, the Federal Reserve note, which was not redeemable in gold or silver, was deemed an "IOU" issued by the banks as an instrument of debt. This enabled the banks to control the value of the dollar by simply backing dollars with Federal Reserve notes and not with gold, thus using debt as a way to inflate real money. The system as a whole, however, was obliged to maintain a 40 percent gold backing for its notes, but even 40 percent in 1913 provided an unequal opportunity for the banks to deflate the real money supply.

The Federal Reserve Act, in addition to introducing a new form of currency, also reduced the various banks' reserve requirements. The Act was to cut the reserve to 12 percent for checking accounts and 5 percent on savings deposits. Prior to 1913 banks had to retain a reserve of 25 percent of their total deposits in cash in the bank's own vaults. Relaxing such reserve standards made it much easier for the banks to create credit.[20]

Opposition to allowing banks to create money as debt and in turn lend that money to the government had been long-standing for opponents saw it leading eventually to a ruinous Federal debt, high interest rates and political instability.

Such an argument was prophetically offered on February 9, 1790 by Georgia Congressman James Jackson, speaking before the First Congress of the United States, when he denounced Alexander Hamilton's efforts to use a funded debt to increase the money supply of the new nation:

Gentlemen may come forward, perhaps, and tell me, that funding the public debt will increase the circulating medium of the country, by means of its transferable quality; but this is denied by the best informed men. The funding of the debt will occasion enormous taxes for the payment of interest. These taxes will bear heavily, both on agriculture and commerce. It will be charging the active and industrious citizen ... to pay the indolent and idle creditor. ... In the proportion that it benefits the one, it will depress the other.

I contend that a funding system in this country will be highly dangerous to the welfare of the Republic; it may, for a moment, raise our credit, and increase our circulation by multiplying a new species of currency; but it must hereafter settle upon our posterity a burden which they can neither bear nor relieve themselves from.

It will establish a precedent in America that may, and in all probability will, be pursued by the sovereign authority, until it brings upon us that ruin which it has never failed to bring. Let us take warning by the errors of Europe and guard against the introduction of a system followed by calamities so general. Though our present debt may be but a few million, in the course of a single century it may be multiplied to an extent we dare not think of.[21]

Credit or the lack of credit would, of course, be one of the major causes of the agricultural depression of 1920. World War I had brought about a general prosperity for the country, with high wages, production bonuses and unprecedented agricultural prices. But because of their suspicion of banks, many people during the war years either held on to their money or placed it in small local banks where they could keep an eye on it.

Meanwhile, the Federal Reserve was trying to encourage the buying of Liberty Bonds as a means to soak up some of the nation's prosperity, but the scheme did not succeed as well as hoped. On the whole there was still an enormous amount of money in circulation at war's end and the Federal Reserve System, acting on behalf of the New York banks, saw as its duty to recapture that money and credit. One method that was immediately apparent was to break the small country banks where much of the farmers' money resided.[22]

Behind Closed Doors

The Federal Farm Loan Board was established to encourage farmers to invest such money in land on long term loans. Inflation was allowed to run its course in 1919 and 1920 so in Europe it would start the drive to cancel out a large portion of the Allied war debt and in this country it helped draw in the excess money. As prices began to skyrocket and workers' and farmers' savings decreased in value, industrialists and land owners became richer and the value of land and manufactured goods surged upward.

In the 1939 Senate Silver hearings, Senator Robert L. Owen, Chairman of the Senate Banking and Currency Committee, described what happened next:

In the early part of 1920, the farmers were exceedingly prosperous. They were paying off the mortgages and buying a lot of new land, at the instance of the Government — had borrowed money to do it — and then they were bankrupted by a sudden contraction of credit and currency which took place in 1920.

What took place in 1920 was just the reverse of what should have been taking place. Instead of liquidating the excess of credits created by the war through a period of years, the Federal Reserve Board met in a meeting which was not disclosed to the public. They met on the 18th of May, 1920, and it was a secret meeting. They spent all day conferring; the minutes made 60 printed pages and they appear in Senate Document 310 of February 19, 1923.

The Senator continues,

The Class A Directors, the Federal Reserve Advisory Council, were present, but the Class B Directors, who represented business, commerce, and agriculture, were not present. The Class C Directors, representing the people of the United States, were not present and were not invited to be present. Only the big bankers were there, and their work of that day resulted in a contraction of credit which had the effect the next year of reducing the national income $15 billion, throwing millions of people out of employment, and reducing the value of lands and ranches by $20 billion.[23]

It was later reported that at this same meeting Paul Warburg, then the Council's President, had a resolution passed and sent to a committee of five members of the I.C.C. asking for an increase in railroad rates. Kuhn, Loeb Co., which Warburg represented, owned a large portion at the time of the nation's rail lines.[24]

Less than two weeks after this secret meeting the Federal government also announced the removal of farm price supports, and the agricultural depression of 1920 was underway.

While manufacturers and merchants were allowed a healthy increase in credits to get them through this contraction of credit, farmers were denied such benefits as the interest rate was raised to seven percent on agricultural and livestock paper. As William Jennings Bryan later wrote in *Hearst's Magazine* in 1923: "The Federal Reserve Bank that should have been the farmer's greatest protection has become his greatest foe. The deflation of the farmer was a crime deliberately committed."[25]

The ensuing inflationary credit binge by industrial manufacturers in addition to the debts incurred during and immediately after World War I gave banks expanded liabilities while their cash tills became increasingly depleted. By June 1930 the total savings and checking accounts in Federal Reserve banks had risen to $32 billion, more than double the 1917 amount, while the cash holdings had declined from $800 million to only $500 million, approximately 1.5 percent of their deposit liabilities.[26]

By initially deflating the currency an estimated $2 billion, which precipitated the panic of the early 1920s, the Federal Reserve Board caused the absorption of the aforementioned $43 billion worth of imports over the next ten years to have a dramatic impact on the country's economic stability and future, particularly in agriculture.[27]

The drive to destroy the nation's "family farm system" of agriculture by ridding it of its millions of farms and farm families through converting real wealth into debt-ridden capital was already moving into high gear.

Chapter Fourteen

Fighting for "Equality for Agriculture"

"Quit talking calamity and make the most of a bad situation."

Warren G. Harding's admonition to irate cotton growers in 1920 as they saw their prices plummet, was typical of the reaction by the business community and the general public to the plight of the nation's farmers in immediate post-World War I America.[1]

In three short years American agriculture had plunged into an unprecedented depression. From November 1919 to the following November market prices dropped by 33 percent and by July 1921 they had fallen 85 percent.[2] Four months later, the USDA estimated the purchasing power of the principal farm crops to be slightly more than half of what they were during the 1910-1914 pre-war period.[3]

Farm debt, which in the previous twenty years had shown signs of lessening, ballooned from $8.5 billion in 1920 to $10.7 billion in 1923. Gross income would fall from near $17 billion in 1919 to less than $12 billion in 1929. Measuring the wage for the labor of the farmer and his family, the figures for the 1920-21 period show that after paying for expenses, interest, rent and taxes the farmers' total was $1.72 billion short of their income, excluding a return on capital investment. In 1921-22 the figure decreased slightly to $797 million.[4]

It came as no surprise to rural America when in 1924 Senator LaFollette reported that over 600,000 farmers had gone bankrupt in the previous three years and that the value of farms had declined by some $13 billion.[5]

As agricultural prices collapsed and nonagricultural prices and wages remained stable, ever widening the gap between farm income and farm costs, farmers began organizing in unprecedented numbers protesting their plight, often violently, and vocally in calling for government price fixing.

Some farmers even appealed to the current folk hero, the most prominent industrialist of his time — Henry Ford for financial aid and help. Writing from South Carolina one cotton farmer demanded of the motor car pioneer:

I want you to lead three million cotton planters as one man. George Washington, Napoleon and Foch led men to fight with guns while our battle will be fought with brain force ...Since South Carolina was the first to secede in 1860, now South Carolina will secede from Wall Street.[6]

Such attempts, however, proved unsuccessful. As one historian has noted:

The difficulty lay in the fact that worried farmers, experiencing hard times, wanted relief at once. Ford offered long-range plans. The underdog sought aid from outside interests; Ford recommended the 'bootstrap' formula of self-help. Farmers begging for charity received good advice. Ford's tips for the day smacked too much of the general palaver cluttering up the farm journals. In short those in distress found little consolation in Ford's admonition to be more progressive, to utilize more mechanical power in farm work, to be efficient, and above all, to be self-reliant.[7]

Resurrecting the "Surplus" Issue

The rest of the nation, meanwhile, paid scant attention to the desperate screams of protest coming from the farmers. What little action was taking place in Washington centered mainly around three general courses of action: A) establishing a nationwide system of government-sponsored farm cooperatives that would attempt to regulate the flow of farm and food products into the market to establish a pattern of orderly marketing characterized by fair and stable prices; B) reinvigorating the export market so farm prices might achieve the same ratio to non-farm prices as existed prior to the war; and C) balancing farm output with market demand by withdrawing farm land from crop production.

Easily the most vexing issue at this time for agriculture, and one that continued to plague it for years to come, centered around the question of "surpluses." Many of the policy decisions that would be made in the future, particularly in the years leading up to World War II, would be based on the assumption that the nation's farmers were overproducing and thereby creating an unwanted surplus of crops. This in turn was allegedly depressing most commodity prices.

Putting Together the "Farm Bloc"

When Congress met in special session in April, 1921 the nation clearly faced still another chapter in its ongoing farm crisis. Representatives from the executive committees of the American Farm Bureau Federation, the State Farm Bureau Federations, the National Farmers' Union and others came to Washington to frame an agenda of individual and joint legislative programs for submission to the new Congress.

At this time the American Farm Bureau first emerged as a political force, and has until this day remained a constant and powerful voice in shaping farm legislation. As Fred Shannon points out:

> Conscious of this distress and discomfort at a time when farmer-labor combinations were threatening to take over the state governments of the Midwest {i.e., the Non-Partisan League in North Dakota}, the new Farm Bureau Federation fearing any radical plan that would iron out the differences between industrial and rural workers, began welding together a small group of ordinarily conservative members of Congress into a farm bloc.

Responding to the AFBF's call for action many farm state members of Congress formed a bipartisan "Farm Bloc," which worked closely with the Farm Bureau Federations, led by their Washington representative Gray Silver, on drafting legislation before disbanding in 1923.

The "Farm Bloc," which quickly achieved control of the Senate Agriculture Committee, succeeded in passing several important pieces of legislation, including the Packer and Stockyards Act, the Futures Trading Act, the Agricultural Credits Act of 1921, which extended the powers of the War Finance Corporation for an additional year, and amendments to the Federal Farm Loan Act, designed to better facilitate its operation.[9] The following year the bloc was instrumental in passing the Capper-Volstead Cooperative Marketing Act of 1922 and on the last day of the session saw its colleagues enact: 1) the Agricultural Credits Act of 1923, which set up a system of intermediate credit banks under the supervision of the Farm Loan system; 2) the formation of a National Agricultural Credit Corporation, and 3) finally amend the Federal Reserve Act in an attempt to liberalize its services to agriculture.

The revival of the War Finance Corp. was designed as a means to finance exports, and establish an emergency tariff, which had been vetoed by President Wilson immediately before he left office. The corporation's powers were also broadened so as to authorize loans for agricultural rehabilitation.

Establishing the Office of Farm Management

In casting about for solutions to the farm problem there developed, particularly within the USDA, a growing tendency to emulate modern corporate bureaucratic models to solve such problems as authority, competence, the division of labor and quality control. A disciple of this mode of thinking was Hency C. Taylor, a University of Wisconsin agricultural economist, who in 1919 was named chief of the USDA's Office of Farm Management.

Taylor saw his task in almost strictly economic terms and restructured his office in a manner that made agronomists professionally unfit to fill the new jobs in his department. Among these office divisions were cost analysis, finance, labor, land economics, economic geography and history, farm life, and farm management.[10]

A thumbnail sketch of each of these departments clearly illustrates the direction Taylor and his associates believed agriculture should be taking:

Farm Organization This department was to provide the farmer and the nation with "the necessary information to hasten the adjustment of farm organization" to the demands of the marketplace, and to provide detailed cost analyses of alternative farm products and their marketability. Shortly after this division made its initial recommendations it was merged with the cost analysis division and became the Department of Farm Organization and Cost Analysis.

Land Economics An "economic classification" of the nation's land was made the primary goal of this department with the classifications to be used in helping "guide the course of land settlement, determining the economically efficient size of farms in different localities, and directing wisely the agricultural energies of the country."

Agricultural History and Geography This department was to make studies on the "trends of agricultural development" which caused "changes in [farm] production and price," and also to discern through historical analysis the extent to which farm settlers acted rationally in response to changes in the marketplace.

Labor Because most agricultural economists at the time believed that farmers no longer would face labor shortages, it was determined that there was no need to plan for farm labor and the committee was promptly disbanded.

Finance Unlike most farmers Taylor did not believe the functions of this department were critical in planning modern agriculture. While the department agreed to study national banking, community banks, taxes, insurance, and finance legislation, its chief concern was the impact of commercial investors and speculators on the patterns of farm development, production and prices.

Farm Life Studies This department, sounding remarkably like the voices heard earlier in the Country Life movement, believed that it could help elite farmers establish "many farm life organizations" that together could "promote a better farming, better living, and clearer thinking."

This same department also voiced a concern that "the more intelligent and able members of the [farm] community" were moving to the cities. These so-called elite farmers were making such a move because the cities offered "the arts and institutions of modern civilization" that had yet to develop in rural America. Left behind on the farms were those "less capable and less cultured" and should this migration pattern continue, the department believed, "cultural and racial" decay would pervade the countryside.

Concern over "rural trends toward racial degeneration in the countryside" was not limited to the Farm Life Studies Department as Harry C. McDean, Associate Professor of History at San Diego State University, relates.

One such occasion prompted Frank Harrison, assistant to Secretary of Agriculture Edwin Meredith, to admonish Taylor privately for speaking "of the inferiority of farm people in general." Taylor was told: "That is a very dangerous thing, especially before a [congressional agricultural] committee ... it is true but I doubt the wisdom of saying it before the committee ... when we are trying to get funds." Harrison claimed too many farm state politicians think like Senator Gilbert N. Haugen and believe 'that"the people out west are just as good as anyone else."[11]

By the fall of 1920 Taylor had gained complete control over all the statistical information issued from the USDA. He believed that farmers "were not getting adequate results" from the Department of Agriculture because the various bureaus provided no economic interpretations of the massive amount of statistics on farm prices and supplies that they issued regularly. How, he asked, were farmers to "act [on all this data] intelligently? Taylor believed they could not without the proper perspective of the agricultural economist.

In 1921 Taylor engineered a "bloodless coup" within the USDA and established a Bureau of Economics, which included the Office of Farm Management, the Bureau of Markets and the Bureau of Crop and Livestock Estimates, with Taylor as the new bureau's chief. Meanwhile, he exerted his considerable influence on Secretary Meredith so that the latter was soon telling Americans that there would be "a greatly expanded effort on the part of the [USDA] and the state colleges and experiment stations in interpreting price situations in terms of what the farmer should do in the management of his farm."

Believing that it was time for "a more concrete and effective national agricultural policy," Taylor convinced Agriculture Secretary Henry C. Wallace in March 1921 that his predecessor's reorganization plan should be immediately implemented so that all economic and statistical information would be gathered and disseminated through his office. Wallace agreed to his recommendation and on July 1, 1922 the Bureau of Agricultural Economics was created. It would later play a major role in shaping agricultural policy in Franklin Roosevelt's New Deal.[12]

A "National Wish" and the Search for Parity

As these structural and policy-shaping changes were developing, growing farmer unrest and the desire within the Congress to take action provoked President Harding to instruct Wallace to call a National Agricultural Conference in Washington, D.C. in January 1922.[13]

While more tactful than in his remarks to cotton growers, Harding showed in his letter to Wallace and in his opening address to 400 representatives of agricultural and related industries attending the conference an administration less than fully committed to helping the nation's farmers.

In his call to Secretary Wallace the President declared:

It is unthinkable that with our vast areas, of unparalleled endowment of agricultural re-

sources, our fertility of soil, our vast home market, and the great ability and resourcefulness of our farmers we should accept the status of a distinctly industrial nation. Our destiny seems to require that we should be a well-rounded nation with a high development of both industry and agriculture, supporting one another and prospering together. It must be, and I feel sure it is, the national wish and purpose to maintain our agriculture at the highest possible efficiency.[14]

Yet in his remarks to the Conference delegates, the President made it clear that he saw the Federal Government giving only limited support to the "national wish."

It cannot be too strongly urged that the farmer must be ready to help himself. This conference would do most lasting good if it would find ways to impress the great mass of farmers to avail themselves of the best methods. By this I mean that, in the last analysis, legislation can do little more than give the farmer the chance to organize and help himself.[15]

Significantly, nearly all the themes that have permeated agricultural policy in the last half century can be found in its recommendations incorporated in the Conference's final report.

The single most significant concept to emerge from this meeting was the work of one man — George R. Peek. Initially, rebuffed by Wallace, AFBF officials and others in Washington, Peek was promised a period of ten minutes to appear before the Committee on Price Relations to present an idea he and his colleague, Hugh S. Johnson, had developed. Peek and Johnson, were President and Vice-President respectively, of the Moline Plow Company of Moline, Illinois. Rather than ten minutes, Peek spoke for nearly an hour and one half.

That evening the Midwestern businessman returned to the conference and in the Committee on Marketing won the unanimous approval of the historic recommendation calling for "Equality For Agriculture," a slogan which has been repeatedly echoed throughout the farm community since that January evening in 1922 in the nation's capital.

The key paragraph of Peek's resolution read:

Agriculture is necessary to the life of the nation; and, whereas the prices of agricultural products are far below the cost of production, so far below that relatively they are the lowest in the history of our country; therefore, it is the sense of this Committee that the Congress and the President of the United States should take steps as will immediately reestablish *a fair exchange value for all farm products with that of all other commodities.* (emphasis added)[16]

Peek's ideas were also reflected elsewhere in the Conference report.

The Conference declares that no revival of American business is possible until the farmer's dollar is restored to its normal purchasing power when expressed in the prices paid for commodities which the farmer must purchase, and the Conference further declares that by right the men engaged in the agricultural field are entitled to a larger return than they have heretofore received for the service they give society.[17]

Stressing the adjustment of farm production to demand, the Conference report continued:

The manufacturer has in the past quickly adjusted his production to price recessions which the farmer has not. When farm production is so large that the product cannot be sold for prices that will maintain a reasonable standard of living on the farms, the supply is too large. We recommend that the farmers and the farm organizations consider the problem of world supply and demand and make comprehensive plans for production programs so that they may be able 'to advise their members as to the probable demand for staples, and to propose measures for proper limitation of acreage in particular crops,' as pointed out by the President of the United States.[18]

Other recommendations to emerge from this Conference included higher tariffs, more foreign credits to facilitate exports, an intermediate credit system for farmers, recognition of farm cooperative-marketing associations and price stabilization through their operations, consideration of a system of crop insurance and government guarantees for agricultural prices.

In Search of Grass Roots Support

Peek's "Equality for Agriculture" concept soon captured the imagination of farm interests in the government. First presented to a group of businessmen in the fall of 1921, and later developed into a pamphlet, *Equality For Agriculture*, the plan's three main points were:

A) A device for making tariffs effective on large export surpluses of agricultural products and restoring the favorable pre-war ratios of agricultural and industrial prices by establishing a fair exchange value for agricultural goods. Fair exchange value was defined as a price "which bears the same ratio to the current general price index as a ten-year (1906-1915) pre-war average crop price bore to the average price index for the same period";

B) Creation of a government corporation which would deal in the selling of a few selected commodities (which had domestic surpluses) to be marketed abroad at world prices; and

C) Financing this system by assessing a nominal charge (an equalization fee) against each marketed unit of the commodity benefitted.[19] How Peek and Johnson developed their idea and how it was finally incorporated into legislation is instructive.[20]

In June 1921 the Chairman of the Joint Congressional Commission of Agricultural Inquiry sent a letter to the AFBF requesting that the various Farm Bureau Federations hold meetings about the current agricultural crisis. From these meetings came a consensus that the reason farmers were not buying machinery, manufactured goods and supplies was because this "rate of exchange" was too far below "par." The AFBF's Secretary J.W. Cloverdale noted in his report of the meetings that the farmer "needs to have the value of the goods he sells placed on a parity with the goods he must buy."

While Peek and Johnson later claimed that they were urged by Farm Bureau officials to develop principles for solving agriculture's current problems, their subsequent "Equality For Agriculture" plan resulted primarily from their own initiative to win grass roots support for such an idea. As the Farm Bureau's J.R. Howard described it,

When the collapse of post-war inflation came in 1921, the hardest hit industry in the country was agriculture and the next was the farm implement industry ... George (Peek) came to a typical conclusion: 'There can't be any business for us until the farmer is on his feet. There is nothing we can do here — let's find out what is the matter with agriculture.'[21]

Peek and Johnson visited the AFBF office in Washington, but were told they first should see Secretary Wallace for he was "supposed to be the spokesman for legislation that would affect the welfare of the agricultural interests." If the plan met with his approval then the AFBF would be available for further discussions. Several subsequent drafts were submitted by Peek and Johnson to the Farm Bureau, but they were found to be too controversial and sent back for reworking.

While Secretary Wallace was not responsible for getting Peek's hearing before the National Agricultural Conference in 1922, he did call a conference of business leaders to discuss the idea. Attending that meeting were Julius H. Barnes, one of the nation's leading grain exporters; Charles G. Dawes, director of the budget; Otto Kahn, Kuhn, Loeb and Company; Fred J. Lingham, Lockport Milling Co.; George McFadden, cotton exporter, Frederick B. Wells, Peavey Elevator Co.; Thomas Wilson, president of the American Institute of Meat Packers; J.R. Howard and Gray Silver, American Farm Bureau Federation; Judson Welliver, from President Harding's staff; Wallace; Taylor; Peek and Johnson.

While Peek and Johnson were seeking support for their ideas the Bureau of Agricultural Economics was quietly proceeding with a series of relevant studies on the implications of the plan. Although the business leaders generally reacted unfavorably to the Peek-Johnson idea, the elder economic statesman, Bernard M. Baruch, encouraged the two midwesterners, believing that the plan offered "power enough," if capably administered, to sustain the purchasing power of American farm products. After a followup conference with a group of economists who were favorably disposed to their basic idea, Peek and Johnson set about revising the first edition of their *Equality For Agriculture* pamphlet to make it more politically acceptable.

In this second edition they did not refer to a specific administrative mechanism for attaining "equality for agriculture," although they did retain the 1906-1915 base period. Rather, they shortened their presentation and concentrated attention on the general problems of agriculture and tariffs. Such a political refusal to deal with the "practical organization" of administering an "Equality For Agriculture" program continues to plague U.S. agriculture to this day.

In a cover letter accompanying their second edition, Peek and Johnson warned of dire consequences if the farm problem was not quickly resolved, and then added rather prophetically: "No graver question has ever been presented in the economic development of our nation and, unless we as a nation can solve this problem, we can look forward to a progressively depressed agriculture with an alarming tendency toward tenantry and eventually peasantry ..."[22]

As Peek-Johnson were attempting to win support for their idea, Nebraska's Senator George W. Norris was introducing a bill in the Senate to substitute a government agency for private processors and middlemen. The Norris-Sinclair bill sought to create a government corporation empowered to buy or lease storage and processing facilities, and to buy, process and sell farm products in raw or finished form. Arguing that the plan would increase farm prices while cutting consumer prices, the Norris-Sinclair bill sought to eliminate many commissions and charges between producers and consumers which had traditionally victimized both parties.[23]

The corporation was to be given $100 million in capital, with authority to sell tax-free bonds up to five times that amount. While supporters saw this legislation as a means to fix prices on a cost-of-production basis, it received no support from the Harding Administration for political reasons that would soon become apparent.

A Timid Congress Grapples With the Farm Problem

New low prices for wheat in the summer and fall of 1923 focused increased attention on the wheat "surplus" problem and spurred Secretary Wallace to bring the "farm question" before a September cabinet meeting. Both before the President and later in a November address to the Chicago Association of Commerce he emphasized that the USDA was considering a plan for restoring farm purchasing power by the withdrawal of exportable surpluses from the domestic market.

The USDA believed that this purchasing power plan could be done by establishing a corporation, which in cooperation with private agencies, would seek to restore the pre-war ratio between wheat and other exportable farm products and other commodities. By arranging for the sale of the surplus to be exported at a price lower than the domestic price, the corporation could distribute any incurred losses over the entire crop. Wallace at the same time was already overseeing the drafting of legislation embodying such a plan.

Meanwhile, his son Henry A. Wallace, seeking to build political support for the Peek-Johnson concept,

was forced "to go to the grass roots and get a resolution brought up from the floor of the Iowa State Farm Bureau convention in December, 1923 (the resolution's committee had refused to bring it out) in order to get the first Farm Bureau organization on record."[24]

On January 10, 1924 the proposals of Secretary Wallace and Peek-Johnson were introduced as a bill in the U.S. Senate by Charles L. McNary of Oregon and in the House of Representatives by Gilbert N. Haugen of Iowa.

Events in the next five years confirmed the earlier suspicions of Senator George Norris that the White House's lack of support for his bill was politically motivated and that the McNary-Haugen legislation was conceived and introduced by the Administration primarily to divert and divide farm support.

Before examining the legislative battles and the evolution of the McNary-Haugen bills it is important to point out, as Chester C. Davis, a one-time member of the Board of Governors of the Federal Reserve System, wrote concerning the development of agricultural policy in the years after World War I:

> Developments of later years reveal some surprising gaps and blind spots in these early post-war analyses of the farm problem. Commission and conference alike seemed unconscious of the clash between their demand that agricultural as well as industrial exports be restored and maintained and their insistence that this nation vigorously pursue a policy of exclusion through higher and yet higher tariffs. Neither the conservative Administration leaders nor the farm forces they called radical recognized that the volume of agricultural exports following the war and up to 1929 was financed in large part by extension of credit abroad — many of the loans not to be repaid.[25]

The first McNary-Haugen bill called for the establishment of a government export corporation, to be capitalized at $200 million, which would buy designated farm commodities in sufficient amount to raise the price to a "ratio price," or fair exchange value. In other words, to bring a commodity up to the current all-commodity index level, the corporation would buy the commodity whenever the price fell below that index level and sell it at the price in the domestic market to anyone ready to buy.

The price would not be fixed, but rather would rise and fall as the all-commodity index rose and fell. When the corporation bought more than it could sell on the domestic market, the excess would be sold abroad with re-imports restricted by tariffs. Any losses on exports were to be covered by the use of vouchers which could be purchased by potential farm product buyers at a slight discount and offered by them as legal tender to cover a portion of the cost of buying a farm commodity. Cash in an amount equal to the export price would be required and the difference between domestic and export prices could be paid by vouchers. Until it was redeemed by the corporation, the farmer could hold the vouchers. Depending on the losses experienced by the corporation, they would generally be at some fraction of their face value.

Actually the farmer would not receive the full ratio price, but something between the ratio and the export price. On the other hand, the corporation would sell the commodity in the domestic market at full ratio price. This would enable the corporation to gain on domestic sales part or all of what it lost on export sales.

Telling Farmers to Go to Hell

The McNary-Haugen bill was the first of five similar pieces of legislation to be introduced under their sponsorship in the period between 1924 to 1928. The House defeated the 1924 version, the second attempt never came to a vote, the third bill was beaten back in both the House and Senate, and the fourth and fifth bills passed both houses in 1927 and 1928 respectively but were vetoed by President Coolidge.

Even before the bills were written, however, the President told Congress in his first annual message: "No complicated scheme of relief, no plan for government fixing of prices, no resort to the public treasury will be of any permanent value in establishing agriculture ... simple and direct methods put into operation by the farmer himself are the only real sources for restoration."[26] Coolidge left little doubt that he believed farmers had to work out their own salvation. The speech, which drew frequent cheers when he discussed agriculture, occasioned Senator Pat Harrison to remark that the section of the President's message he liked best was where Coolidge told the farmers to go to hell![27]

During the McNary-Haugen odyssey, the direction of the bills shifted from tariff reform to marketing and from price raising to price stabilization. Specific references to "ratio price" were dropped in an effort to gain political support from various farm organizations and regions of the country.

A Who's Who of Opposition

There was opposition from cooperatives. Cooperative marketing associations which had developed and flourished along commodity lines after World War I, believed they could restore farm prices to equality with costs through a proper marketing of commodities.

While efforts were constantly made to organize large-scale, even nationwide, cooperatives using legally-enforceable contracts to ensure the loyalty of participating producers, a number of obstacles prevented the establishment of such organizations. While in a few cases "farmers were too numerous, too difficult to organize, and too hard to keep in line to make such an ambitious scheme work on a voluntary basis,"[28] many cooperatives were encountering the same economic oppression from commercial and industrial market forces that the 19th century populists had faced with their fledgling co-ops.

The industrial east and the business community were unalterably opposed to the McNary-Haugen bill. The grain trade launched an aggressive, well-organized and well-financed campaign against the bill. The Chicago Board of Trade flooded the Midwest with propaganda denouncing the bill. The U. S. Chamber of Commerce decried "any proposal for buying, selling, manufacturing or other handling of agricultural products by government agencies."[29]

The agricultural colleges and most economists were generally indifferent or opposed to the bill in the early years of the debate. Official Washington, outside of some members of Congress and a small group close to Secretary Wallace, solidly opposed all but the most orthodox moves by the government to assist agriculture. Typical of that reaction was the denunciation of Representative James B. Aswell. He charged that McNary-Haugen would set "the precedent of socializing and nationalizing the industry of agriculture, which would lead inevitably to the nationalization of all industry ... overriding economic law by statutory laws and thus place our government squarely in the class of the bolshevistic government of Russia." The Louisiana Democrat believed after months of study that the bill was "unsound, unworkable, full of Bolshevism, purely socialistic, indefensibly communistic."[30]

Initial and meager support for the legislation came first from special groups such as the Northwest Wheat Associations, which favored the surplus-disposal plan. Next came selected state units of general farm organizations, and eventually the AFBF, the National Farmers' Union and the Grange, although the latter groups were considerably divided on procedural details.

The Agricultural West vs. the Industrial East

If one accepts the theory, and most historians do, that business interests had an inordinate amount of influence during the Harding, Coolidge and Hoover Administrations, the attitude of the business community toward agriculture and the McNary-Haugen bill was particularly significant. Generally, business disapproved of the legislation, but as years went by and the merits of the bill continued to be debated in the Congress, businessmen were forced to take agriculture's problems more seriously, to study them and look for compatible solutions.

By mid-decade, despite a slight pickup in the farm economy, many farmers were still suffering the lingering effects of the 1920-21 agricultural depression. The purchasing power of urban factory workers in 1925-26 was actually 16 percent higher than in the inflationary period of 1919-20 while farmers' was 19 percent less.[31] An increasing number of foreclosures were recorded after 1922 in a delayed reaction to the economic conditions of the previous two years. In South Dakota nearly 87 percent of the banks went broke in 1924 because of an excessive number of farm foreclosures.[32]

Farmers, seeing what was happening to their land and their livelihood, agreed with George Fort Milton's characterization of their struggle as "the same fight we have had throughout our American political and economic history, a conflict between the industrial east and agricultural west."[33]

Thus, the debate over the problems of agriculture that took place in the United States during the 1920s not only revealed the political and economic goals of the nation's business community, but also put into focus that deep-seated tension between agrarians and industrialists that exists to this day.

Chapter Fifteen

Oh Say to Him, Stuff and Nonsense

Mellon pulled the whistle,
Hoover rang the bell,
Wall Street gave the signal,
And the country went to hell!
- Bonus Marchers refrain

By the end of World War I, two parallel developments had occurred: the evolution of the United States from a debtor to a creditor nation and an end to our pioneering adventure — "manifest destiny". As Chester Davis describes the combined effect:

We now had a preempted continent — the last of the good free land had been taken up, and we were face to face with the problem of a maturing nation. No longer was there a frontier to act as a shock absorber for dispossessed farmers and unemployed from industrial centers, with outside creditor nations ready to take our surplus production in payment on our debts to them.[1]

Faced with this situation, business people recognized that it was imperative to consolidate, as they had already done with the nation's capital and industrial might, a major share of the country's natural resource wealth, *i.e.*, agriculture! This land — "from California to the New York Island, from the Redwood forest to the Gulfstream waters" — was now productive land, harvesting a cornucopia of crops and filled with the promise of unimagined wealth.

So it was that these same "communities of economic interests," who had sought to control the other sectors of the nation's economy, reasoned that it was time to make this land their land. As an abundant, prosperous and rapidly urbanized nation turned to more affluent pursuits only 6.5 million farmers now blocked that goal.

Many who initially supported and later remained dedicated to the passage of the McNary-Haugen legislation saw their struggle as more than just for economic improvement, despite the fact that the roots of the program sprang from Peek and Johnson's business concerns. Indeed, many of the bill's backers were more than alarmed over the growing influence of business and it efforts to industrialize agriculture at the expense of rural America. Like Jefferson they believed that a necessary foundation of a strong America was a healthy and independent agricultural class.

Myths and Reality

Some observers of the American scene at this time believed that agriculture was pretty much independent from the predominant interests of the nation and that farm policies should be based on that fact. A National Conference Board study in 1926 noted that the industrial/business population has "become preponderant not only in numbers, but in interest, organization and influence, "while agriculture has become a relatively remote concern and its welfare largely taken for granted in urban thought."[2]

Yet, as this same report also pointed out,

Farming is more than an industry, the significance of agriculture in the life of the nation is far deeper than this. It touches something vital and fundamental in the national existence. It involves the national security, the racial character, the economic welfare and the social progress of our people.[3]

But, as John Philip Gleason, writing on this period in *Agricultural History*, reminds us:

Still we may conclude that most of this attachment to the Jeffersonian ideal was pure romancing, and that it stemmed from devotion to the philosophy of individualism, rather than from a true appreciation of the farmer's situation. To one leading businessman, the Jeffersonian ideal was such a denatured thing that its values could be preserved so long as the "march of invention" enabled the citizen to provide his family with "open space and fresh air."

The more realistic businessmen held, not that the farmer should be the ideal, but that he should become a "businessman." Farmers, instead of being sturdy and self-reliant, were always crying for help — obviously they needed to learn business mobility and knowhow.

The Iron Age was, in fact, so uncharitable as to declare that the farmer needed a "guardian." The same low opinion of rural intelligence is apparent in the statement of a businessman who said that politicians easily misled the farmer with "a few catch phrases."[4]

During the McNary-Haugen campaign, however, business began to realize that the "farm problem" was here to stay and that it would require close attention.

Initially, the business community viewed the plight of farmers as "unpleasant," but by no means desperate. It dismissed the need for special tariff protection, since farming was not an infant industry and candidly implied that "so-called surplus production is largely a myth." It branded the equalization fee as too complicated, but it reserved its harshest criticism for the legislation's intention to relate the price of agricultural goods to the general level of prices by a base period formula — parity!

"Vicious class legislation" which would result in "confusion, disorder, misery and complete failure" was the way *The Commercial and Financial Chronicle* described this tampering with price relationships. The solution, business argued, was simply to let the price mechanism restore the supply and demand equilibrium that had been damaged by wartime inflation and "overproduction."[5]

Limiting production was seen as a panacea by *The Wall Street Journal*, *The Washington Post* and other metropolitan newspapers. A 1924 *Post* editorial declared: "The remedy is plain: Let American wheat growers quit trying to compete with cheap foreign wheat and cut their production down to home needs."[6]

Ironically, when Wallace had argued for acreage reduction in 1922 it was business and grain traders who opposed the idea. Even the casual observer could see that business and industry did not really care what happened to the nation's farmers so long as prices for food and raw materials remained cheap.

The Andrew Mellon Letter

In 1926 this conflict between agrarian and industrial interests was openly expressed in a warning that the McNary-Haugen legislation might indeed work and would bear unpleasant consequences for American "capitalists."

In a letter to Senators Haugen, L.J. Dickinson and Daniel R. Anthony, the Secretary of the Treasury Andrew W. Mellon argued that the effect of the bill "will be to increase the cost of living to every consumer of five basic agricultural commodities." Then he continued:

> We shall have the unusual spectacle of the American consuming public paying a bonus to the producers of five major agricultural commodities, with a resulting decrease in the purchasing power of wages, *and at the same time* contributing a subsidy to the foreign consumers, who under the proposed plan will secure American commodities at prices below the American level. (emphasis added)[7]

Thus, European labor would then be able to live cheaper than the American laborer, Mellon concluded, and foreign industrial costs would become less than those in the U.S. and thus our manufacturers would soon be undersold by foreign competitors.

Mellon's frank admission that the McNary-Haugen legislation was unsound not because it threatened to raise farm prices but because it threatened to undercut industry's lucrative markets abroad drew immediate criticism. It was pointed out that Mellon and the Coolidge/Harding Administrations were not at all reticent about giving legislative aid to industry, labor and transportation while denying such help to the nation's food producers.

The New York World editorialized that Secretary Mellon had seen the "mote that is in the farmer's eye, but the beam in his own eye he has considered not." Senator Thomas J. Walsh accused the Treasury Secretary of profiteering in 1922 when, after the Congress passed the Fordney-McCumber tariff bill, Mellon's Aluminum Company of America increased the price of sheet aluminum three cents a pound within ten days. Mellon would champion profits influenced by legislative action, Senator Walsh charged, so long as they went to himself or industry generally, but he opposed any government aid to agriculture.[8]

Business Offers Its Solutions

Others in the business community were not quite so straightforward as Secretary Mellon. They expressed concerns about the possibility of higher prices leading to greater production and the eventual dumping of surplus U.S. agricultural goods abroad which would in turn force recipient nations to raise their own tariffs. What would be particularly offensive in such situations, it was argued, is that the U.S. government would be cast as the dumping export agent.

To those who charged that industry frequently practiced such dumping, the National City Bank responded in its *Bank Letter* that dumping could not be justified as a national policy, " . . . even though it may be practiced profitably to some extent in private business."[9]

To be sure, while the business community in general spent a good deal of time denouncing the McNary-Haugen legislation, not all businessmen, particularly in the Midwest and Northern Plains, dismissed the farmers' distress calls. The persistence of the farm problem and a realization of the significance of farm purchasing power eventually brought many business organizations, such as the National Chamber of Commerce, to the realization that at the least a thorough study of agriculture was in order.

It was also becoming apparent that close cooperation between business and agriculture was necessary and that both parties needed to be sensitive to such efforts. *The Nation's Business*, in discussing accusations that business was antagonistic to the farmer, pointed out "when the next farm agitator ascribes sinister motives to a businessman who doesn't agree with his particular form of belief — oh say to him, stuff and nonsense."[10]

Among the numerous remedies put forth by some businessmen was simply reducing agricultural production, although many others felt it was "part of America's manifest destiny" to produce at full capacity. Others argued that farmers needed to balance production with domestic demand.

Crop diversification was also suggested as a panacea, but some denounced it as "heresy." Businessmen who advocated this approach began lending money to farmers to carry out such programs while others were extending credit to agricultural cooperatives, believing that the cooperative movement was a sound way to insure a healthy agricultural system. Business journals ran articles on the many benefits to be derived from crop diversification.

One article in *The Nation's Business*, ineloquently described the joys of diversification into dairying, concluding that " . . . soaring out over the heads of the spellbinders and hell raisers, surging mellifluously into the farthest reaches of the Mississippi Basin is the more powerful argument: 'Moo-oo-oo.'"[11]

As business grappled with the problems of agriculture, though strictly from an economic standpoint, one also began to hear what was at first a muted hint but would soon become a demanding scream — human "surpluses" needed to be eliminated from American agriculture — there were simply too many farmers!

For examples, *The Nation's Business* ran an article in 1926 titled, "Abandoned Farms Don't Worry Me," and *The Commercial and Financial Standard* believed that many farmers forced off the land were simply stupid, lazy, or inefficient. "Inefficient farmers" were not to be coddled; the incompetent were advised to ". . . give up farming, and take jobs in the cities at day labor; such jobs require the minimum of intelligence and yet return a good wage . . ."[12] As we shall soon discover, this "final solution" to the farm problem by many in the business world would ultimately become a cornerstone of future U.S. agricultural policy decisions.

Castigating the "Self Indulgent" Farmer

Businessmen, as Gleason notes, ascribed a certain moral opprobrium to failure in farming. He reports that one study of businessmen's beliefs in the 1920's concluded "that success was the reward of something very closely akin to moral virtue, and that failure was at least *prima facie* evidence of the lack of virtue."[13]

For many businessmen it was only the self-indulgent farmer who was in trouble. Wheat farmers, for example, were one-crop farmers and one-crop farming was the lazy man's way. (Even the farmer's practical desire for an automobile came under attack. A *Nation's Business* editorial observed: "of course, he needs a motor vehicle, or he could not attend the 'movies' four times a week, and the boys could not 'burn up' the roads racing around to parties and fandangos.")

Businessmen in the 1920's also cautioned that the farmer's "self-indulgence" might prove contagious. *The Iron Age* thought it saw such a danger in the "eat more" campaigns that were being touted by some farmers at this time. Seeking to eliminate farm surpluses by asking people to eat more than they needed, and you were handing them "a direct invitation to profligacy in living . . ."[15]

The Commercial and Financial Chronicle sought to elevate this so-called moral discussion a notch by asserting that "in justice" farm prices remain low so that "the pale-faced mother of the tenement" could feed her family.[16]

Equally reprehensible to business was the danger that farmers would come to trust politicians and/or farm organization leaders to help solve the problems that they in the business community were best qualified to

remedy. That the farm situation could be bettered by the Federal government or Congress, as these politicians and leaders believed, was, of course, anathema to these champions of individualism and free enterprise.

Typical of such scorn was a long editorial in *The Commercial and Financial Chronicle* subtitled "Lesson." *Laissez-faire* individualism was the bedrock of the editorial with the gospel of work added as a note of fervor. Alluding to the intention of the founding fathers and explaining the equilibrium maintained by the "immutable laws of being," the editorial solemnly warned that "when politics invades economics it destroys our birthright." Calling for a return of "frugality, tolerance and independence," *The Chronicle* in a rhapsodic finale prayed that "favoring seasons bless the farmer; favoring environment blesses us all; work will bring plenty and peace."[17]

In Praise of "Individualism"

How many businessmen really believed in frugality in the days of ballyhoo advertising and installment buying, as Gleason wonders, is open to question.

> It was no doubt clear to many of them that economic liberalism did not jibe with the facts of life in the industrial world of the 1920's. As a guide to practical action, individualism was dead; but as a myth it was very much alive. Capitalistic practice had completely outstripped the theoretical framework within which it was supposed to take place; individualism remained the businessman's only rationale, outmoded though it was.
>
> When first confronted by the problem in agriculture, a field in which they had no practical experience to guide them, businessmen naturally fell back on their theoretical individualism, and 'solved' the problem by a pedantic application of the laws of economics. Nor could they always remain patient and reasonable; their moral sensibilities, as well as their economic orthodoxy, were outraged. Honesty, industry, initiative, fair play — all these virtues and many others clustered around the doctrinal core of individualism. When the doctrine was violated, businessmen were likely to believe that the violator was not so much misguided as depraved, and their reaction was a moral one.[18]

In witnessing the nation's heretofore "self-reliant" farmers "reneging" on their individualism and calling for assistance from the Federal government in the form of the McNary-Haugen legislation, the business community claimed to be scandalized. At the same time, they soon realized that despite their rebuking, denouncing and condemning such behavior, the nation's farmers still remained undaunted and continued to press the Congress and the President for relief.

For some businessmen this perspective would lead to a search for reasons behind the "farm crisis" and an appropriate response. For others, who refused to broaden their narrow economic and ideological preconceptions, it became the clarion call for an all out economic war against farmers that is still being fought to this very day.

Meanwhile, Back in the Congress . . .

The McNary-Haugen legislation would serve as a rallying point for the coalition of senators and representatives in Washington favorable to the farmers' cause. Due to their coalition building, other farm relief legislation was also put forth at this time, some of it laying foundations upon which agriculture and food policy would be structured for decades. For example, the legal position of agricultural cooperatives and to what degree they were exempt from the provisions of antitrust legislation was clarified in 1922 with the passage of the Capper-Volstead law.

The intermediate credit needs of farmers were also to some extent improved, but still too late for many. The Federal Farm Loan Act, passed in 1916, had greatly increased the availability of long-term farm mortgage credit. However, farmers believed that they still deserved not only credit at rates comparable to those paid by business but also to the establishment of financial institutions which could meet their special needs.

In 1923, therefore, Congress enacted the Federal Intermediate Credit Act establishing 12 intermediate credit banks to rediscount for banks and special lending agencies offering agricultural paper maturing within three years. It was not until Banks for Cooperatives and the Production Credit Corporations and Associations were established and provided for in 1933 under the Federal Credit Administration that the government finally made an attempt to address short-term farm credit problems properly.

Conscious of the mushrooming farm problem, in November 1924, President Coolidge called yet another White House Conference on Agriculture, which held a series of hearings before issuing its report four months later. Although the conference placed heavy emphasis on a Federal Cooperative Marketing Board with broad powers as a means of handling exportable surpluses, its chief "accomplishment" was to exacerbate discontent among farmers since it failed to devise any workable plan for establishing the type of balanced agriculture which it had advocated.

However, a consequence of one of the Conference's many recommendations was to increase support for the McNary-Haugen bill by enlisting the backing of the Cooperative Associations. Backers of the bill took at face value the Conference's suggestion that cooperatives should handle the "surplus problem."

In redrafting the bill, therefore, a provision was written in to enable cooperative associations to administer the export transactions of a particular commodity, backed by the equalization fee, which could then spread the costs to all those producers that presumably would be benefited by the transaction. The modified bill, however, failed to ever reach a vote in the Congress.[19]

New Organizations, New Efforts

As all these various efforts to define a farm policy evolved, new organizations were being formed in the mid-1920's to politically support such legislation. The American Council of Agriculture, formed under the presidency of George N. Peek, after a mass meeting in St. Paul, Minnesota in July 1924, became the rallying point for much of the support for surplus control legislation until the Executive Committee of Twenty-Two was formed in 1926.[20]

Growing out of a conference of governors from 11 Midwestern and Northwestern states, which met in Des Moines, Iowa in January, 1926, this committee primarily fought for the passage of the McNary-Haugen bill until President Coolidge's veto in 1928.

Working together with the governors at this time was the Corn Belt Committee of farm organizations, which was put together at a May, 1925 meeting in Des Moines and was sponsored by the NFU and the Committee of Twenty-Two. These groups, along with a generally hesitant AFBF and Grange, sought to enact necessary farm relief legislation.

Additional support for such measures came in 1926 from previous opponents in the South and West, mainly due to the political give-and-take and clarification surrounding the McNary-Haugen bill, such as mentioned above, and the tireless lobbying efforts of Peek.

After a March conference in Memphis, Tennessee, leaders of the powerful Southern cotton, rice and tobacco commodity cooperatives joined with Western and other farm leaders in Washington on behalf of the bill. Because these Southern leaders, representing associations based on membership contracts, were a strong influence in the national cooperative movement, a joint mass meeting between Southern and Western farmers was held in St. Louis, Missouri in November.

Noting that the McNary-Haugen bill had just met its second House defeat, the group supported legislation that "will enable farmers to control and manage excess supplies of crops at their own expense, so as to secure cost of production with a reasonable profit" and recommended that farmers' organizations

> Make a special study of the effects on agriculture of industrial tariffs and also of the effect of our change from debtor to creditor nation, and especially of its effects on the accumulation of our agricultural surpluses. Our "tariff primers" have taught us that the farmer would get his reward through the demand created by the higher purchasing power of prosperous industrial classes. We demand that the farmer be given the opportunity to promote the national prosperity by his own increased purchasing power through increased prices.[21]

The Idea of a Federal Farm Board

A plan that emerged from those who opposed the surplus-disposal legislative programs before Congress was the creation of a Federal Farm Board to assist agricultural cooperatives in the stabilizing of farm prices. In late 1927, a report by the Business Men's Commission on Agriculture, which was sponsored and financed by the National Industrial Conference Board and the U.S. Chamber of Commerce, advocated such a plan. The plan also received the enthusiastic support of the Harding administration.[22]

Already introduced in the form of an administration-backed bill (Curtis-Crisp) in early 1927, the Commission called for a Federal Farm Board to aid in the stabilization of prices and production in agriculture through advice to farmers on production and marketing and through a system of quasi-official stabilization corporations with power to buy farm products at a price announced before the date of planting.

A thorough revision downward of the tariff, *starting with industrial rates*, was also called for by the Commission. When industry and agriculture reached approximately the same level of protection, the rates would continue to be reduced at an equal rate. Products, however, vital to the country's long-run interests and which required full domestic production (*i.e.*, industrial products) would retain "adequate protection."[23] It condemned "legislative measures designed to artificially raise the domestic level of farm products above the world price level by export bounties, export debentures, or by agencies designed to dispose of surplus products abroad at a loss."[24]

At this same time another report on the farm problem was being issued by the Association of Land Grant Colleges and Universities, but as Chester Davis notes,

Like so many reports of the period [it] was strong on analysis and weak on remedy. It was important chiefly as a belated recognition by agricultural colleges that a national agricultural problem did exist, and that they should be concerned with the development of a national policy to meet it. The discussion of the agricultural situation was revealing; of the tariff, straddling; and of the surplus problem, vague. "The movement toward stabilization and control," it concluded, "may be hastened by favorable and sound types of legislation."[25]

By 1928 the McNary-Haugen legislation had been refined to cover all farm products, instead of a limited number of specific commodities, and it provided for procedures similar to those proposed under stabilization corporations, the use of the controversial equalization fee plan to be used only as a last resort. The bill passed both the House and Senate, but was again vetoed by Coolidge after which the Senate subsequently failed by ten votes to override the presidential veto.

No Friend of the Farmer

It was an election year and agricultural policy unsurprisingly was a major issue in the 1928 campaign, a threatened farm revolt having failed to materialize after farmers were promised early in the campaign a generally favorable farm bill.

When Herbert Hoover defeated the Democrat Alfred E. Smith, in the 1928 presidential election farmers worried about where he would take agriculture. Not only was the former World War I Food Administrator unpopular for his efforts during the war to make minimum prices for wheat the maximum price, but farmers had not forgotten Hoover's 1921 memo to Harding's government reorganization committee. In that communication Hoover stated that,

the functions of the Department of Agriculture should end when production on the farm is complete and movement there from starts, and at that point the activities of the Department of Commerce should begin . . . The Department of Agriculture should tell the farmer what he can best produce, based on soil, climate and cultural conditions, and the Department of Commerce should tell him how best to dispose of it.[26]

Hoover's past and the farm relief question, however, were not as important to the conservative-thinking, largely Protestant, rural areas of the country as Smith's Roman Catholicism and whether the nation should be "wet" or" dry."

Trying to keep its word to ease the farm crisis, the new Hoover administration set up the Federal Farm Board under the provisions of the Agricultural Marketing Act of 1929 and soon raised tariffs by the passage of the Smoot-Hawley Tariff Act.

The Marketing Act's primary purpose was to provide agriculture with a mechanism for the orderly production and marketing of farm products similar to those methods used in other industries. Its major provisions concerned marketing and it established the Federal Farm Board to encourage cooperatives and stabilization corporations, which were to be started and owned by cooperatives. By setting up a $500 million revolving fund under the Board's control the Act sought to unify the marketing process with the support of loans.

While initially attempting to establish a system of orderly marketing procedures, the Board was soon faced with the task of stabilizing commodity prices as the drastic decline in those prices began to take its toll on the economy in the latter half of 1929.

At the outset the Board undertook this stabilization process by making loans to cooperatives so they could hold commodities in storage until the market improved. This was followed by setting up stabilization corporations for wheat and cotton which took over most of the supplies held by the cooperatives, in addition to purchasing stocks of the two commodities on the open market.

Although these stabilization corporations were legally owned by the cooperatives, it was the Farm Board which provided them with financing and assumed the risk bearing. Rapidly declining farm prices, however, provoked heavy losses by the Board and it became apparent that the gains realized by withholding supplies from the market could be realized only if production were somehow held in line with actual market demand, both at home and abroad.

By June 1931 over 257 million bushels of wheat were held by the National Grain Corporation, prompting it to announce that it would not attempt to support the 1931 crop. Some $345 million had already been lost trying to stabilize commodity prices and while some farmers realized limited benefits, speculators managed to make large profits as most of the farm community viewed the new law as a dismal failure.[27]

By the end of the 1920's the wheatlands of Canada, Argentina, Australia and Russia were offering considerable competition to American wheat exports. The top three, in fact, were processing eight times more wheat in 1928 than they were at the turn of the century. World wheat production was rapidly exceeding consumption.

War debts were still being paid off very slowly as European nations could neither buy much-needed American agricultural goods nor sell their own manufactured goods because of prohibitively high American tariffs. Low world prices in wheat and corn continued to determine deflated market prices at home.

Farmers' expenses also kept increasing as the cost of new agricultural technology and science advanced and mechanization continued its appointed mission in working to displace farmers and rural families. By 1930 the percentage of the farm population in rural America had decreased by 5.2 percent from the previous decade to 24.9 percent and from a 1900 level of 60 percent.[28]

It was clear by this time that the onrushing economic collapse had thwarted the Federal government's few farm relief programs as agriculture and the entire national economy was about to plunge into a historic national and worldwide economic and social crisis — the Great Depression.

Chapter Sixteen

A "New and Untrod Path"

"... I got this place 28 years ago when this country was nearly all woods no road at al these years I tryed to stick it out and I only lived her a short while my wife died. I had 2 small cyldren the oldst one 9 and the youngest one 4 years when there mother died and we have been liveing alone all these years the oldest one is now married and the youngest one is still staying with me and he is crippled for life he can just help himself and that is all. and now after going through all these hardshipes we are loseing our home for less than the small some of 200.00 dollars it sure is awfull to have these money men take advantage of the poor. ..."

- Letter from an Anima,
Wisconsin farmer to Milo Reno

No period of modern American history has become so vividly etched in our social and economic consciousness than the Great Depression of the early 1930s. For the people who survived those years of severe economic and physical hardship, particularly in rural America and on the farm, mere mention of that time generates a fear and pain that few of us now living in a more affluent society can imagine.

Impossible as it is to capture in words the degree of human misery during that period, statistics at least begin to show how deep and pervasive the crisis of the late twenties and early thirties was and why "red flags of distress" flew all over the nation.

The post-war slump had seen farm prices remain between 30 and 45 percent above their pre-war level.[1] Yet those prices were so out of line with non-agricultural prices and farm equipment and production costs, that each year hundreds of thousands of farmers could barely meet their bills and eventually were forced to liquidate their farms. When general prices plummeted in 1929 it was primarily due to a series of domestic and foreign financial, industrial, trade and political factors. However, the nature of the agricultural crisis once again centered around the problem of price.

Productivity per man hour during the 1920s went up 43 percent in manufacturing (two and one-half times as fast as the growth in population) while factory wages went up less than 20 percent. It was not the worker nor the consumer, however, who benefited from this productivity in terms of wages and lower prices, but rather it was stockholders and speculators. It was also the

monopolies that profited from the economic policies of the 1920s. By 1930 nearly one-half of the non-banking corporate wealth was held by the 200 largest corporations, which were in turn under the interlocking control of some 2,000 individual executives and financiers.[2]

During the later part of the decade net farm income remained steady at $9 billion, climbing to $12 billion by 1929. The value of farm land, however, decreased from $80 to $55 billion as farm bankruptcies multiplied six fold.[3]

Unemployment and Plunging Prices Stalk the Land

Two schools of thought quickly developed within our administration discussions. First was the "leave it alone liquidationists" headed by Secretary of the Treasury Mellon, who felt the government must keep its hands off and let the slump liquidate itself. Mr. Mellon had only one formula: "Liquidate labor, liquidate stocks, liquidate the farmers, liquidate real estate."

He insisted that, when the people get an inflation brainstorm, the only way to get it out of their blood is to let it collapse. He held that even a panic was not altogether a bad thing.

He said: "it will purge the rottenness out of the system. High costs of living and high living will come down. People will work harder, live a more moral life. Values will be adjusted and enterprising people will pick up the wrecks from less competent people"...

-From "The Great Depression," *The Memoirs of Herbert Hoover: The Great Depression 1929-1941*, The MacMillan Co., New York, N.Y.: 1952.

By the end of the "roaring twenties" the contraction in business, speculative activity, and industrial and consumer demand for farm products here and abroad saw a parallel decline in farm prices. The financial crisis and the breakdown in monetary standards that led to tight control of credit and deep industrial stagnation between 1931 and 1932 had already led to reduction in farm prices.

Domestic industrial conditions were at a prosperity level between 1924 and 1929. Total gross farm income remained fairly stable. However, that all changed in the next several years. A two percent decline in production from 1929 to 1930, which should have resulted in a two to three percent price increase, instead saw prices plunge almost 20 percent and gross income drop by 22 percent. By 1934 industrial production would decline from 1929 by 42 percent in volume and 15 percent in price, yet agricultural production had declined only 15 percent in volume while prices had dropped by 40 percent.[4]

The 1929 financial crisis quickly caused a curtailment in industrial demand, a reduction in the work force, and an accumulation of stocks. Reduced consumer expenditures for food and clothing followed unemployment and decreased consumer income.

By 1932 it was estimated that nearly one third of all persons outside of agriculture were unemployed while millions of other Americans were working part time at reduced wages. (Because the nation had no system for collecting such information precise figures are unknown.)

Prices for farm commodities were now at half their pre-war level. National income and farm income were dramatically affected by this drop in price. In 1929 the national income was $91 billion and farm income was at $12 billion. Three years later the former was down to $55 billion while the latter was at $5 billion. By 1932 farmers were receiving 60 percent less for their crops than they were in 1929 (see Chart 16A). The value and volume of our agricultural exports during this period of time also saw a sharp and comparable drop.[5]

Chart 16A

Average of Prices Received, September 1929 - September, 1932 (percentage)	
At the farm	-58
Grain prices	-69
Cotton	-61
Meat animals	-58
Dairy and poultry products	-51
Farm products-wholesale markets	-50
Non-agricultural products	-25
September, 1932 Exchange Value of a Unit of Farm Products Compared with Pre-war Level (percentage)	
All farm products	56
Bushel of wheat	37
100 pounds of hogs	42
Pound of wool/cotton	50
Pound of butter	72

Input costs added to the farmers's economic burden during these three years, and while prices were dropping 60 percent, aggregate costs were declining only 20 percent. Using 100 as the pre-war base, the 1932 index of average farm costs was up to 140 whereas farm prices were down to 55. The USDA estimated in 1932 that the average farmer, after paying his production expenses, rent, interest and taxes, earned about $230, leaving nothing as a return on investment or for common-labor pay for labor and management.[6]

No Avenues of Escape

With the USDA's emphasis on farm management, the land-grant college complex and Extension Service, many farms were growing bigger, more mechanized — and more productive! One writer called them "capitalistic family farms" and two USDA economists observed in 1929 that "one of the most remarkable changes that has come to American agriculture in this post-war period is the increase in the normal size of the family unit, both in terms of total investment and in total acreages in certain of our farming areas."[7]

Comparing farm mortgage debt with gross income in 1932 shows that it was three to four times as heavy as before the war. Interest on mortgage debt and taxes, which had doubled in 20 years requiring four times as many farm production units to pay for them, ate up 25 percent of the gross farm income in 1932 as compared with just seven to eight percent before the war and 11.2 percent in 1929.[8]

Meanwhile, farm-land values were declining at a rapid pace, reducing not only farmer's equity, but also weakening many of the country's lending institutions. As prices dropped, restrictions on credit hurt hundreds of the nation's farming communities. The inability of farmers to pay off high mortgage interest rates and reduce their principal also resulted in thousands of foreclosure sales, voluntary releases of farm land to creditors, and forced liquidation sales. Many country banks were forced to suspend operations. The FDIC has estimated that an average of 2,277 banks failed each year between 1930 and 1933 with a remarkable 4,000 failures in 1933 alone.[9]

Between 1930 and 1935, mortgage foreclosures, bankruptcy, or delinquent tax sales of farms took as many as one-sixth of all U.S. farms, and many believe that percentage actually masks the real number of the thousands of reportedly voluntary sales that were debt-induced transfers to mortgages.

In Iowa, for example, in 1931 nearly one-seventh of all the farm families in the state were foreclosed while three-fifth of all the farms had to be mortgaged to survive.[10] On one April day in Mississippi in 1932 one quarter of the land in the state had to be sold by sheriffs for satisfaction of mortgages and taxes.[11]

In addition, many hundreds of thousands of farm families were struggling to survive at a lower standard of living where the food and shelter they produced for themselves became the chief reward for their labor and investment. A previous avenue of escape from rural poverty — urban employment — was no longer a viable option. Indeed, the increasing migration of the unemployed from the cities only exacerbated the problems of the American farmer as this population movement reduced the demand for commercial farm products and caused a further disruption of the balance between supply and reduced demand.

A "New Deal" to Rescue Agriculture

Such was the grim scene facing Franklin D. Roosevelt when he was elected President of the United States in 1932.

Two weeks after his inauguration in March 1933, the new president, recognizing the urgency of the crisis, spoke to the Congress in a special message accompanying a bill in which he sought broad discretionary powers to deal with agriculture's problems: "I tell you frankly that this is a new and untrod path. But I tell you with equal frankness that an unprecedented condition calls for the trial of new means to rescue agriculture."[12]

At the heart of FDR's plan was the Agricultural Adjustment Act of 1933, which established the Agricultural Adjustment Administration (AAA), and was built around a domestic-allotment plan. Enactment of the AAA confronted the new Administration with two major tasks: to make a crop allotment plan the major form of farm relief, and to promote long-range programs that would involve far-reaching changes in the way the nation used its land.

Since 1929 when the Federal Farm Board was created it had become increasingly apparent that any attempt to control prices through storage and withholding, without the authority to control production, was futile. By the time the Board announced its withdrawal from the wheat market in June 1931, claiming it could no longer justify wheat purchases, the price on the Kansas City Board of Trade was near 27 cents a bushel, thus undercutting much of the price supporting effect of Board purchases.

These sharp price declines, coupled with a burgeoning debt load and increased taxes, left thousands of farmers financially vulnerable. New Deal historian Arthur Schlesinger, Jr. describes the situation: "A cotton farmer who borrowed $800 when cotton was 16 cents a pound borrowed the equivalent of 5,000 pounds of cotton; now, with cotton moving toward five cents, he must pay back the debt with over 15,000 pounds of cotton."[13]

It was during these fruitless years that M. L. Wilson, a professor at Montana State University, sought to interest Congress and farm leaders in his domestic allotment plan as a means of securing voluntary acreage reduction.[14] In Roosevelt's 1932 election campaign Wilson was able to gain the support for his plan from Roosevelt's "brain trusters," Henry A. Wallace and Rexford Tugwell.

Wilson and Howard R. Tolley, a fellow "social scientist" in the Bureau of Agricultural Economics, had joined forces in 1930 with Representative Victor Christgau, a freshman Minnesota Republican and the first agricultural economist to ever serve in Congress, to introduce an agricultural adjustment bill. Designed to encourage highly efficient and profitable farms, the bill offered help to farmers in determining what commodities to produce so that production could be brought into line with current economic conditions.

The main goal of the bill was to enable farmers to produce crops they were equipped to produce, in the most efficient manner possible, and grow no more than they could sell at adequate prices. A major feature of the bill was to expand research and education in economics and reorganize the USDA in an effort to develop a successful adjustment program.

The bill, as one writer described it, indicated that "Wilson's principal initial interest in farm legislation was not simply to raise farm income; he saw it primarily as a device for national planning, with the people participating and growing in understanding on a grand scale."[15]

Congress, however, failed even to give the bill a hearing. During the 1932 election campaign, the bill met a similar fate although it did produce interest among some groups, including the U.S. Chamber of Commerce.

Selling National Agricultural Planning

Despite his initial setbacks Wilson continued to pursue his idea of better national planning in agriculture while controlling production. He believed such a means far preferable to traditional agrarian demands for "trust busting" which he saw reflecting farmers' fear of business power and their insistence that business leaders change their ways.

Consequently, Wilson's ideas picked up support from members of the business community, including Henry I. Harriman, a New England Power Association executive and Chamber of Commerce president, and R. R. Rogers, assistant secretary of the Prudential Life Insurance Co.

Wilson's ideas also came to the attention of Roosevelt as he was preparing to run for the presidency. In one of his most important speeches during the campaign in Topeka, Kansas, the Democratic candidate spoke of the advantages of agricultural planning "to gain a better and less wasteful distribution of agricultural productive effort" which would point the way "to readjustments in the distribution of the population in general."[16]

It was in the AAA bill that Wilson's dream of national agricultural planning, with its chief feature being the allotment program, was at last realized. In the bill that Roosevelt sent to Congress on March 16, such a domestic allotment plan was spelled out.

For reducing their acreage in four basic crops — cotton, wheat, corn and tobacco — by leasing a portion of their productive land to the government and restricting their output on the remaining land, farmers were to be paid a subsidy. The scale of reduction would vary according to the government's annual estimate of demand. Each farmer would be given an individual acreage allotment. Each crop would have a set minimum price and if the market failed to bring that price, the cooperating farmer would receive the subsidy to make up the difference.

A "processing tax" would also be levied against the millers and packers as a means to finance such a subsidy, as these processors and distributors would enter into marketing agreements that would cover prices, production and fair trade practices. Since the Secretary of Agriculture was to be a party to all these agreements, the processors, in effect, would be licensees of the government. (This latter feature, of course, turned millers, grain traders, meat packers, and cotton dealers and manufacturers into the most vocal and vigorous opponents of Wilson's allotment plan.)

Participating farmers who were left with a crop surplus could dispose of it through the government at an established base price (in the form of a loan). The program was to be voluntary and its administration was to be handled primarily by local elected county committees of participating farmers.

Changing American Agriculture Forever

In one legislative act the economy of rural America was suddenly uprooted from the 19th century and agriculture — a highly individualistic enterprise — was made a collective endeavor. The Federal government was placed in the unique position of attempting to raise the economic status of an entire social class of its citizens. As Schlesinger has written:

> Probably never in American history had so much social and legal inventiveness gone into a single legislative measure ... For another quarter century agricultural policy came up with very little which was not provided for one way or another in the Agricultural Adjustment Act.[17]

Due to the urgency of the crisis the House of Representatives passed the bill in four days. Eastern business interests and conservatives, shocked at the broad powers the AAA gave to the President, particularly the power to impose taxes and the marketing and production agreements, fought the AAA legislation for several weeks before its final passage on May 12. They were joined by several angry farm groups which insisted that Roosevelt's reforms did not go far enough.

Despite such protests, however, good farm legislation was passed in 1933 only because farmers themselves demanded it. As Professor Harold Breimyer points out:

> Distress and protest movements in the country had a lot to do with creating the New Deal's farm laws ... In the final analysis, farm and congressional leaders were willing to gamble on an Agricultural Adjustment Act of 1933 because they were scared.[18]

The AAA of 1933 consisted of three parts: Title I, the heart of the Act which established the domestic allotment program, the marketing and production agreements, and the processing tax; Title II: the Farm Mortgage Act which provided for the relief of farm debt; and Title III: the Thomas Amendment which gave the President powers to inflate the currency.

Title II also called for expansion of federal loan facilities, while reducing interest on Land Bank mortgages from 5.4 percent to 4.5 percent. The new mortgages were to be financed not by expanding the currency, but by issuing four percent federal bonds.

Title III came as a partial concession by the Roosevelt Administration to many in the farm community who saw agriculture's salvation in the putting of more money — greenbacks or their equivalent — into the hands of farmers. Essentially the President was empowered to decrease the gold content in the dollar, accept silver up to $100 million in payment of foreign debts and to expand credit by issuing $3 billion in treasury notes. By acceding to the monetary bloc in the Senate and its farm bloc supporters, Roosevelt reluctantly sanctioned this form of controlled and discretionary inflation. Tugwell summed up the Act from a political perspective:

> For real radicals such as Wheeler, Frazier, etc., it is not enough. For conservatives it is too much. For Jeffersonian democrats it is a new control which they distrust. For the economic philosophy it represents, there are no defenders at all. Nevertheless ... something has to be done. Also there is no alternative.[19]

Although the Roosevelt administration's "New Deal" farm programs received initial enthusiastic support from economists in the land grant colleges, the U.S. Chamber of Commerce and the Grange, the agricultural community itself was less than enthusiastic. However, even the AFBF, acknowledging that some controls on the production of wheat, hogs, cotton and other products were necessary to gain satisfactory prices, came around to grudgingly support the AAA of 1933.

Fighting for Cost-of-Production Prices

The National Farmers Union, believing that the question was how to get more money into the hands of farmers, condemned the legislation. After unsuccessfully seeking a cost-of-production amendment attached to the bill, the NFU argued that acreage control would not decrease production and nothing short of "an army of bureaucrats" could enforce such provisions. When an angry A. N. Young, president of the Wisconsin Farmers' Union, testified before the Senate Agriculture Committee, he issued a dire warning to the lawmakers.

> The farmer is naturally a conservative individual, but you cannot find a conservative farmer today. He is not to be found. I am as conservative as any man could be, but any economic system that has in its power to set me and my wife in the streets, at my age — what else could I see but red?
>
> The fact is today that there are more actual reds among farmers in Wisconsin than you could dream about ... They are just ready to do anything to get even with the situation. I almost hate to express it, but I honestly believe that if some of them could buy airplanes, they would come down here to Washington to blow you fellows all up.[20]

One group of protesters was Milo Reno's Farmers' Holiday Association. Originally intending to call a national farm strike on May 13 to voice the organization's unhappiness with the bill, in the end it simply condemned the legislation as a scheme to deliver independent farmers into the hands of the USDA's Cooperative Extension Service, which it had already labeled a "tyrannical and conceited" bureaucracy.

In championing the principal tenet, Reno argued,

> concede to the farmer production costs and he will pay his grocer, the grocer will pay the wholesaler, the wholesaler will pay the manufacturer and the manufacturer will be able to meet his obligations at the bank. Restore the farmers's purchasing power and you have re-established an endless chain of prosperity and happiness in this country.[21]

Reno, a one-time leader of Iowa's Farmers Union, had organized the Farmers' Holiday Movement as a mocking echo of Roosevelt's bank holidays in 1932. Indeed, a popular poem of the era was:

"Let's call a farmer's holiday,
A holiday let's hold.
We'll eat our wheat, ham and eggs
And let them eat their gold.[22]

Believing that farmers' crops were being taken by the Chicago Board of Trade to speculate with, Reno and the Holiday Movement through demonstrations, strikes and violent confrontations with the law enforcement agencies and the courts, insisted "we will not sell our crops until we obtain the cost of production."

The major instruments of protest became the withholding-of-crop movement and roadblocks which quickly led to dumping actions, and the "penny auctions" of farms in the effort to discourage farm foreclosures sales. Unfortunately, the leadership could not always control the membership and while Reno himself deplored violence, a number of bloody and publicly discrediting confrontations, such as Iowa's "Cow War," took place throughout the Midwest in the early 1930s.

In opposing Roosevelt's "New Deal" for agriculture Reno argued that because farm production costs were rising faster than farm prices any subsidy (such as price supports) would only benefit the large agribusiness corporations. Reno feared that such subsidies would enable large, wealthy growers to mechanize more rapidly and thus continue to enlarge their competitive advantage over family farmers, which, as we shall soon see, indeed took place in the south.

As the University of the Pacific's Donald H. Grubbs reminds us, "even before World War II, the richer agricultural areas had received more New Deal money than the poorer ones; wealthier ranchers and planters had profited more than family farmers."[23] It has been estimated that at this time 50 percent of the nation's farmers received about 15 percent of agriculture's total income and since AAA payments were based on acreage, 75 percent of the program's payments went to one third of the farmers who complied with the program.

"The day for pussyfooting," Reno declared in denouncing the New Deal's agricultural policies, "and deception in the farmers' problems is past. The politicians who have juggled with the agricultural problem and used it as a pawn with which to promote their own selfish interests can succeed no longer ..."[24]

The NFU's cost-of-production principle was based on itemizing by farmers of average production costs of all commodities and arriving at a price for their domestically consumed products that would return to the average operator costs, labor and a reasonable profit. While processors would be required to purchase a percentage of the year's domestically consumed crop at this cost-of-production price, the surplus would be the farmer's own responsibility either to store for future sale or disposed of at the current world price. In a discussion of populism in the 1930s, historian John L. Shover notes that,

While Reno and the N. Wallace argued that the lacked any means of surplus notes that,

more reasons than the plan's impracticab... made it necessary for Secretary Wallace to resist the cost of production proposal. Cost of production was inconsistent with domestic allotment: to have fixed prices on domestically consumed produce at the same time subsidy payments were being made for decreased acreage, would have caused hopeless confusion. If cost of production prices were guaranteed, the domestic allotment system could not function.[26]

By adding the Norris-Simpson amendment to the Senate bill the proponents of the cost-of-production idea sought to give the Secretary of Agriculture power to fix prices at the cost of production level.

John Simpson, NFU's president, told senators that Roosevelt's bill was simply a subsidy to consumers since it would allow them to buy farm products at less than the cost of production. He also argued that the bill would not decrease production, but would rather serve as a green light for farmers to cultivate more intensely and for big farmers and financial institutions, who were repossessing and buying up vast tracts in the farm belt, to reap more large profits by "renting" the land back to the government.[27]

The battle over the Norris-Simpson amendment became bitter, with Senator Arthur Vandenberg reminding his colleagues that "when we mix Ph.D.s and R.F.D.s we are in trouble."[28] The eventual passage of the amendment by the Senate, however, was viewed by many as Roosevelt's first serious legislative setback. But, in the final version of the bill, after the House refused to accept the cost of production concept, the Senate retreated from its previous support and the 1933 AAA became law.

While the AAA was finally approved by the Senate 64-20, Wilson lamented that Congress did "not get the production control idea at all" and it was only Roosevelt's influence that eventually enabled the bill to pass into law. Shover adds,

Inflationist pressure had been channeled; it had not been checked as events in the succeeding

...te. There was fuel for ...the contention that the ...ned a farm plan favored by ...t farmers and substituted a ...ent system endorsed by the ...ommerce and conservative farm ...

...al farm bill confirms the position of ...ew Deal as a moderate, even conserva- ...ram that spurned strong grass root and ...ssional demands for more extreme mea- ...[29]

...ttempt to Exercise Governmental Responsibility

...In seeking to increase income directly for domestic ...onsumption of farm products, and leaving the export surplus to take care of itself, the AAA of 1933 also initiated the idea of nonrecourse loans on farm commodities held in approved storage.

On October 16, 1933 an Executive order established the Commodity Credit Corporation to issue loans to AAA participants at 4 percent interest. The following June, Wallace, now Secretary of Agriculture, proposed that the CCC be made a permanent program, an "ever normal granary" with storage increased in years of abundant crops and low prices, and reduced in years with small crops.

The rationale for all these New Deal farm programs was that past government policy had contributed to overexpansion of agriculture, so it was the responsibility of government to limit farm output and thereby achieve legitimate policy objectives of a fair price and equality for agriculture, placing it in parity with other sectors of the economy.

The Keepers of the Mortgage

Nineteen thirty-three also saw passage of the Farm Credit Act which sought to establish a comprehensive system of federally sponsored credit agencies and give a measure of much needed relief to thousands of farmers facing bankruptcy and foreclosure. By this time nearly half of the nation's farmers who owned their own farms had no mortgage indebtedness. Another one-third had an indebtedness that would have not been burdensome had they been receiving pre-World War I prices for their products and comparable costs of production.

This meant that almost one sixth or over one million farmers were in a precarious debt situation. Because many of these farmers had an accumulation of unpaid taxes, interest, principal payments, notes and open accounts, while the prices they received for their goods continued to drop, it was clear that some sort of rescue operation was desperately needed. The nation could ill-afford the legal rights of all creditors to be exercised.

By 1938 the total debt-acquired farm real estate was worth approximately $934 million. Of that total, life insurance companies owned $612 million; federal and joint-stock land banks, which sold foreclosed farms usually within a year of acquisition, held $194 million; commercial banks owned $56 million; and state-operated rural credit agencies in North and South Dakota and Minnesota held $72 million.[30]

Typical of the companies which held this type of real estate was the Equitable Life Assurance Society, which in 1938 owned near 1.1 million acres valued at $68 million; its mortgage portfolio was almost on an equal basis with its $71 million in farm loans. In 1935 the company created a new department to conduct farm real estate and mortgage operations. Nils A. Olsen, former Chief of the USDA's Bureau of Agricultural Economics was its director, succeeded in 1940 by R.I. Nowell, another USDA employee.[31] It was not the first time nor would it be the last that the revolving door between the Department and corporate agribusiness spun freely.

Unlike other firms which sold their farms on the contract sale method, accepting five to 10 percent of the purchase price in cash, Equitable sold fewer than 50 of its over 6000 farms in this manner. As one company official later explained: "it [Equitable] felt that a *sufficient* cash down-payment, representing the buyer's equity in the farm, should be required so that the property would stay sold." (emphasis added)[32]

Not surprisingly a tabulation of the buyers of these farms revealed that about 40 percent of sales "were to tenants, either on Equitable's property or other farms"; 20 percent were to "adjoining land-owners and *other* well-to-do farmers," and a like percentage to buyers who were classified as "investors, largely local merchants and professional men." (emphasis added) The "total consideration" the life insurance company received from the sale of these farms was $101.6 million in addition to $38.8 million in operating revenues.[33]

The Farm Credit Act of 1933 provided farm loans by the Federal Loan Banks at 50 percent of the appraised normal value of the land and 20 percent of the value of the buildings. Land Bank Commissioner loans could be had when needed, which conceivably could have brought the total loan up to 75 percent of the normal value of land and buildings, the "normal value" defined as the average price of land and buildings in the five year period of 1909-1914.

To implement the Farm Credit Act two new groups of credit agencies were created: a central bank and 12 regional banks for making loans to cooperatives, and a system of 12 production credit corporations to organize, supervise and finance local PCA's that would enable cooperating groups of farmers to borrow from the intermediate credit banks.

Even these new lending policies and procedures, however, were not enough for thousands of farmers. Their debt had been contracted at a time when land values and farm prices had been at a pre-depression level. Now depression farm prices and farm value appraisals foreclosed many farmers' eligibility for re-financing even under these new and relatively liberal lending provisions.

The Plight of the Sharecropper

One sector of American agriculture that saw few benefits from these policies or from the AAA program were tenant farmers and sharecroppers, particularly in the south.

In the south in the early 1930s nearly 25 percent of farm operators and 44 percent of tenant farmers were sharecroppers. While most worked under the standard sharecropping pattern, a new quasi-sharecropping system, developed in Texas in the 1920s, began to appear throughout the southeast. Workers became part laborers and part croppers as they not only worked their own small acreage, but also worked as a day hand on shares unassigned to them.[34]

When the Depression struck the south and southeast many of these "sharecroppers" lost their jobs, as the planters cut back on their workforce. In the past, plantation owners had usually allowed sharecroppers to keep half of the cotton they raised. Under the AAA program the planters were paid to withdraw a third of their acreage from production. The subsidy on each withdrawn acre, however, was not split half and half, but rather eight to one in the landlord's favor.

Racial unrest and labor agitation soon appeared as the first sharecroppers' union was born in Tallapoose County, Alabama in 1931. By 1934, from an idea suggested by the long-time socialist leader Norman Thomas, the Southern Tenant Farmers Union (STFU) was founded in Arkansas by two rural radicals — H.L. Mitchell and his neighbor Clay East.[34]

While committed to a racially integrated union, the STFU was forced to have segregated locals. Nevertheless the STFU made all policy decisions at integrated meetings and had a racially balanced leadership. The union's stated objective was not necessarily racial "progress" in itself, but the elimination of race as an obstacle to building a union. The STFU's bi-racial character, however, made it the object of violence and bloodshed. As Mitchell noted at the time,

> we called it the system. You guys called it the power structure. It's all the same. See, we made an inroad with the whites and blacks here. We had done something that none of these agrarian movements had really done. They had all floundered on this race thing. But we didn't. We didn't flounder on it. We held our principles.[36]

After a December 1934 sit-in at Secretary Wallace's office in Washington, the STFU was promised an investigation into its grievances. At a later rally back in Arkansas celebrating the promised investigation, a young white minister and union organizer named Ward Rogers was arrested for criminal anarchy. Arrests, church burnings, beatings and murder attempts followed as a campaign of intimidation was unleashed against the STFU across the south. Soon the Rogers arrest became the focus of widespread attention and money from throughout the nation began to pour into the STFU.

A general strike by the union in 1935 proved successful, with handbills distributed throughout Arkansas and Missouri and parts of Tennessee, Mississippi and Alabama. Because of the dangers of picketing, workers were simply asked to remain out of the fields and over 5,000 cotton pickers responded to the call. Many landlords capitulated and wages saw an increase from less than 50 cents per 100 pounds to 75 cents or more. Interest in the union grew rapidly, but, like so many other field worker unions, before and after the STFU was

unable to win recognition as the collective bargaining agent for its field hands.

Opposition by the Southern growers to the STFU and the continued violence against the workers, nevertheless, occasioned both federal and state governments to establish farm tenancy commissions to investigate the situation and make recommendations. Some relief legislation was soon passed.

Reacting to the AAA cotton program specifically, the STFU complained about discrimination against tenants; AAA's failure to enforce provisions designed to offer the tenants protection, and the fact that those who ran the federal program shared the landlord's point of view — in fact, often were the landlords!

It was contended that restricting the acreage reduced the plantation's labor force which in turn encouraged a shift from sharecropping to wage labor. In this manner, many planters cheated their tenants out of AAA payments and turned the program into a lucrative subsidy for themselves. Because there was a noticeably lower rate of black migration from the south during the decade and a reduced need for plantation labor, a labor surplus soon developed.

The ensuing breakdown of a significant portion of the south's "way of life" only accelerated the mass black exodus between 1940 and 1950 when over one million men, women and children would leave the area. As we shall discover in the next chapter, some "social scientists" in the Roosevelt Administration were alarmed by the results of the AAA program in the south and subsequently made a number of vain efforts to correct the situation.

The STFU, it should be noted, in later years was to suffer from an internal conflict generated by its "affiliation" with the United Cannery, Agricultural, Packing and Allied Workers, CIO. Although these groups ultimately disaffiliated from the union, the association destroyed the STFU. Mitchell recalls, "in 1937, when we joined the CIO, we had more than 200 locals and when we wound up in that battle we had about 30 or 40 locals, just a handful of people."[37]

As it has so frequently throughout its history, organized labor leadership refused to make a serious commitment to organize farmworkers. "There does not appear," the American Federation of Labor (AFL) stated rather candidly, "to be a financial basis for the organization of a trade union among sharecroppers."[38]

A Moratorium on Debts and Mortgages

The Frazier-Lemke Act in 1933 was perhaps the most crucial piece of legislation passed during this era to help farmers financially survive the Great Depression. Until this time, creditors had an absolute right to claim enforcement. The Frazier-Lemke Bankruptcy Act, passed after some 37 states had already enacted some form of foreclosure moratorium, would later be involved in a series of court battles and redrafted as the Frazier-Lemke Farm Refinancing Act before finally being declared constitutional by the U.S. Supreme Court. It allowed a five-year moratorium on debts and mortgages, while the courts appraised the value of the farmer's property. During or at the end of that period, the farmer could repurchase the property at the new appraised value. Meanwhile, the debtor could retain and use the property with a reasonable rental fee during which time all bankruptcy proceedings would be stayed. At the end of the five-year period the court could have the property re-appraised.

Despite such efforts to unburden the farmer, banks in many rural states were forced to reduce their outstanding loans and to continue to foreclose on farm and chattel mortgages.

One Treasury Department official estimated that in the five years since the start of the Depression the Federal Reserve had curtailed the total money supply by over $6.5 billion. Per capita allotment of bank credit, which included total money stocks, outstanding currency and bank deposits was only $117.73.

However, six states and the District of Columbia were above this national average (*i.e.*, New York, $406.60 per capita); while 41 states were below the national average (*i.e.* Iowa, $63.43 per capita; Kansas, $76.68 per capita; Mississippi, $21.10 per capita). Based on these figures, some farm leaders contended that the Federal Reserve Board had been actively pursuing a policy of restricting bank credit in the farm states so as to offset any benefits the farm community would receive from government payments for reducing its acreage and production.[39]

The Frazier-Lemke legislation replaced $3 billion of that $6.5 billion deficit and was thought by some to have played a major role in breaking the Federal Reserve's strangulation of the economy. It gave farmers and creditors an opportunity, under the supervision of the courts, to arrive at a "voluntary" settlement by extending, reducing or adjusting the creditors' claims. If the creditor balked, the farmer had the option of forcing the creditor into a compulsory debt-adjustment procedure. Since the passage of this legislation, however, the pendulum has progressively swung away from protecting the farmers and back to an almost complete protection of the creditors' right to forced sales.

Frazier-Lemke was violently attacked as a "socialist" measure by lending institutions, which were aided and abetted by the lower courts until the U.S. Supreme Court's decision in 1937. University of Nebraska agricultural economist Ernest Feder describes that attack:

> The political fight against the Frazier-Lemke Act or bills modeled in accordance with its general provisions was led by the large insurance companies, the American Bankers Association, and the Federal Land Bank of Berkeley, California. By and large, agricultural economists took a stand which supported the lending interests. It is a strange political paradox that the farm groups, with the exception of the Farmers Union, were either allied with the lenders or kept aloof, and all of them became disinterested in the problem by 1956. Ironically, the fight in favor of greater protection of farmers through adequate bankruptcy provisions was carried on by bankruptcy experts.[40]

Codifying "Fair Competition"

Farmers pointed to the National Recovery Administration (NRA) as further evidence that Roosevelt's "New Deal" contradicted his economic principles by favoring the industrial East at the expense of the agricultural West. NRA was designed to set up codes of fair competition for various businesses and industries; put a price floor on goods and services, including profits; and give labor the right to organize and bargain collectively. Codes of Fair Competition, which considered the costs of materials, management and labor in setting the minimum prices for goods and services, were designed by the NRA to cover all U.S. business and industry — *except* agriculture.

Farm critics pointed out that here on one hand was the Federal government establishing a floor under the prices of industrial goods and services, including labor, which were based on the cost of doing business while enjoying a margin of profit. On the other hand the government, through the Agricultural Adjustment Act, was establishing a ceiling on the prices of farm products and subsidizing the farmer for part of the difference between the ceiling price level and the cost of production.

The farmers' reward for restricting and curtailing production while receiving this subsidy was supposedly an "abundant life through scarcity." But the consequence of these two economic policies, it was argued, was simply to freeze the disparity between agriculture and industry and accelerate the latter's economic depression.

Here Come the Judges!

It was the U.S. Supreme Court, however, not business nor farmers, which brought these two landmark laws to an end. On May 27, 1935 in *A.L.A. Schechter Poultry Corporation vs. U.S., 295 U.S. 495, 1935* the Court unanimously held that the delegation of powers granted in the NRA exceeded those permissible under the Constitution and thus the Act was invalid.

On January 6 of the following year, the Court in a 6-3 decision in the case of *U.S. vs Butler et al., Receivers of Hoosac Mills Corp., 297 U.S. 1, 1936* ruled that in the Agricultural Adjustment Act of 1933 "the power to confer or withhold unlimited benefits is the power to coerce or destroy ... This is coercion by economic pressure. The asserted power of choice is illusory."

In a sharply-worded dissent, Justice Harlan Fiske Stone argued that the Court's "tortured" interpretation could prevent any number of government efforts to operate effectively. "The suggestion that [the power of the purse] must now be curtailed by judicial fiat because it may be abused by unwise use hardly rises to the level of argument. So may judicial power be abused."

Despite these setbacks Roosevelt and his Administration were already embarking on a new program to aid agriculture and revitalize the nation's economy.

Chapter Seventeen

Liberty vs. Paternalism

"Officer, this spring was the first time I've had a wheat crop in three years and I'm going to harvest it if I have to chase it all the way to Mexico."
- Kansas farmer after being stopped for speeding on a Texas highway towing a combine behind his Model T truck.[1]

Even as Franklin Roosevelt and his "New Deal" legislation began to rekindle the hopes of the American people, farm prices already started showing modest increases. At the same time, however, U.S. production of wheat and cotton declined as carryover supplies started to dwindle.

Serious droughts in the Great Plains, and the early effects of the AAA's crop reduction program, caused wheat production go from 941 million bushels in 1931 to 526 million in 1934 before again climbing to over 600 million in 1936. The temporary crop loss caused the United States to become a substantial wheat importer in 1934, 1935 and 1936.[2]

The terrible droughts of the mid-1930s, had only added to farmers' misery. In 1935 H.S. Person, E. Johnson Coil and Robert T. Beall authored a small book, *Little Waters* which described some of the conditions at that time:

> The soil-erosion specialists tell us that the dust storm of May 11, 1934 swept 300 million tons of fertile topsoil off the great wheat plains; that 400 million tons of soil material are washed annually into the Gulf of Mexico by the Mississippi River; that generally water and wind erosion together each year remove beyond use three billion tons of soil.
>
> ... This is not a loss of income the flow of which can be resumed, but of assets that cannot be recovered, for it takes Nature centuries to make the equivalent of the top soil which has been swept away — at the rate in some places of 3 to 6 inches in a single season.

Called by some "one of the three worst ecological blunders in history," the Dust Bowl was a mere 50 years in the making. In his authoritative investigation, *Dust Bowl: The Southern Plains in the 1930s*, Donald Worster vividly describes this tragedy, and sees more than just nature on a rampage:

My argument ... is that there was in fact a close link between the Dust Bowl and the Depression — that the same society produced them both, and for similar reasons. Both events revealed fundamental weaknesses in the traditional culture of America, the one in ecological terms, the other in economic. Both offered a reason, and an opportunity for substantial reform of that culture...

It came about because the expansionary energy of the United States had finally encountered a volatile, marginal land, destroying the delicate ecological balance that had evolved there. We speak of farmers and plows on the plains and the damage they did, but the language is inadequate. What brought them to the region was a social system, a set of values, an economic order. There is no word that so fully sums up those elements as "capitalism".[3]

Worster adds that "capitalism" has developed an "enduring ethos" that seeks to give the economic culture continuity. The ecological values of that ethos include: nature must be seen as capital; man has a right, even an obligation, to use this capital for constant self-advancement; and the social order should permit and encourage this continual increase of personal wealth.[4]

By the 1920s farming and ranching had become for many a business, the object of which was not necessarily to make a living, but to make money. Just as they objected to the "social controls" that they perceived Roosevelt's New Deal trying to impose on them, they also believed that nature would dare not thwart them in the managing of their business affairs. Thus, these same *laissez-faire* interests continued to plow up the Great Plains extensively, planting their wheat, and creating highly mechanized factory farms that produced unprecedented harvests.

As Worster states, "There was nothing in the plains society to check the progress of commercial farming, nothing to prevent it from taking the risks it was willing to take for profit. That is how and why the Dust Bowl came about."[5]

The Dust Bowl was only an extreme example, however, of the serious drought which threatened the greater part of the nation in the 1930s. If one uses a precipitation deficiency of at least 15 percent of the historical mean to define drought, the only states that escaped the calamity from 1930 to 1936 were Maine and Vermont. Intense heat also accompanied this drought in many areas of the country.

Centered around Liberal, Kansas the Dust Bowl stretched 400 miles north to south and 300 miles east to west. This 151,000 square mile area included western Kansas, southeastern Colorado, northeastern New Mexico and the panhandles of Oklahoma and Texas. It was in this region where the "black blizzards" of the 1930s struck with all their fury.[6]

On April 17, 1935 the famous pilot Laura Engels was forced to make an emergency landing at Alamosa, Colorado after encountering what many believe to be the worst black duster on record. She reported later that somewhere over the Texas Panhandle she sought to climb to 23,000 feet and yet still was unable to avoid the giant cloud of dust.[7]

These 200-mile wide storms, with a 1,000-feet high dust clouds rolling along the ground at speeds of 60 miles per hour, kept some towns in night-like blackness for more than three hours and stretched across Kansas, Eastern Colorado and into Texas and Oklahoma.[8] Dust from storms such as these found its way into the streets of New York and Washington, D.C.[9]

The estimated financial cost of the 1934 drought alone amounted to one-half the U.S. cost in World War I. By 1936 farm losses had reached $25 million a day as more than two million farmers were drawing relief checks.[10] "You could look out the window and watch Kansas go by," was the way one Midwesterner put it to a reporter. "The wind blew everything into old Mexico, except the mortgage," observed another farmer.

Most farmers gladly accepted their relief in the form of federal dollars along with the federal government's inevitable reassurance, solicitation and encouragement. However, when innovative New Deal policies were attempted, many plains people turned hostile. "The fate of the plains lay in the hands of Providence, and Providence, not Washington, would see them come out all right" was a popularly expressed sentiment at the time, notes Worster.

> What the plainsmen needed was hope, of course — but the mature hope that does not smooth over failure, deny responsibility, or prevent basic change. They needed a disciplined optimism, tempered with restraint and realism toward the land. But all that required a substantial reform of commercial farming, which neither Roosevelt nor most of his New Deal advisers were prepared or able to bring about. Even as it evolved toward a more comprehensive program, the New Deal did not aim to alter fundamentally the American economic culture. Washington became and remained throughout the decade a substitute for a benign Providence, trying to give plainsmen their "next year."[11]

As a consequence of the Dust Bowl and the severe droughts of the 1930s, approximately 500,000 farm families were found to be on land unsuitable for agriculture. It was later estimated that from two million to five million acres of sub-marginal land a year should have been retired over this period of time.

The disaster of the Dust Bowl also gave birth to the Soil Conservation Act of 1935 which in turn created a Soil Conservation Service (SCS) under the direction of Hugh H. Bennett, a USDA soil chemist who had been warning about the impending dangers of soil erosion since 1928.

Initially, it was Rexford Guy Tugwell, assistant secretary of Agriculture, who had urged action on soil protection. However, Interior Secretary Harold Ickes was intent on consolidating his hold on such land issues and in September 1933 established the Soil Erosion Service within his own department. Franklin Roosevelt, however, wanted a more ambitious program in USDA and on a weekend in March 1935 when Ickes was in Florida, he had it transferred to the USDA.

This new SCS program stressed the need for contour plowing, crop rotations, fertilization and sectional planting of woodlands. In order to qualify for federal aid, farmers had to comply with the program. With an initial budget of $665,408 the SCS has now grown to an over $700 million federal program.[12]

The Tenancy Question

Between 1930 and 1935 census figures had showed that more than 40 percent of the nation's farms were operated by tenants. In some areas, like the south, the tenancy rate was as high as 60 percent.[13] Since 1900 increasing amounts of capital were required to operate and maintain a commercially successful, non-family type farm. Many farmers, unable to afford such costs, found themselves tilling and cultivating someone else's land. At the same time the laws governing landlord-tenant relationships were inadequate, little if any security of tenure existed, and very often the rental agreements were of such a dubious legal nature that in effect they created a new form of slavery.

The nation was thus confronted with not only the problem of improving tenure arrangements, but how to rescue small, poor, subsistence farms, and how to deal with the migrant farmworker population. A 1937 report drafted by the President's Farm Tenancy Committee described the situation:

> Half a century ago one of every four farmers was a tenant. Today two of every five are tenants. They operate land and buildings valued at $11,000,000,000.
>
> For the past 10 years the number of new tenants each year has been about 40,000. Many change farms every 2 or 3 years and apparently one out of three remains no longer than 1 year.
>
> Thousands of farmers commonly considered owners are as insecure as tenants, because in some areas the farmers' equity in their property is as little as one-fifth.
>
> Fully half the total farm population of the United States has no adequate farm security.

Some believed that one solution to the tenancy problem was to move farmers struggling to squeeze out an existence off of submarginal land and "rehabilitate" them as farmers elsewhere rather than put them on public relief. Others believed that the solution was to create programs that would save a relative few from financial disaster by helping them acquire ownership of the land they were on. The fact that such a solution still left the nation with thousands of displaced rural citizens in a depressed economy is reflected in Murray Benedict's observation that:

> the real need was either to increase the ability of these farmers to produce for the market, or to shift them out of agriculture into occupations where their efforts would be more remunerative. Shifting them out of agriculture was hardly practical when unemployment was still widespread in the cities. Increasing their abilities and resources was to prove a difficult and baffling task.[14]

The President's Committee had listed four major causes of farm insecurity: "economic maladjustment, defective land and credit policies, consequences of fee-simple ownership, and credit disabilities." In turn the Committee suggested two general types of action: "movement upward from rung to rung (of the agricultural ladder) by farmers who are prepared to take such steps" and taking steps that looked to the "increase [of] security on each step of the ladder's various rungs."

"Rural Rehabilitation"

Against such background Roosevelt, in addition to securing passage of the Grazing Act of 1934, created the Tennessee Valley Authority, pushed the enactment of the Soil Erosion Act of 1935 and established the Resettlement Administration (RA) in May, 1935.

In sending his Emergency Relief Act of 1935 to Congress, the President urged the legislators to insert a brief phrase in the Act calling for "rural rehabilitation and relief in stricken agricultural areas." It was from this modest legislative mandate that he issued an executive order creating the Resettlement Administration. The very heart of the resettlement concept was, in the words of its creator, Rexford Tugwell, "the simultaneous attack on the wastage of people and the inefficient use of resources, each of which was so much the cause of the other that they were inextricably linked."[15]

Tugwell, although born on a farm in western New York, received his education and taught mainly in eastern private universities and was a former Columbia University economist. With this background, agricultural historian Richard S. Kirkendall has noted, "his lack of confidence in farm groups extended to those colleges and their extension services, agencies that seemed to be identified with upper-class groups in rural America."[16]

Having so little faith in such "farm leaders," Tugwell assailed the agrarian philosophy that they and many farmers were preaching at this time. He believed that the United States was essentially an industrial nation and that the time had come for an absorption of "a very large number of persons from farms into our general industrial and urban life."[17] Agriculture, he argued, needed governmental action focused on increased technical

efficiency, lower costs and prices, and the conservation of society's interest in the land.

At the same time Tugwell distrusted business leaders, believing that strong government controls were needed, and often opined that the hostility toward the New Deal by these "communities of economic interests" was a product of selfish economic interest. Uncontrolled and unregulated private enterprise, he argued, would lead to a tragically wasteful and destructive use of the land.

USDA's "Impractical Lawyers"

As Undersecretary of Agriculture Tugwell was also unhappy with the direction taken by the USDA in the early years of the New Deal. He believed the AAA was dominated by big farmers and that it discriminated against sharecroppers, tenants, and farm laborers.

He was particularly bitter about the firing of a number of lawyers, headed by Jerome Frank, from the AAA. In 1933 these lawyers had been called upon for an opinion respecting the contract between the AAA and cotton growers. The two parties had been interpreting their contract such that when it said planters were required to keep the same number of tenants as they had on the land in 1933 it meant simply that — the same number. Seeking to maintain the spirit of the original law in providing greater security for low-income groups the attorneys ruled that the contract required landlords to keep the same *people*, not just the same number.

This opinion by Frank and company was immediately denounced in the south by planters, extension agents and politicians. Chester Davis, who headed the AAA at the time, thought the ruling a dishonest distortion of the cotton contract and another in a long series of impractical acts by the department's lawyers.[18] To Davis his agency existed to bring higher prices to commercial farmers, not to reform the Southern social system or the way crops should be marketed. He resented the view that the AAA was "entirely worthless so long as it did not result in a social revolution in the South."[19]

Writing in *The Nation*, Raymond Gram Swing, a popular radio political commentator of the day, argued that the firing of these lawyers showed that the power in agricultural politics clearly laid with the processors, the distributors, and the big producers. Roosevelt, he wrote, was unwilling to make the "frontal attack" needed to take "economic power from the interests in agriculture who hold it and are increasing it."[20]

The Resettlement Agency Attacks Rural Poverty

In viewing this situation Tugwell decided that it was necessary to develop alternative ways of improving the plight of the rural poor while at the same time coordinating the many federal agencies that dealt with the land. As administrator of the Resettlement Agency, Tugwell was initially independent of the USDA, although later in 1936 the RA became part of the Agriculture Department.

By employing a wide variety of activities and making full use of its social scientists, the RA began to attack rural poverty programmatically not just in terms of offering relief, but in seeking to determine its causes.

The RA believed that such programs needed to be devised "because all Americans, not just the rural poor, suffered from poverty in agriculture, for it meant inadequate purchasing power, destruction of land, disease, costly social services, and the like."[21]

Immediately opposition developed from large commercial growers, bankers and businessmen, who saw federal resettlement or rehabilitation of the needy as a challenge to the dominant orientation of farm politics. "I know what's the matter with Harry Byrd," Roosevelt told Tugwell when the Senator objected to a resettlement project in Virginia. "He's afraid you'll force him to pay more than ten cents an hour for his apple pickers."[22]

RA quickly embarked on an effort to assist families in worst-situation scenarios, helping them find new and more economic farms or locating them elsewhere in other occupations that gave greater promise of work and income. The primary object was clear: facilitate the integration of small farms, particularly tenant farms, into the mainstream of American agriculture.

However, Tugwell saw only the most able tenants becoming owners. He wanted government to experiment with long-term leases and large-scale cooperative farms as well as with other types of cooperatives. Advice and loans were to be made to farms which showed signs of recovering while submarginal agricultural land was set aside for use as parks and recreational areas. Real estate operators had for some time been profiting handsomely off drought-stricken land, selling farms that had been abandoned in times of drought to new settlers in recurring periods of land-sustaining rainfall.

Through its farm-and-home program, the RA also sought to help people whose lives had become hopeless because their land could no longer support them. The plan involved making a loan to a family for whom a suitable location had been found. These loans included money not only for farm and personal expenses but also for families to pay the poll tax. This feature was a political bombshell, particularly for farm families attempting to establish themselves in the South.

Such loans were made on the condition that the farmer followed an agreed plan of operation and that his wife agree to make use of the farm's potentialities under the guidance of a home economist. Of the hundreds of millions of dollars subsequently loaned by the government for this program, in the end over 95 percent were returned and with a certain amount of interest.

Conforming to the Prejudices of the "Well-to-Do"

Tugwell's creation existed for two tumultuous years without recognition from the Congress, operating on those funds allotted to Roosevelt for the relief of the depression. After passage of the Bankhead-Jones Farm Tenant Act in 1937, built around the proposals made by the President's 1937 Farm Tenancy Committee, the RA's name was changed to the Farm Security Administration (FSA), its power restricted by the Congress, and its focus directed toward the 1937 Committee's recommendations.

In Tugwell's words, the FSA became "much more in conformity with the prejudices of the well-to-do concerning those who have not succeeded in the competition of economic life." Several years later, in evaluating the resettlement idea as part of the "New Deal" farm policy, he pointed out,

> The critics' objection ... as to the whole idea of resettling people under the guidance of sympathetic experts, centered in the idea that it limited peoples' freedom. That the freedom involved was limited to the right to be dispossessed and to migrate, or perhaps to sink deeper into misery, seemed not to affect loyalty to principle. The government was not a suitable agency for such assistance. Relief might be given; but that workable opportunities should be found and guidance given did not command consent. The one was in the realm of liberty; the other was inadmissible paternalism.[23]

Despite these misgivings FSA figures showed that the net costs to government per family helped by these rehabilitation type of loans was only about $75 a year while the average payment to families in northern cities ran somewhere around $800 on WPA and $350 for rural work relief.[24] Thus, if FSA was viewed only as a relief program it was still a good deal less expensive than if the families had been encouraged to leave their farms for life on the relief rolls in the city.

By 1936 the drought had helped reduce production to the point that cash income from farming had risen from $4.7 billion in 1932 to $8.4 billion, while farm expenses had increased only about $1 billion.[25] Many heavily mortgaged farms were now re-financed and relatively free of debt, either in the hands of creditors or resold to new owner-operators for a lower price and a smaller indebtedness.

Exports and Imports

During these early years of the "New Deal" the policy debate over export subsidies and production controls raged on. As many economists had predicted in 1929 when the Smoot-Hawley tariff bill was passed, it had an immediate and damaging effect on U.S. trade. In the three years after Smoot-Hawley the U.S.'s export trade dropped to $6.7 billion from $9.6 billion, as the total volume of all agricultural exports declined 35 percent between 1927 and 1931. Meanwhile, the nation's import duties were reaching record levels.[26]

It was the supreme irony for many of the nation's farmers that while the Roosevelt Administration was seeking ways to cut back on crop production in the United States the nation at the same time was importing substantial quantities of cheap agricultural goods.

At the same time that the AAA was being approved, Congress also enacted a Special Trade Agreements Act. In the decade ahead these treaties effectively limited American exports by the amount of imports we were willing to accept in payment for our exports. For example, a special trade agreement with Great Britain provided for a competitive market on agricultural products only. It did not provide for a competitive market in industrial goods.

The consequences of these agreements included a flood of foreign agricultural and raw products in the U.S.

throughout the 1930s. The *Statistical Abstract of the United States of 1944-45* shows that from 1933 to 1943 the United States exported a total of $8,723,787,000 in agricultural products while importing a total worth $12,785,725,000.

Similarly, between 1931 and 1939 the equivalent of 23.2 million acres worth of production in wheat, corn, oats, barley, soybeans and cotton alone was imported into the United States From 1928 through 1939 the total value of this nation's agricultural exports was $10.9 billion while the value of those agricultural products imported into the United States was $14.5 billion, of which $7.1 billion were in supplementary imports (crops also grown in the United States).

The percentage of the value of supplementary agriculture imports as related to the total value of agricultural imports during this period ranged from 44.1 percent in 1930 to 56.4 percent in 1936, averaging for the 11 years just over 49 percent per year. In addition, agriculture products accounted for 50.6 percent of the total value of U.S. imports between 1931 and 1939 while they accounted for only 31.2 percent of the nation's total export value.[27]

It is also worth noting in this regard that between 1934 and 1939 alone the United States exported $10 billion in manufactured goods while importing only $3 billion. It has been estimated that if the American farmer had been allowed to produce the amount of agricultural products that we imported during this period of time, it would have required 15 million individuals to produce such a harvest. By utilizing an accepted law of economics, that additional $12 billion of income would have translated into an increase of over $84 billion in national income.[28]

Carl Wilkins, the maverick yet insightful pioneer agricultural economist, has noted that when a manufacturer saw the reduced amount of domestic purchasing power in the late 1920s and 1930s foreign markets became essential:

And, the more that he can be persuaded to look abroad for his markets, the easier it will be to change his whole attitude toward wages... if he can be induced to look abroad for his markets, then wages become merely an item of costs and it is to the manufacturer's interest to reduce them as low as possible.

If they are reduced — and the odium for reducing them, of course, allowed to fall on the manufacturer — then American industry becomes at once a much more profitable investment for the financier, while the foreign goods can flow into Free Trade America to pay the interests on the foreign loans.[29]

Indeed, there is evidence that at this time underproduction, rather than surplus, was a major source of the nation's economic woes.

In 1935 the Brookings Institute published a study titled "Income and Economic Progress" which reported that the United States had a loss of $135 billion in the first four years of the decade. It added that there had

been no surplus production, but rather a very marked underproduction of goods. Quoting a USDA source, the study noted in regards to agricultural production that if everyone had had an adequate diet during this period, the nation could have produced 75 percent more farm products that it actually did.[30]

Battling Over Special Trade Agreements

Nevertheless, many saw production controls as essential to foreign trade during this period. A struggle developed between Wallace and George N. Peek, whom Roosevelt had appointed to head the AAA. Peek advocated high tariffs, individual barter and contract agreements at negotiated prices for the disposal of farm surpluses not marketable at parity prices, and conditional most-favored-nations treatment. Wallace advocated lower tariffs and more free-trade policies.

Many believed that an educational system long dominated by the thinking of exporters and importers of goods — the international cartels — was largely responsible for the economic theory the Roosevelt Administration depended on in its foreign trade matters. Critics of this type of thinking pointed out that the United States had always had more foreign trade with high tariffs than with low tariffs. The demand for the latter came mainly from traders who sought to bring in products to a rich U.S. market and from the five percent of our largest manufacturers who always wanted to import farm products and other raw materials to pay for the exports of their manufactured products.

Eventually, Roosevelt decided in Wallace's favor, and forced Peek to resign. Fearful, however, of Peek's "forcefulness and vocabulary" on the loose outside of his administration, FDR subsequently named Peek as his Special Adviser on Foreign Trade. On June 12, 1934 the Special Trade Agreements Act was signed and became a cornerstone of a new U.S. trade policy. It allowed the President to raise or lower tariffs by as much as 50 percent on unconditional most-favored-nation treatment, meaning that if the United States made a trade agreement with one nation to lower rates on certain imports, it could extend that same treatment to other nations which also gave U.S. exports most-favored-nation treatment.

Divorcing the American Economy From the World Economy

Dating back to the late 1920s there had been increasing concern over the dwindling of world trade and the chaotic situation in international exchange rates, as nations desperately sought to curtail imports and protect their gold reserves while expanding outlets for their products.

By 1932 the flow of foreign investment by the United States had virtually ceased. At this time, the British began to push for a world economic conference. The United States, fearing that such a meeting would deal primarily with the readjustment or cancellation of war debts showed only a mild interest in the meeting and agreed to participate only if neither the war debt or tariff issues were discussed.

While he carefully avoids pinpointing exactly who would have been the major losers if readjustments or cancellations were made on war debts, Murray R. Benedict in his *Farm Policies of the United States, 1790-1950* described the U.S. attitude as "quite unrealistic" because it

was obviously bringing closer the repudiation which later occurred. A concession that would have reduced the amounts owed in proportion to the deflation in prices of commodities would have been in order, since it would have meant repayment of a comparable amount of commodities and services to that which had given rise to the obligations. It was clear, however, that payment in full could not be made, even on amounts so adjusted.

There was little inclination in the United States to recognize these debts for what they were, namely, a part of the United States contribution to the war effort comparable to the sums spent in putting their own soldiers in the field. The expenditures had not gone for building up resources in the borrowing countries which would enable them to make repayment, and our aversion to receiving imports made talk of repayment illogical and naive.[31] (emphasis added)

Subsequently, the London Economic Conference of 1933 failed because the United States showed little enthusiasm for collaborating with the other participants to stabilize currencies. Instead, Roosevelt, who was making a deliberate effort to divorce the American economy from the world economy and was counseled by advocates of a policy based on varying the gold content of the dollar as a means of raising prices, chastised the other nations for entertaining such ideas as currency stabilization. He declared that "the sound internal economic system of a Nation is a greater factor in its well-being than the price of its currency in changing terms of the currencies of other Nations."[32]

The consequences of the inability of the major nations to arrive at any economic consensus in London soon became apparent: exchange values of the various currencies remained chaotic, trade barriers increased and international cynicism and hatred increased as both nationalism and fascism began increasingly to dominate the European political scene.

Searching For Ways to Help Agriculture

Meanwhile, the various agricultural programs initiated by the Roosevelt administration, in conjunction with the nation's general economic recovery and the effect of the droughts, were significantly advancing farm prices. However, in 1937 they began again dropping to less than 100 percent of parity and did not recover until the United States moved towards war three years later. Based on the 1910-1914 period, the parity income ratio rose to 107 in 1935, receded to 99 in 1936 and returned to 107 again in 1937.

Meanwhile, the national economy was still struggling as total income in 1936 was $64.7 billion as opposed to $87.4 billion in 1929. The market value of stocks which

had reached $90 billion in 1929 was now $60 billion (recovering from a disastrous low of $16 billion in 1932). Whereas deflation characterized the economy in 1933, by 1937, after the revaluation of the dollar in 1934, there was genuine concern about inflation as the United States was well on its way to accumulating a vast sum of gold amounting to $17 billion of the world's 1939 stock of $26 billion.[33]

Shortly after the Supreme Court in January 1936 ruled that the AAA of 1933 was unconstitutional, Roosevelt submitted to the Congress the Soil Conservation and Domestic Allotment Act of 1936. This redrafted Act was intended not only to side-step the Court's objections to the 1933 legislation, but also to correct the overcentralization of the AAA. Roosevelt's people pointed out that such changes had been in the planning stage even before the Court's ruling and that the Hoosac decision simply "precipitated as a sudden change that which had been planned as a gradual one."

The new Act aimed "to promote the conservation and profitable use of agricultural land resources by temporary Federal aid to farmers and by providing for a permanent policy of Federal aid to states for such purposes."

Close examination of this act, however, especially compared to the 1933 legislation, evinces a fundamental policy change for American agriculture from a *price* objective to an *income* objective. It was a subtle but important change, the first step towards removing agriculture from the marketplace and attempting to reformulate it structurally so it could be dealt with as a social welfare issue, thereby allowing taxpayers to underwrite it in its times of need.

In the AAA of 1933 a balance between agricultural production and consumption was to be achieved by reestablishing

prices to farmers at a level that will give agricultural commodities a purchasing power with respect to articles that farmers buy, *equivalent to the purchasing power of agricultural commodities* in the base period. (emphasis added)

But, in the 1936 Act that balance would be achieved,

at as rapid a rate as the Secretary of Agriculture determines to be practicable and in the general public interest ... *the ratio between the purchasing power of the net income per person on farms and that of the income per person not on farms* that prevailed during the five-year period August 1909-July 1914 ... (emphasis added)

By basing the parity ratio on the net income of persons on farms as compared with the net income of non-farm persons, rather than on the purchasing power of farm commodity prices compared with the purchasing power of the non-agricultural sector, the Federal government neatly abrogated the marketplace's responsibility to provide farmers with reasonable prices for their goods. The move in effect told farmers that if they wanted to stay in business and accept what the market was willing to offer them for their raw materials, then they must be willing to seek some form of off-farm income or government help to survive.

In the name of Federal assistance for the family farm in America this new legislation had developed into a neat *coup d'etat* for corporate agribusiness.

Crops were to be classified into two general categories: "soil-depleting" (cash crops like wheat, cotton, corn, tobacco and sugar beets) and "soil-conserving" (grasses, legumes and other forage crops that would rebuild and protect soils and which would not contribute directly to the nation's so-called burdensome surpluses).

Payments were to be made to farmers for shifting specified percentages of their "soil-depleting" crops to "soil-conserving" and for approved soil-building practices. Field administration was to be carried out by state agencies and county and community committees on the condition that authorizing state legislation acceptable to the Secretary of Agriculture had been passed and put into effect by the end of 1937.

Funds were to be transferred accordingly and after submission of such soil adjustment programs, payment would be made only after proof that the plan had been carried out. Unlike the AAA of 1933 where the operating funds came from processing taxes, the funding for this program, an amount not to exceed $500 million annually, was to be appropriated by the Congress from the Treasury.

By couching his new legislation in terms of soil conservation Roosevelt gained greater acceptance for his farm policy from Congress and the general public, which were shocked over the Dust Bowl tragedy. At the same time, FDR was able to sustain the momentum for his "New Deal" farm recovery program.

Some Legislative Milestones

In 1936 Congress also took a significant step towards curbing abuses in the marketing of agricultural commodities by extending exchange control coverage to many perishables and amending the Grain Futures Act. This new legislation established the Commodity Exchange Commission (CEC) which required merchants and brokers to register with USDA and to keep adequate records open for inspection by the Department. The Commission was also given new powers to limit speculative trading, prevent fraud and safeguard margin funds and other customer properties.

Another legislative milestone passed at this time was the National Labor Relations Act (NLRA), a long-sought triumph for the labor movement. However, the Act, which firmly established the right to unionization and collective bargaining, exempted agricultural labor from its provisions. For over five decades this exemption has profoundly affected agriculture's integrity and has belied its overall efforts to achieve genuine social and economic justice.

Just as the economy began to show distinct signs of recovery in 1936, a severe recession in the last half of 1937 and early 1938 showed that the nation was still faced with major economic problems. Unemployment doubled, production declined to 1934 levels, the value of listed stocks dropped $20 billion, the Administration abandoned efforts to affect price levels through manipulating the gold value of the dollar, credit was tightened and farm prices declined by 20 percent.[34] Clearly, the economy was not fully readjusted and agriculture was still in dire need of sustained help.

A President Copes With a Faltering Economy

When Roosevelt took office in 1933 the immediate agricultural task was to improve desperately low commodity prices while trying to domestically dispose of a purported accumulated stock of farm goods. The AAA of 1933 was an effort to generate immediate economic relief while reducing production.

In 1936, after historic droughts the previous three years, the focus of legislation was on soil conservation through crop cutbacks, while continuing the effort to transfer income to agriculture. The recession of 1937 and 1938, however, gave dramatic evidence that more permanent solutions were necessary if agriculture was to become a truly healthy part of the nation's economic life.

Some historians have rightly argued that the New Deal was overly concerned with the problems of large commercial non-family type farms and that it failed to give sufficient aid and relief to small, subsistence type farms. This strengthening of corporate style agriculture, rather than cooperative farming, would have two long-lasting consequences.

First, as University of the Pacific historian Donald H. Grubbs points out, large-scale, heavily capitalized, tax subsidized agricultural enterprises of the future, were owned by individuals and/or stockholders who viewed labor simply as an input cost, rather than as a productive factor.[35] Thus labor, capable of furnishing both management and muscle, would be progressively weakened in its effort to pressure middlemen and politicians for equitable compensation for its work.

Second, the New Deal tended to strengthen those established institutions within agribusiness for political reasons, which in turn allowed these same groups to solidify their political and economic power base. Witness, for example, the ascendancy of the Farm Bureau Federations in farm politics while the voices of other farm organizations became fainter and fainter.

The Selling of Income Maintenance to Agriculture

The Agricultural Adjustment Act of 1938 sought to forge a permanent and comprehensive approach that would provide for the adjustment of agricultural production while maintaining an adequate agricultural income. Title I of the Act set forth new amendments to the 1936 Soil Conservation Act; Title II authorized the Secretary of Agriculture to intervene on behalf of agriculture in cases before the Interstate Commerce Commission regarding freight rates on agricultural commodities; Title III concerned loans, parity payments, consumer safeguards and marketing quotas; Title IV concerned Cotton Pool Participation Trust Certificates, and Title V was the new Crop Insurance Act.

The most important section of this act was Title III, which spelled out new policies regarding production control and price supports in addition to redefining parity prices and honing the parity income definition.

As noted, the 1936 Act, in defining parity, referred to the "ratio between purchasing power of the *net income per person on farms* and that of the income per person not on farms." In the AAA of 1938 it reads "*per capita net income of individuals on farms* from farming operations" (emphasis added). Thus, the goal of federal farm policy now permanently became an *income* objective for farmers rather than the farmer-desired *price* objective.

Farmers who could not survive in a changing "free market" ceased to be corporate agribusiness's responsibility; they now became a societal problem, to be cared for and protected by the state.

The 1938 Act also outlined policies for loans from the CCC and specified that figuring allotments to individual farmers would be determined on the basis of acreage allotment in place of the previous base-acreage approach.

If a given commodity exceeded a "normal supply," the Secretary of Agriculture was empowered to establish a quota indicating the amount of the commodity that could be marketed within that year. Any grower marketing in excess of that quota would be subject to a heavy tax. Loans in accordance within the CCC provisions would be made available to cooperators in the plan, providing producers did not reject a quota plan proposed by the Secretary.

The constitutionality of the Agricultural Adjustment Act of 1938 was tested shortly after it became law. In *Mulford v. Smith* tobacco growers seeking to market tobacco in excess of their quotas challenged the validity of the Secretary's promulgation and enforcement of tobacco quotas.

In *Agricultural History*, Ohio State University's Paul I. Murphy, notes that Justice Roberts, who had written the *Butler* decision outlawing the original AAA, reflected the court's altered viewpoint in his *Mulford* majority opinion upholding the 1938 measure.

Roberts stated that the act did not purport to control production. It set no limit upon the acreage which might be planted, and imposed no penalty for the planting and producing of tobacco in excess of the marketing quota. It purported to be solely a regulation of interstate commerce, which it reached and affected at the place where tobacco entered the stream of commerce — the marketing warehouse.[36]

Such restrictions, Roberts pointed out, was valid since "any rule ... intended to foster, protect and conserve that commerce, or to prevent the flow of commerce from working harm to the people of the nation, is within the competence of Congress."[37]

Murphy concludes that Justice Roberts in effect "sanctioned under the commerce power, the type of agricultural regulation unsuccessfully attempted under the taxing power."[38]

In sum, the 1938 act gave the Secretary of Agriculture several ways to control surpluses, which many farm leaders and members of Congress still believed to be agriculture's root problem. Some farm leaders have suggested that the concern over surpluses was unwarranted; indeed was merely an excuse to maintain a low loan rate which in effect would became a ceiling price for most major commodities while government-owned stocks in the "ever-normal granary" would be used to keep prices below that loan rate. This would maintain a two-price system: the loan rate for the cooperating producers, and a lower or "market" price for the non-cooperating farmer.

It was pointed out, for example, that domestic wheat production for the 11 years between 1930 and 1940, according to a summary of USDA statistics, showed the United States not producing enough of the grain for domestic and export use and in fact revealing a deficit for the same period of 15,700,000 bushels.

It was not until the advent of World War II that the reality of the "surplus" question was faced as it became obvious that the nation had no meaningful strategy to deal with crop scarcities. Only abundantly good crop years during the early war years saved the United States and its Allies from a potentially disastrous food crisis.

By the late 1930s, however, the pace of international trade had grown acute as the Depression had brought about severe distress in surplus-producing areas while deficit countries sought to protect their goods with increasingly higher tariffs. Efforts to forge international commodity agreements, particularly in wheat, were short-lived or in some cases singularly unsuccessful.

U.S. exports/imports had improved after 1932 and although 1938 saw a setback, the value of the nation's agricultural exports remained steady from 1932-1938 before declining in 1939. The international trade situation, however, was not helped by the fact that even as the United States still retained a disproportionate share of the world's gold and silver supplies, its protectionist farm price policies still tended to handicap exports.

Against this background of an uncertain domestic economy and a chaotic world trade situation, Americans once again found themselves watching with alarm as another world war, which would soon consume all their energy and resources, began boiling over on the European continent. As it turned out, the most significant economic and social crisis of 20th century America — the Great Depression — was resolved in large part by the nation's most serious international crisis — World War II.

Chapter Eighteen

War and Peace

For centuries civilization has been turning to ever more sophisticated means of violence in its efforts to both promote and curb those extreme cases of nationalistic chauvinism, terrorism and international adventurism which periodically disrupt its peace. Born out of such chaos, are often those technological and economic innovations that ultimately have come to affect agriculture and the business of feeding people. World War II was no exception to that phenomenon.

In America, the global conflict led to the almost complete transition from animal to tractor power. It also brought forth a systematic analysis of agriculture with greater emphasis on mechanization, hybrid seeds, the development of livestock designed to make more efficient use of feed, the increased use of fertilizers, irrigation, chemical poisons, and capital. These dramatic technological developments not only accelerated the nation's ongoing agricultural revolution, but also profoundly affected the structure of U. S. agriculture, causing the rapid expansion in the size and operations of many farms.

USDA's Wayne Rasmussen describes this period in American agriculture as a controversial one.

Within the Department of Agriculture there was a period of controversy over the administration of the new wartime programs. One group urged that the quickest way to obtain increased production was to put resources into the existing structure. Another group urged that small farmers be encouraged to increase production with the idea that there was a greater potential for obtaining additional food and fiber from small farms with limited resources than from the large farms already operating at near capacity. The group favoring putting resources into the larger farms charged that others wanted to use the war effort to change the structure of agriculture. The group favoring strengthening the existing structure won the battle.[1]

The struggle over who would lead the way in obtaining this needed increase in production was only one of the many skirmishes to take place within the USDA during the war years. Linked to the "battle" Rasmussen notes, was the controversy surrounding the Bureau of Agricultural Economics (BAE).

Dismembering the BAE

In attempting to make agricultural planning democratic in method by establishing local planning commit-

tees of farmers and rural citizens, the BAE incurred the wrath of the American Farm Bureau Federation, which rapidly became the acknowledged leader in attacking the government agency.

The AFBF viewed the BAE committees as a threat to its own power in rural America, believing that "the various agricultural programs within a county should be consolidated and should be administered under the direction of the county agricultural agent."[2]

At the same time it was attacking the BAE the Farm Bureau was also becoming disenchanted with the New Deal. Not only did it believe that the administration's programs were characterized by duplication and overlap, but it also contended that the Roosevelt Administration was dominated by urban liberalism, particularly organized labor, and was biased against farmers.

Roosevelt had become preoccupied with the war abroad and former Secretary Wallace was busy with his own political pursuits as the nation's new Vice President. With both men lacking the time to champion their planning programs, the AFBF found itself with a golden opportunity to cultivate powerful friends in the Congress who would later prove to be valuable allies in its attacks on the BAE.

The AAA had also become angry with the BAE because the latter became increasingly critical of the former's activities. A budget cut of a half-million dollars in 1941 further diminished the bureau's effectiveness, especially since Congress added a proviso "that no part of the funds ... shall be used for State and county land use planning."[3]

As the 1940s progressed the BAE became more identified in its critics' minds with the prevailing liberalism, not only agrarian liberalism, with its emphasis upon government assistance for small family farms, but also urban liberalism, characterized by concern for the welfare and civil rights of working people.

In late 1942 and again in 1943 the BAE and the AFBF locked horns. The BAE had presented figures showing that while large-size farms were producing close to their capacity, agricultural production could be increased by ten percent if small family farmers were granted Farm Security Agency loans. The Farm Security Administration's use of these figures immediately drew fire from the Farm Bureau's leadership, who contended that such farmers could not produce a large quantity of food and that better prices were the key to greater production.[4]

A number of sociological studies by the BAE, including those dealing with the impact of local customs on agricultural production, the future of cotton in the

United States, and a California study of two rural towns (to be discussed later), also led to renewed attacks on BAE's creditability and its role within the USDA. At the same time as the Congress was virtually stripping it of all its responsibilities and funds. The bureau was soon relegated to near obscurity.

Price Controls

Despite the changes and the prosperity brought on by increased prices in the early 1940s, yet with the economic disaster that followed World War I still clearly etched in their minds, many farmers tried to think seriously and politically plan ahead for a healthy post-war agriculture economy.

In 1940 the prospect of war and expected shortages in a variety of goods along with higher prices spurred production, increased inventories and generally improved the nation's business climate. Farm prices, however, were still five points below 1937 levels and more than 30 points below the 1929 level. Due in part to the decline in exports, cash farm income was about equal to that of 1937 and approximately 20 percent below that of 1929. Using the years 1924-1929 as a base period of 100, agricultural exports in 1940 stood at 25.[5] The parity ratio, however, in 1940 was only at 80, which aside from 1921 and the Depression years of 1931-1934, had never been lower.[6]

As commodity prices began to rise and as the fear of inflation and labor unrest over wages increased, the FDR administration made a concerted effort to control prices. While the Administration talked of controls, few in Congress wanted to endanger a resurgent farm economy. Legislation introduced with the Administration's support specified that no ceiling was to be put on any agricultural product at less than 110 percent of the parity price, or the October 1, 1941 prevailing market price, or the average price from July 1, 1919 to June 30, 1929, whichever was highest.

Secretary Wickard, arguing for such legislation, pointed out to the Congress that,

> the recent increases in farm prices have been unusually rapid, but I want to make it plain that in my opinion they are not yet out of line, for the simple reason that these are increases from levels which were abnormally low ... One of the merits of the pending bill is its acceptance of the parity principle... There is a perfectly practical and obvious reason for stipulating that no ceilings should be imposed on farm products at less than 110 percent of parity, rather than exactly at parity.
>
> As every farmer knows, farm product prices fluctuate every day ... If ceilings were placed exactly at parity, the daily fluctuations in the market would necessarily all be between parity and some lower figure, and as a result farmers could not possibly average parity.[8]

Only a few short days after the House passed such legislation the Japanese bombed Pearl Harbor and America was officially at war. On January 30, 1942 the Emergency Price Control Act was signed by Roosevelt. Out of this Act evolved the Office of Price Administration (OPA) which throughout the war played a major role in the controversy over farm and food prices.

The year-long delay in passing the Price Control Act had generally been blamed on the fact that many legislators were suspicious of the Administration's attitude toward labor since Roosevelt had not specifically called for a freeze on wages. This ignored the fact that in the immediate past years most industries had been operating at less than full capacity and, as they increased output, they became capable of turning out goods at substantially lower average costs while still paying higher wages.

Although the OPA issued a General Maximum Price Regulation order, it failed to address two major areas: regulating farm product prices and the growing purchasing power of the nation's consumers. Subsequently, Roosevelt sent a message to Congress outlining a seven-point program he termed "our present national economic policy." Speaking to agriculture, Roosevelt pointed out that "to keep the cost of living from spiraling upward, we must stabilize the prices received by growers for the products of their lands."[9]

In comments accompanying this program Roosevelt expressed the need for a correction of the parity formula so that *ceilings* could be placed at parity and the government would be allowed to sell from its own stocks of farm products at market prices. He recommended no change in legislation affecting labor. Congress took little action in implementing Roosevelt's program. Meanwhile, farm prices rose more than eight percent between April and September 1942 while consumer food prices gained only six percent during the same period.[10]

In September 1942, the President again urged Congress to take action on his stabilization program, warning that unless he be given authorization to hold farm prices down to parity, "I shall accept the responsibility, and I will act."[11] He also strongly argued against any recomputation of parity which would put it at a higher level and felt that all benefit payments under the AAA should be included in the parity figure. To placate the farm interests, he recommended,

> that Congress in due time give consideration to the advisability of legislation which would place a floor under prices of farm products ... for one year, or even two years — or whatever period is necessary after the end of the war.[12]

The Steagall Amendment

In October 1942 Congress passed a Stabilization Act which brought about reductions in the levels at which ceilings could be placed on farm products; specifically no ceiling could be applied lower than the parity price for the commodity or the highest price paid between January 1 and September 15, 1942. An escape clause, however, permitted the President to set a price below the indicated level if necessary to correct "gross inequities." The Act also set up tighter controls on wages and the implementation of post-war price-support arrangements.

Prior to the passage of this Act in 1941, Representative Henry B. Steagall of Alabama attached a rider to the CCC authorization bill which stated that any agricultural commodities for which the Secretary of Agriculture asked for increased production as a contribution to the war effort must be provided with support prices at 85 percent of parity.[13] Subsequently, in the Stabilization Act of October 1942 the Steagall Amendment was amended in Section 9 and, in what some commentators have called the most important single action taken during the entire war period, it raised the support level of the Steagall commodities from 85 percent of parity to 90 percent.

It also extended to these commodities the same postwar parity price guarantees (90 percent) that had been specified for the basic crops covered in Section 8 (cotton, corn, wheat, rice, tobacco and peanuts) for the two years immediately succeeding the first day of January following a presidential or congressional declaration that hostilities had ceased. This guarantee of a reasonable parity price would enable American agriculture to maintain an unmatched period of general prosperity for nearly an entire decade.

This Stabilization Act and the OPA's Emergency Price Control Act were also to become the basic statements of price control policy for the duration of the war.

The Appearance of War-time Subsidies

While the inflationary gap — that difference between the amount of spendable income and the value of available goods and services — remained a vexing situation and a constant concern of the OPA, their price controls had a noticeable effect on the economy. During World War I with only limited controls, prices of all items rose 35 percent whereas between 1942-1945 the increase was only ten percent.[14]

A closer look at these costs show that rentals remained stable, dropping two tenths of a point, apparel increased 17.4 percent, furnishings went up 19 percent, fuel and electricity edged up 5 percent and food prices showed a 12 percent increase. During this same period (1939-1944) farmers' net cash income went from $3.2 to $11 billion, much of that amount, however, going into debt retirement.[15]

One of the key tenets in the Administration's plan to maintain a balance between supply and demand in a wartime economy was that cost-of-living items should be kept stable. Government-held and imported stocks were to be manipulated to help achieve such stability while subsidies were to be employed where necessary to offset increased costs or to stimulate production in those areas where greater output was desired. Actually, the war-time demand for farm products was such that, with few exceptions and for short periods of time, prices seldom dropped to support levels.

Agricultural subsidies took the form of payments to processors and importers, in an attempt to keep consumer prices stable. Where it was necessary an effort was made to compensate farmers for increased costs or greater production expenses by paying part of the price in the form of a subsidy while letting the product move in the market at a stabilized price.

Opposition to this subsidy program from within the farm community centered around the claim that such payments were really only subsidies to consumers so they could purchase food cheaply while earning more income. Also, it was argued that such programs increased government expenditures, and were inflationary, whereas increasing market prices was a more realistic approach than commodities supported by subsidies.

Consumers, it was argued, should get accustomed to paying higher food prices in anticipation of the higher base prices during the inevitable postwar price-support programs. Roosevelt countered that the subsidy program was not merely aimed at cutting consumer costs, but was rather a psychological move taken to keep wages and prices in line with general wartime price control measures.[16]

During this war-time controversy over subsidy payments, Congress made several attempts to pass legislation prohibiting the use of any funds for subsidies, price rollbacks or a substitute for raising prices, unless it specifically authorized such payments. Roosevelt promptly vetoed several such bills. By the summer of 1945, therefore, subsidies were paid on 18 different food and agricultural products, or groups of foods, at a cost of approximately $1.6 billion per year.[17] While the subsidy struggle soon died down, it was but the opening salvo in what was to become one of this nation's perennial agricultural policy conflicts.

Acquiring An Arsenal of War-time Measures

Throughout the war, price incentives, the announcement of production goals, and assistance in obtaining the necessary physical resources for maintaining increased food and fiber production were the principal tools employed to expand and guide agricultural production. Critics charged that these war-time price incentives favored commodities already in abundant supply (grains, cotton and tobacco) rather than such products as meat animals, dairy products and oilseed crops which were to be in high demand during the course of the war effort.

Cotton, for example, showed an annual carryover during the war years equivalent to a year's crop at the same time it was making heavy demands for scarce labor and valuable nitrogenous fertilizer. Yet, cotton acreage was dropping by 17 percent as domestic consumption showed only modest increases while foreign shipments were in sharp decline.[18] It was precisely cotton, grains and tobacco, however, which were the ones furthest below the parity figure in 1941.[19]

At the outbreak of the war, the USDA had taken steps to guide production into desired channels by establishing production goals to be administered through national and state committees. Support prices for hogs, dairy products and poultry and the gearing of certain conservation regulations toward raising peanuts on cotton acreage were initiated. Other commodities for which the USDA sought increased output were also supported by passage of the Steagall Amendment. Production goals for many of these commodities would later be established by the War Production Board that was created in January 1942.

In addition to price incentives farm machinery was rationed, local draft boards were instructed to give special consideration to certain kinds of farm labor, and the Secretary of Agriculture was directed to assure that adequate transportation, housing and health facilities be provided for migrant farm workers.

The Secretary was also given jurisdiction over farm wages and salaries for workers earning less than $2,400 a year. Further, an agreement with Mexico was reached on August 4, 1942 whereby workers from that country would be recruited and brought into the United States contractually and on a *temporary* basis. (Twenty-two years later, after years of controversy and human suffering, this highly exploitative *bracero* program was finally terminated.)

By mid-1943 the tools for stimulating and guiding farm production were well in place. Some criticism was voiced that the production goals established by the local and regional committees were too low and that acreage use and output were not geared to keep up with demand. Later, statistics would be cited to show that between 1941 and 1945 the total acreage of key crops increased only 12 percent as overall acreage in crops in 1945 was 5 percent less than it was in 1932.[20]

Reexamination reveals that these goal-oriented committees were uncertain whether to suggest what and how much *should* be produced based on national needs, or establish what *would* be produced given the existing price structure and how changes in that structure would affect production. In the meantime, Congress was shying away from full-scale food production planning, instead seeking to set up parity price legislation which made any selective guidance of resources difficult, if not impossible.

Murray R. Benedict, commenting on this situation, notes that while "the great diversity of American agriculture reduced somewhat the deleterious effects of the parity pricing straight jacket," nevertheless "a response all across the board to the higher level of prices, but largely in the old pattern of relationships between commodities, did not fit too badly the needs of the time."[21]

He goes on, however, to say:

One segment of American agriculture was clearly used ineffectively, namely, the manpower on some 1 to 3 million small, inefficient subsistence farms. These were mainly in areas where large families and small land and capital resources were the rule. Certain individuals in the war agencies urged vigorously a large-scale effort to upgrade the productivity of these farms through enlargement and capital input. But the majority opinion was that the results of such action would be too slow and the contribution to commercial supplies too small to warrant it as a short-term war program. *Furthermore, it seemed evident that the limited national resources in trained personnel could be used more effectively elsewhere.* (emphasis added)[22]

Nevertheless, a valuable contribution to the war effort was made in these areas, Benedict claims, "through the outmigration of manpower not needed on these small-scale farms."

Fighting for the "Slaves We Rent"

As agriculture became more profitable during the course of the war large growers were vitally concerned about their ability to purchase labor, despite the fact that the Tydings Amendment of 1942[23] gave preferential treatment in relation to the draft of any worker found "to be necessary to and regularly engaged in an agricultural occupation ..."[24] About 1.5 million to 1.8 million agricultural workers received deferred status in contrast to the 4.1 million in all nonfarm occupations.[25]

At the beginning of the war the Farm Security Administration had been given responsibility for the placement of agricultural workers throughout the United States, but the beleaguered agency soon came under attack from old and familiar enemies.

The Farm Bureau, the Grange and National Council of Farmer Cooperatives repeatedly expressed dissatisfaction with the FSA's policies in regard to the living and wage standards required for workers imported from Mexico. Claiming that such standards were higher than they were required to maintain for their own workers, the three farm groups eventually succeeded in taking away the FSA's recruiting and placement responsibilities and putting them in the hands of the more compliant Agricultural Extension Service (AES).

From 1943 through 1945 over 152,000 Mexican nationals were used in American fields and orchards, in addition to 60,000 Jamaicans and Bahamians and the 130,000 German and Italian prisoners of war.[26] Despite these figures, however, the number of farm workers in America declined by 8 percent between 1939 and 1945 (400,000 hired workers and 200,000 family workers) as five million people left the farm for urban employment or to join the armed services.[27]

A major cause of this exodus, of course, was the fact that farm workers, as has been their lot throughout the history of American agriculture, had neither the economic and social standing of farmers nor the legal protection afforded industrial workers by federal labor laws.

The Lend-Leasing of U.S. Food

The food these thousands of workers produced and harvested went to three main markets: the military, lend lease programs, and American civilian consumers. While the military's needs were more than provided for, the lend lease shipments were in large measure determined by the available shipping and the ability to move the cargo despite enemy submarine attacks which reduced food supplies to our Allies to dangerously low levels in 1942 and early 1943.

Space requirements also dictated an emphasis on foods with a concentrated nutritional value. While the British produced bulky foods such as wheat, potatoes and vegetables the U.S. lend lease program was shipping abroad dried eggs, canned meat, cheese, dried milk, fats and oils, etc. From March 1941 to December 31, 1945 lend-lease shipments of food to the British Empire totaled $3.4 billion, $1.7 to the U.S.S.R. and $238 million to other countries for a war-time total of $5.3 billion.[28]

During the war, international trade became government trade; private enterprise all but disappeared. Both the United States and many South American governments exercised direct control over all exports and imports. Government purchasing programs were also developed in many countries to prevent undesirable price competition for the limited supplies of food commodities.

Democratizing Food Consumption

Despite the war and the rationing of scarce items Americans consumed a higher volume of food per capita than they had in their entire history. The most notable shift in civilian food distribution occurred as highquality foods, heretofore readily available only to higher income groups, became restricted.[29]

Meanwhile, traditional lower-income people, hard at work, consuming more energy, and now earning much more money in a war-time economy and with little to spend it on besides food, began purchasing more expensive foods such as meat. Despite a rationing system that went into effect in March 1943, American per capita meat consumption increased by 18 percent during the course of the war.[30]

Sugar and coffee were the first commodities to be placed under rationing in 1942, followed by processed foods and meat in 1943. The food rationing and price control programs were both administered by the OPA, while the allocation of food was the responsibility of the War Food Administration. Both farm groups and economists were sharply critical of the two agencies. Farmers objected to having prices held down and to the inconvenience of the rationing system, while the economists wanted spending reduced through taxation and monetary controls to curb inflation.

One consequence of the increased demand for meat was that vast quantities of grain were used to produce such meat while domestic wheat supplies became seriously depleted. Yet, the War Food Administration, once again politically concerned over the possibility of "surpluses" and a repeat of the price declines of 1920 and 1932, continued to bank on the idea that the nation's farmers would keep producing large crops right into the post-war years when both domestic and foreign demand would assuredly be heavy. It was only because 1946, 1947 and 1948 saw such an abundant harvest of wheat that the United States was able to export nearly a billion bushels abroad in the first two years after the war and save the Allies from starvation.[31]

For example, between 1933 and 1936 the average U.S. yield was 12 bushels per acre. If the 1942-1945 yields had been comparable, wheat supplies during World War II would have been 1.3 billion bushels less than they actually were.[32]

The government also contributed to this problem by failing to act on several recommendations for increasing its storage facilities during the war. Without such space it was impossible to accumulate sufficient grain reserves. As a result, the government had difficulty maintaining hog and egg support prices.

Prior to the abundant post-war wheat crops the United States had almost a bare cupboard, with a wheat carry-over of only 280 million bushels on July 1, 1945.[33] Subsequent efforts by the nation's farmers to supply American grain to a starving, war-ravaged world soon saw wheat become the forerunner of a postwar foodprice inflation spiral.

Wartime Prosperity and the Farmer

The war years were clearly good to the American farmer financially, especially compared to the catastrophes of the previous two decades. The parity ratio (the ratio of prices received by farmers to prices paid by them), which had been 77 in 1939 rose to 119 in 1943 before dropping slightly in 1945; the increase matching a similar gain during World War I.[34] The total national income increased by 129 percent with farm income going up 165 percent. Meanwhile non-farm per capita income went from $663 in 1939 to $1320 in 1945, a gain of 99 percent while as farm per capita income increased from $173 to $554, a 220 percent gain.[35]

Despite this prosperity, however, farm prices still lagged behind the hourly earnings of industrial labor. (See Chart 18A)

Chart 18A: Increase in Farm Prices

	Hourly Farm Earnings Percentage Increase	Prices of Labor
1910-14 to July, 1945	106	419
1925-29 to July, 1945	40	99
1935-39 to July, 1945	93	81

Source: Computed from Bureau of Labor and Bureau of Agricultural Economics statistics, *The Farmer in the Second World War*, by Walter W. Wilcox, Iowa State College Press, Ames, Iowa: 1947, pg. 250.

In 1920, farm land prices were indexed at 170 (1912-1914=100). In the following 13 years they dropped to 73, before recovering to 84 in 1940 and rising to 126 with war-time prosperity.[36] Correspondingly, as farm mortgage debt dropped from $6.8 billion in 1939 to $5.25 billion in 1945,[37] it was evident that both farmers and financial institutions were showing remarkable borrowing and lending restraint while farmers were enjoying their most prosperous period of the 20th century.

Upon entering the post-war period, American agriculture seemed financially strong, with bank deposits and currency holdings of approximately $14 billion, up from $3.9 billion in 1940, its total debt reduced from $10 billion before the war to $8.3 billion in 1945, and its real estate valued at $56.5 billion compared to a 1940 value of $33.6 billion.[38]

As Benedict describes it,

Farm population had declined from around 30 million to about 25 million, largely as a result of heavy movement out of agricultural areas *chronically oversupplied* with labor. Aside from the fears of coming reductions in farm product prices, there was little to cloud the horizon of the *main body* of commercial farmers.

Within agriculture there still were great inequalities. The so-called 'poverty fourth' had gained little through war prosperity except that its small and poor farmers were less crowded with *surplus labor* than before. Conditions were now more favorable for *some* consolidation of unduly small holdings, but, as yet, there was little in the way of specific programs for raising the levels of living in this group. This problem was to come *increasingly under study* in the years to follow.

First attention was to be given, however, to measures *designed to maintain the prosperity of the larger-scale, commercial farmer.* (emphasis added)[39]

As Benedict suggests, the major concern of government agricultural planners during the war was less structural than it was a question of how to move agriculture back into a peacetime economy and protect the income of large, commercial farming operations.

In 1943 the USDA's Interbureau and Regional Committees on Post-War Programs first issued a report on "What Post-War Policies for Agriculture?"

The paper listed several major objectives: "adequate food and fiber for all at prices fair to both consumers and producers;" parity income for farmers; parity of public services and facilities for all, better marketing at lower cost; tipping the "scales of public policy" toward family farms that are efficiently operated and yield a "satisfactory" level of living; the operation of such farms under "economic and social conditions that will discourage the exploitation of "family labor;" good land tenure conditions, the reclamation and cultivation of potentially good land, employment and security for part-time farmers and "rural residents;" fertile soils and "luxuriant" forests, a high level of industrial activity; and freer international trade. All this was to be accomplished, the USDA proposed, through "a democratic process."[40]

But a detailed look at a few of these points indicates that the small family farm was clearly being placed on an endangered species list.

Our advocacy of a public policy which favors the family farm does not mean that we favor the retention of all small farms. Farms lacking a resource base large enough to provide a minimum level of living under current and *prospective techniques of production* either should be regarded as part-time farms and their operators given opportunity to supplement their farm earnings with income from nonfarm work, from old-age insurance, or from other sources, or they should be eliminated as farming units as soon as better alternative economic opportunities can be found for the people living on them. (emphasis added)[41]

The report further noted that according to 1943 Census figures the nation had six million farms and "at least two and one-half million of these can probably never be made to fit our definition of family farms."[42] Adding that 84 percent of the nation's farm production for market was produced by only one third of the farms, the report observed that any national agricultural policy should "not seek to ration the rights to produce the output of the most productive third among the remaining two-thirds."[43]

Rather, a policy was called for that sought to increase the output of the "less productive" to the extent that a greater quantity was needed, and "to direct the surplus manpower into productive nonagricultural activities, where better economic opportunities are available."[44]

The report went on to state that "the real goal for a farm family and for agriculture as a whole should be not a parity of *prices* but a parity of *income*." In addition, it reminded farmers that in the 1930s "we became more fully aware of the fact that farm produce is sold *through* and not simply *to* a marketing system."

The report went on to observe that farmers had a real stake in a high level of consumption, which USDA believed could be achieved through full employment if possible "and with governmental aid if necessary." And, it continued, a reduction in "marketing margins can be just as effective in increasing farm income as a rise in prices."

In concluding its recommendations on what agricultural policy after the war "ought to be" the USDA committee, in an attempt to regain the moral high ground, remarked that from an economic viewpoint

the fundamental distinction between a democracy and a dictatorship is in a democracy conflicting group interests are resolved by the peaceful, evolutionary process of *collective bargaining*, whereas the dictatorship resolves them by force and violence. Hence, we believe that to complete the picture of the kind of agriculture we want, *every* farmer should have the opportunity to become an *active* participant in developing public policies and programs, preferably through membership in his own *organizations*." (emphasis added)[45]

Chapter Nineteen

Peace and War

Even before the guns went silent and the bombs stopped dropping, the political, economic and physical devastation of civilization's second world war was apparent to both victor and vanquished. The victorious Allies, however, were poorly prepared to handle the monumental challenges that came with peace: a perceived expansionist policy by the Soviet Union in Eastern Europe; the breakup of the last of the colonial empires by both peaceful and violent revolution; the future political stability of war-ravaged countries; new trade arrangements; and a renewed search for natural resources.

And overshadowing all this chaos was the terrifying light cast upon civilization by the "thousand suns" which burst over Hiroshima and Nagasaki, Japan in August 1945.

Nature also played a significant role in the post-war turmoil, with the failure of the wet monsoon in India, typhoons in Japan and the unusually severe winter months of 1946-1947 throughout much of Europe soon followed by a catastrophic summer drought extending from North Africa to Scandinavia.

It was the United States, therefore, to which the world now anxiously turned for food and industrial equipment. But, with the abrupt cessation of lend-lease even before the conflict in the Pacific was officially over, insufficient personnel, ill-defined plans and poorly formulated policies, the United States was hardly ready to assume such a role fully.

In January, 1946 an alarmed Secretary of Agriculture Clinton Anderson learned that American grain consumption was running so high that the United States might not be able to meet its minimal foreign commitments in the immediate future. Optimistic forecasts for a record corn crop also were reduced by ten percent when the USDA learned that grain had been swollen by useless moisture.[1]

At the same time wheat consumption in the last quarter of 1945 exceeded by 34 percent the amount consumed a year earlier.[2] Meanwhile, the government's previously determined ratio of corn prices to hog prices had been encouraging farmers to feed grain to hogs rather than to sell it on the open market.

The Truman administration, fearful that inflated food prices would wreck its post-war price stabilization plan, refused to raise either the hog or corn prices. However, when the seriousness of the food problems abroad became known to the American people and the fear of "communism" haunted the nation, a series of bonus prices on corn and wheat were announced by a reluctant USDA which, along with other unprecedented food relief measures, averted a global catastrophe.

George C. Marshall's Plan

A major problem for those countries that so desperately needed U.S. foodstuffs and manufactured goods was a world-wide shortage of dollars to buy such items. As a result, Secretary of State George C. Marshall made his famous June 5, 1947 commencement speech at Harvard University, proposing a plan for saving Europe that would later bear his name.

Marshall's plan called for the European nations to project their minimum needs for recovery, estimate what they could contribute toward these goals and then have the United States make up the difference.

While the Soviet Union saw the plan as an act of U.S. economic and military hegemony, Western European nations generally received the program enthusiastically. Soon the Marshall Plan would become the foundation of a new-found prosperity for American agriculture.

"Farm Led and Farm Fed"

During the war years in the United States there had been an unprecedented amount of buying power, and with peace came the removal of restraints on wages, prices, rationing and a call by businessmen, farmers and labor for an easing of the tax load. The nation, already lacking a sound and orderly peacetime plan for the economy, soon saw food prices, which had remained relatively stable from 1943 through 1945, rapidly advance in 1946, going from 131 in 1945 to 187 in September 1948 (1926=100).[3]

This inflationary post-war period, largely due to the policies of the OPA and War Production Board, also saw wages and farm prices increase dramatically. Although it has been referred to by some as "farm led and farm fed," it should be remembered, as Benedict has noted that:

While the rapid rate of *food prices* undoubtedly touched off the upward movement of wage rates, and accelerated it, it is probable that labor, in view of its strong position in a fully employed economy and *with profits at a high level*, would shortly have demanded and obtained substantial wage increases, even if food had remained low. (emphasis added)[4]

The war, the unprecedented export demand due in large part to the Marshall Plan, and a booming domestic market, caused gross cash receipts from farming to rise 163 percent between 1941 and 1948, while total production expenses during the same period went up 150 percent.[5] Unlike after World War I, however, deflation did not stalk farm income at the same time inflation was pushing costs up.

Against this background, an effort was made in the latter stages of the war to develop long-range farm policies which would stabilize food prices and put agriculture on a long-term and sound economic footing.

One of the more noteworthy ideas of this time was put forth by M.W. Thatcher, a founder of what was to become the Farmers' Union Grain Terminal Association (GTA). He proposed the establishment of a National Agricultural Relations Act, modeled after the National Labor Relations Act.[6] A seven-person board (four farmers, a processor, a consumer and the Secretary of Agriculture) would establish farm commodity prices, production quotas, and price insurance fees to be paid by farmers to finance management and administration. It was not until some years later, however, during the Kennedy administration, that Thatcher's idea received serious political consideration.

More Attempts At Long-Range Planning

Three separate, but somewhat similar efforts were also made in the direction of long-range agricultural planning by the Committee on Postwar Agricultural Policy of the Association of Land-Grant Colleges and Universities (ALGCU), the House Special Committee on Postwar Economic Policy and Planning (Colmer Committee), and the National Food Allotment Plan.

The Land-Grant study urged that prices be allowed to seek their natural levels under a more self-regulating economy, with continuance of price controls but gradual liquidation of all artificial production incentives. For times of depression, the committee recommended a subsidization of food consumption, a deferral of farm mortgage payments, and income payments to farmers.[7]

The Colmer Committee's recommendations paralleled the Land-Grant study, urging that price supports be kept to lower current percentages of parity, allowing such supports to become more flexible. Supplemental income payments were, however, recommended as a substitute for market support prices as a means to insure the free flow of products into foreign and domestic markets.[8]

Representative Colmer also called for the improvement of the economic status of that large, low-income group of farmers which had not benefited from the prosperity of the past ten years. Urging that basic adjustments were necessary in agriculture in an effort to stop uneconomic, high-cost types of production, his Committee further recommended facilitating the movement of *unnecessary labor resources* out of agriculture, providing credit for equipping and enlarging small farms and expanding tenant-purchase programs.[9]

The National Food Allotment Plan offered a unique approach to both rural and urban economic and nutritional problems. Aimed primarily at upgrading the diets of low-income families, the Plan called for each family, by paying in 40 percent of its income, to receive coupons or stamps enabling it to purchase an adequate minimum diet.[10]

Although all three of these plans received some attention and provoked comment, the political climate in the mid-1940s was such that they were not given serious, sustained legislative consideration at that time.

R.I.P.: "The Conscience of the New Deal"

Meanwhile, the Farm Security Administration was finally abolished after a five year ordeal in which it had become almost totally emasculated by its old enemies the Farm Bureau and the National Chamber of Commerce and their congressional allies. In the summer of 1946 the Farmers Home Administration Act was passed, establishing in the FSA's place a weak and less controversial agency. The nation had lost what one observer called "the conscience of the New Deal."[11]

After the Bankhead-Jones Farm Tenant Act was signed in 1937 and the Resettlement Administration was transferred into USDA and renamed the Farm Security Administration, the FSA had begun a comprehensive attack on rural poverty. Utilizing a tenant purchase program, a rural rehabilitation program, a resettlement project, and a migratory farm labor program, the FSA flourished despite the political attacks and criticism that came from a broad spectrum of corporate and right-wing organizations.

During the war alone the FSA was responsible for resettling 6,000 farm families from the two million acres the government had acquired for military installations. It also recruited farm operators for the 6,000 farms in the Far West that had been taken from Japanese-Americans after they had been hurriedly and scandalously packed off to internment camps at the outbreak of the war in the Pacific.

For many in government and in the farm community itself the FSA represented, as Sidney Baldwin later reminded us, a challenge to the economic and ideological status quo, to "the southern way of life," and in general to the traditional and increasingly entrenched political power structure in agriculture.[12] Thus, it came as no surprise that in its last five years the FSA's budget was consistently trimmed and its freedom to act curtailed; it was forced to liquidate its resettlement projects; it was vilified as "communistic" and "un-American"; it was charged with everything from wasting public funds to undermining the initiative, individualism and self-reliance of farm families and endangering the "peaceful" relations between blacks and whites. It was also the subject of frequent investigations by both House and Senate committees.

The most creative and determined effort toward genuine land reform by a government agency in the history of rural America was soon forced to pass into history.[12]

Debating A New Farm Bill

When it was recognized in 1946 that without new farm legislation agricultural policies would automatically revert to those of the 1930s, a bipartisan congressional farm bloc, with the Republicans now controlling the House for the first time in 16 years, began a long struggle to find a new farm program equal to the challenges of the 1950s.

The task became even more critical on December 31, 1946 when President Harry S. Truman issued a declaration that hostilities had officially ceased. Under terms of the Steagall Amendment, this signaled that in two years the World War II legislation promising price supports at 90 percent of parity would end.

Thus, a major confrontation loomed within Congress, deepening an already sharp division between corporate agribusiness advocating a "freer" agricultural economy and those determined to maintain a system of security through current close-to-parity price supports.

The two different approaches to the farm problem were subsequently embodied in legislation introduced in the Senate (S.2318) and the House (H.R.6248). The legislation signaled the beginning of a long and bitter fight between the two houses before the Agricultural Act of 1948 was finally approved.[13]

S. 2318 sought to continue the work of the Soil Conservation and Domestic Allotment Act of 1936 by decentralizing agriculture, placing more responsibility on state agencies and furthering educational and research activities within the land grant colleges. Its price support features paralleled those of the Agricultural Adjustment Act of 1938, with support levels ranging from 60 percent to 90 percent of parity, depending on supplies.

Designed principally as a stop-gap measure, H.R. 6248 sought to maintain current price supports, with wheat, corn, tobacco, rice and peanut war-time support prices to be continued at 90 percent of parity until June 30, 1950. Cotton prices were also set at 90 percent, a drop from the previous 95 percent. Steagall commodities were to be supported at not less than 60 percent, nor more than 90 percent.

The eventual Congressional compromise, which was to be the Agricultural Adjustment Act of 1948, included the House bill as Title I, the Senate version, with an effective date of January 1, 1950 rather January 1, 1949, as Title II, and miscellaneous provisions designed to clarify Title II as Title III.

Three of the most important provisions of Title III included a new formula for computing parity, a transitional parity to be used during an interim period of adjustment from the old to the new formula, and a more flexible program of price supports to replace the fixed percentages of parity provided in war and post-war legislation.

In an effort to increase prices at the same ratio for all products the revised parity formula provided that the parity price for any agricultural commodity would be the "adjusted base price" for that commodity multiplied by the parity index as of the date of computation.

The "adjusted base price" in turn was defined as the average price received by a farmer for a commodity during the preceding ten years divided by the ratio of the general level of prices received in this same ten-year period to the general level of prices received from January 1910 to December 1914.

Thus, whereas the old parity formula maintained the relationship between prices of individual farm commodities in the 1910-1914 period unless some other base period was established, the new formula used the relationship of the price of individual farm products to the average price of all farm products from the immediate preceding ten years. However, the average for all farm products under the old and new parity prices formulas was essentially the same — a less than one percent difference.

Transitional parity income was to be computed by establishing the parity price for a commodity by the old formula, with the transitional parity price being five percent less for each calendar year after January 1, 1950 until such time as the price would be lower than that specified in the revised formula.

"Parity income" was now defined as the "gross income from agriculture which will provide the farm operator and his family with a standard of living equivalent to those afforded persons dependent upon other gainful occupation." As applied to the return for any specific commodity for any particular year, parity income was to be

> that gross income which bears the same relationship to parity income from agriculture for such years as the average gross income from such commodity for the preceding ten calendar years bears to the average gross income from agriculture for such ten calendar years.[14]

Vigorously denounced by the cotton and tobacco interests, the provisions for the flexible price support program established prices to "cooperators" on the "basic" commodities to be supported at a level ranging between 60 percent and 90 percent of parity, the latter applying only where there was a percentage of supply of not more than 70 percent. If the normal supply was 130 percent or more the parity price would be 60 percent. Normal supply was defined as 1) the estimated domestic consumption for the preceding year, plus 2) the estimated exports for the current year, plus 3) an allowance for carry-over.

If either acreage or marketing controls were in effect, however, the minimum support level would be 72 percent and the maximum 90 percent of parity. In the event producers rejected marketing quotas on any "basic" commodity, support levels, under the provisions of the 1948 act, could drop to an absolute floor of 50 percent of parity and an absolute maximum of 90 percent. Nonbasic crop (except wool and Irish potatoes) price support levels could not exceed 90 percent.

Advocates of these changes claimed such adjustments would realign support prices so as to discourage the overproduction of cheaply-produced farm commodities, relative to 1910-1914 standards, and encourage production of those crops in short supply. The architects of the 1948 Act conceived it as a way to firmly establish the market place (a market place becoming increasingly dominated by corporate agribusiness) as the determining factor in setting prices and the quantity and quality of production.

After fierce lobbying by conflicting farm groups and considerable political intrigue in the House of Representatives, which earlier, with only three dissenting votes, had supported legislation calling for 90 percent of parity price supports, it was determined that the new law would not become effective until January 1, 1950; thus farmers suffered a reduction in the parity price (from the guaranteed Steagall Amendment's 90 percent of parity) and in their support prices. Shortly after Harry Truman signed this legislation, farm prices began a long slide downward as 1948 and 1949 saw a 14 percent price decline, primarily due to speculator activity in anticipation of the return to higher parity prices in 1950.

Give'm Hell Harry!

Harry Truman's stunning upset of Thomas Dewey in the Presidential election of 1948 and the return of the Democrats to power in both houses of Congress brought renewed efforts to secure higher levels of support while retaining the flexible price-support features of the 1948 legislation. Subsequently, in the Agricultural Act of 1949 the 70 percent-130 percent normal supply range was narrowed to 103 percent-130 percent, and the new parity range was from 70 percent to 90 percent.[15]

To help raise the level of support prices further, additional modifications were made in the procedures for computing and using parity as a price-support criterion. These included wages paid to hired farm labor, interest and taxes in computing the cost of the farm inputs, and subsidy payments.

The 1949 Act also contained a provision that in the ensuing four-year period the parity price of any "basic" agricultural product could not be less than "its parity price computed in the manner used prior to the enactment of the Agricultural Act of 1949." This meant that the old formula would apply only if it computed higher than the new price and the new formula would apply only if it resulted in a higher parity price than the old one. Clearly, this was a significant victory for the cotton, wheat, corn, rice and tobacco farmers.

Five other significant pieces of legislation affecting agriculture were also passed during this period:
• After bitter debate and still another congressional investigation of the FSA, the Farmers Home Administration Act of 1946 was passed. It provided for liquidating all labor supply centers, labor homes, labor camps and resettlement and rural rehabilitation projects previously established for rehabilitation purposes. It also called for the liquidation of the land-leasing and land purchasing associations and all corporations or associations organized for similar purposes funded by various government departments and war-time agencies.
• Although farm credit policy saw little change at this time, the maximum loan that could be made by a federal land bank was increased by legislation from 50 percent of the value of the land plus 20 percent of the value of the buildings to 65 percent of the normal agricultural value of the farm.[16]
• Research funds double existing levels for state agricultural experiment stations and the USDA were appropriated by the Agricultural Research and Marketing Act of 1946. Although it was hoped that the money would be used to confront some of agriculture's more vexing economic problems, in fact most of the funds went to research on marketing and development of the new uses for farm products.[17]
• Title V of the Housing Act of 1949 sought to upgrade and improve the quality and availability of rural housing, a persistent problem since the end of the Civil War. A modest and experimental educational program under the direction of the Secretary of Agriculture was established which stressed appropriate types of construction, design and materials and provided for technical aid in the planning and supervision of repairs, improvements and new construction.[18]
• Farm workers, who had been denied coverage by the Social Security Act of 1937, were recognized in a limited way in the Social Security Act Amendments of August 1950. The amendments stipulated that laborers employed on a farm continuously for over six months would be "covered" by Social Security. In effect, the provision continued to exclude most seasonal and migratory workers.[19]

Charles F. Brannan's Plan

By far the most controversial piece of legislation at this time was a farm program put forth by Truman's Secretary of Agriculture Charles F. Brannan.

Designed primarily to provide a high level price support system that would offer greater protection to small farmers and less to corporate operators, the Brannan Plan was bitterly debated both in Congress and among farmers. The keystone of the Secretary's plan was the Income Support Standard, which further sought to shift the focus of agricultural policy from farm prices to farm income. Brannan stressed:

We have had income criteria in our laws — so-called parity income definitions — but, so far, we have not used them. Since *income* is what finally counts, I think it is time to start relating support prices to an *income standard*. The factor which has discouraged real use of the parity income definition in the past has been the gap between farm and nonfarm income. This is so wide that a program based on real dollar equity looks unrealistic as an immediate objective.

Under the old definition, for example, farmers last year (1948) received 160 percent of the theoretical parity income. But, actually, the average net income of farm people from all sources was only $909 per capita, including the value of home-produced food and income from non-farm sources, compared with the nonfarm average of $1,569. This puts the average farmer's income at less that 60 percent of his urban brother's income. Such a definition of parity seems to me indefensible[20] (emphasis added).

Brannan's Plan established a minimum income goal for agriculture, beginning in 1950, which would have been equal in any one year to the farmer's average purchasing power in the first ten of the preceding 12 years. By utilizing a moving base period, the years immediately ahead would include the prosperous war and post-war years, insuring high price support levels for some time to come.

Brannan argued that "price supports are the farmer's equivalent of the laboring man's minimum-wage, social security, and collective-bargaining arrangements ..."[21] By using such a formula in raising support prices for meat and dairy products in relation to other commodities, farmers would be encouraged to shift production from so-called "surplus crops" like wheat and cotton to feed grains, grasses and meat animals.

Typical of the flood of criticism regarding this element of Brannan's plan was agricultural economist Theodore Schultz's remarks before a University of Missouri agricultural extension conference in December 1949. "It will be necessary to correct the unwarranted optimism of policy makers regarding the value of farm products ... Farm products simply are not worth 90 percent of parity or as much as the Brannan Plan would specify."[23]

Another important section of the Brannan plan was the proposed expansion and revision of the list of "basic" commodities for which price supports would be mandatory. The ten commodities "of prime importance both from the standpoint of their contribution to farm income and their importance to the American consumer family" included corn, cotton, wheat, tobacco, whole milk, eggs, farm chickens, hogs, beef cattle and lambs. Support for nonbasic commodities was to be left to the discretion of the Secretary.

Perhaps the most hotly debated feature of Brannan's program was his proposal that the traditional, but misnamed "free market" set prices, with direct government "production payments" making up the difference between actual and supported prices. To protect against too great an expansion of production and huge production payment expenditures the Agricultural Secretary would have the power to impose production controls on all basic commodities whenever necessary.

Truman's Agricultural Secretary also sought to impose restrictions and conditions on the receipt of such production payments by limiting the size of farms eligible for benefits, encouraging "the family-sized farms" and discouraging "development of extremely large-scale industrial farming."

> According to the 1945 census, about 100,000 of the largest units — fewer than two percent of all farms are selling products valued at nearly one-fourth of all the farm products marketed in this country. This is more than is sold in total by two-thirds of all our farms, including half of our family farms.[23]

The (In)Famous Arvin-Dinuba Study

The validity of Brannan's belief in the family farm system of agriculture and its economic and social value to the rural community had already been attested to in a landmark study by a California social scientist, Dr. Walter Goldschmidt, under the auspices of the BAE.[24]

In 1942 the Bureau of Reclamation expressed justified concern whether the 160 acre limitation principle in the federal reclamation law should be applied to California's burgeoning Central Valley Project (CVP). The BAE was enlisted to help and Marion Clawson, a staff economist, was placed in charge. Clawson and Dr. Paul Taylor of the University of California and the Division of Farm Population designed a study to "determine what difference does it make to the character of rural life if the farm units are large corporate holdings as against family-size units," such as provided for in the 1902 Reclamation law? Dr. Goldschmidt was given responsibility for conducting the study.

A comparative study of Arvin, a town located alongside the mammoth DiGiorgio Corporation, long a symbol of California corporate agribusiness, and Dinuba, a community surrounded by small family-type farms, was undertaken. As Dr. Goldschmidt, now an anthropology professor emeritus at UCLA, explains:

> the research plan that was devised from the outset included two phases. The first was a detailed examination of the two representative communities. From that experience a series of measures of community organization were to be devised that would reflect the quality of life in the towns, based upon data that could be easily attained without questionnaires or interviews. Among the items to be considered were everything from the number of local business enterprises to the rate of teacher turnovers. From this objective data an index was to be formulated that would enable some 24 other small towns in the upper San Joaquin Valley to be rated.[25]

The Arvin-Dinuba study would become the Bible for those arguing in favor of perpetuating the "family farm system" of agriculture throughout rural America. Dinuba was found far superior to Arvin, as the quality of life in each community was directly related to the inequities in landholdings and directly reflected in the difference between the communities' economic, political and social stability.

> Large scale farm operations is immediately seen to take an important part in the creation of the conditions found in Arvin. Its direct causative effect is to create a community made up of a few persons of high economic position, and a mass of individuals whose economic status and whose security and stability are low, and who are economically dependent directly on the few. In the framework of American culture, more particularly that of industrialized farming, this creates immediately a situation where community participation and leadership, economic well-being, and business activities are relatively impoverished.[26]

The small-farm community of Dinuba meanwhile was supporting 62 separate businesses with a volume of trade of $4.3 million, while the large-farm community of Arvin had 35 established business establishments; expenditures for household supplies and building equipment were over three times greater in the small-farm community; Dinuba had a larger dollar-volume of agricultural production; over one-half of the breadwinners in the small-farm community were independently employed, while in the large-farm community less than one-fifth were so employed; public services in the small-farm community were far better; the small farm community had two newspapers while the large-farm community had one, and the small-farm community had twice the number of organizations for civic improvement and recreation. As applied to a small-farm community the 160 acreage limitation principle was found to be justified, indeed highly desirable.

As a postscript to this 1946 study, Isao Fujimoto, a University of California - Davis behavioral scientist professor and his rural sociology students 31 years later sought to continue the work Goldschmidt and his associates had been prevented from completing. They surveyed 130 towns in eight San Joaquin Valley counties to determine the relationship between the control of land and water and the quality of community life.[27]

Comparing three variables — complexity of town services, scale of cropping patterns, and water use — Fujimoto & Co. confirmed Goldschmidt's Arvin-Dinuba findings, namely that areas with large-scale farming and undemocratic water districts had noticeably fewer towns that provided a smaller range of services while towns associated with small-scale family farms had proportionately more elementary schools, dentists, pharmacies and medical specialists.

While the first phase of the 1946 study was completed and reported on, the second, due to the extended controversy surrounding the first, was never completed. Goldschmidt remembers,

I had hoped to calculate a regression curve between these two variables [the size of farms measured by gross acreage and by 'equivalent' acres, based upon the income potential, of diverse crops] but was prevented from making this sophisticated analysis. I have recently reexamined these data and have found that they revealed a most important relationship ... It showed that as the average size of farm increases, the number of persons supported in the rural area and local community declines.[28]

Reaction to the Arvin-Dinuba study was immediate and ominous. Repeated efforts were made to block its publication after the study's completion in 1944. When it finally was issued in December, 1946, due principally to the efforts of Dewey Anderson, the Senate Small Business Committee and committee chairman, James E. Murray, it was on the condition that no mention *whatsoever* be made of USDA's involvement in the study.

Efforts, principally by the American Farm Bureau and its allies, were made in the media and in Congress to discredit the study. As noted earlier, the Goldschmidt study also exacerbated the criticism of the BAE's activities.

In a September 1946 article in *The Nation*, Alden Stevens suggested that the AFBF was the one primarily responsible for getting a provision written into a later USDA appropriations bill which would prohibit any further studies similar to Arvin-Dinuba. He went on to

say that the study "was used to destroy one of the most honest and courageous organizations in Washington, the Bureau of Agricultural Economics."[29] Goldschmidt now recalls:

I wrote a letter to *The Nation* saying that the study was not manifestly responsible for this action ... I am not so sure as I was when I wrote that letter to *The Nation* that the Arvin-Dinuba investigation was not a major factor in the curtailment of the BAE and its subsequent demise.[30]

In fact, the USDA's Appropriations Act for 1947 contains the following codicil:

That no part of the funds herein appropriated or made available to the [BAE] under the heading "Economic Investigation" shall be used for state or county land and planning, *for conducting cultural surveys, or for the maintenance of regional offices.*[31]

Goldschmidt now believes that those who sabotaged his expanded research into a larger sample of communities knew exactly what it would reveal. It was much easier to discount the Arvin-Dinuba conclusions than it would have been to dismiss the results of a much more collaborative and comprehensive study.

Keeping Farmers and Workers Apart

The Brannan Plan's support of a "family farm system" of agriculture was not the only drawback to its many enemies, who finally managed to kill it. The ultimate reasons for its defeat centered on political considerations, especially the fear of Republicans and conservatives that its passage would cement the alliance between farmers and labor which only recently had played a major role in reelecting Truman in 1948.[32]

Thus, the all too familiar pattern that first emerged in the populist era, later to re-surface during the New Deal, was again evident in the Brannan Plan: whenever farmers and labor show genuine signs of building an economic and/or political coalition the various "communities of economic interests" that today dominate corporate agribusiness react with a sense of foreboding and urgency, or what one farm leader has described as "hostility and political terrorism."

It is also no coincidence that these same economic and political forces which have historically tried to destroy trade and industrial unionism are the same elements that have traditionally and consistently depicted the major problem facing agriculture as one of "excess human resources."

It is true that the cost of the Brannan proposal was unknown; even he admitted that he couldn't estimate the cost any more "than the people who came up with the first price-support program involving loans were able to estimate for you then."[33] But cost was not the conservatives' and Republicans' major reason for wanting the plan killed. Rather, the Grand Old Party feared Brannan's plan might have a special appeal to the farm community in the upcoming 1950 Congressional elections. "That the Republicans will fight it is already evident," a *New York Times* report declared, "because as one observer said, 'if the Democrats get it through, they are in for life.'"[34]

By March 1949 farm prices were 15 percent lower than they were at the outset of 1948, while prices paid by farmers were down only two percent from the previous summer. As industrial prices continued to rise, the farmer's purchasing power dropped to its lowest point since 1942.[35] Yet, unlike after World War I when farmers' debt represented 60 percent of the national debt, now in 1949 that debt, estimated at $10 billion (30 percent less than at the end of World War I) was now less than four percent of the nation's total $255 billion debt.[36]

The Korean "Police Action"

As the forties came to a close, however, agricultural economic policies were again at the mercy of the force which so profoundly transformed agriculture at the beginning of the decade — war.

When the hostilities between South Korea and North Korea began in June 1950, many in the United States, already nurtured on a steady diet of anti-communist sentiment, saw the conflict as the possible prelude to a full-scale war with either the Chinese or the Russians. Suddenly there was an upsurge in foreign and domestic demand, largely attributable to panic buying, as many thought that the nation was destined for yet another period of high inflation.[37]

In September 1950 Congress passed the Defense Production Act which included stand-by authority to curb prices and wages. However, it exempted from price control those farm products selling at below parity prices. Apart from the fact that the imposition of price controls were uneven and haphazard (particularly in agriculture), the very price control concept built around the idea of an economy dominated by all-out war mobilization was later recognized as a fundamental mistake. Defense spending at the time never reached a level sufficient to fuel the rampant inflation feared by so many in government.

However, as some critics have suggested, the use of the Korean "police action" as an excuse for all-out war mobilization may have had more subtle economic motivations (rather than being an attempt to heat up the cold war and draw a line in the dirt against "communist aggression").[38]

In December 1951, before a joint session of the American Economic Association and the American Farm Economic Association, Karl Brandt, an economist with Stanford University's Food Research Institute (FSI), neatly summed up some of those motivations in his address on "American Agricultural Policy During Rearmament."[39]

Brandt pointed out that gross farm income rose from $11 billion in prewar years to $38 billion in 1951, while net income from farming increased during the same period from $5 billion to $18 billion, increases which were striking even allowing for inflation. He further noted that the farm labor force had shrunk from 9.6 million in 1939 to 7.5 million in 1950 (monthly average), while the output of farm products in 1951 was 46 per

cent above the prewar (1935-1939) average, with only four per cent more acres planted in crops.

Yet, he reasoned, we still had an economic reserve in agriculture. Roughly three million farms, or more than one-half of what the census enumerated as "farms," were "efficient production units," supplying about 95 percent of the marketed products. Of the remaining 2.8 million "farms," two-thirds were the homes of "part-time farmers and other non-commercial borderline farm people," while the other third or roughly 800,000 small farms were operated by people who were "under-equipped and under-employed on too little land."

Brandt added,

Not by our agricultural policy which acted as a deterrent to that adjustment, but by the opportunities created by industrial development in rural areas, did we make great strides in improving this situation during the war and afterwards, particularly in the Deep South. Yet a long period of further adjustment in utilizing human, natural, and capital resources lies ahead.

The transfer of a part of the farm population by *its free choice and initiative to other more productive jobs* requires a great deal of economic leeway, and the *forced expansion* of our industrial and commercial economy under the impact of defense spending provides this leeway. (emphasis added)

Its utilization for the defense effort calls for two processes: migration from farm to factory, and adjustments in size and equipment of the farms these people leave, as well as development of the managerial abilities of the farmers remaining. This adjustment will increase the productivity of the people transferred to other jobs. To agricultural production it will add a changed output at lower cost but not necessarily increase the proportion of this group in national farm output.

Brandt concluded, therefore,

National defense production policies *must assist* in every possible way the *transfer of more manpower* from under-equipped and too small farm units to other occupations, while *agricultural policy must provide for the improvement of the remaining farms.*" (emphasis added)

Chapter Twenty

"Adapt or Die"

The National Council of Farmer Cooperatives, popularly know as the Co-op Council, has for many years been recognized as one of the nation's premier farm organizations.

During World War II its chief lobbyist and manager in Washington, D.C. was Ezra Taft Benson, who later served as President Dwight D. Eisenhower's Secretary of Agriculture from 1953-1961 and in 1985 became the 13th prophet and president of the Church of Jesus Christ of the Latter Day Saints (the Mormons), itself a $2.1 billion corporate agribusiness establishment with over 928,600 farm-land acres in the United States.

Succeeding Benson at the Co-op Council, which included a broad spectrum of commodity interests represented through scores of affiliates and thousands of co-ops, was John H. Davis. In the late 1940s Davis left the Co-op Council to become Manager of the National Wool Marketing Corporation, a co-op which at that time handled about 95 percent of the nation's wool supply.

With Eisenhower's election in 1952, Davis accepted a post as Assistant Secretary of Agriculture, in charge of price supports and marketing, only to resign that position in 1954 to become the first Director of the Moffett Program in Business and Agriculture, an effort by the Harvard Business School (endowed with $300,000 by the Corn Products Refining Corp., later known as CPC International) to improve relations between farmers and businessmen.

Writing in the January-February 1956 issue of the *Harvard Business Review*, Davis suggested that the time had come for a movement advocating vertical integration as the alternative to "big government programs to help agriculture." He called such a movement "agribusiness." "In the dynamic era ahead the term 'farm problem' will become more and more a misnomer; farm problems will be recognized as being also business problems and vice versa. More precisely, farms problems will be agribusiness problems."[1]

It is fitting that the concept of "agribusiness" came into common usage during the Eisenhower presidency and in the decade of Benson's farm policy, for that conjunction and its economic and political consequences reverberate to this very day throughout the entire structure of American agriculture.

In the twilight of the Truman years and at the dawn of the Benson-Davis era, there began to exist a sharp division within the farm community and between Democrats and Republicans concerning high price supports. Early in 1952 it was a lame duck Truman who asked Congress to repeal the sliding price support scale established in the controversial Agricultural Adjustment Act of 1949.

Congress responded by voting to set price supports for basic commodities at 90 percent of parity through April 1953, unless a producer referendum disapproved of marketing quotas. Immediately prior to the 1952 elections the legislators extended such provisions through 1954.

The Thinkers Speak

At about this time 13 agricultural economists, including chairman O.B Jesness, Murray R. Benedict, Earl L. Butz, Edwin G. Nourse and T.W. Schultz, many of whom would later advise and serve in the Eisenhower Administration, authored a Farm Foundation report, "Turning the Searchlight on Farm Policy, a Forthright Analysis of Experience, Lessons, Criteria and Recommendations," with significant suggestions:

> If the effort to equalize income (of farm and non-farm) groups takes the form of continuous cash supplements or subsidies rather than returns for the market, this means that resources, especially labor resources are being used in agriculture when they could be used more profitably in other lines . . We must, therefore, seek better means for promoting economic equality for agriculture.[2]

The report specifically suggested "free market-clearing prices" (and the scrapping of the parity price formula that had been used in farm legislation since 1932), ready and equal access to capital (*i.e.*, credit) for all producers, free managerial choices (*i.e.*, free from government regulatory control), a safeguard against depression through "stop-loss" direct supplementary income payments if depression occurred, and a separate program for noncommercial farmers. Its suggestions for structural change included,

> educational institutions should provide adequate training for workers of all grades and should use their facilities to urge the movement of farm people away from situations where labor returns in farming fall below that in other comparable occupations ... We need to encourage and develop prompt adaptation and flexible reduction of farmers' efforts to constantly changing conditions ... This principle of voluntary adjustment is basic to our system of free enterprise.

It concluded that,

The basic theme of this report is that our farm policy needs to be realistically shaped to the conditions developing for the future rather than continue as a legacy from the past...

Frankly, we think that the evolution of national farm policies has now brought agriculture into a position of undue reliance on public financial assistance, on efforts to restrict market supplies, and into undesirable political involvement.[3]

But Will You Respect Me in the Morning?

Despite these recommendations, General Eisenhower and his Democratic rival, Governor Adlai Stevenson, both promised during the 1952 presidential campaign to continue high support levels, with Ike at one point suggesting 100 percent of parity.[4] After the Republican victory, however, although still legally and politically bound to keep the 90 percent support level throughout 1954, Secretary Benson quickly began to attempt a quick repeal of the measure.

At a June 19, 1953 cabinet meeting he suggested that the Eisenhower Administration seek a congressional resolution permitting the immediate lowering of price supports. Despite this suggestion and Benson's continuing pressure for such a resolution, Eisenhower refused to heed his Secretary's advice immediately, arguing in typical Ike fashion that "gradualism" was the best policy.[5]

Eventually, however, Benson and the advocates of "flexible price supports" won the day and effectively ended a decade-long period of relative agricultural prosperity. In reflecting on that time ten years later, Representative Harold D. Cooley, Chairman of the House Agriculture Committee told an Independent Bankers Association meeting in 1964:

For 11 consecutive years prior to 1953 the average prices paid to farmers were at or above 100 percent of parity with the rest of the economy. There was prosperity on the farms — and along Main Street. Rural America — the countryside and Main Street — looked secure then and for all the years ahead.[6]

The North Carolina representative went on to point out that the government, with broad cooperation from farmers, supported the prices of major storable crops for 20 years at an actual profit of $13 million, making such profits by selling the commodities — such as wheat, corn, cotton, tobacco, rice and peanuts — that it had taken over during its price-supporting operations.

Those who deprecate the role of the farm program in this great era of farm prosperity emphasize that this period embraced war and postwar years, when the demands for the products of our farms were high, but they ignore the fact the markets, at home and abroad, for farm commodities have been greater in the last ten years than during any period of our history, and they forget that the farm economy collapsed after World War I, and

this did not occur following World War II when the farm program was working.[7]

By way of illustration he recounted to his banker audience that in the ten years between 1953 and 1962 inclusive, while all other segments of the economy had been booming, net income for agriculture had been $25 billion less than in the previous ten years. Meanwhile, the USDA had been spending for all purposes in the previous ten years $35 billion more than in the 1943 to 1952 period. The costs from 1953 to 1962 were almost $20 billion more than all expenditures of the Department in the previous 90 years of its existence.

For 11 years — 1942 through 1952 — farmers had bargaining power in the market place. Supply and demand were in reasonable balance and farmers enjoyed price insurance through the farm program ...

Many farmers have turned against their own program — the program that prevailed during the years of our greatest era of prosperity. *Why, and for what reason, I shall never understand.* Farmers have lost bargaining power in the market place, and 100 percent of parity for agriculture — generally approved and accepted by the public a decade ago — is hardly any more a dream. (emphasis added)[8]

After his address Representative Cooley remarked to one banker that it was the Farm Bureau which had been responsible for gutting the Steagall Amendment farm price support program, the very program many family farmers believed had accounted for their 1942-1952 prosperity.[9] The Farm Bureau had successfully convinced the agricultural establishment's economists and their followers in Congress that the farm price support program of that era was "un-American," and ultimately would lead to socialism, or worse, communism.

The Epistle From the Apostle

Ezra Taft Benson's belief in a highly moralistic, religious-economic laissez-faire philosophy led him to become one of the era's most prominent radical right ideologues, his dogmatism becoming known as "the epistle from the apostle." Throughout the 1950s and 1960s he would become a darling of such militant right-wing organizations as the National Right-to-Work Committee, the John Birch Society, the AFBF and others.

It was just two weeks after he took office that Benson declared:

Freedom is a God-given, eternal principle vouchsafed to us under the Constitution. It must be continually guarded as something more precious than life itself. It is doubtful if any man can be politically free who depends on the state for sustenance. A completely planned and subsidized economy weakens initiative, discourages industry, destroys character, and demoralizes the people ... The future of agriculture and the pres-

ervation of a sound economic system depends on the vigorous re-emphasis of the principles, benefits, and values of private competitive enterprise...
[10]

For understanding the Eisenhower administration's approach to agricultural policy, an even more telling gauge than Benson's public statements is the backgrounds and caliber of those men he choose to surround himself with in the eight years he served as the USDA's Secretary.

"Far Above Cayuga's Waters"
Possibly no one group had a more profound effect on Benson's department at this time than prominent members of the faculty and certain alumni of Cornell University.[11] Discussing this land-grant college complex's influence on farm policy in a series of articles in the *Watertown (N.Y.) Times* in February 1954, Alan S. Emory wrote:

If, some evening a casual stroller in the Nation's capital hears the strains of "Far Above Cayuga's Waters" floating up from the Agriculture Department he need not be surprised. The boys from Ithaca have really taken over. Farm policy in the Eisenhower administration was, to a large extent, taught in the classrooms at Cornell University, organized by the Cornell faculty and furnished to farm groups by Cornell experts.[12]

Emory goes on to describe the Cornell philosophy as one

based on a maximum of freedom from government interference and from high fixed price supports, cheap grain and a preference for big agriculture over the individual farmer ... The Cornellians appear more interested in low prices for raw materials than in increased purchasing power for the farmer. They stress the dangers of regimentation and inform the farmer that "government bureaucracy" and control means "dictatorship."[13]

A few thumbnail sketches of those men from Cornell, who would come to play major roles in directing agricultural policy in the next two decades, helps clarify the motives behind such policy decisions.

Dean William I. Myers, appointed by Eisenhower as a "farmer" to chair his National Agricultural Advisory Committee, had served as head of Cornell's Agricultural College since 1943. In addition to his academic duties Myers served on the Agricultural Committees of the U.S. Chamber of Commerce, the American Enterprise Institute and the American Bankers Association.

Myers was also the Deputy Chairman of the Federal Reserve Bank of New York and served on the board of directors of Continental Can Company, U.S. Industrial Chemicals, New York State Electric and Gas Corp., L.C. Smith & Corona Typewriters, Insular Lumber Co., AVCO

Manufacturing Corp., Food Fair Stores, and Mutual Life Insurance Co. of New York.

Myers' "farm" background was often reflected in his views on the current state of agriculture, particularly relative to price supports. In May 1952 he wrote in *Farm Economics*, published by Cornell University, that flexible supports for storable commodities "at conservative levels might be used as a last resort as protection against serious losses due to low prices during a severe depression."[14]

"Because of their dangers to democratic government and free competitive enterprise," Myers opposed the use of free market prices supplemented by direct payments to farmers. Despite such misgivings by the Chairman of the President's National Agricultural Advisory Committee, in the first three years of the Eisenhower administration the only price support raised via direct payments was wool. As previously noted, 95 percent of the nation's wool supply at the time was handled by the National Wool Marketing Corporation whose manager John H. Davis, Ezra Taft Benson's successor at the Co-op Council, was to become the USDA's Assistant Secretary in charge of price supports and marketing.

Myers also opposed the price ceilings and food rationing that had been conceived during the Korean "police action." He argued that prices should be allowed to do the rationing. Writing in the February 1951 *Farm Policy Forum* the Ithaca agricultural economist and two of his Cornell colleagues argued:

The old method of transferring goods from consumers to the fighting forces was through rising prices. Rising prices curtail civilian purchasing power, making products available for the military forces...
The modern method is through priorities, followed by price fixing, rationing and subsidies, in that order ... From an economic point of view, rising prices are the cheapest way to get the job done since neither manpower nor materials are needed to regulate the machinery. Under this system, no questions are asked as to whose standard of living is to be reduced, nor by how much. The chips fall where they may.[15]

Although recognizing that such action might not be altogether popular with the public, in a unique blend of right-wing economics, jingoism and Social Darwinism, they observed that,

What this nation needs is more of the so-called chiselers who know and understand how high prices stimulate production, create opposition to communism, divert resources from Russia and her satellites and reduce civilian consumption.
They understand that these results are of more importance than the screams of the generals, bureaucrats and professors who must then pay $16 for a tire for their personal autos that formerly cost $10.

James A. McConnell, another Cornell man, became Benson's Administrator of Commodity Stabilization Service, and oversaw the price support and related programs. Just weeks before McConnell's appointment he made it clear to a Syracuse University audience that he viewed those very programs which he would soon administer as undesirable, saying that the United States was "in danger of becoming a state which is predominantly Socialistic in character."[16]

He declared that "the wheat and cotton growers (the biggest recipients of current price support programs) are largely innocent dupes being manipulated by very clever professional Socialists" and that the Brannan Plan had been "the ultimate step in the socialization of agriculture.... Don't think for a moment that the present farm program of high price supports on basic crops will not eventually suck all agriculture into its toil".[17]

Such pronouncements worried midwestern farm leaders, for as the *Watertown Times* pointed out, "McConnell comes from an area largely interested in buying cheap feed from the Corn Belt" and "the emphasis on cheap feed prices stems from the close connection between most of the Cornell men and the Cooperative Grange-League-Federation Exchange (GLF)." In 1953 alone the GLF did over $400 million in trade, much of that in grain.

McConnell, active in many conservative farm organizations and a Cornell trustee, had served for 16 years as general manager of the GLF, one of the country's largest farm cooperatives (its name an amalgamation of the New York State *Grange*, the Dairymen's *League* and the Farm Bureau *Federation*, the co-op's founding organization). One of the directors of the GLF at this time was also Dean Myers.

Immediately prior to leaving for government service McConnell served as Vice President of the Co-op Council. After administering price support programs at the CCC for over a year, he was appointed Assistant Secretary of Agriculture in early 1955, but in charge of the same work. However, within a year he resigned his USDA post and returned to Cornell to teach a course titled "Business in Agriculture."

Mr. Agribusiness

The Cornell man who undoubtedly would have the most profound effect on U.S. agriculture, *Earl L. Butz*, a Cornell student and professor, transferred to Purdue University before becoming Benson's Assistant Secretary. Butz's influence reached its zenith when he became Richard M. Nixon's Secretary of Agriculture in 1972, but as far back as 1954, he publicly declared that agriculture "is now a big business" and that it too "just like the modern business enterprise, must '*adapt or die*'."[18]

Government, for Butz, was the long-standing enemy. In a 1954 address to the American Institute of Cooperatives he noted that while the "modern farmer cooperative is big business, government is the biggest business in America today." He went on to expound that "one of the most critical factors limiting sound agricultural policy formulation in the United States is the relatively low level of economic understanding among our people."[19]

"Members of Congress sometimes vote against their better judgment because they feel they cannot withstand pressures back home for or against a particular policy." He lamented the huge "hoard" of surplus commodities held by the government, blamed them on the price support laws, and urged his audience to oppose the farm adjustment programs.

We need to return more decision-making in agriculture to the individual *farm manager* on his farm *or* to the individual food processor and to reduce the direct participation of government in price making and marketing. (emphasis added)[20]

In 1951, while still at Purdue, Butz wrote a pamphlet for the American Enterprise Association, Inc. titled, *Price Fixing for Foodstuffs*, which attacked both price supports and price ceilings during the Korean "police action." As Wesley McCune points out "a few chapter headings [illustrates] Butz's clever attack on both the effort to increase farm prices and to keep retail food prices from being excessive during wartime:"[21] "Controls Go With High Price Supports," "Rationing and Black Markets Follow Ceilings," "Food is Always Rationed [by purchasing power]," "Subsidized Food is Not Our Birthright," "Price-Freedom is Essential."

Echoing Senator Robert Taft's statement that people could "eat less" when food prices became too high, Butz adds: "If Americans had been content to eat the same quantity and same quality of food per person in 1950 as in 1935-39, they could have purchased it with only 18 percent of their disposable income. It is not the high cost of living that hurts so much as the *Cost of High Living*."[22] Butz, one of the 13 economists who drafted the aforementioned *Turning the Searchlight on Farm Policy*, would often describe the early years of the Eisenhower Administration as a "highly prosperous depression!"[23]

Benson's Economic Advisor

It has been said that Secretary Benson discussed farm policy in terms of freedom and morality; when his point of view needed economic justification he turned to his economic advisor, Don Paarlberg. A Purdue University graduate, Paarlberg received a doctorate in agricultural economics from Cornell in 1946 and returned to Purdue to teach before becoming Benson's special assistant/economic advisor in 1953.

Four years later he was named Assistant Secretary of Marketing and Foreign Agriculture and the following year became an economic advisor in the White House to President Eisenhower. Although he left government service in 1961 to resume teaching at Purdue he would later return to the USDA under Butz.

Paarlberg believed that past farm policy as related to the basic commodities had been only one dimensional — price.

The law established a measuring rod for this one-dimensional approach, called parity. This is like reporting the size of the states of the Union by measuring them in north-south direction only.

In order to attain the one-dimensional price objective the law provided for restrictions on production in the form of acreage allotments and marketing quotas.

Price support policy for the basic commodities during the past 25 years sought to solve the problems of both large-scale and small-scale farm operators with this one-dimensional approach, despite the fact that price has scant meaning if a man has little to sell.

Arguing that agriculture has at least one other dimension — volume, he continues,

In time farm legislation may recognize a fact which students of agriculture have long known — that the economic model for agriculture really is a three-dimensional figure, the three being price, volume and cost per unit. Price times volume minus cost per unit equal net income. It is net income, not price, which is available for spending. And it is net income in which farmers are interested.[24]

Once again the bulk of the nation's farmers were being asked to deflect their attention from questions concerning fair prices for their raw materials to considering other ways to boost their income, preferably outside agriculture, thereby leaving an increasingly number of large, highly-capitalized, high-volume producers free to control prices in whatever market might exist for their crops.

While Paarlberg admitted in 1957 that "most of the dollars put out to support farm prices go to the larger farm operators," he questioned how much higher price supports would help the nation's million and one-half farm families whose total sales were less than $1,000. "His problem is volume, not price. Two hundred percent of parity would not give him a decent level of living... We are now at one of the turning points in agricultural policy. We are about to enter a new dimension — production in volume."[25]

Encouraging "Self-Help Programs for Farmers"
When in early June 1953 Secretary of Agriculture Benson was questioned during a nationwide television program by President Eisenhower about the prospects for the future of farm policy, the influence of his Cornell colleagues was apparent.

Benson maintained that the Eisenhower farm policy should have six objectives: to build up markets; to allow for adjustments in production; to avoid pricing commodities "out of the world or domestic markets"; to guard against holding "an umbrella over synthetic and competing products"; to emphasize consumer research; and to encourage a "self-help program for farmers."[26]

As noted above, Benson's approach was an occasion for growing concern among many of the nation's farmers. The *Des Moines Register's* Washington correspondent reported in February 1954 that:

Eastern farming interests represented by the conservative Ithaca, N.Y. 'crowd' are strongly influencing policy in the Department of Agriculture ... That explains, in part, why [the] Secretary of Agriculture cut dairy price supports ... [and] ... the administration's strong backing for a flexible price support system ...[27]

Although the Eisenhower Administration's first farm program that was finally submitted to the Congress in January 1954 incorporated several of Benson's objectives, it also exhibited Eisenhower's "gradualism."

By relating commodity loans to market needs and by using a "modernized parity" (loosely defined as reducing price supports by 14 percent) "in steps of five percentage points of the old parity per year (effective January 1, 1955) until the change from old to modernized parity had been accomplished," the President sought to initiate flexible and distinct steps in lowering the level of price supports. While "the key element of the new program was gradual adjustment to new circumstances and conditions" the Eisenhower administration's program did make allowances for temporary set-asides of surpluses.

Though controlled by the Republicans, Congress was reluctant to accept the Benson-Eisenhower plan, fearful that the Administration's talk about "flexible price supports" was simply another effort to reduce government's role in agriculture; farm interests both in and outside of government felt that approach would only add to the once again severe economic instability plaguing rural America. Between 1950 and 1954 the Census Bureau was reporting that the number of U.S. farms had decreased by 600,000, leaving the nation with fewer farms than any year since 1890.

Productivity continued its upsurge soon after the Korean "police action," as wheat, cotton and dairy product surpluses began to accumulate in CCC warehouses and storage costs increased, both factors contributing to noticeable depressions in prices.

Another Bill, Another Compromise
After considerable pressure from Eisenhower and Benson's repeated arguments to Congress for "flexibility," the Agricultural Act of 1954, laden with numerous compromises, passed. Price supports for basic crops (except tobacco) were at a rate ranging from 82 1/2 to 90 percent of parity for 1955, the rate to be lowered gradually each year after to a minimum of 75 percent. Surplus set-asides were also mandated with wool not surprisingly receiving special treatment over a four-year period. An attempt to set a two-price system for wheat was unsuccessful in the face of a Presidential veto.

Eisenhower thought this new law to be "the central core of a vigorous, progressive agricultural program,"[28] but Benson, disappointed at not having achieved total success, pointed out that "we had to take what we could get. We *had* to make a beginning somewhere. We had to start at least to reverse the 20-year trend toward socialism in agriculture."[29]

"Sonorous Boondoggling"

Benson's continued persistent attacks against federal assistance to farmers, charging that such programs tended to raise the cost of living among consumers, began to cost the farm bloc valuable allies among urban representatives in Congress. Noted economist John Kenneth Galbraith thought the Eisenhower/Benson approach to the farm problem and the 1954 act to be nothing but "sonorous boondoggling." In a controversial 1954 address to the USDA's Graduate School, the Harvard professor said,

> The tradition of economic analysis in the USDA has long stressed a maximum of guidance by empirical data and a minimum of concessions to ideological nonsense. Attack on this work and the inconvenient truths it throws up has for a decade or more been a Washington political pastime. The new Administration made generous concessions to this evil viewpoint. In writing the new farm program it obviously regarded the judgments of social scientists as dispensable. It turned to its more tractable laymen and men of practical judgment. By an ironic coincidence, at the very moment it was making a historic miscalculation of supply and demand elasticities it was reorganizing the Bureau of Agricultural Economics out of existence.[30]

It is important to understand that at this point in the history of American agriculture a fundamental shift in both priorities and structural concepts was taking place that would dictate the basis for U.S. farm policy right up to the present day.

The nonmetropolitan population was now in the minority, as the number of farmers continued to shrink. By putting in place a set of programs that lumped small farmers together with the nonfarm rural poor, it was relatively easy to disregard small farmers completely as part of the U.S. agricultural structure.[31] The plight of the small farmer was now made to appear as a "human welfare problem," but not one that now should be of any concern to corporate agribusiness.

Although price supports remained the center of controversy at this time other significant agricultural legislation was being enacted. Tax depreciation benefits and Social Security coverage were extended to farmers. The approval of the St. Lawrence Seaway Project saw the advent of lower freight rates for farmers. In addition: the Agricultural Marketing Service (AMS) was established within the USDA; new emphasis was placed on consumer programs within the Agricultural Research Service; Public Law 480 — the Agricultural Trade Development and Assistance Act (later to be known as the Food for Peace program) — was passed, authorizing the sale or barter of surpluses abroad; excess stocks of food and fiber were made available for purposes of national defense through the Mutual Security Act; a school milk program was reinaugurated, and an experimental extension of crop insurance was attempted.

Several conservation measures were also passed encouraging wise storage and use of water, and matching funds for construction of local dams. In addition, $15 million was made available for farmers living in areas stricken by natural disasters.

The Traveling Salesman

Secretary Benson, meanwhile, using his marketing expertise and overcoming a variety of international roadblocks and State Department restrictions, was traveling the world seeking to sell U.S. surpluses abroad. Engaging in all kinds of sales (usually for foreign currency to be spent in that country), barter arrangements and outright gifts in conjunction with foreign aid programs, the United States was reducing its surpluses in wheat by four billion bushels, its dairy products by two and one-half billion pounds, and its cottonseed products by four and one-half billion pounds.[32]

Surpluses, however, continued to be Benson's obsession as the Agriculture Secretary attempted to clean out CCC storage bins while preaching for downward production adjustments to conform with market demands. As a result of such actions, the United States increased its foreign markets for food while farmers at home were growing increasingly angry that they were being sacrificed for Benson's notion of economic efficiency.

Repeated efforts were made by Benson's USDA to force farmers to accept the idea of taking sole responsibility for storing their own grain. In a June 1953 meeting in Des Moines, Iowa, chaired by John Davis, USDA Undersecretary True D. Morse told an invited audience (while farmers picketed outside) that farmers must provide for their own storage space and that if the government should have to provide additional steel bins, he would look upon them as "a monument to stupidity and to the failure of the free enterprise system."[33]

The Secretary's disregard of farmers' criticism was also evident in the words of a confidential report on "Elements of Production Research" which was being circulated at the time within the Eisenhower Administration. "Ill-advised public pressures operating through the legislative branch are chiefly responsible for our departure from a free agricultural economy into one of increasing complexity."[34]

Others Tackle the "Surplus Question"

Among the more interesting suggestions that the Eisenhower Administration received at this time for a solution to the "surplus question," and one it would act upon before discovering its two essential flaws, came from Henry Hazlitt, a trustee of the Foundation for Economic Education and who was also a *Newsweek* columnist. Writing in the national magazine, Hazlitt devoted a series of columns to "The Farm 'Parity' Fraud."[35]

Initially, he declared that "the whole notion of a price 'parity' that ought to be perpetually maintained between farm and non-farm prices [was] absurd." He branded the price support system as "nonsense," "foolish," and "mischievous as could be imagined." Arguing that "the real gain from the Benson program was not that it provided 'flexible' price supports but that it made possible *lower* price supports," he urged the Federal government to get out from under the present program.

By announcing "a halt to further price supports within a year" the government could achieve such a goal. He also questioned whether there was the "political courage" needed in Washington, D.C. to follow such a path.

Finally, in a December 19, 1955 column, Hazlitt proposed a two point plan for carrying out his idea to get the government out from under the program. "The first point may strike some readers as extremely novel, because it is almost nowhere being suggested. This is that Congress *stop all price guarantees and all promises of support-buying of any kind* on any crop that has not yet been planted. ... The second step of my proposed program [is that] the government would *sell its existing surpluses back to the farmers themselves.*"

Hazlitt's proposal was soon matched by a similar AFBF convention recommendation. By the following January the Eisenhower Administration sent such a plan — "using surplus to remove the surplus" — to the Congress. It was promptly rejected by one of Eisenhower's best friends, Senator George Aiken. He pointed out that farmers didn't want a load of surplus commodities and the release of even one bushel of a surplus commodity held by the government would break the market price of that commodity. When the bill was returned from the White House to Congress it had been drastically revised.[36]

Ironically, another Republican president, Ronald Reagan, 26 years later would haul out the second part of the Hazlitt scheme again and call it the Payment-In-Kind (PIK) program and see it rapidly become the most expensive program in USDA's history, costing taxpayers billions of dollars.

Creating a Soil Bank Program

When the Eisenhower Administration and Benson sent to Congress another proposal for reducing surpluses in 1956, they also included a plan for the creation of a Soil Bank program. Designed to provide monetary incentives for retiring both productive and marginal land in either acreage or conservation reserves, the plan was basically economic in nature. By 1958 the Bank's acreage program would get cut back and the remainder of the program would be repealed by 1965.

In 1956, aware that rural income was on the decline in an election year, Congress quickly passed such a Soil Bank program, but not before adding to it a number of its own proposals to help the nation's farmers. The additions included: provisions for support of feed grains; a two-price system for wheat and rice; a dual method of computing parity for wheat, peanuts, cotton and corn; 80 percent of parity for dairy products; set-asides for wheat, cotton, and corn, and compulsory participation in acreage withdrawal programs for eligibility in the price support system.

A Democrat-controlled Congress passed the bill on to the President for his signature. Despite the urging of rural Republicans to sign the measure, Eisenhower, on the counsel of Secretary Benson, vetoed the bill. He contended:

1) The return now to wartime 90 percent supports would be wrong ...

2) The provisions for dual parity would result in a permanent double standard ... for determining price supports...

3) The provision for mandatory supports on the feed grains would create more problems for farmers ...

4) The multiple price plans for wheat and rice would have adverse effects upon producers of other crops, upon relations with friendly foreign nations, and upon consumers.[37]

But, as historians Edward L. and Frederick H. Schapsmeier note,

> The core of Eisenhower's logic, which represented Benson's thinking, was good economics only if one discounted the human element. Political considerations do take into account the needs of people and cost-price squeezes affected farmers more than many other segments of the population. Ike won out, however, and Congress gave him pretty much what he wanted.[38]

The U.S. Chamber of Commerce led the opposition to high price supports. In 1952 the organization's *Washington Report* editorially declared that "these artificial prices keep inefficient farmers in business by concealing their losses. And so, competition for efficient farmers is increased."[39] Later, in 1956, testifying on behalf of Eisenhower's legislation, the Chamber's Dr. Walter B. Garver, an agricultural economist from the University of Minnesota by way of the Federal Reserve Bank of Chicago staff, told a Senate Committee on Agriculture and Forestry that farm income should be higher but that

> some of the nation's farmers must quit farming if farm income is to reach ideal goals ... This could and perhaps should involve the eventual voluntary withdrawal of some of the families from agriculture who cannot achieve comparable status under such a price level.[40]

Another perspective from the business community came from T. V. Houser, Chairman of the Board of Sears, Roebuck and Company. In an address to a 1955 National Institute of Animal Agriculture, Houser discussed the great interdependence of industry with agriculture and urged that so-called marginal farmers be given more training for industrial job opportunities and adequate credit to improve their economic base.

> Can anything constructive for the individual or the nation come out of efforts to maintain such marginal farmers on the land through a system of subsidies, which in effect are relief payments, but quite deficient for that purpose? How much can industry step up its efforts to utilize this reservoir of workers, as the trend toward decentralization continues?[41]

True B. Morse

Such thinking, of course, received the support of the USDA. True B. Morse, Benson's Undersecretary of Agriculture, according to a United Press article, told a

1953 Newspaper Farm Editors Association meeting, "...price support programs tend to keep the inefficient farmer in business instead of allowing the 'normal healthy adjustment' that should take place in agriculture." He said inefficient producers may "either be forced out of business or else 'farm the life out of their farms' to pay the bills." He believed it would "be better if the marginal farmer got out of farming and into industry and his land were turned over to grass or trees or other soil conservation practices."[42]

In subsequent testimony before the House Banking and Currency Committee the following year Morse candidly repeated his views to Representative Wright Patman. The Texas Democrat had been proposing a limitation on the amount of price support a farmer could receive, in an effort to see that family farmers received full price support while letting larger farmers rely more on the open market.

Patman questioned Morse concerning overproduction and its relation, if any, to price supports. The USDA official responded that it was a question of subsidizing inefficient producers or letting "normal adjustments" take place. "You mean, squeeze them out," Patman asked. "Well, would you keep them in?" Morse replied.[43]

In addition to being President of the Commodity Credit Corporation, Morse was put in charge at USDA of a special program to "help" small farmers. This, despite the fact that he often expressed the idea that agricultural problems would not be solved primarily by the government, but that farmers would move forward "toward more security and prosperity by teamwork of farmers and businessmen."[44]

Prior to his entering the Eisenhower administration, Morse had been the longtime president of the Doane's Agricultural Service and Agricultural Institute, whose principal work was farm management and appraisals. At his confirmation hearing Morse noted that,

> because of that intimate contact with agriculture, industrial organizations and financial organizations we felt that we could be of assistance to them. The first that came to us in any large measure were the large life-insurance companies.[45]

If the consequences for many of the nation's farmers had not been so grim, one could now chuckle over Morse's speaking itinerary while at the USDA. Some of his rosier speeches, as Wesley McCune outlines in *Who's Behind Our Farm Policy?*, are included in Chart 20A.[46] By the end of 1955, the parity ratio had dropped to 80 percent, its lowest level since September 1940.

In addition to the Soil Bank legislation in 1956 Congress also enacted a Great Plains program to combat the effects of drought; increased the appropriations for utilization research; granted refunds to farmers on taxes collected for gasoline used in the field; and passed a Rural Development Program for assisting farm families earning less than $1,000 per year. The latter program, however, never really progressed beyond the pilot stage since it lacked the necessary funding to retrain marginal producers in nonagricultural vocations.

Chart 20A: The "True" Gospel

	Date	Prevailing Parity Ratio
"The Solid Future for Agriculture"	6/16/53	94%
"How Farmers Get 100 % of Parity"	2/22/54	91%
"More Profitable Farming Ahead"	10/13/54	88%
"Progress Ahead for Agriculture"	11/16/54	86%
"Agriculture That Is Stable, Prosperous and Free"	3/08/55	86%
"Moving Forward With the Department of Agriculture"	8/25/55	84%

An Era of Complacency and Impotence

The final four years of the Eisenhower farm program paralleled the complacency and impotence that characterized his second term generally. The Democrats, who had managed to retain control of Congress in the 1956 elections (it was generally accepted in political circles that the GOP's lack of success was due primarily to Benson's farm program and rural discontent in the Midwest), were able with the help of some dissatisfied Republicans to thwart the Agriculture Secretary's continued efforts to abolish most price supports.

Ironically, at this time, as has so often been the case, government price supports were primarily benefiting the nation's biggest farmers, whose supporters in the nation's capital were at the same time the most vocal in decrying such supports. In 1959, for example, 56 percent of the nation's farms were receiving only seven percent of such payments.[47]

In the Agricultural Act of 1958, therefore, price supports for most feed grains, in addition to wheat, cotton and tobacco, were made mandatory. Corn farmers were given the option in referendum in choosing either
1) to terminate allotments in 1959 and thereafter, and thereby receive price supports at 90 percent of the average price of the preceding three years, or
2) to keep acreage allotments and receive price support at 75 percent to 90 percent of parity, as outlined in the 1954 act. A 1958 referendum saw corn farmers support the first option, which ended such allotments.

The Democrats, however, were unable to restore full parity. As W. R. Poage, Chairman of the House Committee on Agriculture, and an outspoken foe of Benson later reflected, "there was never any kind of very sound overall alternatives offered and Democratic leadership did resort to a great deal of day to day opposition."[48]

Despite mounting criticism from within his own party, Eisenhower, staunchly defended his Secretary of Agriculture. In his memoirs many years later the Presi-

dent observed that despite the fact that when Benson
arrived at a conclusion it was

> earnestly held and argued, though not always
> with the maximum of tact ... he and I agreed that
> high, rigid government price supports could never
> solve the farm problem, and so I supported his
> every effort and they were honest efforts because
> he was and is a man of unimpeachable integrity
> — to make American agriculture more responsive
> to a free market.[49]

Despite such hindsight, as the Schapsmeirs note,

> amid an atmosphere of rancorous Congres-
> sional hearings and exchanges of public
> charges, agricultural policy soon degenerated
> into an incongruous combination of open
> production and continued price supports.[50]

Chapter Twenty-One

"New Frontiers" and New Challenges

Historian Arthur M. Schlesinger, Jr. reminds us that "as a people, Americans regularly go through seasons of actions, passion, idealism and reform until energies languish. Then they long for respite and enter into seasons of withdrawal, neglect, hedonism and cynicism."[1]

Twentieth century America has certainly adhered to just such a pattern. Its first two decades were demanding, as Americans "were exhorted to democratize political and economic institutions at home and abroad." Those years in turn were followed by a decade-long "return to normalcy." Subsequently, from the ruins of the Great Depression came the New Deal, the Second World War, and Truman's Fair Deal. Then, after the 20 years of such challenge and conflict, the Eisenhower decade spawned a prolonged period of apathy, peopled for the most part by the "silent generation."

The election of John F. Kennedy in 1960 and two subsequent decades of political assassinations, racial riots, campus turmoil, the waging of an immoral and unpopular war in Southeast Asia, the resignation in disgrace of the President of the United States and the taking of 52 American hostages in Iran, would return a bewildered nation to the brink of emotional chaos and political exhaustion, again searching for a political savior, a leader who would reassure it, comfort it, confirm its prejudices.

Thus, with the approach of the 1980s, many Americans turned inward, grew cynical, self-centered and unwilling to accept the increasing burden of renewed social responsibility. It was no accident, therefore, that in 1980 they elected Ronald Reagan to lead the country into the new decade. That election ushered in an era which provoked prominent New York investment banker, Felix Rohatyn, to observe in 1986: "I have been in business for almost 40 years, and I cannot recall a period in which greed and corruption appeared as prevalent as they are today."[2]

Schlesinger also reflects,

Two things happen during the conservative swings of the cycle. One the one hand, rest recharges the national batteries and replenishes the national energies. On the other, the problems neglected in the years of drift become acute, threaten to become unmanageable and demand remedy. Each activist epoch has a detonating issue — a problem growing in magnitude and menace and beyond the capacity of the marketplace to control.

At the turn of the century, the detonating issue was the concentration of private economic power in the trusts; in the 1930s it was depression and mass unemployment; in the 1960s it was racial injustice. As the republic rallies its forces to meet such problems, it develops new agendas and discharges impulses of innovation and reform against social anomalies across the board.[3]

Certainly twentieth century American agriculture has ages of neglect, of drift. Yet, emerging from these same "hard times a travelin'," agriculture has seen the development of "new agendas" and the energetic discharge of "impulses of innovation and reform."

Again, The Question of Price

Throughout the twentieth century, one vexing, inescapable and fundamental problem has plagued American agriculture. Rarely acknowledged, much less dealt with in a realistic fashion, it has been selfishly manipulated by concentrated capital, often dismissed by the public, obscured by world events and perennially camouflaged by government action and inaction.

Price — a fair price to the farmer is now, has been, and will continue to be the number one problem facing American agriculture.

With the advent of the New Frontier, after the election of John F. Kennedy in 1960, there was the initial hope that with a young, progressive Democrat in the White House and his party in control of the Congress the ruinous farm policies of the Eisenhower/Benson years might be reversed, and fair prices for farm products would again become the centerpiece of the nation's agricultural policy debates.

In the previous ten years, over 1.5 million independent farm units had gone out of business. In 1949, 88 percent of all farms with gross farm sales of *less* than $10,000 had 42 percent of the sales. In 1959, 78 percent of these same farms had only 28 percent of the sales. In 1949, 77 percent of all farms with gross farm sales of *over* $10,000 had 21 percent of the sales, while ten years later 17 percent of these farms now had 42 percent of the sales.[4]

Meanwhile, from 1953 to 1961 the gross national product climbed by 42.9 percent and disposable personal income went up 44.7 percent, yet net farm income declined by 7.7 percent.[5] As had so often been the case in the previous six decades, comparing the average farm population personal income per capita in 1962 with the non-farm population per capita income showed a $1,000 gap.[6]

Although total gross farm income increased by 12.9 percent during the Eisenhower/Benson years, farm production expenses jumped 27.5 percent as the total net income for farmers as a percentage of gross income dropped from 37.7 percent to 29.6 percent.[7] Two other figures also reflected the growing disparity between agriculture and the rest of the food economy. The eight year average on agriculture's return to equity was a sickly 2.75 percent, while the food processors' and food chains' return to equity was a healthy 22 percent.[8]

To Feed the Nation and the World

The hope that the nation's farm and food policy was about to receive priority treatment was further buoyed by the fact that Kennedy's first official act as president was to sign a proclamation directing the new Secretary of Agriculture Orville Freeman to expand food distribution to needy persons, promote the greater utilization of food stamps, and enlarge the school lunch program. This effort, however, was only in partial fulfillment of one of the two broad-based food policy goals the new president had set out for himself.

While utilizing the nation's burgeoning warehouse of food to eliminate hunger and malnutrition at home and provide increased food aid abroad as a means of promoting world peace, the Kennedy administration also began to seek out ways to reduce the nation's farm output. By designing programs with stringent production controls and payments to farmers the government sought to rid itself of crop surpluses and expensive grain stocks acquired in the previous decade.

In March, 1961 the tone and direction of the nation's farm policy for the following eight years was set with the signing by Kennedy of the important Emergency Feed Grain Act. The act's threefold purpose was a large-scale diversion of corn and grain sorghum acreage, to encourage farmers in that direction by expanded diversion payments, and to raise feed grain prices. To be eligible for these payments, based at 74 percent of parity, farmers in 1961 had to divert 20 percent of the average acreage they had devoted to corn and grain sorghum in 1959/1960. The national average support rate for corn at the time was $1.20 per bushel and $1.93 per 100 pounds for grain sorghum. Payment for a minimum 20 percent acreage reduction was to be equal to 50 percent of the local support price multiplied by the normal yield of corn for the farm as recommended by a responsible committee and administratively approved. Payments for a 20-40 percent diversion from base acreage were to be equal to 60 percent of the local support price.

This voluntary program was reasonably popular with farmers throughout the decade, as payments were set at generous levels in an effort to attract large numbers of eligible farmers. Meanwhile, the CCC, in an effort to hold prices below loan levels, began releasing corn stocks. While this move was controversial among farm groups, and proved to be expensive for the federal government (costing an estimated $1 billion a year), it was generally recognized as successful in stopping the accumulation of stocks.

The Era of "Holding Actions"

In 1962 many farmers in the western Corn Belt, however, were dissatisfied with the prices they had been receiving for their crops, feed and livestock. In protest they began organizing "holding actions," under the aegis of the seven-year old National Farmers Organization.[9]

First organized in 1955 as a protest against the Eisenhower-Benson farm prices and policies, the NFO, in the tradition of the Farmers' Holiday movement and the Equity Association, believed that concerted action could have a substantial effect on raising farm prices. Its principal organizing technique was to set a target price well above current market levels and then get farmers to sign a membership agreement to "withhold" their products from the market when called upon to do so by the NFO.

On August 28, 1962 after attempting three "limited test holding actions" 20,000 farmers gathered in Des Moines, Iowa to register their approval of an "all-out holding action" to start on August 31. They also sought to publicly register their anger and outrage over a recently published report, *An Adaptive Program for Agriculture*, authored by the Committee for Economic Development (CED) (See Chapter 27).

In the months immediately following the Des Moines meeting there were several other formal and many "wildcat" withholding actions throughout the midwest and south involving hogs and cattle, soybeans, grains, and dairy products. These campaigns reached a peak in January 1968 when another Des Moines rally of 34,500 approved an "all commodity" holding action.

Meanwhile, a milk holding action in 1967 had evoked an anti-trust lawsuit by the Federal government, seeking an injunction to halt the NFO effort. The NFO's action, however, was adjudged legal since the NFO was organized under the Capper-Volstead Act of 1922, which permits farmers to combine in cooperative organizations for purposes that include collective bargaining. The court, however, did issue a restraining order against any violence, which had become an undesirable side-effect of a few of the organization's holding actions.

Just as their milk holding action seemed to be loosing steam, the Meat Cutters and Teamsters began honoring the NFO picket lines in Nashville, Tennessee. Many believe that this action led the Federal government to hold hearings in April to review the levels of fluid milk prices in Midwest markets.[10]

For some time the NFO had been targeting the enrollment of dairy farmers and negotiating agreements with dairy processors to buy under contract from NFO members. The organization believed the latter to be more likely to sign such agreements since markets were more localized and dairy processors were already familiar with purchasing under Federal milk marketing orders.

Arguing for Mandatory Controls

Some members of the Kennedy administration felt that unless the rapid increase in farm production was curbed and something was done concerning chronically low farm prices the ultimate elimination of the family farm was inevitable. It was argued that both free market prices and the high costs of voluntary government control programs were "politically unattractive," and thus strong mandatory controls over farm production and marketing were necessary.

Incorporating such thinking into action the White House sent Congress a proposed bill in late 1961 establishing guidelines for mandatory production control programs. The legislation outlined procedures whereby the Secretary of Agriculture would authorize allotment levels and price supports. Unless the Congress rejected the idea within 60 days after its submission, a commodity program, administered by the USDA's Agricultural Stabilization and Conservation Service (ASCS) at the farmer level, would go into effect on order of the Secretary. Congress rejected this idea, however, since it clearly signaled a considerable shift of power from the legislative to the executive branch of government. USDA then submitted another bill in 1962 which, in an effort to maintain farm income, would have controlled the growth of stocks while holding down government expenditures by establishing a comprehensive supply control system for major farm commodities, including feed grains and dairy products. Not only would the Secretary establish allotment and quota levels, but the producers of a particular commodity would vote in a national referendum whether to approve quotas and related price supports. Quotas would be mandatory, if approved by a two-thirds vote, and a tax or other penalties would be levied against those producers who exceeded their quotas.

The bill, bitterly opposed by the American Farm Bureau Federation and the National Cattlemen's Association and their respective local affiliates, but strongly supported by other farm organizations including the National Farmers Union, failed to win Congress's approval. Narrowly passing in the Senate by 42-38 vote, it lost in the House 215-205 after a number of Democrats defied the Administration and voted against the measure.[11]

In the bill's place the 1961 Emergency Feed Grain Program was extended by the passage of the Food and Agricultural Act of 1962, with provisions for a national referendum to be conducted among wheat growers in 1963 to adopt or reject mandatory controls. The 55 million acre national wheat allotment, which in past referendums had been the minimum, was abolished and the Secretary was left to set the new allotment as low as necessary in order to bring production into line with utilization.

The nation's wheat farmers were presented with two possible plans. The first was to accept marketing certificates equal to the quantity of wheat to be used for domestic consumption and a portion for exports. Support prices for this wheat would be pegged at 65 percent to 90 percent of parity, with the surplus to go as feed and any overplanting of acreage allotments to be assessed a penalty. The second plan would make wheat growers who complied with allotments eligible for price supports at 50 percent of parity (about $1.25 a bushel). There would be no penalty for overplanting, except that such farmers would be ineligible for any price supports.

In what the American Farm Bureau was to call the "freedom to farm" issue, the 1963 wheat referendum soon become a major test of the Administration's agricultural policy. While the Administration and other proponents of the first plan, such as the NFU, argued that to reject the proposal would invite another farm depression, spell the end of the family farm and be a disaster for rural America, the AFBF saw the acceptance of such a plan as "putting the country on the road to socialism, bureaucrats, big government, and the end of the traditional freedoms on which this nation was founded."[12]

In a vote five times as large as any previous farm referendum, over one million of the nation's wheat producers and their wives cast ballots with only 48 percent voting for the first alternative, far short of the two-thirds required for its passage. It was a stunning defeat for the Kennedy administration, requiring a return to the drawing board in an effort to present a new and acceptable farm program in 1964, a presidential election year.

What came out of this process was the Wheat-Cotton Act of 1964 which established a voluntary two-price certificate program for wheat. Complying farmers initially received $2 per bushel for 45 percent of their normal crop production, 70 cents of which came from certificate receipts purchased by processors. Another 45 percent was supported at $1.55 per bushel and the remaining 10 percent was supported at $1.30 per bushel.

After 1964 the domestic portion, 40 percent to 45 percent of normal production, was supported at parity and the balance at $1.25 per bushel. Processors paid 75 cents per bushel for the certificate portion in addition to the $1.25 when the support price was at $2. Eventually the value of the certificates rose as the parity price increased relative to the basic support level. The diversion of land from wheat to soil-conserving uses was also required by complying farmers, for which they received land diversion payments.

Cotton farmers complying with their regular allotments were to have their crops supported at 30 cents per pound and those farmers who reduced their acreage to a smaller allotment level were to receive 33.5 cents per pound. The Secretary was also authorized under the 1964 act to make subsidy payments to handlers or millers sufficient to reduce the effective price of cotton used domestically to the export price level so domestic handlers and textile mills could remain competitive with foreign manufacturers.[13]

These programs in wheat and cotton were to become the basis for the government's farm policy for the remainder of the decade.

Shortly after Lyndon Johnson began his first full term as president, the Food and Agricultural Act of 1965 was debated and passed. Essentially it extended the previously enacted wheat and feed grain programs to 1968 (although in 1968 they were again extended to 1970).

The 1965 act also established a general land retirement effort titled the Cropland Adjustment Program. It authorized the Secretary to enter into five to ten year contracts to retire cropland for conservation uses. Congress specified that payments for such retirement could not exceed 40 percent of the value of probable production on the land, and that the Secretary could not obligate more than $225 million per year for the program.

The 1965 act also addressed the growing accumulation of cotton surpluses. In an effort to eliminate the need for subsidizing cotton used in domestic mills or for exports and at the same time to set cotton payments at an attractive level to bring farmers into the control program, domestic cotton prices could not be supported at more that 90 percent of the world price. As a means to bolster cotton growers' income, federal payments to those growers were to replace price supports.

Studying the Fundamental Restructuring of the Food Industry

In the efforts to reduce surpluses on the farm while at the same time feeding the hungry, it had become apparent to many that the basic structure of our food production and distribution system was undergoing fundamental change. Perhaps the most noticeable change had come in the food retailing industry.

After the end of World War II the supermarket began with increasing speed to replace the smaller neighborhood "mom n' pop" grocery store. In 1948, 27 percent of the nation's food sales were in supermarkets, but by 1963 supermarkets claimed nearly 70 percent of such sales.[14] The early proliferation of these markets came through both internal growth and expansion, following the growing numbers of Americans moving to the suburbs. But, as these wholesale and retail food businesses reached the saturation level a handful of supermarket chains began aggressively acquiring and merging with other smaller chains creating near monopolistic buying and selling practices in many areas.

Alarmed by this fundamental restructuring of the food supply and marketing system and the effect it was having on the economy and government farm programs, in 1964 President Johnson established the National Commission on Food Marketing.

The Commission, consisting of 15 members — the President *pro tempore* of the Senate, the Speaker of the House and the President each appointing five members — would conduct a broad study of the changes that had taken place throughout the food industry in the past two decades, what these changes suggested about future trends, and what was necessary to ensure that the food industry would be both efficient and competitive.

The Commission was also asked to: study and appraise public policy initiatives that would facilitate a more equitable food system; evaluate the effectiveness of government services for the food industry; assess the effects of food imports; and recommend actions by government, private enterprise and individuals. Congress, however, in passing the bill establishing the Commission, unwisely chose to delete the latter mandate.

Despite the fact that the Commission staff compiled many well-researched and competent reports and held well-conducted hearings, the Commission issued no unanimous set of conclusions. This owed to a number of

sharp divisions among the nine majority and the six minority members.[15] (See Appendix D)

In addition to a few general recommendations, four individual members of the majority issued statements, noting: the steady trend since World War II toward increasing concentration in national food store sales; that the imbalance of bargaining power was largely responsible for the deteriorating economic position of producers, small manufacturers and processors; that stronger action to provide protection to producers, distributors and consumers through improved reliability of price determinations and information was necessary; and that adequate and equal representation of consumers through the statutory establishment of an individual consumer agency was needed.

In the minority report, six members of the Commission so strongly disagreed with the "unwise and untenable conclusions" of the majority that they urged the report not even be submitted to the President.

Because there was such a sharp division between the majority and minority members of the President's Commission on Food Marketing neither the Congress nor the White House believed the time was appropriate for new legislation affecting the food industry. Yet, unfortunately while many simply "filed and forgot" the Commission's report, the problems the Commission addressed became more acute and complex.

And Still Another Commission Report Is Ignored

Considering the fact that the Commission's work came when the Johnson Administration was preoccupied with its own war in Southeast Asia while attempting to fend off turmoil at home, it was surprising that the President immediately created by executive order yet another commission to examine the problems of agriculture and the food industry.

On November 4, 1965 the National Advisory Commission on Food and Fiber and the President's Committee on Food and Fiber was established. The 30-member panel appointed by the President was directed to

> make a penetrating and long-range appraisal of our agricultural and related foreign trade policies in terms of the national interest, the welfare of our rural Americans, the well-being of our farmers, the needs of our workers, and the interests of our consumers ... to construct a thorough and searching study of the effects of our agricultural policies on the performance of our economy and our foreign relations ... to prepare a report which will serve as a guide and focus for future decisions and policies in the vast and diverse complex of food and fiber.[16]

Two years later the Commission summarized its findings and issued its recommendations in a report titled, *Food and Fiber for the Future*. (See Appendix E)

The Commission's composition betrayed the tone and direction it was to take. Seven of the thirty members were agricultural economists from the land grant college complex, seven were "farmers" or leaders of farm or cooperative organizations, and the remaining members were from such institutions as General Foods Corporation, Agway, Inc., Archer Daniels Midland Co., Wilson & Co., Deere & Co., Campbell Soup Co., Bank of America, Mechanics and Farmers Bank of North Carolina, the National Cotton Council, etcetera, etcetera. No representatives from the nation's increasingly vocal and active consumer movement served on the panel.

Throughout its report the Commission emphasized that it was time for a major redirection of the nation's food and fiber policy toward a "market-oriented agriculture." Mainly, it advocated taking better advantage of the market's ability to allocate resources and distribute incomes by reducing the overcapacity of farmers through such means as the adjusting of cropland and helping people who would be leaving agriculture to earn more in nonfarm occupations.[17]

The role of the government, however, in assisting these farmers was to be kept at a minimum so as not to interfere with the functioning of the "free market." No attention was given to the National Commission on Food Marketing's concerns about economic concentration in the food industry or the related issues discussed in the earlier report.

The new Commission, however, did recommend a number of positive social and economic measures, including social security for farm people, a federal minimum wage for farm workers, federal protection for farm labor unions and increased rural development programs, including improved social services in such areas and a stated minimum annual income for rural people.

Not unlike the Commission on Food and Marketing, a decided majority-minority division of opinion appeared in the Commission's final recommendations. The nineteen-member majority was composed of four of the seven academic members, the farm and co-op leaders and only two of the industry representatives, while the minority was composed primarily of those Commission members from industry in addition to two academic representatives.

University of Illinois Professor of Agricultural Economics Harold G. Halcrow adroitly summarizes the work of the Commission:

> By avoiding the difficult questions of economic structure and concentration that so divided the Commission on Food Marketing, the Commission on Food and Fiber was able to reduce its differences largely to matters of timing and degree. But, by avoiding these more difficult questions of policy in food marketing, and by emphasizing, instead, the farm and rural problems, it not only drew attention away from the report of the Commission on Food Marketing; it probably contributed to government inaction on crucial matters affecting the food industry. The emphasis helped to veer national policy away from the difficult questions of economic structure and the effectiveness of competition in the food industry.[18]

The Lost Opportunity

As a consequence of the Commission's report and the fact that the Kennedy and Johnson Administrations found themselves deeply embroiled in domestic riots and foreign wars, the promise of a new era in farm and food policy was soon lost. The significant policy-making initiatives that were to emerge during this crucial decade came not from government, but rather were spawned by those movements and groups battling for social and economic justice in the streets and fields of America.

Meanwhile, the food industry was convincing government policy makers that the oligopolistic/monopolistic trends that the Commission on Food Marketing had expressed alarm over were false. Later, with the election of Richard Nixon in 1968, corporate agribusiness claimed a close friend in the White House and felt it had little to fear in the way of regulatory legislation.

At its outset the Kennedy administration recognized to a degree that the hunger problem, both at home and abroad, needed more attention than it had received in the past. But, it was not until 1967-1968 that hunger would really become a major domestic issue. Unfortunately, both the Kennedy and Johnson administrations failed to fully perceive that this issue was part of a much larger problem, one which involved not only hunger, but also one that poignantly illustrated the economic plight of rural America and how government programs for decades had actually exacerbated the poverty of so many of its citizens.

In 1967, the President's Commission on Rural Poverty called attention to this situation, reporting that, "this nation has been largely oblivious to these 14 million impoverished people left behind in rural America ... Instead of combating low incomes of rural people [U.S. agricultural programs] have helped to create wealthy landowners while bypassing the rural poor."[19] By way of example, the 1964 Bureau of the Census revealed that of the nation's 868,908 farmers with sales of $10,000 or more, only 7,036 were nonwhite operators mostly living in the South.[20] Charles Hardin, a member of the Commission on Food and Fiber, had noted that "major programs have been discriminating against the poor farmers since the 1930s."[21] Not only had these programs driven hundreds of thousands of farmers out of business, but they had also been instrumental in bringing about a mass exodus of the poor, unemployed and hungry from rural to urban America.

Looking for Someone to Take the Initiative

Although hunger and malnutrition were concerns of John Kennedy's even as a senator, it soon became apparent that rather than fighting hunger, the main motive of his Administration in distributing large amounts of commodities at home and abroad was to control the escalating expenses associated with the surpluses piled up during the Benson era. By the mid 1960s, the "hunger problem" had become a political and social minefield for the Democrats. As Iowa State political scientist Don Hadwiger points out,

> At least four initiatives seemed in order, given the resources of the [USDA] and the needs of the

nation: to describe the conditions of poverty in rural America, and experiment with remedies; to seek a more equitable distribution of existing program benefits; to institute racial integration in USDA agencies and services; and to develop adequate family food assistance and school lunch programs.[22]

A close look at the plight of rural America, made it apparent to many, particularly those living in rural areas, that agricultural research had become almost solely focused on agricultural productivity while neglecting the idea of enriching rural society. In both letter and spirit the mandate of the Hatch Act, which Congress had used to establish the research arm of the land grant college complex, was ignored if not flouted. The Act had originally provided for research on

the problems of agriculture in its broadest aspects and such investigations which have for their purpose the development and improvement of the rural home and rural life, and the maximum contribution of agriculture to the welfare of the consumer, as may be deemed advisable, having due regard to the varying conditions and needs of the respective states.[23]

As we have already seen, specific efforts to deal with the problems of the rural poor, for example, such as the Farm Security Administration and the USDA's Bureau of Agricultural Economics, quickly became the targets and victims of corporate agribusiness and its colleagues in the Congress and the Farm Bureau.

The USDA, meanwhile, was also shirking its responsibility to deal with rural poverty. In 1960 some 4.8 million rural families lived in substandard housing[24] and while FmHA-subsidized loan activity tripled in eight years, despite inadequate funding and understaffing, the number of annual housing starts and rehabilitations financed during that time was only one percent of the need.[25]

Rural people were not just badly served by the USDA in housing, but in other agency programs as well. In 1964 the USDA made an initial effort to bring some order to the food distribution system by introducing a new food stamp program, which was designed to eventually displace a rather chaotic and inefficient commodity distribution program. However, the program sought primarily to placate the food manufacturing and marketing industry and local governments. By 1967 it was apparent that low-income America was faced with a serious, if not a scandalous, malnutrition problem.[26]

"Hunger USA"

A U.S. Senate Labor and Public Welfare investigation and hearings; a Citizen's Board of Inquiry which produced the milestone report, *Hunger USA*; *Our Daily Bread*, a report decrying the government's school lunch program; a CBS-TV documentary "Hunger USA," which shocked the nation with its indictment of the USDA's food programs, and the Poor People's March on Washington in the summer of 1968 all sought to direct and

focus the nation's attention on the seriousness of malnutrition and hunger in its midst.

While the USDA at this time sought to require all poor counties to have a food program and establish guidelines to insure that free school lunches were available, Secretary Freeman dismissed and decried the criticism begin directed at his department for its tepid response to the general domestic hunger problem.

Nevertheless, at the same time Freeman was busy winning friends in Congress among those representatives who controlled the vast majority of the nation's agricultural and food programs. These included: Allen Ellender, a segregationist, conservative Democrat from Louisiana, who chaired the Senate Agriculture and Forestry Committee; Harold Cooley, a moderate Democrat from North Carolina, chairman of the House Agriculture Committee; W.R. Poage, an outspoken segregationist, conservative Democrat from Texas and vice chairman of that same committee; Jamie Whitten, the "permanent Secretary of Agriculture" to many of his colleagues, and another segregationist Democrat from Mississippi, who chaired the House Appropriations Subcommittee.

As Hadwiger notes:

In Freeman's time the phalanx of southerners dominating each congressional agriculture committee wished to use the resources and jurisdiction of their federal agency to resist the civil rights revolution, and also to resist most aspects of the anti-poverty programs. Even the domestic food-assistance programs were to be used only to dispose of farm surpluses, to maintain a compliant and low-cost work force, and to bargain for urban votes on farm bills. ...

Orville Freeman as Secretary of Agriculture might at some point have challenged these men on these issues. But President Kennedy's first instructions to him were "Placate them," because Kennedy needed southern congressional votes on matters of higher priority than agricultural reform. At a crucial moment years later, Freeman got similar orders from President Johnson. ...

The strategy of relying upon the liberal conscience and public opinion against entrenched power had not worked, at least over the short run.[27]

When Dr. Ralph Abernathy, who had assumed leadership of the Southern Christian Leadership Conference after the assassination of Dr. Martin Luther King, brought the Poor People's campaign to the steps of the USDA in the summer of 1968 the primary purpose was to draw national attention to the plight of hungry and malnourished Americans. But that same campaign also was intent on dramatizing the need to end big farmer subsidies, make loans more available to small farm cooperatives, secure the rights of farm workers to bargain collectively, and end decades of discrimination against black farmers and rural people by immediately implementing the recommendations of the U.S. Civil Rights Commission.

Like most government agencies at the time, the USDA was a white man's institution. As Hadwiger argues,

> on the race issue it was rural southern white, because federal policy for each of the great agricultural regions had been written largely by its own representatives, and few black people farmed outside the South. Black colleges and black extension workers existed mainly to permit an easy exclusion of blacks from the regular system.[28]

In its 1965 study the U.S. Civil Rights Commission bore out this analysis, finding that virtually all employees in responsible positions at the USDA were white. In addition, a combination of government programs and inputs of technology had left blacks progressively worse off than whites with respect to the distribution of program benefits than whites. Such charges against the USDA persist even to the present day.

"There is unmistakable evidence," the Commission report concluded, "that racial discrimination has served to accelerate the displacement and impoverishment of the Negro farmer."[29] Despite some efforts by Secretary Freeman to correct this intolerable situation, much stalling and deceit at the local and state level managed to prolong it.

At the time of the Commission's report, the Extension Service had *no* black chief county extension agents in the United States. In the ASCS, which distributes farm program subsidies at the local level only a few black farmers had been elected to community committees and these committees' only practical function was to serve as an electoral body to select the three-member county ASCS committee. At the time there were only three black county committeemen in the entire country.

It was these inequalities, in addition to the problem of malnutrition and widespread hunger, that the Poor People's Campaign brought to the nation's capital in 1968. But as Hadwiger concludes,

> The USDA administration, when the national spotlight fell upon it, did not come forward to enlighten the American people about poverty, racism and hunger in rural America. It did not wholeheartedly join the black Americans and other liberal groups but kept them at arms length and in retrospect was an instrument in frustrating their efforts to achieve substantial remedies within the system.[30]

Chapter Twenty-Two

Ifs, Ands and Butz

Nineteen sixty-eight saw the end of eight years of Democratic administrations. With the election of Richard M. Nixon corporate agribusiness began to regenerate itself and intensify its efforts to reshape U.S. farm policy permanently both at home and abroad.

Although, the Food and Agricultural Act of 1965 was extended through 1970, after the Nixon victory the AFBF made yet another and more determined bid to end government production controls and to alter the nation's farm policies fundamentally.

Aligned against them was the "Coalition of Farm Organizations" comprised of an unprecedented 25 different farm and commodity organizations seeking to strengthen such controls.[1] The parity ratio was now at 73 percent, the lowest since 1932, and agriculture's return to equity was 3.19 percent as compared to the food processors' and food chains' 20.9 percent.[2] Congress, after conducting numerous hearings and logging thousands of pages of testimony, finally passed the Agricultural Act of 1970, which was so compromised that it seemed to please no one.[3]

The key features of the Act included:
1) Rather than reducing the production of feed grains, wheat and cotton, the land for growing such crops would be "set-aside," meaning that it would be retired for conservation, similar to the system under production controls. However, farmers could still plant that acreage as they chose.
2) Both price supports, which were reduced slightly, and compensatory payments, which were slightly increased, continued to be distanced from parity.
3) Set-aside payments to any one farmer could not exceed $55,000 per year on any one commodity.
4) The target level for wool production was disengaged from parity.
5) All dairy products would become supported.
6) More emphasis would be placed on rural development.

Designed to give farmers more freedom in making production decisions, to support farm income at levels near those of the recent past, to facilitate exports by lower price supports, and to improve the public image of farm programs supposedly by limiting payments to corporate farmers, the 1970 Act was quickly attacked by all major farm groups for various reasons.

Setting the Stage for the Great American Grain Robbery

Immediately following its passage, a series of events unfolded that would clearly set the tone and direction of farm policy for the next six years, one of the most explosive periods in the history of American agriculture.

At the dawn of this new decade the United States faced an economic crisis; the nation's balance of payments was worsening and the value of the dollar plummeting as Washington refused to redeem foreign-held dollars for gold. For the first time in the century, the United States was registering a trade deficit. In 1971, for example, the United States showed a deficit of $2.02 billion, even though agriculture products were still registering a $1.8 billion surplus.[4]

The Nixon administration, realizing the need to respond to this crisis, appointed a Presidential Commission on International Trade and Investment Policy, headed by Albert L. Williams, head of IBM's finance committee.

The committee, which reported to the President the following year, was composed of representatives from several major U.S. corporations, academics and two labor leaders. Corporate agribusiness was well represented by Edmund W. Littlefield, head of the Business Council and a board member of the Del Monte Corp., and William R. Pearce, a vice-president of Cargill Corp., who played a prominent role on the Commission and was responsible for writing much of the final report.[5]

The Nixon's Administration's New Economic Policy (NEP) quickly incorporated the Williams Commission's analysis and policy recommendations. Recognizing that there were costs to maintaining the United States's philosophy of "economic imperialism," the report pointed out "many of the economic problems we face today grow out of the overseas responsibilities the United States has assumed as the major power of the non-communist world."[6]

A major section of the Williams report outlined a strategy for expanding U.S. food exports. The basis for this strategy was the principal of "comparative advantage."

"Comparative advantage" essentially refers to an international division of labor structured around U.S. interests. As authors Roger Burbach and Patricia Flynn observe in their 1975 in-depth report, *U.S. Grain Arsenal*, the Williams Commission believed that the United States had a natural advantage in grain production due to highly favorable soil and weather conditions combined with intensive application of technology and capital, thereby making it a model of "capitalist efficiency."[7]

In the interests of the rational use of the world's resources, the Commission argued, other countries should remove their agricultural trade barriers and end domestic policies that subsidize "inefficient" farmers. "In other words," Burbach and Flynn comment, "they should abandon policies aimed at self-sufficiency and allow the United States to become the world's granary."[8]

With free trade, U.S. exports would be able to penetrate the Japanese and European markets while the Third World countries could rely on their "comparative advantage" in producing labor intensive crops such as fruits, vegetables and sugar for export — thus earning the necessary money to import vital U.S. grain products.

The Williams Commission also believed that to carry out such "free trade" policies, U.S. agriculture would have to be converted into an efficient export industry, phasing out domestic farm programs designed to protect farm income and moving to a "free market" oriented agriculture. This approach was widely supported by corporate agribusiness and would become the cornerstone of the Nixon administration's farm policy.

By devaluing the dollar in August 1971 the United States took the first step in implementing its new export policies. As the president of the National Grain and Feed Association described it: "the NEP was very important in giving U.S. agriculture an advantage due to the devaluation of the dollar."[9]

A crucial element in expanding food exports was the multilateral trade negotiations carried out under the General Agreement on Tariffs and Trade (GATT), a multilateral institution which had grown out of post-war efforts to restructure the international economic system. GATT served as a forum for negotiating trade liberalization.

In 1972 as Peter Flanigan, the head of Nixon's Council on International Economic Policy, was imploring the USDA to develop a strategy for the upcoming GATT negotiations, Cargill's Pearce was appointed the White House's special deputy trade representative. Flanigan's principal target (which to this day remains the basis of the U.S. negotiating position at GATT) was the Common Agricultural Policy (CAP) of the Common Market countries. Burbach and Flynn explain why:

The CAP has been a thorn in the side of U.S. grain exporters since its inception in the mid-sixties. The United States is ... demanding the removal of the Common Market's protective tariff system which effectively prevents U.S. grain exporters from being competitive in the European market ... The United States is also demanding the end to domestic farm support policies in Western Europe which, in the view of the Flanigan report, sustain millions of small and inefficient farmers.

The effect of these support programs (as in the United States) has been to encourage surpluses, which are then exported from Europe with the aid of government subsides. [It was] competition from subsidized European grain exports [that] contributed to the decline in the U.S. share of the world market during the 1960s.[10]

The subsequent passage of the Trade Reform Act of 1974, engineered through the Congress by Pearce,

directed U.S. negotiators to trade off concessions *from* the United States in the industrial sector in exchange for concessions *to* the United States in the agricultural sector. Many believe this action accelerated the decline of many long-time U.S. industries, like steel, which left an unseemly residue in the jobless and abandoned communities of the so-called "rust belts" scattered throughout the northeastern United States.

By the end of 1971 the U.S. dollar was floating, setting off a major realignment of international currencies. Poor growing conditions plagued the Soviet Union, drastically cutting its grain crop. Drought set back grain production in Argentina and Australia. India's monsoon dropped below normal, a serious set-back for that nation's efforts to achieve self-sufficiency in cereal crops; Peru's anchovy catch was a disaster; rice and corn crops in the Philippines were severely damaged by typhoons; and wet fall weather in 1972 had seriously delayed corn and soybean harvests in the United States, followed by a spring of similar weather which also delayed plantings.

By July 1973, in the aftermath of what would become known as the "great American grain robbery" (see Chapter 30) when both the Russians and Chinese purchased massive amounts of U.S. grain, an effort was made by the Nixon administration to limit rapid commodity price increases. The United States also instituted a series of highly-controversial export controls on soybeans and soybean products. The Congress, meanwhile, enacted the Agricultural and Consumer Protection Act, which ultimately belied its title for it brought little, if any, protection to either consumers or farmers.

The Return of Mr. Agribusiness

Juxtaposed against all these developments was the return in 1971 of Earl L. Butz as Richard Nixon's second Secretary of Agriculture, succeeding Clifford Hardin.

As we saw earlier, in the Eisenhower years Butz brought to his post the philosophy that rural America was a place to do business, big business, not a place in which to live. He also believed that corporate agribusiness was the logical force to direct such a venture, "with more highly concentrated capital, higher levels of management, more specialization of labor, and, if you choose, with a higher degree of integration."[11]

A brief review of the life of the new secretary helps explain his philosophy. Throughout his professional career he had served corporate agribusiness well, as an academician and Dean of the Agricultural School at Purdue University; Benson's undersecretary; a director of the Farm Foundation of American Agriculture; and the Purdue Research Foundation, among others, and as a paid member of the board of directors of such agribusiness giants as Ralston Purina, International Minerals and Chemical Corp., Stokely-Van Camp, Inc., J.I. Case & Co. and Standard Life Insurance Company of Indiana.

As one government official at Purdue in the late 1960s told *The Washington Post*'s Dan Morgan: "Butz and a few of his cronies ran the university. They wanted to work with the top ten percent of commercial farmers. They weren't interested in things like rural poverty or small farmers."[12]

Even before he took office, Butz was subject to much criticism for his close ties with corporate agribusiness. Only after considerable Senate debate and a close vote was he confirmed as the new Secretary of Agriculture. He would remain a controversial figure throughout his five years as Secretary until he was forced to resign in 1976 after telling an embarrassing and demeaning racial joke to the press.

Butz would often describe himself to farm audiences as

> your old cowhand on the Potomac. I've always got some fence to mend or a stray to round up, a bull to buy or a calf to clamp, a banker to corner or a trader to sell. And every time it looks like I might settle down for a peaceful night around the campfire, a dozen feisty coyotes howl in the moonlight not far away.[13]

While some might have thought of Butz in such endearing terms, thousands of American farmers and millions of consumers would soon see the Agricultural Secretary more in terms of the "feisty coyote" in the chicken coop.

Butz, an immensely popular speaker on the farm circuit, was a never-tiring advocate of a "cheap food policy," seeing the exodus of farmers from agriculture as a means of "freeing themselves" to find more fruitful vocations and contributing more fully to the nation's prosperity. The greatness of American agriculture, he frequently reminded his audiences, is that 70 years ago U.S. agriculture employed 40 percent of the work force and today hired less than two percent.[14]

The function of today's farmer was simply to "assemble packages of technology which have never been produced by others on a custom basis." By employing such methods modern large scale farming "tended to *eliminate* stoop labor ... and much of the drudgery."[15]

The Agricultural Secretary had some other curious ideas when it came to labor, particularly farm labor, as evidenced in his remarks about banning the backbreaking short-handled hoe used by farm workers to thin, weed and harvest certain crops. The remarks also reflect some of Butz's racial perspectives in addition to a certain anti-urban bias, which appealed to many of his rural audiences.

> In California, *Mexican* farm workers are no longer allowed to use the short-handled hoe they have used for generations; now they are required to use long-handled American-type hoes... this is not because the workers or the farmers want to change, but apparently because the *city people*, driving by, feel more comfortable watching the workers using the kind of hoes that look good through car windows.[16] (emphasis added)

Planting Fence Row to Fence Row

The major tragedy of the Butz years that continues to destroy hundreds of the nation's farm communities today, was his incessant command to farmers to plant "fence row to fence row" ("go borrow, young man, get bigger").[17]

By structuring USDA programs to support the Nixon doctrine of using agricultural products to stabilize the nation's balance of payments, he encouraged land speculation, and by preaching that "planting fence row to fence row" was almost a sacred obligation, Butz must now bear a major responsibility for the plight of thousands and thousands of American farmers who have been forced off their land and into bankruptcy, forced foreclosures, depression, divorce, alcoholism, and suicide.

By 1972, farm income had regained the level it enjoyed ten years earlier, although the return on investment to farmers was only 3.9 percent, compared to the 5 percent return they might have realized from a simple passbook savings account.[18] The cost of farming had increased by 110 percent, farm debt had climbed 355 percent with an average of over 1000 farms going out of business every week.[19] Only 3.4 million persons were employed on the nation's farms in contrast to the 7.1 million there in 1950.[20]

Farm efficiency (output per man hour) had increased by 330 percent since 1952 (as compared with 160 percent in manufacturing).[21] Dependence on mechanical power and machinery had increased from 1940 by 146 percent.[22] Use of chemicals, fertilizers, and chemical poisons had grown sevenfold.[23] The USDA estimated that in 1950 farmers purchased only 20 percent of the materials they used in production. In 1973 that figure was 65 percent.[24] At the same time more than half of the total income reported by farm families in 1970 came from work done off the farm.[25]

Soon after Butz took office these figures became even more dramatic. Because of an unprecedented foreign demand for food commodities in 1973 net farm income skyrocketed, but by 1976 the level was back below that of 1970.[26] Even this brief surge was not without a price, however, as the Federal Reserve Bank of Chicago reported that production expenses in 1974 were "49 percent above the level of two years ago."[27]

The parity ratio, which went from 77 percent to 76 percent during Nixon's first term in office, dropped again to 73 percent by 1975.[28] In addition, during the three year period from 1972 to 1975 agriculture saw a onehalf percent decline in its return on equity while food processors were realizing a 4.3 percent increase. In 1975 alone, the net return on equity for agriculture was 4.7 percent contrasted to a whopping 24.6 percent for food processors.[29]

Paying the Price for Economic Concentration

Consumers also felt the impact of Butz's pro-corporate agribusiness policies. Between 1961 and 1965 the food component of the Consumer Price Index (CPI) showed an annual increase of 1.5 percent, growing to an annual rate of 3.8 percent in the 1965-1970 period. In both of these periods the food inflation rate was equal to or slightly below the entire CPI inflation rate.[30]

In 1971 and 1972 the food inflation rate climbed to 4.5 percent; in 1973 it shot up by an astounding 20.1 percent and the following year went up another 12.1 percent followed in 1975 by a 6.6 percent increase. By September 1976 Americans were spending $70 billion more per year for food than they had spent in 1972.[31] Clearly the gospel of more concentration of capital and the need for tighter integration in agriculture that the Secretary of Agriculture had been preaching for years was now reaping rich rewards for corporate agribusiness.

The idea of more concentration in the food system did not appeal to everyone. Paul W. Barkley, speaking to the 1976 American Agricultural Economics Association, voiced such concern:

> In concentrating, those who make decisions are removed from the resources and are likely to be motivated by the economic forces that influence firm behavior — product prices, profits, internal rates of return, and payoff periods. If agriculture is organized on these lines, the great loss will not be the loss of moral and cultural virtues of family farms but the loss of the capacity of the smallholder system to maintain production in a time of economic adversity.
>
> An agriculture in which resource control is centralized may be more efficient, more productive, and more responsive to the demands of food consumers and may provide higher incomes to persons involved in the ownership of resources used in the production process. However, it does not have the most desirable of all characteristics: guaranteed stability in output.[32]

A contrary viewpoint, however, was taken by the U.S. Chamber of Commerce in response to an effort in 1974 by the NFO to win support for a Family Farm Act.

> It is quite possible that the current wave of state and federal legislation to prohibit farming by major corporations will be counter-productive in an industrialized food system where consumer interests are paramount.
>
> The enactment of such legislation may impose many restrictions on large corporations which would impair the availability of credit and prohibit large corporations from contracting directly with producers to insure orderly supply of quality products for processing and marketing.[33]

The direction of policies like those put forth by the USCC was now being candidly endorsed not only by corporate agribusiness (as we shall see in Chapter 27), but by many policy makers within the Federal government.

Darryl R. Francis, for example, President of the Federal Reserve Bank of St. Louis, stated in a 1970 letter (See Appendix F) that he foresaw in the coming decade the possibility of only 100,000 farms producing the nation's food. In addition, he believed the Federal Reserve's goal should be the control of American agriculture through *debt*, since with modern agriculture's increasing capital costs it was "unreasonable" to expect farmers to liquidate their debts prior to retirement.

By mid-decade both farmers and consumers found themselves at the mercy of a food marketing structure which neither party could control. As Lavern Rison ruminated in verse in *U.S. Farm News*:

THE FARMER GOES TO MARKET:
OUTPUT OLIGOPSONIES

> This little piggy went to market
> Where he brought thirty cents per pound
> But down at the store
> They charge sixty cents more
> Where it averages ninety, I've found.
> The farmer is standing,
> His back to the wall.
> The housewife is serving
> Hooves and all.
> The little guy's deserving
> A better break;
> But somebody
> Somewhere
> Is on the take.
> Ninety less thirty,
> That's sixty for sure.
> Still the housewife gets took
> And the farmer gets poor.
> Tell me, oh sage,
> Where the sixty cents goes.
> Nobody,
> Nobody,
> Nobody,
> Knows.

True, there were several efforts during the early seventies to establish an effective consumer protection agency within the federal government which would give the shopper some leverage in dealing with a near monopolistic food industry, but all were unsuccessful. A coalition of organizations, such as the Grocery Manufactures of America, the National Canners League, and the Farm Bureau, among others, repeatedly thwarted such legislative efforts.[34]

Leaving Farmers to the Mercy of the "Free Market"

Congress sought to placate the growing consumer movement by giving new farm legislation: the misnamed Agricultural and Consumer Protection Act of 1973.

It was neither!

The Act sharply lowered price supports, created incentives for stockpiling, and left the majority of the nation's 1.8 million commercial farms at the untender mercy of the "free market." Effective through 1977 the Act covered all basic and most nonbasic commodities with a system of nonrecourse loans and target price supports to be implemented by combining loans and deficiency payments. No deficiency payments were to be made if the market price for a commodity was above the target price and the Secretary of Agriculture could make such deficiency payments only if market prices fell below the target price. Disaster payments to farmers could now be made only after specific areas had been officially declared such.

Target prices for 1974 and 1975 were set at specific levels and loan rates were to be a third to a fifth lower. Adjustments in 1976 and 1977 would be made on the basis of the index of prices paid by farmers, adjusted for the estimated change in farm productivity. Set-aside payment limits were set at $20,000 per farmer and the

Secretary was directed to implement policies which were "designed to encourage American farmers to produce to their full capabilities during periods of short supply to assure American consumers with an adequate supply of food and fiber at fair and reasonable prices."[35]

As noted, this policy of planting "fence row to fence row" was a key tenet of Butz's farm programs and effectively discouraged land diversion efforts while expanding farm credit and encouraging greater use of expensive farm fuel, fertilizers, farm chemicals and high-priced mechanization.

Meanwhile, the 1973 legislation began removing the federal government from nearly all price support operations and from accumulating or reestablishing a food reserve. In short order, target prices were only about one-half of parity and wheat, corn and grain sorghum prices were generally less than half of the market price, while the loan rate for soybeans was less than a third of the commodity's market price.

In 1975 both Houses in a Democratic Congress passed legislation to raise corn, wheat and cotton target prices. However, the House failed to override Nixon's veto.

As bumper crops were again at hand and the foreign market continued to boom, domestic food prices also continued to accelerate. Alarmed by these developments the AFL-CIO demanded that the fledgling Ford administration intervene and take corrective action. With an eye to the upcoming presidential election Ford announced an embargo on all grain sales to the Soviet Union. Wheat prices promptly plummeted from over $4 per bushel to $2.[36]

Food for War

One program that came under increasing fire during the Nixon-Ford years was the so-called Food for Peace, Public Law 480. Originally designed to relieve U.S. grain surpluses, the program converted food from a human necessity to an international political weapon.

The idea that food should be used for such purposes had been discussed in agricultural circles for some time. In 1949, for example, Austin Kiplinger, who later became editor of the *Chicago Journal of Commerce*, wrote:

The United States must be an imperialist if it is to do its world job properly. 'Imperialism' has become a nasty word, of course, but the facts and the logic of our position are inescapable.

In ABC's, the facts are these: The United States can produce more than its present capacity to consume. Increased consumption at home will sop up some of this excess, but still more excess will remain.

We sell this excess abroad. And since the rest of the world is not up to our standard of production, we must decide what to take in payment. We can let the deficit stand as a debt which probably will never be paid. Or and this is where imperialism comes in — we can take ownership of properties throughout the world, and help run them...

This is not exactly like the older style British imperialism which frequently disregarded the rights of the countries in which Britain traded. But rather than shrinking in fear from the word, "imperialism," we would do better to meet it head-on, and make a virtue of it. Let us distinguish between Russian "despotic imperialism" and American "democratic imperialism"...[37]

As a postscript, thirty-one years later, in answering a letter from Merle Hansen, president of the North American Farm Alliance, Kiplinger acknowledged authorship and added "I think I still subscribe to the basic idea that we should keep our exports strong and that we should not hesitate to take foreign investment in exchange."[38]

Nixon's Secretary of State, Henry Kissinger, also saw the value of using food as a weapon in the early 1970s when it was apparent that the Russians were interested in increasing trade with the United States He would later write that it was

the White House's determination to have trade follow political progress and not precede it. Nixon and I agreed that it was best to proceed deliberately on grain sales (by delaying a trip to Moscow by Secretary of Agriculture Earl Butz until April) ... We would, in short, *make economic relations depend on some demonstrated progress on matters of foreign policy importance to the United States*.[39] (emphasis added)

By the seventies American food policies were widely used to curry political favors at home and abroad while third world regimes were also using food to reward their elite class as well as forestall revolt among their poor. Although the United States was putting almost $1.5 billion a year into the P.L. 480 program, more for food assistance than any other country, its global share of aid based on the Gross National Product was decreasing throughout the decade.[40]

When the Congress became outraged in 1975 after it was learned that more than half of our food aid was going to South Vietnam and other political and military allies who were supporting our dubious objectives in Southeast Asia, it amended the act to ensure that more food went to the poorer nations. However, it is estimated that today, more than 15 years later, 60 percent of our food aid is still linked to foreign policy. As one Washington foreign policy analyst sums it up: "Food is arguably the most political of commodities. At bottom, it's more political than oil, because it is far more basic than oil."[41]

Perhaps the most critical analysis of the "Food for Peace" program came in 1975 with the publication of *The Fields Have Turned Brown: Four Essays on World Hunger*, by Susan DeMarco and Susan Sechler, co-directors of the Agribusiness Accountability Project.

In their report they contended that "simple greed" more than "generosity" had motivated the administration of a food program designed to feed hungry people. In what amounted to a form of "economic imperialism," USDA and the State Department in league with the grain trade and corporate agribusiness used the program:

• "To dispose profitably of farm surpluses, which otherwise might create serious domestic economic problems."
• "To create new, or to expand or protect existing, markets for United States-owner interests."
• "To provide cheap capital for overseas investment by U.S. enterprises."
• "To 'launder', so to speak, military assistance, which might have been challenged if so identified."

One of the most important results of these policies the two women went on to document meticulously, is that U.S. agricultural trade policies forced a change in the eating habits of people in less developed countries and stifled their own agricultural production by making them dependent on U.S. food stuffs.

Such use of food aid as "one of the chips in the poker game of international power politics" partly explains, as DeMarco and Sechler note, "our undignified posture" at the 1975 World Food Conference in Rome, Italy, "where the official U.S. representatives proclaimed the urgent need for a workable food aid program, yet we found ourselves unable or unwilling to commit our share." "So long as the major portion of U.S. food aid is captive to overriding political and commercial concerns, it will do little to advance a goal of long-term food security for the hungry, and, more frequently, will even tend to disrupt that goal."[42]

The Georgia Peanut Farmer Fails to Deliver
When Jimmy Carter from Plains, Georgia became the 39th President of the United States on January 20, 1977 American agriculture was on the threshold of its worst depression since the early 1930s. At the time, 19 percent of the nation's farms were producing 78 percent of the United States's total agricultural output.[43]

During the 1972-1977 period the cost of fertilizer had risen by 253 percent, diesel tractor fuel by over 150 percent, tractors by 100 percent. In 1977 a bushel of wheat that cost $3.55 to raise never brought more than $2.80 in the marketplace;[44] at one time the price had even dropped to a low of $2.03.[45] By 1976 American farmers were making a total national investment of $564 billion and netting only $20 billion in return.[46]

Farmers were realizing only one kind of "wealth" — the value of their land — as the average worth of U.S. farmland between 1972 and 1977 was increasing 15 percent to 35 percent a year.[47] To realize that value, however, farmers had only two options. They could either sell their land and get out of agriculture (a course which many farm policy planners had been urging for decades) or borrow on the land and expand (a course favored by many bankers and financial institutions, such as was urged by Federal Reserve Bank of St. Louis President Darryl Francis).

While thousands of farms each month would take the former route many others took the latter. Consequently, total farm debt between 1960 and 1977 increased 400 percent, more than half that amount taking place in the 1972-1977 period while interest payments as a percent-

age of farmers' net income climbed 20 percent to 40 percent in that same five-year span.[48]

Although Jimmy Carter had promised during his 1976 campaign that "I will support prices equal to at least the cost of production,"[49] it became clear to many farmers soon after the peanut farmer took office that the government would do little to improve farm prices. The 1977 farm bill raised wheat support prices only to $2.90, still 60 cents under the cost of production.[50]

Pointing out that the cost to the federal government in 1976 was nearly $734 million and that projected costs of such farm programs in 1977 would reach $3 billion, Carter argued for a $2.65 a bushel support in an effort to hold annual costs to $2 billion.[51] Despite his veto threat, the Congress passed the $2.90 a bushel limit.

The 1977 Food and Agricultural Act also made it less painful for policy purposes to think of low income farms as distinct from large commercial enterprises. Henceforth, the two classes of farmers would file separate annual reports, thus helping to spotlight the growing difference between the two.

The Tractors Are Coming!!! The Tractors Are Coming!!!
Within days after the 1977 Act passed into law farmers from throughout the country began to take matters into their own hands. From some 600 offices scattered throughout the United States emerged the loosely affiliated American Agricultural Movement (AAM).

Starting with a "stop planting, stop buying" action in Springfield, Colorado and soon spreading across the nation, these small groups of farmers called for a nationwide "farm strike," challenging the USDA's estimates of farm costs and urging their neighbors to also STOP: stop selling, stop planting and stop buying farm input goods.

At the outset, the strike attracted only sporadic media attention, but when the AAM's first tractorcade descended on Washington, D.C. in early December 1977, and another larger one in late January 1978, both the government and the public began to realize the seriousness and depth of the farmers' anger.

Unfortunately, however, the majority of this army of protesting farmers that roared into the nation's capital were political amateurs when it came to imposing their will upon the Washington bureaucracy. Few in Congress gave them serious attention while the Carter Administration dismissed them as "greedy and inefficient farmers" in trouble "because they overextended themselves."

But what these demonstrating farmers were seeking was not more government money as the media so often suggested, but simply a federal law preventing sale of any agricultural commodity at less than 100 percent of parity (later to be modified to 90 percent of parity). Such a law, they argued, would be similar to the minimum wage law which declared at the time that no one could hire labor for less that $2.65 per hour.

The administration, citing USDA cost studies, claimed that such a plan would cost as much as $40 billion.[52] AAM spokespersons, however, pointed out that at parity prices the cost of wheat in a one-pound loaf of bread would only rise from three to five cents and that the potatoes used in a 25-cent bag of potato chips currently cost the manufacturer one quarter of a cent, whereas parity price potatoes would add but another one quarter of a cent.[53]

After disorganization and the uncertainty of where or how to apply political pressure in their initial two assaults on Congress and the White House, the AAM returned to Washington, D.C. in March 1978 with a specific strategy. Two farm bills were currently under consideration; one that would authorize payments to farmers for voluntarily holding land out of production; and one, introduced by Senator Robert Dole, R-Kansas, setting up a sliding scale of production reduction and parity guarantees.

Although neither bill was particularly appealing to the farmers, they decided to back the Dole legislation in the hope of getting a full parity bill in the near future. The two pieces of legislation were eventually combined in an emergency farm bill that narrowly passed the Senate but was soundly rejected in the House. Carter hailed the defeat as "good for our farm policy. It is good for holding down inflation, and it is a very encouraging sign of cooperation between the Congress and the White House in dealing with the nation's very important problems."[54]

A Switch in National Economic Policy

The AAM marches on Washington and the growing hostility shown to Carter and his Secretary of Agriculture Bob Bergland by farmers throughout the country provoked serious economic and political discussion in Washington in 1978. Clearly, American agriculture was in deep trouble. Farm prices were at a depression level, and increasing numbers of family farmers were driven out of business as the destruction of their rural communities continued unabated.

Some economists have suggested that by and large the farmers' distress resulted from the Federal Reserve Board's decision in October 1979 to keep money tight and interest rates high. Although the Board has nothing in its charter giving it responsibility for the general price level, it nevertheless took action in an effort to stem inflation. However, its actions merely advanced the interests of savers and bondholders at the expense of borrowers. Commenting on this situation, agricultural economist Breimyer notes: "The question then arises as to the morality of making a select group of citizens [*i.e.,* farmers] the victims of a sharp change in national policy.[55]

The unquenchable thirst for more land, inspired by the Butz's policy of "planting fence row to fence row," was also a large contributor to farmers' problems at this time. The old farm refrain that "I don't want to own all the land in my county, just that which borders my own property" had particular poignancy in the 1970s.

What many of those farmers who ascribe to such a philosophy often fail to remember, as they go about expanding their land holdings in boom times, was best summarized by Andy Kitmer, an Ontario, Canada dairy farmer:

One of the things they have told us is that 'progress is if you can get enough money to buy your neighbor out.' You're progressing. But then we wonder 'when it's going to be our turn for our neighbor to buy us out?' Then when you buy three neighbors out who can afford to buy you out? The big corporations![56]

The price of U.S. farmland tripled during the decade. This acceleration in land values, as discussed in Chapter Three, was also fueled by speculation in the farm land adjacent to many of the nation's urban/suburban centers. The value of that land increased so quickly that it outpaced inflation, rising faster even than the rate of interest one had to pay on borrowed money. Each year during the 1970s the annual increase in the total value of American farmland exceeded net farm income.[57]

As borrowing increased, debt tripled. Finally, when farm prices began a sharp decline in 1977 and 1978 there emerged grave concern that debt and interest payments would not be paid due to the reduced cash flow and other signs of financial weakness.

Comes "A Time to Choose"

Recognizing the gravity of the crisis at hand and the fact that the Carter administration was in serious political trouble throughout the farm community, Secretary Bob Bergland, at the urging of his Office of Economics, Policy Analysis and Budget staff, took a decisive and much needed step to determine in exactly what direction American agriculture was heading. Speaking before the annual convention of the NFU in Kansas City, Missouri on March 12, 1979 Bergland announced:

I am here to open what I hope will become a full-scale national dialogue on the future of American agriculture. I am not here to present my judgments ... I am here to ask you to begin thinking hard about what kind of agriculture you believe would be in the ultimate best interests of farmers and the nation. And I am seeking your advice on what we should do to get that kind of agriculture ... The time has come to consider where we are and where we seem to be going and to ask ourselves some crucially important questions.

Bergland's invitation was soon followed by a year-long "dialogue on the structure of American agriculture" as he and Project Coordinator, Susan Sechler, Deputy Director of USDA's EPAB, and staff members traveled to ten different regions throughout the country, listening to 210 scheduled participants and 365 "open microphone" speakers, and examining written testimony from over 2,500 other persons, organizations and business firms.[58]

The dominant message that emerged from this "dialogue" was articulated at the outset by Richard R. Wood, Jr., a Maine farmer, who told Bergland:

Forty-three percent of the privately owned land in this country is owned by people 60 years of age or older. Seventy percent is owned by those 50 or older. Inevitably, the next two decades will see massive amounts of our agricultural land change hands so, if we wish to steer the structure of American agriculture in any given direction, now is very nearly our last chance.

... I have been farming on my own for the last 24 and a half years. That coincides almost exactly with the era in which the cries "bigger is better" and "get big or get out" have been heard across the farmlands of America. Farmers have gotten out in droves, some believing what they've been told, some trying to get bigger and failing to find salvation that way ... More than a quarter of a century of increased efficiency and a quarter-century of increasing farm size in quest of efficiency have gotten us tractors on the Capitol Mall. ...

As we consider the structure of our agriculture, remember that we are dealing with the shape of our democracy.[59] (emphasis added)

In January 1981, literally hours before the Carter administration left office, *A Time to Choose: Summary Report on the Structure of Agriculture* was released to the public. The 164-page report not only offered an in-depth profile of American agriculture, but discussed U.S. agriculture both in a global and rural context.

Areas of policy concern included land ownership: soil and water conservation; tax; commodity; credit; public research; extension; trade policy; agricultural labor. The report also contained a series of conclusions and recommendations by Bergland which clarified that,

the future economic climate combined with a continuation of current policies and programs, will continue and even accelerate the shift to large and super-large farms. Therefore, unless present policies and programs are changed so that they counter, instead of reinforce and accelerate the trends towards ever-larger farming operations, the result will be a few large farms controlling food production in only a few years.[60]

Not only was *A Time to Choose* all but ignored by the incoming Secretary of Agriculture John R. Block and the Reagan administration, but the USDA quickly allowed the report to go out of print.

Death Valley Days

Yet, even as Bergland's report was being put together, the Carter White House managed to further damage its already deteriorating relations with the nation's farm community.

After the Russians invaded Afghanistan in 1980, Carter immediately retaliated by declaring a grain embargo, which in the eyes of many farmers further and needlessly eroded an already depressed market for their commodities. As we shall later see, the embargo hurt the Russians less than the U.S. farmers, while it made a handful of multinational grain traders even richer at taxpayers' expense.

Ironically, another victim of the grain embargo was Carter himself, for in 1980 farmers overwhelmingly rejected him and his farm policies in a democracy's court of last resort, the voting booth.

What farmers did not realize at that time, however, was that as bad as the Carter era had been for agriculture the ensuing years under Ronald Reagan would be even worse. During his 1980 campaign Reagan delighted in telling farm audiences how he not only planned to balance the budget and get government out of the "free market," but planned to "make life in rural America prosperous again" and "restore profitability to agriculture."

To the contrary, record harvests and huge surpluses, a reluctance to spend money for short-term programs with possible long-term benefits, a mishandling of federal farm credit programs, extended high interest rates, and a monetary policy which while strengthening the dollar weakened grain export sales abroad, all became the hallmarks of Reagan's "death valley days" for America's farmers. A squandering of political capital in Congress in exchange for favorable tax and spending votes and an unprecedented wasteful defense budget also contributed to the unmitigated farm policy disaster that was the hallmark of the Reagan administration.

After ridiculing the Carter administration for spending nearly $3 billion a year on unprofitable farm programs, the Reagan administration's outlay in its initial three years in office was $34 billion, the most massive federal intervention in the annals of agriculture.

But, ironically, it was the Carter administration which saved Reagan from an even greater financial disaster in the farm economy. During the Georgian's four years a workable farmer-owned grain reserve program had been put into effect. That program, despite all the rhetoric from Reagan and Secretary Block about how government needed to get out of agriculture, saved Reagan and Block from themselves. As Ward Sinclair, *The Washington Post*'s insightful agricultural affairs writer, noted,

When Block refused to set up a strong crop reduction program for 1982, the harvest came out a whopper and surplus problems intensified. Much of that excess corn went into reserve and averted a total price collapse, although it sent federal farm-support loan costs soaring.[61]

Likewise, in 1983 when the administration faced serious problems stemming from a low grain output due to the weather and Reagan's Payment-in-Kind program that gave farmers surplus corn for not planting more of the same grain, the Carter grain reserve program again came to the rescue like the U.S. cavalry in an old Reagan movie.

The reserve [helped] Reagan several ways. It [provided] a source of grains that can be turned over to farmers in the PIK program. [That helped] the White House hold down direct government outlays to farmers in the form of price support loans. Beyond that, the reserve [helped] head off even worse trouble: a dramatic rise in food prices during the 1984 election year.[62]

When John Block left the USDA in January 1986 to accept a post as president of the National American Wholesale Grocers' Association, the number of American farms had dropped in five years by 15 percent, from 2.5 million to less than 2.2 million[63] and Treasury outlays for farm price and income supports totaled $68.2 billion as contrasted with the $16.8 billion spent on farm programs in the five years previous to Block's tenure at USDA.[64]

Clearly, by the latter half of the 1980s American agriculture faced a monumental disaster, unparalleled in the history of its permanent agricultural crisis.

Section Four:

Communities of Economic Interests

"The only way I know to get toothpaste out of a tube is to squeeze, and the only way to get people out of agriculture is likewise to squeeze agriculture. If the toothpaste is thin, you don't have to squeeze very hard, on the other hand, if the toothpaste is thick, you have to put real pressure on it. If you can't get people out of agriculture easily, you are going to have to do farmers severe injustice in order to solve the problem of allocation."

- Kenneth E. Boulding

Chapter Twenty-Three

Farmers as Barriers to the Destructuring of Democracy

He is Free
who knows how to keep in his own hands
the power to decide at each step,
the course of his life,
and who lives in a society
which does not block the exercise
of that power.

- Salvador de Madariaga,
16th Century Spanish Diplomat

Farmers, like most other Americans, perceive, as did James Madison in *The Federalist*, that justice is the proper end of government. Like all other political and social animals, farmers think, talk, act, develop ideas, and use their imaginations. They can be both rational and irrational. And yet, like the rest of us, they continue to seek "justice and truth."

As so many of their urban neighbors do, they have come to believe that their own freedom within the framework of a democratic society is contingent on their government's steadfast commitment to the principals of economic and social justice.

Yet, at the same time, farmers profess a wide variety and sometimes conflicting set of political beliefs and values which often color their concept of exactly what justice is.

Because our sense of justice underlies so many of our goals as a society, we must recognize those particular standards of justice, enunciated throughout history by the likes of Aristotle, Thomas Aquinas and Madison, which have traditionally served as the theoretical guidelines in our policy making process.

Distributive Justice and Commutative Justice

Putting aside the question of whether we as a nation have in fact remained faithful to the notion of rewarding individuals according to their own unique contributions to society, while at the same time offering to each person an equal opportunity to be productive, we continue to *profess* a commitment to distributive justice. It is from our adherence in theory to this tradition that the idea has come of a reward or "justice in exchange," *e.g.*, a fair price, a fair wage, or an appropriate level of income as a societal manifestation of commutative justice.

Yet, when it actually comes to applying the concept of distributive justice we often see a wide gap between what is professed and what is practiced. For example, by

providing direct payments to farmers rather than increasing their price supports we deny farmers in various sales classes distributive justice. Historically, we have distributed government payments, with variations among commodity programs, proportionately to the value of farm sales, thus ever widening the margin between the various classes of farmers and allowing the rich to get richer and the poor poorer.

As noted in preceding chapters the evolution of American agriculture and farm policy has involved a perpetual struggle by farmers to realize both distributive *and* commutative justice and thereby maintain the ability to live and work in a truly just society. As Professor Harold Halcrow describes it:

In the just society, the problem is not only how to define a fair price and select among the measures to achieve it within a given or existing resource structure, thus to achieve commutative justice. The problem is also to define the income distribution that is tolerable and the measures that are appropriate to influence income distribution, thus to achieve distributive justice.[1]

Various and Sundry Beliefs and Values

Aside from their ideal of the just society, farmers have also brought with them to political and economic debates certain other beliefs and values. When we view these beliefs and values in the context of the Jeffersonian and/or the Hamiltonian ideal we bring into sharper focus the causes of much of the confusion and mixed political and economic signals that has been emanating for so long from the agricultural community.

It should be noted that beliefs and values found in the formulation of agricultural policy are not totally unlike those beliefs and values which usually influence our society at large. They include:

Political and social stability As a nation we believe in the rule of law and that social and political change can and should be achieved by orderly and democratic means.

Economic stability To a large measure the nation's general economic stability is dependent on agriculture. To many, agriculture is in fact the linchpin of our economic system. A report by the U.S. House of Representatives Committee on Appropriations in 1958 expressed just such an idea:

A review of economic history of the United States will show that every economic recession in this country has started on the farm. Every recession has been preceded by a period of reduced income to the agricultural segment of our population. Since agriculture is the principal segment of our economy which generates *new wealth*, it is inevitable that a prolonged depression in agriculture will eventually reflect itself in more aggravated economic distress throughout the rest of the economy.[2] (emphasis added)

Economic organization　　　　John M. Brewster has described the values upon which many believe our economic system should be organized. They are the work ethic, the democratic creed and the enterprise creed.[3]

The "work ethic" creed, or what has been referred to earlier as "efficiency," dictates that all things being equal the society prefers the production of more goods and services to less and thus it should strive to use its resources in a manner that will result in maximum output.

From this theory has sprung the democratic creed which says that an individual's contribution to society ought to be measured by that person's contribution to production. Such a value, as we shall discuss later, has been traditionally and usefully underscored by Protestant ethic.

At first reading this value, which implies that all individuals should *not* be treated as equals in the marketplace, appears to contradict another basic American value — that all men and women are created equal. Yet this latter value has been skillfully and pragmatically folded into the so-called "enterprise creed," with the idea that no one should be allowed to have *political* power over another and that all individuals should have an equal opportunity to develop their productive *abilities* to the fullest extent possible.

Economic growth　　　　Our belief that more material goods are better than fewer has by now become so prevalent in American society that we think of it almost as synonymous with "the American way of life." While some believe that no group should be made substantially worse off by this process of "growth," even if they have made no direct contribution to that growth, the dominant thinking among Americans holds that the benefits of growth should be shared in our economy, *in particular* by those sectors which have contributed to such growth in output.

Some economists have proudly pointed to the role agribusiness has played in the country's economic growth by providing an abundant food supply at what have *appeared* to be relatively stable and/or declining consumer prices. Others are more skeptical and argue that farmers in particular have not generally shared in this supposed growth and prosperity. They see current "economic growth" as erroneously determined by simply measuring the GNP, which they believe in fact has made farmers worse off in an absolute as well as a relative sense.

Although many large super-farms have benefited from the present economy by exerting considerable economic and political power, their principal means of success has resulted from a coincidence of their economic interests with those nonfarm elements which now control our entire agribusiness sector. Where these super-farms have come to realize their principal gains, however, has been through external economies of scale — purchase discounts, credit availability, and tax shelter and marketing advantages. Yet, all farmers, even the large operators, have suffered to varying degrees from the continuous ability of commodity purchasers to pursue and implement those "policies and manipulations" which have traditionally and inevitably led to depressed farm prices.

Equal Opportunity　　　　Generally, farmers have been led to believe that equal opportunity in American society can be equated with "equal" income. There is a division of thought within the farm community, however, over whether government should help bring about such economic equality. This division is often complicated not only by the subtleties of the democratic creed — "equal opportunity to develop to the limit of one capacities" and "equal opportunity to enjoy a high standard of living" — but by the fact that most farmers not having fully recognized that equal opportunity in today's marketplace is yet another myth, as discussed earlier.

Sharing our abundance As a people, Americans believe they have been singularly blessed as the "world's breadbasket" and it is incumbent upon them to share their good fortune, but such motives have not always been humanitarian.

Corporate agribusiness's plan to accelerate "economic growth," both here and abroad, and our government's desire to advance "the American way of life" as a means of gaining political stability, if not economic hegemony, have historically and profoundly influenced those very policy decisions ostensibly designed to share U.S. agricultural abundance with the world.

Public action and value achievement Agricultural economist Dale Hathaway, in suggesting that all of the above values and beliefs are not unique to farm communities or Americans in general, also directs our attention to an additional set of values that are of special significance because they often lead to public or group action.[4]

Farmers generally have always believed that if there exists a situation in conflict with their values, situations more consistent with those values should be sought by either group or public action. Farmers are equally reluctant to accept the premise that if their desires are not attained, it is simply because that it was not meant to be. Thus, when faced with the need for necessary action, farmers often conclude that if their private actions fail to bring a desired result the government should then intervene and attain such desired results.

Recognizing these particular beliefs and values and their interaction with the Jeffersonian and Hamiltonian ideals may help explain why American agriculture has been continuously divided among the large commercial, non-family farm type growers and land owners, "dirt farmers," and farm laborers. Such divisions, clearly seen in America's present rural class structure, have been a never-ending source of conflict and struggle throughout our history. They have played a major role in influencing national politics, as well as in developing our domestic and international farm and food policy.

"Commodityism" and "Sectionalism"

Obviously an individual's political beliefs are conditioned by class and income status. In America's political economy the higher one's income the more one's philosophy tends to be identified with the Hamiltonians. The farmer is certainly no exception to that hypothesis.

Madison believed that the "pernicious" effects of factionalism and sectionalism could be considerably mitigated by the size of the republic. As Fred Barbash, points out in *The Founding: A Dramatic Account of the Writing of the Constitution*, Madison was deeply concerned over the variety of selfish interests pursued on a grand scale after the War of Independence:

> The solution was not to abandon republicanism, or to stamp out the liberty people enjoyed to pursue their own interests. Republicanism was not the trouble. The trouble was republicanism operating in small spheres, where it was too easy for factions to gang up. The remedy was "an enlargement of the sphere," the creation of a much larger political arena, with a new power center, in which there would be so many competing groups that none would dominate and none would be dominated. The factions, their influence dispersed through the branches of government, would neutralize one another.[5]

Madison's hopes notwithstanding, "sectionalism" in collaboration with "commodityism" has been a powerful and often divisive political force in American agriculture. Historically, it has been influenced by climatic conditions, the presence of various ethnic groups, soils and most profoundly by the blight of slavery.

Simply by deciding what crops they will plant and what measures they will take to protect and promote such commodities, farmers make a political statement. For when it comes to "commodityism," farmers have always looked to maximize their profits and use their production resources — land, labor, capital and management skill — in the most efficacious manner possible, thus frequently allowing their pocketbooks to dictate their politics.

At the same time, "sectionalism" and "commodityism" have progressively splintered the farm economy by pitting one group of agricultural producers against another, isolating individual farmers and turning them into easy, powerless political prey.

By relentlessly promoting such "isms," national corporate agribusiness agricultural policy planners have effectively shaped farm policy. Also, by promoting "economic efficiency" through agricultural research and making available large amounts of capital while maintaining low commodity price supports, they have created an agricultural system with class privileges for a small number of large landowners who continue to assume increasing economic and political power.

By promoting strategies that encourage farmers to solve their problems individually through increased production and "efficiency" (rather than by class action), agricultural policy-makers have systematically and successfully diminished the collective economic and political power of farmers.

The Federal government, of course, has been a key collaborator in this manipulative process, selectively curbing farmer discontent through varying price supports and placing various "ceilings" and "floors" on selected commodity prices. By helping to create and foster "sectionalism" and "commodityism," government agencies and lawmaking bodies have traditionally served as the veritable handmaiden to corporate agribusiness.

Instruments of Power

Reviewing the instruments of power traditionally available to farmers we see first, their own physical energy and skill (learned mainly from seeing and doing); second, their ability to deal with nature; third, the availability of abundant natural resources, including land and labor and fourth, a loose but definable social unity.

When it comes to discussing power and its role in a democracy and in the lives of farmers, the general public tends to ignore the fact that U.S. agriculture operates within an economic system that is decidedly a political economy. While corporate agribusiness has always looked upon economic power as an end in itself, farmers have frequently sought such power as a means rather than an end in itself.

The view that you cannot have political democracy without economic democracy motivated the agrarian populists over 100 years ago, and it still reverberates throughout the nation's agricultural community. But what exactly is such democracy.

In its purest form democracy means one person/one vote. Generally, however, democracy means "the accountability of decision-makers to those touched by their decisions." In defining it thus, Frances Moore Lappé correctly reminds us that:

> one of the most striking features of our social order is that we restrict the democratic principle to the political arena. In the economic arena, we apply a very different rule: in the marketplace — one dollar/one vote, and in the firm — one share/one vote.
>
> What are the consequences of not extending the democratic principle of accountability into the economic arena? Economic power becomes concentrated and unaccountable. The result is nothing less than the undermining of political democracy itself.[6]

A constant source of farmer frustration, therefore, comes from their legitimate belief that other groups in the political economy have considerably more economic power and constantly use that power to subjugate farm communities. Farmers often see their elected representatives and leaders in collusion with that same power.

As rural sociologists Kevin F. Goss, Richard D. Rodefeld and Frederick H. Buttel point out:

Insofar as the role of the state tends to be that of advancing the interests of the dominant class *as a whole* not any one particular segment such as that of capitalist farmers — state policy toward agriculture has primarily revolved around ensuring the profitability of its inputs, and product marketing components.[7]

One factor which has played an increasingly large part in shaping the course of farm politics, particularly in the last century, has been termed "the political infrastructure of food," more frequently referred to as *agribusiness*. We have already seen that this interlocking system includes farmers, land speculators, credit institutions, the farm equipment industry, the fertilizer, petroleum, chemical, and electrical power industries, the transportation and storage industry, domestic and migrant farm workers, labor unions, packers, processors, food wholesalers and retailers. We shall soon see in upcoming chapters that it also includes the USDA, the land-grant college complex including the Extension Service, and the American Farm Bureau Federation.

A Fanatical "Capital for Labor Substitution Fundamentalism"

As previously noted, agribusiness is now securely amalgamated to the powerful domain of corporate America. In its pursuit of maximum returns on investment it has established as major goals: substituting capital for efficiency and technology for labor; the standardization of the food supply, and the manufacturing and creation of synthetic food.

The substitution of capital for efficiency has come to play a vital role in the metamorphosis of farming into corporate agribusiness. Agricultural policy-makers have almost always shown a distorted reverence for capital as compared to labor. As we have seen, farm labor was long considered an "inferior input." Proposed solutions to America's permanent agricultural crisis repeatedly express this assumption: "the only way to increase income to farm laborers would be to accelerate the outmigration of labor from agriculture."

Yet, there is increasing evidence that the amount of capital utilized by American agriculture is disproportionately large in comparison with other sectors of the economy. Some economists believe that the over-application of non-farm capital and over-investment has caused the lowering of realized marginal returns for farm labor.[8] As corporate agribusiness attempts to devise new methods for shifting the risks of employment and of earning income in food manufacturing onto society, it has come to see that more money can be made *from* farmers than *by* farmers.

Take, for example, the source of most of this capital — the banks. As economist Michael Perelman shows:

Bankers ... know that their business would not fare well in a nation of self-sufficient farmers or even self-sufficient communities. They have no reason to encourage farming practices which could do away with the need for borrowing. On the contrary, the more farmers adopt capital

intensive techniques, the brisker the demand for the commodity banks sell — namely money. Banks also realize that they are dependent on the success of business in general. A general business failure means a general banking failure. Again, capital intensive techniques are in the banks's best interest.

The government has also repeatedly participated in substituting capital for efficiency through the very laws and programs originally designed to alleviate the woes of low-income farm families and foster a "family farm system" of agriculture. The consequence of these "policies and manipulations,"[10] these government programs, supported and encouraged by various and sundry "communities of economic interests," have led to a regressive redistribution of income.

Boris Swerling of Stanford University's Food Research Institute notes that the statistical justification for many commodity programs has been derived from low per-capita estimates of farm income and that these low estimates are primarily due to large numbers of low-income farm people (who themselves receive little from such programs). He concludes, not surprisingly, that these commodity programs have been woefully ill-suited to relieving rural poverty.[11]

Large expenditures by the federal government on farm programs have historically benefited the large commercial, non-family farm type growers. They have also influenced the greater expansion of capital investments in agriculture to displace labor, whether that labor be hired or performed by the farm family.

This substituting of capital for efficiency has further evoked many other serious questions. In 1972, Richard G. Milk, assistant professor of economics at Northeast Louisiana University, posed one such question:

Have our programs, directly and indirectly financed by our federal government resulting in a destruction of 6.5 million job opportunities, been a wise allocation of scarce resources? Many economists feel that in almost any society — if there is a serious choice between policies which will promote maximum employment and those which will promote maximum output — the decision for maximum employment becomes more crucial when unemployment is destroying morale and undermining the society. For a sector like American agriculture, where maximum output is no longer a desired objective, this has special validity.[12]

(With considerable irony Milk concluded his essay by noting that "entirely new approaches are needed for our national farm problem, centering on the human beings involved and not on the maximization of profits of fewer and fewer firms," but he added that "general economists, such as the author, are leaving the field of 'specialty of agricultural economics' because that specialty is now dominated by a fanatical 'capital for labor substitution fundamentalism!'")[13]

Confronting the Struggle Between Poverty and Monopoly

Farmers justifiably have always considered themselves an integral part of agribusiness. They have nevertheless constantly been faced with increasingly narrow political choices to enable them to best meet society's needs for food while at the same time protecting themselves from economic extinction.

Now emerging from what many of their urban neighbors like to call "rural isolation," farmers are rapidly coming to realize that they are important participants in the same economic system as everyone else — a system that is constantly being confronted with the struggle between poverty and monopoly.

Most farmers, for example, have historically feared the organization of industrial workers on the grounds that labor unions' wage demands would drive up the price of farm supplies and equipment, and that the unions desire to insure a "cheap food" supply deprives them of earned income. Farmers, until recently, have also seen themselves almost solely as producers, rather than as consumers subject to the vagaries of a giant food manufacturing system.

Yet as more and more farm families are forced to sell their raw materials at a wholesale price, often cheaper than their costs of production, and are also being forced to buy their own food at excessive retail prices, they are coming to recognize the common concerns they share with so many others outside the farm community, including organized labor.

A glance at most farm magazines or newspapers, now either owned, controlled or beholden to large commercial industrial interests, confirms that in the world of corporate agribusiness today farmers are seen principally as *buyers* rather than *sellers*.

Correspondingly, Talbot and Hadwiger suggest that farmers' political decisions have traditionally been based upon the integration of their particular idealism with Madisonian realism.

> He searches for both truth and power, as he understands them. The picture in his head of the just society has to be reconciled, even rationalized with the desire he has for material advancement. His theology has to be molded to fit into his sense of capitalism; his mind has to reconcile the conflicts, if any, between his heart and his pocketbook.[14]

The manner in which this reconciliation takes place and the various groupings that result from it can readily be seen in the plethora of farm, economic, and political cooperatives, alliances, unions, federations, parties and organizations that American farmers have periodically chosen to associate with in their pursuit of political and economic power.

Although they often differ in the means by which they seek this countervailing, or bargaining power, there is usually a consensus among these groups that collective power is necessary if the "family farm system" is to survive.

A Political Dilemma

Throughout their struggles for such power farmers have asked, and will no doubt continue to ask, "how can I so develop my power situation so that I can be in a position of authority and prosperity and still remain 'free' ... ?" Talbot and Hadwiger reply:

> The farmer's response to this challenge varies with his philosophy and his understanding of science. Because of the weaknesses and inconsistencies in his understanding of both, his ideology comes to be, more than he realizes, full of distortions and inconsistencies.[15]

Out of this ideological confusion has emerged a political dilemma for farmers. Because they have generally been too undisciplined to seize power through group action, they have found it necessary to rely on government intervention to forestall financial ruin.

For the large commercial non-family "growers" this surrender of "freedom" to government has been seen as a "disaster." For them "freedom" has come to mean noninterference by government. The paradox here, of course, is that these large growers, who so frequently and loudly denounce "government give-away" programs, are the same ones who argue that the government should underwrite agricultural research and extension activities and/or take whatever appropriate action is necessary to maintain cheap labor and operating costs.

For the majority of family farmers, however, "freedom" simply means the right to farm without constantly encountering rules and regulations that prevent them from going about their business and earning a decent living. Yet, in rebelling against such *government* "interference" these same farmers often fail to recognize that many of those same federal and state regulations they find so reprehensible were adopted at the behest of their corporate agribusiness masters in a concerted effort to protect the latter's narrow vested interests.

As previously suggested, conflicts over farm policy arise not primarily over the ends, or goals, of the society and the state, but rather because of opposing concepts about the nature of man, the legitimacy of power, and the choice of appropriate instruments of power generally used to achieve those agreed-upon goals.

Choosing Between Two Creeds

Two political creeds have emerged out of this conflict of means: one the democratic creed, and the other the polity creed.

The former professes that *democracy* is the best form of government, that public officials ought to be elected by majority vote, that each citizen be entitled to an equal chance to influence public opinion, and that the minority not only be free to criticize the majority but have the right to try and gain majority support.

The polity creed believes that there are several legitimate claims to power, that a *republic* is the best form of government, that balanced government is the essential core of republican government, that institutions of government must be separated and divided through the allocation of written constitutional power, that one house of a legislature ought to be area oriented, and that the will of the majority be not only deep-seated but of some duration and by agreement of a significant proportion of the governing minorities who have become convinced of the wisdom of such policy.

The conflict between these two creeds is not peculiar to the U.S. political system. What is unique here is that these two national interests seek what is considered one national purpose, embodied in both the Preamble to the Constitution of the United States and the first two sentences in the second paragraph of the Declaration of Independence.

We the People of the United States, in order to form a more perfect union, establish justice, insure domestic tranquility, provide for the common defence, promote the general welfare, and secure the blessings of liberty to ourselves and our posterity, do ordain and establish this Constitution for the United States of America.

And,

We hold these Truths to be self-evident, that all Men are created equal, that they are endowed by their Creator with certain unalienable Rights, that among these are Life, Liberty, and the Pursuit of Happiness That to secure these Rights, Governments are instituted among Men, deriving their just powers from the Consent of the Governed, that whenever any Form of Government becomes destructive of these Ends, it is the Right of the People to alter or abolish it, and to institute new Government, laying its Foundation on such Principles, and organizing its Powers in such Form, as to them shall seem most likely to effect their Safety and Happiness. Prudence, indeed will dictate that Governments long established should not be changed for light or transient Causes; and accordingly all Experience hath shewn, that Mankind are more disposed to suffer, while Evils are sufferable, than to right themselves by abolishing the Forms to which they are accustomed.

As Talbot and Hadwiger point out,

The first source constitutes a statement of basic goals and is widely accepted throughout rural and urban America. The second is a statement of fundamental values which the democratic credalists accept at full face, while the polity credalists concur with it only after the Jeffersonian terminology is given a Hamiltonian interpretation.

Consequently, the national interest has two faces. One is democratic, Jeffersonian, Populistic, and egalitarian; the other is mixed, Hamiltonian, social Darwinist, and qualitarian. Each holds firmly, although not rigidly, to the belief that the national purpose is most closely approximated when their respective concept of the national interest is adhered to by the institutions of government.[16]

When these two different creeds clash, the existing power structure is usually threatened, political conflict occurs, and a politically-charged policy-making process is reborn.

Understanding the Policy-Making Process

In any democratic form of government this policy-making process usually includes several steps. Initially, there is a felt need for change, then the development of a public awareness, public acceptance, a study and analysis of the alternatives, and then depending on the course of action deemed appropriate, either legislation enacted, executive action taken, taxes levied, appropriations passed, or court decisions rendered. Ideally, the constant in this process is the general desire to serve the common good, maintain the general welfare and take the appropriate action necessary to perpetuate both such ends.

To understand this process as it relates to farm policy, however, it is necessary to identify not only the previously discussed general goals of farmers, but also more specific ones. It is also important to understand the means by which such goals are to be attained, who is to implement them and what constraints have been established to limit such a process.

Generally, the specific goals of U.S. farm policy have been food abundance, "efficiency," an equitable income, and the satisfactory protection of natural resources to assure an adequate future food supply. But as Halcrow reminds us, "if these are to be made explicit, someone must decide whether freedom, efficiency, security, or economy shall come first, since there is a conflict among these various systems."[17]

The formation of policy goals, he adds, requires "deliberative judgment about production, economic organization or structure, environmental protection and income distribution."[18] The fact that farm policy planners have for over a century sought to use these means in shaping a concentrated corporate agricultural system under the guise of "efficiency" demonstrates that "someone" has made a "deliberate judgment" as to what "shall come first."

Although relevant economic, political, social and environmental conditions within the society always constrain the application of policy, the limits of such constraints are usually imposed by and through the political system. The most general of all constraints, Halcrow notes, "grows out of people's conceptions of need and of alternatives available to them. There is no really coordinated public policy until there is a felt need to do something specific, and until choices are defined and constraints established according to concepts of cost and benefit."[19]

Repeated examples throughout the history of U.S. agriculture demonstrate that the "people's conceptions of need and of alternatives available to them" have been frequently and consistently skewed and distorted by corporate agribusiness in its successful attempts to impose upon the general public its own self-serving "concepts of cost and benefit."

In addition the decision structure for agricultural policy has in recent years seen a gradual transformation from strictly farm-related interests to the general concerns of a mammoth food and fiber industry tightly controlled by corporate America.

Yet, despite corporate agribusiness's "policies and manipulations," our general ideal of the policy-making process in terms of structure has been portrayed as remaining the same. As Hadwiger and Talbot describe it, it flows from political decisions by farmers and their organizations, through the ballot box where the public registers its "felt needs" to political organizations as instruments of power, to the strategies and tactics of legislation.[20]

In reality, however, by seeking to deprive an ever-dwindling number of farmers such power through *forced* exodus, corporate agribusiness is managing not only to thwart the will of a large number of people, but is also engaged in the systematic destructuring of democracy and removing yet another obstacle to its own quest for additional power.

Federal Policymakers: Proposing and Disposing

Throughout the years U.S. farmers have too often seen Washington, D.C., remote and populated by "bureaucrats," as "the enemy." Probably no one element, other than the weather, has been blamed more often by farmers and agribusiness for America's permanent agricultural crisis than these denizens of the Federal government.

Yet, government is not a faceless bureaucracy, it is rather individuals and groups of people with very special interests and allegiances who are ultimately responsible for the decision making process. Such individuals and groups are not neutral. They have beliefs, values and varying degrees of power. How they influence, use and distribute their power determines to a very large extent how policy is made and how it is applied.

When most people talk about the role of the Federal government in farm policy they first think of the U.S. Department of Agriculture, a cabinet level agency within the Executive Branch of our government. The next arm of the federal government they are liable to single out are the various House and Senate agricultural and appropriations committees and subcommittees.

Yet, as the role of food in our society has been moving from the national into the international spotlight an ever-expanding plethora of executive, legislative and regulatory agencies and committees play an increasingly larger role in shaping the course of American agriculture. (See Chart 23A)

Aphid Knees and Thrips Toes

Each department of the federal government from State to Interior, Defense to Health and Human Services, from the Federal Reserve Board to the Occupational Health and Safety Administration vies to influence U.S. farm policy in its own way. Because the power to influence agriculture is so widely distributed clear tensions within the Executive branch of government and between Congress and the White House often emerge.

For example, take the Office of Management and Budget (OMB). Back in the 1970s, the EPA had become quite concerned that a tremendous chemical poison load was going into the environment merely to assure, in the words of Dr. Robert Van den Bosch, "that we get our pretty produce or to minimize the off chance of an aphid knee or thrips toe surfacing in somebody's broccoli amandine or bloody mary." By bidding for and winning an EPA contract, Van den Bosch, a prominent and outspoken University of California entomologist, set out to study this problem. He prepared a simple questionnaire for California growers designed to examine their chemical poison use patterns under the constraints of cosmetic produce production and "zero" insect tolerances.[21]

Van den Bosch soon learned that the questionnaire he planned to distribute through a subcontractee (the Association of Applied Insect Ecologists (AAIE), California's organization of independent pest control advisors), had to undergo the scrutiny of the OMB. No government agency or contractee can submit a standard set of questions to more than nine members of the public without first obtaining permission from the OMB.

After completing numerous and detailed government forms followed by weeks of silence from both the OMB and the EPA, Van den Bosch learned by telephone that his request was being turned down.

I grunted, "Why?" "Well, they think that AAIE is prejudiced and will run a biased set of interviews because of their pest-control method." I responded, "What method? They use all methods, chemical, biological, cultural, and so forth; they're simply independent pest-control advisers." "Oh! I'll tell OMB that; good-by."[22]

After another period of silence and weeks of a stalemated investigation, Van den Bosch phoned his EPA contact and demanded to be put in touch with someone at OMB. Subsequently nothing happened, so he once again called the EPA.

When my contactor answered the phone, he was obviously very nervous and upset. In fact, he never gave me a chance to ask my questions; he simply said, "Look, Van, please cool it; forget about the interviews; there's a lot of heat coming from OMB. They've sent back word that their man who has over-all control over the EPA budget is in charge of this matter and that he isn't about to deal with anybody; the case is closed."[23]

The California entomologist never did learn the reason for OMB's rejection, but as he later reflected:

Somebody very big had gotten to somebody very big in OMB and they were putting the screws to EPA. It was obvious that the pesticide mafia and, in particular, its food processing family didn't want us talking with growers about impeccable peaches and aphid knees.

I was a bit flattered, too. Heavy Watergate games were being played to frustrate our little investigation of cosmetic produce. We were obviously on the track of something very rotten.

The Corporate Reapers

Chart 23A: Principal Federal Agencies, Commissions, Offices and Departments with Major Food and Agricultural Interests

Agricultural Policy Committee
Overall food policy, chaired
by USDA and participants
from several other
different agencies

Central Intelligence Agency
Indirect influence
Analysis of world agri-
cultural situation

**Commodity Futures
Trading Commission**
Regulates commodity futures
trading

Council of Economic Advisors
Indirect influence
Economic analysis, advice on
general economic policy

**Council on International
Economic Policy**
Indirect influence
General international

Department of Agriculture
most aspects
23 separate agencies

Department of Transportation
Major indirect influence
Highway and rail
regulations

Department of Treasury
Major indirect influence
General economic policy

Domestic Council
Indirect influence
General economic policy
Long range planning

EPA
Major indirect influence
Pollution control

Export-Import Bank
Congress
Financing trade

Department of Commerce
Weather
Fishery

**Department of Health
and Human Services**
Food safety
Nutrition research
Title VII
Nutrition education

Department of Defense
Indirect influence
Water resources programs
Minor food R & D
Major food purchaser

Department of Interior
Land management
Water management
Fisheries

Department of Labor
Worker safety (OSHA)
Rural and migrant workers economic policies

Department of State
Food for Peace coordination
Foreign agricultural
trade policy
Foreign agricultural
attachés

**Interstate Commerce
Commission**
Major indirect influence
Carrier regulation

Library of Congress
Indirect influence
Conducts studies for
Congress

**National Science
Foundation**
Research into food
production and weather

**Office of Management
and Budget**
General economic policy
Budget control

Chart 23A: Principal Federal Agencies, Commissions, Offices and Departments with Major Food and Agricultural Interests, continued.

Farm Credit Administration
Capital credit

Federal Energy Administration
Major indirect influence
Energy allocations and policy

Federal Maritime Commission
Indirect influence
Food exports via seaway
promotion

Federal Reserve
Major indirect influence
General economic policy
Banks located in
agricultural areas

Federal Trade Commission
Enforcement of unfair
trade practices
Trade rules affecting
food labeling and ad-
vertising

General Accounting Office
Indirect influence
Audits agricultural
organizations
Advises Congress on
policies and programs

Office of Technology Assessment
Indirect influence
Conducts studies for
Congress

Organization for Economic Cooperation and Development
Worldwide economic growth
and trade policy
promotion

United Nations (Food and Agriculture Organization - FAO and World Council)
Data collection and
analysis
World wide food policy
promotion

Food and Drug Administration
Food health and safety

International Trade Commission
Import/Export policy
enforcement

Of course, we knew this from what had already turned up in our investigation, but it was a shock to learn how dirty the game can get when powerful people have something to hide.[24]

Compromising Conflicting Beliefs and Values

Before discussing the specific role of the two major determining forces in farm policy, the USDA and the Congress, we must keep clearly in mind that power most readily responds to countervailing power. In a democracy such as ours power most frequently manifests itself in two forms — people and money.

The fact that the past century has witnessed a lessening of the power of American farmers as their numbers have been steadily diminished by design, while certain "communities of economic interests" have grown bigger and more powerful, should serve as another clear reminder of who ultimately is responsible for most agricultural policy in the United States.

Political scientists tell us that despite all the well-meaning pleas for policy decisions based on the "national interest" or the "public good," the primary function of our political process has become the compromising of various conflicting interests in a fashion that *maximizes* the satisfaction of those groups involved in the issues being decided.

For the most part this process is so subtle that it eludes documentation. This is due to the fact that the necessary compromises are often made even before they attract wide public attention since the parties involved realize that such attention will affect the ultimate decisions.

Traditionally, the Congress of the United States has been the arena in which the major decision-making process in agricultural policy takes place, always subject to an increasing variety of political interest groups and representing many different "communities of economic interests." As this process has unfolded, the techniques of influence have not only changed, but the number of other affected government agencies and bodies has also grown.

In allocating the division of labor within the Congress four key committees relative to agriculture include both the House and Senate standing committees on agriculture and each body's appropriations committee. Here we see the blending of raw political power with personality and principle as committee chairpersons often exhibit a wide latitude in creating and destroying subcommittees, rewarding friends and punishing enemies. Although party members frequently approve such changes and the number of subcommittees is limited by the rules of each chamber, the giving and taking away of coveted committee assignments can be both byzantine and brutal.

The one dominant factor, however, in determining which members exercise the most influence and power within each Congressional committee is simply how many years each member has served in the Congress.

Thus, seniority has become the very essence of power within the Congressional committee system. And the only way to maintain that precious seniority is by winning elections. The fact that until recent years the Democrats have pretty much ruled the South while the

Republicans have tended to dominate the rural areas of the Midwest explains in large measure the long-standing composition of most of the House and Senate agriculture and appropriations committees.

What has emerged, is a pattern of policy formulation built on obtaining approval for both substantive policy changes and/or funds for programs from committees dominated by legislators who come from the South and Midwest. These areas specialize in particular crops, the former region in tobacco, cotton and sugar and the latter in grains, and their representatives are quite understandably protective of their constituents' own interests.

Such domination has also precluded influence by committee members from predominantly metropolitan areas. As committee members from the South and the Midwest have through the years gained greater seniority and subsequent power they have also become less subject to the clout of their own political party when party interests clash with the economic interests of the producers they represent.

From the outset, commodity groups have lacked the necessary broad geographical base to allow them to influence farm policy as individual groups. Therefore, they have seen their political influence coming from building coalitions with general farm organizations such as the Farm Bureau, or, in some cases, from within these same farm organizations.

Today, while a formal "farm bloc" may no longer be strong enough to impose its will on an entire legislative body, it certainly can be a formidable obstacle in blocking new legislation, especially if a particular committee chairman or any number of senior committee members disapprove of such legislation. This is particularly true in the House of Representatives. Here members represent much smaller geographic areas, which for decades have been arbitrarily determined by state legislatures where non-metropolitan areas have exercised their greatest control, and/or where often the production of a particular commodity is concentrated.

This type of Congressional power, expressed in various and sometimes devious ways, has always been much in evidence. For example, in 1944 the ill-fated Bureau of Agricultural Economics conducted a race-relations study in rural Coahama County, Mississippi, as one of 71 such studies throughout the South. It concluded,

> There are two dominant features of the culture of the people of Coahoma County — one is Negro-white relations, the other is the plantation system of farming. Almost every phase of the people's thoughts and behavior is influenced by these two complexes. Schools, churches, families, law enforcement, public welfare, and earning a living are all under the domination of the plantation economy. Similarly all of these institutions and activities are carried on within the definitions of white supremacy and racial segregation.[27]

A draft copy ("For Administrative Use") of this study was surreptitiously given to Representative Dan R. McGehee, D-Miss., an influential member of the House

Agricultural Committee, who not only took the study out of circulation, but also downgraded the BAE, reduced its appropriations, and further restricted its activities.[28]

Mastering A Technique

Another way of manipulating power in the Congress is for a committee simply not to report bills that they find unfavorable to the whole House or Senate thus allowing those who control these committees a profound influence on the direction of U.S. farm policy.

Because U.S. agricultural policy is born and bred in this fashion, rather than coming from a "farm bloc" that might provide it with more unity, farm policy has been built around a series of commodity programs acceptable to the representatives of specific areas in which that particular commodity is economically important.

Even corporate agribusiness has decried such methods of determining farm policy. In their historic treatise, *A Concept of Agribusiness*, John H. Davis and Ray A. Goldberg argue that:

The result is that farm organizations, commodity interests, and business associations frequently adopt resolutions which are hastily and poorly thought out. Furthermore, little effort is made through the objective application of research to reconcile differences between groups or to work out the best policy, drawing on the ideas of all interested groups as source material.[29]

While some would argue with Davis and Goldberg's panacea — "well, planned, agribusiness-oriented research studies to be made by highly reputable institutions" — as a means to arbitrate the differences between these commodity groups and general farm organizations, it is true that farm policy has frequently been no more than a patchwork of special interest issues.

In recent years commodity favoritism in Congress has become even more pronounced with the emergence of the political action committees (PACs) — many of them representing specific commodity organizations — which make generous contributions to friendly candidates through campaign contributions and honoraria.

The general public only occasionally focuses on this situation, as in the 1970s when it was shown that much of the money that poured into the Watergate "dirty tricks" coffers came from milk producer and processor PAC's seeking to persuade the Nixon administration to raise milk price supports.

A more recent example of PAC influence was also revealed in September 1986, when the Washington D.C.-based Public Voice for Food and Health Policy released a study showing that since 1983, House members who supported the sugar industry's positions during the 1985 farm bill debate received eight times more campaign money from the industry's PAC's than did opposing legislators.

Some 247 members who voted the industry position on a crucial vote during the debate had received $743,021 since March 1983 from 18 sugar-related PAC's while the 142 opponents got only $85,300, with over a third of that number receiving no money at all. Contri-

butors included Cargill Inc., Archer-Daniels-Midland Co., and Castle & Cooke among others.[30]

In 1988 six major agribusiness organizations and corporations, according to Common Cause, the public interest lobby, were among the top ten givers of honoraria to members of Congress. Leading the list was the Tobacco Institute ($123,400), third was the American Bankers Association ($106,500), fifth was the Connell Rice & Sugar Co. ($84,000), seventh was the Chicago Board of Trade ($71,000), eighth was RJR Nabisco Inc.($69,500), and tenth was the Grocery Manufacturers of America ($67,000).[31]

How PAC money is distributed can be seen, for example, by examining honoraria received from agribusiness by Representative Charles Stenholm, D-Texas. After receiving $27,000 honoraria in 1988, the influential Congressman reported $25,000 for speeches, appearances, etc. in the first five months of 1989.[32] Included among those receipts were:

$2,000 from Grocery Manufacturers of America (1/9);
$2,000 from American Farm Bureau (1/10)
$1000 from National Wool Council (1/11);
$1,000 from National Cattleman's Association (1/29);
$2,000 from National Cotton Council (1/30);
$1,000 from Philip Morris Management Corp. (1/31);
$2,000 from Southeastern Poultry & Egg Association (2/2);
$2,000 from Snack Food Association (2/19);
$2,000 from Associated Milk Producers Inc. (3/30);
$500 from American Butter Institute/National Cheese Institute Inc. (4/10);
$500 from Texas Pork Producers (4/15)
$500 from American Soybean Association/National Soybean Producers Association (4/20);
$1,000 from United Egg Producers (4/20);
$2,000 from Dairymen, Inc. (5/5);
$2,000 from Tobacco Institute (5/9);

Because of the conflicts between particular commodity groups, farm programs frequently must be designed so that when one group is protected others must also be safeguarded in some other way. Lacking this necessary agreement among such widely diverse commodity groups, and because the USDA's organization and actions have usually been built around commodity factionalism, it has been nearly impossible through the years to realize a generally sound program for farmers or even achieve necessary major changes for specific commodities.[33]

Only recently, as the political power of farmers has declined and a viable consumer movement has begun to emerge, have some farmers and farm organizations seen the need to think in a broader national policy context.

However, the general public, subject to the pseudo-economic appeals and daily propaganda of corporate agribusiness, has generally failed to recognize that farmers and consumers have so much in common. Contrary to what the public is constantly being told farmers and consumers are *not* natural adversaries for both groups basically are seeking readily available, nutritious food at a reasonable, fair economic, social and environmental price.

But, as some agricultural economists have pointed out, as long as particular commodity groups have permanent legislation on the books, these special interest groups will maintain the status quo. Only a major change in general farm policy will correct this situation, and that will come only when there is either a drastic change in general farm conditions or a complete reformulation of political power in the relevant decision-making bodies within the Congress.[34]

While various farm organizations, such as the Farm Bureau and the NFO, have sought to formulate just such general farm policy reforms, they have had to compromise many of their positions with these same commodity groups, ranging from the Washington State Apple Growers to the Western Cattleman's Association (as often as not composed, but not necessarily controlled by many of their own members). Thus, they have lacked the necessary overall political muscle to effect fundamental and long-overdue economic and political reform.

Chapter Twenty-Four

Say! Say! USDA! What Have You Done Today?

The husbandman that laboreth must be the first partaker of the fruits.

- St. Paul

It is more than ironic that these very words appear over the portico of the U.S. Department of Agriculture headquarters in Washington, D.C.. Ironic, because a close examination of that department reveals a bloated bureaucracy whose actions have often contributed to the demise of those very "husbandman" that it so proudly professes to protect while at the same time devising and implementing various policies and programs which have only enriched the coffers of corporate agribusiness.

Almost from its inception the U.S. Department of Agriculture has, for a variety of philosophical and structural reasons, been unable to reconcile its roles as a client-oriented agency of the federal government and a major force in corporate agribusiness.

With its founding in 1862 the Department was designed to be exclusively concerned with farmer affairs. Its comprehensive charter mandated that it acquire and diffuse among its farm constituents useful information on subjects connected with agriculture "in the most general and comprehensive sense of the word."

But, almost immediately, as we see in the actions of the department's second secretary, J. Sterling Morton, a trait emerged that became one of the USDA's most dominant characteristics — an overly protective attitude, some would say a clear bias, toward corporate agribusiness.

Among the USDA's early functions was the procuring and the distributing of free, new, and valuable seeds and plants. However, in 1894, in a report to Congress Morton challenged his department's free distribution seed policy.

In light of my experience as a former seedman, however, I consider the free distribution of seeds by this Department as an infringement upon and interference with a legitimate business, and I believe it should be abolished.[1]

Although Congress passed a joint resolution overruling the Secretary, over the years corporate seed interests have succeeded not only in ending USDA's distribution of seeds, but in radically changing the character of seed availability in general.

Ingolf Voegler aptly describes the fate of such "egalitarian" ventures by the USDA:

As long as economic practices such as the seed distribution are not profitable, the state provides these services, but once these activities become profitable, business interests want to take them over and usually the state lets them. By improving agriculture the USDA created a profitable private market for agricultural products and services. In this way, the State subsidizes agribusiness in the name of free enterprise, and taxes from the many enhance the private wealth of a few.[2]

A Growing Force In An Expanding Age

As an institution the USDA rapidly grew from its 1862 beginnings — its first commissioner was Isaac Newton — and was given cabinet status in 1889. Given the hallowed place of agriculture and land in the nation's growth process, its existence and its demand for ever-larger Federal expenditures were seldom seriously questioned until recent years.

The growth of the department soon became enormous as one function spilled over into another, from fact and plant gathering to research, extension, education, regulation, credit, subsidies, storage, conservation, insurance, public distribution of surpluses at home and abroad, rural development.

As its functions multiplied, an enormous bureaucracy came into being. It is important to remember that the USDA is not one vast monolithic executive department. In fact, there are dozens and dozens of small, entrenched departmental fiefdoms spread throughout its ten and one-half miles of corridors in its two main buildings on the Mall in Washington, D.C. and in the hundreds of its offices throughout the United States and abroad. Such groups frequently flaunt and defy organizational analysis.

One succinct insight into the workings of the USDA came after the selection of John R. Norton in 1985 as Deputy Secretary of Agriculture. Shortly after his confirmation one lobbyist described Norton, a 56-year old agricultural "employer" who owns and operates 25,000 acres of irrigated fruits and vegetables in Arizona and California, as a "quick study."

People in our trade are almost shocked by his candor and frankness... but he's walked into an administrative nightmare at USDA. It's tougher for him *because there are so many seasoned people to deal with over there ... well-entrenched people who know the routes, and the routes around the routes.*[3] (emphasis added)

Another lobbyist and GOP political activist added: "You can disagree with Norton on philosophy or principle, but you have to respect his views because he is honest. That's important, *because there's been a lot of slipping-around honesty over at the department the last couple of years.*"[4] (emphasis added)

There is also a certain measure within the USDA of what John Gaus found to be "... useful as explaining the ebb and flow of the functions of government. They are: people, place, physical technology, social technology, wishes and ideas, catastrophe and personality."[5] Or as Charles Kindleberger suggests, "... the course of governmental intervention can be explained less by historical determinism or social-science theorems than as a random process of confusion, muddle, error and accident alleviated by occasional lucid periods of effective action and by serendipity."[6]

Ross B. Talbot and Don Hadwiger, however, suggest a simple equation of several factors or conditions moving in sequence to explain the accession of power by the USDA.[7]

1) With the early rapid growth of American agriculture, rooted in the philosophic and physical fabric of the new nation, came both erratic economic expansion and a considerable amount of agrarian economic and social unrest.

2) Because state and local governments were reluctant and in many cases unable to act on behalf of these troubled farmers the Federal government was called upon to assist in the enterprise. In the early years of the republic, Congress was able to both initiate and process such remedies. By the turn of the century, however, corporate agribusiness interest groups had garnered enough political power to initiate important farm policies themselves while also working with certain of their non-agricultural allies in the Congress.

3) But, by 1933, agriculture had become so complex and encompassing that in order for the government to have any control over its course it needed to invest a strong executive agency — the USDA — with the ability to collect data, evaluate situations, and develop legislation.

In the early years of the New Deal it had become apparent to many in the Roosevelt Administration that the USDA was not, in several important respects, properly serving all the farmers entrusted to its care. New programs were quickly established outside the Department. However, as they gradually became assimilated by the USDA after considerable political pressure from farm groups (principally the Farm Bureau), a complex and confusing administrative pattern developed.

The Resettlement Administration became the FSA after the 1937 President's Committee on Farm Tenancy report; the Soil Erosion Service created in the Depart-

ment of Interior in 1933 became part of the USDA in 1935; the REA, formed in 1935 joined the USDA in 1939; and the reorganization of the independent agencies of the FCA soon brought them too into the USDA.

In an attempt to streamline the USDA and bring a new "democracy" to agricultural administration, a large group of representatives from the land-grant colleges and the USDA came together in Virginia at a former Weather Bureau observation station in 1938 and signed the Mount Weather Agreement. This document sought to define the relationship between the old and new among the Department's programs.

In an effort to stabilize the relationships of power among the old and new in the administrative structure, the Mount Weather document provided for the establishment of a nationwide system of county land-use planning committees, to be set up by each state Extension Service. Each committee was to be composed wholly of farm people, with a subcommittee of local officials of the AAA, the Soil Conservation Service and the FSA. Government officials would compose the state organization with the State Extension director as chairperson, along with a representative of farmers. The purpose of these committees was to coordinate agricultural programs and the planning of land use.

While increased responsibility was given to the Bureau of Agricultural Economics for program planning, an Office of Land Use Coordination was created within the USDA. This concentration of programs and the reorganization of USDA soon provoked a declaration of war by the Farm Bureau, which saw these committees as a threat to its own local and national power.

4) Although the President proposes and Congress disposes, the latter does not and cannot know in sufficient detail how to cope with the bewildering array of technical, scientific and economic areas of modern-day agriculture and the many social problems that such advances have spawned. Therefore, in recent years the lawmakers have found themselves delegating an increasing amount of authority to the USDA bureaucracy.

5) Within our system of checks and balances, approval by the Federal courts is often necessary before legislation can effectively become the law of the land. Since the New Deal era, most farm legislation has neatly fit within the broad constitutional boundaries set by the courts at that time.

The interplay among these five factors has resulted in an agricultural establishment rivaled only by the enormous Defense Department complex within the Federal government. In 1990 USDA had over 90,000 employees and a budget of $62.9 billion.[8]

Getting the Job Done

In a short story authored by the comic Woody Allen a man wakes from a long sleep and discovers that his parrot has been named Secretary of Agriculture.

"Why this should be," writer Christopher Graybill asks? "I don't know, and Mr. Allen probably doesn't either. Some things are just plain funny; and the Secretary of Agriculture is easily the funniest position in the cabinet."[9]

Humor aside, any examination of the functions of the USDA should note the process of political leadership within the department and who sets the tone for its activities.

Through the politics of recruiting — selecting department heads, scientists and bureau chiefs, middle-management decision-making (where college graduates join the bureaucratic establishments), and college recruitment programs — the Secretary of Agriculture has an impressive number of tools to secure the political and economic goals of his Chief Executive's administration.

Setting the right tone for each political regime is important. Personality is probably one of the most crucial factors. Whether the Secretary is an innovator, conciliator, philosopher- ideologist, theologian, pragmatist or any combination is usually the key to the tone of the department's operations.

By way of illustration, listen to two recent secretaries of agriculture respond very differently to the question of how the USDA and government can best help farmers. First, Secretary Bob Bergland, writing in *A Time to Choose*:

> ... in addition to respecting our American belief in private property and the freedom of choice ... other basic goals of our society must guide us, and other beliefs must be respected. These include:
> • Belief in the equal dignity and worth of all.
> • Rewarding the striving for excellence as long as it is not at the expense of others' dignity and survival.
> • Promoting access to opportunity, and equity in the distribution of resources, rewards and burdens.
> • Cooperation and shared responsibility.
>
> Those precepts were nurtured during the two centuries after the first colonists arrived, two centuries during which what became the United States was predominantly agricultural. I believe they still flourish today.
>
> Their roots in that agricultural era are a principal reason why Americans today value farming as a way of life, as well as a business. Those beliefs and values are the common property of city dwellers, suburbanites, and rural residents alike. They must be the basic guideposts of our policy.[10]

Next, Bergland's successor John Block, speaking at Harvard's Institute of Politics and Public Affairs on April 30, 1986:

> The Department of Agriculture does do all kinds of analysis, reporting, projecting, but I don't know, I guess you just have to realize that people have to always remember to look back at history and realize that most everything that goes up must come down and everything that's down, and every dog has its day, and it will go up, and it happens that way.
>
> I don't know why, but there are cycles in all of this and when you are sick you think you'll never get well and when you are well you think you'll never get sick. Those aren't very scientific, but they make a hell of a lot more sense than the stuff you read.

Whether an Agriculture Secretary has sufficient insights into the various scientific and technological aspects of agriculture, the degree of political and ideological support the Secretary has from outside the Department, particularly from the President, and how much *esprit de corps* there is within the department are all important in determining whether the USDA will function smoothly and accomplish its stated goals.

When farmer John Block resigned as the Reagan administration's Secretary of Agriculture to go into private business, Ronald Reagan appointed Richard E. Lyng, a long-time personal friend and party loyalist, who was far more compatible with the President's own political and economic ideology. A former co-director of the farm and food division in the 1980 Reagan-Bush presidential campaign, an Assistant Secretary of Agriculture in the Nixon administration, director of the California State Department of Agriculture during Reagan's first term as governor in the late 1960s, a former president of the American Meat Institute, Lyng, who made his money by his connection to his family-owned seed company which was sold out to Northrup-King which was later purchased by Sandoz, came to the top spot in the USDA with an impressive political background and impeccable corporate agribusiness credentials.

Reagan saw Lyng as "a sound and solid friend" of farmers who moved to administer new farm laws that "will help get farming more into the market economy and rectify some of the things that have been wrong." While Lyng also enjoyed popularity with many members of Congress, others saw him in a less positive light.

"He has such a nice way of telling you to go to hell that you want to hurry up and make the trip," observed Michael L. Hall of the National Corn Growers Association. David Senter of the AAM added,

> He was accessible, but after you met him you didn't feel you accomplished much. He didn't want to change anything ... But one thing about him — you knew where he was at; he was consistent, not moving around the screen. You respect someone who stays the course.[11]

Lyng's loyalty to Reagan was legendary in Washington. He once offered to resign his post in an effort to win the support of a key Republican senator angry at him for making changes in the burley tobacco support program in exchange for the Senator's help in sustaining the president's veto of a controversial highway bill.[12]

Such loyalty, however, was decried by others in the nation's capital. "Lyng defended the Reagan budget that would have ended all of these programs," charged Robert Rapoza of the National Rural Housing Coalition, who frequently was forced to lobby hard simply to retain funding for FmHA low-income housing programs.

What they didn't kill outright, they allowed to die on the vine. For example, three quarters of the way through FY 1987 they spent only 40 percent of their housing money. Millions of people are in bad housing in this country. The facts speak for themselves. No other comment is necessary.[13]

Rapoza pointed to the fact that despite having moved about two million rural families into better housing over the past 15 years, and despite a loan default mark of *less than one percent*, there were still two-plus million rural families living in substandard housing, with inadequate plumbing and drinking water.

The poorest and the most isolated have been left behind. This [Reagan] administration simply wants to get the government out of this business. But there is little history to support their contention that the private sector will take care of this problem ... The FmHA can't even get rural banks to take part in the guaranteed operating loan program for farmers.

The Administration view is that the government doesn't have a role to care for people who can't care for themselves ... If we subsidize someone through the tax code to have a house at the beach and a house in town, it seems fair that we subsidize others to have safe and sanitary housing.

Consumer groups noted that Lyng, in his first years in office, did not go after nutrition and food stamp programs with the same sledgehammer approach taken by his predecessor, and appeared more open and responsive than Block had been during the first six years of the Reagan administration.[14]

In his Nixon years Lyng, however, opposed the WIC nutrition program, claiming it wasn't needed, and once referred to Carol Foreman, USDA's assistant secretary for consumer affairs in the Carter Administration, as "the ayatollah of American agriculture."

Lyng's successor and George Bush's first agricultural secretary was Clayton Yeutter, a 58-year old agricultural economist, cattleman and corn grower who farms 2,500 acres near Cozad, Nebraska, and is no stranger to corporate agribusiness boardrooms. A member of Earl Butz's regime at USDA, Yeutter served in President Gerald Ford's Trade Representative office under Frederick B. Dent. After leaving government at the end of Ford's presidency in 1976 he became president of the Chicago Mercantile Exchange. He later returned to government as Ronald Reagan's U.S. Trade Representative.[15]

A man who always dreamed of being Secretary of Agriculture, Yeutter reportedly turned down a $500,000 a-year job at ConAgra to accept the Reagan cabinet post. But, as *Successful Farming* columnist Gene Johnston noted in an open letter to the new secretary, while acceptance of the post "speaks of your commitment to farmers," still "I have a feeling you'll get together with ConAgra in three or four years, anyway."[16]

While one prominent Washington agricultural consultant Gene Moos believed "we have never had a

secretary of agriculture that has had as complete a qualification as Clayton Yeutter," former USDA under-secretary Carol Foreman believes Yeutter merely demonstrated the qualities of a "terrific poker player" in the early days of his administration.[17]

Others were more severe in their appraisal of the new USDA boss. Representative David Nagle, D-Iowa, called Yeutter's first six months in office "a disaster." "Our worst nightmare would be to have the archenemy of the American farmer as secretary of agriculture, and that's exactly what we have with Secretary Yeutter." A GOP congressman told reporter Tim Warner that Yeutter was more often an adversary than an advocate for farmers.[18]

Yeutter has said that "when governments get involved in agriculture, it is usually the consumer who pays the price," and has long advocated eliminating agricultural subsidies. "Whether one's interest is that of producer, consumer or taxpayer, in all three cases we badly need agricultural trade reform."[19]

Meanwhile, Yeutter actively lobbied to rid agriculture of any kind of quotas that now protect farmers and "distort the free flow" of trade. On an official, taxpayer-paid May 1989 visit to Nebraska ostensibly to inspect drought-ravaged farms he instead used the occasion to attend three state GOP fund-raisers (garnering $15,000) before squeezing in a brief 45-minute stop at a Elwood, Nebraska farm. At a 1989 gathering of the American Seed Growers Association he declared that "the federal deficit would double or even triple if all requests for farm aid were honored." These and other facts lead many critics to ask whether the new secretary was the "farmers' friend or foe?"[20]

Keeping Blacks and Minorities in a "Disadvantaged Condition"

When Richard Lyng took office in early 1986 he not only was faced with the disaster on America's farms, but with major problems in his own agency.

The attempted but unsuccessful firing in June 1986 of Dr. Edith Thomas, an administrator and nutritionist in the USDA's Expanded Food and Nutrition Education Program, clearly showed the laxity and confusion in the Department's own civil rights enforcement programs.

According to the Equal Employment Opportunity Commission of the 58 agencies in the Federal government the USDA with 14.7 percent of its work force considered minority, ranked 52nd in fiscal 1986 in minority hiring.[21] In another study, "The Black Presence in the U.S. Cooperative Extension Service to 1983: A Profile," author Joel Schor notes:

It is an accurate, if simplistic, general statement to characterize the black employee as having from one-half to two thirds the salary as the white counterpart for most of the period, about twice the counties to work as the white counterpart, little or no help from specialists, except usually by special invitation, in other words twice the work for half the pay.

Agents and home agents likewise ran adult and youth groups, usually without the backstopping of 4-H specialists or assistants. And the black agents were held in lower esteem by white farmers as well as agents themselves who frequently referred to them as the "farm" agent to distinguish them from the better compensated county agents and his assistants who were white.[22]

Schor concludes,

> In terms of numbers of farmers, white agents throughout their history were usually in short supply; black agents were even more rare, by a factor of two. The short-handedness of agents, black and white, encased in a segregated setting in the Southern states, meant a loss of potential service to clientele which is too large to quantify accurately. In recent years, the reductions of farmers have made the ratio of farmers/agents more realistic.[23]

There is overwhelming evidence that such racial discrimination still exists within the USDA. In 1985 blacks within the Department numbered 7475 or 13 percent of the full-time employees. As a whole the Federal workforce was 22 percent black.[24]

The number of discrimination complaints filed by black and other minority workers at USDA increased from 1981, when 206 complaints were filed, to 1986 when 379 similar complaints were filed.[25]

In six years with USDA, Dr. Thomas alone had filed 12 discrimination complaints, charging among other things that her superior had refused to let her visit black-land grant colleges so as to provide them with technical assistance while no restrictions were put on her to visit the white land grant institutions. She also told of being referred to by her Department colleagues as a "god damn nigger," "a black bitch," and "dog face."

> There is only one logical conclusion that I can reach as to why my nutrition services have been denied to low-income, black and minority people despite this being a major function of my USDA job. A branch of the U.S. government, motivated by racism, has intentionally adopted a policy of keeping blacks and nonwhite minorities in a disadvantaged condition.[26]

Dr. Thomas's attorney, Joseph Gebhardt, described the situation to the press more bluntly. "There is only one conclusion; people who have a racist ideology manage the Extension Service."[27]

Three other cases of racial bias within the USDA received renewed attention during the Thomas firing controversy.

Discrimination charges against the Agricultural Soil Conservation Service in Arkansas by black farmers and one black conservation service employee, Walter White Jr., were sufficient grounds, several members of Congress believed, for a full-scale investigation of civil rights compliance by USDA in that state.[28]

Claiming that they and women had been excluded from participation in the state's 76 local conservation district boards that oversee the spending of federal and state funds for soil and water conservation, the black Arkansans pointed out that of the 380 local board directors there was only one black and 12 women.[29]

According to the ASCS's own statistics, as of July 31, 1987, only 33 of the nation's 2,520 county directors — 1.3 percent — were black and 25 of the 33 were based in southern states where the bulk of a dwindling black farm population resides.[30]

Defending the current situation, Randy Young, director of the Arkansas governor's state soil and water conservation commission, argued that the reason the commission had taken no action on such charges was "in order not to create a sense of ill will between the districts and the state."[31] In the wake of the charges and after an internal investigation the USDA assigned two ranking SCS officials in Arkansas to new jobs outside the state.

Subsequently, White's home was destroyed by fire. Arson was strongly suspected as a small wooden cross was found behind the house.

Later, in one of five reports prepared by the USDA's Office of Advocacy and Enterprise, it was learned that interviews with department employees in Arkansas turned up perceptions "that many agricultural officials in the north-central part of the state are members of the Ku Klux Klan (KKK)." John J. Franke, Jr., assistant secretary for administration, wrote to Representative Don Edwards, D-Calif., that he was asking the department's inspector general to conduct an immediate inquiry.[32] A subsequent department investigation, however, concluded that no USDA employees in the area were involved with the KKK.[33]

After Representative Patricia Schroeder, D-Colo., and her House civil service subcommittee called upon Lyng in May 1986 to immediately provide further information on many of these charges,[34] the Secretary issued a sharply worded letter to his assistant secretaries and agency heads warning that they would be held accountable for how well the USDA did in eliminating racial discrimination within its offices and programs.

> I will not tolerate discrimination in any form and I expect you to make equality of opportunity and respect for civil rights an integral part of all decisions and processes affecting your work force and programs. All managers and supervisors are to be educated as to their obligations. I want civil rights clearly reflected in the performance decisions you make regarding their future employment with this department ...
>
> Do not take this matter lightly. I expect you to assume personal responsibility ... to correct any program or ... practice that results in inequitable treatment. Failure to do this will be viewed as a grievous weakness in management which, in my view, no other accomplishments can offset.[35]

A Florida study, released after this letter, revealed that that state's ASCS leadership structure was virtually all-white; none of the agency's 41 county ASCS offices were led by blacks and the state office included only one black — a GS-4 mailroom employee who had been previously trained for a county director's job but was not placed. The Florida review also uncovered racial insensitivity on the part of managers; several white country directors referred to black males as "boys" and to black females as "negresses."[36]

The Washington Post's Ward Sinclair also has reported that civil rights specialists at the USDA believed that similar ASCS abuses occurred in other states, particularly in the southeast, but none could be documented because the Reagan Administration's budget cuts severely curtailed the compliance activities of the ASCS's nationwide activities.[37]

"I feel the ASCS is sitting on a time bomb," one USDA civil rights counselor declared. "The entire system operates to exclude blacks; the general counsel has told them they simply could not win any class-action complaint brought on the basis of sex."[38] Congress has also shown concern over charges of racial discrimination involving USDA employees in other Department programs.

Representative Edwards noted that his House Judiciary subcommittee on civil and constitutional rights was receiving "at an alarming rate" new complaints about "very serious race discrimination" in USDA employment practices and program delivery. He specifically cited the failure of the Animal and Plant Health Inspection Service (APHIS) to comply with federal government requirements to draft equal opportunity and civil rights enforcement programs.[39]

APHIS proposed a three year plan in fall 1985 to reach compliance, but it was promptly rejected by the Office of Advocacy and Enterprise (OAE) — USDA's compliance overseer — which then gave APHIS one year to comply with the requirements.[40]

Reverend Jesse Jackson has also charged along with many Southern black farmers that there is "clearly a problem of racial discrimination" in states like North Carolina where of 344 FmHA loans in the spring of 1986, 20 went to blacks, one to an Indian and the rest to whites. "The Farmers Home Administration for too long has reflected the worst of local politics."[41]

As Representative Edwards concludes: "We've been holding hearings on USDA for 15 or 20 years, and we're getting pretty tired of it. It doesn't matter if it is Republican or Democratic Administrations. A lot of people are getting hurt."[42]

More fuel was added to these fires of controversy in April, 1988 when more than 100 black employees of the USDA's Foreign Agricultural Service (FAS) filed a discrimination compliant against the department while also calling for a congressional investigation.[43] They pointed out that the FAS, which promotes U.S. agricultural exports through sales and trade development programs abroad, had 118 employees overseas, only four of whom were black and only 33 of whom were women. These jobs included agricultural counselors and attaches, assistant attaches, trade officers and secretaries; all blacks overseas at the time were trade officers.

The group also decried the fact that no blacks had been promoted above the merit rating system of GS- or GM-13 in the past five years and only six blacks among the FAS's entire 828 employees had reached the 13 level.

In an attempt to thwart such protests the USDA announced later in 1988 that it had drawn up a fiveyear affirmative-action plan that called for upgrading and increasing the number of minority and women employees.[44]

In January 1989 the USDA also announced that it was establishing offices on the campuses of the nation's 17 black universities in an effort to encourage more minorities to enter agriculture and forestry. According to Deputy Secretary Peter C. Myers the offices would help with curriculum development, recruit and counsel students on employment opportunities, and develop new ideas to help small-scale, limited-resource and minority farmers.[45]

Trying to Put Socks on an Octopus

A successful poor people's organization tends to disturb and challenge local societies that have developed organically around a class system in which the poor serve and are controlled by an established group of more powerful and wealthy citizens. To that kind of class structure, self-reliant institutions of the poor and near-poor are threats to traditional social status and established privileges.

-National Committee in Support of
Community Based Organizations

While the Federal government and its agencies are often seen as "deliberate" and "prudent" in investigating charges of racial discrimination within their own structures, their conduct in such matters frequently manifests both a covert form of racism and class prejudice. Such was the situation surrounding the federal government's 1979-1981 "investigation" of the Federation of Southern Cooperatives (FSC).[46]

Since 1967 the FSC, with headquarters in Epes, Alabama, had been attempting to support and coordinate the grass-roots efforts of about 30,000 low income rural families throughout the South by organizing them into 130 housing and agricultural cooperatives in 14 states. Throughout the years the FSC has depended in large measure on federal funding to support its activities. Its then director Charles Prejean was black as are many of its members.

On December 31, 1979, after several weeks of unexpected visits by the FBI to the Federation's Atlanta offices seeking sweeping rather than specific FSC records, a federal grand jury in Birmingham, Alabama subpoenaed Prejean to turn over "any and all documents in connection with federal funding of the FSC and its affiliated cooperatives for the years 1976-79."

The subpoena commenced a 17-month ordeal which would see the FSC, in the words of one chronicler, "locked in a legal and financial limbo" while the government's "investigation" continued. On May 20, 1981 the U.S. Attorney for the Northern District of Alabama, J.R. Brooks, abruptly announced "I have decided to decline prosecution."

Neither Brooks nor anyone else connected with the case offered any explanation why the investigation had been undertaken in the first place, why it had been allowed to drag on for so long, or why it was dropped.

Prior to Brooks' subpoena, the GAO, which conducted a full-scale investigation of the FSC in response to a request by Representative Richard Shelby, D-Ala, whose Seventh Congressional District includes Sumter County where the Federation is headquartered, said it found no evidence of malfeasance. Shelby subsequently made no public effort to reveal the contents of the GAO report either to his constituents or to the Federation.

However, later while the grand jury and the government, including the FBI, were conducting what was at best an "unorthodox investigation" of the FSC, a variety of unfounded rumors about the Federation began to circulate.

As it became more widely known that a grand jury was looking into its activities, the FSC found itself severely restricted in its attempts to raise both public and private funding and maintain its widespread education, organizing and training activities. Many people familiar with the Federation's past activities believed that such a sabotage was the ultimate purpose of the government's entire investigation.

Prejean recalls,

Over the past four years we had been able to raise about $2.5 million a year. At the height of the investigation we were down to less than half that, I think, and some of what was coming in was not new money but simply renewals of earlier grants. So while I can't put an exact dollar figure on losses attributable to the investigation, I can certainly say that those losses were substantial — over a million dollars, I would say, not including the staff time we lost and the costs of our legal defense.

Throughout its dozen years of existence the FSC had been on the cutting edge of the social change movement in the South which, not surprisingly, earned it numerous enemies within the Southern political and economic establishment.

One of the FSC's earliest and most controversial efforts was the forming of the Southwest Alabama Farmers Cooperative Association (SWAFCA), first organized in 1966 by black farmers in a ten-county area, including Sumter. Combining black-power politics with pragmatic economics SWAFCA immediately appealed to over 2,500 farmers who signed up with the co-op in a matter of months.

A number of significant economic victories followed, including a concerted effort to get higher commodity prices for its members which resulted in a 100 percent increase in prices paid to farmers in southwest Alabama for peas and cucumbers. Such success immediately evoked a political backlash as food processing companies, supported by local politicians, began objecting that "uppity blacks" were using Office of Economic Opportunity (OEO) money to overturn the economic *status quo* of southwest Alabama. Despite efforts by Alabama Gover-

nor Lurleen Wallace to veto further federal money away from SWAFCA, OEO director Sargent Shriver's commitment to the co-op persisted and the funding continued.

Another example of the Federation's work was the role it played in organizing the Minority Peoples Council (MPC), formed with the explicit goal of "struggling for 40 percent minority utilization in the present [Tennessee-Tombigbee] Waterway construction jobs, in all training programs, and in the jobs that will follow its completion."[47]

The Tennessee-Tombigbee Waterway was conceived as a means of linking grain elevators of the Midwest and the coal mines of Appalachia with the port of Mobile, and was slated to be the biggest earth-moving operation since the building of the Panama Canal. Although 40 percent of the total population along the path of the Waterway was black, black workers held only 15 percent of the jobs available in the early stages of construction.

Led by a long-time FSC staff member Wendell Paris and other Federation members the MPC, with the assistance of the National Association for the Advancement of Colored People (NAACP) Legal Defense Fund, the MPC soon issued a report documenting a pattern of discrimination in Waterway hiring practices. Later, by helping to file lawsuits against the Corps of Engineers, construction unions, Waterway contractors and state employment agencies the MPC became a focal point for Sumter County hostility.

Much of that anger was directed at Paris, a County native, whose father was the first black man to register to vote when the Supreme Court threw out some of Alabama's discriminatory restrictions in 1946. "My political activism goes way back to my birth," Paris observes.

As one who has worked with Paris, the author can testify to his persistence, effectiveness and dedication as an organizer. He believes in getting jobs for neighbors, assuring that they have the right to vote and that they exercise that right, and that their children are properly educated in their local schools. People like Paris, and Prejean, its director, Ralph Paige, the Federation's 30,000 low income family-members and its 25 dedicated staff people have made the Federation one of the nation's premier and most effective community-based organizations.

With this success, however, came the animosity of county, state and federal government agencies, and many business communities, which culminated in the 1979-81 grand jury probe.

Although the Federation initially furnished the grand jury with over 22 file drawers of records, including 40,000 cancelled checks, the probe continued afield with FBI agents making unannounced visits to co-op members and those who had received FSC training, visiting more than 200 people in five states.

As Thomas N. Bethell described it in his report for the National Committee in Support of Community-Based Organizations, *Sumter County Blues: The Ordeal of the Federation of Southern Cooperatives*, "Federation members had a hard time figuring out how to deal with the agents. Most people tried to cooperate, reasoning as most citizens would — that they had nothing to hide.

But the agents asked questions that made people nervous."

The agents asked such questions as "did you know the Federation was ripping off the government?" implying that certain conclusions had already been reached. Women who had stayed at the Epes dormitory while attending training sessions were asked: "whom did you have to sleep with while you were there?"

As Bethell says, the agents "behavior amazed some people, amused a few, but mostly made people very uncomfortable — about the investigation, about the Federation."

As this "investigation" dragged on through the summer of 1980, the National Committee in Support of Community-Based Organizations was formally organized with Leslie Dunbar, then director of the Field Foundation, as its chairman. Dunbar later wrote:

Our Committee was organized ... to show confidence in the Federation, to give it tangible support, and to defend community-based organizations generally. It was for most of us a new and untried task: how to monitor a federal grand jury investigation.[48]

But, as Bethell commented, "the task was a bit like trying to put socks on an octopus."

After the case was dropped, Dunbar speculated that the FSC story might have had a very different ending if the Federation had been unable to rally support from the outside world.

It would have ... gone like this: an early indictment on some count; a pre-trial period during which the Federation would have been effectively paralyzed; a trial; and then an acquittal for lack of evidence. But in that process, all political debts would have been paid and the Federation made virtually bankrupt and destroyed. We think that the resistance ... pointed out to the government that there were prices to be paid for continuing what it had been led to begin and had had some difficulty letting go.[49]

Today, the Federation of Southern Cooperative/Land Assistance Fund, which now includes the Emergency Land Fund — formed in 1971 to help black land owners across the South hold on to property threatened by creditors, tax collectors and unscrupulous land dealers, and to purchase "primary agricultural" land — continues its work.

In addition to the activities of Emergency Land Fund, the FSC's work includes organizing, developing and sustaining (with technical assistance, training, information and resources) 75 affiliated community-based economic development groups; providing employment and training opportunities; organizing a legal assistance project; building over $3.9 million of assets in 11 member community development credit unions; rehabilitating and building over 440 units of rural housing with trainee-labor; and assisting over 500 small farmers to develop livestock operations on their farms.[50]

Political Favoritism

The Federation of Southern Cooperatives case is only one example of how public pressure can be applied to government agencies to make them fulfill the promise of "equal justice under law." In recent years various government studies and press reports have focused on a variety of other such specific issues, particularly within the USDA.

A 1985 GAO study, for example, sharply criticized the Department for its spotty enforcement of the Animal Welfare Act. It was also learned that the Economic Research Service as late as March 1985 had none of its 400 economists studying the ominous farm credit crisis full-time. Meanwhile, it was reported that in FY 1986 the Department was spending the second highest amount of money of any government agency ($229,132) on bodyguards for its top bureaucrats.[51]

Lyng himself was criticized in the early days of his regime for ordering USDA to pay for a program in Florida by canceling an $11 million soil research project in Iowa. The director's aides later told AgriData News Service that the "emergency" funding was provided at the request of Senator Paula Hawkins, R-Fla., to help in what would prove to be her unsuccessful re-election campaign.[52]

Another political favor by Lyng stirred up even more controversy. He made a two-day trip to Iowa and Nebraska to talk with farmers, thus keeping his promise to help two Republican incumbent congressional candidates who had supported Reagan the previous month when he was seeking a $100 million aid package to help Nicaraguan "contras" overthrow that nation's government.[53]

Divining the Process

No matter how political nor how good an administrator a USDA Secretary might be, the department is so huge and complex that no single person can fully gain control of it. When each of USDA's separate, but loosely connected entities, are viewed as a concentration of a power center within the organizational hierarchy, we begin to understand the sometimes mysterious, sometime unexplainable dynamics of the USDA's administrative process.

But there is another important factor to be considered in analyzing the USDA's policy making functions, *i.e.*, most commodity organizations and other corporate agribusiness interest groups usually have one or more representatives who either once worked in high administrative offices at the USDA or currently work in the department.

In the Reagan administration's first five years alone, for example, we saw among others: Norton, described as "the prototypical western agricultural baron" and former chairman of the United Fresh Fruit and Vegetable Association and Western Growers Association, who after first being appointed a deputy secretary later served for a few days as acting USDA director before quitting in anger under heavy political pressure from Congressional Republicans who wanted a midwesterner in the job; Daniel G. Amstutz, a Cargill Inc. executive from 1954 to 1978, serving as Undersecretary for International Affairs and Commodity Programs; Robert L. Thompson, since 1974 a professor of agricultural economics at Purdue

University and senior staff economist for the Council of Economic Advisors and Assistant Secretary for Economics before returning in January 1987 to Purdue as Dean of Agriculture; Everett G. (Bud) Rank, a large California cotton grower, who was named director of the Agricultural Stabilization and Conservation Service (ASCS) in 1981 and was later ordered to undergo an "ethics orientation" after his farm was awarded over $1 million in PIK program payments from the department he at the time headed; and Vance L. Clark, the retired Bank of America senior regional vice-president in the San Joaquin Valley and a board member of Producers Cotton Oil Co., to head the Farmers Home Administration.

As we shall see in discussing the grain trade, the doors to USDA offices often swing wide for corporate agribusiness and its allies in academia.

Chapter Twenty-Five

Taxpayer Dollars Underwrite the Corporate Elite

Perhaps no function in the 125-year history of the U.S. Department of Agriculture has had a greater role in shaping farm and food policy than its agricultural research and development activities.

As noted earlier, in finding ways to subsidize corporate agribusiness, government, in the name of "free enterprise," has repeatedly taxed the many to enrich the few. No better illustration can be offered than the establishment of publicly-financed and supported agricultural research in the nation's land-grant college complex.

Given the dubious record of the nation's land-grant college complex and its significant role in hastening the departure of thousands of productive, efficient U.S. family farmers from their land, there is something remarkably ironic in the introductory statement of a National Association of State Universities and Land Grant Colleges (NASULGC) 1983 Executive Report.

Prepared in coordination with the American Association of State Colleges of Agriculture and Renewable Resources (with "valuable contributions" from representatives of some 14 different industry, trade and commodity groups, including the USDA's Science and Education division), it declares:

American agriculture — some 20 percent of the nation's gross national product — is seriously threatened by deepening shortages of highly qualified scientists, managers, and technical professionals. Particularly critical are shortages, predicted during the next 10 to 15 years, of individuals with masters and doctoral degrees in high technology agricultural disciplines. The U.S. agricultural system, which increasingly integrates advanced technologies and an intensive capital investment structure, will deteriorate unless positive actions occur.

... The United States must not relinquish its leadership role in agriculture by failing to invest in its ultimate resource — *human capital*[1]

Contrast this declaration with the observation of a prominent land-grant academician, Barry Flinchbaugh, Professor of Agricultural Economics at Kansas State University. Each year, he told the *New York Times*' William Robbins, he asks how many of his students plan to farm. Over the years, the number has declined. In 1984 only about ten of 105 students raised their hands.

But, he added, even that number is "*still too many. The only sensible way to get farmers' income up is to reduce the number of farmers.*[2]

Coping With Ambiguities

Not only did 1862 see the establishment of the USDA and the passage of the Homestead Act, but also the Morrill Act (named after Justin S. Morrill, the Vermont senator who sponsored the bill) which endowed each state with public land to establish and support agricultural and mechanical colleges. From the very outset, however, the Morrill Act contained a two-fold ambiguity.

First, established to support "agricultural *and* mechanical arts" the system's purpose was unclear. Did it mean two separate lines of education or was it simply concerned with the breadth of agricultural education? Did it intend education simply for farmers or for all citizens?

The second ambiguity, as Grant McConnell illustrates in *The Decline of Agrarian Democracy*, was more fundamental.

It lay in the general lack of agreement on the responsibility of education to democracy. Is it the part of education to satisfy whatever demands are made on it? Or does education have an obligation to observe goals and standards that are quite independent of these demands? The issue is large and often intangible, but it becomes urgent when applied to vocational education. Specifically, in agricultural education, should the colleges teach zoology or the care and feeding of farm animals? Should the agricultural colleges created by public act teach what the public wants or what the public ought to be taught? In a sense the issue was compromised when the act of Congress indicated that the goal was vocational education.[3]

Prominent agricultural historian Richard S. Kirkendall also reminds us that "the greatest push for the land-grant system came from critics of the farmers." He adds,

Men such as Justin Morrill maintained that American farmers were not good farmers. Inferior to Europeans, they exhausted the soil and then moved west. Consequently, American agriculture could become incapable of serving American needs, and farmers needed colleges so as to become more efficient and take better care of the land...

The Morrill Act, in other words, was influenced by a vision of America that differed significantly from Jefferson's. The act's vision was linked with the vision of the industrializers. In fact, Morrill worked for tariff protection for American manufacturers as well as land-grants for colleges.[4]

As it was, the land-grant colleges set out to teach common scientific and cultural subjects in an established tradition while seeking to prove their usefulness and to justify the faith that had created them by meeting the needs of farmers. After gaining a certain measure of self-respect, these colleges began to ally themselves with the movement for scientific agriculture, which had begun in the 18th century, and went on to build an educational foundation on which a new organization of agriculture could take place. As McConnell observes:

Education tended toward evolutionary gradualism, and agricultural education tended toward a particularly slow form of gradualism. Educational leaders were oriented toward natural science by training and by proclivity. They regarded themselves as nonpolitical and it may be hazarded that as a group they strongly partook of the ideological suppositions of the existing economic order. Although educational leaders occasionally expressed distaste for this trust or that, on the whole they believed that farmers should play the part of mediators in the conflict between capitalists and workers.[5]

In 1887 the Hatch Act authorized Federal funds to be paid directly to each state to establish agricultural experiment stations in connection with the land grant college. Its mandate was quite specific:

to conduct original and other researches, investigations, and experiments bearing directly on and contributing to the establishment and maintenance of a permanent and effective agricultural industry of the United States, including *research basic to the problems of agriculture in its broadest aspects, and such investigations as have for their purpose the development and improvement of the rural home and rural life and the maximum contribution by agriculture to the welfare of the consumer,* having due regard to the varying conditions and needs of the respective states.

In 1914 the Smith-Lever Act was passed in an effort to extend the teachings of the colleges and research stations to rural people for their general welfare. As Representative Asbury Francis Lever, D-S.C., explained to the House in his report on this legislation, the Extension agent "is to assume leadership in every movement, whatever it may be, the aim of which is better farming, better living, more happiness, more education and better citizenship."[6]

Victimizing Rural America

The stated purpose of the land-grant college complex — state agricultural colleges and universities, experiment stations and the Extension service — was to provide education, research and services to working families and rural communities. Throughout its existence this complex of 75 colleges and institutions has gone about its business as the unquestioned scientific and intellectual father of the America agricultural revolution, a revolution that not only has produced a radical restructuring of the rural countryside, but also has profoundly influenced the nation's urban life.

As one writer has described it:

The achievements of this pioneering federal-state system are ... beyond question. It has produced dramatic conquests of animal disease; perfected seed and animal breeding techniques; stimulated spectacular yield and productivity gains for U.S. farmers; eased the workload with new machinery; fostered improvements in fruit growing and storage; developed health protection and convenience for consumers and the food-processing industry. The examples are endless.[7]

Almost half of the presidents and board chairmen of the organizations in *Fortune Magazine*'s listings of the nation's 500 leading corporations attended state and land-grant universities.

While the nation's land-grant college complex has been growing so influential, however, corporate agribusiness has also been profiting handsomely from its tax-supported education, facilities, manpower and energies. As the University of Missouri's respected professor emeritus Harold Breimyer has observed, "land-grant universities don't sell their souls to private industry — they willingly give them away."[8]

Meanwhile, scant attention has been given by this complex to the many farmers, farm workers, small town business people and residents, and the rural poor, all of whom have become victims of this ongoing, protracted, violent economic and social revolution in American agriculture.

As University of California - Santa Cruz professor of rural sociology William H. Friedland argues, "the university has somewhat mindlessly fallen into a set of procedures that link it to large-scale agriculture" while the "more profound problem is that many researchers think in terms of high technology, rather than low technology."[9]

Recognizing that this tax-paid, land grant complex has come to serve an elite of private, corporate interests in rural America, while ignoring those who have the most urgent needs and the most legitimate claims for assistance, the Washington, D.C.-based Agribusiness Accountability Project set out in the early 1970s to provoke "a public response that will help realign the land-grant complex with the public interest."

After first establishing a Task Force on the Land Grant College Complex, under the direction of Susan DeMarco, this fledgling public interest research and advocacy organization in 1972 issued its now famous report, *Hard Tomatoes, Hard Times*, written by the Project's Director, Jim Hightower.

By examining the complex's past budget requests, its expenditures and its distorted research priorities as reflected in the allocation of scientific man-years, the report vividly detailed and illustrated that while American agriculture is enormously productive, and agriculture's surge in productivity is largely the result of mechanical, chemical, genetic and managerial research conducted through the land grant college complex, corporate agribusiness has largely reaped the benefits of that research.

The primary beneficiaries of land grant research are agribusiness corporations. These interests envision rural America solely as a factory that will produce food, fiber and profits on a corporate assembly line extending from the field through the supermarket checkout counters.

Through genetically redesigned, mechanically planted, thinned and weeded, chemically treated and mechanically harvested and sorted food products moving out of the fields and orchards and into the processing and marketing stages — untouched by human hands — the nation's land grant colleges come closer and closer to corporate agribusiness's "cycle of bigness" ideal: enough capital can buy technological and chemical gadgetry, which in turn can handle more acreage, which will produce greater volume, which will generate more profits, which will buy more gadgetry, which will replace more farmers and workers.

The AAP noted in this regard that taxpayers, through the land grant college complex, "have given corporate producers a technological arsenal specifically suited to their scale of operation and designed to increase their efficiency and profits." The quality impact of such research has been given little attention by the complex; its attitude is best expressed by one of its own, former Purdue University Agricultural Dean, Earl Butz, — "adapt or die!"

How to Squeeze a Grapefruit

Consumers as well as farmers have felt the impact of land grant college complex research bias. Convenience to the processor often outweighs taste for the consumer. In its effort to "sell" the consumer on certain products they may neither want nor need, the complex has used tax money for research and development that instead should have been financed privately.

In what has been properly labeled "research of the absurd" Cornell University, for example, at one time studied how hard a supermarket grapefruit should be squeezed for freshness:

Should you squeeze a product firmly or softly to determine its freshness, such as is commonly done with bread and some fruits? By using a universal testing machine, scientists have determined that a gentle squeeze, or more scientifically, a small deformation force, is much more

precise in comparing textural differences than a firm squeeze or large deformation force.

Purdue University, spent years and thousands of taxpayer dollars developing new athletic turfs for football fields and golf courses while Auburn was experimenting with the "heat-retaining properties" of Astroturf.

In what Ward Sinclair says became "a totem of scorn for Massachusetts farmers," a state university agricultural researcher developed the square ear of sweet corn to satisfy a need that was "obvious": square corn would not roll off dinner plates.

Meanwhile, in Massachusetts, sweet corn has become so prone to pest damage that some farmers reportedly must spray it with chemical poisons 20 times in a growing season. Sinclair observes that "the cry is for help that will keep farmers competitive, reduce toxic chemical use, and produce new crop varieties" rather than research on things like "square corn" with "little apparent day-to-day practicality."[10]

The consumer is also often fooled by public research. Using ethylene gas to produce the appearance of "ripe" tomatoes — tomatoes that are of lower quality with less vitamin A and C and inferior taste, color and firmness — and feeding DES, a carcinogenic growth hormone, to cattle to speed growth are but two of many examples of such land grant college complex technology.

In drafting its report the AAP Task Force made three valid assumptions:

First, if there is to be research for firms that surround the farmer, benefits of that research should flow back to the farmer.

Secondly, no public money should be expended on research that principally serves the financial interests of agricultural input and output corporations — they may be a part of modern agriculture, but they also are very big business and capable of doing their own profit-motivated research.

Finally, anything that is good for agribusiness is *not* necessarily good for agriculture, farmers, rural America or the consumer.

The Agricultural Research Establishment

The determination of the short range research policy of the land grant college complex is the product of Congress's annual budgeting process. However, the substance of that budget is the work of the Agricultural Research Policy Advisory Committee (ARPAC), which reports directly to the Secretary of Agriculture. ARPAC is composed mainly of members from the USDA and the land grant college community and in effect is the nation's agricultural research establishment.

Assuming a major role in ARPAC's policy-making process is the Agricultural Division of the National Association of State Universities and Land Grant Colleges, the home of the land-grant establishment, which in turn is composed of deans of agriculture and extension and heads of state experiment stations. The NASULGC counts among its members 24 of the nation's largest universities, colleges and multi-campus systems of higher education in the United States. More than 30 percent of all students enrolled in institutions of higher learning attend the NASULGC member universities and colleges. In the 1990-91 academic year, total enrollment at the 149 principal state and land grant universities was 2.7 million up from 2.2 million in 1984-85. The number of agriculture and natural resource graduates, however, showed a 39 percent decline between 1978-79 and 1987-88.[11]

The USDA's National Research Advisory Committee also plays a major role in determining research priorities. This 11-person advisory committee is often weighted with representatives from corporate agribusiness and the American Farm Bureau.

While many of these various national advisory committees are dominated by land grant scientists and officials, any "outsiders" usually come from industry. For example, between 1965 and 1969 out of 32 national task forces established to prepare a national program of agricultural research, 17 listed advisory committees containing non-USDA, non-land grant people; all but one ("soil and land use") of the outsiders were representatives of corporate agribusiness.

Other state and local advisory structures within the land grant college complex also reflect the narrow focus of the complex's research. USDA's Roland Robinson points out:

Many of the advisory groups, similar to those of the Department of Agriculture, are established along commodity and industry lines. Consequently they are oriented toward traditional research needs. The rural nonfarmer, the small farmer, the leaders of rural communities and the consumer are not usually represented on experiment station advisory committees.[12]

When Congress holds open hearings each year on appropriations for agricultural research, it is usually the representatives of these advisory and policy committees and their corporate agribusiness colleagues who most frequently appear before the legislators seeking to protect and promote their narrow economic interests. As *Hard Tomatoes, Hard Times* concluded:

Land grant policy is the product of a closed community. The administrators, academics and scientists, along with the USDA officials and corporate executives, have locked themselves into an inbred and even incestuous complex, and they are incapable of thinking beyond their self-interest and traditional concepts of agricultural research.

Following the Money

Controlling advisory committees and testifying before Congress are only two means by which corporate agribusiness plays a major role in determining agricultural research priorities. Corporate executives also sit on many land grant college boards of trustees, purchase research from experiment stations and colleges, hire land grant academics as private consultants, advise and

are advised by land grant officials, publish and distribute the writings of academics, provide scholarships and other educational support, and sponsor foundations that extend both grants and recognition to the land grant college community.

As the AAP researchers pointed out, however, money is the web of the tight relationship between agribusiness interests and their friends at the land grant colleges. It is estimated that the nation's land-grant research network consumes well over $2.39 billion a year in federal, state and private money.[13]

"Industry money goes to meet industry needs and whims, and these needs and whims largely determine the research program of land grant colleges."[14]

Since the prime contributors to the land grant complex are the major chemical, drug and oil corporations, it is no surprise that almost half of industry's research contributions to state agricultural experiment stations go to just four categories: insect control, weed control, plant and animal biology and "biological efficiency."

"Where does the corporation end and the land grant college begin?" the AAP report asks.

It is difficult to find the public interest in that tangle. These ties to industry raise the most serious questions about the subversion of scientific integrity and the selling of the public trust. If grants buy corporate research, do they also buy research scientists and agricultural experiment stations?

"Social Sleepwalking"

Research priorities in the land grant college complex are so skewed that vast areas of study are entirely neglected and forgotten. UC's William Friedland suggests that the complex's research establishment, in its concern to justify the expenditure of public dollars has not only failed to pay attention to the social consequences of its research but has even shaped the rural social sciences to justify the process.[15]

In what he terms "social sleepwalking" he charges that land grant researchers, with their production-oriented approach have in the past ignored a host of important issues.

And the issues put aside have to do precisely with the more humanistic aspects of agricultural research. Thus, while production scientists in agriculture argue that the humanistic elements are taken care of by the profusion of food production, its relative cheapness, its contribution to the U.S. strength and political position in the world, other issues are not only set aside and ignored but, indeed, actually suppressed.[16]

Friedland points to the various "pushes" and "pulls" that play such an important role in determining research priorities. Their existence is not happenstance, but rather the product of conscious actions on the part of political leaders, policy makers, and research administrators who are primarily concerned with maintaining the flow of research dollars.

The shaping of rural sociology has therefore not been fortuitous or accidental. It has not been formed simply by the 'academic freedom' of its participants interested in pursuing interesting intellectual and academic problems. Rather it has been shaped by the pulls of research dollars in some directions and the pushes provided by the impediments, hostilities, and persecutions of deviant individuals who have, indeed, manifested curiosity and critical capacities as academic and scholars.[17]

Another rural sociologist, Isao Fujimoto, from the Department of Applied Behavioral Sciences at the University of California - Davis, emphasizes various factors that frequently determine what area researchers choose to investigate. Such influences can be grouped into four major areas: scientific curiosity, funding, academic socialization and sensitivity to public issues. Each of these areas have subsidiary components, which are often interconnected.[18]

In analyzing the funding factors that influence what gets researched by the scientist, there is first the project. The influences that revolve around that project include faculty, the scientist's department, the college milieu, respective audiences and society. More specifically, such factors as the faculty member's proposal writing and grant hustling skills, the funding support associated with the particular department he or she is in, the ability of the College or University to attract money, the particular priorities and favorites of outside funding agencies, and the societal wish to freeze or release monies, all come into play.

The record of beneficiaries of research in the land grant college complex firmly establishes that it is those *who know how the system works* who have access.

Freedom of inquiry, Fujimoto reminds us, is not contingent only on the scientist's interest and curiosity; it is also affected by the orientation of the department and discipline with which the scientist is associated, the atmosphere of the college — whether it is undergoing new directions or holding to a steady state — the receptivity of available journal outlets that will accept or reject one's written findings and whether or not the scientist's social milieu rewards or ignores intellectual curiosity.

Scientific curiosity gets the scientist into the research system, *funding* determines what is worked on and the process of *academic socialization* affects the strategy taken — especially by the non-tenured faculty.

Research considerations in response to broader societal trends, be they in the food, population or energy crisis or *sensitivity to the concerns* of the consuming public such as questions concerning people displaced by technology, the impact of agrichemicals and a capital intensive agriculture to the quality of life in rural communities, can

sometimes be diversionary at best unless responses are congruent with the overall thrust of the College of Agriculture or the department of which the scientist is a part.[19]

Too often the land grant college complex, when it is convenient and self-serving to do so, takes credit for both direct and indirect effects of its research, but, when it is not in its best interest to do so, it disclaims responsibility for the consequences. For example, in the case of using DES as a growth stimulant in cattle, the developers took delight in the results and basked in its success. But, rather than acting on the problem when it was found hazardous to humans they simply referred it the Food and Drug Administration where a prolonged and costly political battle ensued.

Fujimoto concludes:

The University can not have it both ways — if it claims credit for both direct and indirect benefits, then it should be equally prepared to take responsibility for both the direct and indirect consequences — or at least act to anticipate what might happen. With freedom comes responsibility. If the University is to enjoy freedom of inquiry, attendant to this benefit is the responsibility to anticipate at least the consequences of the fruits of that freedom.[20]

Reaction within the academic community to recent attacks on the land-grant college complex's research priorities have ranged from those, such as the AAP in *Hard Tomatoes, Hard Times*, who see a concerted attempt to destroy the American family farmer, to more moderate criticism such as the observations of Frederick H. Buttel, Associate Professor of Rural Sociology at Cornell University.

While acknowledging that the land grant establishment has developed a "narrow technological path" for agriculture to follow, he expresses reservations whether "appropriate technology," an approach many current land-grant critics have urged the system to undertake instead, "can ensure the persistence or renaissance of the family farm."

I would argue that land-grant research has contributed to the differentiation among farmers and concentration of agricultural assets while also arguing that an equally significant output of the land-grant system may have been cultural rather than technological or purely economic.[21]

Professor Buttel sees the outlook of the land-grant (and the larger public agricultural research) system as one of continued declines in its autonomy in directing the course of technological change in U.S. agriculture.

Stagnation of public funding of agricultural research along with the rapid increase in the research capability of private sector firms will mean that the public agricultural research system will continue to be the minority component of the American agricultural research and development system. Private research will increasingly induce the nature of public sector research, rather than vice versa.[22]

There is also concern that the once sharp distinction between land-grant institutions and other universities and colleges is starting to blur. Carolyn J. Mooney, writing in the *Chronicle of Higher Education* observes:

> With their growing dependence on private fund raising, campaigns to improve quality and better applicants, and aggressive national research efforts, many land-grant universities are looking and acting more like the private research institutions that once mainly educated the elite.
>
> Private institutions, meanwhile, are stepping up their public service roles and focusing more attention on the needs of minority groups and others who previously relied on public institutions. And other public institutions such as urban universities and community colleges are equally concerned with educating a broad range of students and responding to their communities' economic needs.[23]

A 1986 report commissioned by the land-grant association also suggested that the relationship many land-grant universities have with the federal government is becoming as important — more important, in some cases — than their relationships with the states.[24]

Institutional Racism

> The night of segregation would have its deadening effects. These also can be measured in lack of funds and facilities which the 1890 institutions were compelled to endure for most of the twentieth century. It is impossible to measure the indirect effects which were even more profound, such as the costs of needless rural poverty, misery and disease and to the spiritual agony of those Americans who loved and worked diligently for democratic ideals.
>
> -Joel Schor, Historian, USDA/ERS
> Agricultural History and Rural History Branch.[25]

The second Morrill Act of 1890 made additional Federal money available to states for "separate but equal" funding for the establishment of black colleges. Seventeen southern and border states accepted such funds. Since that time, however, these "1890 colleges" have been victimized by an institutional racism that the land grant community continuingly and conveniently ignores.

Historically, the resource allocations that these "1890 colleges" receive from the USDA have been blatantly discriminatory. Even today, these colleges get but a fraction of the amount they deserve, an amount totally disproportionate to that of the white land grant colleges.

The Hatch Act of 1887 provided that Federal research money "shall be divided between such institutions as the legislature of such State shall direct." Later, the McIn-

tyre-Stennis Act, which authorized money for forestry research, gave the power of designation to the governor of each state. And the Smith-Lever Act, which authorizes funds for Extension Service, also turns appropriations over to the land-grant college selected by the State legislature.

The bill's author, Senator Hoke Smith of Georgia, was openly racist in introducing the legislation, declaring that his state would have nothing to do with extension funds if an equitable distribution of funds were required: "we do not ... want the fund if it goes to any but the white college."[26]

It was not until 1967 that the black colleges began receiving money under the federal cooperative extension program. Even with the efforts in recent years to increase the funding for black colleges, USDA continues to thwart the process, as was seen in their "coordination" scheme in 1971; after Congress appropriated an additional $12.6 million to the black colleges, the Department devised a plan whereby the white land grant colleges were to remain in charge of the resources.

The action provoked a letter to USDA from Peter H. Schuck of the Center for Study of Responsive Law and author of a paper "Black Land-Grant Colleges: Separate and Still Unequal."

> The core of the new procedure is a "research coordinating committee." Obviously, no responsible person can be against the coordination of research, and the 1890 colleges are no exception. But the [plan] as established by the Cooperative State Research Service guidelines, is less a device for coordinating research between autonomous institutions than an instrument for the effective control by the 1862 colleges of the research funds intended by Congress for the 1890 colleges.

The effect of the aforementioned $12.6 million can be measured by the fact that in 1971 the 1890 institutions and Tuskegee University were receiving .004 percent of the total CSRS appropriations; in 1972 the percentage was 10.7 percent, and ten years later it was 9.5 percent, an amount less than that given for all the system's special research grants.[27]

Currently, almost half of all black Americans who graduate from college receive their degrees from these historically black institutions. Nearly 90 percent of the students in these colleges rely on federal student-aid programs, twice the number for all college students.[28]

The Reagan administration sought to portray itself as in the forefront of extending more financial aid to black colleges after issuing an executive order in 1981 increasing support for the nation's traditionally black colleges and universities. Subsequently, two reports were sent to the White House by the U.S. Department of Education suggesting that federal aid to black schools had increased markedly.

In 1984, however, Joyce Payne of the National Association of State Universities and Land Grant Colleges complained that the Administration's figures were "highly distorted." She charged that after subtracting large federal grants that went to a few well-known schools, such as Howard University in Washington, D.C., other historically black colleges and universities received but 32 percent, or about $197 million of the $606 million Reagan officials claimed were distributed in 1983.[29]

In 1987 the Congress, recognizing their growing financial plight, increased by 50 percent federal aid to the nation's black colleges and universities. The $73.1 million appropriation compared to the average annual spending bill of $43 million between 1984 and 1986, according to Congressional and Education Department officials. By 1990, USDA's budget allocation to support 1890 land-grant institutions and Tuskegee University was $76.2 million.

It was in 1984 that Ronald Reagan signed into law a $50 million appropriation bill designed to provide basic research facilities in the nation's 17 black land-grant institutions. His signature, however, signaled recognition of only one aspect of a long-standing injustice. The other aspect, as USDA historian Joel Schor has pointed out, the continuation of discrimination on the basis of color and sex "has been virtually ignored by the current administration, and efforts to ensure civil rights compliance have been effectively subverted since 1980. Compliance reviews and the processing of routine civil rights complaints have all but ceased."[30]

Due in large part to the lack of funding, many black land-grant colleges are able to offer only a limited number of graduate programs in agriculture while their white counterparts award doctorates in an array of agricultural areas.

Some argue that the 1890 colleges simply duplicate courses available at the other land-grant institutions in their state. In fact, the 1890 schools must often take a different approach to a particular subject. For example, in addition to focusing on how farmers can more profitably raise pigs, researchers at Missouri's Lincoln University also must include techniques that can be used by farmers who do not have capital to invest or who can not readily borrow money.[31]

Even with the meager federal funds the 1890s now receive there is no requirement, as there is with the white land-grant institutions, that the funds be matched by state appropriations. For example, in Mississippi, Alcorn State University, an 1890 institution has received $2.5 million in federal funds for its extension programs and $135,000 from the state. Meanwhile, 57 percent of Mississippi State's $20 million budget for cooperative extension programs comes from state funds.[32]

The situation on both the federal and state level regarding the black land-grant colleges remains a classic "chicken and egg" dilemma. As one black college administrator explains, "They say we don't receive more grants because we don't have comparable graduate programs. We say we don't have those programs because we don't receive the grants."[33]

What the Extension Service Does

Extension Service was designed to reach the greatest number of people in rural America with the benefits of the land-grant colleges' research and information. A look at its evolution will help explain its failure to abide by its mandate.

In addition to the co-opting of agrarian populism in 1896, when it became a sacrificial lamb on the "cross of gold" issue, it also lost much of its impetus due to a temporary rise in farm prices which began to take place immediately after the McKinley election. Although, as Grant McConnell in his *The Decline of Agrarian Democracy* reminds us, many farmers still believed that the enemy of democracy was the power that the capitalists were fashioning from economic inequality, others were convinced that better prices made the faltering agrarian movement unnecessary.[34]

Also, with the disappearance of cheap, abundant land and the push for acceptance of a new agricultural technology, farmers' dependence on the very commercial and industrial interests they had earlier distrusted tended to blunt their efforts to achieve genuine agrarian democracy.

It was also at this time that these same business interests were rapidly mobilizing and taking the necessary action to prevent any political or economic revival of what they viewed as a genuinely serious threat to the established order. They sought to ensure that any "reorganized agriculture" would be firmly on the side of capitalism. One of the means they determined to obtain this goal was to mobilize in their service one of the cardinal tenets of the American democratic ideal — education.

Because farmers were considered notoriously conservative when it came to adopting new methods of farming, by the late 1800s corporate America realized that farmers would have to be shown the clear advantages of "new farm technology."

In rightly attempting to convince Southern farmers of the advantages of diversified farming as opposed to their traditional and often disastrous dependence on a monoculture system of farming, Dr. Seaman A. Knapp, a former college president and a farm and land company manager, helped establish demonstration farms which, with the backing of the USDA's Bureau of Plant Industry, soon led some farmers to see positive results of new methods.[35]

From Knapp's efforts came the concept of the county agent system, county agent being a contraction of "county agricultural demonstration agent." In 1903 his idea received the backing and financial support of the Rockefeller-endowed General Education Board, which sought to elevate demonstration work to a form of respected education.

Agricultural colleges, however, soon became alarmed over the Board's actions because the stimulus for demonstration work was now coming from groups outside the education community. Soon the Association of American Agricultural Colleges and Experiment Stations (AAACES) established a special section on "Extension," designed to extend more convenient forms of educational programs to those areas where regular courses of instruction were not available.

The complexities of such a system rapidly became apparent to many educators in the nation's agricultural colleges. As these land grant colleges began producing more graduates who would enter government service, the idea of agricultural education as the means to increasing production at all costs and thereby make farming grander in scale and more prosperous to a few began to dominate the thinking at USDA.

Corporate America Discovers Education

Although this "extension" movement grew in the century's first decade, farmers were still reluctant to accept all of the new technology, despite what the educators, the USDA and other interested parties within the government, such as Roosevelt's Commission on Country Life, sought to foist upon them.

Means were soon evolved, to convince balking farmers to make such changes. Local businessmen and bankers, who regularly determined whether farmers would get credit, were placed on the demonstration farm committees and urged to convince their customers to "cooperate" with Knapp's people. Meanwhile, the focus of nearly all farm legislation after 1909, culminating in the passage of the Smith-Lever Extension Act of 1914, was to underscore and institutionalize the county agent system.

Not only was the local business community an enthusiastic supporter of the movement, but soon a large number of national business organizations publicly endorsed and heavily supported the effort. The agricultural committee of the American Bankers Association, for example, reported in 1913:

The majority of the members of our committee have devoted their time to the more essential question of developing educational features, both in schools and on the farms, to enable the farmer and his family to live a broader and happier life and develop the business in which they are engaged to the highest state of efficiency, thereby making them more successful producers, *a better credit risk, and a more contented and prosperous people ...*

Nearly all farmers welcome the cooperation of bankers in furthering their interests, as bankers welcome the farmers in aiding them to *secure a scientific system of currency*. We all have to work together, and no interests ought to work together more than bankers and farmers.[36] (emphasis added)

The obvious references to "a better credit risk", "a more *contented* and prosperous people," and "to secure a scientific system of currency" gives ample evidence that corporate America saw this education movement not simply in altruistic terms but as an important instrument in its concerted effort to eliminate all vestiges of agrarian populism.

Despite general enthusiasm for the Extension Service there were, however, voices of apprehension heard among the colleges. In 1913 Agricultural Dean Eugene Davenport rather prophetically warned a AAACES convention:

Given four or five thousand local agents scattered among the farmers of all the congressional districts and under the practical control of a department which depends for its very life upon annual appropriations by Congress, all operating under the interlocking scheme of the new Lever bill, and we should have had constructed and at work the most gigantic political machine ever devised. That it would be used, there is abundant evidence already at hand.[37]

Form Follows Function

The initial Smith-Lever Act authorized $3.48 million for the Extension Service, with $10,000 to go to each of the then 48 states and the remaining $3 million to be distributed to each state in proportion to its rural population, with the states providing matching funds.

Since 1914, funding for the Extension Service has soared. Today its yearly appropriation is in the hundreds of millions; spending $369.2 million in 1990 to finance the work of 54 state Extension Services and the more than 12,000 county agents serving the nation's 3,150 counties. Funds are allocated to the Extension Service's four major program areas: Agriculture and Natural Resources; Home Economics and Nutrition; 4-H and Other Youth Work, and Community and Rural Development.

While these programs overlap some, each has a specific function within the rural community. Understanding the objectives of each program, in relation to the structure of agriculture today, is crucial in evaluating ES's work.

Agriculture and Natural Resources (ANR)   The largest program area within the Extension Service, ANR historically has focused much more on agricultural production, marketing and business-management programs than on natural resource programs. It consists of a broadly defined set of programs and activities providing "informal education" and technical assistance to agricultural producers, business firms, consumers and the like.

In an effort to meet its main objective of providing "informal education," ANR:

• Collects, interprets and disseminates information by linking farmers and other clients with the research conducted by land-grant universities, the USDA, and other government agencies.

• Teaches agricultural skills and principles and provides other assistance in an effort to help individuals and groups develop the capacity to solve problems.

• Carries out programs designed to help farmers and farm businesses identify and diagnose problems, formulate alternative solutions and locate other public and private sources of assistance.

Home Economics and Nutrition   From 1900 through the 1920s, this program was directed primarily at combatting rural poverty. During the Depression and World War II, the program moved into more remote rural areas and put more emphasis on farm management and home finance skills.

Consumer-education and home improvement programs moved to the forefront of the program's activities through the 1950s. Through the 1960s and into the

1970s, the program relied increasingly on the media to convey its message to urban and suburban families. Focusing on consumer education, child development and family relations, the program started using paraprofessionals to assist with its work.

Today, extension home-economics programs are aimed at providing information on food nutrition, good consumer practices, safe and affordable housing and furnishings, the best use of textiles, human development, and family health and safety.

4-H and Other Youth Work   The first USDA-sponsored agricultural youth club, which was to become known in 1911 as the 4-H Club (for Head, Hands, Heart and Health), was organized in 1907. The youth programs, while not specifically mandated, came as a result of the Smith-Lever Act of 1914. In its earliest days, 4-H was a means of demonstrating new, innovative agricultural technology to dubious farmers in a non-threatening way. Later it evolved into a method of enhancing vocational training for rural and farm youths.

Today 4-H focuses on "Boy and Girl Scout" type activities as well as on providing social and technical training, although it has a somewhat distorted public image as an organization devoted to instilling agricultural skills among farm youths. A joint program of USDA, state land-grant universities and county governments, 4-H also is supported by private citizens, industry and foundations.

Community and Rural Development   Rather than promote a particular philosophy of community development, this program is aimed at helping communities assess their development needs and problems — whether they involve population booms, inadequate housing, the uneven distribution and high cost of health services, unemployment and low wages, lack of safe water and sewer systems or increased competition for natural resources — and to develop their own solutions.

The community itself ostensibly selects the problems to be worked on, makes decisions and takes action to reach the objectives it sets forth. The ES, through staffs located in almost every county in the nation, is supposed to help the community reach its goals. County Extension agents, supported by state specialists with technical knowledge in most major disciplines, are also supposed to provide assistance to local citizens seeking to effect change in their communities.

While ES's priority list looks impressive on paper, an examination of its changes in staff years (SY) from 1971 to 1980 alone show a somewhat different story. For example, in that ten-year period its staff years devoted to agricultural crop production and management increased by 103 percent while human nutrition work declined 42 percent; staff years devoted to agricultural livestock production and management increased 74 percent; staff time directed toward human housing and the home environment decreased by 48 percent. As overall attention to production protection moved up 51 percent, staff time to various people and rural community projects dropped nine percent.

Living Up to the Mandate?

Prior to the 1970s, the Extension Service went about its business without having to prove that it was living up to those objectives outlined above — no one had even dared raise any challenging questions. All that changed with the release of *Hard Tomatoes, Hard Times*. The controversial report raised more than a few eyebrows when it stated:

> Like its other partners in the land grant complex, the colleges of agriculture and the agricultural experiment stations, Extension Service has not lived up to its mandate for service to rural people: The focus of ES primarily is on rural 'clients' who need it least, ignoring the obvious needs of the vast majority of rural Americans.
>
> The rural poor, in particular, are badly served by Extension, receiving a pitiful percentage of the time of extension 'professionals,' while drawing band-aid assistance from the highly visible Nutrition Aides program and irrelevant attention from the 4-H programs.
>
> The civil rights record of ES comes close to being the worst in government, even though the effectiveness of ES largely depends on its ability to reach minorities.
>
> Policy-making within ES fails to involve most rural people, and USDA has failed utterly to exercise its power to re-direct the priorities and programs of the state extension services.

Hard Tomatoes, Hard Times documented these charges with evidence drawn from Extension reports, congressional hearings and interviews with Extension officials. Some of its specific findings were that:

• Extension programs have benefited primarily the largest producers while they have "slighted the pressing needs of the vast majority of America's farmers ..." A 1968 inquiry discovered that the Extension Service devoted more than half of its efforts to farmers in the top 25 percent income bracket. This bias reflects the wishes of State Extension directors who, when surveyed for the inquiry, expressed a preference for a "heavy emphasis on work with highly specialized farms and other commercial farms, cooperatives, farm-product purchasers and processors ..."

• The Extension Service has pushed high-technology agriculture to the detriment of smaller producers. Extension agents have acted as salesmen for the agricultural research, research generated by their colleagues in the land-grant college system, which largely serves the needs of corporate agribusiness and larger producers. By persuading farmers to adopt expensive machinery developed by the agricultural research centers, the Extension Service has supported changes in the structure of agriculture that have driven millions of small farmers off the land and benefited only the largest and most prosperous survivors.

Pete Daniel, agricultural curator at the Smithsonian Institute in Washington, D.C., has written in "Breaking the Land," a 1985 study of the mechanical revolution in cotton, rice and tobacco, that "single-minded pursuit of higher production" by government and private industry created havoc among the South's small farmers and has changed, perhaps forever, the face of farming in that region of the country.

The Extension Service worked with middle-class farmers, people who could buy into mechanized agriculture. The experiment stations worked on science that only those with the money could buy. People on the bottom could not take advantages of the changes.[38]

• The Extension Service, the AAP evaluation added, has had close ties with corporate agribusiness: "... the agents frequently are focused so intently on corporate needs that they literally have become tax-supported extensions of corporate agribusiness." As one example, Extension agents set up workshops and other technical-assistance programs designed to improve the management efficiency of corporate agribusiness firms.

The Extension Service's ties to the agrichemical industry, which has made substantial financial contributions to the Service, have been especially strong. With industry assistance, Extension agents have actively promoted the use of specific chemical poisons and herbicides.

• From its inception, the Extension Service has been intimate with the American Farm Bureau Federation. Many individual chapters of the Farm Bureau, in fact, were direct outgrowths of the local farmer advisory committees formed as a requirement for ES funding. Although the formal ties between the Farm Bureau and the Extension Service were severed in 1954, a close informal relationship persists.

• The Extension Service, as shown in the previous chapter, has been notoriously racist in both its hiring and delivery of services. The U.S. Commission on Civil Rights, in reviewing the compliance of Federal agencies with Title VI (which prohibits racial discrimination in the use of Federal funds), characterized the ES's performance as "grossly inadequate" and "marked by unparalleled procrastination."

In recent years, several minority groups have filed lawsuits seeking redress for the Service's poor record in hiring minorities and dispensing services to them. This failure is particularly shocking in light of the dramatic decline in the number of black farmers in the United States and the continuing lower incomes realized by those black farmers who have managed to hang on.

These ES failures have been attributed partly to the autonomy of county agents and the lack of Federal control. Although statutes give the Federal administrator "final review" of state Extension programs and budgets, that power rarely has been used to overrule or redirect state plans.

"A Marked Lack of Analytical Thinking"

As a result of the controversy and debate following the publication of *Hard Tomatoes, Hard Times*, Congress directed the Secretary of Agriculture to evaluate the "economic and social consequences" of the ES's programs. That report, issued in January 1980, consisted of two main sections. The bulk of the report was an internal assessment undertaken jointly by the USDA and the State Cooperative Extension Services; the remainder presented a critique of that internal evaluation by a specially established "Citizen's Review Panel."

The evaluation itself was largely favorable to the ES. This surprised no one since it was carried out by Extension's own staff under the guidance of Federal and state Extension officials. The Executive Summary praised the basic thrust of Extension work in the area of agriculture and natural resources:

By increasing the rate of adoption of new technology and knowledge generated by research, agricultural Extension programs have contributed significantly to the growth in productivity and efficiency of U.S. agriculture ... *True, these same developments also have led to fewer and larger farms.* But by making technology and new knowledge available to more producers, Extension seems to have helped a large number of producers remain in farming ...(emphasis added)

The evaluation of Extension activities also noted that "medium and large farm operators have more contact with Extension programs than small farm operators: only in recent years has a conscious effort been made to implement programs specifically for small, limited-resource farmers."

Despite such admissions, the critique of the evaluation developed by the independent Citizen's Review Panel (and published in the review's appendix) noted that the report was characterized by "a marked lack of analytical thinking." The panel cited as an example the report's assertion that, because Extension programs rely on voluntary participation, "those farmers least inclined to seek assistance have not been served as well as those who have been motivated and able to ask for and utilize the program."

The Citizen panel asked, "why is the responsibility to become involved in Extension placed on the user and not the provider of services? Doesn't the failure of Extension to reach those unable to ask for and use the program imply a criticism of the program itself?"

Expressing concern that in its review of Extension programs Congress would be misled by the published evaluation, the panel recommended that the document be viewed only as an in-house report.

Later, and quite surprisingly, the USDA's 1981 summary report on the structure of agriculture, *A Time to Choose*, also questioned one of its own all-time favorite shibboleths — the "trickle down theory": "Research and extension programs have been generally targeted towards those large-scale, innovative producers, reasoning that the demonstrated benefits would trickle down to the smaller farmers ... This strategy now needs to be reexamined."

Yet, seven years later, even as a USDA panel studying the future of cooperative extension programs prepared to issue its recommended changes for the program, the Reagan administration was seeking to drastically cut the federal budget for programs affiliated with land grant institutions, arguing that only those that directly help farmers should be financed.

"The ultimate outcome could be that the land-grant system as it exists today will have largely disappeared," one independent report on the future of land-grant colleges concludes. Prepared by the Northeast Regional Council, a planning agency that coordinates agricultural research, teaching and cooperative extension, the study adds: "Enough signals are present to suggest it as a possibility in the smaller, more poorly funded and poorly supported colleges in those states in which production agriculture or forestry are perceived to be relatively unimportant to the state economy."[39]

Despite such gloomy predictions and the variety of aforementioned drawbacks of ES, many of its critics still believe that the Service can be useful. There are millions of people — independent family farmers, farm workers, small-town businesses and governments, non-farm rural people and others — who desperately need its help and services. These, of course, are the people the ES was originally designed to serve, reaching down through county agents and directly into the communities and homes of rural people.

But, as *Hard Tomatoes, Hard Times* has cautioned, reforming the Extension Service so that it truly meets the needs of the small farmer and rural poor will not be easy. It will mean "getting out of the traveling salesmen's sample kit. It will mean a change in attitude at the top, and probably a change in personnel at the bottom. Such a change will not come from within."

Chapter Twenty-Six

The Enemy Within

*"It seems to me that it's a good thing to empha-
size the complete interest of all the rest of the
economy in having relatively few people produce the necessary food. We have done an
extraordinary job in America in getting that
thing done. We want to continue to do it ... ".*
- Allan B. Kline, President,
American Farm Bureau Federations
(1947 - 1955) CBS Radio, March 19, 1949

Listening to the president of the nation's largest
"farm organization" publicly praise the eradication of
millions of farm families appears at first blush a mind-
boggling paradox — until one considers the true nature
of its source. Increasing numbers of American family
farmers are arriving at the long overdue conclusion that
they have no greater enemy than the one within their
own ranks — the American Farm Bureau Federation
(AFBF).

Boasting some 3.3 million "member families" in 48
states and Puerto Rico and an annual budget of $10
million with a staff of 250, this 71-year old organization
claims over 2800 county Farm Bureaus throughout the
nation.[1] Although its critics dispute the claim, the
American Farm Bureau is reportedly governed by voting
delegates to its annual meeting of member state organizations. Each state is entitled to a minimum of one
voting delegate plus one additional delegate for every
15,000 members or "major portion thereof."

In addition to its president, vice president, secretary,
treasurer and general counsel the AFBF has a 25-mem-
ber board of directors, with 21 elected for two-year terms
by the voting delegates of member-state Farm Bureaus.
Its national headquarters are located in Park Ridge,
Illinois, a Chicago suburb, which serves as general
offices for the president, administrative assistant,
general counsel, treasurer and seven of the Federation's
eight operating divisions.

Those divisions, according to the American Farm
Bureau, include:
• *Commodities* A structure designed for farmers and
ranchers to "reconcile differences" between producers of
a wide variety of commodities. Market research and
development receive a "high priority" in this division's
activities. Much of the Farm Bureau's marketing activity
is carried out through its own affiliate, the American
Agricultural Marketing Association.

• *Information* An information program designed to
reach Bureau members, the nonfarm public, and the
media.
• *Member Relations* A number of activities, including
membership and organizational efforts, women's, rural
crime detection, rural health, home and farm safety
programs, political education programs, leadership
training for personnel and volunteer leaders, and Young
Farmer and Rancher programs are coordinated through
this division.
• *Natural and Environmental Resources* This division, with a "professional staff of specialists" in resource
management, farm chemicals and energy, works closely
with the national affairs staff and with State Farm
Bureaus in the preparation of materials on land use,
water rights, conservation programs, pollution control,
wildlife management, farm chemicals and energy conservation.
• *Economic Research* A senior economist and his
associates serve as "advisors" on "economic factors"
affecting Bureau members.
• *Field Services* A director and eight Farm Bureau field
representatives work with state Farm Bureau staff,
leadership and affiliated Farm Bureau economic service
divisions on program and organizational matters.
• *Personnel and Administrative Services* This division
is responsible for personnel administration, supplies and
furnishings and for the operation and maintenance of
"Speedline." The AFBF also operates a very active
National Affairs office in Washington, D.C., headed by
the Bureau's secretary and a staff of registered lobbyists,
which maintains "daily contact" with members of
Congress, legislative staffs and other Federal agencies.

State Farm Bureau affiliated insurance companies
are also connected to the AFBF. The American Agricultural Insurance Company, a Farm Bureau affiliate, is a
multiline, multibillion dollar stock company providing
state insurance companies "reinsurance coverage
against many types of casualty and property risk."
American Farm Bureau Service Company, providing
"group purchasing services" to state FB members under
the SAFEMARK brand, is another Farm Bureau affiliate.
A wide variety of farm input goods and services under
the SAFEMARK brand are available locally to members
in 42 states and Puerto Rico through 3,600 outlets in
2,300 counties.

Keeping Farmers From Figuring Out the Meaning
The Farm Bureau's basic unit is the county Farm
Bureau, which usually consists of informal, subordinate

local units which carry on discussion groups in members' homes. In some states the Farm Bureau's business activities are conducted through the county units, whereas in other counties that unit may be no more than an activity carried on by the county extension agent. The primary objective of the county unit is to attract and hold the interest of members and secure new members. This unit also reportedly retains the largest share of membership dues.

At the next level is the state Farm Bureau Federation which carries on activities similar to the county bureaus, but on a much larger scale. The predominant concerns of the state Farm Bureau are education and legislation.

The American Farm Bureau Federation is at the next level and often acts as a holding company, a federation of federations. It is quite removed from the grass roots, which it so frequently invokes. Its functions include lobbying, publicity and information, organization, research, legal and international affairs, rural youth, and commodity marketing. The American Farm Bureau president is usually the spokesperson for the Federation, assisted by the legislative representative, vice president, the federation counsel, the secretary-treasurer and the board of directors.

Currently, AFBF is led by Dean Ralph Kleckner, the son of an Iowa tenant farmer who now owns a 550-acre farm in the state and was president of the Iowa State Farm Bureau for ten years. He also serves as a member of the board of advisors for Iowa State University's College of Agriculture.[2]

The Bureau's president, whose salary is a reported $100,000 a year, is subject to the control of the board of directors, an elective body picked on the basis of regional representation. When the board is not in session, an executive committee composed of a small number of board members has authority and many believe that this committee actually controls the AFBF.

While policy for the Federation is reportedly determined at its annual convention, critics have charged that the American Farm Bureau's executive committee actually determines the organization's priorities, issues a directive to the state and county federations which in turn "rubber stamp" the proposal (to give it the illusion of having grass roots support) and then "yo-yo" it back up the line of federations to the national office.

As one former woman officer of a county Farm Bureau describes it: "Most people talk to convey a meaning, the Farm Bureau talks to keep you from figuring out the meaning."[3]

By engaging in such a "legislative process" the American Farm Bureau has turned its national convention into nothing more than a week's vacation for a few hundred elite members with a break or two for self-congratulatory pep rallies. In 1984, for example, while many of the nation's farmers, faced with foreclosures and bankruptcy, were expressing bitter outrage over the fact that the "nation's largest farm organization" was publicly demeaning their crisis, the American Farm Bureau waltzed off to its annual convention in Hawaii.

A Jealous Suitor

Critics of the American Farm Bureau have offered several different interpretations of its role in American agriculture.

Some suggest that the Farm Bureau is merely a functionary of the Extension Service, created to serve as a pressure group to extract appropriations from Congress for the ES and thereby cripple or destroy any would-be rivals for farmer loyalty. Another interpretation is that the Farm Bureau is merely used as a vehicle for a few power-hungry mercenary officers, while others claim that the organization is a self-styled tool of corporate agribusiness.

The Farm Bureau's history, structure and power, suggest that it is an exotic mixture of all of these things. It is also an extremely jealous suitor which has sought throughout history to hone a sharply delineated class structure within U.S. agriculture.

Although agrarian populism had been politically disposed of by both the government and the business community at the turn of the century, its influence certainly did not disappear for many farmers still distrusted the guardians of economic power and their paternalism that was masked behind the aegis of "extending education" to the rural countryside.

By the turn of the century, the agrarian populist tradition of protest was being pursued by the Farmers' Educational and Cooperative Union of America, or the National Farmers' Union as it would become known. Founded in 1902, it sought "to secure equity", with a decided emphasis on a "just price" and "parity," and "to discourage the credit and mortgage system," while declaring its determination "to eliminate gambling in farm products by Boards of Trade, Cotton Exchanges and other speculators." Its constitution maintained that farmers were a class of people who must work together and not be drawn into politics as party operatives, which many farmers still saw as the main reason for the 1896 disaster.

While the Farmers' Union sought to strengthen itself, the other veteran of 19th century agrarianism, the Grange, turned its attention to more general legislative issues and, as the nation became increasingly involved in World War I, devoted most of its attention to peace and prohibition.

A number of other farm-oriented organizations also sprung up in the years immediately after the demise of the Populists, such as the American Society of Equity, the Farmers' Equity Union, and the Gleaners.

Stopping "Bolshevism"

No one group of farmers at this time, however, caused as much corporate consternation as the Non-Partisan League, formed in North Dakota in 1915. As previously noted, the League targeted bankers, grain dealers and railroads for bitter invective.

The Non-Partisan League was indeed a class organization with a class program and a class strategy — to capture and make use of the machinery of the state. State ownership and operation of banks and grain elevators so as to end usury and gross exploitation was openly advocated by the League, and achieved a large measure of success in the Northern Plains between 1915 and 1920.

Against this background of fledgling "radical" farm organizations and the emergence of the county agent as a key figure in U.S. agriculture, the AFBF was born.

The Smith-Lever Act had already regularized the county agent system, reduced the status of the land grant colleges as participants in the "extension movement," and established Congress as the arbiter of questions relating to agricultural extension work. To facilitate the AFBF's work, which was primarily education aimed at improving technical productivity, the county agents were directed to work with the leaders and groups of farmers. This required that they also provide organization among farmers.

In 1911, the Binghamton (NY) Chamber of Commerce set up a bureau within its own organization to sponsor a county agent. With the support of the Lackawanna Railroad this business group was called the "farm bureau." USDA soon adopted the name for any group deemed a cooperating county organization.

In these early years the county agent was presumed to be under the direction of the college Extension director, but as local farm bureaus began to federate on a state basis and eventually gave birth to the American Farm Bureau Federation in 1920, this relationship became largely illusory; the real power was transferred from the colleges to corporate agribusiness through Washington.

In addition to the monetary support provided by the Lackawanna, the Rockefeller-backed General Education Board, and other large agricultural input corporations, the Chicago Board of Trade also helped in the formation of these country farm bureaus by providing necessary funding. In 1922, Robert McDougall, the Board's president boasted:

The Board of Trade was a sort of grandfather to the Farm Bureau movement. A cash grant of $1,000 was made to each of the first 100 Farm Bureaus formed, beginning with the one in New York and spreading to Iowa and other Middle Western states.[4]

Typical of the few outcries against this transfer of power was Dr. Clarence Ousley's in 1915:

It seemed to me, from the brief allusion to the subject in the paper by Dr. Galloway, that this Bureau movement was a scheme whereby a progressive body of farmers took advantage of the department and college in order exclusively to utilize the services of the county agent.

If that is what the bureau means, then it is an unwholesome movement. The whole tendency of agricultural education is to benefit the man who is already progressive. It does not reach the man who is in most need, the neglected man, who neglects himself, who does not seek knowledge, and to whom the colleges and the department, through the county agent, should go as a missionary.[5]

During World War I the county agents not only became increasingly involved in commercial activities as part of a growing movement for bureau federation. There was also a shift in the nature of the relationship between them and the Farm Bureau. From the role of an educator and leader they increasingly became "managers" of the various local Farm Bureaus; a government bureaucrat in a private organization. Paradoxically, at the same time, while public funding of their work was increasing (93 percent by 1924), private funding was rapidly disappearing. By 1919 the USDA was so enthusiastic over the movement that Secretary David F. Houston was calling upon farmers to join or form farm bureaus in order to "stop bolshevism."[6]

When delegates from 31 states met in Chicago in 1920 and formally inaugurated the American Farm Bureau Federation, they made it quite clear that their objectives were economic and political: "To keep control of our food products" until they reach consumers, to stop any policy "that will align farmers with the radicals of other organizations," to "stabilize the nation," to "put agriculture into proper relationship with the rest of the world."

"I stand as a rock against radicalism," the Federation's first president, James Howard, proclaimed at the time.[7]

Depression and Remission

Although the AFBF did exercise some of its newfound political power in the 1920s by playing a key role in putting together the aforementioned "Farm Bloc," it refrained from becoming a mass movement among farmers. McConnell explains that through the farm depression of the decade the conduct of the Farm Bureau can be regarded as

the substantial return on the investment in concern for agricultural welfare which business groups had made in the preceding period. These groups may not have understood the exact significance of their own steps, but their measures were effective in diverting farm organizations away from 'radical' channels.[8]

Eventually, the Farm Bureau became engaged in the battle to pass the McNary-Haughton bill. It also joined with agricultural academicians, government bureaucrats and corporate agribusiness in defining "the farm problem" of the era as one of crop surpluses. By the end of the decade its president Sam Thompson had resigned to accept a seat on the ill-fated Federal Farm Board and the organization was well on its way to clarifying its role in agribusiness as furthering the interests of an elite class of large, commercial agricultural producers.

However, in the early 1920s the Farm Bureau had yet to fully define its purpose, being formed less around an idea than a bureaucracy, so it soon became merely a broker of ideas in farm policy, which it remains to the present day. On the other hand, its early efforts to build a base around the cooperative movement were beset by internal factionalism and regional cleavage.

Meanwhile, the bureau became involved in a number of questionable business alliances with chemical companies, cement associations, power and lumber interests, canning jar manufacturers, and grocery chain stores. Such behavior evoked a thunderous denunciation from Nebraska's famed senator George Norris: "The time will come when the rank and file of American farmers will realize by whom they are being deceived."[9]

In his early and unprecedented critical analysis, *The TRUTH About the Farm Bureau*, Dale Kramer characterized the organization's status in the 1920s in words as appropriate for that time as they are for farmers seventy years later:

> And so in the hour of the American farmer's greatest need, with corn at ten cents a bushel, wheat at a quarter, cotton at a few cents a pound, with foreclosures sweeping like a prairie fire across the farm lands, the Farm Bureau leadership was completely bankrupt. They had quit even a pretense of leadership. It was left to others to win the moratoriums, to prove to Washington that the farmers at last demanded action and would have it.[10]

Not So Strange Bedfellows

When Franklin Roosevelt started his journey down a "new and untrod path" for American agriculture, his principal vehicle was to become the Agricultural Adjustment Administration. Because FDR wanted to get his program launched immediately, the USDA determined that it would be most effective to utilize an existing "grass roots" apparatus, namely the Extension Service. While the relationship between the Farm Bureau and the ES had withered somewhat throughout the 1920s, the Farm Bureau now saw the ES as an expedient tool for bolstering its own organizational apparatus.

As the AAA program was implemented, particularly in the South, stories of fraud and influence by the Ku Klux Klan circulated, government checks were diverted to creditors of actual farmers and tenants were excluded from AAA payments. This situation, which came about primarily because the AAA programs in the region were organized under the direction of the large planters with the county agents and the Farm Bureau acting as a means of organization, was a major contributing cause to the aforementioned 1935 USDA "lawyer purge."

McDonnell, in tracing the success of the Farm Bureau in the early years of the New Deal, points out:

> By the decision to use Extension Service in administering the AAA, the [USDA] had helped identify the Farm Bureau with the administration of the program. The results had been, on the one hand, a vast increase in the strength and influence of the Farm Bureau and, on the other hand, a great financial boon to the type of farmers who were the natural clientele of the Farm Bureau.[11]

After the Supreme Court voided the AAA in 1936 the Farm Bureau moved swiftly. Within seven weeks it had presented a soil conservation plan which contained many of the essentials of the AAA plan. After Congress enacted a similar plan, local administration of it was reorganized from the previous locally-controlled associations based on commodities, to local groups consolidated into "county agricultural conservation associations."

This reorganization was a coup for the Farm Bureau. The administrative function was now general and not divided among dozens of different commodity groups. It paralleled the local Bureau structure, and it was more amenable to the direction of the county agents; in some areas, like the south, the county agent became secretary of the local association.

The farm legislation of 1938 gave the Farm Bureau most of what it wanted: soil conservation, acreage allotments (voluntary, with benefit payments), commodity credit loans, marketing quotas, crop insurance, and parity payments. Many of these provisions, however, were euphemisms for direct subsidies to large, commercial producers, further strengthening the FB's efforts to create an elite corps of food producers.

For even as the Farm Bureau was publicly backing many of Roosevelt's progressive measures designed to help farmers, and in some cases taking the credit for them, its real sympathies were with the interests of corporate agribusiness. For example, in the late 1920s the Farm Bureau openly aligned itself with the American Cyanamid Corporation and other large power companies in opposing government development of the Muscle Shoals power plant in Florence, Alabama, originally designed as a means to manufacture cheap fertilizer. However, after the establishment by the Federal government of the Tennessee Valley Authority (TVA), the FB took credit for the government's operation of Muscle Shoals in the 1930s.[12]

Meanwhile, as Roosevelt was attempting to win new rights for labor the Farm Bureau was playing a major role in excluding agriculture and farm labor from the provisions of the 1937 National Labor Relations Act, a militant position it maintains to the present day. In addition, the FB has a long record of helping pass state measures severely restricting organized labor.

In Arkansas, for example, the Farm Bureau worked with Pappy ("Pass the Biscuits") O'Daniel's Christian American Association to enact just such anti-labor legislation. When questioned about its support of such work Bureau President Ed O'Neal told a Congressional committee that it wasn't such a bad idea if farmers joined the Ku Klux Klan since every farmer should join something.[13]

On other fronts too the AFBF became increasingly active on behalf of narrow business interests. When FDR announced his seven-point economic stabilization plan to control inflation at the beginning of World War II, a major emergency farm conference was called in Washington. O'Neal and Eric Johnston of the U.S. Chamber of Commerce served as keynote speakers.

Although their efforts would fail in the Congress, what emerged from this conference was a strategy built around business backing farmers to jack up farm price levels for the duration of the war so business could increase consumer prices without taking the blame.

The defeat of that plan did not deter the Farm Bureau as President O'Neal would work closely during the war years with the Food Industry Committee, whose members represented such corporate agribusiness giants as General Foods, Del Monte, Brookfield Dairy, Pillsbury and Nabisco, H.J. Heinz and others.[14]

This "unholy alliance's" most significant victory would come later when Congress ordered the OPA to let prices of finished cotton goods rise so the "processors can pay farmers parity for cotton." Quite to the contrary, the result was that the cotton mills continued to spin out the huge stocks already on hand from cotton which they had previously bought from farmers at below parity prices. These processors would eventually record profits at five times the peacetime average while market prices remained below parity for farmers. Meanwhile, consumers were being asked to pay tens of millions of dollars extra for their clothing.

"A Poor Man's Department of Agriculture"

No one at this time felt the wrath of the Farm Bureau more than the Farm Security Administration. As noted in previous chapters, the work of the FSA was repeatedly attacked by the Farm Bureau until the agency was legislated out of existence in 1946.

In chronicling the FSA's demise it is important to remember that the New Deal's programs for handling rural poverty were initially vested in the National Industrial Recovery Act, not the USDA. In 1935 the seeds of FDR's rural policy — rural rehabilitation and subsistence homesteads — were transplanted into the Resettlement Administration, which at that time was still independent of USDA. It was only after the passage of the Bankhead-Jones Farm Tenancy Act of 1937 that the Agency was abolished, with its functions incorporated into the newly-established FSA within the USDA.

Thus, the FSA became heir to a number of programs dealing with rural poverty which had been receiving no support from established farm organizations like the Farm Bureau. Its administrative structure was built on direct lines of authority reaching from the county supervisor, through state heads and regional chiefs to the administrator. In contrast to the Extension Service, the FSA was in McDonnell's words, "a poor man's Department of Agriculture."[15] It was even argued by FSA supporters that if the Extension Service had been doing its job properly there would have never been a need for the FSA.

In its efforts to develop new attitudes toward farm labor through such programs as an enlightened management of southeastern and western migratory labor camps (such as the one where the Joad family eventually found refuge in "The Grapes of Wrath"), by insuring that Southern blacks had a share in legitimate government farm programs corresponding to their proportion in the population, and by making loans to midwest co-ops to purchase failed grain elevators, the FSA directly antagonized corporate agribusiness and that class of farmer the AFBF sought to represent.

The elite, large commercial agricultural producer favored by the Farm Bureau who attempted to keep labor docile and cheap, the southern landlord who exploited the land to its absolute limit at whatever human cost, and the giant private grain dealers who had come to monopolize their trade, all saw FSA as a serious threat to the status quo and fought furiously to curtail its work. But there is no doubt that the greatest enemy of the FSA and the instrument which almost single-handedly destroyed it, was the American Farm Bureau, as its numerous and continuous attacks on the agency were directed by its national leadership.

In its early stages, FSA appropriation requests to the Congress received no support from the Farm Bureau. In 1941 the Farm Bureau unsuccessfully attempted to get the Agency's farm and home management services relegated to the ES and its loaning functions to the FCA. But, by getting a rider to an appropriations bill which stipulated that FSA personnel not be covered by Civil Service, the Farm Bureau scored a partial victory. Agency morale was seriously damaged and many resignations soon followed.[16]

Congress, meanwhile, at the instigation of the Farm Bureau, was engaged in a series of damaging FSA investigations, which McConnell describes as "progressively degrading" in character, absent of any "searching investigation into the total operations of Farm Security or the guiding concepts of its administration", and marked by the "readiness with which the committees — and Congress as a whole — allowed themselves to be manipulated by the lobbyists of the Farm Bureau."[17]

FSA Director C.B. Baldwin summed up the nature of the Farm Bureau's attack to one of the many Congressional committees he testified before during these investigations:

It is in this context and only in this context that the current fight to weaken the Farm Security Administration can be understood. The choice before the committee is whether the small independent farmer should be given an opportunity to maintain and improve his status or whether these large interests should be permitted to take advantage of the war situation to accumulate large land holdings and to make laborers out of farmers.[18]

"To Maintain Its Own Power"

The battle over the FSA was actually only secondary in the eyes of Farm Bureau leadership. The real question was, as Grant McConnell asks,

What was the basic policy of the Farm Bureau itself? The answer is plain: the Farm Bureau sought at every point to maintain its own power, which in turn, was based upon its influence over the Extension Service. Farm Bureau power was expanded by using the Extension Service to control other more vital parts of the [USDA's] program[s]. Where such control could not be extended, what remained uncontrolled had to be destroyed.[19]

With its ascendancy to unprecedented power in the late 1930s and throughout World War II, the Farm Bureau

The Corporate Reapers

established and maintained a narrow approach to farm policy and its implementation that has prevailed to the present day.

Appropriating to itself the title of "the farmers voice" and systematically drowning out the voices of its opponents, the AFBF framed farm programs to outsiders as so involved, so varying in methods and administration and with so many complexities that neither the general public nor politicians could ever hope to understand them fully.

By directing its attacks on the administration of agricultural programs, such as the FSA and later the SCS, and trying unsuccessfully to reorganize the USDA in 1940 through its plan of "decentralization," the Farm Bureau sought to solidify its power as a policy maker.

The Bureau's concept of "decentralization" uniquely served its own self-interest. By placing authority and responsibility for combined USDA programs in the hands of local, district and state farmer committees and operating them on the basis of grants-in-aid to the states, the Farm Bureau saw the Extension Service, which in many cases it controlled, as a means of the Bureau's gaining even more power and influence within the rural community.

However, in its efforts to "simplify" administrative coordination the Farm Bureau soon found itself confronted with the pressures of a war-time agricultural economy and the serious policy issues of the post-war debates. When Roosevelt's emergency price control legislation was passed in 1942 the Farm Bureau immediately saw another distinct threat to its power with the Federal government now interjecting itself into a vital and sensitive area of farm policy — the setting of farm prices.

After the war and with the rather curious role it played in fashioning and obtaining passage of the 1948 Hope-Aiken compromise farm bill, the Farm Bureau believed that the formulation of farm policy had been taken out of the hands of the general public and both political parties and was now "bipartisan" in nature. In fact, in a political context, this so-called "bi-partisan" farm policy was but Farm Bureau farm policy.

Thus, the Bureau fought the Brannan Plan so hard, seeing it as a threat to its own existence. Truman's agriculture secretary had taken "bipartisan" farm policy, i.e., Farm Bureau policy, and put it back squarely in the political arena and was receiving support from those very elements in society — family farmers and organized labor — that the Farm Bureau branded as "dangerous" and "anti-American."

By the early 1950s the hue and cry from other farm organizations and some members of Congress concerning the "relationship" between Extension and the Bureau had become so vocal that Agricultural Secretary Benson issued a memorandum in 1954 specifying that no USDA employee should accept the use of free office space or contributions for salary or traveling expenses from any general or specialized organization of farmers. Also, no employee should advocate that any one organization work with the USDA, nor solicit members for any such organization, nor approve contracts with it for the Department.

The rule was weak. In 1963 the Secretary's office was forced to issue an "Interpretation" of the 1954 memo, which was really an amplification of a USDA policy statement in 1945, which was itself a restatement of the incorporation into Department regulations in 1922 of the "True-Howard" agreement of 1921. The 1963 "interpretation" sought to define the prohibited "close relationship" between the ES and the Bureau. It concluded that any funds given by an organization to Extension had to be made to the State University without specification as to use, a situation that already existed in some states to the mutual satisfaction of both the Farm Bureau and the ES.

Although certain formal agreements between the Farm Bureau and the Extension Service have been subsequently terminated, there still exists in many areas of the country a close working relationship between the Farm Bureau and the ES to the degree that many farmers believe one is a function of the other.

Decentralization?

To fully understand the influence and ascent to power that the Farm Bureau has enjoyed in the post-war period, particularly since 1952, it is important to reconsider the role of "decentralization" within the Bureau's overall philosophy. As Grant McConnell explains,

> Decentralization of political organization and government in agriculture today has two effects of great importance. The first is the narrowing of the political base. In theory this narrowing might have taken place on any of a number of different lines, but in fact it has occurred on a basis of class. The already existent lines of class have been sharpened. The second effect is the building of a structure of political power. Decentralization has been an essential condition to this structure. *In effect, the Farm Bureau has become an association of already existing elites in agriculture joined on a basis of class.* The political power of the whole organization has, in turn, served to elevate the position of these elites, even while respecting their mutual differences.[20] (emphasis added)

In the past three and one-half decades the dominant political theme in the United States, with only a slight interruption in the early sixties, has been "less government, more private initiative" or as some cynics characterize it, "capitalism for the poor and socialism for the rich." Nowhere has the call to get "government out of our lives" been more pronounced than in agriculture and more zealously championed than by the Farm Bureau.

Agricultural economist Halcrow reminds us that the main policy interests and major conflicts within the Farm Bureau over the years have centered on price policy and the means or programs by which prices are affected. He outlines the three major periods of such activity.[23]

• Pre-New Deal: The Bureau fought for a number of reforms and was finally persuaded to join the

280

battle for the export subsidy in the form of the McNary-Haughton bill.
• New Deal and Post War Era to 1947: The major policy effort was directed at raising prices.
• Post 1947: This era has been characterized by Farm Bureau efforts to become disengaged from government programs and move agriculture toward a "free market."

By constantly railing against "big government," the Bureau has come to endear itself to many like-minded special interest business groups outside of agribusiness who provide the Farm Bureau with powerful political support when it seeks to block legislation unfavorable to corporate agribusiness.

In a 1984 speech to farmers in Mississippi County, Arkansas, then-AFBF President Robert Delano underscored the corporate agribusiness approach to the "farm problem" that the organization continues to espouse. By asking for lower prices and abolishing commodity storage programs farmers can expect to sell more goods, he told the assembly. Farmers should also learn a lesson from business firms, he added, namely that corporate debt is a continuing debt that is constantly rolled over; therefore, farmers as good business persons should become reconciled to passing their debt onto their children and grandchildren.[24]

Such an attitude helps explain why the nation's family farm system is systematically being eradicated while rural America is rocked by the physical and economic violence stemming from a mounting number of farm foreclosures, forced liquidations and bankruptcies brought on by the "policies and manipulations" of corporate agribusiness.

Meanwhile, in an outright betrayal by "the enemy within," the nation's "largest farm and ranch member-family" organization continues to turn its back to the plight of thousands of its so-called member-constituency.

One state Farm Bureau leader, in opposing any moratorium on Federal farm loan foreclosures, has even lamented: "We hate to see any farmer go broke, but if they can't compete they will go broke. The inefficient ones get weeded out. That's free enterprise. Farmers have to be astute businessmen these days."[25]

And Delano, after reviewing the 1984 election, noted,
I think we can trust the surviving politicians to stop expressing exaggerated concern over the supposed demise of American agriculture and family farming.
... Progress, stimulated by reduced political tapering and lessened regulatory interference with the farming and ranching business, will do more to sustain the family farm than any panaceas offered by vote-seekers campaigning ... to 'save the family farm!'[26]

Plying the "Tactics of a Rural Mafia"

An enduring mystery of the post-war era is that while the AFBF has grown so politically powerful, both within the farm community and in the halls of Congress,

pushing both its legislative agenda while destroying agencies and organizations it saw as a threat, there has been an almost total lack of critical analysis by farmers or their elected representatives about the means and goals the Farm Bureau often employs in its pursuit of political and economic power.

The story of Representative Joseph Resnick, D-NY, and the fate of his 1967 inquiry into the affairs of the Farm Bureau possibly clarifies why we have seen so few "profiles in courage" in evidence in the Congress of the United States in all the years that the Farm Bureau has claimed to speak for the American farmer.[27]

In June 1967, Resnick, Chairman of the House Agriculture Subcommittee on Rural Development, was holding unprecedented hearings on the effects of Federal programs on rural America. The AFBF was invited to testify, but at the initial hearing time expired before the Bureau representative could complete his testimony.

At the following week's hearings and before the completion of the Farm Bureau's representative's testimony, Resnick had uncovered material strongly indicating that the Farm Bureau had a substantial nonfarm membership and that it was conducting widespread and questionable financial and commercial activities. He noted that the AFBF was a gigantic interlocking, nationwide combine of insurance companies with total assets of over $1 billion, which were unrelated to farmers. The Congressman questioned whether the Bureau even had the right to appear before the committee as a representative of the interests of farmers.

Once again, however, time expired before the Farm Bureau could complete its testimony or challenge Resnick's charges, so the Congressman invited the Bureau representative to come back before the committee and complete his remarks.

In the following week, however, Roger Fleming, AFBF secretary-treasurer, dispatched a letter to House Agriculture Committee chairman W.R. Poage, with copies to each committee member, specifying those terms by which he would appear before Resnick to continue his testimony. In effect the letter was what Resnick later called "a blueprint for Agriculture Committee action to silence me and prevent me from making further revelations about the Farm Bureau." In part the letter stated:

In the interest of justice and fair play we urge that the full committee give immediate consideration to the charges made by [Resnick] against the Farm Bureau organization (county, state and national) ... if the Committee does not concur in these charges, then we feel that the Committee should clear the record by adopting a resolution in which it disassociates itself from the attacks on the Farm Bureau made by [Resnick] and by making known to the public at an early date its disposition of this matter.

Within 24 hours of receiving the letter five members of Resnick's subcommittee, four of whom were reportedly Farm Bureau members, issued a statement attacking their Chairman's criticisms of the Farm Bureau with language almost identical to that in the Farm Bureau letter.

Their statement was followed by action unprecedented in the history of Congress. Within 48 hours of receiving Fleming's letter, the full Ag Committee met behind closed doors in executive session and issued a statement declaring that it did "in no manner endorse, condone, or support the personal attack launched by the Chairman of the Subcommittee on Rural Development upon the AFBF."

At the same time the committee was issuing its statement, the Farm Bureau's Fleming was distributing a press release which stated: "This judgment by his Congressional colleagues should make it crystal clear that Congressman Resnick's charges against the Farm Bureau Federation are reckless, unwarranted, and unfounded."

Later, in a speech to the House of Representatives, Resnick reflected:

> While any reading of the committee resolution would make it obvious that Mr. Fleming's statement did not contain a single grain of truth, and was in no way related to the specific and documented charges I have made against the Farm Bureau, not one single member of the committee has risen to criticize him for it ...
>
> [The AFBF] reaction, and the reaction of the Committee on Agriculture is all the more remarkable when we recognize that I am being attacked — not for telling lies about the Farm Bureau — but for revealing the truth. The plain fact is that this powerful organization has at no time denied or contradicted any of the revelations I have made about its operations. But before my subcommittee, they were evasive, tight-lipped, and downright untruthful.

A Bill of Particulars

A review of Resnick's "revelations" today concerning the Farm Bureau's operations in the 1960s has led an ever increasing number of angry and disillusioned farmers to realize that a similar if not identical set of charges could validly be made against the present-day AFB organization. They include:

• The Bureau is not the organization of farmers it claims to be. A substantial portion of its membership — possibly half — has no agricultural interest whatsoever. In 1984, for example, the Farm Bureau added over 41,000 families to its membership rolls while the Census Bureau reported that 399,000 people had left their farms.[28]

• The Farm Bureau has used the American farmer to build one of the largest insurance and financial empires in the United States, whose insurance assets alone total over $1 billion. In 1985 alone its insurance companies recorded annual earned premiums totaling over $3 billion.[29]

• The Bureau has misrepresented itself to the Internal Revenue Service in order to obtain a tax exemption, and to the clerks of both Houses of Congress.

• The directors and officers of the Farm Bureau are also directors and officers of insurance companies directly controlled and owned by the various State Farm Bureaus.

• As a result of these interlocking directorates the Farm Bureau may be in violation of antitrust law.

• The Farm Bureau has taken advantage of its tax-exempt status in order to expand its business activities which cover the fields of insurance, real estate, shopping centers, fertilizer, mutual funds, gas stations, oil wells, grain storage, petroleum refineries, and a considerable variety of other such ventures.

• Because of its widespread commercial interests the Farm Bureau has misrepresented its true nature in its dealings with farmers and in its statements to Congressional committees.

• As a tax-exempt organization the Farm Bureau has been improperly competing in commercial activities with private taxpaying business concerns, thus enjoying an unfair competitive advantage.

• The Farm Bureau has torpedoed American farmers by posing as an organization representing their interests when in fact, the Bureau's widespread commercial activities — which include the operation of businesses which sell to the farmer and buy from the farmer — puts them in a position of representing a point of view antagonistic to the interests of the farmer.

• The Farm Bureau's commercial activities have generated funds which have found their way, illegally, into political and lobbying activities.

A Rustling in the Grassroots

Despite the admonition from his Congressional colleagues, Resnick continued his investigation and attacks on the Farm Bureau. In the meantime, he received hundreds of letters from farmers throughout the country ("one might say that the farmers of America have been my unofficial investigative force in the field") calling his attention to a plethora of questionable Farm Bureau practices.

Charging that the Farm Bureau had done more to prevent the economic and social advancement of rural citizens than any other organization in America, Resnick told the pathetic stories he had heard about the misery of migrant workers and the poverty of rural communities such as Belle Glade, Florida (which in recent years has also become known as "the AIDS capital of the world") where the second largest industry was the manufacture of baby coffins.

> The Farm Bureau is entitled to its full share of the blame for the fact that our rural areas are burdened with the most poverty, highest unemployment, least social and economic development, and poorest health facilities in the Nation. Their crime has not been mere indifference. Quite the contrary. They have intensively fought every attempt to correct these ills.

There is nothing to which the Farm Bureau has dedicated more of its resources, save the dismantling of Federal farm programs, than fighting to destroy attempts by farm labor to achieve economic and social justice.

From legislatively and often times physically preventing the organizing of farm workers to the prohibiting of strikes, from promoting the importation of foreign migrant laborers to denying coverage of social security unemployment insurance to farm workers, from opposing coverage of field workers by minimum wage and hour laws to restricting enforcement of health and safety laws in the fields (*e.g.*, its 1985 platform called for the repeal of the Occupational Safety and Health Act), the Farm Bureau has devoted countless time and effort to resisting progress for farmers.

As recently as 1985 the Texas Farm Bureau voiced opposition to a federal minimum wage for farm workers, and reaffirmed its long-standing opposition to child labor legislation, workers' compensation and unemployment compensation, and the abolition of the back-breaking short-handled hoe.[30]

Here too, the Bureau's vested interests are blatant. In many farm areas, the Farm Bureau has not only operated farm labor camps, but served as a contractor service in providing local growers with seasonal workers. Despite fatal fires in what have been described as "squalid" labor camps and fatal accidents involving overcrowded work buses, the Farm Bureau has consistently opposed legislation to correct such unsafe conditions, claiming each time that such federal or state action would be inappropriate since no "dire emergency" exists.

Nothing typifies the Farm Bureau's attitude toward rural poverty and the people who are forced to suffer such inhuman conditions, better than American Farm Bureau's Charles Schuman's interview with *The St. Louis Post Dispatch* several years ago. First, he defined poverty as,

> a combination of lack of education, training, and lack of ambition ... I don't think the Federal Government can do anything about it except spend a lot of money . . the very things which have made our Nation relatively free of poverty — freedom to work or play, freedom to spend or save, freedom to own a TV set and a Cadillac but live in a shack in order to do so. We are already too far down the road that leads to socialism — a morally decrepit philosophy which destroys the initiative to do better.[31]

Later, in conceding that the United States did indeed have "poverty-stricken families," Schuman asked in *Nation's Agriculture*: "What kind of poverty is this? With abundant educational and job opportunities on every hand, it must be primarily a poverty of the mind and soul — a lack of desire."[32]

In all of its public policy statements, which include positions on everything from pornography to off-track betting, from the libraries of ex-presidents to pay TV, from ROTC to the National Council of Churches, the Bureau never quite gets around to concerning itself with rural poverty.

Moreover, it has openly fought against the establishment of Volunteers in Service to America (VISTA) and attempted to stop the activities of the National Association for the Advancement of Colored People's (NAACP) Legal Defense Fund and the National Migrant Ministry's efforts to assist farm workers and the rural poor. The North Carolina state farm bureau even opposed anti-slavery legislation in 1983![33]

In other areas of agriculture the Farm Bureau has distorted the issues, used scare tactics and opposed pro-farmer legislation that conflicted with its own self-interests. In March 1985, for example, it called on Congress to *defeat* national legislation requiring the Secretary of Agriculture to grant deferrals and forego foreclosures on FmHA loans.[34]

The same year, the Texas State Department of Agriculture (TDA) proposed regulations giving farmers the right to prior notification of aerial spraying of chemical poisons, preventing farm workers from entering fields too soon after the application of these poisons and providing access to toxicological information on such poisons. The proposed regulation did *not* restrict their amount, type or manner of application.[35] Yet, in a concerted campaign against the regulations the Farm Bureau charged that the proposed changes "would prohibit for all practical purposes, the use of pesticides," that the regulations would "shut down agriculture" and prompt high food costs, and that the regulations were "part of a larger effort to socialize agriculture and divert land from private use to state control."

As we shall see when discussing the AFBF's insurance holdings, the Texas Farm Bureaus's stand on chemical poisons has more to do with self-interest than any concern about the state of agriculture or the future of land use.

"Kept Money"

During his investigations, Representative Resnick had sought to show how both Farm Bureau supply and marketing cooperatives ranked "as one of the most gigantic and successful shell games ever practiced." By transferring their tax burden from themselves to their patrons, he charged, these "farm cooperatives" evaded federal income taxes.

The vehicle for such a transfer — worthless dividend certificates — is one many farmers have learned about the hard way. Federal tax laws allowed the Farm Bureau co-ops to distribute such worthless pieces of paper instead of money, and then deduct their face value from the co-op's earnings before figuring taxes.

At the same time the Farm Bureau has used such "kept money" to expand into contract farming and drive independent millers, supply houses, oil dealers, warehouses, and grain elevators out of business. It has likewise made individual farmers captives of the Farm Bureau Co-op and/or its feed companies.

Through this process the Co-ops have been taking over the farm supply and commodity marketing business by buying up and absorbing private independent companies and becoming gigantic businesses with management effectively insulated from the farmer-patron, who by now has little real voice in the decision-making.

The Farm Bureau, Resnick noted, has repeatedly told the IRS that its membership was limited to people who are "engaged in carrying on a farm or farms or who have a major agricultural interest." Yet statistics from 1967 alone in Illinois, a state where the Farm Bureau has its headquarters (often referred to as the "agribusiness pentagon") and its largest state organization, led Resnick to brand the Farm Bureau's IRS claim "an outright lie."

For example, in that year there were 61,000 more Farm Bureau members in the state than there were farms. While USDA statistics for the year showed a 9,000-farm decrease, Illinois Farm Bureau membership showed a 10,681 increase. It has been estimated that fewer than half of the Farm Bureau members are actually farmers.

A recent example of the AFBF's questionable membership claims was in Texas where the TDA estimated that, at most 90,000 people in the state could be earning over half of their income from agriculture, yet the Texas Farm Bureau was claiming 317,000 "member families." It was only in the 1980s that the Bureau first started to enlist associate memberships for its insurance customers and full voting memberships for farmers.[36]

Discussing the Farm Bureau's membership policies, Resnick told many stories he had heard of what some farmers called the "gestapo-like tactics" on the part of the Farm Bureau management; how they waged (in the Bureau's own words) "neutralization" campaigns against ministers who spoke out against them and how members who questioned policy would suddenly find their Farm Bureau insurance policies cancelled.

> The leaders of the Farm Bureau run their organization with the heavy handed tactics of a rural Mafia. As long as the members pay their dues and their insurance premiums, keep the Farm Bureau gas bill paid up to date, and do not run up too sizable a bill at the Farm Bureau's so-called cooperative, they are entitled to all the benefits that membership in the Farm Bureau bestows on an individual. But, if anyone dares to question a policy or voice disapproval loud enough, the wrath of the magnates of the Merchandise Mart will rain down upon him and his.

In the spring, 1969 Congressman Resnick left Washington, D.C. and returned to private law practice. He still harbored, however, a deep and abiding interest in the Farm Bureau. He and former staff person, Samuel R. Berger, decided to co-author a book detailing the activities of the Farm Bureau and attempt to answer those questions that the Congressman's earlier probes had raised. Berger traveled across the country, interviewing hundreds of people and reviewing pages and pages of Congressional documents amassed both during and after Resnick's hearings. Suddenly, at age 45, Resnick died in October 1969.

Berger, however, doggedly pursued the investigation and eventually authored *Dollar Harvest: An Expose of the Farm Bureau.* Chapter after chapter detailed how the Farm Bureau could be accurately described not as a farm organization but as a $4 billion business combine

with interests ranging from insurance to oil, fertilizer to finance, mutual funds to urban shopping centers.

"The farmer has increasingly become the customer, not the constituent, of an organization that today regards agriculture largely as the market for its own goods and services, as the cornerstone of a commercial empire."

Berger showed how the Farm Bureau's political power stemmed first from its huge business earnings that are frequently siphoned off (while the IRS is busy elsewhere) into tax-exempt state and national Farm Bureau chapters to be used for lobbying and other political ventures.

Second, the Farm Bureau's political power was enhanced by the public and the Congress's long-standing acceptance of the Federation as the voice of the American farmer, when in fact a near majority of the membership joined the Bureau only as a prerequisite to buying its insurance.

How To Deal "At Arm's Length" With Oneself

The cornerstone of the Farm Bureau's "service to members" projects for many years has been its business operations in insurance, involving a network of 55 insurance companies with over $3 billion in both total assets and life insurance in force. A revealing insight of how state federations operate their insurance business was provided in 1985 by Mikkel Jordahl in an investigative essay on the Texas Farm Bureau ("Their Business Is Business") in *The Texas Observer*.[37]

The Texas Farm Bureau is sole owner of the Texas Farm Bureau Mutual Insurance Company which had 1984 assets of $61 million. The Mutual Company's investment portfolio also contained out-of-state industrial development and utility company interests to the tune of $11.5 million, with $1.3 million in the financially-plagued and ill-fated nuclear power industry in Washington State.

> Other concerns, according to the 1984 annual statement of the Mutual Company include chemical companies and the oil industry, with over $1 million invested in each. While the TFB lobbies against pesticide regulation, the Mutual Company owns stock in Hooker Chemical of Niagara, Allied Chemical, Monsanto, and Union Carbide.

The State Bureau affiliates also included four insurance companies and one cash fund organization with combined sales in excess of $600 million: the Southern Farm Bureau Life Insurance Co, insured 156,000 Texans; the Southern Farm Bureau Casualty Insurance Company insured more than 450,000 cars in the Lone Star state; and the TFB Mutual Insurance Company covered property damage with over 180,000 policies in effect.

To gain insurance coverage from the various Texas Farm Bureau insurance companies (as is also the case in the other state Farm Bureau companies in the United States) one must take out membership in the Farm Bureau itself. This policy makes it possible for state bureaus like Texas' to realize over $2 million annually in membership fees. Out of the $25 membership fee, the county Farm Bureau retains $15 while $7 goes to the state FB and $3 to the AFB Federation headquarters in Illinois.

One former Farm Bureau insurance agent explained to Jordahl how the Farm Bureau profited from both these memberships and insurance policies:

[Most] county Farm Bureaus and the insurance companies share office space in Bureau-owned buildings. The county organization pays for the upkeep and secretarial help. In return the agents are producing lots of income for that county Bureau. Every time an agent writes some coverage on any of the FB insurance companies, on all premiums there is a remuneration back to the county organization. That may only be a small percentage, but it adds up.

Jordahl goes on to detail how in 1984, in exchange for selling Farm Bureau memberships two of the Texas Farm Bureau's affiliated insurance companies paid a combined total of just under $2.5 million in such remunerations.

The way those memberships are sold is a story in itself. Often the insurance holder is not interested in becoming a member of the Texas Farm Bureau. The agent will therefore agree to waive the county portion of the membership fee and pay the state portion.

The membership technically goes into effect, the businessman gets low-cost insurance minus the membership fee, and the county Bureau collects, say a $50 remuneration from the insurance company. The county is out the state membership fee, but if you subtract that from the $50 remuneration generated by the sale you can see why it was worth their while.

As Berger points out in *Dollar Harvest* this type of arrangement not only benefits the insurance companies, which profit by being identified with the Farm Bureau name, but also reaps both increased membership and money for the Farm Bureau.

Through a variety of corporate techniques, the most common being the interlocking directorate, the Farm Bureau keeps a tight reign on its insurance companies. As a Farm Bureau staff member explained:

The board of directors of the state organization regularly meets at the state headquarters. When they are finished, they adjourn, go around to the other side of the table, so to speak, and call the meeting of the insurance company to order.

Many of the Farm Bureau's insurance companies are affiliated companies and sell stock. However, most if not all of the stock is often owned by the State Farm Bureau or its holding company. Consequently, any stock dividends realized by these insurance companies usually revert to the State Farm Bureau. While the Farm Bureau has claimed that its insurance operations and Bureau activities are perfectly distinct, "the complicated bundle of benefits," as Berger observes, "flowing between business and organization makes such a simple explanation unrealistic. It is most difficult to deal 'at arm's length' with yourself."

How well farmers are served by such a relationship can be gleaned from South Carolina Chief Insurance Commissioner Charles Gambrell's testimony at rate hearings held by the state's Insurance Department in 1967. He accused the Southern Farm Bureau Casualty Insurance Company of embarking on a campaign "to induce, if not force" other commercial insurance companies in the state "to lead the way in raising farmers' rates, so that the Farm Bureau could follow suit, and avoid the stigma of being the first to do so."

It should also be pointed out that the AFBF has its own insurance operation — the American Agricultural Insurance Company. This company is primarily a reinsurance company for the state operations, i.e. an insurance company's insurance company. It is through such operations that Farm Bureau insurance companies are interlocked with a number of major U.S. insurance companies, including Nationwide.

"The Right Wing in Overalls"

One area of AFBF activity that Resnick, Berger and others have found particularly unsettling is the Bureau's close ties with the political far right in the United States.

"What might once have been a conservative, business-oriented organization is now considerably more," the N.Y. Congressman declared in 1968. "By my calculation, the Farm Bureau is the most efficient conduit now in existence for the dissemination of right-wing propaganda." He continued:

The Bureau is a perfect sewer line for transporting right-wing ideology, particularly to our young people. In many states it sponsors annual well-planned, well-financed youth conferences. They go under several names, but most are called 'citizenship seminars', or 'freedom forums.' They last from two to five days. Each county Farm Bureau unit is told to select two or three top students, whom it sponsors.

The Kansas City Star once described such seminars as "a cram course in anti-communism and free enterprise Americanism and political conservatism."

Berger is even more explicit:

The message that these primed audiences of young, eager high school leaders hear at these seminars is the same: pervasive distrust of government; deprecation of civil liberties; a frozen, conspiratorial view of world affairs; a sense of futility about the possibility of easing world tensions and pursuing disarmament; and a *laissez-faire* attitude toward our serious domestic problems. The Farm Bureau's right-wing speakers twist and pervert notions of self-reliance and personal freedom into clubs with which to beat down the destitute.

The parents of these youth and other Bureau members have been repeatedly assured that the speakers and the publications they peddle give young people "a better understanding of the American way of life" and the "present trends jeopardizing the very foundation of our American heritage" by "recognized authorities on the American system" who deplore "spoon-fed socialism."

Because a major target of AFBF for the past several decades has been the power of the Federal government and its role in advocating social reforms, the Bureau has aptly juggled the terms "centralization," "planned economy," "socialism", and "communism" to a degree that they have become interchangeable in the minds of many American farmers. These farmers have become susceptible to the menacing talk of the "international Godless communist conspiracy," "the enemy within," and "the evil empire."

Not only has the Farm Bureau used its economic resources to promote an often vicious, anti-government, anti-civil rights economic and political philosophy, but because of its tax-exemption, the American taxpayers have been picking up part of the bill.

In recent years the Farm Bureau under the banners of the various extreme right-wing extremist shibboleths it espouses has vigorously opposed rural development, improvements in social security, medicare, aid to dependent children, public rural electrification programs, federal aid to education, and the United Nations, to name but a few.

The political philosophy of the Farm Bureau has frequently coincided with the far right's and an affinity has developed. Although it has certainly helped the far right in many practical ways, the Bureau has *formally* affiliated itself with only a handful of recognized far right-wing organizations.

What it has done more effectively, however, is to give far-right speakers and literature respectability, acting as a transmission belt by quoting them favorably in its publications and sponsoring meetings giving the far right a nearly unfettered opportunity to expound its views.

Wesley McCune, a long-time observer of right-wing activities and the author of the two authoritative books, *The Farm Bloc* and *Who's Behind Our Farm Policy*, describes the Farm Bureau's role:

> By avoiding formal affiliation, the Farm Bureau may well have developed a technique much more effective — namely, the soft sell, the moderate repetition, the avoidance of extremist labels, the lecture fee for needy advocators, the geographic distribution of ideas, and above all, the 'respectability' which every speaker or writer needs in order to have audience or impacts.[38]

Throughout the late 1950s, 1960s and well into the 1970s the speakers list and literature tables at various Farm Bureau county, state and national functions often resembled a who's who of the political far right in the United States.

Such organizations and institutions as the Americans for Constitutional Action, the Freedoms Foundation at Valley Forge, the John Birch Society, the National Right-to-Work Committee, the Foundation for Economic Education, among others, have all had informal ties with the American Farm Bureau.

Either through the exchange of speakers, jointly-sponsored meetings and seminars or through Farm Bureau leaders serving in leadership roles in such organizations, the Farm Bureau at the county, state and national level has worked with numerous far right organizations, used their material, and encouraged sympathy for them.

Spawning Seeds of Hate

It would be unfair to blame the AFB entirely for the recent spate of fascist, racist, anti-Semitic vigilante farm groups which have sprung up throughout the United States in recent years, born in frustration and nurtured by a depressed farm economy. However, the Farm Bureau, through its long-standing role as a visible propaganda agent for right wing extremism, certainly made itself the spawning ground for the misdirected, unsocial and violent behavior that currently exists in many of our farm communities. As one Iowa farm leader has warned,

> farmers are victims of the hate propaganda and phony schemes of a surprisingly strong, organized right-wing element. With the farm situation clearly deteriorating and out of control, it is imperative that farmers organize themselves to defend their interests in a manner that is democratic, nonviolent and pluralistic. The alternative is continued growth of the extreme right and a clear threat to the well-being of our rural communities.[39]

The secrecy surrounding the right-wing makes it impossible to know how broad or how deep its roots are in the nation's farm communities, but the Center for Democratic Renewal in Atlanta, Georgia, a private research group which has for many years monitored the activities of the KKK and other such groups, estimates that there are between 2,000-5,000 activists in these groups and between 14,000 and 50,000 sympathizers in the Middle West.[40]

The Washington Post also reported that in 1987 "telephone taps and bugs planted by FBI agents in the home of at least one major American neo-Nazi figure," according to federal court documents, "show an 'underground' of racist and anti-Semitic leaders coordinated bank robberies, commando-style raids on armored cars, counterfeiting, murder and other crimes."[41]

Many of these extremist groups, which include Christian Identity; Posse Comitatus; the so-called Populist Party; the Heritage Library; the Aryan Nations; the Order; the Covenant, Sword and Arm of the Lord, and the National Agricultural Press Association, among others have urged their followers to stockpile weapons, food, ammunition and explosives.

Some have also urged their members to take violent actions against Jews and racial minorities. Other groups offer desperate farmers "phony" loans and legal schemes that purportedly will save their farms from bankruptcy. "Deceiving farmers," says the Iowa farm leader, "diverting them from real solutions, milking them of their money — this is probably the most common damage done by the right wing."[42]

Charging farmers fees as high $1,000 for unorthodox legal advice, individuals such as Lawrence L. Humphrey, the heir to a small banking fortune; George Gordon, a former California dairyman, and Rick Elliott, a Coloradan who publishes *The Primrose and Cattleman's Gazette*, have been traveling throughout farm country selling farmers on *pro se* litigation as a means to forestall creditors.

Pro se simply means that the farmer represents himself in court, basing his arguments on interpretations of Biblical scriptures as "common law," including variations on the theme that banks commit usury by charging interest on loans.[43] (Elliott was indicted on fraud and sentenced to eight years in prison for charges in connection with funds he obtained from associates as backing for his National Agricultural Press Association, an organization which promised to find farmers low-interest loans although there was no evidence that any such loans were in fact found.)[44]

Perhaps the most enduring of these new right wing organizations in the farm belt is the starkly racist Posse Comitatus, which opposes all income taxes and believes that the Federal Reserve is the work of the devil. Author James Ridgeway has described the posse as anarchist.

> The ultimate goal is to get rid of the state, to rear a new generation that can't be traced: children with no birth certificates, who don't go to school, who grow up as true Sovereigns under God and the Constitution.
>
> The idea of Posse is supercharged with religion. Christian fundamentalism has many followers in the farm belt, and premillennialism has taken on new immediacy both because of the economic crisis and because of its popularizing by television preachers who have made the notion of the end times both immediate and highly political.[45]

This theological foundation for the radicalism now seen throughout the nation's farm belt can be traced to "Christian identity theology," which says that white Christians are the true "Israelites" of the Old Testament and thus God's chosen people. They identify the "ten lost tribes of Israel" as the real predecessors of Nordic, British, and American whites and relegate the modern-day Jews to a historically separate kingdom of Judah, thus in a political sense making modern Israel a hoax and deigning the United States God's promised land.

Alarmed by this increase in right-wing hatred that he sees in the rural countryside, former Des Moines Bishop Maurice Dingman has cautioned that "desperate people will look for scapegoats. Farmers are desperate. Therefore they are psychologically and emotionally prey to the hatemongers who would blame the devastating farm crisis on, for example, Jewish bankers." But, he continues, the real solution is to remove the occasion for the hatred by giving farmers a fair price for their production

and to engage in educational programs to dispel such Jewish conspiracy theories.[46]

Typical of the vicious scapegoating of the Jewish people found in many right-wing publications are the words of Jim Wickstrom, a leader of the paramilitary Posse Comitatus, the only right wing group, incidentally, labelled as terrorist by the FBI. Writing in a pamphlet, "The American Farmer: Twentieth Century Slave," he declares:

> The Jew-run banks and loan agencies are working hand in hand foreclosing on thousands of farms ... The Federal government follows a well-regulated plan that goes hand in hand with the Jewish money barons who pay off politicians who control the farm crops ...The farmer sells his hard-earned self-invested crops to the local Jewish governed cooperative, in turn practically giving our crops to the enemy for nothing.[47]

Other targets of these extremists, as detailed in *The Spotlight*, published by Willis Cato and his Liberty Lobby in Washington, D.C., include the Rothchilds "who have always controlled the *Morgan* and *Rockefeller* operations The Rothchilds rule the United States through their foundations, the Council of Foreign Relations, and the *Federal Reserve System.*"[48]

This extremist threat in rural America made national headlines in March 1986 when two candidates, followers of far right-wing activist Lyndon LaRouche, scored stunning upset victories as Democrats in statewide primary elections in Illinois.

LaRouche began his activities in the Midwest in the late 1970s through a variety of front organizations, including the now defunct Parity Foundation, The Schiller Institute, and his National Democratic Policy Committee. Although his efforts in the farm belt diminished in the early 1980s he picked up his activities in that area again in 1983. He now leads what the conservative Heritage Foundation has termed "one of the strangest political groups in American history" as LaRouche has managed to attract a small but fanatical following to his conspiratorial view of the world.

One preposterous scenario spawned from this conspiratorial world view by LaRouche and his followers is an "international oligarchy" that "controls the radical farm protest movement."

> At the top are the ideological controllers, such as the Benedictine pseudo-religious order, which originated with the Egyptian Gnostic cults that penetrated the Catholic Church in the third century. The Benedictines have been caught running the radical activist groups (countergangs) that are now proliferating in the U.S. farm belt ...
>
> These groups insist that the problem with the farm sector is 'over-production' and too much advanced technology. They demand cuts in defense spending in order to pay for the radical restructuring of agriculture. The outcome of their "small is beautiful" program would be the transforma-

tion of the technology-proud American farmer into a serf...

The financing and political control for these grass- roots operations also come ... from the old European oligarchical families, the food cartel companies, and the U.S.S.R... [49]

Unfortunately, LaRouche has succeeded in recruiting some farmers and local farm leaders throughout the Midwest and currently maintains a network of farm followers who sell his newspaper and literature at major farm movement events and who sponsor LaRouche speakers and seminars.

In 1988 LaRouche and six of his top aides were convicted of federal mail fraud and tax-evasion charges. LaRouche himself received a sentence of 15 years. The charges stemmed from his fundraising activities, which prosecutors charged netted more than $30 million in four years.[50] During LaRouche's trial six women testified they had lent LaRouche's organization $481,300 during 1985-86 and not received any money in return. Meanwhile, LaRouche's organization was spending $4.2 million on Virginia real estate and thousands of dollars on elaborate security procedures for LaRouche.[51]

Delving deeply into the activities of LaRouche and others, authors Dennis King, in his book *Lyndon La-Rouche and the New American Fascism* and Kevin Flynn and Gary Gerhardt in *The Silent Brotherhood: Inside America's Racist Underground*, have shown that La-Rouche and his ilk are dangerous, anti-semitic fascists.

And, as the Center for Democratic Renewal's Daniel Levitas, formerly of Prairiefire Rural Action, a farmers' advocacy group that has been tracking LaRouche and other right-wing extremists throughout the Farm Belt, warns,

Far right activists have used our public gatherings and protest events as an opportunity to circulate and recruit, often without being openly confronted or identified. In some instances they have even gained access to the platform. And, in a more general fashion, as the crisis has intensified, the politics of paranoia, anti-semitism and conspiracy have come to significantly influence how we formulate our rural community organizing strategies.

The task remains, however, to construct even more effectively barriers against the influence of anti-democratic forces and to develop a more sophisticated approach towards constructively confronting those forces directly.[52]

Chapter Twenty-Seven

Squeezing the "Toothpaste"

The basic premise of this book is that almost from its inception, American agriculture has been the victim of concerted efforts by various "communities of economic interests" to dispose of its "excess human resources" as a sure way of concentrating the means of production into as few hands as possible.*

There is perhaps, no clearer manifestation of this effort than in the workings of the Committee for Economic Development.

Established in August 1942 by a group of top business leaders, the Committee for Economic Development was designed to "seize the opportunities for unprecedented peacetime prosperity in the postwar era and to avoid the real perils of mass unemployment or mass government employment." It believed that individual employers, "while in no degree relaxing their efforts toward military victory, must begin to plan promptly, realistically, and boldly for rapid reconversion and vigorous expansion after the war."[1]

Through its Field Development Division the CED and communities throughout the United States worked locally with more than 2,900 counties and 65,000 - businessmen in helping over two million private employers plan their postwar production and employment through analytical studies, research papers and seminars.

In 1962 a blue ribbon panel of 200 businessmen and educators, under the aegis of the Research and Policy Committee of the CED issued a report, "An Adaptive Program for Agriculture." It was not the first time nor would it be the last time the CED addressed itself to agricultural matters.[2]

The authors of this 1962 report included many individuals who in years to come would be both the initiators and implementors of government policy: Dale Hathaway, former assistant secretary of agriculture with responsibilities for overseeing the farm price support and other government programs; T. W. Schultz, the prominent University of Chicago economist; Paul Samuelson, Massachusetts Institute of Technology economist; Herbert Stein, one-time head of the Wage and Price Council and a top economic advisor to several recent administrations; and Kenneth Bolding, an influential University of Michigan agricultural economist.

The Adaptive Approach

The CED's 1962 report began by isolating the most serious challenges facing agriculture at the time:

> The common characteristic shared by these [agricultural] problems is that, as a result of changes in the economy, the labor and capital employed in the industry cannot all continue to earn, by producing goods for sale in a free market, as much income as they formerly earned, or as much as they could earn employed in some other use; that is — the industry is using too many resources.

CED immediately informed its readers that: "The movement of people from agriculture *has not been fast enough* to take full advantage of the opportunities that improving farm technologies, thus increasing capital, create." (emphasis added)

Having characterized the "farm problem" as too low a return on investment caused by farmers not leaving agriculture fast enough, the CED report goes on to describe "Three Possible Approaches to the Problem of Agriculture" which would include a *laissez-faire*, a protectionist and an adaptive approach. The CED chose the last "adaptive approach" as its own proposed solution.

> The adaptive approach utilizes positive government action to facilitate and promote the movement of labor and capital where they will be most productive and earn the most income. Essentially this approach seeks to achieve what the *laissez-faire* approach would ordinarily expect to achieve but to do it more quickly and with less deep and protracted loss of income to the persons involved than might result if no assistance were given.
>
> The adaptive approach requires improved knowledge of available employment opportunities, and measures to finance movement and retrain workers; that is, a generally improved labor

---

* "In a richly symbolic act, one response of the federal government to the 1985 farm problem has been the provision of a grant to the state of Iowa for free vasectomies for troubled rural men.

"'Our argument [in seeking the grant],' said one state health official, 'was that this was a particularly good idea in Iowa because of the high unemployment rate and the problems of farmers.' Admittedly, the welfare-state logic here is impeccable: Still too many farmers? Sterilize them!"

— "Produce Good People, Not Just Food," by Allan C. Carlson, Rockford Institute, *The Washington Post*, November 3, 1985.

market. It works best when there is a high rate of economic activity and employment.

Thus, the CED approach was to "adapt" agriculture through the removal of excess "resources" (farmers), and then utilize such "resources" in other sectors of the economy where they could generate a greater return on "investment of resources.

As it was to stress repeatedly, there was a "persistent excess of resources, particularly labor, in agriculture over the quantities that could have earned, by the sale of their product (Labor Power) in free markets, incomes equivalent to what similar resources could have earned in other uses.

Having defined the problem in this manner, the report goes on to look at the causes of this failure of "resources to flow" out of farming, and thus states that it is a "support of prices" that has "deterred the movement out of agriculture."

After a careful explanation of the problem, the CED then went on to spell out its solutions. "The Choices Before Us: (a) leak-proof control of farm production, or (b) a program, such as we are recommending here, to induce excess resources (primarily people) to move rapidly out of agriculture."

The CED's "program for agricultural adjustment" called for "(a) policies and programs to attract excess resources for use in farm production and (b) for measures to cushion the effects of the adjustment on property and people." In keeping with its concern that the program be "large-scale, vigorous, and thorough-going", it proposed:

If the farm labor force were to be, five years hence, no more than two-thirds as large as its present size of approximately 5.5 millions, the program would involve moving off the farm about two million of the present farm labor force, plus a number equal to a large part of the new entrants who would otherwise join the farm labor force in five years.

In spelling out the policies and programs needed to bring about this change the CED focused on a primary strategy of adjusting agricultural prices. As it explained, "the basic adjustment required to solve the farm problem, adjustment of resources used to produce farm goods (farmers), cannot be expected to take place unless the price system is permitted to signal to farmers." The report goes on to recommend that

the price supports for wheat, cotton, rice, feed grains and related crops now under price supports be reduced immediately. The importance of such price adjustments should not be underestimated. The lower price levels would discourage further commitments of new productive resources to those crops unless it appeared profitable at the lower prices. Also, the lower prices would induce

some of the increased sales of these products both at home and abroad ...

Clearly, the CED saw it was time to "squeeze the toothpaste" a little harder!

The "Catalog Marches"

Reactions to the CED proposals were swift and sure. They were sharply attacked not only by Agriculture Secretary Orville Freeman, but also by members of the House and Senate Agricultural committees, who later held hearings devoted primarily to discrediting the CED's "adaptive" approach to the "farm problem."

Among farm organizations both the NFU and the NFO vehemently denounced the idea. Only the Farm Bureau, which found the plan entirely compatible with its goal of creating an elite class within American agriculture, favored the CED proposals.

The publication of the 1962 report had come shortly before an August 1962 NFO meeting in Des Moines, Iowa. As noted, the NFO had been engaging in several "test holding actions" and now some 20,000 farmers were coming together to call for an "all-out holding action" in their effort to bolster depressed farm prices. The recently-released CED report rapidly fueled the determination of the assembled farmers to take direct action on their own behalf against an economic and political establishment they saw as increasingly oppressive.[3] Because Theodore O. Yntema, chairman of the Finance Committee, Ford Motor Co., was also chairman of the CED's Research and Policy Committee, and Theodore V. Houser, director, Sears and Roebuck Co., was a vice-chairman of the same committee and a CED trustee, the NFO called upon farmers to boycott both the Ford and Sears companies in protest.

In seven cities throughout the country there were "catalog marches" where protesting farmers and others piled Sears Roebuck catalogs in front of the company's stores. In some six cities caravans of Ford cars and trucks were driven around the firms plants in protest of the CED report. The impact of the protest soon became apparent as both Sears and Ford publicly announced that they did not officially endorse the report and that the members of the committee were advocates of the plan solely as private citizens.

"A Gross Economic Quantity"

Despite such corporate distancing, it was clear that the CED's "adaptive" approach was looked upon favorably within government circles by those who determined national economic policy. It was probably no coincidence that in 1962 the *Economic Report of the President* carried an added line in its title: "Together with the Annual Report of the Council of Economic Advisers."

Here, the words of CEA authors Walter W. Heller, Kermit Gordon and James Tobin, reflected not only CED's "adaptive" approach to agriculture, but also incorporated some of the suggestions that the same committee had made in previous farm policy position papers, papers which we will examine shortly.

Many more children are born and raised on farms than will be needed to produce the nation's food and fiber. They must be educated, trained and guided to non-agricultural employment... .

Objectives of agricultural policy as it develops in the future should encompass both 1) continuation of agriculture's historic role as a major contributor to national economic growth and 2) equitable distribution of gains in agricultural productivity between farmers and consumers. Achievement of these two objectives will require continued rapid transfer of labor from the farm to the nonfarm sector and reduction in resources devoted to the production, storage, and disposition of surplus production.

The drive by the nation's "communities of economic interests" to rid U.S. agriculture of its "excess human resources" was becoming firmly embedded in the Federal government's approach to farm policy.

Such an approach by the CED, agricultural economists and now the Federal government, treated farmers in the words of Johnson D. Hill and Walter E. Stuerman in their book *Roots in the Soil*, as a "gross economic quantity." They add:

The CED argues from finances to persons, rather than from persons to finances. And they argue about finances on the basis of the myth of a *laissez-faire* economy. Their program boils down to a manipulation of persons in accord with a myth which they, as businessmen — men from the urban-industrial context — cherish and seek to propagate.[4]

The most incisive criticism of the CED approach to the farm problem came from economist Carl Wilken.[5] At the outset, Wilken challenged the CED's authors' assumptions, questioning what *Acres, U.S.A.* publisher Charles Walters, Jr. would later describe as their "foundations for conjectural economics."[6]

Wilken recounted the record of agriculture since the early 1930s to illustrate how the CED's conceptualizations did not explain "the way our economy operates." In fact, he noted, the "have-more-to-buy-manufactured-goods" thesis was static. It could not and did not explain how income was generated and distributed.

Wilken and others had long disputed the idea held by many monetary experts that it is the banks which create real money by making loans since such endeavors were often limited by their own pragmatic judgment of whether they would be paid back.

Realistically, this "limiting factor" in the earning of profits had to be considered tangible in nature if a proper sense of values was to be realized. If economists accepted such a contention, Wilken argued, then they would be forced to call for a policy of high, rather than low raw material prices, or at least raw material prices that were in line with other goods and services, simply because it was the monetization of raw material production which in fact created real money.[7]

Despite such reasoning, Wilkens reminded us, raw material prices have traditionally and intentionally been kept low as a matter of public policy since low prices force the agricultural economy to borrow constantly in order to maintain its production levels. If raw material prices were kept at a parity price, he went on to show, farmers and consumers could *earn* enough to buy the products while more of the real wealth would be kept in circulation. (See Chapter 37) As history has shown, however, excessive debt merely funnels the nation's wealth into fewer and fewer hands.

Most agricultural policy writers, Wilken contended, seem to believe that the economy can function by taking the consumer price level, subtracting transportation, wage, and manufacturing costs, etc. and then giving the raw material producer the leavings, whether it covers his costs or not.

To those who argued that most manufactured high raw material prices would seriously disrupt international trade Wilken pointed out that goods entering the United States from abroad were certainly not being paid for at half the price it cost to produce them. The United States wasn't paying for cheap steel with high priced IBM machines, it was paying for them with cheap food commodities. Cheap raw material prices in the United States also served to keep raw materials cheap in other countries, particularly those Third World nations which the United States was dependent on for cash crops.[8]

In the post-Korean war period foreign markets for U.S. farm products began to disappear while an ever-mounting surplus of the nation's farm goods accumulated. The fact that farm prices were deteriorating while agricultural economists argued for reduced price supports, symbolized to Wilken the fundamental dichotomy facing agriculture.

Instead of correcting the farm price situation and restoring our primary markets, those in charge of government and business instituted the credit expansion to revive the economy. Instead of helping agriculture it merely forced farm prices downward as money was diverted away from the purchase of non-durable goods, 90 percent of which are processed from farm products, to capital goods or goods normally purchased from savings or profits.[9]

Walters has further described this period as one in which

no production x no price = no income was being refuted by the fact that men with international cunning knew how to create debt, buy time, make a profit, buy more time, scuttle the private enterprise system, buy still more time, profit from war, and depart the scene before their legacy came home to roost.[10]

In his testimony before the Congressional committee evaluating the 1962 CED report Wilken prophetically sketched a debt-expansion scenario that is still being played out today:

In 1953 the Korean War ended and our debt expansion dropped back from $46 billion in 1953 to $30 billion in 1954. That was not enough borrowed money to offset the operating loss due to low farm prices, and we immediately moved into the 1954 depression.[11]

He went on to show how the failure to restore farm prices made it necessary to increase the debt injection into the economy each year, and any failure to do so brought on an inevitable slump. He warned that this compounded debt injection would most likely soon become impossible to overcome since it would begin to outrun any physical possibility of repayment.

Wilken also attacked the reoccurring "surplus" syndrome, the concept that importation of four to five percent of a product should be allowed to break the price structure for American producers down to the world level on the grounds that a surplus existed. He refuted such notions by pointing out that at that time there existed a $96 billion inventory in the manufacturing, wholesale and retail trade while farm products were accounting for a mere inventory of $8 billion.

This $96 billion surplus in the hands of American business has not been permitted to break the price. Who is paying the cost? The consumer is paying the cost because the manufacturer, the wholesaler and the retailer must recover the cost of storage and the warehousing of the goods when he marks the price tags on what he has to sell.[12]

Inventory, therefore, remained the key issue for agriculture. As Walters would later write,

Business manipulation, and agriculture's failure to develop arrangements so that each farm could handle its own inventory — and institutional arrangements for agriculture as a whole marketing in an orderly manner now made it possible for businessmen [CED] to write a policy paper that in effect told farmers to go out of business so that others could pluck the leavings.

The Big Squeeze

As noted, many of the authors of the 1962 CED report would go on to serve in positions of farm policy-making power in the Federal government. It is thus unsurprising that, as a 1974 follow-up report by the CED reveals federal policy followed the 1962 Committee's recommendations and succeeded in "squeezing" out an untold number of "excess human resources."

The situation of U.S. agriculture has changed drastically within a decade. In 1962, when the Committee issued the policy statement, "An Adaptive Program for Agriculture," the problems of U.S. farming were mainly related to maintaining farm income in the face of continuing surpluses. The diagnosis was that agriculture was using too many resources; fewer farms and farmers could produce all the output then required or

even more than could be marketed. As a result of these findings, we prescribed programs "for the better use of our resources in agriculture [that], vigorously prosecuted, would enable the people involved in farming to receive higher incomes without government controls or subsidy.

In general, policies of this nature have been pursued by the U.S. government, with the result described in the present statement; namely, that U.S. agriculture today is far more efficient, a far more productive industry.

Thus the CED concluded that its past analysis and recommendations had been fundamentally correct, that the government had faithfully followed its recommendations and that the desired results had been achieved.

As indicated in its introduction to the 1974 report, the CED policy planners believed that enough "excess resources" had been removed from agriculture (primarily through the enforcement of below parity pricing), so the time had come to "stabilize the farm population to maintain production for helping the world food crisis and for keeping food prices down here at home." Thus, the ultimate goal of the CED had been accomplished.

Because of the sustained reduction in farm population, production has become concentrated on fewer farms. As a result, two readily identifiable segments of agriculture have emerged, one geared largely to farming, the other to jobs in the industrial and service economies.

The farm population (4.5 percent) is now so small in relation to the total population that further migration from farms will not be substantial. Annual agricultural employment, which was 4.5 million persons only ten years ago, is now about 3.5 million persons, or only 4 percent of the total labor force, and it is still declining. It represents approximately the optimum farm labor force that this Committee envisaged for the 1970s in its statement "An Adaptive Program for Agriculture."

For the CED the creation of a two-tier system of agriculture, with a few large farms and the majority poor enough for welfare, was now a reality!

This statement examines the vast changes that have taken place in U.S. agriculture in the past decade. The reduction in the number of farms, the great increase in productivity, the industrialization of farming, and the urbanization of rural life has produced two readily identifiable agricultural sectors.

One sector consists of large farms that, although numbering about 25 percent of all farms, produce 80 percent of all food marketings. This group is engaged in the production of the major food and fiber crops such as grain, oilseeds, and cotton. These products of commercial agriculture have been the focus of U.S. agricultural policy over the past 40 years and are now the major crops in world trade.

The other 75 percent of U.S. farms, accounting for only 20 percent of the output, are operated largely by farmers who are increasingly dependent on the industrial and service sectors of the economy to provide supplemental or full-time employment. *Where financial distress exists in this group, it is rooted mainly in general social and economic causes, not in farm prices.* Assistance for these farmers *should be extended not through special support programs, but rather through the same kind of program that should be made available to all disadvantaged Americans, urban or rural* (e.g., *through a national welfare assistance program based on a minimum annual income*).(emphasis added)

The CED's concern here for "disadvantaged Americans" is curious. William C. Frederick, a Professor of Business Ethics from the University of Pittsburgh, writing in the Spring, 1981 issue of *California Management Review*, carefully examined this concern in his essay: "Free Market vs. Social Responsibility: Decision Time at the CED."

Contrasting a June 1971 CED report on "Social Responsibilities of Business Corporations" with a 1979 Committee study, "Redefining Government's Role in the Market System," Frederick shows how the former report invited business to expand its social horizons by thinking of itself as a socioeconomic institution. The latter report, however, addressed itself mainly to the importance of the economic efficiency of markets. He concluded that,

CED's tradition and the extent of opposition to the [1971] statement on social responsibility reveal that it was never entirely comfortable with the prickly subject. Reinforcing its ideological homecoming in 1979 were the ever more intrusive regulatory agencies (OSHA, EPA, FTC, CPSC) with their burdensome and costly bureaucratic trappings. The enduring themes of CED's business philosophy appear to be that profits must prevail over social responsibility, that market solutions are preferred to government-assisted efforts, that government actions must be curbed or "disciplined" to protect the market system, and that social progress is a function of a market-centered economic process.

It is no accident that soon after the CED's 1979 report the nation's business community culminated this "ideological homecoming" by installing Ronald Reagan in the White House.

It's Luther Tweeten Time Again!

The authors of the 1974 CED report, like those who drafted the one in 1962, were well-positioned both inside and outside government to see to it that their recommendations were implemented. For example, the membership of the CED's Subcommittee on Government Farm Policy, which wrote the 1974 report, included individuals from many corporate agribusiness giants:

John H. Daniels, Independent Bancorporation, Chairman;
Joseph W. Barr, Franklin National Bank;
William O. Beers, Kraftco Corp.;
Robert J. Carlson, Deere & Co.;
Robert C. Cosgrove, Green Giant Co.;
R. Hal Dean, Ralston Purina Co.;
Alfred W. Eames, Jr., Del Monte Corp.;
Robert T. Foote, Universal Foods Corp.;
Terrance Hanold, The Pillsbury Co.; and
H.J. Heinz, II, H. J. Heinz Co..

Other individuals who served as advisors to the subcommittee included:

Robert Gray, Stanford University Food Institute;
Hendrik S. Houthakker, Harvard University;
D. Gale Johnson, University of Chicago;
Vernon Ruttan, Agribusiness Development Council;
William R. Pearce, Cargill Corp.; and
Luther Tweeten from Oklahoma State University's Department of Agricultural Economics.

Project director was John A. Schnittker, Schnittker Associates, and later a USDA undersecretary.

Luther Tweeten's role in the formulation of CED's agricultural policies is essentially significant. In addition to being the primary contributor to Secretary of Agriculture Bob Bergland's "1978 Report to Congress on the Status of Family Farms," he has served as an agricultural policy advisor in several recent administrations and continues to be (as we learn in Chapter 36) a key farm policy advisor and author.

Tweeten has always pushed for policies which would create an agricultural system consisting of a large number of small farmers supported primarily by off-farm income and available to supply the necessary inputs to a select number of corporate-financed and capital-intensive large farms. In a March 1983, *Science Magazine* article on "The Economics of Small Farms" he asserts that "evidence provides no basis to accept any of the eight small farm hypotheses."

Defining the "small farm" in a one-dimensional dollars-and- cents manner as one which grosses less than $40,000 per year in sales, and the "smaller-than-optimal" size as one between $40,000 and $100,000 in yearly sales, Tweeten listed eight "more or less conventional assertions" concerning such farms. 1) Small farms provide a higher quality of life. 2) Small farm operators take better care of their soil. 3) Small farms are more energy efficient. 4) Small farms offer an alternative to the trauma of outmigration of farm people to cities. 5) Redirection of publicly supported agricultural research and extension can save the small farm. 6) Federal government programs have hastened the demise of small farms. 7) Small farms provide the social and economic support necessary to maintain vitality of nearby towns and cities. 8) Preservation of small farms is essential to preserve competition and avoid concentration.

In denying that such arguments have any real validity — while totally ignoring a significant body of evidence supporting just such arguments — Tweeten simply assumed the role of a corporate agribusiness propagandist rather than an advocate of scientific inquiry. Unfortunately, however, the views of Tweeten and his CED colleagues have come to shape much of our contemporary thought about farm policy.

Minimizing Farmers' Power

A careful reading of its 1974 report makes the CED's actual strategies and tactics abundantly clear despite its attempts to camouflage its ultimate goals and underlying motivations until the end of the report. There it declares: "The absence of widespread surpluses and economic distress resulting from low farm income has provided an atmosphere relatively free of the political pressures from farmers experienced in the past."

Thus, the real target of the CED was the political strength of the farm community. By enforcing below parity prices and providing for income subsidies, the CED planners acknowledge in 1974 that in a large measure they have already been successful in reducing farmers' political impact.

Indeed, the lessening, if not the complete elimination of the farmers' political power, remains a popular refrain even today, long after the CED's 1974 report. Writing in *The Washington Post* op-ed section on January 22, 1987 Nobel Prize economist Milton Friedman declares:

The sharp decline in the relative size of agriculture in the near century since 1890 has clearly been accomplished by an increase rather than decrease in its political clout. And what is true of the United States is true around the world. Almost without exception, wherever a majority of the population is engaged in agriculture — as in most poor countries in the world -farmers are taxed to subsidize the urban minority. By contrast, wherever only a small minority of the population is engaged in agriculture — as in most highly developed countries — the urban majority is taxed to subsidize farmers.

The reason is straightforward. A group that seeks benefits through political pressure is handicapped by being too numerous and, at least up to a point, benefited by being few. Government can spend a dollar per member of a majority only by collecting more than a dollar from each member of the minority, each of who will therefore squeal louder than each of the majority will applaud. On the other hand, government can spend a dollar per member of a small minority by collecting only a few cents from each member of a large majority — the applause is then far louder than the squeal.

And, Friedman adds,

Agriculture not only provides a striking example of this universal political law, but also suggests that the optimum political coalition may be very small indeed. Over the past three decades, agricultural employment has declined from nearly 6 percent of the adult population to less than 2 percent. At the same time, spending by the De-

partment of Agriculture per person employed in agriculture has multiplied nearly tenfold, from less than $2,000 to nearly $18,000. Political clout indeed.

... We pride ourselves on being ruled by a majority, yet the majority repeatedly accedes to being *fleeced by special interest minorities*. In the main, we become active politically only on behalf of our own special interest. Resolving that dilemma is the major political problem we face in preserving our freedom. (emphasis added)

Mark Ritchie, a former special agricultural trade consultant to the Minnesota State Department of Agriculture, and a long-time rural activist who first alerted thousands of today's farmers to the past policy efforts of the CED in his popular pamphlet, *The Loss of Our Family Farms: Inevitable Results or Conscious Policy*, views this minimizing of farmers' political power as crucial to corporate agribusiness for several reasons.

1) Many farmers have historically aligned themselves with trade unions and urban workers. In addition to the efforts of the agrarian populists and groups like the Non-Partisan League there has been the formation of Farmer-Labor Parties, which held political power in a dozen midwest and southwest states.

These parties were committed to the restriction and control of corporations in their states.

2) Corporate agribusiness in seeking to achieve its three fundamental goals: a) substituting capital for efficiency and technology for labor; b) standardizing the food supply, and c) creating synthetic and manufactured food sees the role of U.S. farmers in producing raw materials as a continual diminishing one.

3) On occasion the political strength of the nation's farmers has resulted in their securing beneficial farm policies, such as parity income. Such policies strengthen farm income and further increase farmers' political power, making it more difficult for corporations to control agriculture in much the same way they now control many other vital U.S. industries.

As noted, CED's early admission that in agriculture "capital could not receive an adequate return on investment" led their planners in 1962 to argue that breaking the power of the farmers was necessary to force a third of them off the land and into unemployment. Once that was accomplished to the CED's satisfaction, maintaining the large majority of those left on some form of government-subsidized welfare would become a secondary task, thus insuring the farmers' political impotence.

"Severe injustices," such as those recommended by Boulding, ranging from below parity pricing to putting farmers into a lifetime of debt, thus became a driving force behind the many policy recommendations offered by the CED and any number of the corporations it represented. In many instances, these same corporations implemented such policies by not only influencing government actions (their policy-makers serving in the government), but also by fostering economic plans which succeeded in "squeezing out" millions of farmers and relegating them to social welfare programs at an enormous expense to the nation's taxpayers.

The implications of this "squeeze play" upon the increasingly important world trade and international economic situation were explored in another of Ritchie's rather sobering articles, "Food Diplomacy: An Historical Precedent," in the July 1983 edition of *Catholic Rural Life.*

Noting that since World War II the United States has had two main "food diplomacy" strategies — the exporting of grains and the highly controlled importing of specific food products like sugar, meat, dairy products, and fresh produce — he goes on to point out that

> before the U.S. government can achieve its primary economic objective, dramatic increases in grain sales to Europe, they must first destroy the European food security policies that encourage domestic production by controlling grain imports. This political objective, the destroying of European farm programs, has taken on an increasingly bitter tone.

While such foreign policy objectives, both economic and political, have thus far failed, the domestic political policy goals — diffusing the anger of hard-pressed U.S. farmers — necessary to achieve those foreign policy objectives have been relatively successful.

> By painting a picture of "unjust policies protecting inefficient farmers," the blame for the low prices falls on farmers, not the academics, industry and government people enforcing the "low price" policies.
>
> If farmers can successfully be confused and diverted towards blaming 'external enemies,' it will be easier for them to forget that their economic crisis is in fact caused by intentionally low price policies of the U.S. government, and by the 'side-effects' of aggressive, destructive U.S. food weaponry, including the recent Russian grain embargo.

Ritchie notes that the current international food policies of Pax Americana frighteningly resemble those of "agricultural cartelization" found in Nazi Germany prior to World War II. The latter was a plan instituted by the major industrialists, the Junkers and the military to dramatically increase food imports from Germany's neighbors, "hooking" them on an economic dependency to the Fatherland.

> Germany's Agricultural Cartelization Programme was the tactic used to create the necessary changes in the agricultural structure to carry out its 'food diplomacy' strategy. Enforced lower domestic prices to achieve dramatic increases in food imports required both politically weakened family farmers and a tightly-controlled centralized industrial-type management over the entire farm economy. Cartelization was the perfect answer.

As we have seen, in the United States the tactic that seemed the most promising to meet the needs of this "tightly-controlled centralized industrial-type management" was the lowering of prices of basic commodities to the "choking point," thereby placing enormous pressures on large numbers of farmers to leave agriculture and politically weakening those who choose to stay.

For Germany, the consequences of those policies as Alfred Sohn-Rethel reminds us so graphically in his classic economic history, *Economy and Class Structure of German Fascism,* were disastrous:

> [In December, 1932] I.G. Farben (the single most important German manufacturing firm) ... accepted the project of Agrarian Cartelization. The winning of I.G. Farben for the policy completed the industrial programme of reuniting the vital sections of German monopoly capital on a common imperialist programme. Now the pre-condition was given for lifting a dictatorial government into power, and this was established on January 30, 1933, under the Chancellorship of Hitler.

Sohn-Rethel goes on to explain that Hitler went forward to develop his own policies to continue the breaking of the political power of farmers by instituting the ominous Farm Inheritance Law. "The Farm Inheritance Law immobilized farming capital in Germany to such an extent that the majority of peasant farmers were quite unable to muster up any more ready credit and had to pawn their actual harvests in order to pay for the barest essentials."

Progress???

Since they first issued their 1974 report the CED's corporate planners have recognized that certain "changes" in strategy were necessary to achieve their goal of restructuring American agriculture. Thus, they adapted in the name of "progress" and "efficiency."

One change they immediately recognized was that if the "toothpaste is thin [in Boulding's words] it will squeeze out of the tube easier." Therefore, supposedly to soften the economic blow to those farmers who resisted moving out of agriculture, Washington began defining their problem as one of "cash flow." In the late 1970s this problem was addressed by inflating land prices, but packaging it as "income" for farmers, in the form of more credit to help "tide them over."

By masquerading what was in effect a growing debt load in the alluring garb of increasing the farmer's "cash flow," this tactic put additional pressure on farmers to produce more and more raw materials. This was ostensibly to meet growing world food demands, but in fact only furthered corporate agribusiness's "cheap food" policy and created enough of a surplus to drive commodity prices to record lows and made it impossible for many farmers to cover even their production costs.

When the bottom inevitably fell out of the land market, many farmers not only found themselves unable to repay their loans, but were also faced with losing many of their principal assets, including their land (often built up over several generations), to banks, insurance companies, farm management firms and large corporations.

Another change in the CED's strategy soon became apparent in its adoption of the "plight of the small farmer" as an issue of national concern. It had discovered that its initial plans to "squeeze out" thousands of these family farms were being stoutly resisted both by a few influential politicians and also by many of the nation's farmers who chose even to accept a meager farm income in a determined effort to both retain and control their small, yet indispensable, parcels of land.

While Tweeten and Co. and others would like us to think that the solution for most of today's farmers is the old Butzist refrain of "free market," "get big or get out," "adapt or die!"; the USDA's *A Time to Choose* saw the situation quite differently. Its 1981 report on the structure of agriculture points out that it is the $40,000 to $100,000 group of farmers who are the ones having "the most difficulty surviving as farmers" despite the fact that they have farms that are "for the most part, large enough to realize most of the efficiencies associated with size, who have little off-farm income, and who, in some cases, do not have sufficient volume for an adequate income."

And most importantly, this uniquely relevant government study stresses: "The changed financial structure of these farms would suggest they are much more vulnerable *because of the increased variability of incomes and returns.*" (emphasis added)

As it goes on to add:

Recent studies reaffirm, for example, earlier findings that the long run average cost curve for farms decreases rapidly as farm size increases, up to a point, and then becomes relatively flat over a wide range in size. It thus appears that most of the primary farms have reached or surpassed the size needed to attain most economies related to size. *The major portion of our food and fiber is thus produced by firms that are beyond the most technically efficient size.*" (emphasis added)

All Hail the "Free Market"

Despite these appraisals and other compatible public and private studies in recent years, the CED mentality, as expressed not only in its 1962 and 1974 reports, but even earlier on, has dominated the farm policy debate for the past four decades. Yet, the CED has traditionally seen the so-called "free market" as the most certain policy for agriculture and one they believe that ultimately will resolve its "disequilibrium" problem.

Many believe that equilibrium in agriculture is achieved when the quantity of resources used in farm production is such that the output of those resources will generate returns equal to their acquisition costs. Likewise, disequilibrium is evidenced by low returns to productive resources (particularly labor) and, when market prices are supported to maintain incomes, output is in excess (surpluses) of that which will clear the market.

In the late 1940s and 1950s groups like the CED and the Twentieth Century Fund argued that the gap be-

tween the equilibrium price and the market price that existed without government intervention was not large.

By the early 1960s, however, the CED recognized the gap had become large and that a return to the "free market" would involve painful adjustments. Past and present price-support programs, which they believed had been responsible for part of the disequilibrium level of "excessive resources" in agriculture, were thus dubbed as the culprit. To cushion the inevitable "short-run income declines" the CED believed that while a return to "market prices" as a guide to present and future "resource allocation" was necessary, special programs would be needed to make such a transition successful.

In 1945 that the CED first issued a paper, "Agriculture In An Expanding Economy," that defined the basic cause of agriculture's troubles as "the excess of human resources engaged in agriculture," and expressed the belief that "the flow of labor from the farms must take place even when farming is enjoying good times."

Exhibiting what would become its decidedly urban bias, the CED proclaimed that "the farm is the seedbed of our population" and "it is the most important source of *new blood for the cities,* whose population does not otherwise sustain itself." (emphasis added) In addressing the "farm problem" the CED also called for a "redefinition" of parity since "the needed standard of measurement cannot be expressed in terms of commodity relationships."

This new definition, it argued, also needed to account for creating conditions favorable to "the enjoyment of at least a fair *minimum standard of realized income* by farm families" and a guide for farm production into the pattern that makes for the "most efficient use of agricultural resources." (emphasis added)

At about the time this paper was published Theodore W. Schultz, Professor of Agricultural Economics at the University of Chicago and a member of the CED's Research Advisory Council, was publishing, under the sponsorship of the CED, his *Agriculture in an Unstable Economy.*

In this book Schultz discussed in detail the significance of "excess labor resources" on farms, the "failure" of price mechanisms to induce shifts of "resources" out of agriculture, the differences between the farm and industrial sectors in "responding" to reduced demand, the importance to farmers of continued "prosperity" in *business,* and a "solution" to the farm problem without resort to price floors or restrictions on output.[15]

In Search of Non-Partisanship

In 1956 the CED made another bold attempt to play a direct role in determining farm policy.

In a paper, "Economic Policy for American Agriculture," after reiterating some of its earlier positions on the source of the "farm problem", the Committee suggested that a "non-partisan" board of representatives (modeled after the Federal Reserve Board) of farmers, food processors and consumers, serving long terms and staggered so as to provide continuity, be established to determine national agricultural policy. Later, in evaluating various proposals designed to change the policy making process in agriculture, agricultural economist Dale Hathaway, would write:

> The intended purpose of such a board [was] to remove agriculture policy from the short-run political pressures. However, it has been pointed out that to a large extent the relevant decision-making groups in the Congress and the Department of Agriculture are not motivated primarily by partisan politics. If the proposed board were chosen from the membership of the commodity interest groups, their access to and influence over farm policy would be strengthened. If it were not, such groups would oppose it.[16]

The CED's 1958 paper, "Toward A Realistic Farm Program," also contains many of the seeds that would spring up in its more widely-read study four years later. In noting that its proposed programs "means getting resources — people and land — out of agriculture and freeing farm prices" the Committee declared that

> the higher average farm incomes resulting from dividing farm incomes among fewer operators will make many farm towns more prosperous. But the flow of people out of agriculture will decrease the trade of other rural towns. This is part of the relocation necessary to a solution of our agricultural problems.

Discussing the special approaches needed to aid low income farmers, the CED pointed out that "the problem of the farmer who is chronically poor is outside the scope of programs designed to assist the commercial farmer." As a means of bettering the conditions of the "poor" farmers the report suggests an approach "based upon the opportunities arising from a growing, high-employment economy" and emphasizes that farmers will need "training and resources for a transfer to more profitable and productive employment."

It should come as no surprise that a committee with over 20 members of the Board of Trustees from farm equipment and implement corporations and 16 other trustees from oil and chemical companies would issue a report advocating a "realistic farm program" that would speak of efficiency in terms of machines and chemicals rather than people:

> Prosperous, larger farms will be efficiently operated farms, making optimum use of fertilizers and of productive equipment. The farms that will be taken permanently out of production are not the farms using significant amounts of either. Except in the short run, our program requires more emphasis upon the redirection of *people* from agriculture to better opportunities elsewhere than it does upon retirement of land.

A Process Feeding On Itself

The CED has not been alone in its approach to solving the "farm problem."

In March 1945 the Agricultural Department Committee of the U.S. Chamber of Commerce in a report, "Variations in Farm Incomes and Their Relation to Agricultural Policies," stated that "from the standpoint of national policy the importance of the larger producing units in the agricultural industry should be recognized." The committee, composed of representatives from Ralston Purina, Armour & Co., Carnation Co., General Electric, Pillsbury, Stouffer Corp., the Indiana State Grange, and the Arkansas Farm Bureau, among others, declared that national policies "should be directed toward the third [two million of the six million farmers in business in 1939] or, at most, the half of the farmers on whom American consumers are dependent for their supply of agricultural products." Dismissing the "low-producing farm units" [an estimated 1.5 million farm families] the Chamber of Commerce report observed:

> There is evidence that in a great many cases its members have become habituated to a primitive environment and prefer it to any other. Often there has been developed little desire for the variety of material things associated with a higher standard of living, if their attainment must be at the cost of that freedom which comes from self-employment and a leisurely mode of life... Very often the ambition, the energy, and the managerial ability, as well as the capital and experience necessary for larger-scale production, are lacking.
>
> Although these farms are definitely of the *family type* and apparently constitute a substantial portion of that type which is supposed to be the backbone of the nation, their limited incomes inevitably create conditions which fall far short of being favorable for the development of a high type of worker and citizen.

Twenty-nine years later the Chamber issued still another report, "The Changing Structure of U.S. Agribusiness and Its Contributions to the National Economy," exhorting U.S. agriculture to "focus on more intensive use of existing resources for increased production." The report warned that "the current wave of state and federal legislation to prohibit farming by major corporations will be counter-productive in an industrialized food system where consumers' interests are paramount." It argued further:

> The food system is predicated on continual reorganization of production by more efficient methods. As an industry expands, it furnishes an enlarged market for the output of other industries which tend to grow and furnish enlarged markets to still others. With potentials for specialization, economies of size, and applications of technology, the process feeds on itself.

Finding ways to get farmers off the land has also been the focus of other groups in the post-war years, such as the American Bankers Association. In 1958 its Agricultural Commission and Economic Policy Commission issued a paper, "The Farm Problem," an attempt by the nation's bankers, through a "factual discussion" of American agriculture, "to give a better understanding of the problems, and a summary of major alternatives."

Noting that the price situation in agriculture was in large measure resulted from "overcapacity to produce in some lines" the report suggested that such lines needed to be "helped to get back into balance." In proposing a remedy — the immediate discontinuing of pricing programs leaving the problem to farmers themselves and the "free market" on one hand and higher supports extended to a larger list of commodities on the other — the bankers affirmed their belief that a proper adjustment would involve land and people.

> Overexpansion simply means that too many resources are being used in some lines ... The productive resources involved are people, land, capital and know-how. There is no logic in proposing that there be a return to outmoded and less efficient methods in order to get rid of surplus capacity. The role of know-how in farming will increase, as it should, in a world of progress. Nor is there prospect that there will be any major cut in the use of capital. Increasing mechanization and new technology will call for more rather than less capital even though farm consolidation leads to more efficient use. Adjustment hence involves mainly land and people.

The report goes on to state that while land resource use needs to be guided by anticipated returns, "it is not good use of manpower to keep more people than are needed in agriculture or in any other line." Farm families, therefore, need to be encouraged to seek "better earning opportunities elsewhere" and such shifts "deserve to be aided and encouraged, not hindered." In making the argument for a shift to larger more "efficient" farms, the ABA commission's study also notes that "banks can aid desirable adjustments by participating in providing needed capital." The report concludes with four possible program alternatives:

1) Maintain or even raise present price supports and related programs and expand them to farm products generally as a long-run governmental function;

2) discontinue government price supports and acquisition of farm products, leaving the pricing and disposal to the farmers and the market;

3) "muddle along as we have been doing in the hope that the situation will right itself ... ", and

4) recognize that the "basic problem is one of too many *productive resources* being assigned to lines in surplus, and attack this problem by public policies aimed at bringing about and speeding — rather than preventing or unduly delaying — *the desired adjustments in resource use.*" (italics added)

In an "epilogue" to their study the bankers add:

> While the purpose of this report is not to outline a specific farm program, alternative four appeals to the Agricultural Commission and Economic Policy Commission as being the one most likely to bring the needed improvement ... The costs to the public of the required adjustments will be considerable; but with an effective program, these are likely to be much less than those which will have to be met if present programs are continued.

Two and one-half decades later, in the midst of a near-record number of small town and rural bank failures and the worst depression in U.S. agricultural history with a record number of farm bankruptcies and forced liquidations, another ABA agricultural task force expressed opposition to any moratorium on farm loan foreclosures.

Speaking for the task force was Brenton Bank of Iowa's president, Robert Brenton, ABA's president-elect. It is not surprising that Brenton, who claimed such a moratorium would "hurt" farmers, give them a false sense of hope, and harm the nation's economic development by raising fears of a depression, would issue such a statement. It was merely in keeping with the family tradition for W. Harold Brenton, the bank's founder, had served both as Chairman of the CED's Agricultural Subcommittee (which issued the 1962 report) and as a member of CED's Research and Policy Committee.[17]

Finally, in 1985 the Trilateral Commission, formed in 1973 by "private citizens" of Western Europe, Japan, and North America "to foster closer cooperation among these three regions on common problems" and "improve public understanding of such problems" by supporting "proposals for handling them jointly and to nurture habits and practices of working together among these regions" issued its own report evaluating trends in current agricultural policy.[18]

Its report, *Agricultural Policy and Trade: Adjusting Domestic Programs In An International Framework*, was authored by D. Gale Johnson of the University of Chicago (and CED fame), Kenzo Hemmi, former Dean of the Faculty of Agriculture at the University of Tokyo, and Pierre Lardinois, Chairman of the Executive Board - Rabobank. In part they concluded,

> The level of farm prices *does* determine to some degree how many *people* will be engaged in agriculture, which leads us to another basic analytical point reflected in the postwar economic history of all our countries. The process of economic growth everywhere requires *that the absolute level of employment in agriculture decline over time.* Farm employment *must* decline given the combination of low income elasticity of demand for farm products (*i.e.*, demand increases more slowly than income in our countries) with productivity change at least as rapid as in the rest of the economy. In fact increases in *labor productivity* in agriculture have generally been *greater* than in industrial employment. (emphasis added)

And in addressing domestic prices the Trilateral Commission report states:

> In sum, the agricultural achievements of the trilateral countries are real and substantial. The cost of food has been reduced as a component of

consumer budgets, agricultural productivity has increased at a rapid pace, *most* of the adjustments in farm employment required by economic growth have now occurred, and the degree of food security has been enhanced with the great expansion of international trade in agricultural products in the past two decades.(emphasis added)

Section Five:

"The Reign it's Plain
is Mainly in the Grain"

"It's hard to imagine a national debate on energy or oil without frequent mention of such corporate giants as Gulf or Exxon. Yet that is what has occurred in the debate on the nation's 'farm crisis,' with names like Cargill, Continental and Bunge seldom mentioned and scarcely recognized as having a critical stake in and likely influence over U.S. agriculture policy."

Mike Dennison, Montana journalist

Chapter Twenty-Eight

Ebenezer Scrooge Was A Grain Trader

"If you want my corn gentlemen, you must meet my quote, plus 5 percent for the delay!"

"That's outrageous Scrooge, you'll be left with a warehouse stuffed with corn."

"Well, that's my affair, isn't it? Buy the corn someplace else, good day sir."

"Scrooge, a moment. We'll take your corn at the price you quoted yesterday."

"Too late! you wait until tomorrow and it will cost you another 5 percent!"

"Damn it Scrooge, it's not fair!"

*"No, but it's **business**!"*

-*A Christmas Carol* by Charles Dickens
CBS-TV, December 22, 1985.

Because they dominate the "business" of moving the world's farm commodities from the fields of agriculturally rich nations to people's tables spanning the globe, large multinational companies like Cargill, Continental Grain, Louis Dreyfus, Bunge and Mitsui/Cook accrue to themselves much of the world's "new wealth," a wealth that some critics rightly argue belongs to the many, not the few.

But for us even to begin to understand how the grain trade has become the major beneficiary of the so-called "free market system" of agriculture, we must first acquaint ourselves with its principal actors and its basic characteristics, as well as its history and how it operates in today's world and domestic food markets.

In 1921 some 36 firms accounted for 85 percent of the United States's wheat exports;[1] by the end of the 1970s just six companies Cargill, Continental Grain, Louis Dreyfus, Bunge, Andre & Co. and Mitsui/Cook — exported 96 percent of all U.S. wheat, 95 percent of its corn, 90 percent of its oats and 80 percent of the nation's sorghum. The top five companies also handled 90 percent of the Common Market's trade in wheat and corn, 90 percent of Canada's barley exports, 80 percent of Argentina's wheat exports, and 90 percent of Australia's sorghum exports. Together, the aforementioned six companies accounted for over 60 percent of the world's grain traffic, including shipments under food assistance programs.[2]

Since the U.S. exports nearly 30 percent of the food grown by its farmers (with U.S. wheat exports averaging 36 percent of the world's wheat exports between 1981 and 1985; corn, 72 percent; soybeans, 52 percent; cotton, 28 percent, and rice, 18 percent and grain accounting for 76 percent of world agricultural trade) the power of the grain trade's elite to control world food supplies is awesome.

The leaders in the grain trade are the two U.S.-based giants, Cargill Corp. and Continental Grain, which each control about 25 percent of the market, followed by Bunge with approximately 15-20 percent, and the Louis Dreyfus Corp., with another ten percent. While the secret nature of the trade makes it difficult to ascertain exact market shares, a 1974 survey by the GAO on grain exporters' opinions of the USDA's Export Sales Reporting System demonstrates the tight concentration in the grain trade.

The survey respondents represented, in terms of sales and exports, almost all of the 316 agricultural export businesses that filed export sales reports with the USDA in 1974. A mere 4.7 percent of the companies accounted for over 60 percent of the total year's sales, while over 81 percent of the companies accounted for only 8.3 percent of the total sales. Another GAO study has shown that from 1974 to 1980, farm cooperatives increased their share but 1.1 percent, while the five largest multinationals lost only 5.3 percent. Firms with Japanese ownership or affiliation gained 4.7 percent, due in large part to the Mitsui & Co.'s purchase of Cook & Co.'s assets in 1978.[3]

Significantly, cooperatives established to sell the grain of farmer-members are almost helpless to offer overseas customers grain from other countries where it may be available at discount rates. In the meantime, these same farm co-ops have frequently come to the aid of the grain companies by storing thousands of bushels of grain until company customers can be found. Thus, many co-ops are not so much *traders*, as *marketers* selling to a small group of elite corporations.

The USDA notes that four out of every five U.S. farmers use cooperatives to either market their products, provide them with supplies or procure needed services. The fact that nationwide co-op membership is approximately 4.1 million indicates that many farmers belong to more than one cooperative. Farmers market 26 percent of their raw products, led by dairy and grain sales, through their various co-ops.

Farm equity in these cooperatives at the end of 1988 was $25.5 billion. USDA's Agricultural Cooperative Service (ACS) also reports that some 4,700 co-ops in 1988 transacted $66.4 billion in business with a net income of $1.68 billion.

The USDA has also estimated that on the average, farm cooperatives sell 70 percent of their export-bound grain not to foreign customers but to the grain trade's elite.[4] Farm co-ops abroad report the same difficulty: when they enter the export market, they must almost invariably compete against the likes of Cargill and Continental for international customers.

While they sell high volumes of grain anywhere to anyone, the majority of the grain trade elite's business comes from transactions conducted in tight secrecy among their own affiliates. There is a second tier of smaller grain trading firms which frequently find themselves used by the trade to substantiate so-called "competitiveness" in the grain business. In fact, these smaller firms are usually forced to rely on the trade's elite for much of their business.

Often, rather than compete with such smaller firms, the larger traders simply buy them out. For example, in 1985 Cargill purchased six soybean processing plants from Ralston Purina, making Cargill the nation's largest soybean processor (with 19 plants throughout the United States). Similarly in 1984, Continental Grain announced that it was assuming the interests in five Texas grain terminals with a combined capacity of more than 30 million bushels from AGRI Industries of West Des Moines, Iowa, a regional grain marketing cooperative. (There are indications that in an effort to survive, many of these "second-tier" companies are attempting to strike back by seeking larger market shares in specific grain-related businesses: hence the 1984 merger of the nation's number five flour miller ConAgra with number four Peavey Corp., creating the nation's largest flour miller with a daily capacity of over 266,000 cwts.)

Chart 28A: Four Firm Concentration in Milling Industry

Flour Milling (61 percent): ConAgra, ADM, Cargill, Grand Metropolitan (Pillsbury).

Soybean Milling (61 percent): ADM, Cargill, Bunge, Agricultural Processors.

Wet Corn Milling (74 percent): ADM, Cargill, Tate & Lyle, PLC (A.E. Staley), CPC.

Dry Corn Milling (57 percent): Bunge (Lauhoff Mills), Illinois cereal Mills, ADM, ConAgra.

Sources: Flour: Census of Manufacturing, 1982, *Milling and Baking News* "Milling Directory for 1990;" Soybean: *Milling and Baking News*, July 13, 1087, Census of Manufacturing, 1982; Wet Corn: *Milling and Baking News*, "Milling Directory for 1990," Census of Manufacturing, 1982; and Dry Corn: *Corn: Chemistry and Technology, 1989*: 352, Census of Manufacturing, 1982.

Former Representative James Weaver, D-Oregon, ex-member of the House Agricultural Committee, once described this increasing concentration within the grain trade in somewhat vivid terms to the Center for the Study of Responsive Law's Andy Moore:

> These companies are giants. They control not only the buying and the selling of grain but the shipment of it, the storage of it and everything else. It's obscene. I have railed against them again and again. I think food is the most — hell, whoever controls the food supply has really got the people by the scrotum. And yet we allow six corporations to do this in secret. It's mind boggling!

Today, the trade's elite are engaged in a myriad of other business ventures, not all grain related. Equally important, most of these companies are privately owned.

Cargill, headquartered in Minneapolis, Minnesota, is principally owned by members of the MacMillan and Cargill families with minority interests held by some of the company's top executives. Continental Grain is headquartered in New York with Michel Fribourg, the fifth generation of the Fribourg family to have owned and managed the company since it was founded in 1813 at Arlon, Belgium, its chief executive officer and president. Bunge headquartered in Buenos Aires, Argentina, is owned by the Bunge and Born families who serve as its chief executive officers. Paris, France is the headquarters of Louis-Dreyfus, which is owned by members of the Louis-Dreyfus family who also serve as its executive officers. Andre, headquartered in Lausanne, Switzerland, is owned and managed by the Andre family. Cook/Mitsui is an amalgamation of the giant Japanese trading firm and Cook Industries, United States.

Because these companies need large amounts of money available to be moved around the world at a moment's notice and without time-consuming paperwork, they argue that it is advantageous for them to remain private, tightly-controlled, family-run corporations away from the prying eyes of stockholders, free of having to file detailed financial reports with federal regulatory agencies, and in the hands of family members who have a vested interest in the firm and who can be trusted.

I've Got A Secret

Because these giant grain traders are so tightly controlled and the decision-making is vested in so few hands, information on their activities is one of the business community's best kept secrets (despite the fact that the trade receives, as we shall see shortly, billions of dollars in local, state and federal taxpayer subsidies). The secrecy that plays such a key role in the day-to-day operations of the grain trade is sometimes carried to absurd lengths.

In 1975 the *Des Moines Register*'s George Anthan sought by telephone information concerning the Louis-Dreyfus headquarters, its officers, affiliates and facilities. Merton Sarnoff, the company's counsel, responding to a question by Anthan on the location of the company's U.S. headquarters, said, "I'm speaking from a New York number" and promptly added, "it's not normally our policy to comment to the media about our business."

Asked if Gerald L. Dreyfus was president of the firm, Sarnoff replied, "I will make an exception," and confirmed that Dreyfus headed the company. Later, however, he noted, "that mention of Gerald is off the record. I should not mention that he's president. It might be embarrassing to me here."[5]

For some time now the degree of secrecy by which the grain trade shrouds its business dealings has been a matter of considerable concern to farmers, government officials, foreign governments, and the press.

Lester Brown, president of the Worldwatch Institute, candidly describes the situation that confronts so many who deal today with the grain trade.

The thing about the grain trade is that it's very difficult for governments to implement their policies when they don't have control of the [food] resources, and in some cases, don't even have the information on the resources. There's an awful lot that happens in the world grain trade that we learn about after the fact and not before. And that's because the companies thrive on information over which they have much greater control than anyone else ...

It's that ability not only to have their own information networks which gives them an advantage in dealing with farmers and others — individual farmers can't maintain that kind of global market intelligence system but when you add to that the Department of Agriculture working with the grain companies [as a source of data] the farmers really don't have a chance ... If prices jump all over the place they really thrive, because they usually know which way they're going to jump before anyone else.[6]

"Stability, gentlemen, is the one thing we can't deal with"

Because consumers want food security with fair and relatively stable prices while the grain trade desires profits based on market instability, the objectives of the traders and the general public frequently conflict. Price fluctuations and speculation have become important tools to grain traders. Unlike the farmer and the consumer, it matters little to the grain trader whether the price rises or falls. The profit lies in the price *spread*. In 1981 testimony before a House Agricultural Subcommittee, reviewing agricultural export issues, Francis Moore Lappé quoted one Chicago Board of Trade official telling a group of corporate agribusiness executives, "stability, gentlemen, is the one thing we can't deal with."[7]

Researcher Oscar Billey Martinson suggests that to ensure an environment of "controlled instability," the grain traders seek as much control as possible over networks of professional organizations and trade organizations; establish numerous links between individual company employees and government agencies and interlocks with the boards of banks and railroads; and ensure corporate representation on regulatory boards.[8]

Today, a handful of large traders dominate the membership of commodity exchanges like the Chicago Board of Trade, the Kansas City Board of Trade and the Minneapolis Grain Exchange and are disproportionately represented on several of the boards and committees that govern these exchanges.

In 1985, for example, Daniel R. Huber, a director of the Chicago Board of Trade and a member of the executive committee of the National Grain and Feed Association, was appointed president of Tradax Gestion, Cargill Corporation's Swiss affiliate. Through such domination, and similar influence among trade associations and other important trade networks, the large grain traders create "a social-economic environment that eliminates or at least reduces uncertainties that confront independent firms."[9]

It is unnecessary, to look for executives from these companies huddled in a smoke-filled hotel suite, jointly making business decisions harmful to the public. The danger comes from indirect cooperation, for as Martinson points out, "to the extent that ... a small minority of firms engaged in the various facets of grain marketing are able to exercise control over commodity exchange (and trade association) governance they constitute an oligarchy."

Oligopolists may make collective coordinated decisions regarding common environmental contingencies via other organizations whose function is to rationalize the economic action of an entire industry or marketing system. When the oligopolists do so they become an oligarchy of organizations which can subvert at least nominally democratic institutions (*e.g.*, the trade associations and commodity exchanges.[10]

By maintaining a system that enables them to make such coordinated decisions and by information control which enables them to operate interorganizational networks that can transmit feedback through the grain marketing system, these traders maintain market power, which Martinson defines as "the capability of influencing prices, quantities and quality characteristics of grain and grain products being marketed."

Myron Just, North Dakota's former Commissioner of Agriculture, described this situation in his state to a 1976 Senate Subcommittee on Multinational Corporations:

The pyramid of power, as I see it, is 30,000 North Dakota farmers selling through about 500 grain elevators in North Dakota, farmer-owned but discreetly Minneapolis-run in my estimation, into one grain exchange which in turn sells mostly to six large exporters. So, you know, the grain moves in that direction. And the marketing power and marketing information really concentrates as it moves on up. You could say that we really have two and one-half million farmers that feed into this thing and that the power really becomes concentrated at the top.[11]

This type of marketing power enables the grain trade elite not only to limit competition, but also to dictate its own terms to producers and consumers. It is frequently assisted by both acquiescent United States and sympathetic foreign governments.

There is a major agricultural myth that grain traders need to buy grain from farmers at inordinately low prices and sell high to foreign buyers if they are to make money. But, as Richard Gilmore points out in his compelling and comprehensive analysis, *A Poor Harvest: The Clash of Policies and Interests in the Grain Trade*:

> The key to profitability in the grain trade is not the price itself but a host of other factors including the variation in price levels for a commodity *at a given point in time*, the spread between cash and future prices, interest rates, the state of the money markets, and transportation costs... Volume is essential to profitability, but not to profit margins on individual transactions...[12]

Because the largest international grain houses are individually the biggest buyers of their own product, the benefits of interaffiliate transactions often outweigh the apparently lower profit margins such contracts entail. Tax considerations and volume, therefore, are more important to the grain trade elite than price differentials. As Gilmore adds, "it is the variation in daily prices registered on the commodity exchanges, along with the ability to purchase and sell huge volumes of grain throughout the world, that is the gold in the grain and not the grain itself."[13]

Cargill: "From Algeria To Zambia" and "Aluminum To Zinc"

A brief profile of the Cargill Corp., the world's largest trader, will help us understand the nature of the grain trade and how its elite exercise such enormous economic and political power.

Cargill's annual sales in 1989 registered at $44 billion which easily ranks it in the top ten of *Fortune's* Top 500 U.S. Corporations. In its 1990 rankings of the nation's largest private companies, *Forbes* magazine, lists Cargill number one, its sales figure over 60 percent greater than that of the second corporation on the list (Koch Industries) and nearly 300 percent greater than the third largest private corporation, Continental Grain.[14]

Food, of course, earns most of the company's revenues. Cargill is the nation's number one grain exporter, number one egg producer, number three meat packer, number three corn miller, number four wheat miller, number one soybean crusher and in recent years has also become a major force in coffee and orange juice concentrate trading.

Cargill employs 46,000 people and has a net worth valued at $2.4 billion.[15] Three family groups within the Cargill and MacMillan family control over 85 percent of the corporation's stock worth an estimated $675 million (the remaining 15 percent of non-voting stock is controlled by company executives).[16]

Country elevators, some 125 in 16 states, are at the core of the Cargill's grain collecting network in the United States Its total of 340 elevators, terminals and subterminals can collect and assemble over 390 million bushels of grain for shipment via railroad and barge to 16 giant export elevators on the Atlantic, Pacific and Great Lakes for shipment abroad.[17] The company also collects grain from six provinces in Canada, France, Brazil, Argentina and Thailand.

Utilizing 430 barges and nine towboats, which operate on the nation's inland waterways; two large boats, that navigate the Great Lakes; 12 ocean-going ships; 1500 covered railroad hopper cars and 1,000 tank cars, Cargill trades, markets and processes commodities through a network of 700 plants and offices in nearly 48 countries.

The advantage of such a transportation system is explained by Duncan Russell, manager of grain marketing for a Cargill competitor, The Andersons of Maumee, Ohio. "In tough times, Cargill has more capacity weighing on it, but it has more transportation options and it's able to respond better to changes in volume."[18]

Indeed, according to Cargill's vice-chairman Walter ("Barney") Saunders, the grain trade in the mid-1980s was running at one-third or less of its total export elevator capacity. "You can imagine what's happened to the margins," he explains and although he claims grain trading remains a profitable business for Cargill he admits, "in the United States we've suffered."[19]

"Where O' Where's Parky Now?"

Cargill's worldwide operations include: sugar trading in Central and South America, Great Britain, Eastern Europe, the Middle East and Asia; cotton, fiber; and rubber trading operations (through its British-based Bowater Corp.) in India, Pakistan, Turkey and several African countries. "We stick to our knitting like Procter & Gamble," claims Whitney MacMillan, chairman and CEO for Cargill. "How many soaps does P. & G. make? In a sense they're all the same. Can you tell the difference between trading soybeans, cotton and rubber? They're all soaps to us."[20]

Cargill can process 300 million bushels of corn every year and produces 25 different kinds of corn syrup and 800 million pounds of corn starch, converting corn from the U.S. sweeteners for candies and other products. Its high-fructose corn syrup operations usually run at 90 percent of capacity, turning out sweeteners for soft drink companies at the rate of 1.5 billion pounds a year, a pound selling for 18 cents.

In Ontario, Canada, Cargill's Shaver Poultry Breeding farms sells layer chicks to egg producers and broiler chicks to commercial feeder-growers in more than 90 countries. The Cargill ad published in *Milling and Baking News* and shown on the next page describes such operations:

"From Algeria to Zambia" and "Aluminum to Zinc" Cargill's 50 lines of business in 46 countries range from agricultural commodities to life insurance, steel, cocoa, molasses, salt, resins, fertilizer, construction, manufacturing equipment, vegetable oils, etc.

One of Cargill's most interesting ventures in recent years has been the exporting of orange juice concentrate from Brazil, the world's second largest agricultural producer and a country that now accounts for 90 percent of the world's export market in orange juice

HOW CARGILL BUILT A FOREIGN MARKET FOR
U.S. SOYBEANS BY STARTING A CHICKEN
BUSINESS FROM SCRATCH

Several years ago, Cargill saw a way to create a
new market for soybean meal in Indonesia. Cargill
sent one of its managers, Parky Parkinson, there
to build a facility for raising chickens. It started
out small, but today Cargill raises 4 million chickens a year in Indonesia. And they eat a lot of
soybean meal. Where's Parky now? He's gone to
Thailand to open up another market for U.S.
soybeans by starting another chicken business ...
from scratch.

concentrate and controls 60 percent of the total world
market. Cargill Citrus Ltd. has joined with two Brazilian
companies — Sucocitrico Cutrale, which supplies much
of Coca Cola's Minute Maid orange juice demands, and
the German-Brazilian firm Citrosuco Paulista, S.A. — to
control nearly 90 percent of the country's concentrate
exports.[21] In 1986 the Brazilian concentrate accounted
for 40 percent of the U.S. market.[22]

Cargill's heavy export traffic in not only orange juice
concentrate but soybeans as well has occasioned it to
open what the *Journal of Commerce*'s James Bruce calls
"a private export corridor in Brazil." From a private $10
million bulk terminal at the Port of Santos the international grain trader plans to move over 444,000 tons of
citrus meal, soybean meal and soybeans annually. In
1984-1985, before plans for the Port of Santos plant
were announced, one percent of the company's world-
wide commodity movement came from its four Brazilian
processing plants with a capacity to process 2.8 million
tons of soybeans per day and 40 million crates of
oranges annually.[23] Some of Cargill's more recent
acquisitions have been the MBPXL Corp., the nation's
second largest beef packer, a Texas seed company, a
New York coffee broker and a British poultry business.
MBPXL, now the Excel Corp., fell short of expectations
in its early years but after the company invested millions
to improve its productivity, seeking to "stabilize" the beef
packing industry through forward contracting and
selling leaner beef, it now produces annual revenues
estimated at $2.6 billion.

Sue Shellenbarger in *The Wall Street Journal* has
suggested:

What Cargill usually sees is a chance to get
bigger, often by buying a bigger share of a particular business or by diversifying into a new face of
agribusiness. The combination of volume and
diversity is hard to beat. Volume helps make
Cargill a low-cost producer ... Diversification
spreads the risk inherent in commodity-price
volatility and gives Cargill a means of weathering
farm slumps that can slice profit margins razor
thin.[24]

According to unprecedented documents obtained by
The New York Times' Steven Greenhouse, which the
company was required to file in 1985 when it sought to
borrow money from public markets in order to take
advantage of low interest rates, since 1981 it had
reinvested 87 percent of its net earnings, with $463.5
million in 1985 alone going into capital investment while
paying out only a meager three percent of its profits in
dividends.[25]

At the core of Cargill's international trading operations is the economic enigma, Tradax International,
based in Panama, but with its center of operations in
Geneva, Switzerland. In *Merchants of Grain*, an exhaustive and benchmark historical study of the grain trade,
Dan Morgan succinctly describes how Tradax operates
and why it is so vital to Cargill's globe-spanning businesses both as a broker and tax conduit.

When Cargill sells a cargo of corn to a Dutch
animal feed manufacturer, the grain is shipped
down the Mississippi River, put aboard a vessel
at Baton Rouge and sent to Rotterdam. On paper,
however, as tracked by the Internal Revenue
Service, its route is more elaborate. Cargill will
first sell the corn to Tradax International in
Panama, which will 'hire' Tradax/Geneva as its
agent; Tradax/Geneva then might arrange the
sale to a Dutch miller through its subsidiary,
Tradax/Holland; any profits would be booked to
Tradax/Panama, a tax-haven company, and
Tradax/Geneva would earn only a 'management
fee' for brokering the deal between Tradax/Pan-
ama and Tradax/Holland.[26]

"Food for Peace" Spells Markets for Cargill

Perhaps the major means by which Cargill and other
members of the grain trade's elite have come to gain
such preeminence in world trade, was a ready-made
sales promotion gimmick fashioned for them by a
compliant U. S. government. Public Law 480 was passed
by the Congress in 1954 as a mechanism for disposing
U.S. farm surpluses. While it euphemistically became
known as the "Food for Peace" program, its political
potential was probably best expressed by one of the
law's principal architects, Minnesota Senator Hubert H.
Humphrey:

I have heard ... that people may become dependent on us for food. I know that was not supposed to be good news. To me that was good
news, because before people can do anything they
have got to eat. And if you are looking for a way
to get people to lean on you and to be dependent
on you, in terms of their cooperation with you, it
seems to me that food dependence would be
terrific.[27]

For Cargill (a long-time friend of Humphrey) and the
other major grain companies, P.L. 480 served as a two-
pronged instrument in its market expansion programs.
It not only enabled Cargill & Company to increase their
own export sales directly, but also to "whet the appe-

tites" of many new markets and open up these countries with P.L. 480 concessional sales so as to be positioned later to make direct commercial sales later.

One ex-USDA official described this process as teaching "people to eat wheat who didn't eat it before, particularly in the Far East,"[28] but a Bunge executive described P.L. 480 much more candidly as the means "enabling the companies to gain entrance into a market at the smallest expense possible."[29]

The program's benefits were most readily apparent when John Block boasted to farmers at the Indiana State Fair before a "Good Morning America" national TV audience that,

we have helped a lot of countries over the years develop their economies and these countries, *most* of them, have become *very* good trading partners for us, in fact, seven out of ten of the recipients of our P.L. 480 aid in years past are now seven out of ten of our *best* customers.

Because of the large surpluses in the 1950s and 1960s, the Commodity Credit Corporation purchased grain to protect commodity prices from falling. The government then paid Cargill and other big grain traders for storage space in their facilities. From 1958 to 1968 Cargill alone received over $76 million in such storage payments. At the same time, whenever Cargill and other traders required grain to cover their own marketing needs they were able to purchase it most readily and conveniently from these same reserves.

By so manipulating CCC reserves in 1956, for example, the grain companies bought most of the government's corn reserves in anticipation of shortages and rising prices. Small country elevator operators and farmer cooperatives complained bitterly to the USDA as the grain companies were able to take advantage of subsequent price rises at their expense. In the end, CCC also lost the sizeable revenue it would have earned had it waited for corn prices to rise before selling its surpluses.[30]

Today, the results of the early years of the P.L. 480 program are manifest: Cargill, Continental, Bunge, Louis Dreyfus and Andre control a variety of export-import facilities, operate large shipping and transportation networks, and maintain a close working relationship with foreign bankers, financial institutions, and government officials.

Wielding the Corporate Axe

As noted, the public rarely has an opportunity to see the manner in which the secretive grain elite conducts its daily business. In recent years, however, Cargill's operations have come under increasing public scrutiny. In 1981 the company pleaded guilty to charges of filing false tax returns in 1975 and 1976.[31] It has also been forced to settle lawsuits alleging that it fixed prices for paint resins and sold contaminated feed to a now-defunct beef producer.[32]

An even more telling example of how a corporation like Cargill operates in today's agricultural economy,

however, came in its crass attempt to influence the 1985 farm bill debate in the Congress.

In late 1984 Cargill announced plans to import nearly one million bushels of Argentine wheat for milling in the United States in what the *Wall Street Journal* described as an "apparent attempt to pressure U.S. lawmakers into changing farm policy ... a political step designed to pressure farm-state Congressmen who may oppose proposed reductions in farm price supports."[33]

The action outraged both farm-state representatives — one called it a "cheap propaganda shot by Cargill" — and farm organizations. The North Dakota Farmers Union board of directors charged that the company was using a "double-headed axe" on the American farmer.

With one edge, Cargill is undercutting our producers to force lower grain prices upon a nation of distressed farmers who desperately need improved income to meet expenses and debt repayment.

With the other edge of the axe, Cargill is swinging its corporate power against U.S. farm policies which already provide too little price protection for our wheat producers. This axe is directly aimed at the 1985 farm bill for the purpose of reducing and eliminating price support loans and target prices.

Officials of this multinational grain merchant have repeatedly attempted to mislead American farmers and the public toward what they call a "market-oriented" farm policy. The Argentine wheat purchase is an example of what their kind of market-oriented farm policy would create. U.S. producers would become a pawn in international trade wars and the sole beneficiaries of such policies would be the international grain merchants.

Every American farmer who does business with Cargill is condoning and encouraging Cargill to continue on its path of gutting farm prices and farm policies.[34]

Texas Agricultural Commissioner Jim Hightower, whose state is a major wheat producer, characterized the Cargill maneuver as

a not-too-subtle statement ... that would have a price busting impact.

It is an insult to the farmers of America who have been the bread and butter of Cargill for years. We'll come right back at them. The American farmer won't sit around and buy their Nutrena feeds, their seeds, their Burros Mills pancake flour. And he might even turn off 'A Prairie Home Companion' [a Cargill-sponsored radio show] on Saturday nights and go out organizing other farmers.[35]

Such criticism soon forced Cargill to announce that it would send its 25,000 tons of Argentine wheat elsewhere, all the while contending that its original plan made economic sense. Farmers and the public, however, had learned a lesson: Cargill was indeed capable of buying grain elsewhere in the world at less cost and bringing it *into* the United States at a profit.

"Nor Are We Anxious to Make Moral Judgments Of Our Own"

Important questions need to be asked about the operations of corporations like Cargill and their crucial role in feeding people at home and abroad.

In 1982 the Joseph Project, a public policy research group sponsored by the Senate of Catholic Priests of the Archdiocese of Minneapolis-St.Paul, sought answers from Cargill to some of the fundamental moral and economic questions relating to hunger, grain and transnational corporations. Interviewing three Cargill executives — William Pearce, vice president for public relations; Robin Johnson, assistant vice president for public relations, and John McGrory, corporate counsel — for its report, *Daily Bread: An Abdication of Power*, Dee Elwood, the Joseph Project coordinator, asked the trio:

You function in three main areas: world market, domestic market, the general area of morality; and therefore, you influence the world economy, the national economy, and starvation in the world. This is an awesome responsibility. What are your priorities among these three? Are they the same in your future plans?

Cargill's answer not only exhibits the corporate agribusiness attitude toward the life-and-death question of who gets fed and who doesn't, but it also underscores the general amoral perspective toward basic human needs that prevails in many corporate board rooms today.

The assumption that there are moral priorities that are offended in serving world or domestic markets as economically and efficiently as possible rests on a confusion about *economic facts.* It is also a highly objectionable characterization of business's role. Before one makes moral judgments and advocates economic actions, one should understand the *economic issues* that are involved.

The business of making moral judgments is both hazardous and potentially irresponsible unless one is fully satisfied that all the facts and causal relationships have been explored ... We are not in a position — given time and other constraints — to provide all the relevant background. *Nor are we anxious to make moral judgments — or moral defenses — of our own ...*

I think the evolution of this [free] marketing system and Cargill's role in it have also played an important role in reducing the incidence and severity of periodic famine or chronic malnutrition. Private entities, however — whether farmers, grain companies or food manufacturers — are not in a position themselves to subsidize food consumption in order to relieve famine.

Such subsidies must come from public institutions (national or international) or from voluntary relief agencies. The private sector can help the world food system work more efficiently and productively, which yields important benefits in reducing the incidence of hunger and malnutrition. *The burdens of inequality by and large must be altered or offset by public rather than private institutions.*[36] (emphasis added)

The Salt of the Bay

The enormous wealth of grain-trading firms, and the fact that most are private corporations unaccountable to outsiders, has given the grain trade untold and often unseen power to influence U.S. government trade and tax policies and gain lucrative federal, state and local financial assistance in hidden subsidies.

Cargill, for example, has leased or built a number of giant grain terminals from Seattle to Buffalo financed primarily by industrial revenue bonds and special state and federal funds. At the same time, it has shown little regard for the communities' best economic interests when these interests conflict with its own corporate goals.

One illustration: In February 1978, in Buffalo, Cargill simply abandoned three grain elevators after refusing to pay property taxes on them for five years, leaving the city with an uncollected bill of $860,000. The city subsequently acquired the property at its own tax sale, but was unable to realize as much money from the selling of the property as the amount Cargill owed in taxes.

Buffalo sought to collect the delinquent tax money from Cargill by taking its case to the New York State Supreme Court. The Court, however, ruled that state law compelled the city to bid on the property at the tax sale and that the same law deemed the delinquent taxes to have been paid when Buffalo picked up the property at the tax sale.

Later that same year, Cargill announced the purchase of Leslie Salt Company in California, which included over 44,000 acres of salt evaporation ponds in six of the nine counties on the San Francisco Bay.

In light of the furor over property taxes in California and the passage of Proposition 13, the Agribusiness Accountability Project wrote to each of the six county tax assessors questioning them as to how much land in their county Cargill would be paying taxes on, what the rate would be and whether the county had any administrative or statutory procedure to prevent Cargill from doing to that county what it did to Buffalo.

The replies all pretty much followed the same pattern as to the county's recourse in such a circumstance. One assessor, however, concluded his letter candidly: "After this long explanation, what I am really telling you is that we would possibly find ourselves in a similar situation as Buffalo, New York." Thus, in a state where property taxes had become the number one political issue, local governments remained uncertain as to how they might go about collecting delinquent taxes in their own counties from the nation's largest private corporation.

On the Road

When grain leaves the farm gate its first stop has traditionally been the local grain elevator. But, the country grain elevator, a long-time center of the rural communities' economic life, is becoming a another mere relic of rural America due to competition from large traders, marketing arrangements, trends in transportation and the growing expense of complying with government safety regulations. In many areas these elevators are now being bypassed, as grain is hauled long distances by trucks to giant subterminal and terminal elevators, which not coincidentally are owned by these same large grain traders.

Many farmers still largely depend on the railroads to deliver their elevator-stored grain, but some recent trends affecting the grain transportation system have forced increasing numbers of country elevators to pay less to local farmers. These trends include: railroads' shifting to unit trains; the closing of many rail branch lines, and various state, national, and rail company plans for a "core" rail system to accommodate an emphasis on exports. An advertisement by Burlington Northern shown here underscores this trend.

Because they often do not have sufficient volume for l25-car, one-commodity unit trains, country elevators are forced to pay higher rail fees simply to reserve hopper cars to move their already stored grain. It is estimated that those elevators able to take advantage of the unit train discount are able to realize a five to 15-cent per-bushel savings in transportation costs.

Not surprisingly, it is the large grain traders who have the volume to contract such unit trains. Reportedly, Cargill and Continental alone operate 25 percent of the nation's grain facilities and have a similar (18 percent) percentage of the aggregate domestic capacity in millions of bushels (See Chart 28B).

The *Grain 1989* profile of the top 100 grain companies includes 3,934 facilities with a storage capacity of over 3.4 billion bushels, up 215.5 million from 1988. Canadian companies and co-ops accounted for 440.9 million bushels of capacity, or 12.7 percent of the total. Of the companies listed, 61 were independent and 29 were cooperatives.

The fact that the grain trade elite have such transportation fee and storage benefits and that the changing configurations in the nation's rail system has worked to their distinct advantage is not surprising given that many members of the boards of directors of these rail companies also often serve on the boards or act as financial consultants to the large grain companies.

Curiously, while the grain trade negotiates with the rail companies 60 percent of the time for special rates in moving its commodities, one of the nation's largest grain shippers, the USDA, has been paying railroads the published — or highest — rates for 90 percent of all its grain shipments, according to a GAO study released in January, 1987 by Representative Byron L. Dorgan, D-ND.

All the big shippers go to the railroads now and negotiate rates. But the [Agriculture Department] people have been asleep at the switch. When railroad deregulation occurred, allowing this to happen, they failed to adjust.

The GAO estimates that in 1985 alone, USDA hauling charges could have been nearly 29 percent lower for many shipments and that negotiations could have resulted in a $6.6 million savings.[38] USDA officials, however, claimed they were unable to bargain for the lower rates because they lacked information on when their grain was to be moved and lacked qualified personnel to engage in such bargaining.[39]

Burlington Northern can start your grain on the road to market.

With over 25,000 miles of track across 25 states and 2 Canadian Provinces, Burlington Northern will start your grain on its way to market.

Our fleet of jumbo grain hopper cars is the largest in the nation. That means we can satisfy virtually all of your grain transportation needs.

Domestically, BN trains will haul your load to the major mills in large metropolitan cities. And we can also carry your grain to feedlots in the Southwest, South Coast and the Texas Panhandle; or poultry-producing areas in the Southeast.

For your export needs, we provide direct rail access to 12 U.S. ports — including the Pacific Northwest, Gulf of Mexico, Great Lakes and the Mississippi Valley an Columbia River systems....

The grain trade also moves many of its own commodities by barge (according to one Department of Transportation estimate, nearly one-half of the grain crop in transit is by water) due to the fact that the Mississippi River is the conduit for an estimated 60 percent of the U.S.'s grain and soybean exports.[40] Although approximately one-half of the U.S. barge fleet capacity is owned by the major grain companies, for years they were the only domestic freight carriers who paid no part of the expense of building or maintaining their right of way.[41]

In 1978, however, the Inland Waterways Revenue Act introduced a fuel tax for "commercial waterway transportation," in an effort to introduce self-financing from tax revenues for construction and maintenance of the nation's vast waterway system.

Such a tax, however, not only gets passed down the line to the producer, eventually bringing about a reduction in the purchase price of commodities, but it also inspires proportionate increases in trucking and rail charges.

This explains why in 1986 the largest eastern railroad company (CSX Rail Corp.) merged its operations with the nation's largest barge operator (American

Commercial Lines). According to Joseph Farrell, president of the American Waterways Operators, Inc., the rail industry's own estimates show that rail lines are forced to charge about $1 billion less per year for shipments by rail because of competition from the waterways industry.[42] By the mid-1980s however, barge rates had collapsed, due to increased competition from the railroads, as barge owners found themselves getting only 25 percent-40 percent of the rates they enjoyed in the late 1970s.[43]

In the fall of 1986, however, river barges owned by 12 grain companies along the Mississippi, Illinois, Missouri and Ohio rivers reaped the windfall of a government program, which according to a GAO study, saw taxpayers spend nearly a dollar a bushel to store some 64.9 million bushels of grain for a four month period. Such fees were sharply higher than those paid by the government for grain inventories in elevators and farm bins, according to the GAO report.[44]

Chart 28B: Top Five Corporate Grain Companies

Corporation	Storage Capacity Facilities	Millions of Bushels
Cargill	397	440
Continental Grain	80	188
Bunge	55+	164
ADM	103	135
ConAgra/Peavey	103	112

(+ Does not include country elevators.)

Five Firm Totals	738	1,059
Percent of Industry	46%	31%
Four Firm Totals	635	827
Percent of Industry	39%	24%
Top Two Firm Totals	477	628
Percent of Industry	25%	18%

Source: "Concentration of Agricultural Markets, September, 1990," by William D. Heffernan and Douglas H. Constance, Department of Rural Sociology, University of Missouri, Columbia, Missouri 65211.

The grain trade has also become adept at speculating heavily in international shipping. Companies buy and sell contracts for shipping space although never intending to use all the space, but nevertheless holding it as a way of keeping options open so as to maximize company profits.

Playing a Hundred Simultaneous Chess Games

Let's take a closer look at some factors that determine the world's grain prices. Dan Morgan begins that inquiry by attempting to answer a simple question: "what is the price of wheat?"

At any moment, there are *hundreds* of prices for wheat all around the United States and throughout the world. The price of wheat depends on its grade and quality, its protein, its location, the availability of ships, railroad hopper cars, barges, and trucks to transport it, the need for it in Europe, and the ability of the buyers to obtain credit and financing. Predicting the price distortions caused by a myriad of variables is the meat and potatoes of grain trading.

Continuing, the *Washington Post* editor emphasizes that "the grain trade is a business of tactics, strategy, bluff and deception... [a] game the public never sees [and one] described as having an intricacy equivalent to that of playing a hundred simultaneous chess games.[45]

Traditionally, we have been told that prices of agricultural goods should be based on the "law of supply and demand" so both here and abroad farmers can make accurate planting decisions and consumers can plan purchases. But in the grain trade, where profits are so dependent on uncertainty, gyrating prices and

supply, fluctuations are repeatedly sending the market false signals. Thus the "law of supply and demand" is subject to the constant manipulation by grain oligopolies and government monopolies.

For example, as we shall see, the grain trade elite claimed to have lost money in the "Great American Grain Robbery of 1972," but they failed to mention, as Gilmore has noted, their profits from transactions with third countries.

In the aftermath of that deal and by the time the market had registered skyrocketing prices, the grain companies had already bought grain at relatively cheap prices to sell later at high profit margins. Slackening demand or mounting surpluses usually find the grain trade buying at bargain prices, but because of the size of their purchases, the net effect is usually higher sales prices. Over the years the grain trade has adopted many tactics to manipulate the prices paid to farmers and charged to customers, and these tactics have had precious little to do with the law of supply and demand.

The practice of purposeful contamination, or "blending," as it is euphemistically known, is but one of the many forms of price manipulation employed by the grain trade. Usually it goes unnoticed, except perhaps at those times when foreign customers start complaining about the quality of their grain shipments.

One such instance was in February 1986 when the Chinese promptly rejected two ship loads of soybeans which had arrived from the United States. Terry Foley of the American Soybean Association was so upset that he sent the following cable from Beijing:

Urgent need for high-level intervention ... Bad problems with U.S. soybean shipment sent to People's Republic of China ... No question damage extensive. Trader, Chinese, USDA-FGIS [Federal Grain Inspection Service] all agree soybeans badly damaged ... Ceroils [the Chinese importer] upset and very angry because they've already paid for them, but quality is so bad that Chinese customers refuse to take them off their hands. [They say] "We don't want them and we're not paying for them. If this is U.S. #2 yellow they can keep them." All here feel their anger is justified ...[46]

A spokesman for Cargill, which loaded one of the two ships, at first denied any involvement with the shipment — "It's not our ship, and we weren't the shipper" — but when told that FGIS records indicated that his company had loaded one ship, he told the *Farm Journal*, "if the FGIS certified the soybeans as #2, we have no comment." The loader of the other ship, Zen Noh, replied,

whatever the system allows is what we do. If it meets the grade we use it. Of course, if beans are damaged, the farmer gets discounted. But if we couldn't blend, the whole system would fall apart. Go to Washington and change the standards if you don't like what you see.[47]

David Senter, a Washington representative of the American Agricultural Movement, describes this industry-wide procedure called "purposeful contamination":

When a farmer goes to a Cargill elevator, for example, and sells wheat or corn or whatever, Cargill docks that farmer for any kind of foreign matter, any kind of dirt, cracked grain, high moisture or anything.

They dock the farmer's price so he takes less for that commodity ... And then when they get to the export facility, each one of these negotiations with foreign countries — one customer might say you can have up to four percent foreign matter, one might be five percent. In other words, each one of these contracts has a certain percentage of foreign matter it allows.

When Cargill loads the commodity on the ship, say, if the moisture content is down at 12 percent, and the contract allows 14 percent, they put water on it as it goes on the ship and bring it up to 14 percent. They can get corn prices for water that they're pumping in. If the foreign matter of the grain they're loading is only six percent and the contract allows eight percent, they will add sand, dirt, screenings, below-grade grain — whatever they have available at that export facility — and bring it right up to the limit with all that trash. All the grain companies operate the same way.[48]

Confirmation of Senter's description is found in a 1982 story in *The Kansas City Times* quoting a Cargill superintendent as stating, "if we've got a real clean load [of grain] we'll make sure we hold it until we can mix it with something dirtier, otherwise, we'd be throwing money away."[49]

In a scathing indictment of these practices Dale McDonald, writing in *Top Producer*, points out that the major grain companies' business is not promoting U.S. grain sales, or improving U.S. export grain quality, or promoting the interests of the American farmer.

Yet the United States meekly allows a few multinational grain companies to virtually set the rules for American grain exports through their domination of our grain quality standards and export capabilities. We have, in effect, placed the future of U.S. grain exports at their mercy. *And their business is not mercy.*[50] (emphasis added)

An eastern Mediterranean government buyer describes how these major grain traders often operate:

When we want to buy, we will contact a company, let's say Continental, stationed in Geneva. They offer grain to us from Argentina, Canada, the United States, from any country. When we are offered both American and Canadian wheat near the same price, we certainly buy the Canadian because it will not be blended. We get what we want. The shipper makes money. But the farmer in the United States is you know, the loser. Do you get my point?[51]

McDonald notes that in 1987 the "American" multinationals set a record as they brought nearly 345,000 metric tons of Canadian wheat into the United States, some of which was feed wheat and "utility" wheat. The importer? "I am not allowed to give out exact figures," a statistician with the Canadian Grain Commission cautioned, "but you are in the ball park with Cargill and Continental. They would get most of it, if not all."[52]

Nicolaas Konijnendijk, formerly with U.S. Wheat Associates and Kansas State University, and now owner of a company in Antwerp — Agro Consulting and Trading — recalls,

Fifteen years ago the business was easy. You had a contract, you got what you wanted, and that was the end of it. But now the big companies push blending to the limits. I think they only want to make a big shipment, deals that your government arranges and pays a bonus for. The result is that the crushers and millers are scrambling, trying to go around the big traders and buy directly from the cooperatives and farmer groups. But that is very difficult to do because the multinationals are so powerful.

He adds that "the problem with a heavily blended shipment is that you only make a sale like that to a good customer once. No one wants to pay for the American blending system."[53]

Critics of the current standards, which have changed little since 1917, note that the rules for storage have not kept up with changes in harvest, storage and shipping technology that often compound the quality problem.

One such critic is the National Farmers Organization's Chuck Frasier.

> Most of the damage I have been able to find stemmed from local elevators and export terminals. Everybody believes he has a chance to add a little foreign material and water, and believe me, they do it. It happens all along the chain. We don't have adequate standards. They are set and dictated by the big companies.[54]

Dan McGuire formerly of the Nebraska Wheat Board feels the time to change the standards is now.

> U.S. grain producers believe that U.S. wheat and other grains are dirtier than grain exported by our competitors, and these producers want Congress to do something about it. There is no mystery as to why the large grain exporting firms and the grain trade oppose changing the standards. *It is primarily a profit motive*" (emphasis added)

Despite all this criticism, however, the FGIS Advisory Committee (composed mainly of industry representatives) has in recent years advised against new rules on insect infestation, against a proposal that would establish an "optimal grade" of export grain, against a rule that would prohibit recombining dust that had been removed from grain, and against a proposal that would prohibit the addition of dockage or foreign material to grain shipments.[55]

Meanwhile, FGIS Administrator Kenneth A. Giles acknowledged that his office seeks to propose plans, endorsed by an industry task force, to better inform buyers about grain quality, but not to reduce foreign materials in the grain. "From a quality standpoint, I would support the idea of no foreign materials in the grain. But if you said there could be no foreign material or moisture, who wants to pay the bill? It would mean more inspectors, more inspections."[56]

Former Iowa Congressman Cooper Evans, who devoted his farewell term to the passage of the Grain Quality Improvement Act, acknowledges that "the exporters will surely try to gut the law." The basic problem, he adds, is that our export grain standards "were written in a manner which virtually guarantees that a buyer can be deceived if a sophisticated grain exporter chooses to do so."[57]

The reckless abuse of "purposeful contamination" and the Federal government's inability to monitor such practices adequately through proper grain inspection standards first came to national attention in 1975 when 16 firms (including nearly all of the grain trade elite, though not Cargill) and 146 individuals were indicted under the Grain Standards Act of 1968, resulting in a total of $1 million in fines, 31 years of prison terms and 111 years of probation.

Not only in grain inspection, but in other areas, the ability of the Federal government to monitor, regulate and balance the grain trade's interests with those of the public has been largely unsuccessful.

In December 1987, for example, some ten years after 54 workers were killed in twin Christmas week grain elevator explosions near New Orleans and Galveston, Texas, the Occupational Safety and Health Administration adopted new safety standards aimed at preventing explosive grain dust from claiming additional lives. In the decade it took for the government agency to promulgate the new standards, 59 workers were killed and 370 injured in 190 other grain facility explosions.[58]

Though concerned that the new standards were so vague that they would prove unenforceable, labor unions expressed surprise that they were issued at all, given the substantial opposition by large grain companies, mills and elevator operators. The unions also immediately charged that the new regulations were watered down by OSHA, under pressure from the Office of Management and Budget, from the strict recommendations made earlier by a panel of the National Academy of Sciences.

"The new standard is clearly a political expediency," Deborah Berkowitz, director of safety and health for AFL-CIO's Food and Allied Service Trades Department, explained, "it's certainly not based on science."[59]

Grain trade regulation has failed mainly because the grain trade capitalizes on the division of national and private interests, by circumventing government regulations, and as Gilmore observes, "governmental efforts to regulate or control grain exports have been frustrated by contradictory policies designed to promote exports, by American agriculture's increasing dependence on foreign demand, and by the oligopoly that dominates the grain trade."[60]

Given such conditions some critics doubt that there can ever be any compatibility between the private control of grain flows and stability in its supply and price. Former Senator George McGovern, in a preface to a report by his Senate Select Committee on Hunger and Malnutrition argues:

> The contention that the world can have [food] reserves held in private hands is fallacious on its face. Private traders are in business to turn investment into profit as rapidly as possible. To expect that a multiplicity of private traders would or should manage the acquisition and release of food and feed grains in a manner which will meet the goals of a conscious reserve policy — to flatten the widest upward and downward fluctuations in market prices and to maintain a steady supply against times of shortage — would be contradictory ... In reality, a [food] reserve in private hands is no reserve at all.

Or, as the great German dramatist and poet Berthold Brecht put it more pointedly: "Famines do occur; they are organized by the grain trade."[61]

The Hidden Subsidies

As we saw earlier, the major beneficiaries of the PIK program were a handful of very large farms, several owned by multinational corporate conglomerates. But the Cargills and Continentals also reaped millions from the program, for with the institution of Ronald Reagan's

PIK program the grain trade's elite were once again being given another turn at the public trough.

In order to meet its payment obligations to producers the USDA had to relocate some of the program's wheat, corn and grain sorghum so these commodities would be locally available to the participating producers. To provide the crops to the areas where they were needed, USDA instituted a program to exchange CCC-owned commodities held at warehouses in surplus counties with privately-owned commodities held at warehouses in or near the deficit areas.

The total number of CCC-owned commodities traded in the PIK program, however, exceeded the quantity of privately-owned commodities that the CCC received by some 5.2 million bushels of wheat, 48.7 million bushels of corn, and 2.6 million bushels of grain sorghum. The difference between the quantity of the CCC-owned grain exchanged and the privately-owned grain received represented the "cost" to the CCC for the private contractors to transfer the grain.

A 1985 GAO report shows that USDA contracted to exchange about 433.7 million bushels of CCC grain for 377.2 million bushels of privately-owned grain. This difference — about 56.5 million bushels — originally cost the CCC about $170 million, based on average loan rates. However, these commodities were actually worth about $191.6 million if valued at the "average major market prices for wheat, corn, and grain sorghum between June and November, 1983, the period in which the exchange contracts were awarded."[62]

Chart 28C shows how well the grain trade's elite fared in this tax-supported program. It is well to recall, however, that profitability in the grain trade is not usually measured by monthly averages, but rather by price fluctuations and volatility on a day-to-day, hour-to-hour, even minute-to-minute basis.

Although the program's exchange rates were set on the basis of bidding among hundreds of firms for the 1259 contracts, the right to provide grain in the deficient areas decidedly favored the grain trade's elite, with their extensive storage and transportation networks.

One Tennessee elevator operator explained:

The major companies will make a killing on corn, particularly in the South. Most corn is stored in the North. There's little in the South, partly because of the drought. Millers and hog-feeders here will have to pay more ... but the [PIK] price to the farmer won't vary much. It is a very lucrative thing. They stand to do very well.[63]

Protecting "Market Flexibility"

By virtually monopolizing the export sales market through their enormous economic power and an abundant storage capacity, the large grain traders can prevent competitors like farm cooperatives, more of

Chart 28C: Payment-In-Kind (PIK) Program

Contractor	Number of contracts awarded	Quanity received by contractors	Quantity provided by contractors	Total Difference	Value (in millions)
WHEAT				(a)	
Cargill	99	24.3 (29)*	21.9	2.4	$ 9.8
Continental Grain	45	14.2 (17)	13.4	0.8	$ 3.3
Bunge	66	10.7 (13)	10.0	0.7	$ 2.9
TOTAL	461	82.4 (100)	77.2	5.2	$ 21.3
CORN				(b)	
Cargill	141	83.3 (26)*	70.3	13.0	$ 43.3
Continental Grain	26	33.7 (10)	28.4	5.3	$ 17.6
Pillsbury	43	35.5 (11)	30.0	4.5	$ 15.0
TOTAL	669	323.8 (100)	275.1	48.7	$162.2
GRAIN SORGHUM				(c)	
Cargill	41	4.7 (17)	4.1	0.6	$ 1.9
Continental Grain	5	3.6 (13)	3.2	0.4	$ 1.2
TOTAL	129	27.5 (100)	24.9	2.6	$ 8.1

Footnotes:

* = Percentage of total quantity received by all contractors.
(a) = Based on average major market price of $4.10 per bushel.
(b) = Based on average major market price of $3.33 per bushel.
(c) = Based on average major market price of $3.12 per bushel.

whose money from foreign sales would likely go to the producers, from engaging in trade abroad.

Engaging in what is sometimes called a "string" of sales before shipment to the final destination, sellers and buyers may ultimately involve scores of international speculators, brokers, and companies, who initiate the string, enter, and later withdraw from the same contract, often securing additional quantities of grain at favorable prices to the traders.

Unverifiable shipping destinations and tolerance regulations, designed to account for changes in freight loads necessitated by unpredictable shipping conditions, are simply another way of achieving "market flexibility" which trader profits so depend upon.

These companies operating worldwide, often through "off-shore" companies, also run their own "commodity exchanges." Because they may either need the grain for a sale or may have lost a sale they expected to make, or simply for pure speculation, they sometimes will trade whole ship cargoes of grain among themselves.

As author Richard Gilmore stresses, grain in today's world takes on real value only when it is marketed, not when it is harvested. Its value in our present economy is more an expression of interacting political and economic forces than its intrinsic worth as food.[64] Thus, no importing or exporting country can operate independent of the United States since an oligopoly of traders, the major two being headquartered in the United States, now controls the flow of grain and grain-related products throughout the entire world market.

Chapter Twenty-Nine

Many Are Called For, But Few Are The Chosen

"The more farmers who go bankrupt, the easier it will be for the surviving farmers to make an honest living. Agricultural Department programs create surpluses that depress the market prices, thus making it harder for all farmers to earn a living. Congress and the department have tried every solution except the obvious one: the free market."

- James Bovard, "Let farms go belly up; we can't afford them, *USA Today*, July 8, 1986.

On a bleak February night in the American farmer's 1985 winter of discontent, ABC-TV news anchor Peter Jennings interviewed Dixon Terry, a young, articulate Iowa farmer in Ames, the site of that day's massive rally by 15,000 angry farmers assembled from around the nation. Terry, who four years later would be tragically struck down by a bolt of lightening on his farm, explained to a national audience the impact of the gathering and what it should mean to the general public, warning that if America's "family farm system" of agriculture was allowed to continue to deteriorate, the nation's food supply would soon be produced and controlled solely by only a few corporate giants.

Unfortunately, Terry did not get the last word, for sitting in Washington, D.C. was ABC-TV's conservative political commentator, George Will. Cynically dismissing the farmer organizer's grim warning, Will pollyanna-ishly observed that there was a third alternative between superfarms and the complete loss of family farms. Farmers, he stressed, rather than being such pessimists should enthusiastically embrace the "free market system" in agriculture.

Will and others of his ilk conveniently overlook the fact that there is no such thing today as a "free market system" in U.S. agriculture.

While modern American agriculture is incredibly diverse, growing everything from apples to zucchini, any discussion about the much-revered "free market system" in agriculture must take into account that grain and grain-related commodities comprise the bulk of the nation's agricultural output. Certainly in that sector of our farm economy there is nothing remotely resembling a "free market."

Consequently, it is no surprise that the most vocal and consistent defenders of agriculture's ill-defined "free market system" are the giant grain traders, that elite group of multinational conglomerates which buy, sell, transport and increasingly process the bulk of the world's grains and its byproducts.

While thriving on market fluctuations and opposing any efforts by government to stabilize prices, these multinational grain traders have fought long and hard both politically and economically against any attempts to limit their ability to profit from the cyclical nature of agricultural trade. As one Congressional aide has described it, "in the United States there's a free market, but freedom exists only for a few and not for the many."[1]

As grain has come to assume an ever-more vital role in the global economy, the power that has accompanied its place in world politics has been slowly shifting from the many hands of the producers to those of its distributors. The giant companies that now dominate the world grain trade are not only well equipped to buy a variety of commodities in areas of surplus and sell them in areas of scarcity, but are also able to store them worldwide until such surpluses disappear.

In addition, these same multinationals have the unique ability to select the most profitable way to sell commodities, either raw or processed, depending on demand, leaving farmers and merchants at the mercy of an oligopolistic market place.

Investigative reporters Roger Burbach and Patricia Flynn explain,

Caught in this system, and at the mercy of the free market, the grain farmer is forced to see export markets as the only condition to maintaining his income and covering his costs of production. U.S. strategists are aware that manipulation of the farmer is essential to the success of their export drive. As [Peter Flannigan, head of President Richard Nixon's Council on International Economic Policy] commented, "farmers must become a main force in the political drive in the United States for internationally oriented policies." For U.S. policy makers, farmers are the necessary cogs in 'on-line production factories' producing the commodity that will keep the U.S. competitive in world trade.[2]

The grain traders, like so many of their other big business contemporaries, have not forgotten recent history. They know all too well from the experiences of their corporate predecessors during the era of agrarian populism that the wrath of many farmers against big business can often be significantly mitigated simply by expanding markets abroad.

Seeking the "Comparative Advantage"

Because deficits and surpluses have been regarded as short-term problems, dwindling returns to efficient producers as aberrations, and expensive, inefficient agricultural systems as necessary to self-sufficiency and food security, the establishment of food reserves and multilateral coordination of agricultural policies have traditionally received scant attention from the general public.

Today, due to frequent unstable economic and agricultural conditions and because the world has come to increasingly depend on a small, limited number of suppliers for much of its grain, these suppliers have a growing interest in developing a coordinated approach to agricultural policies, particularly exports.

Continental Grain's chairman and chief executive officer, Michel Fribourg, has articulated just such an approach.

> The United States should persuade other major food exporters to join in a long-range alignment of national food policies not unlike the efforts recently undertaken to coordinate currency exchange rates and earlier, emergency energy sharing.
>
> First, national support prices, target prices and other government incentives everywhere should be gradually lowered and geared toward efficient farmers only, reducing ultimately to zero the present disparity among national programs.
>
> Second, all government distortions in farm trade, including tariffs, quotas and export and import subsidies, should be gradually eliminated.
>
> Third, all food aid programs for developing nations should be coordinated by donor nations, using food to create jobs and income and opening our markets to enable those nations to earn foreign exchange.[3]

But in the United States, as agricultural economist E. Phillip VeVeen shows us, the real cause of both the environmental and food-price problems in recent years has been the internationalization of U.S. agriculture and the corresponding explosion of agricultural commodity exports:

> Export expansion has been the overriding goal of U.S. farm policy since the late 1960s. To produce these exports, we have heavily taxed the productive capacity of our agricultural system. Further

expansion will accelerate environmental degradation and the depletion of soil and water resources, and will force still higher prices on consumers. If we are to avoid these problems, we must reduce the pressures caused by commodity exports.[4]

Past efforts in this regard have not met with much success, dating back to the International Wheat Agreement of 1933, the first of its kind. Here it was hoped producers would accept export quotas in exchange for importer purchasing commitments. Market shares among nations would be assigned on the basis of average production minus domestic consumption with surpluses subject to an agreed upon export limit. The agreement also contained a uniform pricing system pegged to gold with different prices assigned to different types of wheat, all of which would be convertible into universally accepted units of exchange.

From the outset, however, the plan was doomed, for it lacked any real commitment from its members — control of the flow of trade was politically impossible as long as the principal wheat exporters depended so heavily on exports to relieve their stock burdens. In addition, it soon became evident that a uniform pricing system dependent on government enforcement was impotent as long as export markets were dominated by a few companies.

Another effort was made in 1939 by Agricultural Secretary Wallace, in proposing "the ever normal granary" — the international counterpart to the New Deal's domestic agricultural program.

> As part of the effort to win the peace, I am hoping that what might be called the "ever normal granary principle" can be established for a number of commodities on a world-wide scale. It will be remembered that the fourth point of the eight points agreed upon by Roosevelt and Churchill in the Atlantic Charter mentioned the enjoying by all states, great and small, victor or vanquished, of access on equal terms to the raw materials of the world. To give this lofty ideal a more definite substance should be one of our chief objectives in the months that lie immediately ahead.[5]

In the plan Wallace put forth, stabilization was construed to mean higher export prices and a distribution formula that allocated market shares among suppliers. Reserves and food aid were linked to a mutually accepted quota and pricing system. Subsequently, the 1942 agreement gave the United States a share above its actual share of the world market, provoking Lord Keynes to label it "a fantastic piece of chicanery."[6] The grain trade also vigorously opposed the plan as unnecessary tinkering with the market, even as the European importing countries were denouncing the new agreement as an exporter's cartel.

An important feature of the 1942 agreement was the establishment of an "enforcement" provision. However, it was apparent from the outset that the newly-established International Wheat Council (IWC) was severely limited in fulfilling its purpose. Essential to its task was having sufficient market information, which included timely, accurate price reports from member governments, so it could monitor prices effectively. Yet, as long as members of the agreement continued to rely exclusively on the private sector for export news, the IWC's task proved impossible.

In the years following World War II came the European Recovery Program, which saw the United States becoming the major exporter of grain and lay claim to the role as the world's breadbasket. By 1949, however, it remained apparent that some type of agreement was necessary and a subsequent pact was ratified by the three major exporters (Australia, Canada and the United States) and a substantial number of importing countries.

The agreement provided the United States with a definite export market at prices not lower than the minimum price and established a modest reserve to be either released onto the world market or built up as circumstances required; the latter being designed to reduce price fluctuations associated with changes in supply and also to reinforce the quota allocations.

This act was to have only a minimal impact as the Korean war and shrinking harvests in Europe again depressed supply and increased demand, resulting in high wheat prices as 40 percent of the world's wheat sales took place in the free market. A revised agreement in 1953, which sought to establish a new, higher price range and which caused Britain, the world's largest wheat importer to drop out, was even less effective.

In this period the United States, no longer willing to rely on such agreements to support prices in a time of surplus, devised Public Law 480 as a means of reducing stocks while maintaining a floor under U.S. grain prices.

After a decade of uncertainty and instability in world grain markets, the Johnson administration sought to improve on the 1949 IGA in order to: provide a fair return to wheat growers through a stabilized market; multilateralize food aid; and ensure exporting nations a market in time of surplus and importing nations a reasonably priced wheat supply in times of shortage. The fact that this effort contained no supply management features was its major shortcoming.

It is important to remember that this agreement, like all previous ones, recognized that the growth of the world's grain trade was finite. While consumption most certainly would increase, importing nations would also attempt to produce more for their own requirements, some even becoming exporters. A finite market, however, imposes limits on the extent to which any exporter's share can be increased except at the expense of other major exporters.

Shortly after 52 nations adopted the new IGA in 1967, it not only had the misfortune of being administered in the United States by a non-supportive Nixon Administration, but the grain trade itself began to cut prices, thereby fulfilling their own prophecy that such an IGA would never work.

Harry L. Graham, a former Grange and NFO Washington representative, documented before a Congressional committee how in early 1969 several large shipments of wheat were sold by "someone in the United States" for 19 and 14 cents a bushel below the IGA's floor price of $1.73 per bushel.

In mid-February, Argentina and Australia protested the U.S. sales. Late in February, the USDA called a meeting of farm organizations and the grain trade, forbidding a discussion of the causes of the crisis by the producer groups, but then allowing the Farm Bureau and traders to lambast the IGA for an hour and a half. This caused the producer representatives to protest and insist U.S. policy should be to preserve the IGA and not destroy it.[7]

Life In a Free Trade Fantasyland

After the IGA expired in 1972 it was succeeded by the renamed International Wheat Agreement (IWA), which some viewed as simply a weak gentleman's agreement. At the insistence of the Nixon administration, the new Agreement included no minimum or maximum pricing.

Martha Hamilton, author of the Agribusiness Accountability Project's 1973 report *The Great American Grain Robbery and Other Stories*, correctly points out in discussing the demise of the IWA that

> the world of wheat trading is not a world of free trade. It reeks of price protection, conflicting national interests, political considerations, finite markets, and trade blocks. USDA officials and grain trade representatives seem to come from another world when they argue against putting minimums in the agreement — a free trade fantasyland. U.S. wheat growers, meanwhile, endure the real world pressures of the cost-price squeeze.

When the IWA was before the Congress, most farm groups supported it since they wanted to see the framework kept intact. However, they vigorously protested the absence of maximum and minimum prices. Harry Graham, speaking for the NFO called the agreement,

> a collection of weasel words ... It claims that it provides a framework for continued international cooperation in wheat trade and will contribute to stability in the world wheat market. That is hogwash. We are not in a period of international cooperation in the wheat trade. We are in a period of cutthroat competition ...[This agreement is] of the grain trade, by the grain trade, and for the grain trade. The welfare of American wheat growers and the possibility of increased foreign trade earnings can be damned, and is.[8]

During the IWA debate an alternative repeatedly suggested by opponents of minimum pricing was one with which the grain trade has long beaten farmers and the American public over the head: lower the U.S. market price of grain to the so-called "world price" thus enabling the nation to export more grain at lower prices, increase "farm income," and boost the U.S. balance of payments. As Ms. Hamilton notes, however, that idea "makes sense in a vacuum, but not in the real world in international trade. In the real world, there is no world price reflecting supply and demand."[9] Similarly during the aforementioned hearings Senator Milton Young, R-ND, a member of the Senate Agricultural Committee, observed:

> The world price is a sort of rigged price. It is established largely by Canada and the United States and to some extent other wheat exporting nations. It doesn't make any difference how low the price gets here; it doesn't seem to increase exports.[10]

History has shown that when the United States, as the dominant wheat exporter, moves prices down, other developed countries usually follow in an effort to maintain their own market shares.

Increasing the "world" price of U.S. grain to a level closer to the domestic price would only minimize any need for export subsidy payments such as has been paid out in the billions of dollars since the early 1970s. Moreover, if the domestic price of grain moved up on the basis of an increase in the world price, farm program payments could be reduced and ultimately eliminated. Such increases in domestic prices would have little impact on consumer prices. (It was noted during the IWC hearings that a change of 50 cents a bushel in the price of wheat to the farmer at the time would have resulted in less than a one cent change in the price of a one-pound loaf of bread.[11])

At the IWC hearings, Clarence Palmby, Undersecretary of Agriculture, in arguing for a no-minimum agreement, declared that the IWC would provide an international forum for exporters to keep account of each other's selling policies and subject exporters to "discipline on prices, which does lend some stability and strength to world wheat prices."[12]

Six months later, Palmby's boss, Earl Butz, was telling a Senate Committee "the international market for wheat is in a chaotic condition right now."[13] Today, the IWC still stands, doing little more than ratifying the status quo, including the present pattern of gyrating grain prices. As Gilmore concludes: "That it stands at all, that it remained in place longer than any of its predecessors, is perhaps because it does so little and makes so few demands on its signatories."[14]

The United States, meanwhile, still resists any kind of "fair market share" program in grain trading, such as has been proposed by the EC. As Chart 29A, listing the top 10 world exporters of agricultural commodities, shows the world marketing shares varied slightly, for example, between 1979 and 1988.

It is important to remember that in addition to the fact only a handful of private companies control the movement of the world's grain, nearly 95 percent of all the world's grain trade, according to the GAO, is conducted by state agencies such as the Canadian Wheat Board, the Japanese Food Agency, and the EC.

Despite the fact that the U.S. share of world farm trade is roughly equivalent in value to the combined shares of the next three exporters — France, the Netherlands and Brazil — former Agriculture Secretary Block told the Europeans in 1985 that the United States would continue to pursue "an aggressive farm exporting policy and a firm rejection of unfair trading practices."

> The U.S. government has never believed in dividing up the world market with some sort of market shares. We believe the law of *competitive advantage* should rule. So let us look to the future with bold, new, aggressive policies.[15] (emphasis added)

Recognizing, however, the United States's production capacity and the inordinate economic and political power of the grain trade within the U.S. agricultural community, E.C.'s former Commissioner of Agriculture, Poul Dalsager, resisted such a "free for all" concept. "The Community has an agreement in the General Agreement on Tariffs and Trade (GATT) in which we are working with a so-called *fair share* of the market, and the Community intends to stick to that policy."[16] (emphasis added)

Unmasking the Foreign Trade Myth

"Grain in the United States, and in most other countries, is not merely grown and delivered to market. It is hedged and speculated against, linked to international currency alignments, and even constitutes a source of economic and political warfare. The fact that people eat grain seems incidental."

-Richard Gilmore, *A Poor Harvest*

We live in an age when agricultural exports are touted as both the ultimate salvation of the American farmer and one of the most expedient way for the United States to regain an upper hand in a badly deficient balance of payments. Thus, while government and corporate agribusiness aggressively seek to restructure American agriculture, expanding the average size of farm units, encouraging more concentration in the trading and marketing sectors, and integrating export and import operations, they continue to ignore the long-term consequences of such a policy, all the while masking their activities behind the facade of the "free market system."

As we have seen in past chapters, each prosperous period in American agriculture was followed by rural recession or depression due largely to government policies resulting from fear of inflation. Monetary policies moved toward tight credit and high interest rates, export credit programs got cut and trade relationships were altered. Increased production, encouraged by earlier government policies, no longer had viable markets, only exacerbating all those problems already caused by overproduction.

Reflecting on such conditions, Dr. Scot Stradley, Associate Professor of Economics at the University of North Dakota, pointed out to the 1983 annual convention of the North Dakota Farmers Union that in each of these instances, in the shifting of these policies, "farmers were then told to solve the overproduction problems by turning to the free market."

Chart 29A: Top 10 Nation's Share of Total World Agricultural Exports (percentage)*

Top 15 Nations	1979-80	1981-82	1983-84	1988
United States	18.1	18.7	18.0	14.0
France	7.7	7.6	7.4	9.4
Netherlands	7.0	6.9	6.9	8.7
West Germany	4.5	4.6	4.5	5.8
Australia	3.7	4.0	3.4	3.6
United Kingdom	3.4	3.4	3.2	3.6
Brazil	3.8	4.0	4.6	3.3
Belgium-Luxemburg	2.8	2.8	2.7	3.2
Italy	2.6	2.6	2.4	3.1
Canada	2.9	3.5	3.9	3.1

* = Based on aggregate value of agricultural exports, measured in U.S. dollars.

Source: "Top Export Nations," *Farmline*, USDA, May, 1986; February 1990.

The rhetoric of deregulation and the free market can be a dangerous and powerful tool; because those that advocate it are most often those who do not practice it. Big business abandoned the free-market model with the development of the railroads. Big business is not willing to give up what they have achieved in economic power, which has become a key determinant of pricing.[17]

By promoting the mythology that increased production for export will solve many of our fundamental structural economic problems in agriculture, the grain trade, corporate agribusiness and their friends in government continue to neglect the ever-increasing social and environmental costs discussed in preceding chapters.

A prophetic, detailed and insightful 1987 paper on "The Historical Case For International Commodity Agreements," prepared and written for the Minnesota Department of Agriculture by Farm Policy Analyst Berton E. Henningson, Jr., shows that as far back as World War II the USDA's Office of Foreign Agricultural Relations (OFAR), now the FAO, was arguing against the idea of "free trade" in agriculture and for the establishment of international commodity agreements.

In summary, OFAR's position was that free traders should acknowledge the economic basis for not fully exposing agriculture to free market conditions. Supply and demand functioned imperfectly when applied to agriculture because of the physical constraints which prevented farmers from responding rapidly to changing market conditions. Under a free trade system, the inability of readily shift production in response to declining demand led to periodic price-depressing surpluses which threatened the economic well-being of both inefficient and efficient producers, thus rendering the principle of comparative advantage useless under such circumstances.

OFAR saw international commodity agreements as a means to distribute export market shares equitably, to establish prices fair to both exporter and importer, to regulate reserve stocks, and to maintain production controls designed to balance supply with demand.

Its proposals included provisions for production controls in exporting countries, although restricting supply was not the sole focus. OFAR wanted these postwar agreements to include both producing and consuming countries and to be "directed toward an expansion in world trade and consumption." By bringing the importing countries into such agreements, OFAR intended to also incorporate issues related to consumption.

Wishing to restrain the tendency for commodity programs to become restrictive and for governmental intervention to perpetuate and extend itself, OFAR saw the need for international coordination of national price support programs. Under the guidance of international commodity agreements, producer and consumer nations could arrive at a mutually acceptable set of principles related to fair price levels, market shares, reserve stocks and the expansion of consumption.

But OFAR was ultimately unsuccessful in setting the course of U.S. post-war agricultural export policy. The State Department's influence within the White House was greater and as Henningson points out,

Although OFAR had built a solid case for international commodity agreements, the importing and exporting interests in the State Department ultimately rejected the approach arguing that it conflicted with free trade. In reality, the importers and exporters wanted access to cheap commodities and to export markets at any price in order to increase the profits of the private firms they represented.

Ironically, even though the State Department became the citadel for free traders at the time it never really intended to pursue a policy of perfect free trade. As Henningson concludes,

To capture foreign markets for U.S. exports, the State Department ignored the free traders and instead pursued a policy of creating "artificial demand" through the use of loans and grants to tie foreign economies to that of the United States

From such an interventionist policy came the Marshall Plan, economic assistance programs to developing nations and military assistance programs.

Reflecting on "free trade" policy arguments economic historians Joyce and Gabriel Kolko note:

in the long run perfect free trade in the world economy would hurt the United States far more than it helped it, for European states would again trade with each other, restore their power in the world economy and Third World, and inevitably challenge America's supremacy even in its domestic market.[18]

In addition, some economists like Frederick L. Cannon, director of regional and resource economics for the Bank of America, have properly pointed out that

policies that promote exports in the short run can also increase volatility in the farm economy and be self-defeating in the long run. In addition, such policies may sacrifice the health of rural economics for an improbable return to the expansion decade of the 1970s.[19]

Two lines of reasoning both flawed and historically unsupported have led to an argument that promoting and subsidizing exports will again yield a world dependent on the United States as its major source of food and fiber. At the outset history teaches us that foreign dependence on U.S. farms will always be short-lived.

There is little historical or political basis for the idea that competing nations will reduce farm subsidies and production due to increased U.S. export subsidies. The idea that the U.S. will force reduced production in Australia, Canada, and Argentina by reducing wheat prices while keeping support prices to farmers high has no historical basis.[20]

In addition, export promotion schemes that seek to expand the nation's exports are not the way to insure that rural American will grow and thrive.

Such reasoning ignores three issues critical to the health of the rural economy: Subsidized exports use scarce resources, export subsidies are an inefficient way to reduce surpluses, and export markets are inherently unstable... and unless properly managed can lead to a boom-and-bust farm economy like the one the United States has been experiencing in the past 15 years.[21]

Moreover, contrary to the "free enterprise" myth, the push for exports successfully masks still another way to further concentrate American agriculture's natural and human resources. Walter B. Saunders, Cargill's vice-chairman, told a 1985 National Grain and Feed Association convention in New Orleans:

The fundamental problem with farm policy goes back nearly 50 years to the belief that the best way to protect farm income is to link it to price. That has required us to set up elaborate mechanisms to cut production to meet residual demand. It has led to price support policies that divorce U.S. agriculture from the signals of the market whenever competitive pressures intensify...

But if the 1980s have taught us anything so far, it's that we can't solve the economic problems of the *marginal farmer* through price protection. And attempts to do so spread those financial problems to otherwise *viable producers* ...

Income must become less dependent on unit prices and more dependent of production efficiencies, *diversification* of income sources, better marketing and *greater volume*. Each farmer will have to find the mix that best fits his situation...

These changes place increased stress on farm incomes and equity in the short run. Some of the stress must be relieved in fairness to farmers who cannot bear the full load themselves. *Such relief should focus on the farmer earning most or all of his income from farming.*[22] (emphasis added)

Given Saunders' analysis it comes as no surprise that a 1981 USDA report on "Changes in the International Grain Trade in the 1980s" forecasted that in the coming decade the world's major grain trading nations will be forced by "market behavior" to base their export policies on "political and short-term self-interest rather than on global concerns."[23]

As noted, a host of economic, political, climatic and social variables are at work in the complex world of trading grain and each only adds to greater price fluctuations and an uncertain supply. A less obvious factor, to which Frances Moore Lappé has called attention, is that

the international market in grain is volatile simply because most nations produce 95 percent of what they consume. Since they import only a five percent margin, a very small change in domestic production could either double or eliminate entirely a nation's import needs. But what amounts to a small change in a single nation's production can move prices by as much as 25 percent to 50 percent once the news hits the international market.[24]

There is yet another myth attached to the idea that our grain exports help feed most of the world's hungry people. Figures available through London's Overseas Development Institute show that although the 14 less developed countries (LDCs) traditionally most linked to the U.S. account for only 23 percent of the Third World's population, until the mid-1980s they received 81 percent of all U.S. food aid shipped to the LDCs.[25]

Only since 1983 has there been a shift of U.S. agricultural trade from the United States's traditional customers of Western Europe, Japan and Canada to the LDCs. In 1985 less than 40 percent of the nation's grain and feed exports went to these traditional customers as another 20 percent went to centrally planned markets like the USSR, Eastern Europe and China, while the LDCs imported about 40 percent of the U.S.'s grain exports.[26] Nevertheless, 60 percent of all U.S. agricultural exports go to the 14.2 percent of the world's population that live in our "best customer" countries of Japan, U.S.S.R., Netherlands, Canada, Mexico, Korea, Taiwan, West Germany, Spain and Egypt.

At the same time, while the United States boasts that it is the world's largest *exporter* of food few people are aware that it is also the world's third largest *importer* of food. Between 1984 and 1988 the United States showed a seven percent decrease in its export value while registering a 11 percent increase in import value (See Chart 29B). The increase in imports was more apparent in competitive imports — crops that compete with domestically produced products like meat — than in the noncompetitive imports those which do not compete with U.S. agricultural products like coffee, cocoa and bananas. (See Chart 29C)

For example, in fresh vegetables, compare these USDA percentage increases in imports from 1981 to 1985 to per capita utilization percentages for the same period.[27]

Vegetable	% Import Increase	% Per Capita Utilization Increase
Broccoli	509	31
Carrots	68	7
Cauliflower	32	36
Celery	72	-4
Sweet Corn	1,760	6
Lettuce	231	-1
Onions	95	38
Tomatoes	56	19

A 1986 GAO report, commenting on the fact that U.S. agricultural exports dropped by $17.3 billion between 1981 and 1986 while imports rose by $3.2 billion during the same period, points out that

> between the decline in exports and the increase in imports, the 1986 annual U.S. agricultural trade balance has dropped to an estimated [surplus of] $6 billion, its lowest since 1972 ... Moreover, the most recent three months for which data exist [May, June, July] have seen negative agricultural trade deficits for three months in succession, for the first time in over 25 years.[28]

There is no more graphic example of the brutal consequences of an economy based on an exploitative export-import food policy than the daily headlines from Mexico and Central America. For decades corporate agribusiness has exploited and plundered that region for its cash crops while using the U.S. Marines and the Central Intelligence Agency to insure that these so-called "banana republics" and a docile labor force remained subservient to the export-import policies of their "good neighbor" to the north.

The century-old struggle for economic, political and social independence in that area of the world continues

to take place. In the desire to own their own land, raise their own crops and feed, house and clothe their own people, these struggling nations have sadly become but one more trip wire in needless but ongoing confrontations within the international community.[29]

Reducing U.S. Agriculture to Colonial Status

Apart from the multinational economic and political disaster of U.S. food policy, American farmers and consumers need also to recognize the domestic impact of such export trade. Today, each American farmer, backed by corporate agribusiness, feeds 128 other people, 33.7 of them living overseas. In 1988 production from two of every five harvested acres in the United States was exported, including 76 percent of our wheat, 45 percent of our cotton, 50 percent of our soybeans, 57 percent of our rice and 40 percent of our corn.[30]

Since 1970, domestic exports of non-agricultural products have grown by 405 percent while domestic agricultural exports have increased by 425 percent.[31] Meanwhile, net farm income has been up and down since 1953 while the total value of U.S. exports has continued to climb steadily as the farmers' dependence on exports doubled in just the 1980s. In 1970, for example, the value of farm exports amounted to 14 percent of the farmer's cash receipts from farming; by 1980 it was 30 percent.[32]

Yet, as Chart 29D shows, the American farmer has benefitted little if any financially from such trade.

In fact, the United States has achieved its so-called "comparative advantage" in agricultural trade through cheap farm commodities because as Henningston, testifying for the NFO, told a July 1981 House Agricultural Subcommittee hearing, "we've reduced the U.S. farm sector to a colonial status within the economy through the steady reduction of price support levels and the resulting steep decline in farm income."

> The grain trade figures prominently among the agricultural export expansionists who embrace free trade theory as a tool to promote cheap raw commodities policy. Representatives from multinational grain companies have been instrumental in lobbying Congress to reduce price supports for U.S. grain to the lowest levels in the world. Although the grain companies claimed that price supports had to be reduced in order to expand exports, in truth they wanted access to a low-priced pool of grain which would enable them to seek a competitive advantage *for themselves*.[33]

As their profits from export sales mount, further swelling their corporate coffers, the grain trade's elite have in recent years been hedging their grain trading activities by continued expansion into virtually every other aspect of the food industry, especially the lucrative market of food processing. Thus, Cargill's buying of the nation's second largest beef packer, MBPXL (Excel Corp.), for example, came as no surprise to grain trade observers. The FTC has found that of all the industrial sectors, food processing has had one of the lowest proportions of expenditures on research and develop-

Chart 29B: U.S. Agricultural Export/Import Values, 1984-1988

Exports (Billion dollars)

Commodity	1984	1986	1988
Grains and feeds	$17.4	$9.7	$12.7
Wheat	$ 6.8	$3.3	$ 4.5
Rice	$ 0.9	$0.6	$ 0.7
Feed grains	$ 8.2	$3.8	$ 5.2
Oilseeds and products	$ 8.8	$6.5	$ 7.7
Livestock production	$ 3.5	$3.5	$ 4.9
Poultry production	$ 0.4	$0.5	$ 0.6
Dairy production	$ 0.4	$0.4	$ 0.5
Horticulture production	$ 2.6	$2.7	$ 3.8
Cotton	$ 2.4	$0.7	$ 2.2
Tobacco	$ 1.4	$1.3	$ 1.3
Other	$ 1.1	$1.3	$ 1.4
TOTAL	**$38.0**	**$26.3**	**$35.3**

Imports (Billion dollars)

Commodity	1984	1986	1988
Competitive:			
Dairy & poultry production	$0.9	$0.9	$0.9
Animal & Products	$3.8	$4.1	$5.2
Fruits, nuts & vegetables	$2.7	$3.2	$3.4
Oilseeds & production	$0.8	$0.7	$0.8
Sugar & related products	$1.5	$1.0	$0.6
Wine & malt beverages	$1.5	$1.8	$1.9
Other	$1.0	$1.4	$1.7
Sub-Total	$12.2	$13.1	$14.5
Noncompetitive:			
Bananas & plantains	$0.7	$0.7	$0.8
Coffee (green & processed)	$3.3	$4.4	$2.6
Cooca beans & production	$1.1	$1.2	$1.2
Rubber & allied gums	$0.9	$0.6	$0.9
Other	$0.4	$0.4	$0.5
Sub-Total	$6.7	$7.8	$6.5
TOTAL	$18.9	$20.9	$21.0

* = Forecast

Source: *Desk Reference Guide to U.S. Agricultural Trade FAS*, USDA, Agricultural Handbook, No. 683, January, 1989

the grain trade strengthen individual interests while they weaken others; ultimately, they work to corrode the entire agricultural chain.[34]

Free Trade vs. Fair Trade

The Reagan and Bush administrations' desire to invest even more economic control in the hands of corporate agribusiness is revealed by their concerted efforts to utilize GATT in eliminating necessary farm programs and preventing Congress from exercising future control over production or pricing of agricultural products. GATT was originally designed and signed in 1947 as a multilateral agreement governing the conduct of international trading corporations. It was also intended to provide a framework for consultation and dispute settlement and negotiations on trade issues among the signatory nations. Covering 90 percent of world trade in 1989, it has been engaged in recent years in a new round of negotiations, the Uruguay Round, with agricultural trade topping its agenda.

The United States, for its part, has sought to have all agricultural programs put "on the table," meaning the elimination of all government farm programs that effect price, production, consumption, or trade in any way. This would include dairy and commodity programs, import restrictions on agricultural products and many existing conservation programs. In recent years these programs alone have provided up to 50 percent of net U.S. farm income.[35] (See Chart 29E.)

The only type of government program that would be permitted under the new U.S. proposal would be "decoupled" welfare-type payments to farmers for a five to ten year period while they "adjust" to a "free market" or a "transition" out of agriculture.

ment and one of the highest proportions of advertising to sales.

Viewing the increasing concentration of the grain trade in the hands of a few large, private, multinational corporations, Richard Gilmore sees such conditions remaining "a fact of life throughout the American agricultural economy."

It pervades transportation, grain inspection, the daily activities on the commodities exchanges, and even some actions of government. It affects even the dissemination of information, which is crucial to any effort by farmers to gain a more direct role in marketing of grain and to the U.S. government as it attempts to regulate the grain trade. Structural inefficiencies and inequities in

One need look no further than the drafter of the U.S. proposal — Daniel Amstutz, former Cargill vice-president and chief agricultural trade negotiator for the United States — to discern who its major beneficiaries would be. The measure is promoted worldwide by Cargill, the Fertilizer Institute and other corporate agribusiness groups who stand to benefit substantially from a return to full-scale agricultural production.

In the United States this so-called "decoupling" mechanism for corn, wheat, soybeans, sunflowers, cotton and rice was contained in bills proposed in 1985 by Senators Rudy Boschwitz, R-Minn., and David Boren, D-Okla., and again in 1989 along with Senator David Karnes, R-Neb. The later bill (SB1725) would have cut

Chart 29C: U.S. Agricultural Imports by Commodity

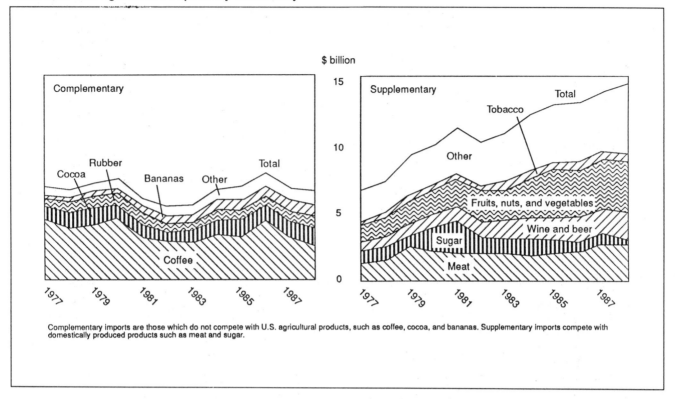

Complementary imports are those which do not compete with U.S. agricultural products, such as coffee, cocoa, and bananas. Supplementary imports compete with domestically produced products such as meat and sugar.

farm price support loans by nearly 30 percent from the 1989 level; replace deficiency payments with welfare-type guaranteed "equity payments" based solely on production history, that would be phased out or reduced over a five-year period; eliminate all supply management programs; place a 50 million acre limit on all land set-asides, and institute marketing loan export subsidies for commodities with CCC loans.

Agriculture trade policy analyst Mark Ritchie notes that such a "decoupling" proposal would have any number of severe impacts on agriculture. It would mean that at least 30 million of the estimated 80 million acres of highly erodible U.S. agricultural land would not be taken out of production; the land would be farmed much more intensively, using more chemicals and fertilizers; farm prices would fall, leaving farmers with less income; conservation features of existing legislation would be eliminated; families currently on the land would be replaced by corporate and/or absentee owners; diversified livestock producers would be replaced by large-scale environmentally unsound feedlots; budget costs would continue at record levels, reducing funds for sustainable agriculture and conservation programs; existing small and medium sized farmers of non-program and specialty crops, some of agriculture's most genuinely efficient producers, would be subject to intense pressure from the shifting of land now in set-asides of other crops into their crops; and the downward pressure on prices in Third World agriculture would accelerate, forcing debtor nations to intensify production in order to keep their export earnings in the face of lower prices and thereby force their own farmers to further "mine their land" and "poach" such areas as the world's already rapidly depleting rainforests.

One alternative to the U.S. proposal to the GATT negotiations came from the European Community. It put forward a plan echoing the early days of the IWA negotiations, that would raise world prices by phasing out all export dumping and establishing minimum reference prices for cereals, sugar and dairy products. The proposal would allow nations to administer domestic farm programs as they determined where necessary to protect food security, promote rural development, protect the environment, consumers and producers.

Clearly, this European approach to the Uruguay Round reflected more sensitivity about food security than the always abundant United States. After encountering hunger and wide-spread shortages in two world wars and wishing to maintain a vital part of their society structured around family farms and villages, the EC has understandably resisted the arguments for recent change put forth by U.S. corporate agribusiness trade interests.

Public opinion surveys among Europeans show such concern. For example, government support for farmers was agreed to be "a good thing" by 59 percent of the general public in one 1988 survey; by contrast, only 28 percent favored such support for steelmakers and 11 percent for the automobile industry. Likewise, 78 percent of the surveyed people accepted having to pay more for "healthier farm products" grown with reduced use of chemical, poisons and fertilizers.[36]

Although the United States initially sought the immediate elimination of all "trade-distorting farm subsidies," international opinion soon forced it to abandon such a position in favor of a "substantial and

Chart 29D: Comparing Decreasing Net Farm Income with the Increasing Value of U.S. Agricultural Exports

Year	Average Net Farm Income (1982 $) (billions)	% of Change	% of Increase/ Decrease in Govern. Payments	Average Value of U.S. Ag Exports (billions)	% of Change	Average no. of Acres Exported (millions)	% of Change
1952-55	49.35			$ 3.22			
1956-59	39.40	- 2.0	+242.8	3.97	+23.3		
1960-63	37.17	-22.3	+ 68.8	4.90	+23.4		
1964-67	36.10	- 2.9	+ 95.0	6.42	+31.0		
1968-71	34.15	- 5.4	+ 28.3	6.77	+ 5.4	22.5*	
1972-73	55.60	+62.8	- 6.9	11.60	+41.6	30.5	+35.5
1974-77	38.77	-30.3	- 237.8	22.52	+94.1	28.7	- 6.0
1978-81	29.30	-24.4	+ 96.0	35.90	+59.4	35.7	+24.4
1982-85	23.70	-19.1	+279.4	35.77	- 0.3	30.7	-14.0
1986-88	36.96	+55.9	+ 98.4	29.83	-16.6	32.3	+ 5.2

*1970-71

Note: Government payments include both cash payments and payments in kind (PIK) for feed grains, wheat, rice, cotton, wool and conservation programs, including Soil Bank programs until 1971 when program was discontinued.

Source: Table 2, Table 12, "Economic Indicators of the Farm Sector. National Financial Summary, 1988," USDA-ERS, ECIFS 8-1, September, 1989 and "Value of U.S. Exports by Major Sector, Fiscal Years Ending 1950-89," *Desk Reference Guide to U.S. Agricultural Trade*, USDA-FAS, Agriculture Handbook No. 683, January, 1989.

progressive reduction" of such subsidies. Carla Hills, chief U.S. Trade Representative, admitted that even though its proposal was couched in new language the U.S. position remained unchanged. "If over time you have substantial progressive reductions you do get to zero," she concluded.[37] "We backed off the stance for the moment," one USDA aide commented in January, 1989, "but we hope to reach that goal during the next 20 months. Our objective is still the same. How we get there has changed for tactical negotiating reasons."[38]

Critics of the U.S. GATT agricultural agenda such as William Dunavent, president of Dunavent Enterprises, Memphis, Tennessee, a major U.S. cotton merchant, believe it is unrealistic to have a market entirely free of government intervention.

If anybody could survive in a free market, we in the United States could do it, but there are too many ideologies and governments around the world for a free market to work. *We don't want free markets, we want fair markets.* Our future is to continue to devote energy and thought to fair trade. Free trade is only a dream that will never come true.[39] (emphasis added)

Many Are Called For, But Few Are The Chosen

Chart 29E: Trade 1991

Trading Partners   All figures in billions.

Rank/Country	U.S. Exports	U. S. Imports	Trade Deficit
1. Canada	$85.1	$91.1	-$6.0
2. Japan	$48.1	$91.6	-$43.5
3. Mexico	$33.3	$31.2	+$2.1
4. Germany	$21.3	$26.2	-$4.9
5. United Kingdom	$22.1	$18.5	+$3.5
6. Taiwan	$13.2	$23.0	-$9.8
7. South Korea	$15.5	$17.0	-$1.5
8. France	$15.4	$13.4	+$2.0
9. China	$6.3	$19.0	-$12.7
10. Italy	$8.6	$11.8	-$3.2

Chart 29E: Trade 1991 (continued)

Top U.S. Exports   All figures in billions.

Item (example)	1990	1991
Agricultural products	$38.7	$38.5
Data-processing and office equipment	$24.7	$26.0
Aircraft	$19.6	$24.2
Electrical machinery (fuses, circuit breakers)	$28.4	$30.0
General industrial machinery (escalator parts)	$15.8	$17.1
Power generating machinery (turbine engines)	$15.8	$17.0
Specialized industrial machinery (bulldozers)	$15.3	$16.6
Vehicle parts (brakes, gear boxes, axles)	$14.5	$14.3
Scientific instruments (dental drill motors)	$12.1	$13.5
Coal, other fuels	$12.2	$12.0

Top U.S. Imports   All figures in billions.

Item (example)	1990	1991
Crude oil	$43.8	$37.2
Electrical machinery (fuses, circuit breakers)	$33.6	$35.1
Data-processing and office equipment	$26.9	$30.1
Clothing	$25.6	$26.2
Telecommunications equipment	$22.2	$23.5
Agricultural products	$22.3	$22.2
New cars from Japan	$19.2	$20.4
General industrial machinery (escalator parts)	$14.5	$14.4
Power-generating machinery	$14.5	$14.2
Car and truck parts	$15.2	$14.1

Source: U.S. Dept. of Commerce, *USA Today*, February 21, 1992

Chapter Thirty

"But It's The Name of the Game"

"Nagle discloses U.S. rejection of Soviet request for more grain."
— Des Moines Register, *April 28, 1989*

"Subsidy On Wheat For Soviet Sales Approved by Bush: One Goal, White House Says, Is Advancing Global Talks to Cut Farm Supports"
— The New York Times, *May 3, 1989*

"Soviets Buying U.S. Grain at Record Pace"
— The Wall Street Journal, *May 4, 1989*

"11-year-low feared for winter wheat harvest"
— USA Today, *May 12, 1989*

"Export Subsidies For Wheat Concern Consumer Groups"
— The Wall Street Journal, *May 8, 1989*

For many Americans these headlines, which began appearing throughout the press in a two-week period in the spring of 1989, were in the immortal words of Yogi Berra, "*deja vu* all over again."

Remembering the consequences of the "Great American Grain Robbery of 1972" some farmers, consumers and politicians seriously questioned whether a nation that was still recovering from disastrous droughts throughout the 1980s and a record low stock of essential grains should be exporting its grain abroad at prices that could only be supported through a government subsidy such as the Export Enhancement Program.

On July 8, 1972, the United States and Russia announced a then unprecedented trade agreement: the United States gave the Soviet Union three-year credit at six percent interest in amounts up to $500 million. In return, the Soviets promised to buy a minimum of $750 million of grain, including a $200 million purchase the first year.

But, by September 1, 1972, over $1 billion of U.S. grain and nearly one-quarter of the nation's wheat crop had been sold to Russia, mostly for cash, in secret negotiations between Russian officials and six large U.S. grain exporters.

Secretary Butz had hailed the sales as a "major break-through for peaceful coexistence between Russia and the United States" But the favoritism and political intrigue surrounding the subsequent public and private negotiations suggest that the billion dollar transaction

could more appropriately be termed a Great American Grain Robbery.

The background of this heist was complex. It involved a systematic program by USDA to deny itself vital grain export data, the joint USDA-grain trade sabotage of the International Wheat Agreement and sporadic efforts to liberalize trade with Russia that had been previously thwarted by right-wing political pressure.

Other key elements were a long-time USDA reverence for the grain trade's elite and a 1971 feed grain sale to Russia in which USDA bought grain at inflated prices with taxpayers' money so it could deliver it cheap to the likes of the Cargill and Continental Grain corporations.

In 1963 the Russians first entered the world grain market in a large way after experiencing a severe crop failure the previous year. Unlike past years, when the Russian people had been asked to restrict their use of grain, the Soviet Union now sought to increase its grain supply with imports.

Much to the consternation of the Kennedy administration, the first major sale to the Soviets was 6.8 million tons of Canadian wheat at a price estimated to be nearly $500 million. Meanwhile, over a billion bushels of unsold U.S. grain lay in storage. President Kennedy had hoped for a change in our trade policy which would both allow U.S. shipments of grain to the Soviet Union and help lessen Cold War tensions. He believed that despite strong anti-Soviet attitudes in the United States there was support for such trade even beyond the farm community.

Mission: "Cram It Down Their Throats"

Since 1949 wheat had been a drug on the world market. For the most part world prices were lower than American prices, the latter being supported by the U.S. government. To keep the nation's export trade competitive the government began compensating grain companies with a subsidy that was the difference between U.S. inland wheat prices and the gateway price foreigners bought the grain for at U.S. ports.

When a grain company made a sale it registered it for compensation with the USDA. This compensation would change as prices varied at home and abroad. If the USDA wanted to "dump" wheat or undersell another country it had only to increase the compensation which in turn enabled the companies to sell the U.S. grain at either "world prices" or at a discount.

In 1963 alone the government aid programs provided financing for $1.5 billion of the nation's total agricultural exports sales of $4 billion. By this time, P.L. 480 had already generated nearly $2 billion in sales for Continental and Cargill alone.

No longer willing to dump U.S. grain surpluses throughout the world the United States was beginning to think of grain in terms of trade rather than aid. The USDA became more aggressive and conducted what Dan Morgan has called

> at times a ruthless campaign to carry out this objective.
>
> The government paid grain companies a large enough subsidy for every bushel they shipped so that companies could offer U.S. wheat at a discount from prevailing world prices. The subsidies came out of the federal budget; the trade off was that the more wheat was shipped abroad, the less the government spent to store unsold surpluses and the more foreign exchange came back into the country. The United States set out to grab away markets from Canada and other competitors. Officially, this was called "making American agricultural products more competitive abroad." Privately, officials acknowledged that the objective in foreign markets was to "cram it down their throats."[1]

By the end of 1963 the United States had negotiated a sale of one and a half million tons of wheat to the Soviets, to be handled by Continental Grain and Cargill, along with a subsidy that amounted to a total of $1.7 million. Ensuing difficulties in locating enough available American ships to transport the grain caused considerable tension between the Kennedy administration and the International Longshoreman's Association, which was objecting to the use of so many foreign carriers in the shipment.

When the Federal Maritime Administration approved Continental's use of additional foreign ships, Theodore Gleason, the union's president, charged that the Administration and Continental were in cahoots to cheat U.S. seaman. In *Newsweek*, Gleason described the government's waffling on a 50-50 shipping promise as "the characteristic pose of two-faced panderers and their scarlet women caught in *flagrante delicto*."[2]

The 1963 sale did not, however, usher in a new era in U.S.-Russian grain trading. Not only was there an ideological bias against such continued large sales, but the maritime union's insistence that American vessels be used made possible future transactions too costly to contemplate.

Ironically, it was during the administration of long-time anti-communist crusader Richard Nixon that trade with the Soviets was renewed. One of the vital but little noticed steps which paved the way into this new trade era came in June 1971, when Nixon quietly removed a requirement that exporters obtain licenses for foreign transactions while also eliminating a standing policy that a minimum 50 percent of expected grain had to be shipped on American vessels.

The Great American Grain Robbery

It was a pessimistic U.S. trade team, however, headed by Butz, Clarence D. Palmby, Assistant Secretary of Agriculture for International Affairs and Commodity Programs, and Clifford G. Pulvermacher, the USDA's chief foreign salesman, which returned from Moscow in early April, 1972. After discussing an increase in grain sales and the possible extension of credit, the Russians flatly rejected Butz's initial offer.

The Russians had sought a ten-year, two percent interest loan. The United States, arguing that such a loan would be unfair to the country's long-time, established world customers, proposed instead the CCC's standard three-year credit terms at 6 1/8 percent.

Palmby later admitted, "I, along with my colleagues from the U.S. government, returned to Washington on April 14 firmly convinced the USSR would *never* buy grain on *credit*." (emphasis added). While Palmby (and Pulvermacher), both with extensive international trade and negotiating backgrounds, may have been skeptical of a credit agreement, they were certainly aware that Russia desperately needed wheat.[3]

A severe Russian winter had killed much of the season's wheat crop, seeded with Besostaja, a high-yielding variety and highly responsive to inputs, but unsuited to survive the bitter cold Ukraine winter. An American Agricultural Attache in Moscow had already reported to Washington in February that an inadequate snow cover threatened some 2.5 million acres of the country's wheat crop. Again in June, after touring the Ukraine and Moldavia, the attaché reported that over 27 million acres of wheat that had been replanted in the spring had also been wiped out by drought. Reports on these disasters were upgraded and highly classified, denying U.S. farmers any knowledge of such dire conditions. The difficulties Russia was having with its wheat, however, were soon manifested on the world's markets as it began to default on sales contracts with other world market customers.

On the international scene, Canada, which had sold wheat to the Russians in the past, was logistically unable to deliver grain at this time in significant quantities as its port and transportation facilities were taxed to capacity. Meanwhile, the United States was preparing to harvest a mammoth 1.6 billion bushels of wheat, of which over one billion bushels would be available for export — an amount that would easily exceed the 1965-66 record high by over 130 million bushels. Thus, the stage was set for lucrative cash sales to the Russians by the grain trades' elite — Cargill, Continental, Bunge, Louis Dreyfus, Cook & Co., Peavey and Garnac (Andre's U.S. subsidiary). Several individuals who were to play vital parts in the unfolding story of the Great American Grain Robbery were also strategically positioning themselves.

The Palmbys Go Shopping In the Big Apple

In March, prior to Clarence Palmby's departure for Moscow, Michel Fribourg, president of Continental Grain, had contacted Palmby about coming to work for his firm as Vice-President for International Trade. After what Palmby later described as "very limited conversations," he and his wife spent several hours in New York (headquarters for Continental) looking at apartments and living conditions.

On May 9, two days prior to informing Butz of his intention to leave USDA, Palmby, a former executive vice-president of the U.S. Feed Grains Council, an organization designed to promote feed grain exports by helping countries set up high-technology poultry and livestock industries, met in Washington with the Russian Deputy Minister of Foreign Trade. No progress, however, was reported on any sales agreement between the two countries. Palmby then accepted Continental's offer the same day he tendered his resignation to USDA. He said he received a firm offer from Continental, "as I recall, somewhere around the first part of May, in that area." On June 8, just a month before the announcement of the first 1972 Russian sale, Palmby joined Continental.

Butz later told the press that, "in our business you operate in a gold fish bowl. If I had known (about the co-op purchase) when we went to Russia, I would not have taken Mr. Palmby on the team." Butz recalled he had discussed Palmby's future with the Assistant Secretary in February, since he realized that Palmby was certainly "the most *merchandisable person* in the Agriculture Department."[4] (emphasis added)

The Revolving Door: Merrily, Merrily It Spins Around

Palmby's hop, however, was not the only one between USDA and the grain trade during this period of time. Replacing Palmby at USDA was Carroll Brunthaver, who prior to his government appointment in 1969, was Associate Director of Research for an affiliate of Cook Industries.

In early 1972, Claude Merriman, USDA's Export Marketing Service's (EMS) assistant sales manager for commodity exports, retired, but June Merriman had become a consultant for Louis Dreyfus Corp. Merriman's successor, George S. Shanklin, came to EMS after serving for seven years as manager of the Washington, D.C. office of Bunge Corp. And, as noted above, EMS General Sales Manager, Carroll Pulvermacher, would also eventually leave USDA to take a job with Bunge.

Meanwhile, a Cargill merchandiser, Charles Turnquist, would also join USDA late in the summer of 1972. Turnquist acted as a consultant to the department's ASC Service while awaiting a civil service clearance for appointment to the post of Deputy Administrator for Commodity Operations. According to one department source, the former Cargill executive spent much of this time checking with exporters on what further government actions might be needed to assure their ability to meet the Russian commitment without taking a loss due to higher grain prices.[5]

As the world wheat situation continued to grow increasingly clear to only a small, select group of shifting USDA and grain trade executives in Washington, New York and Minneapolis, farmers in Texas, Oklahoma, Kansas and other areas throughout the southwest were going about their normal task of harvesting another abundant wheat crop. Many of them, unaware of the rich rewards their crop would soon be reaping for

traders in the marketplace, were selling their bounty for as little as $1.20 - $1.35 a bushel.

The large grain companies were also busy, buying the current wheat crop cheaply and storing its bulk in their massive elevators for later sale. Cargill's storage capacity alone at that time was estimated at 180 million bushels, some 30 million bushels more than Continental's facilities. In fact, a Purdue University study showed as early as 1967 that over 56 percent of the storage capacity in major U.S. grain shipping ports was held by only six grain corporations.

(Grain farmers in Texas, Oklahoma and New Mexico would later file a class action suit on behalf of 60,000 wheat producers against Cargill and Continental alleging the companies "conspired in 1972 to suppress information regarding impending wheat sales to the Soviet Union." They also contended that the conspiracy was an antitrust violation that kept market prices depressed to the benefit of the grain companies. In 1982, however, the U.S. Supreme Court let stand a lower court ruling that the farmers could not sue the major U.S. grain companies.[6])

"Sightseeing" Russian Grain Traders Come to Washington, D.C.

On June 29, a Russian delegation headed by M.R. Kuzmin, First Deputy Foreign Minister of Trade, came to Washington to begin a series of meetings with U.S. officials. The Russians indicated, as Commerce Undersecretary James Lynn later pointed out, that they wanted to pursue negotiations on the basis of the terms the U.S. trade mission to Moscow had offered in April. This was a sure sign to government officials that a major agreement was in the offing. These sessions in Washington lasted until President Nixon announced the two-nation, three-year credit agreement on July 8.

The officials of Exportkhleb, the Soviet state trading organization were also in Washington at this same time. Clarence Palmby, now with Continental, and another company official from its Paris office took a group of the Russians sightseeing in the nation's capital and to lunch in Alexandria, Virginia over the weekend. Palmby claims, however, that "no business" was discussed with the officials at that time. The American exporters would later claim that they were unaware that an official Russian trade delegation was also in Washington at the same time.[7] Undersecretary Lynn, however, stated that the United States did know that a separate Soviet team was in New York negotiating privately with the grain trade.

Palmby recalls that during June he sat in on policy meetings at Continental at which time Soviet crop conditions and "other matters" were discussed. He offered the benefit of his judgment, but "I never negotiated with the U.S.S.R. on the grain deal for Continental."[8]

Using Food to Achieve an "Honorable Peace" in Vietnam

On Monday, July 3, negotiations between Exportkhleb and Continental continued in New York. Two days later the Russians bought an estimated 147 million bushels of wheat from Continental at $1.63 per bushel. Although the sale was for "cash," Secretary Butz stated that there was also a stipulation in the contract that the deal might be handled through credit transactions if credit later became available.[9]

An Associated Press story almost a year later (buried by the news of the rapidly developing Watergate scandal) disclosed that this low, fixed purchase price the Russians eventually paid for the U.S. wheat was part of an agreement between the two countries for Russian silence with respect to the U.S. bombing of Hanoi and the mining of Haiphong harbor.

According to AP, Secretary Butz, the Department of Commerce, the State Department and the White House all reluctantly confirmed the story.[10] Later, Secretary Butz, in a June 1974 speech to the Advertising Council noted,

> Food has become a major force for negotiations in the substantial and solid stride toward world peace which this nation has made in the 1970s. Food was a major force for achieving detente with the Soviet Union. Thus, food was indeed a major weapon in achieving an honorable peace in Vietnam.

The 1972 Russian wheat sale involved $240 million, more than the total dollar amount and double the amount of wheat that the USDA had originally said Russia was prepared to buy in the coming year. Yet, all this was consummated three days before the U.S.-Russia agreement was signed and announced. Later, it would be denied by nearly all parties to an unbelieving public that anybody ever really knew either the size or scope of the Russian sale at that time.

A later review of the events throughout the summer of '72, however, suggest that this U.S.-Russian grain trade agreement might well have been but a smokescreen by the Russians in an effort to buy wheat at cheap prices, since most of their subsequent buying was in wheat rather than other feed grains and was for cash, rather than credit.

Selective Memories

In Kinsley, Kansas, on July 8, only a few hours before Richard Nixon announced the signing of the Russian agreement, wheat farmer Elmer Frick sold his entire 1972 crop of 4,000 bushels for $1.27 a bushel. Frick's plight was typical of farmers throughout the early harvest season. Eight weeks later, after the magnitude of the Russian sale began attracting public scrutiny, those same bushels of hard red winter wheat would bring a farmer $2.14 per bushel. That fluctuation in price, Frick explained, amounted to the difference between being barely able to cover his cost of production and having enough money to pay off all his current farm debts, excepting the mortgage.

Likewise, in Oklahoma, by July 15 over 50 percent of the state's wheat crop was harvested and sold at prices near those paid to Frick.[11] Harvest figures were up to 75% by August 8 as 90 percent of the state's 50,000 farmers sold nearly 80 million bushels at prices below $1.50 per bushel — a total loss approaching $47 million. Elsewhere, throughout the southwest and early-har-

vesting midwestern states, 20 to 25 percent of the 1972 wheat crop had already been sold by the middle of July.

Farmers, pressed with debts occasioned by rising production costs, needed cash. Many of them had inadequate storage facilities on the farm and commercial storage was a costly risk without some assurance of higher prices later. Faced with that situation many farmers were forced to sell their grain immediately after harvest.

Disregarding such realities, a contemptuous Earl Butz, in noting the losses some growers were suffering, observed that "farmers didn't lose money (because of the early sales), they just weren't smart enough to take advantage of the situation."

At a September 9 press conference he also observed that the farmers who sold during the early harvest season "knew precisely as much as we knew. They knew as much as the grain companies ... Some money has been made in the deal. Some trading companies have made it. But it's the name of the game."

Throughout July the Russians continued to make large purchases of wheat from the grain trade's elite. No public announcement followed any of these sales.[12] Later, in testimony before a Senate investigating committee, officials of the major grain corporations told Senator Henry Jackson, D-Wash, that they had indeed alerted the USDA to these large purchases by the Russians. However, Carroll Brunthaver, the person who reportedly took the calls, said he could not remember all of those reported calls and those he did remember contained no unusual news. Bernard Steinweg, Michel Fribourg's brother-in-law and head of Continental's N.Y. grain division, swore before Senator Jackson's Permanent Investigations Subcommittee that he had mentioned an initial sale of four million tons of wheat by Continental in a telephone conversation with Brunthaver two days before the announcement of the sale. Yet, neither Brunthaver nor Butz could recall such a conversation. Butz also claimed he was not aware of the dimensions of the Soviet purchases until *September 19* (almost ten weeks after the public announcement) when Palmby gave a House agriculture subcommittee the details of the sale.

Two subsequently unclassified CIA documents, however, show that the government was well aware of the details of the Soviet sale before it publicly claimed to be. In a August 11 report stamped "confidential," the CIA's director of intelligence told Brunthaver and USDA general counsel, Claude Coffman:

> In July and early August the Soviet Union negotiated further purchases of unprecedented quantities of grain from U.S. companies. These new contracts, taken together with additional orders for Canadian and French grain, place total purchases for fiscal year 1973 at more than 20 million tons.[13]

A second CIA report, classified "secret," sent to Brunthaver on August 31 stated:

Total [Soviet] grain contracts with all countries for delivery during FY 1973 now total 24.2 million tons worth almost $1.5 billion, three times the quantity imported in FY 1972 and more than twice the amounts bought after the disastrous harvests of 1963 and 1965. A recent contract for one million tons of soybeans [this referred to a sale by Cook on August 4] to be used for livestock feed and vegetable oil, brings total purchases of grain and soybeans to about $1.6 billion. *These imports of grain will be largely from the United States 17.5 million tons* — with the remainder from Canada, France, Australia and Sweden ... Negotiations reportedly are continuing for additional contracts.[14]

At his July 8 press conference Secretary Butz had noted that although the Russians would have to buy wheat beyond that already contracted from Canada, "they [the Soviets] have plenty of wheat for now." In early August, however, Morton Sosland reported in his *Milling and Baking News* that a series of mysterious phone calls to the magazine related to him that the Russians were in the U.S. grain market in a *very* big way.

Wheat future activity on the Kansas City Board of Trade also increased dramatically throughout July. *The Wall Street Journal's* Burt Schorr reported on September 18 that the Commodity Exchange Authority was conducting an intensive investigation to determine whether exporters had been placing heavy orders in the closing minutes of trading each day to boost closing prices and occasion a corresponding rise in the wheat export subsidy.

According to one trader for a large flour company, "suspicious last-minute purchases of September contracts occurred on several days in July." He cited "one instance ... when with three or four minutes of trading remaining pit brokers handled orders totaling five million bushels."[15]

Doing the Continental

> "When overseas grain users buy U.S. grain, they deal with many commodity marketing organizations, one of which might be Continental Grain.
>
> "This is in keeping with America's traditional belief in the free market system which reinforces the right of buyers and sellers to negotiate with out undue interference or restrictions.
>
> "Operating in an open market, grain buyers throughout the world compete on equal terms with one another, and with domestic customers, for U.S. grain supplies ..."

An outspoken champion of the "free market," Continental Grain has throughout the years boasted of the virtue of "competing on equal terms" in the world's grain markets. Advertising rhetoric to the contrary, in 1973 the USDA's Commodity Exchange Authority charged Continental with failing to report during the time of the Great American Grain Robbery of 1972 that it owned some 177.5 million bushels of wheat and 168.9 million bushels of corn. CEA Administrator Alex Caldwell termed the company's reporting violations "willful."[16]

Under the law at the time, companies using the grain futures market were required to report their trading to the CEA and provide evidence that they were not exceeding certain Congressionally-imposed limits on speculation. Designed to provide clues to developments within the grain markets, the law had failed to achieve such a purpose during this period of massive purchases as the nation's grain traders engaged in "competing on equal terms with one another."

Continental "emphatically denied that it willfully violated" the Federal law and explained that *clerical errors* were initially responsible for its reporting oversights and that these initial errors got repeated in subsequent reports.[17]

During this time, farmers and grain elevator operators who were "hedging" on the futures markets were absorbing hugh losses in their effort to protect grain prices. As prices continued to climb their contracts, which had already been sold, lost more and more money. Meanwhile, the grain companies, now singularly aware of what was happening in grain markets throughout the world, began "double hedging," *i.e.*, taking the same positions in the futures markets that they were taking in the field, and thus buying all the grain they could before farmers realized what the fundamentals were. The rewards reaped by the grain trade's elite in such "trading," along with the massive government subsidies they would continue to enjoy for several months to come, allowed these staunch defenders of the "free market" system to report earnings as much as six times greater than in previous years.

Protecting the Grain Trade

On July 23 the Russians quietly returned to the United States to buy more cheap American wheat. Crucial to the trade's future plans at this time was USDA's export subsidy policy and the payments it was making to exporters as a means of keeping U.S. wheat export prices competitive in world markets.

Through July and into August the domestic price of wheat keep rising, and each day the government's subsidy program grew more and more lucrative for those firms that had bought wheat cheaply early on from thousands of the nation's unsuspecting farmers.

Protests began to be heard that USDA, by maintaining the net export price and allowing the subsidies to increase, was artificially driving domestic prices. The USDA, however, doggedly defended its subsidy program as essential to keeping U.S. wheat competitive with the world price, failing to concede that the world price had indeed become the American selling price.

At approximately noon on August 24, EMS's Grain Division Director, Charles Pence, began placing calls to a few unnamed members of the grain trade, notifying them that there would be a meeting at the Department the next day to inform them that "there would be a change in export payment policy on sales of wheat," and that the United States could no longer maintain the present export subsidy level.

USDA's Brunthaver later told a House Subcommittee on Grains that he had no knowledge of Pence's "tip-off" calls. Rather, he said, he had asked Frank McKnight, EMS's Assistant General Sales manager, on August 24,

> to notify exporters immediately that a change had just been made in export policy; which, in effect, notified wheat exporters not to assume sales made after the close of business on the 23 of August would necessarily qualify for export payments based on U.S. export prices that had prevailed for the previous ten months.[18]

Whether in fact Pence made it clear to the handful of exporters whom he called that the new policy was retroactive to the close of business on August 23 is open to question. Brunthaver later testified that the decision to make the cutoff date for the special subsidy the 24th, rather than the 23rd, was made until the 25th when USDA decided that some exporters (those who received no calls from Pence on the 24th) might not have been properly informed.

Pence also noted in a *New York Times* telephone interview that when he called the grain companies they "immediately began talking about whether there would be a two-tier system." He told them that he had no such knowledge. But he conceded that he had "already heard from *sources in the trade* that this was what the Department had in mind, even before I knew it."[19]

"We've Got to Call and Warn the Traders!"

On August 24, the domestic price of wheat was near $2.10 and the subsidy a staggering 38 cents a bushel. On the twenty-fifth, USDA announced that all sales made through August 24 (23?) and registered by September 1, would be eligible for a 38 cent subsidy, plus a nine cent retroactive supplement. (In the previous few days, USDA had not changed the export subsidy payment while the domestic price continued to climb.)

With the announcement of the two-tier policy, USDA felt it could not penalize those exporters who had abided by the old policy, so the retroactive supplement of nine cents was to bring the current "world price" plus the subsidy up to a level with the present "domestic wheat price."

The second-tier payment policy was simply an early warning sign to the grain trade that it could no longer depend on the old subsidy policy and that the day of zero subsidy was at hand, and in fact came on September 21. Despite the handwriting on the wall that the change in subsidy policy was doing little to cool off a hot market, USDA apparently still felt it necessary to stick by the program to the very end.

Earlier in the week that the zero subsidy was announced, Brunthaver was questioned about such a possibility by Representative John Melcher, D-Mont., during the House subcommittee hearing. "No," Brunt-

haver replied, "I don't think that it is in active consideration. No."[20]

While the Assistant Secretary was unable to make up his mind in various public statements about whether the Pence calls had benefited the exporters or not, journalist Rich Thomas uncovered one of the more revealing episodes in the entire story of the Great American Grain Robbery in a *Newsweek* report:

> It took the White House Office of Management and Budget to blow the whistle. In a routine audit, director Casper Weinberger was startled by the burgeoning cost of the export subsidies. His crash investigation culminated in a showdown with Carroll Brunthaver ... "My God, you mean we suspend the subsidy?" Brunthaver exclaimed, "We've got to call and warn the traders." Weinberger icily insisted that a public announcement be made.[21]

During the House Subcommittee hearings, Melcher had also asked Brunthaver whether it was proper for the USDA to give verbal assurances on policy to major exporters. "This involves millions of dollars," the Montana Congressman questioned. "Is it customary to do it verbally?" Brunthaver replied that he thought he was simply guaranteeing the firms a continuation of long-standing policy.

Reaping A Windfall In Export Subsidy Payments

Later, after these sales had been completed, the government's General Accounting Office questioned whether the United States had sold its wheat too cheaply:

> There were indications that recent world market conditions suggested that the United States was in a preferred position as a supplier of wheat, and Agriculture may not have had to subsidize sales to the extent that it did... In our opinion, the expenditure of government funds totaling hundreds of millions of dollars dictates that agency officials assure themselves that program objectives are being achieved as economically as possible.

During the week of August 25-September 1, for example, 282,047,694 bushels of wheat were registered for the special subsidy of 47 cents a bushel — 85 percent of that wheat being booked for subsidy payments on September 1. The cost to the American taxpayer: approximately $131.6 million.

One of the major grain exporters which scored a windfall in export subsidy profits with the announcement of the 47-cent policy was the Louis Dreyfus Corp. Sometime in mid-August after two or three days of talks with French representatives of Dreyfus, officials of the Peoples' Republic of China agreed to buy over 14,500,000 bushels of American wheat.

Dreyfus subsequently registered one quarter of the sales on a day the subsidy was 29 cents a bushel. As for the remaining wheat, the company said, the transaction was completed before 3:30 p.m., August 24, thereby qualifying for the special 47-cent subsidy. Dreyfus, however, did not furnish its verifying information on the sale until September 11, as USDA allowed exporters five business days beyond September 1 to provide data verifying a sale on which a subsidy was claimed before August 24. The French firm, therefore, received some $5.8 million in subsidy payments on the China sale, nearly double the amount it would ordinarily have received if they had applied for a subsidy at the time of the sale.

By early September, the Russians had bought nearly 400 million bushels of wheat — half of those sales handled by Continental Grain Co. — from the United States. Domestic prices were near $2.20 per bushel, yet exporters were still receiving over 25 cents a bushel in subsidy payments.

Earl Butz's "Trickle Down" Theory

Amid charges by Democratic Presidential candidate George McGovern of USDA favoritism and the passing on of "inside information," to corporate agribusiness, the House Subcommittee on Livestock and Grains held hearings in mid-September. It was at these hearings that USDA and Butz defended their actions.

Reverting to his now famous "trickle down" theory, Butz pointed out how

the American taxpayer gains from this sale by paying less to store surplus wheat. The grain farmer gains from a stronger market and higher prices. Union members gain from expanded jobs and opportunities. The economy gains from this increased activity and from a sizeable contribution to our balance of trade.

The Agriculture Secretary did not address the fundamental question of whether his department did everything it could to alert U.S. producers to the size and scope of Russia's wheat needs and knowing what it already considerably did about that country's crop failures. Ignoring the facts of world food supply conditions in 1972, Butz blandly told the committee that "it is accurate to say that the eventual size of the Soviet purchases caught everyone by surprise, including the Russians themselves."

Yet Butz maintained that the U.S.-Russian "deal" was "good for everybody but George McGovern." This remark, during a Presidential campaign already marred by a major political scandal that would later lead to a presidential resignation, took on a certain poignancy when a subsequent GAO report revealed that officials of the grain industry had reported gifts of over $158,000 to Richard Nixon's 1972 re-election campaign.[22]

The Grain Trade's "Open and Shut" Defense

The grain trade, meanwhile, was going about its business in an unprecedented manner, given its usually secretive nature, seeking to disprove charges of "excessive" and "windfall" profits by allowing the public a brief glimpse at their financial ledgers.

At a November 2 press conference in Minneapolis, Cargill detailed how it had *lost* money on the Russian sales. The nation's largest private corporation claimed its loss came because of its "need to purchase wheat at rapidly rising prices and at the same time, failure of the government's export differential (subsidy) to keep pace with those rising prices."

Cargill's 14-page financial accounting left several key questions unanswered. In its acquisition costs Cargill did not state whether it computed such costs at a competitive price or an actual rate or how many bushels of the wheat it had sold to the Russians were purchased from its own subsidiaries. What prices did those subsidiaries ordinarily pay for the wheat *they* purchased from wheat growers? Did the stated shipping costs of the wheat include freight charges paid to Cargill's own barge company? Were the large "backhaul" charges included? How many and to what degree did Cargill's *subsidiaries* own wheat futures at the time of the Russian sale? Were any of the purchasing costs of Burris Mills and its significant wheat storage facilities in Texas, bought by Cargill in August, included in its "operating expenses — elevator, office and overhead"?

While Cargill sought to prove a loss on the Russian sale, Continental Grain, although declining to reveal its financial gain, framed a reply that was at least much more candid. "What," John Fialka of *The Washington Star-News* asked a Continental spokesman, "was the grain company's profit on the entire Russian transaction?"

"We couldn't comment on that," the spokesman replied, "it would be difficult to measure in any event because the business is not totally segregated from our other businesses."

Consumers Pay the Bill

In attempting to extol the benefits taxpayers and farmers derived from the Russian sale, Cargill admitted in what would become somewhat of a masterpiece of understatement that "the U.S. consumer may have to pay *slightly* more for food products made from wheat."[23] (emphasis added)

The baking industry in the course of the Russian sale had applied a number of times for an industry-wide exemption from price controls for bread in the face of higher wheat costs. Bakers estimated that costs would force at least a two-cent a loaf increase by spring, 1973. Yet in that same year, wheat farmers shared only four cents on each sale of a 28-cent loaf of bread in the supermarket. An industry spokesman estimated that at least 200 small bakers throughout the United States faced the loss of their businesses due to high flour costs.

In rejecting an industry-wide exemption, the Price Commission noted that any price increase would have to be considered on a company-by-company basis. Subsequently, in a four-week period the Commission gave varying increases to ten large bakers, including ITT-Continental (makers of Wonder Bread) and Pillsbury.

Meanwhile, the sudden depletion of U.S. grain stocks coupled with rising domestic prices for feed grains soon drove meat prices up sharply. The reaction (and actions) of consumers to these high prices sent immediate shock waves throughout the entire food economy which in turn would affect the nation's food prices for several years to come.

As consumers wondered aloud about increased meat and bread prices, world relief agencies also began to express increasing alarm as wheat became more expensive, bottlenecks in shipping developed and the possibility of dwindling grain reserves in 1975 became a very real threat.

Against this background, Kathleen Teltsch in the November 15 *New York Times* noted reports in Washington that the USDA intended to propose a cut of 50 percent (approximately $500 million) in the funds appropriated under Public Law 480. That cutback would also affect the U.S. program for donated food abroad and the liberal terms by which the government sold food to foreign countries.

And Still Yet Another Subsidy

As an enormous amount of grain began to move across the United States's vast transportation network, the Federal government found itself faced with having to provide yet another subsidy to fulfill an October 14 U.S.-Soviet maritime pact which specified that a third of all the wheat shipped to Russia would be in American ships.

The agreement called for U.S. flag operators to be paid over $10 per ton until late January 1973 when the rate schedule was to be reviewed and possibly renegotiated. In the meantime, the Russians paid a minimum of $8.05 a ton, the difference between $10 and $8 coming in the form of subsidies to U.S. shipping companies from the Federal government. Prevailing world-wide ocean charter rates had for years been geared to ships of nations with significantly lower operating costs than the U.S. Merchant Marine.

Until the U.S.-Russian agreement was reached on November 22 only some 56 million bushels of wheat, out of the over 400 million already sold, had already been exported to Russia.

Some Inescapable Conclusions

There are several inescapable conclusions about the Great American Grain Robbery in 1972.

• The United States could have asked for and received a much higher price from Russia because we alone had the wheat the Soviets so desperately needed. In the free enterprise system, the process is called supply and demand.

• USDA has traditionally shown a systematic and diligent favoritism, bordering on reverence, for the grain trade elite, in both the marketplace and the halls of government.

• The wheat sale to Russia was definitely an effort by the Nixon Administration to capture the farm vote in 1972 by attempting to create economic conditions favorable to large commercial-type farmers when the rest of the world was so dependent on the U.S. food supply. Like so many other gambles by the Nixon White House to ensure reelection, this one ultimately wound up cheating the American public.

• At the same time that Cargill and other grain traders were using their control over railroads and elevator facilities to exploit farmers those same farmers were left with no alternative means of moving their own grain, having to accept price discounts of ten to 25 and, in some cases, as much as 50 cents a bushel from these companies.

• While over $200 million of taxpayers' money was spent in a four-month period in subsidy payments, the public was deliberately denied information (under the guise of "trade secrets") by the men and corporations who were depending on that money for personal gain and profit.

John Rainbolt, then counsel for the House Livestock and Grains subcommittee, felt that the Russian sale would cost the public from $2 billion to $2.8 billion, largely in price increases. Subsequent events showed that his prediction was far too conservative.

• In the years prior to 1972, large U.S. stockpiles of grain had a stabilizing effect on the world food market. The Nixon Administration decision to eliminate those stockpiles in one big sale, rather than in an orderly, systematic fashion which would have allowed other nations to compensate and wait for prices to adjust slowly, cut the ground out from under what had been a relatively stable market.

• Wheat prices increased from $60 a ton in the second quarter of 1972 to $211 a ton in the first quarter of 1974, a 250 percent increase. World end-of-the-year wheat stocks had fallen from 50 to 26 million tons between 1971-1972 and 1973-1974, while U.S. stocks fell from 23.5 to a dangerous 5.9 million tons.[24]

• In the words of a 1973 Senate Subcommittee on Investigations report, "The large sales of grain to the Russians are an illustration of how, in pursuit of a worthwhile goal, government programs and officials can go astray. At virtually every step, from the initial planning of the sales to the subsidy that helped support them, the grain sales were ineptly managed. The result was public confusion, waste of the taxpayers' dollars and higher food prices."

• An agency mandated to protect American farmers — the USDA — woefully neglected that job. The Department was found not on the side of the "husbandman that laboreth" but rather aligned with a handful of giant multinational corporations, aiding and abetting the Great American Grain Robbery of 1972.

More Hidden Subsidies

Eight years later still more examples of "hidden subsidies" enjoyed by the grain trade's elite in dealing with the Soviet Union came to light during what was euphemistically termed the 1980 Russian grain embargo.

After the invasion of Afghanistan by the Russians President Carter ordered an embargo on grain destined for the Soviet Union. At the same time the USDA promptly announced the buying back of grain from U.S. trading companies in an effort to cushion the economic impact of the sudden cutoff.

Within months, however, the government resold the grain to the same companies at a loss of almost $500 million in federal funds. Almost immediately after these grain traders repurchased 99.8 percent of these commodities, prices in the marketplace increased sharply, significantly increasing the value of the grain involved.

Later, a USDA inspector general's report showed that the 13 grain exporting firms first boosted the amount of money they received from the government by claiming their profits on the suspended sales would have been relatively small. These firms were to be reimbursed for only the actual costs they had incurred on Soviet bound grain, but later studies showed they received a $2.6 million profit on contracts totalling $2.4 billion.

The Inspector General's study also reported that

there was an unusual amount of shifting from "unknown destination" to "USSR destination" in the two days preceding the announcement of the suspension. Approximately 30 percent (five million metric tons) of total undelivered contracts originally assumed by [the Federal government] were entered into the USDA Export Sales Reporting System as "destination USSR" in the two days preceding the grain suspension.[9]

It should also be recalled that two days prior to the announcement of the embargo one high U.S. official indicated that the President was contemplating trade sanctions against the Soviet Union. Later, it was also revealed that the USDA had information indicating some grain firms in Europe were selling grain to the Russians during the embargo, although it was not known whether the alleged sales involved U.S. firms or their European subsidiaries.[26]

A subsequent 1981 GAO report prepared for Senator Charles Grassley, R-Iowa, pointed out that no illegal shipments had been substantiated, "although 15 cases of alleged illegal shipments had been or were being investigated." The report went on to say that "certain factors" — the fungibility, or interchangeability, of grain; limited U.S. legal jurisdiction; and diplomatic and political considerations — hindered our ability to detect illegal shipments of U.S. grain to the Soviets. Without further explanation, it casually concluded: "It does not appear practical to overcome these limitations."[27]

The report also called into question the CCC's purchase of soybean and soybean product contracts that showed a loss of about $75.5 million. It was claimed that there were further losses to the U.S. Treasury by purchases of wheat varieties not involved in the grain embargo, and through the purchases of grain at prices substantially above market prices, including low-quality grain bought at high prices.

The GAO concluded that the embargo had little if any effect on the Russian food supply as the Soviet Union "substantially offset the loss of U.S. grain by increasing its imports of non-U.S. grain and meat."[28] It was appar-

ent from this report and the later investigations by the USDA that the only party ultimately affected by the 1980 grain embargo was the American farmer, as neither the Russians nor the grain trade realized any substantiated or identifiable economic losses.[29]

"This (GAO) report," Senator Grassley declared, "documents our previous charges that the American people were the real losers through the impulsive, mismanaged implementation of the Soviet grain embargo."[30]

Six years after the embargo, six years after Republican Ronald Reagan had used the embargo to politically bludgeon Democrat Jimmy Carter for precipitating the "farm crisis of the 1980s" the USDA's ERS issued a report, *Embargoes, Surplus Disposal, and U.S. Agriculture*, which concluded:

Embargoes *did not* cause the farm crisis of the 1980s, and an aggressive export subsidy program to reduce surplus commodity stock would *not* have prevented it. The cause more likely rests with radical changes in such worldwide economic conditions as recession, high interest rates, and the value of the dollar ... The longer term 1980 USSR embargo, implemented for foreign policy reasons, *barely* changed U.S. and world trade levels, but did alter trade flows as the USSR replaced lost U.S. exports from other sources. U.S. policies to protect farmers from the cost of the embargo *more than offset* any immediate damage... (emphasis added)

Chapter Thirty-One

Supply and Demand in Agriculture? It's the Pits!

No one enduring myth in American agriculture has taken deeper root than that which says that the law of supply and demand is the determining factor in establishing fair prices for agricultural commodities.

Today, still seeking to recover from a decade marked by bankruptcy, severe financial stress and unstable weather, many of those farmers who survived this latest chapter in America's permanent agricultural crisis have begun to seriously challenge that myth.

As the prices for farm products become increasingly determined by flawed government policy, speculation and greed rather than by supply and demand, farmer's major markets are rapidly being dominated by ever-larger corporate interests. Meanwhile, increasing numbers of major food corporations, seeking to escape the last measure of public accountability, have become private, tightly-controlled firms.*

Victimized by such oppressive market power, farmers are forced to watch virtually helpless as unfair, uncontrolled and wildly fluctuating below cost-of-production prices are bid for the products that so many of them produce each season.

Meanwhile, consumers see themselves progressively paying a higher and more exacting quantitative and qualitative price for corporate agribusiness's rush to bigness. Like so many other things in our daily lives, what we eat has become one more *manufactured* product; simply another "bottom line" item to be processed, packaged, advertised, and marketed, in addition to also being used as still one more weapon in the high stakes game of geopolitical diplomacy.

To many farmers the "engine" of this long train of economic injustices is the commodity trading pits of the nation's major futures exchanges.

It is in these pits where contracts on such raw materials as wheat, corn, soybeans, oats, live cattle, feeder cattle, pork bellies, plywood, and gold, among others, along with treasury bills, stocks, and a variety of demands merge, thus avoiding violent price gyrations or damaging sell-outs, as for example, of the nation's grain supplies which, they argue, would result in famine and "economic anarchy."

In reality, however, what is taking place in the never-ending frenzy of activity that is the hallmark of the "trading pits" of Chicago and elsewhere is that high stakes gamblers are in fact placing bets on what the price of these raw materials and financial instruments will be at some point in tommorrowland and then employing whatever information and "ingenuity" that is available to them in an attempt to cover that bet.*

Chicago writer Bob Tamarkin in his behind-the-scenes look at *The New Gatsbys: Fortunes and Misfortunes of Commodity Traders* explains this unique phenomena from personal experience:

> When you speculated in commodities, you were always on the brink, like climbing a mountain for the sheer adventure and forgetting the danger though it was ever-present.
>
> Uncertainty was precisely why commodity futures markets existed in the first place, feeding on an insatiable diet of interlocking economic and political woes the world over.[1]

Thus, thriving on such instability, the men and women who occupy the nation's various and sundry commodity exchange pits and who regularly trade contracts on agricultural commodities justify their role and that of the futures market with the notion that through the legendary "invisible hand of the market" a fair price is being established for a given commodity.

Yet, even as these same markets continue to grow in size, volume and time, some of the more candid traders who operate in them admit that the ever-popular "invisible hand" is in fact not so invisible.

---

* Seven of the top ten private U.S. corporations in 1989 were agricultural commodity, food, or food related corporations. They included Cargill (1), Continental Grain (3), RJR Nabisco (4), Southland (6), Mars (7), American Financial (8) and Supermarkets General (10). Together these *seven* accounted for nearly 17 percent of all revenues realized by the top *400* private corporations in the United States.

* Encouraged by government policies in recent years, commodity traders have been afforded an ever broader range within which to speculate, such policies have kept loan rates and target prices for crops often lower than the cost of production, while a so-called supply management program has set no real limits on marketing or established an ability to maintain an adequate reserve to compensate for weather scares and crop shortfalls, all resulting in prices being driven down lower than the loan rate while at the same time effectively removing caps on price speculation.

Wayne Cryts, a Missouri soybean producer, who in 1984 led 150 of his angry fellow Midwestern protesting farmers into the Chicago Board of Trade agrees. "Low prices are the farmer's problem and those prices are set right here."[2]

With the disclosure on January 19, 1989 by *Chicago Tribune* reporters Christopher Drew and William B. Crawford Jr. that the Federal Bureau of Investigation in a far-reaching two and one-half year probe headed by U.S. Attorney Anton Valukas had uncovered evidence of widespread fraud on the trading floors of the Chicago futures exchanges,[3] the public belatedly was afforded not only a rare glimpse of whose "invisible" hands actually shape the market, but how the futures market itself operates and who profits and who loses from its activities.

Taming the "Headwaters of Capitalism"

Initially, in any discussion concerning the trading of agricultural commodities in U.S. futures markets a primary focus needs to be directed to that elite few who control the trading of the world's grain (wheat, corn, oats, soybeans and their various derivatives).

Any thorough investigation of the world's grain trade, dominated as it is by Cargill and Continental, and the foreign-owned Louis Dreyfus and Bunge Corporations, will quickly show as discussed earlier that the key to profitability in the grain trade is not the price of grain itself but rather a host of other variables.

Often veiled in secrecy and complexity, such factors as the existing variation in price levels for a commodity at any given time, interest rates, the state of money markets, transportation rates, world-wide weather patterns, and the spread between cash and futures prices all play a paramount role in the way grain is traded and priced throughout the world on a day-to-day basis.

Is it any wonder, therefore, that this global trade in food commodities, which has become over a $60 billion a year business, so aptly conforms to Karl Marx's observation that the circulation of commodities is the headwater of capitalism.[4]

Today, as the world of grain trading becomes riskier and more complicated, such monetary movements have become more tied in with the corporate business of agriculture.

"Virtually all grain transactions," Richard Gilmore, author of the penetrating *A Poor Harvest: The Clash of Policies and Interests in the Grain Trade*, reminds us,

whether they involve purchases of grain originating in the United States or elsewhere, are conducted in dollars. Although a little worn, the dollar remains the international passport currency for grain. With fairly wide daily fluctuations in the value of the dollar, a trader now has to engage in arbitrage — nonspeculative buying and selling of alternate currencies — synchronized with any spot and long futures position he may hold.[5]

"Legalized Gambling Casinos?"

The U.S. "marketplace" in which the business of the buying and trading of grain and a variety of other agricultural and non-agricultural commodity contracts takes place is in different exchanges approved by the Federal government's Commodity Futures Trading Commission (CFTC).

Those exchanges include the American Commodity Exchange (ACE); AMEX Commodity Corporation (ACC); Chicago Board of Trade (CBOT); the Chicago Mercantile Exchange (CME); Chicago Rice and Cotton Exchange (CRCE); Coffee, Sugar and Cocoa Exchange (CSCE); Commodity Exchange, Inc. (COMEX); Kansas City Board of Trade (KCBT); MidAmerica Commodity Exchange (MCE); Minneapolis Grain Exchange (MGE); New York Cotton Exchange and Associates (NYCE); New York Futures Exchange (NYFE); New York Mercantile Exchange (NYMEX); Philadelphia Board of Trade (PBOT); Pacific Commodity Exchange (PCE), and the Pacific Futures Exchange (PFE).[6]

Since 1971, just prior to the introduction of financial instrument futures, 14.6 million future contracts were traded on the major U.S. exchanges, 91 percent of them being agricultural contracts with the remainder largely ones dealing in silver. After rebounding from a low of 19 percent in 1987, mainly due to speculative interest resulting from the nation's drought, agricultural commodity future contracts in 1988 accounted for but 25 percent of the total volume of the 225 million contracts traded.[7]

The most important market activity in agricultural commodities is centered in four principal exchanges: the Chicago Board of Trade, the Chicago Mercantile Exchange, the Minneapolis Grain Exchange and the Kansas City Board of Trade.

A brief profile of each and their primary functions can begin to help us understand their importance and how the grain trade utilizes their services in its pursuit of greater profits.

Kansas City Board of Trade   Principally a cash market, prices quoted on this exchange are intended to represent valid purchase orders at the farm gate, Kansas City is also the center for trading of hard red winter wheat and in 1988 represented 24.6 percent of a four-market total in wheat futures traded.[8]

Minneapolis Grain Exchange   Minneapolis, like Kansas City, is also a cash market, but specializes in durum and dark northern spring wheats and in 1988 claimed 7.8 percent of the wheat futures traded.

Both exchanges, which to a large extent synchronize their purchases and sales to price performances based on trading in Chicago, have also developed additional price categories as changes in trading practices have continued to evolve.

Chicago Board of Trade   If the United States is "the hub of world hedging and speculation in agricultural commodities" then the CBOT is the epicenter of that hub. Founded in 1848 and largely controlled traditionally by floor traders acting in the interests of the grain trade, it now trades 28 futures and future option contracts with a 1988 volume of 118 million contracts traded, averaging 2.4 million contracts traded each day.[9]

With the statue of Ceres, the Greek goddess of agriculture, overlooking its Art Deco building in the heart of Chicago's financial district, the CBOT is the largest of the four exchanges, dealing principally in wheat, corn, and soybeans among a variety of other farm and non-farm commodities.

In 1988, 62 percent of the wheat futures from the four major markets were traded on the CBOT. More importantly, however, the CBOT, once described as "the biggest legalized gambling casino in the world" is where most domestic and worldwide agricultural commodity future prices are in fact established.

During the summer of 1986 when North American Farm Alliance president and Nebraska cattle rancher Merle Hansen was traveling through several southern African nations with the Rev. Jesse Jackson, he made a point of visiting not only with farmers but Ministers of Agriculture of the host countries.

> Sitting across the table from the Minister of Agriculture in Dar es Salaam, Tanzania facing the Indian Ocean almost half way around the world I asked the Minister how he went about determining how prices were set for their farmers. His answer was simple and direct. He said the Chicago Board of Trade.[10]

Chicago Mercantile Exchange   In addition to these major boards of trade and because developments in the past two decades in the international currency markets have come to play such a key role in the trading of agricultural commodities,[11] the CME or the Merc, now ranks as a near co-equal with the nation's major commercial banks as a principal center for currency trading, and is regarded by many in corporate agribusiness as a major force in the grain trade.

An outgrowth of the Chicago Butter and Egg Board formed in 1898, the CME initially evolved from the Chicago Produce Exchange established in 1874 to provide markets for eggs, butter and poultry. Called in its earlier days the "whorehouse of the Chicago Loop's westside" by the more established eastside CBOT members, the Butter and Egg Board became a futures market in 1919 and changed its name to the CME.

It was after Richard Nixon devalued the dollar in 1972, however, severing nearly all links between the dollar and the price of gold, and thereby leaving a freely floating system of international exchange rates, that the CME's stature began to grow.

By 1988 the Merc was trading some 30 futures and future options, including agricultural commodities like cattle, pork bellies and hogs. However, 80 percent of its 78 million contracts traded were financial instruments with an average daily volume of 400,000 contracts traded.[12]

Together the CBOT and the CME now account for over 40 percent of the world's futures and options trading, employing approximately 30,000 people in Chicago.

Guppies Among the Sharks

For many the futures market is extremely complex and difficult to understand. Asa Baber, however, perhaps best captured the essence of this pillar of the "free market system" in the title of his perceptive, witty and in-depth essay on futures trading in the July, 1977 issue of *Playboy*: "The Commodities Market: You've Really Got To Be An Animal: Want to know how to make a small fortune in commodities? Start with a large one."

He writes:

> It is something like [Catch 22's] Milo Mindbender's selling Egyptian cotton, buying Italian grapes, coating them all with chocolate to trade for African gold with the understanding that everyone will get a cut — depending on the price of goats on Crete and the shipping tonnage in the Suez Canal. The logic is there if you want it to be. Surely, this is the bottom line for all economic systems: We subscribe to them and they are reflections of us. They are the mirror, not the cause, of our complexities.[13]

The exchange of future contracts has become a commercial device whereby buyers and sellers seek to shift the risk of future price changes to speculators who assume that risk in the hope of realizing a profit. Through this process both producers and buyers seek to protect themselves from unanticipated commodity price changes.

Or, as grain trader George Andre once remarked, "the secret of success in the grain business is to sell cheaper than you buy and still make money."[14]

Futures markets are overseen by the commodity exchanges, and were originally established to offer a competitive system for pricing grain and a guidance mechanism for their marketing and distribution that would ideally reflect the law of "supply and demand." That goal, however, is repeatedly impeded by market manipulations, by limiting farmer involvement in the hedging system, a system purportedly designed for their benefit, and because those very exchanges where futures are bought and sold have always been venerated as the highest manifestation of the "free market" system and therefore immune to public accountability or interference.

Hiding Their Bushels Under Stacks of Paper

In examining the nature of the farm commodity futures industry it is clear that actual farmer participation, despite claims to the contrary, is limited to a select few since most farmers have come to have little faith in the system.

Wayne Cyrts believes that the Board of Trade fails to acknowledge farmer concern over the unfair trading practices of the speculative seller, as opposed to those who have a legitimate position of ownership of the commodity.

"We have no problem with speculators in the market as long as they have taken a position of production costs similar to that of the farmer, which means they must buy, or be able to produce commodities before they can sell them — period!"[15]

The fallacy of corporate agribusiness's so-called "supply and demand" argument can be seen in figures obtained from the Futures Industry Association and the U.S. Department of Agriculture's 1988 Crop Production Summary. They show that for each bushel of wheat produced by the farmer in 1988, 14 bushels were being traded on commodity exchanges, for corn the ratio was one to 11 bushels, for oats one bushel to eight, the cattle ratio was one pound to eight traded, and for soybeans a staggering one bushel produced for every 41 traded.

A critic of this so-called agricultural "paper blizzard harvest," still called by some the "free market" system, American Agriculture Movement Director David Senter, himself a Texas farmer, believes that immediate steps are needed to curb the manipulation and speculation which affect day-to-day prices. He says,

CBOT speculators are depressing the price of commodities by selling unlimited numbers of futures contracts, regardless of what we can produce or what's in storage. These paper contracts with nothing to back them up should be barred.[16]

Further reflecting on this deification of "the law of supply and demand," one veteran trader told author Tamarkin "it's just a bunch of numbers. And we all know that people use statistics the way dogs use lampposts — for convenience rather than illumination."[17]

The "Long" and "Short" of It

The *futures contract* itself is simply a legally binding standardized agreement to deliver or take delivery of a given quality and quantity (in grain usually 5,000 bushels per contract) of a commodity at an agreed price at a specific date and place.

A *futures option* is a unilateral contract which gives a buyer the *right* to buy or sell a specified quantity of a commodity at a specified price within a specified period of time regardless of the market price of that commodity.

Two of the most commonly used words in the trading of futures are the adjectives "long" and" short." As Elizabeth Withnell, an analyst for the Congressional Research Service explains, a trader who is *long* in the market is one who has purchased a contract obligating that individual to take delivery on a specified date. A trader who is *short* is one who has sold a futures contract obligating delivery on a specified future date.[18]

The purpose of buying and selling futures contracts is not to actually obtain or rid oneself of the commodity itself, but rather for the purpose of "hedging" or "speculating" on future price changes in that particular commodity. It is estimated that of all the commodities traded in the various exchanges less than five percent are ever actually delivered.[19]

"Hedging" is simply a device most often used by commodity dealers, processors, warehouse operators and some farmers who will buy futures contracts themselves to protect against potential losses from future fluctuations in the value of a commodity which must be held in inventory or which must be purchased or sold at a later date.

"Hedging," therefore, supposedly enables individuals to reduce the price risk of transactions in the cash market with transactions involving the same commodity in the futures market while at the same time allowing producers to obtain better prices for their products and processors to eliminate part of the risk in the holding of such commodities.

Despite the fact that there has been some growth in recent years in production volume and the number of contracts traded, farmers, due in large part to problems of liquidity and what for them has been high margin calls, have been "hedging" only a very small percentage of their crops. In 1982, for example, they hedged only one percent of their own production as compared with six percent in 1976.

"Speculating" on the futures market is conducted by scalpers, pit and floor traders and brokers usually representing large brokerage houses, financial institutions and the grain trade. Here individuals who are willing to assume those very same risks that a hedger seeks to avoid are looking for profits derived from various price movements.

But, as author and sometime trader Bob Tamarkin confesses, "as far as I was concerned, there were only two types of commodity speculator: the risk takers and the big risk takers." Yet, as it has been traditionally claimed, these speculators are essential to the market as they frequently provide needed liquidity.

Both the CFTC and the exchanges themselves attempt, sometimes unsuccessfully, to limit the number of contracts which may be held by a speculator in a particular commodity in an effort to avoid any one individual or institution from "cornering" the market. In it's 15-year history, however, the CFTC has acted in a disciplinary manner in only five such price-manipulation cases.[20]

"I Know Who Lost ... It's Important to Know Who Won"

A most recent and celebrated example of such so-called "cornering" of the market came to public attention on July 11, 1989. On that date the CBOT ordered Italy's giant multinational Ferruzzi Finanziaria S.p.A, through its U.S. subsidiary Central Soya Corp., one the nation's three largest soybean buyers, to sell off within a week's time most of its huge future holdings in soybeans that called for the delivery of 23 million bushels by the end of the July contract month. At the time Ferruzzi reportedly held two thirds of the contracts to buy beans and already owned most of the 13 million bushels of a drought-depleted crop of beans to be had in Chicago warehouses.[21]

Thus, Ferruzzi's position, according to the CBOT, was of being capable of pushing up the price of the beans while at the same time squeezing out as much money as possible from those traders who already promised to deliver beans they in fact did not possess. The company, however, countered that the CBOT acted not out of self-regulation, but self-interest, a claim that many other traders supported. Ferruzzi said it was simply seeking to get its hands on as many soybeans as possible in an effort to fulfill its voluminous export orders, principally to the Soviet Union.[22]

Ferruzzi also charged that the liquidation decision stemmed from the CBOT seeking to drive the price of soybeans down in an effort to bail out those traders who held contracts and had bet wrong about the prices called for in those contracts.

Nevertheless, despite the company's protestations and a failed attempted court order to block the CBOT action, Ferruzzi lost millions, later reporting that it expected to lose nearly $100 million in 1989 on its commodity trading business.[23]

But the Italian firm was not the only loser in the deal. Angry soybean farmers saw the liquidation order drive down the price of the crop by over 90 cents in one month's time, the steepest one month dive in five years.[24]

"I know who lost — every farmer in Iowa," charged Representative David Nagle, D-Iowa. "It's important to know who won."[25] An analysis by the Minnesota Department of Agriculture issued three days after the liquidation order indicated that soybean farmers nationwide could already have lost close to $500 million.[26]

The American Soybean Association also expressed anger over rumors that news of the liquidation order was leaked a few hours before the close of trading on July 11, thus giving a selling advantage to some traders.[27]

The second largest private conglomerate in Italy, Ferruzzi Finanziaria S.p.A. first appeared on the American corporate agribusiness scene in 1987 when it purchased Central Soya. On a world-wide basis, it processes over five million tons of soybeans each year, approximately seven percent of the world market.[28]

Founded in 1948 as an "agricultural trading company" it became in 40 years "an industrial system" which in 1988 employed over 100,000 people and had over 500 production plants. With combined revenues of $26 billion and operating in 100 countries throughout the world, the Ferruzzi Group controls not only the Montedison Chemical Company, one of the world's top ten chemical firms with sales over $10 billion, but also has holdings in pharmaceuticals, energy, finance, newspapers, construction, and agribusiness interests.[29]

Under the guidance of one of Italy's most daring and powerful industrialists Raul Gardini, who took over the Group from his father-in-law Serafino Ferruzzi in 1979, the Ferruzzi Financial Group is the European Community's single largest producer of sugar, rice, vegetable oils and starch and has become a big investor in recent years in research concerning nonpolluting "green chemicals" as a means of environmental protection.[30]

The very size of Ferruzzi, however, and the increasingly prominent role it has assumed in recent years in the world soybean market perhaps best explains the underlying reason for the CBOT's actions. According to a scenario developed by Allendale, Inc., a commodity brokerage firm based in Crystal City, Illinois, the CBOT's emergency order was the "tumultuous climax" to a long-simmering feud among Ferruzzi and Cargill and Archer-Daniels-Midland Co., (identified in the Allendale study only as "F," "A" and "C"), the United States's three major soybean traders.[31]

Based on research Allendale had been assembling for months, Ferruzzi, beginning in the fall of 1987 had been buying both soybeans and soybean futures contracts. Initially, this buying spree created allegedly big problems for ADM, who while needing a ready supply of the beans for its many customers, was encountering increasingly more expensive prices resulting from Ferruzzi's aggressive buying practices.

Cargill, however, was at first benefitting from Ferruzzi's buying activities as the Minneapolis firm had ample soybean stocks from which to sell and was thereby realizing handsome profits as Ferruzzi increased its buying of beans. However, when Cargill depleted its stock it too joined ADM in seeking out additional supplies to satisfy customer demand.[32]

Allendale suggests that because they were both being faced with shortages in soybeans it was both Cargill and ADM who complained to the CBOT and prevailed on the Board to issue its July 11 order. As we shall soon see this was not the first time ADM sought disciplinary action on its own behalf vis-a-vis the CBOT and the grain trade. Allendale concludes that Ferruzzi's intent was not to squeeze Cargill or ADM, but simply to amass adequate supplies of beans for its own use and protect its existing supply against future price declines.[33]

"It was an extremely well-researched play by Ferruzzi to gain market share," points out William Biedermann, Allendale's director of research.[34]

The final move by Cargill and ADM "to turn the entire game around," according to Biedermann, came when the two grain traders decided to cease all activity in the July futures contract. The move left Ferruzzi as one of the only major players in the contract and virtually assured that the Italian trader would suffer if and when the CBOT forced it to close out its July position, as the Board ultimately did order.[35]

Cargill would deny that it had requested the CBOT to limit trading in the July contract, however, the company did confirm that for more than a year it "had expressed concern" to the Board about soybean future contract prices.[36] ADM had no comment on a *Chicago Sun-Times* story that the CBOT action stemmed from a complaint by the Decatur, Illinois agribusiness giant.[37]

Traders, meanwhile, generally were reluctant to discuss the role Cargill and ADM played in the CBOT's action. "This is a turf battle," one soybean broker told *The Wall Street Journal*, "they could crush me like an ant."[38]

"Pit Sex"

The actual trading of futures contracts takes place in the commodity pits and rings on the floor of the various exchanges where particular commodity contracts are bought and sold through "open outcry" — voice bids and/or hand signals — by brokers who are either employees of established firms, "locals" or independent brokers.

The *broker employees* usually number the fewest in the pits due mainly to what the *New York Times*' Floyd Norris describes as "some firms saying privately that they fear the way their brokers might be treated by other traders if they were sent into the pits. That feeling is said to be especially strong in some agricultural commodity pits."[39]

The "locals" or *speculators* usually trade for their own accounts and move in and out of the commodity they trade at a rapid rate. It is these "locals" who are generally acknowledged as the ones who provide the market with liquidity. Among the "locals" those who trade large numbers of contracts are know as *position traders* betting on long-term trends, not on the markets minute-by-minute fluctuations.

The majority of the "locals," however, are known as *scalpers* and their task, through the making of hundreds of small trades a day, is to capitalize on the rapid fluctuations of the market. Among the "locals" there are also *spreaders*, who seek to take advantage of the shifting relationships between different commodities or between different delivery months of the same commodity.

Neither the *scalpers* or *spreaders* really care if the market price is up or down for their profits lie in the market's movement. As one "scalper" told Chicago *Reader*'s John Eisendrath, "we need instability and we need inflation."[40]

The independent brokers, although working often for themselves, also execute orders on a commission per contract basis for individual and corporate customers off the floor. It is these independent brokers or order fillers who have been described as the "mechanics of the pits." It is their job to get the best possible prices for their customers and depending on the size of their "deck" of buy and sell order cards. At the same time they can also often control the very flow of the trading action in the pit.

Standing shoulder to shoulder, often for hours at a time in crowded pits, these brokers and traders shout and gesture wildly all in an effort to bid for or buy contracts from other nearby traders. Frequently these pits are so jammed full of traders that it is impossible for one standing on one side of the pit to see or hear those on the other side, often resulting in different prices existing at the same time for the same contract.

"They call it 'pit sex'," according to one Chicago attorney. "They spend more time in physical contact with each other than they do with their wives." [41]

Each of traders in the pit must accept the first offer that meets his or her price with the buy or sell price noted on a small trading card along with the amount traded, the initials of the other trader, shown in big letters on the badges all traders must wear, *and* the time the trade was executed within *30* minutes accuracy.

Later, the exchanges attempt to track all trading times to the nearest minute and computers are used to collect all the trades in a given pit and document the day's transactions minute-by-minute.

As the World Turns

It is in these trading pits where numerous gut-wrenching, heart-pounding dramas of financial success and failure take place each trading minute and day of the year. Tamarkin explains the makings of such stories.

Wheat, corn, soybeans moved in quarter-cent ticks, and each tick was $12.50 per contract. It didn't sound like much, but those fractional cents could add up to mega-bucks if you traded hugh volume, similar to the way grocery chains operate on small markups. If, for example, in a year a trader averaged a quarter-cent profit on 20,000 contracts of wheat (100 million bushels), his annual income would be a quarter of a million dollars.[42]

Harry ("the Hat") Lowrance at the CME was, as Tamarkin describes him, "a glowing example of the kind of money an ambitious order filler could make." He worked the live cattle pit, "earning a mere $2 on average per order he executed. Mere? On an average day he did 1400 orders, grossing $2800 a day. That's an average of $56,000 a month, or $670,000 for an average year." By the time Lowrance was 32 in 1981 he was a multimillionaire.

Many observers have described the nation's commodity trading pits as an anachronism where highly sophisticated information gives way to pure physical and emotional energy, where an unwritten maxim "buy on rumor, sell on fact" is widely accepted.[43] "Trading is 98 percent emotional and two percent intellectual," ruminates Ronald Manaster, a partner in Goodman-Manaster Inc., a Chicago commodities clearinghouse.[44]

But, it is simply not a case of routinely buying and selling contracts, Tamarkin explains, that determines financial success or failure for many traders and order fillers.

In those few moments when the order is received and filled in the pit, all hell can break loose, and the world can turn upside down. Many an order becomes a loss before it hits the pit because the market moves so quickly. It works, of course, the other way, too. Regardless, it's the traders in the pit who have the edge over the public ... and in the crush of a wild closing, when the trading madness reaches a crescendo, many brokers don't have time to write down their transactions. After the trading bell they scramble about, trying to figure out what they have traded and with whom.[45]

Stories like the egg pit trader who accidentally bought ten times the volume intended because of a mistaken hand signal and ended up $200,000 richer and a stake in starting a business that today includes cattle feedlots, oil wells, and a printing company have become the stuff of legends in the Chicago trading pits.[46]

Not A Game For Widows and Orphans

Watching these commodity exchanges in action has been described by the *Washington Post*'s Dan Morgan as "a little like watching men wrestling under a blanket."[47] It is not as the former President of the CBOT once explained, "a game for widows and orphans."[48]

"If you have trouble sleeping, look elsewhere," warns Nancy Dunnan, author of *Dun & Bradstreet's Guide to*

Your Investments 1988. Don't consider commodities, she adds, unless you have six to 12 months living expenses in savings and an extra $10,000 to risk on commodities.[49]

John Train, president of Train, Smith Investment Counsel of New York, has further noted that the commodities market today is a "young man's game" as the psychological and physical battering commodity and option traders take is terrific. "Many live very simply, too absorbed with making money to have time to spend it. They are compulsive plungers, and to relax, often take part of their Wall Street winnings to Las Vegas, where they drop them again."[50]

There is also the possibly of making more money in one month than their fathers made in a year that lures many young people today into commodity trading. New traders "are in for a definite ethical toxic shock," Richard J. Thain, a University of Chicago business-school dean told *The Wall Street Journal.* "The machismo of the exchanges is very strong. Their creed is like pro football — if you get away with it, it's OK."

In his book *The Traders* reporter Sonny Kleinfield shows how most pit traders really have no interest in the physical things they are trading, studying only price movements, and if they are successful, learning mostly through flair to anticipate movements, not through any particular knowledge, but rather from past behavior. He quotes two traders.

One observes:

A broker has public orders and the public are ass holes. So who would you trade with — an ass hole or a trader? The public is always losing money. The public shouldn't be in this business." Another says: "They [the public] don't know what the hell they're doing. It's like meat going through a grinder.[51]

Tamarkin adds,

Against the insiders — those who make their living buying and selling futures contracts on the floors of the nation's commodity exchanges — the public is a school of guppies among sharks. One grim statistic says it all: Nine out of every ten trades made by the public result in a loss.[52]

A Commodity Exchange Authority (CEA) study only confirms that grim statistic for in the early 1970's it found after examining the trading activities of 8782 speculators over a nine-year period only 25 percent of them (2184) had registered a net profit. The major reason for such a large number of losers was that they apparently ignored what many consider the first law of commodity trading — cut losses short, and let profits run.[53]

Operation Hedge Clipper and Operation Sour Mash

It is into this financial maelstrom and the abuses it generates that U.S. attorney Anton Valukas and the FBI began to delve in mid-1986. The undercover operation, designated by the FBI as a "Group 1" investigation,

meaning that it was one of national importance, of very high cost and extended duration,[54] was code named Operation Hedge Clipper and Operation Sour Mash.

Using several undercover FBI agents who posed as floor traders the Federal government gathered hundreds of hours of conversations between their undercover agents and various commodity traders. After the public disclosure of their preliminary investigation the government began issuing subpoenas for the records of scores of traders, brokers and executives suspected of fraudulent trading practices. They also sought to examine documents used in the past by the various exchange's own disciplinary committees.

Early indications were that the government would pursue possible racketeering charges against certain exchange traders.[55] Since it is a fact that there exists among traders in certain commodity pits what the *Wall Street Journal* has termed a certain "wild fraternity," [56] it was thought possible that the government's attorneys would ultimately be able to demonstrate a pattern of collusion to defraud customers.

"Their strategy is to start at the bottom and squeeze each level as hard as they can," observed one lawyer who spoke with the government's prosecutors immediately after the announcement of the investigation. The idea was to convince traders that if they didn't go along early, the consequences would be worse later.[57]

"There are systemwide violations that appear to be occurring on a regular basis," added attorney David Bortman, who is representing at least one defendant. Unwilling to elaborate, however, he added, "it seems that to get along in the system it was necessary to go along with these violations."[58]

And from Wall Street one major firm's executive pointed out, "I think this [the Chicago probe] will be a lot bigger than the insider-trader scandal. The Ivan Boeskys and Drexel Burnhams already had $100 million in their pockets. But in this one, this time they're stealing from the little guy."[59]

Specifically, the types of fraud the government had begun investigating included:

"Bucketing," a type of transaction that was declared illegal by Congress in the 1930's, which essentially thwarts the customer's intention of "buying low and selling high" by paying more than one has to for a contract or making less money on one than they should.

The crudest form of this activity is when the trader simply throws away or "buckets" a customer's order, pocketing the customer's money and walking away from the transaction. A modern version of the practice, however, would be where the broker mails the customer a confirmation notice that, for example, a soybean contract was sold at a market price of $9 when actually the sale was made for $10. The broker pockets $1 and sends the customer $9.

Another form of "bucket trading" is when a broker receives an order from an outside customer to buy a contract at the prevailing market price when the market opens. A price range is recorded by the exchange in the first frantic moments that follows the opening bell. By law, the broker should try to buy the contract for his customer as close to the low figure on the price range as possible, but instead the trader might turn to another broker, and by previous agreement, buy the contract for his customer at two or three cents more, guaranteeing a profit for the other broker.

Yet, the exchange records would later show that the trade was executed within the prevailing price range and there likely would be no questions asked. Likewise, the customer off the floor would have no way of knowing that he had paid more than necessary for the bought contract.

"Bag trading" is a technique whereby a broker conspires with a second broker, known as the "bag man," to sell a customer's contract at the low end of an official price range and to buy it back for a different customer at the high end of the range. The two brokers then split the profits.

"Wash trading" is when brokers enter into trades, either actual or fake, that don't result in any change in a trader's market position, but are engineered solely to manipulate market prices or to arrange transactions that will ultimately reap profits for the broker.

"Front running" is a term used to describe the taking of an *options* position based on *non-public information* regarding an impending large transaction in the underlying commodity that would result in obtaining a profit when the options market adjusts to the price at which the transaction occurs.

"Prearranged trading" is simply trading between brokers in accordance with an expressed or implied agreement or understanding and is a violation of the Commodity Exchange Act. All prices are required to be negotiated in the trading pits of the various exchanges.

"Dual trading" while legal is perhaps the most controversial technique in futures trading and one that critics say must be outlawed since it provides ample opportunity for fraud.

"Dual trading is the same thing as insider trading in the stock market, it simply should not be permitted," declares Representative Neal Smith, D-Iowa, the principal author of legislation that created the CFTC.[60] In 1984 Smith also introduced legislation in the House of Representatives to outlaw "dual trading" and while the House passed the measure it was killed in conference committee after heavy lobbying by the futures industry.

"Dual trading" allows a broker who might receive an order to buy a large number of a certain commodity's contracts (an order that would surely tend to increase the price of that contract) to also buy a few contracts for him or herself at the same time the customer's order is being filled. Then after the price for the contracts increase the broker would immediately sell the contracts at the higher price and make a quick profit even though the broker's customer might not have such an opportunity.

Defenders of "dual trading" argue that the practice makes the market work more efficiently by bringing in more buyers and sellers. "The argument," according to Mark Powers, editor of *The Journal of Futures Markets* and former economist for the CFTC, "was that no one would want to be a broker" handling customers orders on commissions "when they could make more trading for their own account."[61]

A related technique, known as "trading ahead of the customer" and one that is illegal, is when a broker might be watching the price of a commodity vary by one or two cents and while waiting for the opportunity to buy low, a buy order comes in from a customer. By exchange rules the broker must handle the customer's order first, but since the commission for filling a customer's order is less than the broker could make on a personal trade there is always the temptation to not give the customer priority preference.

It is these techniques that were the subject of the government's investigation in addition to possible massive tax cheating by some brokers and traders and illegal drug use.[62]

What made the government's task that much more difficult, however, in its attempt to show fraud in the trading pits was the lack of a seamless paper trail. Although the exchanges time-stamp orders, track prices and compare trades to prevailing prices in the pits all such records, as has already been explained, ultimately depend on the integrity of the member brokers and traders in keeping accurate accounts. Even when the customer might challenge the price, the various frauds cited above are difficult to prove when order volume is unusually high and prices are rising and falling rapidly.

On August 2, 1989 46 traders at the CBOT and the Merc were indicted on charges of illegal trading. (See Appendix K.)

Blowing the Whistle

Before discussing the regulating or lack of self-regulation found in today's future exchanges, it is instructive to examine for a moment who first triggered the government's massive investigation into the practices of the nation's commodity traders and brokers.

For many years farmers and small investors have been periodically complaining about the way the futures markets operated and the unfair status they had in those markets due to their lack of size and access to important trading information. the breaking point came, however, when Dwayne O. Andreas, chairman and chief executive of Archer-Daniels-Midland Corp. became angry over impending disciplinary action by the CBOT on allegations that his firm had engaged in manipulating soybean prices. He openly defied its disciplinary committee and refused to appear before them. Subsequently, he was fined $25,000 for his non-appearance. "That was not an easy thing to do," a former exchange director observed to *The Wall Street Journal*'s Sue Shellenbarger. "ADM is a highly respected member of the Board of Trade and Dwayne Andreas is a big shot."[63]

Indeed, Andreas decided not to get mad, but get even and since he had already expressed displeasure with the way price ranges were established at the open and close of trading and the way final settlement prices were reached, he took his complaints to the federal government and when Dwayne Andreas talks Washington listens!

ADM, the nation's major agricultural processing corporations with 1990 sales of $7.7 billion, has mastered well the technique of what its CEO once termed "living with the vicissitudes of the market."[64]

While becoming the nation's largest soybean processor in the 1970's, for example, when the nation was gripped by an "energy crisis" it was ADM which seized upon the already farmer-proven idea of distilling large amounts of surplus grain into a new domestic fuel called gasohol — gasoline mixed with one-tenth ethanol made from corn. With the generous financial help of the Federal government ADM soon became the nation's leading producer. Subsequently, for almost seven years Congress extended its largesse to the gasohol industry to the tune of more than $1 billion in subsidies and tax breaks enabling ADM to become the Exxon of ethanol, producing some 60 percent of the U.S. total with over $425 million in sales.[65]

"This is probably the most expert tapping of the Federal treasury than anyone can imagine," charged Jack Blum, Washington counsel to the Independent Gasoline Marketers Council. In 1985 Blum successfully managed to get the Federal Trade Commission (FTC) to investigate charges that ADM was engaged in predatory pricing and other unfair trade practices.

> It's crazy. Here you have one company that figures out how to mine the government in order to go into business and then spends a ton of money to keep everybody else out ... Their market control is so complete they're absolutely able to take whatever they want out of the marketplace.[66]

ADM's critics have also charged that the firm has used its market power to ensure that it captures most of the profits to be made from gasohol's growing use by mainly charging different prices in each state, depending on the level of that particular state's subsidies. Andreas' firm has also sought to limit low-cost foreign imports by selectively dropping its prices in the affected areas.

In what critics charged as a "giveaway," the USDA announced in June, 1986 that it was extending still another "subsidy" to ADM in the form of $35 million worth of free corn for gasohol production. Blum characterized the subsidy as

> corporate food stamps for ADM. It's truly amazing. If these guys [ADM] can operate profitably without this, why is the government giving them money? ... Dwayne Andreas has got to be the least likely candidate for food stamps in American history.[67]

Defending ADM and Andreas's actions, Prudential-Bache Securities analyst John McMillian points out, "he is just playing the game. With 92 percent of U.S. farmers participating in government programs, any agricultural company that didn't play the game would be doing a disservice to shareholders."[68]

Other firms receiving such subsidies included A.E. Staley, the Pekin Energy Corporation of Illinois (a joint venture between Texaco and CPC Corp., the New Energy Corporation in Indiana (half-owned by E.F. Hutton), and South Point Ethanol (which is half-owned by Ashland Oil).[69]

Former USDA Secretary Richard Lyng later claimed that he was not aware that ADM had received most of the benefits under the government's ethanol subsidy program. "I knew they were a very large corn refiner, but I didn't know they were the largest ethanol producer. Dwayne Andreas is a good friend of mine, and we get together from time to time. I almost never talk business with Andreas."[70]

ADM in May, 1988 also announced that it had obtained world rights to a British technology for imbedding polyethlene film with corn starch to produce plastic bags that would eventually break down into a fine dust. Market analysts believe that ADM's early move into biodegradable plastics could give it the biggest share of a potential $1.5 billion-a-year market.[71]

Because over the years ADM's Andreas has maintained a close relationships with key political figures in Washington and on Capital Hill, including Hubert Humphrey, Jimmy Carter, former Carter campaign chairman and George Bush's ambassador to the Soviet Union Robert Strauss (who serves on the ADM board), Senate Minority Leader Robert Dole R-Kansas, and others, in addition to the fact that ADM's Political Action Committees (PAC's) have given nearly $300,000 to Democratic and Republican lawmakers since 1979, the company has had few problems enjoying the largesse of the Federal government.[72]

The ADM president, who until 1990 served as co-chairman of the U.S.-U.S.S.R. Trade and Economic Council, first came into the national political spotlight in 1972 when a $25,000 check he gave to one of President Nixon's fundraisers, Kenneth Dahlberg, ended up as a cashier's check in the bank account of Watergate burglar Bernard Barker. It was to become the first solid link between the Watergate break-in and the Nixon campaign committee. Later, when questioned about the fact that the check was his Andreas shrugged it off with the remark, "it was like being crapped on by a bird. It didn't bother me a bit."[73]

There are those that believe, however, that Andreas complaints to the Federal government concerning futures market practices and the willingness to let the FBI use his firm as a cover for two of its investigating agents may ultimately prove to be quite "bothersome" to him and his company.

> "If I were a stockholder in ADM, I would go to the annual meeting and say, "'did any of you clowns think about the ramifications of doing this,'" one veteran trader observed to the *Wall Street Journal*. "The guys in the pit have a long memory. ADM will never be able to buy at the bid again, or sell at the offer. They'll be doing business with the five-and 10-lot traders, and over the years that's going to cost them millions of dollars."[74]

Chapter Thirty-Two

The "Sleeping Pygmy" and the "Chicago Mirage"

The government's investigation of futures contracts involved more than just fraudulent practices by some brokers and traders; it was also about how the exchanges are regulated and the role that the Commodity Futures Trading Commission and the Congress *must* play in regulating such activities.

As noted, the nation's major commodity exchanges have frequently come under considerable criticism for the manner in which they conduct their business and for their lack of self-regulation. For many they have become, in effect, closed societies like so many of their major corporate members.

Thomas Eagleton, a former U.S. Senator from Missouri and ex-Merc governor, has termed the regulation of futures trading a "Chicago mirage" and "something of a myth." In appealing for tougher federal oversight of the exchange he has characterized the CFTC as a "sleeping pygmy" compared with the Securities and Exchange Commission.[1]

"The self-interest of the trading exchange can prevail over the public interest," he points out in underscoring the problems inherent in allowing traders to regulate their own markets. "the Merc is not a private downtown athletic club. It impacts tellingly on the financial markets of the entire free world."[2]

In November 1989 Eagleton resigned from the board of directors at the Merc charging that exchange officials were interfering with a federal commodities prosecution. In what Eagleton termed "the final straw," the Merc choose to challenge the CFTC's charges against one of its own directors and former chairman, Brain Monieson, whose GNP Commodities Inc. firm had been charged with failing to supervise its brokers accused of bilking customers. The CFTC at the time was seeking to ban GNP and Monieson, a former Merc chairman and board member, from the futures industry.[3]

In his letter of resignation Eagleton charged:

Whether the decision relates to open outcry or verbal orders or index arbitrage or floor surveillance or discipline of members or penalties for thievery or education/training of members or, most recently, the Brian Monieson matter, the Merc decision is usually a non-Lincolnian decision of insiders by insiders and for insiders.[4]

The letter went on to point out that "all the Merc power has been brought into action in an attempt to save Monieson's neck." Leo Melamed, "Mr. No. 1 at Merc," Bob Wilmouth, president of the National Futures Association, "a supposed 'regulatory' organization" and USDA Secretary Clayton Yeutter, who formerly served as the Merc's president all became character witnesses, and the Merc's "$1 million per year 'principal outside attorney'," Jerrold Salzman, obtained permission for himself and his firm to represent Monieson before the CFTC.

"As I see it," Eagleton's letter concludes, "the Merc has intruded into the legitimate enforcement affairs of the CFTC, counter to prudent public policy and against the public interest."[5]

Despite the intercession of those individuals named by Eagleton and others Monieson, in one of the harshest penalties ever handed down by The CFTC, was fined $500,000 and banned from the futures business. In addition to those penalties the agency's administrative law judge George Painter also revoked the futures trading registration of GNP Commodities Inc. and fined the firm $500,000.[6]

In his decision Painter noted that the small investors who were cheated were "virtually defenseless" and that "the shame of this case is that GNP and Monieson were so callously indifferent to the wrongs done to their most vulnerable customers."[97]

Eagleton had earlier noted that six times during the 1980's GNP had been warned or fined for various trading violations by the Merc,

which is not exactly known for its zealousness in rooting out wrongdoing... When it comes to a choice between protecting an insider and preserving the integrity of the futures markets, there is no question where the exchange stands... The truth regrettably, is that the public cannot invest in the futures exchanges and be confident that it is getting a fair deal.[8]

Some within the trade have even come to believe that they are entirely above the regulatory process, that the role of the government is that of an onlooker with the authority to regulate best left to the commodity trading boards themselves. Rather than protecting the public, federal agencies have often shown more interest in protecting the trade's elite from their own misjudgments.

Critics charge that because control of the commodity committees on the various exchanges tends to rest in the hands of the large grain traders and other large corporate agribusiness interests, exchange rules primarily deal with membership problems rather than the relationship between the exchange and the customers in general.

Jacob Gross, a Chicago lawyer with a long background in handling commodity lawsuits, describes one of the major reasons it is so difficult to ascertain trading violations on various commodity exchanges.

People who have such knowledge (about trading violations) are reluctant to come forward and identify themselves, because they are part of the process as well. The next day, they may be doing business with the person they have accused ...[9]

Before 1975, American commodity markets were being "supervised" by a weak and understaffed Commodity Exchange Authority. The USDA agency, however, was severely limited in its authority not only by statute, but by a general philosophy within the Department that grain markets should not be tampered with. But the manner in which the grain trade conducted itself during the 1972 Great American Grain Robbery, the political outcry for reform became strong enough that the CEA was abolished and the CFTC was established.

Congress mandated that this new independent government agency police the exchanges, but its meager staff of investigators and attorneys (its first chairman often reminded people that the CFTC had fewer "policemen" than the Rockville, Maryland Police Department) had extreme difficulty monitoring a growing number of commodity exchanges which some people already believed to be "among the world's most complex economic institutions."

In recent years, the CFTC's principal occupation has been to balance the principle of equal treatment for foreign and American nationals with the goal of preserving orderly commodity markets.

Yet, despite its concern for equal treatment, the CFTC claims to have seen no serious market disruptions linked to foreign trader activities in the past decade. (It is not helped by the many ambiguities in existing laws which make it almost impossible to identify the futures positions that foreign subsidiaries have in playing the U.S. commodity market.)

In the CFTC eyes the 1972 Soviet sale was a Soviet problem; the 1973 soybean embargo resulted from a severe shortage in Peruvian anchovies; the 1974-1975 Soviet sales were again a Soviet problem combined with some U.S. government mishandling; the Hunt family's "cornering" of the soybean futures market and the subsequent miscalculations by Cook Industries in soybeans in 1977 were all seen as unrelated domestic events.

The 1980 plunge in grain prices after the Russian grain embargo was viewed as the inevitable result of a political decision, and the 1981 soybean futures miscalculation by Farmers Export Company was but a poor judgment call by management. Reflecting on all these cases, Richard Gilmore rightfully concludes, the CFTC believed "ostensibly, each case arose for different reasons, none of them having to do with unidentified foreign purchases." Yet, he adds, "in fact, they all shared this common problem."

As he underscores in *A Poor Harvest,*

government surveillance is now little more than a *pro forma* exercise. The overly modest reforms called for somewhat reluctantly by the CFTC has been rejected for the most part by the [grain] trade. The whole exercise produced little effective defense against a continued abuse of the system ... CFTC's minimal approach to its regulatory duties did little to foster competition and, if anything, may have passively engendered a greater concentration of the grain merchandising business in yet one more area.[10]

Tension in Bed?

Defending itself against the charges that it has been lax in regulating the activities of the CBOT and CME, the CFTC points out that in 1986 it first cited shortcomings in its own enforcement of market regulations and urged the exchange to increase efforts to uncover fraud in the futures markets.[11] The Commission also complained at the time that the traders who violated the rules were often given only minimum penalties.

Kate Hathaway, a CFTC spokesperson, has termed "ludicrous" the charge that the Commission is "in bed" with the futures industry. It is not a defender of commodity traders, she emphasizes. "There is a great deal of tension between the industry and this commission.[12]

Yet, in 1987 the CFTC brought only 48 enforcement actions for commodity-trading rule violations while the Securities and Exchange Commission (SEC) brought 252 cases for insider-trading and other violations. The CFTC argues that the reason for such a discrepancy is that whereas the SEC had a staff of 749 and a fiscal '89 budget of $142.2 million, it only had a staff of 140 and a fiscal '89 budget of $34.7 million.[13]

It is counter-claimed that the CFTC should make the consumer-investor its top priority. Supporting such a focus is Ted Urban, an attorney and former deputy director of trading at the CFTC, who notes that the difference between the recent Wall Street scandals and the latest futures industry scandal is that the New York scandals were "side deals" where inside information was passed off the floor. In Chicago, he notes, "the fraud is happening on the floor of the trading exchanges, which everyone views as the real heart of the market."[14]

And, as Christopher Lovell, a New York futures attorney who has frequently represented clients before the CFTC, points out, "my clients and others have brought complaints to the attention of enforcement personnel, and those complaints haven't been meaningfully prosecuted." The reason for this lack of vigor, according to Lovell, is that the CFTC has gone especially light on well-connected exchange insiders.[15] The CFTC denies such allegations and points to its recent record of actions against major brokerage firms, exchange insiders and the exchanges themselves.

Shortly after the government's investigation of the futures industry in Chicago became public, but before the Justice Department officially confirmed the investigation, CFTC chairman Wendy Gramm announced that the agency had been "actively involved from the beginning" of the federal inquiry.[16] But, as the *Chicago Sun-Times* "Inside Business" columnist David Greising wondered aloud, "if the commission were involved from the outset, as it claims, it becomes difficult to explain several activities of former chairman Susan Phillips."

When Phillips announced in May 1987 that she was leaving the CFTC she presumably, as it's chairman would have known about the then five-month old unprecedented federal investigation — if in fact the CFTC was involved from the beginning. Yet in January 1988 Phillips became one of the CME's board of governors and in January 1989 was named co-chairman of the Merc panel considering changes following the publicity concerning the exchange scandals.

As Greising notes, "the two Merc assignments would seem to place Phillips in a difficult ethical position if — and it's a big 'if' — the CFTC really were involved in the federal investigation from the very outset." He also quotes one trading source as saying "she must not have known, because if she did, there's no way she could sit on the Merc's board and not say anything."[17] The CFTC's Hathaway declined comment on the timing "we have agreed with our partners in the investigation that we won't disclose information" about dates.[18]

Less than one month after the Chicago scandal began making headlines the CFTC, in its biannual review of enforcement at the CBOT, issued one of its most critical reports ever, claiming that the exchange had essentially been unable to detect fundamental abuses, like noncompetitive trading, trading for oneself in advance of the customer's order and taking the opposite position of a customer's order.

"This report is definitely critical," declared Hathaway, "there is no question that there are a number of exchange practices that need to be improved."[19]

The Commission also expressed dissatisfaction with the CBOT's new computerized system for determining when trades occur. The system, installed in July 1987, was not doing its job, it was reporting inaccurate times because of programming flaws and it was not using all the information available to it.

To make matters worse, the CBOT had no method of verifying how well its computerized system was performing. The CFTC also decried the lack of information being provided to the CBOT by its members. The Commission directed the CBOT to henceforth file monthly enforcement reports so the CFTC could more closely monitor investigations of suspected trading violations.[20]

For its part the CBOT's position was summarized by its President Thomas Donovan, in defending the integrity of the exchange after the FBI investigation became known. "We know we have excellent surveillance systems. We know we have a membership that won't tolerate abuses. We know we have a board of directors who vigorously prosecute disciplinary cases." Such sentiments were immediately echoed by CBOT Chairman Karsten "Cash" Mahlmann. "We have the best exchange in the damn world on price and on integrity."[21]

Although the Board of Trade's 24 directors announced that they would consider a number of proposals (including the institution of a full-time salary of $240,000 a year for its chairman, retroactive to January 1, 1989[69]) to bolster public confidence and demonstrate that the Board could regulate itself, critics viewed the proposals as more cosmetic than substantive.[22]

Among those proposals, some of which were later adopted, were ones to increase the number of people in the enforcement unit and to budget an additional $1 million for computers to monitor trading. The Boards also asked traders and brokers to pinpoint the recording times of trades within a 15-minute interval rather than the current 30 minutes and to be especially precise in recording their timing of trades after the opening and before the closing bells when the exchange is most volatile.[23]

"They're not getting to the heart of the matter: the ability of traders to make trades at prices that are not current," observed Daniel Siegel, a professor of finance at Northwestern University's Graduate School of Management.[24]

The CBOT's refusal to face the growing criticism of its customers concerning the practice of "dual trading" is, according to Daniel W. Basse, director of market research for AgResource Co., a Chicago-based trading advisory service, "like letting the fox watch the chicken house. There are too many conflicts of interest."[25]

Board of Trade President Donovan, however says it would be wrong for the exchange to be "cowed" into banning dual trading. "Eliminating 'dual trading' would have been the easy way out. But it would have destroyed market liquidity and that would have been wrong."[26]

Nearby at the Merc the exchange's most powerful group of brokers — ABS Partners — announced soon after the news of the government's investigation spread that it was banning its individual members from the practice of "dual trading."[27]

While the action was applauded by some, others saw it as yet another discriminatory move against individual or small traders. They argue that barring "dual trading" by *individuals* does not prevent giant commodity firms, like members of the grain trade, from positioning different brokers in the pits to do their bidding so as to manipulate market prices while holding opposite positions in that same market.

As the CFTC continues its push to ban "dual trading" the Congress has also been considering legislation to end such activity. In September 1989 the House in approving a bill 420-0 to strengthen the federal regulation of the futures industry imposed a ban on "dual trading."[28]

An April 1989 *Wall Street Journal* commodity trader survey found that 80 percent of those traders surveyed at the CME believed that dual trading should be banned while 63 percent of those questioned at the CBOT favored such a ban. When traders are allowed to wear two hats, trading on the one hand for their own accounts and on the other hand acting as brokers for the public the potential for abuse is obvious.

"The methods and techniques of manipulation are limited only by the ingenuity of man," remarked a federal judge upon finding Cargill guilty of manipulating May 1963 wheat futures contracts on the CBOT.[29]

The Merc also announced it had appointed a special panel to recommend some of the most extensive changes in its 115-year history.[30] In a letter signed by Leo Melamed, chairman of the executive committee and John Geldermann, chairman of the board, the Merc said that it had uncovered suspected improprieties before the undercover investigation by the federal government was disclosed.

"Our own internal compliance department had already focused on many of the same practices that appear to be central to the federal investigation... These practices will be exposed and the violators brought to justice."[31]

Subsequently, on April 19, 1989 the Merc panel released its long list of recommendations designed to eliminate trading abuses and bolster public confidence in the market. Included among its reforms were a ban on "dual trading;" members of so-called brokers' associations — groups of brokers who band together to share expenses — would be prohibited from trading their own account with another association member. Verbal orders, where exchange members execute trades with one another with little, if any, documentation would also be banned.

The panel's recommendations, however, did not include an endorsement of the one-minute time stamping of trades nor did it call for any further outsider involvement on the exchange's board of governors, both steps many believe necessary if the exchange is to be properly regulated.

The harshest criticism of the U.S. futures markets, came in a General Accounting Office (GAO) report delivered to Congress in February 1989. As the investigative arm of the U.S. Congress the GAO questioned the "intensity" of the futures industry to conduct proper oversight of its practices.[32]

Richard Fogel, GAO's assistant comptroller general urged the Congress to examine whether the system of having the exchanges police themselves is working.

The data certainly raise a number of questions that need to be pursued as to the level of fines and the intensity of the effort of both the CFTC and the exchanges. The first place you've got to look is the commitment of the exchanges. "It gets down to: Are they really serious about doing it themselves?"[33]

In 1984, the GAO noted, 12 traders were sanctioned by the Board of Trade while in 1988 only 13 were sanctioned, despite the fact that the number of contracts traded at the CBOT doubled to 140 million in the same period. At the CME the number of penalties rose from 13 to 105 during the same four-year period while volume almost doubled from 42 million to 78 million contracts.

"We read some cases where the exchanges sent a letter to a person six or seven times saying, 'Geez, you weren't filling out your [order] cards correctly,'" Vogel related. "the question is how many times do you send them a letter before you fine them."[34]

Later in 1989, after the CFTC issued new proposals to tighten exchange trading-floor rules, the GAO issued still another report faulting the new regulations as not strong enough.[35] The CFTC had proposed more frequent collections of trading cards, stricter rules governing contracts opening and closing trading periods, stricter criteria for exchange members who serve on governing boards, and a pilot program to improve floor surveillance.[36]

The GAO pointed out in its September 1989 critique that "even if these rules are implemented, floor participants will still be relied on to provide accurate trading records ... trading times will not be exact, and complete information on trades will not be available."[37] It recommended that the CFTC order the exchanges to "independently, precisely and completely time each trade," and that the timing of the trade should be independent of other trading information supplied by floor traders and brokers. Such information should contain "the precise time the broker receives and records as executed each order, as well as the precise execution times of non-customer trades."[38]

"Weakness in controls over future trading," the report concludes,

provide dishonest floor participants with the opportunity to cheat customers. While detecting every abuse may never be possible, most of the types of the abuses alleged in Justice Department indictments could have been detected and documented with independent, precise and complete timing of trades.[39]

Commenting on the GAO report, Senator Patrick Leahy, chairman of the Senate Agriculture committee, noted that "read along with the recent indictments of 46 Chicago futures traders, [it] argues strongly that major flaws exist in the current system of policing the floors of our nation's futures exchanges. The public is not being adequately protected."[40]

By continuing to place important surveillance and enforcement responsibilities in the hands of the exchanges with only minimal "interference" from the CFTC, the Commission's declared objective of preserving competition actually results in preserving the status quo, which, in effect, has become the antithesis of competition.

The Mother's Milk of Politics

"We're all on trial, to a certain extent. This committee, and the committee in the House ...have a responsibility to examine whether we as legislators have exerted proper oversight."[41]

- Senator Thomas Daschle, D- S.D.

One cannot hold the CFTC solely responsible for its inability to regulate the nation's futures exchanges effectively. The United States Congress must also share a large measure of that blame and shame for its lack of responsibility and resolve in acting against traders and brokers who cheat customers and manipulate market prices to serve their own greed.

As the *Wall Street Journal*'s Brooks Jackson and Thomas E. Ricks write, few governmental bodies have more reason to be embarrassed by the allegations of improper commodity dealings. Hundreds of members of Congress have collected personal fees from the exchanges for visiting the very trading pits where, it now turns out, undercover agents of the Federal Bureau of Investigation were pursuing evidence of criminal activity.[42]

According to Jackson and Ricks, from 1983 through 1987 the traders gave $483,950 in honoraria to federal lawmakers with a total of $130,496 in 1987 alone given to 24 senators and 62 House members. Of the 43 members of the House Agricultural Committee, which oversees the CFTC, 22 members received such fees. The committee's chairman, Representative E. "Kika" de la Garza, D-Texas, received $3000 in such honoraria, however, because the amount exceeded the legal ceiling he donated $1000 to charity.

"Our responsibility is the integrity of the markets and the protection of investors," Representative de la Garza asserts. "We intend to pursue that with all the diligence and forcefulness we can... I could care less how many millions they give or who they give it to."

Defending such honoraria Representative Fred Grandy, R-Iowa, claims that he and his colleagues are paid not to speak at the exchanges but are asked to go for educational purposes. "It's kind of a standard trip for new members of the agricultural committee." The objective of the exchanges, therefore, are "educational." "They're interested in making sure their business isn't restricted." he adds.[43]

Many members of Congress have received substantial campaign donations from various PACs which have been established by the CME, the CBOT and the Industry Futures Association. From 1983 through 1988 these three PAC's contributed some $1.8 million to candidates in three Congressional elections, with 90 percent of those donations going to incumbents.

The top five recipients in the House and Senate included:[44]

HOUSE:

Marty Russo, D-Ill.,	$45,100
Thomas Foley, D-Wash.,	$31,500
Glenn English, D-Okla.,	$28,750
Cardiss Collins, D-Ill.,	$25,500
E. "Kika" de la Garza, D-Texas,	$25,500

SENATE:

Thomas Daschle, D-S.D.,	$29,500
James Jeffords, R-Vt.,	$24,500
Lloyd Bentsen, D-Texas,	$23,500
Alfonse D'Amato, R-N.Y.,	$22,000
Jesse Helms, R-N.C.,	$21,000

Clayton Yeutter, confirmed unanimously as Secretary of Agriculture by the Senate, is a long-time believer in the futures market and one of its more outspoken defenders. It was while he was head of the CME from 1978-85 that ordinary speaking fees were first fashioned into "honorariums" and used as a lobbying tool.[45]

Likewise, a general attitude of hear no evil, see no evil, speak no evil in respect to abuses on the exchange floors has characterized Yeutter's approach to regulation of the exchanges. In 1980 Congressional hearings, commenting on the suggestion that there had been massive unchecked and unnecessary speculation in commodities, he stated: "I would like to know ... how anyone in Government defines unnecessary speculation. I don't believe it is possible to define unnecessary speculation in any manner that has yet surfaced."[46]

In response to the suggestion that it would be appropriate to limit speculative activities to a level conducive to useful commerce, the former agricultural economist replied:

I would like some definition of what speculative activity, what level of activity it (sic) is conducive to useful commerce. It seems to me that we have not yet observed a level of speculative activity that is not conducive to useful commerce. I am not persuaded that anything other than that occurred in the silver case. (*i.e.*, the 1979-80 silver futures market scandal involving the Hunt brothers.)[47]

The access to lawmakers that these PAC's and honoraria provide the futures industry was evident in the months immediately following the October 1987 Wall Street stock market crash. Chicago exchange officials and industry lobbyists began lobbying hard in Washington to prevent any changes in the regulatory system that would effect them.[48]

Again, within hours of the federal investigation of the Chicago futures industry being made public, exchange officials were meeting in the nation's capital with key supporters, such as then House Speaker Jim Wright, D-Texas, and House Ways and Means Chairman Dan Rostenkowski, D-Ill., seeking continued Congressional support in anticipation of the storm of criticism that was likely to come.[49]

Former CFTC chairman James Stone (1979-1981) recalls another example of the industry working through Congress to defeat tight regulation. In 1979 the CFTC voted 5-0 to require the "time stamping" of trading cards within one minute of the execution order in an effort to monitor trading patterns better. The industry, however, opposed the move. Stone recalls,

There was direct lobbying and indirect lobbying through Congress and when it came to the next vote, it was 3-1 against the proposal. The fact is a regulatory agency views itself as a creature of Congress and searches out the congressional will on issues.

It was not until 1986 that the CFTC finally decided on a "time-stamping" rule for all exchanges.[50]

Watching Shadows on the Wall

Asa Baber has warned that a "small investor's" (someone with $20,000 or less to spend) chances of making a profit in the futures market most always depends on a) how much information the investor has to help make a sensible buy or sell, and b) how reliable the commission house and brokers are in looking out for their interests.

Information, of course, is vital to the investor, and it is here where the major grain traders and large brokerage houses have an overwhelming advantage.

The general recognition of how access to information is essential even to enter the futures market, let alone dominate it like so many large corporate agribusiness companies currently do, makes the testimony of Carlos Bradley before a 1974 Senate Committee laughable if not ludicrous. The then president of the Kansas City Board of Trade told the committee:

> There is no such thing as inside information in the grain business. The only potential inside information that might exist would be government reports ... If there are leaks in the government, which we greatly doubt, this is something that should be stopped. But within the trade itself, there is no inside information.[51]

Futures buyers who might be inclined to believe such pap as Bradley's should consider still another Baber admonition.

> When you read press releases from the USDA about what is supposedly the latest word in fundamental information, or when your account executive whispers over the phone that he has just learned the real scoop about cotton yields in Zanzibar, take it all with a dose of caution. The big money people had all that information long ago.
>
> The market has already reacted to it. You are out of sync with the market, suffering eternally from a disease you might call information lag. You will be the last to get the word. Like the person in Plato's cave, you will never see the fires of truth yourself. You are doomed to watching only shadows and reflections dance on the walls of your den.[52]

Further, it must also be remembered that small investors, usually the farthest removed from the trading floor, are generally more vulnerable to trading abuses. As the GAO's Cecile Trop told a February, 1989 Senate Agricultural Committee, small investors "don't have the time or the resources to monitor the markets," or to know when they are simply being cheated out of their money.[53]

"They don't understand the full dynamics of how those guys on the floor can play games," is how Morton Baratz, editor of *Managed Account Reports* has described the plight of the small investor.[54]

Searching For the "Competitive Advantage"

In discussing "the rusting American agricultural chain," Richard Gilmore points out in his authoritative *A Poor Harvest* that ideally the futures market offers a competitive system for pricing grain, but in distribution and marketing the actual record tells a far different story. Farmers' involvement in the hedging system, purportedly designed for their benefit, has remained "severely limited."

Before commodity exchanges came into being farmers were forced to haul their goods over poor roads into large cities and go from merchant to merchant in an attempt to sell their goods — a chaotic system at best. Farmers' victimization under this regiment can be seen from the fact that between 1883 and 1889 two large grain terminals in Minneapolis averaged annual returns on capital investment of 40 percent and 30 percent respectively.[55]

Adding to this early dilemma, nearly all the millers and warehouses were interlocked with the railroad companies. Even though the Chicago Board of Trade was established in 1848 it soon became a mecca for "the worst elements of American free enterprise: greed; the cycle of riches and ruin, boom and bust; corruption."[56]

While the CBT provided at least a public price for all to see in Chicago, which tended to reduce the chances of merchants attempting to cheat farmers, it did spawn "bucket shops" throughout the country where "potboiler operators" would accept bets on the movement of grain prices on the CBOT. These "bucket shops" became so prolific throughout the nation that one federal judge proclaimed that "gambling in grains may be said to be the national pastime."[57]

The twentieth century brought needed reforms. In addition the large grain exchanges throughout the world became connected by new high-speed international communications equipment, which in turn quickly helped open up global markets for U.S. grain.

Yet, despite the revered position that the major grain traders have come to hold within the nation's various commodity exchanges they have on occasion challenged and even defied these same trading institutions when it suited their narrow interests.

Such was the historic case, for example, with Cargill and the Chicago Board of Trade in the 1930s. Faced with a disastrous 1936 corn crop and a 1937 crop that was due to be harvested in October, Cargill began buying up corn for delivery in September. Company suppliers soon found themselves unable to obtain enough corn to fulfill their sales contracts to Cargill.

The CBOT ordered Cargill to sell some of its own reserves to relieve the "squeeze," but the company refused, saying such a sale would collapse prices and cost the company $2 million. The CBOT followed up its plea by halting all trading on September corn futures and banishing Cargill's floor trader. While Agriculture Secretary Henry Wallace was charging the Minneapolis firm with trying to corner the corn market, Cargill quietly began using independent brokers to do its floor trading.

Cargill was later invited back to the pits, but did not accept the offer for several years. Subsequently, the company admitted that it had learned a priceless lesson from the incident: by using independent brokers on a commodity exchange floor it could keep its trading activities even more secret than before and thereby increase its "competitive advantage."

"Merchants of Human Misery"

As the grain trade's elite have gone about acquiring an inordinate influence within the various commodity exchanges one could rightly say that today these exchanges now exist for their own convenience. Dan Morgan, author of *The Merchants of Grain* and others, however, argue that such a system nevertheless "is preferable to secret, privately negotiated forward contracting in which individual farmers would be at a considerably greater disadvantage in negotiating with hugh multinationals."[58]

Despite such arguments, Gilmore has properly concluded that "size, then, is a principal indicator of influence on the exchanges (as well as in other aspects along the agricultural chain) ..."[59]

One such manifestation is the fact that in the 1970's when the commodity markets were booming, many of the large grain companies themselves went into the commodity brokerage business. By establishing their own brokerage subsidiaries they began taking orders from members of the general public who wanted to speculate in the futures markets. Despite the apparent conflict of interest, neither the government nor the CFTC attempted to interfere.

In initiating their own brokerage business, these grain traders have succeeded at getting the banks to recognize that the money deposited on behalf of the brokerage clients should be counted as part of the company balance which, in turn, increases the bank credit available to the company.

Testifying before a House subcommittee in 1973, Harry Fortes, a Chicago lawyer and former vice-chairman of the Chicago Mercantile Exchange, addressed this problem of size in the nation's commodity exchanges.

> Although millions of people have been enticed to their sorrow into the trading of commodity futures only a bare handful of commercial interests and professional pit traders really have the sophistication and know-how to successfully trade in commodities. When properly employed, this expertise serves a valuable economic function...
>
> However, in many instances, this sophistication and know-how simply are utilized by commercial interests and professional traders, acting in concert with sufficient group power and money to squeeze and manipulate a market. ...
>
> Manipulation results in price control, it results in disruption of our free-market price structure, it results in a complete breakdown of the hedge operation to the detriment of the grower and it results in inflated costs to the American housewife in millions of dollars.[60]

Thanks to the ambiguities in existing law, multinational grain traders' futures positions cannot be fully identified. Under such circumstances, these traders can conceal big sales by quietly building up a "long" futures position whose size neither other traders nor the government can divine. This practice in turn provides ample lead time for these same traders, through their subsidiaries, to buy grain at reasonable prices before the market registers an increase in price resulting from a surge in demand.

Describing the consequences of such practices Frank Van Den Broeck, general manager of the trading firm A.M. Achille De Smedt in Antwerp, Belgium and a former Cargill employee, relates:

> The multinationals don't like to trade on cash anymore because there is less time to look for a way to manipulate the shipment. Why else would they always want to sell long futures? That gives them three to four months to play around and look for the cheapest grain. Often you cannot get immediate delivery, they just say it isn't there.[61]

Depending on how long they are able to seal off the news, the companies may well be able to establish all the futures they need for an extended period of time. As one trader told author Tamarkin, "if the H-bomb dropped, traders would want to know if they had time to go long on gold."[62] Such are the facts of life in the commodity trading business.

In 1948, for example, while the U.S. was attempting to feed a food-scarce Europe through the Marshall Plan, the heavy demand for agricultural commodities led to such dramatic run-ups in grain prices on the CBOT that an angry President Truman called the nation's commodity traders "merchants of human misery."[63]

Timed correctly, futures transactions can precede the sales registration with the CFTC and thereby avoid any likely price penalty if the news of such a large export transaction breaks before the company's foreign subsidiary and its U.S. division have time to place their hedges.

In October 1986 even the CBOT was criticized by the CFTC for allegedly permitting its members to report the timing of their transactions improperly. Based on figures for 11 months in 1985-86 the CFTC noted that 32.5 percent of all trades were not reported within the required half-hour period, an unacceptably high inaccuracy rate and one that could "mask possible substantive violations."

As Gilmore stresses:

> If the foreign sales are large enough in the short term, their disclosure can bring pandemonium to the market-place. When this has happened in the past, the large trading houses have rarely been identified as the culprits because, as they explain it, their interests lie with a stable, well-run exchange system.
>
> Nevertheless, the [grain trade elite's] mode of operations is such that the margin of transactions they do not account for is more likely to show wide price variations when their share of the futures market is largest. The [grain trade elite's] interests are certainly linked with a predictable market, but their hedging practices inevitably induce a high degree of market instability.[64]

Take for example the story pieced together by the *Des Moines Register* a few years ago concerning how several large grain companies engineered a series of secret deals with the Canadian Wheat Board which cost American farmers millions of dollars in lost sales.[65]

Canada, accurately foreseeing in the summer of 1976 that a worldwide wheat surplus and lessening export demand would depress prices, agreed to sell several grain firms up to five million tons of wheat, to be delivered in the spring of 1977. Prices were kept secret, but it was believed by USDA officials that the Canadians agreed to sell the grain at a discount.

Also, according to USDA officials, the Canadian Wheat Board agreed to store the wheat in port elevators free of charge until the grain companies decided to ship it abroad. It is thought that the grain companies originally bought the Canadian wheat for 15 to 35 cents below the price in effect at the time for comparable American wheat.

U.S. wheat was selling in Minneapolis late in the summer of 1976 for about $3.36 a bushel. At the same time, May 1977 wheat futures were selling in Chicago for $3.42 a bushel. USDA officials said it was possible that while the grain companies paid Canada from $3 a bushel to $3.20 a bushel, they were able to sell the futures contracts for substantially more.

The grain firms not only protected themselves against the price decline that did occur, but actually received more per bushel from the futures contracts they eventually sold, than from what they had paid the Canadians for the wheat. Thus, they had an assured supply of wheat at an assured price, without the usual grain storage costs. At this same time American farmers were paying about 30 cents a bushel to store their wheat for the year.

Richard Baum of the National Association of Wheat Growers was rightfully critical of the action:

They have the best of both worlds. They're international traders who do most of their business in the U.S., handling U.S. grain. They use the American futures markets to hedge their sales and also they handle our government aid programs such as Food for Peace. But then, they play us against other countries when it's to their advantage.

What I'm saying is that everything they did is legal, but it's not in the best interests of American agriculture ... it's in the interests of the international grain trade.[66]

Playing the Game By the Rules and Regulations?

One Chicago attorney, Jeffrey N. Cole, who was approached by several brokers and traders who feared that they might have been part of the federal government's investigation of the futures industry, observed to the *Chicago Sun-Times* that if all of the allegations raised by federal prosecutors were in fact true,[67] then:
• "The investigation could threaten to bring down an entire exchange" and force "sweeping reforms in the industry."

• Investors may have been cheated out of "hundreds of millions of dollars" in the trading scams.
• The scope of the inquiry "could easily surpass in significance" the insider trading scandal that had already shaken Wall Street.
To many those conclusions came as no surprise.
Former CFTC chairman Stone, now chairman of Plymouth Rock Assurance in Boston, Massachusetts, notes that

people in the business have known for years and years that abuses on the floor, in futures, and in takeovers ... are growing and the culprits, the villains, always felt secure that their crimes were too sophisticated and too expensive to investigate. And therefore they went about them with impunity. The New York and Chicago investigators have, thank goodness, shown them that the public sector is willing to invest time, effort and sophistication to catch them.[68]

In an industry where a sense of fraternity and a set of unwritten rules govern each day's trading, where the most sacrosanct of all those rules has been the trust that enabled one trader to take the word of another as a bond, the inability of the various exchanges to regulate themselves effectively has traditionally remained its achilles heel.

Over 15 years ago, at the conclusion of the House Committee on Agriculture hearings in 1973 which created the CFTC, the Committee Chairman duly noted that

Attempted investigations in regulated exchanges are often characterized by the unwillingness of the investigating committees composed of exchange members to inquire too closely into the possible excesses of their own brethren ... Brokers, customers, and eventually the American economy suffers in the atmosphere of so-called 'self-regulation' where tradition and self-interest has been allowed to displace the public interest.[69]

Despite this warning and others like it throughout the years, the heart of nearly all the major futures market disruptions in recent years has been alleged manipulations. The facts that have emerged from such investigations since the establishment of the CFTC, whether they be in the potato, soybean, coffee, wheat, silver or other market pits, include:
• by virtue of their large cash and futures positions major market participants wield tremendous market power;
• substantial market power is generally a precondition for market manipulation;
• the CFTC has not developed effective measures for prevention of market manipulation and conflicts of interests, and
• episodes such as the 1979-80 silver cornering case are likely to recur in other markets amidst allegations of and conflicts of interest unless

specific rules and regulations are implemented to prevent them.[70]

Dating back to 1922 when Congress first established the Commodity Exchange Act, much rhetoric has emanated from the nation's highest legislative body about the direct responsibility of designated exchanges to prevent market disruption or distortion and to ensure the "economic utility" of futures markets. The 1922 statute was "built on the concern that such noncompetitive conditions can yield artificial prices and inhibit the legitimate hedging use of the markets."[71]

Yet, despite several important revisions of federal regulations governing commodity exchanges since 1922, exchange self-regulation has always been at the heart of the regulatory structure. This in spite of the fact that other important segments of the nation's financial community have come to realize that it is simply not reasonable to expect those same individuals and institutions that have a financial interest in a market to make objective regulatory decisions about those same markets.

Even in the face of periodic scandals, the futures industry adamantly maintains that its board and committee members — including those with substantial market positions — can provide all necessary remedial action.

One aspect of the 1989 Ferruzzi soybean caper, little noted by the nation's press, raised the very questions many critics have had about the role of the exchanges to act without bias in adjudicating matters when they themselves may be holding substantial marketing positions in the contracts involved.

Responding to charges that top officers of the CBOT might have benefitted from its emergency order to Ferruzzi to liquidate its July 1989 soybean contracts, the CFTC issued a preliminary report in August stating that it found no conflict of interest among the CBOT directors.[72]

Two weeks later before a Senate Agriculture committee hearing on the CFTC, it was learned that while the CBOT board vote was 16-1 for the emergency order, with three members not voting, six of the members present worked for firms whose customer accounts benefitted from the Board's action.[73] Only one board member recused himself from the vote due to his personal holdings.[74]

Although CBOT Chairman Mahlmann votes only in case of stalemates, he did participate in the discussion and his firm, Stotler & Co. held a short position of 110,000 bushels of soybeans. Board Vice-Chairman Patrick Arbor's firm, L.I.T. America also held a short position of 420,000 bushels. Another CBOT director, Hal P. Hansen, is president of Cargill Investor Services, a subsidiary of Cargill, and his firm held the largest short position of the six, 910,000 bushels. (Other directors whose firms held short positions included Donald G. Andrew, Shearson Lehman Hutton; Lester Mouscher, Lee B. Stern & Co., and Irwin Smith, Rosenthal-Collins.)[75]

As a postscript to this vote, it should be noted that a year after the CBOT's action, chairman Mahlmann suddenly resigned both his board post and the chairmanship of Stotler Group Inc., the third-largest clearing firm at the CBOT. The resignations came after the CFTC charged Stotler with misusing $5.5 million of funds invested in its pools. Two weeks after the agency's actions the Stotler Group and two of its subsidiaries — Stotler & Co. and Stotler Financial Corp. — were forced by investors in two commodity funds to file for liquidation under Chapter 7 of the Federal Bankruptcy Act.[76]

In his July 31 letter of resignation to CBOT members, a shattered Mahlmann sought to assure his business colleagues that during his four years as CBOT chairman his attention had been dedicated to Board affairs. "I have had no day-to-day management responsibilities [at Stotler] since early 1988, and my position at Stotler was constantly eroding."[77]

The Wearing of Many Hats

Inherent "conflicts of interest" involved in the course of self-regulatory action by the CBOT, the Merc and other exchanges suggests what has been obvious to many over the years. Former Representative Fred Richmond, D-NY, voiced such concern in 1980:

Gentlemen, I am troubled by this whole conflict of interest problem ... I have been in business all my life, and I can't recall a situation where an industry has or wears as many different hats as your industry wears. I can't recall any similar situation where the same organization that runs an exchange also sets its margins, and allows its own board of directors to trade for themselves and for customers. There isn't even an electronic system to guarantee if each trade is made for a specific customer or for the trader himself. It seems to me that your industry is fraught with conflicts of interest.[78]

The potential for conflict of interest in many areas of commodity trading is indeed ever-present. For example, the low margins set by the exchanges not only encourage speculation by major customers, but are also often both a lure and a risk to the small investor. While one might initially put $5,000 down to control $100,000 worth of soybeans, whether one realizes a significant return on their investment depends on what happens to the price. A wrong guess can be financially disastrous as margin calls mount if one is to maintain one's position in the market.[79]

After the October 1987 collapse of the stock market, some called for a greater role by the CFTC in regulating the futures market, arguing that it be given the authority to actually set futures margins rather than just act in emergencies by adjusting levels such as it is presently empowered to do.[80]

In matters such as the setting of margins, as in so many other instances, it is argued that the CFTC has an obligation, explicitly derived from the statute that created the CEA, that "its authority is not limited to situations where action is necessary to *restore* orderly trading, but specifically includes authority to act to *maintain* orderly trading." The law also defines "emergency" to mean "threatened" as well as actual market manipulations and the "cornering" of markets.[81]

Long a major obstacle to any effort to either *restore* or *maintain* an orderly market is the fact that the major regulatory players — the exchanges and the CFTC — do not even agree on the rules of the game.

Such a "disagreement" was evident in the 1979 March wheat contract on the Chicago Board of Trade. At the time the CFTC halted trading in March wheat futures after learning that four traders had acquired nearly all of the contracts calling for delivery of wheat in that month. One speculator alone apparently owned enough grain to satisfy the contract, leading the CFTC to level allegations of market manipulation.[82]

Because of a provision of the CFTC law that prohibited the agency from disclosing individual market positions, only two traders were identified publicly. One was Leslie Rosenthal, a CBOT vice-chairman and head of a commodity brokerage firm, and the other was a partner in Rosenthal's firm. These two and a third speculator held 86 percent of the "open interest" — the number of outstanding contracts for which a futures purchase or sale had to be made unless the commodity was actually delivered — in March wheat, 30 times the "open interest" figure for comparable contracts a year earlier.[83]

After the CFTC halted trading for a day, four days after trying unsuccessfully to close the contract down, the CBOT sued and won a court decision to permit liquidation, or forced closeout of open contracts, and new sales for delivery only, during the last three trading days of the March contracts.

CBOT President Robert Wilmouth claimed that there was no wrongdoing and that the exchange would not take any action against the four. Federal regulators, he added, "misperceived the situation, a misperception made worse by press tendencies to magnify it."[84] However, Gary Seevers, the acting CFTC chairman, later told a Congressional committee investigating the case that the orderly liquidation of the March wheat contracts at lower prices proved that the futures price was artificial rather than a price set by economic forces in the market.[85]

Clearly, in cases like this reflect a divergence of views as to what is the rule concerning "market manipulation." Richard Heifner, in a report to the House Agricultural Committee on the aforementioned wheat emergency, stated:

> The Commodity Exchange Act does not define manipulation or threatened manipulation, but the distinction between the two is important. Actual manipulation involves: (1) dominant or controlling positions in both the futures and cash markets; (2) intent to manipulate; and (3) price distortion. Threatened manipulation does not require that any of the above three conditions actually hold, but only that we have forewarning of their occurrence.[86]

It is clear from the record and the past regulatory decisions of the CFTC that much ambiguity exists between the Commission and the exchanges and that "the rules of the game" need to be more precisely defined.

Looking for the Sharks in a Goldfish Bowl

In order to effectively surveil the futures markets, the CFTC needs comprehensive market information that provides an immediate historical context for evaluating any given market situation. This requires the development of a technically sophisticated and scientifically accurate market surveillance system. Such a system should include the development of objective market performance indicators, which would automatically alert the Commission to any technical market abnormality. The technology, hardware, statistical methodology and most of the necessary market data is currently available and could be combined within a reasonably short period of time to significantly upgrade the Commission's market surveillance system.[87]

Seven years after this 1982 CFTC reauthorization hearing report, and then only after the news of a sweeping federal probe into the activities of the futures industry we are just beginning to see the exchanges enter the computerized age. The CME announced that in late 1989 it planned to join Globex, a world-wide trading system designed by the CME and Reuters Holdings PLC.[88]

Through the use of a computer the fairest price between the bids and offers would be located to determine an opening price. A publicly viewed screen would display an auction process showing the current prices, the last sale and quantity of the last sale, and the quantity of the best bids and the best offers.

There would be another screen for dealers which would indicate the liquidity of the market by showing the ten best offers and their amounts at ascending prices and the ten best offers and their amounts at descending prices.[89]

While Chairman Gramm, in announcing the CFTC's approval of the new system, saw an "innovation of this type as essential if the U.S. is to maintain its competitive edge," Andrea Corcoran, director of the Commission's trading and marketing division, saw it as producing an extremely accurate "audit trail" of the sequence and timing of trades. It would also help regulators track the financial exposure of traders, she added.[90]

The CBOT has announced only that it is studying the possibility of developing a computerized trading system which would permit trading electronically, but just as Globex, only during the hours that the exchange was not open.[91]

Some futures industry spokespersons argue that computers would introduce uncertainty, possibly not hold up in the most complex and high pressure transactions, disrupt the long-tested way of doing things and risk driving participants away and making the market less liquid. Others scoff at such objections and point out that exchange members frequently owe their fortunes to their presence in a market where the public has only limited access to the vital information that is the stuff from which those fortunes are made.

"Those people who control the marketplace," Junius Peake, an Englewood, N.J. marketing consultant who specializes in trading technology, told *The Wall Street Journal*, "be they commodity exchanges or stock exchanges, benefit economically by having uniqueness of information... The fellow in the pits have information you and I in our offices could never have."[92]

"There is no question Globex represents a near-perfect audit trail," observes the Merc's Leo Melamed. "It's the fishbowl and everything that happens is inside it. Computations will be calculated to the nearest nano-second, and in terms of regulatory framework it gets great applause."[93]

Electronic trading, however, "adds another dimension of interconnection, speed and complexity of the network relationships," according to Peter Schwartz, a Berkeley, California consultant serving on a government panel to study security technology. "And the system has already gotten so complex that literally no one understands the interconnections."[94]

As Bob Tamarkin explains it,

In an effort to cope with [the market's] hair-trigger volatility, many analysts and traders have turned to the computer in recent years ... The computer is a mere extension of the chart. The price history of a particular commodity and its trading volume are plugged into a computer that has been programmed to yield the maximum investment strategies for that contract. The information is then applied to a current contract.

However, he cautions, while "their computers work well, it's the human element that seems to short-circuit. The combination of speed and confusion jolts the system."[95]

Indeed, before his "retirement" from the business futures speculator Richard J. Dennis, for years one of the most influential and successful traders in the Chicago markets, confided to the *Wall Street Journal*'s Scott McMurray that computerized trading systems used by a growing number of public trading funds often overwhelmed his own trading decisions.

"You can't beat the system," he said and added that part of his recent losses derived from overriding the trading decisions of his own computer systems, which he painstakingly had developed over the years.[96]

Exposing the "Invisible Hand"

Clearly the time has come for seriously questioning the many perceptions of the futures market that have been held for so long by farmers, investors and politicians, not only in respect to the role the market currently serves, but the regulatory means necessary to make sure it operates fairly and properly.

By way of explaining why his organization contributes so much money to Congressional Political Action Committees, John Damgard, president of the Futures Industry Association, has stated that, "in an industry that is so arcane and has so little grass-roots support, lots of things could have happened to us."[97]

It is precisely here where the reform of the futures industry must begin. For it is the lack of a proper *public perception* that allows the "the invisible hand" the industry always talks about, but never properly identifies, to function.

Therefore, a public understanding of both the role the futures market serves in our economy and the consequences of its abuses is vital if we are to have a genuine economic and political democracy.

As former CME vice chairman Harry Fortes states: "manipulation results in price control, it results in disruption of our free-market price structure, it results in a complete breakdown of the hedge operation to the detriment of the grower and it results in inflated costs to the American housewife in millions of dollars."[98]

Thus, we need a "grass roots" constituency that can both invest in the market with confidence and empower its elected representatives to unmask those "invisible hands" which seek only to satiate their own greed. The market must be regulated to a degree that serves well farmers, all investors and the general public.

A proper public perception of the futures industry also requires jettisoning false perceptions that the presently constituted market is a safe place for farmers to hedge their crops, for investors to reap rich financial rewards, and for the government to let the exchanges regulate themselves without any kind of public accountability.

A proper futures market should be one where traders must buy or be able to produce commodities before they can sell them; a market where the public or the small investor is not held in contempt, but rather has equal access to information that will enable him or her to make wise decisions on whether to buy or sell; where the exchanges come to realize that it is not reasonable to expect individuals and institutions that have a financial interest in a market will make objective regulatory decisions about those same markets.

Farmers and investors deserve a market where an outside regulatory body will give its highest priority to maintaining an orderly market, not just trying endlessly to restore orderly trading. They also deserve a Congress responsive to the public welfare and not willing to sit back and meekly accept the well-worn corporate agribusiness shibboleth that the best market is one that is left to its own "self-regulatory" devices.

To once again echo the words of former House Agricultural Committee Chairman W.R. Poage, D-Texas,

brokers, customers, and eventually the American economy suffers in the atmosphere of so-called "self-regulation" where tradition and self-interest has been allowed to displace the public interest.

Section Six:

Heading Toward the Last Roundup

"Sure, it's chaotic, but chaos is our favorite environment."

**- William (Bill) Haw, president and
chief executive of National Farms, Inc.**

Chapter Thirty-Three

The Big Three's Prime Cut

For nearly two centuries cattle and the colorful lore and legends surrounding their role in American history have held a hallowed place in the nation's annals, immortalized in song, story and film.

Likewise, the very food that these animals produce, from steak to hamburgers, have traditionally been acclaimed as quite literally the main course in the All-American diet. For some, red meat remains to this day *the* culinary status symbol.

Yet, the social and economic costs that have marked the growth of the U.S. cattle and meat packing industry have left indelible marks on our national character.

From the violence of the range wars of our 19th century west to the lawless amassing of huge land-grabbing cattle empires, from the workplace horrors of the infamous turn-of-the-century Chicago slaughterhouses, immortalized in Upton Sinclair's *The Jungle*, to the present-day cartels, cattle production and meat packing has long been and remains one of our economic system's most unruly sectors.

By virtually eliminating the cowboy, closing numerous major cattle markets, and establishing giant cattle feedlot and regional slaughtering facilities, the industry has achieved its three single overriding corporate objectives: the substitution of capital for efficiency and technology for labor, the standardization of its production, and the creation of new consumer products in order to gain ever larger market shares.

Although the cattle and meat packing industry has undergone important structural changes in the eight decades since the publication of *The Jungle*, its basic monopolistic character and the callous disregard it has shown for the health and economic life of its suppliers, its workers and the consuming public remains an ongoing scandal.

Today, cattle and meat packing rank as the largest single component of the food industry with regard to total assets, value added to product, total employees and total business receipts. With $33.8 billion in beef cattle sales in 1987 and with meat marketing sales of $47.3 billion it is the nation's fourth largest manufacturing industry.[1]

Just over ten percent of all the food Americans buy each year is red meat, beef and pork. Consumption of the products has gone from a 1975 high of 138.5 pounds per capita to 119.5 pounds in 1988.[2]

A 1985 Gallup poll commissioned by *American Health*, however, found that 24 percent of the population now eats less meat than in past years due to dietary and health concerns, and the increasing availability of low-cost poultry.[3]

Despite these figures a third of North America is currently devoted to the grazing of cattle; over one-half of the nation's cropland grows livestock feed, and more than half of the potable water consumed in the United States is used to water livestock.

It is calculated that one pound of feedlot-finished beefsteak requires five pounds of grain, 2500 gallons of water, the energy equivalent of a gallon of gasoline, and 35 pounds of eroded topsoil.[4]

And Then There Were Only Three

The U.S. cattle industry has become dominated by just three major packing companies. It is estimated that these three companies — Iowa Beef Processors, Inc. (whose majority stock owner is Occidental Petroleum Corp.), Excel Corp. (formerly MBPXL Corp. and now a subsidiary of Cargill Corp., the nation's largest private corporation), and ConAgra, Inc. — in 1990 slaughtered nearly 80 percent of all fat cattle in the United States.[5] These three alone can slaughter about 23 million cattle a year, a number equal to 82 percent of the 1986 steer and heifer slaughter and 62 percent of the 1986 total cattle kill.[6]

"Right now they are in an atmosphere of intense competition," warns Chuck Hassebrook, a Center for Rural Affairs's policy analyst, however, as he cautions, "they are all trying to get their chunks before anyone else."[7]

B.H. (Bill) Jones, head of USDA's Packers and Stockyards Administration (PS&A), while acknowledging that "we are monitoring for anticompetitive trade practices," points out that "so far there is no evidence that prices are any different than they would have been otherwise. Still I have to feel that three or four bidders in a market are not as good as five or six ... they don't have to collude to know what each other is doing."[8]

As noted, most economists believe that whenever the four-firm concentration ratio goes over 40 percent, firms have a potential to exercise monopoly or monopsony power. Monopoly power is reflected in control over the quantity, quality and price of products sold; monopsony power is seen in the control over the quantity and price of inputs. Generally a four-firm concentration ratio over 65 percent is considered highly concentrated.

Before discussing how Iowa Beef Processors, Excel and ConAgra have acquired such a massive concentration of economic power and how the U.S. cattle industry has evolved into the corporate behemoth that it is today, the economic and social consequences of such growth must first be described.

Dr. John W. Helmuth, chief economist for the U.S. House of Representatives Committee on Small Business from 1979 through 1987, succinctly explains the essence of the problem:

> When a few large firms buy, slaughter and sell the meat products from most of the livestock produced by farmers, those few firms are in a position to control the price they pay for livestock, control the quality of the meat produced, and control the price of the meat products they sell.
>
> Such firms are motivated to pay the lowest possible price for farmers' livestock, produce the minimum quality meat product that consumers will accept, and charge the highest possible price for the meat products they sell. All such activities harm livestock producers.
>
> In such an environment livestock producers receive less than a competitive price for their animals, consumers receive a less than competitive quality product, and pay a more than competitive price for it. In such an environment consumers eat less meat, further harming producers because of shrinking demand.[9]

Shortly after the turn of the century five firms — Swift, Armour, Cudahy, Wilson and Morris — controlled over 60 percent of the U.S. slaughter industry. A 1916 report requested of the Federal Trade Commission (FTC) by President Woodrow Wilson and completed in 1919 showed that there was no longer competition in meat packing. The report called for severe industry restructuring.

After discussions between the U.S. Attorney General's office and lawyers for the meat packing companies, the Consent Decree of 1920 was drawn up which in effect dissolved the "Beef Trust's" monopoly of the meat packing industry. The government's petition which led to this decree indicated that the five major packers had successfully suppressed competition in *both* the purchase of livestock and in the sale of fresh meat.[10]

The following year Congress passed the Packers and Stockyards Act, which sought to restore both competition and fair trade practices to meat packing and prohibit its too few companies from diversifying into other businesses. Nevertheless, by the early 1920's the Big Five had become the Big Four as Morris merged with Armour. Soon after the passage of the P&SA an estimated 2000 packing houses were operating throughout the United States.

Immediately following World War II, at the same time small retail food stores, many with their own butcher shops, were being forced out of business by the large supermarket chains, the meatpacking industry slowly began to return to its monopolistic structure, as its new customers began the search for large and reliable suppliers.

Also, by this time most packinghouses had begun moving away from the traditional large city plants to more compact packinghouses in the Midwest, nearer

their supply of cattle and hogs. By 1969 the move toward consolidation was well under way as the figures below indicate.

By 1988, in addition to the Big Three's 70 percent market share, National Beef Packing Company and Beef-America handled another 9.3 percent among them, leaving just 20 percent of the slaughter to the rest of the nation's meat packers. If these five firms present expansion plans proceed according to schedule, by the end of 1991 they could conceivably be killing 100,000 head a day. Currently, federally inspected slaughter runs between 125,000 and 130,000 a day.[11]

National Concentration of Fed Steer and Heifer Slaughter by the Industry's Four Largest Packers

1972	27.4 percent
1977	32.3 percent
1982	44.0 percent
1986	56.0 percent
1987	68 percent

Source: Packers & Stockyards Administration

In addition to and fueling the rapid growth of IBP, Excel and Conagra during the past 30 years have been the actions of several large non-agricultural corporations which began to acquire already well-established meat packing companies in the 1960s. Subsequently, in their effort to increase the output of their packing-house divisions, and take advantage of readily identifiable brand names on processed meat products, these conglomerates began shifting production activities away from cyclical commodities and toward processed foods.

This buying spree within the industry was highlighted by Esmark's buying of Swift & Co. (now a subsidiary of Beatrice Foods, which previously had bought out Peter Eckrich), Greyhound's purchase of Armour & Co. (which, after later shutting down their own plants, sold them to ConAgra), LTV's purchase of Wilson & Co. (which in turn was later sold to United Brands, which had previously bought John Morrell), General Host's buying of Cudahy, General Foods' acquisition of Oscar Mayer and Hanson Trust's purchasing of Hygrade.

A Changing Structure

On a nationwide basis the overall corporate market shares of the cattle industry do not appear to be high. A 1988 study of slaughtered fed cattle shows IBP with 29 percent, ConAgra with 20 percent and Excel with 18 percent.[12] However, in several key geographic cattle producing regions of the United States, these large packing firms exercise their domination of the market, for today almost all packers buy 80 percent to 85 percent of the cattle they intend to slaughter within 150 miles of their own plants.[13]

Alarmed over this trend toward concentration in the cattle production and meat packing industry back in the 1960's and 70's, Representative Neal Smith, D-Iowa, and his House Small Business Committee launched a series of comprehensive hearings in 1977 which resulted in eight volumes of records and staff studies totalling more than 1900 pages.[14]

In recounting how his committee sought to determine the scope of corporate concentration in this vital segment of our food industry, Representative Smith noted:

Frankly, while we have had some indications of the scope of the problem, we had found it difficult to document and thus it became even harder to arrive at meaningful remedies. USDA had national figures available on cattle production and slaughter, but few regional details existed.

The Committee, therefore, working with USDA statistics, commissioned a study assessing regional trends toward concentration in the beef packing industry. This had never been done before and I can tell you that the results of this study are alarming...

We find, for example, that in certain areas conditions in the meat industry are ripe for large, predatory companies to almost invade a region and drive efficient competitors completely out of business. The study confirms that in certain regions of the country this is just not a healthy industry where free enterprise competitive factors determine which businesses survive.

From 1969 to 1977 the weighted average four-firm concentration for 23 fed cattle marketing states increased from 55.9 percent to 63.2 percent and has continued to increase yearly by two to three percent. In the major cattle producing regions of Iowa, Nebraska and Texas, for example, figures showed that four of the largest packing firms controlled more than 50 percent of the market. In each of 17 of the 23 fed-cattle marketing states, four firms accounted for more than 65 percent of the total steer and heifer slaughter. Two-thirds of all grade and weight purchases were in three states — Nebraska, Iowa and Colorado. And 53 percent of all carcass basis purchases of cows and bulls were in four states — Texas, Iowa, Minnesota and Wisconsin.

In 1960 nearly 40 percent of all cattle were sold directly from feedlot to packer, but by 1984 that figure skyrocketed to 90 percent.[15]

As long as packers continue to control a significant portion of the cattle supply, Smith's studies concluded, they can avoid buying cattle on the free market and thus depress livestock prices when it is to their benefit to do so.

According to a 1986 PS&A Statistical Report, 91.1 percent of the fed cattle marketed were sold directly to the packer, 5.1 percent through auction markets and 3.8 percent through terminal sales. Representative Smith has explained the potential dangers of this trend:

The way it works is that, first, the big packers get bigger. While this is happening, there's more competition for a while, and everybody benefits. Then they get the leverage to nose out others and the ones who drop out aren't necessarily the least efficient ones. Then let's say, you're an Iowa producer and you've been selling to a good, efficient packer, you find he isn't there any more. Temporarily, while the big packer has been driving the other guy out, your cattle were worth more. But then, you pay dearly because there isn't any more competition for your cattle. Packers are going out of business regularly, and it isn't all economics.

It is no surprise, therefore, that the cattle industry is becoming increasingly vertically integrated. Packers now seek to enhance their control of the cattle industry and beef production either through various forms of forward contracting for their supply of cattle or by producing their own beef for slaughter, such as Excel does through Caprock, another Cargill subsidiary.

In the summer of 1988, for example, IBP announced in addition to a contract it already had with National Farms, Inc., one of the nation's largest feeders with lots in Colorado and Kansas, that it had signed a contract with Cactus Feeders, Inc., the United States's largest cattle feeding operation with seven feedyards, a capacity of 333,000 head and annual sales of 800,000 cattle.

These acquisitions, in addition to ConAgra's 1987 purchase of Monfort of Colorado, mean that the nation's three largest packers now "raise" over one fourth of all the cattle they slaughter, or about 17 percent of all cattle slaughtered in the United States. Kevin McCullough, former IBP executive, told *Beef Today* that by 1995 he foresees 30 percent of the nation's cattle being slaughtered by the Big Three in joint ventures with feedlots.[16]

A Colorado rancher explains the impact of this trend. "Whenever the market strengthens to a certain point, they [the packers] quit buying our cattle and they kill cattle out of their own yards. Then they break the market."[17]

The USDA estimates that when packers feed their own cattle or have them custom fed, it can lower the market prices for cattle by 25-30 cents per hundredweight. An increase in cattle fed by packers can depress local prices ten times more than a similar increase in cattle marketed by independent feeders.[18]

A major study upon which Smith relied during his hearings was the "Changing Structure of the Beef Packing Industry" by Dr. Willard F. Williams, the late distinguished Professor of Agricultural Economics at Texas Tech University.

Some of the highlights of that report included:
• While IBP accounted for only 13 percent of the total U.S. steer-heifer slaughter in 1977, they more than doubled their slaughter and share of the total during 1970-1977. By 1978, it slaughtered more than twice as many steers/heifers as its nearest competitor. Later, a 1986 University of Wisconsin study showed that the mere presence of IBP in a meat marketing region reduces cattle prices by 44 cents a hundred-weight.[19]

In May 1988, before a House Judiciary subcommittee, Leonard Litvak, head of a Denver packing firm, told how he not only had been recently forced to close down his operation because two large packers so controlled his area and how at least 15 other small firms near his own had also gone out of business.

"These expansions will lead to the detriment of both cattlemen and the consumer," Litvak warned. "As competition is eliminated, the options of the cattlemen and cattle feeders become more limited and more limited."[20]

• The top four firms in the industry slaughtered one-third of the total in 1977 with seven responsible for 50 percent. Ten percent of the packers controlled 80 percent of industry total steer-heifer slaughter.

• Some regions in the United States saw extremely high degrees of concentration. They included the Pacific Northwest, the Iowa- eastern Nebraska area, Colorado, Kansas and the Texas-Oklahoma Panhandle areas. All of these areas contained plants of the "new breed" and one or more IBP plants were found in each area except Colorado.

• Those regions where no large scale plants of the "new breed" firms were found remained populated with large numbers of medium to small packing firms. California, Arizona, the eastern seaboard and the South all had low levels of concentration.

However, the construction of a long-rumored IBP plant with capacity for 600,000 head annually in Yuma, Arizona, or elsewhere in the Arizona-Southern California area would undoubtedly accelerate the drive of numerous medium to small volume firms out of business in the west. With such a new plant, many believe, the area would also experience excessive slaughtering capacity.

• Excess slaughtering capacity was a striking feature of regions characterized by high levels of packing firm concentration, especially within regions containing IBP plants.

• *Monopoly power does not always involve control of selling prices. It can involve power to influence, control or destroy competitors, possibly by controlling buying prices.*

"We are now at a point where there are some real concerns about the numbers of buyers of cattle from farmers," University of Wisconsin's Bruce Marion told *In These Times*.[21] He also has estimated that with each ten percentage point increase in concentration, farmers earn 10 cents less per hundred pounds, which in today's fragile beef market has become a crucial sum of money.[22]

Our research shows the regions that are moderately concentrated, even though they may have fairly small plants, end up paying better prices to farmers than regions with high concentration and a lack of competition. This tells me the declining competition is at least as important as cost savings through bigger plants. Maybe we'd be better off having ten plants slaughtering 100,000 head rather than three plants at 330,000.[23]

The consumer, as well as the farmer, has likewise been affected. Representative Smith noted during his investigations that of the 83.3 cents a pound increase in 1978 beef prices compared to 1969, 25 cents per pound was due entirely to increased local concentration among steer and heifer slaughtering firms. This 25 cent per pound increase showed up even after accounting for seasonal variations, the effects of inflation in labor costs, inflation in raw product prices and changes in per capita beef consumption.

In June 1984 an update of Representative Smith's earlier report revealed:

• The rate of decline in the number of firms reporting steer and heifer slaughter had doubled since 1979.

• The four largest firms slaughtering steers and heifers had moved past the point (measured by market shares) where earlier testimony had indicated they could assert monopoly power to inflate their selling prices and exert power to depress the price they pay farmers for cattle.

• In the west North Central region, which accounts for over 50 percent of the nation's steer and heifer slaughter, the concentration of economic power, as measured by market shares of the four largest firms, had reached the point where earlier committee testimony indicated control over prices charged and prices paid were at a peak.

• Since 1972, the number of firms reporting steer and heifer slaughter in Iowa has dropped by 50 percent. The market share of the four largest firms slaughtering steers and heifers in Iowa in 1982 was over 85 percent, up 18.5 percent since 1972.

• The growth in market shares and dominance by the four largest firms had been equally dramatic in other leading cattle states such as Texas, Kansas, Colorado, Idaho and Washington.

• At the state level, the top four firm's market share exceeded 90 percent in all the leading boxed beef states.

Corporate Buying Sprees

In recent years no one company has been on a more concerted buying binge within the cattle industry than ConAgra, Inc., an already giant diversified food company. With annual sales of $11.3 billion its two major divisions, ConAgra Red Meat Cos. and ConAgra Agri-Products Cos., have interests in farm chemicals, feed and fertilizer, specialty retailing, global commodity trading, grain processing, poultry, frozen prepared meals and seafood.

ConAgra's stampede to further concentrate the cattle industry began curiously in 1983 when Excel announced its plans to buy Spencer, the nation's third largest beef packer. Monfort, the nation's fifth largest beef and lamb packer and distributor with approximately ten percent of the market, successfully sued to stop the merger arguing that the combination would violate antitrust laws by creating a corporation so powerful that it would further reduce competition in the beef packing industry.

"That scares the hell out of me," cried Kenneth Monfort, the Colorado firm's president.[24] After the Colorado District Court and the Tenth Circuit Court of Appeals found the merger unlawful, Cargill appealed the case to the U.S. Supreme Court. Cargill, the world's largest grain trader contended that Monfort was merely afraid of competition and noted that the nation's anti-trust laws "were designed to protect competition, not competitors."

Not surprisingly, given its desire to rewrite anti-trust laws in favor of large corporate interests, Ronald Reagan's Justice Department, seeing this case as a possible landmark decision, filed a friend of the court brief on behalf of Cargill arguing that "the anti-trust laws would be perverted if they could be used to thwart transactions that would enhance competition."[25]

In December 1986, the U.S. Supreme Court in a 6-2 decision, which in effect approved the merger, restricted the ability of companies like Monfort to file private anti-trust suits to block competitors from merging.

The opinion by Justice William J. Brennan Jr. held that "the antitrust laws do not require the courts to protect small businesses from the loss of profits due to continued competition, but only against the loss of profits from practices forbidden by the antitrust laws."[26] The kind of competition that Monfort alleged in *Cargill Inc. v. Monfort of Colorado Inc.*, Brennan continued "competition for increased market share, is not activity forbidden by the antitrust laws. It is simply vigorous competition."

Justice John Paul Stevens and Justice Byron R. White dissented from the majority, contending that the effect of the court's ruling ran counter to what Congress intended in allowing private companies to use antitrust laws to maintain a competitive marketplace.

Given the statutory purposes to protect small businesses and to stem the rising tide of concentration in particular markets, a competitor trying to stay in business in a changing market must have standing to ask a court to set aside a merger that has changed the character of the market in an illegal way.[27]

It took only three months after the Court's decision for Monfort to announce that it had signed a letter of intent to merge with ConAgra Inc. Based in Greeley, the giant beef packer soon became but one more subsidiary of this new major force in corporate agribusiness.

As one industry publication described it:

With half of Swift [Swift Independent Packing Co. - SIPCO], ConAgra is number two in boxed beef with over $4 billion in annual sales. With the purchase of the remainder of Swift, ConAgra will likely eclipse IBP. When all of ConAgra's meat and poultry holdings are considered, ConAgra is number one.[28]

Indeed, in July, 1989 ConAgra exercised its option to buy the remaining 50 percent of SIPCO for $51.5 million, thus boosting ConAgra's Red Meat Cos. annual sales to $7.5 billion in 1989.[29] Subsequently, in June 1990, ConAgra announced it was purchasing Beatrice Inc. from Kohlberg Kravis Roberts & Co. for $1.34 billion. The sale, which solidified ConAgra's position as

the nation's second largest food processor behind Philip Morris, also placed 15 percent of ConAgra's stock in the KKR "long-term investment" portfolio.

The previously "scared" Kenneth Monfort, who would become president of ConAgra's Red Meat Companies after the Monfort merger, had no trouble in quickly rationalizing his earlier concentration fears.

I thought at the time that it was going to lead to too much concentration — to two-firm concentration. Of course, we fought that all the way through the Supreme Court, and the Supreme Court said we were wrong. So that changed my mind a little. But, in addition to that, it seemed to me that if the industry was going to be concentrated there should be at least three large players instead of just two.

I think three-firm concentration at this level assures the public and producers of adequate competition.[30]

Earlier, in September 1987, ConAgra had purchased a 50 percent interest in Swift Independent Holding Company, the parent company of SIPCO and Val-Agri, Inc. for approximately $51.5 million in cash. The remaining 50 percent was acquired by Elkhorn Enterprises, Inc, based in Elkhorn, Nebraska and owned by Bob Gottsch.[31]

A relative newcomer to the industry, Val-Agri had previously sought unsuccessfully to purchase Swift Independent in 1985 for $135 million. Val-Agri, a subsidiary of Valley View Holdings Inc., was principally owned by Dallas' Edwin L. Cox Jr., the 39-year old son of one of the nation's richest independent oil men. Within a year after it was first organized Val-Agri had an annual processing capacity of over five percent of the total U.S. fed-beef kill. Most of its executives had been hired *en masse* from Excel, the Cargill subsidiary.

Valley View also operated several large Texas feedlots which occasioned a Packers and Stockyards Administration administrator to comment shortly after the firm was inaugurated,

We're well aware that Valley View feeds cattle along with owning a packing firm, but the mere existence of this situation isn't new, and it isn't a violation of our regulations. Only if the two are arranged and operated in a way that restrains competition would we be involved.[32]

After his unsuccessful effort to purchase Swift Independent, Cox formed a partnership, CHS Holding II Inc., which in 1986 accomplished a $135 million leveraged buyout of Swift. In addition to controlling the partnership Cox, according to *The Wall Street Journal*, was "one of the three largest beef packers and the largest pork packers in the country."

Cox also had major feedlot interests and was often one of the largest holders of cattle futures positions.[33] By 1986 the Swift Independent Holding Company had been formed when SIPCO and Val-Agri, Inc. were merged by Cox.

But, by mid-1986 Cox had attracted considerable notoriety when Interfirst Corp., a large southwestern energy lender, attributed part of a $340 - $365 million charge against second quarter earnings to a $80 million line of credit to board member Cox. News of the controversial loan quickly created uncertainty in the cattle futures market and a two-day rally in prices abruptly ended.[34]

Later, in June 1988 Cox plead guilty to violating federal banking laws relating to the loan. Cox admitted he had exaggerated the number of cattle he possessed as collateral for loans he had used to finance his agribusiness interests. Cox was subsequently sentenced to six months in prison, a $250,000 fine and 1,000 hours of community service. Explaining why he was imposing the maximum penalty U.S. District court Judge Joe Fish told Cox that he was one of the few individuals "to appear in my court with the wherewithal to pay such a fine."[35]

Number One And "A Corporate Outlaw"

Although ConAgra and Excel have challenged it for the industry's leadership, the dominant force in cattle slaughtering and meat packing for the past two decades remains Iowa Beef Processors, Inc., headquartered in Dakota City, Nebraska, and until September 1991 was 51 percent owned by Occidental Petroleum Corp.

In 1989 IBP had sales of $9.13 billion with net earnings of $35.3 million. Its working capital in 1987 was $210.4 million, down $67.9 million from 1986.[36] In 1988 its ten beef plants in eight states slaughtered and processed some 9.6 million grain-fed cattle of which over 75 percent were used in its boxed beef-program. Four pork plants in two states slaughtered and processed a record 2.68 million hogs in the first quarter of 1989, as compared with 2.3 million for the same period in 1988.[37] It also began marketing products in the European Common Market and the Far East.

Despite this preeminence for many cattle ranchers and labor unions today IBP stands as a modern-day corporate agribusiness "robber baron."

Within the beef packing industry IBP is looked upon by some as "a laggard in the widespread move to create brand identity around beef."[38] Unlike other major packers, IBP has been selling its beef unbranded to supermarkets, who retail it under their own label. Faced with this challenge IBP began in early 1988 to develop branded beef products, although it claimed that it was not about to rush into markets until it had satisfied itself that a product had good shelf life, cost, and convenience. "Adding value isn't wrapping cellophane around a piece of meat and sticking a gummed label on it," according to IBP's CEO Robert L. Peterson.[39]

Herbert Meischen, Excel's marketing vice-president, disagrees. "To say cake mixes are great just doesn't have the impact of Betty Crocker saying *my* cake mixes are great. The manufacturer is going to have to take the lead or it won't sell."[40]

However, according to the *Wall Street Journal*'s Marj Charlier industry analysts believe that just as IBM waited for the personal computer market to be estab-

lished by others, IBP is big enough to move if a branded-beef market is established.[41]

In the years IBP has grown from a fledgling company to an industry giant, however, there has been the more serious and growing alarm over many of its business practices. It was former Arizona governor Bruce Babbitt who, during the 1988 Iowa Democratic presidential caucuses, branded IBP a "corporate outlaw," singling it out as

a monument to everything shabby and backwards and wrong in the American economy — not only because the company lies and cheats, but because it believes its employees are the problem and not the solution.[42]

It was in September 1977 that a revealing confidential report to the USDA by the National Economic Research Associates, Inc. (NERA), a private consultant firm, warned that IBP's business practices would enable the firm "to exert monopoly power and be in a position to manipulate price" both in the purchase of live cattle and in beef sales.

The NERA and some USDA staff reports later obtained by *The Des Moines Register* also focused on IBP's practice of buying carcass beef from other packing companies which ostensibly were competing with Iowa Beef. Such purchasing, according to one USDA staff analyst, "effectively circumvents" a 1970 federal court action prohibiting IBP from acquiring additional meat packing companies in Iowa, Nebraska, Minnesota and South Dakota.

The practice of buying processed beef from its competitors, the analyst added, "has the same anti-competitive effect on the supply market (live cattle) and in the wholesale market (meat) as a merger that would have been proscribed under federal antitrust laws."[43]

These practices and others led the House Small Business Committee in 1979 to file a brief with the U.S. Court of Appeals in St. Louis, Missouri, stating that it had documents which "show significant, deliberate and repeated violations of this nation's civil and criminal laws by IBP" and that "these violations have resulted in the loss of millions of dollars to the customers and competitors of IBP."[44] Many of the documents were later made public in Congressman Smith's Committee investigation of the structure of the meat industry.

Recalling his early days as an IBP packer buyer, Walt Hackney, now coordinating the National Farmer Organization's livestock forward-contracting program, told *Beef Today* that,

Iowa Beef was really aggressive. We drove green cars and used green pencils because green was the color of money. The symbolism was not lost on the cattlemen: When Iowa Beef drove in, it was bringing money to the farm.

When I left the packing industry in 1974, I knew that I had helped all but destroy a lot of farmer-feeders. The big packers were making a lot of money, but the farmers weren't getting any of it. I felt it was completely needless for farmers to lose all that money just because they couldn't compete with me as a marketer.[45]

Smith's committee had obtained the aforementioned IBP documents following a series of legal maneuvers involving federal courts in Texas and Iowa, with the papers having been taken from IBP by Hughes Bagley, a former company vice-president. "The Bagley documents," the Committee's brief stated, "could also expose past and present high corporate officials of IBP to felony criminal charges for violations of anti-trust laws."[46]

Retaliating, IBP's president Peterson wrote to Smith charging that Bagley, who had been fired by the company in 1975, had perjured himself in Committee testimony; Peterson especially disputed Bagley's description of IBP's early 70's pricing policies.[47]

Bagley in turn sued IBP in 1982 for libel and was subsequently awarded an $8.8 million judgment by a Federal Court jury.

A Labyrinth of Corporate Power

In 1987, 49 percent of the stock in Iowa Beef Processors was sold to the "public" by Occidental Petroleum, saddling the company with $400 million in long-term debt compared with the $81 million in similar debt that it held six years earlier when the giant oil and gas company had acquired it.[48]

Prior to its takeover by Occidental in 1981, however, Iowa Beef Processors' corporate power was solidly interlocked in a labyrinth of economic decision-making and corporate ownership.

The largest single block of the company's stock (18 percent) was held by the California-based Pacific Holding Corp. In addition to controlling IBP, Pacific Holding owned the International Mining Corp., which at the time controlled the largest block of stock in Union Oil Co. of California, and was the second largest stockholder in the Chicago, Rock Island & Pacific Railroad Co.

Pacific Holding Corp., is a wholly-owned private company held by David Murdock of Los Angeles, California, who previously had made millions off a multitude of real estate deals. In that process, Murdock had acquired a personal fortune estimated at $600 million, principally by taking over firms with undervalued assets. When Occidental bought IBP for $800 million, Murdock became the $15.5 billion petroleum conglomerate's single largest stock-holder (4.6 percent).

In fact, as IBP's leadership spoke of the "benefits" that the company's thousands of shareholders would derive from the Oxy sale, three corporate executives Robert L. Peterson, Dale C. Tinstman, and Perry V. Haines, collected a reported $5.6 million. Murdock reportedly made a $35.2 million gain from the sale.[49]

For its part, Occidental was very clear about its intent in purchasing IBP, noting that the move reflected a "logical and deliberate strategy for the 1990's." The company, already involved in fertilizer production and feed supplements, saw the coming years as ones short of food and energy and declared that "Oxy wants to be a significant factor in both."[50]

In 1984, after a feud with long-time friend Oxy chairman Armand Hammer, Murdock sold his holdings to Hammer for a $100 million plus profit.

Since that time another Murdock enterprise, Flexi-Van Corp., has merged with Castle & Cooke, the giant agribusiness firm which now owns Dole food products and other vast agribusiness and real estate holdings in Hawaii and California, including the Bud Antle Corp., one of the world's largest grower-shippers of lettuce.

Besides those individual members of IBP management who held sizeable blocks of company stock prior to its purchase by Oxy, other institutional investors included the National Bank of Commerce Trust and Savings Association and Republic of Texas Corp.

At the same time Republic of Texas Corp was also the single largest stockholder of such agribusiness giants as Safeway Stores Inc. (6.3 percent); Tenneco, Inc. (5.71 percent); the fifth largest stockholder of Southland Corp. (2.15 percent) and Tropicana (3.57 percent), later to become a subsidiary of Beatrice Foods, and Anderson Clayton (.58 percent), later purchased in 1986 by Quaker Oats Co.

Doing Business With "The Cartel"

Typical of the tactics IBP has used in mobilizing its corporate power to gain near monopoly control in the beef packing industry is the way it moved into the Pacific Northwest.

In December 1976 IBP announced that it had purchased Columbia Foods Inc. in the region's Mid-Columbia Basin. By April 1978 it had completed a $14 million expansion project at the plant's Wallula, Washington facility.

Financing for this operation came in part from a $30 million revolving credit and loan agreement IBP negotiated in 1976 with 12 banks, including Citibank ($10 million), Chase Manhattan ($3.25 million), Continental Illinois ($3.25 million), Crocker National ($3.25), First National Bank of Minneapolis ($2.5 million), and five other financial institutions ($7.25 million).

In its 1977 annual report IBP discussed its decision to move into the Pacific Northwest in terms of "a sizeable unrealized potential" in the region for producers, fabricators and markets.

An even and dependable availability of cattle is an essential element in the efficient operation of a modern beef slaughter/processing factory. Such a flow permits better plant utilization by spreading overhead expense over a larger volume of production, thus reducing unit cost.

To ensure "an even and dependable availability of cattle" IBP soon signed a five-year joint venture agreement with Northwest Feeders, Inc., a "cooperative" comprised of six large feedlots in the area headed not so coincidentally by Bob Kemp, one of the founders of IBP.

"The Cartel," as it became known to many Pacific Northwest cattle ranchers, immediately began to supply IBP's Columbia Foods with thousands of head of cattle each week. Close examination of this "Cartel" reveals a side of corporate agribusiness that normally escapes public attention and provides a glimpse of how intricate, tightly controlled, and interlocked the corporations and individuals that produce and manufacture our food have become.[51]

Largest of the feedlots in IBP's joint venture was the McGregor Feedlots, a subsidiary of McGregor Land and Livestock Co., which at the time kept about 45,000 head of cattle on hand year round. John McGregor, the Company's president, also served on the board of directors of Pacific Power and Light and the Seattle First National Bank. William McGregor, the Company's Vice-President, served as a member of the board of governors on the Chicago Mercantile Exchange.

Sitting with McGregor on the Seattle First National Bank board at the time was also a board member from the Burlington Northern railroad company. McGregor's other corporate affiliation, Pacific Power and Light, was also the second largest stockholder of Burlington Northern, a large landowner in the Pacific Northwest leasing thousands of acres for cattle grazing.

The Garst Company, another large Midwest cattle and agricultural operation, solidified still another interlock. Its manager, Mary Garst, sat on the board of directors of International Harvester, Burlington Northern, Northwestern Bell Telephone and the Federal Reserve Bank of Chicago. Another member of the Garst family and a fellow board member also served as an IBP director.

The second largest feedlot involved with Northwest Feeders Inc. was the Simplot Feedlots in Idaho. Its president, J.R. Simplot, whose personal wealth is estimated at $660 million,[52] in addition to owning one of the world's largest privately-held multinational corporations, served on the board of directors of First Security Corp. of Salt Lake City, Utah, a bank very closely allied with the Mormon Church. Simplot's potato operations alone reportedly supplies the McDonald's chain with seven out of every ten french fries its customers consume.

With Simplot on the First Security board were five directors from Amalgamated Sugar; one from American Crystal Sugar; three from U & I Sugar (owned by the Mormon Church), including Continental Grain's Clarence Palmby; one from Consolidated Freightways; and three from the Union Pacific Corp., another giant Western railroad with large land holdings.

In turn, the latter railroad's largest single stockholder was Equitable Life Assurance Society of the United States, which also had two members of its board of directors sitting on the Burlington Northern board.

Evaluating his "Cartel's" agreement with IBP, John McGregor saw the area's cattle market simply being stabilized by the pact. "We have a more reliable week-to-week demand for feeder cattle ... without the agreement we tend to yo-yo the inventory." Other Northwest cattle ranchers, however, angrily disagreed with the Oregon businessman.[53]

Harold Cox, President of the Washington Cattleman's Association and a Pasco, Washington rancher and owner of a 40,000 acre operation, pointed out:

Initially, we were pleased to see Iowa Beef come to our part of the country. But the first thing they did was sign up these six big feedlots. These feeders aren't going to be competing with each other in the marketplace, because any of them that offers a premium price [to cattle raisers] is cutting the profits of all of them.[54]

Art Schuster, a sixth-generation Ellensburg, Washington rancher with 30,000 acres told a *Wall Street Journal* reporter: "There's no question about it. If I had only one outlet to sell my cattle and [that outlet] is Iowa Beef, they'll tell me what I'm going to be paid."[55]

At the time of IBP's initial push into the Pacific Northwest and its attempts to expand its operations in the western United States, many believed that the nation's largest meat packer sought to break into the lucrative California market.

While California had a near 10 percent share of the total U.S. population, its per capita consumption was about 30 percent higher than the national average. Long in the midst of a crisis, the California meat industry saw the very survival of its few remaining small packing plants and cattle feeding business at stake.

According to a survey by the Western States Meat Packers Association (WSMPA) some 129 plants in California, Idaho, Oregon, and Washington, where approximately 85 percent of the total number of beef slaughterers are members of the WSMPA, shut their doors between 1970 and 1980. The state also saw 50 percent of its WSMPA members go out of business during this same period.

It was also shortly after IBP entered into the Pacific Northwest's cattle and beef packing industry, that feedlot operator M.L. Monson of Selah, Washington, observed "we don't quarrel with the Mafia associations or the idea of boxed beef. What we are quarreling with is this arrangement is like General Motors and U.S. Steel combining. It's un-American."[56]

Monson's reference to the Mafia, however, is serious, and only one of the many such controversies that have surrounded IBP's growth.

Striking a Mood

By far the darkest chapter in IBP's history came in the early 1970's with the conviction of the late C.J. Holman, then board co-chairman, for conspiring with a Mafia figure to bribe the company's way into the world's largest meat market — the New York City metropolitan area — through a series of kick-back payments to both union officials and supermarket executives.

In *Vicious Circles: The Mafia in the Marketplace*, a remarkable piece of investigative journalism, former *Wall Street Journal* reporter Jonathan Kwitny, describes this "anatomy of a bribe."

Iowa Beef, though founded only in 1961, already in 1970 dominated the meat industry the way few other industries are dominated by anyone. Since then, in partnership with [Moe] Steinman and his family and friends, Iowa Beef has grown more dominant still. It was as if the Mafia had moved into the automobile industry by summoning the executive committee of General Motors, or the computer industry by summoning the heads of IBM, or the oil industry by bringing Exxon to its knees. Moe Steinman and the band of murderers and thugs he represented had effectively kidnapped a giant business. Its leaders were coming to pay him the ransom, a ransom that turned out to be both enormous and enduring.[57]

He continues,

As a result of the meeting in the darkened suite at the Stanhope Hotel [in New York City] that day in 1970, Iowa Beef would send millions of dollars to Steinman and his family under an arrangement that continued at least until 1978. After the meeting millions more would go to a life-long pal of Steinman and his Mafia friends, a man who had gone to prison for using slimy, diseased meat in filling millions of dollars in orders [by bribing meat inspectors] and wound up on Iowa Beef's board of directors.

Consequent to the meeting in the Stanhope Hotel, Iowa Beef would reorganize its entire marketing apparatus to allow Steinman's organization complete control over the company's largest market and influence over its operations coast-to-coast. In 1975, Iowa Beef would bring Moe Steinman's son-in-law and protege to its headquarters near Sioux City to run the company's largest division and throw his voice into vital corporate decisions.

But, most important, a mood would be struck in the Stanhope that day — a mood of callous disregard for decency and the law. Iowa Beef would proceed to sell its butcher employees out to the Teamsters Union, to turn its trucking operations over to Mafia-connected manipulators, and to play fast and loose with anti-trust laws.[58]

Kwitny concludes,

Because of their hold on Iowa Beef, the racketeers' control of other segments of the meat industry would expand and harden. And as a result of all this, the price of meat for the American consumer — the very thing Currier Holman had done so much to reduce — would rise. Meyer Lansky once said that the Syndicate was bigger than U.S. Steel. When Iowa Beef Processors caved in on that April day in 1970, the Syndicate, as far as the meat industry was concerned, *became* U.S. Steel.[59]

Boxed Beef

A major factor in IBP's ability to reach its number one position in the meat packing industry has been its perfecting of the technology of converting cattle into "boxed beef." In 1979 boxed beef accounted for 44 percent of all fed steers and heifers slaughtered. Six years later, based on P&SA data, it was 77 percent.

Meanwhile, according to May 1988 testimony by Professor Marion before a House judiciary subcommittee, the four largest firms which accounted for 60 percent of the box beef sales in 1979, increased their market share to an estimated 82 percent in 1987.[60] It has also been estimated that IBP alone may well control 35-40 percent of the nation's boxed beef market.

Representative Smith's committee heard testimony from the USDA in 1979 suggesting that while 90 percent of the beef bought by the nation's largest grocery chains would soon be in box form, the so-called increased "efficiencies" of boxing and portion control were nevertheless retained by the controlling corporations, which ultimately resulted in losses for both producers and consumers.

To underscore his point Smith pointed to a study by the FTC's Dr. Russell Parker that concluded if national brand-name advertising of boxed beef products became a reality the monopoly overcharges to consumers could range from $133 million to $178 million in 1979 dollars.[61]

The boxed beef process, pioneered by IBP, sees the carcass cut up in the packing plant and delivered in vacuum-sealed bags to wholesalers/supermarkets. The wholesalers and retailers, therefore, do not have to maintain staffs of butchers to divide carcasses into smaller cuts, but rather a staff of "meat managers," a process which has not only led to the disappearance of many butchers, but also seriously undermined their pay scale.

The box beef phenomenon, while encouraging increased concentration in the cattle and meat packing industry, has also led to less diversified, less stable and environmentally unsound farming practices. Meanwhile, cattle raising and slaughtering has shifted to the Great Plains where most cattle are now raised in giant feedlot operations.

Many of these large feedlots scattered around the nation are now using land for feed crops that should not have been plowed up in the first place. In the areas where they operate, they have badly depleted the groundwater supply and created serious waste management problems. Yet for many of their owners they have become a modern day financial bonanza.

In 1988 the U.S. cattle herd was at a 26-year low, a severe summer drought had raised the feeding of steers by $75, according to Gene Futrell, an Iowa State economist. For cattle-feeding investors, when prices for feed and feeder cattle (steers and heifers about to enter the feedlots from the range) are low and prices for slaughter cattle (animals about to leave the feedlots) are high, such as they were throughout the mid-1980's, returns can be rewarding. *Forbes* reports that Fort Morgan, Colorado-based Agritech investors, who put together cattle-feeding partnerships for Drexel Burnham, put up $100 per head for an animal and borrowed the remaining $600 it took to bring a heifer/steer to its 1,100-pound slaughter weight.[62]

Prior to the 1988 drought, according to Agritech's manager Gary Weisbart, "we've made as much as $55 per head over the previous three years." After tax annual revenues have been as high as 80 percent due to investor's leverage and ability to turn over their investment 2.5 times per year. It is not uncommon to see feedlot owners during such prosperous times owning as much as 30 percent of the cattle in their own feedlots.[63]

When feed and feeder cattle prices rise, however, and slaughter prices drop as they did in 1988, investors can lose as much as $150 a steer. While feedlot owners usually reduce their ownership during such times, they still remain in a position to make money, charging outside investors $35 a head to feed and fatten the cattle in their feedlots. Thus, in both good and bad times the large feedlot owner prospers.

"Sure, it's chaotic," says William (Bill) Haw, president and chief executive of National Farms, Inc., "but chaos is our favorite environment."[64]

Haw also admits that National may even decide at some future date, if the price is right, to sell their farms and feedlots, while still leaving the company with over 100,000 acres of ranchland. The reasoning is that if food shortages should develop in the next decade National could reap lucrative financial rewards from such land, such as it did in 1981 when it sold 40,000 corn-growing acres to Prudential Insurance Co. at top-of-the-market prices.[65]

Taking all these factors into account, it is no wonder that one study of the boxed beef phenomena concluded that it is not much more of an efficient way to market beef than the more traditional methods of merchandising, except where the product must be transported over long distances.

"Thus, the shift westward," as David Moberg reasons in *In These Times*, "and encouragement of large-scale farmers or commercial feedlots that could deliver many hundreds of cattle of uniform size at one time — was not only encouraged by the IBP-style packers but also gave them a further advantage."[66]

That "advantage" and who will ultimately benefit from it has been called into question by many, including Texas Tech's Professor Williams. IBP and Excel, he once observed,

> have brought more efficient methods and have forced their industry to become more efficient. But from the standpoint of competitive pricing, the situation is already deteriorating. The best of all worlds just isn't there. They may reduce costs in the short run, but they're getting to be in a better position to retain those cost savings rather than pass them onto consumers, and they're going to be in a position to do more independent manipulation of the retail price.

371

Chapter Thirty-Four

Hogging the Market

"In the end, farmers will receive lower prices for their cattle and consumers will pay higher prices for their beef products."

It is inescapable that any analysis of the growing concentration of the cattle industry that does not seriously heed late U.S. Senator Edward Zorinsky's, D-Neb. warning is well on the path to condoning economic chaos.

Examining the recent huge price spread between what ranchers have been receiving for their cattle and what consumers pay for the finished product confirm Zorinsky's fear. Comparing the noticeable percentage changes at each level from 1978-1988 vividly illustrate who pays and who profits in today's cattle industry. (See Chart 34A)

These latest available figures, culled from USDA and United Food and Commercial Workers Union (UFCW) reports, show that while output per man hours in packinghouses rose between 1980-1982 and 1986-1988 from 141.9 pounds to 154.6 pounds, a nine percent *increase*, the average hourly wage decreased from $8.98 in 1982 to $8.48 in 1988, a *decrease* of nearly six percent. At the same time the average retail price of red meat per pound went from $2.14 in 1982 to $2.58 in 1988, an *increase* of 21 percent.

Examining the price spreads of both beef and pork (See Chart 34B) between 1978 and the end of 1988, we see that the farm to carcass spread *dropped* by 20.7 percent in beef and rose only eight percent in pork while the spread between the middleman and the retailer skyrocketed 63.7 percent in beef and 140 percent in pork. Meanwhile, retail prices in beef showed over a 41.7 percent rise and pork registered a 26.5 percent rise. These inequities of meat pricing nationally were also the subject of hearings before Representative Neal Smith's 1978 Small Business Committee.[1]

The prices of most meat moving from producer to consumer are based on quotes from the daily publication: *The Yellow Sheet*, published by the National Provisioner Inc. of Chicago. First published in 1923, *The Yellow Sheet* is the most popular of the market news services despite the fact that it provides less information than the others. A primary function of publications like *The Yellow Sheet* is to provide meat dealers with information for determining so-called formula prices.

Formula pricing is an agreement between the buyer and seller to do business on a specified future date based on a price published at that time by a market news service — most likely *The Yellow Sheet*. The remaining sales are negotiated, meaning prices are set in bargaining on the open market. However, as Representative Smith's committee report stresses,

While "formula pricing" through use of *The Yellow Sheet* seemed to be just another evolution in the efficient marketing of meat, this practice has grown to the extent where today 70 percent to 90 percent of all meat trading is done on the basis of prices reported by *The Yellow Sheet*. The ever-increasing number of negotiated trades reported to and by *The Yellow Sheet* has deteriorated to the extent that today there exists a relatively small number of open market negotiated trades [less than 15 percent] which may be establishing the pricing system for the entire industry — a case of the tail wagging the dog.

Critics of *The Yellow Sheet* charge it is not regulated by any government agency and that there are no legal requirements that prices reported to it be accurate or that it report an accurate market. Thus, persons reporting sales or purchases of beef to it reveal only those trades that will benefit their own economic position and enable them to manipulate the market more effectively. Representative Smith's committee studies reveal that approximately 80 percent of the beef and pork prices reported by *The Yellow Sheet* during a 25-day sample period were not supported by entries on the publication's reporter's worksheet.[2]

Aware of these many attacks on *The Yellow Sheet*, the USDA beginning in 1986 through its Market News Service, established the *Blue Sheet*. Designed only as a "basis" for current meat pricing, the *Blue Sheet* collects price information daily, all day and unlike *The Yellow Sheet*, which reports only the *closing* price each day, the USDA publication reports a price based on the *daily range* — a weighted average price.

"We have never promoted the use of our reports as a trading base," according to MNS's chief Jim Ray, adding also that a portion of the meat packing industry still uses *The Yellow Sheet* for their pricing information.

Between 800-1,100 carlots a week (40,000 pounds per carlot) of the now popular fabricated box beef cuts serve as the basis for the *Blue Sheet*'s price determination. Beginning in June, 1990 price information, however, based on carcass weight was no longer collected by the USDA service.

Chart 34A: Producer and Consumer Loss Estmates, Cattle, Hogs, Beef Pork and Processed Meats, 1978-1987 (in billions of dollars)[*]

	Potential Cash Receipts Sale of Cattle[a]	Producer Loss to Lower Cattle Prices[b]	Potential Cash Receipts Sale of Hogs[c]	Potential Producer Loss to Lower Hog Prices[c]	Consumer Loss to Monopoly Overcharge Beef[d]	Monopoly Overcharge Pork Processed Meats[e]
1978	$28.2	$0.52	$ 8.8	$0.16	$0.16	$0.19
1979	35.0	0.65	9.0	0.17	0.17	0.21
1980	31.8	0.59	8.9	0.16	0.19	0.23
1981	29.5	0.55	9.8	0.18	0.20	0.25
1982	29.8	0.55	10.7	0.20	0.21	0.27
1983	28.7	0.53	9.8	0.18	0.22	0.28
1984	30.7	0.57	9.7	0.18	0.22	0.29
1985	29.1	0.54	9.0	0.17	0.22	0.30
1986	28.9	0.53	9.7	0.18	0.23	0.30
1987	33.8	0.63	10.3	0.19	0.24	0.32
TOTAL POTENTIAL LOSS	$5.7	$1.8	$2.1	$2.6		

(a) *Agricultural Statistics*, USDA, pg. 265.

(b) John M. Connor, "Concentration Issues in the U.S. Beef Subsector," *Competitive Issues in the Beef Sector*, Hubert H. Humphrey Institute of Public Affairs, University of Minnesota, October, 1989, pg. 89. Potential loss is calculated using 1.85 percent of cash receipts.

(c) *Agricultural Statistics*, USDA, 1988, pg. 276.

(d) Neal Smith, M.C., (1981) "The Monopoly Component in Food Prices," *Journal of Law Reform*, University of Michigan (14:149-172) See pg. 164. The 1979 estimate of potential consumer loss due to monopoly overcharge in beef is inflated by the Consumer Price Index as used by D. Gale Johnson in "Competitive Position of Beef in the U.S. Meat Sector," *Competitive Issues in the Beef Sector*, Hubert H. Humphrey Institute of Public Affairs, University of Minesota, October 1989, pg. 31-33.

(e) Based on an estimated 1975 overcharge of 1.15 percent of the value of shipments, inflated by the Consumer Price Index for 1978-1987. See Russell Parker and John Connor (1979), "Estimates of Consumer Loss Due to Monopoly in the U.S. Food Manufacturing Industries," *American Journal of Agricultural Economics*, (61:626-639).

[*] Chart taken from "The Impacts of Increasing Concentration in the Meat Industry," by John W. Helmuth. Presented to the Western organization of Resource Councils, Public Education Forum, Indianapolis, Indiana, April 6, 1990.

Over 100 packers and retail chains ofvarying size, according to USDA, are sampled each day so that both buyer and seller prices are factored into each of the *Blue Sheet*'s reports. The reported load, weight, and price are then fed into a computer by some ten MNS reporters.

Although no individual trades are divulged, Ray acknowledges that the reporters sometimes keep written records on various trades during the day so as to track daily price variations, however, these records are destroyed at the end of each day.

"We don't maintain anything that can identify a buyer or seller or what he got for his product," Ray pointed out in a telephone interview with the author.

In further efforts to diminish reliance on a publication like *The Yellow Sheet* establishment of a national electronic marketing system has also been recommended in the past. One system considered was a Chicago firm's that would link buyers and sellers to a central computer through portable terminals. A seller's offer would be flashed immediately to all buyers connected to the system. The information would include weight, quality grade and yield grade of the meat in terms understandable to all trading participants.

Bids would be flashed to the seller, who would complete the transaction electronically in minutes. Then, the price at which a sale was completed would be available nationally so that other buyers and sellers could gauge actual market conditions.

The cattle and meat packing industry's attitude toward such a system was revealed when a report advocating a similar system was produced by a USDA economist, Ralph Johnson of Lincoln, Nebraska, in 1979. It immediately became embroiled in controversy within the USDA.[3] IBP attacked Johnson's report even before its official publication claiming it was "immediately recognized as being biased in favor of electronic marketing and designed more for its attention-getting content than its objective and scholarly analysis ..."[4]

Johnson, in turn, charged IBP with "defaming" him and argued that the opposition by the Company and others within USDA was "due primarily to the anticipated reaction of industry people such as [Robert] Peterson [president of IBP], who has prospered under the present

Chart 34B: Farm to Carcass to Retail Spreads Based on Cents per Pound

	1978	1979	1980	1982	1984	1986		1987	1988
Beef									
Farm to Carcass	8.2	9.7 +18.3%	10.4 +7.2%	10.2 -1.9%	7.6 -25.4%	8.7 +14.5%		7.4 -14.9%	6.5 -12.2
Carcass to Retail	62.6	75.8 +21.1%	82.2 +8.4%	91.8 +11.7%	92.0 unch.	97.6 +6.1%		97.2 -.04%	102.5 +5.5%
Total Spread	70.8	85.5 +20.7%	92.6 +8.3%	102.0 +10.1%	99.6 -2.3%	106.3 +6.7%		104.6 -1.6%	109.0 +4.2%
Retail Price	181.9	226.3 +25.8%	237.6 +5.0%	242.5 +2.1%	239.6 -1.2%	230.7 -3.7%		242.5 +5.1%	257.8 +6.3%
Pork									
Farm to Carcass	31.1	33.8 +8.6%	34.8 +2.9%	3.8 -2.9%	32.7 -3.2%	28.5 -12.8%		30.3 +6.3%	33.6 +10.9%
Carcass to Retail	35.9	43.7 21.7%	41.4 -5.2%	53.6 +29.5%	51.9 -3.2%	67.5 +30.1%		75.4 +11.7%	85.8 +13.8%
Total Spread	77.5	76.2 +15.7%	87.4 -1.7%	84.6 +14.7%	96.0 -3.2%	105.7 +13.5%		119.4 +10.1%	114.0 +13.0%
Retail Price	143.6	144.1 +.3%	139.4 -3.2%	175.4 +25.8%	162.0 -7.6%	178.4 +10.1%		188.4 +5.6%	181.6 -3.6%

Source: U.S. Department of Agriculture

system and would like to keep things just as they are."[5]

Representative Berkley Bedell, D-Iowa, added fuel to the fire by noting that after studying the matter for several months he discovered that Johnson's superiors in Washington at the USDA first attempted to release — under Johnson's name — a "distorted" version of his report, which would have been much more favorable to the beef packing industry. In a letter to then USDA Secretary Bob Bergland, Representative Bedell charged:

My investigation of Dr. Johnson's situation has uncovered further cases which could be construed as research "tampering" apparently catalyzed by individual administrators' concern for the potential political ramifications of a report's conclusions. I find such a possibility extremely disturbing ... [6]

Charles Jennings, chief of the USDA's Packers and Stockyards Administration, also had opposed the public release of Johnson's report, claiming that "the industry would not accept" such a system.[7] In a memorandum to Dr. Johnson's superiors, Jennings recommended that

the proper forum, *if any there be*, for discussion of [his] recommendation would be within the industry, either at some annual convention of producer organizations or some industry symposium, where the regulatory authority is *invited* to give its view on this subject.[8] (emphasis added)

After such statements it came as no surprise that Jennings, a former Washington lobbyist for the American Stock Yard Association and former president of the Kansas City Stockyards Company, shortly after the controversy announced his resignation from his USDA post to accept a position as vice president in charge of public affairs for IBP.

The Supermarket Spread

Glenn Freie of the Meat Price Investigators Association (MPIA), a legal-action group formed by over 500 cattle feeders throughout the United States, recounts the events of the 1970s which many ranchers believe led to the current pricing situation in the meat industry.

Early in 1973, beef prices were relatively high, but by fall *The Yellow Sheet* began reporting a steady drop in the wholesale price (which by simple formula becomes the cattle price).

Even while the wholesale price dropped precipitously, the retail price paid by the consumer remained at record highs. And even as the cattle price remained low for the next four years, the supermarkets' margin or spread increased threefold. One has to admit that the "buying agent for the consumer" was taking a healthy commission.

Neither the consumer nor the producer caused the price break of 1973; it was caused by those who controlled the price mechanism by their concerted power — the supermarkets with the aid of the packers. The short term result was a severe recession, particularly in the cattle industry, and the more recent result has been a dramatic increase in the consumer price of beef.[9]

One example of how large retail food chains and major beef packers manipulate the market came to light during MPIA's legal action against the four top beef packers for price fixing.

Iowa Beef Processors filed an affidavit by its head cattle buyer for the purpose of exonerating itself. What the affidavit actually revealed, however, was that IBP rigidly adhered to *The Yellow Sheet* carcass price in buying cattle.

Further MPIA study showed that IBP was also rigidly adhering to *The Yellow Sheet* in selling processed beef.[10] IBP's chief concern appeared to be that its buyers accurately determine the yield and quality grade of the cattle. Before 1973 cattle prices had been climbing upward toward 100 percent of parity, however, after 1973 they plummeted to a point where in 1985 they stood at 50.5 percent of parity.

With cattle numbers the lowest since the 1960's," according to George Levin, board chairman of the Independent Stockgrowers of America (ISA), "the USDA and industry economists predicted choice slaughter prices at 70 cents a pound plus, by early spring of 1985. Instead choice cattle in April and May slid to the mid fifties with some heavy cattle selling near the mid forties.

That the predictions of 70 cent live cattle proved erroneous is due in large part to food retailers widening their margins at a time when they are paying substantially lower prices for dressed beef. Retailers are paying $12 to $15 less for dressed beef with little perceptive retail price decrease.[11]

The Sturgis, South Dakota rancher also notes that *The Wall Street Journal* was reporting at the time that "beef retailers are currently keeping more than 43 cents of each dollar the consumer spends on beef" while ranchers were going busted producing the animals. By mid-1985 the retail margin was over $1 per pound, giving retailers well over $500 gross profits on the carcass from a 1,200 pound steer.

MPIA has recently developed still more convincing evidence that the nation's entire beef marketing system is manipulated daily not only by large supermarket chains as the *Bray v. Safeway* case in California demonstrated, but also by several large beef packers, in conjunction with several beef brokers and *The Yellow Sheet*.

Glenn Freie of MPIA explains:

The supermarkets control the ultimate consumer demand for beef by the specials they feature in their meat departments. If the wholesale price of beef threatens to move higher they lessen demand for beef by either raising their prices to a level where consumers hesitate to buy, or feature other items, such as poultry, ham, etc. This determines what the housewife will have on her table. This permits the supermarkets to withdraw from the wholesale beef market for periods of time sufficient to allow carcass beef to accumulate and depress the carcass wholesale price.[12]

Large beef packers almost always base their price of live cattle on a strict percentage formula based on the wholesale *Yellow Sheet* price, and directly pass on the decrease in price to the live cattle producer. The live cattle market is thus entirely artificial, according to Freie, and ranchers can do little or nothing to influence the price materially.

The result of this market manipulation by the supermarkets and the packers has resulted in the supermarkets steadily increasing their spread (price they pay for the wholesale beef and the price they sell to the consumer) three to four times in some instances since 1970, and the large packers have increased their spreads (price they sell to the chains and the price they pay for live cattle).[13]

Because in recent years the cattle producer's spread has been so drastically decreased that thousands of producers and many small beef packers have been forced out of business, the beef marketing machinery today remains almost entirely in the hands of the large retail food chains and a concentrated meat packing industry.

"Secret" Signals and Windfall Profits

It was in response to an inquiry from then Secretary of Agriculture Bob Bergland in October, 1977 that the staff of the PS&A, with the assistance of the department's ESCS, prepared a controversial "Beef Pricing Report." Although PS&A administrator Charles Jennings was not in favor of making the study public, and several USDA officials complained that the final report was "toned down" it contained information on the futures market activity of leading packing firms that "nobody has ever seen before outside the regulatory people."[14]

The report, released in December, 1978, showed, after studying a seven-week active trading period on the Chicago Mercantile Exchange in the summer of 1977 that the wholesale price of beef dipped on certain days the price of cattle futures at the CME also dropped.

Officials of the PS&A subsequently acknowledged that the data it had collected raised the possibility that the seven unidentified companies whose records it had studied manipulated the futures market to their advantage.

On July 29, 1977, for example, none of the packers who were trading in futures reported any sales of meat to *The Yellow Sheet.* "When this happens," one USDA official said, "you might expect the trade to perceive a weak market. You expect meat prices to drop."

The reported *Yellow Sheet* meat price did drop from $63.75 per hundred pounds on July 28 to $61.75 the next day. The futures price of cattle also took a dip from $40.20 to $39.50. During the next three days, as *The Yellow Sheet* price of meat remained below what USDA officials called "normal" levels for that period, futures prices also stayed relatively low.

Recalls one USDA official,

We puzzled for some time over the question of why packers would be interested in driving down the price of meat. Then we looked at their futures trading. Since they were selling futures contracts, the lower the price on the exchange, the more money they could make. If these packers had liquidated their futures contracts on July 28, the day before the price break, they would have earned $184,544 less.

In the four-day period the packing firms involved, who held more than 15 percent of the cattle futures contracts at the Chicago exchange, sold 28 percent of their futures contracts, a figure the USDA thought "seemed to be abnormally high."

Representative Smith, in reviewi[...] committee on the subject of cattle fu[...] about 70 percent of those selling su[...] and up to 90 percent of those bu[...] speculators, not producers.

Our studies show that with the advantag[...] inside information large companies can unduly influence the cattle futures so that the typical farmer-hedger can seldom use the market to hedge.

Representative Smith's concern about the role of speculation in the cattle futures' market led Committee staff economist, John Helmuth, to make a careful study of the futures market activity of a group of executives of packing houses, grain companies, feedlot operators and commodity brokers who had showed extraordinary success in the trading of cattle futures.

Helmuth found that in a short period of time a secret "signal" that predicted "with 100 percent accuracy" when prices will fall on the cattle futures market was being utilized by these executives and brokers to earn millions of dollars in profits.

Specifically, Helmuth showed in a 16-month period between January, 1978 and April, 1979, 32 industry insiders made cattle-trading profits of $110 million, each averaging $3.4 million in a business where 90 percent of traders lose money. Some 29 times this "secret" signal was given and each time cattle futures prices dropped within an average of two and one-half days.

Explaining the "secret" signal, Representative Smith noted that when giant corporate feedlots, which raise as many as 50,000 head of cattle and have cheaper operating costs than the small midwestern feeders whose costs are usually reported by the USDA, saw Chicago Mercantile Exchange prices approach USDA figures they could afford to sell first, driving down the price before the small feeders could get into the market.

By selling their cattle futures just before the price dropped they could then buy the contracts back later at a lower price. Smith charged that by following such signals and selling their futures contacts all at once these industry insiders created a snowball effect, successfully forcing down cattle prices.

Such charges of manipulation were promptly and summarily dismissed as "typical Neal Smith demagoguery" by CME President Clayton Yeutter, who later would become the Reagan Administration's chief foreign trade negotiator and George Bush's first Secretary of Agriculture.

In contesting Smith's claim that cattle futures prices could be foreseen by formula Yeutter, in a remark betraying a somewhat Reaganesque attitude regarding public service, suggested that if Representative Smith has "a system that makes those kind of predictions with 100 percent accuracy, he ought to copyright it and make a few million."[15]

Elsie Goes to Market

Further complicating the marketing of beef in recent years was the USDA's "whole-herd buyout" program

...ned to reduce the nation's persistent dairy-surplus ...gram. In 1986 and 1987 the Department spent over ...1.8 billion to pay dairy farmers to slaughter over one million head.

Meanwhile, cattlemen charged that in the first weeks of the program they lost nearly $25 million due to price drops averaging $2 to $3 per hundred pounds.

"This buyout program has totally disrupted normal cattle marketing ... It's just falling apart on us," Chuck Ball, a spokesman for the 230,000 member National Cattleman's Association charged after his group filed a suit in Federal District Court seeking the USDA to suspend the program.[16]

Representative Tony Coelho, D-Calif., who had helped design the original dairy buyout program, later charged the Reagan Administration with deciding to use the program to save money by dumping excess dairy cows on the market early in an attempt to drive down beef prices.

Then when they had to go out and buy beef, as our farm bill required, they could get it cheaper. They bankrupted a lot of people in the process. They hurt innocent people. I'm very upset with the department.[17]

It was only after one million dairy cows had been slaughtered between April and August 1986, that an agreement was finally reached with the USDA which allowed buyout farmers voluntarily to shift the sales of their cattle from the first disposal period to the second or third.

Compounding the dairy situation — high production and low prices — in recent years has also been the emergence of the Bovine Growth Hormone (BGH), a genetically engineered bacteria which after being injected into cows twice a month purportedly accelerates milk yields from 10 to 28 percent.

The growing movement, however, to ban the use of BGH by spotlighting its dire economic and health effects on dairy farmers and consumers has already signaled to Monsanto, the principal producer of the growth hormone, that the production of biotechnology products for agriculture poses certain economic risks.

"I've contended for some time," states Paul T. Leming, of Morgan Stanley & Co.'s Equity Research Department, "that BST is the litmus test of biotechnology products getting into the human food chain."

Conscious of the growing controversy surrounding BGH, banned in 1990 in Wisconsin and the subject of similar attempts in Vermont, Monsanto has sought to employ the scientific community and the FDA to gain farmer and consumer confidence in addition to saturating officials of the American Medical Association (AMA) with favorable propaganda.

For example, one of the company's tactics, according to the *Wall Street Journal*, is to insist on using the more scientific — and sanitized — term Bovine Somatotropin or BST, rather than BGH.

In addition to its own multi-million dollar research facilities, Monsanto also has enlisted the research help of such land-grant universities as the University of Wisconsin, University of Missouri and the University of Vermont in conducting BGH research. Other corporate agribusiness chemical/pharmaceutical companies such as American Cyanamid, Eli Lilly and Upjohn are also investing millions of dollars into BGH research and production.

"In the majority of instances where industry interests are involved," charges Dr. Samuel Epstein, University of Illinois professor of environment and occupational medicine, "the only information available to Congress and decision-makers is either developed inhouse, or by contract with university research arms. This creates an inherent conflict of interest, and a conscious and subconscious effect on those receiving the funds."

Dr. Epstein, one of the first critics of BGH-produced milk, warns that such "cell-stimulating growth factors" could induce premature growth and breast stimulation in infants and possibly promote breast cancer.

Wisconsin Secretary of State Doug LaFollette, in a August 1989 letter to the FDA's Frank Young, has also pointed out that "a few chemical companies are willing to endanger the health of millions of Americans who take for granted the safe, wholesome quality of our milk supply."

Some food companies and food outlets, such as Ben & Jerry's Ice Cream (urging their customers to "save family farms") and Kroger Co. have already refused to use or sell BGH milk in their products and stores.

Other critics of BGH, such as Wisconsin's John Stauber, an associate of Jeremy Rifkin's Foundation on Economic Trends, notes that in the long run, time and money are on the side of the chemical companies. "Companies ... will clean up on this stuff if it gets approved," he charges. "If the cows get sick, they'll make more money selling antibiotics to the farmers. They just can't lose."

The BGH controversy, however, is only one more problem that the nation's dairy farmers have had to confront in recent years. Unprecedented low prices for their product and a corresponding lack of income have seen thousands of dairy farmers driven out of business.

Historically there has been little or no relationship between prices paid to farmers and milk prices paid by consumers. For example, milk prices went up by 29 percent between 1985 and 1990, according to USDA statistics, while the federal support price for milk fell from $12.50 to $10.10 per hundredweight. A GAO report as recent as 1991 has shown that while farmers were showing a 30 percent drop, consumer prices came down a mere 5 percent.

Meanwhile, such corporate agribusiness giants as Kraft, Land of Lakes and Kroger were experiencing record profits. In some areas of the nation, like the northeast, consumers are having to buy their milk from as far away as the upper midwest, adding more than 25 cents per gallon in transportation charges to the cost of their milk.

Thus, dairy farmers throughout the nation in recent years have been seeking *a two tier supply management program* that would provide them with at least the average cost of producing milk and at the same time discourage overproduction. Not only would this help dairy farmers, but it would cut down on government support costs and allow such savings to go into other federal food programs like food stamps and the food supplemental program for Women, Infants and Children (WIC).

The Hamburger, U.S.A Connection

Set against the background of such questionable domestic beef production and price figures is the fact that at the same time millions of tons of beef was continuing to be *imported* into the United States, the government itself was buying and giving away or exporting as much meat as the dairy termination plan produced.[18]

By using USDA statistics Virginia farmers Harold D. Beyeier and Mike Toner developed figures showing that between 1970 and 1986 U.S. consumption of beef exceeded U.S. herd production by nearly 31.2 billion pounds. Using a 59 percent carcass weight factor and a 1,100 pound animal, the 31.2 billion pounds converts into roughly 48.1 million head. Based on a 1970-1986 yearly average, U.S. herd production would have had to increase by slightly more than 3 million head in order to satisfy U.S. consumption.

Further, Beyeier and Toner pointed out that the average live animal *import* of 40.2 billion pounds from 1970 to 1986 translated into 36.6 million live 1,100 pound steer/heifers. If the United States continued to import this same number, they added, U.S. beef producers would likewise continue to be undercut by imports — in spite of the myth that the United States is producing a surplus.

Much of the cattle being slaughtered today is for U.S. hamburger production and imports are no exception. While the U.S. imports roughly six percent of its beef needs, which translates into roughly 40 percent of the world's beef exports, Roy Rogers restaurants and Pillsbury's Burger King fast food chain acknowledge that they have used beef imported from Central America.

Today, both in Central America and South America thousands of acres of environmentally valuable rain forest are being destroyed for cattle grazing. Some of the beef being raised on that land is making its way into our fast food restaurants enabling a handful of U.S. firms to sell hamburgers to the American public five cents cheaper than their competitors.[19] This "hamburger connection," as it has been called, at the same time sees many Latin Americans eating less beef per year than the average U.S. cat eats in the same period of time.

Cattle is not the only case where U.S. consumption exceeds production. Between 1970-1986, Beyier and Toner note, the U.S. consumption of pork exceeded the slaughter by approximately 9.3 billion pounds. Assuming a 71 percent carcass weight factor and an average shortfall of 823 million pounds it would have required almost 3.7 million additional hogs to meet U.S. consumption.

Projecting these production figures for cattle and hogs together and their effect on corn production, the grain now most widely used to feed these animals, would have seen an increase in the demand for corn acreage by nearly ten million acres.

Making Pigs of Themselves

One of the most significant trends in the 1980s in the marketing of meat and related products by large corporations has been the movement into the pork industry by the Big Three beef packers.

With the decline in beef consumption in the late 1970s firms such as IBP, with a 1985 hog slaughtering capacity of 11 million, saw a lucrative pork market as a new way to stuff its corporate coffers and compensate for declining fresh meat revenues.

Soon following IBP into the pork market was ConAgra and Excel. Conagra's entry came through its acquisition of Armour and SIPCO, with a capacity to slaughter over six million hogs; Beatrice, through its acquisition of Eckrich and Esmark/Swift; and SaraLee, which bought up some 16-18 regional companies such as Kahns, Jimmy Dean, Hillshire and Bryans. Cargill's move, through its Excel subsidiary, was less dramatic because it already had laid claim as the United States's largest commercial hog feeder.[20]

While it is estimated that 92 percent of the nation's hogs are slaughtered by eight percent of the plants, plants, the Big Three alone slaughter 30 percent to 40 percent. A Clemson University study has estimated that for every one percent increase in the four largest packers market share, hog prices drop by two cents a hundred weight.[21] And another study by the agricultural consultants, the Helming Group, forecasts that by the year 2,000 four firms will be slaughtering over 70 percent of the nation's hogs.[22]

University of Missouri agricultural economist Glenn Grimes has noted that in 1988 from 70 percent to 75 percent of all pork came from hog farms that sell 1,000 or more butcher hogs yearly, an increase of 120 percent from 1978.[23] In Iowa alone, another study reveals, over 15 percent of the 22.9 million hogs sold annually are not owned by the farmers who care for them.[24]

Marion believes the building of monster plants capable of slaughtering two and one-half to four million hogs per year will accelerate the increasing concentration of hog slaughtering. "As hog buyers shrink in numbers and become more dominant in local procurement markets, the prices paid to hog producers is likely to decline — at least in the long run."[25]

This concentration of the pork industry is further fueled by small pork processors either reducing or phasing out their hog slaughtering activities and buying pork cuts and carcasses from the Big Three. Even Oscar Mayer and Hormel, two major pork processors with recognizable brand names, have already begun closing down their hog slaughtering operations.

Observers, like Professor Marion, believe that because pork processing has generally been more profitable than slaughtering,

it may be only a matter of time before IBP and Excel enter pork processing — probably by buying an existing well-known brand. This could result in specialized pork processors relying on the Big Three for the supply of raw products, but also competing with them in the sale of processed products. Specialized pork processors would then become vulnerable to vertical price squeezes and other competitive tactics by the Big Three.[26]

Pointing to at least one and possibly three of the recent acquisitions by ConAgra and Cargill as violations of Section 7 of the Clayton Act, Marion believes that the federal government's antitrust agencies

are apparently unconcerned about concentrated oligopolies in spite of compelling evidence from a large number of empirical studies that concentrated oligopolies have many of the performance deficiencies of monopolies: high prices, bloated costs and complacency regarding market or technological opportunities.[27]

Dr. John Helmuth agrees, arguing that the Antitrust Division of the U.S. Department of Justice and the PS&A "have failed to meet their responsibilities for adequately enforcing the federal statutes for which they are responsible."[28]

In other areas the Federal government has also helped corporate giants dominate the cattle and pork industry, such as by awarding IBP a $4 million, low-interest loan to develop pork boning and freezing operations at its Columbus Junction plant in Iowa.[29]

"Your giving grants to the worst ones in the industry. Those who are paying the worst wages are doing the least for economic development," charged Iowa Representative David Osterberg, D-Mt. Vernon, upon learning of the federal grant to IBP.[30] Iowa hog producers as well as labor have also expressed reservations about the way IBP has come to dominate the state's pork industry.

Lewie Anderson, former UFCW vice-president, sums up the feelings of many in assessing the future of an industry dominated by the Big Three, thus leading to low prices for producers, low wages for workers and higher prices for consumers.

"We're dealing with real barracudas," he charges. "In my view, they're every bit as ruthless as the packers at the turn of the century."[31]

In northwest Iowa, for example, IBP initially paid a premium for hogs when it opened its Storm Lake plant in 1982. Now that most of its rival buyers have disappeared, according to local farmer Steve McKenna, "they're not paying as well as they used to." In 1988 alone IBP slaughtered 80 percent of the surrounding area's hogs and bought 25 percent of Iowa's total hog production.[32]

Living High Off the Hog

In 1981 key changes in the tax law markedly altered the hog industry. Large capital investors saw golden opportunities in the field as the Center for Rural Affairs in Walthill, Nebraska documented so graphically in its two in-depth reports, *Who's Minding the Corporate Sow?* and *Take Hogs for Example.*

Hog raising buildings were made eligible for investment tax credits and accelerated depreciation that allowed tax write-off savings in five years instead of 15. Such changes in the tax code also encouraged factory-

style hog production firms to use their money immediately instead of in the future.

Ken and Helen Engelmeyer, a Beemer, Nebraska couple, who were marketing about 1,900 hogs annually, saw a disturbing trend in the pork industry as he later explained,

these big corporate operations keep producing the numbers, whether they make a profit or not. They need a market for their tax breaks and they provide it with their buildings, which they can write off in five years. There's no way that smaller farmers like us can compete with that.[33]

A prime example of "hog farmers" that benefited from the 1981 tax code revisions was National Farms of Atkinson, Nebraska, owned by the oil rich Bass family of Texas, whose family fortune is reported to exceed $3 billion.

National markets about 350,000 hogs annually, a number that could be more than doubled if the company successfully completes a $50 million, 18,000 sow hog operation in Greeley, Colorado.[34] This new facility was originally slated to be built in South Dakota, but a locally organized campaign stopped the project. There is now also growing opposition to the plant in Colorado.

In addition to its hog operations, National has nine cattle feedlots with a combined 250,000 head one-time capacity and its 100,000 acres of ranchland that spread from Texas to Nebraska. It is widely believed in the cattle and pork industry that almost all of National's hogs and cattle are sold to IBP.[35]

While U.S. hog farmers averaged $34 a head in 1987, it is estimated that the Basses earned double that amount. The Basses used sophisticated cement holding cells, which for tax purposes could be depreciated over seven years like equipment rather than the 15 years required for buildings. In half the years between 1980-1989 hog farmers generally have experienced hard times. The Basses, however, have realized at least a $15 a head profit.[36]

In addition, comparing computerized records of small (fewer than 100 sows) and large (over 300 sows) hog producers, the *National Hog Farmer* reveals that large producers received $1.45 more for their hogs than the small operators. Also the lower prices charged large producers for soybean meal amounts to a 39 cent per hundred weight advantage in the cost of producing hogs.[37]

The Center for Rural Affairs' tax analyst Chuck Hassebrook notes that investors in the 50 percent bracket have in recent years received more than triple the tax benefits that low income hog farmers in the 20 percent bracket get and, as a result, "the smaller operators are weakened as competitors." He adds,

There is real reason for concern in hogs. Between 1980 and 1982 we lost 30 percent of our pork producers in the United States and USDA has said we'll lose 80 percent of our hog farmers by the year 2000. Yet six major corporations announced expansions that would have sent over one million more hogs to market in 1985.[38]

Concurring with Hassebrook, John Helmuth, after studying both the beef and pork industry while chief economist for the House Small Business Committee, concluded that

> the hog slaughtering industry at the national level in 1982 was in about the same relative position with regard to concentration as the steer and heifer industry was in 1979. [It] appears to be at a crossroad: with one road leading to increased concentration and oligopolistic dominance by a few large firms...[39]

Playing Chicken With the IRS

Tax advantages for large corporations are not only found among the big hogs, but among the chickens as well. Utilizing a tax break created by Congress decades ago to protect and encourage family farms, producers like Tyson Foods, the nation's largest poultry producer with more than $1.9 billion in sales in 1988, Hudson Foods, Inc., the 8th largest producer, and Perdue Farms Inc., one of the United States's largest private firms with over $1 billion in sales in 1988, all have taken advantage of this family farm loophole to defer large portions of their federal tax bills.

The tax code, in defining a family farm as one in which three or fewer families control at least half the stock (both the Hudson and Tyson families control more than half of their company's stock), permits the family farmer to use a cash accounting method which allows for deduction of certain expenses from taxable income when those expenses are incurred. They are permitted, however, to report income later, when they sell their crops or animals. Such a deferral of income reporting, critics charge, amounts to interest free loans from the U.S. Treasury.

Just such a provision enabled the Tysons, for example, to pay no income tax in the 1981-1985 period, using the aforementioned tax break to defer $26 million, more than three-fourths of its tax bill in 1985 alone.

According to the *Arkansas Gazette*, the company and 21 of the nation's other 25 largest corporate poultry producers have been benefiting from this tax deferral. Tyson's general counsel, James B. Blair, notes that the tax break serves as a "shock absorber" against fluctuations in the poultry market.[40]

The fact that Congress kept this "loophole" in the 1986 tax reform bill angered people like Hassebrook. "It was a violation of the trust of family farmers," he charged, "as it was these farmers who supported tax reform through hard times, when no one else backed it, and won on every vote on the issue. "In the end, the corporate farmers won on that issue ..."[41]

Someone's in the Kitchen With Dinah

Not only have corporate chicken farmers reaped lucrative benefits from the nation's tax laws, but they are also rapidly currying the favor of consumers. According to the USDA, from 1982 to 1988, the per-capita consumption of poultry rose from 44.9 to 57.4 pounds while beef per-capita consumption was dropping.[42] (Poultry includes turkey, goose, duck and quail as well as chicken.)

In assessing this phenomena *The Wall Street Journal's* Timothy K. Smith notes:

> And perhaps most significantly, chicken companies have lately increased profit margins by producing scores of what the industry calls value-added items: chicken parts that have been boned or skinned or marinated or otherwise processed for the convenience of consumers. Just as any fool can cook a steak, any fool can now cook a shrink-wrapped chicken breast.[43]

Pounds of Each Food an American Consumes Per Year (Measured by boneless trimmed weight)

| Food | Change in Consumption | | |
	1969	1989*	(1969-1989)
Pork	48	43	- 7.0%
Beef	79	68	- 14.5%
Chicken	28	48	+ 77.0%
Fish	11	15	+ 33.9%

* Forecast
Source: USDA

In fact the "value-added" item that revolutionized the poultry industry was Chicken McNuggets. "Their impact was so huge that it changed the industry," according to ConAgra President George Haefner.[44] Because they have become so widely imitated in the fast-food business chicken nuggets, a $6 billion dollar business,[45] now account for over ten percent of the total U.S. broiler output. (In the United Kingdom, Cargill has become the country's major supplier of the nuggets for McDonald's.)

Industry analysts believe that McNuggets showed chicken companies what could happen if they went beyond selling what is called in the trade, "feathers-off, guts-out birds." In 1980 only one in ten chickens turned out went into processed products, but with the advent of the nuggets, the number zoomed to one out of every three.[46] "The business has matured," according to Holly Farms' vice president Ted Bailey, "we're looking to marketing now."[47]

That "maturity," however, has taken its toll in the past several decades with the disappearance of thousands of small, independent chicken farmers. As *Wall Street Journal* reporter Smith points out:

> Still more efficiency derives from the chicken industry's unusually thorough vertical integration. The biggest producers — ConAgra; Holly Farms; Tyson Foods Inc. of Springdale, Arizona; Perdue Farms Inc. of Salisbury, Md.; and Gold Kist Inc. of Atlanta, Georgia — generally control

everything from the chickens to the feed mill to the trucks to the processing plant. Chicken farmers are merely wardens of the companies' birds, paid to provide housing and labor.[48]

As was so thoroughly documented by Harrison Wellford in his book *Sowing the Wind*, beginning in the 1950's through vertical integration, companies such as Ralston Purina, Holly Farms and Frank Perdue began to consolidate the broiler business, from producing the feed to raising the chicks to packaging the processed parts. In 1969 Frank Perdue revolutionized the broiler industry by creating the first brand-name chicken. By 1987 he alone (reportedly with a little help from "influential friends") controlled over 50 percent of the $800 million New York City and Connecticut chicken market.[49]

In 1982, 127 companies raised and sold chickens. By 1989 there were only 48 companies, but producing 27 percent more chickens, (5.2 billion a year) than were produced in the previous seven years.[50] Together, four producers in 1989 shared 47 percent of the nation's broiler market.

Today, almost all commercial chickens are bred from birds supplied by one of 30 companies. Arbor Acres in Glastonbury, Connecticut alone supplies over 40 percent of the world's broiler market. ISA in Lyon, France and its U.S. subsidiary ISA Babcock, provide birds for two thirds of the international brown egg industry. As journalist Richard Conniff relates "when one researcher told me, 'this is a business of a few winners and a lot of losers,' he wasn't talking about the chickens."[51]

"Chicken Roost Rulers"

Corporation	Market Share
Tyson Foods	24 percent
ConAgra	9 percent
Gold Kist	7.4 percent
Perdue Farms	6.6 percent

Source: Prudential-Bache Securities Inc. *USA Today*, August 2, 1989

As early as 1984 Tyson embarked on a major campaign to buy out other chicken producers. In its 1987 annual report it outlined its goals in terms of making its products as synonymous with chicken as "Kleenex is synonymous with paper tissue."[52]

In fiscal 1989 over half of Tysons $2 billion sales came from the firm's food service division, a major supplier of chicken parts to McDonald's Corp. Abiding by the trade maxim, "segment, concentrate and dominate" which he so succinctly coined, Don Tyson, the company's chairman, has advised would-be competitors to "find your niche and devote your resources to driving out the other suppliers."

Tyson underscores such advice by noting that 80 percent of his company's profits come from products it didn't produce seven years ago.[53] In fact, 30 of the company's 32 plants have come by way of acquisition.[54] Tyson's success, however, has had its costs.

"Tyson is strained by production right now and it needs poultry," according to Napoleon Overton, an analyst with Morgan Keegan in Memphis, Tenn.[55] It is for that reason that Tysons in 1988 began actively seeking to buy Holly Farms, the nation's No. 1 retail producer of fresh chicken.

Tysons was not alone in its lust for Holly Farms, as ConAgra also began feverishly bidding for the company's favors. Had such an acquisition ever taken place ConAgra would clearly have become the nation's largest processor of broilers.

What ensued, however, was a protracted "chicken war" between ConAgra and Tysons, with Holly Farms eventually wooed by Tysons for $1.29 billion — but not before ConAgra received a $50 million payoff from Tysons to end a previous merger pact with Holly Farms. The acquisition immediately raised Tysons processing capacity from one out of every seven chickens slaughtered in the United States to one out of every five.[56]

Even though it already dominates the U.S. broiler industry, Tysons forever continues to look for new ways to increase its market share. The company has 25 scientists who do nothing but slice, dice and conjure up visions of what qualities the ultimate boneless, microwaveable, precooked and seasoned chicken part might possess in the future. One such project is a juggling of genes which would produce a four-breasted, four-winged bird. Don Tyson himself has also suggested exploring the possibility of a "giblet burger," made from chicken hearts, livers and gizzards.[57]

Human Barnyards of "Efficiency"

"Perdue showed everybody how to really market chickens. Now somebody needs to show him how to treat people like human beings."
- Tex Walker, UFCW organizer

In their drive to dominate a $16-billion-a-year chicken industry, the Tysons, ConAgra's, Gold Kists and Perdue's have built empires largely on the backs of hundreds of small subservient contract farmers and thousands of impoverished processing plant workers.

Parlaying expanded production by buying up existing companies, building new processing facilities and contracting more dependent farmers to grow chickens faster and cheaper, poultry productivity has not only outpaced all U.S. manufacturing since 1960, but has become one of the food industry's most profitable sectors.

"In many industries, increased productivity has provided workers with a higher standard of living," points out Bob Hall, research director of the Institute for Southern Studies, "but sharing the profits from the booming chicken business has been one of the last things on the poultry kings' agenda."[58]

Figures developed by the Institute show that in 1960 workers received 2.6 cents of the 43 cents a pound chickens fetched at the store. Twenty years later, they received 3.3 cents — though chicken had risen to 72 cents a pound. Despite the fact that their wages lagged behind the rest of the food industry, their productivity and per-worker contribution to profits dramatically increased, showing a 33 percent gain between 1981 and 1985 alone.[59]

Such increases allow industry giants like Frank Perdue (who boasts not only that "it takes a tough man to produce a tender chicken" but also that he pays his non-union workers 29 cents more an hour more than his unionized competitors) to amass a personal fortune estimated between $200 million and $500 million.

"I grew up having to know my business in every detail," Perdue once told a *Wall Street Journal* reporter,.. "I know I'm not very smart, at least from the standpoint of pure IQ, and that gave me one prime ingredient of success — fear. I mean, a man should have enough fear so that he's always second-guessing himself."[60]

In this thirst for greater productivity and profits, the nation's poultry processing industry has also contributed in a large share to many rural communities' pollution problems. Using an average of 5.5 gallons of water for every bird processed, its industrial waste has for years polluted streams and contaminated wells in many areas of the nation, particularly in the south.

In north Georgia, for example, citizens successfully sued several poultry firms as public nuisances — only to see pro-industry state legislators promptly exempt the poultry companies from such nuisance ordinances.

The greatest cost in the poultry industry's going from what the Institute for Southern Studies has so aptly termed "a barnyard hobby to a giant — and dangerous — engine of efficiency" is the human cost.

With many of the over 150,000 workers in the United States's poultry processing plants thwarted in their efforts to organize and bargain collectively with their employers, their workplaces remain ever so dangerous. Suffering one of the highest rates of injury and illness in American manufacturing, their 18.5-per-100- employee 1986 rate-of-injury was twice that of textile and tobacco workers and even higher than those of miners.[61]

Assembly lines that are constantly accelerated, abnormal temperatures and rapid, repetitive hand motions all contribute substantially to worker skin diseases, crippling hand and arm illnesses called cumulative trauma disorders, ammonia exposure, infections from toxins in the air, stress and back problems.

In the midst of such deplorable conditions the poultry industry continues to invest millions each year in an effort to keep the *chickens* happy. "Birds should be free from pain, from fear, from distress, and from long-term discomfort," implores the *World's Poultry Science Journal.* "They should not be exposed to long periods of boredom."[62]

In the pursuit of such goals Animalens, a Wellesley, Massachusetts firm, has developed special red-tinted contact lens for chickens, which it claims will "lower social stress" among the birds and make them easier to handle and "enhance their productivity." The cost: 20 cents a pair.[63]

"With its gushing flow of profits," observes Bob Hall, "one wonders why the industry doesn't have the 'courage' — to use Don Tyson's word — to slow down its processing lines, treat workers with respect, give their contract growers a measure of security, and still produce a product people are happy to eat."[64]

Chapter Thirty-Five

Efficiency and Ruthlessness

"The most extraordinary aspect of the national furor over The Jungle, with its international repercussions, was that public attention was concentrated almost exclusively upon material regarded by Sinclair as incidental, mere background and local color for his major theme which was the oppression of the Packinghouse workers."[1]

Concerning such initial public reaction to *The Jungle*, Sinclair later wrote in keen disappointment, "I aimed at the public's heart and by accident I hit it in the stomach."[2]

Today, nearly eight decades since the publication of *The Jungle*, the meat packing industry continues to show little empathy for its workers. Meanwhile, a consuming public has become indifferent to the plight of the industry's workers.

Despite the fact that until recently meat packing was highly unionized with wages consistently 15 percent to 20 percent above the manufacturing average, it remains the most hazardous, oppressive and corporately irresponsible industry in America.

Due in large part to organizing efforts in the 1930s and 1940s by the United Packinghouse Workers of America and the Amalgamated Meat Cutters and Butcher Workmen, meat packing workers in the post-World War II era were one of the most highly organized workforces in America. After merging in 1968 the meat packers unions joined with the Retail Clerks International Union in 1979 to form the United Food and Commercial Workers Union (UFCW). Today, about 70 percent of all packinghouse workers are now UFCW members.[3]

Starting with the entry of Iowa Beef Processors in 1961, however, the organized union movement within the meat packing industry began to witness gradual erosion of its power. With the company's specialization and location, its mechanized approach to slaughtering and packing, and the breaking down of traditionally skilled work into less skilled jobs, it began through traditional union-busting tactics to draw upon a broader labor pool with less sympathy toward organized labor. As journalist David Moberg has noted,

Rather than ship carcasses to urban wholesalers or supermarket chains, it cut up the animals and sold "box beef" that eliminated skilled, well-paid urban butchers. It ruthlessly fought the packinghouse union, breaking strikes, signing sweetheart contracts with unions like the Teamsters or National Maritime Union and, where unionized, accepting only contracts below the rates at established packers ... It was efficient and ruthless.[4]

The meat packing industry has long been labor-intensive, making wage scales a major cost factor. In recent years, however, greater innovativeness and tighter cost controls were introduced by the major meat packers. Consequently, lower labor costs have to some degree been passed on to consumers, but there have also been substantial costs resulting from such changes. As Professor Bruce Marion concludes: "Wages and fringe benefits have dropped sharply in industries characterized by unpleasant and hazardous working conditions. The lower costs of the 'new breed' packers have been largely carried on the backs of packing plant workers."[5]

Because it is a nationwide industry the UFCW has always sought to maintain a national structure of wages and benefits, negotiating wage rates through "master agreements" that cover all plants owned by a particular company.

Since IBP has 11 plants in several states with no union contracts and three plants with union membership,[6] it has successfully negotiated contracts for substantially lower wages than those paid by other companies and less than those prevailing for singleplant operations elsewhere.

A comparison in the late 1970's, for example, of labor costs between IBP's plants in Dakota City, Nebraska and Amarillo, Texas and prevailing wage rates in the San Francisco Bay Area for a "five-year journeyman" vividly illustrate this point.

In a more recent example in 1987, IBP was paying a starting wage of $5 per hour and a $7 base wage after two years at its Columbus Junction, Iowa plant. Elsewhere, Farmstead in Cedar Rapids had a base wage of $8.60 while Dubuque's FDL had a base wage of $8.50. By using such advantages IBP has been able to force out smaller packers, ultimately resulting in lower paying jobs replacing better paying jobs.[7]

Union officials have also pointed out that IBP's worker displacement programs have often been subsidized by state and federal funds. For example, the company has received state administered federal job training funds to train new workers after reopening their closed plants at reduced wage levels. At its Madison, Nebraska plant IBP used such funds to train new workers, ones who had replaced former workers with close union ties who had been on strike before the plant closed.[8]

Cost Comparison of Labor Costs, Per Hour

	Amalgamated Meat Cutters San Francisco		Amalgamated Meat Cutters Dakota City IBP	Teamsters Amarillo IBP	
Wages	$ 9.37	Gr. 2	$7.05	Gr. 8	$6.18
Health & Welfare	.895		.376		.376
Pension	.85		none		.25
Vacation Fund	.094		none		none
Tool Allowance	.06		none		none
Sick Leave Fund	.01		.023		none
Hourly Wage & Fringe	$11.279		$7.449		$6.806

Source: "Small Packers threatened by growth of Iowa Beef, House panel told," Mike McGraw, *The Des Moines Register*, May 3, 1979.

Some believe that the U.S. Supreme Court in a March, 1989 decision further fueled such practices by ruling that once a labor strike is settled, companies are not required to fire employees who returned to work during the strike in order to rehire strikers with more seniority.

While the decision was based on the Court's interpretation of the Railway Labor Act, some union officials fear that because the provisions of that Act so closely parallel the National Labor Relations Act (NLRA) non-transportation employers could argue that the decision also applies to their businesses.[9]

Turnover and Stoking the System

The successes of IBP in meat packing not only inspired major conglomerates to buy out small meatpackers, but also proved ruinous to the industry as a whole and added momentum to many of the industry's traditional anti-union activities. Thus, the industry rapidly became heavily weighted with those packers paying lower wages and benefits rather than those packers who retained master agreement contracts. A UFCW report has noted:

Conglomerates used meat-packing subsidiaries as cash cows by demanding enormous cash dividends, unreasonable management fees, and high interest on loans given to packing operations... Between 1970 and 1980, conglomerates made huge profits by selling off assets of packing subsidiaries ... Conglomerates even made money by closing plants in that tax laws allow companies to write off plant closing costs against earnings ...

At a time when the industry was changing quickly and substantial capital investment was desperately needed, the conglomerates were draining packing operations of their capital. Within a decade and a half, the conglomerates had effectively destroyed once soundly run companies.[10]

A union official carries such analysis a step further:

These companies simply cannot make major management and financial decisions without consulting their primary banks. At the same time the established packers have been screaming about low profits, we've seen major investments being made in building additional plants. That has resulted in the industry being about 30 percent overbuilt. Approving the financing for this expansion only makes sense if the real purpose is to put pressure on the union and on the wages of the workers. The banks are heavily involved in this thing.[11]

When Val-Agri, for example, entered meat packing in 1982 its executive vice-president Lanny Binger commented,

We thought there was room for another viable company in the industry right now. The success of any business depends on management, location, and financial backing. We've put them all together and think the timing is right... Frankly, the labor picture was one reason for our timing. Unemployment at present gives us an opportunity to employ experienced, skilled labor.[12]

An "opportunity to employ experienced, skilled" *cheap* labor!

Some meat packing firms, defending their labor practices, have argued that towns in Kansas, Nebraska, Texas and other states where they have opened new production facilities have reaped numerous economic benefits from the employment opportunities these facilities provide. Reporter Ken Ackland of *The Chicago Tribune*, however, found after a careful study of such areas that many of these same so-called "beneficiaries" were suffering from the usual "boomtown" problems of strained physical facilities, rapid inflation and the inevitable social problems that stem from a transient workforce.[13]

An extremely high turnover rate of the workforce — in some areas as much as 43 percent a month or a complete change of the plant workforce in 2.5 months as at one Excel plant — have pitted workers of ethnic minorities against one another. As large numbers of legal and illegal Mexican workers already employed in many packinghouses have to vie with desperate, Southeast Asian "boat people" for work, explosive tensions are created in many of these "beneficiary" communities.

Peggy Hillman is an attorney who in recent years has been involved in organizing efforts among packinghouse workers in the midwest. Employed herself in a Val-Agri plant in Garden City, Kansas. She reflects on her experiences and how it became apparent to her that organizing packinghouse workers is taking on a new dimension as more and more "migrant" workers vie for available jobs.

Turnover stokes the system. The entire employment strategy of these companies is designed to increase turnover. More importantly, for union organizing, the system of turn-over prevents employees from becoming knowledgeable, from becoming more sophisticated, because they're simply not there long enough.[14]

The consequences of this lack of knowledge, she explains, are that workers' compensation is largely unheard of; most injuries, particularly carpal tunnel syndrome and tendonitis, aren't considered injuries so if you lose work, you lose pay; company towns are tolerated with people living in hovels and trailer courts where there is little room and where rents and infant mortality figures are high, and because ignorance breeds hatred racial polarization is extreme. (Child abuse, according to Hillman, increased by 300 percent in Garden City since the meat packing plant came.)

More importantly, these workers have no ties with their community. Their relations with the community are hostile. They're ostracized. They put a strain on the community resources. The hospitals are reluctant to treat indigents. The schools dislike teaching English to Non-English speaking children.

I'm not exaggerating when I say that the day-to-day existence of this new breed of worker is subhuman. The system of turnover flourishes by making the living and working conditions intolerable and by causing the deterioration of small towns.[15]

The effect on union organizing, according to Hillman, is devastating. "They really don't care enough to vote for a union much less to get involved with the union. They are frustrated, but their frustration has not been channeled into anger and their anger has not been channeled into action."[16]

An excellent example of the practices that have become almost epidemic in the meat packing industry occurred in December 1983 when the Greyhound Corp. shut down its 13 Armour Food Company meatpacking plants, eliminating 1500 union members whose earnings averaged approximately $10 an hour. Two days later, the corporate agribusiness giant ConAgra with over 30,000 employees purchased Armour and reopened 12 plants with a nonunion workforce of some 900 employees whose starting pay was $6 an hour.

Eighteen months later the NLRB accused ConAgra of illegally refusing to hire union members and issued a complaint against the company that could result in a rehiring order and a back-pay award of more than $30 million if the company is found guilty of discrimination against its former union employees.[17] As the UFCW has declared:

From 1980 through 1984, UFCW and its packinghouse membership endured bitter circumstances not previously seen in the past four decades. Corporate spin-offs, sales of entire companies, Chapter 11 bankruptcies, threats of plant closings, actual plant closings, a severe recession, meat packers picking up on concessions made in other smokestack industries, and staggering unemployment created deep worker fear of job loss which resulted in a wave of concessions industry wide.[18]

Union-Busting

In its efforts to turn a highly organized industry into a substantially unorganized one, the nation's major meat packers began a two-front attack on the UFCW in the late 1970's. After first seeking to reduce the national wage rate to $6 per hour they also set out to destroy the union's bargaining power.

Despite concerted resistance by the UFCW, lower wages and benefit retrenchment soon became a reality. By 1981 the union had adopted a long-range program to hold concessions to a minimum through negotiations, while at the same time working on a economy recovery plan for its workers. In 1985 wage concessions reached a temporary impasse as wages began to edge up.

The swing in recent years to processed items, the low margins in fresh meats and the competitive edge that the "new breed" of packers have in labor costs have also served to make companies like IBP and Hormel more militant in negotiating with their workers, and in trying to get them to agree to more "competitive" wage levels and working conditions. The UFCW's president William Wynn admitted to *Business Week* in 1985 that his union had been on a "controlled retreat" since 1980.

Efforts to reverse this trend by the 1.2 million member national UFCW have been relatively unsuccessful. Meanwhile, a handful of the union's locals remain engaged in the long and frustrating struggle to not only bring about "economic recovery for all packinghouse workers," but at the same time to reassert original rank-and-file principles to packinghouse unionism.

The recent concerted drive by the "new breed" of meat packers to destabilize unions began in earnest in 1978. At that time the Meatcutters Union lost a bitter and often violent 14-month strike against IBP at the company's Dakota City plant during which the union had attempted to achieve contract "parity" with other major U.S. meat packing operations.

Yet another effort at "union busting" by IBP provoked a long strike in 1982 at the same plant. The Nebraska National Guard was called out to quell picket-line violence after IBP initiated a four-year review process of a National Labor Relations Board ruling determining that the company had indeed previously been engaging in bad-faith bargaining.

As Arthur Hedberg, Jr., a Des Moines, Iowa strike sympathizer noted:

In Poland, when the state calls the army to quell a strike, such action is a blow to freedom and liberty. In Dakota City, Nebraska when the state calls out the army to quell a strike, it is to protect property and stop riots... . It is not justice when an army may be called on to insist that the workers obey the law, and it takes four years to resolve whether a company will obey the law ...[19]

William Schmitz, the UFCW's Local 222 business agent, reminded his union and the public during the strike that "labor's in a butt-kicking contest, and we're all going to get our butts kicked" unless "we change from complacency to militancy ... If this ruthless corporation [IBP] gets away with [destroying the union] ... it will have a ripple effect on unions throughout the country."[20]

True to Schmitz's warning, in the coming months these fights between IBP and the union profoundly influenced the direction of the UFCW in the 1980's. They not only set the tone, but the direction of the union's efforts to control their own locals while at the same time maintain existing contracts with other major meat packers.

According to UFCW figures, the industry lost 49,000 jobs between 1960 and 1984 and at the 1060 packing plants closed between 1965 and 1985, the wages were at the low end of the wage scale. "Wage concessions do not prevent the closing of meat packing plants," the union emphasizes, "the wave of concessions in meat packing ... was initiated not only by packers in financial trouble but by profitable packers as well."[21]

Nevertheless, between 1983-1985 the UFCW negotiated a third of all two-tier wage settlements, 87 out of 261, more than any other union.

The P-9 Affair

That very strategy, however, was starkly called into question on August 17, 1985 when 1500 members of Local P-9 of the UFCW struck the Austin, Minnesota plant of George A. Hormel & Co. in what would become a long, bitter, violent and community-dividing strike.

Refusing to accept a cut of 23 percent in workers' base pay and concessions on seniority, attendance control and plant assignments, the workers of P-9 went on strike. To its surprise, however, Local P-9 encountered a UFCW and AFL-CIO national leadership that refused to back its efforts. Meanwhile, Hormel officials were bringing in strikebreakers through the company gates under the protection of the Minnesota National Guard while firing workers at their other plants who began supporting the Austin strikers.

Since 1980, when the last master contract for the industry established base wages at $10.69 an hour, wages had been repeatedly slashed in Austin with or without union consent. At the major pork packing plants wages ranged from $6 to $10.69 an hour, with most in the $7.75 to $9.50 range. From a peak of $8.98 in 1982 down to $8.24 in 1984 the overall average wage for the first time in many years went below the manufacturing average of $9.17. Worker benefits suffered a similar fate.

Meanwhile, output per worker-hour among meat packing firms was dramatically outstripping all U.S. industries. At the same time, total meat output increased by half, as the average wage per pound of meat produced was only about 4.17 cents, down from a high of 5.11 cents in 1982, an amount roughly calculated at 2.6 percent of meat's retail price.

In arguing against the cuts called for by Hormel, Local P-9 cited *Business Week*'s report that Hormel rated number one in earnings per share among major beef packers. It also had recorded a 1984 profit of $29.4 million and gave its chairman Robert Knowlton a raise of $231,000 from $339,000 to $570,000.

P-9 charged that companies such as Hormel could threaten a community and "hold these communities hostage with their demands on the workers, along with their threats to move." It was necessary, therefore, that these communities "look beyond the Hormel Company to see who has the wherewithal to allow this corporate extortion to exist."[22]

What P-9 soon found in following such a course was that First Bank Systems, with assets of $25.4 billion and net profits of $166.8 million in 1985, either controlled or was linked to 60 percent of all Hormel's stock. The bank system itself, the nation's 38th largest at the time, held 12 percent-16 percent, of the stock and six of its present or retired board members were serving as Hormel Foundation board directors which in turn controlled 46 percent of Hormel's stock.

Further study also showed that First Bank Systems had been expanding its control in the food industry. Figures collected by Corporate Data Exchange, Inc. in 1981 revealed that besides holding stock in Hormel, Systems was also a leading shareholder in such corporate agribusinesses as Peavey, ConAgra and International Multifoods. It was also in the process of acquiring Banks of Iowa while Hormel was in the process of acquiring FDL Foods of Dubuque, Iowa.

Not so coincidentally the Chief Executive Officer of FDL sat on the board of directors of Banks of Iowa. At the same time this acquisition was being processed, the Bank was also attempting to divest itself of 27 smaller community banks within its existing system.

Despite such evidence the UFCW's national leadership continued to oppose any economic campaign to pressure Hormel. At the same time, P-9 was also accusing the UFCW of seeking to discredit its strike by undercutting its bargaining position and its efforts to raise funds to keep it's members on the picket lines. The UFCW countered that Hormel was its best client and that for P-9 to pick on it only undermined efforts elsewhere to maintain current wage levels.[23]

After P-9 refused to call off its strike, the International placed the local in receivership, cut off all strike benefits, offered members "post strike" payments only if they would offer to return to work, and sent a letter to Hormel saying that all UFCW members would return to work unconditionally on September 12, 1986. Unlike the "inexperienced, inflexible local union representatives" of P-9, the letter said, the UFCW was ready to initiate bargaining sessions with Hormel.[24]

The UFCW's course of action throughout the Hormel strike drew criticism from many, including religious observers and labor relations experts. Typical of such reaction was a June 6, 1986 editorial in *The National Catholic Reporter:*

The UFCW's "overall strategy" has not won them the national wage rate they have been working for, nor has it had any apparent effect against plant closings, corporate mergers and the like. In the name of that ineffective "overall strategy" they are undermining working women and men who represent the hands and heart of trade unionism in this country ... Sooner or later there will come a day of reckoning, and those in charge will be called to account.

Undaunted by the UFCW's leaders' receivership action, a large group of P-9 members recertified themselves and continued their struggle against Hormel as "Original P-9."

Destroying 50 Years of Bargaining

The six-year old argument by the UFCW's national leadership that concessions are necessary "to bring about economic recovery for all packinghouse workers" and prevent the meat packing companies from establishing a $6 per hour nonunion industry, continues to attract only a lukewarm reception from the union's rank-and-file (as illustrated by the Austin strike) as meat packers' hourly wages continue to drop.

Not surprisingly, less than three months after the UFCW leadership declared the Hormel strike over, IBP locked out 2,800 of its workers from its Dakota City plant after they demanded a wage freeze for three years. The AFL-CIO in condemning the fact that its employees were forced "to the picket line in a fight for justice and decency for the fifth time in 17 years," pointed out that the wages of the IBP employees were so low that under the existing "two-tier" pay scale "some employees who work full-time are eligible for welfare and food stamps."[25]

Almost 18 months after the Austin strike began, negotiations on a union contract at John Morrell's Sioux Falls plant, home of Nathan's hot dogs, also broke down. *Meat and Poultry* reported in a July 1988 survey that Morrell has slipped from fifth to eighth place in the pork industry since 1979.*

Earlier in 1983, Morrill had cut wage rates by $2.44 an hour at its Sioux Falls plant. Two years later, despite intensive negotiations and after a three-month strike, the UFCW remained unable to restore the cuts and was finally forced to settle on a 25-cent an hour increase. After the January 1987 breakdown in negotiations the union struck again and the company immediately began hiring replacement workers. The strike was soon abandoned, with fewer than 20 percent of the 3000 union workers being called back to work by Morrell.

The following year the Sioux Falls UFCW local suffered another bitter defeat when a South Dakota federal court jury ruled that the local's members violated their contract by refusing to cross a picket line set up by

* John Morrell, is a subsidiary of United Brands (recently renamed Chiquita International Inc.), the modern-day heir of infamous United Fruit Co., which for nearly a century has played a major role in perpetuating the United States's exploitative "banana republic' foreign policy in Central America.

strikers from the Morrell plant in Sioux City, Iowa. Following that verdict in November 1988 another jury awarded Morrell $24.6 million in damages despite the fact that a federal arbitrator had ruled a week earlier that the union members were legally refusing to cross the picket line.

In appealing the jury's award, UFCW's assistant general counsel Nick Clark pointed out that the arbitrator's findings would allow an estimated 1900 union members to return to the jobs they had lost 19 months earlier.[26]

Two years after the Sioux Falls strike collapsed Morrell imposed its own contract on its 2,000 employees, a contract which cut worker's base wages from $9.75 to $8 an hour in addition to curtailing benefits. Although over 99 percent of the workers voted to reject the contract no strike was called.

Jim Lyons, UFCW local president, declared that "this four-year contract virtually destroys 50 years of bargaining" and will ruin the standard of living for Morrell workers in Sioux Falls. But Raoul Baxter, Morrell's executive vice-president, defended the new contract. "If we really wanted to punish them, we would've taken them down to $6, which is the real thing out there."[27]

Despite its recent court and contract victories Morrell has remained the object of various civil suits and government investigations.

In October 1988, eleven current and former Morrell workers filed a suit on behalf of the company's workers seeking $35 million in unpaid wages, overtime and penalties. The workers charged that Morrell had failed to pay its employees for time spent putting on, taking off and cleaning safety equipment. Instead it required its workers to perform said tasks on their meal breaks or before or at the end of their regular work shifts. A U.S. Department of Labor's similar suit against IBP the previous March provided precedent for their suit. In that case the government alleged that the nation's largest meat packer had failed to pay overtime to its workers for installing safety equipment at ten of its 14 plants since April 1, 1985.[28]

The Morrell worker's suit was soon followed by separate government action in March 1989 when the NLRB accused Morrell (and its parent company, United Brands) of illegally scheming to circumvent its union contract by closing its Ark City, Kansas and Memphis, Tennessee packing plants in 1982 and then later reopening them with workers who were paid lower wages. It also charged that the company had "fraudulently concealed" important information about the scheme from the NLRB and the UFCW.

The complaint also sought compensation for the workers for their loses, back pay for all plant employees to make up the difference between the higher wage rates paid before the closing and the lower ones when the plants reopened nine months later, restoration of the Morrell-UFCW master agreement that was wiped out in 1982, and the payment of dues lost to the union.

At the Ark City plant over 750 workers had been receiving a base wage of $11.07 an hour before the plant closed, but after the plant reopened only 200 workers were employed and received only $5 an hour. At the

Memphis facility, before it closed, 400 UFCW members received a base wage of $10.69 an hour; when it re-opened 250 employees got a base wage of $5.50 an hour.[29]

These highly questionable, if not illegal, actions by Morrell and those of other major meat packers not only bring questions of economic justice within the industry into sharp focus, but also raise another important issue regarding the health and safety of the workers.

While the industry has succeeded in finding a profitable use for nearly every part of a steer or pig, the most troubling cost for corporate agribusiness's slaughterhouses has been labor. The fact that steers, heifers and hogs do not come in uniform sizes prevents the packing companies from completely automating their production facilities. Thus, they have resorted to reducing labor costs as a means of remaining "competitive."

The UFCW, however, charges that in their pursuit of larger profits and market shares, meat packing companies (where, as one journalist describes it, "knife-wielding workers stand elbow-to-elbow in a sea of blood as they dismember animal carcasses")[30] have compromised the safety of the workers through job cutbacks and assembly line speedups.

In this regard, Lyle Grate, a 30-year old Morrell worker, who suffers constant pain from an injury he received while working in the Sioux Falls plant, points out that when he started in the hog kill department there were five people cutting about 800 head an hour. When he last worked there, three people were handling more than 1,000 hogs an hour.[31]

Working in "Hellholes"

"A meatpacking plant is like nothing you've ever seen or could imagine. It's like a vision of hell."
- Eleanor Kennelly, UFCW

Throughout the Austin/Hormel strike Jim Guyette, Local P-9's forceful president, continually stressed that "what we are asking for is just to get back what was taken away" *and*, he stressed, the need for Hormel to improve working conditions as well as wages.

Meatpacking is the most dangerous of jobs. At one Iowa Beef plant which has a 5,000 person workforce, the turnover has been over 30,000 workers in the last three years. At Hormel we have a 33 percent annual injury rate. The company paid $5 million in out-of-pocket workers compensation in 1983, and over $6 million in 1984. They are willing to pay these costs, to cut safety corners, and speed up production lines, but they are not willing to deal fairly and honestly with our union.[32]

Dan Peterson, a P-9 contract negotiator, has noted that "safety in the Hormel plant is a serious problem, resulting in one-third lost time during injuries. We have 202 injuries a year for every 100 workers."[33] In 1988, 45,000 people were injured in meat packing plants nationally, 173 injuries every working day, three times above the average for all U.S. factories.[34]

Examples of what Guyette called "the most dangerous of jobs" abound in the meat packing industry.*

In March 1986, for example, Excel Corp. was fined $2,000 for violating Federal safety standards at its Wichita, Kansas facility when an employee died at the plant after being pinned in an intestine cooker.[165] A Storm Lake, Iowa jury in March 1988 awarded $572,000 to Janet Henrichs, an ex-IBP employee whose hand was ripped apart by a fat trimming machine, after it was determined that the accident was caused by improper training. The award was against six plant supervisors.[36]

IBP's meteoric climb to the top is attributable to the fact that it is able to "take cattle apart the way Henry Ford assembled cars" while exacting a high cost in human suffering. IBP's Storm Lake plant, now one of the nation's largest fresh pork operations, slaughters up to 12,000 hogs per day and three million hogs annually. Its Dakota City plant, with a capacity to slaughter and disassemble thousands of head of cattle a day, has been described as a "hellhole" for workers.[37]

Only one other industry — the logging, saw-mill and wood products business — has higher incidences of injuries and illnesses than meat packing. From 1977-1981, a record 20,000 workers were either permanently disabled or killed because of injuries received while working in U.S. meat packing plants. Some 30.4 workers out of 100 are injured on the job or afflicted by an occupational disease each year, compared to the national average of 8.8 for all industry and 18.3 for the food and kindred products manufacturing industry, according to U.S. Department of Labor statistics.

The Occupational Health and Safety Administration has estimated that in some meat packing plants the injury rate has been as high as 85 percent.[40]

In 1985 at IBP's Dakota City plant, by way of illustration, the injury rate was 37 per 100. In 1976 the plant's accident rate was 44.1 per 100 workers, compared to the industry average that year of 34.7. At the Company's Emporia, Kansas plant it was 43.2 in 1977 and at its Amarillo plant, 50.

IBP's main concern, however, has always been output. "Once we push the button in the morning, we don't want the chain to stop. If it stops, it costs money. We want to pump the tonnage through," an IBP vice-president has stressed.[41]

A company nurse, however, takes a very different attitude. "It's a heartless outfit," and after pausing, she adds as an afterthought, "they do have humane ways of killing cattle."[42]

In 1985 the Company's nurses reported that in one three month period there were 1800 injuries at the IBP's Dakota City plant. The Company claimed there were only 162 and it was the latter report, according to UFCW's Health and Safety Director, Deborah Berkowitz,

---

* University of Iowa researchers are engaged in a five-year study of 250 people who work in swine confinement operations after discovering 90 percent of them had respiratory problems.[38] Preliminary indications reveal that they pose significant health risks such as chest tightness, coughing, watery eyes, and running noses after only 30 minutes.[39]

that was submitted to OSHA.

"We Bungled It Badly"

Subsequently, in July 1987 the Labor Department announced a fine of $2.59 million against IBP for 1038 instances of willfully failing to report job-related injuries and illnesses at its Dakota City plant in 1985 and 1986.

Three months later IBP board chairman Peterson admitted to a House Committee that "we bungled it badly" when he testified to another House subcommittee on May 6 that company officials had not been keeping two sets of worker injury records when in fact they had — a key point since the number of such injuries reported determines whether OSHA can make on-site company health and safety inspections.

Claiming that the false statements stemmed from a misunderstanding of questions about when the lists were compiled resulting in "a dichotomy between what one was saying and one was hearing," Peterson admitted to the two sets of records, claiming that his earlier testimony was "inaccurate, but it wasn't perjury." (Committee Chairman Tom Lantos, D-Calif, noted that Peterson had corrected the record "only when the bloodhounds were at your door.")[43] IBP later agreed to pay a reduced penalty of $975,000, the third largest ever collected by OSHA, to settle the $5.7 million worth of fines the government had previously imposed for the meat packer's job safety violations.[44]

Shortly before the OSHA-IBP-UFCW agreement the government agency had announced in October 1988, that John Morrell & Co. was also being fined $4.6 million for "egregious" and "willful" health violations at its Sioux Falls, South Dakota plant.[45] OSHA cited injury rates nine times the industry average and 600 times the rate for all U.S. industries.

OSHA officials said they had "incredible documentation" of injury-causing jobs at Morrell's Sioux Falls plant as investigators for the National Institute of Occupational Safety and Health (NIOSH) had videotaped hundreds of jobs at the plant to determine how they contributed to the injury problem.[46] Union officials had previously pointed to the fact that from May to December 1987 the plant had 1,706 work related injuries and illnesses as compared to 1986's grand total of 1,397. The reason for the increase, the UFCW added, was the hiring of inexperienced non-union workers after their May strike.[47]

Gary Junso, a Morrell vice-president, later acknowledged in an internal company memo that 87 out of every 100 workers in 1987 needed doctor's care for work-related injuries or illnesses.[48]

The most common occupational illness found in meat packing plants today is called cumulative trauma disorder or carpal syndrome, a crippling disease caused by tendons becoming inflamed from stresses and strains stemming from prolonged periods of repetitive motion.[49] NIOSH regards 30 to 60 days as a necessary recuperative time for surgery following the treatment of this disease.

OSHA found that at Morrell in 63 of 180 cases requiring surgery the average time off was 1.1 days, with 27 injured workers not getting any time off.[50]

During the Congressional hearings involving IBP's health violations, Chairman Peterson refused to answer questions about carpal syndrome among IBP workers.[51] Four months later, however, OSHA announced that it planned to look into the above-average injury rates at IBP's facilities for 1985-86.[52]

For some OSHA's recent actions are belated at best. U.S. Senator Paul Simon, D-Ill., chairman of the Senate Subcommittee on Employment and Productivity, believes OSHA's fines "came too late" to help injured workers. The blame for the agency's lax enforcement he declared, "must be laid nowhere else but at the doorstep of the Reagan-Bush administration."[53]

After the announcement of the $4.3 million Morrell fine, 110 members of the U.S. House of Representatives and 11 U.S. Senators wrote to the company's board chairman Milton Schloss questioning his company's commitment to safety and requesting to know what actions he planned to take to improve worker safety.[54]

Schloss, without seeing the letters, immediately charged that they were drafted by the meatpacking unions. "We find it insulting, misleading and question how any member of Congress could blindly sign such a letter without knowledge of the issues involved."[55]

At the same time that members of Congress were sending their letter to the John Morrell Co.,the USDA announced that it was proposing new regulations to target the most troublesome meat and poultry plants for closer federal inspections, while easing up on those with good records.

While the American Meat Institute, whose former president Richard Lyng was the current Secretary of Agriculture, applauded the new proposals, union officials expressed skepticism noting that the USDA plan appeared similar to OSHA's policy of targeting inspections to those companies with poor safety records.

"What we discovered with that inspection program was that companies lied on their records," the UFCW's Allen Zach recalls. "And so inspections [by OSHA] were not done. As a result we've had a tragic increase in safety and health problems [for workers] in meat packing, poultry in particular."[56]

Voicing similar concerns, Kerry Strand, a Hood College sociology professor and an expert on work place conditions, points out that OSHA had been understaffed for a number of years due to the Reagan Administration's deregulation drive.

"To get the most for your dollar you send the inspectors to the big places. In the South you have right-to-work states. Your food processing plants are an example of marginal industries with low profit margins: They operate more or less on a shoestring, which means it comes out of the hide of the workers."

It's a lot like Third World countries where young women either have no jobs or very low-paying, dangerous jobs. It's not a question of we should let them get away with it because otherwise there wouldn't be any jobs. To me, it's what kind of a society are we that we have an economy that survives on the backs of workers.[57]

The National Safe Workplace Institute believes that the U.S. government must share a major responsibility for many of the nation's unsafe workplaces because of its unwillingness to prosecute aggressively companies that violate safety laws and endanger workers. In a July 1988 study it notes that the Justice Department has placed such a low priority on filing criminal charges against health and safety violators that it managed only two successful criminal prosecutions of safety violations between 1980 and 1988.

As Joseph Kinney, executive director of the non-profit Institute, stresses:

> There are at least 100 good criminal cases every year where deaths have occurred and where employers knowingly and willfully violate federal regulations. If the government wants to reduce deaths and injuries, go forward with 50 of those ... It's clear the use of civil fines just isn't working.
>
> Companies simply amortize the [fines] and look at it as the cost of doing business. Put them in jail and you'd get their attention.[58]

Troubling Questions For Consumers

With the appearance of *The Jungle* in January 1906 and the subsequent publishing of such rhymes in the press as:

"Mary had a little lamb,
And when she saw it sicken,
She shipped it off to Packingtown,
And now it's labeled chicken."[59]

and a realization by the public that the canned goods and other meat products it consumed daily were prepared in filth and degradation, meat sales soon plummeted.

Thus, swept by public outrage, a shocked nation, despite efforts by the meat packers to discredit Sinclair's work, quickly saw to the passage of the precedent-setting Pure Food and Drug Act and the Beef Inspection Act within six months of the publication of *The Jungle*.

Today, corporate control and manipulation of beef prices are by no means the only symptoms of an increasingly concentrated meat industry, as recent newspaper headlines show.

United States Would Ease Bone Labeling Rule for Meat

Japan bars drug-tainted U.S. pork

Steroids in Your Hamburger

USDA Proposes Labeling Changes For Meat Products

Growing Demand for Lean Meat Spurs Embryo-Transfer Experiments With Bison

Interest Growing in "Natural Beef"

Overhaul of USDA Meat Inspection Urged

USDA agrees it's responsible for ensuring "wholesome" poultry

Slicing It Thin: Meat Inspection Cuts Proposed by Reagan Are Hot Issue for Bush

While most meat consumed by Americans is safe and wholesome, as the above headlines indicate in recent years many serious questions have emerged regarding the quality of that meat. Such concerns range from microbial infections stemming from organisms such as salmonella, to too much fat in our meat, to chemical residues in animals which can pose serious health risks, to questions about the very quality of our meat inspection system.

A National Academy of Sciences (NAS) panel has called for major changes in the system that assures the quality of U.S. meat and poultry, pointing out that inspection methods have failed to keep pace with technology or new health concerns.[60]

Contrary to the USDA's belief that the Academy's report was generally "upbeat," Carol Tucker Foreman, former assistant USDA secretary for food and consumer services, believed it was "very critical" of the system. "I think the public should be outraged and demand change." Unfortunately, she added, the "Gramm-Rudman compulsion" to save money will likely further reduce the quality of meat inspection and "almost eliminate the chance that it will be done better."[61]

Shortly after NAS released its report which was greeted by criticisms like Foreman's, Gramm-Rudman-Hollings legislation did in fact impose a crippling 4.3 percent budget cut in 1986 on the USDA's meat and poultry inspection system. Personnel was about to be trimmed and a nine-day furlough for USDA's some 9000 inspectors was considered.

Industry representatives, however, met with the Office of Management and Budget and succeeded in getting a last minute release of $5.7 million to prevent such drastic cuts. This release requested by the White House was originally appropriated by the Congress in 1985 in the belief that the Reagan Administration's annual budget request for the Food Safety and Inspection Service was not sufficient.

One Congressional staffer later explained,

> Occasionally there are accounts where the Administration doesn't ask for the amount they need. If Congress appropriates the money they need, the Administration points the finger at Congress for overspending . . In this case we called the bluff of the Administration on meat inspection.[62]

When we recognize that the Reagan Administration sought to systematically dismantle the meat inspection system it becomes clear why such budgetary problems have arisen in the past. As Kathleen Hughes shows in her exhaustive study, *Return to the Jungle: How the Reagan Administration Is Imperiling the Nation's Meat and Poultry Program*, since the first federal meat inspection act was passed in 1906 government inspectors "have waged an often intense tug of war with the meat industry, much of which resents the burden of complying with health and safety standards, but at the same time needs the USDA stamp to market its product."

Yet, just as these questions concerning the quality of the meat supply and controversies like the one that swirled around the United States's $100 million of meat exports to Europe vie for our attention, the grave internal structural problems that persist within the nation's multi-billion dollar meat and poultry industry remain unattended, often ignored.

To view each of these questions and controversies, however, as a singular problem is a serious mistake, for as we have seen throughout this book they are but symptoms of a larger, more complex, and much more ominous issue. That issue, as it is throughout our entire corporate agribusiness structure, is who shall control our food supply and do we want it controlled by a handful of powerful, impersonal, unaccountable corporations?

Or do we want it controlled by a variety of individuals and companies who are motivated not by a bottom line that dictates speed and greed, but rather by individuals and businesses who recognize a reasonable concern for the public interest based on the principles of economic and social justice?

Section Seven:

The Struggle for Economic Equilibrium

"The biggest problem farmers have is that they have to sell their products through a market place that is really a 'raw materials procurement and distribution system': a system that is designed to buy raw materials as cheaply as possible and resell the products on the basis of all the traffic will bear — regardless of cost, efficiency, supply, demand or fair market value."

- Fred Stover, President of the U.S. Farmers Association.

Chapter Thirty-Six

Tapping the Roots

It has been said, only partly in jest, that farmers frequently reach all the right conclusions for the wrong reasons when they assess their plight and the causes of "America's permanent agricultural crisis."

Many factors have helped create the hodgepodge of thinking that exists today in farm communities, including: confusion regarding the term "farm fundamentalism;" how the agrarian ideals of Thomas Jefferson, who believed so strongly in the family farm system, have been corrupted; and how the Protestant ethic has been used by corporate agribusiness and its "communities of economic interest" to divide and conquer rural America.

Almost lost in the cacophony of farmers' self-evaluation is one incontrovertible fact: seldom have farmers' movements, except perhaps for that of the agrarian populists in the late nineteenth century, seen themselves in the context of a fundamental and deliberately constructed gap between the persistent maladjustments of the economic structure of agriculture and social status of rural America on the one hand, and the economic and social status of urban America on the other.

To understand how this gap was constructed we must explore some of those basic characteristics which have become the hallmark of the American family farmer, and which have helped mold and shape those characteristics. We will then be in a better position to evaluate critically the principal attacks being made on our current family farm system.

Who is the Farmer?

While farmers are people with as many different tastes, idiosyncracies and subtleties of character as the rest of us, city dwellers have traditionally underestimated their intelligence. This is perhaps due to rustic speech and mannerisms resulting from geographical isolation. However, modern communications and transportation have significantly narrowed if not eliminated such cultural gaps. In fact, many have come to recognize and admire farmers essential intelligence; their skills in adapting to the environment, self-preservation and individual self-expression.

Ralph Waldo Emerson observed that the farmer is a "slow" person, "timed to nature, not to city watches." Since most land ownership in this country has historically been controlled by those who live timed to "city watches," many family farmers have found themselves powerless, their destinies controlled by economic and political forces not responsive to the farmer's nature.

This powerlessness has also contributed to the perception of many urban dwellers that family farmers belong to a lower or inferior class. For many, the family farmer has now become nothing more than a producer of raw materials for a mammoth food manufacturing system, thus becoming the newest member of the nation's blue collar class.

Farmers sometimes even view themselves in similar terms. As Richard Rhodes, author of *Farm: A Year in the Life of an American Farmer*, sardonically notes one definition of a farmer today might well be "someone who launders Government money for a chemical company."

While authors Richard Sennett and Jonathan Cobb do not specifically discuss the current plight of rural workers in their book *The Hidden Injuries of Class*, they do define a new form of class conflict in America among blue collar workers that certainly applies to farmers:

> Class is a system for limiting freedom: it limits the freedom of the powerful in dealing with other people, because the strong are constricted within the circle of action that maintains their power; class constricts the weak more obviously in that they must obey commands. What happens to the dignity men see in themselves and in each other, when their freedom is checked by class?[1]

Farmers, like the rest of us, are interested in acquiring the knowledge and wisdom necessary to maintain a decent quality of life. But, as we saw earlier in Teddy Roosevelt's Country Life Commission recommendations and Seaman Knapp's introduction of the Extension Service, farmers have always been told that the best route to such knowledge is formal education. Yet Sennett and Cobb remind us:

> Knowledge through formal education they see as giving a man the tools for achieving freedom — by permitting him to control situations and by furnishing him with access to a greater set of roles in life. As things actually stand, however, Certified Knowledge does not mean dignity ... indeed, it is the reverse, it is a sham. What needs to be understood is how class structure in America is organized so that *the tools of freedom become sources of indignity*.[2]

The argument that rural America needs to maintain its own time-tested and traditional elements steadfastly and resist the efforts of the "city" to foist upon it its own self-serving "tools for achieving freedom" is a valid one. As we have seen, the city's so-called Certified Knowledge has frequently tended only to perpetuate those conditions which have given us America's permanent agricultural crisis.

Despite what others may think about their intelligence or purpose in life, most farm families have maintained an abiding faith in the permanence of agriculture which for them has been historically based mainly around land tenure. Even when the return from the land is small or erratic, the land remains. This sense of immutability and the realization that nature will again yield fruitfully, even after the lean years, has not only inspired much patience and confidence in their way of life, but it also has given most farmers a basically optimistic and courageous attitude toward life.

This positive attitude toward their own plight combined with a large measure of healthy skepticism can frequently be seen in the farmers' sense of humor. Farm humor is not, as some believe, inordinately earthy. Rather it reflects the farce of concrete situations faced daily by farmers while seeking to illustrate a serious idea, particularly the economic moral of thrift, self-reliance and industry. Consider what A. C. Townley, founder of the Non-Partisan League, told a 1917 Idaho league meeting about a frustrated farmer trying to cope with staying in business:

He found out that it cost more to raise the beef than he got for it, and he sat there and kept getting madder and madder. Finally he got up, jammed the figures into his pocket and started down the street looking straight ahead. He met a friend, who said: "Hello Bill, what is the matter? Are you crazy?" "No, I am not crazy yet, but I guess I will be." His friend says: "Where are you going?" He says: "I am going down to the end of the street to get my dinner. I am going down to that little restaurant where I can get oxtail soup and tongue." His friend says: "What do you want with oxtail soup and tongue? You can get plenty to eat up here." He says: "I want to get some oxtail soup and tongue today, because that is the only way that I can make both ends meet."[3]

How the World and Society Perceives the Farmer

In a recent directive to company employees, R.E. Sneddon, president of Agricenter International in Memphis, Tennessee ordered that henceforth, the word "farmer" be dropped from his firm's literature. Sneddon, who develops and promotes farm products and who has sought to lobby other agribusiness enterprises to join his effort, believes that the term "agricultural producer" is more appropriate in today's "free market" economy.

"Farmer," he says, "creates a mental image of a guy in bibbed overalls, who comes to town dirty, who is uneducated, [and] who almost has a 'poor white trash' image."[4] Others would have us believe that many of our American farmers are also greedy, grasping, generally reckless and failures as independent businesspeople.

Fortunately, the general public's perception of the American farmer is considerably more positive and accurate than the opposite extremes presented by Sneddon and a small body of the nation's agricultural economists. A February, 1986 CBS News-*New York Times* poll found that 58 percent of those questioned believed that farm life was more honest than life elsewhere in the U.S. and 64 percent thought farmers more hardworking than others in the society. A heavy majority (67 percent) also opined that farm families had closer ties with one another than most other Americans.[5]

Unfortunately, however, negative public notions have contributed immeasurably to a mutual suspicion between urban and rural people and have successfully thwarted beneficial relationships between the two groups. Most of these false images and unwarranted suspicions have been nurtured and exploited for selfish reasons by those self-same "communities of economic interests" that today control corporate agribusiness.

As the Center for Rural Affairs' Marty Strange so sagely observes,

American agriculture needs to be reconciled with its values. I believe that there is fundamental goodness. I still believe in the Jeffersonian notion that the people of the land are decent people. But I do believe that our values have not been well nourished, that instead they have been swapped in the pettiness of economics.

American agriculture, I believe, stands for economic opportunity, social justice, equality, thrift, conservation, modesty, humility, caring for community, belief in family and honesty in business relationships. I think the American family farm stands historically with all of those things.[6]

"All Cannot be Shavers — Some Must be Fleeced."

In today's world of the family farmer we often see social mutuality and equality, rather than individuals tending to conform to the modern themes of industry and thrift. Despite their love of independence, iconoclasts, non-conformists and even innovators find it difficult to overcome the static character of our current social and economic system and thus often find themselves rejected by it.

Because farmers have always fancied themselves as members of the landownership class, they have not only magnified that conservative self-image, but because farm families have traditionally been headed by males, there still exists that certain reinforcement in the general public's mind of the patriarchal landlord figure from a bygone era.

Thus, as a property owner, head of the family and imagined ruler of his own economic destiny, many a family farmer still continues mistakenly to identify himself with the wealthy and dominant class despite the fact that the erosion of the farm economy has consistently been robbing him of real financial or political power.

All family farmers must sooner or later face this crucial question of self-identity, whether they are in fact members of the managerial or the laboring class. For example, the vast majority of farmers in the 1970s who bought additional acreage while the value of their land multiplied, were generally not acting as "greedy farmers," but rather they were following an American tradition as "responsible business people," trying to make the most out of the resources available to them. Unfortunately, their efforts to maximize the use of their resources would lead them a few years later to face choices which would ultimately result in undermining their most cherished hopes and dreams.

James Madison wrote that, "those who hold and those who are without property have ever formed distinct interests in society. Those who are creditors, and those who are debtors, fall under a like discrimination."[7] It was also Madison who, quite wisely, said that "all men having power ought to be distrusted to a certain degree."[8]

For nearly a century now it has been exceedingly difficult for most commercial family-type farmers to accept their evolution into proletarians, producers of raw materials for what has essentially become a oligopolistic food manufacturing industry. Instead, they have doggedly clung to the myth of their independence.

American economist Thorstein Veblen dwelt on this fact in his 1923 essay, "The Independent Farmer." He contended that farmers have mythologically held on to the "time-worn make-believe that they are individually self-sufficient masterless men." While often given to overbroad generalizations, Veblen does raise several valid points respecting the modern farmers' notion of independence.

They have become blinded, he writes, by "the system of business interests in whose web [they] are caught" and have offered their "unwavering loyalty" to the system in which they saw themselves acting like other independent businessmen. Ironically, however, most of these other businessmen were not independent, their units of operation rather were "drawn on a large scale, massive, impersonal, imperturbable and in effect, irresponsible, under the established law and custom, and they are interlocked in an unbreakable framework of common interests."[9]

Farmers, he continues, are surrounded by bankers, railroad magnates and food processors who profit from their

effective collusive control of the market, while the foolish farmer does little more than identify with the very people who are most adept at exploiting him. Some day he, too, will share in the prosperity of the system, at least he so believes. The poor farmer turns a deaf ear to the warning that it is certain that all cannot become rich in this way. All cannot be shavers — some must be fleeced.[10]

It is only very recently that most farmers have come to realize that the production costs and markets for their commodities are determined by factors nearly totally unrelated to the inherent physical or human resources or even the theoretical world demand for such commodities. The fact that there is really no such thing in agriculture today as a "free market" often been overlooked by farmers desiring to integrate themselves into the nation's current economic structure.

Agricultural markets today have become totally dependent on noncompetitive sectors. They are sand-wiched between a tightly co[...] which protects profits by pa[...] and an equally small numbe[...] to play off producers on on[...] against producers on the [...] abandon the ancient idea t[...] unique class thus risks th[...] inferior status.

Because they cling to thi[...] ness, many farmers have [...] absolutist attitude toward [...] generally regarding their workers as merely low-grade economic inputs, much to the glee of corporate agribusiness.

In adopting such a stance, along with those others mentioned above, farm communities have generally felt that there is little or no reason why the laws of nature or humanity should be changed. Their traditional, often fundamentalist, Protestant-ethic religious belief system has only reinforced this basic conservatism.

Addressing this very question in a brilliant Gregory Foundation Memorial Lecture on "The Rural Foundation of American Culture" at the University of Missouri on January 26, 1976, Dr. Walter Goldschmidt observed:

I said earlier that one aspect of the Protestant ethic ... is a belief that each individual's value is established by his accomplishment, and that for that reason each person should be allowed to grow as wealthy and powerful as he can. But this unfettered growth of wealth and power threatens the very social framework out of which it has emerged. It is not an easy dilemma to solve, for it confronts freedom with equality — an age-old issue.

How much freedom? How much equality? Very much is at stake, not only for the farm communities, but for the whole of the American polity.

If, as I have suggested, the growth of corporate control of agriculture is not a product of efficiency, intelligence and hard work — of virtue according to the Protestant Ethic — but a consequence of policies and manipulations, the matter takes on a different character. The task, is to reformulate policies respecting agriculture so that the competitive advantage of large scale operations are removed, so that the ordinary working farmer has an equal chance. If this is done, it may not be necessary to resolve the dilemma between freedom and equality.[11]

Any discussion, therefore, about the shaping of the farm character and that character's impact on the development of U.S. farm and food policy must recognize the importance of the questions posed by Dr. Goldschmidt. How much freedom? How much equality? And, who has primarily benefited from U.S. agricultural and food policy decisions?

Honest answers to such questions are crucial if we are to understand the roots and significance of America's permanent agricultural crisis, and who are the key players in this crisis.

Dr. Goldschmidt's raises regarding
ty are also similar to those philosophical
arguments that have long revolved around
f Thomas Jefferson and Alexander Hamilton.

Farmer's Jeffersonian Character

In their book *The Policy Process in American Agriculture*, Talbot and Hadwiger point out that while Jeffersonians have claimed Thomas Jefferson as their mentor, they also see John Locke as their oracle and Frederick Jackson Turner as a myth-maker and interpreter.

The natural rights of man ("liberty, freedom and equality") were the central themes spelled out by Locke in his *Second Treatise on Civil Government* and enunciated by Jefferson in the second paragraph of the Declaration of Independence: "We hold these truths to be self-evident; that all men are created equal ..."[12]

The genesis of such thinking involved a unique merger of ideas developed during the Enlightenment and the Romantic Movement in Western Europe. From the former came the notion that the ideal world could be found in the natural order of things as opposed to collective restraints on individual actions — and that utopia could be realized by allowing ourselves, because of our acquisitive instincts, to be guided by the invisible hand of the perfect market. Such philosophizing played an instrumental role in the defining of the rights of man, leading enlightened thinkers to exalt the rule of reason and constitutional democracy.

The thinkers and artists of the Romantic period also gloried in the world of nature and the pristine simplicity of rural life, viewing it as a corrective to the "evil contaminants" of civilization, believing that nature purified and enhanced individuals weighted down with the artificial culture of their age. They were also reacting to the Industrial Revolution, contrasting the rural world with the dismal circumstances of the manufacturing centers where the human spirit was crushed by endless toil in a depressing physical environment.

The Jeffersonians drew from the Aristotelian idea that "the first and best kind of populace is one of farmers; and there is thus no difficulty in constructing a democracy where the bulk of the people live by farming."[13] They would fashion what might be called a certain agricultural fundamentalism in their new homeland.

Such fundamentalism involved: support for the independent yeoman; cheap land; the value of personal sweat in conquering a bountiful, but often unyielding natural environment; fee-simple ownership; a hatred of tenancy; a fear of overpopulated cities inhabited by large factories dependent on exploited labor, and a belief in the limited power of government. As Francis Moore Lappé, an authority on food policy, reminds us,

> Certainly the founders of our nation never believed that democracy could be built purely by self-seeking. Nowhere did our Founding Fathers praise individualism, rugged or otherwise. They clearly believed community interests should be paramount over selfish interests. Even James Madison, often viewed as the hard-headed advocate of governance through competition of oppos-

ing interests believed adamantly in the need for what was then known as "civic virtue" — what Montesquieu had defined as the integration of one's own good with the public good. "To suppose that any form of government will secure liberty or happiness without any [civic] virtue in the people is a chimerical idea."[14]

In Pursuit of Liberty and Human Progress

Because there has been so much misunderstanding concerning this agricultural fundamentalism and the role it has played throughout U.S. history we must carefully examine the thought process of its mentor. For while Jefferson's idea of the "chosen people of God" is both exalted and decried in our technological and urban age, many of the basic concepts behind his ideas have been either conveniently ignored or forgotten.

The Jeffersonian thought process, as William B. Wheeler notes in his perceptive essay on "Jeffersonian Thought In An Urban Society," can be divided into three basic categories:[15]

1) Faith: Jefferson's beliefs, from which he derives his basic arguments;
2) Ends: goals which he reasoned to be the timeless aspirations of human beings worthy of pursuit, and
3) Means: the plans and programs designed by each generation to achieve the desired ends of their common faith.

Likewise, the three central aspects of Jefferson's vision were:

a) a belief in the basic goodness and worth of human beings, who were not only reasonable and generally just, but also compassionate and intelligent,
b) that the Creator had bestowed on each person natural rights, which might on occasion need to be defended, but never earned and which came to them regardless of earthly condition, and
c) that the new United States of America provided a unique and unmatchable opportunity for human beings to exercise their God-given rights, to live in peace and human goodness.

For Jefferson, the constant and changeless ends of any human society were clear — liberty and progress.

His notion of liberty included broadly defined concepts of independence, individualism and freedom of the human mind. Societies would be judged by how much freedom each citizen was able to exercise.

Human progress was defined rather generally by Jefferson, sometimes even in different ways. On occasion he saw self-reliance, hard work, independence, equality, love of nature and other like virtues as part, if not the product, of the push West and a basic ingredient in the formation of the American character.[16] On other occasions, Jefferson expressed the idea that human progress was an individual affair, each person improving him or herself economically and culturally until Americans collectively would form the most advanced, finest civilization in which any human being could hope to live.

As a practical thinker and a politician, however, Jefferson knew that *each generation had to formulate for itself* the means to achieve these goals of liberty and human progress. For Jefferson and his time an agrarian republic, a society of family farmers, was the best way to achieve such ends. As Wheeler explains:

Not only was he convinced that the pastoral life was a better means to pursue man's constant searching for liberty and human progress, but the Virginia planter further believed that his faith could *not* be maintained nor his ends achieved in a nonagrarian society. When one examines his anti-urban writings, it is clear that it was not the city *per se* to which Jefferson objected but rather that urban living was a poor (perhaps impossible) method of meeting human needs.[17]

In Jefferson's time three factors made the family farm a popular idea: it was a familiar unit, it made economic sense, and it coincided well with accepted beliefs about the nature of democratic political power.

Agrarian Life and Democracy's Four Basic Qualities

Jefferson preferred rural life as a *means* by which human beings could pursue liberty and human progress. To think that Jefferson believed in the agrarian republic as a goal in and of itself, I believe, is to misunderstand his work.

For almost two centuries we have witnessed the evolving industrialization, urbanization and commercialism of our nation's "family farm system" (as Jefferson forecast). During that time we have also witnessed many attempts to return to the "good ol' days" and the pastoral life of Jefferson's day, rather than a redoubling of the effort to maintain the *faith* and achieve those *ends* which he espoused.

Through the understanding of that latter process we can see not only how the Jeffersonian ideal has been corrupted and misinterpreted and what is necessary to revitalize it, but also how and why repeated efforts by farmers and rural citizens to maintain those ideals have been successfully thwarted by an increasingly industrialized society.

Jefferson saw four basic qualities inherent within the agrarian life as vital to any community or society: namely, retaining control of one's life while nurturing the principle of self-sufficiency, maintaining a homogeneity of interests, a love of naturalism, and the prizing of creativity.[18]

No element in modern society has traditionally projected a more pronounced image of people with fundamental control over their own lives than our farm families. Such control is reflected in many ways, especially the degree of self-sufficiency so often exhibited by farmers and rural people. Because they have the means to produce their own food and the security provided by the land, farmers have frequently seen themselves as relatively independent of the industrial/commercial world. This degree of genuine and/or imagined independence has had not only curious economic, political and psychological overtones, but has also fueled the notion among many that farming is uniquely "a way of life."

Such an acceptance of agriculture as "a way of life" has in turn made farmers doubly distrustful of urban life. They characterize the latter environment as highly centralized and the antithesis of independence, with individuals having little or no control over their own lives and far removed from the land and the majesty of nature.

Aside from the hoped-for wealth from the goods produced each year on their land, the earth itself has always given farmers a sense of oneness. They see themselves as truly sharing in nature's abundance, yet blessed with the rewarding task of taming nature for a common purpose. This shared pursuit of common interests among farmers often involves cooperative efforts (such as participating in the legendary barn buildings) where each individual in the community seeks to complement ideally, rather than compete with one another.

There is a paradox here for while farmers espouse this ideal of solidarity, believing that because farming is the community's major economic activity, they are the ones who must maintain a large measure of control over their own lives it is, in fact, the large and often absentee owners and corporate agribusiness interests who now wield the real economic and political power in many of their rural communities.

Jefferson believed that farmers were more attuned to the rhythms of nature than their urban neighbors. While they have historically had a more acute sense of what Jefferson characterized as "naturalness," their attitude toward nature has, nevertheless, been a strange mixture of environmental traditions.

In *American Environmentalism: Values, Tactics, Priorities*, Joseph Petulla suggests that part of the reason for these "dual and occasionally paradoxical values of environmentalism," found in people like farmers, lies in the origins and history of their expression."*[19]

---

* "Those traditions that have inspired such expressions are called biocentric, ecologic and economic.

"The **biocentric** tradition stems from the primitive feelings which led the ancients to both fear and to respect nature and the power of *mana* — the unknown creator and destroyer of life — within nature. Although this extraphysical force which gave plants, animals and other objects of nature their unique powers has changed its expression throughout the millennia, it can be seen today in both its progressive and conservative forms.

"The **ecologic** tradition, has evolved from ancient Greco-Roman theories of natural law which have come to us through the Christian interpretations of teleology (investigation of the purposes and final ends of nature) of the medieval Scholastics, and from them through the natural philosophies of the eighteenth-century Enlightenment, ending finally in what we know as modern science.

The pursuit of knowledge from the early natural-law philosophers to contemporary scientists has been characterized mostly by the desire to uncover predictable "laws of nature" and to use those laws according to the prevailing religion,

For Jefferson, creativity was a basic quality of agrarian life that was desirable in the pursuit of both liberty and human progress. Again, in this regard farmers have been unique in our society in that they have had the opportunity on an almost daily basis to be part of — as well as witness to — creation, growth, realization, and the enjoyment of the fruits of one's own labor. Wheeler well puts into words what many farmers have probably asked each other many times over the years.

How could it be possible ... that anyone else beside the farmer could establish such an indelible link in the great chain of being, the continuous act of creation? If the creations themselves are not grand (as those of a Carnegie or a Rockefeller or a Morgan), they are not accomplished by an army of laborers or a well oiled mass human machine, but rather by one person who can plan, execute and bask in his successes, however modest.[20]

These four qualities (retaining control, homogeneity of interests, naturalness, and creativity) often overlap in

---

ideology, or dominant class interests.

Finally, the **economic** tradition or our third environmental expression is a modern one and grew out of an attempt to make efficiency a virtue in early capitalistic societies. Max Weber in *Protestant Ethics* and R. H. Tawney in *Religion and Capitalism* illustrated the connections between the principles of Calvinism, Puritanism and other religions on the one hand and the development of the middle class in early capitalism on the other.

Individualistic religions — that is, religions that focused on the individual rather than the particular church — appeared to offer both the mark of holiness and eternal rewards as well to those who, with strict self-discipline, lived up to their societal duties. The individualistic virtues replaced social solidarity, fraternity, and sympathy when 'economic man' was born in the grand alliance between the bourgeoisie and organized religion.

It then took just one short step for moral and political leaders to support economic theories of 'the invisible hand' in which the common good of all could be reached by individual competition. Finally, goodness became identified with efficiency (that is, economic efficiency) and elimination of waste so that even monopoly consolidations and 'economic planning' could be touted as more efficient and therefore morally superior.

Both the progressive and conservative interpretation of these three environmental traditions — biocentric, ecologic and economic — have thus enabled various and frequently conflicting special interests within agriculture to gain added sustenance from a variety of history's religious and/or ideological convictions."

Jeffersonian thought. They are *ideals*. Whether such qualities were or are actual components possessed by all or even a majority of farmers in Jefferson's day or since, as Wheeler notes, is almost beside the point:

the repetition of them by Jeffersonians and farmers alike made them real *in the minds* of Americans from that day to this. Indeed, they have *become real* and have been seen as the components indispensable to any realization of the Jeffersonian creed.[21]

Can Democracy Save the Family Farm?

Repeated efforts by farmers and farm communities throughout our history to preserve and protect a semblance of Jefferson's agrarian republic, however, has become largely a losing battle. This is both due partly to the fact that such efforts have generally been aimed at physical goals (land ownership, conservation, etc.), rather than qualitative ones (retaining control, homogeneity of interests, naturalism, and creativity), but more importantly, because an industrialized-capitalist-oriented society has seen such qualities as inimical to its own well-being and has reacted accordingly.

In a 1948 book, *Farming and Democracy*, A. Whitney Griswold, a political scientist and former president of Yale University properly warned us that

we can expect no democratic miracles from agriculture or any other particular part of our economy. We can expect them only from democracy itself ... The only sure source of democracy in any of these is a national well-spring that feeds all of them, not just a source among farmers, or, as we should say, among some farmers. *The lesson is plain in history. Family farming cannot save democracy. Only democracy can save the family farm* ... (emphasis added)

Griswold also expressed the belief that the family farm's strongest claim on democracy, "the one by which it will either stand or fall as democratic political theory," is that for all its "corruption" by industry, business, and government, it is still "the outstanding form of individual economic enterprise."

He goes on to say,

A family farm of the type and dimensions stipulated by our theory — one "on which the operator, with the help of his family and perhaps a moderate amount of outside labor, can make a satisfactory living and maintain the farm's productivity and assets" — affords scope for a citizen to live and work more or less on his own terms, to develop the initiative and resourcefulness, the sense of responsibility and the self-respect that have always and everywhere been considered among the greatest assets of democracy.

In concluding this thought, Griswold poses the quintessential question:

If we still count them as such, *not symbolically, but concretely and instrumentally,* like our physical resources and our geographical position, we will support family farming as we will all *socially constructive individual enterprise.* The question is, do we really believe in free enterprise in these vital terms?[22] (emphasis added)

Relative to this question, Lappé stresses Jefferson's view that political democracy hinged on a rough equality of condition.

> He intuited that if people's life experiences were greatly different because of great differences in wealth, they simply wouldn't see the world the same way. They couldn't identify with each other. And without that identity any hope for a common purpose was lost.
>
> What would it mean to challenge, as our founders did, the presumption of individual self-seeking as primary? What would it mean to put freedom, democracy and community above the rigid dictates of the market and unlimited private productive property? What would it mean to make these devices *serve* our values, instead of subverting and rationalizing our values to make them fit the dogma?[23]

This question, she believes, should push us to the very frontier of human progress. "It requires letting go of our preconceived notions of capitalism (economic decisionmaking by wealth) and statism (economic decisionmaking by a political elite)."

Dr. John Helmuth, currently Adjunct Associate Professor and Assistant Director, Center for Agriculture and Rural Development, Iowa State University, poignantly underscores that observation in his introduction to the PrairieFire Rural Action publication *Heading Toward the Last Roundup: The Big Three's Prime Cut* when he observes:

> ... when fewer and fewer individuals make more and more of the economic decisions, whether those individuals are in government or big business, the result is anti-competitive, inefficient and harmful to the society as a whole; when more and more individuals make more and more of the economic decisions, the result is more competitive and more efficient and beneficial to society as a whole.
>
> There is even greater irony in that the principal advocates of centralized economic planning — the Soviet Union and Eastern European countries — are abandoning it as an economic failure, at the very time American industries ... are becoming more and more centrally planned by those few firms with greater and greater economic power resulting from ever increasing industry concentration.

The Hamiltonian Ideal

Since the founding of our nation a Hamiltonian tradition has come to rival the Jeffersonian ideal in the attempt to influence, direct and shape the nation's political and economic landscape. As with the Jeffersonians, agrarian fundamentalism has also played a significant role in the Hamiltonian scheme of things, although in its evolution it has been rationalized, conveniently manipulated and often twisted to serve a variety of very specific ideologies and special interests.

Whereas the Jeffersonian ideal sees life in New Testament terms, respecting differences among human beings but emphasizing that the natural equality of individuals will show forth where liberty and human progress abound, the Hamiltonian views life more in an Old Testament framework: a righteous God will cast his favors upon a chosen few.

Edmund Burke can perhaps be thought of as the Hamiltonian's oracle, believing as an Englishman that those who govern should be those who have the sufficient intelligence, breeding and leisure. Despite the fact that so many of his fellow countrymen had fled to this new land to escape the political and religious feudalism of Europe, Alexander Hamilton shared Burke's ideals. As Talbot and Hadwiger show:

> Earned wealth was the label of distinction in the Hamiltonian picture. Whether earned or inherited, however, private property was the hallmark of merit. Those who had the intelligence and the will would, and should, be the principal property-holders in a free society, and they ought to have an influential, if not decisive, voice in public affairs.[24]

For the Hamiltonians, the marketplace was to become the "harsh judge of righteousness," the role of government was to be limited, change would be tolerated only as long as it did not disturb the prevailing distribution of power, heredity was considered more important than environment, the theories of modern social scientists were either pseudo- or, at best, quasi-scientific, and

> philosophy is something that a few academics participate in. It is of little practical value and perhaps leads only to confusion, since the propositions from which the good life proceeds are simple and self-evident. These propositions should be taught, not tested. Institutions of higher education can be trusted in the areas of physical and biological sciences because the elite farmers will use the knowledge therefrom to become more productive. Through a "seeping-down" process, this use of education will eventually be to the advantage of all.[25]

Calvinism and the Protestant ethic also had a significant influence in shaping the Hamiltonian ideal in its direction. That ethic has often been referred to as a transcendental paradox, for how are God-fearing, hard working Christians to know if they will be saved? The answer for the Hamiltonian was simple: success and prosperity in terms of land and property ownership were assuredly proof that "God's grace had been shed on thee."

However, in this Hamiltonian response there is a kind of internal contradiction. As Dr. Goldschmidt observes,

> Central to this ethical system is the belief that success, both in the spiritual and mundane senses, is the proof of virtue. Hence, it is important that the pursuit of success be unfettered, and that the sky be the limit to a person's demonstration of such virtue. This gives approval to the process of individual self-aggrandizement and the amassing of personal fortunes. Thus, despite the egalitarian presuppositions, the system not only allows for, but actually encourages the development of great distinctions in wealth.[26]

An Apostle of "Economic Violence"

"That farmers are poor, that they could not survive without government programs, that food supplies would be inadequate without the programs, that corporations would take over farming without the programs, that the family farm has got to be preserved because it's essential for democracy, or that programs are essential to preserve the rural community: All of these things, all of it is myth. All myth."[27]

- Luther Tweeten

It is this tension between the ideals of Jefferson and Hamilton which has significantly contributed to the sharp ideological and material conflicts we see today within American agriculture. While the nation's agricultural goals have remained constant, the means chosen to gain those ends have frequently sown the seeds of bitter discontent in our fields of plenty.

Among those growing numbers who seek to rationalize, defend and justify the role of corporate agribusiness in America's permanent agricultural crisis no single individual has been more outspoken than Luther Tweeten, Oklahoma State University's regent's professor of agricultural economics. For Tweeten, destroying the nation's family farm system has become a holy and righteous crusade.

By denouncing farm activist groups "on the left" who "eschew violence but espouse conspiracy theories, scapegoating, and onerous forms of farm fundamentalism,"[28] by declaring that "democratic principles do not inherently extend to any sector the right to vote on its economic destiny,"[29] and by admonishing farmers that "their social contract with society" demands that they "accept without violence and with respect for due process, a system that alternatively may provide rich rewards and at other times economic setbacks, even bankruptcy."[30] Tweeten, essentially advocates an agribusiness fundamentalism based on what Rev. Jesse Jackson aptly describes as "economic violence."

He seeks to portray what he calls the "farm political activist movement"[31] as a small group of protestors ("mostly family farmers rather than large industrial-type farmers or part-time small farmers"[32]) enslaved to what

he terms the myths of the "dark side of the farm personality,"[33] which he contends, exhibits "a psychological and ideological climate where paranoia, scapegoating, violence, armed confrontation and fear" have come together. Tweeten, however, clearly reveals the contradictions of corporate agribusiness: publicly mounting a pseudo-defense of the family farm while at the same time attempting to destroy the very system on which the family farm is founded.

When Tweeten proclaims that "the personality of the farm sector is basically healthy and has many of the favorable attributes embodied in the image of the family farm as self-reliant and independent"[34] he is only underscoring what Ingolf Voegler has called the *genuine* myths about the family farm in the United States: that in attempting to capitalize on the "myth as power" concept, farmers have unwittingly become victims of that "family farm" myth so often perpetuated by corporate agribusiness.

That myth, so prominent throughout much of Tweeten's writings, proclaims that the farmer has been his or her "own boss," living the most independent existence possible in a pluralistic society. Such a myth has led farmers to believe they remain the last best examples of American independence, whereas in reality for nearly a century they have suffered a steadily diminishing control over their own lives and the lives of their communities.

We recall Voegler's primary thesis in *The Myth of the Family Farm: Agribusiness Dominance of U.S. Agriculture,*

> The conventional account of contemporary U.S. agriculture is widely accepted because it is based on the national ideal of the family farm derived from the Jeffersonian concept of agrarian democracy and from a small amount of truth. *When a myth is widely accepted, this small amount of truth is perceived as the whole truth!* (emphasis added)
>
> In the United States the myth of the family farm continues to be used for the benefit of a relatively small group of large-scale producers and agribusiness firms, while the vast majority of rural and urban people, believing the myth, pay the economic, political, social and environmental costs of this fantasy.[35]

Voegler also suggests that this "self-reliant and independent" myth of family farmers has been supported by four related myths: the work ethic myth, the free enterprise myth, the efficiency myth and the equal opportunity myth.[36]

Such mutually supporting myths have been sanctified and carefully manipulated by various social scientists and economists (like Tweeten and the "communities of economic interest" he represents) to give family farmers a false confidence in their position while their real political and economic power has been cleverly abrogated by corporate agribusiness.

Any critical examination of these myths exposes the reactionary philosophy that today motivates the corporate reapers in their eradication of the family farm system in America. It also helps us understand how America's permanent agricultural crisis is the product of a variety of extraordinary social and political circumstances, in addition to those unique economic and historical factors already discussed.

Tweeten's Roots of Antisocial Behavior

Believing that social scientists must confront the myths that "may have made life tolerable for many farmers but which also have provided a psychological and ideological climate where paranoia, scapegoating, violence, armed confrontation, intimidation and fear" abound,[37] Tweeten sees a number of "antisocial" roots which have precipitated this "dark side of the farm personality." They include:

1) Frustration over personal and industry economic problems in the 1980s;
2) A basic sense of superiority or "essentiality," in part motivated by "farm fundamentalism;"
3) A strong problem-solving orientation, and
4) More intense social and economic ties by families to farming than ties by others to their industries.

While acknowledging that farmers "have reason to complain" about the "quantum failure of fiscal policy in the 1980s" Tweeten lays the main burden of that failure on real interest and exchange rates and federal deficits, which he suggests are due in large part to over generous subsidies to farmers. He ignores increasing corporate economic concentration in the farm and food sector and the failure of the "free enterprise" system to maintain a fair price for commodities, as having played any role in the most recent chapter of America's permanent agricultural crisis.

> Farm fundamentalism is the belief that farming is not only a superior way of life but also represents the highest ideals of the nation ... [it] holds that the nation's political and social system cannot survive without the type of person the farm way of life produces. In economic philosophy, the ideal holds new wealth derives only from raw materials and that the farmer must prosper for the nation to prosper.[38]

By defining "farm fundamentalism" in a belittling manner Tweeten not only further isolates himself in that land-grant college ivory tower populated by so many agricultural economists, but he also turns his back on a significant body of principles fundamental to the American character.

Life Beyond the Farm Gate

Rather than admiring the strong problem-solving orientation that people have come to associate with the farm character, commentators like Tweeten contend that this too is a root of antisocial behavior reflected in the "dark side of the farm personality."

While acknowledging that farmers are "impatient with intellectualizing and bureaucratic procedures" and "are accustomed to improvising and taking matters into their own hands to create solutions by expedient means," Tweeten ignores the large role that corporate agribusi-

ness has played in fostering such distrust. He condescendingly declares that "the greater economic problems of farmers have roots beyond the farm gate and are less tractable to individual action and initiative than are problems of a sick cow or nutrient-deficient crops."[39]

But, as Tuskegee University Professor Emeritus Booker T. Whatley has already reminded us:

> Farmers must destroy the myth that there is a divine law which states they must lose title to their commodities at the farm gate. We have reached the level of sophistication in this country where everybody is making a profit on agricultural commodities *except* the farmers who produce them.[40]

Tweeten, however, a defender of the Earl Butz school of "get big or get out," not surprisingly decries the need for destroying such a myth.

> I have found widespread support among farm people for two propositions: 1) Washington and the market perennially have not favored them, and 2) they need more political and economic bargaining power to serve the needs of farmers and society. Each point has dubious validity.[41]

What about the concern among family farmers that commodity markets do not favor them and that unless the family farm system is preserved the nation's food production will fall into the hands of a few large corporations with the ability to control food prices? Tweeten dismisses it as "overblown and inconsistent rhetoric."[42]

But Tweeten betrays his real fears and those of corporate agribusiness in general, when he adds that "this incorrect assertion often prefaces the assertion that family farmers must *organize* to control production, *raise farm prices*, and in general find their ultimate economic security in *greater economic bargaining power*."[43] (emphasis added)

In an incredible and ironic litany of reasons why such a quest for market power by farmers has serious drawbacks, Tweeten, totally ignores the role and character of modern day corporate agribusiness (multinational, economically concentrated, and profit hungry by its very nature) and explains away his position:

> First, farmers are too independent and numerous to congeal into the tightly controlled bargaining organization required to affect farm economic outcomes.
>
> Second, the auto and steel labor unions have demonstrated that even powerful bargaining groups are unable to preserve jobs and earnings when domestic industries operate in an open global economy.
>
> Third, given that a facilitative public policy is required for farmers to bargain collectively, the public is unlikely to give any group arbitrary control over food supplies. To do so would place the public at risk and at the mercy of groups whose first concern would be self-interest rather

than safe, abundant, quality food supplies at reasonable prices.[44]

By insisting that the family farm system does not suffer from federal neglect and that farmers do not need more economic and political bargaining power, Tweeten once again demonstrates the validity of a major concern of the agrarian reform movement a century ago: that the nation's "communities of economic interests" remain unalterably opposed to farmers organizing for their own economic and political survival.

Remembering that agrarian populism was characterized by an evolving democratic culture in which people could "see themselves" and therefore aspire to a society conducive to mass human dignity, agrarian populists, like many family farmers today, believed that it was imperative to bring the corporate state under democratic control.

"Agrarian reformers," recalling the words of historian Lawrence Goodwyn,

> attempted to overcome a concentrating system of finance capitalism that was rooted in Eastern commercial banks and which radiated outward through trunk-line railroad networks to link in a number of common purposes much of America's consolidating corporate community. Their aim was structural reform of the American economic system.[45]

The fact that populism thrived for over a decade in the late 1800s by preaching that genuine political democracy was impossible without economic democracy explains why in the century since that "agrarian revolt," corporate America and its mouthpieces like Tweeten have sought to discredit and demean any renewed moves by the nation's farmers to reassert that economic and political power they so forcefully applied in the late 1800s.

"In its underlying emotional impulses," Goodwyn again reminds us,

> populism was a revolt against the narrowing limits of political debate within capitalism as much as it was a protest against specific economic injustices. The abundant evidence that 'great aggregations of capital' could cloak self-interested policies in high moral purposes — and have such interpretations disseminated widely and persuasively through the nation's press — outraged and frightened the agrarian reformers, convincing them of the need for a new political party free of corporate control.[46]

But Tweeten has emphatically rejected the notion of economic democracy.

> Democratic principles do not inherently extend to any sector the right to vote on its economic destiny. To do so without strong safeguards would create economic chaos ... For the most part, such decisions are best left to the imperson-

al workings of supply and demand in the marketplace and to a political system well endowed which checks and balances.[47]

One way corporate agribusiness has historically sought to deny economic democracy to the rural community has been to play off farmers against hired workers. Tweeten argues that "activists" in pressing not only for "an encompassing family farm bargaining organization, but also for unionization of all farm workers, *presumably* motivated by a concern that hired workers are disadvantaged and exploited," would, "however well intentioned deal a serious blow to the economic fortunes of the most disadvantaged workers — an outcome opposite that intended by activists." (emphasis added)

> The effect would likely be displacement of thousands of farm workers by mechanization and by production (especially of fruits and vegetables) shifting to foreign sources. Alternative employment opportunities for displaced low-skill farm workers are few and there is little reason to believe that they are currently employed in other than their best alternative.[48]

As farmers have looked at the society at large and seen the slow drift toward the standardization of work, home, church and school which in the twilight of twentieth century has come to characterize much of urban life, they have grown increasingly wary of that society. They are rightly concerned that this rapidly developing standardization process now threatens their own individualism.

Likewise, many farmers have come to see that they are no longer a world apart from the rest of the society, that they also have access to numerous opportunities through cooperative efforts, that overcoming their feelings of inferiority is a liberating economic, political and social experience, and that their struggles for societal equality need not be waged alone.

This reaching out by farmers beyond the farm gate to unite with those displaced, disadvantaged and exploited fellow victims of the "economic violence" that pervades our modern society not only frightens agricultural economists like Luther Tweeten, but has begun to sound alarm bells throughout the corporate agribusiness community.

Ties that Bind

Perhaps the most intriguing root of the antisocial behavior of the "dark side of the farm personality" that Tweeten disparages is the "intense social and economic ties by families to farming than ties by others to their industries."[33]

Such ties have not only been decried by agricultural economists like Tweeten, but by others as well. In their *Economic Development* textbook, Gerald Meier and Robert Baldwin advise:

> Every specific principle of economic change should be considered alongside a specific princi-

ple of cultural change. For instance, the economic criteria of investment are alone not sufficient guide for investment policy: they must be supplemented by non-economic criteria.

For illustrative purposes, some non-economic criteria for investment might be as follows invest in projects that break up village life by drawing people to centers of employment away from the village because, by preventing impersonal relations, village life is a major source of opposition to change. Such non-economic considerations may reinforce or contradict economic considerations, but they constitute an essential part in any assessment of the requirements for development. (p.357)

They continue,

Economic development of sufficient rapidity has not taken place within the present cultural framework. New wants, new motivations, new ways of production, new institutions need to be created if national income is to rise more rapidly. Where there are religious obstacles to modern economic progress, the religion may have to be taken less seriously or its character altered. (p.356)

By attempting to invoke the Protestant ethic, without specifically labeling it as such, Tweeten has sought to justify the current exalted position enjoyed by those "communities of economic interests" which today dominate corporate agribusiness.

A basic sense of superiority coupled with a belief that merit is neither recognized nor rewarded by

---

Agribusinesses Fund Fight Against Crop-Control Bill

USDA Ex-Officials Head Lucrative Effort

By Ward Sinclair
Washington Post Staff Writer

Some of the country's biggest and most profitable agribusiness companies have mounted a campaign, orchestrated by two former Reagan administration agriculture officials, to defeat legislation that would raise farmers' prices by reducing crop production.

The campaign could generate earnings of $ 250,000 for one-time Agriculture Department officials William G. Lesher and Randy M. Russell, now partners in an agricultural consulting firm. Forces behind the campaign include Cargill Inc., the world's largest grain trading company; Continental Grain Co., the third largest; Monsanto Co., which produces pesticides; International Minerals and Chemical Corp..

would have to pay more for their raw product," he said. "The further down we lower commodity prices under current policy, it's like saying we'll increase the profits of the companies.

"I don't mind these companies making profits — that's the engine of our system," he continued. "But when they make the kind of profits they do and then come in to defeat legislation that will help farmers make a little more money, then that's unconscionable. There's some gouging of the public and a squeezing of the farmers."

Cy Carpenter, president of the National Farmers Union, went further. "This is an absolute insult to the process of democracy as it is designed to serve people. It is a sham and a scandal," he said. "These companies recognize that their profit is substantial and that

---

society leads to frustration. Activists are not revolutionaries; they mostly believe in the American free enterprise economic system, representative democracy, the constitution, and a pluralistic society. That an important contribution to society goes unrewarded despite a basically sound socio-political system must mean a conspiracy exists to thwart prosperity.[50]

Aside from the question of whether agriculture is really part of a "basically sound socio-political system," this alleged paranoia among the "farm political activist movement" must also be addressed.

Listening to how Tweeten defines the "farm political-economic conspiracy theory" of the "farm political activist movement," and his dismissal of the idea that there exists an effort to "thwart prosperity" we should recall Dr. Goldschmidt's thoughts concerning those "policies and manipulations" which have shaped current U.S. farm policy. While many farmers today might choose to *say* that their current plight stems from a "conspiracy," they, in fact, *mean* that they see certain "communities of economic interests" successfully adopting and implementing such "policies and manipulations" to their own selfish advantage.

It is ironic that while Tweeten justifies his critical examination of the "farm political activist movement" by asserting that this "is not to show that farmers are somehow different but rather they are pretty much like other sectors — orchestrating myth and reality to promote self-interests,"[51] he also cynically declares:

Adherents to the political-economic conspiracy theory generally hold that the competitive market system is inherently just and superior in performance to other economic systems but that it has been hopelessly infiltrated and corrupted by those who would exploit the farmer for their own political and economic advantage. Low farm prices have been blamed alternatively on a conspiracy of merchants, bankers, futures markets, railroads, a multinational grain cartel, agribusiness corporations, some ethnic groups, the Rockefeller cabal, and the Trilateral Commission.[52]

Despite what Tweeten and others would have us believe, it is precisely these same "communities of economic interests" (with the exception of "some ethnic groups") whose "policies and manipulations" have for decades been relentlessly "orchestrating myth and reality to promote self-interests" while at the same time exploiting "the farmer for their own political and economic advantage." One can only speculate whether Professor Tweeten would view the *Washington Post*, as yet another sinister vassal of "the antisocial behavior of the dark side of the farm personality," which he so abhors, when it publishes articles like the one shown in the accompanying illustration.

Clearly, it is a mistake to blame the negative personality traits of "farm fundamentalism" and the goals, values and beliefs that underlie such "negative traits" for the psychological and ideological climate which exists today in rural America. Yet, by examining such theses carefully we can help clarify how the nation's permanent agricultural crisis remains a product of a variety of extraordinary social and political circumstances involving a host of government agencies, research facilities, farm organizations, and corporate-sponsored organizations.

Chapter Thirty-Seven

Creating "New Wealth"

At the corner of 42nd Street and Broadway in downtown Manhattan, New York, above signs advertising hamburgers, frankfurters, pizza, Coca-Cola and "tropical fruit drinks," sits a large electronic tote board, methodically flashing the U.S. national debt and each family's proportionate share. On a sunny spring afternoon in 1991 seemingly disinterested New Yorkers gave bare notice as this national debt scoreboard began registering a $3.4 trillion figure with "your family's share" at $53,540.

Even in the time it has taken you to read the above paragraph that clock has increased its tally roughly by $160,000. It continues to rise, second by second, dollar by dollar.

The brainchild of developer Seymour B. Durst, this continuous flashing tally of the national debt is only one more reminder of a grim economic fact that few of our politicians care to confront. As New York journalist Hal Lux has noted,

> If the clock runs and the numbers grow, and the sun still rises, will New Yorkers become blase above excessive spending? Probably, since 42nd Street is a monument to how even the freakish can become routine. Even a 13 digit money meter can blend into the New York skyline.
>
> I salute Mr. Durst and his idea. But, I'm afraid that the only way to get Americans worried about the debt is to ask them to pay it back.[1]

Watching this digital sign glitter among the jungle of various advertisements promoting the ever popular range of what has become our national food menu, one is forced to ask some crucial economic questions.

Is agriculture still this nation's biggest "business." Yes? No! Today, the harvesting of the interest on debts has become a far bigger enterprise in the United States than the harvesting of crops from our fields and orchards.

In 1988 total gross receipts from U.S. agricultural production amounted to $166 billion.[2] By contrast, the total combined public and corporate debt in the United States during the same year amounted to over $11.5 *trillion* dollars.[3] Interest on that debt, calculated at a very conservative 8.33 percent prime rate, would amount to $957 billion. It was not until 1962 that the United States accumulated its first one trillion dollars in public and private debt.

In 1985, for example, the national debt grew by $1.090 trillion as the growth of public and private debt increased 6.35 times as fast as national income in one year. By comparison, in 1950 the total national debt was approximately $300 billion and the interest paid on that debt was $9.4 billion.[4]

At the advent of the "Reagan Revolution" the government's gross federal debt for two centuries was $834 billion.[5] In September 1991, it was estimated by the Bush administration the national public debt had increased by 284 percent.[6]

While the outstanding debt during the Reagan years had grown by 146 percent as of June 30, 1986, the gross interest on the public debt by mid-1986 was an estimated $196 billion, an amount larger than the total federal budget in 1969.[7] By the beginning of 1988, according to a study by economists Rudiger Dornbush, James Poterba and Lawrence Summers sponsored by Eastman Kodak Co., the federal government was paying $586 million *a day* to service its debt, a sum more than the aggregate 1987 earnings of most large corporations.[8]

So, what in fact is this nation's biggest business?

It is the repaying of our public and private debt, which continues to grow 1.95 times faster than the Gross National Product — the combined output of our national goods and services. Furthermore, a person earning the 1985 median income of $33,000 worked an extra one and one-half weeks that year alone just to pay off the interest on the government's debt; 63 percent of that time was spent financing the interest costs on government debts alone accumulated during the first six years of the Reagan presidency.[9]

Contrast this staggering amount of $8.18 per capita per day that it cost to pay off the interest on the national debt with food which cost an average of 97.6 cents per capita per day at the farm level.[10] Every day in 1985 the government paid $512 million in interest on the federal debt, twice the amount it was spending on health, teacher training and employment.[11]

Agriculture, however, remains America's biggest *productive* business. It consumes 30 percent of all of our manufactured goods and, more importantly, produces 70 percent of the nation's *new wealth* created each year from our abundant natural resources and labor.[12]

To many today the dominant dynamic in our national economy is money changing hands. Rather than perceiving money as a convenient medium of exchange making it easier for us to satisfy equitably our many wants and needs (of which food is the most basic), we have instead seemingly adopted a concept that the acquiring of money is an end in and of itself.

In that process, however, we have ignored a certain logic of economics. Initially, every transaction has a debit (a charge) and a credit (money). In all such transactions, save one, the equation thus reads: the individual debited, the individual credited. The only transaction which comes out differently is the one that sees nature's bounty harvested; that transaction reads, the individual debited, nature credited, for the gift of nature is a profit, or social surplus, within the economic system.

When raw materials are harvested from nature they are turned into money, through a pricing system whose equation is production times price equals income. Any operating economy therefore divides itself into two divisions: income and cost. Such income segments in our society include: unincorporated enterprise, corporations, agriculture, and rentals to persons. These four segments have to first earn every cent they can before being used to pay the costs of the economy: wages and capital costs (interest).

Producing what we want requires a continuous supply of raw materials: food and fiber, minerals, timber and energy. As such raw materials are grown and extracted each year from the earth and sea they produce what we call "new wealth." Here lies the key to a healthy economy, for it is here that the actual exchange of money begins.

Take, for example, the growing of wheat. After the farmer has cleared the land, plowed the ground and planted the seed, where there was nothing, wheat is grown — new wealth. The harvested grain is then taken to the miller, where the farmer is paid for the wheat. From such income farmers should be able to pay their workers, their production costs and their families' cost of living expenses.

After the miller has ground the wheat and sold the flour it produces to a bakery the miller's revenue is used to pay the milling company's production costs, including its employees' salaries. The bakery in turn uses the flour to bake bread which is sold to a grocery store which then sells it to the consumer.

Throughout this entire process, of course, money is changing hands, but it is the wheat, not the money, which is the focal point of the process. Ideally, the money earned should not remain stagnant, but rather be used by the people involved to buy other goods and services. Consequently, this money will be constantly multiplying as it makes its way through the marketing process. But because each part in this process depends to a very large extent on the others, a certain balance must be maintained if this economic system is to function properly *and* equitably.

A fair sharing of the national income as it is progressively distributed between the various divisions of labor provides an equitable, reciprocal market for all goods and services produced. These goods can be paid for with the cash (earned income and profits) already received in the annual economic cycle.

The price, for example, that farmers receive from the miller should properly correspond with the buying power of urban workers, which would include, of course, their production costs. *This is what is meant when we discuss the concept of parity: a proper balance among the various parts of our economic system.* If the farmer charges prices that are too high, then he prospers at the expense

of others. If, however, as is now the case, farmers receive too little for their product, then they are victimized by the other sectors of our economic system.

An equitable national income should not be based simply on the number of dollars one can accumulate, but rather on the precision of the distribution of those dollars. As banker Vincent E. Rossiter, Sr. explained it, that distribution depends on economic equilibrium, and economic equilibrium is dependent

> 1) upon that amount of increase in raw material production needed annually to provide the needs and the wants of the modest increase in population, and vital to this factor is 2) the absolute necessity to price this raw material at a floor of 90 percent of parity in order to provide the cash to assure its production and consumption, without the injection of *excessive* debt.[13]

Since most "new wealth" begins with what is produced from our natural resources, of which farming is the largest, it is *essential* that the creators of this "new wealth" receive their fair share of the income, for as their income rises or falls so too will that of all the other parties in the process.

The production of raw materials and the subsequent industrial conversion and ultimate consumption of those materials have traditionally been financed by ever larger bank loans at each step as value is added. The old loans from the previous steps are retired by subsequent new loans obtained by each new handler of the original raw material product.

Meanwhile, raw material production is monetized "as though it were gold" by the commercial banks while the economy is fueled by added loans which increase the total money supply, profits, dividends, wages and salaries, etc. as value is added. When consumers finally spend their money for the finished product, the money that was created in the value added process is used by the retailer to pay back to the bank the money that was borrowed. That would include all previous costs and the profits that were earned in the industrial conversion process.

Thus, all the debt that was created after the original "monetization of the raw material" is completely repaid, leaving the economy with only the "new wealth" created by the monetization of raw materials which were also newly created, in annual cycles, from renewable and exhaustable raw material sources.

Recent farm income figures, however, show that agriculture's share of national income has declined nearly sixfold from an average of 6.63 cents out of each dollar of national income in the 1943-1952 period, to 1.2 percent at the end of 1989. And this during what some have termed the longest period of uninterrupted prosperity in the nation's history. By comparison, from 1929 through 1932, the period of the nation's worst depression, the decline in agriculture's share of national income was only 32 percent![14] (See Chart 37A)

The Struggle for Economic Equilibrium

After a disastrous net farm income figure of $13

Chart 37A: What occurred BEFORE and AFTER Congress Erected the "Anti-Parity Wall" on the foundation established by the Farm Act of 1953

Party	Year	Percentage Share of National Income Earned By Agriculture Annually As Realized For Loans Income		U.S. Commercial Banks Total Loan Volume As Percentage Of Deposits Available Billions (1929-1989)		Total Public/Private Debt As Computed By Net Farm D of C	FRB
Republican	1932	7.2		68.9	<12/31/29	$ 190.0	
Democratic	1932	4.9	< NATIONAL DEPRESSION	53.0		$ 174.6	
(Roosevelt	1933	6.3	Low National Income Share	47.2		$ 168.5	
& Truman)	1939	6.2	< World War II >	28.3		$ 183.2	
	1940	5.5		27.2		$ 189.9	
	1941	6.2	< 90% Parity Price Floor >	30.4		$ 211.6	
	1942	7.4		21.6		$ 259.0	
	1943	7.1		18.1		$ 313.6	
	1944	6.5		16.9	< Historic	$ 370.8	
	1945	6.8	< Comm. Bank Failures End	17.4	Low	$ 406.4	
	1946	8.2	< Historic High >	22.4	(Loan to	$ 379.4	
	1947	7.7	(National Income Share)	26.4	Deposit	$ 417.9	
	1948	7.9		29.7	Ratio)	$ 434.0	
	1949	5.9	< Post War Parity Period >	29.6		$ 448.0	$ 403.2
	1950	5.7		33.7		$ 490.7	$ 429.9
	1951	5.8		35.0	< Korean	$ 525.7	$ 453.2
	1952	5.1	< End of 90% Price Support	36.6	War	$ 556.1	$ 485.7
			< [1942-52 Average: 6.74%]				
Republican	1953	4.2	< "Anti-Parity Wall"* >	38.3		$ 585.5	$ 516.6
(Eisenhower)	1954	4.0		38.2		$ 612.0	$ 543.2
	1955	3.4		43.0		$ 672.3	$ 583.8
	1956	3.0		45.7		$ 707.5	$ 612.6
	1957	3.0		46.6		$ 738.9	$ 643.0
	1958	3.5		45.5		$ 782.6	$ 682.7
	1959	2.6		50.4		$ 846.2	$ 740.4
	1960	2.7		51.2		$ 890.2	$ 779.9
			< [1953-60 Average: 3.3%]				

Chart 37A: What occurred BEFORE and AFTER Congress Erected the "Anti-Parity Wall" on the foundation established by the Farm Act of 1953, continued.

Democratic	1961	2.7		50.2	$ 947.7	$ 827.9
(Kennedy	1962	2.6		53.5	$1,016.7	$ 888.5
and Johnson)	1963	2.4		56.7	$1,089.5	$ 955.4
	1964	2.0		57.2	$1,066.4	$1,028.7
	1965	2.2		60.7	$1,257.6	$ 1,108.6
	1966	2.2		61.8	$1,346.1	$ 1,184.6
	1967	1.9		59.7	$1,443.0	$ 1,265.3
	1968	1.7	< Bank Liquidity Crisis >	61.1	$1,585.0	$ 1,373.8
			< [1961-68 Average: 2.2%]			
Republican	1969	1.8		67.9	$1,723.0	$ 1,490.7
(Nixon and	1970	1.8		65.2	$1,870.0	$ 1,598.9
Ford)	1971	1.7	< Gold Standard Abandoned	64.5	$2,050.0	$ 1,751.7
	1972	2.0		67.3	$2,276.0	$ 1,941.8
	1973	3.0		72.2	$2,532.0	$ 2,180.9
	1974	2.3		72.0	$2,769.0	$ 2,404.7
	1975	2.0		66.4	$2,997.0	$ 2,619.2
	1976	1.4		67.8		$ 2,903.6
			< [1969-76 Average: 2.0%]			
Democratic	1977	1.3		69.5	< Higher than	$ 3,291.4
(Carter)	1978	1.5		74.1	12/31/29	$ 3,761.1
	1979	1.5		80.2		$ 4,240.7
	1980	0.9		75.4		$ 4,654.8
			< [1977-80 Average: 1.3%]			
Republican	1981	1.3	< Bank Failures Begin Again	76.7		$ 5,183.2
(Reagan and	1982	1.0		75.1		$ 5,161.4
Bush)	1983	0.5	< Historic All-Time Low: >	82.8		$ 5,623.0
	1984	1.0	(National Income Share)	89.7		$ 7,195.7
	1985	0.9		91.2		$ 8,243.1
	1986	1.0		89.5		$ 9,431.2
	1987	1.1		94.5		$10,463.4
	1988	1.0		95.5		$11,504.9
			< [1981-88 Average: 0.97%]			
	1989	1.2		98.2	< 9/27/89	$12,533.8

Note: U.S. commercial banks total loan volume excludes investments in U.S government bonds and other securities.

* = 1953 and all subsequent "National Income Share" to and including 1989 lower than the Depression low of 1932.

D of C = Department of Commerce
FRB = Federal Reserve Board

Statistics compiled by: V.E. Rossiter, Senior Analyst, Harrington, Nebraska, January 12, 1990.

billion in 1983, net farm income more than doubled, to $32.7 billion[15] the following year, mainly due to USDA bookkeeping methods which took into account changes in the value of crop and livestock inventories held by farmers during a calendar year. In 1986, the USDA reported that net farm income was up to $37.5 billion, rising to $42.7 billion by 1988 and $53 billion in 1989. Some critics, however, have advised caution in analyzing such figures. "Over 50 cents of every dollar that goes to a corn, wheat or soybean farmer will come from a government check drawn on a deficit account," Iowa's U.S. Senator Tom Harkin points out. "If that's recovery, it's the strangest I've seen."[16]

Some economic apologists have pointed out that the aforementioned decline in agriculture's share of national income is the logical consequence of having fewer but more "efficient" farmers today than three decades ago. Vince Rossiter disagrees:

> The automobile industry lost $4 billion in just one year, very recently. The auto industry solved its problem immediately by "disemploying" 320,000 auto workers. They downsized their plants and substituted robots for people wherever they could to increase the efficiency of auto production, and finally they reduced the size of the car by to 30 percent to 40 percent and doubled and tripled the gasoline mileage available to a buyer, the final beneficiary of all of these improvements. Then did the price of the automobile decline?
>
> No. It doubled. That is exactly where the farm economy is today, farm prices have to double to restore economic equity to agriculture.[17]

"New Wealth" and National Prosperity

When Carl Wilken, mathematician and economist, studied the causes of the Great Depression of the 1930s, he discovered a direct relationship between "new wealth," unemployment and the prosperity of the overall economy. (See Chart 37B) He found that whenever gross farm income equaled approximately one-seventh of the national income the national economy prospered. Further studies have shown that initial earned income from our natural resources multiplies from five to seven times as it progresses through the economy.[18]

Based on such calculations the farmers' share of the national income of $3.2 trillion in 1985, for example, should have been $458 billion, but instead it was only $156.5 billion; a loss to the economy of $302.2 billion. In 1950, by comparison, when the national income was $237.5 billion and farmers were receiving prices comparable to those earned by others in the economy, farm income was $33.1, a fraction over one-seventh of the national income.[19]

The 1943-1952 years are regarded by many as the last sustained period when farm prices were on an equilibrium with the rest of the national economy. If all sectors of the economy had continued to grow at approximately the same rate that they grew in the 1943-52 period, parity advocates argue, there would have been ample profits each year to purchase the goods and services available for cash, which would have been generated in each economic cycle.

By the end of 1985 net farm income would have increased from $16.9 billion on the average from 1943-52, to $88.9 billion in 1985, an increase of 526 percent. During this same time interest income of individuals would have increased from $2.7 billion on the average from 1943-1952, to $16.9 billion in 1985, an increase of 526 percent.[20]

The "conventional wisdom" during the 1943-1952 period, based on supposedly the best economic advice available, was almost indiscriminately to force the price level of commodities down after 1953, abandoning all pretenses of trying to maintain an economic equilibrium.

Consequently, net farm income increased only from $16.9 billion on the average in 1943-52, to $18.8 billion in 1985, a mere gain of 11.3 percent. Concurrently, net interest income of individuals increased from $2.7 billion on the average in 1943-52, to $273.3 billion in 1985, a rise of 10,022 percent![21]

In terms of constant dollars the three years — 1982, 1983 and 1984 — were the worst three years in net return to agriculture since records have been kept. By way of contrast, these same three years were the best years for earnings of interest income of individuals since records have been kept.

Chart 37B: Parity Ratio Compared to Unemployment

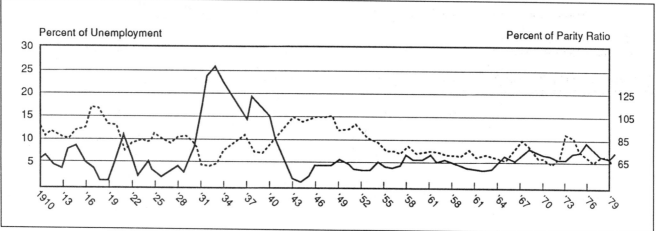

"Conventional economic wisdom" argues that agriculture is no longer a significant economic factor in the national economy, that agriculture provides only 70 percent of the total national production of raw materials, mostly food and fiber, which it will continue to do regardless of price and/or profit, because it has always done so in the past. And, if it fails to do that, cheaply produced farm goods from overseas can always be imported.

Many farmers counter such arguments by pointing out that the United States's so-called "cheap food policy" for the last three decades is responsible for and has brought about this distortion in the nation's economic picture. Not only has that policy resulted in a reduction of agriculture's share of national income in spite of its increased production, but it has also brought about a decline in small business income. That in turn has resulted in a reduction in corporate income and rental income increasing the total dollars of income and profits lost with each annual cycle of the national economy.

A growing number of individuals like Rossiter have pointed out that if the Office of Management and Budget would look carefully it could readily see why the nation is year after year faced with recurring federal budget deficits. The reason is a diminishing wage and salary level.

For example, since 1950 Congress has increased the minimum wage six times. Unadjusted for inflation, the hourly rate appears to be more than four times as high as it was in 1950. But increases in the cost of living have chipped away at the real value of minimum wage jobs. Measured in 1986 dollars — adjusting for inflation — the minimum wage was much higher in the 1960s (See Chart 37C).[23] As Lance Compa, a labor attorney for the United Electrical, Radio and Machine Workers of America, emphasizes:

There may be more jobs, but more and more they're low-paying jobs with short hours, small benefits and bleak futures. We've seen the same thing happen to the American job that happened to the American dollar when it was glutted by inflation — there are more of them around, but they bring home a lot less bacon.[24]

He notes that a third of the new jobs since 1980 are part-time, three quarters have been filled by people looking for full-time work, two-thirds make the minimum wage and 85 percent have no health insurance from their employment.[25]

A Joint Economic Committee report by Barry Bluestone of the University of Massachusetts and Bennett Harison of M.I.T. shows that in the early 1980s low-rate jobs (those at or near the minimum wage — now just under $7,000 a year) increased at twice the rate of the 1970s.[26]

Three-fifths of the eight million new jobs created from 1979 to 1984 paid less than $7,000 a year based on a 1984 dollar). Those people paid no income tax, nor were they buying the products and services in the quantities that half that many people could buy prior to 1979.

Median household incomes and mean family income dropped five percent below 1980 levels despite the infusion of women and teenagers into the work force. Only per capita income levels rose slightly because husbands and wives must now both work to pay their bills while having fewer children.[27]

But, as Compa concludes, "the real problem with the unemployment rate is that we've devalued American employment in order to have more of it. While corporate stock prices soar to new highs, the working class is paying for this situation."[28]

In addition, the nation is faced with the reoccurring fact that escalating public and private debt requires an interest cost that increases the cost of food by 15 percent more than it would have cost had not the interest income of individual sectors of the economy jumped an unprecedented 622 percent from 1952 to 1985.

Likewise, a similar interest cost is factored into everything we buy, and even into our federal income tax. We have incurred an additional $7.1 trillion of public and private debt since 1952, whereas net income of the private enterprise sectors have declined an average of nearly 60 percent since 1952. The relative profit level of business and industry has also declined 60 percent from the average level of profit that prevailed from 1942 through 1952.[29]

Had agriculture's share of the national income averaged the annual 6.63 percent that it did in the 1943-1952 period an additional $4,306.7 billion of gross farm income and net profits of $1,852.0 billion would have been earned by agriculture as its share of the national economy. (See Chart 37E)

Banker Rossiter points out that because this $4,306.7 billion would have been *earned* into the economy it would have come to rest as new wealth and would have increased total savings by that exact amount. These saving would then be distributed throughout the economy as those dollars moved from the farmer to the merchant, to the manufacturer and processor, to the labor force in wages and salaries, to the shareholder in corporate profits, and to the savers in interest income to individuals, in approximately the same ratio that was seen in the economy of 1943-1952.

He concludes,

To contend that the absence of the proven multiplier effect of this "new wealth" flowing through the economy, has nothing to do with the need for the injection of $7.1 trillion of excessive public and private debt into the national economy since 1952, one has to be an orthodox economist, or he is living in that make believe world that has been created for us "by classical economics which deepens disequilibrium to inevitable depression."[30]

It is also interesting to note that if farmers required a return on investment equal to the average achieved in the manufacturing industry and a wage rate equal to the average wage for factory workers, they would need to have five times the income they realized in the Reagan

Chart 37C: Minimum wages over the years

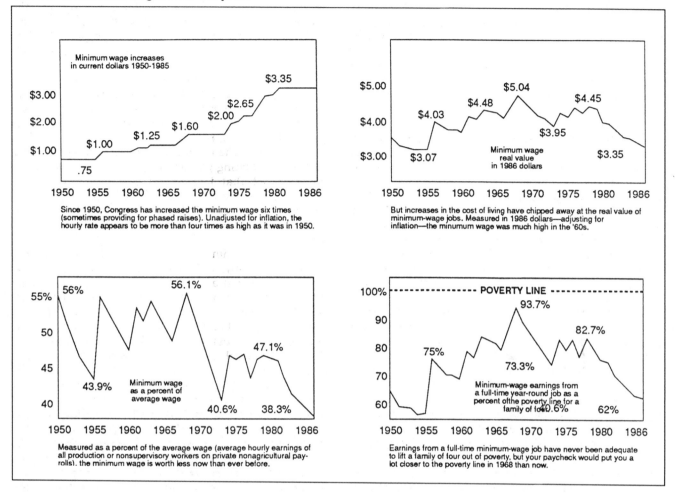

Minimum wage increases in current dollars 1950-1985

Since 1950, Congress has increased the minimum wage six times (sometimes providing for phased raises). Unadjusted for inflation, the hourly rate appears to be more than four times as high as it was in 1950.

But increases in the cost of living have chipped away at the real value of minimum-wage jobs. Measured in 1986 dollars—adjusting for inflation—the minimum wage was much high in the '60s.

Measured as a percent of the average wage (average hourly earnings of all production or nonsupervisory workers on private nonagricultural pay-rolls), the minimum wage is worth less now than ever before.

Earnings from a full-time minimum-wage job have never been adequate to lift a family of four out of poverty, but your paycheck would put you a lot closer to the poverty line in 1968 than now.

years. Such a multiple, it should be noted, does *not* include any costs for management or a return for entrepreneurship!

How does such a loss of income by farmers affect the consumer? Examining per capita expenditures of the consumer dollar for 1980 (See Chart 37F), for example, we see that the shortage of earned national income, caused by years of underpricing many of our agricultural commodities (as well as other raw materials), has required a massive debt expansion.

To most Americans the post-World War II years brought prosperity as well as the era of the "cheap food" policy. We are beginning to realize, however, that this prosperity has not been earned, but borrowed. As the National Organization for Raw Materials (NORM), a nationwide association of persons interested in showing the essential contribution of raw materials income to the national prosperity, points out:

> We are enjoying good times on credit. The indebtedness begins with the raw materials producers again. They're falling short of income, but if they want to stay in business, they need more money. So they borrow. They borrow to invest in new capital goods to increase production and give themselves an edge. But even if they do succeed

and raise production, they get into the same bind once more the next year. Income still falls short of the parity share, and they still need money. So they borrow once again.[31]

Thus, the 6.2 cents (Chart 37F) consumers thought they saved in 1980 by paying less for food than they did in 1950 now accounts for much of the 5.6 cent increase in taxes and the outrageous 30.2 cent increase in interest (much of which is hidden in the price of everything bought from corporate agribusiness as we saw in connection with the Kohlberg Kravis Roberts & Co. buyout of Safeway Stores).

Because our economy, both public and private, has had to borrow so heavily to maintain a semblance of economic equilibrium we now have both government and business vying for infusions of borrowed capital. (See Chart 37G) As financial expertise replaces entrepreneurial capacity fortunes rise and fall with increases and decreases in interest rates.

Some businesses incapable of surviving on their own resources and cut off from affordable funding, stagnate and collapse. Others borrow more heavily, often against their assets, and grow larger, forcing their smaller competitors to either merge or go out of business. In 1984, for example, debt-financed acquisitions and share

Chart 37E: Projected and Actual Agricultural Share of the National Economy

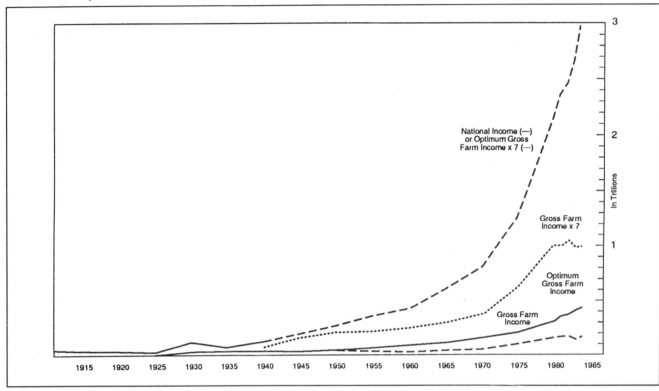

repurchases continued to distort corporate America's balance sheet severely as some $78 billion in equity vanished as companies added a record-setting $169 billion in new debt.[32]

Many individuals today believe that "establishment economics" in the post World War II years has run amok, misusing and abusing the American family farm system. As Rossiter reflects, "it goes back much farther than that, of course, to the early 19th century when David Ricardo conceived the so-called 'law of supply and demand'."[33]

But agriculture is a unique and vital economic resource. As Representative Joe Skeen, R-NM, pointed out in a 1983 letter to *The Wall Street Journal*:

> If a surplus of buggy whips floods the market and lowered prices force buggy whip manufacturers out of business, this is a function of the law of supply and demand.
>
> You cannot apply the same logic to agriculture. The law of supply and demand would dictate that enough farmers be forced out of business to reduce production to only that for which there is a demand. But no one can guarantee that this year, or next year, or the year after, our farmers will be able to produce enough to meet the demand.
>
> We cannot allow agriculture to respond to the law of supply and demand if we are to meet the *necessity of self-sufficiency*. There may be too many farmers today but a series of lean years could prove there are too few. (emphasis added)[34]

Despite such logic, however, American agriculture continues to earn less income than it needs to support itself and must constantly borrow to remain productive. Despite all of its technological innovations, despite being the envy of the world in food production, American agriculture today earns less per acre in real dollars than it did before World War II.

Its ratio of debt to equity since 1950 has nearly tripled. In 1985 alone, as has been shown, farmers' rate of return on equity showed a minus 12.8 percent and a return on assets of minus 8.4 percent. Figures for 1988 show 7.6 percent return on assets and a 8.0 percent on return to equity.[35] Contrast these figures with the food processing industry's 1980-89 *average* of 18.4 percent return on equity.[36] (See Chart 37H)

It is no surprise, therefore, that farm families must rely more and more upon off-farm income to survive. As Chart 37J shows, as recently as 1989 all U.S. farms derived well over 50 percent of their total cash household income from off-farm income.

Coping With A Raw Materials Procurement and Distribution System

As the production of food plays a decreasing role in our economy and its manufacturing plays an ever increasing one, we see farmers earning a diminishing number of dollars for their work. Chart 37K shows how from 1973 to 1988 farm value as a percentage of the retail price for domestically produced foods has dropped dramatically while the retail price of these same commodities has sharply risen.

Take wheat farmers: they now earn less than 5 percent of the consumer's dollar for the grain that goes

Chart 37F: Per Capita Expenditures of Consumer Dollars

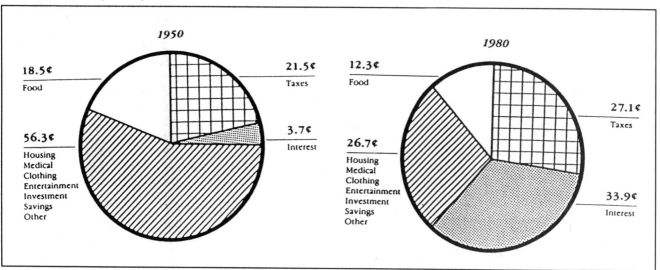

1950

18.5¢
Food

21.5¢
Taxes

3.7¢
Interest

56.3¢
Housing
Medical
Clothing
Entertainment
Investment
Savings
Other

1980

12.3¢
Food

27.1¢
Taxes

33.9¢
Interest

26.7¢
Housing
Medical
Clothing
Entertainment
Investment
Savings
Other

into a 18 ounce box of cereal.[37] At the same time, 9 percent of the cereal's cost goes for advertising and another 6 percent pays for the box. Meanwhile, a company like General Mills will pay a grocer a nickel, more than the farmer gets for the wheat in the cereal, for simply handling the discount coupon found inside the box.

Chart 37G: Farm Parity, Food Costs and Interest Costs

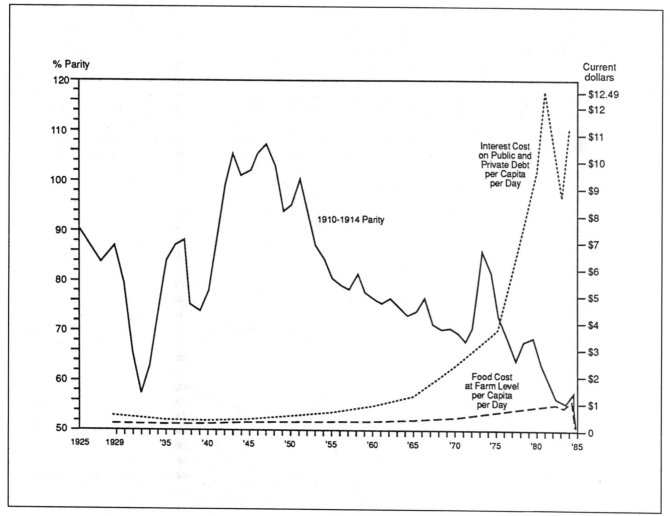

While farmers got disproportionately less of the food dollar from 1970-1989, labor costs at the same time for the marketing of domestically produced farm goods increased by nearly 356 percent; packaging materials went up 328 percent; intercity rail and truck transportation, 258 percent; fuels and electricity, 618 percent; other expenses like depreciation, rent, advertizing, promotion, etc., 293 percent and corporate profits before taxes, nearly 208 percent.[38]

Most agricultural economists and politicians would like the American public to believe that the loss of farm export sales, the lingering effects of the Carter/Reagan Soviet grain embargo and the strength of the dollar abroad were the chief culprits in the declining farm value of our food.

Each of those explanations, though not entirely wrong, are [sic] more politically convenient than accurate," notes Professor Harold Breimyer. Between 70 and 75 percent of the U.S. farm market is domestic, he adds, and that is a fact that a lot of would-be policy makers forget. It's just that when families find their incomes shrinking, they economize on spending for food. They buy as much food as before but they shift from higher-value foods, mainly those of animal origin, and substitute cereals, beans, potatoes and other foods that may be nutritionally adequate, but are less costly.

Not only do consumers spend fewer dollars for food, but the values reaching farmers are cut more. Half or more of the dollars spent for meat, dairy and poultry products go back to farmers. Of money spent for cereals, fats and various other foods, only a small fraction reaches farmers. Farmers are hurt doubly by the change in food buying. ... The various segments of the economy are interdependent. The problems of agriculture cannot be resolved in sectoral isolation.[39]

How all this balances out on the farm and corporate ledger sheets can be graphically seen by just looking at the glaring difference between agriculture, food manufacturers and retail food chains in terms of after-tax profits as a percentage of their equity and their assets.

One explanation of why these margins for the manufacturer and the food retailer are so large comes from Othal Brand, chairman of the board of the McAllen, Texas-based Griffin & Brand, one of the nation's largest growers, shippers, importers and exporters of fresh and frozen fruits and vegetables.

The retail chain markup necessitated by the system is 50 percent. It varies from company to company, but when they say 50 percent-markup, they mean 50 percent of the sales price is marked up. That's a 100 percent-markup over cost. In contrast, we work on one, two or three percent, and if we have a 3 percent at the end of the year, we've had a good year. If we hit 5 or 6 percent, that's a bonanza year.[40]

It is with such markups in mind that farmers must have to check their hearing, put on their glasses and choke back screams of frustration when they listen to and read about retail chains like Safeway Stores, Inc. adopting catchy consumer-oriented slogans such as "you work an honest day, you deserve an honest deal."

These "markups," or as they are now euphemistically termed, "add value" items, as we have seen, are not the main nor are they the only means by which corporate agribusiness reaps profits at the expense of both farmers and consumers. In the past, next to farmers, labor probably is most often singled out as the villain in the disappearance of the consumer's food dollars. But, before food buyers join in such a chorus of denunciation, however, there are some important facts that need to be considered. For example, USDA's Economic Research Service, in noting that in 1985 the farm-to-retail spread rose 5.5 percent, the largest increase since 1982, points out:

As measured by a food marketing cost index, prices of inputs used in handling, processing and retailing food commodities rose by less than one percent in 1985, and presumably accounted for little of the increase in the price spread. The small rise in costs is mainly the result of no change in average hourly labor cost in the food industry.[41]

Where "labor cost" increases do become evident in the food industry is in the continued employment growth among food and beverage manufacturing, preparation and service occupations. Figures developed by the ERS's Denis Durham show that in 1985 a total of around 11 million people were employed in food processing and distribution,

Rates of Return on Farm Assets and Equity

Year	Income*	Real capital	Total	Income°	Real capital	Total
1981-83	1.5%	- 5.8%	-4.2%	-0.7%	- 5.8%	- 6.4%
1984-1986	3.5%	-11.8%	-8.4%	1.5%	-14.3%	-12.8%
1987	5.4%	0.0%	5.4%	4.2%	1.2%	5.4%
1988	4.9%	2.8%	7.6%	3.5%	4.4%	8.0%

* = Excludes returns imputed to operator's labor and management
° = Excludes returns imputed to operator's labor and management and interest on debt

Source: Economic Research Service, USDA

417

Charts 37H: Rates of Return on Assets and Equity (Farm and Food Processing) — 1980-1989

	Profitability Return on Equity		Growth Sales	
Company	10-year average percentage	5-year average percentage	10-year average percentage	5-year average percentage
FOOD PROCESSORS				
Kellogg	38.9	43.7	9.0	13.0
Ralston Purina	33.6	43.0	3.2	4.0
Tyson Foods	27.8	32.7	22.2	28.3
HJ Heinz	23.2	24.9	8.0	6.6
Smithfield Foods	22.9[a]	29.1	24.2[a]	14.0
Dean Foods	22.4	20.9	13.4	14.1
ConAgra	21.9	21.7	36.4	33.5
Lance	21.4	20.8	7.7	5.2
William Wrigley Jr.	20.9	24.4	5.5	9.2
CPC International	20.9	24.7	3.1	3.5
Savannah Foods	20.5	14.6	11.2	13.2
Quaker Oats	20.3	22.8	10.6	13.5
Hershey Foods	20.2	21.1	9.9	6.0
Sara Lee	20.0	20.9	9.6	9.2
Flowers Industries	20.0	20.3	11.3	7.9
Pioneer Hi-Bred Intl.	17.5	14.6	12.6	9.9
Curtice Burns Foods	17.4	16.7	9.9	4.5
Borden	15.8	17.3	5.0	11.4
Campbell Soup	15.4	15.4	9.3	7.9
McCormick & Co.	14.9	12.9	10.8	10.1
Universal Foods	14.8	14.3	9.1	10.0
Gerber Products	14.7	14.5	7.2	4.1
Seaboard	14.1	13.8	NM	39.5
Geo A Hormel	13.5	14.1	5.9	12.3
Intl. Multifoods	13.0	12.2	6.3	11.7
Archer Daniels	12.9	12.9	12.5	8.7
United Brands	9.2	13.7	NM	0.9
American Maize	5.5	4.7	4.7	8.6
Thorn Apple Valley	4.0	2.2	4.2	-3.1
Castle & Cooke	NA	16.6[b]	NA	8.6[c]
General Mills	NA	34.3[b]	NA	5.7
Hudson Foods	NA	39.3	NA	22.5
IBP	NA	NA	NA	7.3
Pilgrim's Pride	NA	35.8	NA	14.4
Whitman	NA	NA	NA	15.5[c]
Medians	20.0	20.3	9.1	9.2
FOOD DISTRIBUTORS				
Marriott	23.3	24.4	19.8	20.4
Super Valu Stores	21.6	19.4	13.3	12.0
Sysco	17.9	16.9	17.8	17.3
Wetterau	16.3	17.7	16.5	12.1
Super Food Servs.	15.7	16.7	7.9	5.2
Fleming Companies	14.2	11.8	17.3	16.1
Nash Finch	13.4	13.4	9.6	13.9
Rykoff-Sexton	12.2[a]	11.9	21.0[a]	26.2
Di Giorgio	5.2	5.2	1.5	NM
Finevest Foods	NA	NA	8.4	6.7
TW Services	NA	12.0	NA	26.0
Medians	15.7	13.4	14.9	13.1

Charts 37H: Rates of Return on Assets and Equity (Farm and Food Processing), continued.

Company	Profitability; Return on Equity		Growth; Sales	
	10-year average percentage	5-year average percentage	10-year average percentage	5-year average percentage
BEVERAGES				
Coca-Cola	26.5	29.3	6.5	3.5
PepsiCo	23.7	27.4	9.9	11.6
Anheuser-Busch	21.5	22.6	15.0	8.3
Brown-Forman	19.5	17.8	15.6	10.9
Seagram	12.6	12.5	7.5	15.8
Adolph Coors	6.2	5.2	8.4	6.3
Coca-Cola Enterprs.	NA	NA	NA	45.5
Medians	20.5	20.2	9.2	10.9
TOBACCO				
UST Inc.	32.4	34.6	11.9	9.4
Philip Morris Cos.	28.4	30.8	17.2	25.6
Loews	24.3	25.6	11.7	18.6
American Brands	19.7	19.5	6.4	10.3
Universal	18.9	18.8	8.1	19.5
Dibrell Brothers	17.2	15.8	3.3	4.5
Culbro	15.2	13.0	12.4	4.5
Std Commercial	11.9	8.6	10.8	17.0
Medians	19.3	19.2	11.2	13.6
Industry medians	18.4	17.5	9.6	10.6
All industry industry medians	14.3	14.3	9.3	10.9
Industry (number of companies)				
HEALTH (39)	18.7	17.8	12.5	12.7
Drugs (19)	20.1	20.7	10.1	11.4
Health care servcs. (9)	15.3	14.8	34.0	14.1
Medical supplies (11)	14.5	16.5	10.9	13.0
FOOD, DRINK & TOBACCO (63)	18.4	17.5	9.6	10.6
Food processors (35)	20.0	20.3	9.1	9.2
Food distributors (13)	15.7	13.4	14.9	13.1
Beverages (7)	20.5	20.2	9.2	10.9
Tobacco (8)	19.3	19.2	11.2	13.6
RETAILING (111)	16.7	16.5	13.3	13.0
Department Strs. (11)	14.4	15.2	9.5	7.3
Apparel (13)	17.7	16.2	14.1	12.6
Drug & discount (22)	16.0	16.1	15.0	14.6
Specialty (31)	17.7	16.8	14.8	18.5
Supermarkets (26)	17.4	17.2	10.8	10.7
Restaurant chains (8)	16.9	15.0	14.5	11.5

NA = not available   NM = not meaningful
a = nine-year average   b = three-year average   c = four-year average

Sources: Forbes; Value Line Data Base Service via Lotus CD Investment.

Chart 37J: Income of Farmers and Farm People from All Sources, 1980-1989 (Billions of dollars)

Year	Cash Receipts From Marketings	Federal Payments to Farmers	Gross[1] Cash Income	Off-farm[2] Income	Net Farm Income After Inventory Adjustment	Total for Family Personal Spending and Investment[3]	Off-farm Income Percentage
1980	$139.7	$1.29	$143.3	$34.7	$16.1	$50.8	68.3
1981	$141.6	$1.93	$146.0	$35.8	$26.9	$62.7	57.1
1982	$142.6	$3.49	$150.6	$36.4	$23.5	$59.9	60.8
1983	$136.6	$9.30	$150.6	$37.0	$15.3	$52.3	70.7
1984	$142.8	$8.43	$155.5	$59.8	$26.3	$65.5	59.8
1985	$144.1	$7.71	$157.2	$55.2	$31.0	$86.2	64.0
1986	$135.2	$11.81	$152.0	$54.5	$31.0	$85.2	63.7
1987	$141.7	$16.75	$164.3	$56.9	$41.3	$98.2	57.9
1988	$150.2	$14.48	$170.4	$57.5	$41.8	$99.5	57.9
1989	$159.2	$10.89	$177.5	$57.5	$46.7	$104.2	55.1

1 Includes cash income from recreation, machine hire and custom work, and forest product sales.

2 Includes non-farm wages, salaries, interest, dividends, rental property, unemployment compensation, social security, etc., but does not include capital gains income from off-farm sources.

3 Net income from farming after change in value of farm inventory, plus off-farm income of farm operator families.

Source: *1990 Fact Book of Agriculture*, Office of Public Affairs, USDA, Miscellaneous Publication #1063, Table 22.

compared with about eight million in 1975.[42] In the words of an unnamed USDA economist in the *Des Moines Register*, which underscores a point all too commonly overlooked by the public (and one conveniently ignored by corporate agribusiness): "One of the things that's happened in our system is that as population growth levels off and the food companies can't keep selling more and more volume, they introduce more exotic convenience products which require more labor and more packaging. We keep putting the same farm products in different forms." Thus it behooves consumers and farmers to look elsewhere when attempting to explain the widening margins of farm-to-retail price spreads, such as was recorded in 1985. We really only need to continue to listen to ERS for such direction. The USDA economist continues:

In general, the more that food is transformed, portioned, cooked, deboned, nutritionally supplemented or specially packaged

Chart 37K: Farm Value as a Percentage of Retail Price for Domestically Produced Foods

Food Item Change	Retail Price 1973-1986	Percentage Change	Retail Price 1980-1988	Percentage
Meats	- 14.8	+ 70	- 11.8	+ 21
Dairy	- 9.2	+ 102	- 23.1	+ 19
Poultry	- 12.6	+ 50	- 9.2	+ 29
Eggs	- 7.9	+ 16	n.a.	n.a.
Cereal & Bakery	- 15.4	+ 155	- 35.7	+ 46
Fresh Fruits & Vegetables	- 7.8	+ 134	unchanged	+ 74
Processed Fruits & Vegetables	+ 0.9	+ 137	+ 21.7	+ 42
Fats & Oils	- 20.2	+ 128	- 20.8	+ 27
Average USDA Market Basket	**- 13.8**	**+ 126**	**- 18.9**	**+ 32**

Source: (1973-1986) *Food Consumption, Prices, and Expenditures: 1963-1983*, USDA-ERS, Statistical Bulletin #713, Table 5A; "Consumer price indexes for all urban consumers, U.S. average," *Agricultural Outlook*, USDA-ERS, March 1987 (1980-1988) Table 2, *National Food Review*, "Food Price," USDA-ERS, April-June, 1989.

after it leaves the farm, the greater the added costs, including labor costs, as the food moves through the marketing chain. When those costs are passed on to consumers, the farm share of the total price goes down. ... With the small rise in the price of inputs, *the widening of the farm-to-retail spread resulted in higher profits margins for some food manufacturers and distributors.*" (emphasis added)[43]

The potato provides an excellent illustration of the aforementioned USDA economist's claim. From 1963 to 1988, the consumption of fresh potatoes per person in the United States dropped from 76.1 pounds per capita to 51.7 pounds, while our consumption of frozen potatoes went from 7.2 pounds to over 47.8 pounds.[44] Yet, when we go into the supermarket to shop for our weekly groceries, we see in the potato what is so frequently happening to so many of our other food products today, mainly the further they get away from the raw product, the more expensive they become. (See Chart 37L)

Fresh potatoes from the field grossed the farmer from three to five cents a pound. Because grain prices became so depressed in the mid-1980s, a growing number of Midwestern farmers, with the lure of forward contracts from potato chip manufacturers enticing them to grow potatoes, began rivaling traditional potato-producing states like Idaho, Washington, Maine, Oregon and California. The immediate consequence of their decision was a surplus of potatoes, lowering prices down to as little as two cents per pound. The transportation, packaging and marketing of those pounds of potatoes, however, brought their cost up to 18 cents a pound for the sack of potatoes that one would buy in the grocery store. After that, the sky was the limit.

Is it any wonder after examining just this one food item, which can increase in price by over 4,450 percent from farmer to consumer, that the food manufacturing and the food retailing industries can each realize a 15 to 20 percent after-tax profit as a percentage of their equity. While Robert Natale, a retail food analyst for *Industry Surveys*, may describe these "wider profit margins" as "resulting from stable or declining wholesale costs and a favorable pricing environment,"[45] Fred Stover, long-time president of the U.S. Farmers Association declares:

> The biggest problem farmers have is that they have to sell their products through a market place that is really a "raw materials procurement and distribution system:" a system that is designed to buy raw materials as cheaply as possible and resell the products on the basis of all the traffic will bear — regardless of cost, efficiency, supply, demand or the fair market value.[46]

Agriculture's Culprit

E. (Kika) de la Garza, D-Texas, is the Chairman of the House Agriculture Committee. In attempting to define the "crisis in the Farm Belt" in the mid-1980s the long-time, self-proclaimed friend of American agriculture declared in a letter to *The Washington Post* that "the heart of the problem is farm income."[47]

Many of America's 2.2 million farmers would disagree, and have attempted to explain to farm politicians like De la Garza that the reason the U.S. agricultural economy remains depressed is precisely because the "farm problem" since the mid-1930s has been repeatedly presented in the form of "inadequate income."

As long as American agriculture's major problem is seen both by economists and politicians as merely lack of income, it will remain relegated to the nation's already growing list of social welfare problems and not treated as a serious economic question in its own right.

But treating it as a social welfare problem not only allows the government to find ways to maintain farmers on the land at a minimal standard of living while they continue to produce raw materials the nation and the world requires at the cheapest price possible, but it also makes it possible for the so-called "free market" to escape nearly all responsibility for achieving national economic stability and equilibrium.

For when all is said and done by the economists, the politicians and the trade experts about the need for improved farm income, or the lowering of high interest rates, or the curtailing or even elimination of government price support programs and subsidies, or the need to counter trade embargoes and foreign competition, the ultimate solution to America's permanent agricultural crisis is, in fact, none of the above.

Rather, as Representative Pat Roberts, R-Kansas, candidly told his colleagues during the debate on the 1985 Farm Bill: "I think there is more of a consensus than people realize. There has been ... months of intensive study, and the problem is pretty well defined. Reducing that to one word, the problem is price!"[48]

Susan Bright, a Centerville, Indiana farm wife and mother has also described the problem succinctly:

> We have no control over our income. We buy retail and sell wholesale. The only way we can increase our income is to produce more. This only adds to our problem. We take more to market and we get less because our efficiency has caused a surplus.
>
> Who else but the farmer is penalized for doing a better job this year than last?
>
> Take away all the farm programs. Don't allow any farm commodities to be sold for less than parity prices. This will put surplus control on the shoulders of the producer.
>
> We will not raise what we cannot sell. Consumers will pay for only what they want and use. No tax dollars will be spent to store surpluses. This will give the farmer a profit from which he will be able to pay his debts and still provide a living for his family.[49]

In a 1982 study, Chase Econometrics Inc., a subsidiary of the Chase Manhattan Bank, warned that there could be no *complete* economic recovery from the decade's earlier recession unless *farm* income was boosted significantly.[50]

Commissioned by the National Association of Wheat Growers (NAWG) the study concluded that the "collapse" of the nation's farm economy was the result "neither of declining productivity nor loss of competitive advantage to foreign competition," but rather record production and "political forces." It noted that the problems of the farm economy were "permeating into the economy in general since the U.S. farmer supports the largest industrial complex in America: the farm supply and food distribution industries," and called for a return of *farm* income at least to the levels of the 1970s when it ranged between 70 percent and 95 percent of parity.[51]

Chart 37L: How Now Brown Potato

Item	Per pound price
Farm value	4 cents
Five-pound sack	18 cents
Canned whole new potatoes (16 ounces)	69 cents
French fried potatoes (5 pounds)	75 cents
Frozen hash brown potatoes (1 pound 8 ounces)	91.2 cents
Tater tots (2 pounds)	$1.07
Frozen scalloped potatoes (12 ounces)	$2.08
McDonald's french fried potatoes (4 ounces)	$2.14
"Ripples" potato chips (8 ounces)	$2.79
Potato chips (11 ounces)	$3.00
Twin Pak potato chips (7.5 ounces)	$3.14
Light potato chips (6.5 ounces)	$4.16
Lunch packet potato chips (12 pack, .5 ounces)	$4.49

Such an increase, Chase Econometrics pointed out, would boost employment by 86,000 jobs and disposable personal income by $4 billion. While higher farm prices would probably raise consumer prices, the study continued, the increase would only be slight. A genuine return to farm profitability would result in a 1.6 percent increase in retail food prices, but the overall inflation rate would go up by only three-tenths of one percent. It concluded that the overall U.S. economy would realize a net positive impact due to an increase in *farm* income.

Small-town bankers agree with their colleagues at Chase. "There isn't going to be a solution unless we get better prices on commodities," claims Bud Gerhart, president of the First National Bank of Newman Grove, Nebraska. "We see the need for mandatory production controls now," says Tom Olson, president of Lisco State Bank in Lisco, Nebraska. Gerhart and Olson both note that in their state farmers and ranchers earned 24 percent less in 1984 and 1983 and 38 percent less than other Nebraskans.[52]

As farmers consistently find themselves unable to realize a fair price for their commodities, bankers see more and more farms going out of business. The consequence? "It's going to be a lot easier for [super-sized] farms to get together and decide on prices," believes Mark Buckley, president of First National Bank of Wilcox, Nebraska.[53]

When Wayne Angell was appointed to the Federal Reserve Board in 1986 he immediately emphasized that he wanted to see the Federal Reserve pay closer attention to commodity prices than it had in the past.[54]

At the time of the release of the Chase study the parity ratio for farmers of prices received to prices paid was 57 percent and the farm debt to asset ratio was 18.7 percent. In September, 1985 the parity ratio had dropped to 49 percent, tieing a June 1932 record, and the farm debt to asset ratio had risen to 23 percent. While prices for farmers had declined by 13 percent during the previous 12 months, grocery prices for food were on the rise by 4 percent.[55]

When one adjusts present-day commodity prices to remove inflation, it became apparent that farmers in 1986 were getting no more than in the worst days of the Great Depression when commodity prices hit an all-time low.

Mike Moeller, a one-time Texas Deputy Commissioner of Agriculture, notes that in 1932 wheat sold for 33 cents a bushel, corn for 30 cents a bushel, rice for a penny a pound, soybeans for $1.60 a bushel and cotton for six cents a pound. In January, 1987 with inflation removed wheat was selling for 38 cents a bushel, corn 23 cents a bushel, rice for $.006 a pound, soybeans for 73 cents a bushel, and cotton for eight cents a pound.[56]

Again, when we speak of parity we are talking about a yardstick, a measuring device. Computing parity, of course, depends on a base year or period — one in which there were no large import invasions, no general imbalance in the economy — a time in which basic storable farm commodities were on a par with wage and capital costs, when the buying power of a crop was on a par with the broad average of the buying power of factory labor, services and the professions.

Although the years 1910-1914 have generally been acknowledged as the parity base period because they represent a time bracket when the dollar stood at 100 percent for every sector of the economy, there have been other periods of time, such as 1943-1952, that would also qualify for this base measuring period.

During those years, for example, farm income was 6.81 percent of the national income compared to .0035 percent of the national income in 1985. Also, during that period despite wasteful war and progressive rebuilding periods, public and private debt increased only $237 billion compared to the ten year period of the Vietnam War when the debt rose by $1,376 billion.[57]

The detractors (and there are many) of the parity concept as a means of measuring farm prosperity point out that parity prices for grain would cause hardship for livestock and poultry producers, that higher farm income would inflate land values and make it more difficult for people entering farming, and that assuring a parity price for farm commodities through loan programs or target payments would be exceedingly expensive for the U.S. Treasury and the American taxpayer.

Merle Hansen, president of the North American Farm Alliance, in answering such objections points out that when price supports were set at 90 percent of parity between 1942 and 1952 through the Steagall Amendment, farmers received 100 percent of parity for those 11 years (90 percent of parity price supports actually yielded 100 percent in the marketplace).

> For 20 years prior to 1953, the government's price support program actually showed a net profit of $13 million, in great contrast to today's expensive programs designed to keep farm prices low.
>
> In spite of the severity of the current attacks on the price support system by the Reagan administration, we must remember that the dismantling of the successful parity program actually began in 1953 through the influence of corporate and banking interests. We have seen a decline in average parity levels with successive presidential administrations.[58]

Tony Dechant, former president of the National Farmers Union, adds:

> If you will examine the years 1942 through 1952 you will find there were no dislocations between livestock and grain economies, no serious inflation of land prices, no skyrocketing consumer food prices, and finally, no inordinate costs to the taxpayers. But, we did have ample food supplies. We had prosperity in the countryside and full employment in the cities.

The long-time farm leader further explains that the parity pricing index, contrary to the claims of its critics, has been updated and modernized almost continuously to reflect changing farm crops, practices, costs and other factors.

> Parity is as up-to-date as antibiotics, anhydrous ammonia, hybrid varieties, and artificial insemination. We contend it is equally as valid to link farm commodity price supports to the parity index as it is to link labor wage rates, salaries of government officials, pensions and retirement benefits, and other public and private contractual obligations to the consumer price index.[59]

Again, when it is said that farmers are receiving 50 percent of parity it simply means that they are getting approximately one-half of the return on the dollar that other segments of the economy are receiving at the time. It should also be noted that the stated parity figure is a broad average, for in some crops, like wheat and corn, the parity figure is lower, while in other commodities like beef cattle the percentage is somewhat higher. Thus, in September 1990 parity prices[60] were

Hogs	57%
Lambs	40%
Dry Beans	41%
All Milk	54%
Beef Cattle	63%
Calves	69%
Upland Cotton	46%
Soybeans	49%
Barley	39%
Wheat	32%
Corn	41%
Grain Sorghum	40%

The dire economic situation farmers faced in the 1980s is graphically illustrated by comparing the parity figures of the 1930-1934 period to the recent past. In the five worst years of the Great Depression the average parity figure was 66 percent; in the 1981-1985 period the average was 56 percent. In the infamous 1932, parity was 58 percent; 53 years later it was barely 52 percent.[61]

Take corn, for example, at 27 cents a bushel in May 1933. It would have taken income from 2,000 bushels to buy a new Chevrolet. On October 16, 1986 at grain elevators in Iowa, that same amount of corn at 96 cents a bushel would have covered only slightly more than one-fifth of the price for a new car from the same company.[62]

"Conventional Economic Wisdom" Peddlers

Luther Tweeten, the Oklahoma State agricultural economist who has served in recent years as a major consultant to the U.S. Department of Agriculture, perhaps best synthesizes those arguments that many of today's agricultural economists offer in their efforts to maintain a historically low level of parity for U.S. farm prices. Tweeten has outlined what is in large measure the conventional economic wisdom guiding this nation's agricultural policies for the past century. After examining the "supply and demand" figures of recent years Tweeten declares:

> The future is unlikely to be dominated by either chronic surplus or shortage of food and fiber. Rather, periods of acute food crisis and acute farm income crisis will appear sporadically to year 2000 and beyond.
>
> The estimated current *excess resource capacity* [ed. too many farmers], a residual from *high prices* in the mid 1970s [ed. when the parity ratio averaged 75 percent], represents fewer *adjustment problems* than did resources in the 1960s [ed. when the United States had 1.7 million more farms]. Then labor was in *excess* by up to 40 percent; currently the *excess* is mostly in *capital resources* [ed. which has been used to substitute for the labor eliminated earlier], that can [now] be reduced in a comparatively short time, although *two or three years of farm prices at the 55-60 percent of parity range* may be required. [ed. since this presentation the parity ratio has averaged 55.2 percent]. Much of the *excess resources* may

be in the middlesize farm classes. (emphasis added)

Noting that the 61 percent parity ratio experienced in 1981 "may not be abnormal, but may be sufficient to induce output in line with demand and provide returns to cover *all the costs of an adequate sized and managed farm in the 1980s*" Tweeten goes on to claim that society need not pay more for its food and fiber. "Farms that account for half of farm output now cover resource costs with prices 54-62 percent of parity." He concludes:

The principal economic problem of the farming industry in the next two decades — instability. A Federal budget out of control will extend the duration of high interest rates, retard economic recovery, *and perpetuate excess capacity in agriculture.*

[Resource] *adjustment* will be especially painful because many such farms have traditionally been the backbone of agriculture, farm organizations and the rural community. (emphasis added)[63]

Reflecting on such long-standing agricultural "economic wisdom," Nebraska banker Rossiter observes that,

those of us who differ with this orthodox economic doctrine are considered virtual idiots by the doctrinaire practitioner. By the same token it is altogether possible, in light of the deplorable economic circumstances that prevail in agriculture and our economy today, that the "practical economist" may have a similar opinion of his orthodox economic counterpart. Fair is fair![64]

Chapter Thirty-Eight

Farmers Seeking Control Over Their Own Destiny

"This madness cannot continue much longer. Let's write a 'farmer bill' not just a new farm bill. Not a cotton program, and a dairy program, but a farmer program that focuses on farmers themselves, instead of bushels and bales and gallons."

At the time, it went relatively unnoticed by the national media and most farm-state politicians. But Texas Agricultural Commissioner Jim Hightower's charge in March 1984 to the 82nd Annual National Farmers Union convention in New Orleans marked the opening salvo in a remarkable three-year legislative effort by thousands of U.S. family farmers to regain a measure of the economic and political power that has been so forcefully in past years wrenched from them:

America's rural economy is headed for a crash because the Reagan administration is dismantling our country's most efficient economic machine — the family farm. I've listened to the president and heard him say that "prosperity has returned." But farmers, rural merchants, agribusiness and others dependent on the farm economy have seen no prosperity.[2]

Describing the effect of America's permanent agricultural crisis on farmers, bankers and consumers alike and how an upcoming battle to write a progressive "farmer bill" required the help of both farmers and consumers, Hightower outlined the direction he believed such legislation should take.

First, start with the farmer's price, cementing a floor at no less than the real cost of production; limit protected price to family farmers.

Second, bring the immediate surplus under control through mandatory production controls.

Third, aggressively seek new export markets, then expand production limits so farmers can produce for those new markets.

Fourth, tap the humanitarian potential of American agriculture by re-establishing an aggressive, well-managed Food-for-Peace program that fairly compensates U.S. farmers to help feed the world's hungry.

Fifth, incorporate soil conservation programs directly into the supply-management and farm benefit programs.

Sixth, write a six-year program that farmers can count on and plan for from one year to the next.

No overnight creation, Hightower's proposed "farmer bill" evolved from two years of intensive meetings with thousands of farmers from throughout the United States, a series of hearings by the Democratic National Committee's Agricultural Council, which Hightower chaired, and a variety of concrete member-debated and supported farm programs put forward by fledgling rural grass roots groups.

In the months following his NFU address, the Texas Agricultural Commissioner's office working in cooperation with Minnesota Agricultural Commissioner Jim Nichols' office, soon developed the technical support needed for such a "farmer program." In March 1985 the Farm Policy Reform Act of 1985 was unveiled. (See Appendix I)

Legislation Designed to Stimulate Recovery Based on Real Growth

On March 23, 1985 in St. Louis, Missouri an historic "Farmer/Labor Solidarity" meeting was held with over 100 major U.S. farm and labor organization delegates from some 17 states in attendance. This meeting unanimously adopted a position paper endorsing the Farm Policy Reform Act of 1985. It also laid the foundation for a new farmer/labor political alliance — the National Coordinating Committee for Farm Policy Reform.

Four national general farm organization presidents (NFU's Cy Carpenter, NFO's DeVon Woodland, AAM's Corky Jones, and NAFA's Merle Hansen) were joined by many state, regional and national leaders of the United Auto Workers, the AFL-CIO and the Teamsters, as well as other state and local labor and farm group leaders. Ken Worley, a UAW official, set the tone of the meeting when he told the gathering: "Working people on the farms and in the factories and offices are joining together in the momentous fight to save our livelihoods and rural America."[3]

On May 7, shortly after this landmark meeting a coalition of rural and urban members in Congress introduced the Farm Policy Reform Act (FPRA) of 1985 in both the House of Representatives (H.R. 2383) and the

Senate (S. 1083). Senator Tom Harkin, author of the Senate bill, declared:

So far, most of the talk in Washington has been for lower prices so we can compete in the so-called free market. There is no free market. We set the world price, and it doesn't make a lick of sense for us to set prices so low we bankrupt our own farmers. The fact is, if we pay farmers a fair price, we might lose a little in sales volume but in terms of dollars, we'll make several billion a year or more off exports than we do right now.[4]

In the House of Representatives, Representative Bill Alexander, D-Ark., Democratic deputy whip and the bill's principal House sponsor added, "This bill would eliminate $10-$15 billion in subsidy payments. Additionally, by matching production with actual demand, it should reduce the amount of money outstanding in federal price support loans by more than $15 billion."[5]

One urban co-sponsor of H.R. 2383, Representative John Conyers, D-Mich., in pledging the support of all 19 members of the Congressional Black Caucus, pointed out,

Economists will tell you if we put a fair price on raw materials like agricultural products, the new income will percolate up through the economy, generating real economic growth all the way. This bill will generate anywhere from $40-$90 billion a year in new economic activity. That means increased demand for all types of products, agricultural and otherwise. That means more new jobs than any tax cut or government jobs program can accomplish. I'm convinced that any real recovery has to start on the farm.[6]

And Representative Lane Evans, D-Ill., who would become one of the bill's leaders in the House Agriculture Committee, also noted,

There's an old and very true saying that recessions are farm led and farm fed. We're told we've got an economic recovery going, but it's being fueled by the biggest deficit-spending spree in our history and by an unprecedented influx of foreign investment capital. Meanwhile, rural America is going bankrupt and unemployment remains about seven percent. By allowing our farmers to make a profit, this bill will stimulate a recovery based upon real growth, not on borrowed money.[7]

Opposition to the bills came immediately from the American Farm Bureau. "Supporters will make a lot of noise, but I don't expect [the bills] to go very far," predicted Farm Bureau president Kleckner. "Congress is to farm bills what little boys are to mud puddles. They just love to hop into them and slosh around."[8]

The Reagan administration and John Block also opposed the farm price increases as called for in the FPRA, claiming that what was needed to boost farm income was simply a system of agriculture based on "market clearing prices." "Market-clearing prices,"

however, as the Hereford, Texas *Agricultural Watchdog* pointed out, was merely another Reaganomics euphemism "because they know they would be shot, hung up and quartered by the nation's farmers if they actually said what they meant — *lower prices* will solve the farmers problems!"[9]

The Texas paper added that the one basic fact about today's economic system that needed to be understood by the public was that agriculture was forced to sell its production at 1948 prices and produce at 1984 costs.

The only conclusion to solving this dilemma is to either *lower* production costs to 1948 levels, *or* raise commodity prices to a level equal to 1984 costs.

To those economists/politicians who oppose supply management and *producer* established prices, we can only say that *all* other industries conduct their business this way. Agriculture is the *only* industry where the *buyer* establishes the price of the commodity. And agriculture is the only industry which is unable to *voluntarily cut production when supplies exceed demand.*

Acknowledging that "farmers realize that they have lots of problems, but one of them *ain't* too much money for their product," the *Watchdog* asked the same question of Reagan & Company, that at the time was being so succinctly expressed by television's sagacious Ernest P. Worrell, "do we look like we got stupid wrote all over our faces, Vern?"

In the FPRA's efforts to lower the overall cost of producing food, it could be seen, for example, that a one percent reduction in interest rates on a one-time total farm debt of $212 billion, would result in a $21.2 billion savings, more than the entire anticipated additional costs to consumers under the provisions of the FPRA. As *The St. Paul Pioneer Press Dispatch* noted in an editorial praising S. 1083, it "makes sense to have people as consumers, rather than as taxpayers, pay the grocery bills."[10] Acknowledging that FPRA might raise food prices slightly for people unemployed, disabled or hurt by Reagan cuts in food stamps and other food assistance programs, FRPA's backers noted that their bill would in fact restore needed food assistance along with incorporating the program revisions long advocated by nutrition experts at a cost of only $4 billion, less than 25 percent of the total budget savings anticipated by FPRA's sponsors.

Supply Management

To those who doubted that FPRA legislation could raise farm prices without government subsidies, its sponsors explained that their plan was possible by first establishing a floor at the average full cost of production using CCC crop loans, and then controlling supply to ensure that the market could function without expensive and price-depressing surpluses.

Since the 1930s the nation's single most successful farm program has been the CCC non-recourse loan program administered by locally-elected committees of the ASCS. This program has allowed farmers to withhold their crops from the market if prices offered by the giant grain corporations fell below a pre-determined level. Farmers pledged such unsold crops as collateral on a loan from the county ASCS, which allowed them to pay their bills until the grain company offered them a reasonable market price.

When farmers are often able to withhold their crops, prices will usually rise above the established target level at which time they can sell the crop and repay their loan with interest. If farmers could use this program to participate in an effective supply management program no surpluses will develop, thus reducing any cost to the government for storage. From 1933 to 1952, when the CCC program included strict supply management, it actually earned $13 million in profits for taxpayers from the interest paid on the loans.[11]

FPRA legislation simply proposed to make use of this already established and proven CCC program by putting a floor under farm prices at the average full cost of production, approximately 70 percent of parity. At the same time, in maintaining a strategic reserve of storable commodities, the CCC would release those reserves on the market only if farm prices rose above 110 percent of parity, thus forcing the "ceiling" price back down.

Some well-meaning but rather myopic critics of the FPRA argued that with higher prices for farm commodities the superfarms and wealthy tax-sheltered operations would get bigger and wealthier and land prices would again skyrocket. However, drafters of the FPRA incorporated a number of specific provisions to address the current land ownership structure crisis, mainly one that had been created by the chaotic conditions of the last decade.

Producers who grew larger than the traditional family farm would be required to absorb an equitably distributed larger share of the set-aside required to balance supply with demand. Also, specific programs to assist farmers who in the past were forced to grow beyond a desirable size (under the Earl Butz and corporate agribusiness dictum of "get big or get out") would be put in place.

Such programs would include debt-rescheduling assistance for farmers wanting to restructure their farms or ranches into smaller, more efficient operations. FPRA also called for the redirection of existing programs, such as the limited resource program of FmHA, to provide immediate emergency assistance and debt restructuring needed to keep families on their land, to resettle families who have already lost their farms, and to help young and low income farmers get started in farming.

Addressing the fear that increased commodity prices will lead to re-inflated land prices, FPRA backers noted that during the late 1970s at precisely the same time that land prices were rising sharply and farm prices were falling steadily, inflation was pressuring investors to seek out any and every hedge to protect their earnings, thus allowing speculators to profit regardless of the level of commodity prices.

With land prices having fallen almost 50 percent in some areas, speculators were beginning to move in again, not because they saw a rise in commodity prices, but because they anticipated a profit from the land itself.

By making it possible for efficient producers to hang on to their land and stabilize their current situation, FPRA sought to prevent large tracts of land from falling into the hands of these same speculators and tax-loss farmers.

By its recognizing four major considerations, the FPRA was also designed to construct an export policy whereby U.S. farmers need not be bankrupt.

1) Exports must profit the entire industry, not just a small number of private grain traders at the expense of farmers and rural businesses;

2) Our export policy needed to be closely tied to our natural resource conservation policy since we could not continue to export a bushel of topsoil with each bushel of corn and jeopardize the food security of our nation for future generations;

3) We needed to consider the impact of our export policies on our political alliances if we expected European and other nations to remain strong friends. We must not continue to attack their national food security policies or undercut them in traditional markets; and

4) It was crucial to understand the impact of our policies on farmers in food deficient nations, especially on their ability to earn enough from their own crops to remain on the land and to invest in resource conservation and increased productivity.

When food self-sufficiency is destroyed in these poor nations the resulting social chaos and rebellion becomes a critical and a potentially catastrophic problem for the entire world community.

Protecting the Soil and Water

The FPRA also saw the sustaining of our natural resources as an extremely high priority. Since the next generation of farmers and the rest of society will depend on such current efforts, the land and water they inherit must be in as good or better condition than when it was received. Toward that end the FPRA proposed:

• Across the board 15 percent set-aside for all producers, with 100 percent cross-compliance requirements, established by the local SCS.

• National Conservation Reserve open to all land in the 3e, 4e, or worse classifications whereby farmers would sign long-term (three to ten years or longer) contracts with the government to retire fragile lands and to put in a permanent cover crop in exchange for up to one-half of their foregone yields in payment-in-kind grain from the CCC.

• Increased funding for the cost-sharing erosion control programs of the SCS along with strict, total prohibitions against "sod busting."

• Equity buy-out provisions to permanently retire irrigation systems in regions where groundwater resources are scarce and at risk from continued deep pumping for crop irrigation.

The Reagan administration's plan of encouraging maximum production promised a renewed stress on the nation's important water supplies both because it was increasing water use and injecting even more chemical poisons into an already-threatened water supply.

Reacting to such problems the FPRA proposed acreage set-asides, especially the most hilly and fragile lands, to help control water run-off and erosion; disincentives to the enormous feedlots and increasingly large "dairy factories" in an effort to reduce high concentrations of animal wastes; assistance to diversified farms by putting cows on hillsides rather than row crops, thereby bringing to the farm manure and vegetation control features; and provisions for buying out farmer equity in irrigations systems in fragile areas, with payments-in-kind.

A True "Market-Oriented Approach"

During the ensuing Congressional committee debates on S. 1083 and H.R. 2383 a couple of relevant studies were introduced which addressed a basic premise of the FPRA, nicely explained by Hal Hamilton in his essay "Barnyard Politics."

Endemic surplus productive capacity inevitably results from the competitive and capital intensive nature of our agriculture. Progressive farm programs always include a system of production quotas or supply management, but the processors and traders of course benefit from the price-depressing results of over-production.[12]

The most important study to come before Congress, however, was a projection by the highly-respected Food and Agricultural Policy Research Institute (FAPRI) of Iowa State University and the University of Missouri relative to the merits of a modification of agricultural policy similar to that approved by a House Agricultural Subcommittee in June 1985 and the provisions contained in S. 1083 and H.R. 2383.

When one examines the contrasting characteristics of the two approaches it is clear not only who would benefit and who would pay for future agricultural programs, but also why S. 1083 and H.R. 2383 were so bitterly opposed by corporate agribusiness. (See Appendix G)

It was Senator Harkin who pointed out in arguing for the passage of S. 1083 that a mandatory supply reduction program such as that embodied in his bill was "a true 'market-oriented approach' (matching supply with anticipated demand)" rather than the Reagan administration's "production only" program which was legislating lower prices, forcing farmers to produce more per given unit and thereby lowering prices even further. Also, recognizing a possible increase in food prices Harkin was quick to note that

Without a doubt, higher commodity prices would mean somewhat higher food prices — about four percent across the board. But isn't food too cheap now? It is time consumers began to pay the real cost of food, rather than continuing to enjoy low government-subsidized prices brought about by our cheap food policy.[13]

Support for supply management legislation also came from the Congressional Office of Technology when in "A Special Report for the 1985 Farm Bill" the government agency presented the results of eight different policy scenarios ranging from a continuation of current policies to high-tech "solutions."[14] The only scenario which showed an increase in the chances of survival for family-sized operations was the "supply control" scenario similar to the dairy program proposed in the FPRA.

Results obtained [showed that] probability of survival was increased for all farms of all regions. The 52-cow Minnesota dairy experienced the largest increase in the probability of survival ... Average net present value increased for all dairy farms. The 52-cow Minnesota dairy increased from negative $77,000 to $22,000 ... Net income from Minnesota dairies was increased by $15,000. These dairies previously had the lowest income.

Farmers to Congress: "It's a Joke!"

When the Congress passed the 1985 farm bill, containing 18 titles including exports, agricultural research, food stamps and conservation among others, at a projected cost of $52 billion, commodity price supports were pegged lower, according to the bill's advocates, in an effort to make U.S. farms goods more competitive abroad.[15]

The bill, called the Food Security Act of 1985 (although Dan McGuire, director of the Nebraska Wheat Board, surely spoke for thousands of U.S. farmers in saying that a more appropriate title would have been the Farmer Reduction Act of 1985), made no attempt to deal with long-overdue structural trends within American agriculture.[16]

The reductions the new law mandated in loan rates, and later in income subsidies, would not only quickly lead to lower farm income, but would soon threaten to cost the Federal government more than $50 billion by 1988, according to Congressional projections, and might even balloon to $70 billion, according to some other budget analysts.[17] It is worth noting again that in 1984 over 15 percent of all federal handouts went to farmers with net worth exceeding $1 million and with the passage of the 1985 Farm Bill this group quickly came to expect, even more in the way of subsidies — which they got.[18]

One such recipient, for example, was Salyer American, a Corcoran, California corporation that was operating one of the nation's largest cotton farms but had not participated in any government farm programs since the land set-aside programs of the early 1970s. After the passage of the new Farm Bill, the company, anticipating a sharp drop in cotton prices, quickly made itself eligible for more than $1 million in federal payments while diverting much of its "idled" land to other crops.[19]

While these massive payments to superfarms have continued unabated, it is well for us to recall Frank Naylor's estimate that only about 17 cents out of every federal dollar now spent in agriculture goes to those full-time family farmers who desperately need help.

Also, as Joe Belden, a Washington-based writer and attorney specializing in rural matters, noted after the passage of the 1985 Farm Bill: "In a terrible irony, this is the most expensive farm bill in history but — by lowering price supports it may still force as many as ten percent of all farmers out of business over the next two years."[20]

The ultimate consequence of the severe loan rate reductions contained in the 1985 bill was best explained by a Missouri farmer, Peter Brewer, who moved to the United States from England in 1983 and began successfully farming 1,800 acres of wheat in Grundy County in the north central part of the state. He immediately found himself faced with a question that so many of his neighbors were already confronting: Does a nation awash in surplus wheat need a campaign to triple its output?

"One hundred-bushel wheat is not the problem," Brewer says. "The problem is the low price that forces farmers to produce more. Every time they lower the federal loan rate, it acts as a floor and pushes prices down that much more. These low prices don't leave much of a margin even for us."[21]

As bad as the 1985 farm bill was, fortunately for thousands of farmers the Reagan administration failed during debate on the bill to secure a one year freeze on existing deficiency payments with later reductions. The Congress did eventually settle on a plan whereby there would be no more than a ten percent cut over the following five years.

During the heated debate in the Senate on the freezing of these payments, the forces to preserve the family farm system of agriculture and those who seek to eradicate its "excess resource capacity" directly confronted each other.

When Senator Richard G. Lugar, R-Ind., introduced an amendment to freeze payments at the current level for a year and then reduce them by five percent in succeeding years, claiming that it would save more than $7 billion over three years, Senator Charles E. Grassley, R-Iowa, correctly reminded his colleagues that "the Lugar amendment makes a political decision, not an economic decision. In my state, 20 to 30 percent of the people who are now in farming are no longer going to be farmers — that [amendment] is a political decision that would remove them from agriculture.[22]

Unsuccessful efforts were also made during the debate on the 1985 bill to target subsidy payments to those farmers who need them most. Kansas's Dan Glickman, a member of the House Agricultural Committee, in introducing one such an amendment, stated:

A subsidy is intended to keep those who are vulnerable alive. So targeting makes immense intellectual sense, as well as practical sense. But it wasn't easy to get institutional forces — the committee, the farm groups to accept it, because it is new and because influential folks representing districts with larger farms didn't like it.[23]

A new "conservation reserve" plan, however, was enacted in the bill, designed to pay farmers for the long-term idling of their most erodible land and bar farmers from receiving Federal farm benefits if they plowed up those erodible lands.

The rejection of the Farm Policy Reform Act of 1985, and the subsequent debate, passage, and reluctant signing of the 1985 farm bill by Ronald Reagan, clearly showed that neither the Congress nor the American public really understood what was at stake in our agricultural economy or in rural America.

"That bill is the legacy of David Stockman," said Tom Harkin, "he set this in motion."[24] Arkansas's Pryor, who had earlier, during the bill-making process urged his fellow committee members not to confuse themselves by reading details of the pending bill, now observed that "comprehending the tax bill and its ramifications is peaches and cream compared to comprehending the farm bill and its ramifications."[25] To which Iowa farmer Dixon Terry responded, "Congress was quibbling over pennies. We're talking about major changes that need to be made. It's a joke!"[26]

Yet another astute and succinct analysis of the legislation was offered by long-time farm journalist and activist, Lem Harris, who observed:

The bill is symbolic of today's Federal administration and Congress. President Reagan wanted to wipe out virtually all farm price support measures and force farm prices to submit to 'market disciplines.'Of course, Reagan's policy means zero bargaining power for several million farm operations, contrasted with monopoly control of farm commodity markets by agribusiness. A "free market" does not exist.[27]

Soon after the 1985 bill was signed, Block used the authority it provided him to announce still more sizeable cutbacks in 1986 federal price supports for some major crops.

In announcing that per-bushel loan rates for wheat were being reduced from $3.30 per bushel to $2.40 and to $1.92 from $2.55 for corn, the USDA argued that subsidy costs would be in the $54 billion range over the 1986-1988 period, reflecting December 1985 market prices and export levels.[28] By July 1986 wheat prices had fallen 20.7 percent to $2.45 per bushel and corn by October had dropped 62 percent to 96 cents a bushel.

Watching this price deterioration many farmers recalled the *Wall Street Journal*'s observation during the farm bill debate: "The sharply reduced price supports will mean lower farm prices but won't necessarily reduce consumer prices. Price cuts for farmers often go to boost profit margins for wholesalers rather than lower retail food prices."

The 1985 Farm Bill not only provided lucrative bonuses for the large multinational commodity exporters, but stuck American farmers and taxpayers with the bill of sale. Consider, for example, a pound of cotton that cost the farmer 87 cents to produce and three additional cents to store. The Federal government purchased that pound from the farmer for 55 cents, plus 26 cents in a direct subsidy; a net loss to the farmer of nine cents a pound. The government then sold that pound of cotton to an export company for 22 cents; a net loss to the taxpayer of 59 cents. The shipper then sold the pound of cotton to Taiwan for 26 cents; a net gain to the shipper of four cents and for Taiwan a 64 cent gain.

Thus, when the total bill is added up we find that with the farmers' loss, the taxpayers' loss, and the shippers' gain we have a net loss to the U.S. economy of 64 cents for each pound of cotton produced for export.[29]

For many farmers, however, the supreme irony of the long debate over the 1985 farm bill was that many of those legislators who opposed the Reagan administration's efforts to dismantle the farm subsidy program would later return to support the Gramm-Rudman-Hollings deficit-reduction bill vigorously. Yet, if ever fully implemented, such ill-advised legislation could have imposed still more drastic cuts in all farm program spending over the following five years.

While major food assistance programs on the domestic side like food stamps and the Women, Infants and Children supplemental food program (WIC) were exempt from Gramm-Rudman-Hollings, such farm and food programs as soil conservation, FmHA loans, foreign assistance programs, etc. were not.

In his proposed Federal budget for 1987 Ronald Reagan asked for an 18 percent reduction in the USDA's budget, a total of $10 billion in farm and food spending program cuts, with the latter programs alone reduced by some $400 million — mostly in food stamp expenditures.

Raymond Daniel, vice president for the food and agricultural group of Chase Econometrics Inc., believed that the Reagan spending estimates of $16 billion related to future Federal price and income support payments in fiscal year 1987 were way off. "The cost of the program could be $25 billion easily if the current farm program isn't changed."[30] But, even Daniel would prove to be way off, as by mid-1986 the Congressional Budget Office (CBO) projected that the cost for the first three years of the program could be $64 billion with the first year alone some 80 percent over budget.[31]

It had been none other than John Schnittker, longtime corporate agribusiness policy maker and former under-secretary of agriculture, who suggested in the first few months after the 1985 farm bill had been in place that it was an ill-conceived patchwork piece of legislation that would cost the taxpayers billions of dollars.

"When we look back in a year or two, it will be a major embarrassment," he declared.[32] One year later he would reflect, "the 1985 Farm Bill has essentially failed. U.S. and world agriculture are in sustained crisis. The administration is trapped in its own rhetoric; Congress is trapped by the nostalgia of old-time farm bills."

"What was needed in 1987," he continued, "is an emergency approach" that would include a "pause" in U.S. price cutting, a phased reduction of production subsidies, decoupling, special attention to the severest farm credit problems and targeting of federal aid to farmers who need it the most.[33]

"Decoupling" generally means that instead of supporting farmer's income on the condition that they participate in federal programs, they would be paid no matter how much or how little they produced. (It was not, as one wag has suggested, a term for a new postcoital position.)

San Francisco Chronicle farm reporter Henry Schacht further explains that "the idea is that farmers would then be free to respond to market conditions rather than federal programs — and presumably make better decisions on how much to produce."[34]

Chapter Thirty-Nine

Scaring Agribusiness
to Death

"We're going to have a tough winter. We're going to continue to see people leave agriculture at a higher level than any of us would like to see."[1]

That warning by outgoing Secretary of Agriculture John Block as the 1985 farm bill awaited the President's signature on a cold, windy December day was more than ironic given the fact that the original farm legislation offered by the Reagan administration in early 1985 was, in the words of one Republican senator, an "out-and-out betrayal" of the American farmer.[2]

Claiming that its proposals would "propel agriculture into a new and more responsible era," the Reagan administration had sought price support loan rates that would have dropped to 75 percent of a three-year average market price.[3] Such a three-year average market price for the 1983-1985 period would have been 55 percent of parity, bringing the Reagan proposed price to 41 percent of parity. Crops could have also been used as collateral on loans up to $200,000, under the proposed plan, with farmers paying interest on amounts above that.

Target price subsidies would have been scaled down, again based on a declining percentage of current average market prices, with a $10,000 limit per farmer by 1988. FmHA would have had to phase out direct operating loans over five years with only guarantees offered to commercial farms or farm credit system lenders to pick up such abandoned clients. Farm program benefits would have been banned to any farmer who converted erodible land that had lain idle to crop production for ten years or more.[4]

Few in Congress took the Reagan proposals seriously. "The administration became almost irrelevant during our markup," Representative E. Thomas Coleman, R-Mo., a key Republican member of the House Agriculture Committee recalls. "I felt from the start that the White House misunderstood the farm-credit situation and the severity of things going on out there."[5]

The USDA, meanwhile, lobbying on behalf of the Reagan bill, became an object of ridicule. Senator Pryor accused the White House of a "flagrant" abuse of power by mobilizing the USDA's nationwide network of employees to lobby for its farm bill. That campaign, according to documents Pryor obtained, included an order lifting the budget restrictions on travel expenditures so USDA staffers could make speeches and address groups throughout the country. News releases were distributed with blank spaces for officials to insert their names following appropriate quotations championing the Reagan farm bill.[6]

USDA efforts to obtain support for the Reagan bill in Congress were, to put it kindly, "uncoordinated." One Department official, for example, sought to lobby Representative Stan Lundine, D-NY, to support an amendment that would scale down peanut supports. Congressman Lundine, however, had already authored just such an amendment, and had been responsible for a similar bill in 1981 which passed in the House by 91 votes.[7] Meanwhile, Deputy Secretary John R. Norton, second in command at USDA, was spending most of his time during the farm bill debate monitoring the progress of immigration legislation. That legislation profoundly affected Norton and other large western produce growers who have come to rely on imported migrant laborers to harvest their crops. (It was Norton, incidentally, who when asked about the plight of the American family farmer responded that "what they want is civil service jobs on the farm. They want to have a guaranteed job making $40,000. It's not the obligation of the federal government to bail out everyone who makes a bad decision."[8])

After passage of the 1985 farm bill, USDA officials expressed disappointment with the efforts of the agribusiness lobby.

"Agribusiness has been, quite frankly, the biggest disappointment," charged Randy Russell, Secretary Block's executive assistant. He went on to speculate that groups that focused on a single commodity, such as corn or wheat, were the most successful, but at the same time admitted that the Reagan bill was a "tactical error" because the measures were "draconian," asking for too much change too quickly.[9]

Curiously, the one-time corporate agribusiness lobby (including the American Farm Bureau Federation) came together to lobby hard during the farm bill debate was during the Senate debate on a referendum amendment which would have allowed farmers a chance to vote on improving farm prices and establishing mandatory production controls.

In a letter to each Senator, this "Farm Coalition Group" declared "we urge that you support the amendment to strike the referendum provision for mandatory government production controls. We would also appreciate your opposition to any other amendments establishing such a referendum."[10]

The letter was signed by a who's who of agribusiness including the American Bakers Association, American Cotton Shippers Association, the American Meat Institute, Biscuit & Cracker Manufacturers' Association of America, U.S. Chamber of Commerce, Chocolate Manufacturers Association, Farm & Industrial Equipment Institute, Florida Phosphate Council, Food Marketing Institute, Independent Bakers Association, Millers' National Federation, National-American Wholesaler Grocers Association, National Broiler Council, National Confectioners Association, National Fertilizer Solutions Association, National Food Processors Association, National Pasta Association, Potato Chip/Snack Food Association, Ralston Purina, and The Fertilizer Institute.

A Pitchfork in the Belly of Air Force One

The Reagan farm bill was not the first time in 1985 that the President gave the back of his hand to hundreds of thousands of the nation's farmers. Earlier in the year he vetoed legislation that would have provided nearly $2 billion in emergency relief to debt-plagued farmers.[11] The action was immediately and angrily denounced by farmers and lawmakers from both political parties.

"There's no point in me planting a crop that I'm going to lose money on," said Douglas Marsh, a Mondovi, Wisconsin farmer and father of five, with a debt of some $450,000, upon hearing of Reagan's action.[12]

"[Reagan's] out to decapitalize rural America," an angry Republican Minnesota State Senator Charlie Berg charged. "He'll reduce the price of farmland and the land will all end up in the Federal Land Bank or the insurance companies."[13]

"Look," said Federal Reserve chairman Paul Volcker in a rather revealing comment, to those farm-state legislators begging for lower interest rates, "your constituents are unhappy, mine [Wall Street, the bond market and banks] aren't."[14]

Kansas' Pat Roberts clearly upset Administration officials before a House Agricultural Committee hearing when he warned that the President should be careful not to fly too low over Kansas on the way to an upcoming California vacation lest he get "a pitchfork in the belly of Air Force One."[15]

Agricultural Committee Chairman de la Garza also voiced his displeasure with the President's action.

> We are concerned, as well we should be, about the budget ... [but] we're talking about the demise of rural America ... the producers in the greatest producing nation in the world. Even if the Administration estimates are correct, we still don't make a dent on the budget. What we're talking about is one extra MX missile.[16] (See Appendix I)

Nebraska farmer-rancher and State Senator Tom Vickers saw the need for farmers and farm state legislators to get "eyeball to eyeball" with the President.

We already know what John Block thinks. He has decided he wants to be the last secretary of agriculture. We know what David Stockman thinks about agriculture, and even his mother doesn't agree... We're afraid that watching "The Beverly Hillbillies" and "Hee Haw" tells [the President] all we wants to know about rural life.[17]

But it was Nebraska's late Democratic U.S. Senator Edward Zorinsky who best summed up the feelings of many when he remarked that "this Administration has done for farmers what Bonnie and Clyde did for banks."[18]

A Fall Farmers' Rebellion Thwarted

Despite a groundswell of support from farmers throughout the nation, despite the studies which showed that a mandatory supply reduction program was the most efficient means toward stemming the crisis in American agriculture, despite the growing and begrudging awareness by many economists that fair prices for agricultural commodities was the central issue within the nation's farming communities, and despite the fact that a small, but determined number of members in both the House and Senate refused to be politically intimidated by the Reagan administration and many of their own farm state colleagues, both S. 1083 and H.R. 2383 were eventually defeated in committee.

Nevertheless, the key feature of the FPRA — mandatory farm production controls — was later introduced as an amendment on the floor of both the Senate and the House during the debate on the 1985 farm bill. Citing a Congressional Budget Office study which declared that "passage of the referendum would ensure that the farm bill remains under budget while raising farm income an estimated 52 percent," the amendment's backers also noted that projected savings of $12.5 billion could be realized by passing the amendment.[19] The savings would come mainly from the elimination of costly direct federal subsidies, which in fact were failing to help family farmers since the bulk of the money was not going to those farmers who needed the most help.

As Dixon Terry, co-chairperson of the National Coordinating Committee for the Farm Policy Reform, summarized the efforts by his colleagues to obtain passage of the Harkin-Alexander "amendment":

> We have put prices and supply management at the center of the national farm policy debate as it hasn't been for three decades. The idea for private equity for farmers and the programs to achieve it have been established as a solid alternative in the minds of many who have been suffering from years of "market oriented" indoctrination by the export establishment.
>
> One thing was disgustingly obvious: the American Farm Bureau Federation, the National Corn Growers, the National Cattleman's Association, the Soybean Association, and others spent thousands of dollars of farmers' money in joining with the National Chamber of Commerce and other corporate interests to lobby for lower farm

prices for the next five years. They had to pull out all the stops and throw everything they had at us to win in the House. It is time this story is told in the countryside.[20]

On October 1, 1985, siding with Representative de la Garza's Agriculture Committee, the House rejected a mandatory farm production control amendment offered by Representative Harold L. Volkmer, D-Mo. The voice vote enabled members to avoid going on the record.

Two days later the House again turned its back in a 251-174 vote on a similar amendment offered by Representative Berkley W. Bedell, D-Iowa. With the solid backing of the Reagan administration and corporate agribusiness, Illinois Representative Edward R. Madigan, the ranking GOP member of the House Agricultural Committee, led the floor fight that culminated in the amendment's defeat. Later, in January 1991, he would be selected by George Bush to succeed Clayton Yeutter as U.S. Secretary of Agriculture.

An alliance of large livestock producers fearing higher feed costs, food processing companies facing higher raw material prices, farm suppliers uneasy over possible reduced sales from production input sales, urban liberals who feared the idea might be too costly for food consumers, outgoing Secretary Block, who had termed the referendum idea the most objectionable feature of the entire farm bill debate, and, of course, the Farm Bureau, all ganged up to defeat the Bedell amendment. Reflecting on the loss the Iowa congressman observed. "I don't believe we can have the middle part of our country collapse and not have it affect all of the country. If the rest of the country gets into the shape we're in, sooner or later we're going to see more willingness to look at alternatives."[21]

On October 8, immediately prior to the House's passage of the 1985 Farm Bill, one last effort was made in the House to get a mandatory production control referendum enacted. After a bitter floor debate Representative Alexander's proposal was defeated on a 368-59 vote. Terry reflects:

We took a beating in the House when the Bedell referendum was struck and when the Harkin-Alexander Bill was later defeated soundly as an amendment. But we did have 174 votes for the Bedell Plan (which was the best indication of our true support due to last-minute complications in the vote on the Alexander bill). That's 172 more than we started with in the spring when the farmers rolled into town with the "radical" idea of raising farm prices.[22]

The House defeat of the Alexander amendment was only one measure of how completely corporate agribusiness carried the day in the final hours of the 1985 Farm Bill's rite of passage.

Earlier in the session, the House had passed an amendment by California's George Miller that barred any federal aid to farmers who did not provide field sanitation facilities for their workers. His amendment called for agricultural employers who employed ten or more workers to provide them with drinking water, hand-washing facilities and toilets in their fields. Yet, on a last-hour roll call vote demanded by Representative Robert S. Walker, R-Pa., the amendment was overturned 227-199.[23]

The mandatory production control amendment in the Senate was destined to meet a fate similar to it's fate in the House. Despite the prediction of Senate Republican Majority Leader Robert Dole, R-Kan., at the outset of the Senate debate that the Harkin Amendment would appeal "to only a handful of his colleagues," it was defeated on November 22 by a 56-36 vote. The Reagan administration had warned the Senate that any such referendum in the Farm Bill would invite an instant veto from the White House.

Harkin, noting the escalating farmer support for his amendment, told the Senate that production controls were the only way to stop the decline in farm prices and bring supply back in line with demand. His proposal, he argued, would cut government costs, put the bill under budget limits and increase net farm income by $8.5 billion, while adding less than a dime a day to the average American's food bill.[24]

Senator Dole dismissed the Harkin amendment as "so bad we don't need much time" for debate. He contended, contradictory evidence notwithstanding, that mandatory controls would price U.S. grain out of export markets and drive up costs for domestic livestock producers.[25]

A later survey by the League of Rural Voters in the spring of 1986, however, showed that an overwhelming majority (64 percent) of 1340 farmers surveyed in 11 Plain states disagreed with Dole and said they favored limiting production if the result would be to receive higher prices for the crops. This poll was later confirmed when over 35 percent of eligible farmers (319,408 ballots) nationally responded to the USDA's informal wheat poll with 57.3 percent saying they favored a mandatory program.[26] Agriculture Secretary Richard Lyng, who openly campaigned against conducting such a survey, puzzlingly termed the poll "inconclusive."[27]

Along with Lyng, the Farm Bureau, the National Fertilizer Institute and the National Grain and Feed Dealers Association launched a national campaign attempting to tell farmers how to vote on the issue. In the course of their effort the Farm Bureau took it upon itself to attack those organizations, such as the Nebraska Wheat Board, that dared voice an opposing opinion.

In a letter to the Nebraska Farm Bureau Federation, Ervain J. Friehe, the state wheat board's immediate past chairman, countercharged that the Farm Bureau and its other coalition members

blatantly failed to present farmers with a balanced range of income, price and export possibilities that could develop under a farmer mandated production control program. Instead, the no-vote coalition presented a radical acreage reduction and wheat price and export scenario, deceiving farmers in the process.

Be assured, however, that the Nebraska Wheat Board understands the difference between the economic interests of the grain trade, the flour miller, the baker and the international grain merchant and that of the wheat producer. This board of directors is not confused about which sector they represent and they clearly display the courage and integrity to stand up for the farmer.[28]

Senator Harkin, in commenting on the "informal" USDA referendum vote, enthused,

in this vote, wheat farmers have turned thumbs down on the current farm program through their vote. They've said that they don't like low prices. They don't like bankruptcy, and they want to earn their income from the market place, not from a government paycheck.[29]

Months later, in the closing days of the 99th Congress, Representative Richard Gephardt and Iowa's Harkin again introduced a "Save the Family Farm Act," a measure that (as the summary in the Appendix I shows) closely paralleled many of the provisions of the FPRA.

As Texas's Hightower noted at the time of the introduction of the Harkin-Gephardt proposal, it "allows farmers to make a profit. It's such a simple concept that agribusiness is scared to death of it."[30]

Having the Last Word

While Congress chose to turn its back on the Food Policy Reform Act and its needed provisions for restoring a measure of social and economic justice to American agriculture, the thousands of farmers and the dozens of farm/labor/citizen coalitions that the FPRA brought forth and which fought so hard for the Act's passage did not suddenly disappear from the political scene when the President signed the 1985 Farm Bill.

At a meeting in Minneapolis, Minnesota two days into 1986, a special campaign strategy meeting with representatives from the National Coordinating Committee for Farm Policy Reform, NAFA, the National Farmers' Fair Credit Campaign, and the National Save the Family Farm Committee was held as a preliminary action in the instituting of a National Rural Crisis Action campaign ("A Price and A Place . . . Justice For Rural America").

Believing that active solidarity among farmers and between farmers and rural and urban supporters was needed to gain the necessary political power to save the family farm system and the nation's rural communities and to insure affordable food for all, the Action campaign recommended increasing unity and taking progressively stronger actions until state and federal governments enacted long-term and emergency legislation which would:

• Reverse the increasing control of food production by giant corporations,
• Increase the viability of family farms,
• Insure the continued availability of affordable food for all people, and
• Accomplish these objectives by setting a floor under farm prices at parity levels, in conjunction with effective supply management.

Later in 1986, after increased public awareness of agriculture's plight in part due to singer Willie Nelson's Farm Aid concerts in Champagne, Illinois and Austin, Texas, funds were realized that enabled some 1,500 delegates, elected in some 500 regional rural caucuses throughout the U.S. in July and August, to attend the United Farmer and Rancher Congress in St. Louis, Missouri on September 10-13.

In three days of meetings and plenary sessions the grassroots delegates attempted to define the severity of the farm crisis and develop an extensive list of "whereas" and "therefore" resolutions concerning farm prices, moratoriums on farm foreclosures, tax incentives for sustainable agricultural practices and soil/water conservation, conservation and the protection of the environment, special land reform measures, importing and exporting farm products, rural community services, rural development and public education on agricultural issues, all of which were approved by a general assembly of the delegates.

"The most important thing to come out of this meeting, in my estimation, " declared Anne Kanten, Congress chairperson and Assistant Commissioner of Agriculture of the State of Minnesota, "is the unity and motivation of these delegates. Some of them saw this congress as their last chance to save their way of life. We have turned their desperation into personal commitments to fight for the integrity of the family farm and rural life."

While the conference heard addresses from Hightower, film star Eddie Albert, Rev. Jesse Jackson, Missouri Lt. Governor Harriett Woods, Wayne Cryts, Representative Richard Gephardt, D-Mo, and Senator Harkin and were even entertained at a special concert by Nelson, many of the delegates felt the most moving and symbolic moment of the congress came when the delegates removed their various farm and organizational caps and donned the white and black congress caps in a remarkable show of unity and solidarity.

Part of the enthusiasm generated at the Congress became evident during the ensuing Congressional elections as four American Agricultural Movement members ran spirited, but unsuccessful political campaigns in Missouri and Texas. Doug Hughes in Missouri's 6th Congressional District, farm activist Wayne Cryts in the state's 8th Congressional District, populist Doug Seal in Texas' 13th Congressional District and Gerald McCathern, AAM's "wagonmaster" — lead driver in their Washington, D.C. tractorcade, in the Lone Star state's 19th CD, all ran as Democrats.

Earlier in primary races Kansas farmer Darrell Ringer was unsuccessful in his bid for the state's Democratic senatorial nominee and California farmer Wayne Myers narrowly lost a Congressional seat race in Northern California.

AAM's David Senter pointed out that these 1986 bids were but the opening salvo in a sustained political campaign on behalf of the farm organization's effort to influence the 1988 Presidential election.

To get the system working for farmers, we have to get farmers inside the system. These guys who are running [in 1986] have been in the struggle and they've learned how the system operates . . . We're already recruiting more candidates for 1988 and we'll have even better representation then.

"Hidden Costs" of "Cheap Food"

"Of 240 million people in the United States, you've got 237 million who are happy because current farm policy is geared toward low food prices. That policy may result in the 2.5 million people in farming not being so happy and not being well off. But even if they organized, it wouldn't have much effect. They're not strong enough to have much of an impact."

- William B. Eickoff
North Carolina Extension Service Economist

In the months of debate which surrounded the passage of the 1985 Farm Bill and subsequent farm legislation the question was repeatedly posed as to how changing current agricultural policy would affect consumers and taxpayers, our farm exports, and the protection of our soil and water. Answering critics who charged food prices would skyrocket if farmers were to receive higher prices for their commodities, it was pointed out that by setting a floor on market prices at average costs of production, roughly 70 percent of parity, such legislation would probably result in a one-time increase of $14.1 billion to the U.S. food system, which would be less than one percent of total consumer food costs per year.

In fact, as Mark Green with Beverly Moore and Bruce Wasserstein point out in *The Closed Enterprise System* there is data to suggest that if "highly concentrated industries were deconcentrated to a point where the four largest firms control 40 percent or less of an industry's sales, prices would fall by 25 percent or more," with the poor realizing an even greater gain since they are being forced to spend a larger portion of their meager incomes on staples like food.[31]

Another fact often conveniently ignored by the apostles of a national "cheap food" policy is that consumers are paying unknowingly many "hidden" high costs to corporate agribusiness for their food, *e.g.*, corn flakes that cost consumers over *$250.00 per bushel*, sees the farmer receiving only a meager $2.65 a bushel.

In addition, there are hidden food "costs" which never appear on that long sales tape stuffed each week into our grocery bag. Absent, for example, is the money food shoppers pay in increasingly high taxes used for government farm subsidies and for those welfare programs that supposedly provide the safety nets for those families and individuals who have been forced off the land and into the cities due to that self-same ill-conceived "cheap food policy."

No more absurd example of such taxpayer financed subsidies can be found than in the Reagan administration's Export Enhancement Program, which in 1987 alone sent $3.2 billion worth of farm goods abroad with subsidies of $1.5 billion.[32]

How were such subsidies put to use? In 1987 while USDA prohibited the sale of millions of cartons of fresh lemons and oranges to Americans it was spending $10 million through its Targeted Export Assistance (TEA) program in Hong Kong, South Korea, and elsewhere to promote U.S. citrus fruits. While it was forcing almond growers in California to abandon 18 percent of their crop, it was also spending $6 million a year advertising almonds abroad.[33]

A May, 1988 GAO report, however, revealed that shoddy administration, inadequate guidelines and safeguards, and abuses by corporate agribusiness were posing serious questions as to how well the USDA's program designed to advertise these goods was actually working. Established by the 1985 Farm Bill, the TEA was created to allow the Foreign Agricultural Service (FAS) to make funds available for overseas market development and product promotion to offset the effects of import quotas and unfair trade practices.

The GAO found that because the larger agribusiness firms and commodity groups had more clout in Washington than smaller farm groups they were able to get the lion's share of TEA funding. In some cases, specifically citrus and almonds, the major industry groups, namely Sunkist Growers Inc. and the California Almond Growers Exchange, a California co-op of 5,500 growers who sell about 60 percent of the U.S. almond crop under the Blue Diamond label, monopolized funding available for their products and then used them for brand name promotions instead of generic market development.[34]

In one instance, the FAS controls were so lax, the GAO reports, that Sunkist Growers Inc., the large California citrus co-op whose membership includes many corporate agribusiness interests, was reimbursed $2.4 million for overseas promotional activities by foreign licensees. The co-op repaid the money to the FAS *after* it was learned that it had not reimbursed its licensees and "was essentially claiming reimbursement for expenditures it never incurred."[35]

The GAO concluded, contrary to the claims of the Reagan Administration that the TEA has played a major role in the recent upsurge of U.S. agricultural exports, "it is difficult if not impossible to confirm the relationship between increased exports and TEA" because of the complexity and variability of international markets.[36]

In their boasting about improved export statistics the USDA also chose to neglect to mention the costs of their new "market-oriented" programs. For example, in 1987 approximately 75 percent of the wheat, 60 percent of corn, and 100 percent of barley, cotton and rice that was exported was federally subsidized.[37] In 1986, the administration spent $12 billion on export subsidy programs for corn, while U.S. corn exports were only worth $4 billion.[38]

Our present system of trade is a "disastrous system," charges farm trade policy analyst Mark Ritchie. "We grew almost a billion more bushels of corn and wheat and earned less money. Meanwhile, on the average farmers earn half of their income from the Government."[39]

But, besides just these export programs, there are also a countless number of other USDA programs, paid for by the taxpayer, which perpetuate administrative policies and government-sponsored research and development designed to enrich corporate agribusiness at the expense of our family farmer system of agriculture.

For example, a May, 1988 General Accounting Office report estimated that farm program costs for the previous 15 years exceeded USDA estimates by more than $46 billion. Such underestimates of the costs of farm programs in the past have necessitated too little money being allocated when Congress draws up its spending plans and thus forces Congress to come back later in the year to make up the shortfalls. In a masterpiece of understatement the report indicated that "although USDA's forecasting methods have generally been developed by highly skilled staff, little attention has been paid to reviewing and evaluating whether these methods work as intended."[40]

On a global scale the Council on International Trade has reported that consumers have been paying billions of dollars yearly to protect agriculture from suffering losses in world trade. Costs such as $63 billion in Western Europe, $34 billion in Japan, and $30 billion in the U.S. were cited in the report.

The Council, a private non-partisan research group, points out that at least one-third of the $147 billion which the world's leading industrialized countries spent in the 1980s to subsidize and protect agriculture was a "dead loss" to their economies. This was because some $50 billion annually was "misallocated to high-cost agricultural production that could be used more efficiently elsewhere," a situation, the report concluded, which slows overall economic growth.[41]

Another curious contrast to the often-heard bromide that the U.S. government subsidizes American farmers to excess was revealed in a 1985 study by Michigan State University's Dr. James Anderson which showed that the farm sector was, in fact, rather heavily subsidizing the military programs of the Pentagon. "In the context of current price levels, the net drain of resources from the farm sector by the federal government is lethal and cannot be halted without freezing and reducing the arms race. Federal budget priorities must insure that military institutions are the servants, not the plundering masters, of the American political economy."[42]

In *Plowing Under the Farmers: The Impact of the Pentagon Tax on America Agriculture* he explained in detail how "even with full allowance for government payments to the agricultural sector, the federal government drained substantially more funds from farm sector states and counties than it returned."

In 25 principal farm states, even after allowing for federal payments and loans to farmers in those states, the Pentagon created a net drain of $31 billion. Of the 1,200 most agricultural counties in those 25 states, 800 or about two thirds suffered a net outflow of taxes due to the Pentagon's tax drain.

Taking Iowa as an example, Dr. Anderson showed that the Hawkeye state carried a Pentagon tax burden of $2.256 billion in FY 1983. In return, the military spent about $549 million on Iowa contractors and salaries for military personnel stationed in the state. For military purposes alone Iowa lost $1.708 billion in FY 1983, which was a net loss per family of about $1,930.

Iowa also bore about 1.2% of the federal tax burden in 1983 for a total tax burden of $9.790 billion. But total federal expenditures in the state for 1983 were only $6.57 billion for a net loss of $3.22 billion. With the Federal government taking out over *$3 billion* more than it put back into Iowa, this major farm state actually *paid* a gigantic subsidy, over half of which went to the Pentagon.

This rapid drop in farm sector equity or capital assets in Iowa, according to Anderson, also reflects this $3 billion outflow. Farm sector equity dropped $33.4 billion, or 40 percent between 1980 and 1984. As we have already seen in the foregoing chapters, the roots of this dramatic drop are in government policies which have kept the prices of commodities below the cost of production, disproportionate military expenditures which continue to deplete farm sector equity, massive land and equipment devaluation, abnormally high interest rates, and the Federal Reserve's policy of "dollar protectionism" which has in effect led to an export tax and an import subsidy that has in turn depressed U.S. grain exports.

Iowa, like so many other farm states, has thus become a victim, not a beneficiary, of federal policy.

Nationally, in the federal budgetary process from 1980 through 1992, outlays for military programs will have increased 54 percent per person, while those for programs for low-income families and children will have decreased by 16 percent.[43]

One did not have to be told that with the increasing activism that was now firmly taking root in rural America as exhibited by the type of organizing activities being carried on by such diverse coalitions as the North American Farm Alliance, the National Family Farm Coalition, and the League of Rural Voters that the hour of decision to once and for all resolve America's permanent agricultural crisis was at hand.

Farmers and their families do not want to exist on borrowed capital, but rather they want to live normal, hard working happy lives by receiving an *earned* income for their labor. *Economic and social justice demands that farmers, like any other individuals in the work place, get a fair price for their product and labor.* Agricultural laborers don't want to exist in slavery and poverty; they want the opportunity to control their own lives, to freely associate with their fellow workers in common cause and to raise their families in a healthful and prosperous community.

The men and women who work in our food and manufacturing plants want the security of a job that pays them a decent, living wage and not the insecurity that tomorrow they may be replaced by a cheaper labor force or that their workplace will be closed and relocated abroad or in another community by some remote, absentee employer whose only interest is the "bottom line."

Consumers want fairly priced, safe, nutritious and healthy food, but not at the cost of economic, environmental or human exploitation in the field, in the factory or in the marketplace.

Epilogue

"In Germany they came first for the Communists,
and I didn't speak up because I wasn't a Communist.
Then they came for the Jews,
and I didn't speak up because I wasn't a Jew.
Then they came for the trade unionists,
and I didn't speak up because I wasn't a trade unionist.
Then they came for the Catholics,
and I didn't speak up because I was a Protestant.
Then they came for me,
and by that time,
nobody was left to speak up."

- Martin Neimoeller

Bringing the Corporate State Under Democratic Control

Epilogue

Bringing the Corporate State Under Democratic Control

A politically self-serving George Bush, asserted in June, 1990 before a group of state Republican leaders in Omaha, Nebraska that there's "nothing but good news for agricultural America."

Supporting this well-worn corporate agribusiness bromide he cited a near-record net farm income for 1989 (buoyed by improved livestock prices and drought-induced higher grain prices), along with the prospects for a multi-billion dollar grain trade agreement with the Soviets. Facts to the contrary, the president somehow believed that in one political speech he could quickly banish the numerous economic and social injustices that have been repeatedly heaped on rural America in recent decades.

Any current examination of the record, however, will show that the president's rosy characterization of the present American agricultural scene is more wishful thinking than a confrontation with reality, For example:

• For decades realized net farm income as a percentage share of the total national income earned by agriculture has been declining. During the decade of the 80's, net farm income averaged $10.3 billion per year in constant 1987 dollars, $2 billion per year less than 1967.

• poverty in rural America, at over 16%, remains three points above the national rate and a mere two points below that of the nation's inner cities.

• By the end of 1990 farm expenses were increasing at their fastest pace in eight years. Meanwhile, the average per year net farm capital investment throughout the previous decade had been showing a noticeable decline at the same time that the Consumer Price Index was steadily rising.

• Corporate profits, expressed in constant dollars, in the food manufacturing industry have nearly tripled in the past two decades.

And that trend in the food industry promises to continue despite the uncertainty of the nation's economic direction as it entered the 1990's. As the *New York Times* H.J. Maidenberg so succinctly observed in his November 29, 1990 "Market Place" column: "As economists argue over whether the nation is in a recession or about to enter one, more investors are seeking safety. Regardless of the state of the economy, they reason, people still eat every day."

• While the most profitable industry in America in the second half of the 1980's, as measure in terms of return on equity, was the food industry, farmers during this same period were averaging less of a return on their equity than if they had invested their money in a passbook savings account at their local bank.

In addition to ignoring these facts Bush & Company also has chosen to dismiss studies such as those conducted by FAPRI. In a 1989 report, based upon such optimistic assumptions as normal weather, projections that U.S. and foreign farm policies would not significantly change, and that there would be no recession before 1996, the FAPRI study projected that inflation adjusted net farm income would fall 43 percent by 1996 while production costs would increase by 24 percent.

Nothing in the subsequent 1990 Farm Bill, which promises only to exacerbate declining farm prices, the budget summit package of over $13 billion in cuts in agriculture programs, nor the continuing and concerted efforts by the U.S. government in the GATT negotiations to completely undermine domestic and foreign price support systems gives one hope that the FAPRI study will prove to be anything but overly optimistic.

Meanwhile, the vast majority of well-fed Americans, no longer saturated with stories of family farms being auctioned off and tearful families losing their economic and social heritage, which appeared with regularity on their evening TV screens and in their newspapers and weekly magazines throughout most of the 1980's, now remain mostly indifferent if not ambivalent to the plight of rural America.

As Brian Ahlberg, former communications director for the National Family Farm Coalition, explains:

The real reason papers and broadcasters no longer run the kind of stories they did in the 1980's is that they consider family farmers history, not news. The media, once a proponent of the family farm ideal, has largely abandoned it, perhaps in fatalistic surrender to the forces which are eradicating independence, personality and community responsibility from its own industry. Such is the predicament of today's family farmers and their supporters. At the very time their vision for American agriculture seems to them most critical and alive, when the social and ecological failure of the corporate food system is most apparent, they are being written out of reality.

440

And legislators, of course, continue to write them out of business.

Countering "The Gamblers in the Necessities of Life"

Clearly, therefore, the time has arrived for a united, well-organized farm/labor/consumer coalition to seriously think about initiating a strategy and/or process designed to bring about a long overdue social, economic and political change in this country and which current circumstances so urgently demands.

Presently, we see not only a lack of focus when it comes to the causes of our major social and economic problems, but precious little progressive leadership exercised when it comes to initiating the necessary social, economic and political changes that are so direly needed. In fact, when it comes to political leadership in our nation there is an incredible void, an almost total absence of what John F. Kennedy once described as "profiles in courage."

As Lawrence Goodwyn in *Democratic Promise: The Populist Moment in America* has pointed out:

The victims of modern culture have tried to view personal resignation and intellectual submission as a form of sophistication and have attempted to sustain their morale by teaching the young not to aspire too grandly for too much democracy. In America the two political names for this narrowed despair are liberalism and conservatism. The language of one is grounded in civic illusion, the other in self-interested complacency...Today, a loyal but disenchanted citizenry, aware that it can do little to affect "politics," endeavors to take what solace it can from pursuit of material goods. But though Americans consume more products today, they are less free than they used to be; and in the privacy of their minds, they suspect it. It is essentially a matter of scale of thought, or more precisely, of scale of aspiration.

We must, therefore, take a lesson from the agrarian populists of nearly a century ago in our approach to present-day politics. Clearly, we need to synthesize those basic economic, social and political issues that we confront today into three fundamental problems, articulating them in a clear, coherent and straight-forward manner.

A) The corporation has become the "dominant institution" throughout the world. It has come to expect that the expansion of its privilege and power should become the main focal point of nearly all of our society's economic, social and political institutions. This growing "corporatist" culture also seeks to impose upon the public a "seller-sovereign" economy, monopolistic and oligopolistic in character, with a goal of creating slavish dependence, not critical capability.

B) People can no longer trust private and public financial institutions to soundly invest, wisely manage or safely care for their money. Rather, with increasing frequency and ease we see these self-same financial institutions transferring their risks, failures, waste and corruption onto an already beleaguered public.

C) Our natural resources (land, water, air, food and fiber) are not only becoming increasingly privatized, but are also being corporately controlled, unfairly priced while at the same time being co-opted and exploited for personal monetary gain. Likewise, these very same natural resources are being abused, endangered, poisoned and with increasing regularity used as geopolitical weapons by those "gamblers in the necessities of life" who repeatedly show little of no regard for the common good or the public welfare.

It is these same three problems, not dissimilar to those raised by the agrarian populists just a century ago, which are today at the root of "America's permanent agricultural crisis."

But, as Goodwyn suggests, despite this reality farmers as well as the general public traditionally have been repeatedly dissuaded as we have seen throughout this book from seriously and actively engaging themselves in correcting these abuses through genuine fundamental social, economic and political change.

Pursuing a Progressive Populist "Declaration of Independence"

Thus, if authentic social/economic/political change is the goal, farmers as well as labor and consumers need to not only assert, but actively pursue that fundamental populist principle that says a society cannot have true political democracy without genuine economic democracy, As Goodwyn reminds us,

the first step is to take control of the past and use it to justify the revolution. American history in that sense begins with the Declaration of Independence. There are 32 paragraphs in that document and 29 of them denounce King George III as a tyrant. It is a classic historical justification of a revolution.

It was in 1873 that the Grangers, with a strong sense of historical precedent rooted in the Jeffersonian tradition, viewed the farm situation as so serious that they drew up and published their own "Farmers' Declaration of Independence."*

In examining that manifesto one can see no reason why such a document in 1990 should not be drafted and debated as the initial step toward articulating the concerns of a family farm/labor/consumer coalition, forcefully restating its basic objectives and mobilizing public opinion (see Appendix J).

People need to understand that the type of culture that a "progressive populist" agenda seeks to create is one that not only receives its validity from our revolutionary past, but is structured around the democratic promise that that same revolution envisioned.

"Congratulating ourselves for past achievements," Goodwyn notes, "is not helpful if such folkways have the practical effect of blinding us to the political implications of the alienation that pervades our daily lives."

---

* "Document No. 14", *American Farmers' Movements* by Fred A. Shannon, Van Nostrand, Princeton, N.J.: 1957, pg. 136-141).

441

Thus, if progressive populists are to successfully counter today's "corporatist" culture they must, as did the agrarian populists of an earlier day, adopt an ideological framework built on *aggressive advocacy* and thereby create about themselves a *movement culture.*

Just as it was a century, ago, the underlying impulses of progressive populism, as Goodwyn notes, must be a revolt against the "narrowing limits of political debate within capitalism as much as it is a protest against specific economic injustices." It was from just such a mass democratic movement, initially generated by a *cooperative* crusade that was to become the heart of the "agrarian revolt," which led to the formation of the National Farmers Alliance and Industrial Union, and from which emerged a political movement that came to be called *populism.*

Agrarian populism was characterized by an evolving democratic culture in which people would "see themselves" and therefore aspire to a society conducive to mass human dignity. In stark contrast to their efforts was the direction they saw being taken by the corporate state in the existing society.

It also clearly recognized the eminent dangers of the "corporatist" culture and believed that it was imperative to bring the corporate state under democratic control. Envisioning a society that "dares to aspire grandly in behalf of their vision of human possibility" Goodwyn adds,

> Observe what happens if we put aside public pretense and apply serious democratic standards to twentieth century life. Democratic social relations; Can we conceptualize a democratic marriage? A democratic economy? A democratic workplace? Can we conceptualize a democratic system of money, credit and exchange at the heart of all our material relations, operating not for the benefit of bankers but for the benefit of society?

By once again looking to the past we can see that the agrarian populists through a series of statements and platforms* sought to offer society a means by which it could reassert the principle *that without economic democracy you cannot have political democracy.*

Their process was both evolutionary and revolutionary and we should be prepared to follow no less a perilous path if we so choose to undertake a similar challenge.

What immediate lessons can we learn from such tactics today? In a July/August 1990 *Mother Jones* essay Ralph Nader summarized such results quite concisely:

> There is nothing to compare to the farmers' drive in Texas during the late 1880s, which signed up 250,000 farmers and led to the early stage of the thirty-year progressive revolt — *still the country's most fundamental political and economic reform*

---

*(Document No. 16 - 19", American Farmers' Movements by Fred A. Shannon, Van Nostrand, Princeton, N.J.: 1957. pg. 146-161)

> *movement since the Constitution was ratified.* And these farmers did it largely on foot and with pamphlets. (emphasis added)

How, without today's communications and transportation facilities, did the farmers manage to cover so much ground, create so many lasting institutions, and elect so many state legislators, governors, members of Congress, and almost the president of the United States? Because they owned what they controlled — the land. And they controlled what they owned — the land. And they aggregated their vote around specific agendas designed to limit the power of the railroads, banks, and absentee "Eastern" financial moguls."

"Stop Mourning, Organize!"

> "Democratic movements are initiated by people who have managed to achieve a high level of personal political self-respect. They are not resigned; they are not intimidated. ... Their sense of autonomy permits them to dare to try to change things by seeking to influence others. The subsequent stages of recruitment and of internal economic and political education turn on the ability of the democratic organizers to develop widespread methods of internal communication within the mass movement. ... If the movement is able to achieve this level of internal communication and democracy, and the ranks accordingly grow in numbers and in political consciousness, a new plateau of social possibility comes within reach of all participants."
>
> - Lawrence Goodwyn, from *The Populist Moment*

As the United State confronts the economic and political morass of the 1990's and keeping in mind that the early 1990's also marks the centennial of the agrarian populist movement, the time has come to disengage ourselves from the endless fratricidal debates that have existed in the past among farmers, farmworkers, labor, consumers and environmentalists. Rather, this period should be viewed as that one propitious "democratic moment" in our lifetimes that we begin to seriously put together a progressive populist movement. Not only does our historical tradition suggest such an effort, but as we see today there exists:

1) a large rural constituency, currently experiencing the reality of almost total disenfranchisement;

2) the "partisan poor," a low-income, less-educated group of voters, two-thirds of them white and a third black who still require and strongly support domestic assistance programs;

3) disenchanted consumers, increasingly angry over being repeatedly victimized by the corporate state's "transfer economy," and who so often find themselves saddled with the continuing costs of corporate mismanagement, inefficiency, and waste;

4) citizens, being poorly served by a government regulatory process, originally designed to promote a "consumer-sovereign" economy, but as Nader has noted, "invariably adopting 'seller-sovereign' priorities," and

5) disillusioned citizen-action groups, who see their own social, economic and political agendas either being outrightly ignored, disregarded and\or co-opted by their own entrusted, elected representatives in local, state and federal governments.

It is time to be bold in our vision if we are going to be about the business of reviving the agrarian populist spirit of the 1880's and 1890's. We need to both think *and* act "globally," but organize locally.

Yes, Joe Hill, we need to quit mourning and start *organizing*!

Rural Americans and family farmers in particular have traditionally associated themselves with the ideals of American democracy as enunciated by Thomas Jefferson, and embodied in the rich historical tradition of agrarian populism. They should not be ignored for the leadership they can and should provide in our nation's continuing struggle for economic and political democracy.

Appendix

A Corporation:

That inglorious device for obtaining individual profit without individual responsibility.

- **Ambrose Bierce**

Reap-er

n. **1**. a machine for cutting standing grain; reaping machine. **2**. a person who reaps. **3**. Also called **Grim Reaper, the Reaper**, the personification of death as a man holding a scythe.

- **Random House Dictionary of the English Language**

Appendix A

Six Myths About Hunger

© 1976 by the Institute for Food and Development Policy

• There is no country in the world where people could not feed themselves from their own resources.

• Food security cannot be measured in grain reserve or production figures.

• A nation's per capita food production can double and yet more people can be hungry.

• Increased prices for agriculture exports could lead to increased hunger.

Are you bewildered by any of these statements? We would not be surprised. For the last several years we have struggled to answer the question "why hunger?" Analyses that call for increasing development assistance or for reducing our consumption so that the hungry might eat left us doubtful. We probed and probed. We agonized over the logical consequences of our findings which seemed to put us in opposition to groups we previously had supported. But eventually we came to an understanding that feels liberating, that gives us energy instead of paralysing us with guilt, fear or despair.

Here we want to share the six myths that kept us locked into a misunderstanding of the problem as well as the alternative view that emerged once we began to grasp the real issues.

Myth One: People are hungry because of scarcity — both of food and agricultural land.

Can scarcity be the cause of hunger when even in the worst years of famine (in the early 70's) there was enough grain alone to provide everyone in the world more than 4,000 calories a day? This figure doesn't even include all the beans, root crops, fruits, nuts, vegetables and grass-fed meat.

What of land scarcity?

We examined the most crowded countries in the world to find a correlation between land density and hunger. We could not find one. Bangladesh, for example, has just half the people per cultivated acre that Taiwan has. Yet Taiwan has no hunger while Bangladesh is considered the world's worst basketcase. China has twice as many people for each cultivated acre as India. Yet in China people are not hungry.

Finally, when the pattern of what is grown sank in, we simply could no longer subscribe to a "scarcity" diagnosis. In Central America and in the Caribbean,

where as much as 70 percent of the children are undernourished, at least half of the agricultural land, and the best land at that, grows for export, not food for the local people. In the Sahelian countries of sub-Saharan Africa, exports of cotton and peanuts in the early 1970's *increased* as drought and hunger loomed.

Myth Two: A hungry world simply cannot afford the luxury of justice for the small farmer.

We are taught that, if we want to eat, we had better rely on large landowners. Governments, international lending agencies and foreign assistance programs have passed over the small producers, convinced that large holders are the key to production gains.

In fact, the small farmer is commonly more productive, often many times more productive, than the larger farmer. A study of Argentina, Brazil, Columbia, Ecuador and Guatemala found the small farmer to be three to fourteen times more productive per acre than the larger farmer. In Thailand plots of two to four acres yield almost sixty percent more rice per acre than farms of 140 acres or more. Other evidence that justice for the small farmer increases production comes from the experience of countries in which the redistribution of land and other basic agricultural resources like water has resulted in rapid growth in agricultural production: Japan, Taiwan, and China stand out.

Myth Three: We are faced with a sad trade-off. A needed increase in food production can come only at the expense of the environment. Farming must be pushed onto marginal lands at the risk of irreparable erosion. The use of pesticides must be increased despite possible risks.

Is the need for food for a growing population the real pressure forcing people to farm lands that are easily destroyed?

Haiti offers a shocking picture of environmental destruction. The majority of the impoverished peasants ravage the once-green mountain slopes in near-futile efforts to grow food to survive. Has food production for Haitians used up every easily cultivated acre so that only the mountain slopes are left? No. These mountain peasants must be seen as exiles from their birthright — some of the world's richest agricultural land. The rich valley lands belong to a handful of elites who seek dollars in order to live an imported lifestyle and to their American partners. These lands produce largely low-nutrition and feed crops (sugar, coffee, cocoa, alfalfa for cattle) — exclusively for export. Grazing land is export-oriented too. Recently U.S. firms began flying Texas cattle into Haiti for grazing and re-export to America franchised hamburger restaurants.

In Africa vast tracts of geologically old sediments perfectly suitable for permanent crops such as grazing grasses or trees have instead been torn up for planting cotton and peanuts for export. In parts of Senegal peanut monoculture has devastated the soils.

It is not, then, people's food needs that threaten to destroy the environment but other forces: land monpolizers that export non-food and luxury crops forcing the rural minority to abuse marginal lands; colonial patterns of cash cropping that continue today; hoarding and speculation on food; and irresponsible profit-seeking by both local and foreign elites.

Still we wondered if people's need for food might not require more pesticide use. In the emergency push to grow more food, won't we have to accept some level of damage from deadly chemicals?

First, just how pesticide dependent is the world's current food production? In the U.S. about 1.2 billion pounds, 30 percent of the world's total, are dumped into the environment every year. Surely, we thought, such a staggering figure means that practically every acre of the nation's farmland is doused with pesticides. U.S. food abundance, therefore, appeared to us as the plus that comes from such a big minus. The facts, however, proved us wrong.

Fact One: Nearly half the pesticides are not used on farmland but on golf courses, parks and lawns.

Fact Two: Only about ten percent of the nation's cropland is treated with insecticides, 30 percent with weedkillers and less than one percent with fungicides. The figures are halved if pastureland is counted.

Fact Three: Non-food crops such as cotton account for more than half of all insecticides used in U.S. agriculture.

Fact Four: The USDA estimates that, even if all pesticides were eliminated, crop loss due to pests (insects, pathogens, weeds, mammals and birds) would rise only about seven percent from 33.6 percent to 40.7 percent.

Fact Five: Numerous studies show that where pesticides are used with ever greater intensity, crop losses due to pests are frequently *increasing*.

Fact Six: Several recent studies indicate great quantities of pesticides applied annually to crop lands are used needlessly.

What about underdeveloped countries? Do pesticides there help produce food for hungry people?

In underdeveloped countries most pesticides are used for export crops, principally cotton, and to a lesser extent fruits and vegetables grown under plantation conditions for export. The quantities of pesticides injected into the world's environment have little to do with its food needs.

The alternatives to chemical pesticides — crop rotation, mixed cropping, mulching, hand weeding, hoeing, collection of pest eggs, manipulation of natural predators, and so on are proven effective. In China, for example, pesticide use can be minimized because of a nationwide early warning system.

In Shao-tung county in Honan Province, 10,000 youths make up watch teams that patrol the fields and report any sign of pathogenic change. Appropriately called the "barefoot doctors of agriculture," they have succeeded in reducing the damage of wheat rust and rice borer to less than one percent and have the locust invasions under control. But none of these safe techniques for pest control will be explored as long as the problem is in the hands of profit-oriented corporations. The alternatives require human involvement and the motivation of farmers who have the security of individual or collective tenure over the land they work.

Myth Four: Hunger is a contest between the Rich World and the Poor World.

The "rich world" versus "poor world" scenario makes the hungry appear as a threat to the material well-being of the majority in the metropolitan countries. To average Americans or Europeans the hungry become the enemy who, in the words of Lyndon Johnson, "want what we got." In truth, however, hunger will never be addressed until the average citizens in the metropolitan countries can see that the hungry abroad are their allies, not their enemies.

What are the links between the plight of the average citizen in the metropolitan countries and the poor majority in the underdeveloped countries? There are many. One example is multinational agribusiness shifting production of luxury items — fresh vegetables, fruits, flowers and meat — out of industrial countries in search of cheap land and labor in the underdeveloped countries. The result? Farmers and workers in the metropolitan countries lose their jobs while agricultural resources in the underdeveloped countries are diverted from food for local people. The food supply of those in the metropolitan countries becomes dependent on maintaining political and economic structures that block hungry people from growing food for themselves.

Nor do consumers in the metropolitan countries at least get cheaper food. Do Ralston Purina's and Green Giant's mushrooms grown in Korea and Taiwan sell for any less than those produced stateside? Not one cent, according to a U.S. Government study. Del Monte and Dole Philippine pineapples actually cost the U.S. consumer more than those produced by a small company in Hawaii.

The common thread is the worldwide tightening control of wealth and power over the most basic human need, food. Multinational agribusiness firms right now are creating a single world agricultural system in which they control all stages of production from farm to consumer. Once achieved, they will be able to effectively manipulate supply and prices for the first time on a world-wide basis through well-established monopoly practices. As farmers, workers and consumers, people everywhere already have begun to experience the costs in terms of food availability, prices and quality.

Myth Five: An underdeveloped country's best hope for development is to export those crops in which it has a natural advantage and use the earnings to import food and industrial goods.

There is nothing "natural" about the underdeveloped countries' concentration on a few, largely low-nutrition crops. The same land that grows cocoa, coffee, rubber, tea and sugar could grow an incredible diversity of nutritious crops — grains, high-protein legumes, vegetables and fruits.

Nor is there any advantage. Relying on a limited number of crops generates economic as well as political vulnerability. Extreme price fluctuations associated with tropical crops combine with the slow-maturing nature of plants themselves (many, for example, take two to ten years before the first harvest) to make development planning impossible.

Another catch in the natural advantage theory is that people who need food are not the same people who benefit from foreign exchange earned by agricultural exports. Even when part of the foreign earnings is used to import food, the food is not basic staples, but items geared toward the eating habits of the better-off urban classes. In Senegal the choice land is used to grow peanuts and vegetables for export to Europe. Much of the foreign exchange earned is spent to import wheat for foreign-owned bakeries that turn out European-style bread for urban dwellers. The country's rural majority goes hungry, deprived of land they needed to grow millet and other traditional grains for themselves and local markets.

Myth Six: Hunger results from maldistribution.

Over and over again we hear that North America is the world's last remaining breadbasket. Food security is invariably measured in terms of reserves held by the metropolitan countries. We are made to feel that the burden of feeding the world is on us. Overconsumption is endlessly contrasted with the deprivation elsewhere. The message is that we cause their hunger. No wonder that North Americans and Europeans feel burdened and resentful. "What did we do to cause their hunger?" they rightfully ask.

The problem lies in seeing food redistribution as the solution to hunger. Distribution of food is but a reflection of the control of food resources. Who controls the land determines who can grow food, what is grown, and where it goes. Who can grow: a few or all who need to? What is grown: luxury nonfood or basic staples? Where does it go: to the hungry or the world's well-fed? Thus redistribution programs, like food aid, will never solve the problem of hunger. Instead we must face up to the real question: How can people everywhere democratize the control of food resources.

We can now counter these six myths with six positive principles:

1. There is no country in the world in which people could not feed themselves from their own resources. But hunger can only be overcome by the transformation of social relationships and only made worse by the narrow focus on technical inputs to increase production.

2. Inequality is the greatest stumbling block to development.

3. Safeguarding the world's environment and people feeding themselves are complementary goals.

4. Our food security is not threatened by the hungry masses but by elites that span all market economies profiting by the concentrating and internationalizing control of food resources.

5. Agriculture must not be used for export income but as the way for people to produce food first for themselves.

6. Relief from hunger comes not through the redistribution of food but through the redistribution of control over food producing resources.

Appendix B

Defining "Communities Of Economic Interests"

A midwestern farmer awakens in the morning, puts on some **Fruit-of-the-Loom** underwear, **Sears, Roebuck** overalls and fixes a **Quaker Oats** and **Pillsbury Pancake** breakfast.

After feeding the livestock soybean meal from the **A.E. Staley Manufacturing Co.** our farmer gets aboard a **John Deere** tractor and begins working the season's crops, applying with **International Harvester** machines the agricultural chemicals recently purchased from the **FMC Corp.**

Near noon after returning home, opening an **IBM**-printed electric bill from **Commonwealth Edison Company** and, if living in Illinois, making a few phone calls via **Illinois Bell Telephone** the farmer discusses with a **Beatrice Foods** buyer a milk sale from a dwindling dairy herd and the sale of some hogs with the **Swift & Co.** buyer, both sales for prices which, if our farmer is lucky, may cover production expenses.

In the afternoon getting into the family car, made in part from **Inland Steel**, and after pulling into the neighborhood **Amoco** station for gasoline, the farmer journey's over to pick up the week's groceries at the **Jewel** supermarket.

Sipping a cold **Dad's** root beer, the farmer discusses with a neighbor the likelihood of the next crop being shipped to market on the **Illinois Central** railroad and what **Peavey Co.**, a giant grain trader, will be willing to pay for such a crop.

After dinner, relaxing in the living room for awhile watching the family **Zenith** TV, the farmer's family visualize themselves in the **TWA** commercial flying off to Europe, sipping soft drinks or a **Cutty Sark** and looking forward to a long-awaited and well-deserved vacation.

The purpose of relating this scenario, first presented by the author to a 1976 Congressional committee investigating a major midwestern bank's attempt to use tax-exempt pension funds to buy up Midwestern agricultural land, was to illustrate the massive influence large corporations and their "communities of economic interests" have come to play in our lives today.

All these aforementioned products and many others not mentioned here were from corporations whose board members sat at the time on the board of directors of just one bank, **Continental Illinois Corporation**, one of the nation's largest banks and agricultural lenders and the same financial institution that was seeking approval at the time of its tax-exempt pension fund scheme.

In 1978, the U.S. Senate Committee on Government Affairs' Subcommittee on Reports, Accounting and Management did a thorough study of the interlocking directorates among 122 major U.S. corporations. The committee and its contractor, the Corporate Data Exchange Center in New York, studied the voting rights in 122 corporations including the nation's largest financial, industrial, transportation, utility and retailing firms, in addition to a number of the country's largest insurance companies and investment complexes.[1] Their survey showed an incredible concentration of decision-making power and a significant pattern of mutual corporate ownership. Not included in their study were the 400 largest private corporations, which in 1988, for example, had combined sales of $523 billion, nearly one-fifth of the combined sales of the nation's largest 500 largest public firms.

Using the Senate study, *The AgBiz Tiller*, in 1978 examined 21 corporations[*] involved in agribusiness, and found a total of 53 direct board-of-director interlocks (one company's board member sits on another company's board) and 1083 indirect board-of-director interlocks (board members from two different companies sit together on the board of a third company) through 801 intermediate corporations (the third company).[2]

What are the implications of this "network" within the American corporate structure?

Every director on a corporate board has a direct fiduciary responsibility to the corporation's owners — the stockholders — for proper management of that company. These board members also have a public responsibility, as set down by appropriate federal, state, and local laws and regulations.

Yet, a 1950 FTC report on interlocking directorates noted:

---

[*] American Stores, Inc.; BankAmerica Corp.; Burlington Northern; Chase Manhattan; Citicorp; Continental Illinois; E.I. Du Pont; Great Atlantic & Pacific Tea Co.; International Harvester; ITT; J.P. Morgan & Co.; Kroger; Mobil; Procter & Gamble; Prudential Insurance; RCA; Southern Pacific; Standard Oil of California; Safeway Stores; Tenneco Inc. and Wells Fargo.

The inherent tendency of interlocking directorates between companies that have dealings with each other as buyers and sellers, or that have relations to each other as competitors, is to blunt the edge of rivalry between corporations, to seek out ways of compromising opposing interests, and to develop alliances where the interest of one of the corporations is jeopardized by third parties . . .[3]

It was Adam Smith, however, who probably best expressed this same thought, but with considerably more candor in his *The Wealth of Nations* when he wrote, "people of the same trade seldom meet together even for merriment and diversion but the conversation ends in a conspiracy against the public or in some contrivance to raise prices."[4]

Interlocking directorates are but only one means by which giant corporations exert a powerful financial influence within the business community. Direct ownership of other corporations, through the voting rights a company possesses by virtue of its managed stock holdings in the other company, is another powerful instrument of control.

Just one statistic demonstrates the enormous size of these aforementioned 122 corporations: the market value of their common stock at the time of the study in 1976 totaled 41 percent of the market value of *all* outstanding common stock in the U.S.. And, concentrated in just 21 institutional investors was the power to vote sizeable numbers of shares of stock in these same 122 of the nation largest corporations.[5]

Even a cursory examination of their ownership figures provokes major questions about the much revered U.S. "free enterprise" system.

For example, Morgan Guaranty Trust was not only among the top five identified stockholders in nearly half (56) of these aforementioned 122 top U.S. businesses, it was also one of the five largest stockvoters in 32 agribusiness companies, often voting large blocks of competing firms such as Coca-Cola/Pepsi; McDonald's/Pizza Hut, and R.J. Reynolds/Philip Morris.

Morgan Guaranty Trust Co. of New York, a subsidiary of the J.P. Morgan & Co., Inc., also according to the 1978 Senate study, out-invested all other major U.S. institutions. It was the prime stockholder in almost one-fourth (27) of the 122 corporations surveyed by the CDC.[6] Morgan, in addition, held the most shares in four of its sister New York banks — Citicorp (3.26 percent), Manufacturers Hanover Corp. (3.88 percent), Chemical New York (3.72 percent), and Bankers Trust - New York Corp. (1.67 percent), and also held the largest single block of stock (2.88 percent) in BankAmerica Corp., world's largest agricultural lender. In turn, Citibank was the No. 1 stockholder of J.P. Morgan & Co. (2.63 percent). Citibank is also, of course, a subsidiary of Citicorp, whose No. 1 stockholder, as noted above, is Morgan Guaranty Trust Co. of New York.[7]

Despite such evidence to the contrary corporate America has long sought to perpetuate the myth that individual stockholders are the cornerstone of their economic foundation. This was illustrated in a television commercial a few years ago when comedian Bob Hope

appeared for Texaco, Inc. and introduced us to the happy faces of a few of the company's 413,661 stockholders, "people just like you and me."[8]

What Hope failed to show us, however, were those "happy faces" of the company's five leading shareholders: (Manufacturers Hanover Corp., Teachers Insurance and Annuity - College Retirement Equities Fund (TIA-CREF), Union National Bank of Pittsburgh, Prudential Insurance Co. of America, and Sarofim (Fayez) & Co. who together at the time were eligible to vote 8.76 percent of Texaco's stock.[9] Texaco's top 25 shareholders (a U.S. corporate who's who) voted 18.6 percent of its stock, a rather formidable figure compared to the 15/100 of a percent a stockholder with ten shares might have. In the not-uncommon situation in which Texaco's 413,661 stockholders held 271,466,000 shares of stock, any small bloc of voters — such as 8.76 percent or 18.6 percent — could without too much effort effectively control the direction of that corporation.

But nobody ever promised corporate stockholders corporate democracy. *The Washington Post*'s, Jerry Knight, in an insightful analysis of stockholder's meetings ("Annual Meetings A Capitalist Farce") correctly points out that,

by their absence, shareholders demonstrate their disdain for the myth of corporate democracy — the capitalist fantasy that investors who buy stock in a corporation own a piece of the rock and therefore have some say in its management.

Corporate elections bear no relation to the political process as practiced in the rest of America. There are no campaigns, no issues, no competing candidates. Elections of officers and directors of American corporations are like elections in Russia: The rulers decide who the candidates will be and the people get to vote yes or no. This curiously coincidental characteristic of capitalism and communism is a sad commentary on corporate democracy.[10]

Business Week's Anthony Bianco adds,

The New York Stock Exchange has all but officially jettisoned the one-share-one-vote principle long considered the foundation of the increasingly wistful notion of 'corporate democracy.' . . . Power has shifted from the corporation not to capital *per se*, but rather to the conduits of capital — to the opportunistic middlemen of Wall Street.[11]

Just how concentrated individual wealth has become was rather dramatically shown in recent studies by a 1986 Congressional study prepared by the Democratic staff of the Joint Economic Committee. Their data was drawn from a survey of consumer finances and wealth conducted in 1983 by the Survey Research Center of the University of Michigan for the Federal Reserve and several other federal agencies.

It showed that in 1983 the top 0.5 percent of American households owned 26.9 percent of all the wealth, up from 25 in 1963, while 9.5 percent registered 44.9 percent of the wealth, as the remaining 90 percent of the nation's households held 28.2 percent, down from 34.9 percent in 1963.[12]

A January 1990 Joint Economic Committee study reveals that between 1979 and 1989 the average family income of the wealthiest 20 percent of the population jumped 14.2 percent while the poorest 20 percent showed a 4.3 percent decline. A Brookings Institute report further notes that the share of the national income of the wealthiest one percent of Americans rose from 8.1 percent in 1981 to 14.7 percent in 1986.

Citizens for Tax Justice, has also concluded that since 1977 the pre-tax income of the lower 60 percent of the nation's taxpayers, adjusted for inflation, has fallen by nearly 14 percent while their taxes have increased by nearly $19 billion. At the same time, the top one percent of all Americans inflation-adjusted income has skyrocketed by 86 percent, while their federal tax burden has dropped by 15 percent. Tax changes since 1977 were worth $93.1 billion in savings to the richest 10 percent in 1990 whereas the remaining 90 percent paid $25.6 billion more.

Some commentators have suggested that as the United States grows older, the wealth is spreading. UCLA sociology professor Maurice Zeitlin, writing in the June, 1978 issue of *The Progressive*, disagreed, noting that in 1860 the top one percent of the population owned 24 percent of the total market worth of everything owned. In 1969, the top one percent owned 25 percent.[13]

Internal Revenue statistics have shown that in 1984 2.8 percent of the adult population with a total net worth — assets minus debts — of $2.4 trillion owned 28 percent of the nation's personal wealth[14] with 26.4 percent of the nation's total personal net worth of $13.1 trillion being in land and real estate and 25 percent in corporate stock.[15] Just under two million people had holdings exceeding $500,000 with only 12.8 percent of the population earning more than $50,000 per year.[16] The fact that our nation's affluence is now concentrated in relatively few hands was neither the intent of our founding fathers who conceived of a land where political *and* economic democracy would exist in tandem, nor was it the dream of those millions of men, women and children who in the past two centuries have worked and sacrificed to help forge a society rich in its vast natural and human resources.

Many now believe that it is this concentrated economic wealth and its influence that is not only seriously destructuring the small business community, but is also dramatically eradicating the family farm system of agriculture in America to a degree unequaled in any other period in our nation's history.

"The Fixers and Dealers of the System"

Obviously, any evaluation concerning the importance and the source of corporate power and current corporate wealth vis-a-vis the world's banking establishment must keep in mind Willie Sutton's poignant answer when asked why he robbed banks? "Because that's where the money is!"

Today, banks are in the words of author Paul Ferris Morrow "the fixers and dealers of the system," or as Bernard A. Weisberger reminds us in a review of Morrow's book, *The Master Bankers: Controlling the World's Finances*, "bankers do more than simply raise the cash: They orchestrate the entire procedure. And of course they are experts at discreetly channeling clients' money away from the grasp of tax collectors."[17]

While most of the nation's 14,473 banks are small, the majority of the money is in the big banks. As of early 1985 some 9567 banks had assets up to $49.9 million and deposits of $191.47 billion, 2623 had assets of $50 million to $99.9 million and deposits of $160.51 billion, and 2283 had assets of $100 million plus and deposits of $1.49 *trillion.*[18]

As of June 30, 1988 the major U.S. bank holding companies and their assets were Citicorp ($205 billion), Chase Manhattan ($96 billion), BankAmerica ($94 billion), J.P. Morgan ($81 billion), and Chemical ($76 billion).[19]

In 1985, 31 foreign banks had more than $1.7 billion each in total assets in U.S. subsidiaries led by Hong Kong & Shanghai Banking Corporation ($23.7 billion), London's Midland Bank PLC ($22.7 billion), Bank of Tokyo Ltd. ($20.3 billion), Tokyo's Fuji Bank Ltd. ($16.6 billion), and the Mitsubishi Bank Ltd. of Tokyo ($15.9 billion).[20] Based on deposits alone at the end of 1987 the world's ten top banks, led by Dai-Ichi Kangyo Bank Ltd. ($275.3 billion), were all Japanese. Of the banks ranked 11th through 25, seven were Japanese, two German, four French, and two British. Among American banks in the top 50, Citibank ranked 28th and Bank of America ranked 48th. In the bank holding category, however, Citibank remained among the world's top ten.[21] The accounting firm of Peat, Marwick, Mitchell & Co. predicts that in the near future we will see between ten and 20 national financial service "retailers" as our major financial institutions.[22]

In fact, there are some both in government and industry that fear the entire U.S. banking system could possibly be built on a "house of cards." By way of illustration they point out that if the Continental Illinois Bank had been allowed to fail in 1984 some 66 banks, with combined assets of $4.8 billion who had uninsured deposits in Continental Illinois that exceeded their net worth, would have failed immediately. Another 113 banks, with total assets of $12.3 billion and with uninsured deposits equivalent to between 50 percent and 100 percent of their net worth, would have also failed.[23] Too big to sell, with $41 billion in assets, Continental was underwritten by the government.

"Our collective judgment," Comptroller of the Currency C.T. Conover later told a House Banking Committee, "was that had Continental failed, we would have seen a national, if not international financial crisis. The dimensions were difficult to imagine. None of us wanted to find out."[24] Felix Rohatyn, the prominent New York investment banker, writing in *The New York Review of Books* before the stock market's Black Monday in 1987, calls attention to the need for preserving the integrity of our financial markets in the context of the mid-1980's Wall Street boom.

The stock market is at an all-time high, while business is relatively slow and major sectors of our economy are in serious difficulty. Furthermore, looking to the future, aside from the devaluation of the dollar, which cuts two ways, we see little or no evidence of a realistic willingness on the part of government to solve our most fundamental economic problems: our budget deficit, our trade deficit and the vulnerability of our banking system.

The financial markets now have a life of their own, seemingly unrelated to any underlying economic realities. The need for productive investments in this country, together with the risks created by the level of existing speculation, makes it more important than ever that the integrity of the financial markets be assured and that capital be used to build and not to speculate.[25]

Compounding this problem of banks saddled with enormous domestic debts, such as currently exists with the banks in the Farm Credit System is the fact that one or several foreign countries — such as Mexico or Argentina — could always default on their debts and possibly provoke a catastrophic effect on the nation's banking industry. According to 1985 U.S. Treasury figures, these major banks had the following percentile exposure, for example, in most of the $24.4 billion that Mexico at the time owed the U.S. alone:[26]

First Chicago	63.7%
Bankers Trust	55.5%
Manufacturers Hanover	54.8%
Chemical Bank	48.6%
Bank of America	48.0%
Citibank	43.5%
Morgan Guaranty	37.6%
Chase Manhattan	34.8%
Continental Illinois	25.9%
Security Pacific	23.9%

In addition, according to a confidential list from federal bank regulators obtained by journalist/researcher Michael Binstein, the nation's ten largest banks in 1985 also held a high level of uninsured foreign deposits. They included Citibank, $53.7 billion; Bank of America, $31.9 billion; Chase Manhattan, $35 billion; Morgan Guaranty, $28.6 billion; Manufacturers Hanover, $21.7 billion; Chemical Bank, $16.2 billion; Bankers Trust, $17.8 billion; Security Pacific, $7 billion; First National Chicago, $14.5 billion, and Continental Illinois, $8.2 billion.[27]

Overextended big banks in this country and abroad tied together through computers and interlocking and over-lapping debts — could conceivably in the near future by losing possibly their most valuable asset — public confidence — collapse. It is said that the Federal Reserve views such a scenario seriously enough that it has considered plans to use the unlimited amounts of money it has or can create to keep such banks, as it did with Continental Illinois, from going under.

Such a tactic, however, would make the U.S. taxpayer the lender of last resort to the world. Some believe that the current predicament many financial institutions and banks are in is due to poor federal regulation. In this regard New York economist Henry Kaufman has pointed out that the quality of federal regulation and regulators has deteriorated. This, he believes, has happened because financial regulatory agencies "have been relegated to a secondary status in the past decade or so." This has resulted in the most competent government workers either going to more visible policy-making agencies, or getting better-paying private sector jobs.[28]

Others see this concentration in the banking industry as not only bad news for depositors but for smaller banks, particularly in rural communities. "Money will be sucked out of rural areas" once the large banks are allowed to move in into interstate banking, claims Luke White, president of Fountain Trust Co. in Covington, Indiana.[29]

Currently state laws governing interstate banking can best be described as a "hodgepodge." Some states welcome banks from outside their borders, others permit only regional inter-state banking. Although in 1985 the U.S. Supreme Court unanimously ruled that neither the Constitution nor federal law prohibits states from banding together to regulate the banking industry, many believe that Congress will ultimately have to rewrite the nation's banking laws to bring any kind of order to the system.[30] If such legislation is not forthcoming, interstate banking may lead to further concentration of lending power, according to F. Hagen McMahon, Jr., executive director of the Independent Bankers Association of Texas. "It goes against the basic philosophy of how the U.S. was built," he argues. "It will mean fewer and fewer people will be making decisions about the economy — and that is simply not good."[31]

A Concentration of Control and Wealth

Not only will the ramifications of further concentration of economic power be felt in banking, but also in the institutional and the corporate investment community.

One of the stark realities of the business world today is that the control of the U.S.'s major corporations has shifted from individual investors to financial institutions — pension funds, insurance companies, foundations, investment companies, educational endowments, trust funds, and banks.

A 1989 Securities Industry Association study has shown that from 1965 to 1989 individual stock ownership of corporations went from 84 percent to 54 percent while institutional ownership has risen from 16 percent to 46 percent.

In the mid 1980s, the nation's top five institutional investors, according to the *Institutional Investor*, were Prudential Insurance ($127.4 billion), Aetna Life & Casualty ($84 billion), Metropolitan Life ($79.4 billion), Equitable Investment Corp. ($78.7 billion), and American Express ($67 billion).[32]

Pat Choate and Juyne Linger in their book *The High-Flex Society* point out that this shift in control will have far-reaching consequences, because individuals and institutions invest in the stock market for sharply different reasons. While individuals usually look for long-term performance from their stocks, institutions seek short-term profits.[33]

Thus, just when U.S. business needs to be making long-term investments to meet global competition, the new owners — the institutions — are pressing for quick results.

Institutions now hold so much equity and are such a powerful presence in stock markets that corporate executives often are at the mercy of their demands. The raw economic power of the institutional investors can be measured in two ways: their stock holdings and their willingness to get rid of stocks that fail to produce quick earnings.

To dramatically illustrate their point, Choate and Linger cite the following (pre-Black Monday) facts:

• By the mid-1980's institutions held more than 35 percent of all equities listed on the New York Stock Exchange (NYSE), double their share in 1960. By 1990 they were expected to own half.
• Institutions owned half to two-thirds of the stock of the nation's 200 largest corporations.
• In 1953, when institutions controlled almost 15 percent of the equities listed on the NYSE their trading activity constituted a quarter of all stock transactions. In 1985 institutional trading constituted near 90 percent of the transactions on the Exchange.
• On the average in 1965 only nine large-block transactions [10,000 shares or more] a day were traded, constituting three percent of the market's daily volume. In 1985 the average number of such daily transactions were more than 2,100, constituting over 51 percent of the volume.
• When individual investors dominated the market in 1965 the turnover rate of stocks was roughly 16 percent a year. By 1985, in the age of the institutional investor, the rate was 54 percent.
• At the 1965 rate it would take six years for the entire value of the stock market to turn over. Twenty years later, it would take a little less than two years.
• In the years 1984 and 1985 corporations spent in excess of $100 billion in stock buybacks as compared with $29 billion in 1983. Had these funds been used to modernize plants and equipment, the total capital investment for corporate America would have been 25 percent higher.
• In a 1985 survey of corporate executives 51 percent said their single overriding objective was "creating shareholder value," while only 18 percent saw their top priority as being the market or industry leader.
• Only four percent of some 308 of the nation's largest institutional investors in a 1985 survey said that in selecting stocks they considered the quality of the company's products.
• The value of corporate equities held by these institutional investors, less than $85 billion in 1970 reached $325 billion in 1983 and in 1985 stood at approximately $500 billion and was projected to be over $1 trillion by 1990.

"The frenzied movement of this much money shapes the priorities and performance of the entire stock market," Choate and Linger observe.

"Fast results and short-term earnings have become the obsessive goal of most American companies. The pursuit of these objectives diverts resources from investment in modern plant and equipment, research, technology and training to clever financial manipulations. It sacrifices market share to high quarterly earnings. And it discourages workers from making long-term commitments to companies."[34]

Wall Street money managers, as authors Mark Green and John F. Berry indicate in their book, *The Challenge of Hidden Profits: Reducing Corporate Bureaucracy and Waste*, put tremendous pressure on corporate managers for short-term profits.

And what easier way to produce quick profits than by a merger? The reason that money managers have so much power is that they manage the investment of pension funds, mutual funds, and the like which control about 60 percent of the stock of Big Board corporations. Their clients pay them for results, so the money managers, in turn, demand results from the corporations.[35]

Several legislative proposals seeking to curb the recent rash of takeovers have in recent years been suggested in Congress, but the threat of a veto by Ronald Reagan, whose economic advisors claimed that takeovers tend to make business more "efficient" and "competitive," forestalled such efforts. "It will be a very difficult debate," according to A.A. Sommer, a Washington attorney who represents the Business Roundtable, a lobbying arm of the corporate establishment.

There is a terrible dichotomy between ownership and management. Management is expected to make long-term plans, undertake expansion, diversify and do what they think is best. That's what they're trained and paid to do. The stockholders . . . don't give one damn about that. Those people are concerned with getting the maximum buck as soon as they can.[36]

But, it must be remembered, as Kenneth Andrews, former editor of the *Harvard Business Review* notes, the corporate raiders and short-term speculators who fueled the 1980s corporate takeover activity are not shareholders in any real meaning of that term. "They aren't responsible owners. Corporate ownership involves responsibility."[37]

In 1982 a study by Hay Associates in conjunction with the Wharton School of 206 corporations questioned this value of diversification by acquisition "after corporations take the first step in diversifying their products, the maximum level of performance attained decreases with every further move forward in diversification."[38] Former Federal Reserve Chairman Paul Voelcker, in expressing alarm over the possibility of "greater financial fragility in the economy," has warned banks to apply "prudent standards" to slow such merger mania. He pointed out that these loans "alter the price and availability of credit" as banks cut off other borrowers or hike rates "temporarily." "We spend our days issuing debt and retiring equity — both in record volume — and then we spend our evenings raising each other's eyebrows with gossip about signs of stress in the financial system. We rail at government inefficiency and intrusion in our markets, while we call upon the same government to protect our interests, our industry, and our financial institutions."[39]

Anthony Bianco concludes that "only when fear overcomes greed will [our] casino society rein itself in,"[40] but author Laurence Shames (*The Hunger for More: Searching for Values in an Age of Greed*) asks,

> can anyone really believe that the greed of the 1980's has been a function of hale high spirits and flush and free-wheeling times? Isn't it more accurate to portray this decade's money frenzy as being motivated by the desire to make one's bundle before the casino closes?
>
> . . . we would be wiser to fess up to our fears and reserve our highest honors for those who meaningfully assuage them by creating wealth that is more widespread. Feeling fear, and not admitting it can only perpetuate the greed that has made the 1980's not only a crass decade but a time when American business sometimes acted against its own best interests.

Reiterating the "Bigness is Better" Gospel

During its almost eight years in office it became increasingly obvious that the Reagan administration sought to ignore the language of the Clayton Act passed in 1914 which says that mergers are illegal where "the effect may be substantially to lessen competition or tend to create a monopoly."[41]

Believing bigness was no longer an anti-trust "problem," Reagan & Co. openly sought to overturn many anti-trust laws that would in the future block such acquisitions. At the same time, the SEC clearly decided not to attempt to control some of the more controversial aspects of corporate takeovers on grounds that "market forces" would correct whatever problems arose.

Whereas William French Smith, Reagan's first U.S. Attorney General and no stranger to corporate board rooms, made it clear at the outset of his close friend's administration that big was not bad, Commerce Secretary Malcolm Baldridge five years later declared that bigness was simply not bad, but was positively good.[42]

In the 1985 annual Economic Report of the President it was stated that "the appropriate government response, if any, should be to ease local adjustment problems rather than to interfere with the takeover process itself." Secretary Baldridge added that "it makes sense to merge and to end up with perhaps fewer but much stronger companies when you talk about worldwide competition." Robert Pitofsky, a former member of the FTC and now with the Georgetown University Law Center, disagrees:

What's going on now is that anti-trust is being made the scapegoat for a wide range of problems in trade which have nothing to do with antitrust enforcement. If American companies are having trouble competing, I don't think it's because they aren't big enough. Making General Motors even bigger isn't going to solve a competitive problem.

Basing antitrust policy on a global market perspective gives too much away. The administration is correct in paying new attention to the impact of international competition in judging merger cases, but they seem to be using international competition as justification for sweeping changes that go beyond what is required . . . A lot of these mergers have nothing to do with increasing efficiency.[43]

TRW Inc. economist Pat Choate, and co-author of *The High Flex Society*, adds, "Corporate managers are so busy trying to preserve themselves that the entire focus of business has turned to short-term payoffs. They're too busy fighting Wall Street to fight Japan. How can anyone concentrate on doing what is needed for long-term competitiveness — spending for plant and equipment, R & D, and job training — when they're so busy battling for survival."[44]

The current anti-anti-trust situation, however, was perhaps best summarized by Arthur Burck, who now heads a merger consulting firm in Palm Beach, Florida and who for over 30 years has written and spoken on merger activity and has himself been the architect of several hundred mergers of small and medium sized firms. In February, 1986, in a wide-ranging interview with *Multinational Monitor* he declared:

> There are no constitutional checks to corporate power and I can foresee if this movement continues we could have such concentration at the top that it's reasonable to foresee that we're going to have a situation where the huge money-center banks can take over and completely dominate our banking industry.
>
> When that happens, what does it mean? It means that if at the same time we're concentrating through deals like General Electric and RCA and many others, if we're concentrating and making larger the huge corporations, a handful of banks will own what might be the controlling blocks of a handful of huge companies that dominate our economy.
>
> Look ahead twenty years. You'll really have concentration of power that is far beyond anything ever imagined by our constitutional drafters — something never envisioned in our constitution — a private power that is something to worry about.[45]

Indeed, John Kenneth Galbraith, the noted Harvard University economist, believes that there's already been "a shift in power to the corporate raider and . . . to the investment houses that manage the exchange of equity for debt." Galbraith believes that if companies keep up buying other companies at their current pace that by the year 2000 we may only have 200 major companies in the U.S.[46]

How lucrative these acquisitions can also be to individuals with "inside information" — confidential information concerning upcoming stock sales and merger plans — has reached scandalous proportions in recent years with the uncovering by the Securities and Exchange Commission (SEC) of major violations. One such case was that of Dennis B. Levine who, the SEC alleges, made in a five year period over $12.6 million in illicit profits by trading some 54 different stocks based on inside information. Among those transactions were a $2.6 million profit on R.J. Reynolds purchase of Nabisco and a $1.2 million profit after Jewel Cos. received a takeover bid from American Stores.[47]

Within a year after the Levine scandal came the revelations that Ivan Boesky, Wall Street's most celebrated and successful arbitrageur, had pleaded guilty to illegal insider trading, and had agreed to pay what some believed a $100 million pittance as a penalty for his activities in addition to accepting a life-time banishment from the American securities industry and agreeing to pleading guilty to one felony count. Boesky, who had been fingered by Levine, had reportedly engaged in more than 40 suspicious purchases of stock in advance of takeover announcements.[48]

While some Wall Streeters might argue that trading on inside information is a "victimless crime," Gordon S. Macklin, president of the National Association of Securities Dealers, sharply disagrees. "The victims are the people that missed out on an opportunity that was captured by someone with a preferred position."[49] Yet, as one old master stock market manipulator in the early 1900's, Daniel Drew, colorfully observed, "anybody who plays the stock market not as an insider is like a man buying cows in the moonlight."[50]

New York Daily News columnist Ken Auletta, author of *Greed and Glory on Wall Street: The Fall of the House of Lehman*, however, believes the problem of inside trading is more endemic than episodic. He points out that in recent years a great growth industry on the Street has become "risk arbitrage," where people bet on the rise, or fall, of stock prices. Today, an estimated $10 billion of capital is in the hands of risk arbitrageurs.

He observes, "investment bankers used to swell with pride when seen as the wise counselors of corporate America. Now it is a badge of honor to be known as a deal-maker. Too often the *deal* becomes an end, not a means."[51]

The issue here is broader than just risk arbitrage. At issue is the value system of Wall Street, a deregulated, in-bred community where high overhead and abundant opportunities to amass wealth propel investment bankers to generate more 'deals,' more fees, more short-term speculation.

The resulting frenzy erodes long term loyalties — to clients, to stocks and even to your own firm, which is a major reason so many private Wall Street partnerships have been sold. Patience, a

virtue we urge on our children or on the poor [*ed. note*: and farmers], becomes the first casualty. Young associates can't wait to get rich. Stock prices gyrate so wildly because the market is now dominated by impatient speculators rather than long-term investors.[52]

In a December 2, 1986 speech to the Urban League of Greater New York Rohatyn succinctly summed up the consequences and challenges faced by the investment community in the 1980's in light of the scandals that pervaded the nation's financial establishments.

Greed and corruption are the cancer of a free society. They are a cancer because they erode our value system. They create contempt for many of our institutions as a result of the corrupt actions of individuals. The continuity of institutions is too important to be sacrificed to the unfettered greed of individuals. *I have been in business for almost 40 years and I cannot recall a period in which greed and corruption appeared as prevalent as they are today* (emphasis added).

. . . the picture of unfettered greed and corruption presently on the covers of national magazines and on the everyday news could unleash a vicious backlash against institutions as well as individuals. Individuals who break the law have to be punished; institutions have to be reformed.[53]

"These scandals are the direct product of the takeover frenzy," according to one Wall Streeter, "whenever you have the kind of activity that a takeover frenzy produces, you begin to attract hungrier people. It becomes like a Gresham's Law: Bad people flock to easy money."[54]

Appendix C

The Nation's 100 Largest Farms

These top 100 farms were ranked according to *Successful Farming* estimates of annual sales from agricultural production. The list was compiled from information publicly available to *Successful Farming* and the information was not intended to be used for any purpose other than the magazine's ranking of the top farms for its readers.

+ Some corporate farms are located in more than one state and in that event the listing here is usually the corporate headquarters.
++ Principal crops, however, some farms may also be producers of other agricultural commodities.

Rank	Farm Name	Sales (Mil.)	Product	State
1	Tyson	1,111	Broilers, Pork	Arkansas
2	ConAgra	1,048	Broilers, Beef	Nebraska
3	Castle & Cooke	800	Vegetables, Fruit	Hawaii
4	Perdue Farms, Inc.	618.8	Broilers, Turkeys	Maryland
5	Gold Kist, Inc.	566	Broilers, Eggs	Georgia
6	Holly Farms	558.3	Broilers	North Carolina
7	Barlett & Company	555	Beef	Maryland
8	Continental Grain	554	Beef, Broilers	Illinois
9	Cargill	528.8	Beef, Turkeys	Minnesota
10	U.S. Sugar Corp.	365	Sugar, Beef	Florida
11	Hudson Foods, Inc.	337.5	Broilers, Turkeys	Arkansas
12	Pilgrim's Pride Corp.	324.1	Broilers, Eggs	Texas
13	E & J Gallo	320	Grapes	California
14	Lykes Brothers Inc.	300	Citrus, Beef	Florida
15	Cactus Feeders, Inc.	275	Beef	Texas
16	J.R. Simplot Company	250	Beef, Row Crop	Idaho
17	Seaboard Farms	223.8	Broilers	Georgia
18	Foster Poultry Farms	219.2	Broilers	California
19	Campbell Soup Co.	215.3	Poultry, Mushrooms	New Jersey

20	C. Brewer & Co., Ltd.	200	Sugar, Macadamias	Hawaii
21	Marshall Durbin Co.	193.3	Broilers	Alabama
22	A. Duda & Sons	190	Citrus, Vegetables	Florida
23	Townsends, Inc	190	Broilers	Delaware
24	Fieldale Farms	183.5	Broilers	Georgia
25	National Farms, Inc.	175	Beef, Pork	Maryland
26	Gottsch FDG Corp.	168	Beef	Nebraska
27	Barret & Crofoot, Inc.	152	Beef	Texas
28	Agri-Beef Co.	150	Beef, Row Crops	Idaho
29	Frito Lay, Inc.	150	Corn, Potatoes	Texas
30	Maui Land & Pineapple	150	Pineapple	Hawaii
31	Swift-Eckrich	148.2	Turkeys	Illinois
32	Zacky Farms, Inc.	146.8	Broilers, Turkeys	California
33	Rocco Enterprise, Inc.	135.8	Turkeys, Broilers	Virginia
34	Friona Industries	125.1	Beef	Texas
35	Cagle's Inc.	122.1	Broilers	Georgia
36	Harris Farms, Inc.	120	Beef, Row Crops	California
37	Gottsch Feeding Corp.	120	Beef	Nebraska
38	Monterrey Mushrooms, Inc.	120	Mushrooms	California
39	Agri-Tech Services	119	Beef	Colorado
40	Jennie-O Foods Inc.	117	Turkeys	Minnesota
41	Sanderson Farms	116	Broilers	Mississippi
42	Showell Farms, Inc.	113	Broilers	Maryland
43	Louis Rich	111.7	Turkeys	California
44	Alexander & Baldwin	111.3	Sugar, Coffee	Hawaii
45	Carroll's Foods, Inc.	110.2	Turkeys, Pork	North Carolina
46	Hitch Enterprises Inc.	108.8	Beef	Oklahoma
47	Norbest	107.3	Turkeys	Utah
48	Foxley Cattle Co.	104	Beef	Nebraska
49	Murphy Farms, Inc.	103	Pork	North Carolina
50	McCarty Farms	101.7	Broilers	Mississippi

51	Simmons Industries	99	Broilers	Arkansas
52	AXTX	98	Beef	Texas
53	T B P Group	97.8	Beef	Texas
54	Cuddy Farms	95.55	Turkeys	North Carolina
55	Schaake	94.5	Beef	Washington
56	George's Inc.	93.6	Broilers, Eggs	Arkansas
57	Wampler Foods, Inc.	88.9	Turkeys	Virginia
58	McElhaney Cattle Co.	86	Beef	Arizona
59	AMFAC-JMB	84.8	Sugar	Hawaii
60	Salyer American Fresh Food	80	Cotton	California
61	Choctaw Maid Farms	78.4	Broilers	Mississippi
62	Granada Corp.	78	Beef, Broilers	Texas
63	Jerome Fairbo Farms	76.05	Turkeys	Minnesota
64	Bruce Church, Inc.	75.3	Vegetables	California
65	Alta Verde Industries	75	Beef, Vegetables	Texas
66	Van De Graff, Inc.	75	Beef	Washington
67	Nash Johnson & Sons Farms	73.65	Turkeys, Broilers	North Carolina
68	Golden Rod Broilers	72.33	Broilers	Alabama
69	Bil Mar Foods, Inc.	72.2	Turkeys	Michegan
70	Allen's Hatchery, Inc.	69.39	Broilers	Delaware
71	Rose Acre Farms	65.63	Eggs	New Jersey
72	B.C. Rogers Poultry	65.55	Broilers	Mississippi
73	Seaboard-ISE America	65.47	Eggs	New Jersey
74	John I. Haas	65	Hops, Tree Fruit	North Carolina
75	Agri-Empire	65	Potatoes, Beef	California
76	Juniata Feed Yards	64.4	Beef	Nebraska
77	MAR-JAC	61.03	Broilers	Virginia
78	Para Cattle Co.	60	Beef	Washington
79	Seven Rivers, Inc.	60	Beef, Pecans	New Mexico
80	Nunes Company, Inc.	60	Lettuce, Vegetables	California

81	Hamakua Sugar Co., Inc.	60	Sugar, Beef	Hawaii
82	Boskovich Farms	59.5	Vegetables	California
83	J.R. Norton Co.	59.4	Row Crops	Arizona
84	Goldsboro Milling	58.8	Turkeys	North Carolina
85	Gress Foods, Inc.	58.77	Broilers	Georgia
86	Peterson Industries, Inc.	58.77	Broilers	Arkansas
87	CAL-Maine	55.25	Eggs, Pork	Mississippi
88	Peco Farms	54.25	Broilers	Alabama
89	Harrison Poultry, Inc.	53.86	Broilers	Georgia
90	Talisman Sugar Corp.	53.72	Sugar	Florida
91	O.D. Foods, Inc.	52.43	Broilers	Arkansas
92	JFC, Inc.	52.17	Broilers	Minnesota
93	Anderson Farms Company	50.3	Rice	California
94	Morrison Enterprises	50	Feed Grains, Beef	Nebraska
95	Berry Company	50	Citrus	Florida
96	Bayview Farms	50	Asparagus, Raspberries	Washington
97	Milton Waldbaum Company	48.45	Eggs	Nebraska
98	Moonlight Mushrooms	48	Mushrooms	Pennsylvania
99	Maple Leaf Farms	47.5	Ducks	Idaho
100	Lone Star	47.4	Beef	Texas

Appendix D

Summary of Recommendations of the National Commission on Food Marketing

The Commission issued no set of conclusions due to sharp divisions that existed between the nine majority and the six minority members. The majority believed:

1) A growing concentration existed within the food industry and that there needed to be more forceful control by the government if the public interest was to be served.

2) Requirements needed to be specified for intended mergers or acquisitions of firms by other firms above a certain size and that a regulatory agency should have the general power to issue a cease and desist order until the economic effects of a proposal could be appraised and evaluated.

3) Each public corporation in the food industry, whose annual sales exceeded a certain amount should be required to report annually to the Securities and Exchange Commission (SEC), for publication, its sales, expenses, and profits in each field of operations in which the annual value of shipments was in excess of a stated minimum.

4) The Robinson-Patman Act, which restricted price discrimination practices such as using loss leaders or below-cost selling to eliminate competition and the using of integrated wholesale firms over independent suppliers to gain further market power, must be strengthened by more effective enforcement.

5) Regulatory jurisdiction over transactions in meat and poultry needed to be made more forceful.

6) More orderly and equitable trading in fresh fruits and vegetables could be realized by strengthening the Perishable Agricultural Commodities Act.

7) Establishing consumer grades on all foods and FDA standards of identity for all foods belonging to a definite product category, improved packaging and labeling to assist consumers in making more accurate appraisals and price comparisons, and forming a centralized consumer agency within the executive branch all would enable consumers to get more satisfaction for their money.

8) Farmers could be better served by more government support for producer cooperatives and bargaining associations; authorizing federal marketing agreements and orders for any agricultural commodity produced in a local area or regional U.S. subdivision; new legislation enabling agricultural marketing boards to be created by a vote of producers for the purpose of joining in the sale of farm products when they first enter the channels of trade; and prohibiting through legislation intermediate parties from obstructing the formation or operation of a producers' bargaining association or cooperative by unduly trying to influence the producers' understanding through false or misleading information or other means.

9) USDA should study the changes in methods and costs of transporting food products, the effects on prices and the location of production; improve the accuracy of its reports on food prices, its price-spread data (with the assistance of the food industry); periodically review the various commissions or other bodies established by the states to increase market demands for food; and improve its market information about market prices and supplies by having the authority to require firms transacting business in foods to report prices, quantities bought or sold, grades and similar information in the forms essential to prompt publication of market news.

10) The Federal Trade Commission needed to investigate the rates for food advertising to determine if various discounts, variations in charges, and ratemaking methods were cost-justified.

11) The Bureau of Labor Statistics should study means by which it could improve the accuracy of its food-price reports.

12) All meat and livestock futures trading should come under the supervision of the Commodity Exchange Authority with consideration also being given to coffee, sugar and other perishable farm foods as well.

The minority argued that:

1) The majority's views on concentration, competition and farm marketing were so badly in error that their adoption as public policy would do lasting damage to the nation's economy.

2) The nation should applaud the impressive evidence gathered by the Commission staff and recognize that much of the analytical material should be read with respect, but that Congress and others should beware of accepting any conclusions.

3) The food industry was not as concentrated as such other industries as steel, automobiles, electrical appliances, etcetera, that it was highly competitive and that ease of entry was not encumbered, especially at the local level.

4) In comparison with other major sectors of the economy the food industry's level of profits were not excessive and that farm to retail price spreads were also not unreasonable.

5) Any requirements for premerger notification would damage competition by limiting the "flexibility" essential for firms to transact necessary business.

6) "Study and reappraisal" of the Robinson-Patman and other anti-trust laws was necessary, there was no evidence that the food industry lacked the proper scrutiny by federal regulatory agencies.

7) The food industry, in responding to consumer demand and preferences, was making excellent progress in continuing to bring high-level, integrated food services to the American public.

8) The majority "conclusion" calling for reporting, surveillance and regulation of the food industry was unjustified and could not be supported since the food industry was offering their services at declining real costs and was contributing substantially to the national welfare and a satisfactory rate of economic growth.

Appendix E

Recommendations of the National Advisory Commission on Food and Fiber

The nineteen-member majority, composed of four of the Commission's seven academic members, the farm and co-op leaders and two of the industry representatives, endorsed:

1) Commodity programs that were consistent with a market-oriented policy and which would not interfere with desirable resource management.

2) Marketing orders, price supports set modestly below a moving average of world market programs, direct commodity payments to implement these price supports, and voluntary supply-management programs and production quotas when necessary.

3) A program for adjusting carryover stocks of major storable farm commodities in order to maintain a reasonable stability of available supplies, with commodity loans and purchase agreements to support price levels to harmonize with the objectives of market-oriented programs.

4) Land use or development programs only when additional farm production was needed.

5) Water use from publicly-financed irrigation projects should be given only to family farms of economically viable size.

6) Public subsidies for capacity-increasing farm practices should be discontinued and the fund redirected toward improving rural life.

7) New legislation in foreign trade to permit reciprocal trade agreements with other countries, reduction and final elimination of export subsidies, substitution of tariffs for quotas to protect affective American producers, discontinuance of authority to impose import quotas on beef and mutton, expansion of East-West trade, and steps to permit U.S. shipping firms to operate at rates competitive with those offered by foreign fleets.

8) Food aid programs for developing countries should be for short-term relief of famine caused by drought or crop failure, whereas long-term multinational aid should be technical assistance to improve agricultural productivity in conjunction with population planning.

The minority, composed primarily of those Commission members from industry in addition to two academic representatives, argued:

1) Commodity programs should be modified to encourage major adjustments to a market-oriented agriculture and then gradually be phased out.

2) Government supply management was inconsistent with market orientation and would interfere with resources moving to more profitable uses and regions.

3) The U.S., following a transition period, should rely on temporary income supplements or a moderate level of price deficiency payments with the income parity concept used only as a gauge and not as a program instrument.

4) Price supports should not be above 90 percent of the five-year average of world market prices and should be gradually phased out in favor of temporary income supplements and/or price deficiency payments.

5) A shift from nonrecourse loans to recourse loans should be made as soon as possible so if market prices fell below loan levels farmers could not liquidate CCC loans without incurring a loss of capital.

6) Direct payments should not be made to achieve parity incomes, particularly if the payments were made on a price per unit of product and independent of the farmer's net income.

7) Acreage allotments and marketing quotas should be gradually relaxed on a specific schedule and eventually abolished.

8) Development projects should not be funded unless they were the cheapest means of getting increased farm production.

9) Subsidies for capacity-increasing farm practices should be discontinued, but that the funds should be redirected, not to rural development projects, but to accomplish a necessary long-term shift of excess cropland to less intensive use, i.e., wheat to livestock grazing.

A Letter from the Federal Reserve

Federal Reserve Bank of St. Louis
P.O. Box 442
St. Louis, Missouri 63166

Darryl R. Francis
President
February 20, 1970

Mr. C. F. Marley, Photojournalist
R.R. 2, Oconee Road East
Nokomis, Illinois 62075

Dear Mr. Marley:

I found your letter of February 10 most interesting. It contains many questions which indicate the deep study you have given to the various topics. I will answer them in the same order in which they were asked. You will understand, however, that other people will have other views relative to these forces which are reshaping our farm economy.

Concerning your first question in which the idea of shooting for 100,000 farms was discussed. I do not believe that we should do something about determining the precise number of commercial farms that will ultimately emerge in this nation. By endorsing the previous speakers' statements relative to the number of efficient farming units that would be required for competitive farm output, I had in view that market forces would continue to reduce the number of farm units in each successive year. I base this conclusion on statistical analysis which shows that the larger farming units are more efficient than smaller units. I think we will continue to produce agricultural technology and that such technology will continue to cause an increase in the average size of farm units. Whether or not we will wind up with more or less than 100,000 farms, I cannot be sure. However, if we permit market forces to make the decision as to the optimum number of farms, the welfare of the nation will be maximized as long as monopolistic forces are excluded.

Concerning the topic of farm prices, it is my belief that only the market place can best determine optimum prices for farm commodities. When farm commodities are scarce, prices will rise in the market place and more resources will flow into agriculture and production is enhanced. Conversely, when farm commodities are plentiful, prices under a free market system will decline and resources will flow out of agriculture thereby

retarding production. I suggest that this method of determining farm commodity and other prices, is the only rational price determining system for either a free enterprise or a socialist type economy.

My discussion was not designed to be in favor of subsidizing farmers or any other sector of the economy. In fact, I am not in favor of subsidies in general. I had hoped to leave the impression that our educational efforts should be designed to make our farm labor force more flexible since in most years throughout the nation's history we have had too many people in agriculture. I believe that we should initiate training programs to make the move from farm to nonfarm vocations much easier than in the past. If we use subsidies for farm people it is more desirable to subsidize the move to nonfarm occupations than our past programs of subsidizing people in agriculture to retirement.

Concerning your inquiry relative to farm assets and debt, it is my view that farmers will bid up assets to some multiple of net incomes. This is the way that nonfarm assets are priced. Thus, I would expect the same general rule to prevail in agriculture. The U.S. Department of Agriculture estimated total farm assets at $298 billion at the beginning of last year. I have little doubt that farm debt will rise rapidly within the next ten years and it may approach the $100 billion suggested figure. It was estimated at $55 billion last year and has been increasing about $4 billion per year in recent years. It seems to me that you may be somewhat low in your estimates of future net farm income. Such income is currently running about $16 billion per year, and I would expect some small increase during the next ten years. If we have a sizeable rate of general price inflation, net farm income may rise substantially. However, I would not expect farmers to go in debt and bid up assets beyond the range that could be handled by expected net income and cash flows. It appears to me that farmers will operate to maximize profits just as any other businessman. In doing so they will probably purchase assets and maintain debt levels that can be serviced without excessive risks.

I do not expect farmers of the future to plan to pay off debt during their lifetimes. I don't know of any other type of business that expects to get free of debt during the life of the present operator. In past years, when farm assets totaled only ten or twelve times expected net income from agriculture, it was not too unreasonable to expect a farmer to liquidate his debts prior to retirement. Today, however, when it takes $500,000 to $1,000,000 to operate an efficient farm, it is asking a great deal for each farmer to liquidate all debt prior to passing the farm on to another operator. Indeed, we would have a wealthy group of retired farmers if such expectations were achieved. It is my view that a farm operator should operate an optimum-sized unit, maintain a maximum net income, and when he gets ready to retire sell his equity to some other individual. I don't see any necessity of a farmer denying himself and his family a reasonable level of family expenditures just to repay debts when he has an adequate net income to service debts and maintain some liquidity for emergencies.

A decrease in number of farm operators, assuming no change in the level of net income accruing to agriculture, will mean that the remaining farmers will have a larger net income accruing to each. It is my contention that as each inefficient producer moves into the nonfarm sector there will be a marginal decline in total farm output and some slight rise in farm prices until adjustments are made on the remaining farms. However, even after the remaining farmers adjust to their new cost and price conditions, I see no reason why total net income accruing to agriculture should decline.

I hope that the above comments are helpful.

Sincerely,

SIGNED:
Darryl R. Francis

Appendix G

Two Approaches: S. 1083 and H.R. 2383

Comparing Two Agricultural Programs

The most important study to come before Congress during the 1985 Farm Bill debate was a project by the highly-respected Food and Agricultural Research Institute (FARI) of Iowa State University and the University of Missouri relative to the merits of a modification of the current agricultural policy similar to that which was approved by the House Agricultural Subcommittee on Wheat, Soybeans, and Feed Grains on June 26, 1985 (shown below in light face) and the provisions of the Farm Policy Reform Act as contained in H.R. 2383 and S. 1083 (shown below in bold face).

NET FARM INCOME
* Net farm income would be 16 percent lower in 1987 and eight percent lower in 1990.
* **Net farm income would be 52 percent higher in 1987 and 605 higher in 1990.**

GOVERNMENT COSTS
* Government costs would increase 39 percent by 1987 but would then decline by 15 percent from current levels by 1990.
* **Government costs would decline to about $1 billion annually and remain at that level.**

VARIABILITY IN FARM PRICES
* Variability in farm prices would increase in both the short and longer run as loan rates no longer would place a floor under commodity prices. However, there would be no change in the variability of net farm income since output variations would tend to offset impacts of price changes on income.
* **Variability of farm prices and net farm income would decline as supply reductions tend to stabilize domestic prices.**

LIVESTOCK INCOME
* Income of livestock producers would increase in the short run, but show little change in the long run after livestock producers adjusted inventories to reflect lower grain prices.
* **Incomes of livestock would be sharply reduced in the short run as inventories were liquidated in response to sharply higher feed prices. After this period of adjustment reduced herd sizes would generate higher prices and return to current levels.**

LAND PRICES
* Land prices would continue to decline reflecting slightly lower farm incomes.

*Land prices for land used by farmers having marketing quotas would increase. Land withdrawn from production would likely decline in value.

PRODUCTION ACREAGE
* Acreage in production would be reduced by about ten to 15 percent as producers participate in voluntary acreage reduction programs.
* **Acreage in production would decline by about 35 percent.**

FARM MACHINERY
* Demand for machinery would not change from current levels as farm incomes would change only slightly.
* **Demand for machinery would increase in the short run as farmers would use increased income to replace worn out equipment. However, reduced acreage would offset income impacts on demand for machinery over the longer run.**

EXPORTS
* Volume of exports of corn, wheat, cotton, and soybeans would increase — especially in the long run in response to lower loan rates and market prices. The value of exports would increase over time although there would be little change in the short run. However, there is considerable uncertainty accompanying these longer term projections.
* **Volume of exports of corn, wheat, cotton, and soybeans would decrease modestly in the short run and decline substantially in the long run in response to higher prices. The value of wheat exports would increase substantially in the short run and continue in the long run for corn and soybeans. However, there is more uncertainty accompanying the longer term.**

FOOD PRICES
* Food prices and consumer expenditures would show very little change in response to this program.
* **Food prices and consumer food expenditures would show little change in the short run as lower livestock prices would offset higher grain prices. However, food prices and expenditures would then increase after livestock herd reductions reduced meat supplies. These food price increases would have the greatest impact on low income customers.**

Appendix H: A Necessary Comparison

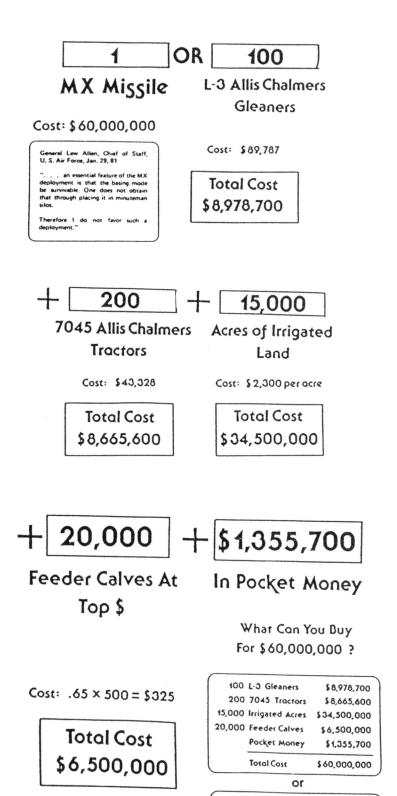

THE MX VS American Agriculture

(A NECESSARY COMPARISON)

THE MX IS HELPING BANKRUPT AMERICAN AGRICULTURE

In this brochure we have itemized what can be purchased with the 60 million dollars it would cost to build **one** MX missile. For the upcoming 1986 budget, the Pentagon is requesting 48 MX missiles at a cost of $5 BILLION dollars. The total MX program cost is estimated at 26-50 Billion.

The MX, for the past two years has been kept in production only because the administration maintains that it is a "WEAPON SYSTEM TO BE USED AS A BARGAINING CHIP WITH THE SOVIETS." The bargaining chip theory has historically been a failure in arms control talks. There is no reason to assume that the MX can now be used successfully as a bargaining chip with the Soviets.

Meanwhile, Congress this year looks to cut agricultural assistance programs that are essential to the survival of many farm operators, as a way to reduce the federal budget. Congressional representatives who continue to support costly, unnecessary weapon systems, such as the MX, are in fact supporting the destruction of the traditional agricultural structure upon which this country was built.

Appendix I

The Family Farm Act of 1987

The Family Farm Act was the result of more than three years of effort by grassroots farm groups across the country to develop a common sense program to help efficient farmers bring their surplus production back into line with demand, get a fair price for their commodities in the marketplace, reverse the economic decline of rural America and slash the cost of federal farm programs.

The bill would have accomplished the following goals:

1. Allow our food producers to earn a living again. The bill would establish commodity price floors at levels which would allow efficient family farmers to earn a reasonable return on their investment and labor.

It initially would establish the price-support "loan rate" for each crop at 70 percent of the current government-calculated "parity price" for that commodity. Using current parity levels as of the beginning of 1987, for reference, the 70 percent formula would have established the price floors listed below; note that in each case the price floors under the Family Farm Act, while considerably higher than current prices, are still significantly lower than the ten-year average market prices of these commodities in the 1970's when adjusted for inflation:

Commodity	Price floors in 1970s	Average prices in (70-79)*
Corn	$ 3.44/bushel	$ 4.34/bushel
Wheat	$ 4.72/bushel	$ 5.84/bushel
Soybeans	$ 8.47/bushel	$ 10.97/bushel
Grain Sorghum	$?? .?? /wt.	$ 7.02/cwt.
Rice	$ 13.44/cwt.	$ 19.93/cwt.
Upland Cotton	$ .86/lb.	$ .92/lb.
Barley	$ 3.14/bushel	$ 3.77/bushel
Oats	$ 2.01/bushel	$ 2.28/bushel
Milk	$ 16.24/cwt.	$ 17.44/cwt.

* In 1967 dollars; annual production volumes were weighed for calculating average price of each commodity for 1970-79 decade. Prices from 1970's do not include any federal subsidy payments also paid on these crops.

In each subsequent year of the program, the price floors would be increased by one percent of parity until, in the 11th year of the program, they reach 80 percent of parity.

The economists at FAPRI — the Food and Agricultural Policy Research Institute at Iowa State University and the University of Missouri — project that the **Family Farm Act** would generate *over $50 billion more in net farm income* during the next five years than the current farm program would.

2. Reduce price-busting surpluses. Mandatory production controls (subject to producer approval in a nationwide referendum) would limit U.S. production of program commodities to the projected amounts needed to meet actual demand, including domestic consumption, export demand, humanitarian need and strategic reserve requirements.

A farmer would only be allowed to market a volume of commodities equal to his/her authorized acres times his/her historic per-acre yield, so in the event of perfect weather and a bumper crop, the excess production would be stored and applied against the following year's marketing quota, thus reducing input costs.

3. Slash farm program costs. With production reduced to better reflect actual demand, producers would receive a fair price for their crops in the marketplace, not from the government. Costly subsidy payments would be eliminated, and with nationwide production requirements adjusted annually, the need for government "purchases" of surplus commodities would be minimized.

4. Target benefits to family farmers. The percentage of acres each farmer would be required to remove from production would be determined by the size of his/her operation.

Small and mid-sized farmers would be assigned the minimum [20-25 percent] set-aside level for each crop. The largest farm operations, on the other hand, would be required to set aside 35 percent of their acreage bases. Those operators in the middle range — relatively large family farm operators, for the most part — would be assigned set-aside levels somewhere between the minimum levels and 35 percent.

This approach contains built-in advantages for its target group, the small and mid-sized family farm operations, while still limiting the average set-aside required of the biggest operators to reasonable levels. A key result of the program is that, by favoring family farmers, it contains a progressive disincentive against expansion beyond the family-farm size, thus discouraging an inflationary land grab by large corporations eager to take advantage of an improved profit picture in agriculture.

5. Increase export earnings. For the past half-century, the world market price for storable commodities has effectively been established by U.S. federal price-support loan levels. The U.S. remains the dominant force in the world agricultural export market, and historical trends, current economic pressures and their own assurances indicate that, once U.S. crop prices are raised, our major export competitors would eagerly follow our lead and raise their prices, as well.

To avert any possibility that competing exporters might attempt to boost their production and increase their market share at our expense, however, the **Family Farm Act** instructs the President to enter into multilateral negotiations with other food exporting nations to increase world market prices and maintain market shares. If an agreement has not been reached after nine months, the Secretary of Agriculture is mandated to use bonus commodities (or, if necessary) cash subsidies to maintain U.S. exports.

To implement the bonus program — the *export hammer* — the Secretary would offer sufficient bonus commodities along with purchased U.S. commodities so that the aggregate per-unit price to our competitor's intended customer would be low enough that we either win the sale or at least make it clear to our competitors that any price-cutting market raid would be unprofitable. In effect, while a multilateral agreement on price and market share would be ideal, we are in a position to end the world commodity price war unilaterally and still maintain our market share while nearly doubling our earnings.

Economists at FAPRI project that U.S. exports of storable commodities would *increase* by more than $10 billion during the first year of the **Family Farm Act** (to $20.6 billion) and would continue rising in subsequent years as prices improve (to $36.4 billion in 1995-96, the last year of the FAPRI projection).

While our export volume of a few (but not all) of these commodities might drop off some initially due to price increase, the higher per-unit returns more than offset (by far) any decline in volume. Additionally, FAPRI projections indicate a steady increase in export volume as well as price in subsequent years of the program.

6. Improve farmer efficiency. Recent farm programs have forced farmers to try to make up in increased volume what they are denied in price, and government and agribusiness promotions have convinced farmers that "efficiency" means maximizing output per acre. The **Family Farm Act**, by specifying up-front the maximum volume each farmer will be authorized to sell at harvest, would immediately redefine efficiency. Rather than the one who *maximizes* his/her use of fertilizer and chemical poisons, the most efficient farmer would be the one who can produce his/her predetermined crop allotment while finding ways to *minimize* his/her input costs.

7. Protect farmers and consumers from disasters. The current myriad of disaster programs would be consolidated into one simplified approach that offers income protection to crop producers and protects both consumers and livestock producers from shortage-induced price increases.

Each producer would contribute a small percentage of his/her crops into a *Federal Disaster Reserve* (FDR). Then, in the event of a disaster, a producer would receive commodities from the FDR to compensate

him/her for disaster-related losses; a producer would absorb a loss of up to ten percent of the production authorized by his/her marketing certificate. Any loss in excess of ten percent would be covered by commodities from the disaster reserve (no producer could receive more than $360,000). The FDR would offer producers substantial protection and at the same time insure that adequate supplies are available in the market.

8. Relieve the farm debt crisis. Debt mediation and restructuring provisions in the **Family Farm Act** will enable many heavily-indebted producers to remain on their land until, with the improved commodity prices established by the bill, they can farm their way out of trouble.

Meanwhile, the improved profit picture in agriculture will reverse the downward spiral of land values, alleviating lender pressure on numerous producers whose plunging collateral value no longer provides adequate security to cover their indebtedness. Important effects would be to reduce or eliminate the need for annual $2-$3 billion federal bail-outs of the Farm Credit System and to restore the viability of much of the $30-$50 billion in farm debt currently considered to be unrecoverable even through foreclosure.

9. Encourage improved conservation practices. When they can afford it, American farmers are the best conservationists in the world. Pride, peer pressure and a clear understanding of their own long-term self interest demand it.

Unfortunately, current U.S. farm policies effectively force farmers to maximize their crop production with intensive use of fertilizers and other chemical poisons, some of which all-too-often run off into nearby streams and rivers or leach into the underground water supply (a major problem in agricultural areas of many states).

In addition, the deteriorating financial situation in U.S. agriculture makes it impossible for many farmers to invest the funds required for adequate soil erosion control projects, with the result that soil erosion is at its highest level since the Dust Bowl days of the 1930's. In short, we are poisoning our water and depleting our soil; we're "mining" our agricultural resources.

In return for the improved crop prices established by the **Family Farm Act**, farmers would agree to reduce their production to levels needed to fill actual projected demand, and locally-approved conservation practices would be required on all land removed from production under the program.

In addition, the crop volume they would be allowed to market would be based upon their past per acre yield history; thus, the **Family Farm Act** would eliminate any incentive to increase yields with additional chemical use and, instead, would reward the efficient producer who can fill his/her production quota with the lowest possible input costs.

Finally, when American farmers are once again earning adequate returns for their production, history demonstrates that they will again become the conscientious stewards of the land and water they've been unable to be under current farm policies.

Appendix J

A Progressive Populist Declaration of Independence[*]

When in the course of human events, it becomes necessary for a class of people, suffering from long continued systems of oppression and abuse, to rouse themselves from their personal resignation and intellectual submission, now heralded as a form of social sophistication; to assume among their fellow citizens, that equal station, and demand from the government they support, those equal rights to which the laws of nature, and nature's God entitles them; a decent respect for the opinions of mankind requires that they should declare the causes that impel them to a course so necessary to their own protection.

We hold these truths to be self-evident: that all men and women are created equal; that they are endowed by their Creator with certain inalienable rights; that among these are life, liberty and the pursuit of happiness. That to secure these rights governments are instituted among the people, deriving their just powers from the consent of the governed; that whenever the powers of a government become destructive of these, either through the injustices or unfairness of its laws or through the corruption of its executive, legislative or judicial system, it is the right of the people to abolish such laws, and institute such reforms as to them shall seem most likely to effect their welfare and happiness.

Prudence indeed will dictate that laws long established shall not be changed for light and trifling causes, and accordingly, experience shows that men and women are more disposed to suffer while evils are sufferable, than to right themselves by abolishing the laws to which they are accustomed.

But, when a long train of abuses and usurpations, pursuing invariably the same object, seeks to impose upon the people a "seller-sovereign" economic order, monopolistic and oligopolistic in character, with a goal of creating slavish dependence, not critical capacity; that, system, under the fostering care of a government "obsequious in its devotion to the purposes of a selfish oligarchy," assumes an almost irresistible influence in the halls of our legislatures. Just as our politics remain gerrymandered to serve the interests of wealth, the people's welfare continues to be scored by our political leadership in terms of financial gain, never about the spirit of our laws or the cherished ideals that embody our history as a people.

Thus, it is the people's right — it is their duty tothrow off such economic and social tyranny, and provide new guards for their future security.

Such has been the patient sufferance of the producing classes in our nation's rural and urban communities, and such is now the necessity which compels us to declare that we will use every means save a resort to violence to overthrow this despotism of monopoly, and to reduce all men and women claiming the protection of American laws to an equality before those laws.

The history of the modern corporate state is a history of repeated injuries and oppressions, all having in direct object the establishment of the corporation as the dominant institution within our society. While reducing the Bill of Rights to little more than a sheaf of commercial paper the corporate state has also carefully contrived to insure that the expansion of its privileges and power will become the main focal point of nearly all of our society's economic, social, and political institutions. To prove this let facts be submitted to a candid world:

It has privatized the nation's natural resources — land, water, air, food and fiber — while controlling, unfairly pricing, and exploiting those same resources for its own personal monetary gain.

It has abused, endangered, poisoned and frequently fashioned our natural resources into geopolitical weapons to further its own narrow interests while demonstrating little or no regard for the common good nor the public welfare.

It has by deifying business imperatives, rather than environmental or social concerns, dramatically increased by means of technological developments, the exploitation and processing of natural resources.

It has through its economic and political power repeatedly influenced government policy and legal institutions to generally support the logic of private enterprise development, promoting and defending individual private property rights over social and environmental concerns, eschewing control of private lands even for purposes of conservation; and providing abundant government assistance for the profitable purposes of corporate agriculture, lumber, oil and mining interests.

It has, while romanticizing family farming as a profession, denigrated the farmer as an individual as it seeks to perpetuate the myth that family farms operate

---

[*] From the works of Thomas Jefferson and all those agrarian populists who have believed and sought to promote his ideas this document is derived.

in an economic system that is both moral and one that rewards individual initiative and effort.

It has, by ceaselessly promoting the "work ethic," the "free enterprise," the "efficiency" and the "equal opportunity" myths made family farmers readily susceptible to (and firm believers in) agricultural programs, services, technologies and research that promotes "efficient," business-like farm management and production, but which in reality simply serves a tightly-controlled economic and political system dominated by corporate capital.

It has by accommodating all major organizational variations within the conceptual "family farm" category, obscured the systematic reasons, particularly the economic and political ones, for operational differences built not on personality, managerial ability or individual effort — the perceived "quality" of processes and resources of production.

It has remained indolent to the general decay of our rural communities and inner-city ghettos by denying the human dignity of millions of men, women and children who have played such a vital and historic role in fashioning our nation's bountiful food system, stripping them unceremoniously of their land, homes, livelihoods, and their heritage.

It has, within the presence of a U.S. political process operating mainly on a crisis basis and seldom capable of making long-term planning decisions, assumed the role of a long-term planner regarding the future direction of our food system; a system now dominated by large corporate interests with their own carefully crafted self-serving agendas.

It has, with the expressed cooperation of the executive branch of the government, staged a concerted effort on behalf of a handful of private corporations intent on monopolizing international agricultural trade, increasing their own market shares, and destroying the family farm system both at home and abroad, yet masquerading that effort in rhetoric about "competitiveness," "flexibility," increased net farm income, abolishing crop "subsidies" and extolling the virtues of a near non-existent world "free" trade.

It has systematically increased the separation of real asset ownership from real asset control as illustrated by the fact that the public owns one-third of U.S. land, but large corporations control their rich resources of timber, oil, gas, copper, iron, zinc, etc. through leaseholds; the citizens own the airwaves, but the broadcasters control them; the workers own over $1.7 trillion worth of pension monies, but the private banks and insurance companies control the investment policy; depositors and policyholders own hundreds of billions of dollars in savings and insurance, but the management of these mutuals control their disposition.

It has demeaned the honest labor of its citizens with burgeoning credit, high interest rates, huge debt loads and a multi-billion dollar national deficit.

It has, motivated by its own narrowly-defined, selfish, financial interests, pitted worker against worker, race against race, culture against culture, man against woman, young against old, class against class.

It has, in the name of greater "productivity" and "cost management," callously endangered the health, safety, and livelihood of thousands of its workers while its executives and managers have remunerated themselves well beyond reasonable and equitable standards.

It has successfully procured the passage of local, state and federal laws designed to put untold millions of dollars into its own coffers while holding taxpayers, labor and entire communities alike hostage to its own commercial and industrial interests.

It has, contrary to the expressed provisions of our Constitution and the spirit of our law, combined its economic and political resources to destroy competition through unjust economic discrimination.

It has created thousands of disenchanted and cheated consumers, angry at being repeatedly victimized by the corporate state's "transfer economy" as they often find themselves saddled with the excessive costs of mismanagement, inefficiency and waste.

It has sufficiently corrupted and neutralized the government regulatory process to the degree that those government agencies and bureaus, designed originally to promote a "consumer-sovereign" economy, have instead adopted the priorities of a "seller-sovereign" economy.

It has continued to benefit economically by its control of patents and the profits emerging from government-sponsored research done in the public's name with taxpayer's funds.

It has repeatedly exhibited its inability to soundly invest, wisely manage or safely care for the monies of workers and consumers, while at the same time asking the public to bear its risks, its own failures, waste and corruption.

It has, at a time when long-time advocates of centralized state economic planning are abandoning such planning as an economic failure, begun creating a society based on centralized corporate economic planning and executed by those corporations with greater and greater economic power resulting from increasing industry concentration.

It has placed government and business decision-making into fewer and fewer corporate hands resulting in anti-competitive and inefficient practices that ultimately have proven to be both harmful and wasteful to the society as a whole.

It has both encouraged and subsidized a "corporatist" political leadership — one not necessarily conservative in nature, but rather one designed to deliver what the elitist element in the corporate state wants, as opposed to a conservative belief which usually follows the dictates of a cautious ideology.

It has, through bribery, "political action campaign" money, and honoraria all designed to intimidate legislators into betraying the true interests of their constituents, bought off so many of our politicians of both major political parties that it is often no longer possible to tell the difference between those parties.

It has successfully coerced politicians, in the name of helping "troubled industries," into creating a huge corporate welfare system composed of hundreds of billions of dollars in tax abatements, tax preferences, grants, inflated contracts, bailouts and a long list of miscellaneous subsidies to industry and commerce.

It has obstructed the administration of justice by injunctions procured from overawed, over-burdened courts, by legal technicalities, by endless numbers of appeals from court to court, with the intent of wearing out or ruining the prosecution, while openly avowing its determination to make it so time-consuming and so expensive for the public to prosecute that it will not dare undertake such an effort.

It has wrapped itself in the flag and claims a devotion to God, country and the public good while encouraging doctrines, values, myths and institutions that have helped create an ideology that transforms a ruling class into a "general interest;" one that seeks to justify existing class relations as the only natural and workable one, while ignoring the close links between the perpetuation of the myth of social sameness and the perpetuation of social wrong.

It has created a mammoth, extravagant and wasteful military-industrial complex which has become not only one of dubious value in protecting world peace, but one that also endangers our national security by depriving the nation of necessary funding for important domestic programs and infrastructural needs essential to our survival.

It has led people into believing that we as a nation can succeed in foreign wars when thousands of parasites, "the gamblers in the necessities of life," use those wars and the threat of such wars for the purpose of exacting exorbitant profits, working not to beat an enemy, but to make more multi-millionaires.

We have not been wanting in our attempts to obtain redress through Congress. Our repeated efforts have been answered only by silence, indifference or attempts to frame laws that shall seem to meet our wants but that are, in fact, only a legal snare for courts to disagree upon and for corporations to disobey.

We have warned our political leaders from time to time of these various and repeated encroachments upon our rights; we have reminded them of the circumstances of our emigration and settlement here; we have appealed to them as administrators of a free and impartial government, to protect us from these encroachments, which, if continued, assuredly will inevitably end in the utter destruction of those liberties for which our fathers and mothers gave their lives, and the establishment of an entrenched privileged class and an aristocracy of wealth.

We must, therefore, acquiesce to the necessity which compels us to denounce the corporate state's moral and criminal indifference to our wrongs, and hold them as we hold many of our leaders and legislators — an enemy to the producer — to the monopolist, a friend.

We, therefore, the producers and workers of several states assembled, given the historic populist tradition that has preceded us, appealing to the Supreme Judge of the world for the rectitude of our intentions, do solemnly declare that we will use all lawful and peaceable means to free ourselves from the tyranny of the corporate state and its monopolistic ideology, and that we will never cease our efforts for economic and political change until every branch of our government gives signification that the reign of greed and corporate subservience is over, and something of the degree of economic and political democracy which the framers of our government sought to inaugurate has taken its place.

That to this end we hereby declare ourselves absolutely free and independent of all past political connections, and that we will give our suffrage only to such men and women for office, from the lowest officer in the state to the president of the United States, as we have good reason to believe will use their best endeavors to the promotion of these ends; and for the support of this declaration, with a firm reliance on Divine Providence, we mutually pledge to each other our lives, our fortunes and our sacred honor. *(Submitted before the Rural Strategy Summit, Kansas City, Missouri on November 8-9, 1990 by A.V. Krebs, Director, Corporate Agribusiness Project.)*

"If there is a flaw in the system ..."

On August 2, 1989 46 CBOT and Merc traders were indicted on charges of illegal trading. With the indictments came the transcripts of numerous conversations secretly taped by government agents which showed futures traders routinely conspiring to make illegal trades and boasting about stealing from the public.

In a pretrial hearing FBI agent Dietrich Volk, known to Merc members by his trader pseudonym Peter Vogel, testified that illegal trading was "systemic and pervasive" on the floor of the Merc.[1]

On one tape John A. Vercillo, a soybean trader, one of 19 people in the CBOT soybean pit indicted on fraud charges, is quoted as saying to FBI agent Richard Ostrom, who was posing as a soybean trader: "Fuck the customers ... We should have the advantage ... That's why we have the membership ... Let them buy a fucking seat for $500,000 and put their money on the line like the rest of us."[2]

Based on the guilty plea of another soybean trader, Micheal Weiser, 21, a former $7000-a-year CBOT floor clerk, the *Chicago Tribune's* William B. Crawford Jr. shows the single theme that ran throughout the government's investigations. Namely, "the routine manner in which Weiser and the others used customer buy and sell orders to settle personal debts, hide income from the IRS and get cash kickbacks from other traders."[3]

The debts incurred by these traders were usually the result of so-called "out-trades," where one trader ends the day owing another trader money because of a trading error made in the frenzied, open outcry atmosphere of the commodity pit.

"In nearly every one of these documents," Crawford adds, "the defendant acknowledged that his actions enriched himself and hurt the trading fortunes of his customers, many of whom did not get the best buy or sell prices for their contracts."[4]

The role of big brokerage firms has also come into question. The results of the federal investigation, according to Richard Dennis, one of the industry's legendary traders who has made more than $200 million trading in futures, show that "there's been a breakdown of the fiduciary responsibility of brokerage firms to mediate between customers and floor brokers."[5]

But Marlyn Jorgensen, an Iowa farmer and head of the American Soybean Association, emphasizes that there are also other and often forgotten victims of past illegal activities in the trading pits of Chicago. "There is fear out in the countryside that the farmers' interests isn't being protected, and something needs to be done quickly to restore confidence in the markets."[6]

Estimating that 90 percent of the big grain elevator companies use the futures market to hedge financial risk and set cash crop prices, Jorgensen points out that if those companies get unfair prices on their trades, farmers might not get the fair price they should when they sell their crops. "If there's a flaw in the system, the farmer is the one who's hurt."[7]

However, despite what appeared to be convincing evidence, the government suffered a major setback in July 1990 when a Chicago jury was able to reach guilty verdicts on only eight of more than 100 criminal counts filed against three Swiss franc Merc futures traders. The jury returned 22 not guilty counts and were deadlocked on 86 counts.[8]

Prior to the jury's findings, 16 of the originally 46 indicted traders from both exchanges had pleaded guilty to fraud and were cooperating with the government's investigation.

What surprised many about the U.S.'s case against the Swiss franc traders was that throughout the seven-week highly-technical trial (where some jurors fell asleep during hours of "mind-numbing" detail) the prosecution failed to produce a single customer to testify that they

477

had been victimized by the alleged illegal activities of the traders. Thus, defense attorneys argued that no customers or brokerage firms had ever complained about those trades that formed the basis for the alleged fraud.[9]

Responding to the controversy surrounding "dual trading," the CFTC staff issued a November, 1989 report that concluded that "dual trading" was not a critical ingredient in maintaining market liquidity.

The amount of "dual trading" does not appear to be higher for low-volume markets, the study noted, and "dual traders" do not provide better execution, nor is their performance in providing market liquidity any better than of exclusive traders.

"Dual traders are not unique super traders, and it seems reasonable that their contribution to the market organization could be substituted for by exclusive traders and brokers," said Steven Manaster, the CFTC's chief economist.[10]

The Commisssion's study also revealed that the vast majority of traders tend to specialize in trading either for themselves or for customers and that only a small number of their trades are dual trades. Although more than 50 percent of all contracts bought and sold during the study period, the CFTC study added, were handled by traders who engage in "dual trading" only 7.4 percent of the trading volume on the exchanges involved dual trades. Therefore, if "dual trading" was banned, Manaster notes, the volume might return to specialists.[11]

Eight of the nation's major future exchanges, including the CBOT and the Merc, immediately attacked the CFTC study. "All of the conclusions of the CFTC study are wrong, misleading or unsupported by the empirical results," one of the exchanges' two reports concluded. Citing work from professors at Duke University and the University of California at Berkeley, the industry report's argue that the CFTC study was based on faulty statistical analysis.[12]

Another and related illegal technique, "trading ahead of the customer," occurs when a broker watching the price of a commodity vary by one or two cents and while waiting for the opportunity to buy low, receives a buy order from a customer.

By exchange rules the broker must handle the customer's order first, but since the commission for filling a customer's order is less than the broker could make on a personal trade, there is always the temptation not to give the customer priority preference.

What made the government attempt to show fraud in the trading pits especially difficult, as pointed out in Chapter 31, was the lack of a seamless paper trail. All records that show exchange time-stamp orders, track prices and how trades compare to the prevailing prices in the pits ultimately depend on the integrity of the member brokers and traders in keeping accurate accounts. Customer challenges to the price withstanding, the various frauds cited above are difficult to prove when order volume is unusually high and prices are rising and falling rapidly.

"It's the old story of garbage in, garbage out," explains one attorney.

> "The entire multimillion-dollar detection systems at the Merc and the CBOT were predicated on the honesty of the trader who provided the computerized system with the information in the first place. Since the trader himself was corrupt, he was, by definition, feeding bogus information into the system, and thus his crimes never showed up."[13]

CHAPTER ONE: Where Have All the Farmers Gone?

1   "Farms bloom again, fears cloud future," by Chuck Raasch and Wendell Cochran, *USA Today*, April 4, 1988.

2   "Federalized Farming," "Review & Outlook," *The Wall Street Journal*, June 7, 1989.

3   Based on figures obtained from the USDA.

4   "As Farms Falter, Rural Homelessness Grows," by Isabel Wilkerson, *The New York Times*, May 2, 1989.

5   "America's Third World," by John McCormick, *Newsweek*, August 8, 1988.

6   "Farmers Rely More on Outside Jobs To Help Balance the Family Budget," Associated Press, *The Wall Street Journal*, May 22, 1989.

7   "Drought stunts growth in income for Iowans," by Jane Norman, *The Des Moines Register*, April 28, 1989

8   "Country life threatened, residents say," by Chuck Raasch and Leslie Werstein, *USA Today*, September 21, 1988.

9   Testimony Before the Democratic Task Force on Agriculture by Jessica Lange, Washington, D.C., May 6, 1985.

10   Testimony Before the Democratic Task Force on Agriculture by Sissy Spacek, Washington, D.C., May 6, 1985.

11   "Growing Up Afraid: Farm Crisis Is Taking Subtle Toll on Children In Distressed Familes," by Wendy L. Wall, *The Wall Street Journal*, November 7, 1985.

12   "The Cost of America's Farm Crisis: For Generations to Come," An Interview with David Ostendorf, *Sojourners*, October, 1986.

13   "As the Heartland Bleeds, Where Is the Church?," "Growing Up Afraid: The Rural Condition Takes Its Toll on Youth," and "Death of a Farm," Papers prepared and written by Joan Blundall.

14   "State of Rural Oklahoma," A Report by Dr. Max E. Glenn, Executive Director, Oklahoma Conference of Churches, September 2, 1986.

15   "Country Blues: Deregulation Raises Prices, Cut Services In Many Rural Areas," by Bill Richards, *The Wall Street Journal*, October 5, 1987.

16   "Finances Sag but Morale Rises as Farmers Band Together," by James R. Dickenson, *The Washington Post*, November 29, 1985.

17   "The Fields of Fear," by Paul Hendrickson, *The Washington Post*, May 30, 1985.

18   "Slain Banker Laid to Rest," by Mary Murray and Jerry Heth, *USA Today*, December 12, 1985.

19   "Coping with stress is extension office's latest crop of advice," by William Ringle, *USA Today*, July 9, 1984.

20   "Protest stops foreclosure of Minnesota dairy farm," *USA Today*, March 19, 1985. "Farm stress: Lightening the load," by Ben Barber and Marjolijn Bijlefeld, *USA Today*, April 4, 1986.

21   "Our Declining Farms," USDA, October, 1983.

22   "Farm Population Lowest Since 1850's," Associated Press, *The New York Times*, July 20, 1988.

23   "Farm Population Drops as Depression Continues," by Keith Schneider, *The New York Times*, August 8, 1986.

24   "U.S. Farm Population Shows Abrupt 7 Percent Decline," United Press International, *The Washington Post*, August 8, 1986.

25   "Farm Population Stable in Size But Lagging in Income, Census Bureau-USDA Reports Shows," U.S. Department of Commerce *News*, January 10, 1986.

26   "The Decline of Black Farming in America," A Report of the U.S. Commission on Civil Rights, February, 1982.

27   "Who's Most Vulnerable to Tough Times in Farming," *Farmline*, USDA, August, 1985.

28   "Number of farmers fell sharply in 1985," *USA Today*, January 10, 1986.

29   "Midwest Hits Bottom For Income," by Spencer Rich, *The Washington Post*, August 6, 1986.

30   "Counties That Depend on Farming," *The Washington Post*, April 18, 1985.

31   "Oil, farm crises hit Okla. sooner," by Julie Morris, *USA Today*, April 10, 1986.

32   *FarmFacts*, Texas Department of Agriculture, March, 1986.

33   "Farmers search for new careers," by Chuck Raasch, *USA Today*, November 1, 1985.

34   "With Farmers' Exodus, Rural Towns Lie Fallow," by Ward Sinclair, *The Washington Post*, March 29, 1985.

35   "Governing the Heartland: Can Rural Communities Survive the Farm Crisis?," A study commissioned by the U.S. Senate Subcommittee on Intergovernmental Relations, Dave Durenberger, Chairman, May 23, 1986.

36   "Farm bill would slash net income, study says," by Don Muhm, *Des Moines Register*, March 27, 1985.

37   "Farm cities thrive while towns suffer," by Chuck Raasch, *USA Today*, January 20, 1986.

38   "It's worse than it has ever been before," by Mark Mayfield and Paul Clancy, *USA Today*, May 16, 1986.

39   "So. Dakotan: 'We're on the skids now'," by Patrick O'Driscoll and Chuck Raasch, *USA Today*, February 22, 1985.

40   "America's Rural Hospitals in Critical Conditions," by Spencer Rich, *The Washington Post*, March 18, 1989.

41   "Washington Warned to Aid Farmers Fast," by Ward Sinclair, *The Washington Post*, January 31, 1985.

42   "Iowa Governor Seeking $91 Million Budget Cut," United Press International, *The New York Times*, September 20, 1985.

43   "'Rural crisis' hasn't stopped yet," by Rae Tyson, *USA Today*, November 4, 1987.

44   "Middle West Journal: Thoughts on Farms from 502," by Andrew H. Malcolm, *The New York Times*, June 30, 1986.

45 *Op. cit.*, Sinclair, March 29, 1985.
46 *Ibid.*
47 "A Chill in Iowa," by Coleman McCarthy, *The Washington Post*, October 13, 1984.
48 *Op. cit.*, Ostendorf, *Sojourners*, October, 1986.
49 "The Changing Structure of Agriculture," *Technology, Public Policy, and the Changing Structure of American Agriculture*, Congress of the United States: Office of Technology Asssessment, Washington, D.C., 1986.
50 "As More Family Farms Fail, Hired Managers Take Charge," by Keith Schneider, *The New York Times*, March 17, 1986.
51 "400 Largest Farms in the United States," *Successful Farming*, January, 1987.
52 *Op. cit.*, Office of Technology Assessment, 1986.
53 "Economic Indicators of the Farm Sector: National Financial Summary, 1985," USDA ERS, November, 1986.
54 "Super Farms: Giants of Agriculture," *Farmline*, USDA, Washington, D.C., February, 1986.
55 "Sen. Melcher Is Smiling Again," by Ward Sinclair, *The Washington Post*, November 2, 1985.
56 "Myths About Farmers From Jesse Helms," by Senators David Pryor and David Boren, *The Washington Post*, November 16, 1985.
57 "Bounty from Uncle Sam," by Janice Castro, *Time Magazine*, August 18, 1986.
58 "Wealthy Farmers Favored," *USA Today*, September 16, 1987.
59 "Loophole Lets Farmers Glean Extra Subsidies," by Ward Sinclair, *The Washington Post*, June 24, 2986.
60 *Ibid.*
61 "Schoolchildren Reap $7000 Farm Subsidy," by Ward Sinclair, *The Washington Post*, October 23, 1985.
62 "U.S. Gives Millions to 10 Farms," by Keith Schneider, *The New York Times*, June 9, 1987.
63 "Subsidy Program Turns Into Bonanza For Big Farmers," by Warren T. Brookes, *San Francisco Chronicle*, October 21, 1986 and "The $50,000 payment limit that isn't," by Marcia Zarley Taylor, *Farm Journal*, August, 1986.
64 *Op. cit.*, Castro, *Time Magazine*, August 18, 1986.
65 "Cotton Interests Received $728 Million in Subsidies," by Ward Sinclair, *The Washington Post*, April 16, 1987.
66 "Lid on Farm Payments Rejected in 12-11 Vote," by Ward Sinclair, *The Washington Post*, September 12, 1986.
67 "The 1985 Farm Bill: Complications stole the show," by Jake Henshaw, *USA Today*, December 19, 1985.
68 "Subsidy Reliance Grows Along With the Crops," by Ward Sinclair, *The Washington Post*, October 23, 1985.
69 "Who Gets Those Farm Program Payments," *Farmline*, USDA, December/January, 1987.
70 "Reagan's grasp of farm economics 'not profound'," by Lauren Soth, *The Des Moines Register*, October 25, 1981.
71 "The Farms Can't Wait," by Sen. Robert Dole (Rep.-Kansas), *The Washington Post*, March 25, 1985.
72 "Farmers' Subsidies Said to Vary Widely Among Crops, Areas," by Ward Sinclair, *The Washington Post*, September 5, 1984.
73 *Farm Payments: Farm Reorganizations and Their Impact on USDA Program Costs*, Briefing Report to Congressional Requesters, U.S. General Accounting Office, GAO/RCED-87- 120BR, April, 1987
74 As quoted in "Green Thumbs: The PIK and Roll and Other Scams From the Farm Belt," by Jeffrey L. Pasley, *The Washington Monthly*, September, 1987.
75 "Farm Payment Abuses May Exceed $2 Billion," by Ward Sinclair, *The Washington Post*, April 2, 1987.
76 "'Farmers' in the Till," by Jack Anderson and Dale Van Atta, *The Washington Post*, October 25, 1987.
77 *Ibid.*
78 "Limits on Subsidies to Big Farms Go Awry, Sending Costs Climbing," by William Robbins, *The New York Times*, June 15, 1987.
79 "Administration Would Tighten Rules for Receiving Farm Subsidies," by Ward Sinclair, *The Washington Post*, March 15, 1987.
80 "Foreigners Get U.S. Farm Subsidies," by Ward Sinclair, *The Washington Post*, April 25, 1987.
81 "King-Size Farm Subsidy for European Prince," by Andrew Mangan, Associated Press, *The Washington Post*, December 10, 1986.
82 "U.S. to Seize Subsidies Due Failing Farmers," by Don Kendall, Associated Press, *The Washington Post*, April 13, 1987.
83 "Farm Programs: An Overview of Price and Income Support, and Storage Programs," Briefing Report to the Hon. Bill Alexander, House of Representatives, U.S. GAO, February, 1988, GAO/RCED-88-84BR
84 "Quotelines: Frank J. Stajcar, farmer, Unionville, Iowa," *USA Today*, July 8, 1986.

CHAPTER TWO: Playing A "Giant Game of Asset Rearrangement"

1   "This Week With David Brinkley," ABC-TV, October 30, 1988.

2   "Kohlberg, Kravis Also Seeks Kroger," by Robert J. Cole, *The New York Times*, September 21, 1988.

3   "Kohlberg, Kravis Cuts Kroger Stake," Associated Press, *The New York Times*, May 5, 1989.

4   "Grand Met Chairman Predicts Pillsbury Will Mount Defensive Recapitalization," by Joann S. Lubin, *The Wall Street Journal*, October 25, 1988.

5   "Burger King Role in Pillsbury Fight," by Eric N. Berg, *The New York Times*, October 27, 1988.

6   "Maxwell Hungers to Widen Philip Morris's Brands . . . ," by Andrea Rothman, *The Wall Street Journal*, October 19, 1988.

7   "Meanwhile, back at the IRS . . . ," by Jonathan Greenberg, *Mother Jones*, May, 1988.

8   "The Hafts' Hunger," by Mary McGrory, *The Washington Post*, December 31, 1987.

9   "Safeway Union Demands a Voice," by Caroline E. Mayer, *The Washington Post*, August 16, 1986 and "Safeway Says It Will Not Bargain," by Caroline E. Mayer, *The Washington Post*, August 19, 1986.

10   "Sold Short," by Jonathan Greenberg, *Mother Jones*, March, 1988 and "Siege At Safeway," by Skip Hollandsworth, *American Way*, March 1, 1988.

11   "What $20 Billion Will Buy Today," by Paul Farhi, *The Washington Post*, October 26, 1988.

12   *Ibid.*

13   "RJR or 1,177,629 Chryslers?, *USA Today*, October 25, 1988.

14   "Deal stocks put Wall Street in a frenzy," by Mark Memmott, *USA Today*, October 25, 1988.

15   "Buyout Specialist Bids $20.3 Billion For RJR Nabisco," by James Sterngold, *The New York Times*, October 25, 1988.

16   *Ibid.*

17   *Ibid.*

18   "Pension Funds Provide Much of Cash in RJR Nabisco Offer," by Anise C. Wallace, *The New York Times*, October 31, 1988.

19   *Ibid.*

20   "What Makes Giant Corporate Buyouts Alarming," Letters-to-the- Editor, by Jean Mayer, *The New York Times*, November 7, 1988.

21   "Supermarket Buy-Out Trend Is Assessed," by James P. Miller, *The Wall Street Journal*, May 24, 1988.

22   "Bankers Defend Buyout Loans but Investors Fret," by Sarah Bartlett, *The New York Times*, October 28, 1988.

23   *Ibid.*

24   *Ibid.*

25   "LBO frenzy may be bubble waiting to burst," by Daniel Kaflec, *USA Today*, October 21, 1988.

26   "Borrowing Binge: Takeover Trend Helps Push Corporate Debt And Defaults Upward," by Lindley H. Clarke, Jr. and Alfred L. Malabre, Jr., *The Wall Street Journal*, March 15, 1988.

27   *Ibid.*

28   "Learning To Live With Leverage," by Christopher Farrell, *Business Week*, November 7, 1988.

29   "The Events That Changed The World of Wall Street," by James Sterngold, *The New York Times*, October 26, 1987.

30   *Ibid.*

31   "The Debt Binge," by Mark N. Varmos and Scott Ticer, *Business Week*, November 7, 1988.

32   "Takeover Boom Is Expected to Benefit Usual Small Circle of Wealthy Law Firms," by Laurie P. Cohen, *The Wall Street Journal*, October 25, 1988.

33   *Ibid.*

34   "A Corporate Milestone: RJR Nabisco Is Biggest Company To Choose Reliance on Private Debt, Not Public Stock," by Sarah Bartlett, *The New York Times*, October 26, 1988.

35   "Top of the News: Are RJR and Philip Morris Putting Stockholders First," Commentary by Judith N. Dobrzynski, *Business Week*, November 7, 1988.

36   "Debating the Nature of U.S. Corporations," by Peter Behr, *The Washington Post*, January 11, 1987.

37   "Takeovers Return to the Old Mode," by Leslie Wayne, *The New York Times*, January 4, 1988; *Op. cit.*, Greenberg, *Mother Jones*, March, 1988, and "Merger wave might drown our economy," by Daniel Kadlec, *USA Today*, March 10, 1988.

38   *Ibid.*

39   Language of the Clayton Act, passed in 1914.

40   "Quotelines," *USA Today.*, June 6, 1985 and "Deal Makers Casting In On Takeover Mania," by Caroline E. Mayer, *The Washington Post*, August 10, 1986.

41   "Fuel for the flames," by Richard Phalon, *Forbes*, November 18, 1985.

42   "When Food Firms Merge, Effects Reach Into Aisles of Supermarkets," by Trish Hall, *The Wall Street Journal*, June 13, 1985.

43   "Heard on the Street: Philip Morris Track Record In Acqusitions Draw Flak," by Randall Smith and Linda

Sadler, *The Wall Street Journal*, October 20, 1988.

44   *Ibid.*

45   "Money Talks: Raiders are wrong," *San Francisco Sunday Examiner*, December 28, 1986.

46   *Op. cit.*, Hall, *The Wall Street Journal*, June 13, 1985.

47   "Philip Morris Says It Won't Impose Strict Policy on Ads if It Wins Kraft," by Joanne Lipman, *The Wall Street Journal*, October 20, 1988.

48   "The Brands With Billion-Dollar Names," by Richard W. Stevenson, *The New York Times*, October 28, 1988.

49   "Market Place: Food Stocks Are Favored," by H.J. Maidenberg, *The New York Times*, December 20, 1986. 50 *Ibid.*

51   *Ibid.*

52   "Space War: Supermarkets Demand Food Firms' Payments Just to Get on the Shelf," by Richard Gibson, *Wall Street Journal*, November 7, 1988.

53   "Kraft Bid Is Just Another Bite in Food-Firm Feeding Frenzy," by Warren Brown, *The Washington Post*, October 19, 1988.

54   *Op. cit.*, Gibson, *The Wall Street Journal*, November 7, 1988.

55   "Philip Morris to Buy General Foods," by David A. Vise, *The Washington Post*, September 28, 1985.

56   "Foodmakers," *USA Today*, November 5, 1987.

57   "As mergers multiply, so do questions," by Jay McCormick, Mark Memmott and Susan Antilla, *USA Today*, October 25, 1988.

58   *Ibid.*

59   "Costly Eating: As Food Prices Surge, Drought is Blamed, But Profits Are Rising," by Robert Johnson and Scott Kilman, *Wall Street Journal*, August 23, 1988.

60   *Ibid.*

61   *Ibid.*

62   "Takeover Mania Could Change Food Products," by Malcolm Gladwell, *The Washington Post*, October 21, 1988.

63   *Ibid.*

64   "Takeover Spree Starts A Speculative Frenzy," by Anise C. Wallace, *The New York Times*, October 25, 1988.

65   *Ibid.*

66   "Brand News: A Philip Morris Merger With Kraft May Limit Product Innovation," by Alix M. Freedman and Richard Gibson, *The Wall Street Journal*, October 20, 1988.

67   *Op. cit.*, Brown, *The Washington Post*, October 19, 1988.

68   "Kraft, Phlip Morris deal a complete meal," by James R. Healey, *USA Today*, October 31, 1988.

69   *Op. cit.*, Brown, *The Washington Post*, October 19, 1988.

CHAPTER THREE: "A Rural Bloodletting"

1   "Farmers get help adapting to new jobs," by Richard Benedetto and Rod Gramer, *USA Today*, May 31, 1985.
2   "Farming pressured from outside," by Hembree Brandon, *California-Arizona Farm Press*, May 25, 1985.
3   "The Biggest Enemy Is Mounting Debt," By Harold F. Breimyer, *The New York Times*, December 30, 1984.
4   "Farm debt staggering, Moore tells members of Nelson County FU," and "NFU president suggests need for new food distribution policy," *North Dakota Union Farmer*, April 26, 1984.
5   "One Point interest increase means $2 billion to farmers," *North Dakota Union Farmer*, May 24, 1984.
6   "Many Quit Farming as Credit Crisis Dims Hopes," by Ward Sinclair, *The Washington Post*, June 3, 1986.
7   "The Outlook: Why the Farm Crisis Is Likely to Worsen," By Henry F. Myers, *The Wall Street Journal*, August 26, 1985.
8   *Ibid.*
9   "Farm Values in Virginia Remaining Stable," Associated Press, *The Washington Post*, August 8, 1985.
10   "Farm Debts' Meanest Squeeze Felt in the Middle," by Ward Sinclair, *The Washington Post*, March 26, 1985.
11   "Farm Bailout Laid to Hill 'Blackmail'," by Ward Sinclair and Helen Dewar, *The Washington Post*, February 6, 1985.
12   "Farmer on the Fed," by Alan Guebert, *Top Producer*, April, 1986.
13   *Op. cit.*, Breimyer, *The New York Times*, December 30, 1984.
14   *Op. cit.*, Brandon, *California-Arizona Farm Press*, May 25, 1985.
15   "The Changing Structure of Agriculture," *Technology, Public Policy, and the Changing Structure of American Agriculture*, Congress of the United States: Office of Technology Asssessment, Washington, D.C., 1986.
16   Source: FmHA, *USA Today*, December 12, 1988.
17   "Iowa Farm Lender's Condition Worsens," *The Washington Post*, December 6, 1985.
18   "Iowa Firm Puts 17 Banks Up for Sale," *The Washington Post*, June 24, 1986.
19   "7.6% of Largest U.S. Banks In Trouble, FDIC Reports," by Kathleen Day, *The Washington Post*, September 13, 1986.
20   "Debt Crisis Tied to 800,000 Lost Jobs," by James L. Rowe, Jr., *The Washington Post*, June 18, 1985.
21   "7 Banks Fail in a Day, Post-Depression Record," by James L. Rowe, Jr., *The Washington Post*, June 1, 1985.
22   "Nebraska Closes Three More Banks," *The Washington Post*, December 20, 1985.
23   "200 Banks Facing Failure This Year," by John M. Berry, *The Washington Post*, May 22, 1987.
24   *Ibid*, and FDIC, "Banks Expected to Have Another Turbulent Year," by Kathleen Day, *The Washington Post*, January 24, 1988.
25   "Farm banks reaping a turnaround," by Dennis Cauchon, *USA Today*, March 2, 1989.
26   "Washington Watch: Bank Failure Costs Rising," by Nathaniel C. Nash, *The New York Times*, January 12, 1987.
27   "Senators Push Bill To Aid Banks Hurt By Bad Farm Loans," by Kathleen Day, *The Washington Post*, March 7, 1986.
28   "The Great Farm-Belt Bank Crisis," by Thomas H. Olson and Weldon Barton, *The Washington Post*, December 30, 1984.
29   "Banks Give Farmers Loans and Pray for Bailout," by Charles F. McCoy and Marj Charlier, *The Wall Street Journal*, June 6, 1985.
30   "Farmers owe FmHA billions," by Mark Rohner and Dennis Camire, *USA Today*, December 12, 1983.
31   "The Decline of Black Farming in America," A Report of the U.S. Commission on Civil Rights, February, 1982.
32   "Penalty Decision Pending at FmHA," by Ward Sinclair, *The Washington Post*, November 2, 1984.
33   "FmHA Wavers on Use of Collection Agency," From News Services, *The Washington Post*, September 5, 1986.
34   "Senators Knock FmHA All Over the Ballpark," by Ward Sinclair, *The Washington Post*.
35   "Wisconsin kitchen band stops forced farm sale," by Jeanne Rohl, *North American Farmer*, February 28, 1986.
36   "FmHA Foreclosures Affected: Class-Action Status Granted to Distressed Farmers," by Ward Sinclair, *The Washington Post*, November 1, 1983.
37   "Coleman v. Block plantiffs: 'Plug loopholes - FmHA 'starves out' farmers," *North American Farmer*, November 18, 1985.
38   "U.S. to Send Farmers Foreclosure Warnings," by Keith B. Richburg, *The Washington Post*, January 2, 1986.
39   "Debt Notices Go To 65,000 Farmers," by Keith Schneider, *The New York Times*, February 13, 1986.
40   "Tightening at FmHA Hits Mississippi Hard," by Ward Sinclair, *The Washington Post*, June 3, 1986.
41   *Op. cit.*, Cauchon, *USA Today*, March 2, 1989.
42   "Changing Fields: More Young Farmers Rent Land They Till Often to Avoid Debt," by Marj Charlier, *The Wall Street Journal*, February 3, 1987.
43   "The Foreclosure Flood," by Kristin Downey, *The Washington Post*, March 19, 1989.
44   "Agency Chief 'Proud' of Performance: USDA Aides Blasted on Farm Loan Policy," by Ward Sinclair, *The Washington Post*, February 3, 1984.
45   "No Relief For Farm Borrowers," by Ward Sinclair, *The Washington Post*, September 18, 1986.
46   "Sowing the seeds of discontent," *USA Today*, March 27, 1986 and "150 Farmers Seek Loan Aide's Ouster,"

by William Robbins, *The New York Times*, March 18, 1986.

47 "The Status of the Farmers Home Administration's Farm Loan Portfolio and Farm Loan-Making Criteria and Policies," Statement of Brian P. Crowley, Senior Associate Director, Resources, Community, and Economic Development Division, U.S. General Accounting Office, Before the Committee on Agriculture, Nutrition, and Forestry, United States Senate, March 11, 1987.

48 "U.S. Writeoff of $2 Billion in Farm Loans," by Ward Sinclair, *The Washington Post*, January 9, 1987.

49 "Eased farm loan payments to add to fed agency's debt," by Mark Rohner, *USA Today*, September 20, 1984.

50 *Op. cit.*, Sinclair, *The Washington Post*, January 9, 1987.

51 "Farm Loan Shrinkage Denounced," by Ward Sinclair, *The Washington Post*, March 12, 1987.

52 "FmHA Revising New Loan Rules After Complaints From Lawmakers," by Ward Sinclair, *The Washington Post*, June 2, 1987.

53 "Judge Orders FmHA to Halt Foreclosures," by Ward Sinclair, *The Washington Post*, June 6, 1987.

54 "U.S. Doubles Write-Off Total Farm Loans," by Bruce Ingersoll, *The Wall Street Journal*, April 14, 1988.

55 *Ibid.*

56 "American Agriculture: Are Hard Times Here To Stay," by Stephen Kindel and Laura Saunders, *Forbes*, August 30, 1982.

57 "Against Farm Credit System: Populist Rebellion," by James Ridgeway, *The Texas Observer*, April 19, 1985.

58 "Farm Credit Bonds, Notes Are Spread Among Investors," by Charles F. McCoy, *The Wall Street Journal*, September 4, 1985.

59 "Interview: Vince Rossiter - Parity and the Matter of Logic," *Acres U.S.A.*, March, 1987.

60 "Farm Lender Posts Record Loss," by Ward Sinclair, *The Washington Post*, February 19, 1985.

61 "GAO Sees Loss Of $2.9 Billion At Farm Credit," by Charles F. McCoy, *The Wall Street Journal*, September 18, 1986.

62 "Farm Credit System Struggles to Reorganize," by Philip J. Garcia, United Press International, *The Washington Post*, August 30, 1987.

63 *Op. cit.*, Sinclair, *The Washington Post*, February 19, 1986.

64 "Farm Credit System Reports Loss of $1.91 Billion in 1986," United Press International, *The Washington Post*, February 19, 1987.

65 "Out of Options: Farm Credit System, Buried in Bad Loans, Seeks Big U.S. Bailout," by Charles F. McCoy, *The Wall Street Journal*, September 4, 1985.

66 "Farm Agency Estimates Loss," Reuters, *The New York Times*, September 17, 1985.

67 *Op. cit.*, McCoy, *The Wall Street Journal*, September 4, 1985.

68 *Ibid.*

69 "Reagan's Farm Debt Fraud," by Merle Hansen, *North American Farmer*, October 3, 1984.

70 "High Anxiety in Congress: Farm Programs, Past, Present and Future," by John M. Russonello, *Food Monitor*, No. 35.

71 "Farm Lender Still Teetering Despite Assistance Pledge," by John M. Berry, *The Washington Post*, March 1, 1987.

72 *Op. cit.*, Ridgeway, *The Texas Observer*, April 19, 1985.

73 *Op. cit.*, McCoy, *The Wall Street Journal*, September 4, 1985.

74 *Op. cit.*, Ridgeway, *The Texas Observer*, April 19, 1985.

75 "Farm Credit Unit Has Loss," Associated Press, *The New York Times*, February 24, 1986, "Omaha Farm District Loses $509 Million," *The Washington Post*, February 22, 1986, and *Ibid.*, McCoy, *The Wall Street Journal*, September 4, 1985.

76 "A Farm Family Fights Back," by William Mueller, *Progressive*, March, 1986.

77 *Op. cit.*, Ridgeway, *The Texas Observer*, April 19, 1985.

78 "Farm Credit System Could Collapse Unless It Reorganizes, Study Finds," by Charles F. McCoy, *The Wall Street Journal*, July 22, 1985.

79 "Rescue Planned For Farm Bank By Loan Agency," by Charles F. McCoy, *The Wall Street Journal*, July 15, 1985.

80 "Two Farm Credit System District Banks Attack Parts of Bailout Plan in Lawsuit," by Charles F. McCoy, *The Wall Street Journal*, September 12, 1986.

81 *Ibid.*

82 *Op. cit.*, UPI, *The Washington Post*, February 19, 1987.

83 *Ibid.*

84 *Op. cit.*, McCoy, *The Wall Street Journal*, September 18, 1986.

85 "Farm Credit System Ready to Paper Over Its Red Ink," by John M. Berry, *The Washington Post*, October 12, 1986.

86 "Farm Credit Action Vowed," by Mike Robinson, Associated Press, *The Washington Post*, February 27, 1987 and "Administration Backs $5 Billion Farm Credit," by Ward Sinclair, *The Washington Post*, June 10, 1987.

87 "Bankers Back Farm Credit System Bailout," by Ward Sinclair, *The Washington Post*, May 14, 1987.

88 "Rescue Operation: Farm Credit System Seems Certain to Win Huge Federal Bailout," by Art Pine, *The Wall*

Street Journal, July 3, 1987.

89   "GAO to Urge Congress to Take Control Of the Struggling Farm Credit System," by Albert R. Karr, *The Wall Street Journal*, April 7, 1987.

90   "Farm Credit System: Back From the Brink," by John M. Berry, *The Washington Post*, June 18, 1989.

91   "Farmers Plan for a Bumper Crop," by Dennis Blank, *The New York Times*, March 6, 1989.

92   "Farm Lender's $36 Billion Losses May Require U.S. Aid, Audit Says," by Nathaniel C. Nash, *The New York Times*, December 21, 1988.

93   *Ibid.*

94   "FCB of Omaha reports 1988 farmland sales," *Ag Week*, December 12, 1988.

95   "Put More Families on Farms," by Ward Sinclair, *The Washington Post*, August 2, 1987.

96   *Ibid.*

CHAPTER FOUR: Sweet Land of Opportunity

1   *1990 Fact Book of Agriculture*, Office of Public Affairs, USDA, Misc. Publication Number 1063, Table 14.
2   "The U.S. Farm Sector in the Mid-1980's," by Donn A. Reimund, Nora L. Brooks, and Paul D. Velde, USDA Economic Research Service, Agricultural Economic Report No. 548.
3   "Corporate Giant Looks Like Grim Reaper to Farmer," by Nick Kotz, *The Sacramento Bee*, November 6, 1971.
4   "Roundup: Foreign Ownership Up," *The Washington Post*, April 8, 1988.
5   "Japan Digs Into American Citrus Groves," by Josh Goldstein, Journal of Commerce, *The Washington Post*, July 20, 1989.
6   "U.S. Farm Land Purchases Spur Some Hostility," by William Celis III, *The Wall Street Journal*, May 19, 1989.
7   "Roll Along Columbia: Corporate Agribusiness in the Mid- Columbia Basin," by A.V. Krebs, Agribusiness Accountability Publications, 1979.
8   "The 1988 Forbes 400," *Forbes*, October 24, 1988.
9   Material compiled from "Foreign Landowners: America Meet Your Missing Neighbor," A Series by Rick Atkinson, Marilyn Cummins, and David Chartrand, *Kansas City Times*, August 28-31, 1979; "Foreign Investors Owners Of Farmland In Area," by Bryce Dustman, *Kirksville Express & News* (Missouri), February 10, 1978; Missouri Secretary of State's Office, and Clerk of the Court, Sullivan County, Missouri.
10   "Erosion in the Vineyard," by Rev. Maurice J. Dingman, *Soujourners*, October, 1986.
11   "Sprouting Leases: Tenant Farming Gains Troubling Proponents of Family Ownership, by Meg Cox, *The Wall Street Journal*, October 6, 1981.
12   "As More Family Farms Fail, Hired Managers Take Charge," by Keith Schneider, *The New York Times*, March 17, 1986.
13   "Doane: Refocusing on intensive farm management," by Mary Thompson, *AgriFinance*, January, 1988.
14   *Ibid.*
15   *Ibid.*
16   "Agricultural Finance: Situation and Outlook Report," USDA Economic Research Service, AFO-27, March 1987.
17   "The Continuing Crisis In Rural America: Fact vs. Fiction," A Research Report Prepared by Prairiefire Rural Action Inc., Des Moines, Iowa, May, 1987.
18   *Op. cit.*, Schneider, *The New York Times*, March 17, 1986.
19   *Op. cit.*, Cox, *The Wall Street Journal*, October 6, 1981.
20   "Insurance Firms Bail Out, Family Farm Advocates Propose Alternatives," by Ken Meter, *Catholic Rural Life*, February, 1988.
21   "Changing Fields: More Young Farmers Rent Land They Till Often to Avoid Debt," by Marj Charlier, *The Wall Street Journal*, February 3, 1987.
22   *Ibid.*
23   *Ibid.*
24   *Ibid.*
25   *Ibid.*
26   *Ibid.*
27   "What Five Families Did After Losing the Farm," by Andrew H. Malcolm, *The New York Times*, February 4, 1987.
28   "Georgia Farmer Valued Land More Than Life," by Dudley Clendinen, *The New York Times*, February 10, 1986.
29   "The Decline of Black Farming In America," A Report of the U.S. Commission on Civil Rights, February, 1982.
30   "The other crisis in rural America: Black land loss," by Ralph Paige, *North American Farmer*, February 28, 1986.
31   "Natural Resources and Rural Poverty: An Overview," by Irma T. Elo and Calvin Beale, National Center for Food and Agricultural Policy, Resources for the Future, Inc., Washington, D.C.
32   *Op. cit.*, Paige, *North American Farmer*, February 28, 1986.
33   "Black Farmers A Dying Minority," by Ward Sinclair, *The Washington Post*, February 18, 1986.
34   *Agricultural Resources: Agricultural Land - Values and Markets*, USDA Economic Research Service, AR-2, June, 1986.
35   *Op. cit.*, Prairiefire Rural Action Inc., Des Moines, Iowa, May, 1987.
36   "Value of Farm Land Continues to Fall," Associated Press, *The Washington Post*, June 17, 1986.
37   "Further decline expected: Land values plummet," *North American Farmer*, January 31, 1986.
38   "Rise in U.S. Farmland Values Likely To Continue," USDA News Release, June 21, 1989
39   *Op. cit.*, *North American Farmer*, January 31, 1986.
40   *Ibid.*
41   "Trillion-dollar national debt equals worth of U.S. agriculture: 'shocking!'," by Don Muhm, *The Des Moines Register*, October 25, 1981.
42   "It's not all doom and gloom," by Chuck Raasch, *USA Today*,

43   "Are Farmers At Fault," by Peter Behr, *The Washington Post*,
44   "Conn.: Investor sees future in farms," *USA Today*, May 24, 1985.
45   "Farmers Seek Investors in Bid to Stay on Land," by Marj Charlier, *The Wall Street Journal*, June 7, 1985.
46   Source: U.S. Department of Agriculture.
47   "Sprouting Leases: Tenant Farming Gains, Troubling Proponents of Family Ownership," by Meg Cox, *The Wall Street Journal*, October 6, 1981.
48   "Agricultural Management Is Big Business In State," by Bob Shallit, January 22, 1984.
49   "The Biggest Enemy Is Mounting Debt," by Harold Briemyer, *The New York Times*, December 30, 1984.
50   "National Agricultural Lands Study," Executive Summary of Final Report, National Agricultural Lands Study, Robert J. Gray, Executive Director, 1981.
51   "Family Farmers Fear Urban Inroads," by Jesus Rangel, *The New York Times*, June 22, 1988.
52   "Farms in the Future? Delaware Must Decide," by Janet Brooks, *The New York Times*, February 19, 1989.
53   "New York Loses 10% of Its Farms in Five Years," by Harold Faber, *The New York Times*, May 21, 1989.
54   Source: USDA, *USA Today*, June 22, 1988.
55   "Farming on the Fringe," *Farmland Notes*, NASDA Research Foundation Farmland Project, Washington, D.C., July, 1986.
56   "Protecting US cropland from urban sprawl," by Jonathan Harsch, *The Christian Science Monitor*, June 9, 1980.
57   *Op. cit.*, National Agricultural Lands Study, 1981.
58   "Texas Loses Farm Land," *American Agricultural Movement Reporter*, December 7, 1984.
59   "Farms' Future on Pennsylvania Ballot," by Associated Press, *The New York Times*, November 1, 1987 and "Election 87: State and Local Races," *USA Today*, November 5, 1987.
60   "In Bucolic Sonoma County, Debate Rages on Preserving Farm Land," by Ward Sinclair, *The Washington Post*, May 14, 1988.
61   *Ibid.*
62   *Op. cit.*, National Agricultural Lands Study, 1981.
63   "The Pastoral Paradox," by Paul Dunphy, *Harrowsmith*, May-June, 1988.
64   *Op. cit.*, National Agricultural Lands Study, 1981.
65   *Op. cit.*, Dunphy, *Harrowsmith*, May-June, 1988.
66   *The Washington Post*, October 6, 1985.
67   "Greed Acres: When the Rich Go Rural," by Jonathan Yardley, *The Washington Post*, April 27, 1987.
68   *Op. cit.*, National Agricultural Lands Study, 1981.
69   "Soil Erosion Threatens U.S. Farms' Output," by Ann Crittenden, *The New York Times*, October 26, 1980.
70   *Farmline*, USDA, August, 1985.
71   "American Journal: Iowa Soil Program Eroding," by Ward Sinclair, *The Washington Post*, February 11, 1985.
72   "The Other Farm Crisis," by James Risser, *Sierra*, May/June, 1985.
73   "Soil Erosion Control on Owner-Operated and Renter Cropland," by David E. Ervin, JSWC, 37:5, 1982.
74   "There's more to John Hancock than life insurance," *North American Farmer*, January 31, 1985.
75   "Let's Protect Our Farm Land," Letters-to-the Editor, Robert Grey, *The Washington Post*, August 31, 1988.
76   *Op. cit.*, Crittenden, *The New York Times*, October 26, 1980.
77   *Op. cit.*, Risser, *Sierra*, May/June, 1985.
78   *Ibid.*
79   "Kansas," *USA Today*, October 9, 1985.
80   "Plains Erosion From the Wind Is Second Worst," by Bruce Ingersoll, *The Wall Street Journal*, June 20, 1989.
81   "Extensive Erosion in Great Plains Tied to Dust Storm Is At Worst Level Since '55," by Bruce Ingersoll, *The Wall Street Journal*, June 27, 1988.
82   *Ibid.*
83   *Op. cit.*, Risser, *Sierra*, May/June, 1985.
84   *Op. cit.*, Crittenden, *The New York Times*, October 26, 1980.
85   *Op. cit.*, Risser, *Sierra*, May/June, 1985.
86   "Erosion Is Called Small Threat to Crop Yields," by Keith Schneider, *The New York Times*, May 16, 1986.
87   *Ibid.*
88   *Ibid.*
89   "Erosion costs USA $6B a year," by Paul Schweizer, *USA Today*, May 7, 1985.
90   "Farmland Conservation: A Major Breakthrough," by Robert Gray, *Food Monitor*, No. 35.
91   "Soil Conservation Plan Stirs a Dust-Up on Hill," by Ward Sinclair, *The Washington Post*, March 20, 1986 and "Secretary Whitten," Editorial, *The Washington Post*, March 24, 1986.
92   "USA Snapshots: Conserving the land," *USA Today*, September 29, 1987.
93   "Conservation Plan Falls Short of Goals," by Ward Sinclair, *The Washington Post*, June 10, 1986.
94   "The Social, Economic, and Environmental Impacts of Agricultural Exports," Testimony of Jack Doyle, Washington Representative, Environmental Policy Center, Before the Department Operations, Research and Foreign Agriculture Subcommittee of the House Agriculture Committee, Washington, D.C., July 8, 1981.

95   "Domestic Food Security and Increasing Competition for Water," by E. Phillip LeVeen, *Food Security in the United States*, Westview Press, Boulder, Colorado: 1984.

96   "Conflicting Laws Sow Crisis," by Ward Sinclair, *The Washington Post*, March 25, 1985.

97   *Ibid.*

98   *Op. cit.*, Doyle, Before the Department Operations, Research and Foreign Agriculture Subcommittee of the House Agriculture Committee, Washington, D.C., July 8, 1981.

99   "Family Farming's Finest Hour," by Marty Strange, Dinner Address, Wisconsin Rural Development Center, Inc., Madison, Wisconsin, March 8, 1985.

100   *Op. cit.*, Sinclair, *The Washington Post*, March 25, 1985.

101   "Nebraska," *USA Today*, January 31, 1986.

102   "Irrigation Without Waste," by Kevin P. Shea, *Environment*, July/August, 1975.

103   "Energy and Irrigation," by John Hostetler and Gordon Sloggett, *Inputs: Outlook and Situation Report*, USDA Economic Research Service, IOS-8, August, 1985.

104   *Op. cit.*, Sinclair, *The Washington Post*, March 25, 1985.

CHAPTER FIVE: Trapped on the Technological Treadmill

1   "The Silos That Don't Hold Wheat," by Ellen Goodman, *The Washington Post*, April 26, 1983.
2   "Nuclear Weapons Locations in the United States," *The Defense Monitor*, Published by the Center for Defense Information, 303 Capital Gallery West, 600 Maryland Ave. S.W., Washington, D.C. 20024, Vol. X, No. 8.
3   "The Bomb Lives," by E. L. Doctorow, *Playboy*, March, 1974.
4   *Ibid.*
5   *Ibid.*
6   *Op. cit.*, Goodman, *The Washington Post*, April 26, 1983.
7   *Op. cit.*, Doctorow, *Playboy*, March, 1974.
8   "Technology," by Sally Hacker, Sociology Dept., Oregon State College, *the second wave*, Spring/Summer, 1977.
9   "Technology: The Treadmill of Agriculture," and "The Treadmill of Technology Changes the Shape of Agriculture," by Eric Van Chantfort, *Farmline*, USDA Economic Research Service, June, 1985.
10 *Ibid.*
11 "Getting Control of the Farm," by Marty Strange, *The Progressive*, September, 1988.
12 *Op. cit.*, Chantfort, *Farmline*, USDA Economic Research Service, June, 1985.
13 *Ibid.*
14 "The Big Farm," by Michael Perelman and Kevin P. Shea, *Environment*, December, 1972;
15 "Sustainable Food Systems - The Potential of Biological Agriculture," by Gil Friend, Plenary Address to Annual Conference, Agricultural Institute of Canada, St. Catherine, Ontario, August 10, 1981.
16 "Parity - That Word Again," by Harold Breimyer, *Economic & Marketing Information for Missouri Agriculture*, Cooperative Extension Service, University of Missouri, February, 1978.
17 "Is farm efficiency lagging," by Lauren Soth, *The Des Moines Register*, September 22, 1980.
18 "Agricultural Report," Tenneco Inc., Houston, Texas, November, 1976.
19 "Economies of Size in Farming," by J. Patrick Madden, Agriculture Economic Report No. 107, February, 1967.
20 "Economies of Size in U.S. Field Crop Farming," USDA Economics and Statistics Service, July, 1981.
21 *Genewatch*, November/December, 1985.
22 "Emerging Technologies, Public Policy, and Various Size Crop Farms," *Technology, Public Policy, and the Changing Structure of American Agriculture*, Congress of the United States: Office of Technology Asssessment, Washington, D.C., 1986.
23 "Table 18 — Components of the marketing bill for domestically produced farm foods," *Food Cost Review, 1985*, USDA Economic Research Service, Agricultural Economic Report No. 559, July, 1986.
24 "Table 27b - Farm Income Statistics," *Agricultural Outlook*, USDA Economic Research Service, March, 1987.
25 "Table 5 - Indexes of retail price, farm value, and farm-to- retail price spread for a market basket of farm foods, and farm value as a share of retail price," *Food Cost Review, 1985*, USDA Economic Research Service, Agricultural Economic Report No. 559, July, 1986 and "Market basket of foods produced on U.S. farms," *Food Costs ... From Farm to Retail*, USDA Economic Research Service, March, 1987.
26 "Assets: The *Forbes* 500s," *Forbes*, April 27, 1987.
27 "*American Banker* Annual Survey of the Top Banks in Agricultural Lending," *American Banker*, November 14, 1986.
28 "Economics: How the family farm can harvest millions," *Business Week*, July 4, 1977.
29 "Big-city lenders' move to farm credit markets," by Don Muhm, *The Des Moines Register*, August 12, 1982.
30 "Big Dutch Bank Helps Increase Farm-Belt Loans," by James L. Rowe, Jr., *The Washington Post*, November 25, 1984.
31 "Farmers in Midwest to get new funding through contact with Netherlands bank," by James Gutman, *Milwaukee Sentential*, September 10, 1982.
32 "Losing Control," Section One, *Community Seed Bank Resource Kit*, Prepared by the International Genetic Resources Programme (IGRP), Published by Rural Advancement Fund International.
33 "Reaping What We Sow: Seeds and the Crisis in Agriculture," by Cary Fowler, *Graham Center Seed Director*, Published by the Rural Advancement Fund, 1979.
34 "The Law of the Seed: Another Development and Plant Genetic Resources," by Pat Roy Mooney, *Development Dialogue*, Published by the Dag Hammarskjold Foundation, Uppsula, Sweden, 1983: 1-2.
35 Plant Variety Protection Office Official Journal, Vol. 8., Index.
36 "Techtalk: Monsanto to plant seeds that secrete pest killer," *USA Today*, July 1, 1985.
37 "Firms create new breed of farming," by Chuck Raasch, *USA Today*, July 2, 1985.
38 "Introduction," *Community Seed Bank Resource Kit*, Prepared by the International Genetic Resources Programme (IGRP).
39 *Altered Harvest: Agriculture, Genetics, and the Fate of the World Food Supply*," by Jack Doyle, Viking Press, New York, N.Y.: 1985.
40 "Players: Jack Doyle - A Warning Voice Amid The Biogenetic Revolution," by Ward Sinclair, *The Washington Post*, March 2, 1987.

41   "Genetic Engineering: Who Will Pay the Costs," by Cary Fowler, *Catholic Rural Life*, November, 1987.
42   "Riding the Farm Boom," *Business Week*, October 27, 1973.
43   "Even These Days, Patricia Leimbach Has Farmers Smiling," by Clare Ansberry, *The Wall Street Journal*, January 17, 1986.
44   "Tenneco-Harvester: Start of trend?" by Gordon Bock, *USA Today*, November 27, 1984.
45   "Harvester to Sell Farm-Tool Division," by Mark Potts, *The Washington Post*, November 27, 1984.
46   "Farm-Equipment Purchase by Ford," *The New York Times*, March 28, 1986.
47   "Farm Reporter: Farm Supply Business Seeing Plenty of Changes in '80s," by Henry Schacht, *San Francisco Chronicle*, January 3, 1987.
48   "Ex-Tractor Firm Seeks Chapter 11," United Press International, *The Washington Post*, June 30, 1987.
49   "Farm Equipment Makers Plowing Rougher Fields," by Mark Potts, *The Washington Post*, July 12, 1987.
50   *Ibid.*
51   "An Uncertain Reprieve for Tractor Makers," by Eric N. Berg, *The New York Times*, December 30, 1990.
52   "Farm equipment makers rebound , too — to a point," by Wendell Cochran and Chuck Raasch, *USA Today*, April 4, 1988.
53   "Table 35 - Average U.S. farm fuel prices," *Agricultural Resources: Inputs - Situation and Outlook Report*, USDA Economic Research Service, ARS, January, 1987.
54   "The Vulnerability of Oil-Based Farming," by Lester R. Brown, *World-Watch*, March-April, 1988.
55   "Pesticides, Agricultural Resources: Situation and Outlook Report," Economic Research Service, USDA, AR-13, February, 1989.
56   USDA Economic Indicators of the Farm Sector.
57   "Fertilizer usage in 1983-84 climbs to 50.2 million tons," *Milling & Baking News*, January 1, 1985.
58   "Summary," *Agricultural Resources: Inputs - Situation and Outlook Report*, USDA Economic Research Service, ARS, January, 1987.
59   "North American Production Capacity Data," *Fertilizer Trends - 1982*, National Fertilizer Development Center, Tennessee Valley Authority.
60   *Op. cit.*, Brown, *World-Watch*, March-April, 1988.
61   *Ibid.*
62   "Biotechnology's Harvest of Herbicides," by Jack Doyle, *GeneWATCH*, November/December, 1985.
63   "Overview of the National Coalition Against the Misuse of Pesticides," Published by the National Coalition Against the Misuse of Pesticides (NCAMP), 530 Seventh Street S.E., Washington, D.C. 20003, October, 1986.
64   Source: EPA, *USA Today*, June 24, 1991.
65   "Squaring the Circle: The Geometry of the Pesticide Trade," Figures compiled from David Weir and and Mark Shapiro's book *Circle of Poison: Pesticides and People in a Hungry World*, Institute for Food and Development Policy, San Francisco, California: 1981, *Not Man Apart*, July/August, 1985.
66   "The Global Pesticide Industry: An Overview," by David Weir, The Dirty Dozen Campaign Booklet, Pesticide Action Network (PAN), San Francisco, California.
67   "'Monster bugs' sneer at eradication efforts," by Wayne Beissert, *USA Today*, February 19, 1987.
68   "Science Notebook: Nature Is Limiting Pesticides' Value, Experts Conclude," by Philip J. Hilts, *The Washington Post*, April 14, 1986.
69   "Pesticides, FIFRA, and the Failure of the Farm As a Profitable Business in the United States," by Erik Jansson, Published by National Coaltion Against the Misuse of Pesticides, Washington, D.C., October 25, 1983.
70   *Ibid.*
71   *Ibid.*
72   "Appendix - Patent Term Extension for Other Industries," Office of Technology Assessment, *Patent-Term Extension and the Pharmaceutical Industry*, OTA-CIT-143, August, 1981.
73   "Germany Beats World in Chemical Sales," by Thomas F. O'Boyle, *The Wall Street Journal*, May 3, 1988.
74   *Op. cit.*, Jansson, NCAMP, October 25, 1983.
75   *Business Week*, June 22, 1987.
76   "Lasso's EPA snags ensnare Monsanto," *USA Today*, November 20, 1984.
77   "Monsanto Working to Develop Plant That Resists Firm's Own Herbicide," by Malcolm Gladwell, *The Washington Post*, May 17, 1988.
78   "Drought, PIK bug insecticide profits," by Charles Koshetz, *USA Today*, May 10, 1984.
79   "Concern Rising Over Harm From Pesticides in Third World," by Marlise Simons, *The New York Times*, May 30, 1989.
80   *Pesticides: Better Sampling and Enforcement Needed on Imported Food*, Report to the Hon. Frank Horton, House of Representatives, U.S. Government Accounting Office, GAO/RCED-86-219, September, 1986.
81   "Pesticides Called Manageable Evil," by Philip Shabecoff, *The New York Times*, May 1, 1987.
82   "Eat Your Vegetables," by Bryan Jay Bashin, *Harrowsmith*, January/February, 1987.
83   "F.D.A. Is Faulted on Imported Food," by Irvin Molotsky, *The New Uork Times*, December 4, 1986.
84   *Op. cit.*, Weir, The Dirty Dozen Campaign Booklet, Pesticide Action Network (PAN), San Francisco, California.

85   *Op. cit.*, Bashin, *Harrowsmith*, January/February, 1987.

86   *Ibid.*

87   *Op. cit.*, Weir, The Dirty Dozen Campaign Booklet, Pesticide Action Network (PAN), San Francisco, California.

88   *Op. cit.*, Simons, *The New York Times*, May 30, 1989.

89   The Dirty Dozen Campaign Booklet, Pesticide Action Network (PAN), San Francisco, California.

90   "Subsidies Blamed For Excess Use of Pesticides in Third World," Associated Press, *The Washington Post*, December 15, 1985.

91   *Op. cit.*, "Squaring the Circle: The Geometry of the Pesticide Trade," *Not Man Apart*, July/August, 1985.

92   *Ibid.*

93   "Nicaragua's Revolution in Pesticide Policy," by Sean L. Swezey, Douglas L. Murray, and Ranier G. Daxi, *Environment*, January/February, 1986.

94   "Seeds of Revolution: New Perennial Crops Are Urged as the Way to Save U.S. Farmers," by Dennis Farney, *The Wall Street Journal*, January 10, 1986.

95   "The Lament of a Nebraska Farm Wife," by Marian Lenzen, *The Los Angeles Times*, March 19, 1978.

CHAPTER SIX: Killing The Environment

1   "Positions to be Examined Concerning National Health," Ben Franklin, April 4, 1769.
2   "Charting the Outlook: Farm Sector Expenditures and Income," *Farmline*, USDA, December/January, 1987.
3   "Farms Deadliest Workplace, Taking the Lives of Children," by Isabel Wilkerson, *The New York Times*, September 26, 1988.
4   "Red River Renegade," by Howard Kohn, *Mother Jones*, June, 1985.
5   "EPA Tightens Restrictions On Widely Used Herbicide," by Cass Peterson, *The Washington Post*, November 21, 1984.
6   Source: Agricultural Marketing Information Service (AGRICOM)
7   "Fertilzers, Pesticides: Working to Control Wastes From Farms," *The Washington Post*, June 1, 1986.
8   "Top 25 farm publication advertisers," *Advertising Age*, September 24, 1987.
9   "Pesticides Finally Top the Problem List at E.P.A.", by Philip Shabecoff, *The New York Times*, March 6, 1986.
10   "Pesticide Laws Said to Increase Some Health Risks," by Cass Peterson, *The Washington Post*, July 14, 1985.
11   "The Global Pesticide Industry: An Overview," by David Weir, Pesticide Action Network International.
12   "Agrichemicals -- Gap widens between researchers, public," by Luis Sinco, *The Packer*, April 6, 1982.
13   "Prospects Fading for Pesticide Law Revision," by Michael Weisskopf, *The Washington Post*, March 6, 1988.
14   "Pesticides in 15 Common Foods May Cause 20,000 Cancers a Year," by Michael Weisskopf, *The Washington Post*, May 21, 1987 and "'Classic Misuse' of Data on Pesticides," by Michael R. Taylor, *The Washington Post*, May 29, 1987.
15   "EPA Moving to Tighten Regulation of Pesticides," by Michael Weisskopf, *The Washington Post*, May 22, 1987.
16   "The Damage at EPA," By Russell W. Peterson, *The Washington Post*, February 18, 1983.
17   "4th Attempt to Alter Pesticide Law Faces Hard Climb on Capital Hill," by Cass Peterson, *The Washington Post*, May 24, 1985.
18   "Changes Urged in Pesticide Controls," by Cass Peterson, *The Washington Post*, April 19, 1985.
19   *Ibid.*
20   "The Nation: A Rare Peace on Pesticide Regulation, *The New York Times*, September 15, 1985.
21   "Pesticide-Law Rewrite Discussed," by Cass Peterson, *The Washington Post*, March 11, 1986.
22   *Op. cit., The New York Times*, September 15, 1985.
23   "Helms Acts to Restrict Pesticide Law Changes," by Michael Weisskopf, *The Washington Post*, August 8, 1986.
24   *Ibid.*
25   "Natl. Pesticide Standard Plan Attacked, Defended," by Lloyd Schwartz, *Supermarket News*, August 11, 1986.
26   "Ex-Officials of Chemical-Testing Lab Found Guilty of Falsifying Results," by Kevin Klose, *The Washington Post*, October 22, 1983.
27   *Op. cit.*, Weisskopf, *The Washington Post*, March 6, 1988.
28   "House Passes Pesticide Law Revision," by Michael Weisskopf, *The Washington Post*, September 21, 1988.
29   *Ibid.*
30   "'Negligible Risk' Policy Replaces Pesticide Ban," by Michael Weisskopf, *The Washington Post*, October 13, 1988.
31   "New Pesticide Policy Leaves Residue of Questions," by Michael Weisskopf, *The Washington Post*, October 24, 1988.
32   *Op. cit.*, Shabecoff, *The New York Times*, March 6, 1986 and "Poisoning The Well," *Environmental Action*, October, 1984.
33   "Getting the Bugs Out," by Carole Sugarman, *The Washington Post*, May 24, 1989.
34   "A New Dust Bowl?" by Ken and Tina Adler, *Environmental Action*, October, 1984.
35   *Ibid.*
36   "California," *USA Today*, April 18, 1985.
37   "Iowa," *USA Today*, March 19, 1986.
38   Interview with Dr. Robert van den Bosch, University of California-Berkeley by the author.
39   Source: Food Marketing Institute survey of 1006 adults, 1985.
40   "Inside: The National Bureau of Standards - Liver Specimens Banked to Track Environmental Changes," by Boyce Rensberger, *The Washington Post*, August 28, 1985.
41   *Pesticides In Food: What the Public Needs to Know*, by Lawrie Mott with the assistance of Martha Broad, Natural Resources Defense Council, Inc., San Francisco, California, March 15, 1984.
42   "U.S. Food Tests Fail to Detect Many Pesticides," United Press International, *The Washington Post*, October 11, 1988.
43   *Ibid.*
44   "Food Industry Is Testing for Toxics To Reassure Consumers on Crops," by Keith Scheider, *The New York Times*, March 27, 1989.
45   "Human milk — as well as cows — became undrinkable," by Matthew Rothschild, *The Multinational Monitor*, May, 1982.
46   "Heptachlor Find Causes Milk Recall," by Cass Peterson, *The Washington Post*, March 11, 1986, "Mothers

fear; farmers suffer," by David Zodrow and Peter Johnson, *USA Today*, March 19, 1986, and "The Human Toll From Tainted Milk," by Michael Weisskopf, *The Washington Post*.

47   *Op. cit.*, Rothschild, *The Multinational Monitor*, May, 1982.

48   Statement of Jay Feldman, National Coordinator, National Coalition Against the Misuse of Pesticides, Before the Committee on Agriculture, Nutrition & Forestry, U.S. Senate, Washington, D.C., May 24, 1983.

49   "Pesticide Safety: Myth & Facts," NCAMP, 1985.

50   *Op. cit.*, Rothschild, *The Multinational Monitor*, May, 1982.

51   "EPA to Ban Pesticide's Use in Food," by Cass Peterson, *The Washington Post*, June 19, 1985.

52   "19 Pesticides, Four on a Strawberry, Found In Sample of Produce," by Cass Peterson, *The Washington Post*, March 16, 1984.

53   "EPA Delays Ban on Farm Use of Suspect Chemical," by Cass Peterson, *The Washington Post*, January 23, 1986.

54   *Ibid.*

55   "Safeway Eliminates Sale of Treated Apples," *The Washington Post*, July 17, 1986 and "Apples Get Clean Bill of Health," by Editors of *Consumer Reports*, *The Washington Post*, October 28, 1987.

56   "Let stand or refused cases: Alar," *USA Today*, April 25, 1989.

57   "Apple prices sink too low to sell them," *USA Today*, June 19, 1989.

58   "Tree Top Inc. Chief Quits in Fight Concerning Alar," *The Wall Street Journal*, June 5, 1989.

59   "Washington," *USA Today*. June 21, 1989.

60   "Avery's Uniroyal Ends Alar Sales in U.S.; Apple Products Imports Still Worry Critics," by Barbara Rosewicz, *The Wall Street Journal*, June 5, 1989.

61   "Many apples still tainted with Alar," by Tim Friend, *USA Today*, May 15, 1989.

62   "EPA Seeking Swift Ban on Plant-Growth Spray," by Cass Peterson, *The Washington Post*, August 29, 1985.

63   "Chronology of Catastrophe," by Sandra Marquardt, *Pesticides and You*, October, 1984.

64   "Get plants into the 20th century," by A. Karim Ahmed, *USA Today*, August 15, 1985.

65   "Bhopal, year later: Could it happen here?," by Peter Johnson and Marilyn Adams, *USA Todat*, December 2, 1985.

66   *Ibid.*, Johnson and Adams, *USA Todat*, December 2, 1985.

67   *Ibid.*

68   "EPA Seeks Fines for New Chemcials," by Cass Peterson, *The Washington Post*, June 18, 1985.

69   "Union Carbide Faces Fines of $1.4 Million on Safety Violations," by Kenneth B. Noble, *The New York Times*, April 2, 1986 and "Union Carbide Fined $1.3 Million," by Michael Isikoff, *The Washington Post*, March 2, 1986..

70   "Supreme Court Upholds U.S. Power To Publicize Pesticide Information," by Cass Peterson, *The Washington Post*, June 27, 1984.

71   "EPA Plans to Require More Data From Pesticides Manufacturers," *The Washington Post*, August 10, 1984.

72   "Toxic Clouds' Can Carry Pollutants Far and Wide," by Michael Weisskopf, *The Washington Post*, March 16, 1988.

73   *Ibid.*

74   "Toxic harvest," and "farmers pass a fatal legacy to their children," by Jane Kay, *San Francisco Examiner*, January 18, 1987 and "Inquiry: We have to get off the pesticide path," Interview with Cesar Chavez by Tom Page, *USA Today*, July 8, 1987.

75   "Monitoring the International Code of Conduct on the Distribution and Use of Pesticides in North America: A Field Survey of Pesticide-Related Working Conditions in the U.S. and Canada," by Marion Moses, M.D., Published by The Pesticide Education and Action Project, P.O. Box 610, San Francisco, California 94101, February, 1988.

76   "American Journal: A Winegrower's Romance With the Past," by Ward Sinclair, *The Washington Post*, March 6, 1988.

77   "Seeds of Revolution: New, Perennial Crops Are Urged as the Way to Save U.S. Farmers," by Dennis Farney, *The Wall Street Journal*, January 10, 1986.

78   Table 36 - Farm production expenses, 1982-1985, *Agricultural Outlook*, USDA Economic Research Service, March, 1987.

79   *The Poverty of Power: Energy and the Economic Crisis*, by Barry Commoner, Knopf, New York, N.Y.: 1976, pg. 172.

80   "Energy and Land Constraints in Food Protein Production," by David Pimentel, et. al., *Science*, November 21, 1975.

81   "Energy and U.S., Agriculture: 1974 and 1978," USDA Economic, Statistical, Cooperative Service, Bulletin No. 632, April, 1980.

82   "Western Perspective," by W.J. Chancellor, *American Vegetable Grower*, November, 1979.

83   *Ibid.*

84   *Op. cit.*, Pimentel, et. al., *Science*, November 21, 1975.

85   *Food Cost Review*, USDA Economic Research Service, Agricultural Economic Report No. 559, July, 1986.

86   "Fuel Priority a 'Must' for Food Field," Food Marketing Institute, *Supermarket News*, August 10, 1981.

87   *Op. cit., Food Cost Review*, No. 559, July, 1986.

88   "Food Costs . . . From Farm to Retail," USDA Economic Research Service, March, 1987.

89   *Op. cit., Food Cost Review*, No. 559, July, 1986.

90   *Ibid.*

91   "Crop Study Finds Severe Ozone Damage," by Jon R. Luoma, *The New York Times*, February 21, 1989.

92   *Ibid.*

93   "Determining crop yield losses from air pollutants," by Patrick M. McCool, Robert G. Musselman, Roberto R. Teso, and Ronald J. Oshima, *California Agriculture*, July/August, 1986.

94   "Air pollution causes moderate damage to tomatoes," by Patrick J. Temple, Kris A. Surano, Randall G. Mutters, Gail E. Bingham, and Joseph H. Shinn, *California Agriculture*, March/April, 1985.

95   "The economic effects of air pollution on annual crops," by Richard E. Howitt, Thomas W. Gossard, and Richard M. Adams, *California Agriculture*, March/April, 1985.

96   "The Toxic Fog," by Jeremy Millstone, *Environmental Action*, May/June, 1987.

97   "Toxic Fog Containing Farm Chemicals May Be Harming U.S. Forests," by Boyce Rensberger, *The Washington Post*, February 12, 1987.

98   "Big Farm Companies Try Hand at Organic Methods," by Keith Schneider, *The New York Times*, May 28, 1989.

99   *Ibid.*

100   "Fears of Pesticides Threaten American Way of Farming," by Keith Schneider, *The New York Times*, May 1, 1989.

101   *Report and Recommendations On Organic Farming*, Prepared by the USDA Study Team on Organic Farming, USDA, Washington, D.C., July, 1980.

102   "Widespread Adoption of Organic Farming Practices: Estimated Impacts on U.S. Agriculture," by Kent Olson, James Langley, and Earl O. Heady, *Journal of Soil and Water Conservation*, January/February, 1982.

103   "Maize Yields and Soil Nutrient Levels With and Without Pesticides and Standard Commercial Fertilizers," by William Lockertz, Georgia Shearer, et. al., *Agronomy Journal*, January/February, 1980.

104   "Organic Farmers Still Harvesting Profits," by Ward Sinclair, *The Washington Post*, September 1, 1985.

105   "Farmers Achieve Natural Balance," by Ward Sinclair, *The Washington Post*, March 1, 1987.

106   "Reaping A Richer Bounty," by Francesca Lyman, *Environmental Action*, October, 1984.

107   "Small-Scale Farmers Harvest Attention," by Ward Sinclair, *The Washington Post*, December 10, 1986.

108   *Op. cit.*, Sinclair, *The Washington Post*, March 1, 1987.

109   *Ibid.*

110   "The Prospects For Small-Scale Farming In An Industrial Society: A Critical Appraisal of *Small Is Beautiful*," by E. Phillip LeVeen, Presented at the Conference "Small Is Beautiful: Economics As If People Mattered," University of California-Davis, February 17, 1977.

CHAPTER SEVEN: Controlling Our Food From "Seedling to Supermarket"

1   *The Bigness Complex: Industry, Labor and Government in the American Economy*, by Walter Adams and James W. Brock, Pantheon Books, New York, N.Y.: 1986.

2   *Economic Concentration: Structure, Behavior & Public Policy*, by John M. Blair, Harcourt Brace Jovanovich, Inc., New York, N.Y.: 1972.

3   *The Food Manufacturing Industries: Structure, Strategies, Performance, and Policies*, by John M. Connor, Richard T. Rogers, Bruce W. Marion, and Willard F. Mueller, Lexington Books, D.C. Heath Co., Lexington, Mass./Toronto:1985.

4   "Contract Production and Vertical Integration in Farming, 1960 and 1970," by Ronald L. Mighell and William S. Hoofnagle, USDA Economic Research Service.

5   As quoted by Daryl Natz, *Feedstuffs*, February 19, 1973.

6   "Corporate Farming, 1969-82," by Kenneth R. Krause, Agriculture and Rural Economy Division, ERS, USDA, Agricultural Economic Report No. 578, December, 1987.

7   Federal Trade Commission letter citing *Case Studies in American Industry*, pp. 432-433 and *Economics and the Public Purpose*, by John Kenneth Galbraith, Houghton Mifflin Co., Boston, Mass.: 1973, pg. 46n.

8   *Op. cit.*, ERS, USDA, Agricultural Economic Report No. 578.

9   *Op. cit.*, Mighell and Hoofnagle, USDA Economic Research Service.

10   "Poultry Peonage," *Sowing the Wind*, by Harrison Wellford, Bantam Books, New York, N.Y.: 1973, pg. 101-124.

11   *Antitrust Policy — an Economic and Legal Analysis*, by Carl Kaysen and Donald T. Turner, Harvard University Press, Cambridge, Mass.: 1959, pg.122.

12   *AgBiz Tiller*, San Francisco, California, Issue No. 2 and "Food giant's recipe: Soup up business," by Darcy Reid Trick, *USA Today*, February 5, 1987.

13   "FTC and Phase II: The McGovern Papers," by Paul D. Scanlon, *Antitrust Law and Economics Review*, Spring, 1972, pp. 33-36.

14   "Structural Adjustment of the Food Industries of the United States," by John M Connor, Staff Report USDA, July, 1982, pg. 78.

15   "Estimates of Consumer Loss Due to Monopoly in the U.S. Manufacturing Industries," by Russell C. Parker and John M. Connor, *American Journal of Agricultural Economics*, November, 1977, pg. 637-638.

16   Figures calculated from corporate annual reports and *Forbes* and *Fortune* magazine's annual corporate reports.

17   *Op. cit.*, Blair, *Economic Concentration*, pg. 46.

18   "Conagra hits new high," *USA Today*, April 10, 1985.

19   "Companies: When competition against sugar turned sour," *Business Week*, November 15, 1976.

20   *Ibid.*

21   "Biodegradable plastics boosts ADM," by Gary Strauss, *USA Today*, May 3, 1988.

22   *Op. cit.*, Blair, *Economic Concentration*, pg. 49.

23   "Beatrice will sell Avis, three others," by Doug Carroll, *USA Today*, October 2, 1985.

24   "Beatrice to Sell $1.45 Billion in Assets," *USA Today*, March 13, 1986.

25   "Beatrice buy-out bestows bounty," *USA Today*, December 2, 1985.

26   "Beatrice Cos. Tries to Sell Itself to Consumers, Investors," by David A. Vise, *The Washington Post*, September 9, 1984.

27   "A smaller spinoff goes public in June," by Jay McCormick, *USA Today*, May 21, 1987.

28   "Companies getting back to the basics," by Constance Mitchell, *USA Today*, April 2, 1985.

29   *Ibid.*

30   "When Food Firms Merge, Effects Reach Into Aisles of Supermarkets," by Trish Hall, *The Wall Street Journal*, June 13, 1985.

31   *Ibid.*

32   *Op. cit..*, Blair, *Economic Concentration*, pg. 58.

33   *Ibid.*, pg 11.

34   Source: 1966 Census of Manufacturing

35   *CDE Stock Ownership Directory - Agribusiness*, Corporate Data Exchange, Inc., Room 707, 198 Broadway, New York, N.Y. 10038, 1979.

36   "Heard on the Street: Castle & Cooke Again Is Drawing Speculation It Might Sell Some Land or Food Businesses," by Linda Sandler, *The Wall Street Journal*, January 15, 1986.

37   "Name-Dropping at the Deli," by John Grossmann, *The New York Times*, June 22, 1986.

38   *Ibid.*

39   Source: *1987 Statistical Abstract*

40   "Beer Brewing in Milwaukee Goes Flat," by Sandra Feustel, *The Washington Post*, February 19, 1985.

41   *Ibid.*

42   *Ibid.*

43   Reported by "Nightline," ABC-TV, October 25, 1985.

44   *Ibid.*

45   *Op. cit.*, Feustel, *The Washington Post*, February 19, 1985.

46   *Op. cit., 1987 Statistical Abstract*

47   "FTC Opposes 2 Soft Drink Mergers," by Peter Bahr and Martha M. Hamilton, *The Washington Post*, June 21, 1986.

48   "Dr. Pepper, Seven-Up to Merge, Creating Nation's Third Major Soft-Drink Maker," by Marj Charlier, *The Wall Street Journal*, March 1, 1988. See also "Dr. Pepper/Seven-Up Stake to be Sold for $600 Million," by Marj Charlier, *The Wall Street Journal*, April 14, 1988.

49   "Pepsi agrees to buy KFC for $850 million," by Betsy Bauer, *USA Today*, July 25, 1986 and "Pepsi beefs up fast- food chicken fight," *USA Today*, September 24, 1986.

50   "Wendy's to Switch From Pepsi to Coke," *USA Today*, October 6, 1986

51   Marketing a Super Idea, 1930," *The Wall Street Journal*, April 27, 1989.

52   Source: *Progressive Grocer, USA Today*, September 21, 1989.

53   Source: Kidder, Peabody & Company, *USA Today*, September 8, 1989.

54   *SN Distribution Study of Grocery Store Sales, 1987*, Fairchild Publications, 1987.

55   "Tightening of Supermarket Antitrust Laws Urged," by Ward Sinclair, *The Washington Post*, May 12, 1988.

56   "Food chains struggling for profits," by Constance Mitchell, *USA Today*, July 30, 1984.

57   *Ibid.*

58   "Stores war is Lucky for grocers," by Daniel Horgan, *USA Today*, March 24, 1988.

59   *Ibid.*

60   "Food Processing Firms Frozen Out in Battle for Space in Supermarkets," by James Asher, Knight-Ridder, *The Washington Post*, April 13, 1986.

61   "For New Food Products, Entry Fee Is High," by Trish Hall, *The New York Times*, January 7, 1988.

62   "The Controversial Costs of Putting Products on the Shelves," by Caroline E. Mayer, *The Washington Post*, April 26, 1989.

63   *Op. cit.*, Hall, *The New York Times*, January 7, 1988.

64   *Ibid.*

65   *Ibid.*

66   *Ibid.*

67   *Ibid.*

68   *Farm Marketing Review, 1989-90*, Commodity Economics Division, ERS, USDA Agricultural Economic Report No. 639, page 169.

69   "Supermarkets of the future are here," by Jefferson Graham, *USA Today*, October 30, 1986.

70   "Fast Food Comes to Supermarkets," by Caroline E. Mayer, *The Washington Post*, October 27, 1986.

71   *Ibid.*

72   *Ibid.*

73   "In-Store Computer Terminals, A Super Marketing Device," by Carole Sugarman, *The Washington Post*, May 28, 1986.

74   "Checking Out the Customer," by Lena H. Sun, *The Washington Post*, July 9, 1989.

75   *Ibid.*

76   *Ibid.*

77   *Ibid.*

78   "Who Wins and Loses in Trend to Fresh Foods," by Robert Lindsey, *The New York Times*, July 19, 1986.

79   *Op. cit*, Asher, Knight-Ridder, *The Washington Post*, April 13, 1986.

80   *Ibid.*

81   "Bigger Stores, Consolidation Ahead: Cetron," by Patrick Geohegan, *Supermarket News*, February 6, 1989.

82   *Ibid.*

83   *Ibid.*

84   "What the little guys sell," *USA Today*, May 16, 1985.

85   *Op. cit., Food Marketing Review, 1989-90*, Appendix Table 27.

86   1984 Southland Corp. Annual Report

87   "7-Eleven Sells Convenience," by John Holusha, *The New York Times*, July 13, 1987.

88   "7-Eleven's Owner in $5 Billion Deal To Sell Company," by Calvin Sims, *The New York Times*, July 6, 1987.

89   "Southland to Buy High's Dairy Stores," by Elizabeth Tucker, *The Washington Post*, November 1, 1986.

90   "Southland To Sell Its Subsidiaries," by David Barron, United Press International, *The Washington Post*, July 7, 1987 and "Southland Corp. To Be Acquired For $4 Billion," by Karen Blumenthal, *The Wall Street Journal*, July 6, 1987..

91   *Ibid.*

92   "Circle K Will Acquire 473 7-Eleven Stores," by Associated Press, *The New York Times*, March 1, 1988.

93   "Convenience Store Chains Face Struggle for Survival As Oil Firms Enter Picture," by Gary Jacobson, *Sallas Morning News, The Washington Post*, June 10, 1989.

94 *Ibid.*
95 *Ibid.*

CHAPTER EIGHT: What Is This Thing Called Food?

1   "Who's who in the Thanksgiving business," by Jim Hightower, *The Texas Observer*, November 17, 1978.
2   "Pondering 'Junk' Food," by Phyllis C. Richman, *The Washington Post*, August 20, 1986.
3   "Chemical Food at the Country Fair," by Ward Sinclair, *The Washington Post*, July 27, 1986.
4   "The March on New Orleans," by Carole Sugarman, *The Washington Post*, March 1, 1989.
5   "How Much Will People Pay to Save A Few Minutes of Cooking? Plenty," by Betsy Morris, *The Wall Street Journal*, July 25, 1985.
6   *Ibid.*
7   "The battle of the trends," *Forbes*, February 9, 1987.
8   *Ibid.*
9   *Op. cit.*, Morris, *The Wall Street Journal*, July 25, 1985.
10   "Faux Food," by Michael McRae, *Harrowsmith*, July/August, 1987.
11   *Op. cit.*, Morris, *The Wall Street Journal*, July 25, 1985
12   "Farm struggle isn't affecting consumers -- not yet, anyway," by Sally Lehrman, *San Francisco Examiner*, March 20, 1986.
13   *Op. cit.*, McRae, *Harrowsmith*, July/August, 1987.
14   "Firms Grow More Cautious About New-Product Plans," by Alecia Swasy, *The Wall Street Journal*, March 9, 1989.
15   "Campbell leads new-product charge," *USA Today*, March 13, 1985 and "Product Proliferators," *The Wall Street Journal*, April 14, 1988.
16   "Are Square Meals Headed for Extinction?" by Betsy Morris, *The Wall Street Journal*, March 15, 1988.
17   *Ibid.*
18   *Ibid.*
19   "Souffle in a Jar -- And a Lot More," by Wendy E. Lane, *The Wall Street Journal*, July 29, 1985.
20   *Op. cit.*, Morris, *The Wall Street Journal*, July 25, 1985.
21   *Ibid.*
22   "Microwave food rivalry is sizzling," by Betsy Bauer, *USA Today*, May 12, 1986 and "Galaxy of Microwave Foods Is Expanding," by Elizabeth Neuffer, *The New York Times*, February 17, 1988.
23   *Ibid.* Bauer.
24   *Op. cit.*, Morris, *The Wall Street Journal*, July 25, 1985.
25   Source: *Entrepreneur*, *USA Today*, December 23, 1987.
26   "Top Credit Card Companies Explore Fast-Food Tie-Ins," by Douglas C. McGill, *The New York Times*, May 1, 1989.
27   "What's New in Supermarket Promotion: Fast Food and Mini- Marts Bite Into Grocers," by Lynette D. Hazelton, *The New York Times*, June 18, 1989.
28   "McDonald's reaches new milestone," by Doug Carroll, *USA Today*, November 19, 1984.
29   "Sad but True: No Place Is Safe From Fast Food," by Jonathan Dahl, *The Wall Street Journal*, May 15, 1986.
30   "50 Billion Sold," by Mark Potts, *The Washington Post*, November 21, 1984 and "Golden Arches Under Fire," by David Streitfeld, *The Washington Post*, June 1, 1987..
31   "Big chains gobble big share," by Robert Getz, *USA Today*, February 27, 1986.
32   "Business Facts," *Chicago Tribune*, February 20, 1990.
33   *Op. cit.*, Dahl, *The Wall Street Journal*, May 15, 1986.
34   Source: 1987 Gallup Annual Report on Eating Out.
35   "Fast food means big bucks," *USA Today*, March 6, 1986.
36   "Why Fast Food Has Slowed Down," by Claudia H. Deutsch, *The New York Times*, March 13, 1988.
37   *Advertising Age*, May 21, 1990.
38   *Advertising Age*, September 28, 1988.
39   *Op. cit.*, Getz, *USA Today*, February 27, 1986.
40   *Op. cit.*, McGill, *The New York Times*, May 1, 1989.
41   *Ibid.*
42   "American Express Chases After the Fast-Food Market," by Barbara Marsh, *The Wall Street Journal*, April 5, 1989.
43   *Op. cit.*, McGill, *The New York Times*, May 1, 1989.
44   *Op. cit.*, Marsh, *The Wall Street Journal*, April 5, 1989.
45   Source: *Nation's Restaurant News*, *The New York Times*, January 9, 1989.
46   "So much fast food, so little time," by Tom Green, *USA Today*, June 28, 1985.
47   "The Way We Shop Now," by Jonathan Yardley, *The Washington Post*, January 24, 1985.
48   "The Fast-Food Factories: MoJobs Are Bad for Kids," by Amitai Etzioni, Professor, George Washington University, *The Washington Post*, August 24, 1986.
49   "Robots to Make Fast Food Chains Still Faster," by Calvin Sims, *The New York Times*, August 24, 1988.
50   *Roadside Empires: How the Chains Franchised America*, by Stan Luxenberg, Viking, New York, N.Y.: 1984.

51   *The Malling of America: An Inside Look at the Great Consumer Paradise*, by William Severini Kowinski, Morrow, New York, N.Y.: 1984.

52   *Op. cit.*, Yardley, *The Washington Post*, January 24, 1985.

53   "Advertising and Marketing: If you're skeptical about ads, you have plenty of company," by Robert Garfield, *USA Today*, May 15, 1985.

54   Source: National survey of 1000 TV viewers each year by Video Storyboard Tests Inc., *The Wall Street Journal*, March 10, 1989.

55   "'Marketing Warfare' Seeks Military Link For Sales Campaigns," by John E. Cooney, *The Wall Street Journal*, April 28, 1978.

56   "Managers Learn Marketing Is War," by Ewart Rouse, Knight- Ridder, *The Washington Post*, November 23, 1986.

57   "Michael Jackson praisin' raisins in ad," by Stuart Elliott, *USA Today*, August 27, 1989.

58   *Advertising Age*, March 12, 1989.

59   Source: Television Bureau of Advertising, Inc.

60   *Ibid.*

61   Source: Television Bureau of Advertising and "Major spending by 100 leading advertisers, *Advertising Age*, September 24, 1987.

62   "The 100 Leading Advertisers - 1986 Edition," *Advertising Age*, September 4, 1986.

63   "FTC and Phase II: The McGovern Papers," by Paul D. Scanlon, *Antitrust Law & Economics Review*, Spring, 1972.

64   "Study Action Guide," *Hamburger, U.S.A.*, American Friends Service Committee, 2160 Lake Street, San Francisco, California, 1980.

65   "Food growers raising bumper ad budgets," by Janet Meyers, *Advertising Age*, September 16, 1985.

66   *Ibid.*

67   "Stars on Their Payrolls, Farmers Entice Americans' Tastebuds," by Ward Sinclair, *The Washington Post*, April 26, 1987.

68   *Op. cit.*, Meyers, *Advertising Age*, September 16, 1985 and "Milk ads pale: Research," by Janet Meyers, *Advertising Age*, July 8, 1985.

69   *Ibid.*

70   "Florida vs. Brazil: The Orange Juice Wars," *The New York Times*.

71   *Op. cit.*. Meyers, *Advertising Age*, September 16, 1985.

72   "Biological Wizardry," by Carole Sugarman, *The Washington Post*, April 19, 1989.

73   *Op. cit.*. Meyers, *Advertising Age*, September 16, 1985.

74   "FTC Alleges Campbell Ad Is Deceptive," by Alix M. Freedman, *The Wall Street Journal*, January 27, 1989.

75   *Op. cit.*, Scanlon, *Antitrust Law & Economics Review*, Spring, 1972.

76   "Rumors Force P&G To Alter Trademark," United Press International, *The Washington Post*, April 25, 1985.

77   "Jack In Box pops up with new name," by Kevin Maney, *USA Today*, May 8, 1985.

78   "Quaker Oats Is Shedding New Light on Jemima," *The Wall Street Journal*, April 28, 1989.

79   "Do You Recognize This Woman?", by Carole Sugarman, *The Washington Post*, May 25, 1986.

80   "50 Years of Ho-Ho-Ho," Associated Press, *The Washington Post*, August 5, 1985.

81   Estimates based on 1982 Census of Manufacturing statistics.

82   "Top 25 network TV advertisers," *Advertising Age*, March 13, 1990.

83   "Plastics Pushing Bottles, Cans Off Shelves," by Sarah Oates, *The Washington Post*, August 25, 1985.

84   "Piles of Packaging," by Cass Peterson, *The Washington Post*, June 7, 1987.

85   "Packaging," *Food Costs . . . From Farm to Retail*, USDA Economic Research Service, March, 1987.

86   "Packaging in Food Marketing," by Anthony Gallo and John Connor, *National Food Review*, USDA, Spring, 1981.

87   "Wrong Turns: Plastic Waste Proliferates," by Cynthia Pollock Shea, *World Watch*, March-April, 1988.

88   "Trends," *USA Today*, June 22, 1984.

89   "New Package May Yield Fresher Produce," by Laurie Hays, *The Wall Street Journal*, October 18, 1988.

90   Food Marketers Find Packaging a Key to Success," by Skip Wollenberg, Associated Press, *The Washington Post*, April 5, 1987.

91   *Ibid.*

92   "How Safe Are Food Containers?", by Will Hitchcock and Rose Marie Audette, *Environmental Action*, October, 1984.

93   *Ibid.*

94   "Luring 'Green' Consumers," by Michael Freitag, *The New York Times*, August 6, 1989.

95   "What's in a (Brand) Name?", by Carole Sugarman, *The Washington Post*, March 10, 1985.

96   *Ibid.*

97   "Marketing Marvels: Ernest & Julio Gallo," by Jaclyn Fierman, *Fortune*, September 1, 1986.

98   "Gallo vs. Gallo: Battle for an Empire," by James Laube, *The Wine Spectator*, October 31, 1986.

99   "Top Three Advertisers by Category," *Advertising Age*, September 24, 1987.

100   "Their Cup Runneth Over," *Forbes*, October 1, 1975.

101   "Forbes 400: The Richest People in America," *Forbes*, October 27, 1986.

102   "FTC Settles Case: Galo Told Not to 'Coerce' Dealers," *San Francisco Chronicle*, May 20, 1976.

103   *Op. cit.*, Laube, *The Wine Spectator*, October 31, 1986.

104   *Ibid.* and *Op. cit.*, Fierman, *Fortune*, September 1, 1986.

105   *Op. cit.*, Sugarman, *The Washington Post*, March 10, 1985.

106   *Ibid.*

107   *Op. cit.*, Sugarman, *The Washington Post*, March 1, 1989.

108   *Op. cit.*, Sugarman, *The Washington Post*, March 10, 1985.

109   *Ibid.*

110   *U.S. Food Spending and Income*, by Alden Manchester, ERS, USDA, Agricultural Information Bulletin No. 618, January, 1981, Table 3.

111   "Appearances Count for Grocer's Private Labels," Caroline E. Mayer, *The Washington Post*, July 19, 1989.

112   *Ibid.*

113   *Op. cit.*, Sugarman, *The Washington Post*, March 10, 1985.

114   *Ibid.*

115   "Of All Energy Used in Agriculture, Farming Itself Takes Only One-Fifth," *Agricultural Outlook*, USDA Economic Research Service, AO-119, May, 1986.

116   "Marketers milk cold-cereal sales," by John C. Maxwell, Jr., *Advertising Age*, September 26, 1988.

117   "Corporate Gumshoes Spy on Competitors," by Elizabeth Tucker, *The Washington Post*, March 30, 1986.

118   "New cereals adjust to adult tastes," *The New York Times*, January 6, 1988.

119   "Brands, products and services by ad spending," *Advertising Age*, May 21, 1990.

120   "Table 93 -- Household Expenditures for food in relation to income, by income group, 1984," *Food Consumption, Prices, and Expenditures - 1985*, USDA Economic Research Service, Statistical Bulleting No. 749, January, 1987.

CHAPTER NINE: Every Trip To The Supermarket -- A Crap Shoot

1   "Croissants, our latest food fad," by Ellen Brown, *USA Today*, November 27, 1984.
2   "Faux Food," by Michael McRae, *Harrowsmith*, July/August, 1987.
3   "What Americans Eat: Nutrition Can Wait, a Survey Finds," by Marian Burros, *The New York Times*, January 6, 1988.
4   *Op. cit.*, Brown, *USA Today*, November 27, 1984.
5   "Table 10 - Foodstore Sales," *Food Marketing Review, 1986*, USDA Economic Research Service, Agricultural Economic Report No. 565, February, 1987.
6   "Human Nutrition, Agriculture and Human Values," by Katherine L. Clancy, *Agriculture and Human Values*, Winter, 1984.
7   "Food Marketers Target Consumer Lifestyles," *Farmline*, USDA, August, 1984.
8   *Ibid.*
9   *Ibid.*
10   "The Food Fabricators," by Ross Hume Hall, *Environment*, January/February, 1976.
11   "Fraud by Scientists Seen Linked To Competition," by Cristine Russell, *The Washington Post*, May 30, 1985.
12   *Op. cit.*, Hall, *Environment*, January/February, 1976.
13   "Building a Better Meal," by Randi Londer, *Discovery Magazine*, "This World," *San Francisco Chronicle*, January 8, 1989.
14   *Guidelines For Food Purchasing in the United States*, by Nick Mottern, Prepared for the Senate Select Committee on Nutrition and Human Needs, Winchester, Virginia, May 12, 1978.
15   *Op. cit.*, McRae, *Harrowsmith*, July,August, 1987.
16   "A taste of the food and drink of 1986," by Karen MacNeill, *USA Today*, January 8, 1986.
17   "McCormick Uses Biotech to Spice Up Research," by Neil Henderson, *The Washington Post*, January 7, 1985 and "A close call," by Janet Novack, *Forbes*, January 26, 1987.
18   *Op. cit.*, Hall, *Environment*, January/February, 1976.
19   "Telling What's In Your Food," Reuters, *The New York Times*, June 1, 1988.
20   *The Food Manufacturing Industries: Structure, Strategies, Performances, and Policies*, by John M. Connor, Richard T. Rogers, Bruce W. Marion, and Willard F. Mueller, Lexington Books, D.C. Heath and Company, Lexington, Mass./Toronto: 1985.
21   Quoted in "The Food Monsters," by Daniel Zwerdling, *The Progressive*, March, 1980.
22   *Op. cit.*, Mottern, *Guidelines for Food Purchasing in the United States*, May 12, 1978.
23   *Op. cit.*, Hall, *Environment*, January/February, 1976.
24   "The Marriage of Food Technology and Nutrition," by Drs. N.W. Tape and Zak Sabry, *World Review of Nutrition and Dietetics*, Vol. 10. 1969.
25   *Op. cit.*, McRae, *Harrowsmith*, July/August, 1987.
26   "Newscience," *Science Digest*, April, 1985.
27   "Feeding at the Company Trough," by Benjamin Rosenthal (D, N.Y.), Michael Jacobson, CSPI, and Marcy Rohm, CSPI, 1976.
28   "Is nutrition sacrificed for convenience?," by Janis Johnson, *USA Today*, September 19, 1984.
29   "Beefing up nutritional information," by Ellen Brown, *USA Today*, October 3, 1984.
30   "Food Labels Often Light on Nutritional Information, by Michael Spector, *The Washington Post*, July 23, 1989.
31   "A failure to digest nutritional facts," by Nanci Helmich, *USA Today*, April 5, 1989.
32   *Ibid.*
33   *Let Them Eat Promises*, by Nick Kotz, Prentice-Hall, Engelwood Heights, N.J.: 1969.
34   "Food and Choice," by Sally Squires, "Washington Post Health," *The Washington Post*, July 5, 1988.
35   "Push Is On for Nutritional Labeling," by Marian Burros, *The New York Times*, March 8, 1989.
36   *Ibid.*
37   *Ibid.*
38   "Labels: The Secret Ingredient," by Carole Sugarman, *The Washington Post*, December 7, 1988.
39   *Op. cit.*, Burros, *The New York Times*, March 8, 1989.
40   "Is Soup Good Food," by Russell Wild, *Environmental Action*, October, 1984.
41   *Op. cit.*, Burros, *The New York Times*, March 8, 1989.
42   "Food Industry in Switch, Backs Nutrition Law," by Carole Sugarman, *The Washington Post*, August 4, 1989.
43   *Op. cit.*, Burros, *The New York Times*, March 8, 1989.
44   USDA Statistics as quoted in "Losing the battle of the bulge," by James Ring Adams and Jeffrey A. Trachtenberg, *Forbes*, November 17, 1986.
45   "New Sweeteners Head for the Sugar Bowl," by Alix M. Freedman, *The Wall Street Journal*, February 6, 1989.
46   "Searle sweetner's success whets Monsanto's appetite," by Michael Felbus, *USA Today*, August 8, 1985.
47   *Op. cit.*, Freedman, *The Wall Street Journal*, February 6, 1989.
48   "A look at the artifical sweetners," *USA Today*, April 17, 1985 and "New Artifical Sweetner Approved," by Philip M. Boffey, *The New York Times*, July 28, 1988.

49   "Most Scientists in Poll Doubt NutraSweet's Safety," by Michael Specter, *The Washington Post*, July 17, 1987 and "NutraSweet sweetens sales," by Dennis Cauchon, *USA Today*, March 24, 1987.
50   *Ibid.*
51   *Food and Drug Administration: Food Additive Approval Process Followed for Aspartame*, U.S. Government Accounting Office, GAO/HRD-87-46, June 18, 1987; *Ibid.*, Specter, *The Washington Post*, July 17, 1987 and "Letters to the Editor: Aspartame - What the Findings Show," by Thomas E. Stenzel, Executive Director, International Food Information Council, *The Washington Post*, August 1, 1987.
52   "FDA Rejects NutraSweet Ban," United Press International, *The Washington Post*, November 25, 1986.
53   "Heavy Use of NutraSweet May Be Harmful, Study Says," United Press International, *The Washington Post*, April 30, 1987.
54   "What's For Diner? Psychologists Explore Quirks and Cravings," by Daniel Goleman, *The New York Times*, July 11, 1989.
55   "NutraSweet: The Debate Continues," by Sandy Rovner, "Washington Post Health," *The Washington Post*, May 19, 1987.
56   *Ibid.*
57   "The Sugar Substitute: The sweet taste we love," by Karen MacNeil, *USA Today*, April 17, 1985.
58   "The Hefty Price of 'Lite' Foods," by Carole Sugarman, *The Washington Post*, February 3, 1988.
59   "Why No Testing of Additives," by Richard J. Wurtman, *The New York Times*, December 23, 1987.
60   *Ibid.*
61   Source: Center for Science in the Public Interest
62   "Salt Hasn't Lost It's Flavor," by Cass Peterson, *The Washington Post*, February 18, 1985.
63   *Op. cit.*, Wild, *Environmental Action*, October, 1984.
64   *Op. Cit.*, Sugarman, *The Washington Post*, February 3, 1988.
65   *Ibid.*
66   *Op. Cit.*, Wild, *Environmental Action*, October, 1984.
67   "Inquiry: Eating Disorders," An interview with Dr. Yoel Yager, Director, UCLA Eating Disorder Clinic, by Mary-Ann Bendel, *USA Today*, May 8, 1985.
68   "Inquiry: Losing Weight," An interview with Dick Gregory by Barbara Reynolds, *USA Today*, October 22, 1984.
69   "Inquiry: Staying Healthy," An interview with Earl Mindell, Co-founder, of Good Earth, a franchised vitamin company, with Barbara Reynolds, *USA Today*, January 2, 1986.
70   "Study Action Guide: Hamburger, U.S.A.: A Closer Look at America's Food System, Produced by American Friends Service Committee, San Francisco, California, 1979.
71   "Suppliers Strained, Buyers Cautious In Midst of Fresh Produce Boom," by Robert Johnson, *The Wall Street Journal*, January 27, 1986.
72   *Ibid.*
73   "The Freshness Illusion," by Bryan Jay Bashin, *Harrowsmith*, January/February, 1987.
74   Source: U.S. Department of Defense
75   *Op. cit.*, Bashin, *Harrowsmith*, January/February, 1987.
76   *Ibid.*
77   *Ibid.*
78   "New York's $6 million broccoli scam," *Tarrytown Letter*, September, 1984.
79   *Op. cit.*, Bashin, *Harrowsmith*, January/February, 1987.
80   *Op. cit.*, Johnson, *The Wall Street Journal*, January 27, 1986.
81   *Op. cit.*, Bashin, *Harrowsmith*, January/February, 1987.
82   *Ibid.*
83   *Ibid.*
84   *Op. cit.*, Johnson, *The Wall Street Journal*, January 27, 1986.
85   *Nutritian and Your Health: Dietary Guidelines for Americans*, USDA and Department of Health and Human Services, Washington, D.C.: February, 1980.
86   "Government Surprises Critics By Sticking to the Official Diet, by *The Los Angeles Times*, *San Francisco Chronicle*, September 25, 1985.
87   *Op. cit.*, Mottern, *Guidelines for Food Purchasing in the United States*, May 12, 1978.
88   *Ibid.* and "Battling Over Food Dye," by Patricia Picone Mitchell, *The Washington Post*, March 31, 1985.
89   *Federal Human Nutrition Research — Need for a Coordinated Approach to Advance Our Knowledge*, U.S. General Accounting Office, Washington, D.C., 1977.
90   *The Role of Health, Education and Welfare in Human Nutrition: Future Directions*," U.S. Department of Health, Education and Welfare, Washington, D.C., November, 1977.
91   *Op. cit.*, Mottern, *Guidelines for Food Purchasing in the United States*, May 12, 1978.
92   "Healthier Eating Through Chemistry," by Carole Sugarman, *The Washington Post*, July 7, 1987.
93   *Ibid.*
94   *Ibid*
95   "Food imports often unsafe, report finds," by Dan Sperling, *USA Today*, July 19, 1989.

96   *Ibid.*
97   "Experts: Our food is safe," by Warren Wheat, *USA Today*, July 19, 1985.
98   "U.S. to Review Food-Safety Efforts," Reuters, *The New York Times*, April 26, 1989.
99   "The FDA has failed to protect consumers," by Nancy Drabble, Public Citizen/Congress Watch, *USA Today*. July 26, 1985.
100   "Watching What We Eat," by Patricia Picone Mitchell, *The Washington Post*, June 30, 1985.
101   "Eating Well: Is That Food Really Safe," by Marian Burros, *The New York Times*, March 15, 1989.
102   *Op. cit.*, Mitchell, *The Washington Post*, June 30, 1985.
103   "Group: Block undercuts nutrition aid program," *USA Today*, August 15, 1984.
104   *Ibid.*
105   *Op. cit.*, Burros.
106   *Ibid.*
107   "The Federal Triangle: USDA Rule Allows 'Junk Food' in Schools," *The Washington Post*, May 28, 1985.
108   "High-Fat Food Pressed on the Young," by Walter Goodman, *The New York Times*, December 29, 1989.
109   "Quick meals for kids to zap," by Anita Manning, *USA Today*, March 15, 1989.
110   "What Are Commercials Selling to Children," by John J. O'Connor, *The New York Times*, June 6, 1989.
111   *Op. cit.*, Goodman, *The New York Times*, December 29, 1989.
112   "'People Are Surely As Smart As Hogs . . .'," by John Shepard, *Environmental Action*, October, 1984.
113   "Block Resigns Agriculture Post," by Ward Sinclair, *The Washington Post*, January 8, 1986.
114   "FDA Slow In Seizing Tainted Food," by Cass Peterson, *The Washington Post*, October 11, 1984.
115   *Ibid.*
116   *Op. cit.*, Bashan, *Harrowsmith*, January/February, 1987.
117   "Radiation & Food At May Forum," by Paul Rauber, *Berkeley Co-op News*, Berkeley, California, May 13, 1985.
118   "Irradiation: What Are the Risks," by Paul Rauber, *Berkeley Co-op News*, December 9, 1985.
119   *Ibid.*
120   "FDA Blessing Is Just A Start," by Carole Sugarman, *The Washington Post*, April 20, 1986.
121   "Glowing In The Fridge," by Judy Licht, *Environmental Action*, October, 1984.
122   "Issue and Debate: Is Radiation the Answer to Spoiled Food?," by Marian Burros, *The New York Times*, April 16, 1986.
123   *Op. cit.*, Rauber, *Berkeley Co-op News*, May 13, 1985.
124   "Tests: Irradiated produce," *USA Today*, September 15, 1986.
125   "Update on Irradiation," by Paul Rauber, *Berkeley Co-op News*, June 17, 1985.
126   *Op. cit.*, Licht, *Environmental Action*, October, 1984.
127   Statement of Robert Alvarez, Director, Nuclear Weapons and Power Project, Environmental Policy Institute before the Subcommittee on Department Operations, Research and Foreign Agriculture of the House Committee on Agriculture regarding H.R. 696: A Bill To Promote The Commercialization of Food Irradiation, Washington, D.C., November 18, 1985.
128   *Ibid.*
129   *Food Irradiation: Federal Requirements and Monitoring*, General Accounting Office, May, 1990, page 5.
130   "California," *USA Today*, February 6, 1986.
131   "Irradiation Is Becoming More Than Food for Thought," by Andrea Knox, Knight-Ridder, "Washington Business," *The Washington Post*, April 21, 1986.
132   "Radiation Company Admits to Safety Vilations," by Alfonso A. Narvaez, *The New York Times*, March 17, 1988.
133   "U.S. Jury Convicts Fromer President of Radiation Firm," by Sanford L. Jacobs, *The Wall Street Journal*, July 14, 1988.
134   *Op. cit.*, Alvarez, Subcommittee on Department Operations, Research and Foreign Agriculture of the House Committee on Agriculture, November 18, 1985.
135   "I just don't like feeling helpless," by Vicki Williams, King Features, *USA Today*, July 26, 1985.

CHAPTER TEN: Breaking The Plains

1   *American Enviornmental History: The Exploitation and Conservation of Natural Resources*, by Joseph M. Petulla, Boyd & Fraser, San Francisco, California: 1977, pg. 10.
2   *Ibid.*, pg. 11.
3   "The Structure of Farming and American History," Wayne D. Rasmussen, "Farm Structure: A Historical Perspective on Changes in the Number and Size of Farms," Committee on Agriculture, Nutrition and Forestry, U.S. Senate, 96th Congress, Second Session, 56-214 0, April, 1980, pg. 8.
4   *The Myth of the Family Farm: Agribusiness Dominance of U.S. Agriculture*, by Ingolf Voegler, Westview Press, Boulder, Colorado: 1981, pg.39.
5   Cited in "Societal Goals in Farm Size," by Philip M. Raup, *Size, Structure and Future of Farms*, Edited by A. Gordon Ball and Earl O. Heady, Iowa State University Press, Ames, Iowa: 1972, pp. 3-18.
6   *Op. cit.*, Petulla, *American Environmental History*, pg 86.
7   *Ibid.*, pg. 108.
8   *American Farmers' Movements*, By Fred A. Shannon, D. Van Nostrand Co., Inc., Princeton, N.J.: 1957, pg. 11.
9   *Op. cit.*, Petulla, *American Environmental History*, pp. 93-94.
10   *Ibid.*, pg. 86.
11   *Op. cit.*, Shannon, *American Farmers' Movements*, pg. 8.
12   *Op. cit.*, Petulla, *American Environmental History*, pg. 84.
13   *Op. cit.*, Voegler, *The Myth of the Family Farm*, pp. 42-45.
14   "Promised Land: A Contemporary Critique of Distribution of Public Land by the United States," by Sheldon L. Greene, Attorney, Greene, Kelley and Tobriner, San Francisco, California, *Ecology Law Quarterly*, School of Law, University of California - Berkeley, Vol. 5, 1976, pg. 713.
15   "Agriculture's Spanish Legacy," *Farmline*, USDA, September/October, 1985.
16   *The Rural Foundation of the American Culture*, by Dr. Walter Goldschmidt, A Gregory Foundation Memorial Lecture, University of Missouri-Columbia, January 26, 1976, pp. 75-79.
17   *Farming for Profit in a Hungry World: Capital and the Crisis in Agriculture*, by Michael Perelman, Allanheld, Osmun, Montclair, N.J.: 1977, pg. 26.
18   *Op. cit.*, Petulla, *American Environmental History*, pp. 192-193.
19   *The Roots of the Modern American Empire*, by William Appleman Williams, Vintage Books, New York, N.Y.: 1969, pg. 90.

CHAPTER ELEVEN: A Populism Born and Bred In Agrarian Revolt

1   *Democratic Promise: The Populist Moment in America* by Lawrence Goodwyn, Oxford University Press, New York: 1976, pg. 26-27.
2   *Ibid.*, pg. 28.
3   "Deflation, Agriculture and Southern Development," by lliam E. Laird and James R. Rinehart, *Journal of Agricultural History*, April, 1968.
4   *American Environmental History*, by Joseph Petulla, Boyd and Fraser, San Francisco, Calif.: 1977, pg. 185.
5   *Ibid.*, pg. 195.
6   *The Roots of the Modern American Empire*, by William Appleman Williams, Random House, New York, N.Y.: 1969, pg. 176.
7   "Inaugural Address of January 9, 1874," by Gov. C.K. Davis, *Executive Documents of the State of Minnesota for the Year 1873*, 3-11.
8   *Op. Cit.*, Williams, pg. 195.
9   *Ibid.*, pg. 208
10   *Sedalia Daily Bazoo*, June 14, 1877
11   *Op. Cit.*, Williams, pg. 228.
12   Rep. John Adam Kasson of Iowa, September, 1881.
13   See *As You Sow: Three Studies in the Social Consequences of Agribusiness*, by Walter Goldschmidt, Allanheld, Osmun & Co., Montclair, N.J.: 1978.
14   *The Myth of the Family Farm: Agribusiness Dominance of U.S. Agriculture*, by Ingolf Voegler, Westview Press, Boulder, Colorado: 1981, pg. 45.
15   *A History of Public Land Policies*, by Benjamin H. Hibbard, University of Wisconsin Press, Madison, Wisconsin: 1965, pg. 380.
16   *Ibid.*, pg. 380.
17   *Op. cit.*, Petulla, pg. 198.
18   "Promised Land: A Contemporary Critique of Distribution of Public Land by the United States," by Sheldon L. Greene, Attorney, Greene, Kelley and Tobriner, San Francisco, California, *Ecology Law Quarterly*, School of Law, University of California - Berkeley, Vol. 5, 1976, pg. 713.
19   *Op. cit.*, Hibbard, pg. 369-370, pg. 389.
20   *Op. cit.*, Voegler, pg. 49.
21   "The Homestead Laws in an Incongruous Land System," by Paul Wallace Gates, in *The Public Lands*, edited by Vernon Carstensen, University of Wisconsin Press, Madison, Wisconsin: 1968, pg. 318.
22   *Op. Cit.*, Petulla, pg. 178.
23   As quoted by Meridel LeSeur in "Plowing Up A Storm," produced by the Nebraska ETV Network, 1985.
24   *Op. cit.*, Voegler, pg. 49-50.
25   *Ibid.*
26   *Politics, Reform and Expansion 1890-1900*, by Harold U. Faulkner, Harper & Row, New York, New York: 1959.
27   *American Farmers' Movements*, by Fred A. Shannon, Van Nostrand Co. Inc., Princeton, N.J.: 1957, pg. 49-50.
28   *Ibid.*, pg. 51.
29   *Ibid.*, pg. 50-51.
30   As quoted in "Plowing Up A Storm," produced by the Nebraska ETV Network, 1985.
31   "The farmers' movement and large farmers' organizations," by Carl L. Taylor, in *Change In Rural America: Causes, Consequences, and Alternatives*, Edited by Rodefeld, et. al., C.V. Mosby Co., St. Louis, Missouri: 1978, pg. 458.
32   *Op. cit.*, Petulla, pg. 203.
33   *Farming for Profit in a Hungry World: Capital and the Crisis in Agriculture*, by Michael Perelman, Allanheld, Osmun, Montclair, N.J.: 1977, pg. 70.
34   Remarks of Minnesota Worthy Master S.E. Adams, National Grange, *Journal of Proceedings of the Session for 1879*.
35   *Op. Cit.*, Williams, pg. 228.
36   *Ibid.*, pg. 358-359.
37   "Grangers and Populists," by Robert W. Cherny, in *Plowing Up A Storm: The History of Midwestern Farm Activism*, A Publication accompanying the 90-minute public television special "Plowing Up A Storm," produced by the Nebraska ETV Network, 1985.
38   As related by Robert W. Cherney in "Plowing Up A Storm: The History of Midwestern Farm Activism," A 90-minute public television special produced by the Nebraska ETV Network, 1985.
39   *People's Party Paper*, January 4, 1894.
40   *Op. cit.*, Goodwyn, pg.
41   *The Populist Response to Industrial America: Midwestern Populist Thought*, by Norman Pollack, Harvard University Press, Cambridge, Mass.: 1962, pg. 77.
42   *Op. cit.*, Goodwyn, pg. xvii.

43 *Ibid.*, pg. 358.

44 *Ibid.*, pg. 611-612.

45 See Goodwyn, pg. 208-211, pg. 590-592.

46 *Rural Citizen*, March 11, 1886.

47 "The Populist Heritage and the Intellectual," by C. Vann Woodward, *American Scholar*, Winter, 1959-60, pg. 65-66.

48 *Op. Cit.*, Williams, pg. 515, 76fn.

49 *Op. cit.*, Shannon, pg. 10.

50 *Ibid.*

51 *Op. cit.*, Petulla, pg. 13-14.

CHAPTER TWELVE: Agriculture's "Golden Years"

1   "Editorial," by Henry Wallace, *Wallace's Farmer*, May 18, 1900.
2   *The Roots of the Modern American Empire*, by William Appleman Williams, Random House, New York, N.Y.: 1969, pg. 90.
3   *Farming for Profit in a Hungry World: Capital and the Crisis in Agriculture*, by Michael Perelman, Allanheld Osmun, Montclair, N.J.: 1977, pg. 29.
4   *Prairie Farmer*, February 10, 24, 1900.
5   *Democratic Promise: The Populist Moment in America*, by Lawrence Goodwyn, Oxford University Press, New York, New York: 1976, pg.524
6   *American Enviornmental History*, by Joseph Petulla, Boyd & Fraser, San Francisco, Calif.: 1977, pg. 262.
7   *Ibid.*, pg. 260.
8   *Ibid.*, pg. 263.
9   *Ibid.*, pg. 284.
10   "The farmers' movement and large farmers' organizations," by Carl L. Taylor, in *Change In Rural America: Causes, Consequences, and Alternatives*, Edited by Rodefeld, et. al., C.V. Mosby Co., St. Louis, Missouri: 1978, pg. 459- 460.
11   *Ibid.*
12   "Report to the President," National Conservation Commission, *Congressional Record*, 60th Congress, 2nd Session, January 22, 1909, Part 2: 1276-1279.
13   *Op. cit.*, Petulla, pg.269-270.
14   *Ibid.*, pg. 284.
15   "The Structure of Farming and American History," by Wayne D. Rasmussen, Chief, Agricultural History Branch, Economics, Statistics and Cooperative Service, USDA, *Farm Structure: A Historical Perspective on Changes in the Number and Size of Farms*, Committee on Agriculture, Nutrition, and Forestry, United States Senate, 96th Congress, 2nd Session, April, 1980, pg. 7.
16   *Ibid.*, pg. 7-8.
17   "Rural Education Reform and the Country Life Commission, 1900-1920," by David B. Danbom, *Agricultural History*.
18   *Ibid.*
19   "Vitalizing A Rural School Course, by Allen S. Woodward, *Education*, May, 1917.
20   *Op. cit.*, Danbom.
21   "Agriculture in the World War Period," by A. B. Genuing, *Yearbook of Agriculture, 1960*, pg. 278.
22   *Ibid.*, pg. 280.
23   *Ibid.*
24   *Ibid.* pg. 281.
25   *Ibid.*
26   *Ibid.*
27   *Agricultural Discontent in the Middle West, 1900-1939*, by Theodore Saloutos and John D. Hicks, University of Wisconsin Press, Madison, Wisconsin: 1951.
28   "Plowing Up A Storm: The History of Midwestern Farm Activism," A 90-minute public television special produced by the Nebraska ETV Network, 1985.
29   *Ibid.*
30   "Why A Nonpartisan League?", Address by A.C. Townley to Mass Meeting at Blackfoot, Idaho, *Non-Partisan League Leader*, December 24, 1917.
31   *Op. cit.*, Genuing, pg. 281.
32   *Ibid.*, pg. 282.
33   *American Pork Production in the World War*, by Frank M.Surface, Chicago and New York, 1926.
34   *Op. cit.*, Genuing, pg. 283.
35   *Ibid.*, pg. 283-284.
36   *Ibid.*, pg. 284-286.
37   *Ibid.*, pg. 286-288.
38   *Ibid.*, pg. pg. 288.
39   *Ibid.*, pg. 285.
40   *Ibid.*, pg. 285-286.
41   *Ibid.*, pg. 289.
42   *Ibid.*
43   *Ibid.*, pg. 292.
44   *Ibid.*, pg. 293.
45   *Ibid.*
46   *Ibid.*
47   *Ibid.*

48   *Ibid.*, pg. 291.

CHAPTER THIRTEEN: An "Interplay Of Economic Forces"

1   *Breadlines Knee Deep in Wheat: Food Assistance in the Great Depression*, by Janet Poppendieck, Rutgers University Press, New Brunswick, N.J.: 1986, pg.3.
2   *American Farmers' Movements*, by Fred A. Shannon, Van Nostrand Co. Inc., Princeton, N.J.: 1957, pg. 84.
3   *Op. Cit.*, Poppendieck, pg. 5.
4   *Ibid.*, pg. 3.
5   *Op. Cit.*, Shannon, pg. 85.
6   *Farm Policies of the United States, 1790-1950: A Study of Their Origins and Development*, by Murray R. Benedict, The Twentieth Century Fund, New York, N.Y.: 1953, pg. 200.
7   *Ibid.*, pg. 201.
8   Statement of Tom Linder, Atlanta, Commissioner of Agriculture of Georgia in Opposition to Trade Treaties Before the Committee on Ways and Means, House of Representatives, Washington, D.C., 1947.
9   Based on figures compiled from *Agricultural Statistics, 1941*, USDA, U.S. Government Printing Office, Washington, D.C., 1941.
10   *Ibid.*
11   *Op. Cit.*, Poppendeick, pg. 10.
12   *Op. Cit.*, Linder.
13   "The Planned Destruction of the Dollar," by James Dale Davidson, *Penthouse*, July, 1980.
14   *Ibid.*
15   *Ibid.*
16   See Eustace Mullins, *The Secrets of the Federal Reserve*, Bankers Research Institute, Staunton, Virginia.
17   "Banks' Stock List Full of Surprises," *The New York Times*, September 23, 1914.
18   "Who Is Behind the Farm Crisis?", Published by the Center for Democratic Renewal, Atlanta, Georgia; Institution for Research and Education on Human Rights, Inc., Kansas City, Missouri, and Prairiefire Rural Action, Des Moines, Iowa.
19   See "Facts About the Federal Reserve System" by Jerry Epstein, Assistant Professor of Economics, Williams College, and "The Power of the Fed: Who really pushes the buttons," by Mark Breibart and Gerald Epstein, *The Progressive*, April, 1983.
20   *Op. Cit.*, Davidson, *Penthouse*.
21   *Annals of Congress*, Vol. 1, February, 1790: 1141-1142.
22   *Op. Cit.*, Linder.
23   From testimony delivered by Sen. Robert L. Owen, Chairman of the Senate Banking and Commerce Committee, to the Senate Silver Hearings in 1939.
24   Testimony delivered by Sen. Brookhart (Iowa) to the Senate Silver Hearings in 1939.
25   William Jennings Bryan, *Hearst's Magazine*, November, 1923.
26   *Op. Cit.*, Davidson, *Penthouse*.
27   *Op. Cit.*, Linder.

CHAPTER FOURTEEN: Fighting For "Equality For Agriculture"

1   "Inflation and Deflation in the United States and the United Kingdom, 1919-1923," by H. W. Macrosty, *Journal of the Royal Statistical Society*, 90:55, 1927.

2   "Henry Ford and the Agricultural Depression of 1920-1923," by Reynold M. Wik, Agricultural History Society and the Mississippi Historical Association, Madison, Wisconsin, April 23, 1954.

3   "The Development of the Parity Price Formula for Agriculture, 1919-1923," by James H. Shideler, *Agricultural History*, July, 1953.

4   Source: *Agricultural Statistics, 1941*, USDA, U.S. Government Printing Office, Washington, D.C., 1941.

5   *Op. Cit.*, Wik.

6   Data compiled by W.P. Kinney, Chicago, August 19, 1924. Manuscript in the Ford Motor Company Archives, Fair Lane, Dearborn, Michigan. Henry Ford Business Correspondence, The Ford-Ferguson File, Accession 380, Box 10, No. 06367.

7   *Op. Cit.*, Wik.

8   *American Farmers' Movements*, by Fred A. Shannon, Van Nostrand Co. Inc., Princeton, N.J.: 1957, pg. 85.

9   *The Farm Bloc*, by Wesley McCune, Doubleday, Doran & Co., Inc., Garden City, N.Y.: 1943.

10   "Professionalism, Policy, and Farm Economists in the Early Bureau of Agricultural Economics," by Harry C. McDean, *Agricultural History*.

11   *Ibid.*, pg. 74.

12   *Ibid.*, pg. 78.

13   *Food Policy For America*, by Harold G. Halcrow, McGraw-Hill Book Co., New York, N.Y.: 1977, pg. 144.

14   "Report on National Agricultural Conference, 1922," National Agricultural Conference, U.S. Congress, 67th, Second Session, House Document 195, pg. 3.

15   *George N. Peek and the Fight for Farm Parity*, by Gilbert C. Fite, University of Oklahoma Press, Norman, Okla.: 1954, pg. 45.

16   *Op. Cit.*, National Agricultural Conference, pg. 10.

17   *Ibid.*, pg. 171.

18   *Ibid.*, pg. 137.

19   *Op. cit.*, Fite, *George N. Peek and the Fight for Farm Parity*.

20   See "Origin of the Base Period Concept of Parity — A Significant Value Judgment in Agricultural Policy," by Robert L. Tontz, *Agricultural History*.

21   *The Blue Eagle from Egg to Earth*, by Hugh S. Johnson, Doubleday, Garden City, N.Y.: 1935, pg. 104.

22   "To All Who May Be Interested in Equality for Agriculture," by George N. Peek and Hugh S. Johnson, Moline, Illinois, April, 1922.

23   "The Development of Agricultural Policy Since the End of the World War," by Chester C. Davis, *Yearbook of Agriculture, 1940*, USDA, pg. 307.

24   Letter to Robert L. Tontz from Henry A. Wallace, Farvue Farm, South Salem, New York, June 12, 1953.

25   *Op. Cit.*, Davis, pg. 303.

26   *Congressional Record*, 68th Congress, 1st Session, December 6, 1923, pg. 100.

27   *Op. Cit.*, Fite, pg. 78.

28   *Breadlines Knee Deep in Wheat: Food Assistance in the Great Depression*, by Janet Poppendieck, Rutgers University Press, New Brunswick, N.J.: 1986, pg. 10.

29   *Nation's Business*, June 4, 1924.

30   *Op. Cit.*, Fite, pg. 92.

31   "Income from Agricultural Production," by L.H. Bean, *Yearbook of Agriculture, 1926*, USDA, pg. 447.

32   "Plowing Up A Storm: The History of Midwestern Farm Activism," A 90-minute public television special produced by the Nebraska ETV Network, 1985.

33   *Ibid.*

CHAPTER FIFTEEN: "Oh Say To Him, Stuff And Nonsense"

1   "The Development of Agricultural Policy Since the End of the World War," By Chester C. Davis, *Yearbook of Agriculture, 1940,* pg. 312.

2   *The Agricultural Problem in the United States,* National Industrial Conference Board, 1926.

3   *Ibid.,* National Industrial Conference Board

4   "The Attitude of the Business Community Toward Agriculture During the McNary-Haugen Period," by John Philip Gleason, *Agricultural History,* April, 1958.

5   *The Commercial and Financial Chronicle,* March, 1924.

6   *The Washington Post,* May 13, 1924.

7   "Mellon to Haugen,Dickinson and Daniel R. Anthony," Reprinted in *Congressional Record,* 69th Congress, Ist Session, June 15, 1926, pg. 11266.

8   *George N. Peek and the Fight for Farm Parity,* by Gilbert C. Fite, University of Oklahoma Press, Norman, Oklahoma: 1954, pg. 192.

9   *Bank Letter,* April, 1925.

10   *Nation's Business,* February, 1927.

11   *Nation's Business,* October, 1924.

12   *Commercial & Financial Chronicle,* March, 1927.

13   *Op. Cit.,* Gleason, April, 1958.

14   "Voices From Across the USA," *USA Today,* February 26, 1985.

15   *Iron Age,* August, 1926.

16   *The Commercial & Financial Chronicle,* July, 1926.

17   *The Commercial & Financial Chronicle,* March, 1927.

18   *Op. Cit.,* Gleason, April, 1958.

19   See *George N. Peek and the Fight for Farm Parity,* by Gilbert C. Fite, University of Oklahoma Press, Norman, Oklahoma: 1954.

20   *Op. Cit.,* Fite, pg. 96-99.

21   "Declaration of Principles," St. Louis Conference on Agricultural Relief, Adopted by Farmer Organization Leaders of Six Southern and Six Northern States in Conference in St. Louis on the Problems of Agricultural Relief.

22   See *Farm Policies of the United States, 1790-1950: A Study of Their Origins and Development,* by Murray R. Benedict, The Twentieth Century Fund, New York, N.Y.: 1953, Chapter 11.

23   *The Condition of Agriculture in the United States and Measures For Its Improvement,* by Business Men's Commission on Agriculture, New York, 1927.

24   *Op. cit.,* Davis.

25   *Ibid.*

26   Memo Herbert Hoover to Brown, October 20, 1921. Files of the Secretary of Agriculture.

27   *Op. Cit.,* Benedict, pg. 260-267.

28   Source: Population Reference Bureau, Inc. as quoted in *The Great Farm Problem,* by William H. Peterson, Henry Regnery, Chicago, Ill.: 1959, pg. 188.

CHAPTER SIXTEEN: A "New And Untrod Path"

1   *Agricultural Statistics - 1950*, USDA, pg. 626-628.

2   *From the Crash to the Blitz, 1929-1939*, by Cabell Phillips, *The New York Times* Chronicle of American Life," The Macmillan Co., London, 1969, pg. 16.

3   *Ibid.*, Phillips, pg. 17.

4   *Breadlines Knee Deep in Wheat: Food Assistance in the Great Depression*, by Janet Poppendieck, Rutgers University Press, New Brunswick, N.J.: 1986, pg. 16-17.

5   "Agriculture and World Crisis," by L.H. Bean, *Yearbook of Agriculture, 1953*.

6   *Ibid.*, *Yearbook of Agriculture, 1953*.

7   "Large-Scale Farming in the United States," by H.R. Tolley and C.L. Holmes, Bureau of Agricultural Economics, USDA, pg. 2-3, Copy in files of Agricultural History Branch, Economic Statistical Cooperative Service, USDA.

8   *Op. Cit.*, *Yearbook of Agriculture, 1953*.

9   *Farm Policies of the United States, 1790-1950: A Study of Their Origins and Development*, by Murray R. Benedict, The Twentieth Century Fund, New York, N.Y.: 1953, pg. 246-247, 279.

10   *American Farmers' Movements*, by Fred A. Shannon, Van Nostrand Co. Inc., Princeton, N.J.: 1957, pg. 88.

11   *Ibid.*, Shannon, pg. 88.

12   As quoted in *The Age of Roosevelt: The Coming of the New Deal*, by Arthur Schlesinger, Houghton Miffin Co., N.Y.: 1959, pg. 39.

13   *Op. Cit.*, Poppendieck, pg. 17.

14   *Food Policy For America*, by Harold G. Halcrow, McGraw-Hill Book Co., New York, N.Y.: 1977, pg. 151.

15   *Social Scientists and Farm Politics in the Age of Roosevelt*, by Richard S. Kirkendall, Iowa State University Press, Ames, Iowa: 1966, pg. 59-60.

16   *Public Papers & Addresses of Franklin D. Roosevelt*, Vol 1, Samuel I. Rosenman, Editor, The Macmillan Co., London: 1938, pg. 699-701.

17   *Op. Cit.*, Schlesinger, pg. 39.

18   "Up the ante on the Farm Bill Fight," by Merle Hansen, *North American Farmer*, October 15, 1985.

19   "The Resettlement Idea," by Rexford G. Tugwell, Paper presented to a joint luncheon meeting of the Agricultural Historical Society and the American Historical Association, Washington, D.C., December 30, 1958.

20   "Reagan May Yet Reap Harvest of Anger," by Haynes Johnson, *The Washington Post.*, March 10, 1985.

21   Radio address of July 20, 1932. "Why the Farmers Holiday" in *Milo Reno: Farmers Union Pioneer*, by Roland White, Iowa City, 1941, pg. 151.

22   As recalled in "Plowing Up A Storm: The History of Midwestern Farm Activism," A 90-minute public television special produced by the Nebraska ETV Network, 1985.

23   "The New Deal and the Roots of Agribusiness: A Statement to the First National Conference on Land Reform," by Donald H. Grubbs, University of the Pacific, San Francisco, Calif., April 25-27, 1973. See also "Western Agriculture and the New Deal," by Leonard J. Arrington, *Agricultural History*, October, 1970.

24   "Years of shame, days of madness," by George Mills, *Des Moines Register Picture*, February 18, 1979.

25   "Populism in the Nineteen Thirties: The Battle for the AAA," by John L. Shover, Paper presented in the Agricultural History session of the Pacific Coast Branch, American Historical Association at UCLA, Los Angeles, California, August 26, 1964.

26   *Ibid.*, Shover, August 26, 1964.

27   *Op. Cit.*, Kirkendall, pg. 56.

28   *Congressional Record*, 73rd Congress, 1st Session, April 11- 12, 1933, LXXVII, Part 2, pg. 1475, 1552-3.

29   *Op. Cit.*, Shover, August 26, 1964.

30   "Farm Loans and Farm Management by the Equitable Life Assurance Society of the United States," by F. J. Skogvold, Paper presented at joint seassion of the Agricultural Historical Society with the American Historical Association, Washington, D.C., December 28, 1955.

31   *Ibid.*

32   *Ibid.*

33   *Ibid.*

34   *This Mighty Dream: Social Protest Movements in the United States*, by Madeleine Adamson and Seth Borgos, Routledge & Kegan Paul, Boston, Mass.: 1985, pg. 33.

35   See *Mean Things Happening in This Land*, by H. L. Mitchell, Allanheld, Osmun, Montclair, N.J.: 1979.

36   *Op. Cit.*, Adamson and Borgos, pg. 37.

37   *Ibid.*

38   *Ibid.*

39   Figures related to Edward S. Kennedy by an official of the U.S. Treasury Department and cited in his *The Fed and the Farmer*, pg. 90.

40   "Farm Debt Adjustments During the Depression - The Other Side of the Coin," by Ernest Feder, *Agricultural*

History, April, 1961.

CHAPTER SEVENTEEN: Liberty vs. Paternalism

1   "Drought Stirs Memories of Dreaded 'Black Dusters'," by Jerry E. Bishop, *The Wall Street Journal*, July 19, 1988.
2   *Farm Policies of the United States, 1790-1950: A Study of Their Origins and Development*, by Murray R. Benedict, The Twentieth Century Fund, New York, N.Y.: 1953, pg. 299.
3   *Ibid.*
4   *Dust Bowl: The Southern Plains in the 1930's*, by Donald Worster, Oxford University Press. New York, N.Y.: 1979, pg. 43.
5   *Ibid.*, Worster, pg. 7.
6   "Drought of '88 Spurs Comparisons to Dust Bowl Era, but Differences Abound," by Keith Schneider, *The New York Times*, July 7, 1988.
7   *Op. cit.*, Bishop, *The Wall Street Journal*, July 19, 1988 and *High Plains Yesterdays* by John C. Dawson, Eakin Press, 1985.
8   *Ibid.*
9   *Op. cit.*, Schneider, *The New York Times*, July 7, 1988.
10 *Op. cit.*, Worster, pg. 12.
11 *Ibid.*, Worster, pg. 43.
12 "An Ill Wind Blows Over the Land, 1935," *The Wall Street Journal*, May 10, 1989.
13 *Op. Cit.*, Benedict, pg. 357.
14 *Ibid.*, Benedict, pg. 357.
15 "The Resettlement Idea," by Rexford G. Tugwell, Paper presented to a joint luncheon meeting of the Agricultural Historical Society and the American Historical Association, Washington, D.C., December 30, 1958.
16 *Social Scientists and Farm Politics in the Age of Roosevelt*, by Richard S. Kirkendall, Iowa State University Press, Ames, Iowa: 1966, pg. 42.
17 "The Placement of Government in a National Land Program," by Rexford G. Tugwell, *Journal of Farm Economics*, January, 1934, pg. 65.
18 Chester Davis to Henry Wallace, February 25, 1936, National Archives Records Group, Secretary of Agriculture.
19 *Ibid.*, Davis to Wallace.
20 "The Purge of the AAA," by Raymond Gram Swing, *The Nation*, February 20, 1935.
21 *Op.Cit.*, Tugwell, December 30, 1958.
22 *Ibid.*
23 *Ibid.*
24 "Planning for Plenty," *Fortune*, October, 1940.
25 *Agricultural Statistics - 1950*, USDA, pg. 628, 636.
26 *Food Policy For America*, by Harold G. Halcrow, McGraw-Hill Book Co., New York, N.Y.: 1977, pg. 153.
27 *Prosperity Unlimited: The American Way*, by Carl H. Wilken, Sioux City, Iowa: 1947, pg. 17.
28 *Ibid.*
29 *Ibid.*
30 *Ibid.*
31 *Op. Cit.*, Benedict, pg 291n.
32 *Public Papers and Addresses, 1933*: Franklin D. Roosevelt, Random House, New York, N.Y.: 1938, pg. 264-265.
33 *United States Statistical Abstract, 1949*, pg. 640-641; *Economic History of the United States*, Second Edition, by Chester Whitney Wright, McGraw Hill, New York, N.Y.: 1949, pg. 792.
34 "The U.S. in the World Economy," U.S. Department of Commerce, Economic Series No. 23, 1943.
35 "The New Deal and the Roots of Agribusiness," by Donald H. Grubbs, A statement to the First National Conference on Land Reform, San Francisco, California, April 25-27, 1973.
36 "The New Deal Agricultural Program and the Constitution," by Paul I. Murphy, *Agricultural History*, October, 1955.
37 *U.S. Reports*, 307:38
38 *Op. cit.*, Murphy, *Agricultural History*, October, 1955.

CHAPTER EIGHTEEN: War And Peace

1   "The Structure of Farming and American History," by Wayne D. Rasmussen, Chief, Agricultural History Branch, Economics, Statistics and Cooperative Service, USDA, *Farm Structure: A Historical Perspective on Changes in the Number and Size of Farms*, Committee on Agriculture, Nutrition, and Forestry, United States Senate, 96th Congress, 2nd Session, April, 1980.

2   M.L. Wilson to C. E. Brehm, Records Group, Secretary of Agriculture, National Archives, Washington, D.C., September 20, 1940.

3   Report 2288; Report 2218; Public Law 674; U.S. House of Representatives, 77th Congress, 2nd Session, *The New York Times*, June 26, 1942.

4   *Social Scientists and Farm Politics in the Age of Roosevelt*, by Richard S. Kirkendall, Iowa State University Press, Ames, Iowa: 1966, pg. 219.

5   *Agricultural Statistics - 1945, USDA, pg. 431; U.S. Statistical Abstract, 1948, pg. 276; Agricultural Statistics - 1949, USDA, pg. 490.*

6   *Farm Policies of the United States, 1790-1950: A Study of Their Origins and Development*, by Murray R. Benedict, The Twentieth Century Fund, New York, N.Y.: 1953, pg. 407.

7   *Ibid.*, Benedict, pg. 408.

8   *The Farmer in the Second World War*, by Walter W. Wilcox, Iowa State College Press, Ames, Iowa: 1947, pg. 122.

9   *Public Papers and Address: Franklin D. Roosevelt, 1942*, pg. 219-20.

10   *Op. Cit.*, Benedict, pg. 414.

11   *Op. Cit., Public Papers, Roosevelt, 1942*, pg. 364.

12   *Ibid., Public Papers, Roosevelt, 1942*, pg. 365-366.

13   See "Agricultural Legislation: An Appraisal of Current Trends and Problems Ahead," by Oris V. Wells, A paper presented at the annual meeting of the American Farm Economic Association, Philadelphia, Penn., December 28, 1946, and *Op. Cit.*, Benedict, pg. 415-416.

14   "General Price Index (GPI) for Moderate Income Families in Large Cities: 1913-1918," *Statistical Abstract, 1949*, pg. 308.

15   *Ibid.*

16   *Op. Cit.*, Benedict, pg. 416.

17   "Food Subsidy Programs for the Fiscal Year 1946," USDA and Office of Price Administration Mimeo., August, 1945.

18   *Op. Cit.*, Wilcox, pg. 64.

19   *Op. Cit.*, Benedict, pg. 432.

20   *Wartime Economic Planning in Agriculture, A Study in the Allocation of Resources*, by Bela Gold, Columbia University Press, New York, N.Y.: 1949, pg. 87.

21   *Op. Cit.*, Benedict, pg. 436.

22   *Ibid.*

23   See "The Concept and Determination of Prevailing Wages in Agriculture During World War II," by Samuel Liss, Farmers Home Administration, USDA, *Agricultural History*, January, 1950.

24   56 Stat. 1018, Sec. 4.

25   *Op. Cit.*, Benedict, pg. 439.

26   See *Migratory Labor in American Agriculture*, President's Commission on Migratory Labor, 1951, and *The Hired Farm Working Force, 1948 and 1949*, Bureau of Agricultural Economics, November, 1950.

27   *Op. Cit.*, Benedict, pg. 440.

28   *Ibid.*, Benedict, pg. 442, 33fn.

29   *United States Consumption of Food in Terms of Fats, Proteins, Carbohyrates, and Calories, 1939-1943*, Tariff Commission, February, 1944, Mimeographed, pg. 18-19.

30   "Consumption of Food in the United States, 1909-1948," USDA, pg. 120.

31   *Op. Cit.*, Benedict, pg. 445.

32   *Ibid.*, Benedict, pg. 447.

33   *Ibid.*, Benedict, pg. 449.

34   *Ibid.*, Benedict, pg. 450.

35   *Agricultural Statistics - 1949*, USDA, pg. 634.

36   "Farm Real Estate Situation, 1943-1946," USDA Circular No. 754, pg. 6-7.

37   *Ibid.*

38   "Balance Sheet of Agriculture, 1946," Bureau of Agricultural Economics, USDA Miscellaneous Publication No. 620, Pg. 5.

39   *Op. Cit.*, Benedict, pg. 459.

40   *What Post-War Policies for Agriculture?*, Report of the USDA Interbureau and Regional Committees on Post-War Programs (1943).

41   *Ibid.*, pg. 6.

42   *Ibid.*, pg. 9.
43   *Ibid.*, pg 12.
44   *Ibid*, pg. 12.
45   *Ibid*, pg. 13.

CHAPTER NINETEEN: Peace And War

1   "The Postwar Famine and Price Control, 1946," by Barton J. Bernstein, *Agricultural History*, October, 1964.
2   *Ibid.*
3   *U.S. Statistical Abstract, 1950*, pg. 279.
4   *Farm Policies of the United States, 1790-1950: A Study of Their Origins and Development*, by Murray R. Benedict, The Twentieth Century Fund, New York, N.Y.: 1953, pg. 463. fn7.
5   *The Farm Income Situation*, Bureau of Agricultural Economics, USDA, August, 1950, pg. 24 and pg. 30.
6   "Collective Bargaining For Farmers," by M.W. Thatcher, *Agricultural Thought in the Twentieth Century*, Edited by George McGovern, Bobbs-Merrill Co. Inc., Indianapolis, Ind.:1967, pg. 305-318.
7   *Postwar Agricultural Policy*, A Report of the Committee on Postwar Agricultural Policy, Association of Land-Grant Colleges and Universities, October, 1944.
8   *Op. Cit.*, Benedict, pg. 470.
9   *Ibid.*, Benedict, pg. 471.
10   *Senate 1331*, 78th Congress, Ist Session.
11   "A Lesson From the New Deal: The Farm Security Administration," by Sidney Baldwin, California State University, A Paper Prepared for the First National Conference on Land Reform, San Francisco, Calif.: April 25-28, 1973.
12   See *Social Scientists and Farm Politics in the Age of Roosevelt*, by Richard S. Kirkendall, Iowa State University Press, Ames, Iowa: 1966; "Professionalism, Policy, and Farm Economists in the Early Bureau of Agricultural Economics," by Harry McDean, Paper presented to Pacific Coast Branch, American Historical Association, University of Oregon, August, 1981; *The Decline of Agrarian Democracy*, by Grant McConnell, Atheneum, New York, N.Y.: 1977.
13   "The Agricultural Act of 1948," by H.C.M. Case, *Journal of Farm Economics*, February, 1949.
14   65 Stat. 1247 at 1251.
15   *Op. Cit.*, Benedict, pg. 478-484.
16   50 Stat. 265.
17   60 Stat. 1082, approved August 14, 1946.
18   60 Stat. 413 at 432, approved July 15, 1949.
19   Public Law 734, 81st Congress, 2nd Session, approved August 28, 1950.
20   "Proposals For Payment Program," by Charles F. Brannan, *Agricultural Thought in the Twentieth Century*, Edited by George McGovern, Bobbs-Merrill Co. Inc., Indianapolis, Ind.:1967, pg. 369-370.
21   *Ibid.*, Brannan, pg. 367.
22   "The Brannan Plan v. the Agricultural Act of 1949," by Theodore W. Schultz, Paper delivered to Annual Conference, Agricultural Extension Service, University of Missouri, December 9, 1949.
23   *Op. Cit.*, Brannan, pg. 366.
24   See *As You Sow: Three Studies in the Social Consequences of Agribusiness*, by Walter Goldschmidt, Allanheld, Osmun & Co., Montclair, N.J.: 1978.
25   *Ibid.*, Goldschmidt, pg. 466.
26   *Ibid.*, pg. 420.
27   "The Communities of the San Joaquin Valley," by Isao Fujimoto, *Priorities in Agricultural Research of the U.S. Department of Agriculture -- Appendix*, Subcommittee on Administrative Practice and Procedure of the Committee of the Judiciary, U.S. Congress, Senate, 95th Congress, 2nd Session, 1978, Part 2, Pg.1374-1396.
28   *Op. Cit.*, Goldschmidt, pg. 466.
29   "Small Town America VII: Dinuba, California," by Alden Stevens, *The Nation*, September 28, 1946.
30   *Op. Cit.*, Goldschmidt, pg. 485.
31   *Ibid.*, Goldschmidt, pg. 486.
32   See *Farm Policies and Politics in the Truman Years*, by Allen J. Matusow, Harvard University Press, Cambridge, Mass.: 1967.
33   *Ibid.*, Matusow, pg. 201.
34   *Ibid.*, pg. 200-201.
35   *Op. Cit.*, Brannan, pg. 363.
36   "The Financial Position of Agriculture," by Jesse W, Tapp, Address to the California Farm Bureau Federation, Long Beach, California, November 15, 1949.
37   *Op. Cit.*, Matusow, Chapter 10.
38   See *The Hidden History of the Korean War* by I.F. Stone, Monthly Review Press, 1952.
39   "American Agricultural Policy During Rearmament," by Karl Brandt, Economist, Food Research Institute, Stanford University, Address delivered at the 64th annual meeting of the American Economic Association, Boston, Mass., December 26, 1951.

CHAPTER TWENTY: "Adapt Or Die"

1   *Who's Behind Our Farm Policy?*, by Wesley McCune, Frederick A. Praeger, New York, N.Y.: 1956, pg. 55.
2   *Turning the Searchlight on Farm Policy: A Forthright Analysis of Experience, Lessons, Criteria and Recommendations*, The Farm Foundation, Chicago, Illinois: 1952, pg. 77.
3   *Ibid.*
4   *Food Policy For America*, by Harold G. Halcrow, McGraw-Hill Book Co., New York, N.Y.: 1977, pg. 171.
5   "Eisenhower and Ezra Taft Benson: Farm Policy in the 1950's," by Edward L. Schapsmeier and Frederick H. Schapsmeier, *Agricultural History*, October, 1970.
6   "Main Street, U.S.A.: A Heritage and A Covenant," Remarks of Rep. Harold D. Cooley (Dem.-N.C.), Chairman, Committee on Agriculture, House of Representatives, before the 30th Annual Convention, Independent Bankers Association, Minneapolis, Minn.: April 10, 1964.
7   *Ibid.*
8   *Ibid.*
9   Conversation between Vince Roositer and Rep. Harold D. Cooley, April 10, 1964.
10   "General Statement On Agricultural Policy by Ezra Taft Benson," Benson Papers, Eisenhower Library, February 5, 1953.
11   *Op. Cit.*, McCune, Chapter 28, "Old School Ties."
12   *Ibid.*, McCune, pg. 289.
13   *Ibid.*
14   *Ibid.*
15   *Farm Policy Forum*, February, 1951.
16   *Op. Cit.*, McCune, pg. 296.
17   *Ibid.*
18   Washington, October 25, 1954.
19   *American Cooperation*, 1955 Yearbook of the American Institute of Cooperation, pg. 21-30.
20   *Ibid.*
21   *Op. Cit.*, McCune, pg.239.
22   *Ibid.*
23   *Ibid.*, pg. 157.
24   "Price Times Units Equals Returns," by Don Paarlberg, *Agricultural Thought in the Twentieth Century*, Edited by George McGovern, Bobbs-Merrill Co. Inc., Indianapolis, Ind.:1967, pg. 417.
25   *Ibid.*
26   Transcript of television broadcast, Adams Papers, June 3, 1953.
27   *Des Moines Register*, February 22, 1954.
28   Statement by the President Upon Signing the Agricultural Act of 1954, *Public Papers of the Presidents of the United States, Dwight D. Eisenhower, 1954*, Washington, D.C., 1960, August 28, 1954, pg. 772.
29   *Cross Fire: The Eight Years With Eisenhower*, by Ezra Taft Benson, Doubleday, Garden City, N.Y.: 1962, pg. 254-255.
30   "A Thurst At 'Sonorous Boondoggling'," by John Kenneth Galbraith, *Agricultural Thought in the Twentieth Century*, pg. 444.
31   "The Family Farm: A Changing Concept," by David Brewster, Economics, Statistics, and Cooperative Service Historian, USDA, *Structure Issues of American Agriculture*, ESCS, Agricultural Economic Report 438, November, 1979.
32   *Op. Cit.*, Schapsmeier, pg. 374.
33   Letter from Fred L. Stover, Iowa Farmers Union to James Patton, National Farmers Union, June 3, 1953.
34   A confidential report, "Elements of Production Research," April 12, 1957, OF 110-N Eisenhower Library.
35   See "Business Tides" by Henry Hazlitt, *Newsweek*, October 24, 1955, December 19, 1955, and January 9, 1956.
36   *Op. Cit.*, McCune, pg. 227.
37   Veto of the Farm Bill, April 16, 1956. *Op. Cit.*, *Public Papers of the Presidents of the United States, Dwight D. Eisenhower, 1954*, pg. 386-388.
38   *Op. Cit.*, Schapsmeier, pg. 376.
39   *Agricultural Bulletin*, U.S. Chamber of Commerce, April 2, 1954.
40   Testimony before the Senate Committee on Agriculture and Forestry, January 19, 1956.
41   Address to the National Institute of Animal Agriculture, Purdue University, April 14, 1954.
42   Newspaper Farm Editors Association, April 24, 1953.
43   United Press dispatch, February 25, 1954.
44   Address to joint meeting of the Macon County Farm Bureau and the Decatur, Illinois Association of Commerce, February 22, 1954.
45   Confirmation hearings before Senate Committee on Agriculture and Forestry, January 27, 1953.
46   *Op. Cit.*, McCune, pg. 165.

47   *Diary Survey*, Bureau of Labor Statistics, Report 448-2, pg. 6.

48   Letter from Rep. W.R. Poage to Edward L. Schapsmeier and Frederick H. Schapsmeier, September 24, 1969.

49   *The White House Years: Mandate for Change, 1953-1956*, by Dwight D. Eisenhower, Doubleday, Garden City, N.Y.: 1963, pg. 354.

50   *Op. Cit.*, Edward L. Schapsmeier and Frederick H. Schapsmeier, pg. 377.

CHAPTER TWENTY-ONE: "New Frontiers" and New Challenges

1   See "Introduction," *The Almanac of American History*, General Editor: Arthur M. Schlesinger, Jr., G.P. Putnam's Sons, New York, N.Y.: 1983, pg. 8-13.

2   "Notable & Quoteable," *The Wall Street Journal*, December 5, 1986.

3   *Op. Cit.*, Schlesinger, pg. 12.

4   Data derived from special tabulations by the Bureau of the Census from 1959 and 1964 Censuses of Agriculture cited in Radoje Nikolitch, *Family-Size Farms in Agriculture*, Economic Research Service Report No. 499, USDA, Table 1.

5   *1976 President's Economic Report*

6   *Farm Income, 1949-1962*, Economic Research Service, USDA, II, 39.

7   "Farm Income Situation," USDA, July, 1976.

8   "Balance Sheet of the Farming Sector," Supplement #1, USDA, April, 1976 and "Farm Income Situation," USDA, July, 1976.

9   "The Great Holding Action: The NFO in September, 1962," by John T. Schlebecker, *Agricultural History*, October, 1965.

10   *Food Policy For America*, by Harold G. Halcrow, McGraw-Hill Book Co., New York, N.Y.: 1977, pg. 223.

11   *Ibid.*, pg. 174.

12   *Ibid.*, pg 175

13   *Ibid.*

14   *Ibid.*, pg.180.

15   *Ibid.*, pg. 176-183.

16   From the President's letter to members of the Commission, January 11, 1966 in *Food and Fiber for the Future*, Report of the National Advisory Commission on Food and Fiber, U.S. Government Printing Office, Washington, D.C., July, 1967.

17   *Op. Cit.*, Halcrow, pg. 183-187.

18   *Ibid.*, pg. 186.

19   *The People Left Behind*, Report by the President's National Advisory Commission on Rural Poverty, U.S. Government Printing Office, Washington, D.C., September, 1967, pg. ix.

20   *1964 U.S. Census of Agriculture*, U.S. Department of Commerce, Bureau of Census, Vol. 2, Chapter 6, Table 25; and Chapter 8, Table 26.

21   *Food and Fiber in the Nation's Politics*, by Charles M. Hardin, Vol 3., Technical Papers for the National Advisory Commission on Food and Fiber, Washington, D.C., August, 1967, pg. 19.

22   "The Freeman Administration and the Poor," by Don F. Hadwiger, Agricultural History, January, 1971.

23   Quoted in *A National Program of Research for Agriculture*, Report of a Study sponsored jointly by Association of State Universities and Land Grant Colleges and U.S. Department of Agriculture, October, 1966, pg. 32-33.

24   *State of Rural Housing in the United States*, Economic Research Service, USDA, 1968, pg. iii.

25   *Op. Cit.*, Hadwiger, pg. 26.

26   See *Let Them Eat Promises* by Nick Kotz, Prentice-Hall, Englewood Cliffs, N.J.: 1969.

27   *Op. Cit.*, Hadwiger, pg. 29.

28   *Ibid.*, pg. 22.

29   *Equal Opportunity in Farm Programs: An Appraisal of Services Rendered by Agencies of the U.S. Department of Agriculture*, U.S. Commission on Civil Rights, Government Printing Office, Washington, D.C.: 1965, pg. 99.

30   *Op. Cit.*, Hadwiger, pg. 32.

CHAPTER TWENTY-TWO: Ifs, Ands and Butz

1   *Food Policy For America*, by Harold G. Halcrow, McGraw-Hill Book Co., New York, N.Y.: 1977, pg. 193.
2   "Balance Sheet of the Farming Sector," Supplement No. 1, April, 1976 and "Farm Income Situation," July, 1976.
3   *Op. Cit.*, Halcrow, pg. 192-194.
4   "The Williams Report," *United States International Economic Policy in an Interdependent World*, Report to the President submitted by the Commission on International Trade and Investment Policy, Washington, D.C., July, 1971.
5   Interview with former Cargill employee by Roger Burbach and Patricia Flynn, NACLA West Agribusiness Project.
6   *Op. Cit.*, Williams Report, pg. 7.
7   "U.S. Grain Arsenal," by Roger Burbach and Patricia Flynn, *NACLA's Latin America & Empire Report*, October, 1975.
8   *Ibid.*, pg. 8.
9   Interview with the president of the National Grain and Feed Association by Roger Burbach and Patricia Flynn, NACLA West Agribusiness Project.
10   *Op. Cit.*, Burbach-Flynn, pg. 8-9.
11   See "Don't Be Afraid of Integration," by Earl L. Butz, *Farmer's Digest*, August/September, 1959, pg. 20.
12   *Merchants of Grain*, by Dan Morgan, The Viking Press, New York, N.Y.: 1979, pg. 147fn.
13   Address before Joint Convention of Nebraska Stock Growers Association and Sandhills Cattle Association, Chadron, Nebraska, June 8, 1972.
14   "Parting Shots: Butz's 'War of Attrition," by T.J. Gilles, *The Farm Journal*, November/December, 1984.
15   "Farmworkers in Rural America 1971-1972," Part 4B, Earl L. Butz, Hearings before the Subcommittee on Migratory Labor of the Committee on Public Works, U.S. Senate, 92nd Congress, Second Session, June 20, 1972, pg. 2566.
16   Speech to the Indiana Farm Bureau Cooperative Association, March 17, 1976.
17   *Op. Cit.*, Gilles.
18   *Op. Cit.*, "Balance Sheet of the Farming Sector," Supplement No. 1, April, 1976 and "Farm Income Situation," July, 1976.
19   "What's Happened to Food Prices?," USDA Office of Communications, April, 1973, pg. 14.
20   Source: U.S. Bureau of Census, Decennial Census of Population & Current Population Reports, U.S. Department of Labor, Bureau of Labor Standards.
21   *Op. cit.*, USDA Office of Communication, April, 1973, pg. 14.
22   "Alternative Agricultural and Food Policy Discussions for the U.S. With Emphasis on a Market-Oriented Approach," by Alex F. McCalla and Harold O. Carter, Paper presented at the Policy Research Workshop on Public, Agriculture and Food, Price and Income Policy Research, Washington, D.C.: January 15-16, 1976.
23   *Ibid.*
24   "The Food and Fiber System — How It Works," ERS, USDA, Agricultural Information Bulletin No. 383, March, 1975, pg. 4 and "Farm Suppliers, Mighty Link in the Marketing Chain," *The Farm Index*, February, 1974, pg. 9-11.
25   Table 27A, Farm Income Statistics, "Agricultural Outlook," ERS, USDA, March, 1987.
26   Source: USDA Statistics
27   "Agricultural Letter," Federal Reserve Bank of Chicago, July 5, 1974.
28   *The Myth of Agricultural Prosperity*, by Frank M. LeRoux, Walla Walla, Washington, 1976, pg. 44.
29   *Ibid.*
30   Bureau of Labor Statistics as quoted in "The Food Gamble," by Hank Frundt, Economics Education Project, Union for Radical Political Economics (UPRE), 1978.
31   *Toward A National Food Policy*, by Joe Belden with Gregg Forte, Exploratory Project for Economic Alternatives, Washington, D.C., pg. 10-11.
32   "A Contemporary Political Economy of Family Farming," by Paul W. Barkley, *American Journal of Agricultural Economics*, December, 1976, pg. 817.
33   "The Changing Structure of U.S. Agribusiness and Its Contributions to the National Economy," Produced by the U.S. Chamber of Commerce, Washington, D.C., 1974, pg 2-3.
34   *Op. Cit.*, Halcrow, pg. 195
35   USDA statistics as quoted to author David Harris in "Bitter Harvest: The Destruction of the American Farmer," *Penthouse*, 1978.
36   *Ibid.*
37   "The Round Table: U.S. Must Accept New World Role As 'Imperialist'," by Austin Kiplinger, *Chicago Journal of Commerce*, March 2, 1949.
38   Letter from Austin Kiplinger, Kiplinger Washington Editors to Merle Hansen, North American Farm Alliance, July 7, 1980.

39   *Op. Cit.*, Burbach-Flynn, pg. 16-18.
40   *Ibid.*, pg. 12-18.
41   "U.S. Food Aid: a Multi-Purpose Strategy Used Least Often to Prevent Starvation," by Adrian Peracchio, *Newsday*, *The Los Angeles Times*, May 27, 1982.
42   "'Misuse' of Food For Peace Told," by James Risser, *The Des Moines Register*, May 19, 1975. See also *The Fields Have Turned Brown: Four Essays On World Hunger*, by Susan DeMarco and Susan Sechler, A Report of the Agribusiness Accountability Project, Washington, D.C., 1975.
43   *Op. Cit.*, Harris, *Penthouse*, 1978.
44   *Ibid.*
45   *Ibid.*
46   *Ibid.*
47   *Ibid.*
48   *Ibid.*
49   *Ibid.*
50   *Ibid.*
51   *Ibid.*
52   *Ibid.*
53   *Ibid.*
54   *Ibid.*
55   "Economic Roots of Farm Distress," by Harold Breimyer, *Catholic Rural Life*, September, 1984.
56   Observation made in conversation with the author.
57   Source: USDA Statistics
58   *A Time to Choose: Summary Report on the Structure of Agriculture*, U.S. Department of Agriculture, Washington, D.C., January, 1981.
59   *A Dialogue on the Structure of American Agriculture*, Summary of Regional Meetings, November 27 - December 18, 1979, U.S. Department of Agriculture, Washington, D.C., April, 1980, pg. 3.
60   *Op Cit.*, *A Time to Choose*, pg. 142.
61   "Carter's Granary Is Saving Reagan," by Ward Sinclair, *The Washington Post*, August 28, 1984.
62   *Ibid.*
63   Source: National Agricultural Statistics Service
64   "Agriculture Chief to Quit; Reagan Hails Block Tenure," by Keith Schneider, *The New York Times*, January 8, 1986.

CHAPTER TWENTY-THREE: Farmers As Barriers To the Destructuring of Democracy

1   *Food Policy For America*, by Harold G. Halcrow, McGraw-Hill Book Co., New York, N.Y.: 1977, pg. 11.
2   "Department of Agriculture and Farm Credit Appropriation Bill," Report No. 1584, U.S. House of Representatives, 85th Congress, 2nd Session, March 28, 1958, pg. 5.
3   "Technological Advance and the Future of the Family Farm," by John M. Brewster, *Journal of Farm Economics*, December, 1958.
4   *Government and Agriculture: Public Policy In a Democratic Society*, by Dale E. Hathaway, MacMillan Co., New York, N.Y.: 1963, pg. 20-21.
5   "A Man for 1987: James Madison: Unsung Hero of the Constitution," by Fred Barbash, "Outlook," *The Washington Post*, March 15, 1987.
6   "The Family Farm: Caught in the Contradictions of American Values," by Francis Moore Lappe, *Agriculture and Human Values*, Spring, 1985, pg. 41.
7   *The Political Economy of Class Structure in U.S. Agriculture: A Theoretical Outline*, by Kevin F. Goss, Richard D. Rodefeld and Frederick H. Buttel, Department of Agricultural Economics and Rural Sociology, Agricultural Experiment Station, Pennsylvania State University, University Park, Penn., October, 1979, pg. 58.
8   "Why Do Farmers Over Invest," by Harold F. Breimyer, *Journal of Farm Economics*, May, 1966.
9   *Farming For Profit In a Hungry World: Capital and the Crisis in Agriculture*, by Michael Perelman, Allanheld, Osmun, Montclair, N.J.: 1977, pg. 90.
10   "The Rural Foundation of the American Culture," by Walter Goldschmidt, Gregory Foundation Memorial Lecture, Columbia, Missouri, January 26, 1976.
11   "Toward Positive Policies for American Agriculture," Vol. 1, by Boris Swerling, Stanford University Food Research Institute Series, Palo Alto, California: November, 1960, pg. 329.
12   "The New Agriculture in the United States: A dissenter's view," by Richard G. Milk, *Change in Rural America*, Isao Fujimoto, et. al, pg. 113-120.
13   *Ibid.*
14   See Chapter Three, *The Policy Process in American Agriculture*, by Ross B. Talbot and Don Hadwiger, Chandler Publishing Co., San Francisco, California: 1968.
15   *Ibid.*
16   *Ibid.*, pg. 344.
17   *Op. Cit.*, Halcrow, pg. 9.
18   *Ibid.*, pg. 10.
19   *Ibid.*, pg. 15.
20   *Op. Cit.*, Talbot and Hadwiger, See Chapter 15.
21   *The Pesticide Conspiracy*, by Robert van den Bosch, Doubleday Inc., Garden City, N.Y.: 1978, pg. 101.
22   *Ibid.*, pg. 102.
23   *Ibid.*, pg. 105.
24   *Ibid.*, pg. 105-106.
25   "The Participants - The Farm Organization," *Government and Agriculture: Public Policy In A Democratic Society*, by Dale Hathaway, MacMillan Co., N.Y.: 1963, N.Y., pg. 217.
26   See *The Farm Bloc*, by Wesley McCune, Doubleday Inc., Garden City, N.Y.: 1943.
27   *Social Scientists and Farm Politics in the Age of Roosevelt*, by Richard S. Kirkendall, Iowa State University Press, Ames, Iowa: 1966, pg. 235.
28   *Ibid.*, pg. 236-237.
29   *A Concept of Agribusiness*, by John H. Davis and Ray A. Goldberg, Division of Research, Graduate School of Business, Harvard University, Boston, Mass.: 1957, pg. 76.
30   "Sugar PAC's Sweeten the Pot," by Ward Sinclair, *The Washington Post*, September 30, 1986.
31   "Paying to hear lawmakers," *USA Today*, July 11, 1989.
32   "Honoraria Scorecard," *The Washington Post*, July 3, 1989.
33   See *The Policy Process in American Agriculture*, by Ross B. Talbot and Don Hadwiger, Chandler Publishing Co., San Francisco, California: 1968, pg. 43-57.
34   *Op cit.*, Hathaway, pg. 197-198.

CHAPTER TWENTY-FOUR: Say! Say! USDA! What Have You Done Today?

1   *The Muth of the Family Farm: Agribusiness Dominance of U.S. Agriculture* by Ingolf Vogeler, Westview Press, Boulder, Colorado: 1981, pg. 196-198.

2   *Ibid.*

3   "New Agriculture Deputy Noted for Being Candid," by Ward Sinclair, *The Washington Post*, August 9, 1985.

4   *Ibid.*

5   *Reflections on Public Administration*, by John Merriman Gavs, University of Alabama Press, 1967, pg. 8-9.

6   *Economic Growth in France and Great Britain, 1851-1950*, by Charles P. Kindjeberger, Harvard University Press, Cambridge, Mass.: 1964, pg. 185.

7   See *The Policy Process in American Agriculture*, by Ross B. Talbot and Don Hadwiger, Chandler Publishing Co., San Francisco, California: 1968, pg. 239-242.

8   *1990 Budget Summary*, USDA, page 3.

9   "Horatio Alger Crops Up in the Cabinet," by Christopher Graybill, *The Wall Street Journal*, February 4, 1989

10   "Forward," *A Time to Choose: Summary Report on the Structure of Agriculture*, USDA, January, 1981.

11   "Secretary's Smooth Style, Pragmatic Politics Ease Tension at USDA," by Ward Sinclair, *The Washington Post*, September 21, 1987.

12   "The Day Lyng Offered to Quit the Cabinet," by Ward Sinclair, *The Washington Post*, September 21, 1987.

13   "For Lobbyist Eyes Have It: Robert Rapoza Pulls Shoestrings For Subsidized Housing," by Ward Sinclair, *The Washington Post*, May 2, 1986.

14   *Op. Cit.*, Sinclair, September 21, 1987.

15   "Expert on Farm Issues, Clayton Keith Yeutter," by Clyde H. Farnsworth, *The New York Times*, December 13, 1988.

16   "Gene Johnston," *Successful Farming*, April, 1989.

17   "Expecting Farm 'Crunch,' Yeutter Looks Overseas," by Arthur S. Brisbane, *The Washington Post*, August 2, 1989.

18   "Yeutter: Farmers' Friend or Foe?" by Jack Anderson and Dale Van Atta, *The Washington Post*, August 18, 1989.

19   "When governments step in, its the consumers who pay," Interview with Clayton Yeutter by Tracy Walker, *USA Today*, April 4, 1989.

20   *Op. cit.*, Anderson/Van Atta, *The Washington Post*, August 18, 1989.

21   "USDA Behind Schedule On Minority-Hiring Plan," by Ward Sinclair, *The Washington Post*, January 17, 1988.

22   "The Black Presence in the U.S. Cooperative Extension Service to 1983: A Profile - An American Quest for Service and Equity," by Joel Schor, Completed Draft, Revised Edition, May 25, 1983.

23   *Ibid.*

24   "Latest Charge of Racism Prompts a Debate," by Lena Williams, *The New York Times*, June 30, 1986.

25   "At USDA, a 5-Year Plan To Fight Discrimination," by Ward Sinclair, *The Washington Post*.

26   "USDA Fires Black Employe After Criticism of Agency," by Ward Sinclair, *The Washington Post*, May 21, 1986 and *Op. Cit.*, Williams, *The New York Times*, June 30, 1986.

27   *Ibid*, Sinclair.

28   "USDA Workers' Bias Charges May Have Made Him a Target," by Ward Sinclair, *The Washington Post*, October 15, 1986.

29   "USDA May Expand Race-Bias Probe," by Ward Sinclair, *The Washington Post*, May 25, 1986.

30   "Old-Boy Network Still Haunts Agriculture's Problem Child," by Ward Sinclair, *The Washington Post*, September 21, 1987.

31   *Op. Cit.*, Sinclair, May 25, 1986.

32   "USDA Seeking Probe of Possible Klan Role," by Mike Robinson, Associated Press, *The Washington Post*, December 18, 1986.

33   "Ag official backs off KKK claim," by Carol Matlack, *USA Today*, December 19, 1986.

34   "Panel Asks Probe of USDA Race Bias Charges," by Ward Sinclair, *The Washington Post*, May 31, 1986.

35   "Statemanship at Agriculture," Editorial, *The Washington Post*, June 14, 1986.

36   *Op. Cit.*, Sinclair, September 21, 1987.

37   *Ibid.*

38   *Ibid.*

39   *Op. Cit.*, Sinclair, May 31, 1986.

40   *Ibid.*

41   "Lyng Opening His Office to Farmers' Feedback," by Ward Sinclair, *The Washington Post*, May 2, 1986.

42   "USDA Hit on Rights Enforcement," by Ward Sinclair, *The Washington Post*, November 6, 1987.

43   "100 Black Employees Accuse USDA of Bias," by Ward Sinclair, *The Washington Post*, April 1, 1988.

44   *Op. cit.*, Sinclair, *The Washington Post*.

45   "USDA Minority Program," *The Washington Post*, January 4, 1989.

46   See *Sumter County Blues: The Ordeal of the Federation of Southern Cooperatives*, A Report by Thomas N.

Bethell for the National Commission in Support of Community Based Organizations, 1982.

47   "The Ditch That Could Change the Country," by David Fairbank White, *Parade Magazine*, August 12, 1984.

48   *Op. Cit.*, Bethell, pg. 16.

49   *Ibid.*

50   "The Federation of Southern Cooperatives/Land Assistance Fund," Pamphlet, FSC.

51   "Agriculture Inspectors Scored For Neglecting Animal Welfare," by Keith B. Richburg, *The Washington Post.*

52   "Lyng Favor to Florida Outrages Iowa," by Ward Sinclair, *The Washington Post*, March 15, 1986.

53   "Promises to Keep," *The Washington Post*, April 3, 1986.

CHAPTER TWENTY-FIVE: Taxpayers Dollars Underwrite the Corporate Elite

1   "Human capital shortages a threat to American Agriculture," Prepared by the President Instruction Committee on Organization and Policy, Division of Agriculture, National Association of State Universities and Land Grant Colleges, 1983.

2   "Many Farm Children Are Preparing For Careers Off Their Families' Land," by William Robbins, *The New York Times*, September 13, 1985.

3   *The Decline of Agrarian Democracy*, by Grant McConnell, Atheneum, New York, N.Y.: 1977, pg. 21.

4   "Up To Now: A History of American Agriculture From Jefferson to Revolution to Crisis," by Richard S. Kirkendall, *Agriculture and Human Values*, Winter, 1987, pg. 6.

5   *Op. cit.*, McConnell, *The Decline of Agrarian Democracy*, pg. 23.

6   "A People and A Spirit," USDA-NASULGC, Extension Study Commission, Colorado State University, Ft. Collins, Colorado, November, 1968, pg. 18.

7   "The Agri-Biz Bonanza," by Ward Sinclair, "Outlook," *The Washington Post*, January 10, 1988.

8   "Prairie Squall: Cross Winds Buffet Land Grant Colleges As States' Need Shift," by Dennis Farney, *The Wall Street Journal*, March 31, 1987.

9   *Op. cit.*, Sinclair, *The Washington Post*, January 10, 1988.

10   *Ibid.*

11   Source: National Association of State Universities and Land Grant Colleges, 1991.

12   "Resource Allocation in the Land Grant University and Agricultural Experiment Stations," by Roland Robinson, *Resource Allocations in Agricultural Research*, University of Minnesota Press, pg. 243.

13   *Op. cit.*, NASULG, 1992.

14   *Hard Tomatoes, Hard Times*, A Report of the Agribusiness Accountability Project on the Failure of America's Land Grant College Complex, by Jim Hightower, Research Coordinated by Susan DeMarco, Schenkman Publishing Co., Cambridge, Mass.: 1973.

15   "Social Science and Humanistic Considerations in Agricultural Research," by William H. Friedland, University of California - Santa Cruz, "Outreach Program of the Land Grant University: Which Public Should They Serve?," Proceedings of a Conference on the campus of Kansas State University, July 14-15, 1978.

16   *Ibid.*

17   *Ibid.*, See also "Social Sleepwalkers: Scientific and Technological Research in California," by William H. Freidland, University of California - Santa Cruz, Research Monograph No. 13.

18   Testimony of Isao Fujimoto, Department of Applied Behavorial Sciences, University of California-Davis, before the California Assembly Sub-Committee on Post Secondary Education, Sacramento, California, April 12, 1977.

19   *Ibid.*

20   *Ibid.*

21   "The Land-grant System: A Sociological Perspective on Value Conflicts and Ethical Issues," by Frederick H. Buttel, *Agriculture and Human Values*, Spring, 1985, pg. 93-94.

22   *Ibid.*, pg. 94.

23   "Land-Grant Institutions Take A Fresh Look at How They Treat 125-Year Old Mission," by Carolyn J. Mooney, *Chronicle of Higher Education*, October 28, 1987.

24   *Ibid.*

25   "Anachronisms or Rising Stars: The Black Land-Grant College System," by Joel Schor, *Agriculture and Human Values*, Summer, 1985, pg. 77.

26   *Ibid.*

27   *Ibid*

28   "Reagan Administration Accused of Hurting Most Black Colleges," by Vivian Aplin-Brownlee, *The Washington Post*, November 4, 1984.

29   *Ibid.*

30   *Ibid.*

31   *Op. Cit.*, Mooney, *Chronicle of Higher Education*, October 28, 1987.

32   *Ibid.*

33   *Ibid.*

34   *Op. Cit.*, McConnell, "Chapter One - The Old Tradition."

35   *Ibid.*, pg. 27-32.

36   American Bankers Association *Proceedings*, 1913 Convention, pg. 60.

37   Association of American Agricultural Colleges and Experiment Stations, *Proceedings*, 1913 Convention, pg. 131.

38   *Op. cit.*, Sinclair, *The Washington Post*, January 10, 1988.

39   *Op. Cit.*, Mooney, *Chronicle of Higher Education*, October 28, 1987.

CHAPTER TWENTY-SIX: The Enemy Within

1   "Ex-Sharecropper in Farm Job," by William Robbins, *The New York Times*, January 17, 1986.
2   *Ibid.*; "Kleckner: Profits should be farmers' goal," by Mary Thompson, *Waterloo Courier*, March 15, 1987.
3   See "The American Farm Bureau Federation," by Rep. Joseph Y. Resnick (Dem.-N.Y.), *Congressional Record*, July 18, 1967, August 17, 1967, September 20, 1967.
4   *Food Policy For America*, by Harold G. Halcrow, McGraw-Hill Book Co., New York, N.Y.: 1977, pg. 227.
5   Association of American Agricultural Colleges and Experiment Stations, *Proceedings*, 1913 Convention, pg. 226.
6   *The Decline of Agrarian Democracy*, by Grant McConnell, Atheneum, New York, N.Y.: 1977, pg. 48.
7   *Ibid.*, pg. 51.
8   *Ibid.*, pg. 56.
9   *The Truth About the Farm Bureau*, by Dale Kramer, National Affairs Press, Falls Church, Virginia: 1950, pg. 7.
10   *Ibid.*
11   *Op. Cit.*, McConnell, pg. 75.
12   *Op. Cit.*, Kramer, pg. 8-9.
13   *Ibid.*, pg. 15.
14   *Ibid.*, pg. 15-17.
15   *Op. Cit.*, McConnell, pg. 89.
16   See *Social Scientists and Farm Politics in the Age of Roosevelt*, by Richard S. Kirkendall, Iowa State University Press, Ames, Iowa: 1966.
17   *Op. Cit.*, McConnell, Chapter Nine.
18   Hearings on Agriculture Appropriation Bill for 1942, U.S. Senate Committee on Appropriations, 77th Congress, 1st Session, 1941, pg. 1016.
19   *Op. Cit.*, McConnell, Chapter Ten.
20   *Ibid*, Chapter Fifteen.
21   "Agriculture: How to Shoot Santa Claus," *Time*, September 3, 1965.
22   *Ibid.*
23   *Op. Cit.*, Halcrow, pg. 235.
24   "Thank you Mr. Delano," by Harvey Joe Sanner, *AAM News*, December 7, 1984.
25   "The Texas Farm Bureau," by Mikkel Jordahl, *The Texas Observer*, April 19, 1985.
26   *Ibid.*
27   In addition to the material on the AFBF specifically footnoted below information on the financial operations and right-wing activities of the Bureau contained in this chapter has been derived principally from the following sources: "The American Farm Bureau Federation," by Rep. Joseph Y. Resnick (Dem.-N.Y.), *Congressional Record*, July 18, 1967, August 17, 1967, September 20, 1967; "Articles on Farm Bureau," Extension of Remarks of Hon. Charles Vanik (Dem.-Ohio), *Congressional Record*, September 20, 1967, "The Right-Wing In Overalls," by Joseph Y. Resnick, *The Progressive*, 1968, and *Dollar Harvest: An Expose of the Farm Bureau* by Samuel R. Berger, D.C. Heath: Heath Lexington Books, 1971.
28   "Top Farm Group to Pick Leader in Tough Times," by William Robbins, *The New York Times*, January 16, 1986.
29   *Op. cit.*, Robbins, *The New York Times*, January 17, 1986.
30   "The Texas Farm Bureau," by Mikkel Jordahl, *The Texas Observer*, April 19, 1985.
31   *St. Louis Post Dispatch*, January 28, 1986; "This We Believe," *Nation's Agriculture*, May, 1964.
32   "What Kind of Poverty?," *Nation's Agriculture*, 1966.
33   *Op. Cit.*, Jordahl.
34   "FB calls for defeat of moratorium," *AAM News*, April 5, 1983.
35   *Op. Cit.*, Jordahl.
36   *Ibid.*
37   *Ibid.*
38   "American Farm Bureau Federation," Group Research Inc., Special Report #15, August 10, 1964; *The Farm Bloc*, by Wesley McCune, Doubleday, Doran & Co., Inc., Garden City, N.Y.: 1943.
39   "Extremists in Farm Belt Are Assailed," by Crystal Nix, *The New York Times*, September 21, 1985.
40   *Ibid.*
41   "'Underground' of Racist Leaders Coordinated Crimes, FBI Taps Show," by James Coates and Stephen Franklin, *The Chicago Tribune, The Washington Post*, December 28, 1987.
42   *Op. cit.*, Nix, *The New York Times*, September 21, 1985.
43   "Self-Help Advisers Profiting From Farmers' Woes," by William Robbins, *The New York Times*, February 18, 1986.
44   "Jury convicts former publisher of theft over unpaid farm loans," by John C. Enselin, *Rocky Mountain News*, May 28, 1986.
45   "The Farm Belt's Far Right: A Historical Overview," by James Ridgeway, *Sojourners*, October, 1986.

46   "Farm and church leaders: Counter right-wing through progressive farm crisis solutions," *North American Farmer*, November 18, 1985.

47   "Anti-Semitism and the Farm Crisis," by Frank Hornstein, *Genesis 2*, May/June, 1985.

48   *Spotlight*, March 25, 1984.

49   "International oligarchy controls the radical farm protest movement," Special Report, *EIR*, March 12, 1985, pg. 24- 25.

50   "LaRouche Sentenced to 15 Years In Prison," by Caryle Murphy, *The Washington Post*, January 28, 1989.

51   "Trial Sheds Light on La Rouche's Financial Deals," by Caryle Murphy, *The Washington Post*, December 5, 1988.

52   "Prairiefire Memorandum," Daniel Levitas, Research Director, May 8, 1986.

CHAPTER TWENTY-SEVEN: Squeezing the "Toothpaste"

1   *Agriculture In A Unstable Economy*, by Theodore W. Schultz, McGraw-Hill Books, New York, N.Y.: 1945, pg. 273.

2   See "The Loss Of Our Family Farms: Inevitable Results or Conscious Policies?," by Mark Ritchie, Center for Rural Studies, Minneapolis, Minnesota, 1981.

3   *Food Policy For America*, by Harold G. Halcrow, McGraw-Hill Book Co., New York, N.Y.: 1977, pg. 219-220.

4   See *Unforgiven: The Biography of an Idea*, by Charles Walters, Jr., Economics Library, Kansas City, Missouri, in cooperation with Citizens Congress for Private Enterprise, Granite Falls, Minn.: 1971, pg. 399.

5   *Ibid.*, pg. 398-403.

6   *Ibid.*, pg. 400.

7   *Ibid.*, pg. 124.

8   *Ibid.*

9   *Ibid.*, pg. 400.

10 *Ibid.*, pg. 373.

11 *Ibid.*, pg. 398-403.

12 *Ibid.*, pg. 401.

13 *Ibid.*

14 "Scapegoating the small farm," by Marty Strange, *Science Magazine*, 1985.

15 *Op. Cit.*, Schultz, *Agriculture In A Unstable Economy*, pg. 273.

16 *Government and Agriculture: Public Policy In a Democratic Society*, by Dale E. Hathaway, MacMillan Co., New York, N.Y.: 1963, pg. 207-210.

17 "Idea of Foreclosure Moratorium Opposed By ABA Task Force," *U.S. Farm News*, March, 1985.

18 *Agricultural Policy and Trade: Adjusting Domestic Programs In An International Framework (1985)*, by D. Gale Johnson, Kenzo Hemmi, Pierre Lardinois, A Report to the Trilateral Commission, No. 29.

CHAPTER TWENTY-EIGHT: Ebeenzer Scrooge Was A Grain Trader

1   Roger Burbach and Patricia Flynn interview with aide to a Senator on the Committee on Agriculture and Forestry as reported in "U.S. Grain Arsenal," *NACLA's Latin America & Empire Report*, October, 1975.

2   "U.S. Grain Arsenal," North American Committee on Latin America's *Latin America and Empire Report*, October, 1975, pg. 10.

3   *A Poor Harvest: The Clash of Policies and Interests in the Grain Trade*, by Richard Gilmore, Longman, New York, N.Y.: 1982, pg. 24.

4   "American Producer Interests and the Grain Trade," by Richard Gilmore, Overseas Development Council, Conference on Agricultural Grain Marketing: What Future Direction for the States?," Statehouse, Topeka, Kansas, July 26, 1978, pg. 5.

5   "Two reports to ease fears about grain exporting," by Lauren Soth, *The Des Moines Register*, August 30, 1982.

6   *Merchants of Grain*, by Dan Morgan, The Viking Press, New York, N.Y.: 1979, pg. 236.

7   "The grain shippers' role in the farm crisis," by Mike Dennison, *In These Times*, March 20-26, 1985.

8   "Big grain exporters shrouded in secrecy," by George Anthan, *The Des Moines Register*, June 15, 1975.

9   Conversation with Andy Moore, Center for the Study of Responsive Law, Washington, D.C. as it appears in *The Big Boys: Power and Position in American Business*, by Ralph Nader/William Taylor, Pantheon Books, N.Y., N.Y.:1986, pg. 311.

10   *Forbes*, December 10, 1987.

11   Source: Dun & Bradstreet

12   "The Richest People in America: The Forbes Four Hundred," *Forbes*, October 26, 1987, pg. 239.

13   "Can farmers beat the multinationals?," *Top Producer*, November, 1987.

14   "For a Grain Giant, No Farm Crisis," by Steven Greenhouse, *The New York Times*, March 30, 1986.

15   "How the merchants of grain are riding out the storm," by Andrew Gowers, *Financial Times*, November 28, 1986.

16   *Ibid.*

17   See "Citrus King: Brazil's Jose Cutrals, Helped by Coca-Cola, Is Taking on Florida," by Roger Cohen, *The Wall Street Journal*, January 22, 1987 and "Revenge of the Frostbelt," *Forbes*, November 5, 1984.

18   "Brazilians Cheer U.S. Citrus Ruling," by James Bruce, *Journal of Commerce*, March 12, 1987.

19   "Cargill Plans Terminal in Brazil," by James Bruce, *Journal of Commerce*, January 6, 1986.

20   "Bigness Counts in Agribusiness, and Cargill Inc. Is Fast Becoming a Commodities Conglomerate," by Sue Shellenbarger, *The Wall Street Journal*, May 7, 1982.

21   *Op. Cit.*, Greenhouse.

22   *Op. Cit.*, Morgan, pg. 203-206.

23   Hearings on Public Law 480 before Senate Committee on Agriculture and Forestry, Washington, D.C., 1957.

24   Roger Burbach and Patricia Flynn interview with George Shanklin, Assistant Administrator, Commodity Export Programs, as reported in "U.S. Grain Arsenal," *NACLA's Latin America & Empire Report*, October, 1975.

25   Roger Burbach and Patricia Flynn interview with aide Washington, D.C. representative of Bunge Corp. as reported in "U.S. Grain Arsenal," *NACLA's Latin America & Empire Report*, October, 1975.

26   "U.S. Grain Arsenal," *NACLA's Latin America & Empire Report*, October, 1975, pg. 23.

27   *Op. Cit.*, Shellenbarger.

28   *Ibid.*

29   "State organizations call for probe of grain corporations," *North Dakota Union Farmer*, January 24, 1985.

30   "NDFU calls for investigation of Cargill wheat deal," *North Dakota Union Farmer*, January 10, 1985.

31   "Cargill Proposed Import of Grain Reaps Criticism," by Ward Sinclair, *The Washington Post*, January 9, 1985.

32   *Daily Bread: An Abdication of Power*, The Joseph Project Report on Hunger, Grain and Transnationals, Sponsored by the Senate of Priests of St. Paul and Minneapolis, Minnesota, 1982.

33   "Hearings to Review Agricultural Export Issues," Statement of Francis Moore Lappe, Before the Committee on Agriculture, U.S. House of Representatives, Subcommittee on Department Operations, Research and Foreign Agriculture, Washington, D.C., July 28, 1981.

34   *Op. Cit.*, As quoted from a monograph "Organization, Scale and Performance of the Grain Trade," in *Daily Bread*, pg. 53-55.

35   *Ibid.*

36   *Ibid.*

37   *Op. Cit.*, Morgan, pg. 234.

38   *Op. cit.*, Gilmore, pg. 59.

39   *Ibid.*, pg. 60.

40   *Op. Cit.*, Morgan, pg. 214.

41   "China spurns soybean shipment," by Dale McDonald, *Farm Journal*, May, 1986.

42   *Ibid.*

43   *Op. Cit.*, Moore, pg. 327-328.

44   *Ibid.*
45   "No Mercy From the Multinationals," by Dale McDonald, *Top Producer*, November, 1987.
46   *Ibid.*
47   *Ibid*
48   *Ibid.*
49   "Debate Grows Over Quality of U.S. Grain," by Ward Sinclair, *The Washington Post*, April 24, 1986.
50   *Op. Cit.*, McDonald, November, 1987.
51   *Op. Cit.*, Sinclair, April 24, 1986.
52   *Op. Cit.*, McDonald, November, 1987.
53   "Safety Rules Set for Grain Elevators," by Associated Press, *The Washington Post*, December 31, 1987.
54   *Ibid.*
55   *Op. cit.*, McDonald, November, 1987.
56   *Op. cit.*, Sinclair, April 24, 1986.
57   *Op. cit.*, McDonald, November, 1987.
58   "Safety Rules Set for Grain Elevators," Associated Press, *The Washington Post*, December 31, 1987.
59   *Ibid.*
60   *Op. cit.*, Gilmore, pg. 4.
61   As quoted in an interview with Susan George, *Multinational Monitor*, March, 1981.
62   "1983 Payment-In-Kind Program Overview: Its Design, Impact and Cost," General Accounting Office, GAO/RCED-85-89, September 25, 1985.
63   "Major Grain Companies Reaping Millions in PIK Program Fees," by Ward Sinclair, *The Washington Post*, September 20, 1983.
64   *Op. cit.*, Gilmore, pg. 22.

CHAPTER TWENTY-NINE: Many Are Called For, But Few Are the Chosen

1   Roger Burbach and Patricia Flynn interview with aide to a Senator on the Committee on Agriculture and Forestry as reported in "U.S. Grain Arsenal," *NACLA's Latin America & Empire Report*, October, 1975.

2   "U.S. Grain Arsenal," North American Committee on Latin America's *Latin America and Empire Report*, October, 1975, pg. 10.

3   "A Global Linking of Farm Policies," by Michel Fribourg, *The New York Times*, July 20, 1986.

4   "Time for a Change in Food Policy," by E. Phillip LeVeen, *Cry California*, Summer, 1981.

5   "Foundations of Peace," by Henry A. Wallace, *Atlantic Monthly*, January, 1942, pg. 37.

6   Cited in *Food: The Growth of Policy: Studies in Administration and Control*, by Richard J. Hammond, Her Majesty's Stationery Office and Longman, London, England: 1962.

7   Statement by Harry L. Graham, former Grange and National Farmers Organization, before Senate Foreign Relations Committee, June 29, 1971.

8   *Ibid.*

9   Statement of Sen. Milton Young (Rep.- N.D.) concerning the Agricultural Act of 1970, Hearings before the Committee on Agriculture and Forestry, U.S. Senate, 91st Congress, 2nd Session, February, 1970, pg. 135.

10   *Ibid.*

11   "Facts and Forecasts for Breadstuffs," by Ray A. Goldberg, *Breadstuffs Seminar: The Southwestern Miller*, Sosland Publishing Co., Phoenix, Arizona, 1972.

12   Statement of Clarence B. Palmby before the 1971 hearings of the Senate Ad Hoc Subcommittee on the International Wheat Agreement, Washington, D.C., pg. 14.

13   Statement on Commodity Reserves and Wheat and Feed Grain Programs by Sec. Earl Butz, Hearings before the Committee on Agriculture and Forestry, U.S. Senate, 92nd Congress, 2nd Session, January 24, 1972, pg. 44.

14   *A Poor Harvest: The Clash of Policies and Interests in the Grain Trade*, by Richard Gilmore, Longman, New York, N.Y.: 1982, pg. 193.

15   "Aggressive exporting part of new policy," *Milling & Baking News*, December 18, 1984.

16   *Ibid.*

17   "Trade is not panacea for solving farm problems," *North Dakota Union Farmer*, December 27, 1983.

18   "Agricultural Exports and the Farm Economy - A Full Accounting Needed," Statement of Berton E. Henningson, Jr., NFO, Subcommittee on Department Operations, Research & Foreign Agriculture, Committee on Agriculture, U.S. House of Representatives, July 8, 1981.

19   "Pushing Exports Is A Recipe For Self-Defeat," by Frederick L. Cannon, Bank of America, *California Farmer*, January 3, 1987.

20   *Ibid.*

21   *Ibid.*

22   "Change needed in agricultural policy," *Milling & Baking News*, April 30, 1985.

23   "USDA predicts grain trade strategies will serve self- interests, not world needs," by Steve Kopperud, *Feedstuffs*, August 3, 1981.

24   "Hearings to Review Agricultural Export Issues," Statement of Francis Moore Lappe before the Committee on Agriculture, U.S. House of Representatives, Subcommittee on Department Operations, Research and Foreign Agriculture, Washington, D.C., July 28, 1981.

25   "Political Weapon Predominates - U.S. Food Aid: A Multi- Purpose Strategy Used Least Often to Prevent Starvation," by Adrian Peracchio, Newsday, *The Los Angeles Times*, May 27, 1982.

26   See "Exports and Trade," *Agricultural Outlook*, ERS, USDA, December, 1985.

27   "Vegetables: Situation and Outlook Yearbook," ERS, USDA, TVS 240, November, 1986 and "Food Consumption, Prices, and Expenditures: 1985," by Karen L. Bunch, ERS, USDA, Statistical Bulletin No. 749, January, 1987.

28   *International Trade: Alternative Trading Practices for International Trade*, Briefing Report to the Chairman, Subcommittee on Department Operations, Research & Foreign Agriculture, Committee on Agriculture, House of Representatives, U.S. Government Accounting Office, GAO/NSIAD-87-90BR, March, 1987.

29   See "Food As A Weapon," *Catholic Rural Life*, July, 1983.

30   "Desk Reference Guide to U.S. Agricultural Trade," FAS, USDA, Ag Handbook 683, January, 1989, pg. 1-2.

31   Source: Bureau of Census, *The Washington Post*, December 12, 1985.

32   *Trading the Future*, by James Wessel with Mort Hantman, Institute for Food and Development Policy, San Francisco, California, 1983, pg. 58.

33   *Op. Cit.*, Henningson.

34   *Op. Cit.*, Gilmore, pg. 141-142.

35   "GATT -- What is it, what will it do?," *Iowa Farm Unity News*.

36   "Europe's farmers get higher supports," by Robert G. Lewis, *The Fauquier Democract*, July 21, 1988.

37   "U.S. Avoids GATT Confrontation Over Issue of Farm Subsidies," by Stuart Auerbach, *The Washington Post*, March 31, 1989.

38   *Ibid.*

39   "Agribusinessmen agree: Free trade not realistic," *Feedstuffs*, February 22, 1988.

CHAPTER THIRTY: "But It's the Name of the Game"

1   *Merchants of Grain*, by Dan Morgan, The Viking Press, New York, N.Y.: 1979, pg. 123.
2   *Ibid.*
3   This chapter has appeared in substantially the same form under the author's name in the appendix to *The Great American Grain Robbery and Other Stores*, by Martha Hamilton, Agribusiness Accountability Project, Washington, D.C.: 1972 and *Food for People Not For Profit: A Sourcebook on the Food Crisis*, Edited by Catherine Lerza and Michael Jacobson, Ballantine Books, New York, N.Y.: 1975.
4   "Butz Rues Palmby's Grain Trip," by Nick Kotz, *The Washington Post*, October 5, 1972.
5   "Wheat Exports Over One Billion Bushels Now Expected in Current Marketing Year," *The Wall Street Journal*, September 5, 1972.
6   "Farmers file suit against grain companies," *Feedstuffs*, October 27, 1980 and "Top court rules for grain firms in '72 wheat sales," by Jonathan Eng, *Feedstuffs*, March 1, 1982.
7   "Ex-U.S. Aide Denies Wheat Deal Windfall," by Nick Kotz, *The Washington Post*, September 20, 1972.
8   "Cargill, Continental Spokesman Defend U.S. Trade Action," by Jack Kiesner, *Feedstuffs*, September 25, 1972.
9   "Butz: No Russia Trip for Palmby if I'd Known About Apartment," by Clark Mollenhoff, *The Des Moines Register*, October 5, 1972.
10   As related to the author in a telephone conversation with the aforementioned Associated Press correspondents.
11   Estimates based on 1972 figures and 1973 prices.
12   *The Des Moines Register*, October 5, 1972.
13   *Op. Cit.*, Morgan, pg. 153-154.
14   *Ibid.*, pg. 154.
15   "Agency Studies Wheat Market for Trades Aimed At Manipulating Export Subsidies," by Burt Schorr, *The Wall Street Journal*, September 18, 1972.
16   *Op. Cit.*, Morgan, pg. 153.
17   *Ibid.*
18   Statement by Carroll G. Brunthaver, Assistant Secretary, International Affairs, and Commodity Programs, USDA, before the Livestock and Grains House Committee, U.S. House of Representatives, Washington, D.C., September 18, 1972.
19   "Butz, Aide Deny Knowing of Tip to Grain Exporters," by E.W. Kenworthy, *The New York Times*, September 15, 1972.
20   "U.S. Drops Subsidy on Export Wheat," by E.W. Kenworthy, *The New York Times*, September 23, 1972.
21   "$150 Million Blunder," *Newsweek*, October 2, 1972.
22   *Op. cit.*, Appendix, *The Great American Grain Robbery and Other Stores.*
23   "Cargill Claims Loss on Russian Wheat Sale of Almost Cent a Bushel, Rebutting Critics," by John A. Prestbo, *The Wall Street Journal*, November 3, 1972.
24   *Op. cit.*, Morgan, pg. 156.
25   "Grain deals during embargo," by George Anthan, *The Des Moines Register*, January 10, 1982.
26   "USDA has information indicating some illegal grain sales to Soviets," by Steve Kopperud, *Feedstuffs*, March 24, 1980 and "Sting seeks dealers diverting U.S. grain," by George Anthan, *The Des Moines Register*, February 15, 1980.
27   "GAO Confirms Multi-Nillion Dollar Loss Through Bungled Soviet Embargo," Press Release from the Office of Sen. Charles E. Grassley (Rep.-Iowa), July 29, 1981.
28   *Ibid.*
29   "Embargoes, Surplus Disposal and U.S. Agriculture," ERS, USDA, Staff Report No. AGES860910, November, 1986.
30   *Op. Cit.*, Grassley.

CHAPTER THIRTY-ONE: Supply and Demand In Agriculture: It's the Pits!

1   *The New Gatsbys: Fortunes and Misfortunes of Commodity Traders*, by Bob Tamarkin, Quill, William Morrow, New York, N.Y.: 1985, pg. 24.
2   "Farmers Protest at Exchange," by Kevin Klose, *The Washington Post*, September 28, 1984
3   "U.S. probes futures exchanges," by Christopher Drew and William B. Crawford, *The Chicago Tribune*, January 19, 1989.
4   *Op. Cit.*, Tamarkin, pg. 22.
5   *CFTC Annual Report*, 1988, pg. 110-111.
6   Based on market figures obtained from the Washington, D.C. office of the Futures Industry Association.
7   "CBOT Volume for '89 Fell 3.3% From '88 Record," *The Wall Street Journal*, January 4, 1990.
8   "See you in St. Louis," by Merle Hansen, North American Farm Alliance, *North American Farmer*, September 5, 1986.
9   *Op. Cit.*, Tamarkin.
10   "The Chicago Markets at a Glance," by Julia Flynn Siber, *The New York Times*, February 21, 1989.
11   "The Commodities Market: You've Really Got To Be An Animal: Want to know how to make a small fortune in commodities? Start with a large one." by Asa Barber, *Playboy*, July, 1977.
12   *Merchants of Grain*, by Dan Morgan, The Viking Press, New York, N.Y.: 1979, pg. 202.
13   "Speculative short selling will draw more protests," *Agricultural Watchdog*, January, 1985.
14   "Free market a mirage; farm safety net vital," by David Senter, *USA Today*, January 24, 1985.
15   *Op. Cit.*, Tamarkin, pg. 123.
16   "Agricultural Options Trading Voted," by James L. Rowe, Jr., *The Washington Post*, October 30, 1984.
17   "Where are the entrepreneurs of the 80s? In the Pits: Futures Trading and the Predator Ethic," by John Eisendrath, *Reader*, Chicago, Illinois, October 14, 1983.
18   "Futures Trading - A Description of the Basic Process," by Elizabeth Withnell, Analyst, Environment and Natural Policy Division, Congressional Research Service, Library of Congress, January 25, 1982.
19   "The Great Soybean Squeeze Puts the Board of Trade in a Corner of Its Own," by Jerry Knight, *The Washington Post*, July 18, 1989.
20   "CBOT Damaged by Its Soybean Intervention," by Scott Kilman and Scott McMurray, *The Wall Street Journal*, July 17, 1989.
21   "Feruzzi Profit Fell 45% in '89 on Soybean Trading," *Wall Street Journal*, May 30, 1990.
22   "Farm Prices Fell 1.4% in August, Led by Soybeans," by Bruce Ingersoll, *The Wall Street Journal*, September 2, 1989.
23   "As Congress Returns, Will CFTC Feel the Squeeze on Soybean Flap," by Bruce Ingersoll, *The Wall Street Journal*, August 22, 1989.
24   "Court Upholds Chicago Ruling," by Eric N. Berg, *The New York Times*, July 14, 1989.
25   "Soybean Prices Leap on Rumor About Ferruzzi," by Scott Kilman, *The Wall Street Journal*, July 20, 1989.
26   "CBOT-AAM Sues Board of Trade," *The AAM Reporter*, December 5, 1989
27   "Ferruzzi's Bold Growth Has Made Big Waves," by Alan Riching, *The New York Times*, July 14, 1989.
28   *Ibid.*
29   *Ibid.*
30   *Op. cit.*, Berg, *The New York Times*, July 14, 1989.
31   *Ibid.*
32   *Ibid.*
33   *Ibid.*
34   *Ibid*
35   "Soybean Scare Fallout Spreads to Other Contracts As Feud Heats Up Between Ferruzzi and Cargill," by Scott Kitman, *The Wall Street Journal*, July6 19, 1989.
36   "Italian Firm Denies Soybean Cornering Bid," by Bill Sing, "The Los Angeles Times," *The Washington Post*, July 13, 1989.
37   *Op. cit.*, Kilman/McMurray, *The Wall Street Journal*, July 17, 1989.
38   "Market Place: The Pits Hang On To Dual Trading," by Floyd Norris, *The New York Times*, February 9, 1989.
39   *Op. cit.*, Eisendrath, *Reader*, October 10, 1983.
40   "Trading pits not for the faint of heart . . . or body," by Matt O'Connor and Gary Marx, *The Chicago Tribune*, February 5, 1989.
41   *Op. Cit.*, Tamarkin, pg. 44-45.
42   *Ibid.*, pg. 125.
43   *Ibid.*, pg. 103.
44   *Ibid.*, pg. 168.
45   *Ibid.*, pg. 55.
46   *Op. Cit.*, Morgan, pg. 220.
47   As quoted by Dan McCurry in an address, "The Light Under A Bushel: Aspects of the Grain Trade in the

U.S.," to the Peoples' Food Conference, Ames, Iowa, June 26, 1976.

48   "Futures: Big wins, big risks," by Dennis Cauchen, *USA Today*, June 8, 1988.

49   "Pit Fighting and Pork Bellies," by John Train, *The Washington Post.*

50   "A Pause to Reflect: Ethics in the Pits," by James Risen, "Los Angeles Times," *Washington Post,* May 6, 1990.

51   *The Traders,* by Sonny Kleinfield, Holt, Reinhart Winston, New York, N.Y.

52   *Op. Cit.,* Tamarkin, pg. 17-18.

53   *Ibid,* pg. 94.

54   "Inquiry on Commodities Is Defended by Officials," by Eric N. Berg, *The New York Times,* January 31, 1989.

55   "Exclusive Club: Probe of 2 Exchanges Shows Wild Fraternity Of Traders in Yen Pit," by Scott McMurray and John Koten, *The Wall Street Journal,* January 26, 1989.

56   "Business and the Law: Commodity Charges Widen Use of Racketeering Statue," by Jurt Eichenwald, *The New York Times,* August 7, 1989.

57   *Op. cit.,* McMurray and Koten, *The Wall Street Journal,* January 26, 1989.

58   "Futures Traders Face Increased Pressure From U.S. as Grand Jury Begins Work," by Robert L. Rose and Jeff Bailey, *The Wall Street Journal,* January 26, 1989.

59   *Ibid.*

60   "Probe forces reform issue on exchanges," by Carol Jouzaitis and Pat Widder, *The Chicago Tribune,* January 22, 1989.

61   "Commodity Sting Focuses on Flaws in Futures Trading," by Jerry Knight, *The Washington Post,* January 29, 1989.

62   *Ibid.*

63   "Grain Maverick: Dwayne Andreas Runs ADM His Own Way, Often Playing Hardball," by Sue Shellenbarger, *The Wall Street Journal,* February 9, 1989.

64   "Biodegradable plastics boosts ADM," by Gary Strauss, *USA Today,* May 3, 1988.

65   "The High-Octane Ethanol Lobby," by Michael J. Weiss, *The New York Times Magazine,* April 1, 1990.

66   "Ethanol Industry Booms Amid New Controversy," by Michael Isikoff, *The Washington Post,* December 8, 1985.

67   "USDA Starts Major Gasohol Subsidy Plan," by Michael Isikoff, *The Washington Post,* June 3, 1986.

68   *Ibid.*

69   *Op. cit.,* Weiss, *The New York Times Magazine,* April 1, 1990.

70   *Op. cit.,* Shellenbarger, *The Wall Street Journal,* February 9, 1989.

71   *Op. cit.,* Weiss, *The New York Times Magazine,* April 1, 1990.

72   "Andreas: College Drop-Out to Global Trader," by Michael Isikoff, *The Washington Post,* December 8, 1985.

73   *Ibid.*

74   *Op. cit.,* Shellenbarger, *The Wall Street Journal,* February 9, 1989.

CHAPTER THIRTY-TWO: The "Sleeping Pgymy" and the "Chicago Mirage"

1   "Board Member At Chicago Merc Upbraids Industry," by Scott McMurray, *The Wall Street Journal*, August 8, 1989.
2   *Ibid.*
3   "Eagleton Accuses Chicago Merc's Leaders and Quits," by Jeff Bailey, *The Wall Street Journal*, Novermber 8, 1989.
4   "Eagleton Resigns Merc Post, Blasts Officials at Exchange," by David A. Vise, *Washington Post*, November 8, 1989.
5   *Ibid.*
6   "Monieson, GNP Barred by CFTC From Industry," by Jeff Bailey, *The Wall Street Journal*, May 29, 1990.
7   *Ibid.*
8   "Chicago's Markets: Corrupt to the Core," by Thomas Eagleton, *The New York Times*, November 14, 1989.
9   ASA, Baber, *Playboy*, July, 1977.
10   *A Poor Harvest: The Clash of Policies and Interests in the Grain Trade*, by Richard Gilmore, Longman, New York, N.Y.: 1982, pg. 130-131.
11   *Op. cit.*, Knight, *The Washington Post*, February 19, 1989.
12   "Government watchdog isn't a pit bull on trading fraud," by Susan Antilla, *USA Today*, January 30, 1989.
13   *Ibid.*
14   *Ibid.*
15   "Cozy Ties: Futures Probes Test Resolve of Congress to Deal With Traders," by Brooks Jackson and Thomas E. Ricks, *The Wall Street Journal*, February 2, 1989.
16   "CFTC muscle-flexing raises conflict questions," by David Greising, *The Chicago Sun-Times*, February 15, 1989.
17   *Ibid.*
18   *Ibid.*
19   "CFTC Criticizes Exchange," by Eric N. Berg, *The New York Times*, February 22, 1989.
20   *Ibid.*
21   "CBOT leaders defend integrity of exchange," by Greg Burns, *The Chicago Sun-Times*, February 10, 1989.
22   "CBOT Proposes to Pay Chairman $240,000 a Year," *The Wall Street Journal*, March 2, 1989.
23   "Commodities Exchange Proposals," by Eric N. Berg, *The New York Times*, February 9, 1989.
24   "Chicago Board Acts on Its Timing," by Eric N. Berg, *The New York Times*, March 4, 1989.
25   *Op. cit.*, Berg, *The New York Times*, February 9, 1989.
26   "CBOT officials stand behind dual trading," by William B. Crawford, Jr. and Sallie Gaines, *The Chicago Tribune*, February 10, 1989.
27   "Chicago Merc Group Prohibits Dual Trading," by Scott McMurray, *The Wall Street Journal*, February 1, 1989.
28   "House Passses Bill Banning Dual Trading," by Charles J. Abbott, UPI, *Washington Post*, September 14, 1989.
29   Cargill, Inc. v. Hardin, 452 F. 2nd 1154, 1163 (8th Cir. 1971), cert. denied 406 U.S. 932 (1972)
30   "Chicago Exchange Appointsd a Panel to Press Reforms," by Kurt Eichenwald, *The New York Times*, January 26, 1989.
31   "CFTC Says It Is Cooperating with FBI Investigation," by Jerry Knight, *The Washington Post*, January 24, 1989.
32   "GAO Questions 'Intensity' of Futures Trade Oversight," by Gregory A. Robb, *The New York Times*, February 24, 1989.
33   "Effort to End Futures Abuses Aimed At Marts," by Thomas E. Ricks, *The Wall Street Journal*, February 24, 1989.
34   *Ibid.*
35   "GAO Faults Rules on Futures Markets," by Jerry Knight, *The Washington Post*, September 8, 1989.
36   "CFTC Moves to Tighten Trading Rules," by Sherie Winston, Knight-Rider, *The Washington Post*, August 30, 1989.
37   "CFTC Plan to Curb Trading Abuses Is Weak, GAO Says," by Kevin G. Salwen, *The Wall Street Journal*, September 8, 1989.
38   *Ibid.*
39   *Op. cit.*, Knight, *The Washington Post*, September 8, 1989.
40   *Ibid.*
41   *Op. cit.*, Ricks, *The Wall Street Journal*, February 24, 1989.
42   *Op. Cit.*, Jackson and Ricks, *The Wall Street Journal*, February 2, 1989.
43   *Ibid.*
44   *Ibid.*
45   *Ibid.*
46   "CFTC Reauthorization," Hearings Before the Subcommittee on Conservation, Credit and Rural Development of the Committee on Agriculture, House of Representatives, 97th Congress, 2nd Session on H.R. 5447,

February 23-25, 1982, Serial No. 97-YY, pg. 753.

47   *Ibid.*

48   "Undercover Probe Targets Chicago Exchanges," by Steve Coll and Ruth Marcus, *The Washington Post,* January 20, 1989.

49   "Chicago Merc Rushes to Protect Expanison Amid U.S. Inquiry," by Scott McMurray, *The Wall Street Journal,* January 27, 1989.

50   *Ibid.*

51   *Op. cit.*, Baber, *Playboy*, July, 1977.

52   *Ibid.*

53   "GAO Questions Ability of CBOT to Detect Trading Floor Abuse," by Reuters News Service, *Investor's Daily,* February 24, 1989.

54   "Fraud probe could rival Wall Street's," by Kevin Johnson, Susan Antilla and Daniel Kadlec, *USA Today,* January 23, 1989.

55   *Op. Cit.*, Morgan, pg. 56.

56   *Ibid.*, pg. 57.

57   *Op. Cit.*, Tamarkin, pg. 175.

58   *Op. Cit.*, Morgan, pg. 57.

59   *Op. Cit.*, Gilmore, pg. 127.

60   *Op. Cit.*, Baber, *Playboy*, July, 1977.

61   "No Mercy From the Multinationals," by Dale McDonald, *Top Producer*, November, 1987.

62   *Op. Cit.*, Tamarkin, pg. 123.

63   *Ibid.*

64   *Op. Cit.*, Gilmore, pg. 131-132.

65   "Secret Grain Deals Could Cost Millions," by George Anthan, *The Des Moines Register*, July 17, 1977.

66   *Ibid.*

67   "How traders got trapped," by Art Petacque, *The Chicago Sun- Times*, January 22, 1989.

68   "But feds' tough tactics draw fire," by Susan Antilla, Daniel Kadlec and Kevin Johnson, *USA Today,* January 24, 1989.

69   *Op. cit.*, "CFTC Reauthorization," pg. 743.

70   *Ibid.*, pg 754.

71   *Ibid.*, pg. 797.

72   "No Conflict Discerned in Soybean Curb," by Eric N. Berg, *The New York Times*, August 26, 1989.

73   "Six CBOT Directors's Firms Retained Short Positions in Ferruzzi Liquidation," by Kevin G. Salwen, *The Wall Street Journal.* September 11, 1989.

74   "Futures Outrage Coming Home to Rest," by Jerry Knight, *The Washington Post*, September 5, 1989.

75   *Op. cit.*, Salwen, *The Wall Street Journal.* September 11, 1989.

76   "Fall From Grace at Board of Trade," by Lee Froehlich, *Washington Post*, September 4, 1990.

77   *Ibid.*

78   *Op. cit.*, "CFTC Reauthorization," pg. 743.

79   "Bored stock players try commodities," by Dennis Cauchen, *USA Today*, May 23, 1988.

80   "Wider Role for CFTC Over Futures Market Weighed," by Steve Coll and David A. Vise, *The Washington Post,* May 14, 1988.

81   *Op. cit.*, "CFTC Reauthorization," pg. 801.

82   "House panel to subpoena records on 4 traders in wheat futures," by James O'Shea, *The Des Moines Register,* March 29, 1979.

83   "Wheat Traders Feel Squeeze in 'Corner' Fracas," by Sue Shellenbarger, Associated Press, *The Los Angeles Times*, April 2, 1979.

84   *Ibid.*

85   *Op. cit.*, O'Shea, *The Des Moines Register*, March 29, 1979.

86   *Op. cit.*, "CFTC Reauthorization," pg. 767.

87   *Ibid.*, pg. 777.

88   "Computers Head Toward the Futures as CFTC Approves Globex," by Thomas E. Ricks, *The Wall Street Journal*, February 3, 1989.

89   "Fraud Investigation Might Bring Futures Pits Into Computer Age," by Michael W. Miller and Matthew Winkler, *The Wall Street Journal*, January 25, 1989.

90   *Op. cit.*, Ricks, *The Wall Street Journal*, February 3, 1989.

91   "CBOT, In a Sign of the Times, May Finally Join Electronic Age," by Sue Shellenbarger, *The Wall Street Journal*, February 6, 1989.

92   *Op. cit.*, Miller and Winkler, *The Wall Street Journal*, January 25, 1989.

93   *Ibid.*

94   *Ibid.*

95   *Op. Cit.*, Tamarkin, pg. 143.

96   "Futures Trader To Quit Field After Bad Year," by Scott McMurray, *The Wall Street Journal*, July 30, 1988.

97   *Op. cit.*, Jackson and Ricks, *The Wall Street Journal*, February 2, 1989.

98   *Op. Cit.*, Baber, *Playboy*, July, 1977.

CHAPTER THIRTY-THREE: The Big Three's Prime Cut

1   Based on figures compiled from the USDA and the Bureau of the Census.
2   "Food Supply and Use,' *Agricultural Outlook*, June, 1991.
3   "We're trimming back on meat," by Janis Johnson and Ellen Brown, *USA Today*, July 17, 1985.
4   "Beef Facts," *Harrowsmith*, May 6, 1988.
5   *Farm to Market Review*, June, 1991, Western Organization of Resource Councils Education Project, Billings, Montana.
6   "Cattlemen are'powerless' to stop meatpacking trend," by Ron DeChristopher, *Iowa Farmer Today*, June 24, 1989
7   "Chance of Price Manipulation Worries Some: ConAgra, IBP, Cargill Dominant in Beef," by William Robbins ("New York Times"), *Omaha Sunday World Herald*, May 29, 1988.
8   *Ibid.*
9   Testimony of Dr. John W. Helmuth before the House Standing Committee on Agriculture, General Assembly of Iowa regarding Concentration in the Meat Packing Industry, Des Moines, Iowa, December 7, 1988.
10   *Ibid.*
11   "Packers Play Musical Chairs," by Steve Kay, *Beef Today*, September, 1989.
12   "IBP keeps tight grip on market," by Dale Kasler, *The Des Moines Register*, September 24, 1988.
13   "Restructuring of Meat Packing Industries: Implications For Farmers and Consumers," by Bruce W. Marion, Professor of Agricultural Economics, University of Wisconsin-Madison. Presented at hearings held by the House Agricultural Committee of the Iowa State Legislature, Des Moines, Iowa, December 7, 1988.
14   See "Small Business Problems in the Marketing of Meat and Other Commodities," Parts 1-5, Hearings Before the Subcommittee on SBA and SBIC Authority and General Small Business Problems of the Committee on Small Business, House of Representatives, 95th Congress, Second Session, October, 1977 - July, 1979.
15   *Op. cit.*, Marion, December 7, 1988.
16   "Concentration in Meat Packing," *CRA Newsletter*, Center for Rural Affairs, Walthill, Nebraska, August, 1987.
17   *Ibid.*
18   "Packers Tighten Grip on Markets," *CRA Special Report #8*, Center for Rural Affairs, Walthill, Nebraska.
19   *Op. cit.*, *CRA Newsletter*, August, 1987.
20   "Tightening of Supermarket Antitrust Laws Urged," by Ward Sinclair, *The Washington Post*, May 12, 1988.
21   "Return of The Jungle," by David Moberg, *In These Times*, July 24 - August 6, 1985.
22   *Op. cit.*, Marion, December 7, 1988.
23   "Interview: A beef oligopoly?" Industry Forum by Kevin Thompson, *Meat & Poultry*, July, 1988.
24   *Op. cit.*, Robbins, *Omaha Sunday World Herald*, May 29, 1988.
25   "High Court Ruling Curbs Challenges to Takeovers," by Al Kamen, *The Washington Post*, December 10, 1986.
26   *Ibid.*
27   *Ibid.*
28   "ConAgra completes Its 50-Percent Purchase of Swift," *Beef*, November, 1987.
29   "ConAgra exercising option to buy SIPCO," by Bartell Nyberg, *The Denver Post*, July 25, 1989.
30   *Op. cit.*, Robbins, *Omaha Sunday World Herald*, May 29, 1988.
31   *Op. cit.*, *Beef*, November, 1987.
32   "Stakes pile higher in the packer poker game," by Nita Effertz, *Farm Journal*, August, 1983.
33   "Cattle Contracts Fall Due to Woes of Edwin L. Cox," by Marj Charlier, *The Wall Street Journal*, June 27, 1986.
34   *Ibid.*
35   "Edwin Cox Jr. Gets Six-Month Sentence on Banking Violation," *Wall Street Journal*, September 8, 1988.
36   "IBP Inc. Struggles to Regain Beef Industry's Leadership," by Marj Charlier, *The Wall Street Journal*, May 3, 1988.
37   "How the Big Three Are Doing," *Beef Today*, Spetmebr, 1989.
38   *Op. cit.*, Charlier, *The Wall Street Journal*, May 3, 1988.
39   *Ibid.*
40   *Op. cit.*, Charlier, *The Wall Street Journal*, February 4, 1989.
41   *Ibid.*
42   *Op. cit.*, Charlier, *The Wall Street Journal*, May 3, 1988.
43   "Iowa Beef monopoly power is possible, studies say," by George Anthan, *The Des Moines Register*, May 12, 1979.
44   "Documents show Iowa Beef violated law, panel says," by George Anthan, *The Des Moines Register*, January 9, 1979.
45   "Strength in Numbers," by Alan Guebert, *Beef Today*, November/December, 1988.
46   "Court lets Smith panel keep Iowa Beef papers," by George Anthan, *The Des Moines Register*, February 8, 1979.
47   "IBP Letter Blasts Smith, Bagley Story," by John Hyde, *The Des Moines Register*, August 3, 1979.

48   *Op. cit.*, Charlier, *The Wall Street Journal*, May 3, 1988.
49   "2 IBP directors disagree with merger plan," by Wendell Cochran, *The Des Moines Register*, July 17, 1981.
50   "IBP, Occidental OK Merger," by Tom Knudson, *The Des Moines Register*, August 13, 1981.
51   For a detailed study of IBP's role in the Pacific Northwest see the author's *Roll Along Columbia: Corporate Agribusiness in the Mid-Columbia Basin*, Agribusiness Accountability Publications, San Francisco, Calif., 1979 Revised Edition.
52   "Simplot boosts Micron stake," *USA Today*, August 14, 1989.
53   "The Iowa Beef Gang Takes Over The Northwest," by Tim Connor, *Spokane Magazine*.
54   "Beef Beachhead: Northwest's Cattlemen Worry About Arrival of Iowa Beef in Area," by Herbert G. Lawson, *The Wall Street Journal*, March 20, 1978.
55   *Ibid.*
56   *Ibid.*
57   *Vicious Circles: The Mafia in the Marketplace*, by Jonathan Kwitny, W.W. Norton & Co., New York, N.Y.: 1979, pg. 252.
58   *Ibid.*
59   *Ibid.*, pg. 252-253.
60   "Tightening of Supermarket Antitrust Laws Urged," by Ward Sinclair, *The Washington Post*, May 12, 1988.
61   *Op. cit.*, Helmuth, Des Moines, Iowa, December 7, 1988.
62   "Calling all hogs," by Phyllis Berman and Dana Wechsler, *Forbes*, September 5, 1988.
63   *Ibid.*
64   *Ibid.*
65   *Ibid.*
66   *Op. cit.*, Moberg, *In These Times*, July 24 - August 6, 1985.

CHAPTER THIRTY-FOUR: Hogging the Market

1   See "Small Business Problems in the Marketing of Meat and Other Commodities," Parts 1-5, Hearings Before the Subcommittee on SBA and SBIC Authority and General Small Business Problems of the Committee on Small Business, House of Representatives, 95th Congress, Second Session, October, 1977 - July, 1979.

2   Testimony of Dr. John W. Helmuth before the House Standing Committee on Agriculture, General Assembly of Iowa regarding Concentration in the Meat Packing Industry, Des Moines, Iowa, December 7, 1988.

3   "USDA official opposes report on meat marketing system," by George Anthan, *The Des Moines Register*, May 24, 1979.

4   *Ibid.*

5   *Ibid.*

6   *Ibid.*

7   *Ibid.*

8   *Ibid.*

9   "Heading Toward the Last Roundup: A Summary Report on Structure, Control and Concentration in the Beef Industry," Agribusiness Accountability Publications, San Francisco, Calif.: 1979, pg. 2.

10   *Ibid.*, pg. 20.

11   "I.S.A. Newsletter", by George Levin, *U.S. Farm News*, June, 1985.

12   *Op. Cit.*, "Heading Toward the Last Roundup," pg. 18-20.

13   *Ibid.*

14   See "Report tells how packers could manipulate futures," by George Anthan, *The Des Moines Register*, October 25, 1978 and "Packers Set Meat Prices, Sell Futures," by George Anthan, *The Des Moines Register*, December 13, 1978.

15   "Cattle Future Market: Signal Helps Speculators, Congressman Charges," by Jerry Knight, *The Washington Post*, February 28, 1981.

16   "Dairy Cow Slaughter Opposed," Associated Press, *The Washington Post*, April 9, 1986.

17   "Making Hay of Subcommittee's Beef," by Ward Sinclair, *The Washington Post*, July 17, 1986.

18   "Agribusiness: 'Twin' beef, dairy industries feud despite their similarities," *The Fauquier Democrat*, August 25, 1988.

19   Source: Rainforest Action Network, 466 Green Street, San Francisco, California 94133.

20   "Swift expansion sets scene for a pork industry brawl," by Gene Erb, *The Des Moines Register*, February 28, 1985.

21   "Concentration in Meat Packing," *CRA Newsletter*, Center for Rural Affairs, Walthill, Nebraska, August, 1987.

22   The Helming Group, Agricultural Consultants, *Farm Journal*, September, 1987.

23   "Limiting farm size like 'shooting self in foot,' expert says," by Don Muhm, *The Des Moines Register*, August 9, 1989.

24   "Reports overdue from some Iowa stock feeders," by Dan Looker, *The Des Moines Register*, September 10, 1989.

25   *Op. cit.*, Marion, December 7, 1988.

26   *Ibid.*

27   *Ibid.*

28   *Op. cit.*, Helmuth, Des Moines, Iowa, December 7, 1988.

29   "Iowa," *USA Today*, December 17, 1985.

30   "IBP keeps tight grip on market," by Dale Kasler, *The Des Moines Register*, September 24, 1988.

31   "Meatpacking: Following a decade of turbulence, packing industry seeks stability," by Gene Erb, *The Des Moines Register*, February 4, 1990.

32   *Op. cit.*, Kasler, *The Des Moines Register*, September 24, 1988.

33   "Small Operators Getting Shouldered Aside," by Ward Sinclair, *The Washington Post*, March 28, 1985.

34   "More Corporate Swine," *CRA Newsletter*, Center for Rural Affairs, Walthill, Nebraska, January, 1989.

35   "Calling all hogs," by Phyllis Berman and Dana Wechsler, *Forbes*, September 5, 1988.

36   *Ibid.*

37   "Efficiency Or Economic Power," *CRA Newsletter*, Center for Rural Affairs, Walthill, Nebraska, December, 1988.

38   *Op. cit.*, Sinclair, *The Washington Post*, March 28, 1985.

39   As quoted in "Return of The Jungle," by David Moberg, *In These Times*, July 24 - August 6, 1985.

40   "Poultry firm paid no taxes," *USA Today*, September 8, 1986.

41   "Sen. Roth Makes Hay With Farm Tax Break," by Sonja Hillgren, United Press International, *The Washington Post*, September 8, 1986.

42   "Food Supply and Use," *Agricultural Outlook*, June, 1991.

43   "Changing Tastes: By the End of This Year Poultry Will Surpass Beef in U.S. Diet," by Timothy K. Smith, *The Wall Street Journal*, September 17, 1987.

44   *Ibid.*

45   "Will the turkey fly this time," by Ruth Simon, *Forbes*, May 18, 1987.

46   "Chicken Empire," by Bob Hall, *Southern Exposure*, Summer, 1989.
47   *Op. cit.*, Smith, *The Wall Street Journal*, September 17, 1987.
48   *Ibid.*
49   *Op. cit.*, Simon, *Forbes*, May 18, 1987.
50   "Poultry firms scramble to cash in," by Lisa Collins, *USA Today*, August 2, 1989.
51   "Superchicken: Whose Life Is It Anyway?," by Richard Conniff, *Discover*, June, 1988.
52   "Tyson Foods Proposes to Buy Holly Farms," by Rick Christie, *The Wall Street Journal*, October 12, 1988.
53   *Op. cit.*, Hall, *Southern Exposure*, Summer, 1989.
54   "For Chicken Biggie Tyson, The Sky Could Be Falling," by Kevin Kelly, *Business Week.*, December 5, 1988.
55   *Op. cit.*, Christie, *The Wall Street Journal*, October 12, 1988.
56   "Tyson has recipe for poultry power," by Harriet Johnson Brackey, *USA Today*, April 20, 1989.
57   *Op. cit.*, Collins, *USA Today*, August 2, 1989.
58   *Op. cit.*, Hall, *Southern Exposure*, Summer, 1989.
59   *Ibid.*
60   *Ibid.*
61   *Ibid.*
62   "Seeing Is Believing," *Southern Exposure*, Summer, 1989.
63   *Ibid.*
64   *Op. cit.*, Hall, *Southern Exposure*, Summer, 1989

CHAPTER THIRTY-FIVE: Efficiency and Ruthlessness

1   "Afterword," by Robert Downs, *The Jungle*, by Upton Sinclair, Signet Classic, New York, N.Y.: 1906, pg. 343-350.
2   *Ibid.*, pg. 349.
3   "The Meat Packing Industry: An Economic Overview," *UFCW Leadership Update*, Vol. 8, No. 4, February, 1986.
4   "Return of The Jungle," by David Moberg, *In These Times*, July 24 - August 6, 1985.
5   Testimony of Dr. John W. Helmuth before the House Standing Committee on Agriculture, General Assembly of Iowa regarding Concentration in the Meat Packing Industry, Des Moines, Iowa, December 7, 1988.
6   "IBP Inc. Struggles to Regain Beef Industry's Leadership," by Marj Charlier, *The Wall Street Journal*, May 3, 1988.
7   "Concentration in Meat Packing," *CRA Newsletter*, Center for Rural Affairs, Walthill, Nebraska, August, 1987.
8   *Ibid.*
9   "Non-Strikers Are Protected by High Court," by Stephen Wermiel, *The Wall Street Journal*, March 1, 1989.
10   *Op. cit.*, Moberg, *In These Times*, July 24 - August 6, 1985.
11   "Union campaign links Hormel and First Banks," *North American Farmer*, May 9, 1985.
12   "Stakes pile higher in the packer poker game," by Nita Effertz, *Farm Journal*, August, 1983.
13   *Op. Cit.*, Moberg, *In These Times*, July 24 - August 6, 1985.. 14 "Section Two - Speeches," by Peggy Hillman, Attorney and Author, General Report, "Solidarity: An Injury To One Is An Injury To All," 1986 National Packinghouse Strategy and Policy Conference, Prepared by Lewie G. Anderson, United Food and Commercial Workers International Union, AFL-CIO, CLC, pg. 18-28.
15   *Ibid.*
16   *Ibid.*
17   "NLRB Acts in Discrimination Case," by Peter Paul, *The Washington Post*, December 10, 1985.
18   See "The Meat Packing Industry: An Economic Overview," *UFCW Leadership Update*, February, 1986.
19   "Back strikers," Letters, Arthur C. Hedberg, Jr., *The Des Moines Register*, August 4, 1982.
20   "Iowa unions urged to help IBP workers," by Jerry Perkins, *The Des Moines Register*, August 20, 1982.
21   "1986 Report on the Meat Packing Industry & Challenges Workers Face," National Packinghouse Strategy and Policy Conference, Chicago, Illinois, November 12, 13 and 14, 1986, pg. II-3, III-3.
22   From a conversation between Jim Guyette and the author in Washington, D.C., on April 18, 1986.
23   "Kirkland Joins In Parent Union's Criticism of Hormel Strikers," by Kenneth B. Noble, *The New York Times*, February 18, 1986.
24   "Austin Under Dictatorship," Hormel Rank-and-File Fightback, P.O. Box 903, Austin, Minnesota 55912.
25   "S.D. meatpackers: Good job's gone bad," by Steve Erpenbach and Wayne Beissert, *USA Today*, May 14, 1987.
26   "Morrell Awarded $24.6 Million From Union," Associated Press, *The Washington Post*, November 13, 1988.
27   "South Dakota Workers Lose 18 Percent of Pay," Associated Press, *The New York Times*, February 21, 1989.
28   "United Brands Co. Unit Cited in Suit Filed by Workers," by Albert R. Karr, *The Wall Street Journal*, October 25, 1988.
29   "United Brands, Morrell Unit Is Accused In NLRB Complaint of Anti-Union Plot," by Albert R. Karr, *The Wall Street Journal*, March 2, 1989.
30   "Major Safety Crackdown on Meatpacking Under Way," by Frank Swoboda, *The Washington Post*, September 21, 1988.
31   "Plains Slaughterhouse a Union Battleground," by Frank Swoboda, *The Washington Post*, August 21, 1988.
32   *Op. Cit.*, *North American Farmer*, May 9, 1985.
33   "P-9 boycott of Hormel endorsed," *North American Farmer*, February 28, 1986.
34   "Iowa," *USA Today*, December 24, 1985.
35   "Burning Questions: Working in America — Hazardous Duty," ABC-TV News, April 20, 1989.
36   "Iowa," *USA Today*, March 28, 1989.
37   "Iowa," *USA Today*, March 15, 1988.
38   "Iowa," *USA Today*, December 24, 1985.
39   "Kansas," *USA Today*, March 13, 1986.
40   "Worker Injuries Highest in Meat Packing," by Bruce Ingersol, *Chicago Sun-Times*, *The Los Angeles Times*, October 18, 1978.
41   *Op. cit.*, Swoboda, *The Washington Post*, September 21, 1988.
42   *Op. cit.*, Ingersol, *The Los Angeles Times*, October 18, 1978.
43   *Ibid.*
44   "Meatpacking Firm Admits to Keeping 2 Sets of Injury Records," by Charles J. Abbott, United Press International, *The Washington Post*, September 22, 1987.
45   "IBP to Pay $975,000 To Settle Charges On Safety, Sources Say," Associated Press, *The Wall Street Journal*, November 23, 1988.

46   "Meatpacker Fined a Record Amount On Plant Injuries," by Robert D. Hershey, Jr., *The New York Times*, October 29, 1988.

47   "Repetitive-Motion Injuries Up," by Frankl Swoboda, *The Washington Post*, October 25, 1988.

48   "South Dakota," *USA Today*, Hanuary 29, 1988.

49   *Op. cit.*, Swoboda, *The Washington Post*, August 21, 1988.

50   See "As Complaints Grow, Doctors Seek Data on Repetitive Motion Injuries," by Gina Kolata, *The New York Times*.

51   "OSHA Urges Record Penalty For Meatplacker," by Albert R. Karr, *The Wall Street Journal*, October 29, 1988.

52   *Op. cit.*, Abbott, *The Washington Post*, September 22, 1987.

53   "Nebraska," *USA Today*, January 25, 1988.

54   *Op. cit.*, Hershey, Jr., *The New York Times*, October 29, 1988.

55   "Meatpacker Is Pressed To Improve Safety," by Frank Swoboda, *The Washington Post*, November 3, 1988.

56   *Ibid.*

57   "USDA Aims at Most Troublesome Meat Plants," Associated Press, *The Washington Post*, Novermber 4, 1988.

58   "Hard Times at Perdue's Plant," by Judy Mann, *The Washington Post*, March 10, 1989.

59   "Study Blames U.S. For Safety Record in the Workplace," by Associated Press, *The Wall Street Journal*, August 18, 1988.

60   *Op. cit.*, Downs, *The Jungle*, Signet Classic, New York, N.Y.: 1906, pg. 348.

61   "Research Links Human Illness, Livestock Drugs," by Cristine Russell, *The Washington Post*, September 6, 1984.

62   "Overhaul of USDA Meat Inspection Urged," *The Washington Post*, July 17, 1985..

CHAPTER THIRTY-SIX: Tapping the Roots

1   *The Hidden Injuries of Class*, by Richard Sennett and Jonathan Cobb, Vintage Books, New York, N.Y.: 1973, pg. 28.
2   *Ibid.*, pg. 30.
3   "Why A Non-Partisan League?" Address to Mass Meeting at Blackfoot, Idaho, *Non-Partisan League Leader*, December 24, 1917, pg. 13-14.
4   "A new image takes seed: agricultural producer," *USA Today*, November 19, 1984.
5   "CBS News - New York Times poll: wide public support for farmers," *North American Farmer*, February 28, 1986.
6   "Family Farming's Finest Hour," by Marty Strange, Dinner Address to Wisconsin Rural Development Center, Inc., Madison, Wisconsin, March 8, 1985.
7   *The Policy Process in American Agriculture*, by Ross B. Talbot and Don Hadwiger, Chandler Publishing Co., San Francisco, California: 1968, pg. 78.
8   "A Man for 1987," by Fred Barbash, "Outlook," *The Washington Post*, March 5, 1987.
9   "The Independent Veblen," Thornstein Veblen, in *The Portable Veblen*, Edited by Max Lerner, The Viking Press, New York, N.Y.: 1948, pg. 398.
10   *Ibid.*, pg. 399.
11   "The Rural Foundation of the American Culture," by Walter Goldschmidt, Gregory Foundation Memorial Lecture, Columbia, Missouri, January 26, 1976.
12   *Op. Cit.*, Talbot and Hadwiger, pg. 22-23.
13   *The Politics of Aristotle*, by Ernest Barker, ed., Oxford University Press, New York, N.Y.: 1946, Book VI, Chapter IV, Section I, Pg. 263. *Ed.Note*: The complete section needs to be read in order to understand Aristotle's position.
14   "The Family Farm: Caught in the Contradictions of American Values," by Francis Moore Lappe, *Agriculture and Human Values*, Spring, 1985, pg. 39.
15   "Jeffersonian Thought In An Urban Society," by William B. Wheeler, *The Agrarian Tradition in American Society*, University of Tennessee, Nashville, Tennessee: 1976, pg. 39-49.
16   *Ibid.*, pg. 41.
17   *Ibid.*, pg. 42.
18   *Ibid.*, pg. 44-46.
19   *American Environmentalism: Values, Tactics, Priorities*, by Joseph Petulla, Texas A&M Press, College Station, Texas: 1980, pg. 18-21.
20   *Op. Cit.*, Wheeler, pg. 46.
21   *Ibid.*
22   *Farming and Democracy*, by A. Whitney Griswold, Harcourt, Brace & Co., New York, N.Y.: 1948, pg. 177-214.
23   *Op. Cit.*, Lappe, pg. 41
24   *Op. Cit.*, Talbot and Hadwiger, pg. 24-29.
25   *Ibid.*, pg. 31.
26   *Op. cit.*, Goldschmidt, Gregory Foundation Memorial Lecture, January 26, 1976.
27   "Beliefs Bound to the Land Hold Firm as Times Change," "Insight," *The Washington Times*, December 7, 1987, pg. 11.
28   "Sector as Personality: The Case of Farm Protest Movements," by Luther Tweeten, *Agriculture and Human Values*, Winter, 1987, pg. 67.
29   *Ibid.*, pg. 70.
30   *Ibid.*, pg. 73.
31   "Farm Activism: A Study in Conflicting Goals, Values, and Beliefs," by Luther Tweeten, Professional paper of the Oklahoma Agricultural Experiment Station, Undated, pg. 2.
32   *Op. cit.*, Tweeten, *Agriculture and Human Values*, Winter, 1987, pg. 66.
33   *Ibid.*, pg. 67.
34   *Ibid.*, pg. 66.
35   *The Myth of the Family Farm: Agribusiness Dominance of U.S. Agriculture* by Ingolf Vogeler, Westview Press, Boulder, Colorado: 1981, pg. 6.
36   *Ibid.*, pg. 7-10.
37   *Op. cit.*, Tweeten, *Agriculture and Human Values*, Winter, 1987, pg. 67.
38   *Ibid.*
39   *Op. cit.*, *Agriculture and Human Values*, Winter, 1987, pg. 67.
40   "Profits for everybody except the producer," by Booker T. Whatley, *USA Today*, July 8, 1986.
41   *Op. cit.*, *Agriculture and Human Values*, Winter, 1987, pg. 67.
42   *Ibid.*, pg. 69
43   *Ibid.*, pg. 69-70.
44   *Ibid.*, pg. 70.

45   *Democratic Promise: The Populist Moment in America* by Lawrence Goodwyn, Oxford University Press, New York: 1976, pg. xvii.

46   *Ibid.*, pg. 358.

47   *Op. cit., Agriculture and Human Values*, Winter, 1987, pg. 70.

48   *Op. cit.*, Tweeten, "Farm Activism: A Study in Conflicting Goals, Values, and Beliefs," Undated, pg. 12.

49   *Op. cit.*, Tweeten, *Agriculture and Human Values*, Winter, 1987, pg. 67.

50   *Ibid.*

51   *Ibid.*

52   *Ibid.*, pg. 68.

CHAPTER THIRTY-SEVEN: Creating New Wealth

1   "I'll Meet You Beneath the National Debt," by Hal Lux, *The New York Times*, March 13, 1989.
2   Appendix Table 1: Farm Income, assets and debt, and returns, "Agricultural Income and Finance: Situation and Outlook Report," ERS, USDA, AFO-33, May, 1989.
3   "This Week With David Brinkley," ABC-TV, October 30, 1988 and Treasury Statement, *The New York Times*, August 20, 1988.
4   Papers and correspondence between the author and Vince E. Rossiter, Agricultural Finance Committee, Independent Bankers Association.
5   "The Growing Federal Debt," Office of Management and Budget, U.S. Treasury Department, *The Washington Post*, August 9, 1985.
6   "Federal Debt Limit Is Set At $2.87 Trillion by Senate," *The Wall Street Journal*, August 7, 1989.
7   "U.S. Falling Deeper Into Debt," by James E. Lebherz, *The Washington Post*, July 13, 1986.
8   As quoted in "Facing the Challenge Ahead," by Hobart Rowen, *The Washington Post*, April 24, 1988.
9   "Another Day Older And Deeper in Debt," by Dale Russakoff, *The Washington Post*, February 14, 1986.
10 *Op. cit.*, Rossiter
11 "Special Report — Behind The Soaring U.S. Deficit," by John Eckhouse, *San Francisco Chronicle*, January 5, 1987.
12 *Borrowing Our Way Out of Debt?*, National Organization of Raw Materials (NORM), 1983.
13 "Even though time has run out for America: There Is No Plan For Agriculture," by V.E. Rossiter, Sr., *Acres U.S.A.*, March, 1983.
14 *Ibid.*
15 "Table 27b - Farm income statistics," *Agricultural Outlook*, USDA Economic Research Service, March, 1987.
16 "USA farms digging out, report says," by Judy Keen, *USA Today*, August 11, 1987.
17 "Dear NORM Member," A Letter From Vince E. Rossiter, Sr., President, NORM, October 15, 1984.
18 *Prosperity Unlimited: The American Way*, by Carl Wilken, Carl H. Wilkin, Sioux City, Iowa: 1947.
19 *Op. cit.*, Rossiter.
20 "If the Truth Were Known," by V.E. Rossiter, Presentation to NORM, Kansas City, Missouri, January 16, 1986.
21 *Ibid.*
22 *Ibid.*
23 "When 'Minimum' Means 'Rockbottom', It's High Time For A Wage Increase," *Update*, Rural Coaliton, Washington, D.C., March, 1987.
24 "American Job Machine Has Begun to Sputter," by Barry Bluestone and Bennett Harrison, *The Washington Post*, May 17, 1987.
25 "So We Have More Jobs — Low Paid, Part-Time Ones," by Lance Compa, Labor Attorney, United Electrical, Radio and Machine Workers of America, *The Washington Post*.
26 *Ibid.*, Bluestone/Harrison, *The Washington Post*, May 17, 1987.
27 *Ibid.*
28 *Op. cit.*, Compa, *The Washington Post.*
29 *Op. cit.*, Rossiter, Kansas City, Missouri, January 16, 1986,
30 *Ibid.*
31 *Op. cit.*, NORM, 1983.
32 "The Casino Society," by Anthony Bianco, *Business Week*, September 19, 1985.
33 *Op. cit.*, Rossiter, *Acres U.S.A.*, March, 1983.
34 "Letters to the Editor - The American Farmer: A Vital Economic Resource," By Joe Skeen R.-N.M.), House of Representatives, *The Wall Street Journal*, February 9, 1983.
35 Table 6: Rate of return on farm assets and equity, "Agricultural Income and Finance: Situation and Outlook Report," ERS, USDA, AFO-33, May, 1989.
36 Source: Donaldson, Lufkin & Jenrette Securities Corp., *Business Week*, Spetmber 25, 1989.
37 *Source:* Goldman, Sachs & Co., 1991.
38 Food Cost Review, Denis Dunham, USDA Economic Research Service, Agricultural Economic Report #636, Table 20, July, 1990.
39 "Farmers' real need: to sell in their big market (U.S.)," by James Flansburg, *The Des Moines Register*, August 1, 1982.
40 "Brand discusses changes ahead for industry," *The Packer*, October 2, 1982.
41 "Farm-to-Retail Price Spread Widens," Food Costs . . . From Farm to Retail, USDA Economic Research Service, March, 1986.
42 "Labor, The Largest Cost," *Food Cost Review, 1985*, USDA Economic Research Service, Agricultural Economic Report, No. 559, July, 1986.
43 "Why Labor Gets More of the Food Dollar Than Farmers," *Farmline*, USDA, October, 1986.
44 "Table 23 - Potatoes, sweetpotatoes, dry edible beans, and dry field peas: Per capita consumption, farm and

retail weights, 1965-1985," Food Consumption, Prices, and Expenditures, 1985, by Karen L. Bunch, USDA Economic Research Service, Statistical Bulletin No. 749, January, 1987.

45   "Survey: Food profits up," *The Packer*, January 22, 1983.

46   "Some Vital Comparisons," by Clarence Sharp, *U.S. Farm News*, October, 1985.

47   "Let's Help Farmers Survive the Crisis," by E. (Kika) de la Garza, U.S. Representative (D.-Texas), Chairman, Committee on Agriculture, *The Washington Post*, September 26, 1985.

48   "Writing Farm Legislation Is Mission Impossible," by Ward Sinclair, *The Washington Post*, April 25, 1985.

49   "We pay penalty for doing better," by Susan Bright, *USA Today*, January 21, 1985.

50   *The Economic Impacts Of Farm Income on the U.S. Economy*, A Special Study Prepared for the National Association of Wheat Growers, Washington, D.C. by the Food and Agriculture Service, Chase Econometrics Inc., Bala Cynwyd, Penn., July, 1982 and "Economists say total recovery hinges on boost in farm income," by George Anthan, *The Des Moines Register*, September 12, 1982.

51   *Ibid.*

52   "Bankers hope for crop price deal," by Tom Petruno, *USA Today*, March 8, 1985.

53   *Ibid.*

54   "Fed Nominee Says He Still Seeks Policy Aimed at Stabilizing Commodity Prices," by Phil Blustein, *The Wall Street Journal*, January 27, 1986.

55   Source: U.S. Department of Agriculture and "Food Supply and Use," *Agricultural Outlook*, June, 1990.

56   *Op. cit.*, Moeller, January 17, 1987.

57   "Lost, 31 Profitable Years: 1952 to 1983," by V. E. Rossiter, Sr., Vice-President, NORM, Kansas City, Missouri, January 19-21, 1984.

58   "Support the Farm Policy Reform Act: Groundwork laid for just farm bill," by Merle Hansen, President, North American Farm Alliance, *North American Farmer*, April, 1985.

59   Letter to James G. Webster, Director, Office of Governmental and Public Affairs, USDA, Washington, D.C. from Tony Dechant, President, National Farmers Union (NFU), April 16, 1979.

60   Agricultural Statistics Board, NASS, USDA, July, 1989.

61   United States Parity Prices for Farm Products and Average Prices Received As Percent of Parity Prices Based on Data for January, 1988, Agricultural Statistics Board, NASS, USDA as quoted in *The NFO Reporter*, February, 1988.

62   "Corn price drops to 15-year low," *USA Today*, October 17, 1986.

63   Luther Tweeten, Regents Professor, Department of Agricultural Economics, Oklahoma State University, March 28, 1983.

64   *Op. cit.*, Rossiter, October 15, 1986.

CHAPTER THIRTY-EIGHT: Farmers Seeking Control Over Their Own Destiny

1   "Hightower criticizes Reagan ag policy," *North Dakota Union Farmer*, March 29, 1984.
2   *Ibid.*
3   "Farm and labor leaders form coalition; discuss farm policy," *North Dakota Union Farmer*, April 4, 1985.
4   "Grassroots farm bill introduced," *North American Farmer*, May 9, 1985.
5   *Ibid.*
6   *Ibid.*
7   *Ibid.*
8   "Farm bill tuneup likely, but no major overhaul," by J. M. Johnson, *The Sacramento Bee*, December 21, 1986.
9   "The Truth About Market Clearing Prices," *Agricultural Watchdog*, January, 1985.
10 "Harkin Proposal: Intriguing farm bill cuts against the grain," Editorial, *St. Paul Pioneer Press-Dispatch*, May 13, 1985.
11 "Groundwork laid for just farm bill," by Merle Hansen, *North American Farmer*, April, 1985.
12 "Barnyard Politics," by Hal Hamilton, Undated.
13 "Harkin's proposal to set a new farm-policy course," by Tom Harkin, *The Des Moines Register*, May 23, 1985.
14 As cited in "Campaign Update: The Farm Policy Reform Act of 1985," by the League of Rural Voters, Minneapolis, Minn., April 10, 1985.
15 "Congress Passes Final Farm Bill," by Ward Sinclair, *The Washington Post*, December 19, 1985.
16 "New farm bill like Robin Hood in reverse," by John McGuire, Nebraska Wheat Board, *North American Farmer*, January 31, 1986.
17 "Senate Farm Bill Said to Cost $5 Billion More Than Project," by Ward Sinclair, *The Washington Post*, October 25, 1985 and "What's Ahead for Business: The Farm Bill - - $55 Billion, And Counting," by Howard Banks, *Forbes*, April 7, 1986.
18 "Paying the Bill: New Farm Law Raises Federal Costs and Fails To Solve Big Problems," by Wendy L. Wall and Charles F. McCoy, *The Wall Street Journal*, June 17, 1986.
19 *Ibid.*
20 "How to Feel Insecure about the Food Security Act of 1985," by Joe Belden, *Food Monitor*, No. 35.
21 "American Journal: British Farmers Show Missouri," by Ward Sinclair, *The Washington Post*, April 6, 1986.
22 "Senate Rejects One-Year Freeze on Farm Subsidies," by Ward Sinclair, *The Washington Post*, October 31, 1985.
23 "Farm Woes Beyond New Bill's Reach," by Ward Sinclair, *The Washington Post*, October 14, 1985.
24 "Stockman Impact Lingers," by Ward Sinclair, *The Washington Post*, November 25, 1985.
25 *Op. cit.*, Henshaw, *USA Today*, December 19, 1985 and "Farm Bill? What Farm Bill?" by Ward Sinclair, *The Washington Post*, June 23, 1985..
26 "Few seem satisfied with'85 farm bill," by Jake Henshaw and Peter Johnson, *USA Today*, November 25, 1985.
27 "New Farm Bill -- Worse Than Before," by Lem Harris, *U.S. Farm News*, February, 1986.
28 "U.S. Reduces Price Supports For 1986 Crop," by Albert R. Karr and Wendy L. Hall, *The Wall Street Journal*, January 14, 1986.
29 "Farm Value in Food Prices," *The Farm Crisis: Causes and Cures*, Prepared for American Agriculture Movement National Convention, Memphis, Tenn. by Mike Moeller, Deputy Commissioner, Texas Department of Agriculture, January 17, 1987.
30 "Reagan Seeks a $10 Billion Cut in Farm Spending," by Keith Schneider, *The New York Times*, February 6, 1986.
31 *Op. cit.*, Wall/McCoy, *The Wall Street Journal*, June 17, 1986.
32 *Ibid.*
33 "Lines Drawn Over Farm Legislation," by Ward Sinclair, *The Washington Post*, December 7, 1986.
34 "What's Ahead for U.S. Farm Policy in '89," by Henry Schacht, *San Francisco Chronicle*, November 24, 1987.

CHAPTER THIRTY-NINE: Scaring Agribusiness to Death

1   "'Tough winter' for farmers," by Mary Kay Quinlan, *USA Today*, December 17, 1985.

2   "In Farm Belt, GOP Senators Keep Reagan Policies at a Distance," by Ward Sinclair, *The Washington Post*, November 30, 1985.

3   "Reagan Plan to Cut U.S. Role in Farming Unveiled by Block," by Ward Sinclair, *The Washington Post*, February 23, 1985.

4   *Ibid.*

5   "Inside: USDA - Administration Plays Small Role Shaping Farm Bill," by Ward Sinclair, *The Washington Post*, October 1, 1985.

6   "USDA's Farm-Bill Lobbying Hit," by Ward Sinclair, *The Washington Post*, October 1, 1985.

7   *Ibid.*

8   "Quotelines," *USA Today*, August 7, 1986.

9   "Few seem satisfied with '85 farm bill," by Jake Henshaw and Peter Johnson, *USA Today*, November 25, 1985.

10   "Fair farm prices and production controls opposed by agribusiness associations," *North American Farmer*, February 28, 1986.

11   "Senate Panel Balks At Agricultural Cuts, Deficit Reduction," by David Hoffman, *The Washington Post*, March 7, 1985.

12   "Veto tangles farmers' futures," by Leslie Phillip and Chuck Raasch, *USA Today*, March 8, 1985.

13   "GOP Trouble on the Farm," by Rowland Evans and Robert Novak, *The Washington Post*, March 4, 1985.

14   *Secrets of the Temple*, by William Greider, Simon & Shuster, New York, NY, 1988.

15   "Inside: the Agriculture Department - From the Hill, It's Raining Pitchforks," by Ward Sinclair, *The Washington Post*, August 21, 1985.

16   "Senate Democrats Reject Farm Pact," by Helen Dewar and Margaret Shapiro, *The Washington Post*, February 22, 1985.

17   "Reagan Warns Farmers," by Ward Sinclair and Kathy Sawyer, *The Washington Post*, February 24, 1985.

18   "Block Moves to Grant Farm-Credit Aid Spurned by Democrats," by Helen Dewar, *The Washington Post*, February 23, 1985.

19   "Saving the Family Farm," by Jim Hightower, *The Washington Post*, October 1, 1985.

20   "Grassroots farmers move full steam ahead on 1985 Farm Bill," by Dixon Terry, *North American Farmer*, October 15, 1985.

21   "Farmer Referendum is Deleted From Bill," by Ward Sinclair, *The Washington Post*, October 4, 1985.

22   *Op. Cit.*, Terry, *North American Farmer*, October 15, 1985.

23   "House Approves Hotly Debated 5 - Year Farm Bill," by Ward Sinclair, *The Washington Post*, October 9, 1985.

24   "Senators Forced into Farm Bill Marathon," by Ward Sinclair, *The Washington Post*, November 23, 1985.

25   *Ibid.*

26   "Farm Policy Study - Year 1986," League of Rural Voters. See also "Washington Asks for Feedback From the Farm." by Keith Schneider, *The New York Times*, July 6, 1986.

27   "Wheat poll success acclaimed in Washington," by Larry Gray, *North American Farmer*, September 5, 1986.

28   Letter to Bryce Neidig, President, Nebraska Farm Bureau Federation, from Ervain J. Friehe, immediate Past Chairman, Nebraska Wheat Board, July 21, 1986.

29   *Op. Cit.*, Gray, *North American Farmer*, September 5, 1986.

30   "Farmers Seeking Crop of Votes," by Ward Sinclair, *The Washington Post*, August 31, 1986.

31   *The Closed Enterprise*, by Mark Green with Beverly C. Moore and Bruce Wasserstein, Grossman, New York, N.Y.: 1972, pg. 14.

32   "Farm Sector Still on Rebound," by Ward Sinclair, *The Washington Post*, January 24, 1988.

33   "Put Agriculture Policy Out to Pasture," by James Bovard, *The Wall Street Journal*, February 4, 1988.

34   "Export Program's Load of Problems," by Ward Sinclair, *The Washington Post*, May 24, 1988.

35   *Ibid.*

36   *Ibid.*

37   *Op. Cit.*, Bovard, *The Wall Street Journal*, February 4, 1988.

38   "Globalizing the Farm Crisis: A Dangerous World Food Situation Demands Education/Action," by Mark Ritchie, *Christian Social Action*, March, 1988.

39   "U.S. Farm Exports Up, With Demand Greatest Since 84," by Keith Schneider, *The New York Times*, January 11, 1988.

40   "Farm Progam Bill Far Above USDA Estimates," by Associated Press, *The Washington Post*, May 10, 1988.

41   "Billions of dollars spent to protect world's farmers," by George Anthan, *The Des Moines Register*, March 12, 1988.

42   *Plowing Under the Farmers: The Impact of the Pentagon Tax on American Agriculture*, by Dr. James R. Anderson, Employment Research Associates, 474 Hollister Bldg., Lansing, Michigan 48933, 1986.

43   "Deep in the Heartland, Deep in Slumber," by Coleman McCarthy, *The Washington Post*, February 28, 1988.

APPENDIX B: Defining "Communities of Economic Interests"

1   *Interlocking Directorates Among The Major U.S. Corporations*, A Staff Study Prepared By the Subcommittee on Reports, Accounting and Management of the Committee On Government Affairs, United States Senate, January, 1978.

2   "Corporate Incest," *The AgBiz Tiller*, San Francisco, California, No. 10, July, 1978.

3   *Report on Interlocking Directorates*, Federal Trade Commission, 1950.

4   *Wealth of Nations*, by Adam Smith, Random House, New York, N.Y.: 1937, pg. 128.

5   *Op. cit.*, AgBiz Tiller, No. 10, July, 1978.

6   *Op. cit.*, Interlocking Directorates, Subcommittee on Reports, Accounting and Management, January, 1978.

7   *Ibid.*

8   *Op. cit.*, AgBiz Tiller, No. 10, July, 1978.

9   *CDE Stock Ownership Directory: Fortune 500*, Corporate Data Exchange, Inc., New York, N.Y.: 1981.

10   "Monday Morning: Annual Meetings, A Capitalist Farce," by Jerry Knight, "Washington Business," *The Washington Post*, February 6, 1984.

11   "American Business Has A New Kingpin: The Investment Banker," by Anthony Bianco, *Business Week*, November 24, 1986.

12   "U.S. Wealth Becomes More Concentrated," by John M. Berry, *The Washington Post*, July 26, 1986, "Obey Releases New Data on the Concentration of Wealth in the United States," Press release from the Joint Economic Committee, Congress of the United States, August 21, 1986, and "Report Overstated Gains of 'Super Rich'," by David A. Vise, *The Washington Post*, August 22, 1986.

13   Maurice Zeitlin, *The Progressive*, June, 1978.

14   "2.8% of Nation, 28% of Wealth," Associated Press, *The Washington Post*, March 8, 1985.

15   "Where the money is," Federal Reserve Board, *USA Today*, November 12, 1984 and "Where the rich invest," CIGNA Corp., *USA Today*, June 4, 1987.

16   *Op. cit.*, Associated Press, *The Washingpton Post*, March 8, 1985.

17   "Book World: Cracking the Bank Job," by Bernard A. Weisberger, *The Washington Post*, March 29, 1985.

18   "Independent banks fight to stay that way," by Tom Petruno, *USA Today*, March 7, 1985.

19   "USA's biggest banks," *USA Today*, October 21, 1988.

20   "Top foreign banks in the USA," American Banker, *USA Today*, March 5, 1986.

21   "Japan's Banks: Top 10 in Deposits," by Nathaniel C. Nash, *The New York Times*, July 20, 1988.

22   "Upheavel Predicted In U.S. Banking System," by Nancy L. Ross, *The Washington Post*, October 20, 1984.

23   "Continental, 100 Banks Seen Linked," by James L. Rowe Jr., *The Washington Post*, September 20, 1984.

24   *Ibid.*

25   "Wall Street Is Riding a Paper Tiger," by Felix Rohatyn, *The Washington Post*, March 8, 1987.

26   "Mexican Debt Threatens U.S. Banks," by Jack Anderson and Dale Van Atta, *The Washington Post*, June 19, 1986.

27   "Big Banks Flush With Uninsured Funds," by Jack Anderson and Dale Van Atta, *The Washington Post*, May 22, 1987.

28   "Full Disclosure for Banks," by Hobart Rowen, *The Washington Post*, March 31, 1985.

29   *Op. cit.*, Petruno, *USA Today*, March 7, 1985.

30   "Court Clears Way for Regional Banking," by James L. Rowe Jr. and Al Kamen, *The Washington Post*, June 11, 1985.

31   *Op. cit.*, Petruno, *USA Today.*, March 7, 1985.

32   "Top 5 institutional investors," Institutional Investor, *USA Today*, September 19, 1986.

33   "Business and the Short-Term Syndrome," by Pat Choate and J.K. Linger, authors of *The High-Flex Society*, *The Washington Post*.

34   *Ibid.*

35   "The Myth of Mergers," by Mark Green and John F. Berry, *Multinational Monitor*, February 15, 1986.

36   "Debating the Nature if U.S. Corporations," by Peter Behr, *The Washington Post*, January 11, 1987.

37   *Ibid.*

38   *Op. cit.*, Green and Berry, *Multinational Monitor*, February 15, 1986.

39   "Merger Maverick: An Interview with Arthur Burck," *Multinational Monitor*, February 15, 1986.

40   *Op. cit.*, "The Casino Society," Bianco, *Business Week*, September 16, 1985.

41   "The Sum and Substance of Antitrust," *Multinational Monitor*, February 15, 1986.

42   "The Reagan Assault on Antitrust," by Eddie Correia, *The Multinational Monitor*, February 15, 1986.

43   "Do All These Deals Help or Hurt the U.S. Economy?," by Norman Jonas and Joan Berger, *Business Week*, November 24, 1986.

44   *Op. cit.*, Burck, *Multinational Monitor*, February 15, 1986.

45   "Takeovers Return to the Old Mode," by Leslie Wayne, *The New York Times*, January 4, 1988; *Op. cit.*, Greenberg, *Mother Jones*, March, 1988, and "Merger wave might drown our economy," by Daniel Kadlec, *USA Today*, March 10, 1988.

46   "Deal Mania: The Restructuring of Corporate America," by Anthony Bianco, *Business Week*, November 24, 1986 and also quoted in "Larry King's 'People;," *USA Today*, July 6, 1987.

47   "Dennis Levine's alleged top ten deals," *USA Today*, June 6, 1986 and "How Inside Knowledge Made, Ruined Career of Dennis B. Levine," by James R. Stewart, Daniel Hertzberg and Scott McMurray, *The Wall Street Journal*, May 15, 1986.

48   "Boesky's World," by Ken Auletta, *The Washington Post*, November 23, 1986.

49   "Inside trading hurst individual investors," by Carl T. Hall, *USA Today*, June 9, 1986.

50   *The New Gatsbys: Fortunes and Misfortunes of Commodity Traders*, by Bob Tamarkin, Quill - William Morrow, New York, N.Y.: 1985, pg. 17.

51   *Op. cit.*, Auletta, *The Washington Post*, November 23, 1986.

52   "Wall Street's Rotten Apples," by Ken Auletta, *The Washington Post*, May 25, 1986.

53   "Notable & Quoteable," *The Wall Street Journal*, December 5, 1986.

54   *Op. cit.*, Auletta, *The Washington Post*, November 23, 1986.

APPENDIX K: "If there's a flaw in the system ..."

1   "Crime at Merc Widespread, FBI Testifies," by Scott McMurray, *The Wall Street Journal*, January 31, 1990.
2   "Traders on Tape, Brag About Illegal Trading," by Scott McMurray, *The Wall Street Journal*, January 9, 1990.

3   "Commodities Brokers' Pleas Show Cheating Was Routine," by William B. Crawford Jr., "*The Chicago Tribune*," *The Washington Post*, November 25, 1989.
4   *Ibid.*
5   "Futures Probe Might Scrutinize Brokerage Firms," by Scott McMurray and Jeff Bailey, *The Wall Street Journal*, August 21, 1989.
6   "For Futures Fraud Victims, Sizing Up Losses Is Difficult," by Carol Jouzaitis and Shawn Pogatchnik, "*The Chicago Tribune*," *The Washington Post*, August 10, 1989.
7   *Ibid.*
8   "U.S. Set Back In Court in Chicago Traders Case," by Scott McMurray, *The Wall Street Journal*, July 11, 1980.
9   "Lack of Victims Hurt Chicago Futures Case," by Scott McMurray, *The Wall Street Journal*, July 11, 1990.
10   "CFTC Finds Dual Trading Not Essential," by Gregory A. Robb, *The New York Times*, November 18, 1989.
11   *Ibid.*
12   "Futures Exchanges to Present Reports Arguing Against Dual Trading Limits," by Jeffrey Taylor, *The Wall Street Journal*, June 14, 1990.
13   *Op. cit.*, Crawford Jr., November 25, 1989.

Select Bibliography

The Bigness Complex: Industry, Labor and Government in the American Economy, by Walter Adams and James W. Brock, Pantheon Books, New York, N.Y.: 1986.

This Mighty Dream: Social Protest Movements in the United States, by Madeleine Adamson and Seth Borgos, Routledge & Kegan Paul, Boston, Mass.: 1985.

Monopoly Capital: An Essay on the American Economic and Social Order, by Paul A. Baran and Paul M. Sweezy, Modern Reader Paperbacks, New York, N.Y.: 1966.

The People's Land, A Reader on Land Reform in the United States, Edited by Peter Barnes for the National Coalition for Land Reform, Rodale Press, Emmaus, Penn., February, 1975.

Toward A National Food Policy, by Joe Belden with Gregg Forte, Exploratory Project for Economic Alternatives, Washington, D.C., 1976.

Farm Policies of the United States, 1790-1950: A Study of Their Origins and Development, by Murray R. Benedict, The Twentieth Century Fund, New York, N.Y.: 1953.

Cross Fire: The Eight Years With Eisenhower, by Ezra Taft Benson, Doubleday, Garden City, N.Y.: 1962.

Dollar Harvest: An Expose of the Farm Bureau, by Samuel R. Berger, D.C. Heath: Heath Lexington Books, 1971.

The Unsettling of America: Culture & Agriculture, by Wendell Berry, Sierra Club Books, San Francisco, California, 1977.

Economic Concentration: Structure, Behavior & Public Policy, by John M. Blair, Harcourt Brace Jovanovich, Inc., New York, N.Y.: 1972.

Economic Report of the ~~President~~ People, An Alternative to the Economic Report of the President, Center for Popular Economics, Washington, D.C., South End Press, Boston, Mass.: 1986.

From the Ground Up: Building a Grass Roots Food Policy, Center for Science in the Public Interest, Washington, D.C., 1976.

Energy for Survival: The Alternative to Extinction, by Wilson Clark, Anchor Books, Garden City, N.Y.: 1975.

Manufacturing Matters: The Myth of the Post-Industrial Economy, by Stephen S. Cohen and John Zysman, Basic Books: 1987.

The Poverty of Power: Energy and the Economic Crisis, by Barry
Commoner, Knopf, New York, N.Y.: 1976.

*The Food Manufacturing Industries: Structure, Strategies,
Performances, and Policies*, by John M. Connor, Richard T. Rogers,
Bruce W. Marion, and Willard F. Mueller, Lexington Books, D.C. Heath
and Company, Lexington, Mass./Toronto: 1985.

CDE Stock Ownership Directory - Agribusiness, Corporate Data
Exchange, Inc., Room 707, 198 Broadway, New York, N.Y. 10038, 1979.

CDE Stock Ownership Directory: No.3 - Banking and Finance,
Corporate Date Exchange, New York, N.Y.: 1980.

CDE Stock Ownership Directory: Fortune 500, Corporate Data
Exchange, Inc., New York, N.Y.: 1981.

The Supermarket Trap, by Jennifer Cross, Berkley Publishing Co.,
New York, N.Y.: 1970.

A Concept of Agribusiness, by John H. Davis and Ray A. Goldberg,
Division of Research, Graduate School of Business, Harvard University,
Boston, Mass.: 1957.

The Fields Have Turned Brown: Four Essays On World Hunger, by
Susan DeMarco and Susan Sechler, A Report of the Agribusiness
Accountability Project, Washington, D.C., 1975.

*Altered Harvest: Agriculture, Genetics, and the Fate of the World
Food Supply*," by Jack Doyle, Viking Press, New York, N.Y.: 1985.

George N. Peek and the Fight for Farm Parity, by Gilbert C. Fite,
University of Oklahoma Press, Norman, Okla.: 1954.

Shattering: Food, Politics, and the Loss of Genetic Diversity, by Cary Fowler and Pat
Mooney, University of Arizona Press, Tucson, Arizona: 1990.

*A Poor Harvest: The Clash of Policies and Interests in the Grain
Trade*, by Richard Gilmore, Longman, New York, N.Y.: 1982.

The Supermarket Handbook, Revised and Expanded Edition, by Nikki
& David Goldbeck, New American Library, New York, N.Y.: 1976.

*As You Sow: Three Studies in the Social Consequences of
Agribusiness*, by Walter Goldschmidt, Allanheld, Osmun & Co.,
Montclair, N.J.: 1978.

Democratic Promise: The Populist Moment in America by Lawrence
  Goodwyn, Oxford University Press, New York: 1976.

*The Political Economy of Class Structure in U.S. Agriculture: A
  Theoretical Outline*, by Kevin F. Goss, Richard D. Rodefeld and Frederick
  H. Buttel, Department of Agricultural Economics and Rural Sociology,
  Agricultural Experiment Station, Pennsylvania State University,
  University Park, Penn., October, 1979.

Industrialization of U.S. Agriculture: An Interpretative Atlas,
  by Howard F. Gregor, Westview Press, Boulder, Colorado, September,
  1982.

Farming and Democracy, by A. Whitney Griswold, Harcourt, Brace &
  Co., New York, N.Y.: 1948.

The Food Lobbyists, by Harold D. Guither, Lexington Books,
  Lexington, Mass.: 1980.

Food Policy For America, by Harold G. Halcrow, McGraw-Hill Book
  Co., New York, N.Y.: 1977.

Food For Nought: The Decline In Nutrition, by Ross Hume Hall,
  Vintage Books, New York, N.Y.: 1976.

The Great American Grain Robbery and Other Stores, by Martha
  Hamilton, Agribusiness Accountability Project, Washington, D.C.: 1972.

The New American Poverty, by Michael Harrington, Holt, Rinehart &
  Winston, New York, N.Y.: 1984.

*Government and Agriculture: Public Policy In A Democratic
  Society*, by Dale Hathaway, MacMillan Co., New York, N.Y.: 1963;

A History of Public Land Policies, by Benjamin H. Hibbard,
  University of Wisconsin Press, Madison, Wisconsin: 1965.

Eat Your Heart Out: How Food Profiteers Victimize The Consumer,
  by Jim Hightower, Vintage Books, New York, N.Y.: August, 1976.

Hard Tomatoes, Hard Times, A Report of the Agribusiness
  Accountability Project on the Failure of America's Land Grant College
  Complex, by Jim Hightower, Research Coordinated by Susan DeMarco,
  Schenkman Publishing Co., Cambridge, Mass.: 1973.

Daily Bread: An Abdication of Power, The Joseph Project Report on
  Hunger, Grain and Transnationals, Sponsored by the Senate of Priests of
  St. Paul and Minneapolis, Minnesota, 1982.

Social Scientists and Farm Politics in the Age of Roosevelt, by
    Richard S. Kirkendall, Iowa State University Press, Ames, Iowa: 1966.

The Traders, by Sonny Kleinfield, Holt, Reinhart Winston, New
    York, N.Y.

Let Them Eat Promises, by Nick Kotz, Prentice-Hall, Engelwood
    Heights, N.J.: 1969.

*The Malling of America: An Inside Look at the Great Consumer
    Paradise*, by William Severini Kowinski, Morrow, New York, N.Y.: 1984.

*Who's Minding the Co-op?: A Report on Farmer Control of Farmer
    Cooperatives*, by Linda Kravitz, Agribusiness Accountability Project,
    Washington, D.C.: March, 1974.

Vicious Circles: The Mafia in the Marketplace, by Jonathan
    Kwitny, W.W. Norton & Co., New York, N.Y.: 1979.

The Myth of U.S. Agricultural Prosperity, by Frank M. LeRoux,
    314 Jones Bldg., Walla Walla, Wash. 99362, 1976.

Food for People Not for Profit, A Sourcebook on the Food Crisis,
    Edited by Catherine Lerza and Michael Jacobson, Ballantine Books, New
    York, N.Y.: 1975.

Agriculture and Energy, Edited by William Lockeretz, Academic
    Press, New York, N.Y.: 1977.

Roadside Empires: How the Chains Franchised America, by Stan
    Luxenberg, Viking, New York, N.Y.: 1984.

Farm Policies and Politics in the Truman Years, by Allen J.
    Matusow, Harvard University Press, Cambridge, Mass.: 1967.

The Bankers, by Martin Mayer, Weybright and Talley, New York,
    N.Y.: 1974.

The Decline of Agrarian Democracy, by Grant McConnell, Atheneum,
    New York, N.Y.: 1977.

The Farm Bloc, by Wesley McCune, Doubleday, Doran & Co., Inc.,
    Garden City, N.Y.: 1943.

Who's Behind Our Farm Policy?, by Wesley McCune, Frederick A.
    Praeger, New York, N.Y.: 1956.

Agricultural Thought in the Twentieth Century, Edited by George

McGovern, Bobbs-Merrill Co. Inc., Indianapolis, Ind.:1967.

*Too Many Farmers: The Story of What Is Here and Ahead in
    Agriculture*, by Wheeler McMillen, William Morrow Co., New York, N.Y.:
    1929.

The Politics of Food, by Don Mitchell, James Lorimer & Co.,
    Toronto, Canada: 1975.

Mean Things Happening in This Land, by H. L. Mitchell, Allanheld,
    Osmun, Montclair, N.J.: 1979.

Merchants of Grain, by Dan Morgan, The Viking Press, New York,
    N.Y.: 1979.

*Everybody's Business - An Almanac: The Irreverent Guide to
    Corporate America*, Edited by Milton Moskowitz, Michael Katz, and
    Robert Levering, Harper & Row Publishers, San Francisco, California,
    1980.

Guidelines For Food Purchasing in the United States, by Nick
    Mottern, Prepared for the Senate Select Committee on Nutrition and
    Human Needs, Winchester, Virginia, May 12, 1978.

*Farming for Profit in a Hungry World: Capital and Crisis In
    Agriculture*, by Michael Perelman, Allanheld, Osmun, Montclair, N.J.:
    1977.

American Environmental History: Second Edition, by Joseph
    Petulla, Merrill Publishing Co., Columbus, Ohio: 1987.

American Environmentalism: Values, Tactics, Priorities, by Joseph
    Petulla, Texas A&M Press, College Station, Texas: 1980.

From the Crash to the Blitz, 1929-1939, by Cabell Phillips,
    from *The New York Times Chronicle of American Life*, The Macmillan Co.,
    London, 1969.

*Breadlines Knee Deep in Wheat: Food Assistance in the Great
    Depression*, by Janet Poppendieck, Rutgers University Press, New
    Brunswick, N.J.: 1986.

*The American Food Scandal: Why You Can't Eat Well on What You
    Earn*, by William Robbins, William Morrow and Co. Inc., New York, N.Y.:
    1974.

Exploring Agribusiness, by Ewell Paul Roy, Ph. D., The
    Interstate, Printers and Publishers, Inc., Danville, Illinois: 1967.

Change In Rural America: Causes, Consequences, and Alternatives,
    Edited by Rodefeld, et. al., C.V. Mosby Co., St. Louis, Missouri: 1978.

The Invisible Farmers: Women In Agriculture Production, by
    Carolyn Sachs, Eowman & Allanhold, Totowa, N.J.: 1983.

Agricultural Discontent in the Middle West, 1900-1939, by
    Theodore Saloutos and John D. Hicks, University of Wisconsin Press,
    Madison, Wisconsin: 1951.

Farmland or Wasteland: A Time to Choose, by R. Neil Sampson,
    Rodale Press, Emmaus, Penn.: 1981.

The Age of Roosevelt: The Coming of the New Deal, by Arthur
    Schlesinger, Houghton Miffin Co., N.Y.: 1959.

The Almanac of American History, General Editor: Arthur M.
    Schlesinger, Jr., G.P. Putnam's Sons, New York, N.Y.: 1983.

Agriculture In A Unstable Economy, by Theodore W. Schultz,
    McGraw-Hill Books, New York, N.Y.: 1945.

The Hidden Injuries of Class, by Richard Sennett and Jonathan
    Cobb, Vintage Books, New York, N.Y.: 1973.

American Farmers' Movements, By Fred A. Shannon, D. Van Nostrand
    Co., Inc., Princeton, N.J.: 1957.

The Jungle, by Upton Sinclair, Signet Classic, New York, N.Y.:
    1906.

Wealth of Nations, by Adam Smith, Random House, New York, N.Y.:
    1937.

Queen of Populists: The Story of Mary Elizabeth Lease, by Richard
    Stiller, Dell Publishing Co., New York, N.Y.: 1970.

The Hidden History of the Korean War by I.F. Stone, Monthly
    Review Press, New York, N.Y.: 1952.

The Policy Process in American Agriculture, by Ross B. Talbot and
    Don Hadwiger, Chandler Publishing Co., San Francisco, California:
    1968.

The New Gatsbys: Fortunes and Misfortunes of Commodity Traders, by Bob Tamarkin, Quill - William Morrow, New York, N.Y.: 1985.

The Changing Structure of Agriculture, Technology, Public
    Policy, and the Changing Structure of American Agriculture, Congress of
    the United States: Office of Technology Asssessment, Washington, D.C.,
    1986.

A Dialogue on the Structure of American Agriculture, Summary of
    Regional Meetings, November 27 - December 18, 1979, U.S. Department
    of Agriculture, Washington, D.C., April, 1980.

Structure Issues of American Agriculture, ESCS, Agricultural
    Economic Report 438, USDA, November, 1979.

A Time to Choose: Summary Report on the Structure of Agriculture,
    USDA, January, 1981.

The Pesticide Conspiracy, by Robert van den Bosch, Doubleday &
    Co., New York, N.Y.: 1978.

*The Muth of the Family Farm: Agribusiness Dominance of U.S.
    Agriculture* by Ingolf Vogeler, Westview Press, Boulder, Colorado: 1981.

Unforgiven: The Biography of an Idea, by Charles Walters, Jr.,
    Economics Library, Kansas City, Missouri, 1971.

Circle of Poison: Pesticides and People in a Hungry World, by
    David Weir and Mark Shapiro, Institute for Food and Development
    Policy, San Francisco, California: 1981.

Sowing the Wind, A Report from Ralph Nader's Center for Study of
    Responsive Law on Food Safety and the Chemical Harvest, by Harrison
    Wellford, Grossman Publishers, New York: 1971.

The Farmer in the Second World War, by Walter W. Wilcox, Iowa
    State College Press, Ames, Iowa: 1947.

Prosperity Unlimited: The American Way, by Carl Wilken, Carl H.
    Wilkin, Sioux City, Iowa: 1947.

The Roots of the Modern American Empire, by William Appleman
    Williams, Vintage Books, New York, N.Y.: 1969.

Dust Bowl: The Southern Plains in the 1930's, by Donald Worster,
    Oxford University Press. New York, N.Y.: 1979.

*Rivers of Empire: Water, Aridity & The Growth of the American
    West*, by Donald Worster, Pantheon Books, New York, N.Y.: 1985.

Index

566

citrus fruits 102, 436
citrus tanker 116
civil liberties 108, 285
civil rights revolution 226
Civil War 141-143, 145, 146, 151, 159, 206
Clancy, Katherine 123, 127
Clark, George 58
Clark, Vance L. 50, 261
class structure 242, 258, 276, 295, 396
Claus Corp. 78
Claybrook, Joan 132
Clayton Act 156, 379, 455
Clemson University 5, 378
Cloverdale, J.W. 172
Co-op Council 211, 213, 214
Coahama County, Mississippi 250
Coalition of Farm Organizations 229
Cobb, Jonathan 396
Coca Cola 37, 57, 106, 307
Coccari, Elena 113
Cochran, Thad 31
Cochrane, Willard 74
cocoa 306, 323, 339, 446, 448
Codes of Fair Competition 188
Coelho, Tony 377
coffee 25, 83, 106, 201, 306, 307, 324, 323, 339,
    355, 446, 448, 459, 462
Coffee, Sugar and Cocoa Exchange 339
Coffman, Claude 331
Cohen, Barbara G. 120
Coil, E. Johnson 189
cold war 209, 328
Cole, Jeffrey N. 355
Coleman, E. Thomas 432
collective bargaining 37, 187, 195, 202, 222
Colleran, Dennis 91
Collins, Cardiss 352
Colmer Committee 204
Colorado 59, 64, 82, 106, 190, 234, 364-366, 370,
    379, 459
Colorado District Court 365
Columbia 68, 84, 109, 188, 191, 311, 310, 368, 446
Columbia Foods Inc. 368
Colwell, Maryanna 6
commercial banks 47, 48, 50, 51, 53, 151, 166, 186,
    340, 405, 409
commercial farming 189, 190, 202
Commission on Country Life 270
Commission on Food and Marketing 225
Committee for Economic Development 222, 289-298
Committee of Twenty-Two 178
Committee on Postwar Agricultural Policy 204
commodity brokers 376
Commodity Credit Corporation 31, 48, 186, 196,
    199, 214-218, 222, 308, 314, 325,
    329, 336, 427, 428, 464
commodity credit loans 278
commodity distribution program 226
Commodity Exchange Act 345, 356, 357
Commodity Exchange Authority 332, 344, 349, 462

Commodity Exchange Commission 195
Commodity Exchange, Inc. 339
commodity factionalism 251
Commodity Futures Trading Commission 339, 341,
    345, 348-352, 354-357
commodity groups 116, 250-252, 263, 278, 436
commodity prices 19, 52, 64, 113, 147, 150, 155,
    161-163, 164, 169, 179, 194, 195,
    198, 204, 230, 243, 259, 295, 308,
    340, 422, 423, 427-429, 468, 472,
    473
commodity storage programs 281
commodityism 243
Common Agricultural Policy 230
Common Cause 251, 437
Common Market 230, 303, 367
communities of economic interest 16, 21, 396, 403
commutative justice 241
Compa, Lance 413
competitive advantage 158, 185, 282, 320, 323, 353,
    398, 422
ConAgra 19, 104, 108, 113, 256, 304, 311, 362-367,
    378-380, 381, 386, 387, 458
ConAgra Agri-Products Cos. 365
ConAgra Red Meat Cos. 365
concentration 15, 18, 19, 21, 28, 41, 45, 47, 56, 57,
    60, 77, 78, 80, 81, 88, 101, 103,
    105, 109, 110, 121, 125, 128, 146,
    154, 221, 224, 225, 231, 232, 254,
    260, 267, 293, 303, 304, 311, 320,
    324, 349, 362-364, 365, 366, 370,
    372, 378, 380, 402, 404, 448, 450,
    453, 455, 462, 475
Confederate currency 146
Confucius 57
Congress 2, 30, 32, 37, 46, 49-55, 68, 69, 76, 79,
    82, 83, 87, 88, 90, 128, 129, 132,
    140, 142, 143, 148, 149, 157, 158,
    163, 164, 166, 167, 169-171, 173,
    174, 176, 177, 178, 182, 183, 185,
    191, 192, 194-200, 205, 206, 208,
    209, 211, 212, 214-216, 217, 218,
    221, 223, 224, 226, 229, 230, 232,
    233, 234-236, 247, 250-255, 257,
    258, 263, 265, 266, 268-270, 272,
    275-284, 293, 297, 307, 308, 313,
    317, 319, 323, 324, 344, 346,
    348-352, 356, 358, 363, 366, 377,
    380, 390, 391, 413, 426, 427, 429,
    430-432, 435, 437, 442, 453, 454,
    463, 468, 476
Congress of International Organizations 187
Congressional Black Caucus 427
Congressional Budget Office 431, 433
Congressional Office of Technology 429
Connecticut 59, 60, 65, 66, 107, 381
Connecticut Mutual 60
Connell Rice & Sugar Co. 251
Conniff, Richard 381
Connor, John M. 101

deficit 22, 27, 48, 51, 55, 188, 196, 229, 233, 256, 314, 318, 323, 404, 412, 413, 427, 431, 453, 475
deflation 65, 161, 168, 194, 204
Dekalb-Pfizer 78
Del Monte Corp. 229, 293
Delaney Clause 88, 131
Delano, Robert 281
Delaware 37, 50, 65, 459, 460
delicatessens 105
delinquent loans 49-51
DeMarco, Susan 233, 234, 264
democracy 6, 8, 17, 20-22, 140, 141, 154, 157, 202, 236, 239, 241, 243, 245, 247, 250, 254, 263, 269, 358, 399, 400, 401-403, 405, 406, 441-443, 451, 452, 476
democratic creed 242, 245
Democratic National Committee's Agricultural Council 426
democratic promise 145, 151, 441
Democrats 31, 142, 143, 153, 158, 174, 179, 184, 186, 206, 209, 211, 217, 218, 221, 223, 225, 226, 250, 287, 336, 435
Dent, Frederick B. 256
depression 17, 19, 25, 27, 28, 45, 48, 50-53, 117, 141, 143, 147, 149, 151, 162, 164, 167-169, 174, 180, 181, 186-188, 189, 192, 196, 198, 204, 211, 213, 214, 221, 223, 231, 234, 235, 242, 270, 277, 292, 298, 320, 409, 412, 413, 422, 423
deregulation 25, 310, 321, 390
DES 265, 267,
Des Moines Register 68, 86, 215, 304, 328, 355, 367, 385, 420
Desert Land Act 149
Detroit 70, 107, 162
Dettman, Geraldine 134
devaluation 47, 230, 437, 453
Dewey, Thomas 206
Diazinon 92, 95
Dickinson, L.J. 176
diet drink 128
dietary fiber 120
DiGiorgio Corporation 207
Dingman, Bishop Maurice 18, 28, 58, 287
Dinuba, California 207, 208
diphenyl 130
direct operating loans 432
direct payments 30, 32, 213, 241, 464
Dirkson, Everett 37
dirt farmers 186, 242
Dirty Dozen 83, 84
disaster payments 232
discrimination 26, 49, 151, 187, 226, 227, 257-259, 269, 272, 386, 398, 462, 475
distributive justice 241
District of Columbia 109, 188
dividend certificates 283
DNA 80
Dobrzynski, Judith H. 38

Doctorow, E.L. 73
Dole, Robert 235, 346, 434
Dole Philippine 447
Dollar Harvest: An Expose of the Farm Bureau 284
dollar protectionism 437
domestic allotment plan 183
Donovan, Thomas 350
Dorgan, Byron 310
Dornbush 408
Douglass, Frederick
Dow Chemical Co. 38, 81, 82
Dow Jones 38
Doyle, Jack 79, 80, 131
Doyle, Mona 130
Dr. Pepper 106
Drabble, Nancy 87
Drabenstott, Mark 48
Drew, Christopher 339
Drew, Daniel 456
Drexel Burnham Lambert 37
dried eggs 200
dried milk 200
dried peas 165
drinking water 89, 256, 434
drought 18, 23, 40, 67, 69, 96, 143, 155, 189, 190, 192, 194, 195, 203, 218, 230, 256, 314, 328, 329, 339, 341, 370, 440, 446, 464
Drug Enforcement Administration 92
drugs 78, 80, 83, 92, 109, 117, 125, 126, 129, 131, 133, 266, 267, 328, 345, 391
Drury, Michael 107
dry beans 95, 423
dry corn 304
dual trading 345, 350, 351
ducks 211, 380, 461
Duff Farm Management Service 59
Duke, James B. 147
dumping 133, 176, 185, 325, 377
Dunavent Enterprises 326
Dunbar, Leslie 6, 260
Dunkelburger, Edward 126
Dunkerton, Iowa 24
Dunnan, Nancy 343
Durst, Seymour B. 408
Durham, Dennis 417
Dust Bowl 67-69, 71, 189, 190, 195, 473
dust storms 68, 189
E.J. Gallo Co. 119
E-II Holdings Inc. 104
Eagleton, Thomas 348
Eames, Alfred W. 293
East, Clay 187
Eastern banks 146, 165, 166
Eastern business 148, 184
eat more campaigns 177
Eckrich 363, 378, 459
ecological values 96, 189
economic concentration 18, 19, 21, 28, 56, 77, 101, 154, 225, 231, 404
economic democracy 17, 140, 243, 405, 441, 442, 452

585

Natale, Robert 421
Nathan's hot dogs 388
Nation's Business 174, 176, 177, 198, 293
National Academy of Sciences 68, 79, 87, 90, 120, 313, 391
National Advisory Commission on Food and Fiber 224, 464
National Agricultural Advisory Committee 213
National Agricultural Conference 171, 172
National Agricultural Conference in 1922 172
National Agricultural Credit Corporation 170
National Agricultural Lands Study 65
national agricultural planning 183
National Agricultural Press Association 286, 287
National Agricultural Relations Act 204
National Alfalfa Dehydrating & Milling Co. 70
National American Wholesale Grocers' Association 237
National Association of Counties 65
National Association of State Departments of Agriculture 66
National Association of State Universities and Land Grant Colleges 263, 265, 268
National Association of Wheat Growers 355, 422
National Association for the Advancement of Colored People 259, 283
National Bank of Commerce 166, 368
National Bank of Commerce Trust and Savings Association 368
national banking system 146
National Broiler Council 433
National Bureau of Standards 89
National Cancer Institute 85, 118
National Canners League 232
National Cattlemen's Association 223
National Chamber of Commerce 176, 204, 433
National Catholic Reporter 387
National City Bank 165, 166, 176
National Coalition Against the Misuse of Pesticides 82, 83, 87, 89, 90, 92
National Commission on Food Marketing 9, 224, 225, 444, 462
National Committee in Support of Community-Based Organizations 259, 260
National Confectioners Association 433
National Conservation Reserve 428
National Coordinating Committee for Farm Policy Reform 426, 435
National Corn Growers 255, 433
National Cotton Council 225, 251
National Council of Farmer Cooperatives 200, 211
National Dairy Board 127
National Democratic Policy Committee 287
National Farmers Alliance and Industrial Union 151, 442
National Farmers Organization 222, 232, 252, 290, 313, 319, 323, 426
National Farmers Union 23, 157, 178, 184, 185, 223, 235, 290, 423, 426
National Farmers' Fair Credit Campaign 435
National Farms Inc. 32
National Farms of Atkinson, Nebraska 379

National Fertilizer Solutions Association 433
National Food Allotment Plan 204
National Food Processors Association 126, 127, 433
National Grain and Feed Association 230, 305, 322
National Grain and Feed Dealers Association 434
National Grain Corporation 179
National Grange 150
National Grape Cooperative 91
National Grocers Association 109
National Hog Farmer 379
National Industrial Conference Board 178
National Institute of Animal Agriculture 217
National Labor Relations Act 195, 385
National Labor Relations Act 1937 278
National Labor Relations Board 386, 388
National Maritime Union 384
National Migrant Ministry 283
National Monetary Commission 165, 166
National Organization for Raw Materials 414
National Pasta Association 433
national planning 183
National Recovery Administration 188
National Reform Press Association 152
National Research Advisory Committee 266
National Research Council 81, 89, 90
national resources 88, 200
National Right-to-Work Committee 212, 286
National Rural Crisis Action campaign 435
National Safe Workplace Institute 391
National Safety Council 85
National Save the Family Farm Committee 435
national security 175, 476
National Soft Drink Association 132
national welfare assistance program 293
National Wool Council 251
National Wool Marketing Corporation 211, 213
nationalism 194
natural gas 94, 95
natural resource wealth 175
natural resources 15, 17, 32, 58, 75, 76, 80, 93, 102, 139, 140, 143, 146, 149, 150, 154, 158, 175, 203, 243, 246, 266, 270-272, 408, 409, 412, 428, 441, 474
Navistar, Inc. 80
Nazi Germany 295
Nebraska 21, 27, 28, 48, 51-55, 64, 66, 69, 70, 84, 85, 96, 107, 173, 188, 256, 260, 278, 313, 340, 364-366, 367, 374, 379, 384-386, 422, 424, 429, 433, 434, 440, 458-461
Nebraska National Guard 386
Nebraska Wheat Board 313, 429, 434
Nedelman, Jeffrey 88
Negro, Adele 6
Nelson, Willie 6, 435
neo-Nazi 286
Nestle Alimentana 103, 106, 113, 126
net farm income 19, 23, 29, 52, 74, 77, 96, 118, 181, 221, 231, 235, 323, 324, 409, 412, 434, 440, 466, 468, 472, 475
Netherlands 32, 77, 321, 320, 323

586

590

THE CORPORATE REAPERS

THE BOOK OF AGRIBUSINESS
A.V. KREBS

"In my 50 years of farming and as a farm activist and even longer as a youngster spending hours listening to farm activists debate and plan actions of the Farm Holiday in the early 1930s, I have never seen a better documented book on the history and meaning of farm struggles than **The Corporate Reapers***.*

"It is an important book to have at your side as a reference book to pencil out important quotes, facts, figures or articles. It is an operator's manual that every person interested in farm, food and land policy needs if we are going to build a national and world community rather than a market, which in the final analysis is choosing whether we are going to live together or die together. It all starts with food and farm policy."

— Merle Hansen, President Emeritus, North American Farm Alliance

"This is a book filled not merely with fact, but with the spirit of Thomas Jefferson, Shay's Rebellion, The Wizard of Oz, *Mary Ellen Lease, Upton Sinclair, Woody Guthrie, Cesar Chavez and Willie Nelson. It's a big book about justice, and it speaks the truth. Al Krebs has poured his life's work into this volume, and it's a work well worth the telling.* **The Corporate Reapers** *will inform you, anger you, broaden your vision and — I hope — fire you up for reform."*

— Jim Hightower, Former Texas State Commissioner of Agriculture

"A veritable almanac of information, **The Corporate Reapers** *details how multinational agribusiness has worked to destroy the family farm. Krebs explains that the decline of the family farm is not a result of the interplay of market forces, but rather of the price-fixing and anti-competitive policies of Cargill, Continental and ConAgra and their allies. The book is a valuable resource for both farmers and consumers who have an interest in preserving the availability of affordable and safe food."*

— Ralph Nader, Consumer Advocate

- -